D0146105

THE OXFORD HISTORY OF THE BRITISH EMPIRE

THE OXFORD HISTORY OF THE BRITISH EMPIRE

Volume I. *The Origins of Empire*
EDITED BY Nicholas Canny

Volume II. *The Eighteenth Century*
EDITED BY P. J. Marshall

Volume III. *The Nineteenth Century*
EDITED BY Andrew Porter

Volume IV. *The Twentieth Century*
EDITED BY Judith M. Brown and Wm. Roger Louis

Volume V. *Historiography*
EDITED BY Robin W. Winks

THE OXFORD HISTORY OF THE BRITISH EMPIRE

Wm. Roger Louis, CBE, D.Litt., FBA

*Kerr Professor of English History and Culture, University of Texas, Austin
and Honorary Fellow of St Antony's College, Oxford*

EDITOR-IN-CHIEF

∾

VOLUME III

The Nineteenth Century

∾

Andrew Porter, Ph.D

*Rhodes Professor of Imperial History,
University of London, King's College*

EDITOR

Alaine Low, D.Phil.

ASSOCIATE EDITOR

Oxford　New York

OXFORD UNIVERSITY PRESS

1999

Oxford University Press, Great Clarendon Street, Oxford OX2 6DP
Oxford University Press is a department of the University of Oxford.
It furthers the University's objective of excellence in research, scholarship,
and education by publishing worldwide in

Oxford New York

Athens Auckland Bangkok Bogotá Buenos Aires Calcutta
Cape Town Chennai Dar es Salaam Delhi Florence Hong Kong Istanbul
Karachi Kuala Lumpur Madrid Melbourne Mexico City Mumbai
Nairobi Paris São Paulo Singapore Taipei Tokyo Toronto Warsaw
and associated companies in Berlin Ibadan

Oxford is a registered trade mark of Oxford University Press
in the UK and certain other countries

Published in the United States
by Oxford University Press Inc., New York

© Oxford University Press 1999

British Library Cataloguing in Publication Data

Data available

Library of Congress Cataloging in Publication Data

Data available
ISBN 0–19–820565–1

1 3 5 7 9 10 8 6 4 2

Typeset by Kolam Information Services Pvt. Ltd, Pondicherry, India
Printed in Great Britain
on acid-free paper by
Bookcraft Ltd,
Midsomer Norton, Somerset

The Editor-in-Chief and Editors of *The Oxford History of the British Empire*
acknowledge with gratitude support from

The Rhodes Trust

The National Endowment for Humanities, Washington, DC

St Antony's College, Oxford

The University of Texas at Austin

FOREWORD

From the founding of the colonies in North America and the West Indies in the seventeenth century to the reversion of Hong Kong to China at the end of the twentieth, British imperialism was a catalyst for far-reaching change. British domination of indigenous peoples in North America, Asia, and Africa can now be seen more clearly as part of the larger and dynamic interaction of European and non-western societies. Though the subject remains ideologically charged, the passions aroused by British imperialism have so lessened that we are now better placed than ever before to see the course of the Empire steadily and to see it whole. At this distance in time the Empire's legacy from earlier centuries can be assessed, in ethics and economics as well as politics, with greater discrimination. At the close of the twentieth century, the interpretation of the dissolution of the Empire can benefit from evolving perspectives on, for example, the end of the cold war. In still larger sweep, the *Oxford History of the British Empire* as a comprehensive study helps to understand the end of the Empire in relation to its beginning, the meaning of British imperialism for the ruled as well as the rulers, and the significance of the British Empire as a theme in world history.

It is nearly half a century since the last volume in the large-scale *Cambridge History of the British Empire* was completed. In the meantime the British Empire has been dismantled and only fragments such as Gibraltar and the Falklands, Bermuda and Pitcairn, remain of an Empire that once stretched over a quarter of the earth's surface. The general understanding of the British imperial experience has been substantially widened in recent decades by the work of historians of Asia and Africa as well as Britain. Earlier histories, though by no means all, tended to trace the Empire's evolution and to concentrate on how it was governed. To many late-Victorian historians the story of the Empire meant the rise of worldwide dominion and Imperial rule, above all in India. Historians in the first half of the twentieth century tended to emphasize constitutional developments and the culmination of the Empire in the free association of the Commonwealth. The *Oxford History of the British Empire* takes a wider approach. It does not depict the history of the Empire as one of purposeful progress through four hundred years, nor does it concentrate narrowly on metropolitan authority and rule. It does attempt to explain how varying conditions in Britain interacted with those in many other parts of the world to create both a constantly changing territorial Empire and ever-shifting patterns of social and economic relations. The *Oxford History of the British Empire* thus deals with the impact of British imperialism on dependent peoples in a broader sense than was usually attempted in earlier historical writings while it also takes into account the significance of the Empire for the Irish, the Scots, and the Welsh as well as the English.

Volume III of the *Oxford History of the British Empire*, as emphasized in the Preface, covers a period that was first and foremost 'Britain's Imperial century'. The territorial extent and the apparently unbounded power of the nineteenth-century Empire fired the imagination of contemporaries and later generations. Yet the Empire in the nineteenth century, though historically distinct, formed only part of the much longer pattern in British Imperial endeavour that can be traced through the four volumes of this *History*.

By the end of the eighteenth century, different interpretations of the meaning of the term British Empire were giving way to a single concept of a British Empire of rule over lands and peoples. This unifying definition would be standard usage throughout the nineteenth century. Yet the comprehensive term, British Empire, encompassed different systems of rule over a great diversity of peoples, as had already become clear in the late eighteenth century. The late-Victorian Empire included self-governing colonies with predominantly white populations, Crown Colonies and Protectorates with non-European subjects, and the British Raj in India as an Empire in its own right.

The nineteenth century also inherited from the earlier era a pattern of world-wide interests that extended far beyond territory under actual British rule. The network of British trade and commerce in areas such as Latin America, the Middle East, and China can be viewed analytically as constituting an 'informal empire' based on naval hegemony and economic power. This is a concept examined in several chapters in both the nineteenth- and twentieth-century volumes. The worldwide British economic system itself reflected an expansiveness brought about by a combination of population growth, industry, finance, technological advance, and the accumulation of scientific knowledge, all of which greatly extended Britain's lead over potential rivals at the end of the eighteenth century.

By the end of the nineteenth century this lead was disappearing. Rival navies as well as empires now challenged the Royal Navy and Britain's Empire. Within the Empire, the rise of nationalism in the colonies of white settlement, Ireland, and India coincided with an emerging sense of national assertiveness in Britain. Colonial nationalism reflected the development of national identities and lingering resentments towards the exploitation or neglect by the 'Mother Country'. These tensions seemed to threaten the structure of the Empire. At the end of the century the British had become more jingoistic, but an important part of the legacy to be carried over into the next century was a sense of vulnerability and insecurity dealt with in Volume IV.

The volumes in the *Oxford History of the British Empire* do not necessarily begin or end at the same point. Historical understanding benefits from an integration and overlap of complex chronology. *The Nineteenth Century*, for example, gives comprehensive treatment to events within the hundred years, but some chapters reach back into the earlier period just as others extend to the outbreak of the First World War. Similarly some developments that began in the late nineteenth century can best be understood in a later context, and some chapters in Volume IV, *The Twentieth Century*, begin in the last decades of the nineteenth century.

A special feature of the series is the Select Bibliography of key works at the end of each chapter. These are not intended to be a comprehensive bibliographical or historiographical guide (which will be found in Volume V) but rather they are lists of useful and informative works on the themes of each chapter.

The Editor-in-Chief and Editors acknowledge, with immense gratitude, support from the Rhodes Trust, the National Endowment for the Humanities in Washington, DC, St Antony's College, Oxford, and the University of Texas at Austin. We have received further specific support from Lord Dahrendorf (former Warden of St Antony's College, Oxford); Sheldon Ekland-Olson formerly the Dean of Liberal Arts, now Provost, at the University of Texas, and, for the preparation of maps, the University Cooperative Society. Mr Iain Sproat helped to inspire the project and provided financial assistance for the initial organizational conference. It is also a true pleasure to thank our patrons Mr and Mrs Alan Spencer of Hatfield Regis Grange, Mr and Mrs Sam Jamot Brown of Durango, Colorado, and Mr and Mrs Baine Kerr of Houston, Texas. We have benefited from the cartographic expertise of Jane Pugh and Mina Moshkeri at the London School of Economics. Our last word of gratitude is to Dr Alaine Low, the Associate Editor, whose dedication to the project has been characterized by indefatigable efficiency and meticulous care.

Wm. Roger Louis

PREFACE

The years 1815 to 1902 were pre-eminently 'Britain's Imperial century', and they provide the core of traditionally triumphalist Imperial narratives. At both dates Britain emerged the victor from major wars. The peace treaties of 1814–15 not only acknowledged Britain's dominance in Europe; they confirmed her conquests made during the wars with France since 1793. Colonies everywhere were thus relieved from fears of attack, political upheaval, and financial loss, and new possessions were converted into fresh bridgeheads for British advance or keystones in the naval defence of Britain's trade. In 1902 the Treaty of Vereeniging, which ended the South African War, from another perspective also coincided with the final phase of Africa's partition. Although victory was bought at a high price, one indicative of future problems, for the moment at least it marked Britain's final emergence as the dominant power in the last colonized continent. Imperial co-operation was manifest in the colonial presence at Queen Victoria's funeral in 1901 and military contributions to the Transvaal's defeat.

However, there is also a 'long nineteenth century', bounded at one end by the events of the 1780s and at the other by those of 1902–14, revealing more of the uncertainties and fluctuations in Imperial fortunes. Peacemaking with a newly independent United States of America, and the reshaping of government for Quebec and British India, from 1782–91, were defensive measures against events which had seemed seriously threatening or uncontrollable. With hindsight, they can be seen as pointers to new connections and influence with both British settlers overseas and the peoples of Asia. Equally, the establishment of Freetown in 1787, of societies in London to promote African exploration and to end slavery, and a penal colony in New South Wales, heralded significant nineteenth-century developments. But resumption of war with France in 1793 left Britain's Imperial future still seriously threatened. Similarly, at the beginning of the twentieth century Britain's renewed sense of isolation and vulnerability to challenges from other imperial powers—Russia, America, Germany—coincided with problems of Imperial defence freshly exposed on India's frontiers and in South Africa; Britain's economic and administrative difficulties encountered nationalist demands in colonial territories. These conditions intensified earlier misgivings, and prompted a reconsideration of Imperial relations and colonial rule which not only anticipated but survived the war of 1914–18.

This, then, is a history integrally related to and overlapping that of the eighteenth and twentieth centuries. In organizing the volume, account has been taken not only of these different chronological perspectives, but of both the enormous growth in recent years of writings on colonial issues, and a much longer tradition of Imperial historiography. Contributors have had to incorporate knowledge and insights accumulated by earlier generations with newer findings and perspectives. Only in this way has it been possible to bring together the British and the Asian, African, and other indigenous aspects of Empire. Although selection has been inescapable, and consolidation and assimilation would not always have been either possible or appropriate, the underlying aim is that of scholarly cross-fertilization and merger rather than segregation. Subjects currently attracting much attention—gender and empire, the role in expansion of 'imperial ideologies', the nature of colonial 'identities', the costs or benefits of Empire—have therefore been generally drawn into broader discussions, rather than isolated in chapters of their own. In this way the isolation or disappearance of important insights may be avoided and the mainstream of Imperial history be continually invigorated and sustained.

The Introduction highlights four themes running through the volume, and uses them to provide a general context for the chapters which follow. They embrace both the 'long' and 'short' centuries, and are divided by theme and territory. In Part I, thematic chapters take up developments underway in the 1790s. Crossing geographical and chronological divides, they discuss those fundamental dynamics of British expansion which encouraged or facilitated the contemplation and eventual exercise of significant influence, domination, and rule overseas. The opening chapters 2–5 illuminate the economic dimensions of British expansion and Empire, and consider continuing debates about the economics of empire. They are followed by three chapters on the nature of British influence and the idea of an 'informal empire' outside territories ruled by Britain. A further sequence explores the scientific, religious, humanitarian, and institutional frameworks which both shaped and were influenced by Imperial expansion. Two final chapters survey the particular difficulties met in maintaining the Empire, and end-of-the-century plans for its reorganization. In this Part too particular attention is given to the place of the Empire in British politics and society.

In Part II, regional chapters, grouped broadly by hemisphere or continent, focus on the main areas of colonial activity. Most begin at the end of the Napoleonic Wars, setting out the phases in the growth of colonial government and the political evolution of the territories concerned, and relating those developments to local social and economic changes. They assess how British preoccupations and rule shaped each region's history, and they pay particular attention to the responses of indigenous peoples to Empire. India has been allotted two chapters, divided chronologically at 1858–60 and each with a distinctive focus, in recognition of its central importance for the Empire. Later rather than contemporary usage has sometimes been preferred—'Canada', rather than 'British North America' widely used before 1867, and 'South African' rather than 'Boer' War. Exceptions in favour of earlier starting dates have been made for South-East Asia (1786), Southern Africa (1795), and Ireland (1801) where continuity seemed to require it. The Irish chapter provides more than a study of the country's ambivalent position under the Union. Together with those on the evolution of colonial cultures in Africa and Asia, it offers an extended discussion of the opportunities opened to colonial subjects as well as the constraints they experienced under British rule.

Andrew Porter

CONTENTS

List of Maps   XV

List of Figures   XVI

List of Tables   XVII

Abbreviations and Location of Manuscript Sources   XVIII

List of Contributors   XIX

1. Introduction: Britain and the Empire in the Nineteenth Century
   Andrew Porter   1

PART I

2. Economics and Empire: The Metropolitan Context   *P. J. Cain*   31
3. Economics and Empire: The Periphery and the Imperial Economy
   B. R. Tomlinson   53
4. British Migration and the Peopling of the Empire   *Marjory Harper*   75
5. Migration from Africa, Asia, and the South Pacific   *David Northrup*   88
6. British Policy, Trade, and Informal Empire in the Mid-Nineteenth
   Century   *Martin Lynn*   101
7. Britain and Latin America   *Alan Knight*   122
8. Britain and China, 1842–1914   *Jürgen Osterhammel*   146
9. Imperial Institutions and the Government of Empire   *Peter Burroughs*   179
10. Trusteeship, Anti-Slavery, and Humanitarianism   *Andrew Porter*   198
11. Religion, Missionary Enthusiasm, and Empire   *Andrew Porter*   222
12. British Expansion, Empire, and Technological Change   *Robert Kubicek*   247
13. Empire and Metropolitan Cultures   *John M. MacKenzie*   270
14. Scientific Exploration and Empire   *Robert A. Stafford*   294
15. Defence and Imperial Disunity   *Peter Burroughs*   320
16. The Political Economy of Empire, 1880–1914   *E. H. H. Green*   346

PART II

17. British Expansion and Rule in South-East Asia   *A. J. Stockwell*   371
18. India, 1818–1860: The Two Faces of Colonialism   *D. A. Washbrook*   395
19. Imperial India, 1858–1914   *Robin J. Moore*   422

20. The Evolution of Colonial Cultures: Nineteenth-Century Asia
    Susan Bayly   447

21. The British West Indies   *Gad Heuman*   470

22. Ireland and the Empire   *David Fitzpatrick*   495

23. Canada from 1815   *Ged Martin*   522

24. Australia and the Western Pacific   *Donald Denoon with Marivic
    Wyndham*   546

25. Southern Islands: New Zealand and Polynesia   *Raewyn Dalziel*   573

26. Southern Africa, 1795–1910   *Christopher Saunders and Iain R. Smith* 597

27. Great Britain and the Partition of Africa, 1870–1914   *Colin Newbury* 624

28. The British Occupation of Egypt from 1882   *Afaf Lutfi al-Sayyid-Marsot* 651

29. Cultural Encounters: Britain and Africa in the Nineteenth Century
    T. C. McCaskie   644

30. Costs and Benefits, Prosperity and Security, 1870–1914
    Avner Offer   690

Chronology   712
Index   743

LIST OF MAPS

1.1. The British Empire in 1815   2
1.2. The British Empire in 1914   3
3.1. World Climatic Regions and European Settlement   54
8.1. China: Treaty Ports and Leased Territories   147
12.1. Communications: Principal Steamship Routes   253
14.1. British Exploration in Africa   301
14.2. The Exploration of Australia   303
15.1. Imperial Defence: Naval Bases, Stations, and Army Garrisons   321
17.1. South-East Asia   373
18.1. Pre-Mutiny India   396
19.1. India: Political Divisions, c.1909   423
21.1. The West Indies   471
23.1. Canada to 1905   524
24.1. Australia: Colonies and Pastoral Settlement   547
24.2. British Possessions and Inter-Regional Migration in the Pacific   554
25.1. New Zealand: Native Peoples and White Settlers   574
26.1. The Expansion of British Control in Southern Africa   600
26.2. The Partition of East and Central Africa   613
27.1. Britain and the Partition of West Africa   646
27.2. Britain and the Partition of Africa, c.1891: International Boundaries
and Areas of Effective Occupation   647
28.1. Egypt and the Sudan   656

LIST OF FIGURES

5.1. Destinations of indentured labourers within the Empire, 1830–1920   89
26.1. Exports of South African produce, 1861–1910   605
27.1. British West African settlements: expenditure, 1848–1890   625
27.2. British trade with Africa, 1870–1903   627

LIST OF TABLES

2.1. Leading British imports and principal suppliers, 1784–1836   33

2.2. Exports of British produce to the Empire, 1814–1913   35

2.3. Empire share in British imports of primary products, 1854 and 1913   43

2.4. Britain's imports from the Empire, 1854–1913   44

2.5. Emigration from England, Wales, and Scotland, 1853–1920   47

2.6. British overseas financial issues, 1865–1914   48

3.1. Pattern of British exports by regions, 1789–1913   58

3.2. Pattern of British imports by regions, 1789–1913   58

3.3. Distribution of capital calls in London, by regions, 1865–1914   59

3.4. Trade in primary products: regional shares, 1876–1913   63

3.5. Expansion of croplands in world regions, 1700–1920   67

3.6. Land converted to regular cropping, 1860–1919   67

3.7. Estimates of world population, 1750 and 1900   68

3.8. Percentage shares of different countries and regions in total world manufacturing output, 1750–1913   69

3.9. Location of world cotton manufacturing industry, 1913   70

3.10. Location of world steel industry, 1913   70

5.1. Overseas indentured immigration to destinations in the British Empire, 1834–1920   89

5.2. Indian overseas labour emigration, 1834–1924   91

5.3. Chinese overseas emigration from Hong Kong, 1854–1880   94

12.1. Distances from Plymouth to selected destinations by sea   254

12.2. Distances from Liverpool, Cape Town, Bombay, and Calcutta to selected destinations by sea   254

12.3. Journey time by sea from England to Cape Town   254

12.4. Journey time from selected ports by sea: routes East   255

12.5. Journey time from England by sea: North Atlantic routes   255

12.6. Journey time from England by sea: West Africa routes   255

21.1. Exports of sugar from the British West Indies, 1820–1899   489

28.1. Egypt's foreign trade, 1885–1913   659

28.2. Egypt's balance of trade and movements of capital, 1884–1914   661

ABBREVIATIONS AND LOCATION
OF MANUSCRIPT SOURCES

Public Record Office, London:

CAB	Cabinet Office
CO	Colonial Office
FO	Foreign Office
WO	War Office

All other abbreviations and manuscript sources will be found in the first reference in each chapter.

LIST OF CONTRIBUTORS

Susan Bayly (Ph.D., Cambridge) is Fellow, Tutor, and College Lecturer, Christ's College, Cambridge University. She is the author of *Saints, Goddesses and Kings: Muslims and Christians in South Indian Society, 1700–1900*, and has forthcoming *Caste, Society and Politics in India from the Eighteenth Century to the Modern Age* for the *New Cambridge History of India*.

Peter Burroughs (Ph.D., London) is former Professor of History at Dalhousie University. His publications include *The Canadian Crisis and British Colonial Policy, 1828–1842*. He is Joint Editor of the *Journal of Imperial and Commonwealth History*.

P. J. Cain (B.Litt., Oxford) is Research Professor at Sheffield Hallam University. He is the author (with A. G. Hopkins) of *British Imperialism: Innovation and Expansion, 1688–1914*; and *British Imperialism: Crisis and Deconstruction, 1914–1990*.

Raewyn Dalziel (Ph.D., Wellington) is Professor of New Zealand History at the University of Auckland. Her books include *The Origins of New Zealand Diplomacy*; and *Julius Vogel: Business Politician*. Much of her recent work has explored the place of women in New Zealand society.

Donald Denoon (Ph.D., Cambridge) was formerly Professor of History at the University of Papua New Guinea and is now Professor at the Australian National University. His books include *A Grand Illusion: The Failure of Imperial Policy in the Transvaal Colony* and *Settler Capitalism: The Dynamics of Dependent Development in the Southern Hemisphere*.

David Fitzpatrick (Ph.D., Cambridge) is Associate Professor of Modern History and a Fellow of Trinity College, Dublin. His works include *Politics and Irish Life, 1913–1921: Provincial Experience of War and Revolution; Irish Emigration, 1801–1921; Oceans of Consolation: Personal Accounts of Irish Migration to Australia*; and *The Two Irelands, 1912–1939*.

E. H. H. Green (Ph.D., Cambridge) is Fellow of Magdalen College, Oxford. He is the author of several articles on British political economy in the late nineteenth and early twentieth centuries, and of *The Crisis of Conservatism: The Politics, Economics and Ideology of the British Conservative Party, 1880–1914.*

MARJORY HARPER (Ph.D., Aberdeen) is Lecturer in History at the University of Aberdeen. She is author of *Emigration from North-East Scotland* (2 vols.). She has edited *Through Canada with a Kodak* and *Emigration from Scotland Between the Wars: Opportunity or Exile* (forthcoming).

GAD HEUMAN (Ph.D., Yale) is Reader in the Department of History at the University of Warwick. His publications include *Between Black and White* and a study of the Morant Bay Rebellion in Jamaica: *The Killing Time.* He has edited books on slave resistance and on labour, and is co-editor of the journal *Slavery and Abolition.*

ALAN KNIGHT (D.Phil., Oxford) FRA is Professor of the History of Latin America, University of Oxford, and Fellow of St Antony's College. His publications include *The Mexican Revolution* (2 vols.); and *US–Mexican Relations, 1910–1940.*

ROBERT KUBICEK (Ph.D., Duke) is Professor of History at the University of British Columbia. His publications include *Joseph Chamberlain at the Colonial Office* and *Economic Imperialism in Theory and Practice: The Case of South African Gold Mining Finance, 1886–1914.* His current interest is the role of nineteenth-century technologies such as steamships and theories of imperialism.

MARTIN LYNN (Ph.D., London) is Senior Lecturer in Modern History at The Queen's University, Belfast. His publications include articles on informal imperialism in the nineteenth century, on West African economic history, and on British business history. He is author of *Commerce and Economic Change in West Africa.*

T. C. McCASKIE (Ph.D., Cambridge) is Reader in Asante History at the Centre of West African Studies, University of Birmingham. His principal interest has been the history and culture of the West African forest kingdom of Asante (Ghana). He has published *State and Society in Precolonial Asante* and has edited *West African Economic and Social History.*

JOHN M. MACKENZIE (Ph.D., British Columbia) is Professor of Imperial History at Lancaster University and Series Editor of *Studies in Imperialism.* He is author of *Propaganda and Empire; The Empire of Nature;* and *The Orientalism Debate.* He has edited *Imperialism and Popular Culture; Imperialism and the Natural World;* and *Popular Imperialism and the Military.*

GED MARTIN (Ph.D., Cambridge) is Professor of Canadian Studies at the University of Edinburgh. He is the author of *The Durham Report and British Policy; Bunyip Aristocracy*; and co-author of *Reappraisals in British Imperial History*. He has edited *The Founding of Australia*; and *The Causes of Canadian Confederation*. He was founding co-editor of the *British Journal of Canadian Studies*.

ROBIN J. MOORE (D.Lit., London) FAHA, is Professor of History at The Flinders University of South Australia. His books include *Liberalism and Indian Politics, 1872–1922; The Crisis of Indian Unity, 1917–1940; Churchill, Cripps and India, 1939–1945; Escape from Empire; Making the New Commonwealth*; and *Paul Scott's Raj*.

COLIN NEWBURY (Ph.D., Australian National University) is former Lecturer in Commonwealth History, University of Oxford, and Vice-Principal of Linacre College. He has written widely on the Pacific, and on West and South Africa. His most recent book is *The Diamond Ring: Business, Politics, and Precious Stones in South Africa, 1867–1947*.

DAVID NORTHRUP (Ph.D., University of California, Los Angeles) is Professor of History at Boston College. He is author of *Trade Without Rulers: Pre-Colonial Economic Development in South-Eastern Nigeria; Beyond the Bend in the River: African Labor in Eastern Zaire, 1865–1940*; and *Indentured Labor in the Age of Imperialism, 1834–1922*.

AVNER OFFER (D.Phil., Oxford) is Reader in Recent Social and Economic History at the University of Oxford and a Professorial Fellow of Nuffield College. His publications on Imperial themes include *The First World War: An Agrarian Interpretation*, as well as articles in the *Economic History Review*.

JÜRGEN OSTERHAMMEL (Dr.phil. habil, Freiburg) a former Research Fellow at the German Historical Institute in London, is Professor at the University of Konstanz. His books include *Britischer Imperialismus im Fernen Osten, China und die Weltgesellschaft*; and *Colonialism: A Theoretical Overview*.

ANDREW PORTER (Ph.D., Cambridge) is Rhodes Professor of Imperial History at King's College, London. His books include *Origins of the South African War, Victorian Shipping, Business and Imperial Policy*, and *British Imperial Policy and Decolonization, 1938–1964*, (2 vols. with A. J. Stockwell). He has been Editor of the *Journal of Imperial and Commonwealth History*.

CHRISTOPHER SAUNDERS (D.Phil., Oxford) is Associate Professor of History at the University of Cape Town. His publications include *The Making of the South African Past*; and numerous articles in the *South African Historical Journal.*

AFAF LUTFI AL-SAYYID-MARSOT (D.Phil., Oxford) is Professor of History at the University of California, Los Angeles. She is the author of *Egypt and Cromer; Egypt's Liberal Experiment: 1922–36; Egypt in the Reign of Muhammed Ali; A Short History of Modern Egypt;* and *Women and Men in Late Eighteenth Century Egypt.*

IAIN R. SMITH (D.Phil., Oxford) is Senior Lecturer in History at the University of Warwick. He is author of *The Origins of the South African War, 1899–1902.*

ROBERT STAFFORD (D.Phil., Oxford) is an Honorary Fellow, History and Philosophy of Science Department, University of Melbourne, Australia. He is the author of *Scientist of Empire: Sir Roderick Murchison, Scientific Exploration, and Victorian Imperialism.*

A. J. STOCKWELL (Ph.D., London) is Professor of Imperial and Commonwealth History at Royal Holloway College, University of London. His publications include *British Policy and Malay Politics; British Imperial Policy and Decolonization, 1938–1964* (with A. N. Porter), *British Documents on the End of Empire: Malaya* (editor). He is Joint Editor of the *Journal of Imperial and Commonwealth History.*

B. R. TOMLINSON (Ph.D., Cambridge) is Professor of Economic History at the University of Strathclyde. He is the author of *The Indian National Congress and the Raj; The Political Economy of the Raj, 1914–1947;* and *The Economy of Modern India, 1870–1960;* as well as numerous articles on the economic, political, and business history of the British Empire.

D. A. WASHBROOK (Ph.D., Cambridge) is Reader in Modern South Asian History and Fellow of St Antony's College, Oxford. He is author of *The Emergence of Provincial Politics: Madras Presidency, 1870–1920;* and many articles on modern Indian history. He has taught at the Universities of Cambridge, Warwick, Harvard, and Pennsylvania.

MARIVIC WYNDHAM (Ph.D., Australian National University) is a Visiting Fellow in the Research School of Pacific and Asian Studies, Australian National University, and teaches Australian cultural history. Her Ph.D. thesis is a cultural biography of the Australian novelist, Eleanor Dark (1901–85).

Introduction: Britain and the Empire in the Nineteenth Century

ANDREW PORTER

At the end of the eighteenth century Britain already stood alongside France, Russia, the Chinese and the Turkish empires, as one of the world's principal states. Thereafter the history of her Empire was bound up with her nineteenth-century record as an expanding Great Power. This was clear in various ways. First, the Empire, even if conceived simply in terms of territory and economic wealth, constantly interacted with the development of Britain's modern capitalist economy at home and overseas. Both grew enormously, but Britain's emergence as the world's richest nation rested on no simple causal relationship with Empire. Secondly, Empire exerted a major influence on Britain's international relations, with Imperial issues and foreign policy frequently inseparable from each other. Britain's possession of an Empire was felt to confirm her Great Power status; protection of that status and her growing presence overseas involved an increasing range of Imperial commitments in Asia, Africa, and the Pacific, which in their turn were as likely to create difficulties as they were to increase Britain's power. Thirdly, developments in Britain's position as a colonial ruler stimulated constitutional and political inventiveness among both rulers and ruled, and gave rise to a growing variety of governmental institutions and practice at home and abroad. Finally, the possession and expansion of an Empire also markedly influenced Britain's 'cultural'—that is, social, institutional, religious, and intellectual—development and her citizens' views of the outside world. It did the same for many of the settler societies and colonized peoples over whom she claimed authority. Imperial and colonial cultures and institutions constantly played upon each other. These four types of relationship provide this volume with its central themes.

In approaching Britain's nineteenth-century Empire, scholars now acknowledge both its complexity and its place in the broader history of indigenous societies outside Europe, as well as the history of international affairs and British domestic change. The nature of empire is no longer taken for granted, and historians show a better sense of proportion in assessing its significance.

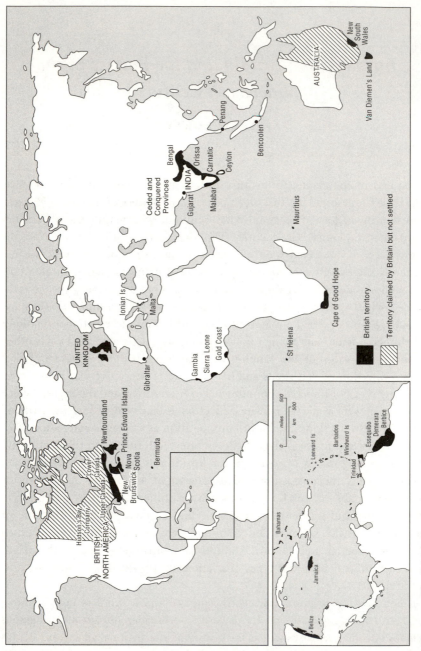

MAP 1.1. The British Empire in 1815

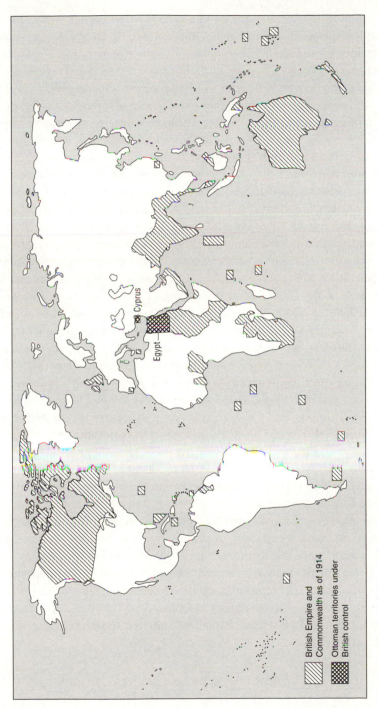

Cyprus

Egypt

British Empire and
Commonwealth as of 1914

Ottoman territories under
British control

MAP 1.2. The British Empire in 1914

Consequently they have developed a keener awareness not only of the strengths but also the weaknesses of Britain's Imperial system. They no longer see in Empire the simple products of metropolitan designs imposed on comparatively inert indigenous peoples. They are much more alive to the varied processes of interaction, adaptation, and exchange which shaped the Imperial and colonial past.

The nineteenth-century Empire was made up of three distinct but overlapping components. An Empire of white settlement, truncated by losses in America, was already growing again by 1800; an Empire in India had expanded enormously since 1756; and an Empire of conquests or wartime acquisitions, the 'dependent empire', was continually added to between 1780 and 1914. These were overseen by no one central department, but by several, whose relative powers, responsibilities, and capacity for effective action steadily changed under the impact of events at home and abroad. A particular feature of this process after 1790 was the increasing divergence between the Empire of British subjects claiming rights abroad, and the Empire of dependent or protected people without such statutory claims. In the first case, Britain's own constitutional experience in which parliamentary authority grew at the Crown's expense, as well as North American and West Indian precedents, shaped from the Canada Act (1791) onwards the tradition and institutions of representative and responsible self-government.[1] The other tradition was that rooted in the Quebec Act (1774) which, applied to the dependent Empire, issued in 'Crown Colony' government and preserved Imperial and colonial executive authority in the hands of Imperial ministers and administrators.[2] This division increasingly paralleled the racial and cultural stereotyping central to Imperial life after 1850, but its inherent contradictions were constantly challenged by Afrikaners, French Canadians, and events in both India and Ireland.

Not surprisingly, perhaps, historians have sometimes reached contradictory conclusions about the importance of the Empire and the pervasiveness of its influence. This is partly because the Empire often merged imperceptibly into a wide range of global British interests which transcended any narrowly territorial view of the world and sources of power or wealth. It is also partly because questions about the 'impact' of either Empire or Britain's presence abroad are ultimately impossible to answer with either precision or confidence. These more cautious but also more sophisticated assessments of the Empire are characteristic of this volume. They represent a significant advance in the study of Britain's classic 'Imperialist' age where estimates of Imperial power are easily exaggerated, and gold, guns, and glory have frequently attracted more than their due share of attention.

---

[1] In Vol. II, see pp. 345; 389 and see below, pp. 185–189.
[2] In Vol. II, see pp. 123; 378 and see below, pp. 185; 188.

The Empire and Expansion

Size, wealth, and population provide striking indicators of how the Empire changed between 1815 and 1914. Of the earlier North Atlantic colonies, the West Indian islands, including the recent wartime additions of Trinidad and what became British Guiana, were still contributing £15.4 million or 17.6 per cent of Britain's trade in 1815, but thereafter rapidly lost their relative importance. A century later their stagnant economies generated trade with Britain of only £6.6 million or 0.47 per cent (1913), even though their population, assisted by the inflow of Indian emigrant labourers, had increased from 877,000 to just over 2 million (1911).[3] Like the thirteen colonies before them, it was British North America that provided in white settlement a pattern for the most valuable expansion of Imperial possessions. With the westward extension of Canadian provinces to the Pacific, the emergence of six colonies in Australia and their political federation in 1901, expansion in Southern Africa and New Zealand, a new collection of white settlement colonies was created. In each, the violent dispossession of indigenous peoples, the spread of emigrants and local-born settlers, investment and economic development, transformed in due course insecure or restricted outliers into self-governing, self-confident 'settler capitalist' societies. A total white population in 1815 of perhaps 550,000 and a correspondingly limited trade were transformed into figures of 18.9 million (1911) and £175 million (1909–13).[4] Rates of growth in the Empire of white settlement compared favourably with those at home, and its component Dominions generated approximately 16.5 per cent of Britain's overseas trade.

Notwithstanding this transformation, India remained of paramount importance in any assessment of Imperial assets. By 1819 the Governors-General Wellesley and Hastings had between them brought together much of what was thereafter to constitute British India. Nevertheless, military conquest extended British control into the north-east (1824–26), north-westwards into Sind and the Punjab during the 1840s, and further into Burma in 1852 and 1885. Further annexations of Indian states were made by Lord Dalhousie (1848–56). Although Indian territorial changes were perhaps less striking than those elsewhere, consolidation of British control steadily increased access to India's immense resources and, especially after

---

[3] Figures here and following are derived from: *Annual Statement of the Trade of the United Kingdom with Foreign Countries and British Possessions. 1913 Compared with Four Preceding Years*, P[arliamentary] P[apers] (1914), LXXXII, Cd. 7401, pp. 20–21, and LXXXIII Cd. 7585, Table 1; B. R. Mitchell, *Abstract of British Historical Statistics* (Cambridge, 1962), Tables 10–12; and *International Historical Statistics: Africa and Asia* (London, 1982), Table B.1; and his *International Historical Statistics: The Americas and Australasia* (London, 1983), Table B.1; Vol. II, p. 433; and see below, chap. by P. J. Cain.

[4] See chap. by B. R. Tomlinson.

1870, enhanced her contribution to the global balancing of Britain's international trade. By annexations and natural growth India's population rose from about 40 million to 303 million (1911). In 1815 her world trade stood at only £8 million but grew to £120 million with Britain alone by 1913. With this expansion there evolved other significant connections, through the financial relations of the Government of India with London, Imperial use of India's military forces, and private investment. Although their value to metropolitan Britain is still hotly but inconclusively debated, at least some individuals or sections of British society benefited considerably from them via official employment, pensions, financial arrangements, shipping, and other services.[5] Few contemporaries would have disputed Sir Charles Dilke's assertion that 'from the larger British Imperial point of view the loss of India would be a crushing blow to our trade . . . It would constitute, moreover, so grave an encouragement to our enemies in all parts of the world, that we might expect a rapid growth of separatist feeling in Canada, South Africa, and Australasia, and a general break-up of the British power.'[6] Prestige, especially in India, joined economic ties as vital bulwarks to survival as a Great Power.

Other newly acquired Asian holdings never matched India's importance, but added to an emerging eastern Empire. Hong Kong, acquired in 1842 and extended in 1898 with the 99-year lease of the mainland 'New Territories', grew steadily both in population and as an entrepôt for the China trade (although rapidly overshadowed by Shanghai). In similarly piecemeal fashion, Singapore, the Malayan mainland, and parts of Borneo (Sarawak, Labuan, and North Borneo) were all incorporated into the Empire's political and economic networks.[7]

In direct contrast to India, the nineteenth-century transformation of the Imperial presence in Africa was territorially immense but—with the exception of the Cape Colony and the Transvaal—economically insignificant. Britain's tiny coastal footholds of 1815 had hardly changed by 1865, Lagos alone being annexed in 1861. In the next fifty years, however, colonial expansion inland brought her territory in every quarter of the continent. By 1911 British Africa embraced 2.8 million square miles and a population estimated at nearly 40 million. By contrast, trade at £44 million (1909–13), of which the Union of South Africa provided some £30 million, accounted for a mere 3.8 per cent of British overseas trade, and only 13 per cent of the Empire's trade.[8]

This economic and territorial network was held together and enabled to function by rapid advances in the means and reliability of communication, for

---

[5] See chaps. by D. A. Washbrook and Robin J. Moore.
[6] Charles Dilke, *Problems of Greater Britain*, 2 vols. (London, 1890), II, p. 3.
[7] See chap. by A. J. Stockwell.
[8] See chap. by Colin Newbury.

instance, by the development of steamships, railways, postal services, and tele-graphs.[9] It was also aided by the spread of the English language, by improved business organization, notably in banking and joint-stock enterprise, by a measure of Imperial and colonial government subsidies for rapid and secure mails, and by the Suez Canal. In 1830 the time taken to travel from Liverpool to New York or from London to Calcutta or Sydney had changed little since the eighteenth century; by 1880 the enhanced frequency and relative cheapness of travel and transport had left that earlier world far behind (Tables 12.1–12.6). The combination of territory, capital, and technology turned migration, in part government-spon-sored but overwhelmingly voluntary in inspiration, into a fundamental feature of colonial economic life and social development. In place of the earlier movement of slaves and emigrants within a North Atlantic system, the nineteenth-century Empire developed as a world-wide arena for the vastly greater movement of British and Asian migrants.[10]

Expansion and the Limits of Empire

Notwithstanding the enlargement of Britain's colonial possessions and their commercial value, they were never capable of satisfying more than part of Britain's needs. Well before 1815 Britain's economy had outgrown its Empire, and the subsequent drive for access to new regions and for freer trade with all partners was widely seen as inevitable and necessary.[11] In many parts of the globe, therefore, British trade and investment underwent striking growth, contributing crucially to metropolitan Britain's wealth and well-being. The importance of these connec-tions was such that revived interest in Imperial Preference and protection, both in Britain and her colonies after 1885, was quite unable to alter them.[12]

The wealth and territorial extent of Britain's Empire was itself also far from an unequivocal source of strength. The integration of world trade, for example, meant that not only Britain but colonies and other commercial partners, hitherto often relatively self-contained, now became parts of more extensive economic systems. Far from offering each other partial protection against economic fluctua-tions, they began simultaneously to experience the same worldwide patterns of boom and slump.[13] Global competition also fed long-standing international rivalries, or spawned new ones. The tasks of defending overseas markets, supplies, extended trade routes, telegraphs, and coaling-stations, therefore became more

---

[9] See chap. by Robert Kubicek.

[10] See Vol. II, p. 13; see Map 12.1 for travel times; and chaps. by Marjory Harper and David Northrup.

[11] See chap. by P. J. Cain.

[12] For discussion of this issue see below, pp. 57–62; and chap. by E. H. H. Green.

[13] S. B. Saul, *Studies in British Overseas Trade, 1870–1914* (Liverpool, 1960).

onerous, even as growth itself held out the prospect of finding resources required to mount such defences. Britain's inescapable dependence on her navy forced governments after 1880 to accept the steady escalation of naval estimates, as the defence of the Empire and of overseas trade once more became virtually inseparable.

Advanced capitalist societies, such as the United States and those of western Europe, found mounting levels of British economic activity compatible with their own unfettered political and economic independence. States in Asia, the Middle East, and even Latin America found it more difficult to accommodate the demand by British enterprise for commercial freedom and unfettered access. This led to tensions which in some cases—notably Egypt—resulted in the imposition of direct Imperial control. Other states maintained their independence but, like China in 1839–42, 1856–60, and 1900, were at intervals subjected to the pressures of war or military intervention and to 'unequal treaties' which limited their economic and territorial sovereignty. Yet others, like Argentina, seemed to manage the impact of British economic expansion well enough, even if they were careful to maintain a complaisant attitude towards British interests.

In such cases, many historians have found inspiration in the concept of 'informal empire', accepting the argument that, at least 'for purposes of economic analysis', it is 'unreal to define imperial history exclusively as the history of those colonies coloured red on the map'.[14] As a result of conscious determination on the part of successive Imperial governments, and of the normal workings of capitalist commerce (the 'invisible hand' of the market), Britain found herself engaged in a wide variety of political relationships with societies overseas. These ranged from colonies where Britain exercised full and effective sovereignty to wholly independent states over whom Britain perhaps could not, but certainly neither needed nor wished to exercise authority. These relations, of course, often changed, and no territory necessarily remained throughout the century at the same point on the spectrum. There was always, however, an intermediate category of territories, some perhaps not yet colonies or possibly no longer so, where Britain nevertheless both wanted and directly or indirectly exercised a dominant political and economic influence. They were areas of control without responsibility, best described as parts of a British 'informal empire', their subordinate position shaped by the workings of 'the imperialism of free trade'.

The value of 'informal empire' for understanding Britain's nineteenth-century global order is nevertheless disputed. Some historians feel the concept raises peculiarly difficult questions. How, for example, does one decide whether or not

---

[14] John Gallagher and Ronald Robinson, 'The Imperialism of Free Trade', *Economic History Review* (hereafter *EcHR*), VI, 1 (1953), p. 1.

an 'imperial' or 'colonial' relationship exists—by consulting contemporary observers or modern statisticians? What kind and degree of influence or control exercised by Britain qualifies a region for inclusion in her 'informal empire'? Some historians acknowledge the concept's value but doubt whether there was ever a systematic preference—official or unofficial—for informal empire, or indeed that it was consciously embodied in the policy of successive British governments.[15] The complexity of Britain's relationships with the extra-European world, and the persistence of this debate, are therefore addressed in several chapters below. The general overview offered in this book from a metropolitan perspective[16] highlights some of the concept's limitations; but it reaches conclusions quite different from those of two local regional studies. In Latin America the scale and impact of the British presence, even if seen as negligible from London, appears to have been often intense and all-pervasive, despite an absence of obvious local protest.[17] In East Asia, despite local success in circumscribing Britain's presence and intervention, deep cultural differences between British and Chinese and the resulting intense sense of humiliation produced a relationship which was seen by the Chinese as undeniably colonial and peculiarly oppressive, and provoked them on occasion to extreme violence.[18] The position in Siam was different again.[19]

The economic expansion which underpinned much of Britain's Empire-building, formal or informal, was such that in mid-century her merchants could confidently claim that 'this country is more than ever the entrepôt for the world'.[20] However, this welcome circumstance was far from simply the result of British initiative or dynamism, and many besides the British benefited from it. The resources of other countries or regions, the adaptability of their people and institutions, as well as their physical environments, combined to shape not only the emerging world economy and Britain's place within it, but also the evolution of her Empire.[21] The strength of local or regional economies was often such that British expansion was conditional on them. British trade was often conducted on others' terms, and frequently assumed only a modest role when compared with the volume of local economic activity. This was especially so in many parts of Asia, where, not only well before but particularly after 1870, intra-Asian trade had its

---

[15] John Darwin, 'Imperialism and the Victorians: The Dynamics of Territorial Expansion', *English Historical Review*, CXII (1997), pp. 614–42.

[16] See chap. by Martin Lynn.

[17] See chap. by Alan Knight.

[18] See chap. by Jürgen Osterhammel.

[19] See below, pp. 380–81, 383–84, 387–89.

[20] C. B. Skinner to C. H. Brown, 18 June 1863, Jardine Skinner Papers, Cambridge University Library.

[21] See chap. by B. R. Tomlinson.

own significant momentum, largely independent of British or other connections. The growth of a global economy in the nineteenth century was driven full-steam-ahead by many different engines. In the offer and export, for instance, of her extensive financial services (banking, insurance, organization of capital invest-ment), Britain was not only integrating new partners into her own expanding economy, but was herself being incorporated by others.[22]

The relationship of economic interest and the Empire was thus widely variable, and never pointed in a single direction. Failure to achieve significant economic growth, or the breakdown of conditions within which British interests could flourish, were variously offered as reasons for British withdrawal or for annexa-tion, as illustrated in parts of West Africa such as the Gambia or the Niger valley. In the British West Indies an unprecedented replacement of colonial self-government by direct rule was the consequence of economic decline and escalating class or racial tensions.[23] Conversely, economic promise contributed both to the assertion of Imperial political controls, as in parts of southern Africa in the 1870s, and to their relaxation, as was the case with the Australasian colonies in the 1850s.

Empire and International Relations

When compared with earlier and later periods, the nineteenth century is some-times viewed as remarkable for the absence of substantial international conflict. After 1815, only in the Crimean War (1854–56) did Britain go to war with another European power, Russia; for no more than brief spells (1842–45, 1896–98) did she come close to war with her ancient enemy France. By European standards it was a century of peace and 'small wars'. Even the South African War (1899–1902) remained essentially a colonial conflict: Britain's European critics muttered belli-gerently on the sidelines but officially refused to become directly involved. Never-theless, although encounters with major competitors were less destructive than those of the previous century,[24] Imperial rivalries shaped British foreign policy, and frequently encouraged territorial expansion on strategic grounds. India and the white colonies were too important for their communications and defence to be neglected.

If, until 1815, France was the power to be feared above all others,[25] after 1815 France, together with Russia, were the two imperial powers of whom Britain had

[22] Shigeru Akita, 'British Informal Empire in East Asia, 1880s–1930s: A Japanese Perspective', in Janet Hunter, ed., *Japanese Perspectives on Imperialism in Asia* (London School of Economics Discussion Paper, 1995); B. R. Tomlinson, 'The Contraction of England: National Decline and Loss of Empire', *Journal of Imperial and Commonwealth History* (hereafter *JICH*), XI (1982), pp. 58–72.

[23] See chap. by Gad Heuman.

[24] In Vol. II, see esp. chaps. 7–9.

[25] In Vol. II, see p. 20.

most cause to be suspicious. Continuing uncertainty about French ambitions partly reflected the legacy of mistrust generated from before 1815. It was reinforced by recurrent French attempts to calm domestic discontent and to restore international prestige by overseas interventions or colonial expansion overseas.[26] Whether by accident or (as British observers, especially after 1870, suspected) design, French activity often seemed to threaten or pre-empt British interests. This was particularly true in the Mediterranean and North Africa, above all in Egypt, scene of Napoleon's strategic thrust towards India in 1798; in New Zealand and Polynesia in the 1830s and 1840s; periodically along the East African coasts from France's position in Réunion and the Comoro Islands (Natal in the 1840s; Zanzibar in 1862 and 1873–74; Madagascar from 1884/85); after 1879 in Senegal, other parts of West Africa, and the Sudan; and occasionally elsewhere, as in the Siam crisis of 1893 and in southern China.

Russia was also viewed with deep mistrust because of her size, the presumed power of her armed forces, and her lack of sympathy with the liberalism of which Britain saw herself as a prime representative. More serious, however, was Russia's territorial expansion, south-westwards to the Black Sea and Mediterranean, south through Central Asia towards Persia, and on the north-western approaches to India. By 1818 these were for British strategists the outer marches of India, to be defended against further external encroachment. No decade passed without serious crises in Anglo-Russian relations on one or other of these three westerly fronts.[27] Russian pressure on China built up in the 1860s and intensified in the 1890s.

Two additional considerations exacerbated British concern with these French and Russian 'threats'. The Franco-Russian alliance following the Treaty of Tilsit (1807) until 1812 provided a persistent reminder of Britain's vulnerability in both Asia and Europe should the two powers combine forces. Their renewed alliance in 1893–94, just as Germany was becoming more aggressively expansionist, brought Britain fifteen years of acute concern for the security of her Indian Empire, and the adequacy of Imperial defences from the North Sea to Hong Kong. As Robert Hart, then Inspector-General of the Chinese Maritime Customs, wrote to his Scottish colleague James Campbell: 'What I long feared is apparently coming: China, between Russia in the north and France in the south, is going to walk arm in arm with them: what will that lead to? Much trouble for England to begin with...'[28]

---

[26] C. M. Andrew and A. S. Kanya-Forstner, 'Centre and Periphery in the Making of the Second French Colonial Empire, 1815–1920', *JICH*, XVI, 3 (1988), pp. 9–34.

[27] David Gillard, *The Struggle for Asia, 1828–1914: A Study in British and Russian Imperialism* (London, 1977).

[28] 24 May 1896, in John King Fairbank, Katherine Frost Bruner, and Elizabeth Macleod Matheson, eds., *The I. G. in Peking: Letters of Robert Hart Chinese Maritime Customs, 1868–1907*, 2 vols. (Cambridge, Mass., 1975), II, p. 1,065.

The British were also alarmed by the fragility of the three non-European empires—Ottoman, Persian, and Chinese—which, together with Afghanistan, occupied so much of the central ground between the main Franco-Russian and British spheres of interest from the western Mediterranean to the China Sea. At best their rulers were regarded as 'inefficient', 'corrupt', often 'brutal' and 'untrustworthy', but 'amenable' both to grudging reform and to diplomatic co-operation in their own self-interest. Such confidence, however, generally waned after mid-century, along with earlier hopes of trade with Persia and Central Asia. Evidence of 'incompetence', 'crumbling central authority', and 'internal disorder' left few but the most visionary believing that ultimate collapse could be more than temporarily postponed by British diplomatic support, the provision of loans, and railway construction. In such volatile conditions, French or Russian interference might rapidly expand into pre-emptive occupation at the expense of British interests and Imperial security.

After the flurry of Russian conflicts with Turkey and Persia between 1826 and 1833, such fears—real or imagined—were never far from officials' minds in Britain and India. To Wellington, the then Prime Minister, Lord Ellenborough, President of the Board of Control, described his 'presentiment that, step by step as the Persian monarchy is broken up, [the Russians] will extend their influence and advance their troops . . . till, without quarrelling with us, they have crept on to Cabul, where they may at their leisure prepare a force for the invasion of India'.[29] Similar fears of French expansion played a part in Palmerston's determination during the Ottoman crisis of 1839–41 to uphold the Sultan's authority and check Muhammad Ali in Egypt, widely seen as France's client. They influenced the calculations which from 1875 led to Britain's occupation of Egypt in 1882 and her continued control thereafter.[30] Britain ensconced in Egypt gained not only local advantage over France and greater security for the Suez Canal route to India, but above all an important lever in negotiating with the Ottoman government to contain Russian expansion into Turkey and the eastern Mediterranean. Cyprus, acquired in 1878, strengthened her further. In 1892 Lord Salisbury, Prime Minister and Foreign Secretary, made the position abundantly clear:

The protection of Constantinople from Russian conquest has been the turning point of the policy of this country for at least forty years, and to a certain extent for forty years before that. . . It is our principal, if not our only, interest in the Mediterranean Sea; for if Russia were mistress of Constantinople, and of the influence which Constantinople possesses in the Levant, the route to India through the Suez Canal would be so much exposed as not to be available except in times of the profoundest peace. I need not dwell upon the effect which

[29]   26 Sept. 1828, quoted in Gillard, *Struggle for Asia*, p. 31.
[30]   See chap. by Afaf Lutfi al-Sayyid-Marsot.

the Russian possession of Constantinople would have upon the Oriental mind, and upon our position in India, which is so largely dependent on prestige.[31]

Sensitive to Great Power concerns, sultans, khedives, shahs, amirs, khans, and kings skilfully played their hands in what became known as 'the Great Game', pitting one power against another in defence of their own independence. While sometimes unable to avoid war, they were frequently successful in holding their own, secure in the knowledge that should any power attempt to gain a disproportionate advantage, other rivals would probably join forces in protest. Rarely did any Great Power thus wish to precipitate a European war. So the Ottoman Sultan was saved on several occasions by Great Power intervention from internal and external threats. In 1839–41, 1854–56, and 1877–78 the British preferred survival of the Sultan's authority to any likely alternative, and found other Great Powers who agreed with them. Occasions when the Great Powers achieved anything like a common front to force a non-European empire into line were few and short-lived, as was illustrated by the despatch of the international force to put down the Chinese Boxer Rebellion in 1901.

The triangular rivalry of Britain, France, and Russia was complicated after 1870 by mounting challenges from new claimants to colonial power. Italy's colonial ambitions in Tripolitania and the Horn of Africa pressed against British interest in the security of routes to India. Germany's developing territorial ambitions, chiefly in west, east, and south-west Africa, and the Pacific, were accommodated by Britain without much difficulty from 1884 to 1890, but subsequent initiatives were more worrisome. Germany's rapid commercial expansion, incursions into the Middle and Far East, her designs on the dilapidated Portuguese and Spanish empires, and above all her conspicuous naval expansion, caused serious alarm between 1895 and 1914. The United States was also becoming a major commercial rival, and her suspicion of Britain's presence in Latin America brought on the dispute over Venezuela's boundaries in 1895. America's naval ambitions in the Pacific became steadily clearer, and her expansionist goals were signalled by her seizure of Spanish territory in the Caribbean and Philippines (1898).

Anxious to avoid war and keen to defend their frontiers and communications along Eurasia's geopolitical fault-line, British governments in search of stability had three principal courses open to them: locally negotiated treaties of alliance, and support—often financial—for buffer states; Great Power diplomacy, perhaps leading to regional partition; or outright conquest. All were used at different times, sometimes singly, sometimes in combination. Afghanistan was a perpetual object of British concern, the focus of conflicting strategies variously advanced by

---

[31] Quoted by C. J. Lowe, *The Reluctant Imperialists: British Foreign Policy, 1878–1902*, 2 vols. (London, 1967), II, p. 86.

Political Agents, Governor-Generals, and Viceroys in India, as well as politicians and their advisers in London. The search for an alliance, agreements in 1855 and 1857, the courting of rivals and offer of subsidies, and two wars (in 1839–42 and 1878–79), left the British little further forward. After 1880 Afghanistan only became less troublesome because Britain and Russia agreed on delimiting frontiers; when their attention shifted to other parts of India's northern frontier, confrontation and crises also moved—to Penjdeh in 1885, the Pamirs in 1891 and 1893–94. But any war likely to pit Britain against another European power was carefully avoided. The diplomacy of global partition was generally successful in delimiting spheres of interest and influence, for instance between Britain and Russia in Persia in 1907, and all the Great Powers in China *c.*1900. Within these spheres Britain imitated her rivals, seeking to consolidate political influence by informal support for selected banks, such as the Imperial Bank of Persia or the Hongkong and Shanghai Bank, or through concessionaries, such as Sir Ernest Cassel.[32]

Similar alternatives were available in the power vacuum that was Africa. Until the 1860s, except in the far south, Britain only teetered on the edges of the continent.[33] European exploration and technological or medical advances only slowly overcame the geographical and environmental difficulties of access to the interior.[34] Economic interest and political pressures, even strategic interest in the Mediterranean and Cape routes to the East, were rarely sufficient to overcome the Imperial government's reservations about involvement far inland.

In West Africa, after abolition of the British slave trade in 1807, commercial activity was sparse, and control of Britain's few settlements passed to and fro between merchants and the Imperial government. Official commitment against the slave trade, expressed in the formalization of Sierra Leone as an official British colony for freed slaves in 1808 and the West African naval squadron to capture slavers, was weighed constantly against the pressures for withdrawal, arising from inadequate revenues, escalating costs, and appalling mortality. Despite the emergence of palm oil as an important trade staple from the late 1820s, the 1821 experiment with centralized administration of the settlements under the British Governor at Freetown lasted only until 1828, and subsequent hopes of organizing British possessions from Fernando Po died by 1834.[35] Mercantile control of the Gold Coast trading forts, surrendered in 1821, was reinstated in 1828 but again reclaimed for the Imperial government in 1843. Further rationalization was

---

[32] David McLean, 'Finance and "Informal Empire" before the First World War', *EcHR*, XXIX (1976), pp. 291–305.

[33] See chaps. by T. C. McCaskie, and Christopher Saunders and Iain R. Smith.

[34] See below, pp. 306–07; *passim.*

[35] R. T. Brown, 'Fernando Po and the Anti- Sierra Leone Campaign, 1826–34', *International Journal of African Historical Studies*, VI (1973), pp. 249–64.

attempted in 1850 with the purchase of the Danish forts and the re-establishment of a Governor separate from Sierra Leone.

Beyond the territorial remit of colonial Governors, the official approach of the early Victorians came to rely on a haphazard array of local treaties and a scattering of British Consuls. On the East African coast, the aims of checking the slave trade, protecting British Indian traders, and providing a counterweight to American and French influence were served by the appointment of a Consul at Zanzibar from 1840, diplomatic support for its Sultan, and a fitful naval presence. From the late 1840s until 1861, before the River Niger was established as the principal artery of trade, a series of British Vice-Consulates attended to the trans-Saharan trade routes between north and west Africa. Captain John Beecroft was appointed Consul for the Bights of Benin and Biafra in 1849, and a further Consul was sent to Lagos in 1853.[36] Nevertheless, despite these commitments, British withdrawal from all but Sierra Leone remained a possibility, as the parliamentary enquiry of 1865 clearly showed.

However, as in Asia and the Middle East so in sub-Saharan Africa, neither withdrawal nor neglect proved possible. Government inertia was overtaken from about 1870 by local conflicts arising from commercial fluctuations and heightened competition; problems of adaptation experienced by local societies; and the interplay of local politics with increasing Great Power rivalry. Again, partition and the exploitation of private business ambitions provided at least some temporary answers, with Britain's diplomatic compromises being gradually hammered into place by military conquest and pacification.[37] Britain's African territories were acquired quickly, in a predominantly reactive process at once unplanned and opportunistic. Contemporaries were more struck by the dramatic episodes of the Scramble, the heroics of Africa's explorers, and the exotic curiosities of its people, than impressed with the substance it brought to the Empire.

The Supervision of Empire

In Britain, no one agency was charged with managing the Empire. Global issues of Imperial rivalry, security, and economic competition were the responsibility in the first instance of the Foreign Office. Diplomacy was conducted through direct ambassadorial relations with a tiny number of capitals (Paris, St Petersburg, Constantinople), and through complex networks of British Ministers, Consuls,

---

[36] A. Adu Boahen, *Britain, the Sahara and the Western Sudan, 1788–1861* (Oxford, 1964), chaps. 7–9; K. Onwuka Dike, *Trade and Politics in the Niger Delta, 1830–1885* (Oxford, 1956).

[37] See chap. by Colin Newbury.

Political Agents, and other diplomatic officials, with lesser states.[38] To the high-political concerns of peace, war, and treaty negotiations were added commercial relations, slave trade diplomacy, issues of extraterritorial rights and jurisdiction, information gathering, and the supervision of Protectorates. Overseen from London, the East India Company and later the Government of India performed similar functions within their own steadily expanding geographical sphere. This took in not only British India's internal and immediate external neighbours (such as Afghanistan or Nepal), but, following British and Indian traders, the Persian Gulf and the further shores of the Indian Ocean. The British Agency established at Zanzibar in 1841 came under the Government of Bombay until 1873, as did ports such as Aden (1839) and Bushire; in the East, Calcutta oversaw relations with the Straits Settlements (1826–67) and with Burma.

Alongside the Foreign and India Offices were the Admiralty and the War Office, responsible for strategic planning and administering the resources available to defend Britain and its possessions abroad. The expansion of British colonies and trade increased demands for troops and ships, and technological changes had to be absorbed if weapons were not to become outdated and if rivals were to be denied any offensive advantage. However, domestic concerns to save money, colonial wishes that Britain should pay, and inter-service competition or professional *amour-propre*, meant that defence policies were normally the variable outcomes of political manœuvres and Imperial disunity rather than victories for long-term planning. London fell back with growing frequency on the use of Indian troops abroad. Effective co-ordination of her armed forces and their integration into broader defensive structures or processes of Imperial policy-making were very slow to develop, notwithstanding the creation of the Cabinet's Colonial Defence Committee in 1885.[39]

The bulk of colonial business, reduced by loss of the American colonies and reshaped by conquests during the French wars, was eventually brought together in 1801 under the Secretary of State for War and Colonies. There it remained until 1854, when responsibilities were clearly redistributed between separate War and Colonial Offices. Able ministers with decided views on how the Empire should be run, such as Earl Grey (1846–52), were rarely attracted to an Office which ranked low in political esteem, and few Secretaries of State stayed long. Capable junior ministers, such as W. E. Gladstone (1834–35), cut their teeth on colonial administration; elderly colleagues—Lord Knutsford (1887–92) and Lord Ripon (1892–95)—passed directly into retirement. Only Joseph Chamberlain (1895–1903) was a household name and gave the Office real political weight. Despite extensive official

---

[38] D. C. M. Platt, *The Cinderella Service: British Consuls since 1825* (Hamden, Conn., 1971).
[39] See chap. 15 by Peter Burroughs; and below pp. 442–43.

patronage, it was also difficult to recruit first-rate administrators or diplomats for colonial service.[40] As a result, colonial business was largely dominated by the Office's permanent officials.

Significant shifts in the Office's work occurred during the century. Administration of the conquered and Crown Colonies, and issues associated with slavery predominated until the 1840s; in the mid-century the problems of white settler colonies and the practice of self-government loomed large; later, the Colonial Office had to cope with the territorial consequences of African and Pacific partitions. Naturally the volume and variety of Colonial Office business (together with the attentions of external pressure groups) increased enormously, but it continued to be distributed among a limited number of inadequately staffed geographical departments. Despite the addition of a General Department in 1870, no officials after 1860 ever attained the wide-ranging mastery of colonial affairs demonstrated by Sir James Stephen as Permanent Under-Secretary (1836–47).[41] Yet even under Stephen, the pressure and diversity of business promoted pragmatism and expediency at the expense of long-term planning and principles. As he put it, 'there cannot be two opinions as to the folly and danger of a Government writing abstract and speculative doctrines—that is usurping the place of Professors and Men of Letters'.[42] The combination of political convenience and administrative practicalities produced a steady relaxation of the Office's supervision of the laws passed in white settler colonies, especially after the Colonial Laws Validity Act (1865). By contrast, in the Crown Colonies it relied increasingly on Orders-in-Council based on advice from the Law Officers of the Crown in London rather than on the consultation of local opinion.

Reactions to the management of colonial business varied widely. Self-government notwithstanding, white colonists continually criticized the Colonial Office, and sometimes other departments, for their intrusiveness, insensitivity, patronizing attitudes, inefficiency, and even, in the Crown Agents' raising of colonial government loans, corruption. The development of the Colonial and Imperial Conferences from 1887, and the creation in 1907 of a Dominions Division separate from those supervising Crown Colonies, involved not only administrative rationalization but concessions to the colonists' *amour propre* and their sense of racial superiority over non-white 'dependent' peoples. However, some colonial subjects were less anxious to escape Whitehall's supervision. Encouraged by Wesleyan

[40] See chap. 9 by Peter Burroughs.

[41] D. M. Young, *The Colonial Office in the Early Nineteenth Century* (London, 1961); John W. Cell, *British Colonial Administration in the Mid-Nineteenth Century: The Policy-Making Process* (New Haven, 1970); Brian L. Blakeley, *The Colonial Office, 1868–92* (Durham, NC, 1972); Robert V. Kubicek, *Joseph Chamberlain and the Administration of Imperialism* (Durham, NC, 1969).

[42] Memorandum, 27 March 1845, C[olonial] O[ffice] 217/189.

missionaries, Tswana chiefs preferred its rule to that by the Cape or the British
South Africa Company:

We came to England to ask the Government of the Great Queen to continue her protection
over us. We have seen the justice and kindness with which the Great Queen seeks to govern
us. We know that her officers sometimes make mistakes, because they are not of our race,
and cannot think our thoughts or understand our customs. But there is no Government
that we can trust as we trust that of the Great Queen...[43]

The Tswana were perhaps in the long term more satisfied than many supplicants
with the settlement of their claims, for it kept them politically outside the Union of
South Africa in 1910.[44] However, there were also those who rejected the niceties of
negotiation. Imperial reliance on collaboration with colonial élites coexisted with
an undercurrent of low-level violence and dissent, and was punctuated with
dramatic outbursts of large-scale protest.[45] The threats to Imperial prestige and
authority posed by the great Indian Mutiny and Rebellion of 1857, the Morant Bay
Rebellion of 1865, the Mahdist regime in the Sudan (1884–98), the Sierra Leone
Hut Tax War (1898), and the South African War (1899–1902), were such as to alter
the practices of Imperial rulers for decades afterwards.

These diverse colonial reactions had to be managed by the Imperial departments in London and by the local agents responsible for the day-to-day conduct of
Britain's colonial rule. The never-ending search for a sustainable balance of
interests was certainly a task that stretched their political inventiveness and
administrative ingenuity to the utmost.[46] Where possible they used control of
patronage, taxation, and public works to win support and consent. Constitutional
devices were tailored to local conditions: representative institutions, up to and
including responsible government in the colonies of white settlement; 'Crown
Colony' government; Protectorates; High Commissions; and chartered companies.
The circumstances in which they were adopted were equally varied. Sometimes
they opened up new political opportunities to colonial subjects. The reverse was
also to be found, not least in India and early colonial Africa. Rule, especially over
indigenous populations, was often unavoidably based on skewed or imperfect
knowledge of local societies, subject to individual caprice or ability, affected by
preoccupation with revenue, security, or prestige and so ill-devised or oppressive,
even if unwittingly. Protest and resistance were often the consequence of serious or

---

[43] To Joseph Chamberlain, 24 Sept. 1895, Frederick Madden (with David Fieldhouse), eds., *Select Documents on the Constitutional History of the British Empire and Commonwealth*, 7 vols. Vol. V, *The Dependent Empire and Ireland, 1840–1900: Advance and Retreat in Representative Self-Government* (London, 1991), V, p. 662.

[44] See below, pp. 620–22.

[45] See below, pp. 405–07, 413, 418–19, 454; 456; 461–67; 678–684.

[46] See, chap. 9 by Peter Burroughs; and Part II of this volume.

sustained British miscalculation; but much of the time a sufficient balance of interests was achieved for Britain's presence to be tolerated by those who carried most weight in colonial societies.

Imperial and Colonial Cultures

Alongside their long-standing preoccupation with the economics and government of Empire, historians have developed comparatively recently an interest in its cultures. By 'culture' is meant the ideas, values, social habits, and institutions which were felt to distinguish the British and their colonial subjects from each other, and which gave to both their sense of identity, purpose, and achievement. Understood in this way, 'culture' clearly influenced and was influenced by expansion, economic practice, and the nature of government; it was also shaped by the encounters of different peoples within the framework of Empire.

Overseas expansion in the nineteenth century continued as much a 'British' undertaking as it had been earlier.[47] In proportion to the size of the populations, Scottish and especially Irish emigration remained far greater than that of the English; their search for employment and opportunities abroad continued unabated.[48] This is of particular interest in the case of the Irish, the nature of whose relationships with Empire throws much light on both Imperial and colonial affairs.[49] However, the significance of Scots to Imperial expansion, and of Empire for Scotland, is hardly less. There has been a long tradition of writing setting out the Scottish contribution to British Imperial enterprise.[50] Among the Empire's migrants as well as its administrators and soldiers, Scots equalled the English in numbers. Everywhere they became steadily more prominent: in the East India Company; in the great trading firms, such as Jardine Matheson (Asia), Balfour Williamson (Latin America), and Mackinnon Mackenzie (Indian Ocean and East Africa); in organizing and manning shipping companies, such as the City, Clan, and Castle Lines, and the British India Steam Navigation Company, as well as in managing and equipping many lesser firms, such as the Irrawaddy Flotilla Company; and in Scottish missions, scattered across the globe.

Far from debilitating Scotland itself, these family and professional connections with Scots overseas invigorated the home economy and society in ways which supported its individuality or scope for manœuvre within the United Kingdom.[51]

---

[47] In Vol. II, see pp. 9; 38–49; 272–74.
[48] See chap. by Marjory Harper.
[49] See chap. by David Fitzpatrick.
[50] See below, pp. 273–74, 289–90.
[51] John M. MacKenzie, 'On Scotland and the Empire', *International History Review*, XV (1993), pp. 714–39.

In a gesture dismissive of those who emphasized the narrowly chauvinist or exclusively Imperial character of missionary enterprise, and simultaneously assertive of Scotland's global role, the World Missionary Conference of 1910 was held in Edinburgh. The smaller Welsh diaspora, much of it from south Wales, has been much less investigated, but both inside and outside the Empire displayed similar characteristics. Local churches, legal institutions, scientific societies, and newspapers held expatriate groups together. St Andrew's Church in Calcutta and the Caledonian Society of Johannesburg had numerous parallels: the 2,000 or so Welsh in the Australian mining town of Ballarat in 1861 soon established their eisteddfod (local festival). For many Welsh and even more Scots and Irish, the Empire was the vehicle through which they expressed their own nationality and contributed to Britain's greatness.[52] Indeed, it can be argued that such particular-isms exported overseas often helped strengthen the Empire. The Irish or Scottish backgrounds of some administrators, such as Sir Richard Bourke (Governor of New South Wales, 1831–38) and Sir William MacGregor (Governor of Lagos, 1899–1904), were associated with a flexible, liberal approach to their role, something as welcome to settlers or Lagosians as it was detested by conservative English expatriate officials.

In one sense the 'Britishness' of the Empire was inclusive, its colonies being conspicuously occupied and ruled by the British rather than merely the English. At the end of the century 'Britishness' was enhanced by improved communications and the relative decline of the United States as an emigrant destination. But the century also witnessed a growing insistence on difference, on the inevitable diversity of the Empire, and a more explicit acceptance of limits to its 'Britishness'. The white colonies shared many common features, especially their overwhelming dependence on agriculture and export trades in staple commodities or raw materials, despite the increasingly urban character and protectionist sentiments of many settlers. Their populations remained very youthful; 20 per cent of Canada's people were under the age of 14 in 1901, 34 per cent of Australia's under 15.[53] Such common characteristics, however, were perfectly compatible with the weakening of British influences. In all settler colonies, the numbers of local-born inhabitants rapidly increased, while the proportion of those with British ancestry fell. The enormous influx of immigrants to Canada between 1895 and 1914 con-tained large numbers of Ukrainians, Poles, Russians, Italians, and Scandinavians, many of them Jews. After about 1840 English-speaking migrants, French Canad-

[52] Ged Martin and Benjamin E. Kline, 'The Welsh and the Empire', in P. J. Marshall, ed., *The Cambridge Illustrated History of the British Empire* (Cambridge, 1996), p. 265; Bob Reece, 'The Welsh in Australian Historical Writing', *Australian Studies*, IV (1990), pp. 88–104.

[53] J. M. Bumsted, *The Peoples of Canada: A Post-Confederation History* (Toronto, 1992), p. 484; Beverley Kingston, *The Oxford History of Australia, Volume 3, 1860–1900* (Melbourne, 1988), p. 116.

ians, and Afrikaners were increasingly left to govern themselves, to organize their own societies, and to work out their own political compromises. In white settler colonies by 1860, the wisdom of separating church and state, political anathema at home, was generally accepted, and controls over colonial trade or land policy had been reluctantly surrendered by London. Within broadly similar constitutional frameworks, the settler communities thus steadily diverged from each other as London's retreat and the working of responsible government gave expression to different constellations of social and economic interests.

Conventional interpretations of this process in the nineteenth-century history of white settler societies have charted a course from the original British settlements, moulded by immigration, economic development and integration, class formation, social diversification, and political evolution via responsible government, to new and distinct Dominions.[54] These were genuinely nation states, culturally emancipated, hankering after self-assertion on the global scene, but still linked to the British Empire by sentimental attachments and acceptable degrees of material dependence. It was a saga wrapped in the warm language of family ties, still studded with the contemporary imagery of mother and children, and reaching its immediate apogee in the mutual sacrifices of the First World War.

Elements of this traditional interpretation remain important, perhaps most evidently in New Zealand, where the white sense of local distinctiveness from Australia, and of domestic progressiveness on many fronts, including welfare and race relations, developed alongside a self-confident acceptance of unusually close Imperial ties. However, most of the chapters which follow might be said to reflect the late twentieth-century's less sanguine views of families as frequently divided if not dysfunctional institutions. The marginalization or worse of women and indigenous peoples in colonial societies, much-emphasized in recent historical research, has further qualified the optimistic perspectives of the older narratives.[55]

There is scant sense of maturity attained, for example, in a Canada showing by 1914 'no indication' of 'moving towards decolonization and full nationhood'. Evidence from Canada—where 'political union did little to overcome incoherent diversity'—of continuing internal disunity and unawareness of shared interests, highly selective and self-serving regard for Imperial solidarity or common principles, and limited capacity or willingness for self-defence, were nevertheless not unique.[56] The overarching sense of identity seems no less feeble in the federated Australia of the early 1900s. Where Canada was overshadowed by the United

---

[54] A. R. M. Lower, *From Colony to Nation* (Toronto, 1946); Donald Creighton, *Dominion of the North* (New York, 1944).

[55] For New Zealand, see chap. by Raewyn Dalziel. In Vol. V, see chap. by James Belich.

[56] See chap. by Ged Martin, esp. pp. 522, 525.

States, many Australians—Queenslanders perhaps most of all—felt threatened by French, German, and American expansion in the western Pacific, and by a growing Japanese or Asian 'threat'. Exclusion and restraint—'white Australia, racial hierarchy, the domestication of women, and the taming of trade unions'—seem to have provided the cement of federation.[57] The same was true of South Africa, where consolidation, having failed in the Anglicized forms projected successively by Lord Carnarvon, Joseph Chamberlain, and Lord Milner, finally emerged from the divisions of English-speaking communities in the form of the Union in 1910 which entrenched the political and economic power of a white, Transvaal-dominated minority for the next eighty years.[58] Except when local crises necessitated appeals to Britain, there was a widespread colonial awareness of having ceased to be unequivocally British, but as yet no clear sense of something distinctive to put in its place.

Critical to ideas of white communal solidarity in these colonial societies, which combined egalitarian political institutions with growing sectional and class divisions, was often less the sense of nationality than the issue of race. At the levels both of Empire and colony, the definition of races (or in the words of Cecil Rhodes, 'civilized men') held enormous potential for justifying rule, generating unity, and for establishing practices of political or administrative exclusion. Some observers thought that racial ties rendered divergence among settler colonies insignificant. Of his tour of the English-speaking world, Greater Britain, in 1866–67, Charles Dilke noted: 'If I remarked that climate, soil, manners of life, that mixture with other peoples had modified the blood, I saw, too, that in essentials the race was always one.' Twenty-five years on, he felt no differently. 'The type of the Anglo-Saxon of the future, growing up in Canada, and in South Africa, and in Australia, may not be everywhere the same . . . but essentially the race continues everywhere to be ours.'[59] From his perspective, race consciousness bred optimism. He believed that the 'world's future . . . belongs to the Anglo-Saxon, to the Russian and the Chinese races; of whom the Chinese in their expansion across the seas tend to fall under the influence of India and the Crown Colonies of Great Britain'.[60]

Racial superiority, increasingly taken for granted from mid-century, thus gave grounds for pride and confidence that the Empire would hold together. This confidence was further strengthened by the frequently noted decline and the anticipated extinction of some indigenous peoples—Maoris, Aborigines, 'Hottentots', and Native Americans—and the existence of those 'dying nations' iden-

---

[57] See chap. by Donald Denoon with Marivic Wyndham esp. p. 548.

[58] See below, pp. 606–07, 615–622.

[59] Charles Wentworth Dilke, *Greater Britain: A Record of Travel in English-Speaking Countries during 1866 and 1867*, 2 vols. (London, 1868), I, p. vii; *Problems of Greater Britain*, II, p. 579.

[60] Dilke, *Problems of Greater Britain*, II, p. 582.

tified by Lord Salisbury.[61] Race-consciousness, in other words, was from one angle both a source and reinforcement of the British character of the Empire. However, few expounded their racial credentials with the patrician detachment of Dilke, Salisbury, or Lord Curzon. Racial ideas encouraged aggressive assertions of difference by Imperial officials as much as colonial workers, by women no less than men, which accentuated the limits to both the Empire's 'Britishness' and heady ideas of common citizenship. Not for nothing did early Indian nationalists complain of the 'unBritishness of British rule' and growing racial discrimination in the administrative and judicial system. Beneath the umbrella of appeals to Britain's obligations and capacity for 'good government', racial feeling prompted an over-ready imposition of authority, exposed too blatantly the force underlying Imperial relationships, and so tended to undermine Empire.

As Governor of the Cape, Sir Alfred Milner, for example, was sensitive to every possible affront to the 'race patriotism' which served him as a religion. He therefore dismissed Transvaal Afrikaners' claims as the pretentions of a 'medieval race oligarchy', utterly inadmissible because involving 'the *permanent inferiority* of men of British race'.[62] The behaviour of white settlers and other expatriates led contemporaries to distinguish between the acceptable and unacceptable faces of race feeling. New Zealanders at war with Maoris provoked Lord Salisbury to observe that there 'is no sounder test of a high and true civilization than its dealings with a race of helpless savages. Its office is to rub off prejudices, and there is no prejudice so catlike in its vitality as the prejudice of race.'[63] That New Zealanders had failed the test, he had no doubt. Gladstone was similarly shocked and depressed by the outcry of Anglo-Indians in 1883 over the judicial reforms in the Ilbert Bill, and among others, Dilke commented at length on the development of racial conflict between white colonial and Asian labour.[64]

Late-nineteenth-century British concern about racialism was prompted by dislike of its crudity and accompanying violence, and by fears about the political dangers of overt discrimination. Only rarely were the underlying premises openly challenged. This reflected how British thinking about race had changed considerably in the course of the century. Humanitarians, religious reformers, and Imperial administrators had been disappointed in their expectations of the transformation and progress of indigenous peoples. Accounts of travel and exploration did little to relieve the gloom.[65] Struck by the slowness of change or

[61] *The Times*, 5 May 1898, p. 7c; 10 Nov. 1898, p. 8f.

[62] Letters to Lord Selborne, 9 May 1898, 17 May 1899, Cecil Headlam, ed., *The Milner Papers: South Africa, 1897–1899*, 2 vols. (London, 1931), I, pp. 232–35, 384.

[63] 'The Story of New Zealand', *Saturday Review*, 7 Jan. 1860, IX, p. 19.

[64] Letter to Lord Northbrook, 15 Dec. 1883, H. C. G. Matthew, ed., *The Gladstone Diaries: Volume XI, July 1883–December 1886* (Oxford, 1990), p. 77; Dilke, *Problems of Greater Britain*, II, pp. 299–313.

[65] See below, pp. 213–14, 216–17; 294–319; 459–61; 491–92.

colonial populations' apparent rejection of much that they had offered, and usually insensitive to the extent of indigenous adaptation, the British gradually abandoned the late-eighteenth-century consensus that the hierarchy of human societies rested on *cultural* not racial differences. Assumptions that human nature was everywhere uniform, and that cultures could therefore be easily transformed, were slowly relinquished. Instead, there took hold a belief in the underlying reality of permanent *racial* divisions, and in the limits which this set to cultural change. The accumulating knowledge of the Asian and African worlds was widely held to support these views, as was the development of new scientific and evolutionary understandings of race. Stereotypes multiplied, and were widely popularized, often in arguments about the inevitability of social-Darwinist, interracial struggles for survival.[66] Expressed, for example, by Benjamin Kidd in terms of the superior 'social efficiency' of the Anglo-Saxon race, they made Imperial rule seem less hopeful and more necessary. This was memorably captured by Rudyard Kipling's exhortation in 1899 to those other Anglo-Saxons, the Americans, to join the British in taking up 'the White Man's burden' of rule over 'new-caught sullen peoples, half-devil and half-child'.[67] They reinforced administrative authoritarianism and reluctance to involve local peoples—especially the western-educated—in colonial government.

For the British, the explicit sense of racial distinctiveness that came to predominate in the second half of the century also had positive aspects. It helped to explain the Empire's growth and justify the costs and exertions to maintain it; it was held to excuse some of Empire's destructiveness and oppression. Contemporaries attributed many Imperial achievements to the progressive tendencies of their race—economic growth, law and order, good government, free institutions and civil liberties, an end to indigenous warfare, protection for the vulnerable, greater respect for women, and the spread of true religion. Such racial awareness, however, also produced its mirror images among the Empire's non-British peoples. In many of them, experience of Empire began to provoke a heightened sense of identity, an enhanced awareness of local potential, and an eagerness to bring out the best in their own societies by adopting the most attractive features of western ways and beliefs.

It is a fascinating, but perhaps ultimately unanswerable, question whether British India, given the range and intensity of the Imperial impact over more than two centuries, was more or less decisively reshaped by the experience of colonial rule than was, for instance, Southern Africa, refashioned in barely fifty

---

[66] See chap. by Robert A. Stafford and chap. by John M. Mackenzie, esp. pp. 282–290.
[67] Benjamin Kidd, *Social Evolution* (London, 1895), esp. pp. 303–29; *A Choice of Kipling's Verse Selected with an Essay on Rudyard Kipling by T. S. Eliot* (London, 1963 edn.), p. 136.

years to the requirements of a modern, urban, and industrialized economy. Two chapters in particular address this encounter, from the African and Asian perspectives respectively.[68] What they reveal is the extent to which colonial peoples almost everywhere chose to select and adapt to their own needs features of British learning, ideas, religious belief, political and other habits, as well as technology and mechanical skills. Together with the worldwide spread of the English language, and the reform and revival of indigenous religions, these developments stimulated not only racial and ethnic consciousness, but the first stirrings of independent 'nationalist' organization.

These changes in colonial cultures meant that the terms on which colonial peoples were prepared to collaborate with the British thus began to change, first in Asia, later in Africa, and especially after 1880. This took place even as the technological gulf between Britain and her dependent peoples reached perhaps its widest extent at the end of the century, and suggests that the relative balance of power between colonizer and colonized can never be measured in material terms alone. As the twentieth century began, British nervousness about the challenge posed by the social and political mobilization of Asian peoples, outside as well as inside the Empire, revealed a sense of the fragility of Imperial control and the limitations of Imperial resources. That events were often seen through racial spectacles only made them less intelligible and more worrying, especially to Europeans in colonies where they were a clear minority. No straightforward evaluation of the consequences of colonial rule is possible, given the 'constantly shifting kaleidoscope of give and take' which characterized the process of cultural encounter and exchange.[69] However, the historian can at least help to give a better understanding of what it may have meant to many non-Europeans individually, and in the longer term to their societies, to have experienced British rule.

Nineteenth-Century Assessments

The variety of economic relationships, the diversity of Britain's presence overseas, the unpredictable patterns of international affairs, the opportunism of nineteenth-century territorial expansion, and the cultural consequences of Empire, all reflect the formative influence of local, peripheral, no less than metropolitan, circumstances. However, while debating endlessly the ethics of Empire, the political wisdom of acquisition, and the practicalities of rule, contemporaries also concerned themselves particularly with what they saw as the measurable assets, gains, and losses of Empire. They tried to offset the economic value of Imperial

---

[68] See chaps. by T. C. McCaskie and Susan Bayly.
[69] See below, p. 665.

trade and investment against the costs of its government and defence, and to assess Empire's value relative to Britain's many other overseas interests. This overarching concern involved conceptual and statistical, as well as political arguments; it has embraced the analysis of economists from Adam Smith to J. A. Hobson, and has continued to intrigue twentieth-century scholars. It is a most fitting subject with which to conclude this volume.[70]

Between 1790 and 1914 there were two periods when these calculations attracted unusual attention. The first was the years 1830–50, which are sometimes held to have seen the end of Britain's *ancien régime*, and during which Britain's shift to free trade was finally confirmed.[71] The second period, approximately 1895–1911, witnessed a powerful challenge to that early Victorian consensus based on support for free trade, laissez-faire, and colonial self-government. International economic and political challenges to Britain had intensified, and the country was unable to sustain its pre-eminence of the 1860s. The case for preserving Britain's position by a programme of Imperial consolidation and colonial development became the centre of a fierce political debate.[72] After 1900 this was related to the many 'lessons' of the South African War, and renewed discussion as to whether Britain was preponderantly an overseas or a European, and therefore continental, Power.

At the heart of the arguments lay—as always—the position of the settler colonies.[73] Distinguished by metropolitan observers in the early 1840s for their social and political insignificance, after 1890 they took on for imperialists everywhere a new importance, in part by reason of their continued growth and prosperity but most of all because of mounting Imperial insecurity and over-extension. On this occasion, however, despite the ever-greater polarization of international politics between 1902 and 1914, there was to be no reordering of the Empire. The wish of the settler colonies to preserve control of their own affairs, the attractions of free trade to the British electorate in 1906, and the weight of the United Kingdom's extra-Imperial interests, were sufficient to defeat the Imperial consolidationists' onslaught.

This was perhaps just as well. Attempts at a new autarchic subordination of tropical colonies to metropolitan needs might have overwhelmed more constructive approaches to their administration; the evidence of local political mobilization in India and Egypt after 1900 suggests that it would also have provoked serious indigenous protest. Centralization at the visible expense of the Dominions before 1914 could have jeopardized those compromises which subsequently

---

[70] See chap. by Avner Offer.
[71] See below, pp. 38; 42; Bernard Semmel, *The Rise of Free Trade Imperialism: Classical Political Economy, the Empire of Free Trade and Imperialism, 1750–1850* (Cambridge, 1970).
[72] See chap. by E. H. H. Green.
[73] See chap. by Avner Offer, esp. pp. 703–10.

enabled co-operation to continue and the Dominions to make vital contributions to Imperial defence and welfare during the First World War. The temporary defeat of the 'constructive imperialists' before 1914 avoided trouble and encouraged more optimistic assessment of Imperial prospects. Future promise was symbolized in the rechristening of colonial Prime Ministers' gatherings at the Imperial Conference in 1911, and the profusion of Imperial architecture associated with Herbert Baker and Edwin Lutyens. Nevertheless, that same defeat reaffirmed the essentials of mid-Victorian approaches to Empire. To many, this particular form of triumphalism also held out little promise for the future, and contributed to a widespread pessimism equally characteristic of the Edwardian years.[74]

Since 1815 an insular people, accepting concepts of authority, exclusiveness, and inequality so essential to Empire, had also espoused a political and economic liberalism which simultaneously undermined those foundations. In a period when national identities were commonly tied to language and were being ever-more sharply defined, the spread of English as a *lingua franca*, like the movement of people and ideas which equally served Britain's Imperial expansion, also opened that Empire to the world. The essential ambiguity of the Empire survived the nineteenth century.

[74] In Vol. IV, see chap. 2 by Ronald Hyam.

Select Bibliography

C. A. BAYLY, *Imperial Meridian: The British Empire and the World, 1780–1830* (London, 1989).

JOHN BENYON, 'Overlords of Empire? British "Proconsular Imperialism" in Comparative Perspective', *Journal of Imperial and Commonwealth History*, XIX (1991), pp. 164–202.

ANTOINETTE BURTON, *Burdens of History: British Feminists, Indian Women, and Imperial Culture, 1865–1915* (London, 1994).

STANLEY CHAPMAN, *Merchant Enterprise in Britain: From the Industrial Revolution to World War I* (Cambridge, 1992).

JOHN EDDY and DERYCK SCHREUDER, eds., *The Rise of Colonial Nationalism: Australia, New Zealand, Canada, and South Africa First Assert their Nationalities, 1880–1914* (London, 1988).

C. C. ELDRIDGE, *England's Mission: The Imperial Idea in the Age of Gladstone and Disraeli, 1868–1880* (London, 1973).

D. K. FIELDHOUSE, *Economics and Empire, 1830–1914* (London, 1973).

L. H. GANN and PETER DUIGNAN, *The Rulers of British Africa, 1870–1914* (Stanford, Calif., 1978).

RONALD HYAM, *Britain's Imperial Century, 1815–1914: A Study of Empire and Expansion*, 2nd edn. (London, 1993).

FREDERICK MADDEN (with DAVID FIELDHOUSE), ed., *Select Documents on the Constitutional History of the British Empire and Commonwealth*, Vol. III, *Imperial Reconstruction, 1763–1840*; Vol. IV, *Settler Self-Government, 1840–1900*; Vol. V, *The Dependent Empire and Ireland, 1840–1900. Advance and Retreat in Representative Self-Government* (New York, 1987–91).

W. DAVID MCINTYRE, *The Imperial Frontier in the Tropics, 1865–75: A Study of British Colonial Policy in West Africa, Malaya and the South Pacific in the Age of Gladstone and Disraeli* (London, 1967).

P. J. MARSHALL, ed., *The Cambridge Illustrated History of the British Empire* (Cambridge, 1996).

ROGER OWEN and BOB SUTCLIFFE, eds., *Studies in the Theory of Imperialism* (London, 1972).

BERNARD PORTER, *The Lion's Share: A Short History of British Imperialism, 1850–1990*, 3rd edn. (London, 1995).

R. B. PUGH, 'The Colonial Office 1801–1925', in E. A. Benians and others, eds., *The Cambridge History of the British Empire*, Vol. III, *The Empire-Commonwealth, 1870–1914* (Cambridge, 1959), chap. 19.

PAUL B. RICH, *Race and Empire in British Politics*, 2nd edn. (Cambridge, 1990).

BERNARD SEMMEL, *Imperialism and Social Reform: English Social-Imperial Thought, 1895–1914* (London, 1960).

JOHN MANNING WARD, *Colonial Self-Government: The British Experience, 1759–1856* (London, 1976).

PETER WARWICK, ed., *The South African War: The Anglo-Boer War, 1899–1902* (London, 1980).

M. E. YAPP, *Strategies of British India: Britain, Iran and Afghanistan, 1798–1850* (Oxford, 1980).

PART I

Economics and Empire: The Metropolitan Context

P. J. CAIN

Despite the loss of the American colonies, Britain was still the greatest Imperial power in the world in the 1790s, a position emphatically confirmed by her victory in the Napoleonic Wars. In the following century the Empire expanded greatly in area on four continents. By 1914 it had become a global phenomenon of immense economic and cultural diversity and by far the largest, most populous and most prosperous of the European Imperial domains. Yet despite its impressive dimensions, the Empire never recaptured the position of importance in Britain's economic life it had held before 1776. Britain's overseas economic relations between 1790 and 1914 spanned the globe: in the latter part of the century around three-fifths of its trade was with extra-European partners, a proportion far greater than that of any other major industrializing power.[1] Imperial economic ties were never more than part of this broader pattern of trade and the associated movements of people and capital. In economic terms, the British Empire always exercised a far greater influence on the mother country than did the overseas possessions of France or Germany: but that influence was not great enough for Imperial considerations to dominate British international economic policy which became infected by the spirit of free-trade cosmopolitanism.

The expansion of trade with the American colonies had been one major reason for the rapid growth in importance of the Imperial element in overseas relations in the eighteenth century. The loss of the colonies in the 1770s converted about one-fifth of Britain's exports from Imperial to foreign trade at a stroke; and, since the emerging United States continued to provide one of Britain's most dynamic markets, growing dramatically as a source of supplies and providing the biggest single outlet for British migrants and capital in the nineteenth century, the rupture had an enduring influence. Moreover, the independence of the American colonies occurred precisely when, as a result of the industrial revolution, Britain's competitive advantage as an international trader was becoming marked in terms of both industry and services, spreading British economic influence across the whole

---

[1] Paul Bairoch, 'Geographical Structure and Trade Balances of European Foreign Trade from 1800 to 1970', *Journal of European Economic History* (hereafter *JEEcH*), III (1974), Tables 5 and 6.

world. In the early nineteenth century the most obvious sign of Britain's international competitiveness was the growth of the cotton industry. In the latter part of the period her industrial leadership was lost, but a global presence was retained by improving her comparative advantage as a seller of international services.[2] This enduring cosmopolitan success provided the context wherein Imperial economic policy was formulated throughout the century.

Building up a picture of the Empire's role in international trade before 1850 is difficult because of the limitations of the available statistics. Imports were recorded at 'official' rather than real values before 1854 and recent estimates of the latter do not allow the Empire's share to be precisely determined. It is clear that, despite upheavals caused by war and blockade, imports from the major developed markets of Europe, the United States, and Latin America accounted for a little over two-fifths of the total between the 1780s and the end of the Napoleonic Wars. Then, as the United States's significance grew, the developed markets increased their share of imports to 60 per cent by 1844–46. As for Imperial trade, assuming that India accounted for three-fifths of imports from Asia and that four-fifths of goods from the West Indies were from islands under British control, the Empire provided roughly 35–40 per cent of imports during the war period. After that the share of the Empire fell. India continued to provide about 10 per cent of total imports after 1815 but the increasing importance of British North America (BNA) and of Australia in British markets was more than offset by the drastic decline in the importance of the West Indies, whose share of imports fell from around 18 per cent to 6 per cent of the total between 1814–16 and 1844–46 as slave emancipation began to work its effects.[3]

The best way to evaluate the significance of Empire is to look at the chief imported commodities of the early nineteenth century and the Empire's contribution to their supply. Of the ten leading commodities imported into Britain in 1784–86, half came from Europe and, of the remainder, the Empire was a major supplier of only three: sugar, which came wholly from the West Indies; raw cotton, also mainly from the West Indies; and manufactured cottons and silks imported from India. Tea came mainly from China as did most of the raw silk imported. By 1834–36 the Empire led the way in only two of the leading commodities. The West Indies was still the first supplier of sugar, though its share had fallen to 80 per cent, and North

[2] For overviews see: Phyllis Deane and W. A. Cole, *British Economic Growth, 1688–1959* (Cambridge, 1962), pp. 28–38; François Crouzet, 'Toward an Export Economy: British Exports during the Industrial Revolution', *Explorations in Economic History*, XVII, 1 (1980), pp. 48–93; Peter Mathias, *The First Industrial Nation: An Economic History of Britain, 1700–1914* (London, 1983), chap. 11.

[3] Ralph Davis, *The Industrial Revolution and British Overseas Trade* (Leicester, 1979), Table 40, pp. 92–93.

American timber had replaced European as market leader. Besides this, Australia was just emerging as an important supplier of wool and India's share of raw silk imports was rising (Table 2.1). Among lesser, though still significant, commodities of Imperial origin were indigo, the bulk of which came from India, and coffee.

To place the Empire's contribution in perspective, it must be remembered that, throughout the first half of the century, its position was boosted by the complex of tariffs and other forms of discrimination which made up what was called the 'Old Colonial System'. The two leading Imperial products of the 1830s, sugar and timber, as well as other important commodities such as coffee, owed their position in the British market to preferences which only began to be eroded seriously in the 1840s.[4] The North American timber trade is the best example of how much

TABLE 2.1. *Leading British imports and principal suppliers, 1784–1836*

Import	£000	1784–86 Supplier
Raw sugar	2,614	West Indies 2,614
Tea	2,587	Asia 2,587
Cotton	1,814	West Indies 890; NW Europe 456
Cotton & silk goods	1,344	Asia 1,344
Silk	1,218	Asia 568; S. Europe 531
Wine	964	S Europe 831
Timber	917	N Europe 671
Iron & ore	702	N Europe 700
Linen goods	672	NW Europe 417; N Europe 255
Flax	563	N Europe 466

Import	£000	1834–36 Supplier
Cotton	14,494	USA 11,332
Raw sugar	7,070	West Indies 5,779
Wool	6,718	NW Europe 3,864; Australia 923
Silk	4,383	NW Europe 1,466; Asia 1,223; China 871
Tea	3,846	China 3,696
Timber	3,832	BNA 2,586
Wine	2,757	S Europe 2,292
Flax	2,613	N Europe 1,754
Hides and skins	1,999	Latin America 724; NW Europe 353; N Europe 327
Tallow	1,962	N Europe 1,883

Source: Ralph Davis, *The Industrial Revolution and British Trade* (Leicester, 1979), Table 57, pp. 110–11, and Table 62, pp. 120–21. The figures for 1784–86 exclude trade with Ireland; China is included in Asia.

[4] On sugar, coffee, and timber preferences see Davis, *Industrial Revolution*, pp. 43–44, 47–49; Sarah Palmer, *Politics, Shipping and the Repeal of the Navigation Acts* (Manchester, 1990), pp. 57–58; Lucy Brown, *The Board of Trade and the Free Trade Movement, 1833–42* (Oxford, 1958), pp. 185–86.

Imperial commerce depended on political power. Fear of dependence upon Baltic timber for naval supplies during the French wars led to high tariffs on foreign wood big enough to allow the Canadian Maritime Provinces to overcome hitherto forbidding transport costs. Canadian timber dominated the market after 1815 and supplied two-thirds of British demand by the 1830s, a demand much increased by rapid urbanization.[5] It only began to lose its position in 1842 when the duties on foreign timber were sharply reduced. They were finally abolished in 1860, after which Canada's share of imports fell steadily.[6]

There are no established statistics for the Empire's share in British exports before 1815. Later data indicates that, although there were sharp annual fluctuations, exports of home produce to British possessions until *c.*1850 averaged around 30 per cent of the total: but the remarkable stability of the global figure hides striking changes in the geography of Imperial trade.[7] In 1815 the West Indies was by far the biggest market for British goods followed by BNA and British Asia (mainly India). By 1840 the West Indies had declined considerably in importance and British North America had been overshadowed as a market by India and by Australia. During the early part of the period cottons were the most rapidly growing export, rising from 6–7 per cent of the total in 1784–86 to 42 per cent in 1814–16, and peaking at 48 per cent in the mid-1830s.[8] At the time of Waterloo, most of these markets were found outside the Empire: Europe, the United States, and Latin America then accounted for about 98 per cent of all exports of cotton goods.[9] After that, rising tariffs in Europe and the United States forced cotton exporters further afield and India became a prominent market for the first time. Sales to India were responsible for three-tenths of the increase in cotton exports between 1820 and 1850, by which date the subcontinent absorbed 18.5 per cent of all cotton piece-goods sent abroad. India's share of all exports to the Empire rose from a sixth to a third over the same period.[10] After 1815, however, the share of underdeveloped countries within the Empire in British exports declined, partly because of the demise of West Indian trade and partly because of the rapid growth of the areas of white settlement. Especially notable was the rise of Australia, an insignificant market in 1815 but one which was growing rapidly long before the famous gold rushes of the 1850s (Table 2.2).

[5] J. H. Clapham, 'The Industrial Revolution and the Colonies, 1783–1822', in *Cambridge History of the British Empire*, II (1940), pp. 219–21.

[6] Robert Livingstone Schuyler, *The Fall of the Old Colonial System: A Study in British Free Trade, 1770–1870.* (New York, 1945), p. 149.

[7] Werner Schlote, *British Foreign Trade from 1700 to the 1930s* (Oxford, 1952), Table 20a, pp. 160–61.

[8] Davis, *Industrial Revolution*, Table 2, p. 15.

[9] Ibid., Table 3, p. 15.

[10] D. A. Farnie, *The English Cotton Industry and the World Market, 1815–96* (Oxford, 1979), chap. 3 and Tables 5 and 6, pp. 91, 98.

TABLE 2.2. *Exports of British produce to the Empire, 1814–1913* (yearly averages)

	1814–19		1854–57		1909–13	
	(£m)	(%)	(£m)	(%)	(£m)	(%)
Australasia	0.03	0.2	9.94	30.5	39.78	24.7
South Africa	0.23	1.7	1.23	3.8	19.56	12.1
BNA (Canada)	2.61	19.9	4.33	13.3	21.23	13.2
Settlement Empire	2.86	21.8	15.50	47.6	80.57	50.0
India	2.29	17.4	10.32	31.7	53.95	33.5
British Asia	—	—	1.76	5.4	12.18	7.6
Africa	—	—	0.79	2.4	7.93	4.9
West Indies	5.93	45.2	2.14	6.6	3.43	2.1
British Europe	2.04	15.6	2.03	6.2	2.87	1.8
Other	—	—	—	—	0.23	0.1
Dependent Empire	10.26	78.2	17.05	52.4	80.60	50.0
All Empire	13.12	100.0	32.55	100.0	161.16	100.0
Empire % of all exports		30.0		30.3		35.4

Source: Werner Schlote, *British Foreign Trade from 1700 to the 1930s* (Oxford, 1952), Table 23, p. 169.

Note: BNA includes Newfoundland throughout. Figures may not add up precisely to totals because of rounding.

The re-export trade, which largely consisted of recycling extra-European imports to the Continent, was badly hit by the defection of America from the Imperial system and, despite a revival during the French wars, re-exports tended to fall as a percentage of imports throughout the early nineteenth century.[11] The Empire's contribution to re-exports may also have declined in so far as freer trade and Britain's industrialization made her the central market for raw materials from all parts of the world. But many of Britain's new acquisitions in the early nineteenth century, such as Hong Kong and Singapore, were collecting points for commodities sent on for re-export, and several Empire commodities figured prominently as re-exports, including Indian silks, West African palm-oil, and most famously, Australian wool.

There is no doubt that Imperial trade provided a large portion of Britain's so-called 'invisible' earnings even after the loss of the American colonies, though it is impossible to estimate these satisfactorily. Britain was already the world's leading provider of international services by 1780 and Empire territories were dependent on the use of sterling and the credit of British merchants in London, Liverpool, and Edinburgh.[12] Before 1850 virtually all Imperial trade was financed by short-

[11] Davis, *Industrial Revolution*, pp. 31–35; Albert H. Imlah, *Economic Elements in the Pax Britannica* (Ithaca, NY, 1958), Table 13, p. 132.

[12] Davis, *Industrial Revolution*, pp. 58–61.

term credit originating in Britain, compared with only one-third of European trade.[13] In shipping, Britain was temporarily hit by the loss of the American colonies since one-third of the Imperial mercantile marine was American-built at the Revolution.[14] After the Revolution Britain continued to rely on a combination of preferential tariffs and the Navigation Acts, which confined Imperial trade to Imperial ships, to boost its shipping income.[15] Canadian timber and West Indian sugar were the principal commodities involved: no less than two-fifths of the tonnage of British ships in the early nineteenth century was engaged in the BNA and West Indian sector.[16] The development of Australian markets under the Navigation Acts also promoted British shipping and helped to forge valuable links with other Imperial and foreign trading posts in the Pacific and Indian Oceans.[17] In trade finance Britain was internationally competitive, but in shipping American and Scandinavian competition was keen and the growth of foreign tonnage entering British ports was very rapid after 1815.[18] Whether the Navigation Acts prevented a further erosion of Britain's position or whether they added to its difficulties by raising costs is a question with, at present, no clear answer.

Britain's economic links with the Imperial periphery also involved migrants from the motherland building up the populations of British North America and Australia and, to a much lesser extent, South Africa and New Zealand. Here again, however, this movement of population to the Empire has to be seen in the context of the counter-attraction provided by the largest and most dynamic newly settled country, the United States.

Approximately 150,000 people emigrated from England and Wales and perhaps a further 30,000–35,000 left Scotland between 1790 and 1815.[19] Revised figures for the period 1815–50 (which exclude Irish emigrants travelling from British ports) suggest that there were about 500,000 emigrants (net of returns) from England

[13] S. D. Chapman, 'The International Houses: The Continental Contribution to British Commerce, 1800–1860', *JEEcH*, XVII (1977), p. 45.

[14] The rapid increase in British-built tonnage soon made up the difference. Vincent T. Harlow, *The Founding of the Second British Empire*, 2 vols. (Oxford, 1965), II, pp. 264–65.

[15] For the origins and development of the Navigation Acts see Vol. I, chap. by Nuala Zahedieh and Vol. II, chap. by Jacob M. Price.

[16] Palmer, *Politics, Shipping and the Navigation Acts*, Table 3, p. 7.

[17] Frank, J. A. Broeze, *Mr. Brooks and the Australian Trade: Imperial Business in the Nineteenth Century* (Melbourne, 1993).

[18] J. H. Clapham, 'The Last Years of the Navigation Acts', *English Historical Review*, XXV (1910), pp. 687–88, 705.

[19] A figure of 140,000 for English emigration is derived from B. R. Mitchell, *British Historical Statistics* (Cambridge, 1988), p. 76, with 10,000 added for Wales. The rough estimate for Scotland is mine based on Michael W. Flinn, ed., *Scottish Population History from the 17th Century to the 1930s* (Cambridge, 1977), p. 443, and Ian H. Adam and Meredyth Somerville, *Cargoes of Despair and Hope: Scottish Emigration to North America, 1603–1803* (Edinburgh, 1995), p. 4.

and Wales and that in excess of 100,000 emigrants left Scotland, representing roughly 7 and 11 per cent of the natural increase of the respective populations.[20] Emigration to BNA was encouraged by fares offered by returning timber ships even lower than those to the United States, a bounty made possible by preferential tariffs and the Navigation Acts.[21] Some effort was also made, both in Britain and on the periphery, to support colonial emigration directly. The attention paid by historians to forms of assisted migration has obscured the fact that only 7 per cent of emigrants received assistance: however, 23 per cent of the migrants to the Empire did need some direct support either from British or colonial sources, and those travelling to Australasia were particularly dependent on aid since the fare was four times that to the United States.[22] Despite these inducements, only one-fifth of emigrants went to the Imperial frontier and four-fifths to the United States, whose economic dynamism far outstripped anything possible in the colonies at the time.[23] The pull of the United States's economy was so strong that emigrants to BNA were often induced to transfer south: in 1841, for example, 20 per cent of immigrant arrivals in BNA went on to the republic.[24] Given the costs of passage and the working time foregone in travelling, the bulk of the migrants were, inevitably, skilled people with some capital behind them.[25] Assistance from British sources enabled some poor people to move, but this did not always meet with approval in the colonies.[26]

The data on British long-term capital invested abroad before 1850 is sparse and may be misleading. Rough estimates of British portfolio overseas investment (holdings of foreign securities by British nationals) in 1854 put the total at between £195m and £230m, and suggest, somewhat improbably, that the Empire's share was nil or negligible.[27] There are no global estimates of direct investments by British firms abroad, though investment of this kind in Imperial territory must have been

---

[20] Dudley Baines, *Migration in a Mature Economy: Emigration and Internal Migration in England and Wales, 1861–1900* (Cambridge, 1985), p. 58 and App. II, p. 299–300.

[21] Charlotte Erickson, *Leaving England: Essays in British Emigration in the Nineteenth Century* (Ithaca, NY, 1994), p. 174–75; Helen I. Cowan, *British Emigration to British North America: The First Hundred Years* (Toronto, 1961), p. 24; M. Gray, 'The Course of Scottish Emigration, 1750–1914', in T. M. Devine, ed., *Scottish Emigration and Scottish Society* (Edinburgh, 1992), p. 21.

[22] Baines, *Migration*, p. 72; Gray, 'The Course of Scottish Emigration', p. 33; Broeze, *Mr. Brooks and the Australian Trade*, p. 123.

[23] Baines, *Migration*, p. 58.

[24] Erickson, *Leaving England*, p. 170.

[25] Baines, *Migration*, pp. 67, 71; Cowan, *British Emigration to British North America*, pp. 28–39; Ian Donnachie, 'The Making of "Scots on the Make": Scottish Settlement and Enterprise in Australia', in Devine, *Scottish Emigration*, p. 146.

[26] For assisted migration, see chap. by Marjory Harper.

[27] See P. L. Cottrell, *British Overseas Investment in the Nineteenth Century* (Basingstoke, 1975), Table I, p. 23; Elise S. Brezis, 'Foreign Capital Flows in the Century of Britain's Industrial Revolution: New

significant. For example, the Canada Company, a BNA land company, was set up with British funds; Scottish capital was invested directly in Australia; and British-based banking firms were beginning to spread through the Empire from the 1830s.[28] Also, in the 1850s British railway enterprise was just taking off in BNA and India.[29] Nonetheless, it is likely that in 1850 only a small portion of Britain's overseas assets were held in the Empire.

It has been argued that the loss of the American colonies revolutionized Imperial policy, ushering in an era of 'free trade imperialism', with the emphasis on 'informal' rather than formal control.[30] In reaction to this, other historians have pointed out that the preferential system lasted until the 1840s and that there was little pressure to change policies before that time.[31] Recent scholarship tells a more complex and confused story of policy evolution.[32] After some initial hesitation, the first reaction to American defection was simply to exclude her from the colonial system, as the Navigation Act of 1786 indicated. Moreover, William Pitt's moves to lower tariffs in treaties with France and Ireland were intended to increase revenues by rationalizing the tariff rather than to break up the colonial system, and businessmen in Britain were at that time more inclined to support increased protection than to demand freer trade.[33] Again, the wars with France after 1793, which resulted in the assertion of British naval dominance,[34] also encouraged some extension of protection, as witnessed by the Corn Laws of 1804 and 1815,[35] and of the preferential system. The shift to British North American timber was only the most spectacular attempt to use preferences to tap Empire sources for supplies in time of conflict.[36]

Estimates, Controlled Conjectures', *Economic History Review* (hereafter *EcHR*), XLVIII, 1 (1995), pp. 46–67.

[28] For an example, see Geoffrey Jones, *British Multinational Banking, 1830–1990* (Oxford, 1993), esp. pp. 18–22.

[29] Daniel Thorner, *Investment in Empire: British Railways and Steam Shipping Enterprise in India* (London, 1950); D. C. M. Platt and Jeremy Adelman, 'London Merchant Bankers in the First Phase of Heavy Borrowing: The Grand Trunk Railway of Canada', *Journal of Imperial and Commonwealth History* (hereafter *JICH*), XVIII, 2 (1990), pp. 208–27.

[30] Harlow, *Second British Empire*.

[31] See D. C. M. Platt, 'The National Economy and British Imperial Expansion before 1914', *JICH*, II, 1 (1973–74), pp. 3–14.

[32] For an overview see P. J. Cain and A. G. Hopkins, 'The Political Economy of British Expansion Overseas, 1750–1914', *EcHR*, Second Series, XXXIII (1980), pp. 471–78.

[33] Harlow, *Second British Empire* I, pp. 519–20, 538–39, 592–616; John Ehrman, *The British Government and Commercial Negotiations with Europe, 1783–93* (Cambridge, 1962).

[34] A. D. Harvey, *Britain in the Early Nineteenth Century* (London, 1978), pp. 302–04.

[35] Ibid., pp. 318–19; Boyd Hilton, *Corn, Cash, Commerce: The Economic Policies of the Tory Governments, 1815–1830* (Oxford, 1977), pp. 15–30.

[36] Davis, *Industrial Revolution*, pp. 48–49; Harlow, *Second British Empire*, II, pp. 283, 286–87.

Simultaneously, however, the pressures for freer trade were also growing in some areas of British operations. The attempt to exclude the United States from the colonial system failed and the dependence of BNA and the West Indies on American shipping and trade was recognized in the Jay Treaty of 1794.[37] After the war of 1812 the British went further and, in 1815, agreed that the heavy duties placed on American shipping in British ports under the Navigation Acts should be reduced provided the United States offered reciprocal concessions. In the 1820s William Huskisson, the highly influential President of the Board of Trade, extended these concessions to a number of European powers, partly to curb the growing influence of American shipping in British ports which had followed the agreement of 1815. His successors acted similarly, and the Acts were continuously relaxed and amended, often under foreign pressure. By 1828, for example, the colonies were allowed to trade in their own ships and those of foreigners with whom they traded directly; and in 1825 and 1833 the list of enumerated goods was reduced.[38]

This shift to freer trade was also reinforced by the success of British industry and commerce during the French wars, which encouraged both governmental and business élites to believe that they would triumph in open competition.[39] This was complemented, in the 1820s, by the dawning perception amongst Tory government leaders that industrialization and population increase meant Britain could no long remain self-sufficient in foodstuffs. Freer trade was necessary to encourage imports which would come largely from Europe and the United States rather than the Empire. The 1822 and 1828 modifications of the Corn Laws were the result of this thinking as were the general reductions in tariffs of the mid-1820s.[40] Rapid growth also created an expanding host of trading interests in the provinces hostile to chartered company monopoly. As a result, the East India Company lost its exclusive hold over the Indian trade in 1813 and over the China trade twenty years later.[41] By the 1830s Britain's global network of trade and, in particular, her flourishing connection with her ex-colonies in America, seemed to give the lie to the traditional notion that trade could only be secured by the use of power.

Neither Huskisson nor his successors, however, had any intention of destroying the colonial system. Rather, all were concerned to make it work more efficiently within a competitive environment. The post-1815 depression, together with the

---

[37] D. L. Mackay, 'Direction and Purpose in British Imperial Policy, 1783–1801', *Historical Journal* (hereafter *HJ*), XVII, 3 (1974), pp. 487–501.

[38] Palmer, *Politics, Shipping and the Repeal of the Navigation Laws*, chap. 3.

[39] Hilton, *Corn, Cash, Commerce*, chap. 2.

[40] Ibid., chap. 4 and pp. 305–06.

[41] D. J. Moss, 'Birmingham and the Campaign against the Orders-in-Council and East of India Company Charter, 1812–13', *Canadian Journal of History*, XI, 2 (1976), pp. 173–88; Antony Webster, 'The

rising protectionism of both European and American rivals after 1820, reinforced the traditional idea that closed colonial markets were assets worth preserving, and these sentiments were strongly felt until the 1840s.[42] Even Robert Peel's tariff-cutting budgets of 1842 and 1845, which lowered some colonial preferences quite sharply, were still compatible with Huskisson's philosophy: as late as 1843 Peel offered the Canadian colonies a preference on wheat to encourage American mid-Western traffic to travel along the St Lawrence seaway.[43] Nor did Peel radically alter the Navigation Acts. Despite numerous modifications in the rules, the principle that Imperial traffic should be carried in British and colonial ships with British or colonial crews, and that the 'long trades' even with countries outside the Empire should be reserved for Imperial shipping, remained largely intact.[44]

Yet by 1860 the Acts had gone and all preferential arrangements with the Empire had been abolished. Why? The great turning-point was undoubtedly the repeal of the Corn Laws in 1846. Peel, like the Tories of the 1820s, became convinced that economic growth and the survival of the established order he represented depended on providing cheap food for the urban areas, and that the Corn Laws were a serious impediment to that.[45] But the timing of Repeal was influenced by the Irish famine and by the ferocious and growing hostility to the Laws demonstrated by the business classes. They resented agrarian dominance and had become convinced that cheap imported supplies of food and raw material were the key to international competitive success now that Europe and the United States were becoming serious industrial rivals.[46] No colonial preference system was compatible with that conviction and, once the Corn Laws were abolished, its days were numbered.[47]

The move to free trade provoked some agonized debates, particularly over the issue of exposing the sugar exports of the slave-emancipated West Indies to the competition of slave-grown sugar from Brazil and Cuba.[48] The most contentious issue, however, was the abolition of the Navigation Acts in 1849. Once commercial

Political Economy of Trade Liberalisation: The East India Company Charter Act of 1813', *EcHR*, Second Series, XLIII, 3 (1990), pp. 404–19.

[42] A. G. L. Shaw, 'British Attitudes to the Colonies, *ca.* 1820–1850', *Journal of British Studies*, IX, 1 (1969), pp. 71–95.

[43] Schuyler, *Fall of the Old Colonial System*, pp. 142–44.

[44] A Consolidating Act was passed as late as 1845. Clapham, 'The Last Years of the Navigation Acts', p. 692.

[45] Hilton, *Corn, Cash, Commerce*, pp. 303 ff.; S. Fairlie, 'The Nineteenth-Century Corn Law Reconsidered', *EcHR*, Second Series, XVIII, 3 (1965), pp. 562–75.

[46] For a useful summary, see Anthony Howe, *Free Trade and Liberal England, 1846–1946* (Oxford, 1997), chap. 1.

[47] For the legislative changes, see Schuyler, *Fall of the Old Colonial System*.

[48] C. Duncan Rice, ' "Humanity Sold for Sugar!": The British Abolitionist Response to Free-Trade in Slave-grown Sugar', *HJ*, XIII, 3 (1970), pp. 402–18. On the Caribbean see below, p. 483.

interests in British North America and the West Indies were clear that they would lose their tariff privileges they objected to the restrictions placed on them by the Acts. Governments were also strongly influenced by threats of retaliation against the Acts from the United States and the European countries which had more liberal shipping regimes. The fading link between naval strength and the mercantile marine also influenced the decision, and there was some concern in shipping circles that the Acts raised shipping costs and undermined the British position in non-Empire trade. In contrast to the Corn Law debate, however, there was no great surge of business support for abolition; shipping interests were divided on the issue, as was business opinion in general. In this delicate situation, the fact that Russell's Whig government depended for its survival on a Cobdenite radical faction which was ideologically committed to abolition may have been decisive.[49] There is no doubt that, in the early days after abolition, the severity of competition in the shipping market rose sharply: two-fifths of the tonnage entering British ports in the 1850s was foreign-owned, compared with three-tenths in the previous decade. After 1860, steam and iron gave the British an edge they had never quite achieved under the regime of wood and sail and the American Civil War undermined the transatlantic challenge. Without these contingencies the British might soon have been tempted to invoke the retaliation clauses which the opponents of reform had insisted be written into the abolition Acts.[50]

The move to free trade was a long drawn out affair which often bitterly divided the business community. The process was undoubtedly slowed considerably by the sluggish growth of British export values after 1815 when continental protection was becoming an alarming reality. By the 1840s, however, the ideological shift towards free trade amongst the political and business élites was unmistakable and the act of faith involved in abolishing the Navigation Acts was the best testament to that. Belief in the efficacy of an open economy also had its effects on emigration policy. By 1850, when gold discoveries were beginning to stimulate a more rapid emigrant flow, free trade sentiment was already undermining the idea of state aid, and officials and politicians were becoming increasingly convinced that their limited interventions merely diverted the stream rather than swelled it. Moreover, the concession of responsible government to the white settled colonies meant that control over land disposal became a local concern. From mid-century, save for some private philanthropy, assistance for emigration became almost entirely a colonial matter rather than a metropolitan one.[51]

---

[49] Palmer, *Politics, Shipping and the Repeal of the Navigation Acts*. For colonial reaction, Schuyler, *Fall of the Old Colonial System*, pp. 177–93.

[50] Palmer, *Politics, Shipping and the Repeal of the Navigation Acts*, Table 11, p. 181 and p. 183.

[51] D. V. Glass and P. A. M. Taylor, *Population and Emigration* (Dublin, 1976) p. 84; Erickson, *Leaving England*, p. 204.

Responsible government in the white colonies was not an inevitable consequence of free trade and was granted, from the late 1840s onwards, for quite independent reasons. Even in the early 1850s it was still assumed by prominent statesmen in Britain that free trade could be upheld in the colonies whatever political changes might occur. Colonial demands for autonomy in the disposal of land and, later, for freedom to impose tariffs were unintended outcomes of the concession of political power to the white frontier and were accepted with reluctance in Britain only because opposition to local claims would cause more trouble than it was worth. In the dependent Empire, where there was no devolution of political control, free trade was actively imposed, most notably in India.[52]

Between 1800 and 1850 the volume of world trade grew by about two and a half times; over the next sixty years it increased tenfold as a truly multilateral network of world trade emerged for the first time.[53] The original impetus to this upward spiral of growth was given by the gold discoveries of the 1850s in Australia and America; but the long-term revolution in transportation was the strongest force making for change. Shipping freights began to fall dramatically long before steam and iron replaced sail and wood on the high seas, a transformation only decisively completed after 1880.[54] In 1840 a mere 5,000 miles of railway had been built, most of it in Britain: by 1920 a global network of 675,000 miles was in place, bringing vast areas of hitherto inaccessible land in touch with the seaboard.[55] In these new conditions the British Empire expanded rapidly in Africa, Asia, Australasia, and North America: but the relative economic importance of British possessions did not change in any fundamental way.

Changes in the nature of trade with the Empire reflected many of those taking place elsewhere in the world.[56] In the mid-1850s the Empire was the leading supplier of three of the ten most valuable imports—wool, where Australia was now dominant, timber, and raw sugar. However, the West Indian share of raw sugar imports was falling rapidly and, like Canadian timber, was just losing its preferential position in the British market. Indeed, free trade led to a reduction in

[52] P. J. Cain and A. G. Hopkins, *British Imperialism: Innovation and Expansion, 1688–1914* (London, 1993), pp. 235, 336–37.

[53] Imlah, *Economic Elements in the Pax Britannica*, Table 27, p. 189; for a more British perspective see Cain and Hopkins, *British Imperialism*, I, chap. 5.

[54] Douglass C. North, 'Ocean Freight Rates and Economic Development, 1750–1913', *JEcH*, XVII, 4 (1958), pp. 537–55.

[55] William Woodruff, 'The Emergence of an International Economy, 1700–1914', in C. Cipolla, ed., *The Emergence of Industrial Societies*, 2 vols. (London, 1973), II, p. 690.

[56] François Crouzet, 'Trade and Empire: The British Experience from the Establishment of Free Trade until the First World War', in Barrie M. Ratcliffe, ed., *Great Britain and Her World: Essays in Honour of W. O. Henderson* (Manchester, 1975). For imports in the 1850s, Davis, *Industrial Revolution*, Table 64, pp. 124–25.

the Empire's share in imports; from the 1850s until the Great War, 1914–18, the contribution of Imperial possessions never rose above one-quarter of the total and sometimes fell to one-fifth. The fall in the Empire's share reflected the fact that, under free trade, Britain became a major importer of manufactured goods. By 1913 they accounted for 25 per cent of all imports and came mainly from Western Europe with the Empire supplying only £23.4m out of a total of £193.6m, or 12 per cent. This dramatic change obscured the Empire's growing contribution to food and raw material imports, which rose to just over 29 per cent in 1913. In that year, the Empire was a majority supplier of four of the ten leading primary imports: wool, still coming largely from Australasia; tea, since the British now preferred Indian and Celanese to Chinese; rubber, from the Malay states; and oil-seeds, in which the West African possessions had a prominent place. The Empire also took a significant slice of the new bulk trades such as wheat (Canada being the principal source), and was the chief supplier of two other key commodities, tin (Malaya) and jute (India) (Table 2.3). In geographical terms, the biggest shift was the rise of Australia and New Zealand, who provided meat and dairy produce as well as wool. In the dependent Empire, the West Indies shrivelled into insignificance as sugar declined in relative importance and foreigners took over the British market; but India's relative decline was offset by the rise of other British Asian territories supplying raw materials, especially Malaya (Table 2.4).

Another key feature of Empire trade after 1850 was the contribution to Britain's re-export business: 30 per cent of Imperial supplies were re-exported in 1913, comprising over one-half of all re-exports. In the case of Australian wool, more

TABLE 2.3. *Empire share in British Imports of primary products, 1854 and 1913*

1854	Import (£m)	Empire share (%)	1913	Import (£m)	Empire share (%)
Grains	22.9	5.8	Grains	105.5	35.3
Cotton	20.2	8.4	Cotton	60.3	3.0
Timber	11.9	55.2	Meat	56.4	24.7
Sugar	9.6	64.7	Wool	34.2	80.2
Wool	6.4	70.6	Timber	33.8	16.2
Tea	5.5	0.7	Butter	24.1	19.0
Oilseeds	2.9	26.5	Rubber	20.5	57.2
Butter	2.2	1.5	Oilseeds	15.9	53.3
Meat	1.7	0.9	Tea	13.8	87.3
Indigo	1.7	95.7	Fruit, Nuts	11.6	14.3
Total imports	152.4	22.4	Total imports	768.7	24.9

Source: Schlote, *British Overseas Trade*, Table 21, pp. 164–65.

TABLE 2.4. *Britain's imports from the Empire, 1854–1913, by origin (yearly averages)*

	1854–57 (£m)	1854–57 (%)	1909–13 (£m)	1909–13 (%)
Australasia	5.12	13.1	56.33	32.6
South Africa	1.23	3.1	10.68	6.2
BNA (Canada)	6.29	16.0	27.26	15.8
Settlement Empire	12.64	32.2	94.27	54.6
India	14.81	37.7	44.84	26.0
British Asia	2.23	5.7	22.67	13.1
Africa	2.28	5.8	5.79	3.4
West Indies	6.45	16.4	2.87	1.7
Brit. Europe	0.82	2.1	1.82	1.1
Other	—	—	0.43	0.3
Dependent Empire	26.60	67.8	78.41	45.4
Total	39.24	100.0	172.68	100.0
Empire % of all imports		23.9		24.9

Source: Schlote, *British Foreign Trade*, Table 23, p. 168.

Note: BNA includes Newfoundland throughout. Figures may not add up precisely to totals because of rounding.

was re-exported than retained.[57] As for exports of British goods, the changes both in the nature of trade, and in the Empire's part in it, were fewer. In the third quarter of the century the Empire's share fluctuated between 26 per cent and one-third of the total: thereafter it stabilized at around 35 per cent. The balance between white colonial and other Imperial outlets underwent remarkably little change. The emergent Dominions took about one-half of exports throughout. Markets in Australia and New Zealand grew rapidly after 1850 but were badly affected by prolonged depression in their economies from the mid-1880s; the compensation came from South Africa, after the gold discoveries of the 1880s, and from British North America during the wheat boom after 1900. In the dependent Empire, India remained the major market for cotton goods and continued to take one-third of all Imperial exports. However, sales to the newly acquired parts of the Empire in Africa and Asia proved disappointing (Table 2.2). Overall, the Empire steadily became a more important market for staple commodities such as pig iron and iron goods, and also for cottons, taking just over half of each category by 1913. By then, India and the emerging Dominions absorbed £72m out of £186m of Britain's leading export, cotton textiles.[58]

[57] S. B. Saul, *Studies in British Overseas Trade, 1870–1914* (Liverpool, 1960), pp. 223–25. Re-exports were usually between 12 and 15% of imports by value: Imlah, *Economic Elements in the Pax Britannica*, Table 21, p. 170.

[58] Schlote, *British Overseas Trade*, Table 25, pp. 172–73. For India as a market for cotton goods, Farnie, *English Cotton Industry*, Tables 5 and 6, pp. 91, 98.

There is no doubt that the Empire provided an important shelter for British exports hit by European and US tariffs and suffering from competition with newly industrialized countries in the wider world. In the emerging Dominions, international trade per head of population was much greater than in comparable newly settled countries like the United States, Argentina, and Chile. Although there was some competition, institutional and cultural links with Britain gave the latter a powerful edge, an edge reinforced by the modest preferences given her in the twenty years before the War.[59] In Australia, New Zealand, and South Africa, the British took the lion's share of the market for manufactures as well as dominating services. The crucial importance of the Imperial factor is evident from a brief comparison of Australia with Argentina in 1913. British imports from Argentina at £42.5m were higher than from Australia (£38.2), but exports to the former, in which foreign competition was intense, were only £23.4m compared with £37.8m for Australia.[60] Even in Canada, where the United States had geographical and cultural advantages, Britain's influence was sufficient to ensure that she supplied one-third of the Canadian imports in which she was directly competitive with the United States and other rivals in 1913.[61]

In the dependent Empire, trade levels were largely determined by British authority in everything from law to tariffs. Here, where the role of the state was much greater, British governments and officials saw to it that their purchases went to the mother country.[62] Apart from the Malay states and West Africa, the new territories added to the Empire after 1880 proved disappointing to British business: but had they remained independent, or been absorbed by another European power, they might have been even less valuable as markets. Britain's favourable position in Imperial markets may have had long-term disadvantages: some historians have argued that Britain's ability to offset European competition by relying on the Empire encouraged continued investment in old industries such as textiles and thus contributed to relative economic decline.[63] However, it is worth noting that, although the share of the Empire in exports increased sharply in the 1870s, it remained fairly stable thereafter when relative industrial decline was becoming marked.

As for emigration and capital exports, flows to the Empire increased rapidly after 1850 and became a larger component of the broad stream of international factor

---

[59] Saul, *British Overseas Trade*, pp. 215–26, 229; I. W. McLean, 'Anglo-American Engineering Competition: Some Third Market Evidence, 1870–1914', *EcHR*, Second Series, XXIX, 3 (1976), pp. 452–64.

[60] Mitchell, *British Historical Statistics*, p. 507.

[61] D. C. M. Platt, *Latin America and British Trade, 1806–1914* (London, 1972), pp. 105–14.

[62] W. Arthur Lewis, *Growth and Fluctuations, 1870–1913* (London, 1978), p. 121.

[63] Saul, *British Overseas Trade*, p. 220.

movement from Britain without ever becoming the dominant part of it. Falling freight rates, greater speeds, and more extensive international communication induced a rising share of the British population to emigrate. Increased mobility and greater information also made return migration much more feasible, with the result that something like 40 per cent of emigrants returned home.[64] Consequently, figures of outward passenger movement after 1850 are not accurate indicators of long-term emigration, but they are useful in giving a broad picture of emigrant destinations. Between 1853 and 1920 there were over 8 million outward passenger journeys from England and Wales and over 1.5 million from Scotland to extra-European destinations, with the Scots showing a greater tendency to emigrate than their neighbours.[65]

Of the grand total of 9.7m passengers, 4.3m (44.5 per cent) sailed for the United States, 2.4m for BNA (24.1 per cent), 1.7m for Australia and New Zealand (17.5 per cent), and 670,000 to South Africa (6.9 per cent). The United States took over 55 per cent of emigrants between 1860 and 1900 when the western frontier was unfolding, and a considerable number of emigrants to BNA at that time probably moved on to the republic later. But Australia was the favoured destination in the gold rush decade of the 1850s, and BNA became dominant after 1900 when the wheat frontier swept across the 49th parallel. South Africa also became a significant target for emigrants after 1870 when diamonds and gold were discovered (Table 2.5). Under the stimulus of the transportation revolution and Britain's growing demands for cheap foodstuffs and raw materials, the white Imperial frontier expanded very rapidly after 1850. Although in terms of wealth and population the burgeoning Dominions remained small in comparison with the United States, the ratio of British immigrants to total population was much greater there than in the republic. Particular regions in Britain also developed strong economic and cultural links with parts of the Empire which encouraged a steady stream of migrants: Cornwall's connection with Australia was a case in point, as was the Scottish tradition of emigrating to North America.[66] As before 1850, most emigrants left unassisted except for relatives' remittances but the natural attractions of Empire were supplemented to some degree. In Britain, emigrant funds were now raised only by a few charitable agencies, but migration to the white Empire was boosted by help from the periphery. Canadian governments used recruiting agents in Britain and about 100,000 people were assisted to

[64] Baines, *Migration*, pp. 59–60, 77, 134–35.

[65] See Baines, *Migration*, Apps. 4 and 5, pp. 301–06. For causal factors, see the introductory essay in Devine, *Scottish Emigration and Scottish Society*.

[66] For an early study see Ross Duncan, 'Case Studies of Emigration: Cornwall, Gloucestershire and New South Wales, 1877–86', *EcHR*, Second Series, XVI (1963), pp. 272–89. See also the comments of Baines, *Migration*, pp. 159–60, 210–11.

TABLE 2.5. *Emigration (outward passenger movement) from England, Wales, and Scotland, by destination, 1853–1920* (000s)

	USA	BNA	Australasia	South Africa	Other	Total
1853–60	230.8	58.7	273.1	12.7	—	575.3
1861–70	441.8	90.2	184.4	12.1	24.9	753.4
1871–80	637.9	152.2	241.5	46.7	58.0	1,136.3
1881–90	1,087.4	257.4	317.3	76.1	86.0	1,824.2
1891–1900	718.7	176.4	116.2	160.0	110.6	1,281.9
1901–10	837.5	793.2	218.9	269.8	213.8	2,333.2
1911–20	379.3	822.0	352.6	94.1	180.8	1,828.8
1853–1920	4,333.4	2,350.1	1,704.0	671.5	674.1	9,733.1

Sources: Dudley Baines, *Migration in a Mature Economy: Emigration and Internal Migration in England and Wales* (Cambridge, 1985), Tables 3.3 and 3.4, pp. 63–64; and N. H. Carrier and J. R. Jeffrey, *External Migration: A Study of the Available Statistics, 1815–1950* (London, 1953), pp. 99–100. Figures for South Africa include Irish emigrants before 1877, but the numbers involved are small.

emigrate as a result.[67] Australian governments were much more active in attracting migrants to offset the relatively high cost of passage. Of the gross figure of 800,000 migrants to Australia between 1860 and 1900, one-half were assisted and a similar proportion were aided in the boom of 1910–14.[68] The typical emigrant in the late nineteenth century was an urban dweller responding to the pull of economic opportunity abroad.[69]

One of the most notable features of British economic history after 1850 was the sustained outflow of capital. Although there is not a complete consensus, most experts agree that the amount of assets held by Britons abroad reached about £700m by 1870 and had risen to $4bn by 1914.[70] A considerable portion of the investors were the traditionally wealthy, with the bulk of the funds coming from London and the South-East of England: provincial industrialists usually kept their money at home, though Lancashire and South Scotland proved exceptions. The returns, conservatively estimated at £200m per annum by 1913, fertilized a growing service sector in South-East England which, with the City of London's financial and commercial businesses at its centre, became the most dynamic and innovative

[67] Baines, *Migration*, p. 86; Stephen Constantine, 'Empire Migration and Social Reform, 1880–1950', in Colin G. Pooley and Ian D. Whyte, eds., *Migrants, Emigrants and Immigrants: A Social History of Migration* (London, 1991), pp. 66–70.

[68] Baines, *Migration*, pp. 63–64, 86–87; C. M. H. Clark, *Select Documents on Australian History, 1850–1900* (Sydney, 1955), p. 257; David Pope, 'Empire Migration to Canada, Australia and New Zealand, 1910–29', *Australian Economic Papers*, VII (1968). For emigrants' motives, see chap. by Marjory Harper.

[69] Baines, *Migration*, pp. 82–84, 279–82.

[70] See Cain and Hopkins, *British Imperialism*, I, pp. 173–79 and references therein.

part of the British economy after 1850.[71] The finance raised for overseas purposes between 1865 and 1914 was largely lent to regions of new settlement, and financed the railways and other public utilities which opened up these areas to international trade.[72] The 37.6 per cent (£1.5bn) of foreign investment placed in the Empire was faithful to this pattern: three-fifths of it went to the white settled frontier in Australasia, Canada, and South Africa, and the bulk was spent on infrastructure. The Empire's share rose slightly after 1900, stimulated by the Colonial Stock Act of 1900 which gave trustees permission to invest in a range of Imperial concerns.[73] Between 1860 and 1890 the principal Imperial borrower was Australia, but financial collapse and depression in the 1890s reduced inflows to a trickle until just before the First World War. In Edwardian times the biggest Imperial outlet was British North America, its great wheat boom attracting about £250m of British capital. Of the remaining investment in Empire, 20 per cent went to India often to finance railway development in the early part of the period. Despite its vast extension in the nineteenth century, the rest of the dependent Empire was responsible for only 10 per cent of Imperial investment or 4 per cent of foreign investment as a whole (Table 2.6).

TABLE 2.6. *British overseas financial issues, 1865–1914* (Capital called up: 5 year totals: £m)

	Foreign	White settled Empire	India	Dependent colonies	All Empire	Total
1865–69	87	16	31	6	53	140
1870–74	131	31	13	2	46	177
1875–79	62	63	25	1	89	151
1880–84	224	91	24	7	123	347
1885–89	291	110	30	8	148	439
1890–94	219	82	24	7	113	332
1895–99	185	63	27	23	113	298
1900–04	216	129	25	25	179	395
1905–09	484	196	47	29	272	757
1910–14	559	263	42	47	352	911
1865–1914	2,458	1,045	287	156	1,488	3,946

Source: Davis and Huttenback, *Mammon and the Pursuit of Empire: The Political Economy of British Imperialism, 1860–1912* (Cambridge, 1986), Table 2.1, pp. 40–41. These are Davis and Huttenback's intermediate estimates.

[71] Cain and Hopkins, *British Imperialism* chaps. 3, 5 and 6; Lance E. Davis and Robert A. Huttenback, with assistance from Susan Gray Davis, *Mammon and the Pursuit of Empire: The Political Economy of British Imperialism* (Cambridge, 1986), chap. 7.

[72] Matthew Simon, 'The Enterprise and Industrial Composition of New British Portfolio Foreign Investment, 1865–1914', *Journal of Development Studies*, III, 3 (1967), pp. 280–92.

[73] David Jessop, 'The Colonial Stocks Act of 1900: A Symptom of the New Imperialism?', *JICH*, IV, 2 (1976), pp. 154–63.

Was capital pushed or pulled overseas? Judging by the Australian experience in the 1880s, capital from Britain was first pulled in to service the huge infrastructural boom of that decade for which home savings were inadequate. The same phenomenon occurred during the Canadian wheat boom after 1900: the boom began by using domestic resources but had to be supplemented by large drafts of British capital as it increased in intensity. However, at its peak the Australian boom of the 1880s attracted 'over-investment' financed by 'overly abundant' British savings; and a similar phenomenon took place in Canada before the First World War. A more pervasive 'push' factor was the steady decline in returns on safe British investments like government paper and railways which forced gentlemanly investors to look abroad after 1870.[74]

Flows of capital and of emigrants to the white settled Empire were closely correlated. In the Canadian boom after 1900, for example, the domestic economy soon ran up against shortages of both labour and capital, which were then attracted from abroad by higher returns.[75] The movements of factors of production also exhibited the so-called 'long swing', cycles of around twenty to twenty-five years from peak to peak. In Britain there were three huge foreign investment booms, accompanied by large outflows of emigrants, in the early 1870s, the late 1880s, and 1906–14, with corresponding downswings in the late 1870s and 1890s, when home investment replaced foreign and migrant flows fell to low levels.[76] Within the Empire the long swing was most evident in Australia, where the huge influx of population in the gold rush of the 1850s was 'echoed' in the early 1880s, triggering an investment boom which pulled in capital and labour from Britain and which set up a further echo in the upswing of 1910–14.[77] Similar long swings can be detected in Canadian growth. But the effects of the long swing in the Empire were somewhat blurred by British investors' tendency to shift funds there when other overseas markets failed them, as in the late 1870s.[78]

Assuming a 5 per cent average return on investments,[79] Imperial capital assets probably realized about £75m in return income for Britain in 1913. This 'invisible' income from investments was supplemented by other sources, notably shipping which was dominated by British firms, and by trade credits, insurance, and other

---

[74] Michael Edelstein, *Overseas Investment in the Age of High Imperialism: The United Kingdom, 1850–1914*, (London, 1982), chaps. 11 and 12.

[75] John Archibald Stovel, *Canada in the World Economy* (Cambridge, Mass., 1959), pp. 104–24.

[76] Cottrell, *British Overseas Investment in the Nineteenth Century*, pp. 35–40, 57–65.

[77] A. C. Kelley, 'Demographic Growth and Economic Change in Australia, 1861–1911', *Explorations in Entrepreneurial History*, V (1967–68), pp. 207–77.

[78] Saul, *British Overseas Trade*, pp. 112–24.

[79] Imlah, *Economic Elements in the Pax Britannica*, p. 180.

services financed in the City of London and through the medium of sterling. Assuming that half of Britain's earnings in 'business services' came from Imperial trade, say £60m, then total invisible earnings from the Empire were around £135m in 1913. Taking into account a small surplus on the balance of trade, Britain thus had a huge balance-of-payments surplus with the Empire. This surplus played an important role in maintaining the viability of the system of multilateral trade and payments which emerged out of a complex of smaller trade groupings after 1870, with Britain at its centre and sterling as its monetary dynamic. In effect, Britain paid its growing debts in Europe and America with credits earned in the newly settled and underdeveloped world, a large part of which was within the Imperial domain. India's role in this complex web of transactions has been particularly noted, as has that of the Malay states and Australia: but, especially when invisible income is included, most parts of the Empire made some contribution.[80]

Throughout the 'long nineteenth century', Empire played a role in British international economic affairs which was far too big to ignore but never big enough to dominate either events or policy. The globalization of British trade and factor movements shattered the old colonial system inherited from previous centuries; it also stifled the possibility of replacing it with a new one after 1880, even though Britain's industrial leadership was now under threat. By then, recognition of the 'kith and kin' factor in the Dominions, and of the effects of political control in India and the dependencies, had convinced some ardent imperialists that Britain could meet the growing competition of Europe by abandoning free trade and creating a protectionist regime to encourage greater trade with the Empire and to induce more British migrants and capital to stay Imperial. However, the number and the diversity of the interests dependent on free trade after 1850 made any fundamental change in economic policy implausible before 1914. A new Imperial policy would only have been acceptable if the enthusiasts could have shown that the Empire connection was capable of far outstripping the foreign in importance. But this could only have happened if, collectively, the white settlements had been able to emulate the United States in population and wealth, and this was never more than a dream.[81] It is also arguable, with a certain degree of hindsight, that the stability of the international financial system rested upon Britain's continued loyalty to free trade before 1914. Sterling was the key currency of the whole of the international system, not merely the Imperial section, and making sterling universally available was essential to its success: free trade was a means of ensuring

[80] Saul, *British Overseas Trade*, chap. 3.
[81] See below, pp. 362–67; Peter J. Cain, 'The Economic Philosophy of Constructive Imperialism', in Cornelia Navari, ed., *British Politics and the Spirit of the Age: Political Concepts in Action* (Keele, 1996).

that debtors could always have access to the currency by selling in the British market.[82] However, while maintaining free trade, Britain might have improved its trading position by favouring the emergent Dominions in other ways. Given that white settlers were such good customers, it might have paid Britain to encourage more of its capital and labour to migrate to the colonies and to build up their population and wealth. Such was the hold of free-trade sentiment that this was never likely to appear on the political agenda. Despite widespread fears of 'over-population', unemployment, and social unrest in the late nineteenth century, governments of all shades of opinion refused to assist migration to the colonies;[83] and, apart from the minor diversions caused by the Colonial Stock Act and by Chamberlain's ability, when Colonial Secretary between 1895 and 1902, to wring a small amount out of the Treasury for Imperial development projects, interference with the capital market was avoided.[84]

The global nature of Britain's international relations and her centrality in the world's economic system provided the context in which the Empire, as an economic entity, was understood in this period. The cosmopolitan reach of her industry, commerce, and finance was also one of the fundamental reasons why the terms 'empire' and 'imperialism' were not necessarily synonymous in Britain between 1790 and 1914. Whether Britain added to her 'formal' Empire an 'informal' Empire of dominance exerted through economic strength is a matter of great dispute: but the dispute undoubtedly has its origins in the fact that the extent of British economic influence in the world in the nineteenth century always ranged far beyond the boundaries of sovereign control.

[82] Cain and Hopkins, *British Imperialism*, pp. 177–78; Saul, *British Overseas Trade*, pp. 220–21.

[83] Howard LeRoy Malchow, *Population Pressures: Emigration and Government in the Late Nineteenth Century* (Palo Alto, Calif., 1979), esp. chaps. 8 and 9.

[84] For Chamberlain see below, chap. by E. H. H. Green.

Select Bibliography

DUDLEY BAINES, *Migration in a Mature Economy: Emigration and Internal Migration in England and Wales, 1861–1900* (Cambridge, 1985).

P. J. CAIN and A. G. HOPKINS, 'The Political Economy of British Expansion Overseas, 1750–1914', *Economic History Review*, Second Series, XXXIII (1980), pp. 463–90.

—— *British Imperialism: Innovation and Expansion, 1688–1914* (London, 1993).

P. L. COTTRELL, *British Overseas Investment in the Nineteenth Century* (Basingstoke, 1975).

FRANÇOIS CROUZET, 'Trade and Empire: The British Experience from the Establishment of Free Trade until the First World War', in Barrie M. Ratcliffe, ed., *Great Britain and Her World: Essays in Honour of W. H. Henderson* (Manchester, 1975).

LANCE E. DAVIS and ROBERT A. HUTTENBACK with the assistance of SUSAN GRAY
    DAVIS, *Mammon and the Pursuit of Empire: The Political Economy of British Imperialism,*
    1860–1912 (Cambridge, 1986).

RALPH DAVIS, *The Industrial Revolution and British Overseas Trade* (Leicester, 1979).

T. M. DEVINE, ed., *Scottish Emigration and Scottish Society* (Edinburgh, 1992).

MICHAEL EDELSTEIN, *Overseas Investment in the Age of High Imperialism: The United*
    Kingdom, 1850–1914 (London, 1982).

D. A. FARNIE, *The English Cotton Industry and the World Market, 1815–96* (Oxford, 1979).

VINCENT T. HARLOW, *The Founding of the Second British Empire,* 2 vols. (Oxford, 1965).

B. HILTON, *Corn, Cash, Commerce: The Economic Policies of the Tory Governments, 1815–*
    1830 (Oxford, 1977).

ANTHONY HOWE, *Free Trade and Liberal England, 1846–1946* (Oxford, 1997).

ALBERT H. IMLAH, *Economic Elements in the Pax Britannica* (Ithaca, NY, 1958).

SARAH PALMER, *Politics, Shipping and the Repeal of the Navigation Acts* (Manchester,
    1990).

D. C. M. PLATT, 'The National Economy and British Imperial Expansion before 1914',
    Journal of Imperial and Commonwealth History, II (1973–74), pp. 3–14.

S. B. SAUL, *Studies in British Overseas Trade, 1870–1914* (Liverpool, 1960).

WERNER SCHLOTE, *British Foreign Trade from 1700 to the 1930s* (Oxford, 1952).

ROBERT LIVINGTONE SCHUYLER, *The Fall of the Old Colonial System: A Study in*
    British Free Trade, 1770–1870 (New York, 1945).

3

Economics and Empire: The Periphery and the Imperial Economy

B. R. TOMLINSON

The terms 'core' and 'periphery' are widely, if rather loosely, used in the literature on the economic history of the Empire in the nineteenth century to distinguish the industrial economies of Europe, notably Britain, from the primary producing economies of other continents.[1] Such terms demonstrate the interdependence between the manufacture of industrial goods in Europe and the supply of food and raw materials from other parts of the world that became the dominant feature of the global economic system over the course of the nineteenth century. During the late eighteenth and early nineteenth centuries Europe traded extensively with Asia, Africa, the Americas, and the Caribbean, exchanging manufactures and metals for exotic foodstuffs, textiles, slaves, and precious metals. By the 1870s, with a mature manufacturing economy established in Britain, with industrialization proceeding rapidly elsewhere in Europe and North America, the needs of the core economies changed fundamentally, and a new wave of expansion took place in the periphery as a result. Industrial Europe required new sources of staple foodstuffs for its urban populations and raw materials for its factories. Over the next forty years the process of economic change became the most intense that the world had known. To fuel this expansion, Europe's relations with overseas economies altered significantly, stimulating rapid territorial expansion and economic growth in those regions where European settlers, capital, and commodities could most easily be employed. The result was to change the physical characteristics of these areas, as well as their economic fortunes and human histories. As one recent survey of environmental history has pointed out, the two 'paramount' reasons for 'the transformation of the earth' in the modern period have been 'the explosive increase of European population and its movement overseas, and the rise of the

---

[1] These terms also usually imply some imbalance in political and economic structures, with the 'core' being able to exert both economic and political power over the periphery. For these reasons, as well as because of their unusual economic structures, the United States and Japan straddle these categories during the period.

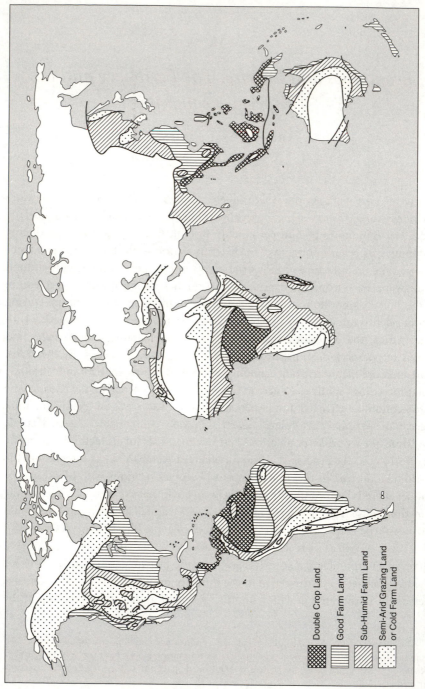

Map 3.1. World Climatic Regions and European Settlement

Double Crop Land

Good Farm Land

Sub-Humid Farm Land

Semi-Arid Grazing Land
or Cold Farm Land

modern capitalist economy and its evolution into industrialism'.[2] Both these
phenomena peaked during the second half of the nineteenth century, and both
were closely linked to British Imperial expansion in the periphery.

Britain—the pre-eminent industrial and Imperial economy of the age—obtained
her supplies of food and raw materials globally in the nineteenth century. In the
periphery her suppliers can be divided into two broad categories, determined by
their suitability for colonization by European organisms, technology, values, and
production methods. These were the 'capitalist neo-Europes' of the empty lands
of the western and southern hemispheres, and the 'tropical periphery' of Asia,
Africa north of the Zambezi, the Caribbean, and much of Central and South
America.[3] The neo-Europes were the temperate regions of the New World that
European settlers had colonized since the sixteenth century, bringing with them
the staple food crops, domestic animals, weeds, pests, and pathogens of Eurasia.
These areas came to prominence in the international economy after 1850 as
colonization, fuelled by the demand requirements and supply capacities of industrial Europe, imposed an alien ecology and alien patterns of land use in a process of
ecological imperialism.[4]

The concept of ecological imperialism points up the intensity of the colonizing
experience in the temperate zones of the Americas and Oceania (Australia and
New Zealand). Conventional accounts of the economic history of the nineteenth
century usually emphasize the autonomous role of the United States, and under-
play events in other regions of recent settlement, except for the Cape. It is true that
economic and political relations in these latter regions moved along fairly predictable and one-dimensional lines, yet in environmental terms the changes in

---

[2] Michael Williams, 'The Relations of Environmental History and Historical Geography', *Journal of Historical Geography*, XX (1994), p. 12.

[3] The term 'capitalist neo-Europes' is based on Crosby's concept of 'ecological imperialism': Alfred W. Crosby, *Ecological Imperialism: The Biological Expansion of Europe, 900–1900* (Cambridge, 1986) and also draws on Denoon's notion of 'settler capitalism': Donald Denoon, *Settler Capitalism: The Dynamics of Dependent Development in the Southern Hemispheres* (Oxford, 1983). The concept of the 'tropical periphery' is based on the work of Sir Arthur Lewis: see W. Arthur Lewis, *Growth and Fluctuations, 1870–1913* (London, 1978). The notion of a distinctive tropical periphery is also important in analyses of nineteenth-century imperialism such as Ronald Robinson's, see his, 'Non-European Foundations of European Imperialism: A Sketch for a Theory of Collaboration', in Roger Owen and Bob Sutcliffe, eds., *Studies in the Theory of Imperialism* (London, 1972), pp. 117–40.

[4] 'Ecological imperialism' was certainly not 'natural' and was often not easy. European domestic animals thrived best with European plants to eat, but this required a wide range of small but far-reaching adaptations of the local environment—it took more than thirty years to establish adequate numbers of bumble-bees in New Zealand to pollinate the red clover that had been imported to improve the pasture, for example. In the 1880s successfully imported live bumble-bees could be sold in New Zealand for 9s. (45p) each: Bill Clark, 'Shipping Bees to Australia and New Zealand', *Cambridgeshire Bee Keeping Association Newsletter* (Spring, 1994), pp. 11–13.

these areas that followed colonization were more intense and far-reaching than anywhere else in the world. It was the speed and completeness of these changes that made possible both the rapid progress of European colonization, and the pattern of economic activity that resulted from it.

In the tropical periphery, by contrast, similar progress was impeded by an environment hostile to European settlers and technologies, in which dense settlement and ecological adaptation by other races and cultures had already taken place. Problems of Imperial political control and economic development in Asia and Africa gave rise to severe difficulties in the second half of the nineteenth century. Environmental problems that European technology was not able to solve—such as organizing intensive rice cultivation in monsoon Asia, or coping with a particularly vicious disease environment in parts of Africa—shaped the economic and social history of these regions.[5] To establish capitalism in such places required a strong local response that could modify, refine, and adapt European technologies and social relations of production. In the conditions of nineteenth-century imperialism, such a response was rare.[6]

The neo-European region of the nineteenth-century periphery was made up of the United States, British North America (Canada), Australia, New Zealand, South Africa, Argentina, Uruguay, and Chile. These territories all enjoyed mainly temperate climates, and were 'empty' in the sense that the native peoples were ultimately unable to mount an effective resistance to capitalist colonization. The pre-European inhabitants of these lands were not necessarily 'primitive' or ecologically unbalanced. However, they certainly were not capitalist, and they did not, for the most part, employ the arable or pastoral farming techniques of Europeans. The exercise of Imperial power was an important element in the opening up of all of these territories, and force was used against both foreign rivals and recalcitrant natives. The neo-European economies all grew rapidly between 1790 and 1913, all had close ties to Britain during the nineteenth century, and all relied on overseas (largely British) exports of capital, manpower, and enterprise to expand their economies. In return they produced primary produce for export to the industrial countries, especially to Britain which was the industrialized country with the smallest food and raw-material supplying base, and the largest surplus of mobile capital and population. These exports were usually of commodities that were familiar to Europeans, being temperate food and raw material crops that replaced local supplies that had been exhausted or were now inadequate.

---

[5] For the conservationist response of colonial regimes to dramatic changes caused by economic expansion in many tropical areas by the 1830s, see Richard H. Grove, *Green Imperialism: Colonial Expansion, Tropical Island Edens, and the Origins of Environmentalism, 1600–1860* (Cambridge, 1995).

[6] Japan is the obvious exception to this generalization, but she was the least colonized of the major Asian economies.

The United States was the most important economy outside Europe throughout the nineteenth century. The American economy was already a special case by the middle of the century, not least because of the rapid and distinctive growth that had resulted from the close links between the cotton-growing areas of the South and the Lancashire cotton industry.[7] With the re-establishment of an effective central political authority after the Civil War (1860–65), the United States could progress to her own manifest destiny of industrialization and overseas expansion, and her national economy broke free from dependence on supply-and-demand factors originating in Europe. As a result, a secondary semi-autonomous 'core' region of industrial capital and labour had developed in North America by the 1880s that provided an independent dynamic for an extended regional specialization within the domestic economy. By 1900, if not before, Canada was being pulled along in the wake of the United States, and relied heavily on inputs of American, as well as British, capital and commodities. The settler colonies of the southern hemisphere, especially South Africa and Australia, underwent some industrialization in processing primary produce and manufacturing consumer goods for domestic consumption, but when sustained growth boosted demand for investment goods and infrastructure, they were dependent on imported capital and machinery.[8] Despite their economic success, all the neo-European economies of the regions of recent settlement relied on London's role as a lender of last resort and a purchaser of distress goods in times of economic difficulty to overcome balance-of-payments and currency crises throughout our period. Thus when, as in 1890, 'Britain caught a cold, the periphery caught pneumonia', and the subsequent domestic recovery in Britain based on repatriated gold caused deep depressions elsewhere, even in the United States.[9]

The classification of Britain's trading partners into neo-European and tropical countries (Tables 3.1 and 3.2) reinforces the point that the process of industrialization tended to increase, in relative terms, the importance of the temperate zones of recent settlement to British external economic activity over the course of the nineteenth century. Table 3.3 demonstrates that British capital was mainly employed in the empty lands of the neo-European periphery in this period, while

---

[7] Robert O. Keohane, 'Associative American Development, 1776–1860: Economic Growth and Political Disintegration', in John Gerald Ruggie, ed., *The Antinomies of Interdependence: National Welfare and the International Division of Labor* (New York, 1983), pp. 43–90.

[8] For a useful chronological account of the pattern of investment and the business cycle in the neo-European periphery, Michael Edelstein, *Overseas Investment in the Age of High Imperialism: The United Kingdom, 1850–1914* (London, 1982), pp. 288–311.

[9] Brinley Thomas, *Migration and Economic Growth: A Study of Great Britain and the Atlantic Economy,* 2nd edn. (Cambridge, 1973), chap. 15, esp. pp. 276–77.

TABLE 3.1. *Pattern of British exports by regions, 1789–1913* (%)

Annual averages	Europe	Neo-Europes	Tropics
1789–90	47	23	30
1797–98	30	31	38
1830–32	40	25	34
1845–47	44	23	33
1856–58	35	29	36
1871–73	46	23	31
1891–93	35	40	25
1911–13	35	41	24

TABLE 3.2. *Pattern of British imports by regions, 1789–1913* (%)

Annual averages	Europe	Neo-Europes	Tropics
1789–90	52	8	40
1797–98	42	8	49
1856–58	35	27	37
1871–73	41	34	26
1891–93	44	35	21
1911–13	41	35	24

Source: Calculated from B. R. Mitchell, *Abstract of British Historical Statistics* (Cambridge, 1962), Tables 10 and 11.

Notes: Europe includes Turkey. Neo-Europes = United States, British North America, Australasia, Argentina. Tropics = West Indies, Asia, Africa, Central and South America.

most analyses of the global pattern of migration suggest that emigrants from both Europe and Asia mainly went to the neo-European lands, with the United States by far the most-favoured destination.

The economic history of the tropical periphery during the nineteenth century was somewhat different from that of the neo-European colonies of settlement. Britain, like other European countries, had engaged in significant amounts of intercontinental trade in the late eighteenth century, largely from Asia and the Americas. In this period most of her imports consisted of finished consumer goods such as tobacco, furs, spices, sugar, coffee, tea, and manufactured fine textiles. Also important were supplies of precious metals, notably the gold and silver from South America that built up the war-chests of the eighteenth-century powers and provided the remittances to pay for Europe's trade deficit with Asia. Demand for luxury consumer goods rose in the late eighteenth century as a consequence of rising incomes and

TABLE 3.3. *Distribution of capital calls in London, by regions, 1865–1914*

	Total £m	%
Europe	349.7	12
Neo-Europes total	1,630.7	56
United States	679.2	23
Canada	141.8	5
Australia and New Zealand	362.3	12
South Africa	131.9	5
Latin America*	315.5	11
Tropics total	945.5	33
India	239.1	8
Rest of Asia	203.4	7
Rest of Pacific	9.2	1
Rest of Africa	178.3	6
Latin America*	315.5	11
Grand Total	2,925.8	100

Source: Calculated from Lance E. Davis and Robert A. Huttenback with the assistance of Susan Gray Davis, *Mammon and the Pursuit of Empire: The Political Economy of British Imperialism, 1860–1912* (Cambridge, 1986), Tables 2.9A and 2.9B

Notes: *Latin America total not broken down in source. Assigned half to neo-Europes (Argentina, Uruguay, Chile), and half to rest of Latin America and Caribbean. Sub-totals are rounded. Grand total and percentages calculated from unrounded totals.

consumption, and this may have provided a powerful motive for Imperial expansion in the pre-industrial era.[10]

At its peak, in the 'second British Empire' that attempted to centralize control and management of British overseas interests in Africa, Asia, and Oceania between 1780 and 1800, Imperial economic activities in tropical areas had provided a significant bolster to the economic and social power of the landed and business élites of Regency England. However, the extent of economic interdependence between Britain and the extra-European world in the late eighteenth and early nineteenth centuries should not be exaggerated.[11] Such involvement was intense for particular groups of merchants and investors, such as those associated with the

[10] J. R. Ward, 'The Industrial Revolution and British Imperialism, 1750–1850', *Economic History Review* (henceforth *EcHR*), XLVII (1994), pp. 44–65.

[11] C. A. Bayly, *Imperial Meridian: The British Empire and the World, 1780–1830* (London, 1989). For a summary of the role of Asia, Africa, the Caribbean, and Latin America in the world trading systems of the seventeenth and eighteenth centuries, see Michael Chisholm, 'The Increasing Separation of Production and Consumption', in B. L. Turner II and others, eds., *The Earth as Transformed by Human Action: Global and Regional Changes in the Biosphere over the Past 300 Years* (Cambridge, 1990), pp. 87–112; see also in Vol. II chaps. by P. J. Marshall on Asia, J. R. Ward on the Caribbean, Jacob M. Price on the Imperial economy and David Richardson on the slave trade.

East India Company, with the Caribbean sugar economy, or with the American tobacco industry, but overall it was rather narrow in its penetration of both the metropolitan and the peripheral economies. The economic rationale of Britain's formal and informal Empire in the eighteenth century had been based heavily around the exploitation of tropical resources of goods that could not be found in Europe—largely luxury finished consumer goods such as sugar (West Indies and Indonesia), cotton manufactures (India), and silk and tea (China). In some areas these goods were produced directly by European investment and enterprise using local or imported labour—as in the sugar plantations of the Caribbean, for example—and in others European officials and merchants tried to command supplies from local artisans and peasants through control of access to land, credit, and trading networks. In much of Asia, however, Britain and other European powers secured their supplies of local goods, and the profits of their Imperial expansion, by 'service' activities—especially by playing an intermediate role in finance, transportation, and the political protection of inter-regional trade.

The industrialization of the British metropolitan economy built up direct links with tropical economies in the periphery, through the expansion of both plantations and peasant production backed up by imported capital and infrastructure, that were much stronger and more wide-ranging than anything that had gone before. The most important products imported from the tropics after 1860 were essential raw-material inputs into the industrialization process (rubber, vegetable oils, minerals), or formerly exotic foods (sugar, cocoa, tea) that had now become staples. With the exception of the export of cotton textiles to India, the flows of goods and capital from the core to the tropics went into roughly the same activities as in the neo-Europes—the supply of capital and equipment to facilitate the production of raw materials and minerals for export, chiefly through the construction of railways and other areas of infrastructure.

As in the neo-Europes, economic expansion in the tropics in the nineteenth century was chiefly based on movement of capital, goods, and people, and the opening up of frontier regions such as Assam, the outer islands of Indonesia, and eventually the Kenyan highlands. Japan, the wealthiest, most inventive, and most productive Asian economy at the end of the eighteenth century, was the only national economy outside the neo-European periphery that had emerged significantly out of a dependent status by 1913.[12] Elsewhere in Asia some regional specialization of economic activity took place, supplying non-European labour and food-grains (rice) to food- and labour-deficit areas producing industrial raw materials for export to Europe. The regional economy of South, East, and South-

[12] Yet even she was the heaviest tropical borrower of British capital in the decade before the First World War.

East Asia centred on Malaysian rubber, Burmese and Thai rice, and Chinese and India capital and labour is a good example of this.[13]

One crucial difference in the tropics was that the new economic activities fostered by colonialism were dependent on supplies of local labour, not immigrants of European stock. Since Asian and African peasants expected standards of living and real wages that were much lower than those of European farmers and settlers, and the productivity of labour, land, and capital was lower in the tropics than in temperate zones, pressures to raise rates of economic growth and development were less intense in the tropics than in the neo-Europes. Arguably, these differences determined the pattern of tropical development until well into the twentieth century.[14]

By the mid-nineteenth century British investors, businessmen, and officials were trying to bolster economic activity in the tropics that would be complementary to that of the metropolis. Over the course of the nineteenth century as a whole, about half of Europe's imports from the tropics consisted of food products, and less than one-third of industrial raw materials.[15] In general, Britain and the other European powers set out to create a neo-European social, ecological, and economic setting in their tropical possessions, based on private property rights in land, settled agriculture, and primary product extraction, to encourage the manufacture and export of goods produced under the influence of capitalism. This, it was thought, would make populous local societies easier to rule, and would enable European powers to secure the economic rewards they sought from imperialism. However, the control of Europe-centred capitalists over the local economies in the tropics was never as complete as it was in the neo-Europes. There were few European settlers in the tropics. Agricultural production there was chiefly organized by local peasants, with some contribution from European planters — but these latter created a society very different from the settler-capitalism of the temperate zones. It remains true that the process of nineteenth-century economic expansion saw industrial capitalism engulf other systems of production and exchange in the tropical periphery, just as much as in the neo-Europes. However, the impact of this process was less intense in the tropics than in the regions of recent settlement,

---

[13] A brilliant sketch of this regional economy is given in Christopher J. Baker, 'Economic Reorganization and the Slump in South and Southeast Asia', *Comparative Studies in Society and History*, XXIII (1981), pp. 324–46.

[14] One estimate is that the average yield per acre of grain in the tropics was 700 pounds per acre, as against 1,600 pounds per acre in Britain. To attract European immigrants the neo-Europes had to offer a standard of living (based on real wages or returns to agriculture) higher than that of the European urban working class; in the tropics, by contrast, expanding agricultural regions had only to offer a standard of living higher than that enjoyed by the most deprived of Indian or Chinese peasants. Lewis: *Growth and Fluctuations*, pp. 188–93.

[15] Paul Bairoch, *Economics and World History: Myths and Paradoxes* (London, 1993), chap. 5.

largely because there was much more resistance to be overcome, and because their environment was less responsive to European technology.

The British Empire, formal and informal, was never a hermetically sealed economic system. Therefore we cannot measure the extension of the British economy overseas simply by investigating the progress of production, trade, and investment in those territories which had become part of the formal Empire by 1913. Throughout the nineteenth century Britain was the world's richest single consumer market for food and raw materials. Chief among her imports were food-grains, especially wheat, other foodstuffs such as meat and dairy produce, animal and vegetable fats, sweets and stimulants, and industrial raw materials, notably fibres such as cotton, wool, and jute, as well as rubber, timber, hides and skins, some metal ores and specie. Former luxuries such as tea and sugar became common items of diet following the growth of urbanization and increase in working-class incomes in the last third of the nineteenth century, while wheat, the 'superior' food-grain of peasant agriculture, became the staple cereal of mass consumption.[16] In the 1870s such primary produce made up three-quarters of Britain's imports by value; although this proportion fell slightly thereafter, it was still about two-thirds in 1913.[17]

While Britain was thus a major driving force in expanding the international economy over the course of the nineteenth century, she was not alone in that role. The economic forces that determined expansion in territories under London's political control were equally important elsewhere in the world. Continental European economies supplied some of the men, money, and markets that were needed to transform economic relations in North and South America, Asia, and Africa during this period, as did some of the colonists and indigenous peoples of the periphery themselves. For Europe as a whole, the trade deficit in primary produce (Europe's share of world imports minus her share of world exports) was substantial in the 1870s, and diminished only slightly over the next forty years (Table 3.4). In the same period, the share of world exports of primary produce supplied from the peripheral economies outside the European core remained roughly constant. For these reasons, the world economy of the late nineteenth century became a system for the multilateral exchange of goods, services, and

---

[16] Average weekly per capita consumption of sugar increased from 0.7 pounds in 1860 to 1.2 pounds in 1880, and remained at about that level until 1913; consumption of tea increased from 0.8 ounces in 1860 to 1.4 ounces in 1880, and then rose again to 2.1 ounces by 1913; consumption of wheat was between 6.2 pounds and 6.6 pounds over the period: Mary MacKinnon, 'Living Standards, 1870–1914' in Roderick Floud and Donald McCloskey, eds., *The Economic History of Britain Since 1700*, Vol. II *1860–1939*, 2nd edn. (Cambridge, 1994), Table 11.6.

[17] Avner Offer, *The First World War: An Agrarian Interpretation* (Oxford, 1989), Table 6.1.

TABLE 3.4. *Trade in primary products: regional shares, 1876–1913*

Region	1876–1895		1896–1900		1913	
	Imports %	Exports %	Imports %	Exports %	Imports %	Exports %
UK and Ireland	29.7	3.1	25.8	3.9	19.0	6.2
NW Europe*	39.3	22.6	45.0	27.6	43.1	25.2
Other Europe	11.2	20.2	10.4	18.1	12.3	14.7
USA and Canada	7.2	16.1	8.5	18.7	11.3	17.3
Rest of World	12.6	38.0	10.3	31.7	14.3	36.6

Source: A. G. Kenwood and A. L. Lougheed, *The Growth of the International Economy, 1820–1990*, 3rd edn. (London, 1992), Table 10a.

Notes: *Includes Finland, Sweden, Norway, Denmark, Germany, Belgium, the Netherlands, Switzerland, and Austria.

capital that included both tropics and temperate zones. The networks that made up this system were not exclusively Imperial ones, and many areas of the world that were not part of any formal empire played a crucial role in them.

The process by which a multilateral balance-of-payments system was established after 1870 is well known: by the closing decades of the century Britain was able to earn payments surpluses with the tropical countries, which she used to meet, in part, her deficits with the rest of Europe and North America. Continental Europe, in turn, used surpluses with Britain to meet deficits with the 'great plains' economies of Canada, Argentina, and Australia, while these economies were in deficit with the United States, which was in turn a net importer from the tropics.[18] Less obvious, but more wide-reaching, were the multilateral flows of factors of production—capital, labour, skills—that enabled most parts of the world to take part in the expansion of the international economy after 1870. While the industrialized core supplied emigrants, capital, and capital goods to the periphery in return for primary produce and investment income, some areas of the periphery specialized in exports of food, raw materials, and surplus labour to each other as well as to the core. By this means some of the poorest, most land-scarce regions of the world, such as the coastal strip of south-eastern India and some parts of southern China, were able to import food by exporting labour to the new rice-growing areas and the mines and plantations of South-East Asia, which supplied remittances that enabled those left behind to supplement their income. Migration by 'target earners' or 'birds of passage', who intended to return home eventually, and whose earnings were remitted to support others, represented an important element in the labour market of the Atlantic economy, particularly among the

[18] S. B. Saul, *Studies in British Overseas Trade, 1870–1914* (Liverpool, 1960), chap. 3.

increasing numbers of migrants from southern Europe who crossed to North and South America in the late nineteenth century.[19]

The global reach of European capitalism, spearheaded by the expansive forces in the British economy in the mid- and late nineteenth century, is unquestioned. But is it much harder to identify and measure the nature and extent of the economic expansion that resulted from this process in the non-European periphery. Conventional assessments of national economic growth in the nineteenth century are heavily dependent on indicators of the spread of modern industrial capitalism such as railway mileage, coal production and consumption, and foreign trade.[20] However, such indicators are of limited use in measuring expansion in the periphery, since they are not appropriate for non-capitalist, non-industrial economies. They measure only one type of economic growth, and are based on assumptions about production and exchange not necessarily appropriate for measuring the performance of the systems in many parts of the world. In the nineteenth century colonial economies were usually imposed on other economic systems which had proved their effectiveness in meeting the needs of the local inhabitants, but which were not based on the principles and practices of industrial or financial capitalism.

To the extent that economic growth in tropical economies was fuelled by the escalating demand for food and raw materials from Britain and the rest of the industrial core, the standard indicators of the progress of trade, investment, migration, and infrastructure have some use. One recent summary has suggested that, with the volume of world trade in tropical exports growing at 3.6 per cent per year from 1883 to 1913, exports were the key to initiating 'intensive growth' even for colonial territories. According to these calculations, twenty-three non-European developing countries passed a decisive turning-point on the road to intensive growth, of whom twenty-one would be tropical countries by our definition.[21]

---

[19] On Asian migration, Lewis, *Growth and Fluctuations*, pp. 181–88 and Baker, 'Economic Reorganization' *passim*; on the Atlantic economy, Dudley Baines, 'European Emigration, 1815–1930: Looking at the Emigration Decision Again', *EcHR* XLVII, 3 (1994), pp. 525–44.

[20] S. Kuznets, *Economic Growth and Structure* (London, 1965) and *Economic Growth of Nations* (Cambridge Mass., 1971). For data based on more recent research, Angus Maddison, *Phases of Capitalist Development* (Oxford, 1982).

[21] Lloyd G. Reynolds, *Economic Growth in the Third World, 1850–1980: An Introduction* (New Haven, 1985), pp. 31–35. The list of developing countries, with the approximate date of their turning points, is as follows: Chile (1840); Malaysia, Thailand (1850); Argentina (1860); Burma (1870); Mexico (1876); Algeria, Brazil, Japan, Peru, Sri Lanka (1880); Colombia (1885); Nigeria (1890); Ghana, Ivory Coast, Kenya, Taiwan (1895); Cuba, Philippines, Tanzania, Uganda, Zimbabwe (1900); Korea (1910). Reynolds follows Kuznets in distinguishing 'extensive' growth, in which population and output are growing at roughly the same rate, from 'intensive' growth, in which there is a rising trend of per capita output caused by increased productivity. For a rather different picture see W. Arthur Lewis, ed., *Tropical*

However, such optimistic assessments of tropical development before 1914 rest on a number of implausible assumptions. The linkages between foreign trade in primary produce and wage-levels and productivity elsewhere in such economies were often weak, with enclaves emerging to serve the export market that had little impact on the bulk of producers.[22]

It is therefore hardly surprising that rates of growth of output, productivity, and welfare were much lower in the tropics than in the regions of recent settlement.[23] The existence of a large pool of underemployed labour in tropical agriculture held down wage levels on plantations and in mines, while few of the profits of such operations were invested in peasant agriculture. Where peasant crops were exported directly, skewed institutions and interlinked markets often increased the risks and limited the rewards that small producers obtained from the system. Furthermore, export-led agricultural expansion in Asia and Africa often caused major political upheavals and exacerbated structural problems of employment and resource allocation, associated especially with de-industrialization of hand-powered textile manufacturing, and the clearance of forests for arable cultivation. The obvious example here is that of colonial South Asia, where the effect of British colonial control in the first half of the nineteenth century was to create a peasant-based, arable rural economy in place of a much more fluid economic system based around local states, armies, and centres of handicraft manufacture. During this process of economic 'expansion', settled agriculture was also imposed on forest areas and systems of common grazing rights, disrupting non-arable patterns of rural economic and social activity.[24]

The revolution in commodity demand which transformed the global economy in the nineteenth century required massive changes in land use throughout the world, and therefore calculating such changes by mapping the agricultural frontier is probably the best way to measure the process of economic expansion in the non-European periphery taken as a whole.[25] The expansion of agricultural settlement was undoubtedly the most important feature of this, since even mineral

---

Development, 1880–1913 (London, 1970), and J. R. Hanson, Trade in Transition: Exports from the Third World, 1840–1900 (New York, 1980).

[22] The Japanese economy was an exception. S. Sugiyama, Japan's Industrialization in the World Economy, 1859–1899 (London, 1988), chap. 4.

[23] In these regions, too, the development of neo-European economic systems had severely negative effects on many of the indigenous peoples.

[24] B. R. Tomlinson, The Economy of Modern India, 1860–1970, New Cambridge History of India, III. 3 (Cambridge, 1993), chap. 2 passim. On the impact of Imperial expansion on Indian forests in the nineteenth century, see Madhav Gadgil and Ramachandra Guha, This Fissured Land: An Ecological History of India (Delhi, 1992) chaps. 4 and 5.

[25] This argument is based on John F. Richards, 'Land Transformation', in Turner and others, eds., Earth Transformed, pp. 163–78.

exploitation often depended on prior land clearance for use as pasture or arable.[26] This expansion took many different forms in different parts of the world, from the plantations of colonial Asia to the ranching systems of the New World, to smallholder or peasant family farms in every continent that provided the basic unit of grain production. The data available are unreliable, but some informed guesses can be made. One estimate (Table 3.5) suggests that the world's croplands increased by 376 million hectares between 1850 and 1920, a rise of 70 per cent in seven decades. An alternative estimate (Table 3.6) involves an even steeper rise, with the net land area converted into regular cropping increasing by 432.2 million hectares between 1860 and 1919. Both these tables indicate, as we would expect, that by far the largest absolute and relative increases in cropped land occurred in the frontier regions of the periphery that were being opened up by European enterprise in this period, notably in North America and the Russian steppes, with some increases also in South America and Australasia. The figures in the second column of Table 3.6, which shows land converted away from crop use, demonstrate that there was very little urbanization outside Europe and, to a lesser extent, North America. These tables also suggest that some expansion of agriculture was taking place in the tropical regions of Africa and Asia, with a particular spurt in South-East Asia in the second half of the nineteenth century. Any analysis of economic expansion on the periphery must incorporate the opening up new lands to plantation and peasant agriculture in countries such as Burma, Thailand, and Malaysia, as well as the more usual story about European emigration and colonization in the western and southern hemispheres.[27]

Map 3.1, which shows the classification of the world's climatic regions and ecological zones as developed by the school of geographical determinists headed by C. Warren Thornwaite and Ellsworth Huntington, illustrates this analysis of the process of expansion into the periphery during the nineteenth century.[28] Thornwaite's categorization of the world's climatic regions suggested that the world's ecology could be defined in terms of its suitability for various crops, with 'good farm land' found only in Europe west of the Urals, central and southern China, the temperate lands of Latin America, the south-eastern and south-western tips of Australia, the Cape area of South Africa, the whole of New Zealand, and the

---

[26] On links between expanding agricultural frontiers and gold discoveries in Australia, South Africa, and the American West in the nineteenth century, G. Blainey, 'A Theory of Mineral Discovery: Australia in the Nineteenth Century', *EcHR*, XXIII (1970), pp. 289–313 and Barry Eichengreen and Ian W. McLean, 'Supply of Gold under the Pre-1914 Gold Standard', *EcHR*, XLVII, 2 (1994), pp. 288–309.

[27] Anne Booth, 'The Economic Development of Southeast Asia: 1870–1985', *Australian Economic History Review*, XXXI (1991), pp. 20–52.

[28] For a convenient set of maps of this type, Colin Clark, *Population Growth and Land Use* (London, 1967), pp. 144–47, Table IV.6 and Diagram IVA (i)–(iii). For a statement of the determinist argument, see Ellsworth Huntington, *Mainsprings of Civilization* (New York, 1945).

TABLE 3.5. *Expansion of croplands in world regions, 1700–1920*

Regions	Area in million hectares %						% change	
	1700		1850		1920		1700–1850	1850–1920
Tropical Africa	44	(17)	57	(11)	88	(10)	25.9	54.4
North Africa/Middle East	20	(7)	27	(5)	43	(5)	35.0	59.3
North America	3	(1)	50	(9)	179	(20)	1,566.7	258.0
Latin America	7	(3)	18	(3)	45	(5)	157.1	150.0
China	29	(11)	75	(14)	95	(10)	158.6	26.7
South Asia	53	(20)	71	(13)	98	(11)	34.0	38.0
South-East Asia	4	(2)	7	(1)	21	(2)	75.0	200.0
Europe	67	(25)	132	(25)	147	(16)	97.0	11.4
Russia/USSR	33	(12)	94	(18)	178	(19)	184.8	89.4
Pacific developed countries	5	(2)	6	(1)	19	(2)	20.0	216.7
Total	265	(100)	537	(100)	913	(100)	102.6	70.0

Source: B. L. Turner II and others eds., *The Earth as Transformed by Human Action: Global and Regional Changes in the Biosphere over the Past 300 Years* (Cambridge, 1990), Table 10.1.

TABLE 3.6. *Land converted to regular cropping, 1860–1919* (millions of hectares)

Region	To crops	From crops*
Africa	15.9	—
North America	163.7	2.5
Central America and Caribbean	4.5	—
South America	35.4	—
Middle East	8.0	—
South Asia	49.9	—
South-East Asia	18.2	—
East Asia	15.6	0.2
Europe (excluding Russia)	26.6	6.0
Russia	88.0	—
Australia/New Zealand	15.1	—
TOTAL	440.9	8.7
NET AREA	432.2	

Source: Turner and others, eds., *Earth Transformed*, Table 10.2.

Note: * These estimates are based on the progress of urbanization; it is not possible to estimate what percentage of agricultural land went out of cultivation for other reasons.

regions of the United States and Canada east of the Mississippi and south of the Great Lakes, plus the Pacific coastal strip from California to Vancouver. Thus, the regions outside Eurasia which favoured dense settlement and intensive agriculture were identified as precisely those lands which European settlers, accompanied by emigrants from India and China and by African slaves, had colonized since the sixteenth century. The great migratory flows of the nineteenth century completed this process, so that by 1914 the only favourable parts of the world that Europeans did not dominate were those parts of Asia that had already been densely populated before 1600.

The definition of 'good farm land' and 'favourable climates' used by that generation of geographical determinists undoubtedly has a strong Western cultural bias, but this only confirms the point of our argument.[29] 'Favourable' areas were defined as those that northern Europeans found most suitable, and in which the main food-plants and domestic animals of Eurasian agriculture could flourish. Such lands as were still 'empty' in 1800—largely those of the Russian steppes, North America, Australasia, southern Africa, and the southern cone of Latin America—provided the most fruitful ground for European economic expansion in the nineteenth century. The estimates we have for the world's population and its geographical distribution in the nineteenth century support this argument. As Table 3.7 makes clear, the increase of human population in these frontier regions between 1750 and 1900 meant that the percentage of the world's population of European descent (those living in North America, Central and South America, Europe, Russia, and Oceania) increased significantly, from around one-quarter to two-fifths of the total between 1750 and 1900. Only 4 per cent of ethnic Europeans were living outside Europe and Siberia around 1800; by 1914 this proportion was more than one-fifth.[30]

TABLE 3.7. *Estimates of world population, 1750 and 1900*

Region	1750		1900	
	millions	% of total	millions	% of total
Rest of Africa	50–80	(8)	90–120	(7)
North Africa/South-western Asia	35–50	(6)	93–100	(7)
North America	2–3	(0.3)	82–83	(6)
Central and Southern America	13–18	(2)	71–78	(5)
China	190–225	(27)	400–450	(30)
South Asia	160–200	(23)	285–295	(20)
Rest of Asia, including Japan	64–85	(10)	154–170	(11)
Europe	120–135	(17)	295–300	(21)
Russia	30–40	(5)	130–135	(9)
Oceania	2	(0.3)	6	(0.4)
TOTAL	735–805	(100)	1,165–1,710	(100)

Source: Turner and others, eds., *Earth Transformed*, Table 6.1.

[29] For summaries of more recent environmental history and its cultural concerns, see the special issue of *Journal of Historical Geography*, XX, 1 (1994) and Robert W. Kates, B. L. Turner II, and William C. Clark, 'The Great Transformation', in Turner and others eds., *Earth Transformed*, pp. 1–17.

[30] Dudley E. Baines, *Emigration from Europe, 1815–1930. Economic History Society, Studies in Economic and Social History* (Basingstoke, 1991), pp. 11–12.

For these reasons, it is easy to see why the economic forces that were unleashed by European expansion in the nineteenth century were so much more successful in transforming the economies and societies of the neo-European regions of recent settlement than they were in developing the tropical countries that had been central to the world economy of the seventeenth and eighteenth centuries. The available estimates of product and income in peripheral economies are very tentative, but the data suggest strongly that the inhabitants of North America and Oceania (Australia and New Zealand) enjoyed comparatively high per capita incomes during the last third of the nineteenth century, while the United States and Canada achieved the largest absolute and per capita growth rates in the world after 1870.[31]

Whatever the dimensions and consequences of increases of output of primary produce in the tropical periphery in the second half of the nineteenth century, little structural change had taken place in these economies by 1914. Measurements of industrialization in the periphery in this period are fraught with difficulties, but some orders of magnitude are suggested by Tables 3.8, 3.9, and 3.10. Table 3.8 shows the transformation that occurred in the distribution of world industrial production with the development of mechanization, and the supplanting of handicrafts

TABLE 3.8. *Percentage shares of different countries and regions in total world manufacturing output, 1750–1913*

	1750	1800	1830	1860	1880	1900	1913
Europe	23.1	28.0	34.1	53.6	62.0	63.0	57.8
UK	1.9	4.3	9.5	19.9	22.9	18.5	13.6
Germany	2.9	3.5	3.5	4.9	8.5	13.2	14.8
France	4.0	4.2	5.2	7.9	7.8	6.8	6.1
Italy	2.4	2.5	2.3	2.5	2.5	2.5	2.4
Russia	5.0	5.6	5.6	7.0	7.6	8.8	8.2
Neo-Europes	0.1	0.8	2.4	7.2	14.7	23.6	32.0
United States	0.1	0.8	2.4	7.2	14.7	23.6	32.0
Tropics	76.8	71.2	63.3	39.2	23.3	13.4	10.2
Japan	3.8	3.5	2.8	2.6	2.4	2.4	2.7
China	32.8	33.3	29.8	19.7	12.5	6.2	3.6
India	24.5	19.7	17.6	8.6	2.8	1.7	1.4

Source: Calculated from Turner and others, eds., *Earth Transformed*, Table 4.32.

Note: These figures include handicrafts as well as industrial manufacturing.

[31] It seems unlikely that any economy in Asia or Africa achieved an annual rate of growth exceeding 0.5% (except for Japan, where GDP per capita grew at just under 2 % between 1870 and 1913). A. G. Kenwood and A. L. Lougheed, *The Growth of the International Economy, 1820–1990*, 3rd edn. (London, 1992), pp. 19–21. Per capita incomes rose rather more slowly in Australia and New Zealand than in the Americas, but this was because they were already so high in 1860.

TABLE 3.9. *Location of world cotton manufacturing industry, 1913 (%)*

Country	Consumption of raw cotton	Location of spindles	Location of looms
Europe	49.7	69.1	66.5
United Kingdom	18.7	38.8	28.7
Germany	8.3	7.8	8.2
Russia	7.8	5.3	7.6
France	4.8	5.2	3.8
Neo-Europes	27.4	22.6	25.9
United States	26.9	22.0	24.8
Tropics	19.2	7.9	7.1
India	8.3	4.2	3.3
Japan	7.6	1.6	0.7
Brazil	2.4	0.8	1.8
Unclassified	3.7	0.4	0.5

TABLE 3.10. *Location of world steel industry, 1913 (%)*

Country	Location of output of finished steel products
Europe	60.5
United Kingdom	12.5
Germany	30.3
France	6.0
Russia	5.4
Belgium	3.6
Neo-Europes	39.0
United States	39.0
Tropics	0.5
Japan	0.5

Source: W. S. Woytinsky and E. S. Woytinsky, *World Population and Production: Trends and Outlook* (New York, 1953), pp. 1,065–68 and Table 471.

as the dominant mode of manufacture. Table 3.9 confirms that while cotton textile manufacture was diffused somewhat through the tropics by 1913 (although not beyond the United States in the neo-European areas), no economy outside Europe, with the exception of the United States, had yet developed a steel industry significant in global terms.

Over the course of the nineteenth century a broadly based international economic system was created, based around the social, technical, intellectual, and moral structures generated in the core areas of European capitalism. The whole world was opened up to western science and classificatory systems, which led the search for products to consume and spread capitalist concepts of utility worldwide, with arable land-systems being imposed on hunter-gatherers, notions of private property supplanting community entitlements, and law replacing custom. The imposition of control over territory—the establishment of 'territoriality' that facilitated the extraction and consumption of commodities in which Imperial economic expansion played a key role—was part of this process.[32] Economic imperialism may be defined as the use of power to determine relations between actors who are bound together mainly by political or economic institutions that have been imposed from outside, and who lack a common, internally generated sense of moral or cultural solidarity. The result may be to divert the economic choice of local people away from their perceived self-interest in a process of informal imperialism. Alternatively, by the exercise of formal control it may determine the economic institutions and policy of a colony, securing the interests of the metropolis, or providing favourable access to public goods for particular groups within local society who have an affinity with the Imperial power, such as settlers, expatriate businessmen and colonial officials, and their indigenous allies. The effect of such actions within the subordinate or colonized economy makes it easier to extract resources without providing payment for them in the form of social investment. The opportunity to do this is often given to favoured groups of nationals and outsiders, selected on the basis of their ethnic composition or political significance rather than their social need or economic potential.

The expansion of the British Imperial economy during the course of the nineteenth century illustrates the relationship between power structures and economic relationships in a number of important ways. Overall, it was no part of Britain's Empire but the United States which was the most important destination for European migrants and capital in this period, although her own development remained less dependent on foreign trade and international capital flows than most. Within the territories linked to London by political ties, the regions of recent settlement were the most rapidly growing and most important markets for trade, capital, and migrants, and their role increased steadily as Europe's need for food and raw material imports to fuel the process of industrialization intensified after 1870. By contrast, the economies of Asia, Africa, the Caribbean, and Latin America played a relatively less important role in the Imperial enterprise. India and, to a lesser extent, China, Japan, and some parts of South-East Asia were the only major

[32] For the concept of 'territoriality' and its importance to the formation of political and social concepts of space in the modern world, Robert David Sack, *Conception of Space in Social Thought: A Geographical Perspective* (London, 1980), p. 167. For the way such concepts have been used by political geographers, see Peter J. Taylor, *Political Geography: World-Economy, Nation State and Locality* (London, 1985), esp. chap. 4.

regions of the world other than those settled by Europeans that became heavily involved in the global system of industrial capitalism between 1860 and 1913. India's central place in the international economy was largely determined by her intense bilateral economic relationship with Britain, based on her capacity to import Lancashire cotton goods and other British manufactures, service heavy debts for civil and military expenditure, and supply European markets for tea, jute, cotton, wheat, and other primary products. The broader regional economy that developed to link parts of South, South-East, and East Asia together in the exchange of labour, capital, raw materials, and industrial goods, and that led to the opening up of new land for plantations, peasant agriculture, and mining, was also significantly dependent on the export of industrial raw materials to the West.[33]

The economic expansion of the periphery in the nineteenth-century Imperial system was largely driven by the resource needs of European industrial economies. Such resources were secured, in large part, by the export of crucial factors of production from the European core itself. Great Britain, especially Ireland and Scotland, was a major supplier of emigrants from the 1840s onwards, mostly to the United States, with smaller numbers in most decades bound for Canada, Australia, and New Zealand. Capital exports from London financed much of the development of infrastructure in the regions of recent settlement, and firms based in London were also heavily involved in mining and other extractive processes in many parts of the periphery. British investors supplied a large share of the funds used to build houses, docks, and storage facilities, to buy machinery and equipment, and to develop transport networks (predominantly railways). In theory, peripheral economic expansion could have consisted of British investors buying equipment from British manufacturers to enable British migrants to grow crops and to extract primary produce to ship back to supply the British factories and their workforce. In practice, there were various leaks from this closed model, but it is true that, up to the 1880s at any rate, much of the supply of factors of production, as well as much of the demand for the goods produced in the peripheral economies, came from the industrial core and especially from Britain.

Since economic expansion in the periphery relied heavily on a narrow range of inputs from the core, variations in rates of growth can in part be explained by the particular technical and ecological contexts of different regions. The fertile and mineral-rich areas of the Americas and Oceania were especially suited to economic expansion under nineteenth-century conditions:

Apart from peoples' willingness and ability to move to these new lands, the key factors in opening them up included an increased knowledge of their natural resources—land,

---

[33] For the business network that underpinned this regional economy, Rajeswary Ampalavanar Brown, *Capital and Entrepreneurship in South-East Asia* (London, 1994).

minerals, climate, and so on—and their economic accessibility, which largely depended on the availability of cheap and adequate transport. Also important was a sufficiency of capital to clear and work the land and exploit its mineral wealth. In all respects the Americas and Oceania were particularly fortunate, for they possessed a variety of natural resources, which, for the most part, were easily accessible and capable of development by known techniques requiring moderate amounts of capital. In Asia and tropical Africa, on the other hand, the opening up of new lands and the development of new sources of raw material was a much slower process than elsewhere. Climatic and topographical difficulties, inadequate knowledge, and institutional resistance to change provided the main obstacles to development in these regions.[34]

In general, the economies of Asia, Africa, and much of Latin America required very substantial inputs of investment to overcome institutional inadequacies and market imperfections—much larger than the core economies of nineteenth-century Europe could or would provide.

The fact that the industrial capitalism of western Europe provided the chief stimulus to the spread of international and inter-regional economic exchange during the second half of the nineteenth century does not mean that large areas of Asia, Africa, and Latin America had no economic history of their own. The local reaction and response to capitalist intrusion was vitally important in determining the eventual outcome of economic expansion in different parts of the periphery, and can be categorized in a similar way. While European emigrants to the western and southern hemispheres 'came to the new lands with "capitalism in their bones"',[35] the indigenous social, political, and economic systems of the tropical periphery could not adapt so easily to the requirements of industrial capitalism, especially where this was bundled up with the exercise of formal or informal imperialism, as for example in West Africa, and Egypt. Only in Meiji Japan were internal conditions favourable to rapid economic expansion and structural change, resulting in the establishment of a self-sustaining growth process reinforced by political independence.[36]

Two centuries after 1790 the most dynamic forces in the global economy are once again outside Europe and its hinterland in the New World, as several national economies in East and South-East Asia have followed Japan into rapid expansion with a global reach coupled to the growth policies of a 'developmental state'. The

---

[34] Kenwood and Lougheed, *Growth of the International Economy*, pp. 18–19.

[35] Paul Baran, *The Political Economy of Growth* (London, 1957), p. 273; Kenwood and Lougheed, *Growth of the International Economy*, pp. 18–19.

[36] On Japanese economic development in this period, P. Francks, *Japanese Economic Development: Theory and Practice* (London, 1992) and R. Minami, *The Economic Development of Japan: A Quantitative Study* (Basingstoke, 1986). Even here there was considerable political upheaval as a result of capitalist development, both before and after the Meiji Restoration of 1868.

pattern of international economic growth and integration established in the world before mechanized industrialization has begun to reassert itself, so that the distorting effect caused by the easy spread of industrial capitalism from Europe to the neo-European lands can be seen more clearly. In this sense, the nineteenth century (which would have to be extended to about 1950) was an exception to the normal balance of forces between European and non-European economies in the world. Today it is Asian capitalism, rather than that of industrial Europe and North America, that shows the developing countries of the world their future, and that points up the limitations of the economic expansion outside Europe wrought by nineteenth-century imperialism.

Select Bibliography

C. A. Bayly, *Imperial Meridian: The British Empire and the World, 1780–1830* (London, 1989).

P. J. Cain and A. G. Hopkins, *British Imperialism: Innovation and Expansion, 1688–1914* (London, 1993).

Colin Clark, *The Conditions of Economic Progress*, 3rd edn. (London 1957).

Alfred W. Crosby, *Ecological Imperialism: The Biological Expansion of Europe, 900–1900* (Cambridge, 1986).

D. K. Fieldhouse, *Economics and Empire, 1880–1914* (London, 1973).

Tom Griffiths and Libby Robin, eds., *Ecology and Empire: Environmental History of Settler Societies* (Edinburgh, 1997).

David B. Grigg, *The Agricultural Systems of the World: An Evolutionary Approach* (Cambridge, 1974).

J. R. Hanson, *Trade in Transition: Exports from the Third World, 1840–1900* (New York, 1980).

Daniel R. Headrick, *The Tools of Empire: Technology and European Imperialism in the Nineteenth Century* (Oxford, 1981).

Leland Hamilton Jenks, *The Migration of British Capital to 1875* (New York, 1927).

A. G. Kenwood and A. L. Lougheed, *The Growth of the International Economy, 1820–1990*, 3rd. edn. (London, 1992).

W. Arthur Lewis, *Growth and Fluctuations, 1870–1913* (London, 1978).

S. B. Saul, *Studies in British Overseas Trade, 1870–1914* (Liverpool, 1960).

J. R. Seeley, *The Expansion of England* (London, 1883).

Brinley Thomas, *Migration and Economic Growth: A Study of Great Britain and the Atlantic Economy*, 2nd edn. (Cambridge, 1973).

B. L. Turner II and others, eds., *The Earth as Transformed by Human Action: Global and Regional Changes in the Biosphere over the Past 300 Years* (Cambridge, 1990).

Eric R. Wolf, *Europe and the People without History* (Berkeley, 1982).

4

British Migration and the Peopling of the Empire

MARJORY HARPER

'British emigrants do not as a body care whether they go to lands under or not under British rule, and cross the seas . . . at the prompting not of sentiment but of interest.'[1]

> If you leave the gloom of London and you seek a glowing land,
> Where all except the flag is strange and new,
> There's a bronzed and stalwart fellow who will grip you by the hand,
> And greet you with a welcome warm and true;
> For he's your younger brother, the one you sent away,
> Because there wasn't room for him at home;
> And now he's quite contented, and he's glad he didn't stay,
> And he's building Britain's greatness o'er the foam.[2]

The disparity between dismissive views of the relationship between emigration and Empire and portrayals of British migrants' umbilical attachment to their flag is one of many paradoxes in the complex mosaic of migration. Those who sponsored emigration not only walked the tightrope of promoting Imperial colonization while discouraging emigration to foreign destinations, notably the United States of America; they also wrestled with contradictory accusations, emanating from centre and periphery respectively, that they were stripping Britain of the brain and sinew of its population yet filling the colonies with paupers, social misfits, and political malcontents. Competing and overlapping theories and schemes of migration proliferated as new destinations were opened up, as British philanthropists and speculators filled the vacuum created by Colonial Office indecision and non-intervention, and as settler colonies acquired increasing control of their own immigration policies. But migration was much more than a subject of impersonal political debate for the 22.6 million individuals who left the British Isles between 1815 and 1914. Their life-changing decisions were shaped perhaps less by governments' and emigration societies' policies than by local

---

[1] Charles Dilke, *Problems of Greater Britain*, 2 vols. (London, 1890), I, p. 26.
[2] 'The Younger Son', in *Collected Verse of Robert Service*, 2 vols. (London, 1960), I, p. 70.

circumstances and the private inducements they received from family, friends, and community through multiple regional networks. Nineteenth-century migration was thus the product of an extremely complex web of influences, which both created a restless, rootless population and also provided an outlet for it in an expanding world within and beyond the British Empire.

Emigration has been a subject of public and political debate since at least the mid-eighteenth century. Opposition then centred on the damaging repercussions for the nation's prosperity and security of depleting its economic and military manpower, particularly from the Scottish Highlands and Ireland, which were losing their most industrious, rather than their surplus, population across the Atlantic. By 1815, however, popular ideas of mercantilism were giving way to those of Malthusianism, as a rapidly rising population, reinforced by a tide of demobilized soldiers, threatened to create massive unemployment, disrupt poor relief, and provoke social conflict. Migration therefore came to be perceived in seventeenth-century terms, not as a threat but a safety valve which—if adequate state funding was forthcoming—would rid Britain of a redundant and potentially dangerous element in its population. Malthusian ideas remained in vogue until economic revival in the 1830s prompted a more positive attitude towards Empire settlement, the focus shifting from domestic problems to the need for systematic colonization of Britain's possessions. Edward Gibbon Wakefield, leading advocate of the new policy, vehemently opposed 'shovelling out the paupers', and the National Colonization Society, founded in 1830 to promote his views, devised a scheme whereby revenue from land sales in the Antipodean colonies would be used by those colonies to finance the passages of eligible settlers. For three decades Wakefield's theories influenced official attitudes towards Empire settlement without compromising the state's non-interventionist stance on emigration, but economic depression again in the 1870s brought renewed lobbying from groups which claimed that state-funded emigration would solve immediately the twin problems of overpopulation in Britain and labour shortage in the colonies. Although it was 1922 before the Empire Settlement Act reached the statute book, the combination of organized lobbying with growing concern for Imperial unity and opportunity ensured that the emigration debate remained as vibrant at the end of the nineteenth century as at its beginning.

Although particular migration policies were dominant at different periods, these were never unanimously endorsed, and disagreements continued to stimulate debate. Mercantilist concern at the 'epidemic desire of wandering'[3] in the late eighteenth century was fuelled by the successful recruitment campaigns of a

---

[3] Samuel Johnson, *A Journey to the Western Islands of Scotland*, ed. R. W. Chapman (Oxford, 1924), p. 87.

growing number of emigration agents, and by the British government's reluctance to condemn Imperial emigration wholeheartedly after losing the thirteen colonies, as it began to see some virtue in bolstering its vulnerable northern frontier against American aggrandizement. Malthusian policies were also criticized as expensive, ineffective, or from a different perspective, negative responses to Britain's socio-economic problems.[4] Colonial accusations of emigrants' unsuitability, and their refusal to accept Britain's unwanted population, became more strident with the growth of self-government and when Malthusian philosophies revived in the late Victorian depression. Wakefieldian orthodoxy was also attacked for promoting an exclusive policy which robbed Britain of the flower of its population while denying assistance to the most needy.[5] The government's consistent priority, as in all matters, was throughout to avoid positive intervention, while broadly sanctioning Imperial colonization and discouraging emigration to the United States. Legislation—either to impede or encourage an exodus—was infrequent and largely ineffective, particularly in respect of state-funded colonization, which remained a major bone of contention throughout the nineteenth century. Equally controversial were the six Passenger Acts which regulated the conditions of migrant shipping within the Empire. Passed between 1803 and 1855, they were designed to protect migrants from hazard and abuse in port and on the voyage. Unfortunately, the legislation was rendered largely ineffective by defective supervision and sanction on the part of the Colonial Office's overworked agents; improvements after 1850 were due less to legislation than to the combination of declining migration and the introduction of steamships.[6]

Despite the overwhelming popularity of the United States, reinforced by Irish and continental migration through Liverpool from mid-century, British emigrants played a prominent part in the peopling of Canada and the Antipodes. British North America—cheap, familiar, accessible, and too near the United States to warrant Imperial government-subsidized migration—attracted a steady flow of independent settlers, supplemented by the recipients of private and charitable assistance, and boosted from the 1890s by assiduous agency activity. The first significant flicker of interest in Australia in 1838 was due to a combination of the Canadian Rebellion, 1837, and the full implementation of bounties; gold discoveries in the 1850s and 1860s brought a more sustained influx to both Australia and New Zealand, reinforced by agency propaganda and the availability of assisted passages by nomination; and the Antipodes maintained their popularity until the

    [4] e.g., *Westminster Review*, VI (Oct. 1826), pp. 342–73; Charles Buller, 6 April 1843, *Parliamentary Debates* (Commons), col. 522.

    [5] R. Torrens and others, 1 March 1870, *Parliamentary Debates* (Commons), cols. 1002–77.

    [6] Oliver MacDonagh, *A Pattern of Government Growth, 1800–60: The Passenger Acts and their Enforcement* (London, 1961).

Canadian government launched its highly effective advertising campaign in the 1890s. Migration to the more distant Empire depended heavily on sponsorship as well as specific economic incentives. South Africa's fleeting popularity at the end of the century was due to mineral discoveries and assisted settlement after the South African War, while a smaller, steadier movement to the West and East Indies comprised mainly 'career migrants'—planters, administrators, and missionaries, with a notable upsurge of movement to India for about six years after the Mutiny.[7]

The multifaceted character of migration, as well as its extent and direction, was dictated largely by the diverse circumstances of the migrants. Some had no choice. Between 1788 and 1853 approximately 123,000 male and 25,000 female convicts were transported to New South Wales and Van Diemen's Land (Map 24.1), many for persistent offences involving theft.[8] Over 88 per cent arrived after 1815, half being sent for seven years, and a quarter for life. Most came from England, where prison overcrowding was particularly acute, but of the quarter who came from Ireland, around a fifth were political and social rebels, and a quarter of all Irish transported were women. Only about one in twenty convicts was of Scottish origin, Scottish judges being more reluctant to impose sentences they believed savage and life-threatening.

Transportation, along with distance, cost, land speculation, and lack of precedent for European settlement impeded free migration to Australia, and in the 1820s convicts outnumbered free settlers by about three to one. During the 1830s that position was steadily reversed, as money from land sales was used to subsidize the passages first of women and then also of artisans and agricultural labourers under two bounty schemes introduced by the Colonial Office and the New South Wales government in 1832 and 1836 respectively. Government bounty migrants were chosen and despatched under the auspices of agents employed by the Colonial Office to disseminate information, protect migrants, and charter ships. From 1837 naval surgeons were employed as selecting agents, and T. F. Elliott was appointed Agent-General, overseeing both the surgeons and sub-agents based at ten major British ports. The reforms were intended to tackle colonial accusations that the Colonial Office's main interest was to relieve British pauperism, and that slack selection had led to an influx of dissolute women and too many men ignorant of the skills they professed. These accusations had provoked the parallel colonial bounty scheme, under which colonists bought bounty orders for specified categories of migrants, who were then selected by agents in Britain and brought

---

[7] For discussion of migration statistics see chap. by P. J. Cain.

[8] L. Robson, *The Convict Settlers of Australia* (Melbourne, 1981), p. 9. From 1850 to 1867 Western Australia, at its own request, received 9,668 male convicts in the teeth of opposition from eastern Australia, where the system was coming to an end.

out to Australia in privately engaged ships, the colonists obtaining a refund for their outlay if the migrants were approved on arrival.

Financial crisis in New South Wales led to the total suspension of assisted migration in 1842–43, and again in 1845–47. When assistance was renewed, temporarily in 1844 and more permanently in 1848, it was largely under the control of the Colonial Land and Emigration Commission in London. Appointed in 1840 to replace Elliott, the Commission administered migration on behalf of the overburdened Colonial Office, and curtailed colonial influence on bounties until its status was eroded by the attainment of responsible government. During the second half of the century migrants were assisted to the Antipodes under three complementary schemes: selection, nomination, and land order. About half were chosen by agents in Britain according to colonial labour requirements and were given assistance from the land fund according to their age and occupation. The appointment of Australian recruitment agents in Britain in the 1850s and 1860s spawned colonial policies of assisted passage and settlement based on nomination, particularly in Victoria and New South Wales, where many settlers took advantage of the scheme to be reunited with relatives and friends. Meanwhile Queensland, which pursued an active immigration policy after becoming a separate colony in 1859, favoured the granting of land orders to those who either paid their own passages or had them paid by friends or employers, and gave assisted passages to eligible migrants who subsequently qualified for land orders. New Zealand, in receipt of migrants since 1839, had by the late 1850s also developed a structure of subsidized passages and land grants, promoted by British-based provincial agents and co-ordinated after 1871 by an Agent-General, located in London. Farmers, agricultural labourers, and domestic servants were given particular encouragement, and migration made steady progress, notably in Otago and Canterbury (Map 25.1), where solid Scottish and English foundations had been laid by Free Church of Scotland and Anglican settlements respectively from 1848 and 1850.[9]

Assistance for migrants to British North America was spasmodic, small-scale, and stimulated by expulsive domestic factors rather than Canadian inducements. Imperial involvement was restricted largely to the decade after 1815, when, in order to strengthen the Canadian frontier, approximately 6,640 migrants, largely impoverished Irish farmers, Scottish handloom weavers, and discharged soldiers, were given free passages and land grants. However, by 1827 escalating costs, questionable results, and economic revival in Britain had overridden the recommendations of a Select Committee that state-funded migration should be formalized and

---

[9] Assisted migration to the Antipodes is examined in Marjory Harper, *Emigration from North East Scotland*, Vol. I, *Willing Exiles* (Aberdeen, 1988), pp. 278–83.

extended.[10] Not until 1888 was the government again involved in sponsoring migration, when in a half-hearted response to the Napier Commission's assertion that state-directed migration was the only solution to Highland overpopulation and unrest it allocated £10,000 towards resettling 100 Hebridean crofting families in Canada.[11]

Assisted migration to Canada was organized primarily by individuals, commercial companies, and charitable societies. From 1803 to 1815 the Earl of Selkirk brought approximately 1,100 Highlanders, mainly victims of clearance, to Prince Edward Island, Upper Canada, and Red River, and between 1803 and 1823 Colonel Thomas Talbot settled 12,000 impecunious migrants on an extensive grant at Lake Erie (Map 23.1).[12] The government's experiments also involved an element of proprietorial colonization, particularly in the Breadalbane migration of 1819 and in Peter Robinson's settlements of 1823 and 1825. By the mid-1820s, however, commercial enterprises such as John Galt's Canada Company—followed a generation later by the railway companies—were beginning to eclipse private individuals as sponsors of migration. Meanwhile, those who could not afford commercial terms turned to philanthropic societies which mushroomed in response both to the new public confidence in migration as a remedy for domestic ills and the Imperial government's refusal to finance a regular removal of paupers. Over 15,000 destitute weavers in West-Central Scotland belonged to around thirty emigration societies in the 1820s, but although the Canadian immigration authorities reported substantial arrivals of pauper weavers, both then and when the societies re-emerged in the 1840s depression, they were the minority which had scraped together the fare from private donations, church collections, and their own meagre savings.[13]

Landlord-assisted migration became a common—and notorious—feature of the nineteenth-century transatlantic movement. Some, like the 500 paupers sent to Canada by the Earl of Egremont from his Sussex estates between 1832 and 1837, were well-supported and successful. For others, assistance was essentially a euphemism for compulsion, particularly in the Highlands, where landlords whose

[10] *First Report from the Select Committee Appointed to Enquire into the Expediency of Encouraging Emigration from the United Kingdom. P[arliamentary] P[apers]* (1826) (404), IV, 1, pp. 3–4.

[11] *Report of the Commission of Inquiry into the Condition of Crofters and Cottars in the Highlands and Islands of Scotland, PP* (1884) [C 3980], XXXII, pp. 97–108. See also Wayne Norton, *Help Us to a Better Land: Crofter Colonies in the Prairie West* (Regina, 1994).

[12] Talbot's initial 5,000-acre grant grew to 65,000 acres after he began to claim extra land in payment for each family he settled. *Dictionary of Canadian Biography,* Vol. VIII, *1851–60* (Toronto, 1985), pp. 857–62.

[13] Helen I. Cowan, *British Emigration to British North America: The First Hundred Years* (Toronto, 1961), pp. 44–45, 61–62, 132–33, 209; *Annual Reports of the Agents for Emigration in Canada for 1841, PP* (1842) (373), XXXI, pp. 6–7, 18.

hostility to migration evaporated when their estate development policies failed began to harness assisted emigration to clearance, in an attempt to reduce over-population on their properties. Their initiatives multiplied after the withdrawal of Australian bounty schemes in 1842 and when it became clear that the Imperial government intended to ignore a Select Committee's advice in 1841 that extensive state-aided emigration was a prerequisite for any permanent improvement in the Highland economy. After famine swept the region in the mid-1840s the roll-call of landlord-assisted migrants arriving at Quebec grew to over 10,000 in the decade 1846–56, with 4,048 arriving in 1851 alone,[14] but their settlement was punctuated by bitter complaints from Canadian sources about the deficient provision for reloca-tion made by several landlords. One of the worst offenders was John Gordon, proprietor of South Uist and Barra, nearly 2,000 of whose tenants were dependent on public assistance in Quebec in 1851, and whose widow and successor, Lady Emily Gordon Cathcart, was also to implement controversial Canadian coloniza-tion schemes in the 1880s and 1920s.[15]

Assisted migration after 1850 was nevertheless dominated by national and provincial charities and self-help groups—over sixty of them in 1886—which aimed to find colonial outlets for Britain's surplus female population, and dest-itute children, as well as the unemployed. Female migration to Australia had been promoted since the early 1830s, in order to redress gender imbalance, then in the 1840s Irish Poor Law Unions began to send women to Canada as well. In 1850 the London Female Emigration Society sent its first contingent of working women to Toronto, and between 1862 and 1892, as colonial conditions continued to improve, Maria Rye's Female Middle Class Emigration Society made interest-free loans to about 400 women, mainly teachers and governesses, bound for Canada, Austral-asia, and South Africa. After 1880 nearly all national and local societies came under the umbrella of the British Women's Emigration Association, although the pro-moters of South African colonization continued to work independently until the formation in 1919 of the Society for the Oversea Settlement of British Women. The familiar justification of female migration—that it 'civilized' the colonies while reducing the chronic surplus of women in Britain—was reinforced after 1880 by economic depression at home, eugenic arguments, and the upsurge of imperial-istic sentiment. Recruits were 'missionaries of Empire',[16] encouraged to migrate not only to find employment but, more importantly, to become wives of British settlers and mothers of a future British colonial generation.

[14] T. M. Devine, *The Great Highland Famine: Hunger, Emigration and the Scottish Highlands in the Nineteenth Century* (Edinburgh, 1988), p. 206.

[15] *Quebec Times*, 1851, quoted in J. Murray Gibbon, *Scots in Canada* (London, 1911), pp. 131–32; Norton, *Help Us to a Better Land*, pp. 3, 7, 17, 88.

[16] Ella Sykes, *A Home Help in Canada* (London, 1912), p. 304.

From 1869 the London feminist Maria Rye also pioneered juvenile migration, as did the Scots-born evangelical Annie Macpherson. Thereafter assisted migration was increasingly incorporated into the rescue and rehabilitation work of philanthropists concerned with child welfare, in the belief that it would solve practical and moral problems alike, and that their city-born recruits—once established in the morally restorative rural colonial environment—would become 'the bricks with which the Empire would be built'.[17] Between 1870 and 1914 the best-known operator, Thomas Barnardo, sent 31,031 children overseas, 28,689 to Canada and 2,342 to Australia, while William Quarrier and his successors despatched to Canada 35 per cent of the 20,000 children taken into the Orphan Homes of Scotland between 1870 and 1930. A further 10 per cent went from English workhouse schools, financed by parish guardians, and most 'home children', after a brief sojourn in a receiving home, were recruited into colonial households as cheap agricultural labourers and domestic servants.[18]

William Booth too shared the vision of an Empire populated with sound—if surplus—British stock, and assisted migration was incorporated into his tripartite scheme, launched in 1890, to rehabilitate the 'submerged tenth' of Britain's population.[19] Booth claimed that the international network of his Salvation Army made it ideally suited to supervise both the selection of colonists and their relocation, and although no overseas colony was established as intended, the Salvation Army soon became the largest emigration agency in the British Empire, promoting and administering the migration—almost exclusively to Canada—of 200,000 working-class men and women by 1930. Although most paid their own fares, a loan fund administered by the Army's Emigration Department assisted the impecunious to cross the Atlantic in specially chartered vessels. Labour bureaux operated during the voyages to secure work for the migrants before they landed, and the Army also arranged protected passages for the dependants of married men whom it had sent to Canada in advance of their families to prepare a new home.

It is not surprising that assisted migration was controversial. Australian bounties were offered to migrants whose skills would further the colonies' development, but the recipients included, for example, large numbers of destitute Highlanders fleeing from the 1836–38 famine, and the sometimes licentious female inmates of English and Irish workhouses. The removal of redundant women, destitute children, urban artisans, and ambitious agriculturists from late Victorian Britain was criticized in the Empire as a renewed evacuation of unadaptable paupers and misfits. At the same time, British employers bemoaned the loss of domestic and

---

[17] Gillian Wagner, *Children of the Empire* (London, 1982), p. xv.

[18] See Marjory Harper, 'The Juvenile Immigrant: Halfway to Heaven, or Hell on Earth?', in C. Kerrigan, ed., *The Immigrant Experience* (Guelph, 1992), pp. 165–83.

[19] *In Darkest England and the Way Out* (London, 1890), pp. 146–55.

farm servants, and socialists challenged the ethics of exporting socio-economic problems instead of providing welfare at home. Disillusioned migrants complained about misleading promises of land, employment, or status offered by fraudulent agents. At the other end of the economic scale, colonial resentment of arrogant, ham-fisted remittance men, whose wealthy families had paid them to emigrate and subsidized them to stay overseas, was manifested primarily in verbal ridicule but sometimes in a refusal to entertain English migrants' employment applications.[20]

Voluntary migration—unimpeded by the regulations of governments and societies—demonstrates even more clearly the influence of migrants' circumstances and ambitions on the volume, direction, and character of the exodus. Private encouragement and practical assistance from family, friends, and community, transmitted primarily by letter and remittance but occasionally through visits home, were of inestimable and enduring importance in stimulating secondary migration and directing patterns of settlement. Pioneer sheepfarmers in Eastern Australia in the 1830s sometimes preferred to hire employees through family contacts, rather than the haphazard allocations of the bounty systems; managerial recruitment for sugar, coffee, and tea plantations in the West and East Indies was achieved through private networking rather than public advertisement; Canada's chief immigration agent frequently commented in mid-century on the large numbers who came out to join earlier arrivals, who 'in many cases have been enabled by their industry to acquire the means of paying the passage of remaining relatives'; and in 1857 James Adam, a Scottish pioneer migrant who revisited Britain as Otago's first provincial emigration agent, orchestrated an exodus of 4,000, of whom 800 were related to earlier settlers and often had their fares paid by the pioneers.[21]

The services of an agent could be a potent catalyst, particularly for migrants who lacked personal contacts overseas. Agents had been involved in the migration business since its inception, and in the first half of the nineteenth century the extensive importation of Canadian timber provided the opportunity for an army of shipowners to offer a wide choice of transatlantic passages to migrants at steerage prices of around £4 per head. As steam eclipsed sail and embarkation became centralized on a few large ports after 1850, provincial booking agents,

---

[20] Patrick Dunae, *Gentlemen Emigrants: From the British Public Schools to the Canadian Frontier* (Vancouver, 1981).

[21] Harper, *Willing Exiles*, pp. 288–97 and 330–39; Report of A. C. Buchanan for 1859: *Emigration* (*North American Colonies*), PP (1860) (606), XLIV, p. 11. In his reports for 1843 and 1855 Buchanan noted that three-quarters of arrivals at Quebec had come out to join relatives. *Emigration*, PP (1844) (181), XXXV, p. 6 and *Emigration* (*North American Colonies*), PP (1857) (14), X, Sess. 1, p. 14); James Adam, *Twenty-Five Years of Emigrant Life in the South of New Zealand* (Edinburgh, 1876), pp. 38–39.

representing the interests of major shipping companies, became the linchpins around whom migrant transportation revolved, not only arranging passages but also responding to pressures exerted by professional colonial agents to publicize assisted-passage and settlement schemes by arranging literature distribution, lectures, and interviews. Rival colonies tried to secure business by offering these part-time agents a commission of up to £1 per head on eligible recruits—generally agricultural workers and domestic servants—in an increasingly competitive race to populate the Empire with useful British stock.

While paid, professional agents were an integral part of Wakefieldian selection procedures from the 1830s, Canada did not launch a co-ordinated campaign to compete with Australasian—and American—propaganda until after Confederation. Canada's first official agent, English migrant Thomas Rolph, was appointed as a temporary itinerant lecturer from 1839 to 1842 to revive Canada's flagging reputation after the Rebellion, but it was 1854 before the newly created Bureau of Agriculture allocated any money to publicize migration. Five years later an information office was opened in Liverpool; following Confederation, resident and itinerant agents were strategically stationed across the British Isles to promote Canada and inspect departing migrants; and from 1872 these provincial agencies were supervised by a London office, headed by Canada's newly appointed High Commissioner from 1880 to 1899 and by a special Emigration Commissioner thereafter. Agents, who were expected to maintain an office and submit regular reports to headquarters, distribute written advertisements and government-sponsored publications, conduct illustrated lecture tours and personal interviews, counteract the activities of rivals, and supervise the work of booking agents, were carefully chosen with reference to local needs, connections, and knowledge of procedure. For instance, W. L. Griffith, sent from Manitoba to North Wales in 1897, was a Welsh-speaking native of Bangor, whose cousin controlled a syndicate of Welsh newspapers and was therefore a useful ally in the propaganda war; Thomas Grahame, appointed to Glasgow in the same year, had previously been a purser with a transatlantic shipping line; and John Maclennan, appointed in 1907 to cover northern Scotland, was a Gaelic-speaking Canadian of Highland descent.[22] A federal injection of 4 million dollars in the decade after 1896 gave agency activity an even higher profile, as the Canadian government and transcontinental railway companies became concerned to populate the vast western prairies for reasons of national unity and economic viability. It was a timely decision, for it coincided with an upsurge of enthusiasm for Canada and Dominion settlement in the British Isles.

---

[22] National Archives of Canada, RG 76, C7302, vol. 146, file 34688; C4660, vol. 5, file 41, part 1; C10294–5, vol. 405, file 590687.

Agency activity did not go unopposed. In addition to the familiar, polarized claims, emanating from Britain and the colonies respectively, about the export of the élite and insufficiently rigorous selection procedures, there was intercolonial antagonism and even rivalry between federal and provincial representatives of the same countries. Apathetic or over-enthusiastic booking agents could create problems for the professional agents, who relied heavily on these shopkeepers and businessmen to overcome local conservatism, and make practical arrangements on their behalf. The frequency with which bonus claims were disputed reflects the temptation faced by booking agents to recruit indiscriminately, sacrificing quality to quantity for the sake of a commission, while more seriously, migrants sometimes fell victim to fraudulent promises. Yet for all their faults, agents—amateur and professional—increasingly became the cornerstone of Imperial migration, translating an unfocused restlessness into a concrete decision to migrate through their lectures, advertisements, and personal persuasion, and facilitating the migrant's removal by arranging the passage and perhaps securing land or employment in the new location.

By the close of the nineteenth century migration had been woven inextricably into the fabric of British life and public debate, and had made a significant demographic and cultural impact on both donor and receiver societies. The famine-induced exodus from Ireland relieved congestion and permitted consolidation of smallholdings into economically viable units, but left a legacy of ineradicable bitterness and continuing depopulation, also evident—to a lesser degree—in Highland Scotland. Scotland's loss of around 61 per cent of natural increase between 1853 and 1930 reinforced a well-established and self-conscious culture of diaspora. By the end of the century there was throughout Britain a trend away from the exodus of farming families and craftsmen towards the departure instead of young, unskilled urban adults, travelling alone, but increasingly as sojourners, whose temporary migration became more feasible as the steamship revolution shrank the world.[23] Yet a vital recurring feature in the kaleidoscopic history of migration was the determination of many migrants, despite their variable backgrounds, aspirations, and experiences, to recreate overseas a national or regional identity which could then be used to enhance economic opportunities, mitigate dislocation, and voice nostalgic, jingoistic—or occasionally revolutionary—sentiments. Through practising endogamy, forming religious and secular societies which reflected their origins, and patronizing ethnic hostels, as well as fostering chain migration supported by remittances, many English, Welsh,

[23] Dudley Baines, *Migration in a Mature Economy* (Cambridge, 1985), pp. 62, 88, 129; N. H. Carrier and J. R. Jeffery, *External Migration: A Study of the Available Statistics, 1815–1950* (London, 1953), pp. 19, 53. By 1914 around 70% of English and Scottish migrants were under 30, and in the half-century before 1914 inward passenger movement averaged around 45% of outflow.

Scottish, and Irish migrants successfully—and sometimes aggressively— implanted their individual national identities overseas, particularly within an Empire over which they often claimed proprietary rights.[24] Apart from Fenians, republicans, and others for whom migration represented revolt against Britain, the imperialism which was often a crucial component of migrants' national identity—particularly at the end of the century—may well have impeded their assimilation and the development of colonial nationalism. It also suggests that, whatever the domestic difficulties which impelled the migrants overseas, their destinations were often decided less by interest than sentiment, although they were probably less inspired than their British-based supporters with the vision of 'building Britain's greatness o'er the foam'.

[24] Ross McCormack, 'Cloth Caps and Jobs: The Ethnicity of English Immigrants in Canada, 1900– 1914', in J. M. Bumsted, ed., *Interpreting Canada's Past*, 2 vols., Vol. II: *After Confederation* (Toronto, 1986), pp. 175–91.

Select Bibliography

DUDLEY BAINES, *Emigration from Europe, 1815–1930* (Basingstoke, 1991).

N. H. CARRIER and J. R. JEFFERY, *External Migration: A Study of the Available Statistics, 1815–1950* (London, 1953).

W. A. CARROTHERS, *Emigration from the British Isles, with Special Reference to the Development of the Overseas Dominions* (London, 1929).

HELEN I. COWAN, *British Emigration to British North America: The First Hundred Years*, revised edn. (Toronto, 1961).

T. M. DEVINE, *Scottish Emigration and Scottish Society* (Edinburgh, 1992).

CHARLOTTE ERICKSON, ed., *Emigration from Europe, 1815–1914: Select Documents* (London, 1976).

DONALD FLEMING and BERNARD BAILYN, eds., *Perspectives in American History*, Vol. VII, *Dislocation and Emigration: The Social Background of American Immigration* (Cambridge, Mass., 1973).

D. V. GLASS and P. A. M. TAYLOR, *Population and Emigration: Government and Society in Nineteenth-Century Britain, Commentaries on British Parliamentary Papers* (Dublin, 1976).

MARJORY HARPER, *Emigration from North East Scotland*, Vol. I, *Willing Exiles*, Vol. II, *Beyond the Broad Atlantic* (Aberdeen, 1988).

H. J. M. JOHNSTON, *British Emigration Policy, 1815–1830: 'Shovelling out Paupers'* (Oxford, 1972).

OLIVER MacDONAGH, 'Irish Emigration to the United States of America and the British Colonies during the Famine', in R. Dudley Edwards and T. Desmond Williams, *The Great Famine: Studies in Irish History, 1845–52* (Dublin, 1962), pp. 319–90.

——— *Emigration in the Victorian Age: Debates on the Issue from Nineteenth-Century Critical Journals* (Farnborough, 1973).

HOWARD L. MALCHOW, *Population Pressures: Emigration and Government in Late Nineteenth-Century Britain* (Palo Alto, Calif., 1979).

A. G. L. SHAW, *Convicts and Colonies* (London, 1966).

HUGH TINKER and others, *The Diaspora of the British* (London, 1982).

5

Migration from Africa, Asia, and the South Pacific

DAVID NORTHRUP

After the British Isles, the most important source of overseas emigrants within the nineteenth-century Empire was British India. In addition, substantial numbers of Africans, Chinese, and Pacific Islanders entered various parts of the Empire. Before 1860 nearly all of these migrations were to supplement former slave populations in tropical sugar plantation colonies, but thereafter a growing share went into plantation labour in colonies that had never known slavery as well as into mining and railway construction. Tropical migration was an integral part of the Empire's expansion, strongly linked to the development of new colonies and subsidized European emigration in the southern hemisphere.

Most Asian, African, and Pacific immigrants were recruited on long-term labour contracts. They either arrived at their destinations already tied to specific employers or were allocated to employers immediately after arrival. Some contracts were in the form of debt bondage, that is, a long-term obligation to a recruiter or employer to repay the cost of passage and advances by wage deductions. Many others entered into formal contracts of indenture, obliging them to work for a specified period of time (typically five years), although no formal debt was incurred. Unlike European indentured servants of earlier centuries, they received wages in addition to free passage overseas and often had the right to free return. Because indentured migrations were subject to close official supervision and to careful record-keeping, their details are better known than other tropical migrations.[1]

Once established the scale of indentured migration into the Empire remained quite stable at 150,000 or more per decade from 1841 until 1910 (Fig. 5.1). However, destinations changed markedly over time. Mauritius received most indentured labourers up until 1866, when it was surpassed by the British Caribbean colonies, principally British Guiana and Trinidad (Table 5.1). After 1890 most immigrants went to newer African and South Pacific colonies. British settlers in Natal began importing indentured labour from India in 1861. Queensland sugar growers

---

[1] The principal discussions of tropical migration are listed in the Select Bibliography.

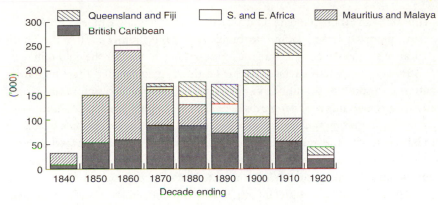

FIGURE 5.1. Destinations of indentured labourers within the Empire, 1831–1920, by decade

Source: David Northrup, *Indentured Labor in the Age of Imperialism, 1834–1922* (Cambridge, 1995), Table A.2.

TABLE 5.1. *Overseas indentured immigration to destinations in the British Empire, 1834–1920*

Destinations	Africans	Indians	Chinese	Pacific Islanders	Totals	%
Mauritius		451,786	816		452,602	31
Malaya		130,000			130,000	9
British Guiana	14,060	238,740	13,533		266,333	18
Trinidad	8,854	143,939	2,645		155,438	11
Jamaica	11,391	36,412	1,152		48,955	3
Other British West Indies	5,027	10,363	574		15,964	1
Natal		152,184			152,184	10
Transvaal			63,695		63,695	4
East Africa		39,437			39,437	3
Queensland			5,130	62,542	67,672	5
Fiji		56,000		26,460	82,460	6
Total	39,332	1,258,861	87,545	89,002	1,474,740	100
%	3	85	6	6		100

Source: Northrup, *Indentured Labor*, Table A.2; Walter Look Lai, *Indentured Labor, Caribbean Sugar; Chinese and Indian Migrants to the British West Indies* (Baltimore, 1993), Table 5.

recruited South Pacific Islanders from 1863. The Colonial Sugar Refining Company of Sydney first brought indentured labourers to Fiji from Pacific islands in 1864 and from India beginning in 1879 (Map 24.2). Other kinds of plantations and mines also tapped these labour sources. Ceylon coffee plantations and Burma rice plantations drew large numbers of Indians. Coffee, sugar, and rubber plantations

in the Malayan Straits Settlements attracted both Indians and Chinese. British East
Africa imported Indian labour to build the Uganda railway. After the South
African War (1899–1902) the Transvaal brought in Chinese for the gold mines.

Although the pull of overseas labour needs strongly dictated these migration
patterns, the push of conditions in the source regions was also significant. Nearly
all African emigrants were people displaced by the suppression of the Atlantic slave
trade. The migration peak in 1851–60 (Fig. 5.1) reflected the exceptional exodus of
Indians following the Indian Mutiny of 1857–58; the peak in 1901–10 was due to the
unsettled conditions that drove nearly 64,000 Chinese to leave their country
during the last years of the Ch'ing empire to work for low wages in the Transvaal
gold mines. Despite their different origins, destinations, and forms of recruitment,
tropical emigrants had much in common with emigrants from Britain in their
aspirations, mode of transport, and permanent settlement abroad. The differences
in the destinations and status of the two groups were due as much to Imperial
policy as to inherent circumstances.

Tropical labour migration arose to meet slavery's decline. In the British Caribbean
a labour shortage that developed when slavery was abolished in 1834 became acute
after the end of the period of apprenticeship there in 1838.[2] Freed people either
refused to work as long and as hard as they had been forced to do under slavery or,
in the case of most women and many men, rejected plantation labour completely.
Meanwhile, African 'recaptives' whom British patrols had rescued from slave ships
were accumulating in liberation depots in the West African colony of Sierra Leone,
on the mid-Atlantic island of St Helena, and at some Latin American locations.
Until 1840 British officials opposed allowing these 'liberated Africans' to emigrate
overseas from Sierra Leone, except as military recruits, lest such migrations be
seen as a disguised revival of the slave trade. Thereafter that policy was reversed
in order to alleviate the worsening labour shortages in the British Caribbean
colonies and stem the mounting expense of maintaining the growing liberated
population.

When recruitment efforts in the early 1840s produced few volunteers, Sierra
Leone authorities adopted measures to stimulate emigration. They discontinued
settling-in allowances in 1844, gave labour recruiters free access to newly arrived
recaptives, whom they kept isolated from local residents who might describe
conditions in the West Indies adversely. Under these circumstances, the number
of emigrants from Sierra Leone to the West Indies rose to an annual average of
1,500 in the late 1840s. Even more were recruited from the depot on St Helena,
which had insufficient land and water to accommodate liberated Africans perman-

---

[2] For discussion of Apprenticeship system see below pp. 476–79.

ently. However, the supply of African recruits fell off rapidly as the Atlantic slave trade was brought to an end at mid-century.

Far larger and more enduring than the flow of free Africans was the migration of Indians that began to Mauritius and was later extended to more distant locations (see Table 5.2). After their African slaves were emancipated, Mauritian planters were confident that all future labour needs could be met from India. By the end of apprenticeship on Mauritius in March 1839, private recruiters had supplied a labour force of some 25,000 Indians, most newly arrived under five-year contracts of indenture. Planters in the British West Indian colonies also turned to India, one British Guiana planter organizing the transport of 396 Indians on two ships in 1838.

Imperial authorities, however, soon balked at continuing Indian immigration unless the conditions of recruitment, transport, and employment in the colonies improved. They suspended indentured migration to Mauritius in 1839, but the stickier issue was whether to permit further recruitment for the West Indies. Lord John Russell, Secretary of State for the Colonies, in February 1840 expressed his unwillingness to support 'any measure to favour the transfer of labourers from British India to Guiana...which may lead to a dreadful loss of life on the one hand, or on the other, to a new system of slavery'. The majority report of the investigators of the Mauritius trade, released in October 1840, concurred: 'We are convinced...if West Indian voyages be permitted, the waste of human life and

TABLE 5.2. *Indian overseas labour emigration, 1834–1924*

Principal Destinations	Indentured	Free of Indenture
Mauritius, 1834–1910	455,187	
Réunion, 1841–82	74,854	
British Guiana, 1838–1918	238,861	
Trinidad, 1845–1917	149,623	
Jamaica, 1845–1915	38,595	
Other British West Indies, 1838–1915	11,152	
French Caribbean, 1853–85	79,089	
Dutch Guiana, 1873–1916	34,503	
East Africa, 1895–1922	39,437	
Natal, 1860–1911	152,932	
Fiji, 1879–1916	61,015	
Burma, 1852–1924		1,164,000
Ceylon, 1843–1924		2,321,000
British Malaya, 1844–1910	130,000	1,624,000
TOTAL	1,465,248	5,109,000

Source: Northrup, *Indentured Labor*, Table A.1, Map 6.

misery that will fall on the Coolies under the name of free labourers will approach to those inflicted on the negro in the middle passage by the slave trade.'[3]

Humanitarian opposition to Indian labour migration to the West Indies soon crumbled in the face of stronger agendas, however, just as it had to liberated African migration. The collapse of British plantations for lack of labour would dash reformers' hopes of convincing French and American authorities that slave emancipation was not the road to ruin. Moreover, it was difficult for Britain to champion the virtues of free labour while denying Indians the right to sell their labour overseas. Once Indian immigration was allowed to resume into Mauritius in 1843 under government surveillance, its extension elsewhere soon followed. The first shipload for the West Indies left Calcutta in January of 1845. Bans on immigration into Natal and Réunion were lifted in 1860 and into the French West Indies in 1865. Indentured Indian immigration was permitted into Dutch Guiana in 1873, into Fiji in 1879, and into East Africa in 1895. Including less-closely regulated immigration into Ceylon, Burma, and the Straits Settlements, the annual emigration from India rose during the last quarter of the nineteenth century from an average of 300,000 to over 425,000. This does not include the considerable labour migration underway within the vast Indian Empire, including indentured migration to the tea estates of Assam.

Yet acquiescence in overseas migration did not signify official disregard of the conditions of their recruitment and of their treatment overseas—nor of their transport, as is considered later. As the exodus from India grew, inspection and supervision improved. At sub-depots where potential recruits were first collected, magistrates verified that they understood and assented to the terms of the contract before sending them on to the coastal depots in Calcutta or Madras. There the recruits received medical examinations and were questioned again about their agreement to the terms of the contract. One-third of those registered in a sub-depot were eventually rejected as unfit or changed their minds before signing a contract and sailing overseas. In British colonies, the welfare of indentured labourers was supervised by Protectors of Immigrants and, as numbers grew, by Agents-General of Immigration and various sub-agents. In foreign colonies, British consular officials were charged with monitoring the welfare of Indian immigrants. A series of commissions in the 1870s and afterwards investigated shortcomings and recommended corrective measures.

The system was far from perfect, even allowing for the inevitable growing-pains in so large an operation. Not all officials were of the highest character and many

---

[3] Hugh Tinker, *New System of Slavery: The Export of Indian Labour Overseas, 1830–1920* (London, 1974), p. vi; *Report of the Committee appointed . . . to Inquire into the Abuses Alleged to Exist in Exporting Bengal Hill Coolies and Indian Labourers*, P[arliamentary] P[apers] (1841), XVI (45), p. 295.

were compromised by conflicts of interest. Recruiters and medical personnel in India were under pressure to process large numbers of recruits quickly, which led to lapses and compromises. Protectors in the colonies could be worn down by the resistance of powerful employers and their allies in the colonial governments.

Yet some problems originated with the recruits, who, in their eagerness to be accepted, concealed illnesses and claimed to understand what they did not. Despite subsequent information to the contrary, many recruits seem to have clung to distorted or exaggerated visions of opportunities and conditions overseas that they heard from the Indian recruiters who scoured the markets, bazaars, and temples for likely candidates. Many seem to have passed through the screening process with vague or erroneous notions of where they were going and what they might expect there.

Such circumstances reflect the degree to which emigration was due to the strong push of social and economic misery. Most Indian emigrants came from two areas feeling strong demographic and economic pressure—the Gangetic Plain of northern India and the environs of Madras in South India. Although ambition motivated some, desperation best explains the emigration of many others. Population pressure, periodic famines, political upheavals, and changing economic conditions drove large numbers of Indians out of their ancestral villages and into the global labour market. The degree to which British rule was itself responsible for the rising tide of misery that drove Indians into overseas migration is a matter of some debate. While a simple delineation of the underlying causes of emigration may not be feasible, it is clear that some spurts of Indian overseas migration were due to specific political and ecological events. Besides the disruptions associated with the Indian Mutiny of 1857–58, periodic famines served to overcome resistance to long-term emigration. Not surprisingly, many emigrants were from the social and economic margins of Indian society, but during the peak decades of the trade emigrants represented a cross-section of rural India. Migrants to Fiji, for example, came from 260 identifiable social groups.

India supplied the greatest number of new labour recruits, but since the early nineteenth century some tropical British colonies had sought immigrants from China. Before mid-century most Chinese went to Singapore and other parts of South-East Asia, but the addition of Western ships and port facilities at Hong Kong from 1842 greatly increased the size and scope of Chinese emigration. Of the 550,000 Chinese who sailed from Hong Kong between 1854 and 1880 (see Table 5.3), nearly two-fifths went to the United States of America, a third to South-East Asia, and 22 per cent to Australia, mostly under a form of debt bondage known as the 'credit-ticket system'. Nearly 18,000 indentured Chinese labourers reached the British West Indies from various ports between 1853 and 1884, a modest number compared to the 240,000 that were indentured to Cuba and Peru during that

TABLE 5.3. *Chinese overseas emigration from Hong Kong, 1854–1880*

Principal Destinations	Indentured	Free of Indenture	Total
United States, 1854–80		224,355	224,355
Australia, 1854–80		118,543	118,543
South-East Asia, 1855–80	730	185,379	186,109
New Zealand, 1871–80		5,191	5,191
Canada, 1865–80		2,394	2,394
British Guiana, 1858–78	6,808		6,808
Cuba, 1856–58	4,991		4,991
Peru, 1869–70	763		763
Surinam, 1866–69	1,869		1,869
Hawaii, 1865–77	789	2,331	3,120
Tahiti, 1864–65	1,035		1,035
India, 1864, 1875	2,370	15	2,385
TOTAL	19,355	538,208	557,563

Source: Calculated from Arnold J. Meagher, 'Introduction of Chinese Laborers to Latin America: The "Coolie Trade", 1847–1874', unpublished Ph.D. dissertation, California, Davis, 1975, p. 108A and Table 4.

period. Although emigration was illegal under Chinese law until 1860, Chinese brokers or 'crimps' combed the impoverished masses in the coastal ports for recruits to deliver to private Western firms. The many victims of deception, debt, and kidnapping among them were rarely detected by inspectors. Chinese and Western concern over gross irregularities sharply curtailed indentured immigration to the Americas after 1874, but 5.75 million Chinese immigrants poured into the Straits Settlements between 1881 and 1915[4] and, for a brief period from 1904 to 1907, the Transvaal recruited 64,000 northern Chinese for its gold mines.

The spread of plantation economies also brought the islands of the South Pacific into the labour trade in the early 1860s. As in China, Pacific Island recruitment initially involved a large amount of kidnapping and deceptive practices. However, as demand grew, the voluntariness of the labour recruitment was closely monitored by British colonial officials. In all, 89,000 Melanesians and Micronesians went to Queensland and Fiji, principally to cultivate sugar. Pacific Islanders experienced particularly appalling mortality in Australia and Fiji from being exposed to unfamiliar epidemiological conditions. For example, the death rate during the first year for those arriving in Fiji in 1880 was 145 per thousand. As they became acclimatized, mortality dropped to 42 per thousand in the second year and 27 in the third. Despite such chilling losses, the desire for Western goods and adventure continued to lure Pacific Island labourers to Queensland until the recruitment ended in 1904 and to Fiji until 1911.

---

[4] See below, pp. 384–86.

Admittedly different in their origins, destinations, and terms of recruitment, the tropical immigrants of the nineteenth century have also been dealt with separately from contemporary European immigrants for less defensible reasons.[5] One misleading proposition put forward by some modern historians is that the tropical migrations had more in common with the African slave trade than with free European migrations. This line of analysis accurately conveys the concerns of contemporary British officials and humanitarians: the undeniable fact that early indentured immigrants replaced or supplemented liberated slaves and performed the same kind of work under distressingly similar conditions. In addition, it highlights the deception or coercion used in the recruitment of many early African, Indian, Chinese, and Pacific Island labourers, practices captured in the crude nicknames used for such recruitment—'blackbirding' in the South Pacific, the 'pig trade' in China, and the 'coolie trade' in both China and India. However, most tropical migrants differed substantially from slaves in their willingness to emigrate as well as in the terms of their recruitment, transport, and working conditions overseas. Most tropical emigrants departed of their own free choice, hoping to achieve a better life abroad or at least to escape the painful circumstances at home. Although tropical labourers' lives overseas may have been harsher than those of European immigrants and filled with greater disappointments, theirs was less a new system of slavery than an old system of free labour revived to suit imperial needs in an industrial age. For these reasons, much greater understanding of tropical immigration comes from comparing it with contemporary European immigration.

The once-common distinction between tropical 'sojourners', who intended to return home at the end of their contracts, and European 'settlers', who were committed to permanent residence in a new land, is likewise greatly overstated. In fact, large proportions of both European and tropical immigrants initially dreamed of returning home after accumulating wealth abroad. Many in both groups did return home, whether wealthy or not, but where conditions permitted a similar proportion of both chose to settle abroad permanently. Not surprisingly, the rate of repatriation to India and China from nearby South-East Asian colonies was quite high. White-preference policies also forced the repatriation of most Pacific Islanders from Australia and of the Chinese from the Transvaal, but elsewhere in the Empire tropical immigrants settled permanently in large numbers. Virtually all indentured Africans stayed on in the West Indies and blended into the black population established there by the slave trade. Indians also stayed on in

---

[5] See Tinker, *New System of Slavery*; Johnson U. J. Asiegbu, *Slavery and the Politics of Liberation, 1787–1861: A Study of Liberated African Emigration and British Anti-Slavery Policy* (London, 1969). Adrian Graves, *Cane and Sugar: The Political Economy of the Queensland Sugar Industry, 1862–1905* (Edinburgh, 1993).

large numbers. By 1920 Indians had displaced Africans as the principal inhabitants of Mauritius, outnumbered Europeans in Natal, formed one-third of the population of Trinidad, and were two-fifths of the inhabitants of British Guiana and Fiji. Chinese established large communities, above all in parts of South-East Asia but also in North America. Despite Canadian restrictions on Chinese immigration after the completion of the Canadian Pacific Railway in 1885, some 15,000 lived there in 1900.

The proportion of women also distinguishes most groups of tropical immigrants into British colonies from sojourners and increases their resemblance to European immigrants. British officials initially doubted that any circumstance would induce Asian women and families to emigrate, but regulations that required a minimum proportion of Indian women on voyages to the West Indies were in fact fulfilled. Without such a provision fewer men would have been willing to stay abroad for the ten years necessary to merit a free return passage, and many fewer Indians might have chosen to remain abroad. In 1853, at the instigation of the British Colonial Office, a minimum of one female for every three males was required among Indian immigrants to Mauritius. Three years later that proportion was extended to British Guiana. From 1868 the proportion of female immigrants was raised to 40 per 100 males (except for Mauritius which remained at 33.3 : 100) and was strictly enforced. Concerted efforts by British agents raised the proportion of women to 20 per 100 men among Chinese recruited for British Guiana. No specific effort was made to recruit women in the Pacific Islands, where only about 6 women per thousand men went to Queensland or to Fiji.[6]

It is now clear that differences in economic circumstances, geography, and Imperial policies were responsible for directing most European immigrants to other temperate destinations, while African, Asian, and Pacific Islanders went largely to tropical ones. By global standards nineteenth-century Britain was an area of high prevailing wages, so that its emigrants naturally chose destinations in developing parts of the world with even higher prevailing wage rates. In contrast, in Asia, Africa, and the South Pacific wages were either very low by global standards or were not even monetarized, making them attractive to plantation economies that could not hope to attract high-cost European labour. In addition, most British emigrants were within relatively easy reach of their preferred destinations in North America, whereas a large proportion of tropical migrants faced voyages of several months to reach a place willing to employ them. The cost of a

---

[6] Tinker, *New System of Slavery,* p. 205; Pieter Emmer, 'The Great Escape: The Migration of Female Indentured Servants from British India to Surinam', in Shula Marks and Peter Richardson, eds., *International Labour Migration: Historical Perspectives* (Hounslow, 1984), pp. 248, 250; Brij V. Lal, *Girmitiyas: The Origins of the Fiji Indians* (London, 1969), pp. 104–06.

passage across the Atlantic amounted to only half of the per capita annual income of European areas, whereas a passage to the West Indies cost 3 to 10 times the per capita annual income in East or South Asia. As a result, most tropical immigrants had no choice but to accept the free passage and low-wage contracts that distant plantations or mines were willing to offer.[7]

The effect of these practical differences was accentuated by policies that required tropical migrants to repay the costs of their passages while underwriting those of British emigrants. In the rare case of indentured European immigrants to the tropics, such as the famine-stricken Portuguese from Madeira, the conditions of servitude were customarily waived or eased. For example, in 1857 the Governor of British Guiana justified imposing no indenture on the Portuguese whose passage that colony's government paid, while simultaneously imposing one on Indian and Chinese immigrants, by his belief that the Portuguese did not require to be compelled to work.[8] Similarly, British immigrants to distant colonies in southern Africa, Australia, and New Zealand (or even to Canada) regularly received government-subsidized passages that had no onerous restrictions attached. Many countries and colonies also promoted European settlement to 'whiten' their populations under the guise of maintaining 'civilized' standards, while excluding or expelling non-European immigrants.

Attention to such politically constructed differences between the tropical and temperate immigrants needs to be balanced by attention to the politically constructed similarities between them with regard to maritime passenger travel. Both groups of voyagers benefited from the rapid growth in the size and speed of ocean vessels in the nineteenth century. Indeed, indentured tropical immigrants generally travelled in ships that were larger than the immigrant vessels of the North Atlantic. By the third quarter of the century vessels from India to the West Indies averaged nearly 1,000 tons and some were double that size. Chinese emigrants to the British West Indies sailed on vessels averaging 870 tons.[9] Although Europeans emigrating to North America were much more likely to travel on steamships than were tropical emigrants, this was largely due to the fact that steam vessels did not become efficient enough to compete with large sailing ships on long runs across

---

[7] This analysis depends on Stanley L. Engerman, 'Coerced and Free Labor: Property Rights and the Development of the Labor Force', *Explorations in Economic History*, XXIX (1992), pp. 1–29; David W. Galenson, 'The Rise and Fall of Indentured Servitude in the Americas: An Economic Analysis', *Journal of Economic History*, XLIV (1984), pp. 1–26; Colin Newbury, 'Labour Migration in the Imperial Phase: An Essay in Interpretation', *Journal of Imperial and Commonwealth History*, III (1975), pp. 234–45; Teodor Shanin, 'The Peasants are Coming: Migrants Who Labour, Peasants Who Travel and Marxists Who Write', *Race and Class*, XIX (1978), pp. 277–88.

[8] Governor Wodehouse to H. Labouchere, 6 June 1857, *Papers Relating to Immigration to the West Indian Colonies*, PP (1859), XVI [1st Session 2452], p. 232.

[9] Northrup, *Indentured Labor in the Age of Imperialism, 1834–1922* (Cambridge, 1995), pp. 80–103.

two oceans until the early twentieth century. But on shorter runs in the tropics this difference was less pronounced. For example, Indians made considerable use of the British India Steam Navigation Company established from Calcutta to Rangoon in 1861, and of other steamship lines that later served the Indian Ocean basin.

Another important change in sea travel shared by both sets of immigrants after 1828 was the development and implementation of strict regulations regarding crowding, sanitation, and accommodation on British maritime vessels. In 1840 ships from British possessions whose routes crossed the equator had to provide 15 square feet of berth space per passenger with headroom of at least 5.5 feet and no more than two tiers of berths. These rules applied to vessels carrying indentured Indians and Africans as well as to the Chinese shipped from Hong Kong. During its existence from 1840 to 1873 the Colonial Land and Emigration Commission supervised both British and indentured passenger movement, issuing detailed regulations to improve emigrants' health and safety and overseeing their enforcement. Spurred on by high passenger mortality associated with Irish famine victims and cholera epidemics in the British Isles, new Passenger Acts by 1855 required more headroom and reduced passenger densities to no more than fifty adults per 100 tons burthen. The application of these rules on British ships from China was regularly evaded in the early 1850s, but the Government of India saw to it that enforcement was quite strict on vessels from their ports. Conventions signed with France in 1860 and 1861 required French vessels to observe the same regulations as British carriers in return for allowing French colonies equal access to Indian labour.

Despite such regulations, passengers on long voyages through the tropics continued to suffer high rates of illness and death, for example, an average mortality of 20 per thousand per month among Indians travelling to the British Caribbean in the period 1851 to 1870. Although this was about one-third the mortality on nineteenth-century slave-trade voyages, it was substantially higher than losses on European immigrant vessels in that period. The difference had less to do with inferior sanitary facilities, food and water, and medical care, than with the presence of highly infectious diseases such as cholera which spread quickly under the crowded conditions of the long tropical immigration voyages. Before 1875 official efforts to control infection were frustrated by the logistics of processing large numbers of people, the emigrants' deliberate concealment of their illnesses, and the limitations of contemporary medical knowledge. However, stricter screening, increasingly detailed regulation of shipboard usages, and improvements in medical practice produced a steady decline in deaths at sea after 1875 to under 10 per thousand for Indian voyages to the West Indies and under 5 per thousand on Indian voyages to Mauritius, Natal, and Fiji as well as on the voyages of Pacific Islanders and of Chinese to the Transvaal.[10]

Limited space prevents consideration of the conditions of labour in the various colonies. These were everywhere extremely arduous, although doubtless mitigated for non-European as for European migrants by the gradual formation of the new local communities and myriad forms of labour organization and resistance. Nevertheless, the view of several official investigating commissions was that, despite some regrettable lapses, indentured labour was free labour not slave labour. The last and broadest of these commissions reported emphatically in 1910: 'Our unhesitating opinion, after examining the best and most authoritative evidence that we could obtain on the subject, is that whatever abuses may have existed in the more remote past, no such charge can be substantiated against the system as it at present exists and has been in practice during the past 20 or 30 years.'[11] Yet within a decade the indentured labour system largely came to an end. In some colonies the number of new immigrants who took up permanent residence eliminated the need for further immigration. The decline in the sugar plantation economy in many places curtailed labour demands. Policies of white preference ended Pacific Islanders' immigration to Australia and restricted the entry of Indians and Chinese in southern Africa. Most fundamental was the decision of the Government of India to ban the remaining indentured labour trade from March 1916 in response to growing Indian nationalist protest.

[10] Fred H. Hitchins, *The Colonial Land and Emigration Commission* (Philadelphia, Pa., 1931), pp. 119–53; Ralph Shlomowitz and John McDonald, 'Mortality of Indian Labour on Ocean Voyages, 1843–1917', *Studies in History*, VI (1990): Table 16; David Eltis, 'Free and Coerced Transatlantic Migrations: Some Comparisons', *American Historical Review*, LXXXVIII (1993), pp. 271–72; Northrup, *Indentured Labor*, pp. 84–103.

[11] *Report of the Committee on Emigration from India to the Crown Colonies and Protectorates*, PP (1910), XXVII [Cd. 5192], p. 23.

Select Bibliography

JOHNSON U. J. ASIEGBU, *Slavery and the Politics of Liberation, 1787–1861: A Study of Liberated African Emigration and British Anti-Slavery Policy* (London, 1969).

SURENDRA BHANA, *Indentured Indian Emigrants to Natal, 1860–1902: A Study Based on Ships' Lists* (New Delhi, 1991).

MARINA CARTER, *Servants, Sirdars and Settlers: Indians in Mauritius, 1834–1874* (New York, 1995).

P. C. EMMER, ed., *Colonialism and Migration: Indentured Labour Before and After Slavery* (The Hague, 1986).

ADRIAN GRAVES, *Cane and Sugar: The Political Economy of the Queensland Sugar Industry, 1862–1905* (Edinburgh, 1993).

ROBERT L. IRICK, *Ch'ing Policy toward the Coolie Trade, 1847–1878* (Taipei, 1982).

BRIJ V. LAL, *Girmitiyas: The Origins of the Fiji Indians* (Canberra, 1983).

A. J. H. LATHAM, 'South-East Asia: A Preliminary Survey, 1800–1914', in Ira Galzier and Luigi de Rosa, eds., *Migration Across Time and Nations: Population Mobility in Historical Contexts* (New York, 1986), pp. 11–29.

K. O. LAURENCE, *A Question of Labour: Indentured Immigration into Trinidad and British Guiana, 1875–1917* (London, 1994).

WALTON LOOK LAI, *Indentured Labor, Caribbean Sugar: Chinese and Indian Migrants to the British West Indies, 1838–1918* (Baltimore, 1993).

SHULA MARKS and PETER RICHARDSON, eds., *International Labour Migration: Historical Perspectives* (Hounslow, 1984).

ARNOLD J. MEAGHER, 'The Introduction of Chinese Laborers to Latin America: The "Coolie Trade", 1847–1874', unpublished Ph.D. dissertation, University of California, Davis, 1975.

CLIVE MOORE, JACQUELINE LECKIE, and DOUG MUNRO, eds., *Labour in the South Pacific* (Townsville, Queensland, 1990).

DOUG MUNRO, 'The Pacific Labour Trade: Approaches, Methodologies, Debates', *Slavery and Abolition*, XIV (1993), pp. 87–108.

DAVID NORTHRUP, *Indentured Labor in the Age of Imperialism, 1834–1922* (Cambridge, 1995).

PETER RICHARDSON, *Chinese Mine Labour in the Transvaal* (London, 1982).

KAY SAUNDERS, ed., *Indentured Labour in the British Empire, 1840–1920* (London, 1984).

MONICA SCHULER, *'Alas, Alas, Kongo': A Social History of Indentured African Immigration into Jamaica, 1841–1865* (London, 1980).

RALPH SHLOMOWITZ and LANCE BRENNAN, 'Epidemiology and Indian Labor Migration at Home and Abroad', *Journal of World History*, V (1994), pp. 47–67.

HUGH TINKER, *A New System of Slavery: The Export of Indian Labour Overseas, 1830–1920* (London, 1974).

6

British Policy, Trade, and Informal Empire in the Mid-Nineteenth Century

MARTIN LYNN

To focus solely on colonial possessions in examining Britain's expansion overseas in the nineteenth century is to ignore the multifaceted nature of Britain's international position.[1] The increases in foreign trade, in the balance of credit abroad, and in the numbers of emigrants settling overseas in these years were but part of a wide-ranging expansion of British society that also took military, naval, religious, and cultural forms and spread far beyond the territorial holdings of Britain's Empire. The naval officer in the Atlantic, the missionary in Africa, and the trader in China were as much agents of potential British influence as the colonial administrator in India. Yet the nature and significance of this influence, its impact, and the British government's role in sustaining it remain elusive.

This chapter examines, from a metropolitan perspective, the government's approach to the expansion of British influence beyond the territorial Empire in the mid-nineteenth century and the nature of the relationship that developed between Britain and several regions where such expansion occurred. Its focus is primarily economic, not because other forms of British expansion—cultural, religious, demographic or political—were unimportant, but because commercial and financial intervention was recognized at the time as critical to reshaping such areas in Britain's interests, however those interests were ultimately defined. It offers a general assessment of both Britain's success in this reshaping and the degree to which, in these years, the British economy in practice asserted its influence over such regions outside the colonial Empire.

British expansion overseas between 1820 and 1880 was extensive, and its nature a major point of controversy at home. For contemporaries the question was how far expansion overseas should be welcomed, given its implications for domestic society and politics. Expense, economy, retrenchment, the 'condition of England',

---

[1] John Gallagher and Ronald Robinson, 'The Imperialism of Free Trade', *Economic History Review* (hereafter *EcHR*), Second Series, VI (1953), pp. 1–15.

and corruption were but some of the issues tied up in this. While much of the argument focused on Britain's existing colonial holdings and reform of the relationship between these and Britain itself, discussion also addressed the nature of Britain's influence beyond the colonies and its impact on the British economy.[2]

What is striking about this debate is the way it was accompanied, at least from the middle decades of the century, by a sense of confidence within many parts of British society about the country's place in the world. Palmerston, the then Foreign Secretary, articulated this clearly in 1848 with his view that Britain led the march of civilization. 'I may say without any vain glorious boast...', he claimed, 'that we stand at the head of moral, social and political civilization. Our task is to lead the way and direct the march of other nations.'[3] Such confidence in Britain's place in the world reflected an optimism that the globe was being 'renovated' and 'improved', and that British interests were at the heart of this. The objective of the Empire, stressed a Commons' Committee report of 1837, was for Britain to afford the peoples of the world 'the opportunity of becoming partakers of that civilization, that innocent commerce, that knowledge and that faith with which it has pleased a gracious Providence to bless our own country'.[4]

Such sentiments came accompanied by numerous calls for the further expansion of British interests overseas. The ostensible aim was what Palmerston termed 'world bettering', yet intertwined with this were clear and acknowledged intentions to benefit British economic interests as well.[5] The nature of these geopolitical ambitions is perhaps best known in George Canning's renowned words of 1824, that 'Spanish America is free and if we do not mismanage our affairs sadly, she is English', a statement suggesting belief that the world was moving Britain's way and rightly so.[6] The expansive ambitions implicit in these attitudes were more broadly applied to the globe as a whole. The early nineteenth century saw calls to open up China to British economic interests; to search for a second India in Africa; and to expand British commerce in South-East Asia and the Middle East.

Free trade, defined in the broadest sense of allowing the free play of the market, was seen as central to this process of expansion. Free trade was the vehicle for 'world bettering' as well as for the expansion of British economic interests overseas. It was the means whereby Britain's role in the wider world could best be

[2] Bernard Semmel, *The Rise of Free Trade Imperialism* (Cambridge, 1970).

[3] In 1848, quoted in W. Baring Pemberton, *Lord Palmerston* (London, 1954), p. 141.

[4] *Report from the Select Committee on Aborigines (British Settlements) P[arliamentary] P[apers]* (1837) (425), VII, p. 76.

[5] Donald Southgate, '*The Most English Minister': The Policies and Politics of Palmerston* (London, 1966), p. 147.

[6] Quoted in H. W. V. Temperley, 'The Later American Policy of George Canning', *American Historical Review*, XI (1906), p. 796.

shaped. Yet the value of this expansion overseas and the place of free trade in it remained controversial, particularly early in the century. In origin the debate about free trade was an argument about the nature of Britain's domestic society, the place within it of land, commerce, industry, and finance, and the role of the State in economic affairs. However, the overseas dimensions to this were clearly considerable. The benefits of free trade were seen as twofold. First, it would stimulate the growth of British manufacturing. It would help other countries to earn sterling through increased exports of food and raw materials to Britain and would enable them to buy more British manufactures. It would encourage the international division of labour, and enhance Britain's comparative advantage in the world economy. Free trade, in short, would enable Britain to become and remain 'the workshop of the world'.

Tightly coupled to this was a second idea, of capitalism as a moral force. Free trade would help civilize the world through the spread of enterprise and the work ethic. This was related to ideas of progress towards a moral goal, defined largely in terms of British cultural norms. The spread of British trade and investment overseas was thus seen as good in its own right; it brought with it enterprise, progress, and civilization. Free trade would encourage moral regeneration, allowing economically 'backward' nations to develop their resources and throw off outdated élites while encouraging the development of capitalist classes through the moral dimensions of industry and capital accumulation. This was seen as being to the benefit of the areas on the receiving end of British intervention, whether or not they realized it. That this might also be to the gain of British economic interests was regarded as incidental, since free trade, it was argued, was to the benefit of all. In this sense free trade became the quintessential characteristic of the early Victorian view of the world, combining moral commitment with material self-interest.

Free trade was thus a principle that involved British economic expansion overseas and implied an important role for the British government in the encouragement of this. The issue was more complex however. On another level, free trade was a philosophy that implied Britain needed neither colonies nor its government to be involved overseas at all. For some observers, indeed, it was associated with what are often labelled 'little Englander' ideas. Richard Cobden, the politician whose name, along with those of Adam Smith and *The Economist* (established in 1843 to promote free trade ideas), is virtually synonymous with free trade, criticized the holding of colonies. The sectional interests embedded in the 'old colonial system' were to Cobden as much part of the corruption and misgovernment of Britain as those embedded in the Corn Laws of 1815. Such figures argued that in a free-trade world colonies would be redundant. Countries would trade with or borrow from Britain because it was in their self-interest to do so, irrespective of political ties. Colonies, therefore, far from benefiting Britain, were costly, wasteful, and above all unnecessary. Thus adherents of free trade supported moves to grant self-government to Britain's colonies of settlement while Cobden criticized Britain's role in India as a 'career of spoliation and wrong'; it would 'be a happy day when England has not an acre of territory in Continental Asia'.[7]

Advocates of free trade such as Cobden and John Bright further implied there was a very limited need for the government to intervene overseas at all. Free trade was 'God's diplomacy', said Cobden, arguing that war and international conflict would be redundant in a free trade world.[8] The mutual interdependency generated by commercial self-interest meant that free trade would ultimately eradicate the occasion of war and military intervention; war and preparation for war, argued Cobden, was part of that aristocratic misgovernment that had held Britain in thrall too long. Hence his criticisms of Britain's intervention to support the Ottoman empire against Russian designs in the 1830s, and of Britain's intervention in China in the late 1850s. Free trade was for Cobden, 'the only human means of effecting universal and permanent peace'; it was 'the grand panacea', bringing prosperity to all, encouraging an international division of labour to everyone's benefit, creating economic interdependence and rendering international conflict a thing of the past.[9]

Such views have led some to see in the triumph of free trade ideas after 1846 an attitude of 'anti-imperialism', critical of the Empire's existence, and of the costs and complications of British intervention overseas. Yet few in practice held such a position. Hardly any can be termed 'little Englanders' in this period with any accuracy, and certainly not Cobden; as Huskisson, the Colonial Secretary, stressed in 1828, 'England cannot afford to be little'.[10] All accepted the need to maintain Britain's interests overseas and that the State had a role in so doing; the issue was rather how best to do this. Few, for example, argued seriously for relinquishing colonies, not least because of their perceived role as a population safety-valve; Edward Gibbon Wakefield and the 'Colonial Reformers' pressed for a new relationship with colonial possessions, not their abandonment. Most accepted the need to maintain the colonial connection but argued that self-government was the more effective way to do this; self-government did not mean separation.

---

[7] Richard Cobden to H. Richard, 21 May 1856, in J. A. Hobson, *Richard Cobden: The International Man* (London, 1919), p. 144; Richard Cobden to John Bright, 22 Sept. 1857, in John Morley, *The Life of Richard Cobden*, 2 vols. [1879], 2nd edn. (London, 1881), II, p. 213.

[8] Hobson, *Richard Cobden*, p. 246.

[9] Cobden to Henry Ashworth, 12 April 1842, in Morley, *Richard Cobden*, I, p. 230; quoted in Donald Read, *Cobden and Bright: A Victorian Partnership* (London, 1967), p. 110.

[10] Huskisson's Speech on the Civil Government of Canada, 2 May 1828, in William Huskisson, *Speeches*, 3 vols. (London, 1831), III, p. 287.

Criticisms of the costs and corruption seen in 'the old colonial system' were not the same as calls for withdrawal from colonies; rather, they were calls for a more effective relationship to maintain Britain's interests overseas. Similarly arguments for the abandonment of India were conspicuous by their rarity; even Cobden accepted the manipulation of Indian tariff policies in British interests.[11]

Thus the triumph of free trade ideas in the mid-nineteenth century did not in practice imply an end to government intervention overseas in defence of British economic interests. Rather, the issue was how best should such intervention be undertaken and how far, in practice, should the government go in its support of those interests. Certainly the gaining of free trade treaties to open up a region's commerce, encouragement for the spread of trade, and the general promotion of free trade principles were accepted as central government aims. Yet there were limits to the government's role, particularly when it came to supporting private interests. First, public duty should never become confused with private gain. In Palmerston's words, 'it is the business of the Government to open and to secure the roads for the merchant', but no more.[12] Indeed, one influential study of Foreign Office policy in this period suggests that *laissez-faire* and free trade were taken literally by a Foreign Office that defined its role in 'securing roads' before the 1880s very narrowly.[13] Hostile to supporting individual bondholders or traders, it was only prepared to intervene on behalf of British economic interests overseas where such interests reinforced existing British political concerns. Secondly, the free trade treaties the Foreign Office pushed for were restricted to 'equal favour and open competition' for all powers. Their function was to open up markets to outsiders, protect British traders and financiers under international law, and guarantee that British trade and finance would receive equal treatment with that of other European states. The 'Open Door' was open for everyone. There was no policy here of obtaining exclusive privileges for Britain.

British policy was less selfless, however, than might appear. The government did not need to go beyond the 'Open Door' to obtain exclusive privileges in this period; the British economy's success made it possible to entertain ambitions of dominating large areas of the globe almost by default. Given the favourable international situation and that Britain's industrial and financial lead was so great, opening an area to outside influences by treaty was often sufficient to ensure that British trade and finance, rather than any rival's, would be

---

[11] A. G. L. Shaw, 'Introduction', in A. G. L. Shaw, ed., *Great Britain and the Colonies, 1815–65* (London, 1970), pp. 19–21.

[12] Palmerston to Auckland, 22 Jan. 1841, Broadlands Papers, University of Southampton Library. I am grateful to the Trustees of the Broadlands Papers and to Her Majesty's Stationary Office for permission to quote from this correspondence.

[13] D. C. M. Platt, *Finance, Trade and Politics in British Foreign Policy, 1815–1914* (Oxford, 1968).

paramount in that region. Opening economies to outside commerce by promoting free trade was *de facto* a policy of expanding British influence.

The assumptions implicit in this approach underlay much of British policy towards the wider world in the mid-nineteenth century. One can see this particularly in the career of Lord Palmerston, (Foreign Secretary 1830–34, 1835–41, 1846–51, and Prime Minister 1855–58 and 1859–65). Palmerston repeatedly used force to extend such principles overseas. He was not an ideological free trader—indeed, he was slow to accept repeal of the Corn Laws—and much of what he advocated came under fierce criticism, even to the extent of Commons motions of censure, from Cobdenites. Nor can his overseas policy be characterized as one simply designed to spread free trade principles. Nonetheless, Palmerston was strongly influenced by economists such as Adam Smith and David Ricardo and, like most of his time and class, he came to share the assumptions of the free trade advocates about Britain's place in the world and the government's role in sustaining it. More crucially perhaps, he was ready to exploit the influence of free trade supporters by appeals to the moral principles of free trade ideas.

Palmerston's primary interests as Foreign Secretary concerned Europe, but his actions extended far beyond that continent. 'The sun never sets upon the interests of this country', he stated in 1843.[14] He recognized too the changing shape of these interests. 'The rivalship of European manufacturers is fast excluding our productions from the markets of Europe and we must unremittingly endeavour to find in other parts of the world new vents for the produce of our industry... Abyssinia, Arabia, the countries on the Indus and the new markets in China, will at no distant period give a most important extension to the range of our foreign commerce.'[15]

There were inconsistencies in Palmerston's approach to the expansion of British influence in the wider world, and much of his apparent policy was simply rhetoric for domestic consumption. Yet underlying his interventions in regions as different as Africa and China was one consistent thread. What has been termed 'Palmerstonianism' represented, for the wider world, a policy of expanding British interests overseas by force wherever necessary, justified by appeals at home to moral imperatives.[16] In Palmerston's view, a universalist notion of progress based on British cultural norms, applicable to all societies across the globe, was tied to the need to hasten the march of civilization—defined by the principles of enterprise, capital accumulation, and individual property ownership—through the judicious use of force. That some societies were 'backward' was, in his view, a temporary

---

[14] Lord Palmerston, 1 March 1843, *P[arliamentary] D[ebates]* (Commons), col. 192.

[15] Palmerston to Auckland, 22 Jan. 1841, Broadlands Papers.

[16] R. J. Gavin, 'Palmerston's Policy Towards East and West Africa, 1830–1865', unpublished Ph.D. thesis, Cambridge, 1959, p. 1.

phenomenon due to environmental circumstances. Decisive action was required to remove these barriers to progress, and it was Britain's role to lead the way in this.

This was a project for, in David Livingstone's words, the 'renovation of the world' which required, in effect, Anglicization.[17] Trade, Christianity, education, and constitutional principles were all vehicles whereby this was to be achieved, but trade, as even Livingstone admitted, was the primer. As trade flourished, so societies would come to see the benefits of capital accumulation and civilization and would respond to the opportunities thus created by commercial contact with Britain. 'Commerce is the best pioneer of civilization,' stressed Palmerston. Free trade would, in his view, lead 'civilization with one hand, and peace with the other, to render mankind happier, wiser, better'.[18] Thus the aim of British policy overseas was to facilitate trade and to develop markets by opening up a region to outside contact. That this would benefit Britain through facilitating British trade and investment and finding new sources of raw materials for the British economy was freely acknowledged. The campaign against the slave trade that Britain led was not just to remove a 'foul and detestable crime', said Palmerston: 'virtue carries with its own reward ... These slave trade treaties ... are indirectly treaties for the encouragement of commerce.' So he argued that Britain's pressure against Brazil over the slave trade was 'greatly advantageous to the Brazilians, not only by freeing them from a grievous crime, but by very much improving their general condition'.[19]

In practical terms this required mutually beneficial links between the commercial classes of Britain and the recipient society. Such linkages would best be established through the free trade treaty that opened up an area to what Palmerston saw as the civilizing effect of foreign trade and investment. Opening up was the aim, for this would ensure British influence and the development of the region along lines that suited British interests; for Palmerston colonial Empire was immaterial but influence was certainly the desired result. The free trade treaty was thus a major weapon in Palmerston's schemes. Yet the problem was, as he realized, that such ties were difficult to establish and would not readily develop on their own. In this sense his was a much more pragmatic view of the world, and the potentialities within it for British trade, than was Cobden's stress on free trade as 'God's diplomacy'. Not least of the blockages to free trade recognized by Palmerston were the recalcitrant élites of African, Asian, and Latin American societies which relied on what he saw as privilege, corruption, or superstition to hold down enterprising groups. This could be seen most obviously in the case of the slave

---

[17] I. Schapera, ed., *Livingstone's African Journal, 1853–56*, 2 vols. (London, 1963), II, pp. 243–44.

[18] Lord Palmerston, 16 Feb. 1842, *PD* (Commons), col. 619.

[19] Lord Palmerston, 10 Aug. 1842, *PD* (Commons), cols. 1251–52; Palmerston to Crampton, 17 Feb. 1864, quoted in Harold Temperley and Lillian M. Penson, *Foundations of British Foreign Policy from Pitt to Salisbury* (1938; London, 1966), p. 304.

trade in Africa, where ruling élites used the traffic to preserve power and thus held back the economic potential of the continent. Such élites had to be reformed or removed, for both moral and practical reasons, and this might require forceful intervention or the threat of it. Once displaced, new groups could then be found to maintain connections with British trade through mutual self-interest.

Thus the British government had to use force, utilizing what Macgregor Laird, the West African traveller and shipping magnate, described as 'the moral power of the 24 pounder', to establish these links.[20] This was necessary to remove opponents and to open up such regions to the march of progress as expressed in the form of British trade and investment. Palmerston thus welcomed the use of naval power against China in 1846–47. 'These half-civilized governments such as those of China, Portugal, Spanish America, require a dressing every eight to ten years to keep them in order', he noted in 1850.[21]

Palmerston did not necessarily want annexations in order to reach his goals. Colonies had a role but were not important for their own sake; on the contrary, he felt, 'the value of such appendages is . . . much over rated'.[22] Hence his rejection of a colony in Abyssinia in the 1840s: 'all we want is trade and land is not necessary for trade; we can carry on commerce very well on ground belonging to other people.'[23] Hence too his rejection of an occupation of Egypt in 1859, comparing it in a well-known passage to the estate owner in the north of England with a residence in the south who did not thereby need to own all the inns between the two: 'all he could want would have been that the inns should be well kept . . . furnishing him with mutton chops and post horses.'[24]

None the less, commercial security could make intervention necessary. Britain did need, for example, to back up free trade treaties by establishing strategic bases to sustain British influence in a region. He was therefore willing to annex Aden in 1839 and Lagos in 1861. Not the least advantage of such bases was their role in relation to rival European powers. This was not because Palmerston felt their trade should be excluded from areas of British interest. On the contrary, provided it did not involve exclusive privileges, trade with other European powers was welcome as further encouragement of progress and 'world bettering': 'there is room

---

[20] Quoted in Philip D. Curtin, *The Image of Africa: British Ideas and Action, 1780–1850* (London, 1965), pp. 457–58.

[21] Minute by Palmerston, 29 Sept. 1850, on F[oreign] O[ffice] Memo of 26 Sept. 1850 on Consular Establishments at Foochowfoo and Ningpo, FO 17/173.

[22] Quoted in Kenneth Bourne, *Palmerston: The Early Years, 1784–1841* (London, 1982), p. 624.

[23] Minute by Palmerston, 30 Aug. 1847, on Plowden to FO, 28 Aug. 1847, FO 1/4.

[24] Palmerston to Cowley, 25 Nov. 1859, quoted in The Hon. Evelyn Ashley, *The Life of Henry John Temple, Viscount Palmerston, 1846–65*, 2 vols. (London, 1876), II, pp. 124–25.

enough...for...all the civilized nations of the rest of the world...[Britain] would see with pleasure every advance of commerce in Africa, provided that such commerce was not founded on monopoly.'[25] Thereafter the threat of force had to be kept ready to maintain the trade connections that had been created. The naval squadron sailing offshore was thus essential for the 'most exemplary drubbing' that Palmerston saw as occasionally necessary.[26] Similarly, Political Agents, such as Consul John Beecroft in the Niger Delta, Walter Plowden in Abyssinia, or Sir John Bowring in China, were necessary to monitor a region and facilitate British trade and investment.

The opening of a region through the free trade treaty—backed up by naval or consular force as required—in order to create economic linkages to the benefit of Britain, and the 'regeneration' of that region through the resultant trade and investment, were thus the twin aims of 'Palmerstonianism'. This policy of forceful intervention to spread market capitalism overseas received much criticism from Cobdenites and others who thought it reckless and unnecessary, but it clearly struck a chord with large sections of the British public. It was a policy that fitted the self-image of the commercial classes and indeed, more broadly, British perceptions of their place in the world. It resonated too with crude ideas of British patriotism, as the reaction to his 'Don Pacifico' speech of 1850, asserting British subjects' rights to protection overseas, showed. Palmerston's greatest skill lay in his ability to cast his overseas policy before the British public in terms of moral imperatives.

The centrality of free trade ideas in British ambitions for the wider world in these years can be seen in several regions outside the colonial Empire that were particularly the focus of British economic interest: Latin America, China, the Ottoman empire, and parts of Africa. British ambitions in Latin America were clear, at least before the 1860s: in Castlereagh's words, it was the 'opening to our manufactures of the markets of that great continent'.[27] The collapse of Spanish and Portuguese rule clearly offered possibilities to a power like Britain that could dominate South American waters and that had already been establishing an important presence in the region's commerce, but this required governmental action. Thus, it has been argued, between the 1830s and the 1860s the British government pursued an interventionist policy in Latin America designed to remove barriers to the intrusion of British trade and finance, to eradicate the slave trade, and to protect British

---

[25] Minute by Palmerston, 20 Dec. 1850, on Colonial Office to FO, 15 Nov. 1850, FO 2/4.

[26] Palmerston to Davis, 9 Jan. 1847, quoted in (The) Rt. Hon. Sir Henry Lytton Bulwer (Lord Dalling), *The Life of Henry John Temple, Viscount Palmerston*, 3 vols. (London, 1870–74), III, pp. 376–78.

[27] Memorandum by Castlereagh, 1 May 1807, in Marquess of Londonderry, ed., *Correspondence, Despatches and Other Papers of Viscount Castlereagh*, 12 vols. (London, 1848–53), VII, p. 321.

economic interests.[28] Officials intervened on numerous occasions. For example, in 1845, as in 1806–07, British forces intervened in the River Plate. British forces were also used in the landing at Callao in 1839 and the Mexico intrusion of 1861–62. On other occasions the mere presence of the Royal Navy was sufficient to obtain compliance, as off Peru in 1857 on behalf of bondholders, and against Chile in 1863. British pressure helped the creation of Uruguay, while Palmerston used the navy to threaten Brazil over the slave trade in 1848–49. From the 1830s to the 1860s the government clearly showed its willingness to intervene assertively in Latin America to open 'the markets of that great continent'.[29]

The aim was not to seize colonies but rather to secure the institutional framework to keep markets open. Numerous free trade treaties with Latin American governments were signed by Britain to achieve precisely that. One such was in 1825 with Argentina; another in 1834 was used to insist on a reduction in Peruvian tariffs; one with Brazil in 1810 gave Britain preferential duties until 1844. Other pressures were exerted to open inland waterways to outside trade. These actions were generally successful in both opening up Latin America to free trade and to achieving economic benefits for Britain: by the 1850s Britain was well established as the main trading partner of the region. Latin America took around 10 per cent of total British exports between 1850 and 1913 and around 10 per cent of British imports, figures second only to India's in Britain's trade. Equally, British financial involvement in Latin America increased with British investment growing from some £30m in 1826 to around £81m by 1865. Overall, there was clearly a considerable British economic presence in the continent by the 1880s.[30]

Similarly in China, British ambitions were to open this potential market of a quarter of humankind to British economic intrusion. Again the hope was that 'world bettering' and British economic ambitions would go hand in hand. The British government's involvement in the region grew sharply, with repeated interventions between the 1830s and 1860s. Chinese reluctance to open their economy to the 'foreign devils' from the West clashed with Britain's ambitions for free trade and demands for recognition and equal status. Such clashes culminated in the so-called Opium War of 1839–42, the seizure of Hong Kong, and the attempt to open China's economy to western trade and finance through the Treaty of Nanking (Nanjing) in 1842. The resulting five 'treaty ports', the 'concessions', and the principle of extra-territoriality were central to British ambitions in China. A further assault on China was launched in 1847 and again, this time with French

---

[28] Rory Miller, *Britain and Latin America in the Nineteenth and Twentieth Centuries* (London, 1993), pp. 67, 243–44.
[29] Memorandum by Castlereagh, 1 May 1807, in *Correspondence of Viscount Castlereagh*, VII, p. 321.
[30] See chap. by Alan Knight.

involvement, between 1856 and 1860, culminating in the establishment of further treaty ports and concessions.

These assaults were accompanied by an influx of western influences into China and the growth of British trade. British traders such as Jardine Matheson and Co. exploited the advantages gained in these treaties and took up important positions in the Chinese economy. Like other western enterprises, they operated with special privileges (such as exemptions from local taxes or extra-territorial legal rights), and the aid of compradors, or local merchants, that such firms employed at the interface with the local economy. British advisers took up positions within the Chinese administration, others helped construct arsenals and shipyards. Of most consequence was Robert Hart, who in 1863 became head of the Chinese Imperial Maritime Customs (IMC). The IMC collected the Chinese customs revenue and ostensibly, was an arm of the Ch'ing (Qing) government. In time, however, as these revenues became pledged to repay loans from western banks Ch'ing control over the customs became diluted; similar processes concerned the salt administration. Perhaps most significantly, the existence of the IMC prevented the Ch'ing imposing protective tariffs. Thus Britain's ostensible policy of opening Ch'ing economy to western trade and finance through free trade masked a deeper commitment to the economic penetration of the country. And, for the British at least, it seemed to work. British trade (imports and exports combined) of around £4m in 1830 rose to nearly £15m by 1860. Palmerston expressed satisfaction in 1845, stating that 'a greater benefit to British manufactures could hardly be conceived'; Lord Elgin, British High Commissioner and envoy to China, was categorical following his actions in 1858: 'we have broken down the barriers' to China's economy.[31]

The Ottoman empire was a further region where Britain entertained political and economic ambitions. Leaving aside the Balkan provinces of the empire, two areas were of particular importance to Britain: Turkey itself and Egypt. The strategic importance of Turkey, primarily because of concerns about the route to India, can be seen in British involvement in its defence against Muhammad Ali, ruler of Egypt, in 1839 and against Russia in 1853–56 during the Crimean War. Britain's aim was to gain a breathing space whereby Ottoman administration, its army, and its economy could be reformed and its independence thereby preserved. It was, said Palmerston, of 'utmost importance' to Britain to keep the Ottoman empire an independent state.[32]

---

[31] Quoted in Southgate, *The Most English Minister*, p. 146; Elgin to Shanghai Merchants, 18 Jan. 1859, *Correspondence Relative to the Earl of Elgin's Special Missions to China and Japan, 1857–1859*, c.2571, PP (1859) (Second Session), XXXIII, p. 458. See chap. by Jürgen Osterhammel.

[32] Lord Palmerston, 11 July 1833, PD (Commons), col. 579.

The ultimate aim may have been strategic, but economic penetration was the means to achieve this. In some ways Britain was successful. From the 1830s through to the 1880s Britain was establishing herself as the major external power in the region, aided by Stratford Canning as Ambassador (1825–29, 1842–58) in Constantinople. This can be seen most clearly in the free trade treaty of 1838, the Convention of Balta Liman, signed between the Ottomans and Britain and then extended to other powers. This treaty was designed to open up Turkey's economy to western, more particularly British, penetration and was recognized as a significant British success. Such penetration, it was believed, would regenerate the ossifying Ottoman empire, a process Palmerston believed would need just ten years of peace. The treaty established a tariff regime effectively outside Ottoman control, exempted foreign traders from internal customs duty, and eliminated state monopolies. By abolishing such monopolies it removed a major source of revenue from the government and forced it to consider foreign loans. When added to existing privileges under the 'Capitulations' for Europeans within the empire, which placed them effectively above the law and which were extended in 1867 to include rights to hold land, the thrust of British ambitions was clear.

Turkey's trade, particularly with Britain, grew considerably after 1838. There was a great increase in agricultural production, particularly wheat and cotton, for export, the other side of which was a sharp rise in cotton textile imports. This was particularly clear between 1840 and 1870, the decisive stage in foreign textile inroads into the Turkish economy. Britain's share of Ottoman imports and exports grew, doubling to nearly a third of the total between 1830–32 and 1870–72. British financial involvement with Turkey also mounted, especially from 1854. The first major loan to the Ottoman government came in that year, followed by thirteen other foreign loans over the next twenty years. Central to this process was the Ottoman Bank, established in London in 1856 and, from 1863 as the Imperial Ottoman Bank, responsible for the issuing of Ottoman currency. These loans came at a high price and increasingly were used to repay earlier debts. When this was not achieved, the Ottoman government was forced to raise funds from local merchants at high rates in order to repay its loans. The end result of this indebtedness came in the 1870s, with the Ottoman government going bankrupt in 1875.

As British ambitions to regenerate Turkey's economy through free trade ran into difficulties, Egypt grew in strategic and economic importance, particularly after the opening of the Suez Canal in 1869 and as illustrated by Benjamin Disraeli's purchase of the Khedive's shares in the Canal company in 1875. Britain's aims were to counter French influence in Egypt by opening its economy to British enterprise. Thereby, felt the Earl of Clarendon, later Foreign Secretary, Britain could secure 'the overland communication with India...the progress of civilization and the development of the commercial resources of the East'.[33] Under Muhammad Ali (1805–48), Egypt had experienced considerable economic growth. His moderniza-tion policies focused on protection and a strong state sector in the economy: government-run factories produced textiles, sugar, glass, and paper, while the state monopolized exports. With increased agricultural output, particularly in cotton, their centrepiece from the 1830s, these initially successful policies were under-mined by the 1838 treaty: it seriously affected Muhammad Ali's state-run factories, and demolished state monopolies, compelling Egypt's rulers to rely increasingly on foreign loans. Large-scale borrowing ensued, particularly from British sources, accompanied by an influx of westerners protected under the Capitulations. As in China, indigenous jurisdictions were increasingly eroded under western pressures.

Britain gained from this by developing as Egypt's main foreign trade partner, particularly in the second half of the century. By the 1880s she took 80 per cent of Egypt's exports and provided 44 per cent of her imports. As the major lender to the Egyptian regime, by the early 1870s Britain held the chief share of the public debt. Much of these loans was spent on public works, particularly railways, to match the ambitions of Egypt's rulers; but much too was spent unproductively on repaying previous loans, and wasteful empire-building in the south. When revenue failed to increase fast enough to meet obligations, the result was bankruptcy in 1876. This watershed in Egypt's history witnessed the establishment of a financial admin-istration under European control to organize Egypt's revenues and debt repay-ments. Although Britain occupied the country only in 1882, from 1876, with the establishment of outside financial control, Egypt effectively lost control of her affairs to foreigners.[34]

Tropical Africa too held an important place in the British government's designs. Here British commercial and political involvement grew markedly in these years. Again British aims centred on the spread of free trade—usually couched in terms of the moral imperatives of the anti-slave trade campaign—which became critical to ambitions of regenerating the continent and developing an important trading partner for British industry. This 'dream of tropical wealth' meant that particularly during the period from the 1840s to the 1860s, and notably under the impact of Palmerston, a growing British involvement on both sides of the continent—in areas as different as the Niger, Dahomey, Abyssinia, and Zanzibar—was encour-aged.[35] Here consul and anti-slaving naval officer worked to support the British presence in the form of trader and missionary. Palmerston encouraged expedi-tions to the Niger in 1841 and 1857; the mission to Dahomey in 1850; the assault on

---

[33] Memorandum by Clarendon, 14 March 1840, in Rt. Hon. Sir Herbert Maxwell, *The Life and Letters of George William Frederick, Fourth Earl Clarendon*, 2 vols. (London, 1913), I, p. 190.

[34] See chap. by Afaf Lutfi al-Sayyid-Marsot.

[35] Curtin, *Image of Africa*, p. 60.

Lagos in 1851 and its annexation ten years later; the creation of a Consulate at Massawa in 1847; and the actions against the Zanzibar slave trade in the early 1840s. The abolition of slave trading on both sides of the continent would be followed, it was hoped, by a surge in legitimate trade leading to economic rewards for Britain and the march of civilization for Africa.[36]

Between 1815 and 1880 British policy-makers intervened frequently in these four regions to support British political and economic interests. In all of them ideas of 'world bettering' and British economic benefits were tightly intertwined in the shape of market capitalism. The seizure of colonies was largely—though by no means entirely—eschewed and the emphasis was placed on establishing positions whereby British influence could be increased and the region's economy opened up to outside trade and investment via the free trade treaty. Where necessary this was undertaken by force, with the seizure of bases such as Hong Kong and the establishment of naval power like the anti-slaving squadrons off West and East Africa, used to maintain British leverage. From such points, Consuls and Political Agents could promote the provisions of free trade treaties and facilitate the spread of British trade and investment into their respective regions, thereby creating a burgeoning realm of British influence overseas.

In assessing the consequences of these actions, contemporary policy-makers and others certainly perceived the expansion of British influence across the globe to be immensely effective. For Herman Merivale, Professor of Political Economy at Oxford University, the British were 'masters of every sea and colonists of every shore, there is scarcely a nook which our industry has not rendered accessible', while for an observer such as W. S. Jevons in 1865, unfettered commerce had made 'the several quarters of the globe our willing tributaries'.[37] The optimism implicit in these views reflected the deeper belief that the spread of British trade and finance represented progress, improvement, and regeneration for the world. It reflected too a confidence that providence was on Britain's side and that the expansion of British influence overseas was right, inevitable, and pre-eminently beneficial to all parties.

Insistence on free trade principles to open regions of the world to British economic penetration undoubtedly worked, at least on one level. From Aden to Buenos Aires, from the Yangtze (Yangtzi) to Zanzibar, free trade principles were assiduously promoted by British officials, where necessary at the point of a gun-

---

[36] See chap. by T. C. McCaskie.

[37] Herman Merivale, *Lectures on Colonization and Colonies* (London, 1861), quoted in Semmel, *Free Trade Imperialism*, p. 1; W. Stanley Jevons, *The Coal Question* [1865], 3rd edn. (London, 1906), p. 410; quoted in Ronald Hyam, *Britain's Imperial Century, 1815–1914: A Study of Empire and Expansion*, 2nd edn. (London, 1993), p. 87.

boat. The resultant opening of local economies to Britain's merchants and financiers undoubtedly brought her benefits. Yet it is possible to see, in ways which
contemporaries like Jevons did not, significant limits to the access Britain secured
and the influence she established in these regions. In retrospect it is clear that,
while Britain achieved much, confidence in the regeneration of so-called backward
areas by tying their economies to the needs of Britain through free trade reflected
far more the persistent over-optimism of early Victorian society rather than the
developing realities of world politics.

The qualified impact of British economic influence can be seen in Latin
America, the area where Britain might be said to have asserted her interests
most effectively. Certainly the promotion of free trade encouraged Latin America
along lines of economic development that suited Britain. Yet looked at from
Britain the results of intervention in the region did not match Canning's ambitions, at least before the 1880s: 'South America was indeed free but she was not, in
the mid-Victorian period, English.'[38] Although the view from parts of Latin
America itself might have seemed very different, and while British economic
interests in Latin America grew during these years, what is striking is the limits
to this growth, and the limits to the leverage it gave: it did not, before 1880, make
the region, as Jevons put it, a 'tributary' of the British economy. Indeed, rival
merchants and financiers had begun to move into British Latin American markets
with remarkable ease by the end of the century.

Limits to dependency on Britain arose from the fact that, while its value might
seem impressive, the volume of British trade in the continent remained limited
before the 1870s. Low population levels, restricted purchasing power, and a poor
communication infrastructure meant that British trade did not have the impact
often imagined: indigenous craft industries were not entirely destroyed by British
imports in these years, nor did British traders replace local entrepreneurs in the
regional economy. Equally, Britain's investments in Latin America grew significantly in this period, but this did not give an unqualified hold over Latin
American economies. Countries could default, as Peru did on its loan of 1853 and
Argentina on the 1824 loan. Similarly, British-owned railway firms and utilities
might try to assert their powers in the market, but found local politicians adept at
extracting concessions in turn; such bargains as were struck between British
capital and local governments were never one-sided. The relationship between
Britain and Latin America remained one where local regimes were well able to
assert their own interests. Study of the Peruvian guano industry, the major
supplier to British agriculture in the middle of the century, for example, shows

---

[38] P. J. Cain and A. G. Hopkins, *British Imperialism: Innovation and Expansion, 1688–1914* (London, 1993), p. 312.

just how restricted was the influence British interests could exert over prices against a determined government.[39] From the metropolitan point of view there were considerable limits to British political influence in the region before 1880. Military interventions were often 'fruitless' and the British learnt the lesson of 1845 of just how counter-productive these could be.[40] Likewise, the leverage Britain gained over tariffs was limited. In practice Latin American governments retained considerable tariff autonomy even at the high-tide of free trade in the mid-century, and undoubtedly remained 'the essential mediators' in the relationship with Britain.[41]

This was even more the case in China. British aggression never achieved the optimistic ambitions that Palmerston and Elgin entertained in the 1840s and 1850s. Britain failed successfully to impose its will on China in these years, a fact Palmerston recognized with his belief that repeated military assaults were necessary. The Chinese economy responded only weakly to these incursions: Britain gained only limited benefits from China in these years. Her trade grew, but remained very small as a proportion of both Britain's total world trade and the Chinese economy; indeed, in this sense the high point in British trade with China lay in the very early 1800s (see Table 2.1 p. 33). Thereafter, China occupied a declining place, failing to keep up with the broader growth of British trade overseas.

The reason for this again lay in market resistance to western inroads. In China, these remained largely limited to the relatively few treaty ports. Chinese firms stood up well to western competition. Being closer to the market, they had many advantages over their western competitors. They could stress 'buy Chinese' sentiments, enjoy better labour relations, and utilize their knowledge of local tastes while compradors exploited western merchants' weaknesses to their own advantage. No more than Latin America's, were Chinese crafts destroyed by western imports. Outside the treaty ports most Chinese relied, as they always had done, on local handicraft products. Foreigners continually complained about the difficulty of penetrating the Chinese market.[42]

Behind this lay the fact that the population had little disposable income; demand for western goods was small and foreign trade remained only a fraction of internal Chinese trade throughout this period. The high costs of transport were

---

[39] W. M. Mathew, 'The Imperialism of Free Trade: Peru, 1820–70', *EcHR*, Second Series, XXI (1968), pp. 562–79.

[40] Peter Winn, 'British Informal Empire in Uruguay in the 19th Century', *Past and Present*, LXXIII (1976), p. 108.

[41] Miller, *Britain and Latin America*, p. 243.

[42] Eugene Lubot, 'The Revisionist Perspective on Modern Chinese History', *Journal of Asian Studies*, XXXIII (1973), p. 96.

a further barrier. Even tax exemptions for Westerners were often ignored by local officials who could apply the 'squeeze' in other ways; Chinese competitors would, in any case, obtain similar exemptions. Important local trades like that in soybeans, for instance, remained beyond western penetration. There were, in short, major impediments in the Chinese market which western traders failed to break down in these years and which made it difficult to create an economy linked to the wider world as a producer of raw materials and purchaser of finished manufactures. The size and impenetrability of China were such that the hopes of Palmerston and Elgin proved grossly over-optimistic.

In the Ottoman empire, British economic inroads remained no less limited and Palmerston's aims to regenerate Turkey through free trade achieved little. Once again local resistance to external economic ambitions needs to be stressed for the period before the 1880s. The impact of the treaty of 1838 has been 'overstated'.[43] British trade with Turkey was something of a disappointment in the middle of the century, reaching only £3m out of a total of some £200m of British imports and exports in 1850. Indeed, the impact of foreign trade as a whole on Turkey remained limited, amounting only to some 6–8 per cent of total Ottoman production and only 12–15 per cent of agricultural production by the 1870s. Most of Anatolia was little affected by western trade before the 1850s; local crafts throughout the Empire were then still in a strong position. Similarly with finance. Foreign investment in the Empire remained limited before the 1870s, and it was hardly British financiers who benefited from the increased indebtedness of the Ottomans thereafter: 'French financiers . . . completely routed the British at Constantinople', at least before 1900.[44] British disappointment with the leverage it was able to establish over Turkey was as great as that felt over China.

It might be argued that the significance for Turkey of the period before the 1880s was that it saw the creation of linkages to the world economy which were of importance later. Yet Ottoman integration into the world economy was very slow, not least due to resistance by the central bureaucracy to the demands of outside powers and its capacity to play off one power against another. Intra-Ottoman internal trade grew, while such railways as were built were of restricted length and impact, and foreign trade remained of importance only in limited areas of Anatolia. Britain failed to make inroads into the Turkish economy sufficient to reverse the ossification which raised increasingly serious strategic concerns in Whitehall in the 1880s and 1890s.

Even in Egypt, which took on a new importance after 1869, it is easy to exaggerate Britain's success before 1885 in achieving its ends. Again, the economic arm of

---

[43] Sevket Pamuk, *The Ottoman Empire and European Capitalism* (Cambridge, 1987), p. 19.
[44] Platt, *Finance, Trade and Politics*, p. 185.

British power found it difficult to break down local barriers. Despite western imports, village cloth production in Egypt survived right through the century, not least because population increase provided a growing domestic market. Khedive Ismail created state sugar factories in the 1870s that were more successful than critics allow. Intra-Ottoman trade provided expanding opportunities quickly seized by Egyptian merchants. There was no absolute diminution in local economic activity in the face of western penetration; imports largely satisfied the demands of the foreign population rather than eroding local manufacturing. With few exceptions, 'foreign competition had not, as yet, basically altered the structure of local production'.[45] This indeed, from the British point of view, was the problem, and the crisis of 1876–82 in Egypt marked the failure of the attempt to promote British interests in the country by regenerating its economy from a distance.

In tropical Africa too, the ambition to force open the economies of the region was of only limited success before the 1870s. Schemes to regenerate the continent through trade and investment ran aground with the various expeditions sent to the Niger. Here, as often on that continent, white dreams remained dependent on the realities of black Africa. Economically, British trade achieved few inroads into tropical Africa before the last decades of the century. Africa clearly did not wish to be 'regenerated' on British terms; slavery proved immensely difficult to root out. Politically, Britain found it difficult to impose its will on West and East Africa and its 'paramountcy' in these areas, if such it was, proved paper thin when challenged after 1885. Local societies retained their autonomy, and Britain's successes in asserting her influence remained dependent on local élites' willingness to tolerate the British presence, usually to suit their own agendas. Lord Salisbury may have felt confident in 1890 of British power in Africa surviving 'without . . . the inconvenience of protectorates or anything of that sort', but policy-makers had to move quickly to secure British interests once the Scramble began.[46]

In the mid-nineteenth century British economic and political influence overseas expanded considerably. Latin America, China, the Ottoman empire, and Africa experienced growing British involvement, economic, political, and military. The theme of these years is of a Britain attempting to negotiate relationships with such societies to her own benefit, with the free trade treaty playing a central role. At its simplest, the aim was thereby to increase British economic interests in that region, although in some cases this underpinned strategic ambitions. This aim was achieved, but the broader goal of 'regenerating' societies and thereby creating regions tied as 'tributaries' to British economic interests was not attained.

---

[45] Roger Owen, *The Middle East in the World Economy, 1800–1914* (London, 1981), p. 149.
[46] Lord Salisbury, 10 July 1890, *PD* (Lords), col. 1265.

This deeper ambition proved much more problematic, because the aim to reshape the world through free trade and its extension overseas owed more to the misplaced optimism of British policy-makers and their partial views of the world than to an understanding of the realities of the mid-nineteenth-century globe. In essence two problems remained unsolved. First, the volumes of trade and investment the British were able to generate with these regions remained limited before 1880. In the case of China, for example, the figures failed even to match the growth of British trade generally. In other regions, while British trade grew, its significance as a proportion of local economic activity remained restricted before the end of the century. This related to the second difficulty. Local economies and local regimes proved adept at restricting the reach of British trade and investment. Local impediments to foreign inroads, the inhabitants' low purchasing power, the resilience of local manufacturing, and the capabilities of local entrepreneurs meant that these areas effectively resisted British economic penetration, both before 1880 and long afterward. The result was that the links Britain achieved in these areas remained limited; large parts of the wider world did not wish to be 'regenerated' by British trade and investment.

This raises broader questions as to the exact nature of the relationship Britain established with these areas of the globe. For John Gallagher and Ronald Robinson the nineteenth century was a period in which they identified an 'imperialism of Free Trade', where British policy-makers were committed to the creation of an extensive, expanding, informal Empire, outside the boundaries of the formal colonies, in order to defend British interests overseas. 'By informal means if possible, or by formal annexations when necessary, British paramountcy was steadily upheld', they wrote in often-quoted words, stressing the continuity in British policy through the century.[47] For Gallagher and Robinson, the end result was indeed an informal empire under British control, with regions such as South America, China, Ottoman Turkey, and others under British sway. These regions became as much part of a British Empire as, say, the Australian colonies, where conversely the policy of reducing formal metropolitan controls reflected the same preferred reliance on 'informal means' of maintaining British paramountcy. Other historians, however, believe such ideas seriously exaggerate both the British government's willingness to intervene overseas before the 1880s, and its success in establishing more than a very superficial paramountcy over parts of the wider world.[48]

In the mid-nineteenth century such linkages with these regions as successive British governments did achieve through the promotion of free trade are less impressive, in retrospect, than they might initially appear. There are conceptual

[47] Gallagher and Robinson, 'Imperialism of Free Trade', p. 3.
[48] D. C. M. Platt is the most notable. See Platt, *Finance, Trade and Politics*.

limitations in using metaphors such as 'informal empire' or 'informal control' to understand Britain's relations with these areas. The metaphors not only distort what should be seen as a more ambiguous, fluid, and infinitely graded continuum of influence between Britain and the wider world. They are also unhelpful in implying—though this is moving beyond the scope of this chapter—that this influence simply reached one way, from Britain into the world outside. Relations between Britain and the wider world, in these years at least, need to be seen in a much more pluralistic and mutually permeable fashion.

It is far better to approach these regions in terms of the fluctuating degrees of British influence that was established in them, considerable or limited as it might be at different times, and the varying success Britain gained thereby in achieving her ambitions. In a country such as Egypt, for instance, British expansion and intervention led to inescapable territorial expansion rather than informal control. Elsewhere British paramountcy remained elusive. That Britain established a commercial or financial presence in a region did not mean, necessarily, that she gained either economic or political paramountcy over it. Only at the highest level of abstraction can Latin America, China, Ottoman Turkey, and Africa in the mid-nineteenth century be described as parts of a British informal empire.

After 1880 a much greater British and European presence overseas came into being. Britain's own economic penetration of the regions surveyed here was much more marked, and British policy much more determined in defence of its economic interests. However, Britain's limited inroads before that date had also helped open the way for powerful economic rivals between 1880 and 1914. Any continuing wish by policy-makers to create an informal empire was overshadowed by greater vulnerabilities in Britain's position, the heightened willingness of other powers to challenge British interests, and a far greater readiness on the part of all powers to assume direct governmental control. Changing circumstances led the British government to recognize that the ambitions of the mid-nineteenth century were based ultimately on over-optimistic views of the willingness of the wider world to respond to the British economy, and on over-confident assessments of Britain's capacity to bring that about. The gulf between intention and reality, even at the height of Britain's power, should not be forgotten.

Select Bibliography

PETER CAIN, 'Capitalism, War and Internationalism in the Thought of Richard Cobden', *British Journal of International Studies*, V (1979), pp. 229–47.

P. J. CAIN, *Economic Foundations of British Overseas Expansion, 1815–1914* (London, 1980).

P. J. CAIN and A. G. HOPKINS, *British Imperialism: Innovation and Expansion, 1688–1914* (London, 1993).

JOHN GALLAGHER and RONALD ROBINSON, 'The Imperialism of Free Trade', *Economic History Review*, Second Series, VI (1953), pp. 1–15.

R. J. GAVIN, 'Palmerston's Policy towards East and West Africa, 1830–65', unpublished Ph.D. Thesis, University of Cambridge, 1959.

RONALD HYAM, *Britain's Imperial Century, 1815–1914: A Study of Empire and Expansion*, 2nd edn. (London, 1993).

WM. ROGER LOUIS, ed., *Imperialism: The Robinson and Gallagher Controversy* (New York, 1970).

PETER LOWE, *Britain in the Far East: A Survey from 1819 to the Present* (London, 1981).

OLIVER MACDONAGH, 'The Anti-Imperialism of Free Trade', *Economic History Review*, Second Series, XIV (1962), pp. 489–501.

D. MCLEAN, 'Finance and "Informal Empire" before the First World War', *Economic History Review*, Second Series, XXIX (1976), pp. 291–305.

RORY MILLER, *Britain and Latin America in the Nineteenth and Twentieth Centuries* (London, 1993).

PETER MORRIS, ed., *Africa, Asia and Central America* (Exeter, 1984).

COLIN NEWBURY, 'The Semantics of International Influence: Informal Empires Reconsidered', in Michael Twaddle, ed., *Imperialism, the State and the Third World* (London, 1992), pp. 23–66.

ROGER OWEN, *The Middle East in the World Economy, 1800–1914* (London, 1981).

D. C. M. PLATT, *Finance, Trade, and Politics in British Foreign Policy, 1815–1914* (Oxford, 1968).

——'The Imperialism of Free Trade: Some Reservations', *Economic History Review*, Second Series, XXI (1968), pp. 296–306.

——'Further Objections to an "Imperialism of Free Trade", 1830–60', *Economic History Review*, Second Series, XXVI (1973), pp. 77–91.

BERNARD SEMMEL, *The Rise of Free Trade Imperialism* (Cambridge, 1970).

A. G. L. SHAW, 'Introduction', in A. G. L. Shaw, ed., *Great Britain and the Colonies, 1815–65* (London, 1970), pp. 1–26.

H. L. WESSELING, 'Imperialism and Empire: An Introduction', in Wolfgang J. Mommsen and Jürgen Osterhammel, eds., *Imperialism and After: Continuities and Discontinuities* (London, 1986), pp. 1–10.

7

Britain and Latin America

ALAN KNIGHT

'Spanish America is free,' George Canning, the Secretary of State for Foreign Affairs, exulted in 1824, 'and if we do not mismanage our affairs sadly, she is English.'[1] Now almost a cliché, the quote has regularly served to justify including Latin America within Britain's notional informal empire. Historians of empire, protagonists of dependency theory, and Marxist theorists from Lenin onwards, have all in their different ways seen the fall of formal Iberian imperialism in the New World as the prelude to British informal imperialism.[2]

How valid is this view? First, British *formal* imperialism, characterized by territorial possession, was not unknown in the Americas south of the 49th parallel. Bits of Central and South America were painted red, but almost by definition these were not bits of *Latin* America.[3] Tiny though they were compared to the great expanses of the continent or the British Empire, they generated local concerns, relating to security, frontiers, contraband, and they occasionally excited local ambitions, mild versions of the 'sub-imperialism' which powered British expansion elsewhere. Trinidad and British Guiana provoked conflicts with Venezuela and, indirectly, with the United States; British Honduras, whose existence galled Guatemala, was seen by visionary British officials as a pivot for naval and commercial power on the Central American isthmus.[4] In contrast, the Falkland Islands, seized by Britain in 1833, remained a diplomatic dead letter for nearly a century.[5]

---

[1] Wendy Hinde, *George Canning* (London, 1973), p. 368.

[2] John Gallagher and Ronald Robinson, 'The Imperialism of Free Trade', *Economic History Review*, VI, 1 (1953), pp. 1–14; Philip J. O'Brien, 'Dependency Revisited', in Christopher Abel and Colin M. Lewis, eds., *Latin America, Economic Imperialism and the State* (London, 1985), pp. 40–69; Anthony Brewer, *Marxist Theories of Imperialism* (London, 1980), chap. 7.

[3] British Honduras and British Guiana, while part of the Central and South American mainland, were never effectively controlled by the Iberian empires; lacking the historical and cultural prerequisites of *Latin* America, they are conventionally bracketed with the Anglophone Caribbean.

[4] G. E. Carl, *First Among Equals: Great Britain and Venezuela, 1810–1910* (Syracuse, NY, 1980), pp. 93–97, 108; Joseph Smith, *Illusions of Conflict, Anglo-American Diplomacy toward Latin America, 1865–1896* (Pittsburgh, Pa., 1979), pp. 205–08.

[5] H. S. Ferns, *Britain and Argentina in the Nineteenth Century* (Oxford, 1960), pp. 227–33.

Apart from these limited, territorial possessions, the British sometimes entertained grander schemes of expansion, displaying (formal) imperialist motives which spurred policy even if they ultimately proved fruitless. But what schemes? Whose motives? British influence and policy emanated from various sources. Whitehall's concerns were not those of the men on the ground, or the men on the bridge. Local representatives—diplomats, consuls, businessmen, naval officers—saw things differently; they lacked the big picture, and responded to immediate local pressures. The Olympian detachment and budgetary caution of Foreign Secretaries such as Castlereagh or Salisbury were denied both to proconsular officials like Strangford in Brazil or Chatfield in Central America, deeply immersed in local politics, as well as naval commanders pitched into local civil wars, blockades, and revolutions. During the turbulent 1840s, Mandeville, British Minister at Buenos Aires, disobeyed Whitehall, and Purvis, commanding the British flotilla in the River Plate, disobeyed Mandeville.[6] Even companies had their local cowboys, practitioners of business 'sub-imperialism', like the British bankers who—demonstrating the timelessness of their trade—played the money market in Brazil in the 1880s: according to one historian, 'their home offices were dead set against exchange speculation, but the local managers sometimes indulged in this heady game'.[7]

Even where territorial possession—actual or potential—was absent, the pursuit of British interests could still involve local political meddling. Economic relations went beyond the dispassionate mediation of the market,[8] and diplomatic relations involved distinct hierarchies of power, in which the threat of coercion was present. For example, the economic imbalance characterizing Anglo-Uruguayan relations in the later nineteenth century might not, of itself, constitute 'imperialism' (consider, for example, Anglo-Danish relations). But British political and military efforts to establish Uruguay as an independent buffer state between the hostile republics of Argentina and Brazil, and thus to keep the Plate open to British commerce, would, by virtue of its coercive, interventionist, and political nature, constitute some sort of imperialism, even though the goal was not Uruguayan annexation but Uruguayan survival.[9] Similarly, British coercion of Mexico in the 1860s or Venezuela in the 1900s, though devoid of territorial ambition, might be

[6] David McLean, *War, Diplomacy and Informal Empire, Britain and the Republics of La Plata, 1836–53* (London, 1995), pp. 40–41, 46, 55.

[7] Richard Graham, *Britain and the Onset of Modernization in Brazil, 1850–1914* (Cambridge, 1968), p. 98.

[8] I do not pretend that 'the market' is a fair, open, and neutral arena, but wish to distinguish roughly between relations conducted within that arena and those involving a substantial degree of 'extra-economic coercion'.

[9] Peter Winn, 'British Informal Empire in Uruguay in the Nineteenth Century', *Past and Present*, LXXIII (1976), pp. 100–26.

termed 'imperialist' since it went beyond the pacific mediation of the market and involved a form of international 'extra-economic coercion'.

Furthermore, British involvement of this kind—political and coercive but non-territorial—was common, though concentrated in certain times and places. It responded to diverse motives and interests. Again, metropolitan caution often contrasted with peripheral aggression. Whitehall was generally reluctant to despatch gunboats. They were costly, unpredictable, and needed elsewhere. Gunboats could not coerce landlocked Andean republics, or even sprawling, self-sufficient prairies.[10] Nevertheless, local coercion and political involvement were common. Consuls, businessmen, and naval officers lobbied, lent weight to local factions, paid bribes, and influenced political outcomes: treaties, tariffs, even (it was said) wars and revolutions. Sometimes the very fact that the British were thought to mix in local politics had an impact, whether in reality they did or not; the fear of foreign intervention had a phenomenological effect in the periphery which Anglo-centric scholars, conning Foreign Office archives, may overlook.[11] Above all, British interests consistently sought out local 'collaborating élites', and some non-élites, who could serve their cause: generals and ministers; lawyers and native businessmen; judges, officials, and local political bosses; labour recruiters, foremen, bandits, and revolutionaries.[12] Indeed, abstinence from formal political control placed a huge premium on such informal collaborative networks and encouraged, among other things, the resort to widespread corruption: the high-mindedness of the Indian Civil Service could not be replicated in self-governing republics, where graft was both a fact of life and a necessary lubricant of collaborative mechanisms. For this reason, 'informal empire' was a two-way street, a construction of peripheral as well as metropolitan interests.

But if collaboration was freely extended, if Latin Americans did business with the British not out of fear but choice, what is left of 'imperialism'? It is here that 'dependency' proves useful. 'Dependency' implies no *formal* subordination of satellite to metropolis. Subordination may arise from economic imbalance and—a possible corollary—ideological or cultural 'hegemony'. A monopsonistic buyer may not need to deploy 'extra-economic coercion' against an economic client: Britain, apparently, could manipulate Argentina because the British market was crucial for Argentina to an extent that the Argentine market was not crucial

---

[10] As José de San Martín, the liberator of South America, politely reminded the Foreign Office during the abortive coercion of Rosas: San Martín to Dickson, 28 Dec. 1846, F[oreign] O[ffice] 6/128.

[11] Rory Miller, *Britain and Latin America in the Nineteenth and Twentieth Centuries* (London, 1993), p. 48; Graham, *Britain and the Onset*, p. 103.

[12] David Rock, *Politics in Argentina, 1890–1930* (Cambridge, 1975), pp. 3, 6; Marshall C. Eakin, 'Business Imperialism and British Enterprise in Brazil: The St John d'El Rey Mining Company Ltd., 1830–1960', *Hispanic American Historical Review*, LXVI (1986), pp. 723, 727.

for Britain.[13] As the British Consul at Angostura asked in 1839, when a 'fool' Venezuelan suggested that a ban on British exports to his country would lead to riots in British industrial towns, 'what is all the trade of Venezuela? Not equal to the sale of many London shopkeepers.'[14] Similarly, a rich creditor could crack the financial whip over a weak debtor without resorting to coercion; in Argentina, 'a quiet word of advice where it mattered from a prominent [British] banker... was enough to influence proposed legislation'.[15] Certainly, considerations of credit-worthiness and business confidence could impose harsh constraints on Latin-American government; structuralists would go further and discern an enduring dependency created by the unequal terms of trade between periphery and metropolis.[16] Whether economic imbalance or cultural dependency qualify as 'imperialism' is a moot theoretical point, but clearly they coloured Anglo-Latin American relations throughout the nineteenth century and beyond.

For those relations were not purely political or economic. The British came bearing not only guns and gifts but also intangible ideas: economic liberalism, parliamentarism, monarchism, anti-slavery, Protestantism, sport, racism, perhaps even the 'gentlemanly' ethos which, some argue, was integral to British capitalism.[17] Indeed, as Adam Smith knew and the new 'institutional' economics rightly stresses, economic activity does not take place within an ethical and cultural vacuum; the market is neither amoral nor anomic. The British presence in Latin America, therefore, involved ideological and cultural proselytization; the dissemination, sometimes enduring, sometimes ephemeral, of British attitudes, ideas, and cultural practices. Indeed, the best way to create congenial collaborating élites was to convert them to the British way of life, especially with regard to business practices. Since immigration from Britain was scant, 'prefabricated' collaborators were in short supply. Latin Americans were not Canadians or Australians. But they could learn. The fall of the Argentine dictator Rosas in 1852 brought to power a new civilian political élite which, a British merchant observed, 'had [in exile] come into contact with a more advanced civilization and learned in adversity to appreciate constitutional order and industrial development. Henceforth... they predisposed large numbers of their countrymen to defer to... the intelligent portion of the foreign residents whose interests had been engrafted into those of

[13] Roger Gravil, *The Anglo-Argentine Connection, 1900–1939* (Boulder, 1985).

[14] Carl, *First Among Equals*, p. 38.

[15] Callum A. MacDonald, 'End of Empire: The Decline of the Anglo-Argentine Connection, 1918–1951', in Alistair Hennessy and John King, eds., *The Land That England Lost: Argentina and Britain, A Special Relationship* (London, 1992), p. 81.

[16] Winston Fritsch, *External Constraints on Economic Policy in Brazil, 1889–1930* (Basingstoke, 1988), pp. 31, 61; Gravil, *Anglo-Argentine Connection*, p. 95.

[17] P. J. Cain and A. G. Hopkins, *British Imperialism: Innovation and Expansion, 1688–1914* (London, 1993), pp. 22–37 and *passim*.

the country.'[18] Such 'deference' and 'engraftment', where they could be achieved, offered the best way of wedding Latin American élites to British interests: it was more secure, durable, and decorous than either the crude coercion of the gunboat or the sordid strategem of the bribe.

Like nineteenth-century China, the Iberian empires of the eighteenth century were seen by British commercial interests as potentially valuable markets, ripe for exploitation but ringed by decaying imperial ramparts. If Portugal allowed a measure of legitimate trade—the British shipped slaves to Brazil in return for gold and cotton—Spain maintained and, from the 1770s, reinforced her mercantilist monopoly. But this reassertion of imperial power came to an end with the wars of the 1790s. Transatlantic communications were broken; foreign, especially British contraband, flooded into Spain's American colonies, and following Napoleon's invasion of the Iberian peninsula in 1808 insurgent movements challenged Spanish authority from Mexico to Buenos Aires. While British merchants took advantage of these opportunities—by 1810 Lima was glutted with contraband British goods—the British government pursued objectives that combined, not always comfortably, commercial self-interest and geopolitical advantage. Between 1796 and 1808, while Spain was allied with France against Britain, the latter pursued its traditional policy of carrying the war to the enemy's colonies. Buenos Aires and Montevideo were seized in 1806–07, and plans were afoot for a *coup de main* against Spain's prize colony, Mexico, when the Napoleonic invasion of Spain radically changed the strategic scene. Now the happy combination of colonial warfare and pacific commercial penetration had to change. Spain became an ally; official colonial subversion, which British conservatives had never liked, was curtailed; and dreams of imperialist expansion in the Americas were temporarily laid to rest. This did not end British involvement in the epic struggle for Latin American independence. If the British government remained ambivalent, British merchants trafficked in arms, freelance mercenaries flocked to the insurgent colours, and Lord Cochrane commanded the infant Chilean navy in its victories over the Spanish fleet. Unofficially, therefore, the British contributed to the continent's emancipation from Spanish rule, which was consummated in the early 1820s.

The British government now faced both a *fait accompli* and a tricky dilemma: commercial advantage and liberal sentiment argued for prompt recognition of the new republics; but monarchical and conservative sympathy for Spain dictated otherwise, since, as Canning put it, recognition 'sanctions...a revolutionary principle [and]...exposes [King George IV] to the risk of having a coconut-

---

[18] William Latham, quoted by Charles A. Jones, 'British Capital in Argentine History: Structures, Rhetoric and Change', in Hennessy and King, *Land That England Lost*, pp. 70–71.

coloured minister to receive at his levee'.[19] Castlereagh and Canning opted for incremental commercial recognition—allowing Latin American ships into British ports, despatching Consuls to the new republics—but political recognition had to wait until the later 1820s, when fear of advancing French and US influence forced the British hand and overcame conservative scruples. In Brazil a different sequence unfolded. There was no mass insurrection, no bloody break with the imperial metropolis. Threatened by Napoleon, protected and prompted by Britain, the Braganza royal family fled to Brazil. Trade was liberalized and the British secured a highly favourable commercial treaty. In 1821–22 the Braganza dynasty bifurcated, when Pedro I proclaimed Brazil's independence, founding a new world empire which endured to 1889. Brazil thus won its independence by means of a peaceful, monarchical transition, aided and abetted by British diplomacy and maritime power; as a result, for the next generation Brazil displayed an unusual combination of political stability and successful British economic penetration.

With the collapse of Spanish mercantilism—and well before Britain recognized the new republics—British goods and investment began to flow to Latin America. By the mid-1820s British exports to Latin America totalled £5m (13 per cent of total British exports), of which textiles comprised about three-quarters. The chief recipients were Brazil, which alone took between a third and a half of British exports, and Argentina, where British goods swiftly percolated through the porous *porteño* economy: by 1820 church images were to be found 'dressed in coarse English cloth'.[20] The early 1820s, when commercial euphoria ran high, also saw a spate of investments, primarily government loans, as well as direct investment, particularly in mining. Cornish miners came to work the silver veins of Mexico's Real del Monte, where they left a legacy of blue-eyed children and a rare local delicacy, the *pastí*.[21] For a time, Latin America promised a bonanza: Disraeli wrote prospectuses and Palmerston dabbled in Peruvian stocks. But the balloon soon burst. Latin American markets were shallow, cities small, and the huge, under-populated rural hinterland generated scant demand for imported manufactures. The Argentine gaucho was 'a person without wants', content to inhabit a filthy hut, consume fresh beef, and seat himself on a steer's skull.[22] Labour was shiftless and unreliable, transport slow and costly. It was cheaper to ship goods from Liverpool

---

[19] Hinde, *George Canning*, p. 369.

[20] Francis Bond Head, *Journeys Across the Pampas and Among the Andes* (1826; reprinted, Carbondale Ill., 1967), pp. 16, 39. The extent of early British market penetration is much debated: Miller, *Britain and Latin America*, pp. 40–42, 74; Graham, *Britain and the Onset*, pp. 84–85; D. C. M. Platt, *Latin America and British Trade, 1806–1914* (London, 1972), pp. 12–22. 'Porteño' refers to Buenos Aires.

[21] Robert W. Randall, *Real del Monte: A British Mining Venture in Mexico* (Austin, Tex., 1972); the Cornish legacy is based on eyewitness accounts.

[22] Head, *Journeys Across the Pampas*, pp. 14–15.

to Buenos Aires than from Córdoba to Buenos Aires.[23] The lack of transport and capital made it difficult, though not impossible, to develop profitable exports, thus to acquire the foreign exchange needed for the purchase of foreign commodities. Only Brazil and, to a degree, Argentina proved capable of sustaining exports in the immediate post-independence period.

Political stability also proved elusive outside Brazil and Chile. The independence wars left a legacy of praetorian violence and local banditry; bloated military budgets swallowed up government loans; and entrepreneurs, foreign and domestic, were at the mercy of warring factions who taxed, fined, and extorted in response to Hobbesian political—rather than Weberian economic—imperatives.[24] In many regions, especially the old colonial heartlands of Mexico and Peru, the regulated corporate economy survived independence: free trade, espoused by minority urban and intellectual élites, was repudiated by artisans, local merchants, and backwoods traders, all of whom stood to suffer from cheap foreign imports. In Lima, Bogotá, and Puebla a loose protectionist coalition formed, hostile to free trade and foreign immigrants (especially Protestants), capable of influencing the shifting *caudillo* politics of the era towards a crude but effective economic nationalism, sometimes tinged with xenophobia.[25]

In such unpropritious circumstances British loans were soon exhausted, and the markets for British goods dried up. By the mid-1820s imported manufactures were piling up, unsold, in the warehouses of Buenos Aires, Lima, and Rio; at Rio a bulk consignment of ice-skates was handtooled into door latches—a triumph of Brazilian ingenuity over British ingenuousness.[26] Initial hopes were dashed. Although the volume of British exports to Latin America increased, their value remained static from the 1820s to the 1840s.[27] While Latin America, particularly Brazil, became a significant market, especially for cotton textiles, it was hardly a bonanza, and British mercantile capitalism, frustrated by topography, instability, and outright local opposition, proved incapable of reducing Latin America to 'dependency'.

It is no paradox to note, however, that this early period of relative economic inertia, roughly 1820–50, was also the heyday of British imperialism defined in terms of official pressures and interventions. Since peaceful commercial

---

[23] Randall, *Real del Monte*, chap. 7, pp. 5–22, 56–57; H. S. Ferns, *Argentine Republic, 1516–1971* (Newton Abbot, 1973), pp. 32–33.

[24] Platt, *Latin America*, p. 58; Carl, *First Among Equals*, p. 16; Ferns, *Britain and Argentina*, pp. 85, 168.

[25] Paul Gootenberg, *Between Silver and Guano Commercial Policy and the State in Postindependence Peru* (Princeton, 1989), chap. 3; Guy P. C. Thomson, 'Protectionism and Industrialization in Mexico, 1821–54: The Case of Puebla', in Abel and Lewis, *Latin America, Economic Imperialism and the State*, pp. 125–46.

[26] Desmond Gregory, *Brute New World: The Rediscovery of Latin America in the Early Nineteenth Century* (London, 1992), pp. 47, 157–58; Platt, *Latin America*, pp. 25, 47, 51.

[27] Miller, *Britain and Latin America*, p. 74.

penetration was slow, and collaborating élites were, at best, incipient, it fell to the British government, as Palmerston put it, to 'open and secure the roads for the merchants'.[28] This is not to say that British policy was coherent, concerted or, still less, successful.[29] Absence of mind characterized Britain's modest Latin American imperialism as it did its more grandiose efforts elsewhere. But the thrust of policy between independence and mid-century was, comparatively speaking, belligerent, interventionist, and meddlesome.

The evidence in regard to the British government is substantial, though contradictory. Policy-makers were wary of involvement in a remote area characterized by endemic political instability. While Castlereagh (1807) certainly favoured 'the opening to our manufactures of the markets of that great Continent', he considered territorial conquest a 'hopeless task' and feared that, by conniving at patriotic insurgency against Spain, Britain might 'in destroying a bad government, leave them without any government at all'.[30] But such cautious sentiments, though reinforced by the failure of the 1806–07 occupation of Buenos Aires, did not uniformly permeate the British 'official mind'. On the contrary, during the fifty years following the American Revolution Britain, far from espousing Cobdenite principles of pacific free trade, was fully prepared to flex its *ancien régime* muscles in pursuit of commercial and strategic advantage—aggressively opening up new markets, forestalling economic and military rivals, pursuing grand geopolitical designs, fostering a bullish patriotism at home and an 'imperial revolution in government' in the colonies, from Ireland to India.[31] Sometimes such 'forward' policy was sanctioned by London; sometimes it was the work of British representatives at the periphery. Either way, the result was a series of pressures and policies for which, as regards intention if not outcome, the adjective 'imperialist' seems appropriate.

Thus, in 1806 Commodore Sir Home Popham, fresh from his empire-building exploits at the Cape, sailed across the South Atlantic and seized Buenos Aires. 'Buenos Aires at this moment forms part of the British Empire', proclaimed *The Times*.[32] Montevideo fell in 1807 and plans were made for an attack on Chile.

---

[28] Ibid., p. 49.

[29] McLean, *War, Diplomacy and Informal Empire*, p. 190, argues that the lack of either mercantile unanimity or clear government strategy invalidates the notion of British informal imperialism. However, interventionist, 'informal imperialist' actions speak louder than words, plans, or blueprints (which were not entirely lacking anyway); and it is in the nature of *informal* imperialism that it should be to a degree reactive and improvised. Gallagher and Robinson's famous dictum—'trade with informal control if possible; trade with rule when necessary' ('The Imperialism of Free Trade', p. 13)—I take to be an *ex post facto* historical induction, not an explicit guiding principle of British policy.

[30] Miller, *Britain and Latin America*, p. 35.

[31] C. A. Bayly, *Imperial Meridian: The British Empire and the World, 1780–1830* (London, 1989).

[32] Jonathan C. Brown, *A Socioeconomic History of Argentina, 1776–1860* (Cambridge, 1979), p. 48.

Popham, indeed, envisaged a seizure of 'all [the] prominent points' of South America, which would confound Britain's enemies, advance British trade, and confer 'popularity and stability [upon] any government that undertook it'.[33] Conquest did not presage an enlightened Cobdenite regime; while the conquerors respected local social hierarchies, they looted the city's bullion. In Britain's brief rule at the Plate, one historian has observed, 'we can discern more than a trace of the old Adam of mercantilist politico-economic methods'.[34] The failure of the Plate expeditions justified Castlereagh's caution, but did not end British aggression and interference. In the 1820s, when Argentina and Brazil fought for control of the Banda Oriental, Britain played midwife at the birth of the Republic of Uruguay. In 1833 Britain seized the Falklands. In 1843 Aberdeen despatched a fleet to the Plate as part of a clumsy Anglo-French coercion of the Argentine dictator Rosas, designed to ensure the independence of Uruguay and free navigation of the Paraná–Plate river system.[35] Such actions involved both metropolitan and, *a fortiori*, peripheral initiatives, the latter facilitated by slow and unsure transatlantic communications. During the Uruguayan imbroglios of the 1820s and 1840s British representatives at Rio and Buenos Aires regularly exceeded official instructions, displaying a contempt for both troublesome local natives and money-grubbing British merchants. Similar proconsular initiatives were evident during Frederick Chatfield's long residence in Guatemala (1834–52) and, intermittently throughout the century, in turbulent Venezuela.[36]

But the contrast between peripheral activism and metropolitan restraint should not be exaggerated. The British government clearly took advantage of its mentorship of the Braganzas to secure a privileged commercial treaty with Brazil; and similar treaties were concluded with most of the infant republics and subsequently maintained in the teeth of criticism.[37] The Brazilian treaty also embodied a commitment to end the slave trade, upon which Brazil's plantation economy depended. Thereafter, British efforts to curtail the trade vitiated Anglo-Brazilian relations for over forty years.[38] Whatever British motives—and the argument for altruistic or cultural, rather than instrumental or economic, motivation seems strong—the suppression of the slave trade, ultimately successful, involved regular interception of vessels plying the trade to Brazil and constant intervention in

---

[33] Ferns, *Britain and Argentina*, p. 19.

[34] Ibid., pp. 50–51.

[35] Ibid., pp. 250–80; McLean, *War, Diplomacy and Informal Empire*, p. 49 ff.

[36] Mario Rodriguez, *A Palmerstonian Diplomat in Central America: Frederick Chatfield Esq.* (Tucson, Ariz., 1964); Carl, *First Among Equals*, pp. 32, 106.

[37] Carl, *First Among Equals*, chap. 3; John Lynch, *Argentine Dictator: Juan Manual Rosas, 1829–1853* (London, 1981), pp. 67–68; Graham, *Britain and the Onset*, pp. 82, 107–08.

[38] Leslie Bethell, *The Abolition of the Brazilian Slave Trade* (Cambridge, 1970).

Brazilian political and judicial processes. To a lesser degree, the British exerted emancipationist pressure on the Spanish dependency of Cuba, where, in the 1840s, the outspoken Consul David Turnbull was blamed for incitement to slave rebellion.[39] However high-minded the goals, British methods were interventionist and hence, by certain criteria, imperialistic.

The aggressive policies of Britain's 'imperial meridian'—products of endemic instability at the periphery as well as great power conflict in Europe—long survived the Napoleonic Wars. Latin America's political travails and economic torpor irked the British, who readily dismissed its government as venal, its people as idle, mongrel, and priest-ridden: stereotypes which survived well into the twentieth century.[40] After the brief bonanza of the 1820s commercial hopes were disappointed, and tougher measures were entertained, both on paper and in practice. In a thorough Foreign Office review of 1841, the problems of instability were rehearsed, and the lost potential of the great Latin American market was lamented. Britain, it was concluded, had to promote order, thereby boosting trade and enhancing domestic—British—welfare (an early intimation of the logic of social imperialism already evident in Commodore Popham's reasoning).[41] Merchants could not go it alone: 'the Merchant thinks but of the time present . . . the Government of a country, on the other hand, looks not only to the present but to the future: how national interest can best be promoted permanently.' The solutions were bold: offensive and defensive alliances with Latin American states such as Uruguay; vigorous protection of British residents; the deployment of British naval power; the hypothecation of Latin American customs revenue to fund support for friendly governments; the consolidation of territorial footholds such as the Mosquito Coast of Nicaragua; and the acquisition of new footholds such as San Francisco (California) which, if purchased from Mexico, would 'secure to Great Britain all the advantages of the finest port in the Pacific for her commercial speculations in time of peace, and in war for more easily securing her maritime ascendancy'. San Francisco, of course, soon became a prize of United States continental imperialism rather than of British thalassocratic power. But the aggressive impulses of the 'official mind' of the 1840s were translated into official policy: with Aberdeen's blockade of the Plate, lesser interventions in Venezuela, and of course the assault on China, 'an obvious precedent' for Latin American policy.[42]

---

[39] Arthur F. Corwin, *Spain and the Abolition of Slavery in Cuba, 1817–1886* (Austin, Tex., 1967), pp. 77–81.

[40] Ferns, *Britain and Argentina*, pp. 57, 270; Gregory, *Brute New World*, *passim*.

[41] 'Memorandum on British Trade', 31 Dec. 1841, in FO 97/284, usually cited as the Murray Memorandum. D. C. M. Platt, *Finance, Trade, and Politics in British Foreign Policy, 1815–1914* (Oxford, 1968), pp. 321–23, strives overmuch to minimize its typicality and importance.

[42] MacLean, *War, Diplomacy and Informal Empire*, pp. 198–99; Ferns, *Britain and Argentina*, pp. 252–53, 272.

But there was more to British imperialism than the official mind. Private interests conducted 'forward' policies of their own, combating the hostile conditions they encountered on the ground. Ideally, this involved cultivating collaborating élites with whom they could do profitable business, and who would perform the necessary political spadework of establishing stable regimes conducive to trade and investment. Commercial treaties, pressed by the British government, were a start; but they were not sufficient—sometimes not even necessary—conditions for mercantile success.[43] Mutual self-interest, sometimes allied to cultural emulation of Britain, was the strongest cement of collaboration; where that was lacking, the British resorted to lobbying, bribery, and threats. On Mexico's west coast, where contraband was rife and commerce subject to the whims of petty officials ('of a very low and ignorant disposition'), British Consuls, usually merchants and necessarily political operators, chose to adopt 'a high and decided line of conduct', which involved threats, bribery, and naval back-up. As one put it, 'acting as a pioneer brought my authority to be respected', to the advantage of British commerce.[44] In war-torn Peru, British merchants and Consuls (*consules sin cañones*, 'cannonless consuls', as they ruefully called themselves) felt threatened by local mayhem and neglected by a distant Whitehall.[45] But they did not sit on their hands. On the contrary, they were politically active: they supported the free-trading Bolivarians in the 1820s, and, subsequently championed the short-lived union of Peru and Bolivia under Santa Cruz. They lobbied for free trade laws, skirmished with rival US representatives, and railed against Chilean influence, which was strong, protectionist, and anti-foreign. 'Overseas interests intervene[d] massively in Peruvian affairs in a push for free trade... British interventions in trade politics appear sporadic, yet most approximated a genuine neoimperial [*sic*] strategy.'[46]

But these efforts enjoyed scant success. In Peru, as in Mexico, Central America, and Venezuela, British interests could not overcome the formidable social, political, and geographical barriers of the time and place. Greater success was achieved, as the trade figures suggest, in Argentina and Brazil, which produced viable exports, earned the foreign exchange necessary to purchase British goods, and possessed political systems capable of sustaining commerce. In Brazil, a stable monarchy enjoyed Britain's blessing and sought to emulate British practice—a

---

[43]   Miller, *Britain and Latin America*, pp. 38, 61.

[44]   E. Barron to C. O'Gorman, 1 Aug. 1830, FO 203/44; John Mayo, 'Consuls and Silver Contraband on Mexico's West Coast in the Era of Santa Anna', *Journal of Latin American Studies*, XIX, 2 (1987), pp. 402–03.

[45]   B. H. Wilson to Aberdeen, 27 Aug. 1842, FO 97/284.

[46]   Gootenberg, *Between Silver and Guano*, pp. 18–19.

two-party system, a constitutional monarch, and a taste for liberal progress in society, economy, and culture. Brazilian capitalism acquired a gentlemanly veneer, though the bedrock of the economic system, especially the crucial export sector, was the ungentlemanly institution of slavery, which British companies utilized, *faute de mieux*.[47] In Argentina British capitalism found its first durable collaborator in the dictator Rosas: a blonde, blue-eyed British gentleman in appearance, a quintessential ruthless Latin American *caudillo* in practice.[48] Even here, the incipient relationship was prejudiced by the clumsy intervention of the 1840s, which revealed that coercion could destroy commerce more surely than it could compel collaboration.[49]

Successful collaboration, these early examples suggest, was vital for British interests to prosper; but collaboration did not require regimes or practices modelled on metropolitan lines, whether in Latin America, West Africa, or the Malay states. British interests were politically blind: in Brazil they owned slaves in defiance of British abolitionism; at Buenos Aires they deplored metropolitan attempts to coerce Rosas, to the point where British volunteers manned Argentine shore batteries against the Royal Navy.[50] They asked no more than a functioning regime, of whatever political hue, capable of maintaining peace, order, and respect for basic capitalist principles of property and contract. The decorous monarchy of Brazil was preferable to the rough *caudillos* of Spanish America, but liberal scruples were expendable and *caudillos* a necessary evil: 'I dislike and condemn the System of Rosas, as all Liberal men must do,' wrote the British Chargé d'Affaires in Buenos Aires, 'but I conceive it would be a great Evil should he be vanquished, as this system gives protection to life and property, more particularly that of Foreigners, and it is based on Order.'[51] During the early nineteenth century these desiderata were rarely met, British commercial hopes faded, and British officials strove, usually with scant success, to remedy the deficiencies. Hence the recurrent treaties and blockades, threats and blandishment. Early Victorian imperialism involved strong-arm methods and may be rightly regarded as 'a sufficient political function of the function of integrating new regions into the expanding economy'; in short, it was a political reflex, tactical, variable, and opportunistic, of the underlying growth of the British industrial economy.[52] However, the success of informal imperialism was patchy: both political intervention and commercial penetration

---

[47] Graham, *Britain and the Onset*.

[48] Lynch, *Argentine Dictator*, p. 297.

[49] McLean, *War, Diplomacy and Informal Empire*, p. 188.

[50] Graham, *Britain and the Onset*, p. 184; Ferns, *Britain and Argentina*, pp. 269, 273–74.

[51] Gore to Palmerston, 4 Jan. 1852, quoted in Ferns, *Britain and Argentina*, p. 288.

[52] Gallagher and Robinson, 'The Imperialism of Free Trade', p. 5.

were, as Platt argued, less thorough and effective than Robinson and Gallagher believed.[53]

With time, however, a sea-change took place. Latin American economies became more receptive to foreign trade and investment. The old vicious circle of political instability and economy stagnation gave way to a virtuous circle of stability and 'development'.[54] Rough *caudillos* were supplanted by more decorous dictators and, better still, by urbane civilian oligarchs linked to the export trade. When, in 1852, Barings sent a representative to Buenos Aires with a brace of pistols for the new president, he sold them to a British naval officer rather than offer them to the 'learned Doctors of Law and peaceful Civilians' who now held power; 'the era of the *caudillos* has passed away: thank God', he concluded.[55] Though premature, his comment was broadly correct. Increasingly through the later nineteenth century, collaboration did not need to be coerced; it was now freely given. British interests in Latin America now burgeoned, but in a relatively apolitical way, without needing the clumsy intervention of metropolitan governments to smooth their path. Their intrinsic economic assets, coupled with a more congenial socio-political climate, ensured at least a good chance of success. Thus, as British trade and investment grew, British interference and intervention declined. 'Business imperialism' or Latin American 'dependency' advanced, but the advance owed more to peripheral transformation than to metropolitan threats. The sequence fits very comfortably within Ronald Robinson's 'excentric' theory of informal imperialism: 'mutually attractive business transactions' supplanted 'the interference of the imperial state'; 'as a country's links with [the] international economy tightened, imperial intervention slackened'.[56]

The timing, sequence, and particular characteristics of this transition varied. But common patterns of the virtuous circle are clear: burgeoning exports generated foreign exchange and elicited foreign investment in infrastructure (ports, railways, telegraphs); economic growth encouraged urbanization and, with time, a domestic market and a more cosmopolitan and technocratic culture; governments could raise more revenue (and pocket more bribes), thus enhancing political stability and encouraging further trade and investment.[57] British interests, though crucial, were not the first movers. They contributed to, but did not engender, the

---

[53] Platt, *Finance, Trade and Politics*, chap. 6.

[54] 'Vice' and 'virtue' are, of course, highly subjective; this transformation was virtuous in terms of British interests, most Latin American élites, and conventional calculations of GDP. See chap. by B. R. Tomlinson.

[55] Ferns, *Britain and Argentina*, p. 283.

[56] Ronald Robinson, 'The Excentric Idea of Imperialism, with or without Empire', in Wolfgang J. Mommsen and Jürgen Osterhammel, eds., *Imperialism and After: Continuities and Discontinuities* (London, 1986), p. 274.

[57] Platt, *Latin America*, pp. 68–72; Miller, *Britain and Latin America*, pp. 67, 94, 97 ff.

transformation, whose speed, timing, and character were peripherally determined. Export growth was vital, as the pioneering cases of Brazil and Argentina had demonstrated. Peru was carried from *caudillesque* chaos to civilian, free-trading boom on a tide of stinking guano.[58] Chile enjoyed a short-lived boom in cereals, followed by a more durable phase of export-led growth based on nitrates, and later copper. Cuba, still under formal Spanish rule but receptive to British trade and investment, was the last exemplar of the Antillean cycle of sugar booms. Brazil became the world's greatest coffee producer, followed by Colombia, Venezuela, and Guatemala. Mexico, a prey to domestic conflict and foreign invasion, developed late, with the railway and export boom of the Porfiriato (1876–1911). And, the outstanding case, Argentina advanced through a series of export cycles (wool, cereals, beef) which made it a pre-eminent export economy, with a per capita income exceeding that of many European countries: a sort of South American Australia.

Britain figured in this transformation as a market, trading partner, and source of investment, both direct and indirect. British exports, stagnant at around £5m per annum through the 1840s, rose to £14m in 1860 and £55m in 1913 (comprising 10 per cent of Britain's total exports). Textiles represented 70 per cent of exports in 1860, only 31 per cent in 1913. British imports from Latin America rose faster, reaching £76m in 1913. The Brazilian trade, the old linchpin of British commerce, grew absolutely but declined relatively; Mexico and Peru ceded ground to the southern cone, especially Argentina, whose economic intimacy with Britain was unique, paralleling that of the Dominions.[59] British investment rose from £81m in 1860 to £1,180m in 1913, with government bonds (76 per cent of the total in 1860, 38 per cent in 1913) giving way to direct investment in railways (34 per cent in 1913), public utilities (12 per cent), and banking and insurance (8 per cent). By 1913 Argentina took 41 per cent of Britain's Latin American investment, compared to Brazil's 22 per cent and Mexico's 11 per cent, making Argentina a recipient of British capital roughly on a par with Australia and South Africa.[60] Swathes of the Latin American economy now came under British control: the railways of Argentina and central Mexico; the public utilities of Buenos Aires, Rio, and Recife; major merchant houses in Chile, Venezuela, and Peru; mines in Brazil and Mexico, later

---

[58] Gootenberg, *Between Silver and Guano*, pp. 80–91, 140–41.

[59] Miller, *Britain and Latin America*, pp. 75, 108, 111; Platt, *Latin America*, p. 111; S. B. Saul, *Studies in British Overseas Trade, 1870–1914* (Liverpool, 1960), p. 219. For the Argentina–Australia parallel and Latin American–Dominion comparisons, see Donald Denoon, *Settler Capitalism: The Dynamics of Settler Capitalism in the Southern Hemisphere* (Oxford, 1983).

[60] Miller, *Britain and Latin America*, pp. 120–24; Irving Stone, 'British Direct and Portfolio Investment in Latin America Before 1914', *Journal of Economic History*, XXXVII, 3 (Sept. 1977), pp. 690–722; Michael Edelstein, *Overseas Investment in the Age of High Imperialism* (London, 1982), pp. 39–40, 102–04.

petroleum in Mexico and Venezuela, and banks and insurance companies throughout the continent.[61]

The growth of British trade and investment carried social and cultural consequences. There was no mass migration to South America as there was to North; the biggest British community—Argentina's—numbered 40,000 in 1914, but in a foreign population of 2 million, half of them Italians.[62] Furthermore, while some British expatriates intermarried and naturalized (they included several major mercantile families—such as the Mexican Barrons, Chilean Edwards, or Venezuelan Boultons—who in the course of the nineteenth century effectively relinquished 'British' status), others remained resolutely British, preserving an Anglocentric lifestyle within the confines—sometimes the physical confines—of company towns (mines, nitrate *oficinas*, oilfields), which possessed their own clubs, churches, and cemeteries.[63] Indeed, as trade gave way to direct corporate investment, associated with such 'enclave' activities, as well as public utilities, so British assimilation tended to decline and local popular resentment to increase.[64]

Despite their scant numbers and cultural aloofness, however, the British managed to transmit ideas, words, customs, fashions, and games to the host society. As early as the 1820s Rio had its Red Lion and Jolly Tar pubs; fifty years later the diminutive railway serving Recife's sugar factories was grandiloquently styled the Great Western of Brazil.[65] Argentina's railway boom brought a spate of British names—another Great Western, a Great Southern—and British seamen and railway-builders introduced football to South America: if the Central Uruguay Railway Cricket Club left no permanent trace, its footballing counterpart, Peñarol, became one of Uruguay's great footballing dyarchy (Montevideo Wanderers enjoyed a less celebrated history), and erstwhile company teams, such as River Plate, flourished across the estuary in Argentina, where Englishisms (e.g. *el córner*) peppered sporting Spanish and the *Buenos Aires Herald* applauded this 'peaceful conquest of British customs'.[66] Several South American teams, such as Brazil's Fluminense, had distinctly élite origins, reflecting British influence among

[61] D. C. M. Platt, *Business Imperialism, 1840–1930: An Inquiry Based on British Experience in Latin America* (Oxford, 1977), offers a good selection of cases.

[62] Andrew Graham-Yooll, *The Forgotten Colony: A History of the English-Speaking Communities in Argentina* (London, 1981).

[63] Miller, *Britain and Latin America*, p. 80; Carl, *First Among Equals*, pp. 68–73. See the argument between Eugene W. Ridings, 'Foreign Predominance Among Overseas Traders in Nineteenth-Century Latin America', and Carlos Marichal, 'Foreign Predominance Among Overseas Traders in Nineteenth-Century Latin America: A Comment', *Latin American Research Review*, XX, 2 (1985), pp. 3–27, and XXI, 3 (1986), pp. 145–50.

[64] Jones, 'British Capital', pp. 72–73. For a classic enclave, see Eakin, 'Business Imperialism'.

[65] Gregory, *Brute New World*, p. 170; Graham, *Britain and the Onset*, p. 70.

[66] Tony Mason, *Passion of the People? Football in South America* (London, 1995), chaps. 1, 2.

oligarchic and rising middle-class groups, some of whom, such as the Brazilian abolitionist Jaoquim Nabuco, confessed to a proud 'Anglomania' which no evidence of British drinking and brawling could apparently shake, and which was reflected in correspondence, lifestyle, and reading: Adam Smith, J. S. Mill, Samuel Smiles, Darwin, Spencer, Carlyle, and Sir Walter Scott. (The Argentine liberal Sarmiento spent half his salary on English lessons and claimed to have read sixty Scott novels in as many days.)[67] In Buenos Aires, above all, élite Argentines and Anglo-Argentines played polo, shopped at Harrods, employed English governesses, and were educated at Anglophone schools, if not at Eton itself.[68] Cultural ties thus paralleled, and no doubt reinforced, commercial relations, tightening the bonds of collaboration. While South America would not expend blood on behalf of the British Empire, it yielded treasure and, so long as liberal Anglophile oligarchs ruled, displayed an intangible politico-cultural sympathy which, by the 1900s, contributed to the 'Atlantic orientation' of Britain's grand strategy.[69]

The British economic presence in Latin America was therefore important for Britain and crucial for Latin America. Did this constitute 'imperialism'? The contrasting adjectives—'important' and 'crucial'—say something about the unequal relationship. The banking crisis at Baring Bros. in 1890 sent a frisson through the City but threatened to bankrupt Argentina; while Lord Salisbury could airily dismiss talk of official British 'regeneration of Argentine finance', President Pellegrini was struck to the quick: 'rather than suspend service on the debt,' he declared, 'I would renounce the presidency.'[70] Even if private bankers, rather than the British government, mounted financial rescues—the 'structural adjustment' programmes of the day, emanating from a 'London consensus'—they imposed tough terms on straitened creditors.[71] Peripheral Latin American economies were therefore more vulnerable than the richer and more diversified British metropolis. In particular, the fragility of export booms (Peruvian guano, Brazilian rubber) demonstrated the dangers of *desarrollo hacia afuera* (export-led development) which accompanied thorough immersion in global markets. Investment booms similarly revealed the dependency of Latin America: lending followed Eurocentric rhythms; and, since there were more borrowers than lenders, the latter enjoyed a tactical advantage.[72]

---

[67] Graham, *Britain and the Onset*, pp. 107, 178, 196; John King, 'The Influence of British Culture in Argentina', in Hennessy and King, *Land That England Lost*, p. 160.

[68] Alistair Hennessy, 'Anglo-Argentines and Others', in Hennessy and King, *Land That England Lost*, pp. 11–12, 27.

[69] Avner Offer, *The First World War: An Agrarian Interpretation* (Oxford, 1989), pp. 136–37, 244 ff.

[70] Miller, *Britain and Latin America*, pp. 62–63, 154.

[71] Fritsch, *External Constraints*, p. 31; Graham, *Britain and the Onset*, pp. 103–06.

[72] Miller, *Britain and Latin America*, pp. 121–22; Carlos Marichal, *A Century of Debt Crises in Latin America, 1820–1930* (Princeton, 1989).

If, in broad, macroeconomic terms, Britain enjoyed, and Latin America suffered, a skewed dependent relationship, this generalization demands infinite qualification. First, there were British losers as well as winners. If a few mines and
railways, such as Brazil's St John d'El Rey and the San [*sic*] Paulo Railway Co., were
moneyspinners, many were failures. Of some 400 British mining enterprises in
Latin America, less than twenty made profits.[73] The first spurt of British mercantile enterprise in Latin America brought 'immense profits for a few, but disappointment and bankruptcy for most'.[74] Sporadic financial crises hit Latin
American governments, but they also resulted in losses for British creditors.
And, while the global division of labour differentially affected Latin Americans—peasants, Indians, artisans tended to lose; élites, landlords, and urban
bourgeoisies benefited—the same was true, to a lesser degree, in Britain where,
for example, British consumers enjoyed cheap Argentine beef and grain, but where
British farmers and farm labourers went to the wall; or where Cornish copper
mines were put out of business by Chilean competition.[75]

Moreover, British economic hegemony was contested. As a manufacturer and
exporter, Britain depended heavily on its pioneering textile industry, which
powered its initial thrust into Latin American markets. By the late nineteenth
century textiles had declined in importance, in part because of incipient import-
substitution industrialization in the major Latin American countries, and new
export lines had become more important: coal, steel, machinery, later electrical
goods, chemicals, and automobiles. Britain never enjoyed equivalent dominance
in the manufacture and export of these, the products of the second industrial
revolution. By 1914 both Germany and the United States had emerged as major
rivals in Latin American trade. Germany had overtaken British commerce in
Venezuela and was fast catching up in Chile; German merchants controlled 20
per cent of Brazil's coffee trade and 60 per cent of her rubber exports; German lager
had now supplanted English Bass.[76] The United States became commercially
dominant in Cuba, Mexico, and Colombia, took more of Brazil's exports (especially coffee) than Britain, and in terms of direct investment had a growing stake in
Venezuela (oil), Chile (copper), and Peru (oil and copper). Even in Argentina,
which most resembled the politically tied economies of the Dominions, US
interests controlled 43 per cent of the grain market (compared to Britain's 33 per

[73] J. Fred Rippy, *British Investments in Latin America, 1822–1949* (New York, 1977), p. 32.

[74] Miller, *Britain and Latin America*, p. 79.

[75] Ferns, *Britain and Argentina*, pp. 488–89; Willam W. Culver and Cornel J. Reinhart, 'Capitalist
Dreams: Chile's Response to Nineteenth-Century World Copper Competition', *Comparative Studies in
Society and History*, XXXI (1989), pp. 722, 724, 730.

[76] Bill Albert, *South America and the First World War* (Cambridge, 1988), pp. 20, 79; Graham, *Britain
and the Onset*, pp. 113, 301–04.

cent) and 60 per cent of the meat trade (to Britain's 31 per cent).[77] The First World War decisively accelerated this process of US market penetration and capital export.

Foreign competition alarmed the British government and prompted new trade-promotion initiatives. Some historians have therefore discerned a more interventionalist, even 'imperialist', turn in British policy during the last quarter of the nineteenth century, the age of the 'new imperialism'. Some talk of a 'scramble for Latin America'.[78] This seems semantically risky, confusing radically different forms of 'intervention' and 'imperialism'. During the early nineteenth century the British government intervened politically and even militarily in Latin America, trying to foster conditions congenial to British interests. Outside Brazil, success was limited. But during the later nineteenth century—and the timing varied from place to place—conditions improved, albeit little thanks to British government efforts. By now most Latin American states were open and welcoming to foreign trade and investment; increasingly, they were controlled by civilian and technocratic élites, such as Peru's Civilistas and Mexico's Porfiristas, who had supplanted the wayward warlords of earlier times and now happily collaborated with foreign capital.[79]

The perceived need for British intervention, for the exercise of imperialism as 'a sufficient political function of the process of integrating new regions into an expanding economy', diminished or disappeared altogether. Why send warships to the River Plate when President Pellegrini staked his high office on defending Argentina's credit? Intervention and intimidation did not cease altogether: a particularly recalcitrant tyrant such as Venezuela's Castro, a throwback, in part, to the *caudillos* of earlier times, might experience half-hearted chastisement at the hands of the British government.[80] But in general the British government—itself, since the 1840s, a champion of *laissez-faire* liberalism—preferred a hands-off policy. As Salisbury stated in 1891, at a time of political and financial crisis in South America, Her Majesty's Government was '[not] in the least disposed to encroach on the function of Providence', partly because Providence was, so far as Britain was concerned, working well enough in Latin America, partly because Britain was busily encroaching on its function elsewhere in Africa and Asia.[81]

Thus a review of British reactions to Latin American 'local crises' *c.*1860–1914 reveals that, *pace* certain conspiracy theorists, Britain tended *not* to intervene on

---

[77] Albert, *South America*, pp. 14, 67.

[78] Cain and Hopkins, *British Imperialism*, pp. 285, 312–13.

[79] Gootenberg, *Between Silver and Guano*, pp. 84–85; Albert, *South America*, pp. 32–33; Alfred Tischendorf, *Great Britain and Mexico in the Era of Porfirio Díaz* (Durham, NC, 1961).

[80] D. C. M. Platt, 'The Allied Coercion of Venezuela, 1902–03: A Reassessment', *Inter-American Economic Affairs*, XV (1962), pp. 3–28.

[81] Ferns, *Britain and Argentina*, p. 465.

behalf of bondholders and companies in the region: Britain withdrew swiftly from the allied coercion of Mexico in the 1860s; avoided involvement in the Paraguayan War (1865–70) and the War of the Pacific between Chile and Peru (1879–81); declined to intervene in the Chilean civil war of 1891 or the Brazilian rebellions of 1892–94; and avoided any serious *démarches* during the Mexican Revolution (1910–17).[82] This record of relative inactivity contrasts, of course, with Britain's forward policy elsewhere, notably in Africa, where local crises—such as Egypt, 1882—provoked direct intervention leading to occupation.

The contrast derives from two factors. First—a negative 'metropolitan' argument—Britain saw no major strategic interest in Latin America. Policy-makers no longer dreamed of securing San Francisco; US supremacy in the Caribbean area was accepted; the bipartisan approach to the question of a trans-Isthmian canal—evident in the Clayton-Bulwer Treaty of 1850—had given way to a resigned acceptance of US hegemony, which was reinforced by the Venezuelan boundary dispute of 1895, the US occupation of Cuba in 1898, and the subsequent US interventions in Central America and revolutionary Mexico.[83] However much they might dislike US policy as crude, clumsy, aggressive, duplicitous, or hypocritical, the British could not bring themselves to jeopardize Anglo-American relations by captious opposition. Some local representatives such as Lionel Carden, Minister to Mexico in 1913–14, sought to stand up to the Yankees; but such attempts at emulating the 'sub-imperialist' policy of early-nineteenth-century Proconsuls like Strangford and Chatfield were naive, anachronistic, and abortive.[84] The geopolitical imperatives which fuelled British expansion in Africa were lacking in Latin America; when it came to defending vital sea-lanes and canals, it was the United States, obsessed with Caribbean security, which, *mutatis mutandis*, played the imperialist role in the western hemisphere.

The second—positive peripheral—argument reasserts the causal primacy of trends within Latin America. If, by the 1900s, most republics possessed viable governments, keen for foreign—but not necessarily British—trade and investment, there was little need for dramatic initiatives. In contrast with the early period, Latin America had now produced collaborating élites who, for reasons of

---

[82] Miller, *Britain and Latin America*, pp. 63–67; Graham, *Britain and the Onset*, pp. 306–11; P. A. R. Calvert, *The Mexican Revolution, 1910–14: The Diplomacy of Anglo-American Conflict* (Cambridge, 1968). British interests on the ground—freelance entrepreneurs in Paraguay, nitrate interests in Chile, merchants in Brazil, oil companies in Mexico—possessed their own lively—but far from unanimous—political preferences; they often engaged in local politicking, and sometimes deplored British government policy; but they could determine neither what that policy would be, nor what outcome would ensue from these 'local crises'.

[83] Smith, *Illusions of Conflict*, chaps. 4, 7.

[84] Friedrich Katz, *The Secret War in Mexico: Europe, the United States and the Mexican Revolution* (Chicago, 1981), p. 189.

self-interest, economic rationality, and ideology, were willing and able to provide a congenial framework for British commercial interests. The 'internalization of British values', even the 'uncritical mimicry of European fashion', were now pervasive, at least among Latin American élites.[85] That did not, of course, produce carbon copies of Westminster democracy. The latter, like cricket, required decades of *formal* imperial rule, as in the British Caribbean or British India, for the rules to be learned, the institutions established, the benefits appreciated. Mutually beneficial economic collaboration required, instead, a lower cultural common denominator: a basic consensus on the values and practices of capitalism; respect for property and contracts; state intervention to bolster the market (transport, communications, tariff, fiscal, and currency reform); and the elimination of obstacles to capital accumulation (labour shortages, corporate village lands, nomadic Indians, bandits, and bushwhackers). These desiderata could be achieved with or, more commonly, without democracy, by 'gentlemanly' or, more commonly, 'ungentlemanly' methods. But they were major undertakings. They involved state-formation, since without a viable state there could be no sustained accumulation; and they required constant social control, especially of the dissolute lower orders—the 'dangerous classes' and 'lazy natives' who prejudiced the smooth workings of the market. Not surprisingly late-nineteenth-century Latin American élites, in collaboration with British capital, replicated many of the policies of contemporary colonial states: they recruited new professional armies and police forces; they repressed peasant and indigenous protest; they dragooned labour (Roger Casement exposed comparable atrocities in the Congo, then the Amazon); they taxed, enumerated, and, to a degree, educated; they moved immigrant labour across oceans and international boundaries; they built infrastructure (ports, railways, telegraphs) and introduced preventive medicine; and they did all this with frequent invocations of 'Progress' and frank references to racial stereotypes. These striking parallels should perhaps not surprise us; both colonial and independent Latin American states were, *grosso modo*, 'sufficient political function[s] of . . . integrating new regions into the expanding economy' (of course, they were much else besides). But whereas in Africa strategic and local conditions obliged the British to undertake the political spadework themselves, in Latin America a satisfactory division of labour was tacitly agreed: local élites ran the shop, while Britain supplied goods and credit.

In this light, the so-called 'scramble for Latin America' bears little resemblance to the 'scramble for Africa'. The latter involved a wholesale carve-up, annexation, and profound social, economic, and cultural transformation. In Latin America the equivalent transformation was a longer, slower process, involving four centuries of

---

[85] Fritsch, *External Constraints*, p. 124, referring to Brazilian mimicry of British financial orthodoxy.

Iberian colonization, followed by one of independent state-building. British
commercial penetration, important though it was, capped half a millenium of
colonialism—Iberian and later 'internal'—and could therefore afford the luxury
of an increasingly apolitical and disinterested role, rather as in the case of the
Dominions.[86] But, having renounced territorial annexation and direct rule, Britain had to rely on commercial and financial prowess in order to retain economic
hegemony in the region. Latin America was therefore the key test of British
international competitiveness.[87]

Financially, Britain survived tolerably well until 1914, although the United States
was by then dominant in the Caribbean and challenging in northern South
America. But commercially Britain was already in decline, losing market share
to Germany and the United States, even in the old bastion of the southern cone. Of
course this reflected a global reversal in industrial power, which subverted Britain's
brief, unsustainable, mid-Victorian hegemony. But it also reflected Britain's
inability to use political muscle and, loosely, imperialist methods, to offset commercial decline in Latin America, as she could in the formal Empire. The late
Victorian Latin American 'scramble', therefore, involved for Britain worried
reports on trade, enhanced commercial intelligence, sporadic missions to the
continent, and attempts, of varying success, to tie trade to finance. Germany
and the United States were, *mutatis mutandis*, involved in similar efforts. This
was a pacific 'scramble' compared to the bloody partition of Africa; and it is a
'scramble' which, with rather different players, continues today, long after the
dissolution of Britain's formal Empire.

The external challenge of commercial rivals was, by the turn of the century, also
matched by domestic challenges mounted by dissident Latin Americans. If, in the
formal Empire, state-building and market penetration elicited protest, so too, in
independent countries undergoing comparable transformations, aggrieved
groups targeted incumbent élites and their foreign collaborators; sometimes,
those élites had to decide whether to continue collaborating or throw in their
lot with nationalist and populist critics. Three main forms of protest stood out:
that of roughly middle-class, educated, urban, white-collar groups (themselves
products of capitalist development and state-building—Latin American 'babus', if
you like); and that of popular groups, including first, artisans, peasants, and
Indians prejudiced by commercialization (roughly, 'declining' groups), and second, the 'new' working classes, products, again, of capitalist development, who
worked on the docks, railways, mines, factories, and plantations of the 'modern'

[86] Denoon, *Settler Capitalism*; H. S. Ferns, 'Argentina: Part of an Informal Empire?', in Hennessy and
King, *Land That England Lost*, pp. 49–50, 55.
[87] Saul, *British Overseas Trade*, pp. 33–34, 38–39.

sector, and who by the 1900s were beginning to flex their organizational muscles. These patterns of protest, which can be loosely subsumed under a 'nationalist' label, varied greatly from country to country. Traditional protest concentrated in the Indian highland regions of Peru, Bolivia, and Mexico; here, the British presence was weak (native landowners were the dominant class) and popular uprisings, of which Mexico's Zapatista revolt was the most sustained and successful, rarely targeted British interests. 'Modern' protest, both middle class and popular, concentrated in areas of greater British presence, by both sector and country. In the cities, particularly those of the southern cone, consumers complained about British trains, trams, and public utilities; and a new, growing proletariat, incipiently unionized, toiled in British mines, steamships, and meat-packing plants. Indeed, foreign ownership of export industries—Chilean mines, Argentinian slaughterhouses, Venezuelan oilfields—arguably played a key role in early labour mobilization, which was sometimes spurred by the high-handed, arbitrary, and racist attitudes of British management.[88] Nationalist labour mobilization exploded in the post-war period; but by the 1900s there were early stirrings, for example, in Chile's nitrate fields, which tended to produce a common front of worried British employers and their no less worried élite collaborators.[89]

But middle-class nationalist critiques of foreign, usually British, penetration clearly antedated the war: with polemicists such as Bunge in Argentina and Encina in Chile; and, more important, with broadly based middle-class protest movements, which attained power in Uruguay (the Batlle administration, 1905–11) and in Argentina following the victory of Irigoyen's Radicals in the 1916 election. Batlle, in particular, implemented policies of social reform and economic nationalism which, while they did not rupture the old Anglo-Uruguayan nexus, questioned its tenets and earned him the cordial dislike of British businessmen and officials.[90] Even oligarchic élites had to take note. Railway regulation, which responded to domestic complaints, was established in Mexico and Argentina well before 1914; Brazil's coffee valorization programme represented a major state initiative to force up prices to the advantage of domestic producers.[91] The dragon of *dirigisme* was fitfully stirring after a slumber of several decades; the guns of August would guarantee his awakening.

---

[88] Charles Bergquist, *Labor in Latin America* (Stanford, Calif., 1986).

[89] Michael Monteón, *Chile in the Nitrate Era* (Madison, 1982), pp. 95–107; Miller, *Britain and Latin America*, p. 173.

[90] M. H. J. Finch, 'British Imperialism in Uruguay: The Public Utility Companies and the *Batllista* State, 1900–30', in Abel and Lewis, *Latin America*, pp. 250–66.

[91] Winthrop R. Wright, *British-Owned Railways in Argentina* (Austin, Tex., 1974), pp. 76–88; Fritsch, *External Constraints*, pp. 13–16.

By 1914, therefore, Britain faced serious challenges to her established position in Latin America. Financially pre-eminent in most, though not all, of the continent, she now deferred geopolitically to the United States in the north, and was rapidly losing her commercial supremacy elsewhere. Having renounced political intervention, Britain had to compete in a relatively 'fair field with no favour', lacking the political privileges which were the rewards of formal Empire. In a sense, Britain's 'imperialist' role, if 'imperialist' it was, had run its course. Britain had helped, first, to batter down the walls of Spanish mercantilism, and then to erect new structures conducive to capitalist development, though not necessarily to gentlemanly—still less, democratic—politics. For several decades Britain was the chief foreign beneficiary of that process, but by the turn of the century other beneficiaries were clawing back her lead and Latin American élites were ready to play the foreign field. In Latin America, as in her domestic industrialization, Britain enjoyed the temporary advantages of forwardness; but, having helped make Latin America stable, capitalist, and productive, Britain had no political monopoly on the fruits of those advances—which, by 1914, were increasingly being contested by both vigorous foreign competitors and nascent Latin American nationalists.

Select Bibliography

CHRISTOPHER ABEL and COLIN LEWIS, *Latin America: Economic Imperialism and the State* (London, 1985).

LESLIE BETHELL, *The Abolition of the Brazilian Slave Trade* (Cambridge, 1970).

DONALD DENOON, *Settler Capitalism: The Dynamics of Dependent Development in the Southern Hemisphere* (Oxford, 1983).

MARSHAL C. EAKIN, *British Enterprise in Brazil: The St John d'El Rey Mining Company and the Moro Velho Gold Mine, 1830–1960* (Durham, 1989).

H. S. FERNS, *Britain and Argentina in the Nineteenth Century* (Oxford, 1960).

PAUL GOOTENBERG, *Between Silver and Guano: Commercial Policy and the State in Postindependence Peru* (Princeton, 1989).

RICHARD GRAHAM, *Britain and the Onset of Modernization in Brazil, 1850–1914* (Cambridge, 1968).

DESMOND GREGORY, *Brute New World: The Rediscovery of Latin America in the Early Nineteenth Century* (London, 1992).

COLIN M. LEWIS, *British Railways in Argentina, 1857–1914* (London, 1983).

DAVID MCLEAN, *War, Diplomacy and Informal Empire: Britain and the Republics of La Plata, 1836–1853* (London, 1995).

CARLOS MARICHAL, *A Century of Debt Crises in Latin America, 1820–1930* (Princeton, 1989).

RORY MILLER, *Britain and Latin America in the Nineteenth and Twentieth Centuries* (London, 1993).

D. C. M. PLATT, *Latin America and British Trade, 1806–1914* (London, 1972).

——*Business Imperialism, 1840–1930: An Inquiry Based on British Experience in Latin America* (Oxford, 1977).

R. W. RANDALL, *Real del Monte: A British Mining Venture in Mexico* (Austin, Tex., 1972).

MARIO RODRIGUEZ, *A Palmerstonian Diplomat in Central America: Frederick Chatfield, Esq.* (Tucson, Ariz., 1964).

JOSEPH SMITH, *Illusions of Conflict: Anglo-American Diplomacy Towards Latin America, 1865–1896* (Pittsburgh, Pa., 1979).

ALFRED TISCHENDORF, *Great Britain and Mexico in the Era of Porfirio Diaz* (Durham, 1961).

PETER WINN, 'Britain's Informal Empire in Uruguay in the Nineteenth Century', *Past and Present*, LXXIII (1976), pp. 100–26.

WINTHROP R. WRIGHT, *British-Owned Railways in Argentina* (Austin, Tex., 1974).

8

Britain and China, 1842–1914

JÜRGEN OSTERHAMMEL

Empire in the Far East was more than a metaphor for commercial supremacy in the China Seas. Ever since Henry Dundas dispatched Lord Macartney to the Court of the Emperor Qianlong in 1792, China figured in grand designs of market conquest and global influence. With the exception of emigration, the same forces of expansion at work elsewhere made their appearance in East Asia. Great hopes for mercantile gain, for the salvation of heathen souls, and for the spread of European-style modernity were pinned to the most populous country on earth. British soldiers and diplomats, merchants and bankers, missionaries and scholars were active in China as soon as the country became accessible as a result of two Anglo-Chinese wars: the Opium War of 1840–42 and the 'Arrow' War of 1856–60.[1] Step by step, a system of international treaties was established that turned large parts of China into an uncolonized extension of Empire (see Map 8.1). The treaties guaranteed rights of access to and of residence in a number of major Chinese cities (transformed into 'treaty ports'), personal security of foreign citizens from the alleged 'barbarity' of Chinese justice, a uniformly low tariff, and a privileged treatment of foreign goods in transit through the customs-ridden Chinese interior. They also opened up China's rivers and coastal waters to the unchecked activities of foreign shipping companies.

Moreover, China excited the British imagination. All sorts of orientalist clichés and racial stereotypes were projected upon China and the Chinese. Some of them, for example, the spectres of a 'yellow peril' and of Asiatic stagnation and decadence, emerged from contemplating the Middle Kingdom: a civilization once admired but increasingly feared and despised. From the mid-nineteenth century, China formed an integral part of the military, economic, and mental history of European and, in particular, of British imperialism.

As China was never turned into any Great Power's colony, its relations with Britain can be narrated in terms of conventional diplomatic history, emphasizing British

---

[1] For China's foreign relations, Immanuel C. Y. Hsü, *The Rise of Modern China*, 5th edn. (New York, 1995).

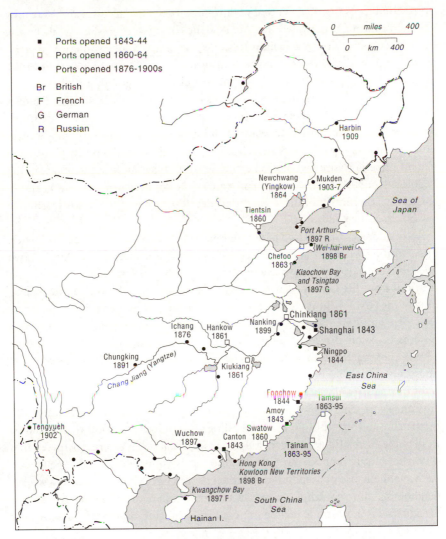

Ports opened 1843-44
Ports opened 1860-64
Ports opened 1876-1900s

Br British
F French
G German
R Russian

0   miles   400
0   km   400

Harbin
1909

Newchwang
(Yingkow)
1864

Mukden
1903-7

Tientsin
1860

Port Arthur
1897 R
(Wei-hai-wei
1898 Br

Chefoo
1863

Kiaochow Bay
and Tsingtao
1897 G

Sea of
Japan

Chinkiang 1861

Nanking
1899

Shanghai 1843

Ichang
1876

Hankow
1861

Ningpo
1844

Chungking
1891

Chang Jiang (Yangtze)

Kiukiang
1861

East China
Sea

Foochow
1844

Tamsui
1863-95

Tengyueh
1902

Wuchow
1897

Canton
1843

Swatow
1860

Amoy
1843

Tainan
1863-95

Hong Kong
Kowloon New Territories
1898 Br

Kwangchow Bay
1897 F

South China
Sea

Hainan I.

MAP 8.1. China: Treaty Ports and Leased Territories

perceptions and strategies and the intergovernmental contacts between the two countries.[2] A different approach tells the story of China's entrance into the family of nations.[3] In this perspective, China was gradually forced to abandon its policy of Sinocentric isolationism and was taught to respect the conventions of international conduct as they had evolved in Europe since the Renaissance and were now expanding throughout the world. After 1860 the Ch'ing (Qing) court, weakened by the tremendous Taiping Rebellion (1850–64), accepted China's inferior international status and allowed Britain to lead in incorporating the country into the modern world's political and economic structures. Although Britain did not disguise its own interests and on numerous occasions clashed with what Chinese rulers perceived to be their own good and that of their country, the British presence, according to this view, in the end promoted China's early modernization. It is interesting to note that such an interpretation, until recently pilloried as blatant imperialist apologetics, is beginning to find favour with historians in the People's Republic of China. Some consequences of imperialism are now acknowledged as early contributions to economic development and to a realistic Chinese awareness of the wider world.

A third approach, preferred here, attempts to focus on the *local* British presence, its institutional context and its effects on indigenous society and economy. Two questions are especially worth examining: What was 'imperial' about Sino-British relations from the Opium War to the time of the 1911 Revolution and the beginning of the First World War? And did the material British presence in China in any way form an interconnected whole, a system that could be seen in parallel with systems of colonial rule? If given a precise meaning, the concept of 'informal empire', not sanctioned by universal scholarly consensus, can help to answer these questions. 'Informal empire' is defined here as a historical situation of some stability and permanence in which overt foreign rule is avoided while economic advantages are secured by 'unequal' legal and institutional arrangements, and also by the constant threat of political meddling and military coercion that would be intolerable in relations between fully sovereign states.[4] It is crucial to see that 'informal empire' implies more than economic asymmetry, cultural dependency, or the sporadic use of preponderant influence by a Great Power towards a weaker neighbour. 'Informal empire' rests on the three pillars of: (1) legal privilege for foreigners; (2) a free trade regime imposed from outside; and (3) the deployment

---

[2] Peter Lowe, *Britain in the Far East: A Survey from 1819 to the Present* (London, 1981).

[3] Gerrit W. Gong, 'China's Entry into International Society', in Hedley Bull and Adam Watson, eds., *The Expansion of International Society* (Oxford, 1984), pp. 171–83.

[4] Elaborated in Jürgen Osterhammel, 'Semi-Colonialism and Informal Empire in Twentieth-Century China: Towards a Framework of Analysis', in Wolfgang J. Mommsen and Jürgen Osterhammel, eds., *Imperialism and After: Continuities and Discontinuities* (London, 1986), pp. 297–98.

of instruments of intervention such as the gunboat and the 'imperial' consul.[5] In China, some kind of British informal empire existed from the first treaty settlement of 1842 which concluded the Opium War, until the destruction of the treaty port system by the Japanese in December 1941. By that time, however, only the key legal privilege of extraterritoriality (foreign exemption from Chinese jurisdiction) continued to be of vital importance. Other features of informal empire had already disappeared or had attenuated during the preceding years.

In contrast to Japan, Britain was never a fully articulated colonial power on the East Asian mainland. Hong Kong, that bridge between South China and the Indo-Malayan world, came to be a minor ornament of Empire, but its transformation from a regional entrepôt into an economic centre of global importance occurred only after the suppression of capitalism in mainland China in 1949 and the following years. British rule over the Chinese, as in Hong Kong, in central Shanghai, and also Singapore, was confined to fluid, comparatively modern urban environments that had largely been created by the European invasion itself: frontier cities in zones of inter-cultural compromise. Only in Hong Kong's New Territories, acquired in 1898 with a population of some 80,000, and in the small leased territory of Wei-hai-wei with its 150,000 inhabitants, located on the northern coast of the Shantung promontory, did British administrators come in touch with the 'real' China, the settled world of the Chinese peasant. The man who left a strong imprint on both possessions, first as Colonial Secretary in Hong Kong and later as Civil Commissioner of Wei-hai-wei, James Stewart Lockhart (1858–1937), a Scottish scholar-mandarin and subtle practitioner of indirect rule, may well be regarded as a next-to-perfect embodiment of that exceptional thing: British colonialism in East Asia.[6]

Soon after the opening of the Middle Kingdom to free trade in 1842 it was felt not only that foreign merchants should enjoy extraterritoriality, but that special residential areas should be set aside for them in the major open ports. These 'Concessions' were areas leased from the Chinese government by a foreign power, which paid a trifling ground rent and sublet plots to its own nationals. The foreign Consul was the highest executive and jurisdictional authority. By 1878 the British had acquired such urban micro-colonies in six treaty ports. Their size ranged from 25 acres in the tea-exporting Yangtze port of Kiukiang (Jiujiang) to more than 1,000 acres in the North Chinese metropolis of Tientsin (Tianjin).[7] None of them,

---

[5] For the legal aspects, N. A. Bootsma, 'Herstel van soevereine rechten. Semi-koloniale landen en Europese expansie in Azië, 1890–1945', *Tijdschrift voor Geschiedenis*, CIV (1991), pp. 24–44.

[6] Shiona Airlie, *Thistle and Bamboo: The Life and Times of Sir James Stewart Lockhart* (Hong Kong, 1989).

[7] Fei Chenkang, *Zhongguo zujie shi* [History of the Foreign Concessionary Areas in China] (Shanghai, 1991), pp. 427–28. See also the detailed collective work *Lieqiang zai Zhongguo de zujie* [The Concessionary Areas of the Great Powers in China] (Peking, 1992).

not even the Concession at Tientsin, became really important as a bridgehead for the commercial penetration of the interior. In Tientsin, characteristically, there was twice as much British-owned land outside the Concession as in it. And the Concession at Hankow (Hankou), the great emporium on the middle Yangtze River, which boasted 'the finest Race and Recreation Club in the world',[8] was returned to China in 1927 without palpable losses for British business. Perhaps the strongest effect of the Concessions was the negative one of provoking Chinese indignation.

The British presence at Shanghai was of an entirely different order. At its quantitative peak in the early 1930s of 13,000 British residents in the entire Republic of China, 6,500 lived in the International Settlement, 2,500 in the neighbouring French Concession, and perhaps 1,000 in the Chinese-governed sector of Shanghai; at the same time the British population of Hong Kong amounted to more than 14,000. In contrast to Hong Kong, Shanghai had been a town of some commercial substance, especially in the cotton trade, when it was opened as a treaty port in 1843.[9] Nevertheless, its rise to the position of China's largest city, a crucible of economic and social modernization and the primary operating centre of Western economic interests in the Far East, was a direct consequence of the restructuring of China's foreign trade since the 1840s. Shanghai and Hong Kong partly rivalled and partly complemented each other. Hong Kong remained slightly more important than Shanghai as a destination for ocean-going traffic, and it continued to surpass Canton (Guangzhou), the old trading post of the pre-Opium War period, as the commercial magnet for South China. Still, in all other respects it was overshadowed by its rival in the North. The gap between the two cities widened even more after 1895, when the Sino-Japanese Treaty of Shimonoseki permitted foreign manufacturing industry in the treaty ports, thereby inaugurating Shanghai's industrialization, partly at the expense of Hong Kong. Only in the 1950s did Hong Kong regain the industrial momentum it had briefly attained in the 1880s. It has been estimated that in 1929 77 per cent of British direct investment in the whole of China was located in Shanghai, as against only 9 per cent in Hong Kong and 14 per cent elsewhere.[10]

Most of this wealth was concentrated in the International Settlement. This foreign enclave, after its final extension in 1899, occupied 8.66 square miles, about 6 per cent of the area of Greater Shanghai, at the heart of the city. It was never a colony in any technical sense, yet it can be regarded as something like the

---

[8] H. G. W. Woodhead, *The Yangtsze and Its Problems* (Shanghai, 1931), p. 106.

[9] Linda Cooke Johnson, *Shanghai: From Market Town to Treaty Port, 1074–1858* (Stanford, Calif., 1995), chap. 6.

[10] C. F. Remer, *Foreign Investments in China* (New York, 1933), p. 395. No such estimates exist for earlier periods.

most important asset of British formal Empire in East Asia. Chinese sovereignty over the Settlement was never officially suspended; there was no treaty between Britain or any other foreign country and the Imperial Chinese government that confirmed the alienation of Chinese rights. Legally, the foreign presence in Shanghai rested on nothing but a generous interpretation of the principle of extraterritoriality and on an agreement (the original 'Land Regulations'), concluded in 1845 between the first British Consul and the local mandarin, to set aside a piece of land within which British subjects were permitted to buy or rent land from private Chinese owners. Since in theory all land was supposed to be held by the Chinese Emperor, the foreign owners obtained deeds of perpetual lease, for which they paid the Chinese government a minuscule land rent. The Chinese state did not profit in any way from the skyrocketing of land values that occurred from the 1880s onwards.

On this slender legal basis rose the edifice of foreign Shanghai. Its political system was unique.[11] Although the British Consul-General, with the Royal Navy behind him, may have been the most powerful man in Shanghai, he did not exercise the same executive functions as his colleagues at Tientsin or Hankow. The highest authority within the Settlement was the Shanghai Municipal Council (SMC). Its members were elected annually by those ratepayers who could meet the qualifications for the franchise: a small minority not only among the Settlement's entire population of 1.12 million (in the mid-1930s), but also among the 39,000 foreign residents.[12] The SMC was a virtually sovereign body, accountable to no outside authority. It promulgated its own laws ('bye-laws'), taxed foreigners and Chinese alike, maintained its own municipal bureaucracy and police force, and managed several profitable public utilities. Representatives of the wealthy Chinese bourgeoisie of merchants, bankers, and retired officials who ran large parts of the Settlement's economy and owned a substantial share of the land within its borders were admitted to the Council as late as 1928. From 1881 to 1928 the Chinese labouring masses were kept out of the Recreation Ground (now Huangpu Park)—a source of much nationalist indignation.[13] (In Hong Kong, special residential areas were reserved for Europeans until 1941.) The common people of Shanghai never came to benefit from even the rudiments of colonial paternalism and modern ideas of trusteeship. The considerable successes in urban modernization and medical improvement achieved during the second half of the nineteenth

---

[11] F. C. Jones, *Shanghai and Tientsin: With Special Reference to British Interests* (London, 1940).

[12] Population figures from *Annual Report of the Shanghai Municipal Council, 1935* (Shanghai, 1935), pp. 50–51.

[13] Robert A. Bickers and Jeffrey N. Wasserstrom, 'Shanghai's "Dogs and Chinese Not Admitted" Sign: Legend, History and Contemporary Symbol', *China Quarterly*, CXLII (June 1995), pp. 445–46.

century did not entirely bypass the Chinese majority.[14] But they had been chiefly motivated, as many Chinese well understood, by the desire to create a tolerable environment for expatriate residents. In Shanghai, foreign big business succeeded where it failed in Hong Kong (and, after 1921, conceded defeat),[15] in achieving *de facto* self-government in a racially stratified society. The British predominated among the foreign oligarchy even after 1915, when the Japanese outnumbered them among the Settlement's foreign population. As late as the 1930s, six of the SMC's nine members were Britons. Almost all responsible positions within the municipal administration were occupied by British citizens. The Chinese could be forgiven for referring to the International Settlement, cosmopolitan as it was in its social composition and cultural outlook, as the 'English Concession' (*ying zujie*).

The rule of British private business, if not of British officialdom, over central Shanghai was built up by the gradual arrogation of governmental functions. The case of the International Settlement shows that not all British positions in China derived directly from the modern form of 'capitulations': the treaties Chinese nationalists came to call 'unequal' because only one party appeared to derive any benefit from them. There are numerous other examples of extra-treaty usurpations, especially in situations where the local authority of the Chinese government had broken down. British control of China's premier modern coal mine, the Kaiping colliery near Tientsin, came about in 1900, when foreign interests exploited the momentary financial weakness of the government-sponsored company and the unstable political conditions prevailing in North China at the height of the Boxer Rebellion.[16] No mining concession in the Kaiping area was ever granted to the British. Apart from the extraterritorial rights of its British and Belgian employees, no treaty privilege could be defended in connection with the Kaiping colliery. In 1912 it transformed itself into the Kailan Mining Administration (KMA), a British dominated Sino-foreign joint venture which accounted for about one-fifth of the coal production in China proper (that is, Manchuria excluded).

On the other hand, various advantages secured on paper were never enforced or utilized. Thus, several of the well-publicized concessions won by British firms and subjects during the international scramble for railway and mining rights around the turn of the century were never taken up. The reasons were lack of capital, insurmountable engineering difficulties, or resistance by the Chinese local élite

---

[14] Kerrie L. Macpherson, *A Wilderness of Marshes: The Origins of Public Health in Shanghai, 1843–1893* (Hong Kong, 1987).

[15] G. B. Endacott, *Government and People in Hong Kong, 1841–1962* (Hong Kong, 1964), pp. 134–45.

[16] Ellsworth C. Carlson, *The Kaiping Mines, 1877–1912*, 2nd edn. (Cambridge, Mass., 1971), pp. 57–74.

and its followers in the designated mining districts. Such concessions were only temporarily relevant as pawns in the diplomatic game. Part of Britain's informal empire existed only on paper.

There was thus a constant tension between legal privilege and its actual fulfill-ment. Sometimes public treaties and private agreements remained a dead letter. In other cases might, not right, accounted for British gains. Yet on the whole, the importance of the treaties stands beyond question. Until their negotiated abroga-tion in November 1943 they ensured that relations between Britain and China differed, at least formally, from normal patterns of modern international inter-course. China remained a country of impaired sovereignty. The treaties were the legal infrastructure of informal empire. They had three main effects: First, their most-favoured-nation clauses internationalized treaty privileges almost automat-ically and contributed to the working of the 'open door', that is, of equality of opportunity in the economic penetration of China. Secondly, the treaties con-ferred upon their beneficiaries advantages their indigenous competitors did not enjoy. The most important of these was non-economic: protection against the arbitrariness of the Chinese state. Thirdly, as soon as nationalist ideas and senti-ments emerged in China, the treaties provided an ideal focus for anti-imperialist critique and agitation. Imperialism was not merely perceptible as the sum total of specific abuses. It could be pinned down as a theory and doctrine enshrined in glaringly unjust documents of international law. The revision and eventual aboli-tion of the Unequal Treaties formed a point of consensus for schools of Chinese nationalism that otherwise quarrelled bitterly.

The treaty system stamped British presence in China with an overwhelming legalism. Even if the number of truly important treaties was much smaller than the 1,182 'unequal' agreements counted by Chinese historians,[17] by the turn of the century the treaty system had assumed an almost impenetrable complexity. Diplomats despaired of mastering the details, big foreign firms employed special-ized legal advisers, and bright Chinese lawyers began to challenge the foreign powers on their own juridical ground. However, the basic outlines of the treaty system were clear enough. The original goal of the early Victorians had been to push forward the trading frontier in what was believed to be one of the world's most promising markets. The early treaties had been imposed on the Chinese empire in the aftermath of its military defeat between 1842 and 1860. Although they were flagrantly unequal in putting unilateral limits on Chinese sovereignty, in some respects they appealed to traditional Chinese practices of managing unruly strangers, for example, the preference for dealing with them collectively through

---

[17] Zhang Zhenkun, 'Lun bupingdeng tiaoyue' [On Unequal Treaties], *Jindai shi yanjiu*, 1993, No. 2, p. 1. This enormous figure includes agreements with private foreign companies.

their headmen. Thus, the early treaty system expressed a certain convergence of interests between East and West. Above all, the British government and the Chinese state shared a common desire for regular trading procedures. Both wanted order and abhorred the turmoil created by smugglers, pirates, and unruly merchants. From the perspective of the British official mind, the treaty system was therefore no *carte blanche* for commercial freebooters. The treaties enshrined the sublime principle of Free Trade. They were meant to 'lift up' backward China and to accustom it to the 'standard of civilization' in international conduct.[18] Consequently, the right of access to the Manchu throne, the creation of a kind of foreign office (the Zongli Yamen), and the establishment of diplomatic relations were part and parcel of the treaty settlements. The treaties postulated 'the rule of law in the service of trade'.[19] Though of European origin and without a Chinese equivalent, this principle was double-edged in application. If necessary, respect would have to be demanded also from members of the foreign trading community.

The policy of introducing free trade by international treaty into a civilization where commerce had never enjoyed legal protection and where foreign merchants were not readily welcomed required the deployment of considerable instruments of intervention. They formed the second prong of informal empire. The treaties had to be upheld by a watchful and determined diplomacy and, in the final resort, to be backed up by force. They were the result of war and required the omnipresent threat of violence, however veiled in daily practice. Gunboat diplomacy, which can be defined as 'the use or threat of limited naval force, otherwise than as an act of war, in order to secure advantage, or to avert loss . . . against foreign nationals within the territory or the jurisdiction of their own state',[20] was the indispensable complement of legal privilege. The Royal Navy on the China Station stood by to protect British nationals from rebellious violence in one of the world's most turbulent countries. Between the naval operations against the Taiping Rebels in 1862 and the Boxer Intervention of 1900, most cases in which it went into action concerned the suppression of piracy, sometimes at the request of local Chinese officials. But the navy was also ready to put heavier kinds of pressure on the regional Chinese authorities within its reach. The last gunboat operation, causing considerable civilian losses, was conducted in July 1930 during the defence of Changsha, the capital of Hunan province, against the advancing Red Army.

Even more important than the naval commander in invigorating the informal empire was his civilian counterpart, the Consul. Calling in the navy was the

---

[18] Gerrit W. Gong, *The Standard of 'Civilization' in International Society* (Oxford, 1984), pp. 130–63.
[19] Richard J. Smith, John K. Fairbank and Katherine F. Bruner, eds., *Robert Hart and China's Early Modernization: His Journals, 1863–1866* (Cambridge, Mass., 1991), p. 117.
[20] John Cable, *Gunboat Diplomacy,* 3rd edn. (Basingstoke, 1994), p. 14.

Consul's ultimate weapon. Normally, he was expected to master difficult situations with his own resources: skill and the magic of character. The early Consuls of the heroic period up to the end of the Taiping menace in 1864, men like the formidable Sir Rutherford Alcock (1809–97), were empire-builders, establishing a British presence in adventurous conditions and in the face of an often hostile Chinese environment. Their successors could settle down to the routine task of making the treaty regime work. Since the posting of a British Minister to Peking in 1861, unresolved local disputes were to be referred to the Legation, which would then hold the Imperial government responsible for the misconduct of provincial and local officials. Consular wars had to be avoided. Even so, the men on the spot enjoyed considerable discretion and, given the vastness of the country and its poor communications, local crisis-management continued to be indispensable.

Imperial Consuls were no mere registrars and purveyors of good offices. They were quasi-diplomatic operators within an increasingly disintegrating empire. Securing specific advantages for British business was among their less important duties. As a rule, at least until the 1890s, they tended to act 'like referees in a football match, trying impartially to ensure that Chinese authorities and British merchants observed the treaty rules for the commercial game'.[21] From the beginning of the British presence to its very end, merchants in the treaty ports accused the Foreign Office and its consular representatives of weakness and passivity. Reproaches of this kind were inevitable. The legalism of the treaty system placed the Consul in an awkward position between Chinese officials and British expatriates. On the one hand, it was his duty to punish British criminals, discipline unruly sailors, and rein in people who deliberately provoked the Chinese and then clamoured for consular support. Missionaries were especially unpopular with Consuls because they frequently disregarded treaty provisions and Chinese sensitivities. Many of them created disagreeable *faits accomplis* and expected the Consuls to bail them out.

On the other hand, Consuls were obliged to protest against Chinese infringements of the treaties even if no specific British interests had been harmed. This insistence on legal positions *in abstracto* often led to fruitless pedantry and unnecessary confrontations with Chinese authorities. A further consequence of legalism was the abuse of treaty privileges by a certain number of Chinese. British citizenship was harder to obtain than that of other treaty powers. There was no British parallel to the case of Du Yuesheng, the prince of the Shanghai underworld, who enjoyed extraterritoriality as a Portuguese subject. But it was almost impossible to prevent British (or Indian) stooges from lending their names to shady Chinese firms. Such *liehang* ('inferior firms') abounded in shipping. Difficult

---

[21] P. D. Coates, *The China Consuls: British Consular Officers, 1843–1943* (Hong Kong, 1988), p. 171.

situations arose, for example, when Chinese vessels flying the British flag were attacked by pirates and claimed consular protection. It could not easily be refused.

The British consular network in China was the largest in the world, a direct consequence of a Foreign Office ruling of 1869 that a consulate ought to be established at every treaty port. Such an ambitious aim could not be entirely fulfilled, for by 1914 as many as ninety-two places had been opened to foreign trade, ten of them voluntarily by the Chinese government. Even so, a consulate was usually maintained wherever the Imperial Maritime Customs (IMC) stationed one of its commissioners. This was the case in about forty Chinese cities. Since the vast majority of them remained quite irrelevant for British trade, the ramified consular network was an expensive luxury.

The twin-like coupling with the IMC was no coincidence. Both the Customs and the Consulate were creatures of the crusade for Free Trade. A predecessor of the IMC had been set up in 1854 as a joint Sino-foreign undertaking. Its original purpose was to guarantee the regular collection of customs duties after rebels of the Small Sword Society (Xiaodashui) had destroyed the Shanghai custom house.[22] The IMC proper was a creation of (Sir) Robert Hart, its long-serving Inspector-General (1863–1908). Hart joined the Chinese consular service as a student interpreter in 1854. His organization of the IMC was internally patterned on the British consular service as well as on the Indian Civil Service. The IMC was a career bureaucracy under the autocratic direction of the Inspector-General, who was solely responsible to the Zongli Yamen. Although a Chinese government agency, in its higher echelons it was entirely staffed by lavishly paid foreigners. Of 1,382 non-Chinese (from nineteen nations) employed in 1906, 738 were Britons.[23]

Hart was undoubtedly the most influential foreigner in nineteenth-century China and the only one who ever obtained a high rank in the Chinese state bureaucracy. He considered himself at the same time a loyal servant of the Chinese Emperor, a patriotic Briton (he was born in Ulster), and chief guardian of the internationalist trade regime that had been installed by the treaties. Hart was sincere, when he confessed, 'I want to make China strong, and I want her to make England her best friend'.[24] He was impervious to complicity with individual

---

[22] Katherine F. Bruner, John K. Fairbank, and Richard J. Smith, eds., *Entering China's Service: Robert Hart's Journals, 1854–1863* (Cambridge, Mass., 1986), pp. 161–68.

[23] Hosea Ballou Morse, *The Trade and Administration of the Chinese Empire* (Shanghai, 1908), pp. 363–64.

[24] Hart to J. D. Campbell, 16 Oct. 1881, in John K. Fairbank, Katherine F. Bruner, and Elizabeth M. Matheson, eds., *The I. G. in Peking: Letters of Robert Hart, Chinese Maritime Customs, 1868–1907* (Cambridge, Mass., 1975), I, p. 389.

British merchants whose typically ignorant disdain of things Chinese he utterly despised. Although he advised half-a-dozen British ministers in succession, he was careful not to take orders from the Legation. During his term of office the IMC restricted its activities to the assessment and collection of customs duties and did not interfere with the disposal of revenue. It did not collaborate with foreign banks and never exercised direct financial control over China. Hart's IMC did not form a proper part of the British or any other national informal empire in China. Nevertheless, there was no stronger support for the treaty system. The IMC stood for incorruptible propriety and the open door in the conduct of China's foreign economic relations. Through harbour engineering, improvement of shipping lanes, pilotage, and commercial intelligence of a very high standard it also provided vital logistic support for foreign traders. The main beneficiaries were those who controlled the lion's share of Chinese foreign trade: the British.

Resulting from administrative rationalization and the elimination of irregular exactions ('squeeze'), the IMC made available to the Chinese treasury a much larger amount of revenue than a continuation of the pre-1854 customs arrangements would have produced. It thus strengthened the Manchu dynasty, especially during the moderately reformist phase between 1862 and the Sino-French War of 1884–85. In this way, Hart's service contributed to one of the long-term objectives of Britain's grand policy towards China. This policy remained remarkably constant. After the dynasty had been humbled but preserved during the period from the Opium War to the Taiping Intervention, London wished to see in Peking, as Sir Edward Grey put it in 1911, 'a strong and stable government which would ensure conditions favourable to trade'.[25] Ideally, the regime in Peking would be amenable to British influence and guidance, but strong enough to ward off internal rebellion and chaos and to resist demands from other powers. As early as 1862, Sir Frederick Bruce, the first Minister to the Ch'ing court, had prophetically observed: 'The weakness of China, rather than her strength, is likely to create a fresh Eastern Question in these seas.'[26] The maintenance of informal empire required a central authority capable of transmitting pressure from the top downward through the hierarchy. Troubles had to be resolved with a minimum of British effort and cost and without risk of being drawn into territorial dominion. A second India had to be avoided under any circumstances. When in doubt, even the colonial interests of Hong Kong were subordinated to broader Imperial concerns. The British government, normally, was careful to keep a healthy distance from the less-than-gentlemanly traders on the China coast. Four larger concerns, above all, seemed worth defending in China: the lives and property of respectable British citizens, the

---

[25] Quoted in E. W. Edwards, *British Diplomacy and Finance in China, 1895–1914* (Oxford, 1987), p. 158.
[26] Quoted in J. S. Gregory, *Great Britain and the Taipings* (London, 1969), p. 112.

sanctity of the International Settlement at Shanghai, the prestige of Britain as China's senior self-appointed 'foreign friend', and the treaty-based internationalist free trade regime.

Ironically, the most visible group among the British in China was one that many Consuls tended to regard as a nuisance: the missionaries. Since all missionaries, by the very nature of their project, posed a revolutionary challenge to the traditional order, they provoked Chinese reactions of unusual bitterness. The Chinese local élite and the common people were perfectly capable of distinguishing between Roman Catholicism (*tianzhujiao*) and Protestant Christianity (*jidujiao*), but they usually missed the differences between British missionaries and those of other nationalities. The Sino-French Treaty of 1860 had removed almost all obstacles to missionary activities anywhere in China. By 1890 Protestant missionaries resided in all provinces of China. The missionary enterprise as a whole was, by and large, rejected by the Chinese people, especially by the educated élite.[27] It does not seem as if British missionaries behaved in a particularly offensive way. But they too challenged the local élite's monopoly of social leadership, interfered with traditional religious practices, and split village communities into minorities protected under the umbrella of a widely defined extraterritoriality and majorities who now had to shoulder a proportionally heavier burden of expenses for festivities and ceremonies and sometimes even of taxes. While the Protestant mission, in contrast to the centralized Roman Catholic Church, never became a veritable *imperium in imperio*, the link between the missionary presence and foreign coercion became apparent to non-Christians whenever they had to foot the bill for the local indemnities exacted following anti-Christian riots. Tensions exploded in the Boxer Uprising of 1900. During the 1880s many missionary societies stepped up their valuable philanthropic, medical, and educational work in the great cities. The British concentrated their efforts on Hong Kong, where a small group of Christian reformers rose to prominence among the well-to-do Chinese citizens. Elsewhere, the British never matched the commitment of the American Protestants. None of the major missionary universities in Peking and Shanghai was British, and British cultural influence on the westernized élite of the early twentieth century remained limited, strikingly out of proportion to Britain's economic stake in China.

Although the institutions of informal empire evolved to be more than mere instruments of commercial expansion, trade remained the *raison d'être* of the British presence in China, at least throughout the nineteenth century. In spite of a growing regional diversification of Chinese foreign trade, by 1914 Britain and the

---

[27] Paul A. Cohen, 'Christian Missions and their Impact to 1900', in John K. Fairbank, ed., *The Cambridge History of China* (Cambridge, 1978), X, pp. 560–73.

British Empire (excluding Hong Kong) were still China's leading trading partners, if only by a slight margin over Japan. Simultaneously, Britain was the most important investor in the Republic of China, with about 38 per cent of total foreign investment.[28] Investment had assumed an important role after the epochal year of 1895, when China's military humiliation by Japan inaugurated a new stage of imperialism in East Asia.

To what extent can the British *economic* presence in China be regarded as an *imperial* presence? In what way was a natural economic asymmetry between the workshop and financial centre of the world and an agrarian country amplified by non-economic power differentials and the infrastructure of informal imperialism? What can be said about the impact of the British presence on the Chinese economy?

These questions can only be answered with some uncertainty. One reason for this is a lack of reliable statistical data. Even more important, the cosmopolitan character of the entire foreign establishment in China makes it difficult to isolate a particular British factor. This cosmopolitanism can be found on various levels. Except during periods of high international tension, the powers, represented by the Diplomatic Body in the capital and by its lower-level counterparts, the Consular Bodies in the treaty ports, frequently acted in unison to put pressure on the Chinese authorities. The joint intervention of the United States, Japan, and six European countries against the anti-foreign Yihetuan ('Boxer') movement in 1900 was a thoroughly co-operative venture, and the Draconian Boxer Protocol of 1901 was the dictate of an (internally less than harmonious) united front of the powers. Some of the principal imperialist institutions were British in their general cultural orientation, but international in composition. This is true for the IMC as well as for the International Settlement at Shanghai. Even the apparently national realms of control were less watertight than is often supposed. The spheres of interest demarcated around the turn of the century did not effectively exclude third-country competitors: German firms, for example, were very active in the 'British' Yangtze Valley, and the British government consented to French and Belgian participation in the financing of railways in Central China. At the outbreak of the European war in August 1914, the open secret that, at Tientsin, Germans owned land in the British Concession turned into a public embarrassment. At the same time, the Hongkong and Shanghai Banking Corporation (HSBC), which had financed German firms almost since its foundation in 1864, lost four of its twelve directors because they were German.[29] And the largest Western manufacturing

---

[28] Remer, *Foreign Investments*, p. 76.

[29] Frank H. H. King, *The Hongkong Bank in the Period of Imperialism and War, 1895–1918: Wayfoong, the Focus of Wealth* (Cambridge, 1988), p. 552.

enterprise on Chinese soil, the British-American Tobacco Corporation (BAT), shifted almost imperceptibly from American to British majority control by the mid-1920s.

The British profile is most clearly discernible during the earliest decades after the opening of China. Until the 1880s British business went almost unchallenged on the China coast. Its biggest success was the development of Shanghai. Shanghai was not only a funnel for goods into and out of Central China. It also became important as a market in itself. The growing foreign community created a demand for luxury imports and local services. This was supplemented by the purchasing power of Chinese businessmen, landowners, and retired officials who had withdrawn from the insecure interior to the safe haven on the coast. The Chinese in general were comparatively conservative in their tastes and consumption habits. They took more slowly to Western goods than the creole élites of Latin America or the Japanese during the Meiji era. Chinese wealth was traditionally invested in land. This now applied to Shanghai. The emergence of an urban real estate market in the International Settlement and land values that shot up from the 1880s on turned central Shanghai into one of the most valuable pieces of territory in Asia.[30]

Beyond the major territorial enclaves, the most spectacular British success story was shipping on the Yangtze and along the coast between Hong Kong and the South Manchurian ports. Before the age of the railway, steam shipping was the driving wedge in the Western penetration of China. The steamship made its first fateful appearance in China during the Opium War. In the 1860s American interests in civilian shipping were strong. Thereafter, the British flag predominated. The two leading steamship lines belonged to the major general-purpose China houses: Jardine Matheson & Co. ('Ewo') and Butterfield & Swire ('Taikoo'). Their combined share of the freight and passenger market was as high as 60 per cent in 1880 and dropped to around 35 per cent by 1937. Since 1873 competition was offered by the semi-governmental China Merchants Steam Navigation Co., and in the early twentieth century also by a number of smaller Chinese private lines. The British shipping companies were strong without ever obtaining a monopoly. Intense rate wars required stabilizing agreements on various occasions between 1877 and 1935.[31] The Ewo and Taikoo lines could only prosper because they attracted Chinese customers. They were thus more than mere auxiliaries of British import–export business. Much of their most lucrative business was transporting staple goods (rice, raw cotton, salt, etc.) within China. Some of the advantages enjoyed by foreign companies, for example, their superior capitalization and

---

[30] Zhao Jin, 'Zujie yu Zhongguo jindai fangdi chanye de dansheng' [The Concessions and the Birth of Modern Real Estate Business in China], *Lishi yanjiu*, 1993, No. 6, pp. 97–108.

[31] Zhang Zhongli, Chen Cengnian, and Yao Xinrong, *Taigu jituan zai jiu Zhongguo* [The Taikoo Group in Old China] (Shanghai, 1991), pp. 63–64.

organization, were of no immediate 'imperial' nature. Still, extra-territorial protection should not be underestimated as an additional asset. Many Chinese passengers and shippers, especially in the early twentieth century, preferred security under foreign flags to the risk of having the ships they were using attacked by pirates or commandeered by local militarists.[32] Steam shipping did not destroy pre-industrial junk traffic. On the contrary, in many regions it stimulated traditional means of transport. It served as a vehicle of modernization and brought great benefits to the Chinese economy. However, it is difficult to see the positive effects of foreign ownership. Not even technology transfer and personnel training played a role. Up to the 1940s, the foreign shipping companies employed hardly any Chinese in senior positions on board.

British merchants found it difficult to gain footholds in the China market. Great expectations were constantly disappointed. Opium imports from India, mostly handled by British firms, peaked in 1879 at a quantity of 5,000 tons and declined thereafter due to massive import substitution.[33] Towards the end of the century the province of Szechwan alone was said to have produced 15,000 tons per annum. Cotton goods, chiefly piece-goods, superseded opium as the principal item of China's legal imports in 1885. They accounted for 66 per cent of direct British exports to China in 1852 and 57 per cent in 1912.[34] China was an important market, but not the El Dorado hoped for at the time of the Opium War. In 1896, an exceptionally good year, it absorbed 8 per cent of the exports of the British cotton industry, against 27 per cent for India and another 8 per cent for the rest of Asia.[35]

By the 1890s British merchants no longer participated in the distribution of their goods 'up-country'. The situation at Ningpo, one of the five original treaty ports, was symptomatic. As early as 1870, it was alleged that Chinese merchants had 'monopolized' the trade in cotton goods in the town and the surrounding province of Chekiang and were able to offer the same British cloth at lower prices than British traders on the spot.[36] Thirty years later, not one British cotton importer remained active west of Shanghai. The entire trade had passed into the hands of country-wide indigenous merchant networks. The British importers in Shanghai, Hong Kong, and Tientsin had been reduced to the status of commission agents of the Chinese cotton guilds. They lacked immediate contact with their customers and had no control over retail prices. Above all, they could do nothing

[32] Zhu Jianbang, *Yangzijiang hangye* [Shipping on the Yangtze] (Shanghai 1937), pp. 146–47.

[33] Hsiao Liang-lin, *China's Foreign Trade Statistics, 1864–1949* (Cambridge, Mass., 1974), p. 52, Table 2.

[34] E. Manico Gull, *British Economic Interests in the Far East* (London, 1943), p. 53.

[35] D. A. Farnie, *The English Cotton Industry and the World Market, 1815–1896* (Oxford, 1979), p. 91, Table 5.

[36] Inspectorate General of Customs, *Reports on Trade at the Treaty Ports in China for the Year 1870* (Shanghai, 1871), p. 59.

against the chains of brokers and middlemen typical of Chinese trade. When Japanese importers developed cost-cutting facilities for direct distribution, British products found themselves seriously disadvantaged. Freedom from the burdens of up-country distribution made life easy for the import houses on the coast. But it also made them dependent on the loyalty of the Chinese merchants, whom nobody could prevent from looking for supplies elsewhere.[37] The import agencies watched helplessly when British cotton exports to China contracted after the First World War and collapsed in the early 1930s. One of the main reasons for this disaster was import substitution. It began with the slow emergence of a Chinese cotton industry after 1890 and intensified with its rapid development from 1915 onwards. Early on, British firms participated in this movement: Jardine Matheson & Co. opened cotton mills in Shanghai in 1895, 1907, and 1914. Yet British investment was soon overtaken by the expansion of a cotton industry in Chinese and Japanese hands. In 1914, 24 per cent of all spindles in China were installed in British mills; by 1936 their share had dropped to 4 per cent.[38]

The abortive conquest of the Chinese cotton market highlights the limitations of informal empire. The treaties and all the consular and naval might behind them could not make the Chinese richer than they were and could not compel them to buy cloth that was expensive and often unsuited to their needs. Manchester exports never dislodged the home-woven product and finally lost in competition with the output of modern mills in the treaty ports. The treaty-stipulated exemption from certain transit duties and provincial taxes did not provide the expected edge over indigenous supplies. In many cases it could not be enforced at all. No Consul was able to keep track of the myriad ways in which British imports were spread all over China. The vicissitudes of the market slipped through the net of informal empire. On the whole, British (and, for that matter, any foreign) physical penetration of the Chinese interior remained strictly limited until the last decade of the nineteenth century.[39] The treaties opened the interior Chinese market for Western goods but not, in effect, for Western merchants. Trade expansion did not surpass the general tendencies of an age of world-wide commercial growth.

The rise of the coastal enclaves would have been unthinkable without the wars of 1840–60 and the resulting treaty system. Their internal development in the ensuing decades owed much to the initiatives of Chinese merchants and the exploita-

---

[37] Arno S. Pearse, *The Cotton Industry of Japan and China: Being the Report of the Journey to Japan and China* (Manchester, 1929), p. 222.

[38] Chao Kang, *The Development of Cotton Textile Production in China* (Cambridge, Mass., 1977), pp. 301–02, Table 40.

[39] See the valid, if somewhat exaggerated, arguments in Rhoads Murphey, *The Outsiders: The Western Experience in India and China* (Ann Arbor, 1977), esp. chaps. 7, 9, 10.

tion of Chinese labour. A small class of Chinese in Shanghai and Hong Kong grew rich as compradors bridging the economic and cultural gap between the foreign establishment and its indigenous environment. They invested part of their profits in Western firms, availing themselves of extraterritorial protection. A kind of mixed Sino-foreign mercantile capitalism unfolded on the China coast.[40] There is a danger, however, that too much is made of such a symbiosis of different commercial civilizations. The worlds of Western and Chinese business met, at least until the 1880s, in a common penchant for short-lived speculation, without blending easily into solid structures. Business styles fused reluctantly. Western ideas of contract and Chinese, ideas of reciprocity and local solidarity did not merge. The widespread use of 'pidgin', a debased mixture of English and Chinese, symbolized the shallowness of the inter-cultural compromise. Both in the International Settlement and in Hong Kong, the emerging Chinese bourgeoisie was informally incorporated into the power structure, but for a long time was not admitted to formal participation.[41]

The Crown Colony differed from Shanghai in one essential point: its very existence as an urban community was due to British initiative. Hong Kong's early population was entirely composed of immigrants. For a long time Hong Kong essentially remained a community of temporary sojourners.[42] Many Chinese, however, arrived to stay and formed the nucleus of a slowly maturing social structure. A 'coolie class' grew in conjunction with expanding foreign trade, shipping, and the germs of industry. By the turn of the century it had evolved into a veritable proletariat that was learning to voice its own interests.[43] The Chinese Revolution of October 1911 inaugurated a period of intense labour protest that raised earlier forms of social unrest to higher levels of organization and was to last up to the late 1920s. From the 1880s on the pre-eminence of Hong Kong's first-generation notables and community leaders was challenged by younger businessmen, professionals, and members of a new intelligentsia who absorbed Western ideas and attitudes and took a keen interest in political events beyond the borders of the colony. National questions rather than local issues came to dominate public debates. Hong Kong's own political development had been arrested at an early stage. As early as 1855, Governor Sir John Bowring, a Philosophical Radical of Benthamite persuasion, had attempted to introduce an element of truly

---

[40] Hao Yen-p'ing, *The Commercial Revolution in Nineteenth-Century China: The Rise of Sino-Western Mercantile Capitalism* (Berkeley, 1986).

[41] For Hong Kong, see Chan Wai Kwan, *The Making of Hong Kong Society: Three Studies of Class Formation in Early Hong Kong* (Oxford, 1991), pp. 105–14.

[42] H. J. Lethbridge, *Hong Kong: Stability and Change* (Hong Kong, 1978), p. 2.

[43] Xu Shengwu, Liu Cunkuan, and others, *Shijiu shiji de Xianggang* [Hong Kong in the 19th Century] (Peking, 1994), pp. 393–405.

representative government into the colony's constitution. His proposal to have unofficial members of the Legislative Council directly elected by propertied voters irrespective of race was, however, repudiated by the home government.[44] Hong Kong politics remained as undemocratic and exclusive as the government of the International Settlement at Shanghai.

Both city-states encapsulated colonial societies in which racial hierarchies were superimposed upon patterns of social order owing little to direct foreign initiative. The junior British clerk was a sahib, the wealthy, respectable Chinese merchant or comprador was not. Power, status, and colour (the Chinese had not been considered 'yellow' until early in the nineteenth century) correlated in ways characteristic of colonialism all over the world. While *informal* empire was hardly perceptible for ordinary Chinese, apart from patriotically alerted members of the élite, *formal* Empire in Hong Kong and Shanghai was an experience shared by hundreds of thousands of colonial subjects. To the extent that the indigenous population derived economic benefits from the foreign presence, they were gained under the shadow of racial discrimination and cultural humiliation.

The equilibrium of the classic treaty system was upset around the turn of the century. The legalism of the preceding period was replaced by a more robust approach. Watching the activities of the Powers in their own country, Chinese intellectuals felt understandably attracted to a Social Darwinist view of the world. Three events underlined the weakness of the Chinese state and contributed to the foreigners' collective advantage: the defeat of 1895, the Boxer fiasco of 1900, and the collapse of the monarchy in 1911. After each of these major turning-points, China was further deprived of sovereign rights. The instruments of foreign intervention were strengthened. Garrisons were established to protect the Legation Quarter at Peking and other strategic spots in North China; 3,000 troops were stationed at Tientsin alone. In the International Settlement at Shanghai, the Mixed Court, yet another extra-treaty invention of the early 1860s, was taken over by the Consuls of the eighteen treaty powers. Henceforth, foreigners sat in judgement over Chinese cases in which no foreign defendants or plaintiffs were involved. The Court applied what it took to be the laws of China according to Western rules of procedure. Shanghai turned into a paradise for Western lawyers, since no case would be heard without foreign counsel.[45]

Most importantly, the IMC changed its character from an impartial duty-collecting agency to a tool of international financial control. From November

---

[44] Frank Welsh, *A History of Hong Kong* (London, 1993), p. 216.
[45] Thomas B. Stephens, *Order and Discipline in China: The Shanghai Mixed Court, 1911–27* (Seattle, Wash., 1992), pp. 51, 109, 111.

1911 on, the customs revenues were transmitted to an international commission of bankers at Shanghai, who represented China's foreign creditors. Only after the ironically named Custodian Banks had satisfied their own demands was the Chinese government allowed to petition the Diplomatic Body for the gracious release of the 'customs surplus'.[46] Sir Robert Hart's achievement was thus turned upside down and the IMC, now renamed Chinese Maritime Customs (CMC), transformed into something like a *caisse de la dette* politically independent of the Chinese state, if administratively still its subordinate agency. Chinese governmental finances never came, as Egypt's did, under *complete* foreign financial control. But the important salt revenues too were administered under their own Custodian Bank system as a result of the international Consortium's Reorganization Loan to President Yuan Shih-k'ai (1913).[47] Security for foreign credit was now equated with a direct grip on the collateral.

In all this, the specifically British element is difficult to identify. The policy of the British government and the British banks can, of course, be studied separately and has been analysed in exhaustive detail.[48] But the rivalry between the powers must be seen within a wider systemic framework of Chinese subjugation. Financial imperialism was the most significant aspect of that subjugation in the 1895 to 1914 period. The London capital market led the world and the HSBC continued to be the *primus inter pares* among the foreign banks in Hong Kong and Shanghai. As a co-operative project under British leadership, financial imperialism has to be discussed in general terms.[49]

A foreign financial presence can be considered imperial if market superiority *vis-à-vis* a non-European country is secured through or strengthened by a general asymmetry in terms of political and military power. In China between 1895 and 1914 this was the case on five counts:

(1) The huge Boxer Indemnity (£67.5 million in gold at 4 per cent per annum, payable until 1940) and several other loans for financing war indemnities were the results of military conflict between China and the Great Powers.

(2) Under extraterritoriality and other treaty privileges, foreign banks in China operated beyond the reach of the host country's government. They were immune to Chinese financial policy.

---

[46] Stanley F. Wright, *The Collection and Disposal of the Maritime Customs Revenue since the Revolution of 1911* (Shanghai, 1925), pp. 1–7. See chap. by Afaf Lutfi al-Sayyid-Marsot.

[47] An excellent account of the Reorganization Loan is Boris Barth, *Die deutsche Hochfinanz und die Imperialismen: Banken und Außenpolitik vor 1914* (Stuttgart, 1995), pp. 386–409; S. A. M. Adshead, *The Modernization of the Chinese Salt Administration, 1900–1920* (Cambridge, Mass., 1970), pp. 82–89.

[48] Above all, F. H. H. King, *History of the Hongkong and Shanghai Banking Corporation*, 4 vols. (Cambridge, 1987–91).

[49] Wolfgang J. Mommsen, 'Europäischer Finanzimperialismus vor 1914. Ein Beitrag zu einer pluralistischen Theorie des Imperialismus', *Historische Zeitschrift*, CCIV (1977), pp. 17–81.

(3) The big overseas banks acted in close collusion with their home governments in an intimacy unknown before 1895 and again after the First World War. The HSBC operated as the financial arm of the British government. The relationship between banks and governments was even closer in France, Germany, Japan, and Russia.

(4) Although groups and consortia of foreign banks never succeeded in completely excluding outsiders and thus obtaining a stranglehold on China's external finances, they came close to establishing an oligopoly which China found hard to evade. China possessed capital, but no modern domestic capital market to mobilize it, and so remained dependent on external capital supply. It was thus in a weak position to challenge the often-unfavourable loan conditions offered by the foreign banks.

(5) The seizure of securities such as customs and salt revenues and a few other indirect taxes would have been impossible under the rules and conventions of normal international relations. Before 1893 the Ch'ing dynasty had contracted a number of small loans. None of them had involved the pawning of government income. The loans after the Sino-Japanese War, however, came invariably in conjunction with political shackles such as the undertaking, linked to the Anglo-German 5 per cent Sterling Loan of 1896, to guarantee European dominance in the customs administration during the currency of the loan (thirty-six years).[50]

The largest part of foreign finance was used for railroad construction.[51] After several false starts, the age of the railway began in earnest in 1897. By 1914 9,568 kilometres of track had been laid.[52] Ten per cent of these were in undiminished Chinese ownership and had been constructed without foreign funds by Chinese engineers. Thirty-nine per cent were based on *colonial* concessions, financed, built, and operated by foreigners. Japan, Russia, France, and Germany constructed railways under such conditions. In Manchuria this form of railway building predominated. Britain possessed (from 1907) only the 36 kilometres of the Kowloon Railway from its southern terminal to the Chinese border: a trifling piece when compared to the 1,721 kilometres of Russia's Chinese Eastern Railway in Manchuria. Britain had no appreciable formal stake in Chinese railways.

The remaining 51 per cent of railway mileage was based on *financial* concessions. In these cases the lines remained Chinese property, and their revenues went to the Chinese government. The loan agreements, however, stipulated all kinds of

---

[50] J. V. A. MacMurray, ed., *Treaties and Agreements With and Concerning China, 1894–1912*, 2 vols. (New York, 1921), I, pp. 55–59.

[51] Clarence B. Davis, 'Railway Imperialism in China, 1895–1939', in Clarence B. Davis and Kenneth E. Wilburn, Jr., eds., *Railway Imperialism* (New York, 1991), pp. 155–73.

[52] All data are based on Mi Rucheng, *Diguozhuyi yu Zhongguo tielu, 1847–1949* [Imperialism and the Chinese Railways] (Shanghai, 1980), pp. 362–63, 670.

foreign control: pledging not only operating profits, but also other government revenues; access to mining rights; supply of construction materials and rolling stock by the creditors and their agents at above-market prices; appointment of foreigners to higher engineering and administrative positions; autocratic powers of the foreign engineers-in-chief, and so on. Until 1936 China was unable to obtain railway loans without such strings attached. Britain occupied the leading position in Chinese railway financing. By 1914 41 per cent of the credit sums disbursed to the Chinese government for railroads had originated from British sources.[53]

Railway financing offered greater scope for Chinese negotiators, some of whom were by now highly able diplomats with a sure mastery of detail, than did indemnities and big political loans. In 1908 Chinese diplomacy, supported by an increasingly vocal public opinion, scored a notable success in obtaining terms for the Tientsin–Pukow railway that restricted foreign interference to an extent unknown in the past.[54] But the older, much less favourable agreements remained in force. On the eve of the First World War an overwhelming proportion of China's state railways was still managed by British, French, and Belgian engineers and administrators. Most railways south of the Great Wall can be counted an addition to the informal empires of Britain and France: they were under some measure of foreign control without being outright colonial possessions. British beneficiaries of Chinese railway expansion included the banks, individual bondholders, expatriate staff, exporters of matériel, and the British collieries in China which found new customers. It is impossible to prove that British-financed railways facilitated British trade in China. If they did, their contribution must have been slight. British goods enjoyed no preferential treatment on these lines. None of them traversed a region that had not hitherto been served well by steamers and traditional means of transport. The railway conquered China only slowly. In 1936 freight traffic on China's railways amounted to 14.6 billion ton-kilometers as opposed to 33.5 billion ton-kilometers in India.[55] British involvement with Chinese railways reflected mainly financial and political considerations and not the old hopes of tapping a huge mass market. Railway financing, therefore, was characteristic of the intermediate and rather brief period of Europe-dominated high finance. After the First World War no effort succeeded in reviving the golden days of Chinese bonds.

The years 1911 and 1914 were dates of equal significance in the history of Britain's special position in China. The collapse of the *ancien régime* in the Revolution of

[53] Chen Hui, *Zhongguo tielu wenti* [Problems of Chinese Railways], new edn. (Peking, 1955), p. 77; E-tu Zen Sun, *Chinese Railways and British Interests, 1898–1911* (New York, 1954).

[54] Lee En-han, *China's Quest for Railway Autonomy, 1904–1911: A Study of the Chinese Railway-Rights Recovery Movement* (Singapore, 1977), p. 181.

[55] Thomas G. Rawski, *Economic Growth in Prewar China* (Berkeley, 1989), p. 208.

1911, after a brief period of last-minute reforms, freed all foreigners from residual restraints and exposed the young Republic to unprecedented rapacity. Ever since the second treaty settlement of 1860, the Manchu rulers and their Chinese officials had proved their worth as reluctant, but reliable collaborators. If extravagant dreams of a boundless China market did not come true, it was not the Ch'ing dynasty's fault. Attempts to rebuild a Ch'ing-type collaborative relationship with Yuan Shih-k'ai, the strong man of the early Republic, failed when the dictator died in 1916. The erosion of the political centre after 1911 and especially after 1916 weakened or even removed the mechanisms of foreign pressure and Chinese compliance that had ensured the functioning of informal empire for more than half a century. Anarchy required different imperial strategies. The outbreak of the First World War did not immediately affect the British position in China, but had important indirect repercussions. It released the energies of Chinese industry and thus invigorated an important competitor. It also encouraged Japan to cast off her earlier inhibitions and to pretend to a hegemonic position on the East Asian mainland. The following period was to be marked by a boost in Chinese as well as Japanese assertiveness.

Select Bibliography

PAMELA ATWELL, *British Mandarins and Chinese Reformers: The British Administration of Weihaiwei (1898–1930) and the Territory's Return to Chinese Rule* (Oxford, 1985).

ROBERT A. BICKERS, 'Shanghailanders: The Formation and Identity of the British Settler Community in Shanghai, 1843–1937', *Past and Present*, CLIX (May 1998), pp. 161–211.

MING K. CHAN, ed., *Precarious Balance: Hong Kong between China and Britain, 1842–1992* (Hong Kong, 1994).

P. D. COATES, *The China Consuls: British Consular Officers, 1843–1943* (Hong Kong, 1988).

E. W. EDWARDS, *British Diplomacy and Finance in China, 1895–1914* (Oxford, 1987).

JOHN K. FAIRBANK, *Trade and Diplomacy on the China Coast: The Opening of the Treaty Ports, 1842–1854*, 2 vols. (Cambridge, Mass., 1953).

——'The Creation of the Treaty System', in John K. Fairbank, ed., *The Cambridge History of China*, X (Cambridge, 1978), pp. 213–63.

GERALD S. GRAHAM, *The China Station: War and Diplomacy, 1830–1860* (Oxford, 1978).

HOU CHI-MING, *Foreign Investment and Economic Development in China, 1840–1937* (Cambridge, Mass., 1965).

FRANK H. H. KING, *The History of the Hongkong and Shanghai Banking Corporation*, 4 vols. (Cambridge, 1987–1991).

EDWARD LeFEVOUR, *Western Enterprise in Late Ch'ing China: A Selective Survey of Jardine Matheson and Company's Operations, 1842–1895* (Cambridge, Mass., 1968).

PETER LOWE, *Britain in the Far East: A Survey from 1819 to the Present* (London, 1981).

Jürgen Osterhammel, *China und die Weltgesellschaft: Vom 18 Jahrhundert bis in unsere Zeit* (Munich, 1989).

——'British Business in China, 1860s–1950s', in R. P. T. Davenport-Hines and Geoffrey Jones, eds., *British Business in Asia since 1860* (Cambridge, 1989), pp. 191–216, 279–88.

E-tu Zen Sun, *Chinese Railways and British Interests, 1898–1911* (New York, 1954).

Jung-fang Tsai, *Hong Kong in Chinese History: Community and Social Unrest in the British Colony, 1842–1913* (New York, 1993).

Wang Jingyu, *Shijiu shiji xifang ziben zhuyi dui Zhongguo de jingji qinlüe* [The Economic Invasion of China by Western Capitalism in the Nineteenth Century] (Peking, 1983).

Frank Welsh, *A History of Hong Kong* (London, 1993).

Stanley F. Wright, *Hart and the Chinese Customs* (Belfast, 1950).

L. K. Young, *British Policy in China, 1895–1902* (Oxford, 1970).

9

Imperial Institutions and the Government of Empire

PETER BURROUGHS

Fundamentally, the British Empire was concerned with power. But power had to be converted into systems of authority, exercised by agents through bureaucratic structures. Not all these instruments of influence and control were arms of the state. In certain circumstances, commercial organizations and missionary societies could embody and uphold Imperial authority. Nevertheless, the management of a global empire required a network of governmental institutions at home and overseas, bureaucratic channels evolved to implement metropolitan directives and meet colonial challenges. Constantly obliged to adjust to circumstance and opportunity, pressures and constraints, Britain's governance of Empire involved dynamic processes, not static structures and inert constitutional frameworks, as some earlier imperial historians imagined. Even routine administration was a two-way process of communication and accommodation. Unlike the Spanish and the French, the British never attempted to rule colonies directly from the metropole; neither their resources nor their inclinations pointed towards centralized direction, and the colonists themselves, to varying degrees, encouraged a tradition of devolved authority and local systems of association. At the core of Imperial administration, therefore, lay a continuous interplay between mother country and colonial communities, between centre and periphery, a series of essentially bilateral relationships which entailed constant negotiation rather than the imposition of rule and the acceptance of subjection.

Another enduring characteristic of British administration was that it tended to be reactive rather than initiatory, with governmental authority lagging behind, not leading, overseas expansion. The familiar slogan, 'trade followed the flag', is misleading in the sense that the bureaucratic standard-bearers of British rule usually trailed in the wake of traders, missionaries, explorers, and settlers, and were charged, like firefighters or troubleshooters, with tidying up the chaos left by private entrepreneurs and trying to impose some order and regularity. Even with territories which the Crown formally acquired by conquest or cession, Governors trod in the footsteps of soldiers and diplomats, and often had to accommodate alien institutions as well as peoples inherited from France, Spain, or Holland. Only in British settlement colonies might administrative arrangements occasionally precede or accompany the first migrants. In 1829, for example, the Colonial Office sanctioned a new colony on the Swan River in Western Australia, and a few years later agreed to a fatally flawed, hybrid form of government devised by the South Australia colonizers. Yet even when the British flag had been hoisted, the Imperial policy-makers' task of crisis management was exacerbated by the continued delegation of authority to local officials and the free range accorded independent agents which allowed crises to develop. These might easily saddle the Imperial government with fresh, unwelcome responsibilities unless the extension or consolidation of colonial control was resolutely withstood.

Because the assertion and discharge of Imperial authority tended to be reactive, with officials in London possessing only slight control over commitments forced on them by circumstance and the actions of distant subordinates, the scale and complexity of governing the Empire steadily increased during the nineteenth century. By the 1890s the Empire encompassed a quarter of the globe's land area and one-fifth of its population. Rather than constituting one empire, this conglomeration of large land masses and territorial fragments comprised several empires—pluralistic and singular in their individual dealings with Britain. Although collectively the Empire might embody a global economy and signify British world power, as a political entity it was loosely held together, despite the entanglements of redtape and the mesh of communications. Lord Milner was not alone in regretting its 'total want of any permanent binding force, or rational system'.[1] Enthusiasts periodically talked of turning it into something more tangible and firmly united, perhaps through the mechanism of federation, but the British dominions remained, as Adam Smith had described them in 1776, 'not an empire, but the project of an empire',[2] a unity and an aspiration lodged in the imaginations of Britons. F. S. Oliver complained in 1906 that the Empire was not 'a political fact, but only a phrase, an influence, or a sentiment'.[3]

Among the various objectives of Imperial policy-makers in managing the Empire's constituent territories, the prime imperative—and major anxiety—remained the preservation of security and loyalty. Many colonies faced actual or potential external threats from foreign rivals or ambitious neighbours; British ministers worried constantly about a Russian incursion into India and American designs on Canada. What materially enhanced the security of Britain's scattered possessions

---

[1] Milner to Sir Clinton Dawkins, 4 Jan. 1902, Cecil Headlam, ed., *The Milner Papers*, 3 vols. (London, 1933), II, p. 288.

[2] *An Inquiry into the Nature and Causes of the Wealth of Nations* [1776], R. H. Campbell and others, eds. (Oxford, 1976), II, pp. 946–47.

[3] *Alexander Hamilton: An Essay on American Union* (London, 1906), p. 481.

after 1815—and temporarily eased the pressures on Imperial administrators—was the relative peacefulness which afflicted international relations and the absence of any European nation strong enough to challenge the global superiority of the Royal Navy. This exceptional interlude faded in the 1870s with the rise of Continental powers harbouring colonial ambitions. Meanwhile, continuous threats to colonies' security arose from endemic instability on their frontiers and in adjacent border regions, most noticeably in Asia and southern Africa. Even more demanding, officials in London and overseas had to guard against internal subversion or disorder and cultivate the acquiescence of assorted populations in British rule, if not their collaboration with the authorities and loyalty to the Imperial connection. The use or threat of force by itself was insufficient permanently to overawe or pacify millions of subjects and, as discussed later, various strategies were devised to promote internal tranquillity. These did not, however, prevent frequent, unpredictable eruptions of unrest throughout the Empire, confronting administrators with an incessant stream of crises, emergencies, and small wars.

A second aim of Imperial rule was the promotion of colonial prosperity. Though disdainful of narrowly commercial priorities, British ministers acknowledged a responsibility for colonists' material well-being. 'Civilization', often defined by Victorians in terms of 'improvement', 'progress', and 'regeneration', had an economic dimension which infused the outlook of officials, who also recognized that flourishing economies would be better able to sustain financial independence of the British Treasury and taxpayer. While commercial activities were chiefly and ideally left to private enterprise without government interference or support, in certain respects and on some occasions the state strove to foster economic development. In addition to control of tariffs and currency, fiscal and monetary policies, government intervention embraced infrastructures, communications, and most prominently the management of land and labour. Championing the superior long-term interests of the wider community, future generations, and the Empire at large against those of the monopolist and the speculator, the state sought to regulate the acquisition of Crown lands in Australia, British North America, and elsewhere. Most ambitiously, the Colonial Office in 1831 adopted as part of Imperial practice the leading principles of Edward Gibbon Wakefield's theory of systematic colonization with respect to restrictive land scales and assisted emigration to Australia, in a bid to shape the colonies' patterns of land use, landownership, and economic development according to a doctrinaire blueprint. Colonial slavery and the transportation of convicts were discontinued in favour of both free and indentured labour.[4]

---

[4] Peter Burroughs, *Britain and Australia, 1831–1855: A Study in Imperial Relations and Crown Lands Administration* (Oxford, 1967). See chaps. by Andrew Porter, Marjory Harper, and David Northrup.

Official temptations to intervene and regulate were greater in the institutional fields. Again, a sense of trusteeship reinforced the notion of good government, with its ideals of law and order, economy and efficiency, as well as settled expectations of how society ought to be organized. It might include private property rights, the rule of law, trial by jury, a free press, education in 'citizenship', arenas for public discourse, and some measure of popular consent to government, even if not representative institutions. More expansively, contemporaries associated Imperial rule with Britain's 'civilizing mission', to which the character of government was everywhere both fundamental and definitive. When it came to translating such worthy objectives into action, however, problems at once confronted policy-makers in London and their agents on the spot. At a time when the responsibilities and bureaucratic resources of the British state were limited, and advocates of *laissez-faire* wanted to reduce its role still further, it was no easy matter to determine either how far and in what ways government should regulate the lives of colonial subjects, or what forms of intervention would be appropriate and efficacious.

The paternalist stance—whether authoritarian or liberal in form—generally espoused by Imperial administrators involved both negative and positive initiatives. Colonial élites and those commanding local authority, though often valuable as collaborators, had to be prohibited or discouraged from pursuing oppressive or unduly selfish policies at the expense of the inhabitants at large. This was a varied and problematic remit which might necessitate executive intervention or merely advice and exhortation. Colonial Secretaries regularly claimed that the disadvantages of distance and imperfect local knowledge were more than offset by the Department's command of superior wisdom, accumulated experience, and impartial, panoramic views. Occasionally local legislation was disallowed; in a last resort Parliament might act. Whatever the chosen instrument, the Colonial Office thought it essential to be vigilant and ready to pounce in the case of Crown Colonies which lacked the supposed safeguards of representative institutions, and where Imperial officials stood *in loco parentis* for the interests of the wider community. They also felt a genuine humanitarian concern for indigenous peoples, who should not be left wholly at the mercy of exploiters, though uncertainty reigned in Whitehall about the fate awaiting aboriginal races and about the constructive part officials might play in assisting missionaries in the task of 'improvement'. In settler colonies, the Imperial authorities faced the dilemma of whether to retain an expensive obligation or rely on white inhabitants to administer 'native policy'. The Duke of Newcastle asserted that 'it was one of the paramount duties of a good Government, in carrying out colonization, to interfere as far as possible to prevent those cruelties and horrors that had been perpetrated in the early days of our Colonies where there were a number of aborigines'.[5] Nevertheless, evidence from British North America, Australia, New Zealand, and South Africa suggests that the necessity for Imperial intervention was only fitfully acknowledged and ineffectually exerted.[6]

In other circumstances, trusteeship and paternalist guidance might be more constructively asserted but involved a choice between two alternative prescriptions: assimilation or diversity. Were Britain's interests and duty best met by transplanting British institutions or by allowing colonial inhabitants to maintain traditional laws and customs and fashion their own arrangements? The question might be complicated by rival political and economic imperatives, as the practitioners of indirect rule in Africa discovered. Throughout the tropical colonies with non-European peoples, the dilemma of either preserving indigenous institutions in order to promote stability or Anglicizing those societies in order to modernize their activities had constantly to be confronted and was difficult to address. The emphasis given the competing principles of assimilation and pluralism therefore varied according to local circumstances; it also fluctuated over time as political ideas and cultural fashions changed within Britain itself. Was human nature intrinsically the same everywhere and were non-European societies therefore amenable to transformation by the workings of law, education, and free trade? Or did differences of history, culture, and race constitute enduring factors that administrators had to recognize and accommodate?

India provided a major arena for this contest. Because of the need of 'liberal' Britain to legitimate autocratic rule, the sense of trusteeship was more highly developed—and more agonizingly appraised—there than elsewhere in the Empire, though it produced diverse and incompatible responses. The strategies of governance for the Raj were also profoundly shaped by the coexistence of conflicting assumptions concerning the underlying similarity or enduring difference of British and Indian society. These impulses produced complex, varied, and constantly shifting patterns of administration, especially when combined with the military and fiscal exigencies of a garrison state. An early administrative respect and tolerance for what were understood to be traditional Indian customs, laws, and religion were subsequently somewhat modified by calls from assorted utilitarians, liberal reformers, and evangelicals for the wholesale Anglicization of society. After the shock of the Indian Mutiny in 1857, however, enthusiasm for rapid Westernization was officially replaced by a deliberate distancing of British authority from the regeneration of Indian society and by a more pronounced insistence on Indian 'difference'. Sir Charles Wood, Secretary of State for India,

---

[5] 26 July 1858, P[arliamentary] D[ebates] (Lords), CLI, col. 2102.
[6] See chaps. by Donald Denoon, Raewyn Dalziel, Ged Martin, and Christopher Saunders and Iain R. Smith.

acknowledged that the 'mistake we fell into, under the influence of the most benevolent feelings, and according to our notion of what was right and just, was that of introducing a system foreign to the habits and wishes of the people'. Henceforth, 'we ought to adopt and improve what we find in existence and avail ourselves as far as possible of the existing institutions of the country'.[7]

Elsewhere, the urge to assimilate was still more sporadic and often ineffectual, the occasional rhetorical outburst seldom being translated into action. Wilmot Horton denounced 'the Dutch laws of the Cape of Good Hope, or the Spanish laws of Trinidad, which he declared it scandalous for an Englishman to be subjected to, as being contrary to all his feelings and prejudices. For himself, he would never flinch from the proposition that all our colonies should be Anglicized rather than preserved in their original form'.[8] Yet, as Under-Secretary at the Colonial Office, Horton did little to translate such sentiments into Imperial practice in the conquered and ceded colonies. Officials at the colonial department generally acknowledged diversity and pluralism. French Canada aroused most support for assimilation but, again, bold words by William Huskisson and Edward Ellice far exceeded official deeds. The chief impetus for Anglicization came from the English élite in Lower Canada, not the authorities in London, just as it was English officials at the Cape like Henry Ellis who in the 1820s sought to change Dutch laws and institutions, an enthusiasm later repeated by Milner after the South African War.

In the case of settlement colonies, commentators at home and overseas might refer to the emulation or export of British forms of government, when it suited their interests. Generally, however, Imperial administrators doubted the possibility of reproducing a British constitution in very different societies and alien environments. Most would have agreed with James Stephen that any 'analogy' with the Westminster model was 'formal and nominal, rather than real'. Local forms 'must be matters of compromise and of adaptation to the particular conditions, character, wants and resources of the place'. Moreover, even 'the closest parallelism in forms' would 'often involve the widest deviation in substance'.[9] As a commission of inquiry in Malta sensibly remarked: 'To graduate our ideas of the perfection of Government by the approximation it bears towards our own, is a mode of reasoning as unjust, as it is erroneous; but it is an error, into which Englishmen are too apt to fall'.[10]

---

[7] 13 Aug. 1860, *PD* (Commons), CLX, col. 1196, and quoted in Thomas R. Metcalf, *The Aftermath of Revolt: India, 1857–1870* (Princeton, 1964), p. 136. See chaps. by D. A. Washbrook and Robin J. Moore.

[8] 2 May 1828, *PD* (Commons), XIX, col. 332.

[9] Stephen to Rice, 30 June 1834, C[olonial] O[ffice] 323/50; minute by Stephen, 19 June 1847, CO 323/63.

[10] Report of Commission of Enquiry into the Affairs of Malta, 1812, p. 12, CO 158/19.

As contemporary comments imply, the imperatives and aims that underlay Britain's governance of the Victorian Empire were subject to persistent constraints and pressures—financial, bureaucratic, intellectual, and political. Throughout the century the opinion prevailed among politicians and commentators that, whatever the Empire's benefits, its administration and defence imposed unduly onerous burdens on the British Treasury which ought to be reduced. This conviction persisted even when Britain became affluent enough to afford such expenditure, so deeply was the obsession with economy embedded in the Victorian political consciousness. In addition to the obvious financial concerns of taxpayers, retrenchment was stimulated by the political goals of greater accountability and efficiency in government. This linkage, first stressed by parliamentary radicals in the 1820s, had profound and constructive implications for Imperial policy-makers. Routine pruning of colonial budgets and avoidance of new expenditures which might be condemned in the Commons had to be supplemented by the more ambitious reform of Imperial bureaucratic and colonial institutions. This was pursued most productively in the settlement colonies where self-government entailed self-reliance in the fields of administration and internal security.

The management of a global empire was also profoundly affected by bureaucratic realities. Vast distances and slow communications meant that it took months to exchange correspondence with colonies—a year or more in the case of Australia—during which interval circumstances could easily drift out of control and instructions be overtaken by events. Even when the flow of information was speeded by clipper ships, then steamships and telegraphs, the fundamental bureaucratic problem remained the continuous adjustment of Imperial preferences and local practice. The mediating role was necessarily delegated to the men on the spot, principally the Governors, Proconsuls, and Viceroys who operated at the key point of interaction between directives emanating from London and pressures generated by conditions on the periphery. These Imperial agents have been described as 'a kind of pointsman on the railway of thought between two stations', who acted as 'a half-way relay station that could charge up, or scale down, the impulses transmitted in either direction'.[11] As these metaphors imply, local officials played a decisive role in determining the strength and the course of Imperial rule in particular territories. They exercised considerable latitude of authority and were notoriously difficult to control, distance blurring the line between discretion and indiscretion. Far from being subordinates, many masterful individuals had their own agendas and ambitions; often they acted independently,

---

[11] John Benyon, *Proconsul and Paramountcy in South Africa: The High Commision, British Supremacy and the Sub-continent, 1806–1910* (Pietermaritzburg, 1980), p. 335; also his, 'Overlords of Empire? British "Proconsular Imperialism" in Perspective', *Journal of Imperial and Commonwealth History* (hereafter *JICH*), XIX (1991), pp. 164–202.

disregarding directives or exceeding instructions with cavalier exuberance and frequently with impunity. The century provides innumerable examples: Governors Lachlan Macquarie in New South Wales and Lord Charles Somerset at the Cape, equally disdainful of orders and legality; Sir Harry Smith, cast by the Colonial Office in the late 1840s as the saviour of South Africa, who turned out to be a flamboyant, expansionist megalomaniac; Sir George Grey, sent back to New Zealand as a troubleshooter in the 1860s, but high-handed and deceitful; Sir John Pope-Hennessy, an eccentric, disputatious Irishman, disobeying instructions in Labuan, Hong Kong, and Mauritius as keenly as Lord Lytton over Afghanistan in 1878; Cromer in Egypt and Curzon in India, pasha and potentate.

The authorities in London could and sometimes did admonish errant Governors, occasionally disown their actions, and even recall them; but weary acquiescence was a more common response, reflecting both a reluctance to reject the advice or countermand the actions of forceful men on the spot, and an admission of impotence. As Stephen remarked of Governors in 1830: 'Though not perhaps men of very large capacity, their proximity to the scene of action is an advantage which in this case would more than compensate for every other incompetency. Had I the understanding of Jeremy Bentham himself, I should distrust my own judgement as to what is really practicable in such remote and anomalous societies.'[12] 'I fear there is no alternative', Herman Merivale conceded, 'except to shut our eyes to proceedings which seen at this distance wear a most extravagant aspect.'[13] Waywardness may have been less widespread than incompetence; Colonial Secretaries repeatedly complained about the lack of qualified, reliable administrators. Military men, favoured after the French wars, were gradually replaced by civilians, but Earl Grey at mid-century desperately raided the ranks of MPs and directors of railway companies for individuals of ability and sound judgement. Such appointees received no training, and generated no collective professionalism as did the covenanted Indian Civil Service. For servants of the Raj, what mattered was character and such personal qualities as self-sacrifice and public-spiritedness. Yet even in post-Mutiny India, British officials were very thin on the ground, the whole subcontinent of 200 or 300 million Indians being overseen by some 2,000 Europeans. Similarly, in southern Uganda during the 1890s British authority was asserted over 3 million people by only twenty-five officials.[14] This slender control on the periphery was matched by bureaucratic fragmentation in Whitehall.[15]

[12] Stephen to Twiss, 25 Aug. 1830, CO 111/98.
[13] Minute on FitzRoy to Grey, 7 Feb. 1853, CO 201/463.
[14] Figures given in Bernard Porter, *The Lion's Share: A Short History of British Imperialism, 1850–1995*, 3rd edn. (London, 1996), p. 46, and Ronald Hyam, *Britain's Imperial Century, 1815–1914: A Study of Empire and Expansion*, 2nd edn. (London, 1993), p. 310.
[15] See above, pp. 17–19.

Imperial policy-makers were also subjected to domestic political pressures, but
parliamentary legislative intervention was nevertheless rare and decidedly a last
resort. In the light of lessons drawn from the American Revolution, Parliament's
supreme authority had to be exercised sparingly. As Sir Robert Peel explained in
1839: 'That transcendental power is an arcanum of empire which...should be
veiled, and brought forward only in the utmost extremity of the state, where other
remedies have failed, to stay the raging of some moral or political pestilence. It
should not be produced on trifling occasions, or in cases of petty refractoriness, or
temporary misconduct.'[16] If this forbearance was shown, William Huskisson
declared in 1828, 'standing aloof, as we do, from the party feelings and local
jealousies...our decision will be the more respected; first, as coming from a
high and competent authority; and next, on account of our manifest impartial-
ity'.[17] This remained a fond delusion of British parliamentarians, and sits uncom-
fortably with the fact that colonial issues were regularly exploited for domestic
party purposes.

To deal with awesome global responsibilities, Imperial administrators developed a
range of strategies and techniques of management. In an emergency, or as a final
resort, force might be required to quell internal disorder and uphold legitimate
authority. But as the South African War, and on a lesser scale the Indian Mutiny,
graphically demonstrated, Britain possessed too few soldiers to hold down large
areas of the Empire forcibly; while the Canadian rebellions of 1837 were less
threatening, the possibility of US intervention raised justified anxieties about
war engulfing North America. Sometimes lesser eruptions of internal unrest,
communal violence, or sectarian rioting necessitated the employment of troops.
Increasingly during the century, regular public-order duties were discharged by
civilian police forces, recruited locally and thought to be less provocative than
soldiers, though the military-style, armed gendarmerie, part-fashioned after Irish
patterns, blurred this distinction.[18] While the threat of coercion underpinned
Imperial sway—detachments of troops being considered emblematic of British
power held in reserve—the resort to armed force was an admission that ordinary
means of administration had failed. As Cromer explained,

There is truth in the saying, of which perhaps we sometimes hear rather too much, that the
maintenance of the Empire depends on the sword; but so little does it depend on the sword
alone that if once we have to draw the sword, not merely to suppress some local effer-
vescence, but to overcome a general upheaval of subject races goaded to action either by

---

[16]   3 May 1839, *PD* (Commons), XLVII, cols. 767–68.

[17]   2 May 1828, ibid., XIX, col. 302.

[18]   See David M. Anderson and David Killingray, eds., *Policing the Empire: Government, Authority and
Control, 1830–1940* (Manchester, 1991).

deliberate oppression, which is highly improbable, or by unintentional misgovernment, which is far more conceivable, the sword will assuredly be powerless to defend us for long, and the days of Imperial rule will be numbered.[19]

Lord Roberts might claim that Britain's dominion in Asia and Africa depended on 'Respect based on fear; remove the fear and the respect will soon disappear'.[20] But the viability of colonial governments ultimately rested on goodwill and co-operation rather than on enforced obedience.

British administrators, therefore, pragmatically sought accommodation with indigenous and emigrant societies. Although direct rule and authoritarian Governors sometimes held sway, officials armed with Crown authority, acts of Parliament, or executive fiat still had to confront and resolve the practical problems of enforcement and observation. This was pursued chiefly through mediation with indigenous élites or collaborating groups possessing local influence, where these could be identified, recruited, and relied on. By this strategy British rulers associated with and exploited, as well as legitimized and sustained, local power structures and networks of authority. Their success goes far towards explaining the longevity and relative stability of the British Empire. Without indigenous co-operation, whether voluntary or enforced, a mere handful of British officials could never have governed so many millions.

Such arrangements afforded mutually beneficial bargains, but were also precarious and constraining for both parties. On the one side, the British had to accept limitations on their local control and freedom of action if collaborators were to be kept content. Indeed, in circumstances like those in early-nineteenth-century West Africa, local élites retained the upper hand, while in South India indigenous power at the village level frustrated, even silently corroded, British administrative structures. The traditional Imperial tactic designed to mitigate such dependency was 'divide and rule', shifting patronage among competing élites, especially if distinct 'communities' could be identified or different levels of administration—country-wide, provincial, and local—became involved in government.

On the other side, Imperial endorsement gave collaborating groups and indigenous power structures a reinforced or new-found legitimacy, and often conferred privileges as the rewards of association, whether patronage appointments or favourable allocations of land and labour. Sometimes the Imperial alliance brought readier access to Western education or Christianity, technology or investment. In return—and although British rule was generally light and made few

---

[19] 'The Government of Subject Races', *Edinburgh Review*, CCVII, 423 (Jan. 1908), p. 2.

[20] Roberts to Minto, 17 May 1907, Minto Papers, quoted in David Dilks, *Curzon in India*, 2 vols. (London, 1969), I, p. 103.

demands—local élites might have to endure periodic pressure and intervention aimed at upholding metropolitan interests, promoting reformist initiatives, or preserving internal stability. Collaborators might also face tactical difficulties in reconciling their retention of traditional sources of local authority with their performance of Imperial services, particularly the implementation of unpopular policies. As clients and dependants, they had to ensure a degree of stability and popular acquiescence in British rule, lest the withdrawal of metropolitan support fatally loosened their grip on local power. While a repressive employment of colonial authority and the law might serve to calm small-scale or temporary discontent, élites could not afford to alienate large masses of fellow subjects, and this reality placed a premium on skilful mediation and brokerage. To this end, they might exploit the deference due to status, the authority commanded by privilege, or the contentment generated by economic prosperity and benefits, material and intangible, which could accrue from membership of a mighty global empire. Rhetoric, symbols, and ceremony were employed to link various levels of self-awareness, civic dignity, or nascent patriotism with the Imperial relationship. Isolation and widespread apathy, too, among millions of British subjects played a part in sustaining the Imperial enterprise.[21]

As was to be expected in a multifarious empire, diverse environments and circumstances produced different types of collaborators, patterns of association, and power relationships. In the North America settlement colonies, the metropolitan government at first deliberately cultivated social élites and political oligarchies—French seigneurs, English merchants, Loyalist lairds, and timber barons. By the 1830s, however, these élites had in some provinces lost local support and Imperial favour, and the Colonial Office tried to identify and enthrone new collaborators through the mechanism of fully self-governing representative Assemblies, although the French majority in Lower Canada complicated the tactical shift of patronage. Similarly in South Africa, ethnic diversity and uncertainty about the reliability of the Dutch made it difficult to line up satisfactory collaborators, especially outside the Cape colony. In the sectional societies of eastern Australia, forged from ex-convicts, free immigrants, and native-born, the oligarchy of economically dominant graziers afforded the authorities effective, if demanding, coadjutors until their monopoly, enhanced by self-government in the 1850s, was challenged by urban and agrarian interests. The leaders of British settlers in New Zealand seemed cast as natural collaborators, but hostilities with the Maori, involving massive British military commitments and expenditure, eventually generated disillusionment in London with local politicians until they assumed full responsibility for the colony's internal affairs. In the West Indies, the

---

[21] See above, pp. 17–27.

earlier reliance on white planters as Imperial agents was abandoned with the final triumph of anti-slavery in 1838, and thereafter London lacked reliable collaborators in the free but segmented societies of the Caribbean, despite the existence in many of them of representative institutions until the 1860s.

In dependencies elsewhere British administrators strove to collaborate with local rulers, whether Indian princes, Malay sultans, or African chiefs, who continued to exercise 'traditional' authority under some form of British supervision, and to mobilize support from amongst indigenous élites whose social status or economic clout enabled them to act as agents of an Imperial power in dealings with the populace at large. Indigenous merchants, traders, and sometimes financiers were incorporated into Britain's global economy, just as sepoy soldiers and later 'martial races' were recruited to sustain an alien military presence. In the vital subcontinent of India, the British relied on Indian magistrates and clerks for the local administration of justice and the collection of revenue, but the strategy for recruiting collaborators changed in emphasis during the nineteenth century. At first the aim of James Mill, Macaulay, and other reformers had been to train a Western-educated élite who would supplant the traditional leaders of Indian society, acting as intermediaries and diffusing enlightenment among the mass of the population. Macaulay hoped 'to form a class who may be interpreters between us and the millions whom we govern; a class of persons, Indian in blood and colour, but English in taste, in opinions, in morals, and in intellect'.[22]

Especially after 1857, however, faith in Westernization and the new élite gave way to a determined search for those the British considered 'natural leaders' of traditional Indian society, who had seemingly retained the people's loyalty during the troubles, and who might now function as the agency of future order and best safeguard against perennial fears of loss of control.[23] India's princes, as rulers of quasi-independent states, were thus integrated into the Imperial order with a recognized status and special privileges. British administrators also cultivated the collaboration of landlords as the leaders of Indian rural society. As an official of the Punjab government explained in 1860,

Dearly bought experience may teach us that political security is not necessarily attained by just laws, equitable taxation, and material progress... If there is a body scattered throughout the country considerable by its property and rank it will for certain exercise great influence whether its position be hereditary or not. If this body is attached to the state by timely concessions... and obtains a share of power and importance, it will constitute a strong support to the existing Government... [Nothing] is more to be feared than that which threatens a foreign rule from the ignorance and indifference of its alien subjects,

[22] Education minute, 2 Feb. 1835, quoted in G. O. Trevelyan, *The Competition Wallah* (London, 1864), p. 422.

[23] See chap. by Robin J. Moore.

when unattached through their natural leaders and held in allegiance only by military force.[24]

Indian landlords may have been ill-suited to fulfil the assigned role of English gentry, but they were thought by the British to possess a traditional status and authority in the localities which made their participation in the Imperial enterprise more valuable and reliable than that of an urbanized educated élite.

Indeed, in India and elsewhere throughout the late-Victorian Empire, a revulsion occurred against educated and Westernized members of indigenous societies who threatened to overturn the 'difference' sustaining British superiority. Fearing loss of control, Lord Salisbury thought that such misfits as the Bengali 'babus' 'cannot be anything else than an opposition in quiet times, rebels in time of trouble'.[25] If not disparaged as discontented agitators, such individuals were dismissed by British officials as superfluous, given the new strategy of ruling in collaboration with traditional Indian élites. With Western ambitions as well as Western acculturation, some 4,000 Indians served in the uncovenanted Indian Civil Service by 1868, but their advancement to senior posts was slow and unwelcome.[26] Those who became associated with the fledgling Indian National Congress after 1885 were discounted as unrepresentative of the population at large. Since talk of self-government and nationhood seemed a dangerous delusion, such people offered no attraction as potential collaborators of the Raj, as did their counterparts in settler societies. Experience drawn from India was reinforced by a general hardening of racial attitudes from the 1860s, so that in Africa too local inhabitants were less trusted in business and less involved in administrative functions. In 1873 Lord Kimberley thought it better in West Africa to 'have nothing to do with the "educated natives" as a body. I would treat with the hereditary chiefs only.' In 1886 Augustus Hemming, head of the African department at the Colonial Office, condemned 'educated natives' as 'the curse of the West Coast'.[27]

British administrators also occupied an ambivalent position, as reflected in their attitudes towards and engagement with local communities. On the one hand, many consciously pursued separateness and drew distinctions, whether racial, social, or educational. Even in British settlement colonies, Governors and expatriate staff might keep leading inhabitants at arm's length and sometimes disparage local customs and proclivities. In Asia and other dependencies, the studied

---

[24] Secretary of Government Punjab to Secretary of Government India, 30 April 1860, quoted in Metcalf, *Aftermath of Revolt*, p. 165.

[25] Salisbury to Lytton, 9 June 1876, Lytton Papers, quoted in Anil Seal, *The Emergence of Indian Nationalism* (Cambridge, 1968), pp. 133–34.

[26] See Metcalf, *Aftermath of Revolt*, pp. 271–81.

[27] Minute by Kimberley, 22 Feb. 1873, CO 96/104; minute by Hemming, 24 July 1886, on Griffith to Granville, 14 June 1886, CO 96/174.

remoteness from indigenous societies was more marked, and historians have advanced the notion of the 'other' to encapsulate British feelings of contrast between their own 'modern' and 'civilized' society and 'backward' non-European peoples. The British in India retreated into the all-white club with its customs and formalities designed to assert and uphold a consciousness of beleaguered difference, moral ascendancy, and the mystique of rule. Physical distancing to keep the threatening Indian world at bay was expressed in the bungalow residence, the civil lines or cantonment, and the hill station. Yet, just as proclaimed 'mastery' over India coexisted with a sense of vulnerability and unease, so separation from a seductive subcontinent and its teeming millions could never be wholly successful.

At the same time, British administrators deliberately strove to cultivate the association of indigenous and emigrant communities with the Imperial enterprise by viceregal display, military parades, public ceremony, and the outward symbols of British civilization. In this task they were assisted by missionaries and educators, both as individuals in the field and through networks of societies and auxiliary branches. Governors orchestrated the hospitality of Government House with levees and balls; dates in the Imperial calendar, such as the monarch's birthday, were publicly observed, and in 1904 the Imperial enthusiast Lord Meath launched Empire Day; special events like royal tours and jubilees or days of thanksgiving were celebrated. Sometimes indigenous symbols and local ceremonies were imperially embraced: in Ceylon custody of Buddha's sacred tooth symbolized British authority, while in Malta British troops participated in Catholic religious processions. If local customs were not exploitable, traditions might be invented to sustain Imperial authority, one notable example being the spectacular pageantry of the Indian durbars, their Mughal precedents suitably transformed by elaborately planned ritual into Victorian extravaganzas. In the Imperial assemblage of 1877 Lord Lytton sought to associate India's 'feudal nobility' with the British Crown by exploiting medieval fantasy, complete with princely banners sporting coats of arms and the symbolic rendering of homage. As the Viceroy remarked, 'the further East you go, the greater becomes the importance of a bit of bunting'. To the special order of knighthood, the Star of India (1861), was added the Order of the Indian Empire (1877), linking the princes at Delhi to the Empress at Windsor. Curzon's Coronation Durbar in 1902 similarly acknowledged the high status of Indian notables.[28] In these sundry ways, common participation in the global enterprise of Empire might be stressed, various levels of patriotism encouraged, and identities cultivated, though these might in time be turned against Imperial control.

[28] Quoted in Thomas R. Metcalf, *Ideologies of the Raj* (Cambridge, 1995), p. 77; also Bernard S. Cohn, 'Representing Authority in Victorian India', in Eric Hobsbawm and Terence Ranger, eds., *The Invention of Tradition* (Cambridge, 1983), pp. 165–209. See also chap. by Robin J. Moore.

Recent writers have emphasized another technique of management and point of contact: the designs of British officials to underpin Imperial rule by the collection and organization of 'colonial knowledge'. Effective intelligence-gathering was essential to the successful exercise of British power in the military and political spheres. More controversially, it also had cultural and epistemological dimensions. As in India in the late eighteenth and early nineteenth centuries, the British could sometimes tap existing indigenous networks of communication and information exchange. In the absence of substantial numbers of European settlers or planters, the British were obliged to draw their knowledge of the people and the country from Indian agents, such as writers, runners, and various 'native informants'. This joint involvement in communications was part of the collaborative process, and colonial knowledge the continuing, adaptable product of Imperial and indigenous contributions rather than a one-sided creation of British imagining and imposed conceptions of Indian society and culture, as the Orientalists would have it.[29]

At the same time, in India as later in Africa, the British built new structures of knowledge that relied less on traditional informants than on European understanding of alien peoples and places. They sought to 'know' the subjects and societies they ruled by studying religions, cultures, and institutions, and by conducting surveys of lands and censuses of population. These investigative endeavours might be characterized as disinterested intellectual inquiries, since the collection and ordering of empirically verifiable information were contemporary British enthusiasms, as evidenced in the decennial census, the statistical table, and the colonial Blue Book. Nevertheless, this accumulating body of knowledge was bound to produce an imperfect grasp of a country's past and social structures. What distorted British understanding most, scholars argue, was the urge to classify information in categories and ordered hierarchies which reflected the preconceptions and purposes of European administrators, caught up in the unequal power relationships of imperialism, rather than 'objective' Indian realities based on dispassionate observation. Convenient categories of religion, community, tribe, and caste (though not class) were superimposed on India; artificial labels like 'criminal tribes' and 'martial races' came into use.

The 'conquest of knowledge' was closely linked, not only with the impact of Imperial rule, but also with the growth of the colonial state. Just as in Britain the compilation of 'scientific' data was often regarded as the necessary preliminary to administrative action, so overseas the codification of laws and languages, the classification of peoples and artefacts, became overtly associated with the creation

[29] See Bernard S. Cohn, *Colonialism and Its Forms of Knowledge: The British in India* (Princeton, 1996), and C. A. Bayly, *Empire and Information: Intelligence Gathering and Social Communication in India, 1780–1870* (Cambridge, 1997).

of the state in colonial communities where knowledge was power (an interesting inversion abroad of the Victorian notion that useful knowledge would empower the working classes). By statistical surveys and other bureaucratic devices, officials in India might define groups who could be recruited to the services of the Raj and identify those who merited coercive treatment. With institutional knowledge British administrators and their successor élites in settler societies intruded governmental authority and the law into private spheres in order to regulate and regiment disorderly inhabitants. In the early convict colonies in Australia the local authorities subjected bond and free to close surveillance and intensive policing; in mid-Victorian Canada bureaucratic knowledge and cadres of educational inspectors aimed to produce conditioned citizens and docile electors who would contentedly leave respectable men of property to operate self-governing institutions.

Political institutions were the most prominent instrument of British rule. They were the legal embodiment and channels of Imperial authority; their structure and operations both reflected and shaped the nature of colonial societies as well as the distribution of power within them. The framework of government also provided an arena for the debate of public affairs and for negotiation among competing interests. Throughout the Empire such processes involved two interrelated issues: the balance to be struck between metropolitan and local control; and who was to exercise authority in colonial communities. By the nineteenth century two broad patterns of government had emerged, one inherited from the earlier American empire, its precedents and practices, the other created in response to the territorial gains from international warfare and more recent British migration. The former tradition of colonial self-reliance operating through representative Assemblies had been adopted for Nova Scotia (1758), Prince Edward Island (1773), and New Brunswick (1784), and after 1791 the Canadas, though the powers of Governors and executives were nominally strengthened in the light of the American experience. In the conquered, ceded, and later settled colonies, however, more authoritarian regimes were established, involving Governors working initially with advisory Councils and then with nominated Executive and Legislative Councils, the latter pattern coming to be known as Crown Colony government. This versatile innovation was designed for communities whose populations seemed unsuited to elective Assemblies: alien Europeans in Quebec (before 1791), Malta, the Cape, and Mauritius; convicts in New South Wales and Van Diemen's Land; and indigenous peoples, for whom the British authorities felt a special responsibility, in Trinidad, Ceylon, and later New Zealand (until 1852).

Representative government was rightly regarded in London and on the periphery as a more responsive and mature political system but it did not always operate harmoniously, as experience in British North America in the 1830s and New South Wales after 1842 aptly illustrates. Its functioning presupposed forbearance and co-operation among the various agencies. In small and fairly homogeneous communities, like those of the Maritime Provinces, this was facilitated by cosy understandings between Councils and Assemblies which did not come under serious strain until mid-1830s. In eastern Australia, as later at the Cape, deeply felt grievances could produce a genuine or manufactured unanimity of protest. In many colonies, however, divisions and fragmentation were more evident. There opinion tended to be polarized and politics confrontational because representative government, so successful in empowering élites, also cultivated oligarchies: the 'Family Compact' of merchants, Loyalists, and Anglicans in Upper Canada; the 'Chateau Clique' of English-speaking merchants and bureaucrats in Lower Canada; the 'squattocracy' of New South Wales. The resultant contests pitted élites, entrenched in the Councils, against the 'outsiders', working through the Assembly, who themselves aspired to monopolize power and patronage. Factionalism and feuding were exacerbated because assemblymen were powerless to remove councillors and, at the same time, were not themselves subject to the potentially sobering responsibilities of office, while councillors, appointed either *ex officio* or effectively for life, could afford to ignore unpopularity. Until the 1840s no mechanisms or conventions were adopted for resolving the collision of authority and constitutional deadlocks, to which this political system was liable when subjected to stress in a colonial context.

The confrontational nature of politics both reflected and was aggravated by the economic, social, religious, and ethnic divisions that characterized settler societies. Commercial interests set merchants against farmers as in the Canadas, or pastoralists against agriculturists as in eastern Australia. Social distinctions in New South Wales differentiated between bond and free, immigrants and native-born, urban and rural inhabitants. In Upper Canada, the disputed rights of recent 'unnaturalized' American immigrants to own land, exercise the franchise, and hold public office wracked provincial politics in the 1820s, as the ruling élite played the loyalty card. During the following decade religious privilege became a major divisive issue in that colony's multi-confessional society. Ethnic antagonisms exacerbated political contests at the Cape, eased somewhat by the exodus of Afrikaner farmers into the interior, and far more acutely in Lower Canada, where a French agrarian Assembly confronted English-dominated Councils favouring commercial enterprise, British immigration, and land settlement on the basis of freehold tenure. Unpopular policies, whether originating locally or devised in London, implemented by élites on such matters as clergy reserves, land companies, banks, and canals alienated much local opinion, and everywhere discontent was generated most by exclusive definitions of citizenship.

By the late 1820s and 1830s, however, oligarchies in North America were beginning to lose their grip. Repressive measures against critics were insufficient to stamp out local unrest. Equally significant, ruling élites gradually forfeited the confidence and backing of the metropolitan authorities as effective Imperial agents. Unlike their Tory predecessors, Whig ministers, coming into office in 1830, evinced broad sympathy with the attack on monopoly, exclusionism, and religious privilege. Championing consent of the governed as the basic principle, they were prepared in settler colonies to move towards self-reliance through a planned, orderly devolution of authority. Nevertheless, being cautious, moderate reformers averse to constitutional innovation, the Whigs experienced paralyzing difficulties deciding what measures were necessary and practicable for restoring harmony in the Canadas. They resorted to modest tinkering with the Councils and some concession of financial control to Assemblies, but the stumbling-block remained a reluctance to empower a francophone Assembly lest this provoked separation and civil war, even intervention by the United States.

No solution to these puzzles was devised before internal dissensions in the Canadas erupted in rebellions in 1837–38. This provided the British authorities with the opportunity and the necessity of redrawing the structures of government, but much uncertainty and difference of opinion persisted, which were not at once removed by Lord Durham's celebrated mission and report of 1839. Eventually, political advance was sought through the Union of 1841 and a subsequent devolution of authority which facilitated local self-government operating under Cabinet conventions known as responsible government. Colonial politicians, enjoying the legitimacy of popular consent for their exercise of executive power, now provided acceptable collaborators who could be left to their own devices in matters of internal administration.

This was a signal development in Imperial governance. It opened the way towards resolving the political conundrum posed at the time of the American Revolution—namely, how could colonial self-government be successfully reconciled with Imperial unity? Such an outcome was by no means inexorable or straightforward. It emerged haphazardly out of conflict, dialogue, and institutional adaptation. It was neither reluctant Imperial concession to nationalist demands, nor planned transfer of Britain's political practice on the Westminster model. It was, however, an arrangement susceptible of extension to other settler societies as time and circumstance permitted, not just within British North America—Nova Scotia (1848), Prince Edward Island (1851), and New Brunswick (1854)—but more widely to Australia and New Zealand in the mid-1850s, and later the Cape (1872) and Natal (1893). This greater diversity and flexibility in Imperial administration opened up a longer process of political evolution encompassing distinct stages through which maturing communities would normally pass, at different speeds according to differing circumstances, from Crown Colony status to full self-government.

Metropolitan administrators might sometimes be interventionist, but few wanted Imperial relations to rely permanently or customarily on authoritarian regimes or on direct rule from Whitehall. As a modest advance during the early 1830s in Crown Colonies outside British North America, the Governor's advisory council was replaced by nominated Executive and Legislative Councils in Western Australia, the Cape, Trinidad, Mauritius, and Ceylon, thus bringing them in line with New South Wales and Van Diemen's Land (1825). These illiberal constitutions were regarded as a temporary, regrettable necessity, since they violated the rights of British subjects and were insufficiently responsive to local opinion.

Nevertheless, a host of difficulties arose when it came to advancing Crown Colonies to representative government. British ministers claimed that they alone possessed the authority and the vision needed for determining the timing and the extent of constitutional change in any given instance. They had also to satisfy themselves that colonial communities were ready to profit from an enlarged participation in government and would exercise responsibly the elective institutions they were granted. It was no use transferring political power to colonies that were economically backward or lacked financial self-sufficiency: for them, 'a miniature British constitution' would be 'the grossest of absurdities'.[30] In societies divided by race, religion, or nationality, or by legal status into bond and free, the surrender of political control to powerful minorities or selfish oligarchies would sanctify misrule and sacrifice the interests of the inhabitants at large for whose welfare the British authorities felt a moral responsibility. Such criteria were cited in the 1830s to refuse representative institutions in Trinidad and convict New South Wales, in 'St Lucia and Mauritius, where French minds would misunderstand, and French fervour would pervert the privilege—in the Cape, which is a Country of Wastes, and impervious tracts, and dispersed occupancies—and in Ceylon, which is a different world altogether', for the result would be 'incessant controversy and confusion'.[31]

By the late 1840s and 1850s a concatenation of circumstances had induced British ministers to revise earlier assessments of the eligibility of settlement colonies for self-governing institutions. Events in British North America played a major part in this process. As the Duke of Newcastle acknowledged, 'all will agree as to the extreme difficulty of withholding political privileges from bodies of men to whom the maxims now prevalent in British domestic policy afford so strong a right to claim them, and of keeping our fellow subjects in Australia on a different

---

[30] Stephen to Howick, 11 Jan. 1836, Grey Papers, University of Durham.
[31] Stephen to Twiss, 25 Aug. 1830, CO 111/98.

political footing from those to whom those rights have been fully conceded in America'.[32] As the pace quickened, the original leisurely timetables were hastily foreshortened in most settlement colonies of the mid-nineteenth century, as they were to be a century later in Asia and Africa. Planned decolonization tended to become a headlong rush. The Colonial Office clerk, Gordon Gairdner, complained in 1857 that 'the Home Government appear simply to have receded before the pressure which they were not prepared to withstand'.[33] Once British North America had forced open the gateway to self-government, Australians and New Zealanders were able to make a final dash for local autonomy, securing both representative institutions and responsible government in virtually one leap between 1850 and 1856.[34] They then set about making local sovereignty a reality by eroding residual Imperial authority—Crown lands, fiscal and commercial policy, and internal security—and by forging the political frameworks of the nations they were in the process of building. The Colonial Office might still advise, warn, and cajole, but its power of intervention was practically confined to the disallowance of local legislation, a latent resource very seldom employed, especially after the Colonial Laws Validity Act (1865) had severely reduced the instances in which disallowance could be exercised.

Different considerations applied at the Cape, where issues of race relations and military defence were complicated by the presence of Afrikaners within and beyond unstable borders. In the early 1850s the Colonial Office conceded representative institutions, including the innovation of an elective upper house. But continuing sporadic conflict among the diverse peoples of southern Africa and the constant threat of major frontier wars, which only Britain commanded the resources to meet, remained powerful arguments against granting full self-government for which there existed no insistent local demand.[35] By the early 1870s, however, British ministers keen to cut commitments and costs decided to force the whites at the Cape to adopt responsible government by threatening to withdraw the Imperial garrison. In this instance, British involvement persisted because of overriding strategic concerns, heightened by the discovery of mineral wealth, and continuing turbulence on indeterminate frontiers.

Developments in the West Indies, meanwhile, demonstrated that constitutional progress was neither automatic nor irreversible. In Jamaica and other islands the ancient system of representative institutions gradually broke down under tensions created by the transition from slave to free societies. Against a background of economic decline in the sugar plantation industry, aggravated by the inadequacies

---

[32] Newcastle to FitzRoy, 4 Aug. 1853, CO 202/63.
[33] Gairdner to Grey, 28 Nov. 1857, Grey Papers, University of Durham.
[34] See chaps. by Donald Denoon and Raewyn Dalziel.
[35] See chap. by Christopher Saunders and Iain R. Smith.

of free labour and Britain's imposition of free trade, and of simmering social disorders, the planters steadily lost their political dominance. As disputatious Assemblies were infiltrated by 'men of colour' independent of the plantation economy, the planters recognized their predicament. It needed only the occasion of the rebellion at Morant Bay in 1865 for the Jamaica Assembly to relinquish its legislative independence in exchange for the security of direct government by the British Crown.[36] In the ensuing years all the small islands of the Lesser Antilles with representative institutions (except Barbados), where the trend towards single mixed chambers was already gathering force, followed Jamaica down the path of constitutional regression.

Aside from representative and Crown Colonies and India, other areas of British economic penetration or strategic value involved policy-makers in administrative decisions, if not fresh responsibilities. While the conduct of commercial activities in many 'spheres of influence' did not require political action, sometimes the state had to intervene to safeguard freedom of trade by resort to regular diplomatic techniques of treaties, consular representations, and occasionally gunboats. Throughout the century, and particularly from the 1880s, pressures for metropolitan political intervention were regularly generated by circumstances on the periphery: the instability or decay of indigenous institutions in weak states under the impact of European commercial penetration; the acquisitive designs of competing colonial powers; the ambitions of individual administrators, soldiers, missionaries, and other sojourners; and the expansionist machinations of British colonial subjects such as the 'sub-imperialism' of Australians and New Zealanders in the Pacific and Cape colonists in southern Africa. These challenges repeatedly forced Whitehall into making agonizing assessments: whether or not the national interest or chronic disorder overseas necessitated annexation, as occurred in New Zealand (1840), Lagos (1861), and Fiji (1874). Sometimes paramountcy might be exercised through indigenous rulers, as in East Africa through the Sultan of Zanzibar, and in the protected Malay states where from 1874 the Sultans accepted British resident 'advisers'.[37] Elsewhere, to evade costly responsibilities, officials in London gradually formulated the amorphous, elastic concept of the 'protectorate'. This proclaimed Britain's effective paramountcy in a designated territory but stopped short of formal annexation and a declaration of sovereignty, and at least initially entailed minimal administrative arrangements. Although most Protectorates soon became indistinguishable from Crown Colonies, this

---

[36] See W. P. Morrell, *British Colonial Policy in the Mid-Victorian Age: South Africa, New Zealand, the West Indies* (Oxford, 1969), chaps. 12–14. See also chap. by Gad Heuman.

[37] See chap. by A. J. Stockwell.

jurisdictional experiment in Africa and the Pacific afforded an interim or transi-
tional form of administrative supervision and an alternative strategy of management initially under Foreign Office control.

The origins of Protectorates lay less in the imperatives of economic expansion
than in a concern to uphold order and regularity. In particular, the Imperial
authorities felt forced to take cognizance of the conduct of British subjects abroad,
not so much to 'protect' them and vouchsafe the birthright of English justice, as to
check their propensities to crime and lawlessness, especially participation in
African slave trading and illicit labour traffic in the Pacific.[38] In the absence of
clear British precedents and comprehensive rules of international law, these questions of extraterritorial jurisdiction were difficult to resolve. Matters were further
complicated by rivalry between the Colonial and Foreign Offices and by the
necessary involvement of departmental legal advisers and the law officers of the
Crown, whose opinions were often vague, ill-informed, and contradictory. Contemporary notions of a Protectorate and the duties of the protecting state were
hazy, and particular uncertainty surrounded the extraterritorial application of the
English doctrine of sovereignty to non-European areas. During discussions concerning Fiji, Frederick Rogers expressed these misgivings: 'A protectorate is sometimes proposed. I do not quite know what this means. I suppose it is an intimation
to the world—that nobody then must assume sovereignty over these Islands or
make war on them—but if they have any grievance against them they must apply
to us ... I do not myself very much like this kind of thing.'[39] Knatchbull-Hugessen
described a Protectorate as 'a very absurd as well as a curious state of affairs; it
involved all the responsibility, without the advantages of annexation. Indeed, he
had never been able to find out exactly what a protectorate meant.'[40] Doubts and
confusion persisted until the mid-1880s, when diplomatic exchanges associated
with the Berlin Conference and heightened colonial competition stimulated more
positive thinking, and produced what one writer has called 'jurisdictional imperialism'.[41]

As developments in West Africa from the 1840s illustrate, the British government adopted two approaches to chronic disorder and extraterritoriality. One
method was to exploit the Foreign Jurisdiction Act of 1843 which covered the
activities of British nationals in such countries as the Ottoman empire, Japan,
China, and later Siam (1856) and Zanzibar (1866). The Foreign Office was

---

[38] See chap. 10 by Andrew Porter.

[39] Minute, 19 Oct. 1870, on Canterbury to Granville, 12 Aug. 1870, CO 309/94.

[40] Minute, 17 April 1871, on Kennedy to Kimberley, 29 March 1871, CO 267/310, and 25 June 1872, *PD*
(Commons), CCXII, col. 209.

[41] W. Ross Johnston, *Sovereignty and Protection: A Study of British Jurisdictional Imperialism in the
Late Nineteenth Century* (Durham, NC, 1973), *passim*.

especially drawn to this employment of consular jurisdiction. In 1872, for example, a West African order in council defined Consuls' magisterial powers to regulate the conduct of British subjects and the merchants' courts of equity in the Niger delta.[42] Meanwhile, where convulsions or irregularities disrupted areas bordering existing British enclaves, special acts of Parliament empowered Governors to exercise extraterritorial jurisdiction over British nationals. A Cape of Good Hope Punishment Act of 1836 vainly asserted authority over British subjects, including Boer trekkers, beyond the colony's boundaries in an area south of the twenty-fifth degree of latitude. The Colonial Office inclined towards this method of empowering Governors, and periodically from 1846 vested those at the Cape with diplomatic and supervisory responsibilities as High Commissioners in adjacent territories. In Sierra Leone and in the Gold Coast when the forts reverted from the African merchants to the Crown, the Coast of Africa and Falklands Act of 1843 proclaimed—on the basis of treaty, grant, usage, or sufferance—British jurisdictional authority in places adjacent to the coastal forts and settlements. Although it sanctioned colonial courts to try offenders, the Act's failure to define the extent of administrative powers or territorial limits allowed local officials to expand control over hinterlands and small African states or political units whose voluntary submission or acquiescence amounted to a tacit recognition of British protection. In 1861 an act extended the laws of Sierra Leone to neighbouring territories and the West Africa Settlements Act of 1871 provided for the punishment of crimes committed within twenty miles of the boundaries of settlements or adjacent 'protectorates'.

Greater irresolution surrounded the handling of similar problems in the vast area of the Pacific, particularly because the islands occupied a shadowy position in international law as sovereign states. Often British officials drew an unthinking distinction between the identifiable political structures of Africa and Asia and the more unsophisticated societies in the Pacific which often seemed to lack recognizable rulers capable of making internationally valid treaties that would be enforceable. On occasion, however, when it suited Imperial purposes, the theory of indigenous sovereignty was cited and acted on, as in the Treaty of Waitangi (1840) with Maori chiefs and the cession of the Fiji Islands accepted in 1874. Cultural assumptions and legal confusions militated against the ready resort to Protectorates in the Pacific, and until the 1880s policy-makers in Whitehall continued to hope that indigenous governments might provide a satisfactory framework of order, if bolstered by British Residents or Consuls and naval patrols. The main step towards the exercise of extraterritorial rights was the appointment

---

[42] See Martin Lynn, 'Law and Imperial Expansion: The Niger Delta Courts of Equity, c.1850–85', *JICH*, XXIII (1995), pp. 54–76.

of the Governor of Fiji as High Commissioner for the Western Pacific. A Pacific Islanders Protection Act (1875) and a subsequent Order-in-Council (1877) vested him with limited powers over British subjects in all places 'not being within the jurisdiction of any civilized Power', an experiment crippled by lack of resources and disregard of foreign nationals and indigenous islanders.[43]

British thinking about Protectorates was clarified by proceedings connected with the Berlin Conference of 1884–85.[44] The international attempt to define the authority and minimize the conflict of European powers in Africa raised questions of sovereignty, extraterritoriality, and what constituted 'effective occupation'. Officials in London discovered that German and French legal theory embodied different, and potentially inconvenient, views on these jurisdictional issues and drew no distinction between annexations and Protectorates. Although the conditions agreed at Berlin for establishing future occupations and recognized authority in Africa were congenially vague, intensified international competition thereafter prodded Britain into a more robust, even interventionist, stance to stake out claims on the ground and pre-empt rival designs. Specific conflicts might be alleviated by diplomatic agreements, but some semblance of 'effective authority' had to be created if the Powers were to recognize and respect British spheres of interest. Following the Anglo-German Agreement of 1886, for example, which partitioned New Guinea, Britain felt compelled to declare Protectorates over the Gilbert and Ellice Islands (1892) and the Solomon Islands (1893) as 'a matter of convenience, enabling us to shuffle off what may prove to be unnecessary for us to hold but the system is not without inconvenience'.[45] At the same time, the proliferation of European ventures in Africa and the Pacific exposed the inability of indigenous regimes to provide stability and withstand both the impact of more intense economic exploitation and the unrestrained initiatives of Imperial agents. To check commitments and expense, British ministers pursued two courses: revival of the chartered company as a quasi-official agency and a seemingly cheap form of paramountcy, already being discharged by the British North Borneo Company (1881); and reinvigoration of consular activity which pointed towards the creation of Protectorates.

In West Africa, ministers declared a Protectorate in the trading zone of the Niger delta in 1885 as an initial, temporary expedient while they turned for assistance to

---

[43] See W. David McIntyre, 'Disraeli's Colonial Policy: The Creation of the Western Pacific High Commission, 1874–1877', *Historical Studies Australia and New Zealand*, IX, 35 (1960), pp. 279–94; and his *The Imperial Frontier in the Tropics, 1865–75* (London, 1967); Deryck Scarr, *Fragments of Empire: A History of the Western Pacific High Commission, 1877–1914* (Canberra, 1967). See also chap. by Colin Newbury.

[44] Stig Förster, Wolfgang J. Mommsen, and Ronald Robinson, eds., *Bismark, Europe and Africa: The Berlin Conference, 1884–1885 and the Onset of Partition* (Oxford, 1988).

[45] Minute by Fairfield, 7 Dec. 1892, on Thurston to Ripon, 1 Oct. 1892, CO 225/39.

George Goldie, a commercial entrepreneur, whose National African Company was busy concluding treaties with riverine chiefs which gave it a convenient predominance in the hinterland. After hesitation about creating a commercial monopoly with extensive political powers, a charter was granted to a revamped Royal Niger Company (1886) which undertook to dispense justice, enforce treaty rights, and devote customs revenues to administrative purposes. In the Oil Rivers, however, the government was obliged to establish a more elaborate consular jurisdiction which led in 1893 to the Niger Coast Protectorate. That year Gambia became a Protectorate, as did Sierra Leone in 1895.

A similar dual pattern emerged in East Africa, where German and French advances stimulated British anxiety about Egypt's security and heightened the strategic importance of the Nile Valley. When a diplomatic Agreement in 1886 provisionally divided a swathe of eastern Africa into British and German zones of interest, officials in London resorted initially to the Imperial British East Africa Company (1888) to uphold Britain's claims. After a definitive arrangement with Germany in 1890 had secured a vital corridor between the Indian Ocean and the Upper Nile, the Cabinet turned from an ailing private enterprise to Protectorates over Uganda (1894) and the rest of British East Africa (1895). The Agreement of 1890 also recognized a British Protectorate over Zanzibar and in Nyasaland the British Central African Protectorate (1893). To safeguard Britain's strategic position at the Cape and encircle the Afrikaner republics, a Protectorate was created in Bechuanaland (1885) and Cecil Rhodes's British South Africa Company (1889) received a charter to occupy and administer at its own expense territory that was to become the Rhodesias.

These proceedings in Africa undermined assumptions of politicians and lawyers like Lord Halsbury that a 'Protectorate furnishes a convenient middle state between annexation and mere alliance',[46] and that the rights and obligations of a protecting power differed from those of complete sovereignty. During the 1890s such distinctions were eroded, both in practice and in theory, as British jurisdiction in Protectorates was enlarged in the interests of security, justice, and efficiency and assimilated to German and French patterns. Increasingly, Protectorates came to be administered as if they were colonies—and some were indeed redesignated as such—trends symbolized by the transfer of the Foreign Office's responsibilities to the Colonial Office between 1898 and 1905. This process was marked by two principal developments. Hitherto the law officers had steadfastly insisted that jurisdiction could not be asserted over foreign nationals in Africa and the Pacific. But disagreement with Germany over the status of foreigners in New Guinea, coinciding with doubts about jurisdiction in the native states of India, produced a

---

[46] Memo by Halsbury, 28 March 1890, FO 97/562.

consolidated Foreign Jurisdiction Act in 1890, under which the consent of foreigners to the exercise of such authority was presumed.[47] This deliberate evasion of thorny jurisdictional issues was overturned in 1891 when the Colonial Office outlined for Bechuanaland a more positive and Continental view of a protecting power's responsibilities for the safety and conduct of other Europeans. As its instigator, John Bramston, argued: 'This protection includes the repression of crime and disorder among white men, which the native chief is of himself powerless to repress, and the establishment of a judicial system for dealing with such crime appears to be one of the attributes of sovereignty which the protecting Power acquires.'[48] This innovation was routinely transferred to the Pacific in 1893 and extended to British East Africa in 1896.

More significant in the long term was the assumption of jurisdiction over indigenous peoples in a Protectorate, whether or not treaties or consent were secured. Drawing on earlier precedents, this was legally endorsed in Sierra Leone and the Gold Coast in 1895 and then adopted in East Africa and elsewhere. According to Bramston,

the principle which governs these cases is, that the existence of a protectorate in an uncivilised country carries with it a right on the part of the protecting Power to exercise within that country such authority and jurisdiction—in short, such of the attributes of sovereignty—as are required for the due discharge of the duties of a Protector, for the purpose not only of protecting the Natives from the subjects of civilised Powers, and such subjects from the Natives and from each other, but also for protecting the Natives from the grosser forms of ill-treatment and oppression by their rulers, and from raids of slave dealers and marauders.[49]

By the 1890s, without the formality of annexation, the British authorities and local agents were freely establishing in Protectorates rudimentary frameworks of government involving courts, taxation, military 'pacification', displacement of indigenous rulers, and the issue of certificates for land titles which paved the way for Crown land rights and appropriation by European settlers.[50]

These moves towards political control were reinforced by the radical, innovatory views of Joseph Chamberlain at the Colonial Office from 1895 that the state must take the lead in developing the Empire's estates by public loans to create infrastructures and administrative agencies to refashion indigenous economies by

---

[47] See Colin Newbury, '"Treaty, Grant, Usage and Sufferance": The Origins of British Colonial Protectorates', in G. A. Wood and P. S. O'Connor, eds., *W. P. Morrell: A Tribute* (Dunedin, 1973), pp. 75–80.

[48] 'Memorandum as to the Jurisdiction and Administrative Powers of a European State holding Protectorates in Africa', Feb. 1891, No. 410, p. 5, CO 879/34.

[49] Bramston to Cardew, 16 Oct. 1895, No. 497, pp. 51–52, CO 879/43.

[50] See Newbury, '"Treaty, Grant, Usage and Sufferance"', pp. 82–84.

land reform, regulated labour, and direct taxes. Chamberlain was not alone in
urging greater intervention, particularly in West Africa; officials and others with
Asian experience advocated extension of the 'Indian model' to Africa. The autonomy and sovereignty of indigenous rulers should be overthrown because they
were unequal to the task of modernization. Colonial officers should go beyond
giving advice and direct African chiefs in the management of domestic affairs.
Frederick Lugard, later the champion of Indirect Rule, at first pursued a highly
interventionist, forceful, and expensive regime in Northern Nigeria, even to the
point of proposing to introduce Muslim Indian clerks, labourers, and soldiers.[51]
Such designs were defeated by a combination of African resistance, symbolized by
the rebellion in Sierra Leone in 1897–98 against a hut tax, and hostility from
Liverpool merchants, British moralists, and sceptics within the Colonial Office.
The department came to reaffirm that securing African consent and avoiding
discontent were overriding imperatives, best maintained through the traditional
courses of non-intervention and collaboration.[52]

It was in this context that Indirect Rule emerged after 1900 as a much-publicized
technique of Imperial management. There was nothing new about the tactic of
preserving indigenous institutions and acting through the agency of local rulers.
As Goldie and his company had shown, this was a pragmatic response to the
problem of controlling huge tracts of territory with scarce resources of personnel
and revenue. Nevertheless, Lugard developed the practice in Northern Nigeria and
elevated an expedient into a principle, one given a moral justification for its
supposed benefits to subject peoples. This theorizing might seem a departure
from British pragmatism, but the Lugardian concept of Indirect Rule was essentially an idealization of pragmatism and a rationalization of comparative impotence. Although it was to become the orthodox philosophy of colonial rule
throughout tropical Africa, the method had many variants, with local circumstances and metropolitan drift being more influential forces. Some colonies lacked
sufficiently hierarchic societies or identifiable chiefs; others adopted a prefectoral
system under which chiefs and headmen were colonial appointees and directly
subordinate to white district officers; in Kenya and Southern Rhodesia the arrival
of European immigrants introduced a complicating factor. Nevertheless, stripped
of its moral gloss and un-British dogma, Indirect Rule exemplified and perpetuated in the new century the essential features of earlier administration of the
Victorian Empire: limited liabilities and minimal management based on accommodation more than compulsion, on collaboration more than confrontation.[53]

---

[51] In Vol. IV, see chap. by John W. Cell.

[52] See Ronald Robinson, 'European Imperialism and Indigenous Reactions in British West Africa,
1880–1914', in H. L. Wesseling, ed., *Expansion and Reaction* (Leiden, 1978), pp. 151–60.

[53] In Vol. IV, see chap. by John W. Cell.

Select Bibliography

DAVID M. ANDERSON and DAVID KILLINGRAY, eds., *Policing the Empire: Government, Authority and Control, 1830–1940* (Manchester, 1991).

C. A. BAYLY, *Indian Society and the Making of the British Empire* (Cambridge, 1988).

PHILLIP A. BUCKNER, *The Transition to Responsible Government: British Policy in British North America, 1815–1850* (Westport, Conn., 1985).

JOHN W. CELL, *British Colonial Administration in the Mid-Nineteenth Century: The Policy-Making Process* (New Haven, 1970).

W. ROSS JOHNSTON, *Sovereignty and Protection: A Study of British Jurisdictional Imperialism in the Late Nineteenth Century* (Durham, NC, 1973).

PAUL KNAPLUND, *James Stephen and the British Colonial System, 1813–1847* (Madison, 1953).

MARTIN LYNN, 'Law and Imperial Expansion: The Niger Delta Courts of Equity, c.1850–85', *Journal of Imperial and Commonwealth History*, XXIII (1995), pp. 54–76.

W. DAVID MCINTYRE, *The Imperial Frontier in the Tropics, 1865–75: A Study of British Colonial Policy in West Africa, Malaya and the South Pacific in the Age of Gladstone and Disraeli.* (London, 1967).

THOMAS R. METCALF, *Ideologies of the Raj* (Cambridge, 1995).

—— *The Aftermath of Revolt: India, 1857–1870* (Princeton, 1964).

W. P. MORRELL, *British Colonial Policy in the Mid-Victorian Age: South Africa, New Zealand, the West Indies* (Oxford, 1969).

—— *British Colonial Policy in the Age of Peel and Russell* (Oxford, 1930).

COLIN NEWBURY, '"Treaty, Grant, Usage and Sufferance": The Origins of British Colonial Protectorates', in G. A. Wood and P. S. O'Connor, eds., *W. P. Morrell: A Tribute* (Dunedin, 1973), pp. 69–84.

RONALD ROBINSON, 'European Imperialism and Indigenous Reactions in British West Africa, 1880–1914', in H. L. Wesseling, ed., *Expansion and Reaction: Essays in European Expansion and Reaction in Asia and Africa* (Leiden, 1978), pp. 141–63.

—— and JOHN GALLAGHER, with ALICE DENNY, *Africa and the Victorians: The Official Mind of Imperialism* (London, 1961).

DERYCK SCARR, *Fragments of Empire: A History of the Western Pacific High Commission, 1877–1914* (Canberra, 1967).

JOHN MANNING WARD, *Colonial Self-Government: The British Experience, 1759–1856* (London, 1976).

10

Trusteeship, Anti-Slavery, and Humanitarianism

ANDREW PORTER

Throughout the nineteenth century, territorial conquest, white settlement, commercial growth, economic development, and above all issues of slavery and the slave trade, raised questions about the ethics of economic exchange, the politics of equal rights or racial differences, and the purpose of Imperial power. It was often and widely assumed that Imperial authority had no object other than the narrowly defined organization and defence of Britain's insular interests. Nevertheless, how far those interests required governments' intervention overseas was always debatable, even in wartime. Still more contentious was the idea that British interests might depend on direct action to advance the interests (however defined) of indigenous peoples. There were even those prepared to argue that possession of Empire, wealth, and power brought obligations, irrespective of British interests, wherever opportunities existed to promote the welfare of less fortunate societies.

These passionate public debates spawned powerful pressure groups. From the 1780s until the First World War they significantly influenced the approach of colonial and Imperial authorities to Britain's role in the Caribbean, India, Africa, and the Pacific. Although the immediate results of so much righteous fervour were often disappointing, its indirect and long-term consequences were considerable. By the 1840s, humanitarianism had become a vital component of Britain's national or Imperial identity and, along with missionary work, channelled much female activity into public and Imperial enterprise. In the mid-nineteenth century, the apparent failure of humanitarian expectations reinforced pessimistic views of 'non-European' capacity and racial hierarchies. By the early 1900s, however, humanitarians' continued watchfulness and criticism of Imperial governments contributed to a positive re-evaluation of non-European cultures and a new scepticism about colonial rule.

Speaking in Parliament on the East India Bill in December 1783, Edmund Burke offered an eloquent statement of Britain's obligations as the possessor of power over other peoples:

all political power which is set over men, and...all privilege claimed...in exclusion of them, being wholly artificial, and...a derogation from the natural equality of mankind at large, ought to be some way or other exercised for their benefit.

If this is true with regard to every species of political dominion, and every description of commercial privilege,...then such rights or privileges, or whatever else you choose to call them, are all in the strictest sense a *trust*; and it is of the very essence of every trust to be rendered *accountable*; and even totally to *cease*, when it substantially varies from the purpose for which alone it could have a lawful existence.[1]

Burke's interpretation of Imperial trusteeship was conservative and defensive. He wished to prevent British subjects who acquired power abroad from abusing it for their own private advantage and to the moral or material detriment of Britain and India. The East India Company's government, 'one of the most corrupt and destructive tyrannies that probably ever existed', and its servants, 'the destroyers of India', should be reined in by Imperial controls so that Indians should again enjoy what he understood as their traditional rights and freedoms. His object was restoration by means of reform, with Britain preventing the recurrence of abuses and correcting the systemic problems of Company government by a parliamentary act 'intended to form the *Magna Charta* of Hindostan'.[2]

To protect traditional societies which against their will had either come under British control or were threatened by the unbridled activities of British subjects, seemed a restricted ambition. It was appropriate to an eighteenth-century society, where government functions were limited, and which was only slowly accepting the idea of Imperial control over non-Western societies. It nevertheless remained central in what came to be recognized as the humanitarian approach to Empire and overseas influence. For nineteenth-century governments, reluctant to adopt open-ended responsibilities and keen to limit the endlessly rising costs of direct Imperial intervention even inside Britain's own colonies, it had another advantage. When pressed into action, governments found the idea of 'protection' convenient because it combined a politically acceptable degree of action with at least the prospect of minimal expense. It naturally found favour in the face of competing claims on government revenues. It could calm conscience and avoid accusations of cynicism or indifference.

India also provided the inspiration and setting for an alternative approach to the responsibilities of Empire. Although Fox's East India Bill fell, Pitt's India Act (1784) created a structure capable of meeting Burke's aims. However, the reshaping of Britain's government for India fuelled the ambitions of groups anxious not merely to protect but to transform Indian society. The idea gained ground that

[1] *The Speeches of the Right Hon. Edmund Burke*, Vol. V, *India: Madras and Bengal, 1774–1785*, ed. P. J. Marshall (Oxford, 1981), p. 385.

[2] Ibid., pp. 441, 439, 386.

British power and influence should be used, as it were, positively, to promote Indians' best interests by improving Indian society, however oblivious most Indians might be of their need for such changes.

Several currents of thought ran together here. Active Christians developed strong and well-publicized criticisms of India's decadence and depravity. Of particular importance were Anglican evangelicals intimately involved in promoting missionary work, such as Charles Grant (proprietor and Director of the East India Company, and friend of William Wilberforce, Henry Thornton, and others in the Clapham Sect [3]), or Sir John Shore, Governor-General in India and later, as Lord Teignmouth, on the committee of the Church Missionary Society (CMS). Grant supported the reforms of the 1780s, but was convinced that in Indian conditions honest, just government could work only if joined with Christianity and Western knowledge. His message, that without moral reform political change would achieve nothing, was developed in two influential studies: *A Proposal for Establishing a Protestant Mission in Bengal and Behar* (1787) and *Observations on the State of Society among the Asiatic Subjects of Great Britain* (1792). Grant had no doubt that 'we may... govern our Asiatic subjects more happily for them than they can be governed by themselves', by blending Christianity with European skills and know-how.[4]

Other reformers shared Grant's confidence in Britain's capacity for good and progressive government, incorporating and uplifting Indians in the process. They too believed that human nature was everywhere fundamentally the same. They went further than he did in their conviction that progress and prosperity could be advanced by rational thought or systematic administration. Placing less weight on the contribution of Christian belief and ethics, they attributed more to Western scientific knowledge and education. Scottish experience and learning in history, philosophy, and political economy contributed greatly to such principles as expressed in the work of Indian administrators from Lord Cornwallis to Sir Thomas Munro.[5] Scottish ideas were reinforced by English criticisms of Indian society and emphasis on the curative potential of rational administration linked to law reform and a good judicial system. Practical illustrations may be found in Richard Wellesley's foundation of Fort William College (1805) to train a new civil service; in the work of James Mill, Benthamite and author of the influential *History of India* (1819); and in William Bentinck's work as Governor of Madras (1803–07).

---

[3] The Clapham Sect was an informal group of wealthy, influential families living near and worshipping in Clapham parish church, south-west of London.

[4] Ainslie Thomas Embree, *Charles Grant and British Rule in India* (London, 1962), pp. 142–43.

[5] C. A. Bayly, *The New Cambridge History of India*, II. 1, *Indian Society and the Making of the British Empire* (Cambridge, 1988); Burton Stein, *Thomas Munro: The Origins of the Colonial State and His Vision of Empire* (Delhi, 1989).

For Bentinck, 'there is, indeed, no engine of civilisation more powerful than the equitable administration of wise laws'.[6]

The two conceptions of 'trusteeship' differed substantially. Burke focused on British laws to restrain the activities of British subjects; indigenous freedoms were to be preserved by restricting the incursions of outsiders. India's administrators justified their own direct intervention by devising laws to channel the activities of Indian subjects; indigenous freedoms were to be extended by allowing the wise paternalism of responsible outsiders. Grant's insertion of Christianity offered a bridge between the two, with official support for missions and education assisting the process of transformation while mitigating the extent to which government directly imposed change. All, however, agreed on the need to secure property and freedom of exchange, and took as their touchstone the happiness and well-being of indigenous peoples. Of course, those interests were variously defined by differing British views of what was acceptable in local society, what worthy or capable of being reformed, and what intolerable. Sometimes these definitions or criteria were agreeable to Indians, but even if they were not (as was often the case), objections frequently went unheeded.

Eighteenth-century enlightened thinking thus influenced Britain's renewed expansion after 1790 in important ways. Debates about Imperial-colonial policy confirmed the ruler's duty of benevolence or obligation to accept responsibility for the well-being of the Empire's subjects. Influential members of Britain's political and administrative élites shared that commitment in varying degrees. It became likely that where those responsibilities were flouted or ignored, public attention would be alerted, and calls heard for wrongs to be righted. Blinkered expediency or neglect as the unprincipled outcome of British expansion stood a greater chance of being checked. Finally, certain activities were acknowledged as inadmissible and illegal within any area where Britain's control or even influence prevailed.

Notwithstanding India's importance, no issues did more to make principles of Imperial trusteeship explicit, implant them in the public mind, and compel Imperial and colonial governments to act upon them, than those of the slave trade and slavery itself. By the 1780s the intellectual argument against slavery had been won, in that it was no longer generally regarded as defensible on grounds other than material expediency. Its economic efficiency was questioned. It was represented as irreconcilable with secular ideas about the proper end of government and the constitution of legitimate authority; its existence defied notions of

---

[6] John Rosselli, *Lord William Bentinck: The Making of a Liberal Imperialist, 1774–1839* (London, 1974), p. 135.

government as being in the interest of the governed, promoting subjects' happiness, and resting on their consent. It had also come to be seen as incompatible with a properly Christian existence. Slave-ownership, for example, conflicted with the obligations of charity and evangelization; slave status removed the liberty for moral choice and ethical behaviour. For British evangelicals especially, slavery and sin were regarded as synonymous, equally individual and national evils to be rooted out.

However, widespread antipathy to slavery coexisted with a substantial interest in its continuation. In particular, Britain's involvement in the African-Atlantic slave trade, her commerce in tropical commodities from the West Indies, her capital investment in shipping, the plantation economies of her colonies, and the prospects for future growth in the West Indies, all continued to flourish. Dislike of slavery was also compatible with attitudes of accommodation towards it, if not of toleration. Nonconformist missionaries, for example, caught between the injunctions of their Societies to avoid political involvement under threat of disconnection, and their loneliness in colonies where officials and planters alike regarded them as subversive, often found no alternative to compromise. Early anti-slavery activists such as Thomas Clarkson and Granville Sharpe thus faced a daunting task in converting an amorphous humanitarianism into the precise terms of Imperial measures of trusteeship.

Prime necessities were, of course, to rally influential friends and mobilize public enthusiasm in ways which would persuade those in authority, notably Cabinet ministers and MPs. Anti-slavery views drew immense support from transatlantic religious networks, notably those of Quakers and Methodists, whose members were sometimes well-to-do but rarely influential outside their own circles. Of critical importance, therefore, was the formation in April 1787 of the Abolition Society in London, and its support by William Wilberforce (MP for Yorkshire) and the Clapham Sect. Their material resources and political weight were essential complements to the broader movement now expressed in the formation of local abolition societies, the petitioning of Parliament, the dissemination of information, and provincial campaigning. In 1788 Sir William Dolben's bill restricting the shipping of slaves, and the Privy Council's Committee of Enquiry, not only stimulated parliamentary debate but were followed in 1792 by the House of Commons' resolution in favour of the gradual abolition of the slave trade, and thereafter by annual motions designed to secure that commitment.

The literature available on the nature and achievements of the anti-slavery movement, on the dynamic kaleidoscopic alliance of reforming interests which propelled it, and its engagement with government and colonial interests is impossible to summarize briefly. Nevertheless, the movement's main phases of development are clear.[7] Its rapid parliamentary progress between 1787 and 1792 gave way to prolonged frustration, as war with France seriously impeded further action. The argument for delaying, until peace was restored, what all parties agreed would be a far-reaching measure, was endorsed in a parliamentary resolution in 1795. Popular agitation for this as for other reforming causes was severely curtailed by fears of radical revolution and the restrictive legislation from 1795 onwards. Pitt's government was preoccupied with the war, divided internally, and consequently reluctant to take up a contentious issue which lacked the Crown's support. Humanitarians' shortage of effective economic arguments for abolition remained a serious weakness. Not until the disappearance of Addington's ministry in 1804, the major shift in the fortunes of war following France's naval defeat at Trafalgar, a temporary glut of sugar, and the political upheaval which brought the Ministry of All Talents into office was progress possible. Renewed popular agitation, the development by abolitionists of arguments which presented ending the trade as damaging to the French and part of wartime strategy, and the abolitionist sympathies of Whig ministers underpinned the legislation of 1805–07 which ended British involvement in the trade.

The results of abolition were far less striking than humanitarians had hoped. Others took up the trade in Britain's place, and British diplomats were felt to have failed when the peace settlements of 1814–15 produced no general abolition treaty. Continuing clandestine participation necessitated introducing stiffer penalties for British slavers in 1811, and capital punishment in 1824. Slave conditions in the Caribbean colonies appeared unaffected, suggesting widespread evasion of the restraints on the trade. New strategies were therefore devised: humanitarians battled to establish effective colonial registers of slaves. From 1823 they increased demands for direct Imperial intervention, even in colonies with their own Legislative Assemblies, to secure improved conditions for the slaves. Continuing colonial resistance and slave discontent, most graphically illustrated in rebellions like that of 1823 in Demerara, destroyed the remaining patience of Imperial ministers and humanitarians alike. When T. F. Buxton, Wilberforce's successor as leader of the parliamentary movement and the Anti-Slavery Society, seemed insufficiently aggressive, provincial activists such as James Cropper and Joseph Sturge made the running. From 1827, with the assistance from the *Anti-Slavery Reporter* and increasing numbers of women and children, the petitioning of Parliament greatly increased, and at the urging of the ever-more independent Agency Committee, radical abolitionists busied themselves at parliamentary elections. As the superior efficiency of free labour finally emerged as conventional

---

[7] Roger Anstey, *The Atlantic Slave Trade and British Abolition, 1760–1810* (London, 1975); David Brion Davis, *Slavery and Human Progress* (New York, 1984); Robin Blackburn, *The Overthrow of Colonial Slavery, 1776–1848* (London, 1988).

wisdom, adding a 'capitalist' argument to the humanitarian armoury, so 'Immediatism'—emancipation now—took hold.

The appointment of a Whig ministry in November 1830, the return of more MPs committed to reform or emancipation, and erosion of the West Indian interest at the elections of 1830 and 1832 favoured the abolitionists. Still more so did the Jamaican rebellion of December 1831, followed as it was by fierce retribution against the slaves, attacks on missionaries blamed for the mayhem, and the destruction of their chapels.[8] As in 1823, the evangelical and nonconformist world was fully roused, as were other humanitarians. Petitions to Parliament favouring immediate emancipation outstripped those for parliamentary reform. The first proposals for a bill came from Lord Howick at the Colonial Office in summer 1832, and an act was passed the following August. Slaves in Britain's colonies were emancipated as from 1 August 1834; subject to varying periods of 'apprenticeship' to their former masters, all would be completely free in 1840. Slave-owners were compensated for their loss of property in slaves from a fund of £20 million established by the government and paid for by metropolitan taxpayers.

The implications of this bald outline for the relationship of humanitarian activity and Britain's Imperial experience are several. As with the definition of trusteeship concerning India, so too the development of an anti-slavery movement had a symbiotic relationship with Empire. Had British slaving and slave-ownership not existed in a context where British authority could plausibly be asserted to restrain it, British humanitarianism would have lacked such clear direction and purpose. Abolitionists could cajole and threaten, but without a government willing and capable of acting, humanitarian outcries were ineffectual. Empire provided the sphere within which benevolent government action was most readily conceivable, with the result that humanitarians rarely questioned the continued existence of territorial Empire, and throughout the century frequently supported extensions of British authority if that would serve their purposes. In practice, their assumptions about universal rights necessitated removing limits to Imperial sovereignty. In the same way, imperialists pointed to their association with humanitarian policies as further justifying the maintenance and expansion of colonial territory. With abolition and emancipation behind them, despite the limitations of both measures, humanitarians were always able to believe in the possibility of success; the tradition of Wilberforce, Buxton, and Sturge had to be maintained, and their achievements might be repeated. After 1833 governments, always under pressure from conflicting interests, could express their sympathy with humanitarian goals even when disinclined or unable to promote them effectively.

---

[8] See below, pp. 231; 475–76.

Humanitarians' dependence on the Imperial government took many forms. Their tasks of persuasion and exchanging information were eased by the emergence of a single department responsible for colonial affairs in 1801, and the employment there of sympathetic officials such as James Stephen or Henry Taylor. Stephen, legal adviser from 1814 and eventually Permanent Secretary (1836–47), proved invaluable in his detailed review of colonial legislation, his advice to ministers, and in alerting abolitionists to worrying issues. Others, however, such as R. W. Hay, Stephen's predecessor, seemed far less amenable; even ministers could be ineffectual, including Lord Glenelg, notwithstanding his impeccable credentials as a concerned evangelical.

Even well-disposed governments could seem to humanitarians intolerably cautious, prompting suspicions of obstruction or insincerity. Successive ministries were notoriously reluctant to break with constitutional convention and intervene directly in the affairs of the legislative colonies. After years of colonial obstruction and even as Lord Liverpool's Cabinet agreed to experiment with an Order-in-Council laying down the programme of 'amelioration' for slaves in the Crown Colony of Trinidad, George Canning refused to legislate for islands like Jamaica: 'no feeling of wounded pride, no motive of questionable expediency, nothing short of real and demonstrable necessity, shall induce me to moot the awful question of the transcendental power of parliament over every dependency of the British Crown. That transcendental power…ought to be kept back…It exists, but it should be veiled.'[9]

Canning's argument was at once principled and expedient. The constitutional right to self-government, once granted, should not be withdrawn lest the result be arbitrary or despotic rule. Secondly, colonial resistance might leave the Imperial government no alternative but retreat or compulsion; worse still, attempted compulsion might fail. Even in the early 1830s, when clearly neither persuasion nor threats would secure serious amelioration, there was considerable reluctance to grasp this nettle. Westminster's Emancipation Act itself was drawn up for colonial legislatures to enact for themselves, with such detailed local changes as were needed. Throughout the 1830s Jamaica, for example, continued to exploit with a bitter zeal the openings for resistance this provided. Indeed, relations became so bad that in 1838 suspension of its constitution and direct Crown Colony rule was contemplated. Although Melbourne's government held back for fear of parliamentary defeat, its reluctance to take the final step illustrates the fundamental and persistent political obstacles to the attainment of humanitarian wishes.

[9] 16 March 1824, House of Commons, cited in George R. Mellor, *British Imperial Trusteeship, 1783–1850* (London, 1951), p. 92.

Governments in London were often unable to do more than mediate between humanitarian demands and the alternative desires of others at home and abroad who cared nothing for such sensitivities or, if they did care, nevertheless rated other matters more important and pressing. Imperial and colonial authorities always had to consider at what point dictation would become counter-productive. The prospect of colonial revolt, the assumption of direct rule in the face of a recalcitrant local population, were not to be lightly contemplated; they might defeat the end in view—either by so souring relations that all Imperial authority became a target for subversion, or most extremely by breaking the Imperial tie and so removing the basis for intervention. In many parts of the West Indies in the 1830s, for example, it became virtually impossible in jury trials to obtain convictions of whites for crimes against blacks. Law, traditional property rights, individual civil rights, and ethical convictions were all in dispute.

These problems are illustrated by the deep dissatisfaction of many humanitarians with the Act of Emancipation itself.[10] Why should slaves not be freed completely? Was not 'apprenticeship' slavery by another name? What justification could there be in compensating slave-owners for their past evil-doing at the expense of those who had never held slaves? Of course, there were answers to such objections. But for many British emancipationists their real victory came not in 1833, but only after another round of agitation and Parliament's premature ending of 'apprenticeship' schemes from 1838.

The legal ending of slavery in Britain's colonies threatened to deprive the popular emancipation movement of its *raison d'être*, and to reduce humanitarian activity to a few limited voluntary projects, or occasional interventions in aspects of colonial administration and Imperial diplomacy. Among the consequences of abolition were Britain's maintenance of a naval squadron on the West African coast, and a diplomatic commitment to extend by international agreements her powers to stop vessels suspected of slaving under foreign flags. Emancipation implicitly committed British authorities to a continuing process of legal review, to ensure that colonial substitutes for slavery were not created surreptitiously; in India, a special case exempted from the 1833 Act, the East India Company would have to be held to its obligation to phase out indigenous forms of slavery. While governments showed no signs of abandoning these activities, there was little place for popular activity or interest in the detail of official exchanges. Other humanitarian ventures, such as the African Association and British African Colonization Society, maintained a fitful existence or petered out altogether.[11] The same

[10] See below, pp. 474–78.
[11] Philip D. Curtin, *The Image of Africa: British Ideas and Action, 1780–1850* (London, 1965); Rhodes House Library, Oxford, MSS.Afr.S.1629.

problem of financing Sierra Leone which had caused the Sierra Leone Company to abandon it to Imperial control in 1808 was also causing the British government to feel lukewarm toward this humanitarian legacy. Humanitarian leaders, therefore, took steps to sustain and redirect popular enthusiasm by adopting new issues, reviving older ideas in new forms, and institutional readjustment.

As the political reform and slavery debates receded, the mid-1830s saw determined attempts to redirect humanitarian efforts towards peoples untouched by the Atlantic slave trade but nevertheless suffering severely from uncontrolled British expansion. Where once India had loomed large, by 1830 the Khoisan and Bantu peoples of southern Africa, Australian Aborigines, New Zealand's Maoris, and Pacific islanders were attracting attention. The elements of the general problem were clear: British traders, established settlers and new emigrants, seamen, and others in these regions were increasingly in conflict with the indigenous peoples. Under conditions where greed, ignorance, and fear outweighed goodwill; where neither party recognized or understood the political authority and social conventions of the other; where distant governments could not enforce their will, even if they possessed the nominal legal right to do so; where the liquor, arms, and opium trades flourished; there, lawlessness, the right of the strongest, retaliation, and revenge flourished. Where colonial frontiers were ill-defined or non-existent, the geographical extent of British colonial authority even over British subjects was uncertain. Tales of atrocities multiplied and were magnified in the telling, further increasing the general insecurity.

Moved by events in southern Africa, where the Imperial government finally reversed the Cape Governor's decision to retain Queen Adelaide Province after the war of 1834, the House of Commons was persuaded to have a committee examine the whole problem in 1836–37. The evidence taken convinced the committee that 'the effect of European intercourse ... has been, upon the whole, hitherto a calamity upon the native and savage nations', that Europeans were generally at fault where conflicts occurred, and that immediate government intervention was essential. Non-intervention and the absence of regulation served no national interest. 'On the contrary, in point of economy, of security, of commerce, of reputation, it is a short-sighted and disastrous policy. As far as it has prevailed, it has been a burthen upon the empire.' Moreover,

The British empire has been signally blessed by Providence, and her ... advantages, are so many reasons for peculiar obedience to the laws of Him who guides the destinies of nations. These were given for some higher purpose than commercial prosperity and military renown. ... He who has made Great Britain what she is, will inquire at our hands how we have employed the influence He has lent to us in our dealings with the untutored and defenceless savage; whether it has been engaged in seizing their lands, warring upon their people, and transplanting unknown disease, and deeper degradation, ... or whether we have, *as far as we have been able*, informed their ignorance, and invited and *afforded them the opportunity of becoming partakers* of that civilization, that innocent commerce, that knowledge and that faith with which it has pleased a gracious Providence to bless our own country.[12]

The Report was paternalistic in tone, and took for granted Britain's self-evident superiority. Nevertheless, it was deeply critical of the consequences of British neglect and expatriate activities; well aware of the practical difficulties of legislation and enforcement; and worried about principles of equity as between different cultural groups. Given the appalling prospect that, without intervention, conditions would deteriorate as emigration increased, and noting that British strength often rendered indigenous groups unable 'to resist any encroachments, however unjust, however mischievous, which we may be disposed to make', the Committee tried to define the principles of a system which would as far as possible 'enforce the observance of their [indigenous] rights'.[13]

In its recommendations, the Committee's intentions were clear. 'Whatever may be the legislative system of any Colony, we...advise that, as far as possible, the Aborigines be withdrawn from its control', and placed in the 'more impartial hands' of Imperial executive officials. All labour legislation and contracts should be regulated so as to preserve the freedom, if people wished, to sell 'their labour at the best price, and at the market most convenient for themselves'. Acquisition and sales of land should be controlled to guarantee just returns, not least opportunities for 'religious instruction and education', for native inhabitants. Reflecting the importance of missionary evidence to the Committee, emphasis was placed on the role of missions as mediators between the British and local peoples. The Report aimed less at imposing Imperial structures or British culture than at adjusting as peacefully as possible 'the disparity of the parties'.[14]

These recommendations should not be dismissed as merely rhetorical or cosmetic. The Report identified clearly the areas and issues which were to preoccupy British administrators throughout the century. In the light of solutions canvassed at the time, its failure to take more seriously the possibility of further restricting or even prohibiting land transfers may seem short-sighted. However, such a course was precluded by belief in its practical impossibility, as well as confidence in the likelihood and advantages of assimilation. Other ideal alternatives were also seen as impractical. Although 'the safety and welfare of an uncivilized race require that their relations with their more cultivated neighbours

---

[12]   *Report from the Select Committee on Aborigines (British Settlements), Parliamentary Papers* (1837), VII (425), pp. 74–76.

[13]   Ibid., p. 3.

[14]   Ibid., pp. 77–78.

should be diminished rather than multiplied', British citizens could not be confined to barracks anywhere within the Empire. Even officially negotiated treaties were 'rather the preparatives...for disputes than securities for peace', given 'the superior sagacity which the European will exercise in framing, in interpreting, and in evading them'.[15] Britain's strength and Imperial authority were often incapable of translation into the precise and competent exercise of power. At the time, the Committee's carefully considered suggestions were regarded as imperfect but the best available.

The gap between humanitarian ambition and achievements is now sadly apparent; then, however, many contemporaries were sanguine. The lessons of the anti-slavery campaign were reapplied, in Thomas Hodgkin's establishment of the Aborigines' Protection Society (APS) in 1837. Like the Anti-Slavery Society, it was a voluntary body to investigate abuses, publicize them, and hold governments to their responsibilities by embarrassing revelations and political pressure. Indeed, a later Secretary, H. R. Fox-Bourne, regarded its purpose as the implementation of the 1837 Report. The Report itself was soon followed by that most striking of Victorian attempts to forestall further disasters, the annexation of New Zealand. Its call for action found further echoes in the acquisition of Natal in 1843, a response to Afrikaner expansion in the Great Trek, and in the re-establishment of British control on the Gold Coast. Under the Foreign Jurisdiction Act (1843) the Crown was allowed to acquire judicial powers by agreement with foreign rulers in territories not belonging to Britain.

Buxton, in his attempts to redirect humanitarian energies, appealed to the same benevolent instincts but in a peculiarly evangelical form. He shared the evangelical view that mobilizing public conscience and government power behind humanitarian causes should not only eradicate sin but atone and make reparation for past wrong-doing. Atonement involved not acts of contrition alone, but the performance of good works from which the doer might also benefit. Here lay the possibility of marrying Christian duty with secular self-interest, something the humanitarian coalition had already shown could become politically unstoppable.

In 1789 Wilberforce had begged Parliament to 'make reparation to Africa...by establishing a trade upon true commercial principles, and we shall soon find the rectitude of our conduct rewarded by the benefits of a regular and growing commerce'.[16] Fifty years later Buxton redeveloped this appeal in *The African Slave Trade* and *The Remedy*.[17] He reinforced it with the wisdom of hindsight: naval suppression of the trade was 'too feeble'; legitimate trade would not supplant

---

[15] Ibid., p. 80

[16] Klaus E. Knorr, *British Colonial Theories, 1570–1850* (1944; London, 1963), p. 378.

[17] Published separately in 1839, Buxton combined them in *The African Slave Trade and Its Remedy* (London, 1840).

slaving without direct intervention to provide security; after much trial and error, staples—certainly palm-oil, possibly cotton—now existed as a basis for trade.

Legitimate commerce would put down the Slave Trade, by demonstrating the superior value of man as a labourer on the soil, to man as an object of merchandise; and if conducted on wise and equitable principles, might be the precursor, or rather the attendant, of civilization, peace, and Christianity, to the unenlightened, warlike, and heathen tribes who now so fearfully prey on each other, to supply the slave markets of the New World. In this view of the subject, the merchant, the philanthropist, the patriot, and the Christian, may unite . . .[18]

For the moment at least Buxton was right because his arguments proved persuasive. Divisions among humanitarians provoked the collapse of the Anti-Slavery Society. Sturge founded the British and Foreign Anti-Slavery Society (BFASS) in April 1839, overtly pacifist and inclined to focus on American slavery. To support his own vision, Buxton formed the African Civilization Society (July 1839), and carried Quakers, Baptists, Wesleyans, and Scottish Presbyterians with him. The government also supported Buxton, anti-slavery sentiment and parliamentary need for humanitarian votes outweighing ministers' privately expressed concerns at the likely costs and expansive consequences of embracing tropical Africa in a network of treaties, land purchases, trading, and peacekeeping expeditions. As a result the slave-trade suppression squadron was increased, and the Whigs agreed to fund a major expedition up the Niger to make treaties and consider territory for agricultural and commercial settlements inland.

The expedition was in many ways a fiasco. Leaving Britain in May 1841, by mid-October it had retreated in disarray from the Niger with forty of the 145 whites dead from fever. The Whig ministry fell, and in 1843, with the Niger settlement abandoned, the African Civilization Society was dissolved. Buxton died in 1845. These consequences, however, were not entirely disastrous for the humanitarians. They simplified the politics of the movement, leaving Sturge and the British and Foreign Anti-Slavery Society to inherit the earth and divide their concerns with the Aborigines' Protection Society. They also confirmed the wisdom of those politicians like Palmerston who combined humanitarian sentiment with a recognition that government support could only be such as was compatible with other British interests and would receive sustained political support.

The increased naval vote survived, and commercial diplomacy, underpinned by successive consular appointments from Zanzibar to the Pacific, was linked to the continuing diplomatic negotiation of anti-slave trade treaties with rulers everywhere. With annexations in the Pacific and Africa, these measures also helped keep France at bay, an international rival soft on slavery and Roman Catholicism. This modest, severely practical approach at least held the Buxtonian coalition—

---

[18] Thomas Fowell Buxton, *The African Slave Trade and its Remedy*, p. 306.

merchants, philanthropists, patriots, Christians—together, even if harnessing their energies in different proportion. Moreover, it implicity accepted the fundamental humanitarian points that the war against slavery and the slave trade should be a significant ingredient of British policy, and could only be so if government concern extended beyond formal colonial possessions. Anti-slave trade diplomacy, described by Aberdeen in 1842 as a 'new and a vast branch of international relations', seemed capable of making useful gains, and the new treaties with Portugal (1842), France and Zanzibar (both 1845) were enthusiastically welcomed.[19] This approach set the continuing framework for the humanitarian movement's activity in goading government and influencing Imperial policy.

Although the 1840s opened promisingly, the achievements to 1870 were often disappointing. Earlier conventional wisdom was either disproved or at least seriously questioned. In West Africa, legitimate trade was not driving out the slave trade—and not simply because it lacked strength or appeal, as Buxton had argued in 1839. The balance of advantage against the slave trade was frequently unclear, and Britain's use of force to decide the issue increased. It became difficult for humanitarians to sustain their optimistic belief that a temporary push with government assistance would everywhere tip the balance in favour of free and prosperous enterprise. Slavery and the trade in Africa remained an intractable and—if travellers' reports were believed—growing problem, unamenable to existing British naval and diplomatic activity. The greater efficiency of free over slave labour was not borne out by the Caribbean colonies' experience, and the terms available for free labour were often unattractive to freed slaves and indigenous people. The consequence for the British and Foreign Anti-Slavery Society was a decade of debilitating argument as to whether or not colonial produce should continue to receive preferential treatment in Britain's markets, or be compelled to compete on a free and equal basis with slave-grown produce from elsewhere. The Free Traders' victory by 1854 indicated a loss of commitment to the West Indian cause.

This internal dispute was only one of several which disrupted the anti-slavery lobby. Tactics and geographical focus were also at issue. The greatest division lay between those believing that the slave trade and Africa should be their prime concern, and those following Sturge, who targeted slavery itself and preferred to join forces with American abolitionists. Lesser arguments about methods—the use of violence against traders, economic blockade or sanctions—only exacerbated divisions. Split over essentials, the British and Foreign was hardly well

---

[19] Gerald S. Graham, *Great Britain in the Indian Ocean: A Study of Maritime Enterprise, 1810–1850* (Oxford, 1967), pp. 106–07, 117, 215.

equipped to pursue other issues beginning to demand attention, such as contract or coolie 'labour'. Recruitment of liberated Africans and Indian labourers for employment in Mauritius, Natal, and West Indian colonies grew steadily from the 1840s, and was easily open to abuse.[20]

Occasionally the Society successfully rallied parliamentary support. On the coolie question in 1842–43 and 1849–50, for instance, it achieved modifications in Mauritius's, British Guiana's, and Trinidad's administration of the system. The general picture by the 1860s, however, was one of indecision, ineffectiveness, and declining membership, with increasing reliance on the connections and resources of the great and good among British Quakers, the Buxton, Gurney, and Barclay families.

The position of the Aborigines' Protection Society was no better. Hodgkin, another Quaker as well as ethnologist and professional physician, remained Secretary until 1866, but seems to have had neither time nor contacts sufficient to his increasingly complicated task. By the end of the 1840s it was clear that Imperial initiatives were having only limited and temporary success. The Aboriginal Protectors appointed in New South Wales and Western Australia (1838–39) after ten years had evidently failed. In New Zealand the early optimism soon evaporated. Confidence was only partially restored by Governor Grey (1846–52), and at the expense of shifting to an overtly assimilationist policy towards the Maori. Moreover, the conflict over land purchases from Maoris remained unresolved, and Grey's ability to negotiate with them, as well as his administrative command, proved beyond his successors.

For those pinning their hopes on the principles of the 1837 Report, however, there were still more fundamental obstacles. Prominent were democratic political institutions and the growth of colonial self-government. Ironically, the same representative electoral practices which enabled the humanitarians to put pressure on the Imperial government to act, once transferred to the colonies worked against humanitarian aims. This came as no surprise in the mid-century. West Indian Assemblies had fought to ward off amelioration and circumvent the Emancipation Act; the Cape Colony's less popularly based Legislative Council tried the same in its 1834 Vagrancy Act. For these reasons the 1837 Report, and by then also the Imperial government, had favoured removing such matters from popular control; but the line proved impossible to hold. The Imperial authorities found the political demand for settler self-government undeniable. Although in Natal responsible government was delayed on the humanitarian ground that such a small white community could not be trusted with power over blacks, this was exceptional. Before 1870 all settler colonies had acquired sufficient financial power

---

[20] See below, pp. 90–93, 95–96, 98; also p. 553.

to enable them to shape policy towards indigenous populations more or less as they wished. Expenditure on native peoples called for in 1837, and to some extent institutionalized by a Governor such as Grey both in New Zealand and the Cape, was cut to the bone. Legislation, carefully framed to avoid Imperial disallowance, and embodying employment conditions or qualifications for political involvement akin to those in Britain, established patterns of labour law and political rights favourable to white minorities. Everywhere indigenous customary rights to land were steadily extinguished.

Justifications for this determined departure from the intentions of the 1830s were developed in ways reconciling it with what were still seen by Victorians in all walks of life as the preferred, if not the actual, priorities of Imperial policy. W. E. Gladstone, formerly a member of the 1836–37 Aborigines' Committee, spoke for many in arguing that, given the limits to Imperial power and the undesirability of compulsion, the best defence for indigenous rights was normally the greatest degree of local self-government.[21] Settler societies, once made wholly responsible for the consequences of their own decisions, would rapidly establish good relations with native populations and neighbouring states. War would not pay, and swords beaten into ploughshares would cultivate general prosperity. Self-government with free trade would reconcile political rights and acceptable economics.

Making a virtue of political necessity did not automatically make Gladstone right, and distinguished figures such as Earl Grey vigorously dissented. In New Zealand the removal of Imperial troops took place only after they had fought the settlers' war which placed Maoris beyond the pale and facilitated the final great land confiscation. At the Cape too, pacific instincts blossomed reluctantly when local odds favoured settlers or when, as a hardened Colonial Office observer put it, 'a little war would be excellent for trade'.[22] In practice, peace and injustice could cohabit far more easily than Gladstone implied.

What constituted 'justice' or 'the best interests' of indigenous peoples, emancipated slaves, or indentured labourers was also being debated and redefined. Various mid-century developments combined to erode the earlier general optimism about non-Western peoples' capacity and to undermine support for the relatively generous approach of 1837. The humanitarians' position was weakened by material decline in the West Indies, the small numbers of missionary converts, the unwillingness of indigenous communities to absorb British ideas or commercial habits, and by what observers interpreted as the violent rejection of British ways evident in the Indian Mutiny, the Maori Wars, and the Morant Bay Rebellion. Disappointment and developing ideas about insurmountable racial and cultural differences

[21] Paul Knaplund, *Gladstone and Britain's Imperial Policy* (London, 1927), pp. 86–91.
[22] R. G. W. Herbert to Lord Carnarvon, 10 April 1874, B[ritish]L[ibrary] Add. MSS 60791.

caused even the compassionate to adjust their sights downward, and the confident (for instance, among the missions) to work to a longer time-scale. To those less thoughtful, humanitarian goals and talk of equal rights seemed unrealistic or irrelevant.

In mid-century the humanitarian movement became temporarily but essentially the creature of habit. It had lost the drive, energy, and political weight of its days as a popular movement. Its activities were now those of small, quite well-informed pressure groups, developing their official and political connections. The two societies often reacted vigorously, but could not influence the outcome of large events such as the Maori Wars, and contributed little to mobilize the public outrage provoked by Governor Eyre in Jamaica in 1865.[23] Individual activists, such as the missionary James Long, fighting in the 1860s for labourers' rights against the powerful indigo planters of Bengal, often went unsupported.[24] However, popular protest on behalf of black Jamaicans, or enthusiasm for the anti-slavery cause and the North in the American Civil War, provided important reminders that humanitarian convictions were far from moribund. They added point to official diplomacy, the expansion of consular appointments, and continued oversight of Britons abroad, particularly in tropical regions. They reinforced the perception by other countries of Britain as committed irrevocably to the anti-slavery cause and sustained the prospect of renewed and vigorous campaigns.

The North's victory in the Civil War in America and abolition in 1865 returned the anti-slavery lobby's main interest to areas where British opinion and Imperial authority could make themselves felt. The slave trade of East and Central Africa, dominated by Arabs working from Zanzibar and as far afield as the Persian Gulf, attracted particular attention. David Livingstone's career and death near Lake Bangweulu in 1873 contributed greatly to this, partly by its encouragement of English and Scottish missions. After initial failure inland, the Universities Mission to Central Africa was re-established at Zanzibar, and under Bishops Steere and Tozer began to extend towards Lake Nyasa. The Church Missionary Society revived its Mombasa mission, and in the late 1870s Scottish churches scattered themselves around Lake Nyasa itself.

This combination of a new focus, and the re-engagement with the missions' help of the religious public, so important in the 1820s and 1830s, was complemented by changes of personnel in both societies. At the British and Foreign in 1870 Sturge invited the Revd Horace Waller on to the executive committee. Waller, a founding member of the Universities Mission, active member of the Royal

---

[23] Bernard Semmel, *The Governor Eyre Controversy* (London, 1962).
[24] Geoffrey A. Oddie, *Social Protest in India: British Protestant Missionaries and Social Reforms, 1850–1900* (Delhi, 1979).

Geographical Society, friend of Livingstone and editor of his *Last Journals* (1874), was well connected and indefatigable.[25] At the Aborigines' Protection Society the Secretary, F. W. Chesson, long overshadowed by Hodgkin, became full time in the same year. Similarly energetic, developing extensive liberal, parliamentary, and journalistic connections, he too made an essential contribution to his Society's revival. The two Societies collaborated closely from 1870 onwards.

In East African matters the British and Foreign Anti-Slavery Society usually took the lead. It carefully watched the 1871 parliamentary committee on the slave trade and organized much of the pressure on Gladstone's ministry which in 1872–73 produced the new anti-slavery treaty with Zanzibar; it was active in Disraeli's embarrassment in 1875–76 over Admiralty regulations about handling fugitive slaves. On this issue Sturge and Waller spent much time addressing public meetings, approaching the Foreign Office, mobilizing parliamentary support, coaching MPs for their speeches, and above all in sustaining a fundamentally non-partisan coalition.[26] There was also the constant gathering of up-to-date information, badgering the Foreign Office about slave trade suppression, and cultivating new figures interested in the region, such as William Mackinnon and King Leopold of the Belgians.

The Aborigines' Protection Society was active in several traditional areas. The Pacific labour traffic and Queensland's recruiting for its plantations was already creating concern when, in November 1871, news reached England of the murder of Bishop Patteson of the Melanesian Mission by islanders at Nukapu, in the Solomon Islands in September, apparently in revenge for recruiters' outrages. Church and missionary societies' outcry joined the Society's continuing publicity and deputation work, and their united agitation produced the Pacific Islanders Protection Act (1872). With the Wesleyan Methodists and interested parties at the Colonial Institute, the Society then organized much of the campaign during 1872–73 which nudged Gladstone's Cabinet towards annexing Fiji. In West Africa, following the Asante War, APS and British and Foreign Anti-Slavery Society work in the summer of 1874 forced a reluctant Colonial Office and Cabinet to commit themselves to abolishing domestic slavery and other involuntary servitude on the Gold Coast. The retention of the Gambia under British control also owed much to the APS, for Chesson brought the Gambia Committee together in summer 1875 and played a strong Protestant card to avoid French Catholic rule.

These activities repeated on a smaller scale those of the abolition and anti-slavery societies in their heyday. They were well-tried staples of effective lobbying:

[25] Dorothy O. Helly, *Livingstone's Legacy: Horace Waller and Victorian Mythmaking* (Athens, Oh., 1987).

[26] Horace Waller, Diaries 1875–76, Yale University Divinity School, MS Group 72/19–20.

information gathering; collaboration with or mobilization of interested parties among the missions or merchant communities; links with societies such as the Royal Geographical; cultivation of all-party support from younger radicals such as Charles Dilke and solid figures like Arthur Kinnaird or Sir John Kennaway; and playing on the personal sympathies of ministers such as Kimberley. With their smaller resources, however, the societies were necessarily more dependent than their predecessors on making themselves useful as well as pushing in the offices of state, and they perhaps reacted to events more often than they took the initiative.

The chief difference, however, between the pre-1840 and post-1870 decades reflected the humanitarians' final abandonment of visions of sweeping transformations in indigenous societies. The middle-class constituency on which they always significantly depended was by the 1870s increasingly well-established and conservative. General humanitarian impulses were very real. However, vigorous protests at Turkish atrocities and, later, at Britain's own concentration camps during the South African War, were not matched by the same ready involvement on behalf of non-Europeans as had occurred two generations before. This was not simply the consequence of mid-century disillusionments; nor was it that the aims of Buxton's African Civilization Society no longer seemed desirable, especially as arguments favouring biological racial differences attracted wide support. It was their feasibility which seemed increasingly doubtful. The persistence of slavery, the perennial need to stop authorities backsliding, the sheer recalcitrance of problems also had a profound cumulative effect. They not only discouraged optimism about African or Maori capacity to cope with white culture, but taught humanitarians to be thankful for small gains and to emphasize protection above all.

Between 1870 and 1914, therefore, notwithstanding the larger funds and membership of the British and Foreign, British humanitarianism came to adopt the goals of the Aborigines' Protection Society. With the slave trade and slavery both declining, abolitionists considered more the consequences of emancipation and the development of what have since been named 'new forms of slavery'. The partitions of Africa and the Pacific progressively closed off many external frontiers where British subjects confronted independent peoples. Humanitarians' attention inevitably converged on problems in territories directly under colonial control, and they generally accepted the traditional APS preoccupation with property as the guarantee of indigenous rights and freedoms. The death of H. R. Fox-Bourne, APS Secretary, removed the final obstacle to a natural merger of the two Societies in June 1910.

In these circumstances relations between the institutionalized humanitarian lobby and government became ever closer; the lobby adopted the role of watchman, briefed to recall government to its obligations whenever it neglected its position as 'trustee'. Of course humanitarians were encouraged in this by the help they had always received from sympathetic individual officials, and in places policy was closely attuned to their goals. In India, for example, legislative curbs on the free market were introduced after 1875 to protect peasant landholding. However, sensitive to what government could and could not do, the societies tailored their recommendations accordingly, rather than reconsider their methods or the interests of those needing assistance. Representatives of the societies went with those of chambers of commerce, missions, and private syndicates, to all the major international conferences of the period, notably the Berlin West Africa Conference (1884–85) and the Brussels Slave Trade Conference (1890).[27]

The modesty of humanitarian expectations and absence of independent thinking is evident on South African questions. Until the 1870s the Aborigines' Protection Society enthusiastically supported a conventional policy of federation as the key to prosperity and a uniform, liberal 'native policy'. However, events in Natal and on the Cape frontiers after 1875 brought a complete change. The Society now argued for Imperial intervention, the establishment at least of protectorates, and opposition to chartered company administration, as did many others, including the missionary John Mackenzie, the Wesleyans, and Joseph Chamberlain. Despite their shift away from the 'civilizing' mission, humanitarians' paternalism persisted in assumptions that indigenous cultures should be protected because they were vulnerable *per se*, and that Britain's Imperial authority could be trusted to be impartial. Bechuanaland excited much popular concern when three paramount chiefs threatened by the British South Africa Company visited Britain in the autumn 1895.[28] On the later issue of Chinese labour, imported to assist South Africa's recovery after the war of 1899–1902, APS opposition rested on the conditions under which the scheme operated—areas of British official responsibility—as well as its bad influence on Africans. On each occasion the informed experts of the BFASS and APS moved after the event, swimming with the general tide of humanitarian concern.

Ultimately the combination of limited resources and the search for abuses cramped the potential of humanitarian leaders. In constantly calling the Imperial government to its duty, they unwittingly fostered a negative conception of trusteeship, confirming the reality of 'the white man's burden' rather than searching for ways in which it might be lightened. By the turn of the century, however, new, more positive thinking was beginning to emerge from quite other quarters.

[27] Suzanne Miers, 'Humanitarianism at Berlin: Myth or Reality?', in Stig Förster, Wolfgang J. Mommsen, and Ronald Robinson, eds., *Bismarck, Europe and Africa: The Berlin African Conference, 1884–1855 and the Onset of Partition* (Oxford, 1988), pp. 333–45.

[28] Neil Parsons, *King Khama, Emperor Joe, and the Great White Queen: Victorian Britain through African Eyes* (Chicago, 1998).

New ideas emerged when, like Buxton in the 1830s, people again reconsidered the future of the tropical world. With declining hopes for development under the combined stimulus of free trade and non-European initiative, thought had turned to alternatives. These included direction by Europeans, either through private enterprises with official endorsement and *de facto* monopoly powers like chartered companies, or directly under Imperial government control in the interest of more widely diffused benefits. However, neither the record of Britain's chartered companies nor state-directed enterprise, such as Chamberlain favoured, commanded general support.

In developing further possibilities the Congo Reform Association was of particular importance.[29] The later 1890s saw disquiet developing as evidence mounted that King Leopold was administering the Congo Free State in ways quite contrary to international undertakings made at Berlin and Brussels. Reports multiplied, revealing discrimination against missions other than those of Belgian Catholic orders, restrictions on trade not controlled by Leopold's agents, and exploitative and vicious methods adopted to gather tropical commodities on which the state's revenues depended. The Congo basin was becoming difficult of access to those seen as 'outsiders', and was being administered in Leopold's exclusive interests. Leopold's persistently aggressive diplomacy to extend the conventional boundaries of his territory pointed in the same direction.

Given his political and social influence, Leopold's bland assurances were adequate to prevent criticism by governments which, having settled the Congo's future in 1885, had no wish to reopen this internationally contentious issue. After APS agitation, Edmund Morel, with great difficulty despite experience in West African shipping, uncovered damning evidence of the rapaciousness of the Congo authorities and the atrocities committed against the Congolese. Convinced that the regime should be called to account but rebuffed in official quarters, Morel published *Red Rubber* (1904) and, with extraordinary energy, mounted a public campaign. Conceived by Consul Roger Casement and led by Morel in alliance with Dr Harry Guinness and John and Alice Harris of the Congo Balolo Mission, with the aid of Liverpool merchants, the churches, and missionary supporters, the Congo Reform Association was ultimately successful in forcing Leopold to relinquish control to the Belgian parliament in 1908.

Morel's single-minded crusade had its parallels with those of Clarkson, Sharpe, Wilberforce, and Sturge; but also its particular problems. The British government, while aware of the truth, was reluctant to act lest its own colonial record be questioned or the European balance of power be tipped in Germany's favour.

---

[29] Kevin Grant, ' "A Civilised Savagery": British Humanitarian Politics and European Imperialism in Africa, 1884–1926', unpublished Ph.D. dissertation, University of California, Berkeley, 1997.

There was international suspicion of selfish ambitions on the part of objectors. Moreover, before 1904, as Morel later wrote: 'As for any real Public Opinion on the subject, it is no disloyalty to Fox Bourne's memory to say that it did not exist...the very catholicity of his sympathies was a source of popular weakness ...and the Aborigines Protection Society of which he was the life and soul, was notorious for criticising every European Government (often quite rightly) in its dealings with subject races.'[30]

To overcome these obstacles Morel relied on his journalistic talents, religious networks, and publicity especially by Baptists and Quakers, and an ability to recreate conditions which had contributed to anti-slavery's early-nineteenth-century achievements. A single issue, the Congo, was combined with a clearly defined outcome—ending Leopold's rule. An alliance of different interests was forged. Crucial, said Morel, was 'appeal to national honour, which meant that the Public, and especially the philanthropic and religious Public, whose aid Stanley had enlisted with such effect in the early eighties in securing British adhesion to King Leopold's enterprise, must be vividly reminded of the very special national responsibility which rested upon England and Englishmen in the matter'. He played up the danger of Leopold's activities to Britain's neighbouring territories, and the immorality of the Free State's commercial monopoly in breach of commitments at Berlin. He also brought to his analysis a vision of what might be if Africans were freed from oppression, guaranteed their land and the profits of its produce, and allowed to develop their own interests. Morel's was 'an appeal addressed to four principles: human pity the world over; British honour: British Imperial responsibilities in Africa: international commercial rights *co-incident with and inseparable from native economic and personal liberties*'.[31]

The persuasiveness of the Congo's appeal also reflected both the continuing significance of Nonconformist commitment to principles of freedom and religious conversion, and the extent to which after 1895 a more positive re-evaluation of non-Western cultures was taking place.[32] Morel had a greater faith than most in Africans to conduct their own affairs. Nevertheless, travellers such as Mary Kingsley, analysts of Imperial economics such as J. A. Hobson, and missionaries and anthropologists were also arguing that the potential of these cultures to change was much greater than generally supposed. The Colonial Office grew hostile to chartered companies and, after 1903, more wary of tropical development

---

[30] Wm. Roger Louis and Jean Stengers, *E. D. Morel's History of the Congo Reform Movement* (Oxford, 1967), pp. 55–56.

[31] Ibid., pp. 63, 68. Henry Morton Stanley, explorer and discoverer of David Livingstone in 1871.

[32] Bernard Porter, *Critics of Empire: British and Radical Attitudes to Colonialism in Africa, 1895–1914* (London, 1968); Ronald Hyam, *Elgin and Churchill at the Colonial Office, 1905–1908: The Watershed of the Empire-Commonwealth* (London, 1968), chaps. 10–12.

schemes which might deprive Africans in particular of their own labour and land rights. Colonial administrators as diverse as Sir William MacGregor and Norman Leys reinforced the message.

There were thus signs of changing emphases and new directions in the development of Britain's humanitarian tradition before 1914. The momentum regained in the early 1870s was sustained, and the willingness of the extensive humanitarian public to rouse itself was periodically displayed. Popular expressions of humanitarian concern were nevertheless enthusiastic and haphazard—opposing the Portuguese at the time of the Anglo-Portuguese Treaty of 1884, strongly supportive of British protection for a continued missionary presence in Uganda in 1892—rather than sustained and clearly focused. This reflected the preferences and a certain lack of imagination on the part of the second tier of activists—the committed organizers of the two principal societies, the British and Foreign and the Aborigines' Protection Society—who favoured a detailed, day-to-day working relationship with government. Their mode of operation was not easily linked to the development of popular agitation. However, given Britain's continued expansion, the societies' organizers needed their wider support to provide finance and vital information, while the broader range of supporters always needed those who could focus their outrage on government in ways which would secure effective action. The two sides of the movement began to draw together again in the context of renewed concern over European activities—arms and opium trades, plantations, mining, labour traffic, the consequences of African partition—and a less ethnocentric approach to the needs and qualities of indigenous societies. In its activities from 1904 to 1913 the Congo Reform Association demonstrated the revived potential of this combination for sustained and effective campaigning.

The 'trusteeship' which Morel's campaign supported and the British government finally endorsed was essentially hybrid. It echoed Burke's restraint. It still reflected the pessimism of later Victorians in offering little to Western-educated colonial subjects. Free trade retained its place, albeit more as a buttress to indigenous status than the moral agent of social transformation. Nevertheless, in acknowledging the need and possibility for indigenous social or economic change, in reasserting acceptable standards of colonial practice especially in the legal definition and protection of individuals' rights, and in reminding colonial governments of their international responsibilities, it offered pointers to the future. The roots of Britain's later colonial development and welfare policies are varied, but to a significant degree they embodied the modification of late-nineteenth-century ideas of European-directed development under pressure from supporters of Britain's older humanitarian traditions of anti-slavery and trusteeship.

Select Bibliography

H. ALAN C. CAIRNS, *Prelude to Imperialism: British Reactions to Central African Society, 1840–1890* (London, 1965).

JOHN CELL, 'The Imperial Conscience', in Peter Marsh, ed., *The Conscience of the Victorian State* (Syracuse, NY, 1979), pp. 173–213.

DAVID BRION DAVIS, *The Problem of Slavery in Western Culture* (Ithaca, NY, 1966).

SEYMOUR DRESCHER, *Capitalism and Antislavery: British Mobilization in Comparative Perspective* (London, 1986).

——'Whose Abolition? Popular Pressure and the Ending of the British Slave Trade', *Past and Present*, CXLIII (1994), pp. 136–66.

JOHN GALLAGHER, 'Fowell Buxton and the New African Policy, 1838–1842', *Cambridge Historical Journal*, X (1950), pp. 36–58.

RAYMOND HOWELL, *The Royal Navy and the Slave Trade* (London, 1987).

ROBERT A. HUTTENBACK, *Racism and Empire: White Settlers and Colored Immigrants in the British Self-Governing Colonies, 1830–1910* (London, 1976).

WILLIAM ROGER LOUIS, 'Roger Casement and the Congo', *Journal of African History*, V, 1 (1964), pp. 99–120.

CLARE MIDGLEY, *Women Against Slavery: The British Campaigns, 1780–1870* (London, 1992).

SUZANNE MIERS, *Britain and the Ending of the Slave Trade* (London, 1975).

KENNETH D. NWORAH, 'The Aborigines' Protection Society, 1889–1909: A Pressure-Group in Colonial Policy', *Canadian Journal of African Studies*, V, 1 (1971), pp. 79–91.

——'The Liverpool "Sect" and British West African Policy, 1895–1915', *African Affairs*, LXX (1971), pp. 349–64.

PAUL B. RICH, *Race and Empire in British Politics*, 2nd edn. (Cambridge, 1990).

H. C. SWAISLAND, 'The Aborigines' Protection Society and British Southern and Western Africa', unpublished D.Phil. thesis, Oxford, 1968.

HOWARD TEMPERLEY, *British Antislavery, 1833–1870* (London, 1972).

DAVID TURLEY, *The Culture of English Antislavery, 1780–1860* (London, 1991).

BRIAN WILLAN, 'The Anti-Slavery and Aborigines' Protection Society, and the South African Natives' Land Act of 1913', *Journal of African History*, XX (1979), pp. 83–102.

SUSAN M. K. WILLMINGTON, 'The Activities of the Aborigines' Protection Society as a Pressure Group on the Formulation of Colonial Policy, 1868–1880', unpublished Ph.D. thesis, University of Wales, Lampeter, 1973.

11

Religion, Missionary Enthusiasm, and Empire

ANDREW PORTER

Christianity's expansion as part of British culture and activities overseas in the nineteenth century was unprecedented in scale. Emigrants and temporary expatriates, such as merchants and officials, frequently carried their faith abroad with them. Anglicans, Presbyterians, Roman Catholics, and other denominations recreated their churches overseas and adapted them to new environments in the process. In a parallel movement, driven especially by voluntary Protestant missionary societies founded in the 1790s, evangelical Christians and the missionaries they supported overseas—some 10,000 by 1900—set out to convert the extra-European world. Imperial control and colonial societies were consequently influenced in a multitude of divergent and ambiguous ways.

Home and colonial governments supported ecclesiastical expansion wherever it was likely to buttress their authority and promote social order. However, religious dynamics proved unpredictable and often at odds with Imperial needs. In the white settlement colonies, a religious establishment at first seemed desirable. However, more even than in Britain, the growth of denominational conflict forced politicians and officials to conclude that only a policy of religious neutrality would serve their purpose. Finding such state support as they received inadequate and constricting, churchmen too distanced themselves from political authorities. By mid-century the formal separation of church and state was occurring, with the result that religious influences began to shape Imperial ties and colonial identities in less obvious ways.

By contrast, Imperial authorities with few exceptions initially distrusted missionary enterprise, and missions rejected all political involvement. Both sides, however, learned gradually that co-operation had its uses. Missions won extensive popular support at home and, inescapably dependent on their hosts, often acquired considerable influence with non-European communities. They could therefore not be ignored, and might be turned to Imperial advantage. Missionaries came to regard secular authorities in a similarly utilitarian way. British missionary enterprise thus sometimes provided channels through which Imperial controls followed; at other times it delayed annexation and colonization, or even subverted

Imperial authority. In many places (sometimes on purpose, often unintentionally) Christians and their churches provided powerful stimuli for local resistance and opposition to colonial rule.

Settlement of North America's affairs in the 1780s required not only a new military order but practical answers to serious constitutional and political questions. These questions centred on securing British sovereignty, respect for continued British colonial rule, and loyal acceptance of political obligations, without exciting colonial discontent. Political radicalism, such as disrupted the old colonial system and disturbed metropolitan Britain after 1790, was regarded by British leaders as inseparable from religious dissent. Not surprisingly, solutions to the problems of Empire were therefore felt, like those at home, to require reinforcing ties between established religion, especially the Church of England, and the state.

William Knox, of the Society for the Propagation of the Gospel (SPG) and Under-Secretary of State for the Colonies (1770–82), asserted in 1786 that 'the Prevalence of the Church of England in those Colonies is the best Security that Great Britain can have for their Fidelity and attachment to her Constitution and Interests'.[1] Few influential men were as forthright, but his general sentiment was found broadly agreeable. Ministers and bishops felt their earlier haphazard attention to the religious life of the colonies had been disastrous. To nurture such links as survived after 1782, it was felt necessary to provide ecclesiastical leadership for Anglicans remaining in the United States. In neighbouring Quebec, and the Maritime Colonies which had received more than 30,000 Loyalist refugees, entrenchment of an officially supported Anglicanism was regarded as constitutionally essential and a wise response to local needs.

These expedient responses were reinforced by the widespread support in Britain herself for linking church and state. The establishment of Anglicanism appropriately expressed both faith and duty, and served as a reminder of the divine origins of society and state as well as the mutual obligations of subjects and sovereign. The English, Edmund Burke wrote in 1790, 'do not consider their Church establishment as ... something ... they may either keep or lay aside, according to their temporary ideas of convenience. They consider it as the foundation of their whole constitution, with which, and with every part of which, it holds an indissoluble union.'[2]

Imperial authorities in London, therefore, acted readily to establish a fully fledged colonial church. The high-Anglican Loyalist Charles Inglis was made

---

[1] Vincent T. Harlow, *The Founding of the Second British Empire, 1763–1793*, 2 vols. (London, 1964), II, p. 738.

[2] Quoted in J. C. D. Clark, *English Society, 1688–1832: Ideology, Social Structure and Political Practice during the Ancien Regime* (Cambridge, 1985), pp. 254–55.

Bishop of Nova Scotia in 1787, with responsibilities including New Brunswick, Newfoundland, and Cape Breton, and as part of the 1791 settlement of the Canadas Jacob Mountain took up the new bishopric of Quebec in 1793. These were government appointments, and subordinate to the Archbishop of Canterbury's authority, unlike previous arrangements whereby colonial clergy were placed under the Bishop of London.

Inglis, Mountain, and the Lieutenant-Governors also pressed unsuccessfully for another diocese in Upper Canada. This refusal to multiply bishoprics reveals other Imperial calculations. Building up effective ecclesiastical structures was costly everywhere. Parliament was prepared to see grants to colonies used for church building and episcopal salaries, and even occasionally contributed specifically for these purposes. In 1804 £3,040 or 42 per cent of the Imperial grant to Nova Scotia went to support the religious establishment.[3] Further metropolitan assistance came from the Society for the Propagation of the Gospel. But these were seen as temporary resorts. Although Imperial grants might create a useful dependence on Britain, far more was anticipated from the growth of self-supporting religious hierarchies, developing their own endowments with colonial Assemblies' support, securing assistance from local congregations, and training local candidates as clergymen. Religious establishments would sustain Empire most effectively if fully integrated into colonial society.

When the ecclesiastical establishments of British North America were revised in the 1780s, government intention was therefore to increase substantially the Crown or public land provided in every parish to support Anglican ministers. The acreage for an adequate endowment was highly contentious, but the Canada Act (1791) laid down conditions for the amount to be set aside as 'clergy reserves'. Land values were expected to rise as the colonies developed, making possible the reduction of grants from civil authorities while assisting the maintenance and expansion of the churches. Bishops were encouraged to develop church schools and higher-level colleges, thus cultivating a committed Anglican population, an educated élite, and an adequate clergy.

Additional features were designed to make the settlements more acceptable to local opinion. Colonial bishops' jurisdiction was everywhere confined to a narrow range of ecclesiastical affairs. Although this still left many points over which civil and religious authorities could clash—for instance, the administration of church lands, or marriage and burial licences—the church's power to intrude on colonists' day-to-day lives was minimized. Imperial rejection of pleas for the early introduction of a full church hierarchy, with its deans, archdeacons, and cathedrals, tended

---

[3] Judith Fingard, *The Anglican Design in Loyalist Nova Scotia, 1783–1816* (London, 1972), p. 212, n. 47.

in the same direction. Such appendages could be left to develop as local wishes and capacity allowed.

In principal, therefore, new or revived colonial churches, increasingly under the leadership of colonial bishops, were acknowledged as indispensable adjuncts to the civil authorities. Where possible the Anglican church, when necessary its closest equivalent, was relied on to underpin the Imperial connection, to provide moral leadership, social cohesion, and education on a scale suited to the colony in question. This pattern of church–state relations, framed for British North America between 1784 and 1793, was applied and adapted throughout the colonial Empire until the 1830s.

Following the Jamaica disturbances in 1796 clerical salaries were raised to elicit greater effort; and after the Demerara rebellion (1823), bishoprics were set up in Jamaica and Barbados, not least, it was claimed, to strengthen the new policy of ameliorating the position of slaves by providing more churches and education. In India, with renewal in 1813 of the East India Company's charter, the first Anglican diocese was established in 1814 based at Calcutta, with a geographical remit later extended to New South Wales. Officials expected the new bishop and his three archdeacons, supported from state funds, to organize more systematic ecclesiastical and educational provision for British expatriates, and to supervise or discipline the growing number of Anglican missionaries and their converts. The disciplining of Dissenters where necessary would be left to the Company or other colonial authority. These arrangements reflected more a concession to public opinion by the Imperial government and East India Company than a feeling either that the supply of Company chaplains was insufficient, or that the Anglican church should become a missionary church directed towards Indians themselves.

Where populations were much smaller than Canada's, resources to support Anglican expansion more limited, and Governors' powers far greater, Imperial governments remained content with only minimal provision. The First Fleet sailed for New South Wales in 1788 with troops and convicts but no chaplain. For a population perceived as largely irreligious and perhaps irredeemable, but none the less tightly controlled, a few chaplains were long thought sufficient. They included the redoubtable Samuel Marsden, assistant chaplain in 1794 and for many years both magistrate and sole chaplain. Colonial expansion prompted appointment of an archdeacon in 1824, and in 1825 new land regulations required at least one-seventh of each county be set aside to support Anglican churches and schools. Administered by a new Church and Schools Corporation, this had all the appearance of yet another 'Anglican design'. At the Cape of Good Hope after 1805 the colonial authorities contented themselves with encouraging revival of the Dutch Reformed Church by recruiting Scottish Presbyterian ministers. In the 1830s new colonial dioceses were contemplated for Sydney and Cape Town, but by then ideas about the ties of imperial church and colonial state were starting to change.

Applied unevenly, imperial principle also encountered resistance. The endowment of Protestant clergy with reserved lands, and preference for the Church of England, reflected desires to counterbalance the well-endowed Roman Catholic hierarchy of Quebec and to stall the progress of dissent and irreligion. Like his contemporaries in Britain, Bishop Mountain deplored the 'itinerant and mendicant Methodists . . . whose preaching is calculated only to perplex the understanding, & corrupt the morals & relax the nerves of industry, & disolve [*sic*] the bonds of society'.[4] Yet in every colony the mushrooming reality of denominational diversity was inescapable. Many Loyalists migrating to Nova Scotia were Presbyterians or Dissenters, as were emigrants from Britain to the Canadian provinces; the religious affiliations of transportees to the Australian colonies were equally varied, and included numerous Roman Catholics.

Colonial churchmen, keen to exploit endowments, staff parishes, and extend Anglican education, often felt themselves an unreasonably hampered minority. The problem of finding able and energetic clergy developed early and plagued colonial churches throughout the century, partly because salaries and career prospects offered limited incentives. Administrative incompetence or corruption often resulted in the loss of reserved land, and the slow pace of development meant that reserves rarely yielded the anticipated income.

In these circumstances, as an important arm of the 'establishment', Anglican leaders naturally defended their rights in the political arena. Mountain and John Strachan, Archdeacon of York (Toronto), differed only in degree from the milder Inglis or Charles Stewart, Mountain's successor in Quebec. All were members of the Legislative Councils, working to enhance their church's position. They were often successful, sometimes with the overt support of sympathetic Governors. In 1813 Inglis secured an additional 37,000 acres for the Church of England to make good earlier losses. Mountain won Governor Sir James Craig's support for his educational policy. With Lieutenant-Governor Maitland's backing in 1819, Strachan had the Anglicans' interest in administering the clergy reserves for their sole advantage embodied in the Clergy Reserves Corporation. Anglican intentions to control higher education were announced in the foundations of the symbolically christened King's Colleges (Windsor, 1789; Fredericton, *c.*1825), and the university at Toronto in 1827. Outside British North America, only Cape Town's South African College escaped Anglican control.

Anglican political involvement, however, only stimulated political conflict driven by the denominationalism it was intended to marginalize. Colonial

---

[4] Gerald M. Craig, *Upper Canada: The Formative Years, 1784–1841* (Toronto, 1963), pp. 165–66.

Governors often failed to combine their backing of high Anglican views with political astuteness, just as victorious or defensive clerics failed to demonstrate religious magnanimity. Presbyterians, also members of an established church (the Church of Scotland, since 1707), justifiably insisted on their equal claim to endowment. Dissenters (or Nonconformists) resented the colonial replication of Britain's own Anglican privilege and discrimination.

The legitimacy of such grievances and the value of protest were easily increased. In their weary attempts to lower the political temperature, or from a pragmatic belief that, when Anglican pretensions outstripped Anglican resources, even Nonconformist religion was better then none, or by genuine gestures of even-handedness, colonial officials often supported Anglicanism's rivals. As Methodist preachers were allowed to conduct marriages by licence, as non-Anglican clergy were appointed magistrates, or received allowances of land or stipends, so a wider sense of entitlement and conviction of right grew. Wherever non-Anglicans were strong, particularly in the British North American Assemblies, movements for political and ecclesiastical reform interwined. Anglican resistance to such developments was weakened by divisions in the church's own ranks, between senior and junior clergy, or over financial, doctrinal, and liturgical issues. Exaggerated claims of Anglican achievement and denigration of other denominations, such as Strachan indulged in when visiting England in 1825, only worsened matters.

An articulate, vigorously supported colonial alternative to the Anglican linking of Imperial church and state was thus progressively elaborated, first in British North America then elsewhere. After 1815 those who wished either to preserve the *status quo* or to strengthen the Church of England's ties with the state declined in numbers or conviction. As in the 1780s and 1790s, however, so in the 1820s and 1830s readjustment of colonial arrangements owed much to parallel changes inside Britain. This is no place to review British social and political developments, including repeal of the Test and Corporation Acts and Catholic Emancipation in 1828–29, which heralded greater equality of civil rights, or the decade of ecclesiastical reform which changed the relative status of the Anglican church as an institution. Nevertheless, their consequences for the colonies as for Britain were profound. They represented metropolitan confirmation of a message most colonists already accepted, namely, the incompatibility of Anglican dominance with continued colonial order and good government; and they recognized the need to place rivals on a more equal footing with Anglicans. With Anglican privilege everywhere coming to seem less a source of strength than an incentive to disaffection, the route to colonial reform was opened.

Although in 1790 the Anglican church was regarded as a defence for Britain's colonial authority, paradoxically the close ties between church and state meant that it was neither a missionary church nor one sympathetic to missionary enterprise. Since their foundation, the Society for the Promotion of Christian Knowledge (SPCK: 1698) and the Society for the Propagation of the Gospel (1701) had financed small numbers of colonial clergy, garrison chaplains, and school-masters for the Britons overseas. Missionary work with indigenous peoples, however, was incidental, the product of occasional personal initiatives, for ex-ample, by 'pious chaplains' such as David Brown or Daniel Corrie in India. Such efforts never matched those of the Moravians, or Methodist activity in the Caribbean from 1786, and were overshadowed by the enterprise of voluntary lay missionary societies, newly established in the 1790s as part of a broader evangelical and social reform movement.[5]

In that decade there appeared the Baptist Missionary Society (BMS: 1792); the London Missionary Society (LMS: 1795, originally non-denominational but eventually Congregational); and the Anglican Church Missionary Society (CMS: 1799). Methodists extended their operations, and in Scotland the Glasgow and Edinburgh Societies were both formed in 1796. Lay and Nonconformist activity was especially remarkable. Henry Thornton observed of the LMS in 1795, 'what a striking thing it is that a Bishop of London [Beilby Porteous] is hardly able ... to scrape a few hundred Pounds together for the Missionary Plans in his hands among all the people of the Church Establishment & that £10,000 shd be raised in such a few days by the Irregulars who are also so much poorer a Class of People than the others'.[6]

The institutional Anglican church was slower to act: missionaries smacked too much of 'Methodism' or the embarrassing and dangerous excesses of religious 'enthusiasm', and they were disliked for their ignorance or low social standing. There were no evangelical bishops to support the Church Missionary Society until Henry Ryder became a vice-president in 1815, and the Revd Sydney Smith spoke for many in 1808 when mocking missionary pretensions in the *Edinburgh Review*: 'The wise and rational part of the Christian ministry find they have enough to do at home ... But if a tinker is a devout man, he infallibly sets off for the East.'[7] Other powerful arguments against missions to non-Europeans included the practical or theological inappropriateness and impossibility of the task itself, and the threat to Imperial security from colonial subjects provoked by proselytization.

By the 1830s, however, the missions had not only impressively extended Britain's global presence, but had won widespread public acceptance and even official

---

[5] Boyd Hilton, *The Age of Atonement: The Influence of Evangelicalism on Social and Economic Thought, 1795–1865* (Oxford, 1988).

[6] Elizabeth Elbourne, 'The Foundation of the Church Missionary Society: The Anglican Missionary Impulse', in John Walsh and others, eds., *The Church of England, c.1689–c.1833* (Oxford, 1993), p. 247.

[7] *The Works of the Reverend Sydney Smith* (London, 1839), pp. 136–37.

support. The Church Missionary Society's early shortage of volunteers, causing them to rely on German Lutherans, had given way to steady recruiting of men less likely to attract scorn. Its income averaged £58,655 per annum, and came from a wide social and geographical area. Overseas, the London Missionary Society was well established in the western Pacific and South Africa, the CMS in Sierra Leone and India, the Baptists in Bengal and the West Indian colonies. Methodist and Presbyterian missions were also similarly scattered and poised for a new phase of expansion.

There were no simple connections between this religious expansion and a specifically British influence and Empire overseas. Although critical of non-Christian cultures, missionary thinking was profoundly egalitarian: 'race' was immaterial, humans everywhere corrupt yet equally open to conversion and redemption. Britain's missions led a wider transatlantic and European under-taking, making common cause with Danes, Swedes, Germans, and Americans, with the Moravian and Basel societies and the American Board of Commissioners for Foreign Missions.[8] These powerful ecumenical and international undercur-rents were reinforced by the societies' determination to avoid involvement with trade, government, and politics. The missions began by explicitly distancing themselves from expanding colonial rule, wary of its chauvinism, secular author-ity, and often flawed commercial ambitions. Throughout the century, however, such detachment was easier for theorists or organizers to assert than it was for missionaries overseas to apply.

Private trade was persistently problematic. Given Indian precedents, mission organizers reasonably feared its potential for exciting conflict. Yet many mission-aries felt their own survival, quite apart from the future of their families and their work, necessitated trade. Marsden struggled vainly to persuade Church Mission-ary Society employees in New Zealand to take communal organization and subsistence agriculture seriously.[9] In the Cape Colony Dr John Philip felt pushed into trade by cuts in the London Missionary Society's budget and the need to preserve his converts' independence of settler society. Not only in the isolation of mission stations were favours from local traders or ships' captains valuable. In Britain, commercial money always played its part in subscriptions to missionary societies. The private fortunes of the evangelical Clapham Sect and the establish-ment of the Sierra Leone Company for trading purposes rescued the evangelicals' first West African settlement, the 'Province of Freedom', in 1790–92. In the 1880s and 1890s involvement in trade and the permissible extent of compromise with

[8] Roger H. Martin, *Evangelicals United: Ecumenical Stirrings in Pre-Victorian Britain, 1795–1830* (London, 1983).

[9] *The Letters and Journals of Samuel Marsden, 1765–1838*, ed. John Rawson Elder (Dunedin, 1932), pp. 232–36, 410–12.

commerce were no less problematical. Disputes over private commerce, especially in alcohol, intensified clashes between white CMS missionaries and Sierra Leonean agents on the River Niger, and the Society itself relied heavily on the goodwill of the Royal Niger Company, Britain's administrative proxy north of the river delta.[10]

Involvement with Imperial government was equally difficult to avoid. Areas already under British rule inevitably attracted missionary attention. Observing British India in 1814, the East India Company's chaplain Thomas Thomason felt that 'we have annihilated the political importance of the natives, stripped them of their power, and laid them prostrate, without giving them any thing in return'. He therefore supported missionaries and an Anglican ecclesiastical establishment to improve the consequences of British rule. His fellow chaplain, Claudius Buchanan, was sure that such a religious establishment needed no continuing government support, but was no less keen to justify it as attaching colonial subjects to their government.[11] All missionaries required authorization to preach and conduct services. Although being licensed 'By permission of His Excellency the Governor' left most Anglicans unperturbed in the absence of a bishop at Cape Town, Nonconformist missionaries always found it irksome. Everywhere the pressure to conform to official requirements was very real, the alternative being perhaps expulsion or imprisonment. John Smith died in 1823, unjustly imprisoned in Demerara for his work with the slaves.

If missionaries hankered after freedom but found the ties of British expansion inescapable, British authorities wanted to restrain missions but came to accept the value of allowing them greater scope. Opposition, especially to Nonconformist missionaries, was strongest regarding India, and religious neutrality or the restraint of evangelical enthusiasm were at first widely supported. Charles James Fox felt in 1793 that 'all systems of proselytisation [are] wrong in themselves, and . . . productive, in most cases, of abuse and political mischief'; Sir George Barlow, witnessing the disturbances among native soldiers at Vellore in 1806, was convinced that 'preaching Methodists and wild visionaries disturbing the religious ceremonies of the Natives will alienate the affections of our Native troops'.[12] Nevertheless, although excluded from certain areas—Surat or Mysore—their position slowly improved. Local resistance to their work taught

---

[10] Christopher Fyfe, *A History of Sierra Leone* (London, 1962); E. A. Ayandele, 'The Relations between the Church Missionary Society and the Royal Niger Company, 1886–1900', *Journal of the Historical Society of Nigeria*, IV (1968), pp. 397–419.

[11] Rev. J. Sargent, *The Life of the Rev. T. T. M.A.* (London, 1833), p. 223; Claudius Buchanan, *Colonial Ecclesiastical Establishment: Being a Brief View of the State of the Colonies of Great Britain, and of her Asiatic Empire, in Respect to Religious Instruction,* 2nd edn. (London, 1813), pp. 37–39, 100–24.

[12] P. S. E. Carson, 'Soldiers of Christ: Evangelicals and India, 1784–1833', unpublished Ph.D. thesis, London, 1988, pp. 35, 75.

missionaries to remain on good terms with officials if possible. While administrators such as Thomas Munro or Stephen Lushington continued hostile, others
like Governor Nepean (Bombay, 1812–19) and Travancore's Residents were often
sympathetic.[13] Missionaries impressed colonial observers by their perseverance,
evident good intentions, translation and educational work, and their scholarship.
Support in Britain grew still faster. The rising output of missionary publications,
the work of the British and Foreign Bible Society, and local missionary associations all helped improve the missions' image, and contributed to the government's
endorsement of their work in the 1813 and 1833 revisions of the East India
Company's charter.

Official fears of missions declined as their common interest in the transformation of colonial society became evident. William Bentinck (Governor-General in
India, 1828–35), for example, disliked the narrow intolerance of extreme missionary lobbyists, but shared the moderate evangelicals' real commitment to missionary enterprise. As he reminded Charles Grant in 1833, 'it is Christianity, the whole
Christian Church, whose cause in this heathen country we are to cherish'.[14] In
India this shared ground was symbolized in two ways. Episcopal support for
missionary work steadily grew, and in Daniel Wilson (Bishop of Calcutta,
1832–58) the Church Missionary Society had an ardent supporter. Approaches to
education also converged, in the support for English-language education from
both T. B. Macaulay and the Scottish missionary Alexander Duff.

Missionary activity outside India also helped change perceptions of their role.
At Freetown, a community largely composed of liberated slaves from many
different parts of West Africa, the Church Missionary Society and Wesleyans
became indispensable. The education, religion, and common language they provided, together with their political authority as magistrates or village superintend-
ents, did much to make the colony governable.[15] The obstruction missionaries
met from local whites in the colonies of the Caribbean or the Cape, and their
persecution by planters during the Demerara and Jamaica rebellions of 1823 and
1831, greatly increased metropolitan respect and sympathy.

This convergence of missionary opinion with that of officials and a wider public
focused on the increasingly explicit association of Christianity, commerce, and
civilization. The Baptist William Carey's famous pamphlet of 1792 drew attention
to British mercantile expansion as pointing the way to the fulfilment of Isaiah's
prophecies, 'that *navigation*, especially that which is *commercial*, shall be one great

[13] Ibid., chap. 8.
[14] John Rosselli, *Lord William Bentinck: The Making of a Liberal Imperialist, 1774–1839* (London,
1974), p. 213.
[15] See chap. by T. C. McCaskie.

mean of carrying on the work of God'.[16] Twenty years later, the upheavals of the Anglo-French wars and the disruption of Catholic nations so contrasted with Britain's 'state of comparative rest and growing prosperity' and continued missionary expansion, that the London Missionary Society's founder asserted, 'This land seems peculiarly destined to be the instrument ... to carry his salvation into the ends of the earth'.[17] Wealth, stability, and expansion indicated a divinely ordained, providential role for Britain. This evangelical interpretation married neatly with the growing confidence and assertiveness of Britain's governing classes contemplating the extension of British rule in India and her European pre-eminence. By 1830 missions both claimed and were accorded a place in a refurbished British national identity, as vital contributors to that 'Protestant worldview which allowed so many Britons to see themselves as a distinct and chosen people'.[18]

Leading politicians became more tolerant of denominationalism as awareness grew that Imperial preference for Anglicanism might be politically imprudent, but they remained convinced that the encouragement of religion was essential to society's well-being. Toleration did not generally mean indifference. Thus, Whig reforms in the 1830s reflected the importance still attached to a national church, and were intended to improve the Church of England's ability to compete with Nonconformity. So it was in the colonies. Episcopal appointments and the creation of sees remained Imperial prerogatives; although parliamentary grants to North American clergy were phased out, Imperial finance still contributed to bishops' salaries; the laws and usages of the Church of England, as interpreted ultimately by the Judicial Committee of the Privy Council and the authority of the Archbishop of Canterbury, remained intact. Just as steps towards responsible government did not signify a retreat from Empire, so a looser relationship between church and state did not weaken the view that the church helped bind the whole together.

By 1840, however, dissatisfaction with Whig measures had spread far beyond those opposed in principle to state control. Colonial bishops could not discover precisely what were the operative laws of the Church of England, and in the absence of ecclesiastical courts, had no means of enforcement. Pleas for bishoprics, to embrace new British annexations and lead the church's missionary activity, produced only three new sees (Madras, 1835; Bombay, 1837; Australia, 1836), all over-large and underfunded. British activities in the Pacific seemed quite

---

[16] William Carey, *An Enquiry into the Obligations of Christians, to Use Means for the Conversion of the Heathens* (Leicester, 1792), p. 68.

[17] Thomas Haweis, *A View of the Present State of Evangelical Religion Throughout the World: With a View to Promote Missionary Exertions* (London, 1812), esp. pp. 13, 24.

[18] Linda Colley, *Britons: Forging the Nation, 1707–1837* (London, 1992), p. 368.

uncontrolled by regular political or ecclesiastical influences. Colonial interdenominational conflicts constantly reminded the Anglican church of its opponents'
strength. New South Wales's Church and Schools Corporation was abolished after
only eight years; in the Canadas, battles for control of the clergy reserves continued. Ill-served by government, insecure in colonial Assemblies, keen to defend
their holdings and combat Nonconformity, churchmen therefore took matters
into their own hands.

Every church party believed expansion essential, for colonial church growth and
Anglican missions to the wider non-European world were now seen as essential
and inseparable. Anthony Grant, Oxford's Bampton Lecturer in 1843, plainly
captured this remarkable change in ecclesiastical outlook. Following 'the wonderful expansion of the Empire of Great Britain, whereby, through her colonies, she is
brought into contact with almost the entire heathen world...it is no longer a
question whether the heathen shall be left to themselves...the Church [must]
extend herself with the extension of our Empire, even to prevent our country from
becoming a curse to the pagan world, even, also, to save our countrymen from
lapsing into a state of apostate infidelity, more fatal than pagan darkness'.[19] The
Anglican church must act, or others less qualified would do so.

So church finally moved ahead of state, sponsoring the Bishops in Foreign
Countries Act (1841), the 'Jerusalem Act', two years before the Foreign Jurisdiction
Act. More important, the bishops, following the Bishop of London's initiative, and
with considerable High Church support, established a Colonial Bishoprics Fund.
This movement contributed almost immediately to George Selwyn's consecration
as Bishop to the newest colony, New Zealand, and in the 1840s to the foundation of
a further fourteen dioceses. In 1848 St Augustine's College, Canterbury, was
established to train colonial clergy.

Selwyn's experience confirmed Grant's exposition. Before 1850 he was seriously
overstretched, torn between Maori or settler and developing his Melanesian
mission, and worried about Roman Catholic and Nonconformist rivals. Like his
friends W. E. Gladstone and Samuel Wilberforce (William Wilberforce's son),
Selwyn felt the answer lay in consecrating more 'missionary bishops' like himself.
Reflecting the contemporary revival of High Churchmanship, this attitude was
also inspired by ideas about the early church and contemporary experience of
westward advance in America. Instead of marking the final stage of church
formation in a settled society, bishops should be leaders consecrated to build up
the church, often from nothing. They would make possible the Church of England's survival in existing colonial societies and its entrenchment in new regions.

---

[19] *The Past and Prospective Extension of the Gospel by Missions to the Heathen*, 2nd edn. (London,
1845), pp. xi, xvi.

This episcopal role had important consequences for the relationship of the Anglican church and Empire. As Grant's lectures suggested, the church's role should be less to support state authority than to scrutinize its exercise of power and moderate the broader processes of expansion. Furthermore, if the church was to be built from scratch, compete with rivals, and be planted beyond colonial frontiers, it would need unrestricted freedom to acquire property, establish its hierarchy and deploy its priests, regulate its liturgy, and discipline members. The existing difficulties of the colonial churches and the new roles being devised for them thus pointed towards episcopal independence, ecclesiastical self-government, and the divorce of church and state.

Powerful interests everywhere resisted such conclusions—among them, colonists eager to preserve ties with Britain, Imperial politicians protective of their patronage, evangelicals seeing a tractarian or ritualist plot to corner the colonial field, and Anglican leaders fearing colonial churches might break with the Church of England. However, after Gladstone took up the issue at the Colonial Office in 1845–46 the reformers gradually gained ground. Successive attempts were made to legislate at Westminster. The idea of ecclesiastical independence as a natural corollary of colonial self-government won growing support in the colonies themselves. Colonial governments everywhere withdrew from religious involvement, not only with Anglicans but all denominations. Bishop Selwyn, for example, found his salary halved in 1855 when the reformed New Zealand Parliament refused to shoulder the Imperial government's share. Finally, in 1856–57 local legislation from Victoria and Canada, effecting for the first time separation of church and state, received the royal assent in London.[20]

Colonial church independence, by reducing political contention surrounding colonial Anglican activity, almost certainly strengthened colonial Anglican churches while allowing important ties with England to persist. The Church in South Africa, for instance, remained heavily reliant on non-governmental funds from England. Everywhere clerical and episcopal appointees continued to come from Britain. Moreover, new pan-Imperial arrangements soon emerged. Colonial bishops attended the first of many Lambeth Conferences in 1867, confirming that their churches would voluntarily retain ties with Canterbury. They continued to acknowledge the spiritual authority of the Archbishops of Canterbury, and developed the habit of frequent consultation and co-operation which thereafter lay at the heart of the Anglican communion.

A similar flexibility characterized other denominations, which also retained powerful links with the metropole, their absence of pretensions to establishment

---

[20] E. D. Daw, *Church and State in the Empire: The Evolution of Imperial Policy, 1846–1856* (Canberra, 1977).

notwithstanding. Thus, religious sentiment and ecclesiastical allegiances contributed to the late-nineteenth-century movement for closer Imperial unity, but were able at the same time to accommodate the growth of colonial particularisms. There were always those, in the Anglican case bishops of the American Protestant Episcopal Church and their British friends at the Lambeth Conferences of 1897 and 1908, ready to remind forgetful colleagues of the distinctions between church and Empire.

Increasingly, mid-Victorian missionaries also operated far outside the formal Empire. A surge of missionary activity occurred between c.1836 and 1844, and another wave at the end of the 1850s. Like that of the 1790s, these movements profited from growing popular awareness of the wider world, the knowledge and sense of opportunity provided by British expansion, and periodic religious revivals. Supporters showed the same evangelical preoccupations: a powerful sense of obligation linked to personal experience of conversion; hostility to 'idolatry' (which for Protestants embraced Roman Catholicism as well as, say, animism or Hinduism); desire to save the 'heathen' from eternal punishment; and optimistic belief in a divinely ordained plan assured of success. Mission support was spurred on by the growth of publications, ranging from outstanding popular books, including those by John Williams and Robert Moffat, to periodicals like the Church Missionary Society's *Intelligencer*.[21]

Specific events, however, prompted the timing and direction of particular advances. In West Africa, a mounting exodus of converts from Sierra Leone back to their homelands interacted with requests from African rulers for missions to be stationed in their country. Consequently, the Church Missionary Society and Methodists both settled in Abeokuta (south-west Nigeria). The idea that missionary activity offered recompense for earlier wrongs done to Africans was a powerful element in the vision linking Christianity and legitimate trade which underpinned the Niger Expedition (1841–42). Following emancipation, West Indian converts and missionaries pressed for expansion into West Africa, with the result that what became the United Presbyterian Church mission was established at Calabar in 1846, and the Baptists settled in Fernando Po in 1843.

The expectation that commerce, 'civilization', and Christianity would advance together also manifested itself in the missions' enthusiastic welcome for the outcome of the Anglo-Chinese War (1839–42). The opening of 'treaty ports' allowed missions for the first time to operate in China. Further conflict in 1857–58 and the Treaty of Peking (1860), again extending missionary privileges, coincided with

---

[21] *A Narrative of Missionary Enterprises in the South Sea Islands* (London, 1837); *Missionary Labours and Scenes in Southern Africa* (London, 1842).

other events to heighten public enthusiasm for more determined missionary efforts. The recent rebellion in India, religious revivals in Britain during 1859, David Livingstone's Central African experiences, recounted during his visit to Britain in 1857–58, and his advocacy of Christianity linked to true commerce as the answer to Africa's continuing troubles, had a startling impact.

Missionary work was often planned as long-term, focusing on schools and the introduction of English and vernacular literacy, as essential foundations of Bible study, religious understanding, and cultural change. Schools ranged from the grand Scottish establishments such as Wilson's High School and College at Bombay, or James Stewart's Lovedale in the eastern Cape, to the tiniest of gatherings in missionary homes. 'Without such schools, how can the people learn to read? and if they cannot read of what use will it be to send Bibles and tracts among them? We therefore think that it is the duty of the missionaries, in subordination to the great work of preaching to establish such schools wherever they can be set up', wrote William MacFarlane from Darjeeling in 1871.[22] Emphases shifted, over time and between different societies, as to the balance of preaching and teaching, and the level at which education could be best provided. However, elementary vernacular and higher English-language instruction were often both available if resources permitted.

Before 1870 this dominant approach rested on the theological proposition that evidence of conversion would include the cultural transformation of indigenous society; although only God knew its timing, this outcome would herald the millennium of Christ's rule on earth. Theological belief was reinforced by practical requirements in the field. Even the earliest missionaries found reliance on indigenous assistance shading quickly into belief that native agents offered the best means of propagating the Gospel. Thus, Bishop Grant, appointed to the new diocese of Victoria in 1849, founded a college in Hong Kong; like his predecessors in Auckland, Freetown, and Calcutta, he hoped to attract and foster local élites to pass on the Christian message.

Ideas about mission strategy evolved rapidly in the 1840s as organizers such as Henry Venn, the new Church Missionary Society Secretary, and his contemporary Rufus Anderson at the American Board in Boston looked ahead to what would succeed the missionaries. Against a background of limited progress in most fields, missionary mortality, and painfully inadequate home funds, the rapid creation of indigenous churches made much sense. Between 1848 and 1851 Venn's ideas on promoting as quickly as possible self-governing, self-supporting, self-propagating native churches were largely crystallized. By 1850 they seemed a natural

---

[22] Cindy L. Perry, 'The History of the Expansion of Protestant Christianity among the Nepali Diaspora', unpublished Ph.D. thesis, Edinburgh, 1994, p. 73.

development when, from Calcutta to Calabar, native agents were already being widely used.

From 1852, however, Venn went further, seeking to have native bishops head the new churches, move the missionaries on to fresh openings, and avoid the subordination of indigenous congregations either to missionaries or to white colonial and missionary bishops.[23] The consecration for the Church Missionary Society in 1864 of the Yoruba freed slave, Samuel Crowther, as Bishop of the Niger was a notable step in this direction. Shortly before, the same drive to open up Africa had also been differently expressed in the formation of the Universities' Mission to Central Africa (UMCA), a direct response to Livingstone's call, and in the departure in 1861 of its Scottish bishop, Charles Mackenzie, for the Zambezi.

Despite their common Anglicanism, these two initiatives represented a choice faced by all denominations between fundamentally different approaches to missionary expansion. In Crowther's case, the object was to complete the process of building the mission and the church, by appointing a local head rooted in local society—even if Crowther was temporarily regarded as the Society's appointee and part subject to its control from London. Mackenzie, however, once endorsed by the Universities Mission, was supplied with funds and, as a bishop, left to his own devices. Far from inheriting a going concern, Mackenzie was a local head brought in from outside to found the local church. Both strategies, however, embodied the mid-century's broad confidence in the progress of Christianity and westernization, dissociation of churches from political power, transfer of religious authority away from Britain, and its extension of the faith far beyond the confines of either formal Empire or that 'Greater Britain' which was capturing imaginations by the late 1860s.

Missions, nevertheless, still often supported not only British commerce and culture but direct political control or intervention. They interpreted India's 1857 rebellion as a sign that the government should abandon neutrality and instead vigorously support Christianization. Echoing Dr John Philip some fifty years before, the Revd John Mackenzie in 1878 was convinced: 'The only real question is—will the Europeans in South Africa advance northward by haphazard blindfold, and with outrage and blood . . . or will [the home government] master the problem, no longer regard this movement as an evil, but arrange for it and control it?'[24] In Uganda, Britain's takeover in 1894–95 was welcomed by missions for the security it brought, and after the Boxer Rising in China most missions relied on government to obtain indemnity for the damages they had suffered.

---

[23] C. Peter Williams, *The Ideal of the Self-Governing Church: A Study in Victorian Missionary Strategy* (Leiden, 1990), chap. 1.

[24] A. J. Dachs, 'Missionary Imperialism in Bechuanaland, 1813–1896', unpublished Ph.D. thesis, Cambridge, 1968, p. 209.

Christians frequently viewed the opportunities offered by British expansion as providentially designed to support world-wide conversion. The tendency for missions and government to support—even exploit—each other's concern for matters like prestige and security almost certainly grew after 1870, especially in the setting of Africa's partition. Some officials, not necessarily mission supporters, none the less admired many consequences of their work and tried to implant what they regarded as Christian values. Harry Johnston in 1890 enthused over the fact that missions 'strengthen our hold over the country, they spread the use of the English language, they induct the natives into the best kind of civilization and in fact each mission station is an essay in colonization'.[25] In late-century conditions of international competition, rivalries with Islam and Roman Catholicism, and indigenous resistance, some missionaries were equally effusive, seduced by the prospect of conversions following at last from Imperial use of force. Contemplating Britain's campaign against Asante in 1895, one Wesleyan felt: 'Although not necessarily avowed Christian men in every instance, yet the officers of the two services serving under Her Majesty's flag represent Justice and Humanity', and was convinced that 'the British Army and Navy are to-day used by God for the accomplishment of His purposes'.[26]

Similar tendencies to exalt British authority also existed within the missions after 1875. Missionaries uneasy about Venn's policy for local churches were numerous by 1890, and received much more support from headquarters. A watershed was reached when disputes within the Niger Mission provoked Bishop Crowther's resignation in 1892. Similar clashes happened in other missions, likewise strongly affected by contemporary changes in British evangelicalism. Influenced by American revivalist thinking about conversion and its consequences, missionaries found indigenous converts' lifestyles and existing mission structures seriously wanting. Consequently the promotion of indigenous Christians was increasingly restricted. Even in Uganda, where a thriving, financially strong Christian community was supported by the Anglican Bishop, Alfred Tucker, the Church Missionary Society sided with conservative missionaries and refused a new constitution for the church. It hoped instead that 'the English-speaking race may have the honour of leading the way in a policy of Christian Imperialism'.[27]

It is often argued that the missionary movement and expansion of Britain's Christian denominations represented distinct forms of cultural and institutional 'imperialism'. Despite small numbers of converts, their presence and teaching

---

[25] Roland Oliver, *Sir Harry Johnston and the Scramble for Africa* (London, 1957), p. 182.

[26] Dennis Kemp, *Nine Years at the Gold Coast* (London, 1898), pp. 232–34.

[27] Williams, *Ideal of the Self-Governing Church*, p. 247; John Wolffe, *God and Greater Britain: Religion and National Life in Britain and Ireland, 1843–1945* (London, 1994), pp. 213–25.

undermined customs and self-confidence, eroded respect for traditional authorities, and created social and political conflict. Thus weakened, non-western
societies succumbed to the broader pressures of Western expansion; internal
collapse and significant cultural changes opened the way to direct colonial rule,
with continued missionary control of education and the churches. In reality,
however, the relation of religion and Empire was rarely so clear-cut.[28]

Missionary work was always vitally dependent on local peoples. However strong
the metropolitan enthusiasm for evangelism, William Carey relied on Indian
advice for his epic translations, just as Livingstone, in combining the roles of
missionary and traveller, required African mediators. The careful negotiation of
rights of residence, the continuing need to remain acceptable, were problems all
missionaries faced. To overstep the mark, or misjudge the local setting, could be
fatal. John Williams, killed at Erromanga in 1839, Bishop Hannington in Uganda in
1885, and James Chalmers on Goaribari Island in 1902 appeared as 'martyrs' to
appalled supporters at home; but they also illustrate starkly the power of local
people to accept, condition, or reject the missionary presence. Preaching and
teaching met universally selective responses, being regarded with varying degrees
of enthusiasm or indifference. Missions were most often popular for their secular
teaching, the trade they might attract, practical skills such as medicine, and their
influence with other Europeans or local neighbours. They were naturally opposed
by those to whom their presence seemed to threaten important local beliefs,
political authority, or social conventions.

No stark dichotomy between 'colonizer' and 'colonized' conveys either the
range of local responses to Britain's missionary presence or the extent of missionary adaptation to local cultures. All parties engaged, consciously and uncon-
sciously, in a constant process of mutual engagement and two-way translation,
even while unqualified dislike, conservatism, and incomprehension could easily be
found on all sides. The frustration and powerlessness so commonly felt among
missionaries, indicates not simply the zealot's unreality but the effective pragmatism of indigenous responses to unwanted Western cultural control or domination.
Much as missionaries, for example, berated caste divisions in India, compromise
with the reality was inescapable, as critics from Bishop Wilson onwards found to
their disappointment.[29]

The positive, liberating effect of much mission work is inescapable. Missionaries' schools, their development of literacy and use of the printing-press, their

[28] Andrew Porter, ' "Cultural Imperialism" and Protestant Missionary Enterprise, 1780–1914', *Journal
of Imperial and Commonwealth History*, XXV, 3 (1997), pp. 367–91.

[29] Duncan B. Forrester, *Caste and Christianity: Attitudes and Policies on Caste of Anglo-Saxon
Protestant Missionaries in India* (London, 1980); Geoffrey A. Oddie, *Hindu and Christian in South-
East India* (London, 1991).

encouragement of English and vernacular languages, introduced not only the accoutrements of Christianity but skills and knowledge. Evangelists could not control the use made of a Christian education, any more than they could restrict the impetus given by Christianity to the reform and revival of indigenous religions. Recipients of mission education by 1914 were everywhere among the most effective and articulate critics of Britain's presence and the mainstays of embryonic nationalist movements. Scholars now also appreciate that conversion itself never meant simply the imposition of Western 'civilization'. It often provided deeply felt religious consolations unavailable in indigenous systems of belief. While it cut some converts off from their roots, it brought converts and others degrees of security or independence, and opportunities for advancement in their own societies that were otherwise unobtainable. This followed from the fact that converts everywhere were drawn above all from the poor and disadvantaged sectors of indigenous societies.

The contribution of the churches to metropolitan understanding had similarly profound and ambivalent implications for Empire. On the one hand, Christian denunciations of extra-European societies' degradation or savagery were commonplace throughout the century. These bleak images balanced by rosy prospects, reported or conjured up in order to generate support for missions, probably helped entrench unfavourable stereotypes in the public mind. Missionary biographies, travels, and periodicals were popular reading, and often contained misperceptions masquerading as authoritative accounts. Thus, Robert Moffat wrote quite erroneously of the Tswana, 'No fragments remain of former days, as mementos to the present generation, that their ancestors ever loved, served or reverenced a being greater than man. . . . While Satan is obviously the author of the polytheism of other nations, he has employed his agency, with fatal success, in erasing every vestige of religious impression from the minds of the Bechuanas.'[30]

However, denigration was only part of the picture. The general movement of missionary thinking in the three decades before 1914 favoured a more open appreciation of other religions. Missions' sense of urgency always reflected acceptance of the fundamental similarity of human nature. As pessimism about non-western abilities grew apace with acceptance of racial hierarchy or the evolutionary obliteration of ethnic groups, missionary views often offered an important counterpoise. Even the most popular missionary literature, through concern with grace, conversion, and redemption, kept alive prospects of change and improvement as well as notions of equality. Moreover, there were always those who detested the deceits and misrepresentation of publicity. In New Guinea, James Chalmers shrank from 'the begging friar business and the telling of excited pointed

---

[30] Moffat, *Missionary Labours*, pp. 243–44.

tales', feeling it 'a pity to overstate facts, to make "striking" missionary speeches. I know a little of the tendency to make a great deal of a little, but I also know its evil effects.'[31] Careful investigation of indigenous societies was the only way forward.

Missionaries often showed genuine curiosity, a scholarly bent, and desire to grasp the reality of non-western societies. The search for aspects of indigenous belief offering openings for the Christian message could be transformed into knowledgeable, sympathetic approaches to indigenous culture; missionaries' constant wrestling with problems of translation and exposition produced cumulative, sometimes dramatic, shifts in perspective. Questions about the Flood by Bishop Colenso's Zulu assistant, William Ngidi, interacted with wider debates about biblical criticism in 1860–61; and Colenso's consequent admission, 'my labours in *translation* have compelled me to . . . take a totally different view of [the Hebrew scriptures] from what I once did', was the prelude to an Empire-wide controversy.[32] For reasons still unclear, some missions, like the Universities Mission to Central Africa, and individuals, such as Chalmers, were more responsive than others to indigenous beliefs. This was most thoroughly expressed in the doctrine of 'fulfilment' as developed by J. N. Farquhar in India, relating Christianity to the realization of fundamental aspirations and potential in Hinduism.[33] By 1914 missions were trying hard to include in their volunteers' training systematic introductions to extra-European societies.

Missionary scholarship was by no means only theologically directed, often flourishing despite missionaries' own limited education. Residence, prolonged observation, knowledge of vernaculars, and close contacts gave missionary observations depths unmatched by early armchair ethnologists and most travellers. Successive London Missionary Society and Church of Scotland missionaries in China and India produced distinguished literary, historical, and theological works; the anthropologists A. C. Haddon and J. G. Frazer were significantly indebted to evangelists such as Chalmers, and John Roscoe in Uganda.[34] Evangelical dynamism at the end of the nineteenth century, as of the eighteenth, continued to influence external perceptions of British expansion and Empire, to extend British knowledge, and shape British understanding of the outside world.

The many-sided nature of that influence is often insufficiently recognized. Knowledge may, of course, assist colonial control, and theologies of 'fulfilment'

[31] J. M. Hitchen, 'Formation of the Nineteenth-Century Missionary Worldview: The Case of James Chalmers', unpublished Ph.D. thesis, Aberdeen, 1984, pp. 56, 61–62.

[32] Jeff Guy, *The Heretic: A Study of the Life of John William Colenso, 1814–1883* (Johannesburg, 1983), chap. 7, pp. 90–91, 105.

[33] Eric J. Sharpe, *Not to Destroy but to Fulfil: The Contribution of J. N. Farquhar to Protestant Missionary Thought in India before 1914* (Uppsala, 1965).

[34] A. F. Walls, 'The Nineteenth-Century Missionary as Scholar', in *Misjonskall og Forskerglede: Festskrift til Professor Olav Guttorm Myklebust*, ed. Nils E. Bloch-Hoell (Oslo, 1975), pp. 209–21.

presupposed a superior revelation. However, missionaries grappling with extra-European realities were frequently hostile to Empire and westernization, or sensed their irrelevance to the missionary task. The devout but superficial optimism of Thomas Haweis, surveying Christian prospects in the Pacific in 1795, was short-lived.[35] By the late 1820s missionaries better acquainted with corrupt European activities were arguing that these should be kept at bay until Christianity had established itself, small numbers of missionaries and converts alone were insufficient to win through. Before 1840, this 'Christianity first' strategy was associated with South Africa and the Pacific, where prospects for containing British expansion still seemed realistic.

Hopes for an alliance of Christianity, legitimate commerce, and cultural expansion flourished in the mid-century, but subsequently again seemed less persuasive. Reflective observers felt the association of Christianity with other forms of expansion or authority had produced limited results—in South Africa, India, New Zealand—and had failed—in Africa and the Pacific—to check the destructiveness of unbridled competition and traffic in opium, arms, alcohol, and labour. Christianity was being discredited in the process. Missionary strategies explicitly dissociated from Western ways and significant social transformation began to take hold, especially after Dr J. Hudson Taylor founded the China Inland Mission (CIM) in 1865. He rejected permanent mission stations, missionary bureaucracy, and elaborate funding, emphasizing instead adaptation to local conditions, peripatetic evangelism, and, preferring areas remote from Europeans, reliance on divine provision and protection. By 1890 the CIM was the largest of all British missions. Other societies followed suit to tap this exploding enthusiasm among rapidly growing numbers of young, middle-class volunteers, many of them university students, many of them women. Having recruited just eighty-seven single women in its first eighty years, the Church Missionary Society took on another 230 between 1880 and 1894.

This new fashion illustrates again the independence of religious dynamics, and was profoundly subversive of British influence and control. It derived much force from resurgent pre-millennial thinking among evangelicals anxious to hasten Christ's second coming and the end of the world. Always present in missionary circles, these ideas were greatly stimulated by American enthusiasts such as Charles Finney and, after 1885, A. T. Pierson or John R. Mott, leaders of the widely influential Student Volunteer Movement. They abandoned ideas of working for world conversion through ecclesiastical institutions or broader Imperial structures, for a much more immediate goal. Their watchword, 'the evangelization of the world in this generation', left limited room for older generations of

---

[35] *The Evangelical Magazine*, July 1795, pp. 261–70.

missionaries and converts, who now seemed worldly and lethargic, lacking the dynamic commitment signalling true Christian rebirth.

This combination of radicalism, new strategies, and novel criteria for conversion was manifest, for example, in Robert Arthington's Congo initiatives. Many missionaries, both High and Low Church, were relieved to leave behind an increasingly secular and doubt-ridden British society. From Northern Nigeria G. W. Brooke wrote of his own efforts: 'I see no hope given in the Bible that wickedness in this world will be subdued by civilization or preaching of the gospel—until the Messiah the prince come. And to hasten that time is, I believe, the function of foreign missions...I therefore should be inclined to frame any missionary plans with a view to giving the simple gospel message to the greatest number possible of ignorant heathen in the shortest possible time.'[36]

The gap between intentions and consequences nevertheless affected missionaries who rejected Empire and Western ways quite as much as those who clung to them. Local confrontations provoked by Brooke on the Niger, contrary to his intentions, encouraged a strengthening of Church Missionary Society controls from London over many of its missions. Simultaneously, like all moves appearing to perpetuate missionary control, this stimulated local resentment. Many indigenous Christians pressed for greater self-government, or broke away from denominational connections to form their own independent churches. From the 1880s onwards, notably in British colonial Africa, such movements presented a substantial challenge to Western authority.

Among British missionaries, the same essentially anti-imperial spirit revived enthusiasm for interdenominational or ecumenical co-operation. Present at the birth of the modern missionary movement, this ambition survived intensified domestic religious rivalries between 1820 and 1880. In the field it was assisted wherever rivals found space to avoid each other, and as needs increased to agree distinct spheres of activity, so did consciousness that denominational conflict bred disrepute and compromised the basic faith. The consequences of this awareness can be seen before 1914. In Kenya, from 1908 to the Kikuyu Conference of 1913, local missionaries worked hard to establish the basis for a united African church which would transcend their own divisions. Presbyterians and Congregationalists brought into being the United Church of South India in 1908. The integration of British missions into a strongly international movement was also abundantly clear in the World Missionary Conferences held at New York in 1900 and Edinburgh in 1910.

[36] To the Revd A. C. D. Ryder, 14 Sept. 1886, Church Missionary Society Archives, Birmingham University Library, F/2.

Colonial developments conspired to divide British missions and governments. To colonial officials in post-partition Africa, still conscious of their vulnerability but nevertheless strengthening their legal and administrative controls, missionary activities could seem positively unhelpful. Harry Johnston's optimism was replaced by echoes of Indian official worries as governments tried to restrict missions in Islamic areas—the Sudan, Egypt, Northern Nigeria. In China the strong anti-missionary features of the Boxer Rebellion provoked official criticism of the societies and suspicions that, but for them, much blood, treasure, and influence could have been saved.[37] More generally, missions found aspects of colonial rule irksome, for example, in education where, much as they welcomed government financial aid, they resisted attempts to control the content of schooling. Sympathizing with their converts, missionaries were increasingly critical of colonial policies in matters of tax, labour, and the defence of settler interests or certain traditional authorities.

The expansion of Christianity from Britain after 1780 not only paralleled the growth of British influence and Empire, but clearly interacted with it at many points. The contribution of the religious laity, clerics, and missionaries to Britain's knowledge and understanding of other peoples was immense, ranging from sophisticated historical and linguistic scholarship to the crudest perpetuation of stereotypes in innumerable missionary panegyrics. In its global expansion evangelical Christianity reflected the relative balance of material power: its geographical reach came to match its universal creed. Britain's own society was transformed in the century before 1914, broadening its sense of national 'mission', diverting much of its charity to religious causes overseas, and developing new respect for missionary enterprise. Christian heroes were adopted, such as Bishop Patteson of Melanesia, and their achievements institutionalized at home and abroad, as at Selwyn College in Cambridge and the Gordon Memorial College in Khartoum. It is nevertheless impossible to speak in any straightforward way of 'religious', 'ecclesiastical' or 'missionary' imperialism. Such hard-and-fast categories are almost meaningless.

Much as they wanted, Imperial authorities and Anglican leaders could neither re-create the Church of England overseas nor bend it to state purposes. Colonial opinion and lack of resources enforced far-reaching adaptations to local circumstances, and reluctance to forego Anglican privilege only advanced the process of change. Growing ecclesiastical resentment of government policies at home simply reinforced demands for the colonial separation of church and state. Few denominations wished to take Anglicanism's place and none succeeded, because to most people the privatization of religion and governments' support for non-

---

[37] 'Lord Salisbury and Foreign Missions', *The Times*, 20 June 1900, p. 10b.

denominational education increasingly seemed preferable. By 1860 all denominations had accepted the necessity for local self-support and self-government.

These were lessons which missionaries and their societies gradually learnt in their turn. Experimentation and adaptation to local conditions were inevitable, in language, liturgy, and church organization. As they occurred, the extent to which a 'British' metropolitan religious culture was being exported, let alone imposed, became increasingly attenuated. At the height of the so-called 'new imperialism' of the late nineteenth century, the influence of non-British strains of Protestantism, millennial or eschatological speculation, scepticism about Western civilization, and greater attentiveness to the values of indigenous cultures combined to make British evangelicalism increasingly less nationalist and chauvinistic. Missions might build in British style, but their location, and activities inside the buildings frequently depended on indigenous wishes, freedoms normally unavailable in Britain, and North American inspiration. High Church ritualists, for example, felt freer of Low Church scrutiny, and women assumed an uncommon prominence in the organization of missionary work. This does not suggest that the religious cultures of the formal and informal empires were necessarily less Imperial for being distinct from both their British and local origins. The argument is rather that religion and Empire frequently mingled, but were as likely to undermine each other as they were to provide mutual support.

Select Bibliography

J. F. ADE AJAYI, *Christian Missions in Nigeria, 1841–1891* (London, 1965).

E. A. AYANDELE, *The Missionary Impact on Modern Nigeria, 1842–1914* (London, 1966).

ROSS BORDER, *Church and State in Australia, 1788–1872: A Constitutional Study of the Church of England in Australia* (London, 1962).

HANS CNATTINGIUS, *Bishops and Societies: A Study of Anglican Colonial and Missionary Expansion, 1698–1850* (London, 1952).

JEAN and JOHN COMAROFF, *Of Revelation and Revolution: Christianity, Colonialism, and Consciousness in South Africa,* Vol. I (Chicago, 1991).

JOHN WEBSTER GRANT, *Moon of Wintertime: Missionaries and the Indians of Canada in Encounter since 1534* (Toronto, 1984).

NEIL GUNSON, *Messengers of Grace: Evangelical Missionaries in the South Seas, 1797–1860* (Melbourne, 1978).

ADRIAN HASTINGS, *The Church in Africa, 1450–1950* (Oxford 1994).

M. A. LAIRD, *Missionaries and Education in Bengal, 1793–1837* (Oxford, 1972).

DIANE LANGMORE, *Missionary Lives: Papua, 1874–1914* (Honolulu, 1989).

JOHN S. MOIR, ed., *Church and State in Canada, 1627–1867: Basic Documents* (Toronto, 1967).

PATRICK J. O'FARRELL, *The Catholic Church and Community: An Australian History*, 3rd revised edn. (Kensington, NSW, 1992).

ROLAND OLIVER, *The Missionary Factor in East Africa*, 2nd edn. (London, 1965).

STUART PIGGIN, *Making Evangelical Missionaries, 1789–1858: The Social Background, Motives and Training of British Protestant Missionaries to India* (Abingdon, 1984).

ANDREW PORTER, 'Cambridge, Keswick and late Nineteenth-Century Attitudes to Africa', *Journal of Imperial and Commonwealth History*, V (1976), pp. 5–34.

—— '"Commerce and Christianity": The Rise and Fall of a Nineteenth-Century Missionary Slogan', *Historical Journal*, XXVIII (1985), pp. 597–621.

WILLIAM L. SACHS, *The Transformation of Anglicanism: From State Church to Global Communion* (New York, 1993).

BRIAN STANLEY, *The Bible and the Flag: Protestant Missions and British Imperialism in the Nineteenth and Twentieth Centuries* (Leicester, 1990).

ALAN M. G. STEPHENSON, *Anglicanism and the Lambeth Conferences* (London, 1978).

T. E. YATES, *Venn and Victorian Bishops Abroad: The Missionary Policies of Henry Venn and their Repercussions upon the Anglican Episcopate of the Colonial Period, 1841–1872* (Uppsala, 1978).

12

British Expansion, Empire, and Technological Change

ROBERT KUBICEK

Technological changes, whatever their origins, have often been turned to imperial purposes. The chariot and stirrup were important empire-building tools in antiquity, as were the sail and gun in the early modern period. Military innovations in weapons and organization were instrumental in expansion before 1800.[1] Thereafter, however, tools crucial to achieving economic advantage and political domination rapidly proliferated. The advent of steam and electrical power, and developments in metallurgy and chemistry provided new means for coercion and movement. Moreover, the tools underwent significant if unco-ordinated development. Soldiers used the musket (a smooth-bore, single-shot muzzle-loader with powder ignited by exposed flintlock) at the beginning of the century, the rifle (a breech-loading repeater accepting metal cartridges activated by internal hammer) at its end. Transport reduced travelling times (see Tables 12.1–6) and carried bulky cargo to distant markets. Communication devices exchanged information in days, then hours.

Nevertheless, while general trends may be clear, there are difficulties in pinpointing when a version of a tool had become sufficiently diffused and effective to institute change in behaviour and relationships. It is hard to decide, for example, when cost-effective, metal-hulled, propeller-driven, ocean-going vessels become sufficiently numerous to make a difference to the connection between technology and empire. Even more elusive are the prevailing norms and values which shaped the use of such inventions, especially since they may themselves have been altered by technology.

Contemporaries were not unaware of the new power sources suddenly available to them. Karl Marx was sufficiently sensitive to their force to be considered by some as a technological determinist. The imperial historian, J. R. Seeley, thought that steam had given the 'political organism' a 'new circulation', that electricity had

---

[1] Geoffrey Parker, *The Military Revolution, Military Innovation and the Rise of the West, 1500–1800*, 2nd edn. (Cambridge, 1990).

provided a 'new nervous system', and that the two innovations had made a 'Greater Britain' both possible and necessary. Some Victorians and Edwardians protested against the damage inflicted on the landscape by steam shovels and the harm to humans from exploding boilers, but many more took immense pride in this increased human capacity to alter environments.[2]

Twentieth-century commentators have generally assigned technological innovation a pervasive if variable function. Some regard 'all technologies' as 'extensions of our physical and nervous systems to increase power and speed'. Such an increase 'in any kind of grouping of any components whatever is itself a disruption that causes a change of organization'. For others, 'It is useless to rail against capitalism. Capitalism did not create our world; the machine did.'[3] Historians of the British Empire have argued that nineteenth-century Europeans generally, and Britons particularly, distinguished themselves from and claimed a superiority over others on the basis of their mastery of science and technology, and have stressed how mid-Victorians saw themselves as 'the titans of technology'. Late-Victorians were caught up in 'a runaway technological revolution' which fuelled a colossal arms race.[4] The most prolific writer on technology and Empire has argued that the new tools 'of the nineteenth century ... shattered traditional trade, technology, and political relationships, and in their place they laid the foundations for a new global civilization based on Western technology'.[5]

This chapter argues that various technologies, especially when combined, enhanced the state's abilities to expand and dominate. They also affected the timing of the Imperial state's expansion, and featured significantly in the dynamics of commercial and industrial capitalism. In both the formal and informal Empire, in temperate and tropical colonies, their transfer gave Imperial agents more scope for intervention. However, other peripheral groups, including indigenous resistance movements and local entrepreneurs, gained access to them as well. Technologies empowered the metropole but also, to some degree, strengthened the periphery. They may have cemented Imperial connections, but they could

---

[2] G. A. Cohen, *Karl Marx's Theory of History* (Oxford, 1978), pp. 145–46; J. R. Seeley, *The Expansion of England* (London, 1880), pp. 61–62; James H. Winter, *'Secure from Rash Assault': Sustaining the Victorian Environment* (Berkeley, forthcoming).

[3] Marshall McLuhan, *Understanding Media* (London, 1964), p. 90; Jacques Ellul, *The Technological Society* (London, 1965), p. 5.

[4] Michael Adas, *Machines as the Measure of Men: Science, Technology and Ideologies of Western Dominance* (Ithaca, NY, 1989); James Morris, *Heaven's Command: An Imperial Progress* (Harmondsworth, 1979), p. 195; William H. McNeill, *The Pursuit of Power: Technology, Armed Force and Society Since A.D. 1000* (Oxford, 1983), pp. 277–78.

[5] Daniel R. Headrick, *The Tools of Empire, Technology and European Imperialism in the Nineteenth Century* (New York, 1981), p. 177.

destabilize them as well. Technology transfer also led diverse peoples to pursue the same material ends by employing similar techniques.

Considerable continuity characterized the diffusion and application of technologies in Imperial activity during the half-century to about 1830. Transport efficiencies were still achieved at home and abroad using old technologies, with human and animal muscle and wind power the prime movers. More extensive use of copper sheathing to protect ships' hulls assisted British dominance in tropical waters. Transferred hydraulic expertise added canals to waterways like the St Lawrence and reclaimed irrigation works in northern India. Some new technologies were absorbed gradually. The displacement of horse-pulled canal boats and coastal sailing vessels by steamers was a long drawn-out process, but steam power on rails was a more precipitate development. Introduced in England in the 1820s, it became extensive and pervasive there in the 1830s and 1840s and shortly thereafter throughout the North Atlantic region. At home its potential for Empire was quickly recognized. As a key invention of the industrial revolution it prompted, along with the clock, a rethinking of humankind's relationship to time and space. The clock measured and allotted activities and the locomotive expanded and speeded them up. Meanwhile domestic productive power increased dramatically as mining and manufacture were mechanized. Increased capacities both to produce and consume 'gave the British a new cutting edge overseas'.[6]

Among the many tools of Empire which empowered both the state and the private sector none was more significant than the steamship. Indeed, its potential was initially overestimated. As a ship owner put it in 1844, 'steam has been a spur to everything'. Administrators in West African backwaters in the 1830s and 1840s demanded steamers as indispensable to operations and as essential and necessary to the 'civilizing mission'. The state, in the form of the Admiralty, was slow to adopt steam, but even the Royal Navy began in 1841 to replace sailing vessels in the anti-slavery squadron. Low-pressure boilers that corroded quickly and consumed coal excessively did not prevent the private sector from sending steamers abroad. Macgregor Laird dispatched steamers up the Niger in the 1830s and 1840s, with disastrous results. The East India Company tried to introduce steamers to the trade routes of the Indian Ocean and sent the *Nemesis*, a Laird-built steamer, to the South China coast. This iron-hulled paddle wheeler played a key role in subduing resistance along the Pearl River during the Opium War of 1839–40. In so doing it enabled local officials to drag the Imperial state into helping merchants gain access to local markets. In 1836 a government-backed expedition descended the Euphrates by steamer in a premature attempt to establish steam navigation on its

---

[6] Adas, *Machines as the Measure of Men*, pp. 21–68; J. R. Ward, 'The Industrial Revolution and British Imperialism, 1750–1850', *Economic History Review*, Second Series, XLVII (1994), pp. 44–65.

waters. Substantial state aid in the form of mail contracts also enabled venture capitalists to establish expensive ocean-going steamship enterprises. By 1850 subsidized lines organized to run to schedules were operating in the North Atlantic, the West Indies, South America, and the Mediterranean—with an extension by way of the Suez isthmus and Red Sea to India and China, and the western Pacific.[7] But the masts of these steamers were a more pronounced feature of their silhouettes than their funnels, an indication that steam power was still a supplement to and not yet a replacement for sails on ocean-going vessels.

British ordnance, by contrast, still offered only limited advantage on both land and water in the 1840s. It was insufficient to prevent disaster in the First Afghan War and only marginally significant against the Sikhs, where both sides had similar muskets, artillery, and effective organization. Small arms, powder, and shot from Europe poured into West African polities, where coastal states installed cannon in their war canoes. Imported firearms continuously disrupted the eastern frontier at the Cape; in New Zealand, conflict between Maori and Pakeha escalated. In each case indigenous adaptation meant that both sides possessed muskets.[8]

The Great Exhibition at the Crystal Palace in 1851 expressed the enormous possibilities for the increase in wealth and dominion presented by technological innovation. A world exhibition with products from many places, it featured displays from various parts of the existing Empire as well as the products of contemporary Britain with a potential role overseas. These included clocks, model steam engines and bridges, and the latest locomotive, 'all green and polished brass, brand-new from the Swindon railway works', earlier versions of which had already been transported overseas. Neither private capital nor the Imperial factor fully controlled 'the transfer of high transport technology [which] had a certain free wheeling momentum of its own'.[9]

This assessment had particular relevance for India. Railway construction began there in 1850. Significant public works had already begun as the British built

[7] Sarah Palmer, *Politics, Shipping and Repeal of the Navigation Laws* (Manchester, 1990), p. 2; Robert V. Kubicek, 'The Colonial Steamer and the Occupation of West Africa by the Victorian State, 1840–1900', *Journal of Imperial and Commonwealth History*, XVIII (Jan. 1990), pp. 9–32; Headrick, *Tools of Empire*, pp. 17–57; Freda Harcourt, 'British Oceanic Mail Contracts in the Age of Steam, 1838–1914', *Journal of Transport History*, Third Series, IX (March 1988), pp. 1–18.

[8] Brian Bond, ed., *Victorian Military Campaigns* (London, 1967), pp. 33–69; Byron Farwell, *Queen Victoria's Little Wars* (London, 1973), esp. pp. 4–11, 37–60; Joseph E. Inikori, 'The Import of Firearms into West Africa, 1750 to 1807: A Quantitative Analysis', *Journal of African History* (hereafter *JAH*), XVIII (1977), pp. 339–68; Shula Marks and Anthony Atmore, 'Firearms in Southern Africa: A Survey', *JAH*, XII (1971), pp. 517–30.

[9] Morris, *Heaven's Command*, p. 198; R. E. Robinson, 'Introduction', in Clarence B. Davis and Kenneth E. Wilburn, Jr., eds., *Railway Imperialism* (Westport, Conn., 1991), p. 2.

irrigation schemes to increase arable acreage and counter the effects of cyclical drought. But according to the rhetoric about the application of steam power, including that of the Governor-General, Lord Dalhousie, locomotives and steamers would be a greater boon to both Britain and India. By 1860 1,000 miles of track had been laid; by the early 1870s more than 5,000. Then government-supervised private enterprise had built a transcontinental network linking Bombay by way of Delhi with Calcutta, and Madras with Bombay. It was an impressive technical feat, though its costs may have been excessive.[10] British engineers were keen on replicating or improving in a very different environment what had worked back home. Moreover, investors were guaranteed 5 per cent. The railway integrated India into the world economy as an exporter of cash crops and an importer of manufactured goods. It also fastened British rule more firmly on the subcontinent by transporting Imperial rulers, their armies, and their messages. Railways featured still more prominently in the settlement Empire. Local agendas in eastern British North America and south-eastern Australia determined both where lines would run and their technical specifications, in the process making them integral to the economic and political development of the colonies. At this stage in their transfer abroad, railways initially empowered the Imperial agents of the tropical Empire, while in the temperate settlement Empire they served more rapidly to strengthen local interests.

The compound engine, employing steam at higher pressure and thereby redu-cing fuel consumption, freed ocean travel from several constraints and was, therefore, a significant part of steamship development in the mid-Victorian period. Along with the iron hull, which allowed for much greater size than wood, and the surface condenser, which sharply reduced boiler failure, the speed, dependability, and carrying capacity of ocean-going vessels were sig-nificantly increased and running costs substantially reduced. Linked to rail net-works at ports, they made it much easier for Britons to achieve or contemplate even further overseas initiatives.

The telegraph had the same effect. 'Telegraphic communication', as the Victor-ians called it, was 'the first invention to bring electricity to the service of man'. Its development featured two systems. Overhead wires provided a grid for the rapid flow of information on land, complementing that offered by the railways, and were widely used in both Britain in the 1860s and India. There in 1869 the system generated more than 480,000 internal telegrams. Undersea cables, the second system, were laid to link land networks.[11] Imperial administrators and private entrepreneurs took extraordinary risks to extend their reach, believing them to have become essential. Engineers tried in 1858–59 to link Britain, following the

[10] Ian J. Kerr, *Building the Railways of the Raj, 1850–1900* (Delhi, 1995).
[11] See Vol. IV, Map 1.2.

Mutiny, to India by way of a cable laid in the Red Sea. So convinced was the cost-conscious Treasury of the new technology's potential that it agreed to allocate government funds for its construction. The cable failed. The British taxpayer lost £862,000. In 1870 lines across Mesopotamia linked to cables in the Persian Gulf and Indian Ocean finally provided a tolerable connection. By 1872 Hong Kong could be reached through sea cable by way of Singapore or through land and sea by way of Russia. Cables to Port Darwin and land lines to Adelaide and beyond put Australia on the net in 1872. But at this juncture overseas telegraphic communication was expensive and undependable. Until cable construction and laying was sufficiently perfected and lines duplicated, interruptions in service were commonplace. Messages were coded, cryptic, and not infrequently unintelligible. The Colonial Office continued to send despatches by scheduled steamer as the preferred means of prompt communication (Map 12.1).[12]

The Suez Canal was somewhat ahead of its times. Built with Egyptian labour mobilized by the khedive as well as locomotives and steam shovels, it opened in 1869. Its capacity to handle traffic was limited until it was deepened and steamships were built that could use it efficiently. British tonnage passing through the waterway was less than 300,000 in 1870, about 2,000,000 in 1875, almost 3,500,000 in 1880, and over 5,300,000 in 1890.

The continued updating and mechanization of the British arms industry in 1858 produced rifled muskets made of interchangeable parts, and reached production levels of more than 100,000 per annum by 1863. These small arms were used to re-equip and thereby make more lethal British military contingents abroad, but their transfer had other repercussions. In India, rifles supplied to sepoys using cartridges greased with animal fat were the catalyst for simmering discontent to erupt into rebellion. Muskets and rifles, many of them obsolescent cast-offs, also continued to be shipped abroad and fell into the hands of groups bent on challenging the British presence in West Africa, on India's North-West Frontier, and in Western Canada. In New Zealand the Maori developed trenches and bunkers to minimize the effect of artillery barrages and, coupled with accurate musket fire, managed to fend off infantry assaults. They were defeated because they were outnumbered, not because they lacked adequate weapons.[13]

---

[12] Jeffrey Kieve, *The Electric Telegraph: A Social and Economic History* (Newton Abbot, 1973), p. 13; John W. Cell, *British Colonial Administration in the Mid-Nineteenth Century: The Policy-Making Process* (New Haven, 1970), pp. 220–253; Kenneth Stanley Inglis, 'The Imperial Connection: Telegraphic Communication Between England and Australia, 1872–1902', in A. F. Madden and W. H. Morris-Jones, eds., *Australia and Britain: Studies in a Changing Relationship* (Sydney, 1980), pp. 21–38.

[13] Russell I. Fries, 'British Response to the American System: The Case of the Small-Arms Industry After 1850', *Technology and Culture* (hereafter *TC*), XVI (1975), pp. 307–403; James Belich, *The New Zealand Wars and the Victorian Interpretation of Racial Conflict* (1986; Auckland, 1988), pp. 292–98.

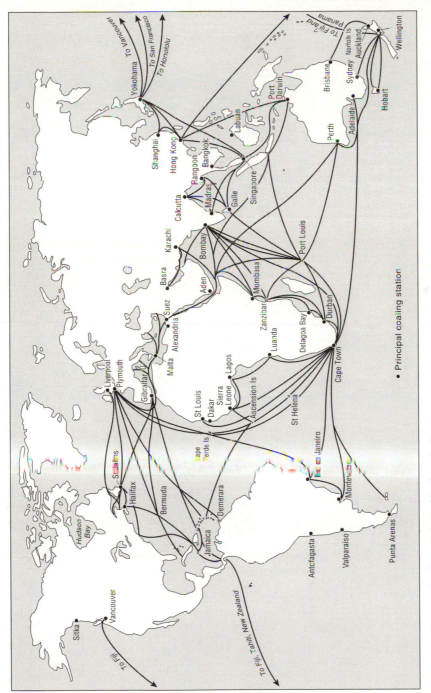

MAP 12.1. Communications: Principal Steamship Routes

TABLE 12.1. *Distances from Plymouth to selected destinations by sea* (in miles)

Destination	via Cape of Good Hope	via Suez
Cape Town	5,800	
Bombay	10,450	6,000
Colombo	10,150	6,490
Calcutta	11,380	7,710
Singapore	11,350	8,050
Hong Kong	12,790	9,490
Shanghai	13,540	10,240
Yokohama	14,220	10,920
Melbourne	11,870	10,670
Sydney	12,340	11,200
Wellington	12,910	12,110

TABLE 12.2. *Distances from Liverpool, Cape Town, Bombay, and Calcutta to selected destinations by sea* (in miles)

From	To	Miles
Liverpool	Quebec	2,625
	New York	3,043
	Jamaica	4,026
Cape Town	St Helena	1,700
	Southampton	5,950
	Mauritius	2,280
	Aden	4,250
	King George's Sound	4,720
Bombay	Aden	1,650
	Zanzibar	2,510
Calcutta	Singapore	1,630

TABLE 12.3. *Journey time by sea from England to Cape Town* (in days)

Year	From Devonport, Dartmouth, Southampton, London	One way	Round trip
1857		42	89
1867		37	—
1872		30	
1873		28	
1876		26	
1888		20	
1893		19	

TABLE 12.4. *Journey time from selected ports by sea: routes East* (in days unless otherwise stated)

Year	From	To	One way	Round trip
1820	London	Calcutta (sail)	5–8 (months)	
1825	Falmouth	Calcutta (steam assisted)	113	
1852	Southampton	Singapore	45	
		Shanghai	57	
		Sydney	75	
1855	Southampton	Alexandria	14	33
	Suez	Calcutta	24	56
		Bombay	14	35
	Bombay	Singapore	15	
	Bombay	Hong Kong (via Singapore)	20	
	Singapore	Sydney	28	
1895	Naples	Adelaide	32	
1897	Brindisi	Bombay	14	
		Shanghai	33	
		Adelaide	30	
1904	Brindisi	Adelaide	27	

TABLE 12.5. *Journey time from England by sea: North Atlantic routes* (in days)

Year	From	To	One way
1819	Liverpool	New York	27
1861			13
1863	Southampton	Jamaica	18
1895			15

TABLE 12.6. *Journey time from England by sea: West Africa routes* (in days)

Year	From	To	One way	Round trip
1857	Liverpool	Sierre Leone	18	}79
		Fernando Po	32	
1866		Sierre Leone	15	}71
		Fernando Po	25	
1883		Sierre Leone	16	}89
		Fernando Po	35	

Note: These figures have been compiled from Imperial and Colonial governments' Mail Contracts, General Post Office timetables, and contractors' returns printed for Parliament. In the delivery of mails the spread of railways complemented the mounting speed and regularity of steam-assisted, sail-assisted, and finally full-steam shipping. By the 1880s mails despatched overnight from London to Brindisi by rail were shipped the following day. Like emigrants and armed forces, they arrived at ports increasingly linked by railways to the colonial hinterlands.

While the steamship, land-sea telegraphy, and weaponry assisted in varying degrees British exploitation of global resources, these and other devices also fostered the creation and transmission of powerful images of peoples and places. In conjunction with techniques used to produce books and newspapers, they provided for the extensive dissemination of evocative travel literature and provocative reports of 'crises' on the periphery of Empire. In the 1860s 'the concept of mechanization' began to 'make an impact on letter-founding, type composition and bookbinding'. At the same time mechanical paper making cut costs and increased production. In 1800 Britain produced 11,000 tons of paper; in 1860 100,000 tons, of which 96,000 were mechanically made. Production costs per pound of paper halved; books became cheaper. In the late 1860s and early 1870s newspapers began to employ the rotary press which used continuous rolls of newsprint to produce quickly a large number of copies. These, containing telegraph reports from abroad and distributed throughout the country by trains running rapidly on tight schedules, transformed the means by which messages were exchanged.[14]

During the mid-Victorian period a number of individuals appeared whose accomplishments were both initiated and disseminated by the evolving technologies. Most famous was the explorer and missionary David Livingstone. Shallow-draft steamers were essential to his abortive attempt to unlock the Zambezi; steam printing enabled a wide public to receive and respond to the accounts of his exploits. *Missionary Travels and Researches in South Africa*, published in 1857, quickly sold 70,000 copies at a time when anything over 10,000 was considered a best-seller. There were scientists too with a practical bent and an eye for Empire. Sir Roderick Murchison launched expeditions using newly available communications and transport to acquire topographical data, as well as the telegraph and the press to mobilize support when President of the Royal Geographical Society. Lord Kelvin, more self-effacing but perhaps an even more significant figure, developed telegraphic, directional, and sounding devices of great importance to the maintenance of Britain's hegemony on ocean routes.[15]

Technologically minded entrepreneurs, as well as investors and merchants, contributed to Imperial expansion. Thomas Brassey constucted railways in Canada, Argentina, Australia, and India. Laird, a Liverpudlian, had pioneered ocean and river steamer technology, but John Elder and William Denny, Clydeside

---

[14] S. H. Steinberg, *Five Hundred Years of Printing*, 2nd edn. (London, 1978), pp. 275–78; T. Brown, 'The Treatment of the News in Mid-Victorian Newspapers', *Transactions of the Royal Historical Society*, Fifth Series, XXVII (1977), pp. 23–29; Alan J. Lee, *The Origins of the Popular Press in England, 1855–1914* (London, 1976), pp. 60–62.

[15] Tim Jeal, *Livingstone* (London, 1973), p. 163; See chap. by Robert A. Stafford; Crosbie Smith and M. Norton Wise, *Energy and Empire: A Biographical Study of Lord Kelvin* (Cambridge, 1989).

shipbuilders, made Glasgow second only to London as the city of the Empire. Along with magnates such as Donald Currie (who also arranged for politicians to cruise free aboard his ships), Samuel Cunard, Alfred Holt, and William Mackinnon, who organized shipping lines around their steamers, and John Pender, who created the Eastern Telegraph Company which dominated sea-cable telegraphy, these entrepreneurs constituted a most formidable if disparate group. All these builders and owners used the tools of Empire to advance their careers and companies. Along with explorers and other professionals, they also received state aid. Livingstone obtained grants as well as transport for his adventures in Southern Africa. Murchison obtained funds to find promising geological formations, while Holt and Pender acquired subsidies for their shipping and telegraph enterprises. Brassey did not always profit from his overseas projects but colonial revenues financed them. The dogmas of *laissez-faire* were in theory the touchstones of governmental, financial, and industrial action. Successive governments, however, were persuaded that technological and economic imperatives required an interventionist approach to safeguard British interests.

After 1875 Imperial activity, driven by policy and interest but assisted by technological innovation and diffusion, rapidly escalated. The tools to move goods, people, and information as well as to extend and solidify domination became more efficient and more widely dispersed. So did inventions to farm, fish, forest, and mine. Meanwhile, habits and notions rooted in past practice were altered as time came to be measured precisely and in smaller intervals, as attainable speeds increased, as access to space eased. In 1873 Jules Verne sent the fictional Phileas Fogg around the world in eighty days: in 1889–90 the American journalist Nellie Bly actually made it in seventy-two. Meanwhile, the world, because of advances in communications, came to be divided into twenty-four time zones one hour apart.[16]

Private railway contractors, backed by guaranteed investor dividends, more than quadrupled tracks in India to 24,000 miles by the end of the century. At the same time Canada emerged as a North American transcontinental polity. Steel rails provided Montreal and Toronto with a western hinterland to develop. In South America a rail net spread into the interior, enriching Buenos Aires and giving substance to Britain's informal imperialism. Elsewhere in the southern hemisphere railway politics assumed an important role. In Australia, a promise to extend rail lines ensured the continent's westernmost colony would become a state in the federal Commonwealth. In South Africa, where Cape Town and Durban competed to monopolize traffic into the Orange Free State and the

[16] Stephen Kern, *The Culture of Time and Space, 1880–1918* (Cambridge, Mass., 1983), chaps. 1 and 8.

Transvaal, and where the latter obtained an outlet to the sea through Portuguese territory, railway politics held back federation and contributed to conflict.

In tropical Africa, 'railway imperialism' attended by visions of transcontinental links (the French imagined east–west, the British north–south lines) came to a climax with the building of the Uganda railway. Its economic potential was limited, its strategic function questionable; yet both political parties, Liberals and Conservatives, committed themselves to it and the British taxpayer met the £5.5m bill. Through extending and consolidating Empire, 'railway imperialism' attracted Asians and Europeans into the African hinterland adding to the future likelihood of ethnic tension.

With steel replacing iron as the preferred material for boiler and hull construction, with engines running more economically through the adoption of triple and even quadruple expansion, with ships becoming more purpose-built (to carry, for example, frozen meat or petroleum), and with their owners fashioning much larger corporate structures to cope with these changes, Britain's maritime hegemony, once substantial, now became pervasive. British tonnage passing through the Suez Canal almost tripled between 1880 and 1910 to more than 10 million per annum. The Peninsular and Oriental (P&O) steamship company's vessels designed both to carry cargo and passengers and to exploit the Suez Canal, increased in gross tonnage from 4,000 in 1870 to 7,500 by 1895. The European diaspora generally, and British emigration to temperate zones in particular, were significantly facilitated by this revolution in steamer traffic. Also much enhanced was British access to tropical climes, their journeys facilitated by 'posh' ('port out, starboard home') accommodation even if marred by the prevalence of coal dust, especially when loading fuel. Colonial cities were transformed as expatriate and hinterland peoples were attracted to them, and as harbours were deepened, quays lengthened and warehouses were built.[17]

Getting into hinterlands where roads were non-existent and railroads not yet built often meant going upriver. Here the shallow-draft steamer came into its own. The state and private sector became much entwined in its diffusion. The naval screw-driven gunboat, built in numbers for the Crimean War and adapted to force open the China trade, was upgraded and distributed to various stations, becoming both an instrument and symbol of Imperial control. To cite one better-known incident among many, a gun vessel, HMS *Goshawk*, launched in 1873, was used in 1887 to kidnap a local ruler and palm oil merchant, Jaja of Opobo. Less remarked upon but equally important were the navy's sturdy, wooden-hulled, side-wheel survey ships. These provided the navigational charts that saved many private

[17] Frank Broeze, 'The External Dynamics of Port City Morphology: Bombay, 1815–1914', in Indu Banga, ed., *Ports and Their Hinterlands in India* (New Delhi, 1992), pp. 245–72.

steamers from disaster. Colonial officials and entrepreneurs also acquired stea-mers for coastal and inland work. These might be stern-wheelers with 'tea-tray' hulls, as described in Joseph Conrad's *Heart of Darkness*, a simple launch such as C. S. Forester's *African Queen*, or the ingeniously designed vessels, with twin screws set in tunnels to cope with unknown currents and snags, which served on the Nile expedition or featured in Frederick Lugard's specifications for his state-of-the-art steamer on the Niger. Government vessels could carry traders, as they did in West Africa and along the coast of Ceylon. Government could subsidize steamers, as it did on the waterways of British Guiana, or even commandeer them, as it did on the Lagos lagoon and the Irrawaddy. In India, where river steamers had run since the 1820s, they were not entirely displaced by the railway. They were instrumental in getting the tea of Assam to market. For the Colonial Office their diffusion was a priority. As one of its long-serving senior bureaucrats put it, in an emergency a steamer 'might prevent a scare from developing into a disaster'. On the other hand, for the man on the spot looking for opportunities to extend his jurisdiction and enhance his career, 'having a light draught steamer of average speed, capable of carrying arms and soldiers, cannot be over-rated'.[18]

During the late nineteenth century Europe became thoroughly wired. By 1882, for example, Great Britain, France, and Germany possessed more than 28,000 telegraph offices which in that year transmitted some 77 million messages. Ocean cables also proliferated. Extensions included a cable down Africa's east coast via Zanzibar and Lourenço Marques to Durban in 1879; prompted by Imperial disaster in the Zulu War, it was hastily connected overland to Cape Town. West coast outposts from St Louis to Bonny, and including Dakar, Bathurst, Freetown, Accra, and Lagos, were linked to Europe in 1886 as trade and the French challenge grew. Extended southward by way of Luanda, this route gave Cape Town a second line to Europe in 1889; a third by way of Ascension and St Helena was completed in 1900. The Treasury, though initially averse, perhaps remembering the Red Sea débâcle of 1859, relented when pressed by the Colonial Office and the Dominions to subsidize a cable from Vancouver Island to Australasia as part of an all-red route. Though of some strategic significance, the Pacific Cable laid in 1902 was largely the result of lobbying by Dominion entrepreneurs. Cables were duplicated or triplicated and more sturdily constructed. Transmission was much improved, for example, by introducing the new system of duplex telegraphy that permitted simultaneous sending of messages in both directions from each end of a conduct-ing line. Charges, which once made all but brief messages prohibitive, were

---

[18] Robert V. Kubicek, 'The Role of Shallow-Draft Steamboats in the Expansion of the British Empire, 1820–1914', *International Journal of Maritime History*, VI (June 1994), pp. 86–106; Percival Griffiths, *A History of the Joint Steamers Companies* (London, 1979); Minute by Robert Herbert, 17 Dec. 1886, C[olonial] O[ffice] 96/176/22336; Dispatch by F. W. Evans, 23 Sept. 1886, CO 147/57/19151.

substantially reduced by increased volume and the introduction of efficient codes and ciphers. Messages to Cape Town cost eight shillings and ninepence per word in 1890, five shillings in 1896. Bombay could be reached for four shillings.[19]

The contemporary expert Charles Bright referred to the linked ocean cables, aerial wire, and buried land cables carrying thousands of messages daily as 'the world's system of electrical nerves'. The establishment and use made of links between Africa and Britain are suggestive of the way these 'electrical nerves' featured in Imperial activity. An east coast African line emerged out of a Cape initiative begun in 1873 to obtain either a sea or land link by way of Egypt. Especially influential were the Imperial government's belief that the telegraph would give it effective means to contain chronic conflict south of the Limpopo, and the lobbying of Pender's Eastern Telegraph Company (ETC) which was becoming a dominant player in global cable communications. Also in 1873 the Colonial and War Offices pressed for a west coast cable which, they thought, would be of great value in ensuring the success of the Asante expedition and in preventing the need for such sorties in the future. Speedier communication with agents and more prompt deployment of locally stationed armed forces (whose number could, it was thought, even be reduced), would quell unrest before it escalated. Because local revenues were insufficient to subsidize such an undertaking, since commercial activity did not warrant it, and as the Treasury refused to consider Imperial financial backing, the project was pigeon-holed for almost a decade. Then, when a British cable company with concessions from the Spanish and French governments went ahead with a version of the scheme, the Treasury agreed to provide most of the subsidy for a subsidiary of the Eastern Telegraph Company to do the job. This enabled the ETC to make an agreement with its competitor and the west coast ended up with two cables to Europe, one by way of the Cape Verde Islands, the other by way of the Canaries. Strategic calculations and assumptions that a more effective, and cheaper British presence to preserve the status quo would result, had moved officials to support more cable laying. Railway and steamship imperialism was buttressed by cable expansion.

It is nevertheless unclear that this rapidly expanding communication system gave the Colonial Office greater control over events on the periphery. The Office received telegraphs by ETC messengers who carried them to Whitehall from their headquarters in the City. At night they were left in a letter-box to be retrieved by resident clerks and handled by the same registration and minuting procedures

---

[19] Eastern Telegraph Company confidential memo to the Colonial Office, 13 March 1900, CO 323/458/8207; CO 96/109/10366; P. M. Kennedy, 'Imperial Cable Communication and Strategy, 1870–1914', *English Historical Review*, LXXXVI (1971), pp. 728–52; Charles Bright, *Submarine Telegraphs: Their History, Construction and Working* (London, 1898), p. 167.

as dispatches. As late as 1899 the Colonial Secretary, Joseph Chamberlain, appeared at the telegraph company's door demanding to know what had happened to a cable expected from South Africa. These practices and incidents suggest that the Office was, even by 1900, still inclined to adopt the telegraphic medium as an adaptation of rather than as a replacement for the dispatch.

The Foreign Office, by contrast, used the telegraph as 'the predominant means of communication' and reduced ambassadorial discretion significantly. Colonial Governors were not so readily restrained. An analysis of telegrams exchanged between the Office and two West African colonies, the Gold Coast and Lagos, is instructive. In 1887, the first full year of telegraphic communication, the Office sent forty-five cables and received seventy-eight. A decade later the figures were 251 and 409. In these exchanges the Office was reactive, especially to reports of French activity in neighbouring territories. At the same time, men on the spot used the telegraph most frequently to relieve a chronic problem: illness and death from tropical diseases, which continued to decimate personnel. Now when officials went down with fever, telegrams could elicit prompt replacements by 'the next steamship'.[20] Cables and local land lines also provided the administrator with much quicker access to the means of coercion. Constabularies or regiments in other West African colonies, as well as naval gunboats which might be elsewhere on the station, could be summoned more promptly. A cryptic telegram calling for immediate Imperial support to deal with conflict conveyed far more sense of urgency than a dispatch arriving weeks after the event, particularly since it was the Colonial Office view that prompt intervention would limit the extent of involvement.

In South Africa, on the eve of the Zulu War, the Secretary of State for the Colonies had wondered if he could use the telegraph to control his Governor on the spot. Here too the periphery sent more telegrams than it received. In 1887, for example, the Colonial Office sent thirty-five telegrams to its agents in the Cape and Natal and received forty-three in return. Administrators fashioned telegrams to get authorization for their preferred agendas while the Colonial Office sought assurance that all was quiet, especially when the press, publishing cables it received, reported Afrikaner raids into Swaziland, for example. In the next decade telegrams failed the premier of the Cape, Cecil Rhodes, in a last-minute attempt to curb his impetuous crony, Dr Leander Starr Jameson. When some of the conspirators' messages came to light, they discredited Chamberlain. Alfred Milner, the man on the spot, used the cable in 1898–99 to help rush the Colonial Office and the

[20] Raymond A. Jones, *The British Diplomatic Service, 1815–1914* (Waterloo, Ontario, 1983), pp. 125–38; correspondence registers for Gold Coast: CO 343/11; 343/14 and Lagos: CO 421/5; 421/8 and counts conducted in the General Department: CO 323/447/1249 and CO 323/497/1321.

Cabinet into preparing an ultimatum for the Transvaal. Even Lord Salisbury thought Milner's view was 'too heated'. The activist agent had also made South Africa an issue in the media, leaving the Cabinet with few options.[21]

Improved communications certainly facilitated the global growth of Imperial economic activity, but whether cables and telegraphs strengthened Imperial dynamics is less evident. In drawing the Imperial state into more intimate working relations with the private sector, they certainly strengthened the Eastern Telegraph Company. In participating in construction of the Pacific Cable, opened in 1902, the ETC provided support for Dominion ambitions even as it completed an Imperial network around the world. In South Africa communications improvements again strengthened sub-imperialist objectives and fostered conflict. Elsewhere, for instance in China, private ambitions for telegraphic extensions drew Imperial agents into imbroglios set off by cable companies pressuring indigenous authorities for landing rights.[22] When it came to men on the spot, the late-nineteenth-century response to this technology saw the periphery more able to prompt the centre into action.

In 1890 the man who was soon to become Viceroy of India was in Baku on the western shore of the Caspian Sea. He had steamed there by vessel through the Black Sea and travelled by locomotive over Transcaucasia, the latter part of a rail link completed in 1882 to deliver oil to Batum. George Nathaniel Curzon had also steamed even further eastward across the Caspian and along Trans-Caspian railways. Facilitated incidentally by British industrialists and engineers, this transfer of technologies by Russia, of which Curzon had first-hand experience, made him particularly keen to participate in the 'Great Game' of Imperial rivalries in Central Asia. The possibility that steamer and locomotive would funnel Russian empire-building into Afghanistan stimulated the Raj to snake lines from the Indus plains to and even through the historic passes of the North-West Frontier.[23]

Medical advances allowing civil and military personnel, businessmen, and missionaries easier travel and safer tours of duties emerged as a major influence in empire-building comparatively late in the period. In 1893 Burroughs, Wellcome

[21] Lady Victoria Hicks Beach, *Life of Sir Michael Hicks Beach*, 2 vols. (London, 1932), I, p. 103; Telegrams to and from South Africa, Jan.–Dec. 1887, CO 879/26/337; Robert Blake, 'The Jameson Raid and "The Missing Telegrams"', in Hugh Lloyd-Jones and others, eds., *History and Imagination* (London, 1981), pp. 326–39; Robert V. Kubicek, *The Administration of the Colonial Office: Joseph Chamberlain at the Colonial Office* (Durham, NC, 1969), p. 109; A. N. Porter, *The Origins of the South African War: Joseph Chamberlain and the Diplomacy of Imperialism, 1895–1899* (Manchester, 1980).

[22] Jorma Ahvenainen, *The Far Eastern Telegraphs: The History of Telegraphic Communications between the Far East, Europe and America before the First World War* (Helsinki, 1981), pp. 91–157.

[23] Sarah Searight, *Steaming East: The Hundred Year Saga of the Struggle to Forge Rail and Steamship Links Between Europe and India* (London, 1991), pp. 176–225.

and Co. placed an advertisement in a guide to health care for Europeans in Africa by Thomas Heazle Parke, a medical officer in both the Gordon and Emin Pasha relief expeditions of the 1880s. He had treated Henry Morton Stanley for various ailments, including stomach cramps. The advertisement listed the medicines in handy tablet form contained in a chest that it advised no traveller to be without. These included quinine, rhubarb, opium, and ginger. Parke, who supplied an endorsement, also listed more than forty drugs, ointments, and powders as well as more than a dozen instruments and applications which should be stocked. Europeans abroad were more likely to die from disease than their home-bound compatriots, but by the late nineteenth century medical technologies had reduced death rates considerably. None the less, West African diseases—especially malaria, even after quinine was used as a prophylactic—continued to take their toll. Army cantonments had long been rife with contagious diseases and steamers and railroads moved epidemics about with deadly effect. The application of germ theory, the knowledge that insects transmit malaria and sleeping sickness, advice on diet, the use of residential segregation and ship quarantine—these developments finally showed significant results only in the early twentieth century.[24]

Such breakthroughs also nurtured what has been loosely called 'engineering imperialism'.[25] The civil engineers abroad played a significant if insufficiently emphasized role in transferring infrastructure and disturbing the status quo. For example, the Bradford firm of Samuel Pearson and Son, the world's largest contractor in the 1890s, constructed canals and railways in Mexico, docks in Canada, and a dam in Egypt. The mechanical engineer and the marine engineer had been essential for the running and maintenance of steam-driven transport. Mining engineers also applied expertise with significant results. The 'rush that never ended' in Australia, mineral extraction in Ontario and British Columbia in Canada, and gold mines in the Gold Coast all evolved as the consequence of the export of machinery and processes that required engineers. Tin-mining in Malaya had been pioneered by Chinese migrants, but their technologies began to be displaced by Western high-pressure water pumps and bucket dredges. Nowhere were the results of transfers of men and machines as destabilizing as in South Africa. There, Cecil Rhodes got a start on the diamond fields controlling steam pumping machines in the diamond quarries of Kimberley. In addition to modern weapons, telegraphs, and railways, South Africa absorbed new mining techniques. The goldfield which developed after 1886 could not have been exploited without 'blasting gelatine' invented in 1874; the MacArthur Forrest cyanide process

---

[24] Thomas Heazle Parke, *Guide to Health in Africa, With Notes on the Country and Its Individuals* (London, 1893); Roy MacLeod and Milton Lewis, eds., *Disease, Medicine and Empire: Perspectives on Western Medicine and the Experience of European Expansion* (London, 1988), pp. 1–60.

[25] R. A. Buchanan, 'The Diaspora of British Engineering', *TC*, XXVII (July 1986), pp. 501–24.

patented in 1887; and steel alloys, essential for dies and shoes in the mortar boxes of mills' stamps, produced in quantity only after about 1880'.[26]

Steam trawlers yielded and tin cans distributed more of the oceans' fish. Mechanization and barbed wire also made possible and even profitable agricultural activity in sparsely settled temperate lands. Combine-harvesters for the wheatlands of Canada and mechanical sheep-shearing devices for Australasia reduced costs already lowered by cheap transport. These developments made for volatile politics as urban and rural interests competed for advantage and, in seeking the ear of London, complicated Imperial relations.

Engineering mastery of earth and water was nowhere more evident in the Empire than in the irrigation canals of India. As noted above, British canal-building had begun before railway technology was introduced. Far less funding went into the former than the latter, and with contradictory results. While irrigation enabled Indian peasants to bring otherwise barren lands into production and ease cyclical famines, this technology was also a vehicle for the transfer of tropical diseases. In time, canal-watered land was subject to salination and consequent loss of fertility. Meanwhile, steam-run machinery extracted logs and milled lumber, contributing to extensive deforestation in North America as well as South Asia.[27] Some contemporaries were sensitive to such depredation, and the India Forestry Service, for example, with its reserves played a vital role in conservation. However, most celebrated such Imperial developments as irrigation works and railway networks in, for example, the festivities marking Queen Victoria's Diamond Jubilee in 1897. The leading advocate of railways, docks, and other infrastructure for the tropical Empire was Joseph Chamberlain, whose appearance on the national and Imperial stage had been made possible by his roots in Birmingham manufacture.

While the agents of Empire spread tools abroad for their own purposes these inventions were also taken up by others. These transfers served to stiffen resistance but also to exacerbate divisions among indigenous groups, sometimes to British advantage. Egypt's pretensions in the Sudan, its proto-nationalist movement led by the army of Arabi Pasha before 1882, and Afrikaner ambition beyond the

---

[26] Robert V. Kubicek, *Economic Imperialism in Theory and Practice: The Case of South African Gold Mining Finance, 1886–1914* (Durham, NC, 1979), pp. 51–52; Simon Katzenellenbogen, 'Cyanide and Bubbles: Patents and Technological Change in Gold and Non-ferrous Metals Treatment', in Klaus Tenfelde, ed., *Sozialgeschichte des Bergbaus in 19. and 20. Jahrhundert* (Munich, 1992), pp. 519–38.

[27] Elizabeth Whitcombe, *Agrarian Conditions in Northern India: The United Provinces Under British Rule, 1860–1900* (Berkeley, 1972); Ramachandra Guha, *Unquiet Woods, Ecological Change and Peasant Resistance in the Himalayas* (Berkeley, 1989); Richard H. Grove, *Green Imperialism: Colonial Expansion, Tropical Island Edens, and the Origins of Environmentalism, 1600–1860* (Cambridge, 1995).

Orange River prior to 1899 may be seen as indigenous initiatives made possible by arms obtained in Europe. Arab penetration of East Africa and the Congo basin, whether viewed as indigenous or expatriate activity, or as a state-making as well as a trading endeavour, was also dependent upon European arms. West Africa's forest states received large quantities of flintlocks. West African Sudanese polities supplemented flintlocks with breech-loaders and even repeaters during the final stages of resistance. In the same way, belated 'self-strengthening' undertakings by modernizers of the Manchu establishment built ordnance factories to arm China against both internal challenge and external aggression.[28]

In numerous armed clashes between British invaders and local peoples—worldwide between about 1875 and 1907—both sides had modern weaponry. The Zulu, smashed by British weapons at Ulundi, had very few small arms, but the Sotho, possessed of considerably more, had been involved in 'gun wars' with Cape colonists. The most spectacular arms caches were found in Ethiopia and the Transvaal. Menilik's forces at Adowa in 1896 possessed more than 14,000 muzzle-loaders, a similar number of rifles and carbines, as well as millions of rounds of ammunition and the occasional machine gun. The Boer republic, on the estimates of the War Office Intelligence Department, by mid-1899 had seventy artillery pieces, thirty-one machine guns, 62,950 rifles, 6,000 revolvers, and sufficient ammunition 'for a protracted campaign'. At the Battle of Omdurman Kitchener's forces (transported by rail and river steamer) had fifty-five machine guns. Sudanese resisters had only two, but were equipped with an extensive arsenal of field artillery.

Destabilizing weapons transfers were not confined to Africa. Conflict in the vast reaches of the Argentine pampas, rebellion in western Canada, and resistance on the North-West Frontier (sustained by gun-running enterprises out of the Persian Gulf) found various combinations of weaponry in the hands of locals and conquerors, where the former, though at a technological disadvantage, could often offer significant resistance. Too much explanatory power has been derived from Hilaire Belloc's poetic reference to 'Whatever happens, we have got | The Maxim Gun, and they have not'. A more revealing assessment of the 'little wars' of Empire is perhaps conveyed by Sir Henry Newbolt: 'The sand of the desert is sodden red— | Red with the wreck of a square that broke— | The Gatling's jammed and the

[28] Howard Bailes, 'Technology and Imperialism: A Case Study of the Victorian Army in Africa', *Victorian Studies* (Autumn 1980), pp. 83–104; P. M. Holt, *The Mahdist State in the Sudan, 1881–1898* (Oxford, 1958), pp. 2–3; David Levering Lewis, *The Race to Fashoda, European Colonialism and African Resistance in the Scramble for Africa* (New York, 1987), pp. 62–72; Michael Crowder, ed., *West African Resistance: The Military Response to Colonial Occupation*. 2nd edn. (1971; London, 1978), p. 27; Thomas L. Kennedy, *The Arms of Kiangnan: Modernization in the Chinese Ordnance Industry, 1860–1895* (Boulder, Colo, 1987), pp. 99–160.

colonel dead, | And the regiment blind with dust and smoke...' Though the
Mahdi wanted Gordon taken alive, he was killed at Khartoum by a bullet from the
gun of a Sudanese soldier who did not know who he was.[29] As the South African
War (1899–1902) also showed, technological advantage could still only too easily
be outweighed by human blunders, mechanical failure, and local knowledge of
climate and terrain.

Although the diffusion of metropolitan technology was largely controlled by
Imperial authorities and entrepreneurs, local initiative was important. Weapons,
as noted, were acquired by indigenous resisters. Others accepted the Imperial
presence because it offered technologies which improved their own condition. In
temperate-zone colonies, officials and capitalists, with agendas sometimes at odds
with Imperial priorities, acquired many tools to ease transport and increase
production. Egyptian khedives were keen on, what often proved to be financially
precarious, modernization. Imperial objectives governed Indian railways, but the
indigenous population flocked in their millions to crowded stations to participate
more readily in religious pilgrimages and family reunions, and they used the postal
system, which piggybacked extensively on the railways. The railway also shaped
Indian economic and political life. Indian contractors and labour built the lines: it
was not unusual for some 200,000 men, women, and children to be employed
annually on construction. Indian entrepreneurs used the lines; so would nationalist leaders. Thus, indigenous economic and political groupings with which the
Raj had to collaborate were defined in part by railway developments. Even though
Imperial authorities in India discouraged such transfers, native entrepreneurs
successfully imported textile-making equipment. They also formed a steamship
service, the 'Mogul Line', for the pilgrim traffic to Mecca, and were involved in
coastal steamer traffic. The Tata family laid the foundations of an iron and steel
industry. Despite little encouragement from the British and constraints in their
own culture, Indians sought either abroad or in local institutions to acquire
modern medical and technical education. Bombay and Bengal established technical institutes, with the British-trained geologist Paramatha Nath Bose becoming
the first rector of the latter. The locally owned China Merchants Steam Navigation
Company by 1880 had six steamers on the Yangtze. The British-based Irrawaddy
Flotilla Company found it necessary to buy out a local challenger, and the Burmese
monarch obtained his own steamer. So did the khedive of Egypt, the sultan of
Zanzibar, and the ruler of Sarawak. Governments in Argentina, China, Haiti, and
Queensland acquired steamers to strengthen their ability to control. Meanwhile,

---

[29] John Ellis, *The Social History of the Machine Gun* (London, 1975), pp. 94, 105–06; Douglas H.
Johnson, 'The Death of Gordon, A Victorian Myth', *Journal of Imperial and Commonwealth History*, X
(1982), pp. 285–310.

stokers, deckhands, pilots, even engine operators drawn from diverse cultures were essential for their maintenance and operation.[30]

Missionaries too were often tolerated for the technologies they transferred. These included alphabets, medicines, printing presses, even shovels, which were seen as materially useful but also capable of enhancing status and power. The case of Lewanika, ruler of the Lozi, is instructive. Adapting missionary initiatives, he constructed extensive drainage canals along the Zambezi watershed to serve both economic and political objectives. While African communities resisted some measures introduced to improve public health, they accepted and adapted others.[31] Indigenous acquisition of expatriate tools was, of course, a double-edged initiative. It might strengthen autonomy, but more often it paved the way for more pervasive alien influence.

The intensified or 'new' imperialism, a much-debated phenomenon of the later nineteenth century, has been seen as a product of a particular stage of finance capital, of the rise of ethnic antagonisms fuelled by racist beliefs, and the geopolitical priorities of the 'official mind'. While these causal factors need not be dismissed, their explanatory powers pale if compared with the transformations wrought by technological innovations. These profoundly stimulated a mind-set already disposed to think about Empire in terms of what was possible, desirable, and (morally speaking) defensible. In their developmental stages before about 1870 they were too costly and unreliable to provide the empowerment visionaries contemplated. In later decades, to most colonizers and many colonized they became more affordable and dependable symbols of a progress rooted in Western knowledge.

By then they also had become more uncontrollable and unpredictable in their effects. Local collaborators could use them to develop their own agendas, especially in the temperate settlement Empire. In these neo-Britains, peoples were strengthened politically and economically by the transfer of technologies. Peoples in the tropics were able, to a certain extent, to use these same tools to resist colonial constraints and alter their material conditions. The wide diffusion of Western weaponry allowed indigenous groups to resist and create imbalances that attracted intervention. Indigenous groups adapted other technologies such as writing, medicines, and steamers. Simultaneously, these devices strengthened the capacity of local Imperial agents, civil and military, to be proactive and less amenable to

---

[30] Daniel R. Headrick, *The Tentacles of Progress: Technology Transfer in the Age of Imperialism, 1850–1940* (New York, 1988); Poonam Bala, *Imperialism and Medicine in Bengal* (New Delhi, 1991).

[31] Gwyn Prins, *The Hidden Hippopotamus: Reappraisal in African History: The Early Colonial Experience of Western Zambia* (Cambridge, 1980); Megan Vaughan, *Curing Their Ills: Colonial Power and African Illness* (Cambridge, 1991).

metropolitan control. Tools to control and shape what had been annexed increasingly fell within the budgets of outposts with modest revenues. The colonial state could more easily raise and equip native troops and lay on infrastructure such as wharves, graving docks, water transport, and rail and telegraph lines.

Maps, another tool of Empire, produced for Victorians and Edwardians comforting and satisfying projections of their nation's numerous possessions. These maps showed how the vast territory was linked by cables, sea routes, and rail lines. However, these depictions of British power and wealth abroad also failed to disclose an important contradiction. Technological innovations had drawn distant places together but had, at the same time, furthered the growth of local nodes of activity less amenable to control than the maps suggested. The diffusion of nineteenth-century, especially late-nineteenth-century technologies, unleashed discontinuities which both abetted and challenged British Imperialist initiatives. From a global perspective this diffusion was also fashioning precedents in which mankind pursued increasingly similar means to sustain material existence. Whether these had to do with using the environment, sustaining life, and communicating or quarrelling with or dominating each other, the techniques employed increasingly differed less in kind and more in degree.

Select Bibliography

JORMA AHVENAINEN, *The History of the Caribbean Telegraphs Before the First World War* (Helsinki, 1996).

DAVID ARNOLD, ed., *Colonizing the Body: State Medicine and Epidemic Disease in Nineteenth-Century India* (Berkeley, 1993).

J. E. CLARKE and F. STORR, *The Introduction of the Use of Mild Steel into the Shipbuilding and Marine Engine Industries* (Newcastle, 1983).

PHILIP D. CURTIN, *Disease and Empire: Military Medicine in the Conquest of Africa* (Baltimore, 1997).

LANCE E. DAVIS, ROBERT E. GALLMAN, and KARIN GLEITER, *Technology, Institutions, Productivity, and Profits in American Whaling, 1816–1906* (Chicago, 1997).

JOHN A. EAGLE, *The Canadian Pacific Railway and the Development of Western Canada, 1896–1914* (Kingston and Montreal 1989).

J. FALCONER, *Sail and Steam: A Century of Seafaring Enterprise, 1840–1935, Photographs From the National Maritime Museum* (London, 1993).

BASIL GREENHILL, ed., *Conway's History of the Ship: The Advent of Steam, the Merchant Steamship Before 1900* (London, 1993).

JOHN S. GUEST, *The Euphrates Expedition* (London, 1992).

DANIEL R. HEADRICK, *The Invisible Weapon: Telecommunications and International Politics, 1851–1945* (New York, 1991).

STEPHANIE JONES, *Trade and Shipping: Lord Inchcape, 1852–1932* (Manchester, 1989).

JOHN B. LYONS, *Surgeon-Major Parke's African Journey, 1887–89* (Dublin, 1994).

ROY MACLEOD and DEEPAK KUMAR, *Technology and the Raj: Western Technology and Technical Transfers to India, 1700–1947* (New Delhi, 1995).

JEREMY MOUAT, *Roaring Days, Rossland's Mines and the History of British Columbia* (Vancouver, 1995).

DIANNE NEWELL, ed., *The Development of the Pacific Salmon-Canning Industry* (Vancouver, 1989).

WALTER NUGENT, *Crossings: The Great Transatlantic Migrations, 1870–1914* (Bloomington, Ind., 1992).

PETER N. STEARNS, *The Industrial Revolution in World History* (Boulder, Colo., 1993).

IAN STONE, *Canal Irrigation in British India: Perspectives on Technological Change in a Peasant Economy* (Cambridge, 1984).

JAN TODD, *Colonial Technology: Science and the Transfer of Innovation to Australia* (Cambridge, 1995).

LANGDON WINNER, *Autonomous Technology: Technics-out-of Control as a Theme in Political Thought* (Cambridge, Mass., 1977).

13

Empire and Metropolitan Cultures

JOHN M. MACKENZIE

The British were not an imperially minded people; they lacked both a theory of empire and the will to engender or implement one.

(Max Beloff)[1]

So vast and yet so detailed is imperialism as an experience with crucial cultural dimensions, that we must speak of overlapping territories, inter-twined histories common to men and women, whites and non-whites, dwellers in the metropolis and on the peripheries, past as well as present and future ... Nearly everywhere in nineteenth- and early twentieth-century British and French culture we find allusions to the facts of empire ...

(Edward Said)[2]

These quotations represent extremes in debate about the relationship between metropolitan cultures and Empire. For Beloff, and others of his and earlier generations, Imperial status did not necessarily imply public interest or concern. Overseas colonialism and domestic culture could be largely separated. Empire was essentially centrifugal, the radiating outwards of supposed moral and material benefits. If Imperial events occasionally stimulated popular excitements, these were jingoistic aberrations to be decried, not discussed.[3] More recently, literary critics have joined Said in arguing that imperialism is a ubiquitous, pervasive element throughout the literature of the late eighteenth to the mid-twentieth centuries.[4] Although concentrating upon 'high' literary culture, their implication is that such obsessions filtered down into other areas of popular culture.

---

[1] Max Beloff, *Britain's Liberal Empire*, 2 vols. (London, 1969; 1989), I, p. 19.

[2] Edward W. Said, *Culture and Imperialism* (London, 1993), pp. 72–73.

[3] John M. MacKenzie, ed., *Imperialism and Popular Culture* (Manchester, 1986), pp. 1–2; John M. Robertson, *Patriotism and Empire* (London, 1899).

[4] Edward W. Said, *Orientalism* (London, 1978) and *Culture and Imperialism*; Patrick Brantlinger, *Rule of Darkness, British Literature and Imperialism, 1830–1914* (London, 1988); and works surveyed in John M. MacKenzie, *Orientalism: History, Theory and the Arts* (Manchester 1995), chaps. 1 and 2. For a critique of colonial discourse analysis, Nicholas Thomas, *Colonialism's Culture: Anthropology, Travel and Government* (Princeton, 1994).

This chapter considers both this debate, and the scale of the problem, which recent work has shown to be much larger than envisaged by either Beloff's concern with an Imperial theory or Said's literary interests. 'Metropolitan cultures' can be divided horizontally and vertically. There are the cultures of different classes, of the aristocracy, bourgeoisie, and the masses, the latter usually viewed as the social milieu of 'popular culture'. There are also the cultures of the various components of the United Kingdom, the English, Welsh, Scots, and Irish, each with their own histories, supposedly contrasting national characteristics, and relationship to Empire. To these may be added (though not discussed here) the cultures of immigrant groups, representing the cultural interpenetration of mother country and colonial territories.

Class and region, of course, intertwine in complex ways. Landed Highland Scots sought to recoup their fortunes through Empire. Younger sons of the upper classes, not least members of Ireland's Protestant ascendancy, often officered the armed forces and secured advancement through colonial campaigns. Many Imperial interests were essentially bourgeois, but distinguishing the nineteenth century is the middle classes' success in co-opting members of other social groups into their concerns. Cities economically bound up with Empire—London, Birmingham, Liverpool, Manchester, and Glasgow—were often settings for the development of Empire-related pressure-groups and leisure interests. Scots and Irish sought to position themselves in a global Imperial context which helped them avoid being swamped by the English, and even the Welsh with less emigration to the Empire had many economic and religious interests in it.[5] Women also identified opportunities in the social causes and religious and political campaigns of Empire.[6]

An Imperial Culture?

It would be surprising had possession of a vast Empire left the cultures of the metropolitan state virtually unaffected. Yet historians have largely ignored such concerns until recently, for several reasons. Researchers have usually been devoted to official archives, and sources derived from the public records are relatively silent on cultural matters, even if their originators were inevitably influenced by such

---

[5] John M. MacKenzie, 'On Scotland and the Empire', *International History Review*, XV, 4 (1993), pp. 714–39; Keith Jeffery, ed., *An Irish Empire? Aspects of Ireland and the British Empire* (Manchester, 1996); Gwyn A. Williams, *When Was Wales? A History of the Welsh* (Harmondsworth, 1985), pp. 124–25, 201, 220, 223–24. See chap. by David Fitzpatrick, and on Wales p. 20.

[6] From an expanding literature, Nupur Chaudhuri and Margaret Strobel, eds., *Western Women and Imperialism: Complicity and Resistance* (Bloomington, Ind., 1992); Ann McClintock, *Imperial Leather: Race, Gender and Sexuality in the Colonial Contest* (London, 1995); and Clare Midgley, ed., *Gender and Imperialism* (Manchester, 1997).

contexts. Secondly, historians have been more interested in cultures of dissent rather than conformity, in working-class resistance and intellectual critique rather than the cultural convergence which seems to characterize the Imperial age in the nineteenth century.[7] Thirdly, the works, stimulated by the South African War, of the liberal economist and journalist J. A. Hobson have long influenced historians. Their debate has been primarily concerned with the economic dimensions of imperialism, but also has cultural implications.[8] In *The Psychology of Jingoism* Hobson seemed contemptuous of the malleability, even gullibility, of popular culture, views unlikely to endear him to social historians or working-class sympathizers.[9]

Many twentieth-century British historians have reacted against both Hobson's polemics and studies by Marxist commentators who built upon his insights. Since Imperialism lost its intellectual respectability, between 1918 and 1939, there has been an inclination to play down the domestic cultural and political effects of Empire.[10] The burning Imperial rhetoric of the Liberal Imperialists of the 1890s and 1900s has been dismissed as mere political opportunism,[11] and the undoubted popular enthusiasms of the 'New Imperialism' seen as brief, spasmodic events.[12] It has also been suggested that the public excitements of the South African (Boer) War were essentially the product of the lower middle class, while the working classes concentrated on hard-headed domestic concerns.[13]

However, the pervasiveness of Empire in entertainment, education, and social activity in Britain demonstrated in recent scholarship reveals cultural practices as inseparable from the political and economic dimensions of imperialism: they both reflected and sometimes actively shaped the instruments of such domestic inheritance of Empire. They offer vital clues to the attitudes of different social classes and individuals; the relationships among them; the flow and ebb of Imperial ideas; and the origins of manipulative forces (if any) within the nation and the state. Cultural practices also illuminate the interaction of the full range of metropolitan cultures and attempts to weld them into a more cohesive Imperial whole. As these concerns

---

[7] Bernard Porter, *Critics of Empire: British Radical Attitudes to Colonialism in Africa, 1895–1914* (London, 1968); John Belchem, *Industrialisation and the Working Class* (London, 1990).

[8] J. A. Hobson, *Imperialism: A Study* (London, 1902); D. K. Fieldhouse, *The Theory of Capitalist Imperialism* (London 1967); Porter, *Critics of Empire*; Andrew Porter, *European Imperialism, 1860–1914* (Basingstoke, 1994), pp. 10 and 62–63.

[9] J. A. Hobson, *The Psychology of Jingoism* (London, 1901), and *The War in South Africa: Its Causes and Effects* (London, 1900).

[10] e.g. A. J. P. Taylor, *English History, 1914–45* (Oxford, 1965) and Henry Pelling, *Popular Politics and Society in Late Victorian Britain* (London, 1979).

[11] H. C. G. Matthew, *The Liberal Imperialists* (Oxford, 1973), p. 151.

[12] D. K. Fieldhouse, *Economics and Empire, 1830–1914* (London, 1976), pp. 75–76.

[13] Richard Price, *An Imperial War and the British Working Class* (London, 1972).

with class and community have widened, the debate has also been carried back in time. Discussions about an Imperial culture once concentrated on the second half of the nineteenth century, era of the 'New Imperialism', the period when entertainment and media became susceptible to new technologies and mass-market techniques, apparently rendering Empire more accessible to a larger public.[14] Imperial excitements were readily identifiable and the popular psychology seemed as susceptible to analysis as the 'official mind'. It is now apparent, however, that widespread cultural expressions of Empire can be identified at least from the late eighteenth century.

Consideration of the metropolitan cultural life of Imperialism is closely connected to discussions about the character and objectives of Imperial rule, but it sets up more extensive rhythms than the often short-term concentration of political controversy. All periods of Imperial activity witnessed acrimonious debates about the necessity or otherwise of the extension of rule, the principles and practices of Empire, and the agencies through which they were implemented. The very word 'imperialism' passed through many changes in meanings and resonance (positive and negative) in the course of the nineteenth century.[15] But amid this maelstrom of intellectual and political activity there were also cultural continuities: a sense of Britain's national destiny and purpose, often heightened through repeated representations of outsiders; and, increasingly, a projection of moral purpose and an alignment of patriotic forces, which together built up an emotional distinctiveness (often expressed in the language of superiority) in respect of both the peoples of Empire and other European nations. Through all of this run interlocking elements of nationality, class, and race. Hence, although it is conventional to identify differing periods in the development of Empire's manifestations through the 'long century', cultural activity seems to represent a certain continuity.

Empire, the British State, and Cultural Continuity

There is little doubt that possession of Empire was significant in forging a sense of 'Britishness' in the late eighteenth century. The British may well have constructed their identity by contrasting themselves with their French neighbours, but this was heightened by the long global duel with France.[16] The Scots were also perhaps

---

[14] W. Hamish Fraser, *The Coming of the Mass Market* (London, 1981); H. John Field, *Toward a Programme of Imperial Life: The British Empire at the Turn of the Century* (Oxford, 1982); Hugh Cunningham, 'The Language of Patriotism, 1750–1914', *History Workshop*, XXII (1981), pp. 8–33, and 'Jingoism in 1877–78', *Victorian Studies*, XIV (1971), pp. 429–53.

[15] R. Koebner and H. D. Schmidt, *Imperialism: The Story and Significance of a Political Word, 1840–1960* (Cambridge, 1964).

[16] Linda Colley, *Britons: Forging the Nation, 1707–1837* (London, 1992).

crucial to this new identity, and although Britain was often referred to as England, from the early eighteenth century the Empire was never anything other than British, a setting for common action by the component populations of the British Islands.[17]

News of colonial activities circulated fairly widely. History painters, who had previously depicted events mainly from the past, took to portraying such moments as Wolfe's death at Quebec in 1759, the acquisition of the Bengal *diwani* by Robert Clive in 1765, and the succession of wars against Tipu Sultan, ruler of Mysore in the last two decades of the century. Such paintings appeared in highly public places, such as buildings in the Vauxhall and other gardens on the South Bank of the Thames, or circulated in engravings. After Captain Cook's death in Hawaii in 1779 he too became the subject of paintings, engravings, and poems.[18] Such Imperial paintings represent a significant strand in British popular art until the early twentieth century. The work of landscape artists (such as Thomas and William Daniell, who visited India between 1786 and 1793 and published their magnificent volumes between 1795 and 1808) was reproduced in engravings throughout the century. Even more influential were paintings of the defining moments of Empire, Imperial campaigns, and its soldiery and heroes. Sometimes these were painted well after the events depicted. Sir David Wilkie completed his vast canvas of General Sir David Baird discovering the body of Tipu Sultan in 1838, commemorating an event from the Mysore wars in 1799. Lady Elizabeth Butler painted *The Remnants of an Army* in 1879, illustrating the British disaster of 1842 in Afghanistan. Others, like the Indian Mutiny paintings of Frederick Goodall and Henry Nelson O'Neill and G. W. Joy's celebrated depiction of Gordon's death at Khartoum, were painted soon after the events. By the end of the nineteenth century photography was beginning to play a similar role and received wide circulation through the press, postcards, cigarette cards, and advertising.[19]

Visual materials were also used to promote the religious and humanitarian concerns of Empire. These illustrate not only a degree of cultural continuity but also the manner in which different social classes and regions of the country could be swept up into major issues of the day. Just as Protestantism was an important marker of 'Britishness' in the late eighteenth century, so was evangelicalism and its

---

[17] George Kirk McGilvary, 'East India Patronage and the Political Management of Scotland, 1720–74', unpublished Ph.D. thesis, Open University, Scotland, 1989; G. J. Bryant, 'Scots in India in the Eighteenth Century', *Scottish Historical Review*, I, 14 (1985), pp. 22–41.

[18] Bernard Smith, *Imagining the Pacific: In the Wake of the Cook Voyages* (New Haven, 1992), chap. 10.

[19] Brian Allen, 'From Plassey to Seringapatam: India and British History Painting, c.1760–c.1800', in C. A. Bayly, ed., *Raj: India and the British, 1600–1947* (London, 1990), pp. 26–27; John M. MacKenzie, 'The Art of Empire', in P. J. Marshall, ed., *Cambridge Illustrated History of the British Empire* (Cambridge, 1996), pp. 296–315. James Ryan, *Picturing Empire: Photography and the Visualisation of the British Empire* (London, 1997).

related humanitarian complex a significant element in Imperial culture. The Society for Effecting the Abolition of the Slave Trade, founded in 1787, was largely middle class, but pioneered techniques that were to embrace a much wider spectrum of the population in the nineteenth century. Effective use of tracts, pamphlets, books, petitions, lectures, powerful visual images and related artefacts soon made slavery a cross-class issue. The propaganda success of this movement influenced domestic political campaigns such as Chartism and the Anti-Corn Law League.[20] It notably drew upon the energies of women and stimulated the remarkable working-class boycott of American cotton in Lancashire in the early 1860s.

At a time when considerable sectors of the population gave time to the education and entertainment as well as spiritual uplift available in the churches, humanitarian concerns permeated the missionary movement. The Victorians became particularly interested in how exemplary lives could illustrate the social and spiritual objectives of these movements and provide moral touchstones to a contemporary generation. William Wilberforce, David Livingstone, and Charles Gordon were all hero-worshipped for their work against the slave trade. Missionary memoirs and biographies, from Robert Moffat in the 1840s to Mary Slessor in the early 1900s, became a popular aspect of publishing. Moreover, evangelical activity offered a milieu where women could express themselves more freely than in many other walks of life. They became steadily more involved in missionary recruitment, fund-raising, and propaganda.[21] The professions increasingly open to them, namely, teaching and nursing, were important routes to work within the Empire overseas, and a source of support at home. Women churchgoers in the city of Glasgow, for example, were active in the Ladies' Colonial Association and the Ladies' Association for the Advancement of Female Education in India in the later decades of the century.[22] Here women were doing much more than acting as auxiliaries in the Imperial endeavour: they were creating significant means of self-expression and independent action, often related to their (albeit culturally and racially slanted) concerns about the position of women in other societies.

From the late eighteenth century a tradition of highly topical theatre began to concentrate on exotic peoples and events. Portraits were painted of Omai, a

[20] J. R. Oldfield, *Popular Politics and British Anti-Slavery: The Mobilisation of Public Opinion Against the Slave Trade, 1783–1807* (Manchester, 1995); R. Coupland, *The British Anti-Slavery Movement* (London, 1933); Douglas A. Lorimer, *Colour, Class and the Victorians: English Attitudes to the Negro in the Mid-Nineteenth Century* (Leicester, 1978).

[21] Clare Midgley, *Women Against Slavery: The British Campaigns, 1780–1870* (London 1992), and 'Anti-slavery and Feminism in Nineteenth-Century Britain', *Gender and History*, III, 3 (1993), pp. 343–62.

[22] Stana Nenadic, 'The Victorian Middle Classes', in Hamish Fraser and Irene Maver, eds., *Glasgow*, Vol. II, *1830–1912*, (Manchester 1996), p. 288.

Tahitian brought to London by Captain Cook, and he was the subject of theatrical performances on the London stage.[23] One such was John O'Keefe's pantomime *Omai, or a Trip Round the World*, which ran in London and the provinces to capacity audiences between 1785 and 1788. A play about Tipu Sultan, *Tippoo Saib or British Valour in India*, appeared on the London stage in 1791. It included 'a battle dance and a representation of an English and Indian Grand Martial Procession'.[24] It was the first of several dramatic portrayals of Tipu which appeared in 1792, 1799, and 1838. The events of the Napoleonic wars were similarly staged, sometimes in spectacular settings, using aquatic displays, horses, and other animals.[25] By the 1820s the fascination with India of such Romantic poets as Byron, Shelley, De Quincey, and Coleridge was communicated to the theatre and a sequence of popular melodramas was performed on the London and provincial stages.[26] Pantomime, another dramatic form which developed great popularity, also began to use exotic characters, often people from the East associated with Imperial expansion.[27]

The particular conditions of the London and provincial theatre, notably the prevailing censorship, helped emphasize these interests. Domestic political and class conflict, depictions of the royal family and politicians, references to the Irish problem or biblical subjects and religious controversies were all banned.[28] Consequently, plays involving geographical discovery, Empire and war, portrayal of other peoples, and the creation of spectacular fantasy worlds were particularly acceptable. Thus, popular melodrama which in the past had usually derived its effects from the interplay of upper and lower classes, sometimes highlighting moral dilemmas inherent in exploitative social and economic relations, turned overseas in order to produce the same effects, thus externalizing class into race. In this period the audience was being offered exciting new information, fantastic visions of the East which, although sometimes set in East India Company territories, perhaps had more to do with oriental fascinations than Imperial issues.

---

[23] Bernard Smith, *European Vision and the South Pacific, 1768–1850: A Study in the History of Art and Ideas* (1969; London, 1985), pp. 114–16.

[24] P. J. Marshall, 'Taming the Exotic: The British and India in the Seventeenth and Eighteenth Centuries', in G. S. Rousseau and Roy Porter, eds., *Exoticism in the Enlightenment* (Manchester, 1990), p. 56; Heidi Holder, 'Melodrama, Realism and Empire on the British Stage', in J. S. Bratton and others, *Acts of Supremacy: The British Empire and the Stage, 1790–1930* (Manchester, 1991), pp. 129–49.

[25] Derek Forbes, 'Aquatic Drama', in David Bradby and others, eds., *Performance and Politics in Popular Drama* (Cambridge 1980), pp. 90–112; Michael Booth, *Victorian Spectacular Theatre, 1850–1910* (London, 1981).

[26] Holder, 'Melodrama, Realism and Empire'; Michael Booth, *English Melodrama* (London, 1965); Nigel Leask, *British Romantic Writers and the East: Anxieties of Empire* (Cambridge, 1992).

[27] David Mayer, *Harlequin in his Element: The English Pantomime, 1806–36* (Cambridge, Mass., 1969).

[28] John Russell Stephens, *The Censorship of the English Drama, 1824–1901* (Cambridge, 1980).

In many of the early-nineteenth-century plays, interracial couples (almost always a white male and an Asian female) featured prominently: audiences seem to have been fascinated by the crossing of racial lines. The conflict between good and evil, lying at their core, was normally worked out among indigenous factions with Europeans intervening only to promote the victory of truth and justice.[29] An enduring European figure in many plays was 'Jack Tar', a working-class naval hero, invariably seen as rough and rowdy at home but heroically moral abroad. Until about 1850, Tar often fought for interracial harmony and assisted the victory of noble indigenous figures. Later, the increasing concern with the technological and moral superiority of Britain over other parts of the world was expressed by him in chauvinistic language and violent events.

The Indian Revolt of 1857, the Zulu War of 1879, the death of General Gordon at Khartoum, and events in southern Africa in the 1890s and during the Boer War were all staged both in London and the 'provinces' in highly popular plays. In these later works alleged racial differences tended to be presented much more starkly.[30] However, it has been suggested that even this material is highly ambiguous, identifying a 'concentration upon the expiation of Imperial guilt by the sacrifice and return to life of the hero'.[31]

The truly distinctive theatrical form of the later nineteenth century was, however, the music hall. This developed from traditional entertainment in pubs and 'song and supper' saloons, mainly in working-class areas. By the 1870s licensing policies were creating a divide between drinking and the provision of variety shows, and there was a country-wide explosion in theatre building. Music halls sprang up in almost every town and similar entertainments were provided in all of them.[32] Patriotic song scenes, featuring uniformed performers, the showing of the flag, and even representations of Britannia and Queen Victoria, invariably formed a significant part of such shows. The 'tableau vivant' was another characteristic form, sufficiently respectable to appear in church halls as well as theatres. These tableaux often featured well-known patriotic and Imperial events, re-created in frozen dumb-show. Sometimes they followed a well-known painting, thus providing an additional spark of visual recognition for the audience, or took up a key moment in the Indian Mutiny, or Gordon's death.

---

[29] J. S. Bratton, 'British Heroism and the Structure of Melodrama', in Bratton and others, *Acts of Supremacy*, pp. 18–61.

[30] Holder, 'Melodrama, Realism and Empire'.

[31] Bratton, 'British Heroism', p. 58.

[32] Peter Bailey, *Leisure and Class in Victorian England: Rational Recreation and the Contest for Control, 1830–85* (London, 1978); R. Mander and J. Mitchensen, *British Music Hall* (London, 1965); G. J. Mellor, *The Northern Music Hall* (Newcastle upon Tyne, 1970).

Celebrated singers performed patriotic songs in the most famous London and provincial halls, gaining considerable fame and fortune as a result. Lesser-known imitators carried this material to remoter theatres, while the songs gained further publicity via sheet music for home performance, and concert parties at seaside resorts and in the parks of the larger municipalities. The most famous of these songs was G. W. Hunt's 'By Jingo', source of the word 'jingoism', and performed by G. H. Macdermott during the Russo-Turkish crisis of 1877–78. This represented aggressive nationalism, but there were countless others with more specific Imperial content,[33] one such, again by Hunt, relating to the Afghan crisis of 1879:

> The Afghan Wolf may friendship make
> With cunning Russian Bear,
> But the Indian Tiger's wide awake
> And bids them both beware!
> The prowling foe on plunder bent
> By this should surely know
> The British Lion's not asleep
> As in the years ago.
> The dusky sons of Hindostan
> Will by our banner stand.
> Australia, aye, and Canada,
> Both love the dear old land!
> No foe we fear—we fight for right!
> No day we e'er shall rue
> If England, dear old England,
> To herself be only true.

This representation of countries as animals was extremely common, not only in songs but also in contemporary cartoons. It helped, perhaps, to heighten a sense of power and aggression. The appeal to the White Dominions to stand together with the mother country against a supposedly common foe was also a frequent refrain. In the music halls Tommy Atkins became the equally celebrated military equivalent of Jack Tar.[34] One song from 1894 featured Tommy fighting throughout the Empire:

> And whether he's on India's coral strand,
> Or pouring out his blood in the Soudan,
> To keep our flag a flying, he's doing and a dying,
> Every inch of him a soldier and a man.

[33] Penny Summerfield, 'Patriotism and Empire: Music Hall Entertainment, 1870–1914', in Mackenzie, *Imperialism and Popular Culture*, pp. 17–48.

[34] Kipling, of course, popularized Tommy Atkins as a generic name for the British soldier, though it originated *c.*1815 when it was used as the name on the specimen enlistment form.

This kind of material led Hobson to portray the music hall as a fount of patriotism, a 'potent educator' of 'mob passion', 'appealing by coarse humour or exaggerated pathos to the animal lusts of an audience stimulated by alcohol into appreciative hilarity'.[35] Many historians have found this seriously overdrawn. However, more recent research indicates that such entertainment was indeed enormously popular in both the working-class halls of London's East End and the middle-class theatres of the West End and wealthier suburbs. Even if Hobson's language is excessively lurid, patriotic shows, prominently featuring Imperial material, were undoubtedly immensely popular from at least the 1870s to 1914. Although much of this material was also satirized, satirical versions themselves tend to indicate the considerable fame of the original rather than undermine its sentiment.[36] Perhaps the underlying comic aspect of many of these songs helped deflect some of the violence and aggression, stressing instead the ambiguities and complexities of the Imperial relationship.

Theatrical fascination with the spectacular character of Imperial activity was matched in visual entertainments which also inspired a considerable following. Exotic animals and peoples were both displayed in commercial shows,[37] but more people probably encountered such diversions through the painted panoramas, dioramas, and cosmoramas shown throughout Britain.[38] The panorama, dating from the 1780s, originally presented a 360-degree image, like a vast theatrical set (and indeed scene painters often executed them) to be viewed from a central gallery. More sophisticated successors offered huge continuous tableaux either as a canvas which was gradually unfurled or on painted boards slid into place by elaborate systems of rollers. The Battle of the Nile appeared on a panorama in 1799, soon followed by the fall of Seringapatam. Thereafter all major military actions were displayed, including events of the Indian Mutiny, the bombardment of Alexandria and the Battle of Tel-el-Kebir during Britain's invasion of Egypt in 1882, and the action at Omdurman in reconquering the Sudan in 1898. Distinguished painters and set designers—David Roberts, John Martin, Frederick Catherwood, and Augustus Earle—were all celebrated for their panoramas.

As the century wore on, many assumed exploratory and didactic purposes: trips around the world, the Overland Mail to India (presented with the assistance of the P&O shipping company), journeys to Hong Kong and later across the Canadian Pacific and Trans-Siberian Railways. Material on emigration, particularly to

---

[35] Hobson, *Psychology of Jingoism*, pp. 1, 3, 9.
[36] Lawrence Senelick, 'Politics as Entertainment: Victorian Music Hall Songs', *Victorian Studies*, XIX (1975), pp. 149–80.
[37] Richard D. Altick, *The Shows of London* (Cambridge, Mass., 1978).
[38] Ralph Hyde, *Panoramania: The Art and Entertainment of the 'All-Embracing View'* (London, 1988).

Canada, Australia, and New Zealand, was disseminated in this way, and there were vast views of eastern cities such as Bombay, Benares, Delhi, and Hong Kong. A Delhi artist even produced spectacular images of the Mughal Emperor's durbar procession in 1815. Panoramas can be seen as a highly successful bridge between high art and popular entertainment. They represented major technical advances in perspective, optics, and efforts at a fresh representation of the world. Displayed everywhere in dedicated buildings, they were a significant means whereby an Imperial people could visualize and encompass within their own imaginations the scale of conquest and command of the outer world. The art critic, social commentator, and supporter of Imperialism John Ruskin greatly approved of them. He described a panorama building in Leicester Square, London, as an 'educational institution of the highest and purest value', worthy of government support as a beneficial 'educational instrument'.[39]

The Indian Revolt of 1857 as an Ideological Turning-Point

While there was considerable continuity in these cultural expressions of Empire, it is also apparent that significant shifts took place in the last decades of the nineteenth century. What had earlier seemed fresh and exotic, full of intriguing potential, became more a battleground not only among empires but also between technical and moral systems. A heightened sense of conflict, a greater anxiety about British capacity to survive and prosper, but also more powerful convictions of cultural superiority and moral worth ran through later projections of Imperialism in these metropolitan cultures. Why had this happened? We can perhaps find answers in the actual events of Imperial rule, in the growing sense of international competition, and in growth of the mass market and the universal search for public acceptability.

One of the most significant ideological turning-points in this cultural metamorphosis came with the Indian Revolt or Mutiny of 1857. Thereafter, this was seen as a great moral watershed, a defining moment of Empire when it faced its greatest test and survived. It also contributed to a progressive heightening of racial attitudes in Imperial culture. The murders of white women and children were particularly shocking to Victorian sensibilities. The Mutiny appeared not only to call forth exemplary heroism, but also to indicate that Indians had rejected policies of Western assimilation. Such racial ideas were further exacerbated by controversy over the brutal suppression by Governor Eyre of the Jamaica Revolt of 1865.[40]

[39] Hyde, *Panoramania: The Art and Entertainment of the 'All-Embracing View'*, p. 28.
[40] See below, pp. 486–87.

Many Victorians, convinced of the supposedly progressive moral and economic effects of Empire upon indigenous peoples and ex-slaves, regarded such resistance as evidence of ingratitude and unwillingness to accept Imperial benefits. Such attitudes were inevitably reflected in the popular culture of the time. Moreover, if the term 'New Imperialism' has meaning, it lies not least in the development of pseudo-scientific racism, the codification of Imperial thought, and the development of the relationship between Empire and education, societies, and exhibitions.

The Mutiny certainly helped transform the army's reputation, already enhanced by the Crimean War; troops became heroic saviours of the besieged avengers of British honour. In the development of Imperial history paintings, it was the Mutiny which helped to create a tradition of grand and sentimental Imperial canvases by such artists as Goodall and O'Neill.[41] The Mutiny also helped generate the atmosphere of hero-worship so characteristic of late-nineteenth-century imperialism. The military leaders of its suppression, figures such as Sir James Outram (the 'Bayard of India' as he was dubbed in a conscious invocation of the medieval Crusades), Herbert Edwardes (whom John Ruskin described as a 'military bishop'), Sir Henry Lawrence (dying while besieged in Lucknow), and above all Sir Henry Havelock became evangelical knights, defenders of the faith as well as the Empire.[42]

Religion, heroism, and Empire were conjoined in a potent mix. Nineteenth-century heroes, most notably Livingstone and General Gordon, were essentially religious figures, portrayed as moral titans facing dark forces which martyred them in a Christ-like sacrifice. The churches and missionary societies were not the least sources of the popular culture of Empire. Moreover, it was perhaps the Mutiny which transformed that powerful evangelical figure Samuel Smiles from a radical, self-improving, working-class propagandist into one who used Empire as a prime source of moral uplift and self-help.[43] He certainly made much of the Mutiny heroes (Campbell and Havelock both had relatively humble social origins), and of David Livingstone whose reputation was contemporaneously being forged in Africa.[44] The Indian Revolt may also have helped transform Ruskin into

[41] J. W. M. Hichberger, *Images of the Army: The Military in British Art, 1815–1914* (Manchester, 1988); Paul Usherwood, 'Officer Material: Representations of Leadership in Late Nineteenth-Century British Battle Painting', in John M. MacKenzie, ed., *Popular Imperialism and the Military* (Manchester, 1992), pp. 162–78.

[42] John M. MacKenzie, 'Heroic Myths of Empire', in MacKenzie, *Popular Imperialism and the Military*, pp. 109–38.

[43] Angus Calder, 'Samuel Smiles: The Unexpurgated Version', *The Raven, Anarchist Quarterly*, V (1989), pp. 79–89.

[44] Samuel Smiles, *Self Help* (London, 1859). A photograph of Livingstone provided the frontispiece of all later editions of Smiles's best-selling work.

the fervent imperialist of his inaugural lecture as Slade Professor at Oxford in 1870.[45]

The military myths of the Mutiny fed into the visual, theatrical, and fictional representations of Imperial action in the later part of the century. They also contributed to the tradition of Christian militarism, which helped enhance the reputation of both army and navy and was reflected in the founding of youth organizations with their military forms and an Imperial patriotism as part of their moral training. The Salvation Army first appeared in 1878, and cadet corps sprang up in the public schools and even spread to working-class districts. The Boys' Brigade was founded in Glasgow in 1883; by 1896 there were over 700 companies in Britain and many soon appeared in the Dominions and colonies. The Anglican Church Lads' Brigade followed in 1891, the Nonconformist Boys' Life Brigade in 1899, and there were Jewish and Catholic equivalents. Many other organizations (such as the Boys' Empire League, the Boys' Naval Brigade, and the Boys' Rifle Brigade) stressed Imperial patriotism with rather less attention to the religious dimension. The Imperial context was given a new twist with the founding of the Boy Scouts (soon followed by the Girl Guides) in 1907 by the hero of the Siege of Mafeking in the South African War, Sir Robert (later Lord) Baden-Powell. He created the most popular youth organization of modern times, and through it brought an Imperial frontier vision (represented in its uniform of shorts, shirt, and broad-brimmed hat, and its emphasis on the outdoors and natural observation) to the training of the young.

The Culture of the New Imperialism

The shifting tone of Empire is observable in the tradition of Imperial exhibitions. The first Great Exhibition, at the Crystal Palace in Hyde Park, London, in 1851, was concerned with the relationship between arts and industry and with world-wide commerce. It represented Britain at the peak of its global economic power displaying Imperial products intermingled with foreign exhibits.[46] In the 1862 Exhibition in South Kensington this Imperial content had grown considerably. India had no fewer than 7,000 exhibits and thirty other colonies also took part, but it was still portrayed as an international exhibition featuring the trade of all nations.

However, from the 1880s the exhibitions became explicitly Imperial and continued so until the Glasgow Empire Exhibition of 1938. In 1886 the London

---

[45] 'Inaugural Lecture', in E. T. Cook and A. Wedderburn, eds., *The Works of John Ruskin*, 39 vols. (London, 1903–12), XX, pp. 17–43, and 'The Two Paths', *Works*, XVI, pp. 261–65, where Ruskin, in a series of lectures delivered in 1858, indicates his revulsion from the Mutiny and revaluation of Indian art.

[46] Paul Greenhalgh, *Ephemeral Vistas: The Expositions Universelles, Great Exhibitions and World's Fairs, 1851–1939* (Manchester, 1988).

Exhibition was known as 'the Colonial and Indian', an Imperial emphasis continued through many provincial expositions, for example, in Glasgow (1888, 1901, and 1911), Wolverhampton (1902), Bradford (1904), Edinburgh (1908), Liverpool (1913), and Newcastle (1929). In London, exhibitions were so popular that they were mounted commercially by the remarkable Imre Kiralfy. Among his many exhibitions were the Empire of India (1895), the Greater Britain (1899), the Imperial International (1909), and the Coronation (1911). A second, official, Coronation Exhibition was held at the Crystal Palace at Sydenham. The whole movement climaxed with the great Empire Exhibition at Wembley in 1924–25.[47] One might view this growing concentration on Empire as yet another symptom of British relative decline. As other nations industrialized, and Britain became apparently more dependent on her Empire, the Imperial connection became the most important focus for these public displays of wealth and power.

These exhibitions featured the products, trade, technology, and cultures of mother country and colonies. The declared objective of the 1886 'Colinderies' (as the Colonial and Indian Exhibition was known) was 'to give to the inhabitants of the British Isles, to foreigners and to one another, practical demonstration of the wealth and industrial development of the outlying portions of the British Empire'.[48] In fact, this and other exhibitions tended to concentrate on Britain's industries' and colonies' potential as suppliers of markets, raw materials, and foodstuffs. As temporary museums of industry, science, and natural history, they also included anthropological and folk display, emigration bureaux, musical festivals, and art galleries. An important element in the later exhibitions (especially Kiralfy's) was a vast funfair, which increased their great popularity. But visitors who moved from the funfair into the other exhibition arenas cannot have failed to sense the extraordinary economic and administrative, military, and cultural power they were designed to represent.

Yet the exhibitions also represented a cultural (if not yet an economic) retreat from free trade and the *laissez-faire* liberalism which had sustained the British since the 1840s. From the 1880s their message was that the British, as a world-wide family of white settler territories and colonies, should stick together in a supposedly complementary economic system.[49] In this, they revealed an awareness of growing continental protectionism, European imperial rivalries, and endemic bouts of industrial depression. As with so much to do with Empire, they were enshrining a number of myths. It was already clear that the Imperial system was far from self-sufficient or internally complementary. Not until the serious slumps of

---

[47] Exhibitions also took place throughout the Empire, in, for example, Sydney, Calcutta, Bombay, Johannesburg, and Wellington. See Vol. IV, chap. by John M. Mackenzie.

[48] F. Cundall, ed., *Reminiscences of the Colonial and Indian Exhibition* (London, 1886), pp. 1–2.

[49] cf. pp. 348–57.

the inter-war years did the message of Imperial exhibitions seem to match the economic and political mood.

The exhibitions represented a sharpening sense of Imperial conflict and the need for new forms of mutuality in the British Empire; they also indicated a heightening of racial consciousness. The most intriguing (and most frequently commented upon) displays were the 'native villages' that commonly appeared. There was nothing exclusively 'British' about these: they featured peoples from the British, French, and even Russian empires, supposedly inhabiting their traditional dwellings, and displaying craftsmanship, cooking, and sports for visitors' edification. They became a form of ethnic 'peep-show', simultaneously illustrating 'backwardness' and alternative lifestyles. Many Indians came to demonstrate their crafts at the Colonial and Indian Exhibition and several were painted (mainly by Rudolf Swoboda) for Queen Victoria—the paintings are now hung outside the durbar dining room at Osborne House. At Kiralfy's Greater Britain Exhibition in 1899 South African peoples (including Zulu, Sotho, and Swazi) re-enacted scenes from their recent history. A Somali village (stressing the martial nature of Somalis) appeared at several subsequent exhibitions, and also toured seaside resorts. This was a cross-empire fascination, two of the most popular shows being of Dahomeyan and Senegalese villagers first displayed at the Jardin d'Acclimatation in Paris.[50]

Missionary and other societies put on smaller-scale exhibitions in many localities, illustrating their work but also displaying the artefacts and lifestyles of peoples in the Empire. This was the popular and propagandist end of the ethnographic displays mounted in national and private collections, in London (the British Museum and the Horniman Museum), and elsewhere such as Oxford (the Pitt-Rivers Museum), and Liverpool (the Joseph Mayer collection).[51] Smaller ethnographic collections appeared widely in municipal museums and the country houses of those associated with travel or Empire. Such collections illustrated the full range of human taxonomies, paralleling the classification which had gone on throughout the century of new discoveries in botany, entomology and zoology. Although such human materials had been collected since the days of Elizabethan exploration, the process quickened in the eighteenth century and peaked in the period between 1880 and the First World War.

Museums distinguished clearly between the art and artefacts of the 'civilizations' of Europe and the ancient Mediterranean world and those of other peoples.

---

[50] Michael A. Osborne, *Nature, the Exotic and the Science of French Colonialism* (Bloomington, Ind., 1994); William H. Schneider, *An Empire for the Masses: The French Popular Image of Africa, 1870–1900* (Westport, Conn., 1982).

[51] Annie E. Coombes, *Reinventing Africa: Museums, Material Culture and Popular Imagination in Late Victorian and Edwardian England* (London, 1994).

Such 'ethnic' materials were increasingly used to illustrate concepts of social evolution according to stages of 'development', from hunting and gathering, through pastoral and agricultural modes, to commercial and industrial systems. Thus, other peoples were organized into categories which derived authority from their air of scientific objectivity but essentially reflected Europeans' views of themselves. Charles Darwin's two great works, *The Origin of Species* (1859) and *The Descent of Man* (1871), came to underpin much of the ethnography and pseudo-scientific racism of the period (as they did much of later-nineteenth-century intellectual life and in ways largely unintended by Darwin himself). Herbert Spencer, among others, applied Darwin's theory of 'natural selection' to human societies, reinforcing older ideas that 'primitive' peoples, and some supposedly static 'advanced' societies, were liable to extinction if they failed to adapt to the modern world. Such 'social Darwinian' ideas became central to much popular culture, including advertising, juvenile literature, and school textbooks.

Schools were indeed another important medium for the projection of an Imperial culture. While the Empire's development was treated in some early geographical texts, only after the Education Act of 1870 did the significance of Imperial rule in the formation and development of the British state become truly prominent in the large numbers of school texts, on British history, world geography, and the development of English language and literature, which were produced until the 1950s.[52] Many were influenced by Sir John Seeley's *The Expansion of England* (London, 1883) and by the school of Imperial geographers that emerged late in the century. However, there was no state control of the production or use of such texts and a wide variety were in circulation at any moment. They offered various shades of opinion about Empire (though none expressed outright criticism) and their emphases subtly changed to match contemporary Imperial objectives. Many included racial ideas influenced by such notions as climatic determinism and social Darwinism. The reformed English public schools are often seen as the main forcing-ground for this type of material, but state educators both in Britain and the Empire often set out to emulate them.[53]

The re-invention of other cultures at exhibitions and their placing in the scale of human history in school texts was strongly influenced by the emerging discipline of anthropology.[54] Practitioners of this new approach to the study of humankind seldom did fieldwork, but pursued their researches by reading the travel accounts

[52] Kathryn Castle, *Britannia's Children: Reading Colonialism through Children's Books and Magazines* (Manchester 1996).

[53] J. A. Mangan, *Athleticism in the Victorian and Edwardian Public School* (Cambridge, 1981); J. A. Mangan, ed., *'Benefits Bestowed'? Education and British Imperialism* (Manchester, 1988), and *Making Imperial Mentalities: Socialisation and British Imperialism* (Manchester, 1990).

[54] George W. Stocking, *Victorian Anthropology* (New York, 1987).

of others. They also provided questionnaires for people who did visit colonial territories: missionaries, military officers, and administrators. Many travellers were also notable amateur anthropologists, whose works had a wider circulation than those by writers considering themselves professionals. Mary Kingsley, who travelled in West Africa between 1893 and 1895, followed the tradition of Livingstone in including anthropological accounts as well as colonial economic theory and natural history in her books.[55]

When anthropologists did become field workers, from about 1900, they usually worked within Imperial structures, utilizing the authority gleaned from power, offering advice to rulers and helping to train officials. Anthropology, in consequence, has often been seen as a discipline owing its origins and early development to dominance by Europe of much of the outer world. Nevertheless, although heavily influenced by Darwinism, anthropological discourse was not monolithic. It was riven by controversy, amply reflected in the organizations founded to support ethnographic study. The Ethnological Society of London, founded by Thomas Hodgkin in 1844, retained many of the humanitarian interests of its founders, but racial determinists influenced by Robert Knox (whose *Races of Man* was first published in 1850) founded the Anthropological Society of London in 1863. These two strands of ethnographic study re-established their uneasy partnership in the Anthropological Institute in 1871.[56] Such differences of interpretations however, were seldom inimical to the development or practice of Imperial rule.

Like anthropology, many physical and life sciences were similarly affected by, and in turn influenced, the contexts of power in which they grew up. Well into the twentieth century such disciplines retained a fundamental belief in scientific and technical progress rooted in Imperial ideas of the beneficent spread of Western science. In the nineteenth century they were associated with the extensive development of societies, professional associations, and a considerable amateur membership; their lectures and publications had a much wider public interest than the purely professional. Thus, they became significant channels through which scientific developments associated with imperialism were disseminated to wider audiences. There is space here to consider only one of the most influential interests, the geographical societies.

---

[55] Dea Birkett, *Mary Kingsley: Imperial Adventuress* (Basingstoke, 1992); Mary Kingsley, *Travels in West Africa, Congo Français, Corisco and Cameroons* (London, 1897), and *West African Studies* (London, 1899).

[56] Christine Bolt, *Victorian Attitudes towards Race* (London, 1971); Lorimer, 'Race, Science and Culture: Historical Continuities and Discontinuities, 1850–1914', in Shearer West, ed., *The Victorians and Race* (Aldershot, 1996), pp. 12–33.

The origins and development of the Royal Geographical Society (RGS) are considered elsewhere.[57] However, the wider growth of geographical societies is emblematic of the broadening social base of such interest, the emergence of regional bodies with their own agendas, and the stimuli offered, for example, by the Scramble for Africa. The social composition of the early RGS was aristocratic and upper middle class, its prime interests in travel and exploration.[58] But from the 1870s greater interest was shown in both the development of commercial geography and the emergence of a more strictly scientific discipline. Although the RGS remained a strikingly Imperial body, it was now riven by controversies with class, professional, practical, and even gender bases.[59]

Pressure for change came from those who felt the discipline should be severely practical, concentrating on the economic potential of overseas territories, especially for metropolitan industry and trade. Moreover, some argued, geography was too London-dominated; it needed to expand into the provinces, there to be utilized and propagated by practical men of business. Plans for a geographical society in Manchester, begun in 1879, finally bore fruit in 1884. It was founded by prominent local politicians, businessmen, clergy, and professional people, active in what has sometimes been called 'municipal imperialism'. An excellent example was the wealthy merchant J. F. Hutton; highly influential in the Manchester Chamber of Commerce, he was concerned, along with many others, to overcome cyclical depression in the Lancashire cotton and related trades, and was involved in schemes for colonial rule in East and Central Africa. At the society's opening meeting the explorer and journalist H. M. Stanley stressed the importance of such societies to the survival of an Imperial state; to do his job properly every clerk in the industrial, commercial, and shipping offices of provincial cities should have some understanding of the geography of Empire.[60]

In the next few years geographical societies swiftly followed in Scotland (the Royal Scottish, with four branches in Edinburgh, Glasgow, Aberdeen, and Dundee), Newcastle, Liverpool, Hull, and Southampton. They all sought to create popular local memberships (including women, not admitted to the RGS in

[57] See chap. by Robert A. Stafford.

[58] D. R. Stoddart. 'The RGS and the "New Geography": Changing Aims and Changing Roles in Nineteenth-Century Science', *Geographical Journal* (hereafter *GJ*), CXXXXVI (1980), pp. 190–202; D. R. Stoddart, *On Geography and its History* (Oxford, 1986).

[59] Morag Bell and Cheryl McEwan, 'The Admission of Women Fellows to the Royal Geographical Society, 1892–1914: The Controversy and the Outcome', *GJ*, CLXII, 3 (1996), pp. 295–312.

[60] John M. MacKenzie, 'Geography and Imperialism: British Provincial Geographical Societies', in Felix Driver and Gillian Rose, eds., *Nature and Science: Essays in the History of Geographical Knowledge* (London, 1992), pp. 49–62, and 'The Provincial Geographical Societies in Britain, 1884–1914', in Morag Bell, Robin Butlin, and Michael Heffernan, eds., *Geography and Imperialism, 1820–1940* (Manchester, 1995), pp. 93–124.

London until some twenty years later), hold lectures by distinguished visitors, issue publications (including semi-scholarly journals), promote the discipline in universities, teacher-training colleges, and schools, and offer prizes for explorat- ory and educational work. Outside London, only the highly successful Scottish society also financed exploration. Research on their early years has indicated the close association of these societies and the 'New Imperialism'. All were concerned with the cyclical depressions of these years, the international competition repre- sented in Africa's partition, the expansion of knowledge to assist trade, the wide dissemination of Imperial information, and with influencing both governments and voters.

Their success was mixed. Both the Manchester and Scottish societies established firm local foundations, and survive to this day. The Royal Scottish, in particular, contributed significantly to Scotland's reputation as a scientific community pur- suing its own interests at home and abroad, for example, in Antarctic exploration. The others rapidly lost members before and during the First World War, and despite attempts at resuscitation in Liverpool and Newcastle between the wars, they all disappeared, following the many other societies associated with Empire which rose and fell in the late nineteenth century. Perhaps their greatest success was in helping to establish the importance of geography in schools. They also brought together geography teachers and academics (who had formed a national body in the Geographical Association of 1894) and often created essay prizes for geography students. In this work they mirrored that of the Royal Colonial Institute, founded in London in 1868 and active in promoting Imperial studies in universities and schools.[61]

Although Imperial pressure groups' fortunes mirror the changing concerns of Empire, other means of propagating Imperial ideas had a longer life and deeper social penetration. This is perhaps particularly true of visual imagery such as advertising, engravings, and (from the 1890s) photography in newspapers and journals, as well as popular and official publications of all sorts. Various develop- ments influenced the wide propagation of such ideas. The later nineteenth century has been seen as the first age of consumerism, reflected in the development of the modern mass market with all its extensive advertising, packaging, and devices (such as tea and cigarette cards) designed to maintain brand loyalty.[62] Many of these reflected patriotic pride, symbols of Empire and the excitements of Imperial events as well as racial ideas. New printing techniques made newspapers, maga- zines, and books cheaper and more commonly available. Modern studies of these

---

[61] Trevor R. Reese, *The History of the Royal Commonwealth Society* (London 1968), pp. 80–92.
[62] Jan Nederveen Pietersee, *White on Black: Images of Africa and Blacks in Western Popular Culture* (New Haven, 1992); Robert Opie, *Rule Britannia: Trading on the British Image* (Harmondsworth, 1985).

humble, yet ubiquitous materials indicate that Imperial ideas of all sorts were extensively propagated through them. High literacy rates also made them widely accessible. Even as early as the 1840s, between two-thirds and three-quarters of the working class were fully literate. Between 1870 and 1900 the estimated literacy rate of England and Wales rose from 80 per cent to 97 per cent, and of Scotland from 90 per cent to 98 per cent.[63]

Like theatrical productions, such publications were seen as uplifting, likely to discourage crime or social dissent. They offered instruction about the wider world: they propagated sympathetic views of the military, the royal family, Empire-builders, and missionary endeavour. They contributed to an adventure tradition containing, in the view of many contemporaries, patriotism and moral uplift. For this reason a powerful consensus can be found among religious societies involved in publication—such as the Society for the Promotion of Christian Knowledge, and the Religious Tract Society, which published the *Boy's Own Paper* from 1879 and the *Girl's Own Paper* from 1880—and the writers and publishers of many other juvenile journals, Empire annuals, vast numbers of popular novels, as well as school texts. Publishers (notably Blackie) produced books with Imperial themes for use in the expanding prize and present market for the young. Sunday schools and corporation day schools actively disseminated the works of such authors as W. H. G. Kingston, R. M. Ballantyne, and G. A. Henty. The circulations of journals and novels with Imperial content were remarkable. Both the *Boy's* and *Girl's Own Paper* sold 200,000 copies per week from the start; their estimated readerships exceeded 600,000 by 1914. Novelists like Sir Henry Rider Haggard maintained their immense popularity until the Second World War and beyond, their works continuously in print throughout the century.[64]

These publications heightened a sense of national identity, of the common purpose of Empire. Yet within that British framework there were also regional responses. The relationship of Ireland with the Empire was peculiarly complex, as is shown elsewhere in this volume.[65]

For the Scots, too, Empire offered remarkable opportunities. In many respects Scottish national pride was nourished by the opportunity to extend her independent church, educational system, and other aspects of her civil society into Imperial territories.[66] Migration established many links, particularly as Presbyterian churches and Caledonian and Burns societies in settlement colonies helped to

---

[63] Joseph McAleer, *Popular Reading and Publishing in Britain, 1914–1950* (Oxford, 1992), p. 14.

[64] Jeffrey Richards, ed., *Imperialism and Juvenile Literature* (Manchester, 1989); McAleer, *Popular Reading*, pp. 20, 209, and *passim*; Joseph Bristow, *Empire Boys: Adventures in a Man's World* (London, 1991), pp. 72–106; 107–25.

[65] See chap. by David Fitzpatrick.

[66] MacKenzie, 'On Scotland and the Empire', pp. 732–37.

maintain close religious and cultural connections.[67] Scots took intense pride not only in the work of missionaries and explorers such as John Philip, Robert Moffat, and David Livingstone, but also in the ministers, doctors, botanists, engineers, and teachers their universities supplied to the Empire.[68] Scots were also prominent in environmental and forestry work. Scottish regiments, merchant houses, and shipping lines (although many moved their headquarters to Liverpool or London) were invariably identifiable as distinctively Scottish. These relationships were emphasized in the major exhibitions held in Glasgow and Edinburgh between 1888 and 1911, as well as in missionary and learned societies.

While they lacked such a pronounced sense of cultural nationalism, the English regions also had their distinctive economic and social connections with Empire. Study of the relations of particular cities with the Empire, such as Birmingham, Manchester, and Liverpool,[69] is revealing not only economic and social influences but effects upon the architecture, planning, and design of provincial cities as well as London itself. It should not be forgotten, also, that textiles, carpets, furniture, and the very plants in parks and gardens all exhibited the influence of far-flung Imperial territories. It was difficult to escape the visual impact of Empire in the shops of Britain.

An Imperial Public?

In the sources surveyed above, developments can be traced in public attitudes not only to Empire but to the emigrants and officials who colonized and ran it, the naval and military arms of the state, and the monarchy. The later nineteenth century witnessed the retreat of republicanism in Britain, and elevation of the monarchy into an institution endowed with patriotic and Imperial symbolism and enjoying a world-wide significance. This may have originated under George III, but undoubtedly, with the great climax of the Diamond Jubilee in 1897, Queen Victoria came to represent almost an incarnation of Imperial Britannia herself.

---

[67] R. A. Cage, ed., *The Scots Abroad* (London, 1985).

[68] John D. Hargreaves, *Academe and Empire: Some Overseas Connections of Aberdeen University, 1860–1970* (Aberdeen, 1994), esp. pp. 5–32 and 114–17. Richard H. Grove, *Green Imperialism: Colonial Expansion, Tropical Island Edens and the Origins of Environmentalism, 1600–1860* (Cambridge, 1995), *passim*; Grove, 'Scottish Missionaries, Evangelical Discourses and the Origins of Conservation Thinking in Southern Africa, 1820–1900', in *Journal of Southern African Studies*, XV, 2 (1989), pp. 163–87; John M. MacKenzie, *Empires of Nature and the Nature of Empires: Imperialism, Scotland and the Environment* (East Linton, 1997), pp. 65–70.

[69] For Birmingham, Catherine Hall, 'Rethinking Imperial Histories, the Reform Act of 1867', *New Left Review*, CCVIII (1994), pp. 3–29; M. H. Port, *Imperial London: Civil Government Building in London, 1850–1915* (London, 1995); Jane M. Jacobs, *Edge of Empire: Postcolonialism and the City* (London, 1996).

An Imperial ideology, a potent mixture of patriotism, excitements in adventure and colonial warfare, reverence for the monarchy, a self-referencing approach to other peoples, admiration for military virtues (represented also by renewed interest in medieval chivalry), and a quasi-religious approach to the obligations of world-wide power, came to dominate many aspects of, especially, popular culture. Throughout society sporadic excitements turned patriotism into jingo-ism, ethnic self-regard often shaded into outright racism, and Imperial self-right-eousness was capable of being transformed into extreme bellicosity. The ideological messages conveyed by this material were nevertheless also complex and conflicting. Notwithstanding anxiety and apprehension in the writings of Edwardian politicians and intellectuals, central characteristics of the popular cultural approach to Empire survived to resurface in the inter-war years.[70]

Nevertheless, historians have continued to be sceptical of the notion that Imperial ideas and enthusiasms penetrated deeply into the consciousness of the British public. Many societies, such as those connected with Imperial Federation in the 1880s, were short-lived and unsuccessful. Voters were influenced by hard-headed domestic concerns: the Imperial Preference issue seemed to demonstrate that colonial sentiment was likely to be subordinated to anxieties about dearer food. Emigration patterns to 1914 show that the United States was more attractive than the Dominions and colonies. Men were seldom eager to enlist in the army except when driven to it by unemployment and economic distress. The complex concept of social imperialism has been much discussed, but never convincingly applied to the period between 1870 and 1914. Later, the British reacted with relative equanimity to decolonization, experiencing little of the national trauma suffered by France or Portugal.

Yet the cultural expressions of Empire were undoubtedly highly pervasive. The framers and receivers of metropolitan culture were unlikely to adopt what was inimical to the populace. Imperial culture almost certainly represented a powerful interaction among the classes, illustrated in the eagerness of the suppliers of entertainment and popular literature, commercial advertisers, and the founders of youth organizations to attach themselves to it. The public, largely uninterested in specific Imperial principles and policies, were none the less fascinated by Empire's existence, its racial connotations, and the superior self-image which it offered in respect of the rest of the world. Imperial ideology was a significant aspect of late-nineteenth-century nationalism.

Empire also represented an area of convergence, not only between 'high' (as represented, for example, by Rudyard Kipling and Edward Elgar) and popular culture, but also among the political parties. Although politicians hotly debated

---

[70] This argument is developed in Vol. IV, see chap. by John M. Mackenzie.

Imperial issues, they tended to coalesce on fundamental aspects of Imperial and patriotic rhetoric. The Liberals produced a group of influential Liberal Imperialists. The Fabians and later the Labour Party promoted ethical imperialism rather than anti-imperialism. Even the radical left, in the shape of H. M. Hyndman's Social Democratic Federation, was initially imperialist.

There are perhaps several powerful—and hitherto largely unnoticed—reasons for this: the existence of structures for disseminating Imperial ideas and images, the exceptionally long period over which they had been entering the British consciousness, their recognized role in consolidating the British state, and the opportunities they presented for a national common ground (however fraught individual issues might be). Hence, moments of Imperial and domestic danger tended to produce bellicose responses heavily laden with Imperial rhetoric. From the late eighteenth century, the public encountered ideas about Empire through news of overseas successes (and reverses), heroic journeys like those of Captain Cook, and the appearance of exotic people in their midst. Anti-slavery propaganda spread its tracts and images very widely, and the theatre repeatedly tackled Imperial themes. Many also heard of such issues from Christian preachers. Others—seamen, traders, and soldiers, for example—often had at least a passing experience of Empire at first hand.

In the nineteenth century the media expanded considerably: the theatre, sermons, tracts, and visual materials such as panoramas were joined by an illustrated press, social campaigns associated with Empire, exhibitions in churches, mechanics' institutions, and local museums, the music hall, national exhibitions in London and elsewhere, local societies, the schools, youth organizations, juvenile literature and journals, and many other forms of entertainment and advertising. Of course, work, family, income, health, and daily survival loomed largest for most people in Britain, but none the less Empire constituted a vital aspect of national identity and race-consciousness, even if complicated by regional, rural, urban, and class contexts. The complex ideological web of social Darwinism, and racial, monarchical, and militarist ideas continued to influence education, the socialization of the young, the integration of the United Kingdom, and the public attitudes which fed into national experiences well into the twentieth century.

Beloff and Said are perhaps both right—and both wrong. The British did not form a theory of empire because their Empire was so complex and culturally dominant that they did not need one. Yet, though it was all about them, a constant source of celebration and self-regard—as well as anxiety—its cultural presence was different from that envisaged by Said. It was more extensive and more popular, yet in some respects structurally less significant. Though it produced much cultural common ground, it also stimulated intense controversy.

Select Bibliography

THOMAS G. AUGUST, *The Selling of the Empire: British and French Imperialist Propaganda, 1890–1940* (Westport, 1985).

MORAG BELL, ROBIN BUTLIN, and MICHAEL HEFFERNAN, eds., *Geography and Imperialism, 1820–1940* (Manchester, 1995).

PATRICK BRANTLINGER, *Rule of Darkness: British Literature and Imperialism, 1830–1914* (London, 1988).

J. S. BRATTON and others, *Acts of Supremacy: The British Empire and the Stage, 1790–1930* (Manchester, 1991).

KATHRYN CASTLE, *Britannia's Children: Reading Colonialism through Children's Books and Magazines* (Manchester, 1996).

ANNIE E. COOMBES, *Reinventing Africa: Museums, Material Culture and Popular Imagination in Late Victorian and Edwardian England* (London, 1994).

H. JOHN FIELD, *Towards a Programme of Imperial Life: The British Empire at the Turn of the Century* (Oxford, 1982).

PAUL GREENHALGH, *Ephemeral Vistas: The Expositions Universelles, Great Exhibitions and World Fairs, 1851–1939* (Manchester, 1988).

DOUGLAS A. LORIMER, *Colour, Class and the Victorians: English Attitudes to the Negro in the Mid-Nineteenth Century* (Leicester, 1978).

JOHN M. MACKENZIE, *Propaganda and Empire: The Manipulation of British Public Opinion, 1880–1960* (Manchester, 1984).

—— *Orientalism: History, Theory and the Arts* (Manchester, 1995).

—— ed., *Imperialism and Popular Culture* (Manchester, 1986).

—— ed., *Popular Imperialism and the Military* (Manchester, 1992).

—— ed., *David Livingstone and the Victorian Encounter with Africa* (London, 1996).

P. J. MARSHALL, ed., *The Cambridge Illustrated History of the British Empire* (Cambridge, 1996).

J. R. OLDFIELD, *Popular Politics and British Anti-Slavery: The Mobilisation of Public Opinion Against the Slave Trade, 1783–1807* (Manchester, 1995).

JEFFREY RICHARDS, ed., *Imperialism and Juvenile Literature* (Manchester, 1989).

EDWARD W. SAID, *Culture and Imperialism* (London, 1993).

BILL SCHWARZ, ed., *The Expansion of England: Race, Ethnicity and Cultural History* (London, 1996).

KATHRYN TIDRICK, *Empire and the English Character* (London, 1990).

14

Scientific Exploration and Empire

ROBERT A. STAFFORD

Throughout the nineteenth century Britain sustained a programme of scientific exploration linked directly with her Imperial and trading interests. It played an important role both in shaping and expressing her culture. Although official commitment to exploration remained sporadic and efforts were rarely systematic, the continuity of British exploration is striking, and its purpose and style remained remarkably consistent. Britain maintained a higher level of exploratory activity than any other Great Power, making the promotion and popularity of exploration a powerful indicator of the strength of Britain's expansionist drive from the 1790s to the First World War.

Exploration can be defined as goal-directed research that creates knowledge in the laboratory of the wilderness. The explorer plays the same role in this regard as the scientist or inventor, increasing the capital of whatever group gains access to the new information. Exploration is an act of intervention that alters perspectives, probabilities, and processes in its parent culture and those that become its objects. People on the receiving end usually felt this most acutely, but Europeans were also aware of their intrusive impact on alien environments and cultures and realized that they themselves were being ineluctably altered by contact. The explorer was the catalyst that started the reaction, the agent of Europe's inevitable confrontation with peripheral lands.

Since the fifteenth century European exploration and imperialism had developed in the same cultural milieu as science, technology, the extractive industries, and the arts, all of which expressed the drive for wealth, control, and knowledge of the natural world. By the late eighteenth century exploration was a self-imposed expectation of the Great Powers. Particularly after Cook's voyages, the Enlightenment's voracious appetite for facts provided a powerful stimulus to discovery.[1] The comprehensive researches of Alexander von Humboldt added new rigour to this scientific enterprise by demonstrating that discrete data from different disciplines could be correlated to construct theoretical models with wide predictive

---

[1] In Vol. II, see chap. by Glyndwr Williams.

value regarding natural processes and patterns of distribution. The power and confidence bequeathed to Britain by industrialization, grafted on to the scientific curiosity sanctioned by the Reformation, combined in the nineteenth century to intensify the nation's expansionist tendencies until they dominated most aspects of culture.[2]

The Organization of Exploration: Metropole and Periphery

The Royal Navy played a major role in managing British exploration during the first half of the century, controlling the world-wide marine charting effort, formalized with the foundation of the Admiralty's Hydrographic Department in 1795, that became one of the outstanding cartographic accomplishments of the Victorian age.[3] The great explorations that characterized the period from 1790 to 1830 were largely maritime coastal reconnaissances. During this era the Admiralty organized voyages of discovery that served a subsidiary training function during lulls in the hostilities with the French, whose achievement in hydrography Britain surpassed only in 1850. Like the Ordnance Survey maps of Britain, the celebrated Admiralty charts codified scientific, strategic, and commercial intelligence, constituting a significant investment in national expansion. For the premier naval, colonial, and maritime trading power, they were a necessity: they made the seas safe to travel. Because of the tradition begun by Joseph Banks[4] of assigning naturalists to naval surveying expeditions, a great deal of scientific research was accomplished during the course of the hydrographic endeavour. Such posts enabled Charles Darwin, Joseph Hooker (later Director of Kew Gardens), Joseph Jukes (later Director of the Geological Survey of Ireland), and Thomas Huxley (later Professor at the Royal School of Mines) to establish their reputations. The amateur tradition and decentralized structure of British science thus linked with official initiatives and resources in the cause of exploration.

In 1830 the Royal Geographical Society (RGS) was founded in London by a small group of enthusiasts led by John Barrow, Second Secretary of the Admiralty from 1804 to 1845. Its goals and membership were based on those of the African Association, established by Banks in 1788 to promote exploration in Africa and elsewhere, and the Raleigh Club, formed by supporters of exploration who seceded from the Travellers Club in 1826. Like earlier geographical societies set up in Paris (1821) and Berlin (1828), the RGS sought to promote scientific exploration over-

---

[2] Stephen Kern, *The Culture of Time and Space, 1880–1918* (Cambridge, Mass., 1983); Edward W. Said, *Culture and Imperialism* (London, 1993).

[3] G. S. Ritchie, *The Admiralty Chart: British Naval Hydrography in the Nineteenth Century* (London, 1967).

[4] In Vol. II, see pp. 247, 249; 566–67; 573–74.

seas, presenting the results as maps and memoirs in its *Journal* and *Proceedings*.[5] From its inception, the cartographers, military officers, colonial administrators, scientists, politicians, diplomats, and travellers who managed the RGS explicitly linked the Society's activities with Imperial affairs.[6] Most of the early papers were contributed by the Admiralty and the Colonial, Foreign, and Indian Offices. The annual addresses of RGS Presidents, like the memoirs, were replete with the language of national expansion, assumptions of moral and technological super-iority over other races, expressions of a natural theology that saw design in human settlement patterns and environmental adaptation, and assertions of Britain's right and duty to act at will around the world. Geography at the RGS was conceived and practised in an ideological and institutional matrix that enmeshed the goals of science and the nation in the practicalities of Imperial rule.[7] In the widest context, the initiatives of the RGS represented an overseas extension of the wave of quantification, classification, and improvement that transformed Europe as a corollary of industrialization.

The RGS managed to secure partial government sponsorship for several early expeditions, such as Robert Schomburgk's to British Guiana in 1831–35 and William Ainsworth's to Armenia and Kurdistan in 1838–40. Disappointing results, however, soon forced the Society to shift to a secondary role in co-ordinating rather than funding explorations. Naval officers, meanwhile, played a key part in Arctic exploration from 1820 to 1850, an endeavour driven as much by the urge to redeem the quest's chief martyr, Sir John Franklin, who perished in 1847, as to conclude the search for a North-west Passage. In roughly the same period, naval officers took part in steamship explorations of the Niger and Zambezi rivers in Africa that were driven by humanitarian pressure to encourage legitimate com-merce and supplant the slave trade. The Niger voyages culminated the series of explorations inspired by Mungo Park, another geographical martyr patronized by Banks's African Association. The Zambezi initiative arose from the celebrity of the missionary David Livingstone. The Admiralty's Hydrographic Department played a central role in these undertakings, the line of succession running from Banks through Barrow to Francis Beaufort and John Washington, official Hydrographers in the periods 1829–55 and 1855–63. Barrow dominated naval exploration and most

[5] Hugh Robert Mill, *The Record of the Royal Geographical Society* (London, 1930), remains a more informative source than Ian Cameron, *To the Farthest Ends of the Earth: The History of the Royal Geographical Society, 1830–1980* (London, 1980).

[6] D. R. Stoddart, 'The R. G. S. and the "New Geography": Changing Aims and Roles in Nineteenth-Century Science', *Geographical Journal*, CXLVI (1980), pp. 190–202.

[7] David N. Livingstone, 'The History of Science and the History of Geography: Interactions and Implications', *History of Science*, XXII (1984), pp. 271–302; in this volume, see above, pp. 285, 286–88.

of Britain's terrestrial exploratory effort from Banks's death in 1820 until his own retirement in 1845.[8] These scientific officers wielded great power in Britain's geographical community. Holding posts in the RGS, Royal Society, British Association for the Advancement of Science, and other learned organizations, they ensured that the Senior Service's interests were attended to on most expeditions. As the great rivers were charted, however, and exploration of continental interiors became the only way to reduce the *terra incognita* further, the Admiralty lost its paramount geographical influence. The way was open for another institution to fill the void: the RGS only required determined leadership to enable it to realize the hopes of its founders.

At the RGS, the naval retreat was largely completed by 1850, when Sir Roderick Murchison, building on the work of other reformers, took firm control of Britain's specialist geographical institution and transformed it into the nation's—indeed, the world's—undisputed directorate of exploration. Murchison had already had three careers before he focused on geography: as a soldier, a fox-hunter, and a geologist who defined the Silurian, Devonian, and Permian stratigraphic systems. Like Humboldt, Murchison believed geology and geography were sister sciences, and his military and hunting background rendered him particularly interested in landforms and geography. Murchison not only saw the data provided by geography as critical to the advancement of all sciences, but as crucial to the commercial, military, and philanthropic endeavours of Europe, and Britain in particular. The key to his passionate interest in geography, as that of Victorians in general, was the map. As a spatial science of relationships, geography not only provided topographical base maps upon which scientific data could be recorded, but it codified information of immense value to everyone involved in managing outcomes based on interaction with the physical world. Maps provide a symbolic language that can legitimize the political power and territorial imperatives of those who deploy it. While Murchison and his colleagues understood the significance of maps as intellectual weapons, they spoke of them publicly as objective, value-neutral tools produced for the common good.[9]

Murchison was an ardent patriot who saw his geological tours as military campaigns, relied on imperial metaphors to describe the spread of his stratigraphic designations around the world, and supported the expansion of Britain's Empire throughout his career as a pillar of the scientific establishment. Murchison believed that the natural sciences played an important role in furthering British interests and that the nation had an obligation to support her scientists. His

---

[8] Christopher Lloyd, *Mr. Barrow of the Admiralty: A Life of Sir John Barrow, 1764–1848* (London, 1970).

[9] J. B. Harley, 'Maps, Knowledge and Power', in D. Cosgrove and S. Daniels, eds., *The Iconography of Time* (Cambridge, 1988), pp. 277–312.

forceful character, indefatigable zeal, extensive social connections, and Imperial proclivities went far to ensure that the relationship between British science and Britain's Empire was mutually advantageous.

Murchison, perhaps more keenly than any contemporary savant, felt the connection between science and Empire. While his work to establish this connection found occasional expression through his offices in the Royal Society, Geological Society, and British Association, his most concerted efforts were channelled through the RGS. As his stratigraphic career flagged for want of continental masses to subdue in the early 1850s, he moved to align the RGS more closely with national needs. Many other public figures recorded similar feelings, but several first-rank scientists, including Darwin, Lyell, Huxley, Joseph Hooker, and Alfred Wallace, shunned Murchison's reconstituted RGS as a promotional farce insulting genuine science. Still, even these critics, as well as other proponents of exploration who did not advocate Empire, willingly used the influence of the RGS to raise funds for research. Conflicting agendas were thus subsumed under a blend of Imperial, humanitarian, and scientific rhetoric: Murchison's genius was to package proposals in language that balanced the factions. In part, he sought to popularize exploration in order to secure official funding for a series of expeditions that satisfied the public's thirst for adventure, the scientists' demand for data, the merchants' desire for details about new markets and sources of supply, and the government's need for objective information upon which to base diplomatic and Imperial decisions. At the same time, the RGS provided Murchison with a new vehicle for his insatiable ambition to win social rank through national service. His assumption of command at the RGS also coincided with his engineering of the British Association's recognition of geography as an independent science—again, the motive was to feed and tap public interest in geography for the benefit of all sciences.

Having set geography's house in order and installed himself as its presiding presence, Murchison completed a complementary manoeuvre in geology that cemented his position as the unassailable leader of the mid-Victorian exploration drive. In 1855 he was appointed Director-General of the Geological Survey of Great Britain. The first Director-General, Sir Henry De la Beche, acting in the manner of his counterpart Sir William Hooker, Director of Kew Gardens, had established the Survey in 1835 to delineate the kingdom's geological structure and mineral deposits on Ordnance Survey maps. De la Beche had performed a good deal of Imperial work, employing the Survey's Museum of Practical Geology to evaluate colonial ore samples, testing overseas coals to facilitate the navy's global deployment of steamships, and founding geological surveys in overseas dependencies. As with the RGS, the Survey gave Murchison a foundation, and again he erected an edifice of decidedly Imperial style. Not only did he accomplish far more colonial geology than his predecessor, partly because the mid-century gold rushes dramatically raised expectations of mineral wealth, but he used the Survey's Royal School of Mines to supply geologists for RGS-sponsored expeditions. These forays provided valuable geographical information while allowing Murchison, by proxy, to map the strata of new regions and test his own geological theories. The colonial surveys enabled Murchison to promote the extension of topographical and geological mapping throughout the Empire. Colonial geologists and botanists also accomplished much original exploration in the course of research largely directed from London. Their results were fed back to the 'centres of calculation', contributing to Europe's preponderant knowledge of peripheral regions,[10] though important theories as well as data issued from the colonial frontier where scientific principles were constantly honed against exotic phenomena. In geology, botany, biology, ethnography, and astronomy, colonial and expeditionary access conferred substantial advantage on British scientists. Indeed, so adept were British scientific leaders, such as Banks and Murchison, at exploiting the research opportunities created by Empire that they can be thought of as 'sub-imperialists' who transformed the physiology of the Imperial state in the manner of symbiotic parasites that create niches for themselves in return for services to their host.

Through institutional power and social prestige, Murchison dominated British exploration from the early 1850s until his death in 1871, standing forth unquestionably as the key figure between the death of Banks and the First World War. Murchison's career spanned the transition between gentlemanly amateurs who worked through informal networks based on the scientific societies, and trained professionals employed by specialized government departments. The influence of learned societies linking officialdom and science in support of exploration outlasted Murchison, and new Empire-wide networks developed around the geological surveys, botanical gardens, natural history museums, and universities that were gradually installed in the colonies. Yet Murchison's leadership coincided with the high noon of Victorian prosperity, so that he was able to engineer a brilliant burst of exploration on the basis of the interest in overseas opportunities generated by the cycle of great gold rushes, the success of free trade, and the anti-slavery movement.[11] Following Murchison's death, other presidents with direct links to the Empire led the RGS into the twentieth century, but none approached his success in promoting exploration. Though rising Imperial sentiment swelled RGS membership and the Society briefly experimented with direct support of

[10] Bruno Latour, *Science in Action: How to Follow Scientists and Engineers Through Society* (Milton Keynes, 1987), chap. 6.

[11] D. H. Hall, *History of the Earth Sciences during the Scientific and Industrial Revolutions* (Oxford, 1976), pp. 160–90, correlates exploratory activity with economic fluctuations.

imperialistic ventures in Africa,[12] the era of primary exploration was ending by the 1880s, Britain's capacity for action was increasingly constrained, and the RGS itself, under the pressure of geography's evolution into a rigorously defined discipline, was transformed into a specialist scientific society. As a result, it was purged of its fashionable, political, and military factions and the attendant ideologies of imperialism, racism, and environmental determinism that had helped express the social utility of this heterogeneous science during its infancy.[13] Thus, while an appreciation of the RGS is critical to understanding the motives and mechanisms behind nineteenth-century British exploration, the Society's Imperial role actually lessened in proportion to the rise of overt imperialism. Except for the poles, the explorers had nearly worked themselves out of a job by the late 1880s, an eventuality Gladstone foresaw as early as 1864, when he remarked to the RGS: 'Gentlemen, you have done so much that you are like Alexander, you have no more worlds to conquer.'[14] The four main regions in which British exploration focused during the century were the Arctic, Australia (Map 14.2), Africa (Map 14.1), and Central Asia. The rest was essentially a piecemeal mopping-up operation.

Official explorers invariably carried detailed instructions drawn up by their sponsors. Until the 1840s such instructions for maritime or riverine Imperial expeditions were usually written by Barrow at the Admiralty. The Colonial Office wrote its own directives, providing general desiderata to be modified by specific local instructions for colonial explorations. For expeditions beyond the Empire, the Colonial Office issued detailed orders direct from London. Again, because of his connection with the African Association, the ubiquitous Barrow wrote the instructions for the expeditions to the Niger hinterland that completed Park's work. Explorers on official service were given the full support of the Imperial government, including naval passages, diplomatic and consular back-up, and aid from colonial and Indian administrations. In the colonies, unclaimed territories, and poorly explored sovereign nations, a good deal of discovery was also accomplished by unofficial British explorers who usually enjoyed the sanction, if not the financial support, of the Imperial or colonial governments. Scientists such as Alfred Wallace likewise received official help while working in remote regions like the Dutch East Indies.

As the RGS gained effective control of British Imperial exploration in the late 1840s it became the chief authority for drafting expeditionary instructions. To ensure co-ordination among all interest groups, the RGS solicited research suggestions from the Colonial or Foreign Office, the Royal Society, and government

[12] R. C. Bridges, 'The R.G.S. and the African Exploration Fund, 1876–80', *Geographical Journal*, CXXIX (1963), pp. 25–35.

[13] Stoddart, 'R.G.S. and the "New Geography"'; Livingstone, 'History of Science'.

[14] *Proceedings of the Royal Geographical Society*, XIV (1869–70), pp. 214.

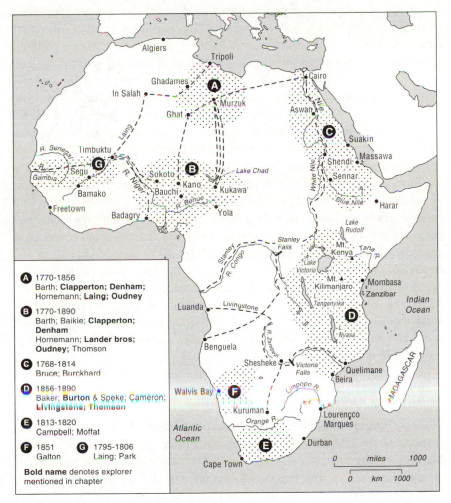

Algiers
Tripoli
Ghadames
Cairo
In Salah
A
Murzuk
Aswan
Ghat
C
Suakin
R. Senegal
Timbuktu
Massawa
R. Gambia
Segu
G
Sokoto
Lake Chad
Shendi
Sennar
Bamako
Bauchi
Kano
Kukawa
Harar
Freetown
Benue
Badagry
Yola
Lake Rudolf
Laing
R. Niger
B
White Nile
Blue Nile
Nile
Stanley Falls
Mt. Kenya
Tana R.
Stanley
R. Congo
Lake Victoria
Luanda
Livingstone
Mt. Kilimanjaro
Mombasa
Zanzibar
L. Tanganyika
D
Indian Ocean
Benguela
R. Zambezi
L. Nyasa
Shesheke
Victoria Falls
Quelimane
Beira
Walvis Bay
F
Limpopo R.
Kuruman
Orange R.
Lourenço Marques
Atlantic Ocean
Durban
E
Cape Town
MADAGASCAR

A 1770-1856
Barth; **Clapperton; Denham;**
Hornemann; **Laing;** Oudney

B 1770-1890
Barth; Baikie; **Clapperton;**
Denham
Hornemann; **Lander bros;**
Oudney; Thomson

C 1768-1814
Bruce; Burckhard

D 1856-1890
Baker; **Burton** & Speke; Cameron;
Livingstone; Thomson

E 1813-1820
Campbell; Moffat

F 1851   **G** 1795-1806
Galton   Laing; Park

Bold name denotes explorer
mentioned in chapter

0   miles   1000
0   km   1000

MAP 14.1. British Exploration in Africa

scientists such as the naval Hydrographer, the Directors of Kew Gardens and the Geological Survey, and Sir Edward Sabine, a specialist in terrestrial magnetism.[15] Emphases in instructions varied with the region and objective, but they generally called for methodical instrumental observation, map-making, written narrative, collection of botanical, geological, zoological, and ethnological specimens, weather recording (temperature and barometric pressure), and inquiry into native languages, customs, population distribution, productions, and trade patterns. Explorers were directed to update their journals daily, trusting nothing to memory. Those travelling outside the British sphere were instructed to send out frequent dispatches, including tracings of maps, to preserve their work from accidents such as Alexander Gordon Laing's murder near Timbuktu in 1826.[16] Explorers were also enjoined to respect native mores, avoid violence, distribute gifts, trade fairly, and cultivate a good name for whites.

Even at this level exploration was profoundly exploitative, for it took hostages in the form of data used to inform decisions about territories made without the knowledge or consent of their inhabitants. The concentration of scientific and commercial data in Europe helped tip the balance of power against the indigenous peoples of other continents, whose control over their destinies could be eroded as surely by map coordinates and museum specimens as by steamships, bullets, and treaties of cession. Natives themselves understood something of this, as was demonstrated by instructions to Dixon Denham, Walter Oudney, and Hugh Clapperton on their mission to the Niger interior in 1822–25 (Map 14.2), to avoid shocking the Africans by blatantly collecting natural history specimens,[17] and the concealment by Richard and John Lander of their interest in the course of the Niger from suspicious local rulers.[18]

Changes in the metropolitan context in which exploration evolved were variously expressed in peripheral regions. In Australia the voyages of Cook, Flinders, Vancouver, and the French had surveyed most of the coastline by 1805 (Map 14.2). While charting continued under captains such as Philip Parker King and John Lort Stokes until the 1850s, few mysteries remained except possible river discoveries. The focus of activity moved inland once the Blue Mountains of New South Wales were crossed in 1813. The two expeditions of 1817–18 led by John Oxley, that colony's Surveyor-General, started a series of explorations by army officers such as Charles Sturt, surveyors like Thomas Mitchell, and bushmen such as Edward

---

[15] John Cawood, 'The Magnetic Crusade: Science and Politics in Early Victorian Britain', *Isis*, LXX (1979), pp. 493–518.

[16] 'The Letters of Major Alexander Gordon Laing, 1824–26', in E. W. Bovill, ed., *Missions to the Niger*, 4 vols. (Cambridge, 1964–66), I, pp. 123–390.

[17] 'The Bornu Mission, 1822–25', in Bovill, ed., *Missions to the Niger*, II, pp. 20–21.

[18] Robin Hallett, ed., *The Niger Journal of Richard and John Lander* (London, 1965), p. 118.

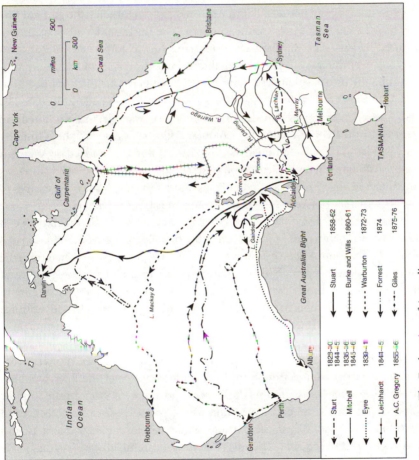

MAP 14.2. The Exploration of Australia

Eyre that revealed the broad outline of the interior by the 1860s. These expeditions were usually the initiative of individual colonies seeking to discover new areas for settlement and to understand the continent's topography. The Colonial Office sanctioned the expenditures and wrote the general instructions, including guidelines about interaction with Aborigines. This remained the pattern until the 1860s, when exploratory management as well as initiative shifted to the colonies in parallel with their assumption of responsible government. In this period open competition broke out between South Australia and Victoria for the glory of first traversing the continent from south to north. The Burke and Wills Expedition, organized by Victoria's Royal Society, illustrates how colonial scientific institutions took over the role of their metropolitan progenitors in sponsoring exploration within the British voluntarist tradition.[19] The Imperial factor continued to be felt in Australian exploration, though it was increasingly mediated by the RGS. The North Australian Exploring Expedition of 1855–56, for example, was promoted and organized by the RGS, funded by the Colonial Office, supported by the Admiralty (aided by Victoria) which seconded its Government Botanist, and led by Augustus Gregory, Assistant Surveyor-General of Western Australia.[20] The strategic interests of the Imperial government centred on ascertaining the north coast's resources to promote settlement as well as trade and communications with Asia.

In Canada and Cape Colony, settler enterprise, even more than the initiative of colonial governments, drove exploration in the first half of the century. In Canada, Colonial Office control again gave way to local management except when Imperial issues that transcended individual colonies or affected global strategy were at stake. Examples are the Palliser Expedition of 1857–60, which surveyed a railroad route to British Columbia to knit together Britain's North American possessions, and the North-West American Boundary Commission of 1858–63, which delimited the international border west of the Rockies. Since the British took the Cape in 1795, southern African exploration was left largely to missionaries, hunters, trekkers, and prospectors operating from Cape Colony and later the Boer republics without government assistance. Yet the Imperial government threw its full support behind Livingstone's Zambezi Expedition of 1857–63 because of its objectives to undermine the East African slave trade while developing new markets and resources for British industry. The government was careful, however, to dissociate itself from Livingstone's colonizing schemes.[21] In New Zealand, missionaries and surveyors of Wakefield's company led the way before sheep graziers, prospectors,

[19] Alan Moorehead, *Cooper's Creek* (1963; Melbourne, 1985).

[20] A. C. and F. T. Gregory, *Journals of Australian Explorations*, 2nd edn. (1884; Victoria Park, Western Australia, 1981); J. H. L. Cumpston, *Augustus Gregory and the Inland Sea* (Canberra, 1972).

[21] Tim Jeal, *Livingstone* (New York, 1973), pp. 184–94; Robert A. Stafford, *Scientist of Empire: Sir Roderick Murchison, Scientific Exploration, and Victorian Imperialism* (Cambridge, 1989), pp. 172–82.

and government geologists took the initiative. The motives of colonial epicentres in sponsoring exploration were more parochial than those of London. Expansion and political consolidation were key considerations; scientific research was less important than development, extraction, and trade. Colonial exploration focused on agricultural and pastoral lands, timber, minerals, and routes for stock droving, river navigation, and railways. After the rushes in California and Victoria, gold became a prime goal because of its capacity to initiate self-sustaining economic growth.

India, typically, went its own way about exploration. The Great Trigonometrical Survey, permanently founded in 1818, remained the main vehicle for Indian initiatives, accomplishing much external exploration in the Himalayas as well as mapping British possessions in the subcontinent. The topographical maps produced by the Survey constituted an important aid to British rule, comparable to the railway or telegraph in their elaboration of a space-time grid that enabled the marshalling of the information, troops, and resources necessary to subdue and govern the vast territory. As in Britain and the colonies, these maps were also used by India's Geological Survey, permanently established in 1851, to lay down the territory's structure and mineral resources. The explorations beyond the frontiers provided valuable intelligence about tribal areas, mountain passes, and the shrinking No Man's Land between the British and Russian spheres of influence. They also enabled the Indian authorities to try to funnel the trade of Central Asia. Much of this work was done by the 'pundits', native officers of the Survey who carried out a breathtaking series of covert explorations between 1865 and 1875. India, too, developed voluntarist associations such as the Asiatic Society of Bengal (1784) that sponsored and rewarded scientific activity, complementing the initial botanical (1786–Calcutta Botanical Gardens), geological, and forestry (1847–Bombay Forest Department) establishments of the East India Company.

The Indian Navy also performed a great deal of primary exploration, completing hydrographic surveys from the East African coast to the Straits of Malacca between 1770 and the mid-nineteenth century. The Company's policy of introducing steamboats on the Indus and Ganges and deploying them in punitive campaigns throughout its sphere[22] also necessitated the charting of the major rivers of southern Asia. Valuable palaeontological and zoological collections made on these missions were transmitted to the metropolitan scientific societies, providing important data for the debate on the progression of life. Perhaps the best example of such steam-powered exploratory work was the survey of the Tigris–Euphrates river system carried out by Captain Francis Chesney, RA, during

---

[22] Daniel R. Headrick, *The Tools of Empire: Technology and European Imperialism in the Nineteenth Century* (Oxford, 1981).

1835–37 to ascertain its suitability as a new route to India. The scheme proved a failure, largely due to technological advances favouring ocean-going steamships, but a wealth of political, commercial, and scientific data was gleaned and an enduring British presence established. Expressing the logic by which exploration often led to intervention, Chesney advocated the establishment of trade depots as 'points of support' for British efforts to increase the region's commerce.[23] Chesney's work, like that of other British expeditions in Ottoman territory and the trans-Himalayan zone, highlights the political and military value of geographical information about sensitive zones, and how exploration often blended into espionage.

Britain took the lead in opening 'the Dark Continent', focusing successively on the Niger, the interior of southern Africa, the Central Lakes, and the Nile. Except the series of West African explorations conducted by the Colonial Office between 1818 and the 1830s and several Niger voyages organized by the Admiralty, much of Britain's African exploration was overseen by the Foreign Office in conjunction with the RGS. Murchison's close relationship with Lord Clarendon during the 1850s was instrumental in this regard. In the case of Macgregor Laird's steam exploration of the Niger in 1832–34, which sought to capitalize on the trade potential revealed by Richard and John Lander, attacking the slave trade and spreading Christianity were adduced as additional benefits from the introduction of British commerce. The Admiralty provided this private expedition with a naval lieutenant to survey the river; Laird, in turn, extracted a pledge that no information from the chart produced would be divulged without his company's permission.[24] Twenty years later the navy returned the favour, allowing Laird's trading agent to accompany William Balfour Baikie's government-funded Niger expedition.[25] By the 1850s the lesson of quinine as a malarial prophylactic had been learned: Baikie's voyage proved Europeans could maintain their health in tropical Africa. By the 1890s female explorers such as Mary Kingsley were also adding laurels to Britain's record of African discovery,[26] though women were not admitted as RGS Fellows until 1904. As noted, southern Africa was largely explored as a result of local colonial initiative. The Central Lakes and the Nile tributaries were explored to solve the mystery of the Nile's source, but as the scale of Arab slaving operations in East Africa was revealed, humanitarianism and the promotion of

---

[23] Francis R. Chesney, *The Expedition for the Survey of the Euphrates and Tigris*, 2 vols. (London, 1850), II, pp. 601–02.

[24] MacGregor Laird and R. A. K. Oldfield, *Narrative of an Expedition into the Interior of Africa by the River Niger*, 2nd edn., 2 vols. (1837; London, 1971), I, p. 11.

[25] William Balfour Baikie, *Narrative of an Exploring Voyage up the Rivers Kwora and Binue*, 2nd edn. (1856; London, 1966), p. 5.

[26] Dea Birkett, *Mary Kingsley: Imperial Adventuress* (Basingstoke, 1992).

legitimate commerce were again deployed to encourage further activity that created the preconditions for annexation. International rivalry for discoveries remained muted before the 1880s, when the quickening pace of annexation in Africa and the shrinking size of untracked regions created friction between European powers.

The Explorers: Styles, Methods, Impacts

While for the most part untiring in following their instructions, explorers interpreted their marching orders according to their own lights. Such ambitious, often flamboyant men were relatively unlikely to be restrained by official dictates once their quests led them beyond Europe's reach. The personalities and motives of explorers were as varied as one might expect in such a broad-based, long-term cultural activity, but discernible patterns emerge. The most significant was the shift during the mid-nineteenth century from the old model of the explorer as self-effacing, duty-driven national servant to a larger-than-life celebrity whose sensational exploits acted out both personal obsessions and public fantasies. George Vancouver exemplifies the first type, Richard Burton the second. Most explorers were serving or former military officers; a few were professional scientists. Many built careers as colonial administrators or diplomats on the foundation of their service in the cause of discovery. Their ability to move between professions by seizing opportunities created by Britain's overseas activities illustrates the larger cultural context of expansionism in which both exploration and empire flourished.

The explorer in the field had to be a man or woman of many parts to accomplish his or her goals—leader, emissary, pathfinder, hunter, observer, collector, recorder, cartographer, and often artist. Unlike their naval counterparts, overland explorers were immersed in alien environments for months or years, having no choice but to get along with indigenous peoples. Sturt believed success came by 'steady perseverance and unceasing attention, by due precaution and a mild discipline'.[27] Eyre admitted that the leader was always lonely and anxious, since one false step or bad judgement might endanger the party or ruin its chances of success.[28] Rarely was the explorer alone: in colonial settings he was accompanied by assistants, native guides, and scientific collectors. Explorers in tropical Africa required bearers because of the susceptibility of draft animals to sleeping sickness and the necessity of carrying trade goods, gifts, and supplies. Many complained of their

[27] Charles Sturt, *Narrative of an Expedition into Central Australia*, 2nd edn., 2 vols. (1849; Adelaide, 1965), I, p. 148.
[28] Edward John Eyre, *Journals of Expeditions of Discovery into Central Australia*, 2nd edn., 2 vols. (1845; Adelaide, 1964), I, p. 24.

impedimenta, Joseph Thomson lamenting 'the dreadful incubus of a caravan'.[29] There was also the strain of maintaining one's dignity amidst crowds of curious natives who had often never seen a European before.

Much of the explorer's energy was dedicated to the day-to-day logistics of moving through the country and dealing with subordinates, animals, equipment, and natives. Terrain and climate were constant issues, as were, depending upon circumstances, disease, water supply, food for man and beast, shelter, and steam fuel. But getting there and back were not enough: concerted scientific work was required to bring new regions within Europe's ken and ambit. The pattern of scientific expectation evolved from eighteenth-century precedents, and the explorer's equipment reflected these requirements. His standard gear—essentially the means for land navigation—included a telescope, a compass for travel and mapping, a sextant for making astronomical observations to determine latitude, chronometers to determine longitude, an artificial horizon, used in conjunction with the sextant for taking altitudes, a barometer to determine altitude by atmospheric pressure, and thermometers to record temperature and determine altitude by boiling point. Other equipment might include surveying chains to measure actual distances travelled, a pedometer to measure approximate distances, a theodolite to measure horizontal angles for triangulation and mapping, sounding lines for determining river and lake depths, and a hygrometer to measure humidity. More specialized research might demand a microscope, blowpiping apparatus for chemical analysis of minerals, or instruments to record terrestrial magnetism and compass deviation due to a ship's iron hull.

Explorers were beset with endless problems maintaining their instruments. Compasses were lost, barometers were broken, chronometers changed rates or stopped, instruments split from heat, their glasses were sandblasted by ferocious winds, thermometers calibrated for English temperatures burst in desert climes, and natives begged precious mercury that was, in Clapperton's words, 'like asking me to part with my heart's blood'.[30] In perhaps the most humourous juxtaposition of scientific order and wilderness recalcitrance, W. B. Baikie had his African crewmen trample the grass at an observation site in order to clear a space for his instruments, only to find he had chosen a hippo track whose owner nearly bowled him over lumbering back to the Niger.[31]

Ever resourceful, explorers improvised and endured, completing an astonishing range of research under the most trying conditions. Accurately fixing positions remained the *sine qua non*. Some colonial explorers went further as they entered

---

[29] Joseph Thomson, *To the Central Africa Lakes and Back*, 2nd edn., 2 vols. (1881; London, 1968), I, p. ix.

[30] Bovill, *Missions to the Niger*, IV, p. 630.

[31] Baikie, *Narrative of an Exploring Voyage*, pp. 136–37.

the void beyond mapped districts, surveying baselines and triangulating to determine co-ordinates that were then measured by chaining and checked by celestial observation. Similarly, altitudes taken by instruments were verified by geometric calculation. Explorers were guided in such activities by procedures as well as instructions, the Admiralty publishing its *Manual of Scientific Enquiry* in 1849 and *Instructions for Hydrographic Surveyors* the following year.[32] Paralleling the shift of power in expeditionary organization, the navy's manual was superseded in 1854 by the RGS's *Hints to Travellers*, which soon achieved world-wide fame.[33]

Not all explorers found science stimulating. The more individualistic tired of the daily round of observations, preferring to engage directly with the landscape and people, and revert to subjective, circumstantial reportage. Differences in approach were sometimes striking even between colleagues. On the Bornu Mission, the leader Denham spent his time hunting, recording impressions, commenting on African women, and even accompanying an Arab slave-raiding party, while Oudney, one of the Scottish naval surgeons so conspicuous in Victorian exploration, made comprehensive scientific observations and collections that constituted the chief results of the mission.[34] Similarly, on the Palliser Expedition across British North America, it was the geologist James Hector, another Scottish doctor, rather than John Palliser, a wealthy big-game hunter turned explorer, who accomplished the most significant discoveries.[35] Some explorers, like Charles Sturt, managed to balance their leadership and scientific roles, while others, such as McDouall Stuart, minimized observations to push through to their goals. Scientific leaders, however, could become so engrossed by fieldwork that expedition management suffered. After the Scottish naval surgeon W. B. Baikie assumed command of the Niger expedition of 1854 when its leader died, he busied himself collecting specimens while a serious confrontation with his sailing master was brewing.[36] Joseph Thomson, on the other hand, who had been trained in geology and made substantial contributions to several disciplines, admitted that 'scientific cares' spoiled the charm of new scenery.[37] When life itself was at stake, even exacting observers sometimes had to jettison instruments, collections, and journals.

The highly processed data gathered by the explorers were introduced into Imperial culture through scientific societies, newspapers, and museums,

---

[32] John Herschel, ed., *A Manual of Scientific Enquiry* (London, 1849); Ritchie, *Admiralty Chart*, p. 198.

[33] Royal Geographical Society, *Hints to Travellers* (London, 1854).

[34] Bovill, 'Bornu Mission'.

[35] Irene M. Spry, *The Palliser Expedition: An Account of John Palliser's British North American Expedition, 1857–1860* (Toronto, 1963).

[36] Baikie, *Narrative of an Exploring Voyage*, pp. 47–53, 92.

[37] Joseph Thomson, *Through Masai Land*, 3rd edn. (1885; London, 1968), p. 203.

influencing attitudes towards distant territories and peoples. The RGS remained the key institution in this process, shaping the make-up and agendas of outbound expeditions and mediating inbound results. Exploration and its narration, which represented new lands by word, map, and illustration, taught Britons to think about, act in, and finally absorb these areas into their consciousness. Exploration thus became an important part of the process of imperialism, for even when it did not lead directly to annexation, it enclosed vast tracts of the periphery, including their inhabitants and resources, within Europe's purview.

Nineteenth-century exploration favoured the taxonomic, spatially oriented field sciences such as geology and botany because their data could be easily and profitably collected. It was no coincidence that these were the very disciplines required to sustain colonization and commerical penetration of new territories, in that they listed resources and suggested use patterns. Indeed, the rise during the heyday of free-trade expansion of bio-geography, the study of the distribution of organisms,[38] prefigured the development of formal imperialism's characteristic socio-political science—geopolitics.[39] The times called forth the appropriate sciences, which in turn supported the culture that nurtured them.

Exploration literature, a stream of growing significance in national culture, expressed the initiatives of the field sciences and contributed to the vision of Empire that was a major component of Britain's will to rule abroad. While the novel and the historical narrative opened history to the Victorian middle-class, exploration and travel literature made geography available, so that the British public learned the entire world, in both time and space, was accessible for objectification, appropriation, and use. The explorer's text was authoritative and highly subjective, but what and how he chose to describe were constrained by the expectations of his own culture. By reshaping the periphery through the conventions of European representation, science, like literature, helped create what Edward Said terms 'structures of feeling',[40] sets of attitudes that sustained Empire by incorporating its exotic lands and inhabitants into metropolitan consciousness. While Said's theory remains controversial because of its assumed dependence on fictional interpretation, first-hand evidence supports it, not least from the scientists, who were frequently active proponents of Empire for ideological as well as professional reasons.[41] On a practical level, scientific exploration helped British

---

[38] Janet Browne, *The Secular Ark: Studies in the History of Biogeography* (London, 1983); Robert A. Stafford, 'Annexing the Landscapes of the Past: British Imperial Geology in the Nineteenth Century', in John M. MacKenzie, ed., *Imperialism and the Natural World* (Manchester, 1990), pp. 67–89.

[39] Kern, *Culture of Time and Space*, pp. 223, 239.

[40] Said, *Culture and Imperialism*, p. 14.

[41] Stafford, 'Annexing the Landscapes'; Adrian Desmond, 'The Making of Institutional Zoology in London, 1822–36', *History of Science*, XXIII (1985), pp. 153–85, 223–50; Livingstone, 'History of Science'.

colonists feel at home in their 'neo-Europes'[42] by providing dimensions and explanations for alien environments, as well as strategies for exploiting them. Exploration literature, like the novel, thus portrayed colonial and unannexed territories as 'realms of possibility'[43] and, by maintaining a tradition of British engagement, became a key element of the 'official mind' of imperialism.[44] The narratives, as much as the explorations they chronicled, constituted acts of possession that legitimized and encouraged territorial control.

The logic of geographical discovery undertaken in an atmosphere of utilitarian improvement or redemption often led explorers to propose schemes to develop the territories revealed. The meaning and use of travel literature had already evolved during the Enlightenment from an emphasis on gathering and disseminating information to interpreting and applying it.[45] By 1850 this process had so accelerated that the Christian belief that natural resources exist to be employed for man's improvement had been overtaken by dramatic growth, through technology, in Europeans' power to remake the world. The two traditions fused in the conviction that man was destined to master nature. This drive, in turn, encouraged the development of the civilizing mission, which sought to improve native societies along rational lines.[46] Most explorers and scientists worked within a framework of environmental determinism that allowed them to lament the passing of native peoples before the European advance while justifying the process by analogy to the struggle for survival between species. Explorers and policy-makers were therefore predisposed to continue dialogue with particular places. Explorers usually eschewed outright annexation, but many advocated trading, settler, and missionary activities that made intervention more likely. Baikie, for example, while stating 'I am no advocate for endeavouring to acquire new territory' on the Niger, followed Chesney in encouraging the establishment of permanent depots to facilitate commerce and realign regional trade patterns in Britain's favour.[47] Thomson noted that his exploration of Masai Land led almost inevitably to its coming within Britain's sphere of influence.[48]

[42] Alfred W. Crosby, *Ecological Imperialism: The Biological Expansion of Europe, 900–1900* (Cambridge, 1986).

[43] Said, *Culture and Imperialism*, p. 75.

[44] Ronald Robinson and John Gallagher, with Alice Denny, *Africa and the Victorians: The Official Mind of Imperialism* (London, 1961; new edn., 1981).

[45] Barbara Stafford, *Voyage into Substance: Art, Science, Nature, and the Illustrated Travel Account, 1760–1840* (Cambridge, Mass., 1984).

[46] Michael Adas, *Machines as the Measure of Men: Science, Technology, and Ideologies of Western Dominance* (Ithaca, NY, 1989), pp. 70, 212.

[47] Compare Baikie, *Narrative of an Exploring Voyage*, pp. 394, 456, and Alexander Nzemeke, *British Imperialism and African Response: The Niger Valley, 1851–1905* (Paderborn, 1982), pp. 47–135.

[48] Thomson, *Through Masai Land*, pp. ix, 8.

Wherever they penetrated, explorers carried a British yardstick of scenery. As Said remarks, 'English places have a kind of export value':[49] the same was true of English stratigraphic sections which, like English manufactured goods, became recognized as patterns world-wide.[50] Explorers filled their descriptions of new landscapes with comparisons to those of the British Isles and the language of Romanticism, even seeing 'ruinous cathedrals and castles' in African dunes[51] and regretting Australia's want of 'bold or fantastic features, by which the imagination is excited and curiosity enhanced'.[52] Park-like scenery remained the ideal because it combined the beautiful with the tame and useful. The more perceptive explorers were sensitive to the interplay of landscape and emotion and the aesthetic dialogue between nature and civilization, waste and verdure. Similarly, their comments about space evinced a value system based on European concepts of size, regularity, and control. Hugh Clapperton described the plantations of Sokoto as being 'as neatly fenced as if they were the property of Englishmen', while the Landers pined for neat English cottages, complaining that African mud huts 'banish every favorable impression'.[53]

Because of homesickness, outraged sensibilities, or the imperative to convey intelligible images of outlandish places, the explorers thus projected a vision of the home islands on to new lands abroad, conquering them by an act of comparative imagination that began the process of reshaping them into something familiar enough to accept and enjoy. The explorers also carried a full battery of literary reference, so peripheral territories could be storied by analogy to stock scenes from literature—itself a canon often shaped by expansion and Empire. Illustrating this two-way trade in images that supplanted or expropriated native cultures, thereby embedding stereotypes facilitating European domination, the Landers compared an African ceremony to restore the eclipsed moon to a scene from *Robinson Crusoe*, noting that it only wanted a cannibal vignette to complete it.[54] Reversing the comparison between reality and art fifty years later, H. Rider Haggard recycled the physical features from Joseph Thomson's *Through Masai Land* to create a fictitious African topography for *King Solomon's Mines*.[55] The European imagination learned to encompass the world's diversity through the literature of exploration, which presented the periphery as a frontier for acting out both old and new challenges.

[49] Said, *Culture and Imperialism*, p. 94.
[50] Stafford, *Scientist of Empire*, p. 19.
[51] Walter Oudney's words: Bovill, *Missions to the Niger*, II, 188.
[52] Paul Edmund De Strzelecki, *Physical Description of New South Wales and Van Diemen's Land*, 2nd edn. (1845; Adelaide, 1967), p. 55.
[53] Bovill, *Missions to the Niger*, IV, p. 774; Hallett, *Niger Journal*, p. 184.
[54] Hallett, *Niger Journal*, p. 168.
[55] Thomson, *Through Masai Land*, p. xii.

While explorers generally saw what they were conditioned to see, many found the wilderness frightening and oppressive. Laird noted that the stillness of the forest of Sierra Leone 'chills the heart, and imparts a feeling of loneliness which can be shaken off only by a strong effort'.[56] Thomson, on the other hand, described his 'perfect ecstasy' in the forests of East Africa—the 'ideal of my dreams', where 'everything was strange, and grand, and colossal!'[57] Again, their differing reactions may be attributable to the half-century between them, though individual sensibilities play a part. Laird, writing in the mid-1830s, inhabited a world replete with ancient forests, in which nature still held sway over much of the planet, settlement frontiers were opening, and the maps of several continents still labelled vast areas *terra incognita*. His outlook—essentially a holdover from eighteenth-century sensibility—only saw nature as beautiful where it was tamed and useful. Thomson, in the early 1880s, lived in a world of closing frontiers, shrinking blank spots, and wild nature retreating everywhere before triumphant technological man. He had the luxury and (perhaps unconscious) sensibility to celebrate the value of something disappearing as rapidly as indigenous peoples—primeval wilderness capable of awing humans.

The numinous, dream-like quality of Thomson's experience suggests two further linkages. First, the new appreciation for wild nature and empty space coincided with the discovery of the unconscious and exploration of the irrational or intuitive as alternatives to inductive reasoning. As world-wide exploration dispelled the 'glowing hues of fantasy' that had beckoned Thomson to Africa,[58] the quest for untracked territory moved to the inner *terra incognita* of the human mind. The ritual baptisms in which several explorers indulged upon reaching their goals, such as MacDouall Stuart at the Timor Sea or Thomson at Lake Nyasa,[59] suggest that exploration represented a journey of discovery into the self, a plunge into the wellsprings of the soul, as much as geographical research. Secondly, absorption in overseas wilderness represented a form of time travel: the experience had not been available in western Europe for centuries. Conrad captured all of these themes in *Heart of Darkness*, with its focus on emptiness, timelessness, and implacable nature. The similarity between his description of the tropical forest and Thomson's is striking.[60] By the 1880s it was only in remote regions like the Congo or the East African highlands that such themes could still be acted out.

[56] Laird and Oldfield, *Narrative of an Expedition*, I, p. 181.
[57] Thomson, *To the Central African Lakes*, I, pp. 51–52.
[58] Thomson, *Through Masai Land*, p. 7.
[59] J. MacDouall Stuart, *Explorations Across the Continent of Australia*, 2nd edn. (1863; Adelaide, 1963), p. 57; Thomson, *To the Central African Lakes*, I, pp. 259–61.
[60] Compare Thomson, ref. 57, with Joseph Conrad, *Heart of Darkness* (1902; Harmondsworth, 1973), p. 48.

In the final decades of the century, therefore, the periphery came to represent an alternative to the confusing, suffocating restraints of modernist Europe, where urbanization and technology had transformed the very dimensions of life and thought. The cultural reactions to this trend—geopolitics, preservation of wilderness, exploration of the unconscious, fascination with the primitive—were paralleled by the politics of imperialism, the impulse to claim more space.[61] Yet British Imperialism went further in its acquisitiveness than expropriating land to commandeer the future. It also sought, through the willing aid of geology, to lay claim to the earth in depth, adding the lower portion of the third dimension to this grand Cartesian plan for enclosure. Similarly, Britain's upsurge of enthusiasm for mountaineering during the second half of the century, another activity closely linked to geography and Empire, represented the conquest of height, complementing geology's annexation of the subterranean world. The process of cultural appropriation reached backward within the fourth dimension as well, where stratigraphy and palaeontology helped annex 'deep time', beyond the past revealed by history and archaeology.[62] The British mind, therefore, balanced in dynamic tension between the dual concepts of the periphery as a primitive playground for the imagination and another locus for development. Imperialism was compatible with both these ideas, for it appropriated territories and their potentialities in order that Britons might transform them, thereby reliving the European experience in new settings that provided opportunities to avoid past mistakes. The role colonies played in the growth of European environmental consciousness and the vehemence of ideological debates about colonial development index the profound psychological ambivalence that lay behind this dialectic.[63]

The intoxication with space found expression not only in Imperialism, but in public interest in exploration, the mania for maps, emigration, and an outpouring of novels of Empire that chronicled the claustrophobia of the home islands and the reaction—greed for land and a longing for freedom to act in an unregulated landscape.[64] The explorer was the archetype of this fantasy of escape on to a larger stage where the ego could assert itself on an heroic scale. Exploration, like Empire, offered renewal for the race and the individual in reliving the immemorial saga of conquering nature, aided by the science and technology that proved the superiority of Europeans and their right to rule. Just as the rising curve of British

---

[61] Kern, *Culture of Time and Space*, pp. 4, 92.

[62] Stafford, 'Annexing the Landscapes'.

[63] Richard H. Grove, *Green Imperialism: Colonial Expansion, Tropical Island Edens and the Origins of Environmentalism, 600–1860* (Cambridge, 1995); John M. Mackenzie, *The Empire of Nature: Hunting, Conservation and British Imperialism* (Manchester, 1988).

[64] Kern, *Culture of Time and Space*, p. 166. Novels of Empire are thoroughly treated in Susanne Howe, *Novels of Empire* (New York, 1949) and Patrick Brantlinger, *Rule of Darkness: British Literature and Imperialism, 1830–1914* (Ithaca, NY, 1988).

exploration during this century charts Britain's economic, technological, and military dominance, it also indicates the rise to power of the middle classes. While the landowning classes supported exploration because it generated strategic, scientific, and prestige dividends, the middle classes provided the real impetus behind the nation's investment in overseas discovery. Middle-class scientists, military officers, merchants, and financiers, working through institutions like the RGS and the British Association that represented the community of interest between the traditional élites and rising economic groups, pushed the hardest for exploration and stood to gain the most from it.

While its material goals were obvious, the middle class also needed mental space that was unavailable in Britain's constricted landscape, where every acre was locked into the pattern of control that expressed the hegemony of the traditional élite. Through the technology, science, and organizational abilities that symbolized its ascendancy, the middle class seized on the overseas wilderness as its own fiefdom, calling new worlds into being to redress the balance of the old. Exploration, like the missionary movement, colonization, and the growth of commerce, was largely an assertion of middle-class goals, methods, and values through horizontal expansion. Leaving the finite fields of the occupied home islands, the explorers forged into the seemingly infinite jungles, deserts, forests, and prairies overseas. There they discovered room to create new Britains, built from scratch to middle-class design. They painted a picture of unbounded scope for improvements of every kind, from exploiting virgin resources to civilizing savage natives.

As their treatment of scenery suggests, explorers were often tense and despondent. They fought back by naming things, symbolically claiming alien territories by representing them with English terms. This act of supreme ego—a demonstration of control that had nothing to do with actual sovereignty—stamped new lands with the image of Europe, beginning the process of wresting them from the control of indigenous peoples.[65] Naming was at once an act of cultural imposition and of despoliation. It connected previously unknown places with European history, notifying other powers that Britain had some claim upon them by right of discovery. British explorers generally named geographical features and dedicated their narratives according to the Imperial social hierarchy: royalty first, followed by Cabinet-level sponsors, metropolitan department heads, colonial Governors or patrons, officers of the explorer's own service or institution, admired scientists or authors, mentors, friends, and relatives. Literary characters and places were also commemorated, and European place-names freely reused. For some, naming was an opportunity to remember and repay; for others, it was an act of

[65] Paul Carter, *The Road to Botany Bay: An Exploration of Landscape and History* (Chicago, 1987).

vengeance against hostile environments.[66] For Thomson, replacing 'uncouth' African names with English ones was simply a relief.[67]

Thomson and many other explorers saw discovery as co   1est.[68] Claiming ceremonies, like naming, expressed this scientific equivalent of Imperial expansion. Maritime explorers had long claimed uncharted islands and coasts, but as the discovery frontier moved inland, policy changed to acquisition only where required, and explorers limited themselves to reaffirming British ownership of unvisited portions of recognized claims. In this respect exploration evolved from actual into symbolic conquest, though its cultural significance remained as high. As harbingers of European civilization, explorers developed an entire set of triumphal rituals: naming, claiming, self-baptism, flag-raising, toast-drinking, observing holidays, carving or burying records of achievement, recovering the possessions of martyred predecessors, and partaking of European foods upon their return. Ceremonial etiquette even evolved for meeting other whites in outlandish locations. James Stewart of the Livingstonia Mission introduced himself to Joseph Thomson at Lake Tanganyika 'according to the African salutation *à la mode*—"Mr. Thomson, I presume?" '[69] Such incidents became tropes in exploration literature that merged into mainstream culture, reflexively reinforcing the commitment to expansion. The behaviours ratified by the explorers, as well as their activities, overlaid a web of European association on new lands.

Explorers lost no opportunity to impress indigenous peoples with the superior power of Europeans. Much of this display centred on demonstrations of science and technology, which in the industrial era supplanted religion as key criteria for measuring human capacity. This transformation in attitudes also expressed the rise to power of the middle class, as well as its growing dominance of exploration. While the middle class was neither uniform nor unique in its scientific outlook— explorers continued to be recruited from the gentry—bourgeois intermediaries like John Barrow were instrumental in propagating the new doctrine that material achievement offered the most accurate gauge of civilization. Barrow served as an editor for John Murray, the premier English publisher of geographical narratives who, like Barrow, was a founder and Council member of the RGS. Through many articles in Murray's influential *Quarterly Review*, Barrow also tutored the public in interpreting exploration. Parvenus who made their careers by understanding science and technology thus drew upon and shaped the work of explorers, redefining the relativities between cultures to reflect their own values.

[66] e.g. John Oxley, *Journals of Two Expeditions into the Interior of New South Wales*, 2nd edn. (1820; Adelaide, 1964), pp. 91, 257.

[67] Thomson, *To the Central African Lakes*, I, pp. 148–49.

[68] Ibid., I, p. 211.

[69] Ibid., II, p. 4.

It was natural, therefore, that explorers exhibit the technical means that enabled their travels, including complex technics such as steamboats, guns, and scientific instruments, and objects as mundane as fireworks and magnets deployed simply to awe and entertain. Their mapping and observational activities were particularly stark demonstrations of cultural superiority, for native peoples often could not understand them. As with primeval environments, explorers often felt that in visiting indigenous cultures they were travelling millennia into the past, confronting ancestral stages of their own culture. The shock of peering into this ancient mirror forced Europeans to question industrial progress, but the disparities revealed easily confirmed the validity of Britain's choices. The decompression required to enter cultures with neither a clock-based sense of time nor a time-based work ethic usually produced frustration equivalent to a mental attack of the bends. Non-European spatial perceptions were similarly rejected.[70] Because quantification was central to industrialism and science, explorers not only used it to evaluate other cultures, but became uneasy when failed instruments left them in the same state of helpless inaccuracy as indigenes. One reason for the phenomenal popularity of the explorer in this era was that he 'voyaged at or beyond the frontiers of technology', demonstrating that the few remaining places not accessible to steam and telegraph could nevertheless be penetrated with a minimum of modern equipment.[71] Explorers were among the élite few who could take full advantage of the global transport systems;[72] for their place-bound audience, much of the excitement of their adventures lay in the disjunction between racing out to the jumping-off point backed by all the logistical might of Britain, and then slowing to the crawl of horse, camel, or safari as they entered unknown lands where Europe's writ did not yet run.

The explorers functioned as living projections of Europe, fired into the void of the peripheral wilderness like modern scientific probes into deep space. They delivered a sharp sense of what the new worlds overseas felt like, reimporting into Britain the colours, sights, sounds, smells, variety, and uninhibited behaviours conspicuously lacking in the culture of physiological denial codified in industrialism's Gospel of Work. The lands revealed by exploration offered an enticing antidote to the cult of the machine—a return to nature and the primitive. At the same time, they offered the lure of new worlds to conquer. This bifocal vision goes far to explain the great vogue of exploration narratives in the nineteenth century: they offered both escape into alternative worlds that were *real*, and psychological respite from the repression of Victorian mores. Audiences allowed themselves to

---

[70] Adas, *Machines as the Measure of Men*, pp. 177–97, 245–49, 259–64.

[71] E. J. Hobsbawm, *The Age of Capital, 1848–1875* (1975; New York, 1979), p. 62.

[72] R. A. Buchanan, *The Power of the Machine: The Impact of Technology from 1700 to the Present*, 2nd edn. (1992; Harmondsworth, 1994), p. 123.

enjoy explorers' escapades because they were conducted as scientific exercises with the full panoply of brass instruments, assumptions of white superiority, moral high-mindedness, and commercial perspective. Audiences did not respond to the work of scholars like Burton who, chameleon-like, shifted into the worlds they discovered. They favoured instead bluff authors like Lander or Thomson, who told an adventure story as straightforwardly as they accomplished their goals. The public's favourite, however, remained Livingstone, the martyr who suffered more, and seemed to enjoy it more, than any other explorer.

Victorian British culture was pervaded by geographical knowledge and metaphors that reflected the nation's powerful expansionist urge. While Britain's literate middle class demonstrated a seemingly insatiable appetite for exploration narratives,[73] the teaching of geography languished before the Devonshire Commission of 1870–75 recommended the establishment of a national curriculum, long the pattern on the continent. Yet by 1886, when the RGS published the Keltie Report on geographical education in Britain, no evidence of a general improvement in standards could be detected.[74] Britons' appetite for geography sprang not from schooling, but from direct engagement with commercial, Imperial, and philanthropic endeavours overseas, and more especially from identification with national heroes who were enlarging Britain's sphere in the world. Exploration exemplified the cultural importance of geography more clearly than any other contemporary activity. In the actions of the explorer in the field, in the style and workings of the Royal Geographical Society, in the content and texture of the narratives, maps, and art that conveyed the results of exploration, the emphasis on control of space is paramount. Exploration and Empire sprang from the same motives and mutually supported each other in defining, exploiting, and acquiring territory. Mapping the world and subjecting it to scientific inventory were principle accomplishments of nineteenth-century European civilization. These activities resulted from the same drive for expansion, power, and global connectivity that fuelled imperialism, free trade, emigration, the missionary movement, and the construction of world-wide transport and communications networks. Science operates within the same paradigm of control as technology. In Victorian Britain, they fused with exploration and Empire in support of an aggressive culture that sought to export its achievements for the betterment of Greater Britain. Scientific exploration led this movement, feeding information into metropolitan culture that facilitated the creation, maintenance, and expansion of Empire. Gladstone was more prescient than he knew: exploration and the cultural power of geogra-

---

[73] e.g. David Livingstone's *Missionary Travels* (London, 1857) sold 70,000 copies in eighteen months.
[74] Stoddart, 'R.G.S. and the "New Geography"'.

phy waned precisely as Empire reached its zenith. The once-actual realms of fantasy—mapped, annexed, and bureaucratized into banality—were then internalized in art and other symbolic forms. Yet during the Victorian heyday of British expansion, science and Empire reached their most perfect congruence in the activity of exploration, an acquisitive quest for knowledge that conferred power over new territories while sculpting metropolitan culture to support its use.

Select Bibliography

J. N. L. BAKER, *History of Geographical Discovery and Exploration* (New York, rept. of 2nd edn. of 1937, 1967).

MORAG BELL and others, eds., *Geography and Imperialism, 1820–1940* (Manchester, 1995).

IAN CAMERON, *To the Farthest Ends of the Earth: The History of the Royal Geographical Society, 1830–1980* (London, 1980).

PAUL CARTER, *The Road to Botany Bay: An Exploration of Landscape and History* (Chicago, 1987).

ALFRED FRIENDLY, *Beaufort of the Admiralty The Life and Times of Sir Francis Beaufort, 1774–1857* (London, 1977).

ROBIN HALLETT, ed., *Records of the African Association, 1788–1831* (London, 1964).

CHRISTOPHER HIBBERT, *Africa Explored: Europeans in the Dark Continent, 1769–1889* (London, 1982).

PETER HOPKIRK, *The Great Game* (London, 1990).

JOHN KEAY, ed., *The Royal Geographical Society History of World Exploration* (London, 1991).

CLEMENTS MARKHAM, *Memoir of the Indian Surveys* (London, 1871).

—— *The Fifty Years' Work of the Royal Geographical Society* (London, 1881).

HUGH ROBERT MILL, *The Record of the Royal Geographical Society* (London, 1930).

G. S. RITCHIE, *The Admiralty Chart: British Naval Hydrography in the Nineteenth Century* (London, 1967).

JANE ROBINSON, *Wayward Women: A Guide to Women Travellers* (Oxford, 1990).

ROBERT ROTBERG, ed., *Africa and its Explorers* (Cambridge, Mass., 1970).

DONALD SIMPSON, *Dark Companions* (London, 1975).

ROBERT A. STAFFORD, *Scientist of Empire: Sir Roderick Murchison, Scientific Exploration, and Victorian Imperialism* (Cambridge, 1989).

R. V. TOOLEY, *The Mapping of Australia* (London, 1979).

DEREK WALLER, *The Pundits: British Exploration of Tibet and Central Asia* (Louisville, Ky., 1990).

15

Defence and Imperial Disunity

PETER BURROUGHS

Safeguarding a global Empire posed British governments with intractable problems and agonizing choices throughout the nineteenth century. In addition to balancing the often-conflicting demands of home defence, protection of scattered colonies against external aggression and internal lawlessness, and security of the interconnecting routes and communications, policy-makers had to decide whether these imperatives should be treated separately or knitted together in a seamless strategy of 'Imperial defence'. Whatever the preferred approach, they had to determine the respective roles of army and navy amidst much inter-service rivalry. Finance was also central, and frequently decisive: the adjustment of unavoidable commitments and acceptable funding, the distribution of costs between British and colonial taxpayers, the desire of politicians and public for defence on the cheap. Seeking to juggle these various elements, British governments successively pursued three different 'strategies'. In the years after 1815 military garrisons overseas commanded priority (Map 15.1), with home defence and the Royal Navy taken for granted. From the late 1840s the perceived threat of a French invasion kindled doubts about the navy's ability to guarantee insular security and encouraged concentration on 'fortress' Britain, secured by fortifications and troops brought home from colonies of settlement, now vested with self-government and self-reliance. By the late 1870s another pattern began to emerge, one which sought to integrate Britain and colonies into an overall strategy of Imperial defence, although the navalist bias towards sea power and centralization operated against such a design.

This diversity of response reflected in large measure the variable climate of international relations and changing contemporary assessments of the dangers threatening Britain and its world-wide interests. Until the 1870s British industrial and naval supremacy was enhanced effortlessly by the absence of serious challenge from other nations. During this 'peculiar interlude', retrenchment and disengagement could be pursued without jeopardizing security. Thereafter, the rise of industrializing foreign competitors with colonial ambitions altered the international context. British ministers and their professional advisers responded

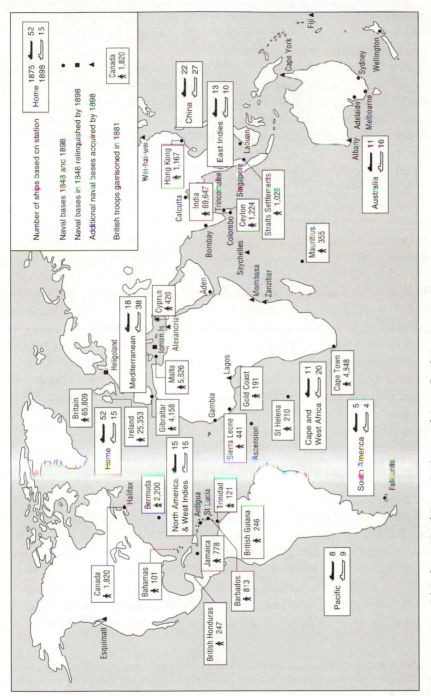

Legend:

Number of ships based on station: Home — 1875: 52, 1898: 15

Naval bases 1848 and 1898 ●
Naval bases in 1848 relinquished by 1898 ■
Additional naval bases acquired by 1898 ▲

British troops garrisoned in 1881: Canada ⚓ 1,820

Map labels (bases, stations, garrisons):

- Canada ⚓ 1,820
- Esquimalt ▲
- Halifax ●
- Bermuda ⚓ 2,200
- Bahamas ⚓ 101
- Jamaica ⚓ 778
- British Honduras ⚓ 247
- Barbados ⚓ 813
- Antigua
- St Lucia
- Trinidad ⚓ 121
- British Guiana ⚓ 246
- North America & West Indies — 1875: 15, 1898: 15
- Pacific — 1875: 8, 1898: 9
- South America — 1875: 5, 1898: 4
- Falklands
- Home — 1875: 52, 1898: 15
- Britain ⚓ 65,809
- Ireland ⚓ 25,353
- Heligoland ■
- Mediterranean — 1875: 18, 1898: 38
- Gibraltar ⚓ 4,158
- Malta ⚓ 5,526
- Ionian Is ■
- Alexandria ▲
- Cyprus ⚓ 420
- Aden ●
- Gambia
- Sierra Leone ⚓ 441
- Ascension ●
- Lagos
- Gold Coast ⚓ 191
- St Helena ⚓ 210
- Cape and West Africa — 1875: 11, 1898: 20
- Cape Town ⚓ 4,848
- South America — 1875: 5, 1898: 4
- Mombasa ▲
- Zanzibar ●
- Seychelles
- Mauritius ⚓ 355
- Bombay ●
- Calcutta ●
- India ⚓ 69,647
- Wei-hai-wei ▲
- Hong Kong ⚓ 1,167
- China — 1875: 22, 1898: 27
- East Indies — 1875: 13, 1898: 10
- Trincomalee ●
- Colombo ●
- Ceylon ⚓ 1,224
- Singapore ●
- Labuan ●
- Straits Settlements ⚓ 1,028
- Cape York ▲
- Australia — 1875: 11, 1898: 16
- Albany ●
- Adelaide ●
- Melbourne ●
- Sydney ●
- Wellington ●
- Fiji ▲

MAP 15.1. Imperial Defence: Naval Bases, Stations, and Army Garrisons

by groping towards a more co-ordinated strategy which entailed greater emphasis on the Royal Navy, a slackening of financial constraints, and bids to conjure co-operation from self-governing colonies.

Within these global dimensions, two defence debates proceeded in parallel, only occasionally intersecting. One was centred on the security of India and was embedded in British diplomacy. It reflected nagging, overblown fears of a Russian invasion across the North-West Frontier, a region periodically convulsed by hostilities with border tribes and not stabilized by British conquests of Sind (1843) and the Punjab (1849) (Map 18.1). Rather than invasion, however, the cardinal concern of the vast garrison (by mid-century some 45,000 European and 230,000 Indian troops) was internal security: to uphold the rule of the Raj by coercive power and massive bluff against the kind of indigenous challenge that erupted in 1857. What Lord Salisbury called 'an English barrack in the Oriental seas' nevertheless also acted as a reservoir of military manpower for employment elsewhere. Indian troops served in Arabia (1821), Burma (1824–26), and Aden (1839), and after mid-century were often sent increasingly far afield.[1] India's defence depended on secure communications, especially the route through the Middle East, which gave the Mediterranean bases, and later the Suez Canal, crucial significance in an overarching strategy that remained remarkably consistent and uncontroversial throughout the century. But what chiefly placed India outside much animated public discussion of defence was the unique arrangement whereby the Indian Army was financed by local revenues, consuming up to half the annual budget, such was its priority. This self-sufficiency also gave the East India Company and then the India Office, as well as the military authorities in India, greater administrative autonomy and freedom from Treasury control than the Colonial and War Offices enjoyed elsewhere in the Empire.

The other focus of British debate, preoccupied with financial more than strategic considerations, involved Britain's non-Asian possessions. Numerous overseas bases, many of them small islands, served as staging posts and vital links in the chain of transmarine communications, a function which, until the 1880s, was taken for granted rather than regularly discussed. Most prominent and contentious were the settlement colonies, principally in British North America and Australasia, whose sizeable British populations and relative wealth ensured them an influential role in the changing patterns of colonial defence. Yet unity of action proved as elusive as an integrated strategy of Imperial defence. Over the years the course of the Empire's defence and governance frequently converged but never

---

[1] Quoted in Sir Charles Lucas, *The Empire at War*, 5 vols. (London, 1921–26), I, p. 56; for details of Indian troops sent overseas after 1858, see below, pp. 442–43 and for the East India Company army see Vol. II, p. 202.

exactly coincided. Whereas security ideally demanded co-ordination, colonial administration remained fragmented in Whitehall and entailed bilateral relationships between Britain and individual colonies. The voices and aspirations of communities enjoying representative institutions had to be heeded in London, but their particular interests did not necessarily match those of Britain or the Empire at large. Issues touching security were enmeshed with political and economic dealings between local and Imperial authorities: sometimes this facilitated agreement on defence; often it encouraged disharmony. A further complication arose from the ambivalence of outlook on both sides: just as colonial sensibilities coexisted with Imperial sentiment, so British self-sufficiency jostled with collaborative impulses. These themes and cross-currents will be traced through the three phases which characterize arrangements for the defence of the nineteenth-century Empire.

Between 1815 and 1846 British thinking on defence continued to reflect notions derived from the previous century. The Royal Navy still functioned as the nation's shield against invasion and protector of global commercial interests, as oceanic highways were riveted by a world-encircling network of island bases and mainland entrepôts. 'Our policy', Lord Castlereagh explained in 1816, 'had been to secure the empire against future attack. In order to do this, we had acquired what in former days would have been thought romance—the keys of every great military position.'[2] The navy also acted as an instrument of foreign policy: warships restrained the expansionist designs of France and Russia, especially in the crucial Mediterranean corridor; gunboats occasionally backed British diplomatic or commercial ventures with a show of force, as in South America and China; naval squadrons suppressed piracy and African slave trading and guaranteed the openness of the seas. During these decades and beyond, despite incidents and alarms, no foreign powers were able to challenge Britain's maritime mastery; indeed, they acquiesced in British overseas pretensions and self-appointed policing role, made the more palatable by the shared benefits of free trade. The result was an exceptional period of international peace when Britain's pacific approach to global trading relations, backed by industrial muscle, commanded general acceptance. What was later dubbed *Pax Britannica* reflected an unwillingness on the part of European competitors to question one nation's unassailable naval supremacy.

While the Senior Service retained a prime role in colonial defence, it was supplemented by a substantial military presence throughout expanding territorial domains. Since the Seven Years War (1756–63), the practice had developed of stationing British troops in each new acquisition: twenty-two colonies in 1793

---

[2] 4 March 1816 P[arliamentary] D[ebates], XXXII (Commons), col. 1104.

had grown to thirty-four by the 1820s, and stood at forty-five in 1846. In some areas, especially the North-West Frontier of India and Canada, garrisons were intended to forestall aggression by a foreign power. Unstable frontier regions, as in Asia and southern Africa, had to be watched over and sometimes subdued or extended by conquest. Policing duties, particularly in ethnically diverse communities, might encompass disturbances, open revolt, and even internecine warfare, feared in the West Indies during the era of slave emancipation and later realized in New Zealand. Such Imperial burdens constituted the major commitments of a British army which was not expected to fight a large-scale war in Europe. Despite the obligations of home defence, the Victorian army was an Imperial force in function, organization, and prevailing ethos.

Both navy and army were constrained by public and parliamentary insistence on retrenchment, which affected all aspects of government spending and the policies of all ministries after 1815. Many Britons agreed with the Select Committee on Finance in 1818 that 'finances recruited during peace, and...all practical savings of expense and consequent diminution of burdens' were as vital to security as 'ships and stores and military arrangements'.[3] The passion for economy derived partly from fiscal considerations and taxpayers' reluctance in peacetime to support 'bloated establishments'. It was also nourished by reformers who designated 'wasteful' expenditure the enemy of probity, efficiency, and good government, vague but influential notions of a political culture of middle-class liberalism which prolonged the quest for economy far into the age of Victorian affluence. Expenditure on the armed forces was both highly visible as the largest component of public spending, and highly vulnerable in the absence of major crises abroad.

Between 1816 and 1834 naval estimates fell from £9.5m to £4.5m, for an authorized complement of 27,000 seamen and marines, while capital ships in commission declined from eighty to fifty-eight. Army estimates slumped from £43m in 1815 to £8m in 1837 and the establishment from 233,952 to 87,993 soldiers. By 1846, however, naval spending had risen to £8m, with 45,000 in the service, and that on the army to £10m, now with 100,600 men.[4] Despite the persevering pursuit of retrenchment, therefore, economizers still had plenty of scope for reining back defence spending. Hitherto, the response of the two services to financial constraints had been to discharge mounting overseas commitments at the expense of domestic defence. The number of ships required for detached duties on foreign stations—sixty-three in 1817, 104 in 1836, and 129 in 1848—was achieved by diminishing the navy's presence in home waters. Of the 103 infantry regiments

---

[3] P[arliamentary] P[apers] (1818) (57), III, p. 69.
[4] PP (1816) (53) and (32) XII; (1834) (17), XLII; Army Estimates (1837) (47), XL; (1846) (59), XXV; (1847) (47), XXXV.

in the 1830s, seventy-nine might be stationed abroad or in transit, and only twenty-four in Britain preparing for eventual embarkation. In 1846, twenty-three of the 112 battalions were located in India, fifty-four elsewhere in the Empire, and thirty-five in the British Isles.[5]

This imbalance in the deployment of troops and ships aroused grave public and ministerial concern in 1846–47, and again in 1852–53, when scares of invasion were sparked by construction of the French naval base at Cherbourg and alarmist pronouncements that 'steam had bridged the Channel'. What turned temporary panic into longer-term remedial action was the wide-ranging review of Britain's defence strategy conducted in 1846 by Earl Grey, a reforming head of the War Office in the late 1830s and now Colonial Secretary. His proposals for reconciling expanding commitments with tight budgets and scarce resources, embodied in a landmark Cabinet paper of October 1846, envisaged a decisive shift in the deployment of military manpower. Instead of soldiers scattered across the Empire, easy communications by steam permitted a greater concentration of troops at home. In future the security of dependencies had to depend more on naval power, rapid responses to emergencies by the despatch of expeditionary forces, and routine reliance on colonial corps or militia. The reduction of garrisons in settlement colonies neatly dovetailed with Grey's policy of devolving political authority: self-defence was the corollary of self-rule. Imperial bases like Malta and Bermuda would remain a British expense, but self-governing communities should undertake internal policing duties and maintain barracks and other military installations.[6]

However sound and settled the objectives, Grey recognized the need for cautious presentation and flexible timing. The clamour in Parliament and press against colonies as financial burdens caused him considerable anxiety, for 'the economical fever is very strong upon John Bull at this moment'.[7] A precipitate transfer of military responsibilities might appear to give countenance and momentum to scepticism about the Empire; yet cutting defence spending overseas was essential to creating a more palatable, enduring Imperial relationship. Colonial sentiment, as well as differing states of security, had also to be considered. Thinking it least controversial to begin with secure, prosperous, and lightly taxed Australians, Grey announced in 1846 troop reductions and the transfer to local management of barracks and military works. 'N.S. Wales kicked a good deal at

[5] Paul M. Kennedy, *The Rise and Fall of British Naval Mastery* (London, 1976), pp. 170–71; *PP* (1851) (564), VII, pp. 741–42.

[6] 'The Army', 17 Oct. 1846, C[olonial] O[ffice] 885/1.

[7] Grey to Elgin, 16 Nov. 1848, in A. G. Doughty, ed., *The Elgin–Grey Papers, 1846–1852*, 4 vols. (Ottawa, 1937), I, p. 252.

first,' he admitted, 'but the people are beginning to understand that they cannot have the advantages without the burthens of self-Government.'[8] In Canada, Grey proceeded more circumspectly. With a population that included French Canadians and Irish Catholics, and a mercantile community dissatisfied with the removal of preferential tariffs, fragile colonial loyalty must not be undermined by conveying the impression that Britain no longer possessed the will or the ability to provide protection, and that an unwelcome shift of responsibilities for defence was a prelude to severing the Imperial connection. Rioting over the Rebellion Losses Act (1843), which many felt rewarded French Canadians for their treason in 1837, and an upsurge of annexationist sentiment in 1849 underscored the need for caution; but within two years Grey had determined to extend to Canada similar arrangements concerning troops and installations to those already applied in Australia.

Grey's strategic design of 1846, embraced by his successors in office, is chiefly significant as a statement of long-term intent, its immediate achievements being limited and dependent on capricious local circumstances. In the Australian colonies, a force of over 5,000 British troops in 1846 fell below 1,800 by 1852, while the Canadian garrison, which had totalled 16,000 in 1841, steadily declined over the ensuing years to a low of 2,800 by 1856, when deteriorating Anglo-American relations prompted the despatch of five regiments. In the West Indies, despite protests by local legislatures, the Colonial Office gradually reduced by a quarter in the mid-1850s a force of 6,000 men by concentrating scattered detachments. While warfare in southern Africa had obliged Grey to augment British regulars to 9,000 men, these were cut by a third in 1854 following cessation of hostilities, the grant of representative institutions at the Cape, and conventions with the Boer communities.[9] The persistence of intermittent fighting precluded an early reduction in New Zealand's small garrison.

After military calculations had been thrown into disarray by the Crimean War (1854–56) and the Indian Mutiny (British forces in India were increased by a third to 60,000 and sepoy numbers prudentially halved to 120,000 in a reconstructed Indian Army),[10] renewed consideration of colonial defence costs led in the late 1850s to a second phase in troop withdrawals from self-governing colonies. Now a sharper divergence of opinion emerged. Behind the practical questions of strategic deployment and financial responsibility lay a speculative controversy over the nature of future Imperial relations. Previously, the moderate, qualified stance of Grey and his successors had been in the ascendant, with their belief that devolu-

[8] Grey to Elgin, 25 Oct. 1850, in ibid., II, p. 721.
[9] *PP* (1854) (117), XLI, and Report from the Select Committee appointed on Colonial Expenditure... (1861) (423), XIII, p. 367.
[10] See below, pp. 427–29.

tion of management in matters of internal security, judiciously pursued, was wholly compatible with sustaining Imperial unity in an altered, more acceptable, and therefore more enduring form. They had not envisaged the complete abandonment or total abnegation of British obligations for the defence of colonies urged by a small but vocal minority of Cobdenites and sceptics. Britain, as an Imperial power, had to maintain the security of overseas possessions, not just by naval strength, but also by military garrisons at key bases and token units strategically stationed elsewhere as emblems of a massive force held in reserve for any emergency.

By the late 1850s and 1860s, however, more rigorous views came into greater prominence. In Parliament, a phalanx of 'colonial reformers' advocated the recall of British troops, irrespective of particular local circumstances and colonial wishes. They believed that Britain might disengage herself almost entirely from the obligations of defence and still preserve Imperial ties based on sentiment and common interests. These opinions also infected official circles, commanding open support at the War Office and the Treasury and among individual Cabinet ministers, including both Gladstone and Disraeli as Chancellors of the Exchequer, as well as covert sympathy among some permanent staff at the Colonial Office, though that department's policy remained ostensibly wedded to Grey's design. The debate which raged between 1859 and 1870 was less about ends than about means and timing: both sides favoured 'self-reliance' but differed over how best to cultivate it among colonists; both championed 'economy' but disagreed over how to apply it appropriately. In this domestically centred debate, finance and political relationships bulked larger than strategic considerations; the defence of individual colonies was left to future local exertions, or to chance. This was not a defence strategy but the absence of one: colonists were somehow expected to fill the vacuum left by British military withdrawal. Ironically, despite the predominance of moderate counsels in the shaping of colonial defence policy during the 1860s, circumstances overseas effected the virtual triumph of the thorough-going approach by 1870.

The issue came to the fore in 1859 because of practical problems experienced by the War and Colonial Offices in co-ordinating their responsibilities for Empire defence, redefined during the Crimean War. Under the prompting of John Robert Godley, a 'colonial reformer' now assistant Under-Secretary, the war department criticized current policy and proposed more demanding, rigid guidelines. In 1857–58 Britain's military spending overseas amounted to £3.9m, towards which colonies contributed only £378,253, 'a state of things' with 'no parallel or precedent in the case of any other organised community of which the history is known'. While the Empire's security relied principally on naval supremacy, and key Imperial bases required military garrisons, British soldiers should be withdrawn from all other dependencies. Internal policing should be left wholly to local management, forces, and funds, 'there being no ground for drawing any distinction between a Colony and an independent nation in this respect'. For protection against aggression Britain was obliged to provide assistance, but colonies should pay towards external defence at a uniform rate, regardless of vulnerability or resources. This arrangement, the War Office believed, would 'stimulate the patriotism, self-reliance and military spirit of the Colonists' and 'show that we rely on their loyalty and attachment and nothing else'.[11] Officials at the colonial department condemned such 'doctrinaire', unworkable proposals. The Empire's diversity precluded any 'single maxim' or 'self-acting rule' for calculating payments towards military expenses. While colonies should help to defend themselves, Britain could not be indifferent to their internal tranquillity, nor take such a minimalist view of her proper responsibilities as the concerned Mother Country of an integrated Empire. Moreover, small military garrisons symbolized British power in reserve and signalled a resolve and a capacity to defend its possessions in a last resort.[12]

An interdepartmental committee comprising Godley, T. F. Elliot of the Colonial Office, and George Hamilton from the Treasury discussed these issues during 1859–60, and so divergent did their views remain that Elliot wrote a dissenting memorandum to Godley's report. In March 1861 the disagreement among officials spilled over into the parliamentary arena. A Select Committee on Colonial Military Expenditure was secured by Arthur Mills, a 'colonial reformer' who adopted a moderate stance, as did most committee members and witnesses examined. The report, reflecting this balance of opinion, distinguished between Imperial bases, whose defence rested with Britain, and colonies proper, where responsibility 'ought mainly to devolve upon themselves', with British ministers applying the principle to particular cases with discretion and flexibility. Overseas garrisons should be further reduced, but not necessarily withdrawn completely.[13] In March 1862 the House of Commons accepted without a division Mills's resolution:

That this House (while fully recognising the claims of all portions of the British Empire to Imperial aid in their protection against perils arising from the consequences of Imperial policy) is of opinion that Colonies exercising the rights of self-government ought to undertake the main responsibility of providing for their own internal order and security, and ought to assist in their own external defence.[14]

---

[11] Godley, 'Military Expenditures in the Colonies', 2 Oct. 1858, W[ar] O[ffice] 33/6; Hawes to Merivale, 14 March 1859, CO 323/255; Report of the Committee on Expense of Military Defences in the Colonies, 24 Jan. 1860, PP (1860) (282), XLI, pp. 574–83.

[12] Merivale minute, 16 March 1859, Lytton minute, 19 March 1859, CO to WO, 26 May 1859, CO 323/255; PP (1860) (282), XLI, pp. 574–83.

[13] PP (1861) (423), XIII, pp. 73–75.

[14] 4 March 1862, PD, CLXV (Commons), col. 1060.

This resolution represented a tightening-up of the policy initiated by Grey, and the addition by the Commons of the pregnant final phrase gave it wider implications. Yet the failure to differentiate precisely between Imperial and local obligations was a tacit acknowledgment that defence still straddled areas of jurisdiction, a fact strikingly demonstrated during the 1860s by events in New Zealand and British North America.

Uncertainties over the division of responsibilities for internal security were highlighted in New Zealand and settled only after protracted controversy and an acute crisis in Imperial relations. With the outbreak of the Taranaki War in 1860, heralding a decade of almost continuous fighting in the North Island, several awkward questions arose: was this an Imperial or a colonial war? Whose interests did the conflict serve and the British troops protect? How far should the Imperial authorities commit men and money to dealing with a local emergency which white inhabitants of a self-governing colony ought themselves to tackle, and in future avoid by more judicious proceedings towards the Maori? By 1860 settler assertiveness and Maori resistance had undermined Britain's ability to mediate or do justice to the conflicting interests: either it could assert a residual oversight of 'native affairs' and bear the military and financial costs of wars it deprecated; or it had to accept the logic of responsible government, oblige colonial ministers to handle internal security, and hope that the discipline of having to face the consequences of their own actions would discourage confrontation. As Gladstone had earlier remarked, neatly combining economy with morality, 'the burdens of war were the providential preventives of war, and operated as a check upon the passions of mankind'.[15] Nevertheless, it took the Imperial authorities a decade to resolve this conundrum.

At first it seemed appropriate for Britain to help New Zealanders bring the current hostilities to a speedy termination before throwing them on their own resources. But the fighting dragged on inconclusively and local politicians displayed an aggravating reluctance to embrace the duties of self-reliance. As British involvement grew from one regiment in 1860 to 18,000 troops in 1864, the ministerial dilemma intensified and Parliament became more restive, especially when the New Zealand government requested a loan guarantee of £3m. With mounting misgivings about the purpose, conduct, and expense of the war, successive Colonial Secretaries exhorted the colonists to redouble their exertions and warned of early troop withdrawals. Eventually, in 1864 Frederick Weld's government adopted a policy of 'self-reliance', under which colonial ministers would assume full charge of Maori affairs and raise a local defence force. This welcome development led to the recall of five of the ten British regiments in 1865 and four

---

[15] 15 April 1851, *PD*, CXVI (Commons), col. 266.

more the following year. The final disengagement, however, was not so harmo-niously completed. When fighting flared anew in 1868–69, pleas by Edward Stafford's ministry to retain the remaining troops, whatever the price, were rejected by the Colonial Office: 'I think we must harden our hearts', remarked Lord Granville.[16] The last regiment of British regulars departed in 1870, even before the hostilities ceased.

This stubborn, unfeeling stance provoked an outcry in both New Zealand and Britain and placed relations between the two countries under a severe but tem-porary strain. The contents and brusque tone of Granville's despatches created anger and resentment in the colony, where anti-British comment in the press and motions of censure in the legislature predicted secession from the Empire. The fracas soon subsided, in part because commissioners sent to London secured a loan of £1m to promote immigration and public works. Britain thus extricated herself from military involvement in New Zealand's internal security, and while some contemporaries interpreted this as indifference to Empire, or even a covert plot to dissolve it, Granville himself claimed that he had only carried to fruition long-established policy. What, however, gave some substance and plausibility to his critics' charges was that the scuttle from New Zealand coincided with the recall of the Imperial legions from British North America.

Questions concerning Britain's responsibility for the defence of self-governing colonies against external aggression had an urgent reality in Canada during the 1860s, when Anglo-American relations were strained by the Civil War, and later the Fenian border raids. The British government's military advisers, chiefly the influential Colonel W. F. D. Jervois, repeatedly considered how best the security of Canada could be safeguarded. According to the political mood of the moment, their recommendations varied with respect to the troops required—British reg-ulars and colonial militia or volunteers—the dispersal of Imperial units or their concentration at Montreal and Quebec, the value of fortifying these fortresses, and the naval force needed on the Great Lakes. Liberal and Conservative ministers responded to assorted advice with irresolution and divided opinions. Some doubted whether Canada could be effectively defended against a well-organized American assault; most conceded that so long as British regiments were stationed there, something had to be done to place them in a defensible position. Cost was a key factor for the politicians. At least until 1868, the Cabinets of Palmerston, Russell, and Derby had a majority in favour of essential expenditures, though often reluctant to act. A more rigorous minority line was taken by Gladstone, who begrudged spending on the misconceived task of defending Canada, and who thought that self-governing colonies 'should cease to have the sentiment and

---

[16] Granville to Sir Frederick Rogers, 29 Sept. 1869, CO 209/212.

habits of mere dependencies' and should, through military self-reliance, 'ascend to the condition of free communities'. The American Civil War provided 'the golden opportunity' and 'almost a necessity' to 'shift the centre of responsibility from this metropolis to the capital of Canada'. The same view was expressed by Disraeli: 'what is the use of these colonial deadweights which *we do not govern?* ... we should withdraw the great body of our troops, and foster a complete development of self-government'.[17]

Whether or not local self-reliance was stifled by the continued British military presence, the readiness of Canadians to protect themselves formed a vital element in any Imperial plan of disengagement. With varying degrees of exhortation and success, British ministers persistently strove during the 1860s, through joint consultations in Canada or in London, to secure and extend colonial contributions of men and money. At moments of severe crisis the Canadian government responded, as in 1861, calling out 38,000 militia in addition to increased numbers of volunteers. In 1862, however, the Militia Bill was defeated, a 'reprehensible and provoking' action which the Colonial Secretary condemned as 'unbecoming feebleness' when no Imperial force could defend the country 'without the efficient aid of the Canadian people'.[18]

In these circumstances, ministers became keen to encourage closer union among the North American provinces as a way of strengthening their defences against annexation by the United States and allowing Britain to escape from an impossible military commitment. Once Canadian politicians had embraced a project of Confederation in 1864, the Imperial government gave them positive backing. A larger political entity with a developing sense of nationhood would be better able and more willing to uphold its territorial integrity, as well as less likely to arouse the aggressive instincts of its republican neighbour, a threat sharpened by the North's victory in the Civil War. Even so, Canadian leaders visiting London to clinch Confederation complained that British enthusiasm for disengagement and scepticism about the Imperial connection betrayed a churlish want of fellow-feeling.

Whatever the future prospects for Canada, Confederation in 1867 opened the way for British military withdrawal. An incoming Liberal government in 1868 made troop redeployment a central purpose of its army reforms, which included short-service enlistment and linked battalions—one serving overseas, the other

[17] Gladstone memorandum, 'Defence of Canada', 12 July 1864, B[ritish] L[ibrary] Add. MSS. 44, 599; Disraeli to Derby, 30 Sept. 1866, quoted in William Flavelle Monypenny and George Earle Buckle, *The Life of Benjamin Disraeli: Earl of Beaconsfield*, 6 vols. (London, 1910–20), IV, pp. 476–77.

[18] Newcastle to Monck, 21 Aug., 20 Dec. 1862, minute, 28 June 1862, on Monck to Newcastle, 10 June 1862, CO 42/634; see also Kenneth Bourne, *Britain and the Balance of Power in North America, 1815–1908* (London, 1967), pp. 257–70, 284–95.

based in Britain as a source of reliefs and focus for reserves. Edward Cardwell, the Secretary for War, hoped to save £2.3m by reducing the army establishment from 137,500 to 126,000 men and concentrating more soldiers at home by halving colonial garrisons to 26,000 men (though 70,000 British regulars and 140,000 sepoys remained in India). He reassured Canadians that their 'true defence' lay in membership of an Empire 'under the aegis' of Britain: every foreign nation knew that 'war with them is war with England'. Although the Duke of Cambridge, the Commander-in-Chief, fought an unrelenting rearguard action against this policy of 'colonial desertion'—an evasion of, not a solution to, the problem of Canadian defence—events hastened towards a denouement despite further Fenian raids and concern over American intentions.[19] By 1871 all British troops had been withdrawn, except at the Imperial naval bases of Halifax, and Esquimalt on the west coast, where they remained until after the South African War.

Mid-Victorian naval policy followed a parallel and similar pattern: redistribution haphazardly driven by economy at home and circumstances abroad. In the navy's case, the full impact of retrenchment and the reappraisal of commitments were delayed until the 1860s. Until then, the invasion panics, coupled with unease about France's naval ambitions, possibly in alliance with Russia, fuelled British naval expansion and higher spending. These tendencies were reinforced by technological developments, because the emergence of the large steam ironclad stimulated both alarm and expenditure. Despite conservatism and technological uncertainty, the Admiralty experimented with steam-powered vessels of superior speed and firepower designed for pursuit and coastal offensive operations. Meanwhile, Palmerston's assertive, meddling diplomacy and resort to gunboats meant the growing deployment of naval forces in non-European waters. By the early 1860s, twice as many ships (some 140) were dispersed on foreign stations as in 1835, including sixty-six vessels on the China Station and a transatlantic squadron augmented from twenty-three to forty-one ships at the start of the American Civil War.[20]

From about 1862, however, or symbolically with Palmerston's death in 1865, the initiative passed to Gladstone, and his determination to slash defence spending ensured a reassessment of the Royal Navy's commitments and deployment. In some respects this process had begun with the invasion scare of 1859, which had prompted massive expenditure on the fortification of major British ports and proposals to concentrate a larger fleet in home waters by scattering fewer vessels around the world. Such a strategic redistribution also depended on changes in the

[19] 11 March 1869, *PD*, CXCIV (Commons), cols. 111–17; also Bourne, *Balance of Power*, pp. 295–304.
[20] C. J. Bartlett, 'The Mid-Victorian Reappraisal of Naval Policy', in K. Bourne and D. C. Watt, eds., *Studies in International History* (London, 1967), pp. 190–94.

conduct of British foreign policy. By the late 1860s the international scene in Europe and beyond facilitated this shift, and potential naval rivals—France, Russia, and the United States—had their attention otherwise occupied. In such propitious circumstances, when security could be purchased cheaply, the governments of Gladstone and Disraeli pruned naval spending, partly through the construction of fewer ironclads, but chiefly by reductions in the non-European squadrons, aided by a foreign policy of greater restraint. The task of redistribution was tackled with vigour by Hugh Childers, the Liberal First Lord. Instead of the routine, permanent dispersal of naval forces across the globe, he favoured greater concentration in home waters of mobile reserves or 'flying squadrons' which, especially with the expanding network of submarine telegraphs, could be speedily despatched to any location where British interests or prestige had to be upheld. In the decade after 1865 the number of ships serving on non-European stations fell by 40 per cent and manpower was halved to 11,000. Naval estimates decreased by a quarter to under £10m, the largest savings under all heads of public expenditure, and the total establishment was cut from 47,000 to 34,000 men.[21] Broadly speaking, this pattern of naval policy prevailed until the mid-1880s.

Because British security was adequately safeguarded by these dispositions and naval dominance remained unchallenged, no grand strategy of defence evolved. Unsure about the future of the large ironclad and the type of fleet required, the Admiralty was too immersed in grappling with technological change to reflect on the broader strategic implications. Politicians tended to regard the Royal Navy, not as a single force to command the seas, but as an assortment of units employed for various particular services. No co-ordination of military and naval policies was attempted or envisaged, and the Imperial dimension of defence was hardly considered in the preoccupation with British interests. One isolated gesture, made principally to the Australian colonies, was the Colonial Naval Defence Act of 1865, which permitted the commissioning of colonial warships and the recruitment of naval personnel as part of the Royal Navy. A measure of future rather than immediate significance, it too aimed at possible economies, not strategic planning, and as such typically reflected the impulses and priorities of mid-Victorian defence policies.

During these years of unchallenged supremacy, a few experts expressed concern about the lack of public debate on a national strategy in the age of steam, the poverty of strategic thinking, and the contemporary fixation with land defences and fortifications. In 1867 John Colomb, an officer in the Royal Marine Artillery,

---

[21] Cf. *Navy (Distribution of Forces)*, PP (1867–68) (167), XLV, pp. 638–39, and *Navy Estimates for the Year 1874–75*, PP (1876) (225), XLV, pp. 522–23; also PP (1874) (20), XXXVIII, p. 3.

published a pamphlet, *The Protection of our Commerce and Distribution of our Naval Forces*, which was to have a profound impact on British defence policy. Starting from the premise that the uninterrupted flow of commerce afforded the key to national survival, he identified the complementary roles of the navy as the protective shield and the army as the spearhead of attack. In the event of war, the Royal Navy would form the front line of home defence, keep open the lines of commerce and communication which bound together the Empire as an interdependent complex of communities, and secure many colonial possessions against external assault; the army would protect British ports from desultory raids, garrison India, and reinforce strategic bases overseas from which strikes against enemy territory might be launched. In this and subsequent writings, Colomb advocated an Empire-wide strategy of defence, and though later identified with the 'blue water school' of naval strategists, he recognized the partnership of the two armed forces in an integrated system of 'Imperial defence'. As for colonies, they might form local squadrons and contribute to the common protection of oceanic trade, but a centralized naval command was imperative.

At first these ideas failed to shake public indifference. By the late 1870s, however, a more threatening international climate caused ministers and their defence advisers to fear that the process of concentration had been carried to a dangerous excess, undermining Britain's margin of security. The Russian war scare of 1877–78, and more distant rumblings of the Second Afghan War, as well as the revival of French maritime and colonial activities, saw the tide turn with respect to naval policy and Imperial defence. British anxieties were as much commercial as diplomatic, and fears of beleaguerment replaced fears of invasion. The necessity for Britain to live by trade in an increasingly competitive world had grown more urgent as the advantages gained by earlier industrialization ebbed away and the country became dependent on imported foodstuffs. An expanding merchant marine (roughly one-third of the world's tonnage, carrying half its seaborne trade) would be highly vulnerable in wartime to commerce-raiding by swift enemy cruisers—so naval propagandists argued. At the same time, Britain's naval supremacy might now be jeopardized because coaling stations and operating bases were too few, too dispersed, and too defenceless to afford the required sustenance and security.

These weaknesses were highlighted in several creatively alarmist departmental investigations in the late 1870s which led to the appointment in 1879 of a Royal Commission chaired by Lord Carnarvon to inquire into 'the defence of British possessions and commerce abroad'. Despite the exclusion from its remit of home defences and the four Imperial fortresses—Gibraltar, Malta, Halifax, and Bermuda—the Commission produced the first comprehensive study of Imperial defence. Recognizing a crucial link between trade and security, its reports of

1881–82 emphasized the volume and value of inter-Imperial seaborne commerce (estimated at £367m a year, with Empire shipping and cargoes afloat worth £900m), its vulnerability in wartime, and the defencelessness of many shore establishments across the Empire. The navy's effectiveness depended on the development of a network of over 150 secure bases world-wide, with repair facilities and ample stocks of coal, since 'the strategy by which a naval force is to obtain the command of a given sea will resolve itself very much into a question of coal supply'. The Commission also advocated reinforcing the Royal Navy in an emergency with fast steamers from shipping lines and mail companies which might in wartime carry moderate armaments, transport troops and supplies, and act as monitors or communications vessels. Its reports refrained from apportioning the costs involved in enhancing the security of what eventually came to be classified (according to the degree of protection afforded) as 'defended ports', 'coaling stations', and 'harbours of refuge', but suggested that colonies should defend their own commercial ports and might reasonably be expected to contribute to local naval squadrons maintained for the benefit of all.[22]

The Carnarvon Commission marked a turning-point in official policy. It sketched a system of Imperial defence based on naval power, embracing both Britain and colonies, combining central command and local contributions. During the 1880s the government accordingly took hesitant steps to improve inter-departmental co-ordination in Whitehall and consultation with the emerging Dominions, as through the Colonial Defence Committee (1885), a pale forerunner of the Committee of Imperial Defence (1902). Such collaboration proved no easy task. Naval arrangements had to recognize that 'the sea is one', a strategic reality affecting the composition, deployment, and command of the fleet not readily reconciled with the political polycentrism of the Empire. No conflict arose while colonists confined their activities to harbour security, providing floating batteries, blockships, and coastal sloops; but general naval defence relied on ocean-going vessels ready, if necessary, to operate outside the territorial limits of any particular colony and as part of a wider strategy drawn up in London. It remained to be seen whether localization and colonial participation could be satisfactorily combined with centralized direction and unity of command.

Although the Commission's findings were kept confidential, they harmonized with the public mood as Imperial naval defence became the subject of lively debate. Reacting to a more hostile world, Britons not only rediscovered the Royal Navy but turned to settler communities as allies whose resources would materially underpin British global power. Colonial self-reliance might now be

---

[22] *Proceedings of the Colonial Conferences, 1887*, Vol. II (Appendix), *PP* (1887) (c.5091–I), LVI, pp. 917–18, 931–32.

transmuted from disengagement to involvement. This call for assistance signalled a change in British attitudes to Empire often noted by historians of the period: in the sphere of defence, it reflected pragmatic calculation, tinged with anxiety. The desire for consolidation and the heightened awareness of common dangers and shared interests—even of a Greater Britain of satellite nations—were most overtly expressed by the movement for Imperial federation which burgeoned in the 1880s. Defence formed a prominent purpose in all blueprints of political union and an area where centralized structures might be particularly appropriate and acceptable, now that 'distance has been almost abolished by steam and electricity', as the historian J. R. Seeley remarked.[23] Nevertheless, the Imperial Federation League (1884), like its successor the Imperial Federation (Defence) League (1894), failed to gain a grip on public opinion, while governmental discussions of defence exposed an ambivalent outlook: ministers and officials wanted the material aid of the self-governing colonies without sharing with them control of policy-making, planning, or operations. More constructively, the government recognized the vital strategic importance of creating an efficient and secure network of submarine cable communications, and under persistent pressure from the Colonial Defence Committee and the service departments, an 'All Red Route' was gradually constructed, linking every part of the Empire without touching foreign soil.[24] This world-wide web braced Britain's military and economic power, but the easier exchange of views and information between London and colonial capitals did not, as the federationists hoped, foster Imperial cohesiveness or co-operation.

In the colonies too, the 1880s saw more active public discussion of Imperial defence, though differences in geographical location and strategic exposure produced diverse responses. Preoccupied with a transcontinental boundary, Canada felt no pressing need for its own naval vessels. Canadian politicians claimed that they could best contribute to Imperial defence by developing the country's resources and building a railway to link two oceans. At the Cape, the presence of the British base as yet discouraged local initiatives. It was principally in Australasia, therefore, where isolation on the exposed fringes of Empire generated the most naval activity. The sense of insecurity was accentuated by the upsurge of French and German colonial enterprise in the Pacific, which also excited the colonists' desire to pre-empt or shape the division of territorial spoils. Irritation with apparent British indifference to the intrusion of European powers into adjacent waters stimulated regional moves to closer co-operation through Inter-Colonial Conferences and the Federal Council of Australasia (1883), a harbinger of eventual federation. While these events also inclined politicians to study local defences and

---

[23] J. R. Seeley, *The Expansion of England* (London, 1883), p. 64.
[24] See Vol IV, Map 1.2.

increase naval expenditure, sensitivity about needs and status made them wary of paying for enhanced naval protection without controlling the deployment of the additional ships.

These matters surfaced at the Inter-Colonial Conference in 1881, where members recommended expenditure on improved land defences at major ports and requested the Admiralty to augment the Australian squadron—'at the exclusive charge of the Imperial Government'.[25] Soon afterwards Victoria purchased three vessels for harbour defence, and New Zealand offered to contribute towards a cruiser assigned to its coastal waters. Welcoming these initiatives, the Admiralty was compelled to consider with urgency what supplementary role Australasian governments might play in naval defence and how best to regulate these incipient colonial navies. Initially, in 1884, the First Sea Lord, Sir Astley Cooper Key, envisaged port defence ships owned by individual colonies but placed under Royal Navy control. When this proved unacceptable, an alternative was successfully negotiated by Rear-Admiral George Tryon, appointed Commander of the Australian Station in 1885. In return for a fixed annual subsidy from the colonies, the Admiralty would supply extra manned ships, serving under a Royal Navy commander, which would not be permitted to leave Australian waters, even in wartime, without the colonial governments' consent. The First Lord in the new Conservative ministry in 1885, Lord George Hamilton, endorsed Tryon's recommendations. The Admiralty acknowledged that this localization of naval forces, designation of duties, and method of financing entailed departures from the traditional insistence on mobility as essential to the effective use of sea power. But a surrender to Australian opinion seemed prudent lest the colonies should otherwise start acquiring fleets of their own. Haggling continued over the costs of five cruisers and two torpedo gunboats, matters being finally resolved at the Colonial Conference in 1887. With Canada and the Cape remaining tight-fisted, the Australian colonies agreed to pay £126,000 a year and New Zealand £20,000 for two ships stationed in its waters. The conference failed, however, to address the wider issues of Imperial defence. Having secured Antipodean money under the pretext of protecting Australasian floating trade, and having thus breached Britain's exclusive responsibility for sea-going defence, British officials showed no inclination to discuss with colonials the principles and implementation of naval strategy.

The Australian Naval Agreement of 1887 was ratified by the various legislatures, producing some heated exchanges and much misunderstanding about Imperial co-operation. Critics in New South Wales and Victoria feared being sucked into Britain's European quarrels and condemned the naval force as an instrument of

---

[25] *PP* (1887) (c5091–I), LVI, p. 817.

British rule in an independent colony. In Queensland opponents castigated an expensive deal stitched up in London, whereby Australians were expected to tax themselves for Imperial purposes. More moderate nationalists were prepared to accept the agreement as an interim expedient until Australia made its own arrangements for defence, and in this spirit they could join with Imperial-minded advocates of greater Empire unity. In New Zealand such difficulties and diversity of opinion did not arise, and it was easy for British ministers to attribute the forging and ratification of the agreement to Imperial loyalty, and to discern in this a mood favourable to closer co-operation. As Sir Henry Holland, the Secretary of State for the Colonies remarked: 'We do not regard this question in the light of a mere bargain between the mother country and the colonies, but as the starting point of a new policy—the first step towards a federation for defence which will not only add strength to the Empire, but tend to find its members in a closer union.'[26]

The need for colonial assistance was underlined by the ministry's decision to launch an expensive programme of naval construction in the late 1880s. In 1884 revelations in the *Pall Mall Gazette* by its editor, W. T. Stead, concerning British naval weaknesses and the rapidly expanding fleet of French battleships excited considerable public alarm. Although the strength of foreign navies and the threat they posed were exaggerated, the popular outcry stung the government into action. In 1885–86 expenditure on shipbuilding almost doubled to £3.6m, and after an official inquiry had discovered continuing deficiencies, the Naval Defence Act of 1889, designed to uphold a 'two-power standard' of superiority, authorized expenditure of £21.5m over five years on ocean-going fighting ships, not coastal assault vessels—a victory for the 'blue water' propagandists. In 1894, amidst renewed agitation, a further five-year programme was approved. Spending continued to rise as construction costs spiralled with larger battleships and rapid technological change. Naval estimates of £11m in 1883 climbed to £18.7m in 1896, and £34.5m in 1903. Even so, the Royal Navy's relative numerical superiority declined: in 1883 Britain had thirty-eight battleships to the forty of other countries; in 1897 the ratio was sixty-two to ninety-six.[27]

Contemporaries found grounds for both apprehension and reassurance in the pronouncements of a clutch of naval strategists. Their Bible was *The Influence of Sea Power upon History* (1890), written by A. T. Mahan, an American naval captain, which appeared to enunciate immutable strategic rules, valid for the future as for the past, concerning the role of navies in international relations. Mahan stressed

---

[26] Quoted in Richard A. Preston, *Canada and 'Imperial Defense'* (Durham, NC, 1967), p. 104. For colonial views, see Donald C. Gordon, *The Dominion Partnership in Imperial Defense, 1870–1914* (Baltimore, 1965), pp. 78–97.

[27] Statistics taken from Kennedy, *British Naval Mastery*, pp. 193, 209.

the value of transmarine commerce, underpinned by secure communications and key bases, but what crucially mattered was a concentration of armed might where it would be most effective. A large battlefleet stationed in European waters would best protect the British Isles, command the world's oceans against rival navies, and clear the seas of commerce-raiders. As an island nation, too, Britain could focus on naval strength and ignore the military contests of land powers, a familiar theme now refurbished as the navalist strategy of the 'blue water school' which downgraded the soldiers and fortifications of the 'bricks and mortar school'. Navalists like Mahan thus equated Imperial defence with British sea power and adopted a centralist stance which not only rendered defence preparations almost exclusively a British responsibility, but also had a stultifying effect on Britain's relations with self-governing colonies. Navalist thinking, and future wars visualized as decisive clashes of battlefleets far out at sea, ran wholly counter to the coastal warfare which had hitherto dominated British experience and naval policy; it also envisaged no collaborative role for colonists, except as financial donors to the Royal Navy.

These navalist tenets, widely championed by leading public figures, sections of the press, and such organizations as the Navy League (1894), were profoundly influential in the 1890s and beyond. They raised public awareness of defence matters, though skewing the debate excessively towards the navy. 'The panic mongers are abroad', a correspondent to the *Daily News* complained in 1893, 'and venerable Admirals are joining juvenile politicians in their attempts to prove that the British fleet, if it has not already gone to the dogs, is at least on its way to them.'[28] At the same time, navalist doctrines undermined both the overall, integrated concept of Imperial defence advocated by the Carnarvon Commission and closer collaboration between Britain and the Dominions. The Australian Naval Agreement, symbol of the co-operative phase during the 1880s, stood condemned as strategically misconceived and practically irrelevant. Despite the jingoistic fervour in Britain and a resurgence of talk about Imperial federation, the debate about defence now sidelined colonies. Ministers and professional advisers, for their part, remained unconcerned to foster greater naval co-operation through policy initiatives or more unified structures.

The Colonial Conference in 1897 exposed these contradictions and the differences in outlook between Britain and the Dominions. Espousing the cause of Imperial unity, Joseph Chamberlain told delegates that the time might be at hand 'when the Colonies will desire to substitute for the slight relationship which at present exists a true partnership', perhaps through 'a great council of Empire'. But he warned that with 'the privilege of management' would come 'the obligation and the responsibility', including a share of defence expenditure. Britain currently

[28] Quoted in Arthur J. Marder, *The Anatomy of British Sea Power* (New York, 1940), p. 174.

spent some £35m a year, over a third of national revenue, on armed forces maintained, not 'exclusively, or even mainly, for the benefit of the United Kingdom', but as 'a necessity of empire'. Although colonial contributions to the British navy were as yet 'absolutely trifling', the colonies were 'still children, but rapidly approaching manhood', and now was the time to begin cultivating the 'principle of mutual support' and 'a truly Imperial patriotism'.[29]

The Colonial Secretary's effusive sentiments and appeal for naval co-operation failed to elicit a positive response. He was not assisted by untimely criticisms from Admiralty spokesmen, directed against the restrictions on the movement of ships of the Australian auxiliary squadron under the 1887 agreement. The Premiers retorted that legislatures would not vote funds if admirals controlled the deployment of subsidized vessels, lest these be removed from Australian waters in time of war. G. J. Goschen, the First Lord of the Admiralty, reluctantly acquiesced, describing the present arrangement 'from a political point of view worth maintaining' but, reflecting the impact of navalist thinking at the department, reprobated any naval strategy based on 'hugging the shoreline', since in wartime the Royal Navy must be 'aggressive' and mobile. Colonial leaders displayed no greater enthusiasm for extended subsidies. The Premiers of Australia and New Zealand refused even token grants towards the general defence of the Empire. For Canada, Sir Wilfrid Laurier adamantly shunned naval commitments. Only the Cape rose to the occasion and offered the Royal Navy a cruiser, a gift later converted into an annual payment of £30,000. As Goschen assured the premiers with respect to subsidies: 'Though I do not mean to say that it assists us to any great extent, it does produce between the Admiralty and the Colonies certain ties which we value, and which I should be very sorry to do anything to loosen?'[30]

In reality, these ties were both slight and strained by attitudes prevailing on the periphery and in the metropole. Politicians in autonomous colonies viewed co-operation in naval defence with wariness or indifference: 'the strategic arguments of the naval imperialists' made little headway against 'the political arguments of the colonial nationalists'.[31] Such circumstances were not conducive to forging the administrative structures essential to closer collaboration. The reservations expressed in colonial capitals were echoed in London. Although Chamberlain talked expansively about 'a true partnership' and shared management of Empire, neither he nor the Admiralty was ready in practice to vouchsafe colonial governments a voice in shaping the priorities, formulating the policies, or supervising the conduct of naval defence. The Royal Navy, for its part, displayed little interest in

---

[29] *Proceedings of a Conference between the Secretary of State for the Colonies and the Premiers of the Self-Governing Colonies, at the Colonial Office, London, June and July 1897*, PP (1897) (c8596), LIX, pp. 535–38.

[30] Ibid., p. 548.

[31] Preston, *Canada and 'Imperial Defense'*, p. 118.

cultivating colonial navies or naval reserves. On one principle only could all parties agree: that naval defence of the Empire had to remain a British responsibility. Any departure from this safe common ground exposed Imperial disunity.

Yet this was not the whole story. The military dimensions of safeguarding the Empire re-emerged in the late 1870s, accompanied by considerable popular enthusiasm for the army, though no upsurge in enlistment. Rivalry from foreign powers with expansionist or colonial ambitions led to the intermeshing of defence and diplomacy, exemplified by Disraeli's 'forward policies' in the Middle East and Afghanistan and Salisbury's subsequent annexations in Africa. In North-West India, the longest land frontier in the Empire, and one unsettled by periodic skirmishes with border tribes, the prospect of warfare intensified with the surge of Russian military activity and railway building in Central Asia and territorial encroachment on buffer states like Afghanistan and Persia. The Indian authorities took the menace seriously, though they were not averse to fuelling the Russophobia in order to enhance the army's profile in Imperial strategy and counter the navalist influence. What General Roberts, the Commander-in-Chief (1885–93), feared most was that a Russian incursion across the North-West Frontier, or even a minor military reverse, would undermine British prestige and supposed invincibility in the eyes of Indians sufficiently to trigger an internal uprising. 'At the best,' he gloomily predicted, 'we could only expect the natives to remain passive, while the first disaster would raise throughout Hindustan a storm, compared with which the troubles of 1857 would be insignificant.'[32] For twenty years after the Russo-Afghan clash at Penjdeh in 1885, British military planners wrestled with the seemingly insoluble difficulty of meeting the threat to security. One response was increased regional recruitment of 'martial races' from the Punjab and Nepal as a more reliable force against Russian troops than the sepoys traditionally enlisted from diverse Hindu communities whose continued collaboration might prove fragile. In 1893 the three presidency armies were amalgamated and General Kitchener introduced further organizational reforms a decade later. But as his forecasts of the number of troops required to repel an invading army escalated alarmingly, ministers were prompted to pursue a diplomatic solution of the frontier emergency, realized in the Anglo-Russian entente of 1907.[33]

Meanwhile Russian designs on the Ottoman empire had revived the Eastern Question, emphasized the crucial importance of Egypt and the Nile Valley to communications with India, especially after the opening of the Suez Canal in 1869,

---

[32] Quoted in Rose Louise Greaves, *Persia and the Defence of India, 1884–1892* (London, 1959), p. 197.

[33] See Sneh Mahajan, 'The Defence of India and the End of Isolation: A Study in the Foreign Policy of the Conservative Government, 1900–1905', *Journal of Imperial and Commonwealth History*, X (1982), pp. 168–93.

and drawn British administrators and soldiers into Egypt and the Sudan in the 1880s. These activities formed part of the Scramble for Africa as Britain, like her European competitors, staked out territorial claims by conquest or annexation, undertook punitive expeditions, and suppressed signs of resistance, lawlessness, or insurrection among peoples as diverse as the Asante (1873–74, 1895–96), the Zulu (1879), the Boers (1881), and the Matabele (Ndebele) (1893, 1896–97). For all the advantages of firepower, disciplined troops, and naval support, these distant campaigns against indigenous warriors and the ravages of nature placed severe strains on military organization, matériel, and above all manpower. Despite the employment of locally recruited auxiliaries and of Indian troops in some instances, General Wolseley and other commanders had to 'bleed' regiments at home for men to complete expeditionary forces. Cardwell's reforms, deranged by the demands of an expanding, unstable Empire under challenge, attracted critical scrutiny. Professional soldiers, Parliament, and press agonized over a dangerous weakening of home defence and administrative shortcomings, as yet partly obscured by the success of British arms in the small colonial wars of Africa and Asia.

In Britain's military dealings with the Dominions, the 1890s witnessed more constructive activity than in naval affairs. The Colonial Defence Committee and local authorities exchanged information and discussed defence plans; an interchange of military personnel took place; British officers, paying inspection visits overseas or serving as General Officer Commanding of the militia, provided expert advice and exhortation. But military collaboration was frustrated by the lack of forward planning in Whitehall and by the hesitations and sensibilities of colonial governments. Even after the Hartington Commission in 1889–90 had attempted to improve administrative structures, the War Office was ill-equipped to oversee colonial defence, co-ordination with the Admiralty was minimal, and divided responsibilities were aggravated by tensions between civilian politicians and military advisers. Despite the strain placed by wars in Africa and Asia on the resources of the British army, the potential Imperial role of colonial land forces remained unclear and little progress was made towards incorporating any of them, including the West Africa Frontier Force, into a pattern of Imperial defence, even as auxiliary troops or emergency reinforcements.

For their part, colonies were likely to show more concern about land defence than coastal security, given local interests and spending priorities, but their planning in peacetime betrayed a lack of urgency and a sensitivity about British involvement. Following a tour of inspection by Major-General J. Bevan Edwards to advise on the better integration of the Australian colonies' defence arrangements, a scheme of what was termed federal defence sparked debate during the 1890s, but it became uneasily entangled with the fluctuating fortunes of the political federation movement. Attempts in Canada to render the militia more effective were offset by friction between politicians and Imperial professional advisers over control of military power and the amount of expenditure required. Although some colonists volunteered for service with British expeditionary forces in the Sudan, the militias or partially paid units which had emerged in the self-governing colonies were neither in size, nor composition, nor mobility suited to wider Imperial purposes, and colonial governments did not envisage them playing such a role.

At the outbreak of the South African War in 1899, however, the preferences of politicians were pre-empted by the actions of their constituents. While New Zealanders expressed few qualms about the war's justification, and Australian criticisms were muted, in Canada the government feared entanglement in unwanted responsibilities of Empire and heeded the hostility or indifference of French voters. Yet even tardy governments were drawn into military participation by the spontaneous surge of volunteers. Despite disagreements over the type of troops required, their terms of service and rates of pay, and their organization as separate contingents, the self-governing colonies eventually contributed some 30,000 men (16,000 Australians, 8,300 Canadians, and 6,500 New Zealanders), together with 50,000 recruited within the South African territories.[34] While only a fraction of the 450,000 soldiers engaged in the conflict, the authorities in London saluted this tangible demonstration of Imperial solidarity by colonial communities willing to come to Britain's aid at a time of crisis. Indeed, advocates of federation drew fresh hope from the display of Imperial sentiment and the spirit of co-operation in wartime.

Much of this was wishful thinking, and the experiences of the war were misleading, its lessons ambivalent. Popular enthusiasm among Imperially minded colonists was not equalled by continuing governmental interest in recruiting, equipping, and funding troops for a distant conflict that remained localized in its dangers and impact. The official commitment was limited, qualified, and diminishing. At the same time, participation, prowess, and pride fostered national sentiment and identities, of which Imperialist fervour was but one manifestation. Colonists also had to recognize that nationhood might mean involvement in international disputes, planning for defence that went beyond local security, and development of military forces that reliance on Britain had hitherto postponed. For Britain, too, the South African War exposed the limitations of 'Imperial defence' according to prevailing theory and practice. The navalist doctrine of sea power had been vindicated to the extent that the Royal Navy had helped to keep

---

[34] *Report of His Majesty's Commissioners appointed to inquire into the Military Preparations and Other Matters connected with the War in South Africa, PP* (1904) (1789), XL, p. 76.

the war localized and free from foreign intervention and had maintained communications and supplies unimpeded. But for an Imperial power, naval supremacy was by itself insufficient; an army was as vital a part of national defence and strategic planning as a navy. The length and severity of the war, and British military reverses, also revealed fundamental defects in the army's ability to field a large, trained, well-equipped force, with the necessary leadership, staff officers, plan of campaign, and adaptability. Such evident unpreparedness and military difficulties against small Boer communities led many contemporaries to ponder uneasily on the implications should Imperial Britain become embroiled in a major European war.

Select Bibliography

C. J. BARTLETT, *Great Britain and Sea Power, 1815–1853* (Oxford, 1963).

—— 'The Mid-Victorian Reappraisal of Naval Policy', in K. Bourne and D. C. Watt, eds., *Studies in International History* (London, 1967), pp. 189–208.

JAMES BELICH, *The New Zealand Wars and the Victorian Interpretation of Racial Conflict* (Auckland, 1986).

KENNETH BOURNE, *Britain and the Balance of Power in North America, 1815–1908* (London, 1967).

DAVID FRENCH, *The British Way in Warfare, 1688–2000* (London, 1990).

DONALD C. GORDON, *The Dominion Partnership in Imperial Defense, 1870–1914* (Baltimore, 1965).

GERALD S. GRAHAM, *The Politics of Naval Supremacy: Studies in British Maritime Ascendancy* (Cambridge, 1965).

DANIEL R. HEADRICK, *The Tools of Empire: Technology and European Imperialism in the Nineteenth Century* (New York, 1981).

PAUL M. KENNEDY, *The Rise and Fall of British Naval Mastery* (1976; London, 1991).

B. A. KNOX, 'The Concept of Empire in the Mid-Nineteenth Century: Ideas in the Colonial Defence Inquiries of 1859–1861', *Journal of Imperial and Commonwealth History*, XV (1987), pp. 242–63.

ANDREW D. LAMBERT, 'The Royal Navy, 1856–1914: Deterrence and the Strategy of World Power', in K. Neilson and E. J. Errington, eds., *Navies and Global Defense: Theories and Strategies* (Westport, Conn., 1995), pp. 69–92.

JOHN M. MACKENZIE, ed., *Popular Imperialism and the Military, 1850–1950* (Manchester, 1992).

ARTHUR J. MARDER, *The Anatomy of British Sea Power: A History of British Naval Policy in the Pre-Dreadnought Era, 1880–1905* (New York, 1940).

PHILIP MASON, *A Matter of Honour: An Account of the Indian Army, its Officers and Men* (London, 1974).

DAVID E. OMISSI, *The Sepoy and the Raj: The Indian Army, 1860–1947* (London, 1994).

RICHARD A. PRESTON, *Canada and 'Imperial Defense': A Study of the Origin of the British Commonwealth Defense Organization, 1867–1919* (Durham, NC, 1967).

N. A. M. RODGER, 'The Dark Ages of the Admiralty, 1869–85', *Mariner's Mirror*, LXI (1975), pp. 331–44, LXII (1976), pp. 33–46, 121–28.

DONALD M. SCHURMAN, *The Education of a Navy: The Development of British Naval Strategic Thought, 1867–1914* (1965; Chicago, 1984).

EDWARD M. SPIERS, *The Late Victorian Army, 1868–1902* (Manchester, 1992).

HEW STRACHAN, *Wellington's Legacy: The Reform of the British Army, 1830–54* (Manchester, 1984).

16

The Political Economy of Empire, 1880–1914

E.H.H. GREEN

> My policy... is entirely based on my firm belief of its necessity if we are to keep
> the Empire together. Rhodes was absolutely right: if we cannot find a practical
> tie we shall insensibly drift apart.
>
> (Joseph Chamberlain)[1]

In 1883 J. R. Seeley famously remarked in *The Expansion of England* that 'we
seem...to have conquered and peopled half the world in a fit of absence of
mind'.[2] The significance of this celebrated aphorism is that it was an eloquent
statement of belated British acknowledgement of the Empire's existence. The
point Seeley was making, echoed almost one hundred years later in another
Cambridge historian's comment that, apart perhaps from India, 'there was no
such thing as a British Empire',[3] was that although Britain had by the late nineteenth century come to hold vast territorial possessions, this had not been the
result of a conscious, systematic plan. Equally important, although many Britons
were aware and even proud of their nation's Imperial position, there existed no
design for turning these sprawling territories into a coherent structure—in Seeley's view, the British Empire had no theme.

Publication of *The Expansion of England* was Seeley's personal attempt to
heighten Imperial consciousness in Britain, and the success of the book, which
sold half a million copies in the 1880s and went into several editions, appeared to
vindicate his efforts. That *The Expansion of England* found a receptive audience
was due to a general awakening of interest in Empire and the question of Imperial
organization. From the early 1880s on the role and function of the Empire was
examined in detail by both government institutions and other organizations, with
the result that the relationship between Britain and its Dominions and colonies
was reconsidered at several levels. One prominent development was the establish-

---

[1] J. Chamberlain to E. B. Iwan-Muller, 11 Dec. 1903, E. B. Iwan-Muller Papers, B[ritish] L[ibrary],
Add. MSS, 51 316.

[2] J. R. Seeley, *The Expansion of England* (1883; London, 1897 edn.), p. 10.

[3] Ronald Hyam, *Britain's Imperial Century, 1815–1914: A Study of Empire and Expansion*, 2nd edn.
(London, 1993), p. 1.

ment of regular high-level meetings between Britain and the self-governing colonies. The first Colonial Conference met in 1887, and five similar conferences were convened before the First World War, providing an increasingly important forum for policy discussions on matters ranging from Imperial defence and trade to the laying of the 'all red route' of transoceanic cables[4] and the Imperial penny post. Of course not all Imperial activities had a high public profile, but a most strenuous public effort to reconsider and reshape Imperial relations was made by organizations and individuals committed to what is best termed 'constructive imperialism'.

The term 'constructive imperialism' was first used by the English historical economist[5] W. A. S. Hewins[6] in 1899. He defined it as 'the deliberate adoption of the Empire as distinguished from the United Kingdom as the basis of public policy', in order to realize 'the splendid dream of a progressive, organized Empire'.[7] Five years later Hewins helped to produce a more precise definition. By that time he had become the leading economic adviser to the campaign for Imperial Preference launched by Joseph Chamberlain in May 1903, and was a member of the organizing committee of the Compatriots' Club. The Compatriots, a group of one hundred Empire enthusiasts[8] interested in 'the purely Imperial and constructive side of the Chamberlain movement',[9] defined their object thus— 'to advance the ideal of a United British Empire and to advocate consistently those principles of constructive policy on all constitutional, economic, defensive, and educational questions which will help towards the fulfilment of that ideal'.[10]

Although the actual term was not used until the turn of the century, the basic parameters of constructive imperialist thought were established in the 1880s. The activities of the Imperial Federation League (IFL), founded in 1884, provided the earliest attempt to promote closer Imperial relations and systematic organization of the Empire. For the IFL, like the Compatriots, the ultimate goal had been to bring about 'the permanent unity of the Empire'[11] by strengthening institutional links between Britain and the colonies and by developing close military and commercial bonds within the Empire. The break-up of the IFL in 1893 was an

---

[4] See above, pp. 259–62.

[5] G. M. Koot, *The English Historical Economists* (Cambridge, 1986).

[6] W. A. S. Hewins (1865–1931), first Director of the London School of Economics, from 1903, and Conservative MP, from 1912.

[7] W. A. S. Hewins, *The Apologia of an Imperialist*, 2 vols. (London, 1929), I, pp. 56, 57.

[8] E. H. H. Green, *The Crisis of Conservatism: The Politics, Economics and Ideology of the British Conservative Party, 1880–1914* (London, 1994), pp. 161–62, 339–40.

[9] L. S. Amery to B. Kidd, 4 March 1904, Benjamin Kidd Papers, Cambridge University Library, Add. MSS, 8069.

[10] Rules of the Compatriots Club, copy in Arthur Steel-Maitland Papers, Scottish Record Office, Edinburgh, GD 193/129/133x.

[11] Minutes of the First Meeting of the IFL General Committee, 18 Nov. 1884, IFL Papers, B[ritish] L[ibrary] Add. MSS, 62778, ff. 1–5.

early setback for the development of constructive imperialism, but discussion of
the issues the IFL helped to raise continued both in Britain and the colonies after
its demise. Hence, when Hewins presented his lectures in 1899 and when the
Compatriots defined their objectives they were drawing upon a well-established
current of ideas. That the first decade of the twentieth century witnessed a
campaign which brought constructive imperialism to the centre of public debate
in both Britain and the colonies was thus hardly surprising. Writing almost thirty
years after Joseph Chamberlain had inaugurated the crusade for Imperial unity
based on preferential trade within the Empire, Austen Chamberlain remarked that
'the immense echo of my father's speech in May 1903 is inexplicable unless it is
appreciated that the train was already laid'.[12] The tariff reform campaign provided
a rallying point for those who sought to fulfil Hewins's 'splendid dream', but it was
as much a symptom as a cause of an ongoing debate within and between Britain
and the colonies over the Empire's future, in particular over the desirability of a
more formal Imperial structure.

The constructive imperialist argument for Imperial unity was in part a response to
changes in the international environment. From the mid-1870s the growing
industrial and military strength and increasing overseas activity of, in particular,
Germany, France, the United States, and Russia meant that Britain was no longer
the sole genuinely global power. In Britain and the colonies official awareness of
this new problem was manifest in a number of important developments, principally relating to defence policy. At both the centre and periphery of Empire there
was a growing sense that neither could survive alone, and the idea of closer
Imperial co-operation on questions of Imperial defence enjoyed a steadily increasing appeal in the late nineteenth and early twentieth centuries.[13]

Many in both Britain and the colonies would have agreed with Adam Smith's
dictum that defence was more important than opulence, but some felt it equally
essential to secure the economic future of the Empire. For constructive imperialists the solution to the new challenges facing the Empire was the Empire itself.
Drawing on fashionable currents of evolutionary thought, constructive imperialists contended that the emergence of imperial powers indicated that God, or
perhaps Darwin, was on the side of big battalions. Constructive imperialists saw
the unification of Germany, Italy, and the United States, and the apparent reinvigoration of Russia, as symptomatic of an evolutionary trend in favour of large-scale
states. For Seeley the implications of this trend were clear, namely, that the

---

[12] To B. Dugdale, 4 March 1931, Joseph Chamberlain Papers, Birmingham University Library, JC 18/
18/22.

[13] See above, pp. 333–34; and below, pp. 704–08.

forces 'which make vast political union possible tend to make States which are on the old scale of magnitude unsafe, insignificant, second rate',[14] an argument echoed by Joseph Chamberlain, who declared in May 1902 that 'The days are for great Empires and not for little States.'[15] It followed that, as Alfred Milner put it, 'the time is coming...when the United Kingdom *alone* will be hard put to retain its place amongst the foremost nations of the world', and hence constructive imperialists urged both the statesmen and peoples of the Empire to 'learn to think imperially'.[16] What 'thinking imperially' meant was partially explained in 1903 by the then First Lord of the Admiralty and former Under-Secretary of State for the Colonies, Lord Selborne, who stated that 'if this country is to maintain herself in the years to come in the same rank with the US, Russia and Germany, the unit must be enlarged from the UK to the Empire'.[17] This was a *partial* explanation in so far as its emphasis was on the survival of the United Kingdom, but for constructive imperialists, including Selborne, the key point was that although 'the maintenance of the Empire must depend to an overwhelming degree upon the power and wealth of the island', it was also the case that 'the power and wealth of the island must depend upon the maintenance of the Empire'.[18] An Imperial problem demanded an Imperial solution.

At first glance there was an inconsistency in the constructive imperialist argument, in that if evolution was tending to produce Empire states then surely the British Empire would coalesce 'naturally'—where was the need for *policy*? The IFL summed up this problem with its reaction to the calling of the first Colonial Conference, when it noted that 'the action of the laws of political development as exemplified in such orderly, though almost unconscious growth, emphasizes the need for the deliberate adoption of [the] federal principle [in the Empire]':[19] at one and the same time, it seems, there were *laws* of development and yet also a need for deliberate, conscious action. The resolution of this seeming paradox is that whilst constructive imperialists saw the trend towards Empire states as the predominant evolutionary path, they also argued that it was not the only one. In their view Empires did not just happen, they had to be *made* by people who recognized their importance. Hence, when Hewins defined constructive imperialism he singled out *laissez-faire* liberalism as its antithesis, on the grounds that

---

[14] Seeley, *Expansion of England*, p. 88.

[15] J. Chamberlain at Birmingham, 16 May 1902, in J. L. Garvin and J. Amery, *The Life of Joseph Chamberlain*, 6 vols. (London, 1929–68), IV, p. 177.

[16] Lord Selborne at Handsworth, 4 Jan. 1905, *The Times*, 5 Jan. 1905.

[17] To E. G. Pretyman, 19 Sept. 1903, Selborne Papers, Bodleian Library, Oxford, MSS Selborne, 73, ff. 5–9.

[18] J. L. Garvin, 'The Principles of Constructive Economics as Applied to the Maintenance of the Empire', in *Compatriots Club Lectures* (London, 1905), p. 44.

[19] IFL, Annual Report, 24 March 1887, IFL Papers, BL Add. MSS, 62779 (my emphasis).

Empires could be 'un-made' if their peoples, and especially their leaders, failed to appreciate the need for Imperial consolidation in the struggle with other Empires.[20] *Laissez-faire* liberalism was deemed incapable of grasping this for two reasons. First, the words and deeds of Cobden, Bright, and 'Little England' Liberal governments had shown that its adherents were opposed to the very notion of Empire, and second, it was inherently antagonistic to *any* conscious government action. In the constructive imperialist schema the 'visible hand' of the human will was vital if the Empire was to be organized. In this last context the Social Darwinism of constructive imperialism was often strongly flavoured with Idealism. The British Empire was depicted as an entity with the *potential* to realize a genuinely Imperial form, but it required an act of will for the *idea* of Empire to be made *real*. Hence it was necessary for decision-makers in Britain and the colonies to develop an Imperial consciousness in order that the Empire could realize its as yet only partially formed essence.[21]

The constructive imperialist stress on the need for conscious direction of Britain's Imperial destiny implied a deliberate break from the 'imperialism of free trade' and an extended, positive role for the British State. The most obvious, early manifestations of this aspect of constructive imperialist thought were the arguments of the Imperial Federation League and the National Fair Trade League (NFTL) for Imperial tariff arrangements in the 1880s.[22] Any suggestion of tariffs was itself heretical in a nation where free trade was regarded as more an article of faith than an economic policy. But it was not only the idea that government should interfere with trade flows that made the IFL and NFTL's call for closer economic links with the Empire subversive of established political-economic orthodoxy. In 1864 the liberal economist J. E. Cairnes had written that 'We do not ask—we certainly do not receive—any commercial advantage from the Colonies which are not equally open to the whole world, which we should not equally command though the political connection were severed tomorrow'.[23] His view outlined a tradition of liberal economic thought on the commercial value of Empire which had been expressed in the work of Smith, Nassau Senior, and J. S. Mill, and which

---

[20] Hewins, *Apologia*, I, p. 58. One reviewer remarked of the *Compatriots Club Lectures* that 'In their opposition to laissez faire... the contributors... are fully agreed', *Economic Review*, XV (1905), p. 364.

[21] The most explicit and influential Idealist contribution to constructive imperialist thought was made by the Canadian George Parkin in *Imperial Federation* (London, 1893). Other Idealist contributions were made in Canada by G. M. Grant, the Principal of Queen's University, and Colonel G. T. Denison, a doyen of the Canadian IFL. In Britain constructive imperialists who drew heavily on Idealist concepts were the historical economists William Cunningham, W. J. Ashley, and Hewins, and the Conservative politicians Alfred Milner, Leo Amery, Arthur Steel-Maitland, and George Wyndham.

[22] Sydney H. Zebel, 'Fair Trade: An English Reaction to the Breakdown of the Cobden Treaty System', *Journal of Modern History*, XII (1940), pp. 161–85 and Zebel, 'Joseph Chamberlain and the Genesis of the Tariff Reform Movement', *Journal of British Studies*, VII, (1967), pp. 131–57.

[23] J. E. Cairnes, *Essays in Political Economy* (London, 1873), pp. 311–12.

was to be reiterated by Henry Fawcett, Thorold Rogers, Goldwin Smith, W. S. Jevons, Alfred Marshall, and J. A. Hobson.[24] However, underpinning the Leagues' argument for closer Imperial trade relations was the assertion that the colonies were important for Britain *because* they were colonies and were therefore more secure, stable, and potentially more valuable markets. The British state was urged to acknowledge that the world was dominated by tariff-protected Empire states, and to adjust accordingly its stance on the regulation of Imperial trade.

Late-nineteenth-century arguments for Imperial tariffs were early examples of unofficial agencies propounding constructive imperialist ideas. But there was an episode of official constructive imperialism in the 1890s which also had important implications for the role of the British state. Joseph Chamberlain was the chief actor in this episode during his tenure of the Colonial Office from 1895 to 1903, and the focus of events was his development programme for Britain's tropical Empire. In March 1895, shortly before the general election which was to bring him into the Cabinet as Secretary of State for the Colonies, Chamberlain argued that 'it is not enough to occupy certain great spaces of the world's surface unless you can make the best of them—unless you are willing to develop them'.[25] Once in office this was precisely what Chamberlain set out to do, seeking to use public revenues or loans to finance the development of colonial infrastructure. Chamberlain's period in office saw the passage of the Colonial Loans and Colonial Stocks Acts of 1899 and 1900, and a large number of irrigation, sanitation, and railway and harbour construction projects carried out under the aegis of the Imperial government. In 1896 work was begun in Nigeria on building a rail link from the port of Lagos to the Northern interior. Likewise, 1895 saw the commencement of the Uganda railway to link the hinterland of East Africa to the port of Mombasa. The overall scale of these development projects remained small in relation to the enormous expanse of British territory. The limitations were largely the responsibility of the Treasury, which constantly objected to the expense of Chamberlain's schemes.[26] Had it not been for the fiscal constraints imposed by the 'Gladstonian garrison' in Treasury Chambers, Chamberlain's schemes would doubtless have had a larger effect. As it was they provided a testimony to Chamberlain's energy and brought about a significant transformation of the economies of, for example, Lagos, British Guiana, Cyprus, and the Gold Coast.[27]

[24] J. C. Wood, *British Economists and the Empire* (London, 1983), pp. 1–180.

[25] J. Chamberlain in Birmingham, 15 March 1895, in Garvin and Amery, *Chamberlain*, III, p. 19.

[26] Richard M. Kesner, *Economic Control and Colonial Development: Crown Colony Financial Management in the Age of Joseph Chamberlain* (London, 1981), *passim*.

[27] Ibid., pp. 216–17; Michael Havinden and David Meredith, *Colonialism and Development: Britain and Its Tropical Colonies, 1850–1960* (London, 1993), pp. 70–90.

But it was not simply the direct impact of the development projects which made Chamberlain's period at the Colonial Office significant. Chamberlain's time as Colonial Secretary accelerated and confirmed a tentative trend for greater government responsibility for economic management and development of the Empire. Until the last quarter of the nineteenth century the preferred method of Imperial government was to devolve responsibility upon private concerns. Even the partition of Africa had been, wherever possible, left to private companies. But through the 1890s, and especially after 1895, the Imperial government increasingly underwrote or replaced private enterprise. Hence, after years of difficulties, the assets of the Imperial British East Africa Company passed to the government in 1895 and the East African Protectorate was established. The British South Africa Company had its autonomy curtailed by Westminster, and even the relatively successful Royal Niger Company was brought under closer supervision and superseded by colonial rule in the newly created colony of Nigeria in 1906.[28] Some in government were resigned to rather than enthusiastic about this trend. When presented with the Mombasa railway plans in July 1895 Lord Salisbury commented that it would have to be financed and constructed under the direction of Indian Public Works. This, he argued, would be preferable to contracting the scheme out to a private company because although 'this mode of proceeding is often dignified by the name of "trusting to private enterprise"', it was the case that 'it cannot be adopted except with the offer of a guarantee from Government', and this rendered 'the use of the words "private enterprise"... a ridiculous misapplication of language'.[29] For Joseph Chamberlain, however, such developments were to be welcomed as part of a more rational exploitation of Britain's Imperial resources. Chamberlain's proposals to 'improve' or develop Britain's 'undeveloped estates' in the Empire were in this respect part of a larger debate about how best to meet challenges to Britain's Imperial position and the growing problems of Britain's maturing economy. That after Chamberlain's tenure of the Colonial Office 'the development issue was fixed permanently on the British government's agenda'[30] was not simply a legacy of Chamberlain's charisma and energy. It was an indication of a shift in both policy and general outlook that was taking place in the late nineteenth and early twentieth centuries—a move towards accepting a more active role for the state in shaping Britain's social, economic, and Imperial development. Chamberlain's battles with the Treasury over colonial development were one aspect of a broader attempt to break the ideological as well as the fiscal shackles of the Gladstonian minimal state. That 'private enterprise' was deemed no longer

[28] Richard M. Kesner, *Economic Control and Colonial Development: Crown Colony Financial Management, passim,* pp. 70–82.

[29] To Sir Michael Hicks-Beach, 26 July 1895, Salisbury Papers, Hatfield House, Hertfordshire.

[30] Havinden and Meredith, *Colonialism and Development,* p. 90.

capable of carrying the burden of Imperial responsibility placed question-marks against the adequacy of *laissez-faire* as anything like a governing maxim either for the Empire or more generally. Chamberlain's development policies gave practical expression to the view that the active agency of a self-conscious Imperial state was essential to the future prosperity and indeed the very survival of the British Empire.

For government to learn to think imperially was one thing, but the encouragement of a genuine Imperial consciousness was also seen as necessary in order to head off internal disruption of the Empire. In his famous speech of 15 May 1903, the opening oration of the tariff reform campaign, Joseph Chamberlain warned his audience: 'Make a mistake in your Imperial policy—it is irretrievable. You have an opportunity, you will never have it again.'[31] Chamberlain's urgency reflected concern that the self-governing colonies were growing increasingly independent. This concern first arose in the 1880s, and grew continuously. Canada's 'National Policy', inaugurated by the government of J. A. (later Sir John) Macdonald in 1879, had introduced high tariffs on manufactured imports, including Britain's, and these were extended in the 1880s and 1890s.[32] By 1911 Canada had negotiated trade treaties with Austria-Hungary, Switzerland, Japan, France, Germany, Italy, the Netherlands, and Belgium, and there was lurking fear that a trade agreement or even commercial union between Canada and the United States was a possibility.[33] Indeed, the Canadian trade negotiations with the United States in 1910–11 induced near panic in constructive imperialist circles.[34] The individual Australian colonies took tariff initiatives in the 1890s, and by 1907 the Deakin administration had placed high tariff barriers around the recently formed Australian Federation.[35] Similar tariff barriers also appeared in Southern Africa and New Zealand. This apparent desire on the part of Britain's self-governing colonies to decide their own commercial priorities was seen as symptomatic of a creeping colonial nationalism.[36] To a degree this was accepted as inevitable, even laudable—a sign of the growing maturity of some of Britain's one-time dependencies—but the

---

[31] At Birmingham, 15 May 1903, in C. Boyd, ed., *Speeches of the Right Honourable Joseph Chamberlain*, 2 vols. (London, 1914), II, p. 128.

[32] R. C. Brown, *Canada's National Policy: A Study in Canadian–American Relations* (Princeton, 1964); G. Williams 'The National Policy Tariffs: Industrial Underdevelopment Through Import Substitution', *Canadian Journal of Political Science*, XII (1979), pp. 333–68; Michael Bliss, *A Living Profit: Studies in the Social History of Canadian Business, 1883–1911* (Toronto, 1974).

[33] J. Chamberlain to Lord Lansdowne, 10 Nov. 1887, in Brown, *National Policy*, p. 150.

[34] For the grave 'dangers to Imperial Unity threatened by these developments', Tariff Commission Memorandum, 'The Problems of the Imperial Conference and the Policy of Preference', 18 May 1911, Tariff Commission Papers, London School of Economics, TC/MM46.

[35] J. A. La Nauze, *Alfred Deakin: A Biography*, 2 vols. (New York, 1965), II, pp. 410–26.

[36] R. Jebb, *Studies in Colonial Nationalism* (London, 1905).

constructive imperialist fear was that it could become a powerful 'centrifugal force' undermining and ultimately fragmenting the Empire.

Imperial unity was thus both a means and an end for constructive imperialists. They felt that only a united Empire would have the strength and resources to match the threat of rival imperial powers, and that general recognition of this fact would hold the Imperial structure together. But the question remained as to *how* the elements of the Empire could be made to recognize that unity was their true interest. Here Imperial trade was seen as the key to Imperial unity. In an increasingly protectionist world an intra-Imperial trading system was to provide guaranteed markets for both British and colonial producers. In its most sophisticated guise, as developed by the tariff reform campaign after 1903, this was to be achieved through a system of reciprocal tariff preferences between Britain and the colonies. The colonies were to offer preferential treatment to British manufactured imports, whilst Britain would offer preference to colonial food products. The economic case for such an arrangement was based on the argument that intra-Imperial trade was the tale of the future. Certainly it was difficult to gainsay that the Empire was a large and growing market for British exports. By 1914 Imperial markets were taking 51.7 per cent of British cotton exports, 33.5 per cent of woollens, 45 per cent of non-textile manufactured goods, and 48.2 per cent of pig iron and metal goods. Likewise, Britain was the main market for colonial produce. For example, between 1875 and 1914 Britain took slightly more than half of Canada's total exports, most of them agricultural products. By 1909 Canada alone was supplying about 15 per cent of Britain's wheat flour, and 10 per cent of beef imports, and Australia and India were also important suppliers of foodstuffs to Britain.[37]

Critics pointed out that Imperial trade was not as great as Britain's trade with other nations, but the constructive imperialists' argument was not based on total value and volume alone. They contended that although the volume of Britain's foreign trade was higher, colonial trade, especially with the self-governing colonies, was growing faster. Imperial markets were presented as markets with a future, as opposed to older markets where tariffs and import substitution precluded any growth of British or colonial trade.[38] The *kind* of goods the colonies imported from Britain was also deemed important, in that Empire markets were reckoned to consume 'almost exclusively our fully manufactured goods'.[39] Last but not least,

---

[37] John Eddy and Deryck Schreuder, 'The Edwardian Empire in Transformation and "Decline", 1902–14', in Eddy and Schreuder, eds., *The Rise of Colonial Nationalism: Australia, New Zealand, Canada and South Africa First Assert their Nationalities, 1880–1914* (Sydney, 1988), p. 27. Williams, 'National Policy', pp. 355–56; Avner Offer, *The First World War: An Agrarian Interpretation* (Oxford, 1989).

[38] Sir Vincent Caillard, *Imperial Fiscal Reform* (London, 1903), pp. 31–32; Brown, *National Policy*, p. 218.

[39] Tariff Reform League, *Speakers' Handbook* (London, 1908), p. xvi.

Imperial trade was deemed superior because its freedom from foreign control made it more secure and, equally important especially where food was concerned, strategically reliable in times of emergency.[40]

That *preference*, in the form outlined above, dominated the early-twentieth-century campaign for Imperial unity was largely due to two factors. First, the only colonial goods that Britain imported were foodstuffs and raw materials. Hence, if Britain was to introduce a new commercial policy that favoured the colonies then it had to be based on tariffs on such goods. Secondly, preference was the only policy acceptable to the colonies. In the 1880s and 1890s the colonies made it quite clear that they would not accept Imperial free trade or a *zollverein*, for the simple reason that they wished to protect their 'infant' industries against British imports.[41] This was recognized by constructive imperialists in Britain. At Glasgow in October 1903 Joseph Chamberlain told listeners that the colonies were 'all protective countries' because they were not content 'to be what the Americans call a "one horse country" with a single industry and no diversity of employment'.[42] Constructive imperialists were most anxious to demonstrate that the structure they envisaged was not simply 'big Little Englanderism'.[43] They grasped that preference was the only viable policy, with the Tariff Commission noting that, '[t]he development of the autonomous powers of the self-governing Colonies has made it necessary that any commercial arrangement with them should be the result of negotiations between the Imperial and the several colonial Governments as representatives of co-ordinate British States each having special regard to its own national interests as well as the interests of the Empire as a whole'.[44] The argument for preference represented an acknowledgement that a new conception of Empire economic relations was necessary if Imperial trade was to provide a basis for Imperial unity. This point was established by W. A. S. Hewins, who in February 1907 told the Conservative party leader Arthur Balfour that mercantilist conceptions of the colonies were no longer valid. 'The colonies', Hewins wrote, 'had a definite place in this [mercantilist] system. But it was a subordinate place, both economically and politically...they were to supply...raw materials...

---

[40] Green, *Crisis of Conservatism*, pp. 196–97.

[41] For example, the remarks of the Queensland and Tasmanian representatives, at the Imperial Conferences, *Proceedings of the Colonial Conference, 1887*, Vol. I, C. 5091, LVI, P[arliamentary] P[apers] (1887), p. 1; *Report by the Right Hon. The Earl of Jersey, GCMG, on The Colonial Conference at Ottawa, with the Proceedings of the Conference and Certain Correspondence*, C. 7553, PP (1894), LVI, p. 337.

[42] 6 Oct. 1903, in Boyd, ed., *Speeches*, II, p. 159.

[43] Eddy and Schreuder, 'Edwardian Empire', pp. 23–24.

[44] The Tariff Commission was a body called together by Chamberlain in 1904 to formulate a 'scientific tariff'; 'Colonial Preference and Imperial Reciprocity', Tariff Commission pamphlet, 22 July 1908, TC MM 35.

which we could not produce and take in our manufactures.'[45] In Hewins's view mercantilist notions had to be replaced with a genuinely reciprocal relationship which would take into account 'recent developments both within and without the Empire'.[46] It was just such a relationship that Joseph Chamberlain sought to define in Birmingham in 1905, when he had argued that 'the British Empire is not an Empire in the sense in which that term has been applied before. The British Colonies are no longer Colonies in the sense in which that term was originally applied to them . . . We are sister States in which the mother country by virtue of her age, by virtue of all that has been done in the past, may claim to be first, but only first among equals.'[47] This was a vision of Empire based on the creation of a system in which no State would be subordinate to another, and ultimate loyalty was to lie with the Empire conceived as an organic entity. Hence, when Leo Amery asked in 1910 'What do we mean when we speak of Imperial unity?' he answered himself by saying 'we mean that all its [the Empire's] members should remain citizens of a single world State with a duty and loyalty towards that State, none the less real and intense because of the co-existence with it of a duty and a loyalty towards the particular nation or community within the Empire to which they belong'.[48] Imperial Preference was to be the commercial system that embodied the economic aspects of this new relationship.

But if Imperial Preference was to provide a tie of general economic interest which would override particular interests and bind the Empire together, it was not the only tie designated for this task. In the constructive imperialist schema consanguinity was as important as cash. Writing in 1904, George Wyndham, the Conservative government's Chief Irish Secretary, argued that 'the remedy against exaggeration of National sentiment' lay in 'preferring . . . the two ideas of Empire and Race'. Empire was vital because 'the State must be large enough in contour to fire the imagination of all its citizens with faith in the future', and in a world dominated by large-scale states only an Empire could instil such faith.[49] Encouragement of racial pride was essential because it was healthier than encouraging national pride, which could easily lapse into a narrow chauvinism.[50] Because nationality was not 'co-extensive with Race',[51] racial pride did not prevent loyalty on the part of members of a particular race towards the nation in which they

[45] Hewins to Balfour, 18 Feb. 1907, Balfour Papers, BL Add. MSS, 49779, ff. 61–70.

[46] Ibid.

[47] 27 July 1905, in Boyd, ed., *Speeches*, II, p. 329.

[48] L. S. Amery, 'Imperial Unity', a speech to the Chatham Club, 15 July 1910, in Amery, *Union and Strength* (London, 1912), p. 2.

[49] G. Wyndham, *The Development of the State* (London, 1904), pp. 51, 11.

[50] Ibid., p. 48.

[51] Ibid., p. 47.

happened to dwell. So, when Wyndham declared 'let pride be in Race, patriotism for the Empire', he harmonized 'universal allegiance' to the Empire and race with the 'particular sentiment' of individual (colonial) nations.[52]

As Irish Secretary, George Wyndham was very familiar with the problem of containing national aspirations within an Imperial framework. But his remarks are also of interest because the concept of 'race loyalty' which he discussed at length in 1904 was central to the constructive imperialist project of Empire. In May 1903 Joseph Chamberlain made it clear that when he discussed the Empire he wished to consider 'only our relations...to that white British population that constitutes the majority in the great self-governing Colonies of the Empire': at Glasgow that October he stated that the aim of Imperial Preference was 'to consolidate the British race'.[53] The Compatriot editor of the *Observer*, J. L. Garvin, spoke of the British Empire as 'a dominion that should be secured by the preponderance in numbers of the race that holds it', whilst Alfred Milner spoke of the Empire as 'these new lands of immense promise inhabited by men of our race'.[54] Whenever the notion of Imperial Preference appeared, the theme of racial unity was never far behind.

By equating Imperial unity with racial unity—and only white settler, self-governing colonies featured prominently in constructive imperialist literature and statements—it was possible to avoid an overstress on separate national, and particularly British, interests. The notion of the Empire as a racially unified polity complemented the constructive imperialist description of the Empire's unity of economic interest. Just as Imperial Preference was to blend national and Imperial economics, so the idea of 'the Race' was to allow for separate national identities within the broader framework of a supra-national identity. In this way constructive imperialists built up arguments designed to show that 'the existence of Empire is reconcilable with the self-development of all its parts,[55] and that there was 'no incompatibility between...national patriotism and the wider patriotism of Empire'.[56]

By 1910 constructive imperialism had developed into a cogent and subtle doctrine. Yet, in spite of the best efforts of Joseph Chamberlain and his cohorts, the constructive imperialist project failed, and the 'splendid dream' of a united Empire did not become a reality. In many respects the reason for the failure of the constructive imperialist project was simple: it did not gather enough support.

[52] Ibid., pp. 49, 58.

[53] Boyd, ed., *Speeches*, II, pp. 2, 142.

[54] Garvin, 'Economics of Empire', p. 57; Milner at the Authors' Club, 2 Dec. 1912, in *The Nation and the Empire*, p. 490.

[55] B. Wise, 'The Problem of Empire', in Lord Malmesbury ed., *The New Order* (London, 1908), p. 101.

[56] A. Milner at Vancouver, 9 Oct. 1908, *The Nation and the Empire*, p. 310.

At first glance this may seem strange, in that from the 1880s on there was an increasing groundswell of opinion both in Britain and the colonies in favour of Imperial unity. Business opinion in Britain appeared particularly sympathetic. Evidence gathered by the Royal Commission on the Depression of Trade and Industry in 1885 indicated that many chambers of commerce wanted closer commercial relations with the Empire,[57] and in March 1887 the annual meeting of the Associated Chambers of Commerce passed the first of several motions over the years calling for Imperial federation.[58] Individual trade associations were equally vocal. Between 1889 and 1894 the Liverpool Chamber of Commerce organized several special meetings to stress the importance of colonial commerce, including one addressed by the IFL's 'star' speaker G. R. Parkin, the leading Canadian advocate of federation.[59] In the 1880s and 1890s the Birmingham Chamber passed motions almost annually arguing that 'the future prosperity of British commerce must depend on increasing our commercial relations with our colonies',[60] and these sentiments found frequent echo in chambers as diverse as Blackburn, Bradford, and London.[61]

Interest in Imperial unity was not confined to the business community. By the late 1880s the IFL had established branches throughout Britain, and its literature was widely disseminated. Included in the IFL membership were one hundred British MPs, and its longest-serving President, Lord Rosebery, was to become Prime Minister in 1894. Further evidence of Imperial federation becoming entrenched in Britain's political culture was provided by the National Union of Conservative Associations, which debated and supported motions in favour of federation and/or preference at its annual meetings from the mid-1880s on. Although the IFL broke up in 1893, Imperial federation and attendant questions of Imperial relations continued to play a prominent part in British public debate, and Joseph Chamberlain was more than justified when he declared at the 1897 Colonial Conference that 'the idea of federation is in the air'.[62]

---

[57] *First Report of the Royal Commission Appointed to Enquire into the Depression of Trade and Industry, 1886*, Appendix A (questionnaires to Chambers of Commerce), C. 4621, pp. 73–113, *PP* (1886), XXI, 1.

[58] 'The Lords of Trade and Imperial Federation', *Imperial Federation*, II, no. 3, March 1887, p. 51.

[59] Special meetings on 16 Dec. 1889; 19 Feb. 1890; 18 Nov. 1891; and 30 Nov. 1892; Imperial federation was also discussed at ordinary meetings: Liverpool Chamber of Commerce papers, Liverpool Central Library, 380 COM 1/2, ff. 61–2, 380 COM 1/3, ff. 3–4, 54, 82.

[60] G. H. Wright, *Chronicles of the Birmingham Chamber of Commerce, 1813–1913* (Birmingham, 1913), pp. 314–411.

[61] Blackburn Chamber of Commerce, *Annual Report* (Blackburn, 1893), p. 17. For Bradford and London, and other chambers, see William G. Hynes, *The Economics of Empire: Britain, Africa and the New Imperialism, 1870–95* (London, 1979), pp. 109–29.

[62] *Proceedings of a Conference between the Secretary of State for the Colonies and the Premiers of the Self-Governing Colonies, at the Colonial Office, London, June and July 1897*, C. 8596, *PP* (1894), LIX, p. 631.

Nor was it only in Britain that the argument for Imperial unity gained ground. In March 1888 a branch of the IFL was established in Toronto, and by the early 1890s the cause of federation appeared to be well established in Canada. The 1891 Canadian general election saw the Conservatives, led by Sir John Macdonald, raise the 'Empire loyalty' banner against the 'Continentalist' argument for closer commercial relations with the United States.[63] The great Conservative victory led Macdonald's government to seek to consolidate support by securing benefits for the 'loyal' vote, and an address was sent from the Canadian Parliament to the Crown in April 1891 pressing for the introduction of a scheme of Imperial Preference.[64] Later that year Macdonald, still anxious to make progress on this question, wrote to W. H. Smith, Leader of the House of Commons in Lord Salisbury's government in Britain, expressing the hope that if the British Conservatives won their forthcoming election, 'which Heaven grant!' [then] some Imperial policy can be formed and carried out'.[65] Macdonald's death in late 1891, and the Liberal party's victory in the British general election of 1892, dashed hopes of immediate progress, but the Canadian government continued to press the Imperial case.[66] Indeed, the general popularity of the preference cause in Canada appeared to be confirmed when the Canadian Liberal party, having triumphed in the 1897 general election, 'stole the clothes' of the Conservatives: they unilaterally reduced tariffs on British goods by 25 per cent after the 1897 Colonial Conference, gave West Indian sugar a similar preference in 1898—a purely Imperial gesture— and gave Britain a further 8 per cent preference at the 1902 Imperial Conference. By the early years of the twentieth century Canadian enthusiasm for Imperial preference seemed deep-rooted.

The question of Empire was less prominent in other self-governing colonies, but there was still sympathy for closer Imperial relations. At the Colonial Conferences of 1887, 1894, and 1897 there were calls from the Cape Colony, Tasmania, Queensland, Victoria, and New Zealand for Imperial Preference. By 1902 the Australian Commonwealth had decided to grant Britain an at that point unspecified preference, whilst New Zealand offered Britain a 10 per cent tariff reduction and the Cape and Natal offered 25 per cent.[67] Such actions as these seemed to indicate that enthusiasm for Imperial unity was, if anything, greater in the colonies than in Britain, and certainly there were few who summed up the constructive imperialist position more succinctly than Alfred Deakin, who told the Australian

---

[63] G. T. Denison, *The Struggle for Imperial Unity* (London, 1909), pp. 96–98.

[64] Brown, *National Policy*, pp. 209–13.

[65] 8 Nov. 1891, in ibid., p. 213.

[66] Ibid., p. 230 and C. 7553, *PP* (1894), LVI, p. 337.

[67] *Papers Relating to a Conference between the Secretary of State for the Colonies and the Prime Ministers of Self-Governing Colonies, June to August, 1902*, Cd. 1299, *PP* (1902), LXVI, p. 451.

Parliament in 1904 that the Empire's position was 'unstable, untrustworthy, impermanent and requires to be replaced, gradually, but surely, by a fuller and more complete organization'.[68]

The development in both Britain and the colonies of a body of support favouring closer Imperial relations, especially in the commercial sphere, posed some problems for 'official' opinion in Britain. The introduction of Imperial Preference as requested by the colonies would have demanded a sea-change in British commercial policy. Britain had negotiated a series of most-favoured-nation treaties with other states; offering the colonies privileged access to the British market would have entailed abrogating those agreements. Equally important, from the repeal of the Corn Laws in 1846 Britain had eschewed tariffs for anything but revenue purposes, and the idea of introducing any taxation on imports of basic foodstuffs (in order then to be able differentiate between colonial and foreign suppliers) was regarded on all sides as politically dangerous or even suicidal—the assumption being that the British electorate would not accept 'stomach taxes'. Yet, if governments were concerned about taking action, there was also the question of whether they could afford *not* to act. In February 1891 a memorandum to the Conservative Cabinet stated that there were sound arguments against Imperial Preference, but it also pointed out that 'the persistent demand of the colonies for preferential fiscal arrangements may... become politically embarrassing'. On the one hand British reluctance to implement Imperial Preference was, the memorandum pointed out, 'interpreted in the colonies as indifference to commercial union itself' and constant refusals were likely to fuel separatism. Examining the scene in Britain, the memorandum noted that 'the existence of the Imperial Federation League, and the support given to it, and to the Colonial Institute and Imperial Institute, show the strength of feeling at home in favour of a consolidation of the Empire', and this, it was concluded, could not be ignored forever.[69]

By the end of the 1890s Joseph Chamberlain, Secretary of State for the Colonies since 1895, was increasingly of the view that the issue of Imperial organization should not be ignored. At the 1897 Colonial Conference Chamberlain encouraged talk of federation and commercial union. He also made it clear to his Cabinet colleagues that Britain should respond to colonial requests by abrogating its trade treaties with other states, noting that he was 'perfectly willing to risk the wrath of Germany [because] the question of Imperial policy involved in the Canadian preferential offer is so important'.[70] But if Chamberlain was moving rapidly

---

[68] 8 Dec. 1904, in La Nauze, *Deakin*, II, p. 477.

[69] 'Commercial Union Between the United Kingdom and the Colonies', Memorandum by R. G. to the Cabinet, 9 Feb. 1891, CAB[inet] [Office] 37/29 (7).

[70] J. Chamberlain, Minute of 3 June 1897, C[olonial] O[ffice] 42/847.

towards a strong constructive imperialist position before 1900, it was after that date that he became fully committed to such a stance, and was prepared to devote all of his energies to the cause of Imperial unity.

The event which finally convinced Chamberlain, and many others, that Imperial organization was both essential and practicable was the South African War. Apart from the fact that the term itself was coined during the war, the South African crisis was important to constructive imperialism for three reasons. First, the fact that the mightiest Empire ever known took four years, lost thousands of lives, and spent millions of pounds subduing 'a little people, few but apt in the field' was a great shock. Alfred Milner, who as High Commissioner had, along with Chamberlain, done most to shape British policy in South Africa before and during the war, argued in January 1902 that 'the condition of South Africa today is a most bitter commentary on our supposed Imperial strength. Here is a single Colony, not by any means one of the largest in the Empire, in which a bare majority of disaffected people is able to disorganize our whole South African policy... and threaten the foundations of the Empire itself.'[71] It was no coincidence that Chamberlain launched his crusade for Imperial unity soon after 'Joe's War' had revealed these problems. In many respects the tariff reform campaign was born on the veld.

A second, more positive, aspect of the war that gave impetus to constructive imperialism was the voluntary support Britain received from the self-governing colonies. Writing to Lord Beauchamp in 1900, Chamberlain noted that 'whatever may have to be recorded in this war there is one great inestimable gain: the bloodshed has cemented the British Empire, and the sense of unity is stronger than it has ever been before.'[72] Three years later Chamberlain restated these wartime sentiments in the opening speech of the tariff campaign, declaring that 'we have had a war—a war in which the majority of our children abroad had no apparent direct interest. We had no hold over them, no agreement with them of any kind, and yet, at one time during this war, by their voluntary decision, at least 50,000 Colonial soldiers were standing shoulder to shoulder with British troops.'[73] Looking at the war from this perspective the *National Review* was able to argue that 'the South African War opened a new epoch in our history'; although 'the crisis revealed the unpleasant fact that Great Britain had scarcely a foul weather friend in the civilized world', it had been the case that 'the hostility of the foreigner had been superabundantly compensated by the grit and determination of the

---

[71] To C. Dawkins, 4 Jan. 1902, Milner Papers, Bodleian Library, Oxford, MSS Eng. Hist. c. 68, ff. 4–6.
[72] 5 March 1900, in Garvin and Amery, *Chamberlain*, III, p. 629.
[73] Boyd, ed., *Speeches*, II, p. 127.

Colonies'.[74] The South African War seemed to demonstrate that colonial nation-alism need not be an insuperable obstacle to Imperial unity.

Lastly, within the United Kingdom the war seemed to provide evidence of widespread popular support for the Empire. Contemporaries of all political shades saw events such as the mass celebration of the relief of Mafeking and the Conservative victory at the 'Khaki' election of September 1900 as indicative of mass enthusiasm for imperialism. Pro-Boer Liberals such as J. A. Hobson were profoundly depressed by the apparent ease with which the masses had fallen prey to the 'mass psychology of jingoism', but Conservative commentators were also persuaded of the force of what Lord Salisbury called the 'jingo hurricane'. The maintenance of Empire appeared to be an electoral trump card, and hence Joseph Chamberlain's attempt to play it more decisively after 1902. In the wake of the South African War the constructive imperialist 'moment' appeared to have arrived.

The great problem for constructive imperialism was, however, that wartime enthusiasm for Empire proved less substantial in peacetime, and Imperial Pre-ference proved less popular than had been hoped. At various levels support for the Imperial cause proved to be incoherent and difficult to mobilize. In the United Kingdom the business community's support for Empire was highly selective and fragmented. In the 1880s and 1890s there had been many expressions of enthusiasm for improved Imperial trade relations, but there had also been very little agreement as to how to bring this about. There were strong differences of opinion both between and within chambers of commerce over the merits of Imperial Prefer-ence,[75] and the only issue which seemed to generate agreement was the damaging impact of, and thus the need to remove or reduce, colonial tariffs.[76] The break-up of the IFL in 1893 had occurred because, when charged with producing a concrete scheme, the fault-lines in its membership and constituency had rapidly emerged, with the result that it had become, as its Secretary put it, 'a house divided against itself'.[77] In spite of continued concern over Britain's economic situation, divisions of opinion over the Imperial economy were still rife in Britain's business commun-ity in the early twentieth century. Thus, when Chamberlain launched the cam-paign for Imperial Preference large sections of industrial and commercial opinion opposed his scheme, with the cotton, coal, and shipbuilding industries and the banking interests of the City of London proving especially hostile. These sectors associated their interests with the maintenance of free trade and a fostering of links

[74] L. J. Maxse, 'Episodes of the Month', *National Review*, CCLXXVII (March 1906), p. 8.

[75] Green, *Crisis of Conservatism*, pp. 32–33.

[76] *Correspondence Respecting the Canadian Tariff*, C. 5179, *PP* (1887), LVIII, 1, containing protests from many different Chambers of Commerce.

[77] H. O. Arnold-Forster to IFL Council, 24 April 1893, IFL Papers, BL Add. MSS, 62780.

with the international economy in general rather than with the Imperial economy in particular, and for the cotton trade there was added concern about Imperial Preference opening the way to Indian tariffs. None of these interests could be deemed 'anti-imperial; they were simply resistant to the constructive imperialists' particular definition of the Imperial economy.

Business interests in the colonies were also wary. The Canadian example illustrates the problem particularly well. By the early twentieth century constructive imperialism seemed to have established a firm base in Canada, but there were limits to Imperial enthusiasm. The preferences granted to Britain in 1897 and 1902 seemed to indicate a desire to foster closer Imperial economic ties, but the British Board of Trade noted in 1902 that 'Canadian policy remains protectionist in spite of the preference to British goods ... the Canadian tariff ... discourages the importation of manufactured goods ... [and] Although ... British goods enjoy a preference compared with the *same* goods imported from other countries, the average *ad valorem* rate of duty on British imports *taken as a whole* is still higher than the average duty levied on all imports, ...'[78] This was hardly surprising given Canadian opinion on the matter. In 1902 Robert Borden, Macdonald's successor as leader of the Canadian Conservatives, stated that he did not wish to deal with the Imperial question 'by accepting a tariff which will shut up mills in Canada and give increased profits and outputs to some manufacturers in Yorkshire',[79] and he also noted that his party was deeply divided on the issue of Imperial Preference.[80] These concerns and divisions in the supposedly pro-Empire Canadian Conservative party reflected concern in the Canadian constituencies. After the introduction of the 1897 preferences the Canadian Manufacturers' Association had emphasized that tariffs must contrive to offer genuine protection against *all* imports, and the Association's journal warned in 1903 of 'sacrificing on the altar of Imperial sentiment the industries which are the bulwark of Canada'[81] Scepticism in the industrial east meant that support for Imperial Preference was strongest in the rapidly expanding western farming provinces of Canada, aware of Britain's importance as a market for their produce, but perhaps also influenced by a large and recently arrived British immigrant population in those regions.[82] At any rate the Canadian position on Imperial Preference was by no means one of unequivocal support, but was marked by complex patterns of diverse interest and opinion. In fact, pro-Empire views were arguably more an indication of anti-Americanism than

[78] Cd. 1299, p. 85, *PP* (1902), LXVI, p. 451.
[79] Canadian House of Commons, 18 March 1902, cited in Robert Craig Brown, *Robert Laird Borden: A Biography*, 2 vols. (Toronto, 1975), I, p. 63.
[80] Borden to J. Stairs, 24 March 1902, cited in ibid., p. 64.
[81] Bliss, *Living Profit*, p. 107.
[82] Ibid., *passim*; P. Berton, *The Promised Land: Settling the West, 1896–1914* (Toronto, 1984).

Imperial enthusiasm. G. T. Denison remarked in 1909 that 'it was not until the Commercial Union [with the United States of America] movement alarmed the people...that the cause of Imperial Federation became a strong and effective influence upon the public opinion of Canada',[83] and there was much to be said for this argument. Certainly it was at times when closer links with the United States were mooted, such as in 1910–11, that 'federationist' opinion surfaced most strongly in Canada. The joy with which constructive imperialists in Britain greeted the victory of Borden's Conservatives in the Canadian election of 1911 was thus largely misplaced. While Borden played the Imperial card in 1911, in a campaign dominated by opposition to reciprocity with the United States, he also reassured Canadian businessmen there would be no downward adjustment of tariffs for Imperial ends. Indeed, Borden made it clear that any Imperial tariff initiative would have to come from Britain.[84] The Imperial link may have been important in constructing a distinctive Canadian national identity in a North American context, but this did not necessarily indicate a commitment to constructive imperialism.

If business élites in both Britain and the colonies proved to be less than unanimous in their support for constructive imperialism, it was also the case that mass support was also largely absent. This was a particular problem in Britain, where in three contests (1906, and January and December 1910) the electorate remained unconvinced that their interests would be served by Imperial Preference. The 'wild clatter of the bread tax', and the association of tariffs and Imperial Preference with defence of propertied privilege, fatally weakened the electoral appeal of constructive imperialism.[85] The British electorate was either indifferent to Empire or quite discriminating as to its value and role. Much the same was true in the colonies. In Australia the Labor Party and trade unions showed no enthusiasm for Imperial Preference, perhaps in part because some keen federationists insisted that only 'the best sort' were Empire enthusiasts,[86] whilst, as noted above, Canadian enthusiasm was also conditional. None of this prevented either the British or colonial masses from rallying to the Empire's defence in great numbers in 1914. There was general support for the Empire *in extremis*, but this was not translated into support for a *particular* project of Empire.

This last point is important, for although constructive imperialists tended to depict opponents as 'anti-imperialist' or 'anti-Empire', this was not the case. In Britain some of Joseph Chamberlain's effective opponents were the Liberal Imperialists, most notably H. H. Asquith. Nor was this a simple party-political

---

[83] Denison, *Struggle for Imperial Unity*, p. 97.
[84] Brown, *Borden*, I, pp. 232–33.
[85] N. Blewett, *The Peers, The Parties and the People* (London, 1972).
[86] La Nauze, *Deakin*, II, pp. 509–10; C. S. Blackton, 'Australian Nationality and Nationalism: The Imperial Federationist Interlude, 1885–1901', *Australian Historical Studies*, VII (1955), pp. 1–16.

division, for a number of prominent Conservatives questioned the constructive imperialist vision of Empire. Conservative free traders, such as the sons of the great Lord Salisbury, Lords Hugh and Robert Cecil, the one-time Proconsul of Egypt, Lord Cromer, and the editor of the *Spectator*, John St Loe Strachey, opposed Imperial Preference with the maxim 'No Free Trade—No Empire'.[87] At the heart of the free trade argument against constructive imperialism was the contention that it would disrupt, not unite the Empire. Winston Churchill, who in 1904 left the Conservative Party as a consequence of his opposition to Chamberlain's initiative, put this argument most eloquently at the 1907 Colonial Conference, arguing 'that [tariff] preferences, even if economically desirable, would prove an element of strain and discord in the structure and system of the British Empire. Why, even in this Conference, what has been the one subject on which we have differed sharply? It has been this question of preference ... the principle of preference is positively injurious to the British Empire, and would create, not union, but discord.'[88] Constructive imperialists were chided for trying to base the Imperial relationship on questions of 'sordid materialism' rather than sentiment.

Nor was this the only problem. Constructive imperialist discussion of the Empire concentrated purely on the white self-governing colonies, and placed emphasis on racial unity as a basis for Imperial harmony. This seemed to indicate indifference to the territories and peoples of British India, Africa, Asia, and the Caribbean. Yet, a supposed *raison d'être* of the British Empire—what stamped *Britishness* upon it—was the duty to provide good governance of 'subject peoples' and the idea of racial harmony. Equally important was the simple fact that one territory rarely mentioned by constructive imperialists, India, was the economic jewel in the Imperial Crown. Hence the irony of John Morley, derided by constructive imperialists as the archetypal Liberal 'Little Englander', pointing out that those who '[blew] the imperial trumpet louder than other people ... would banish India, which is the most stupendous part of the Empire—our best customer among other trifles—into the imperial back kitchen'.[89] Even within the self-governing colonies there was the question of the large French population in Canada, and the even more evident issue of harmonizing Briton and Boer in Southern Africa. The 'white Australia' policy of the Australian federation provided an isolated example of the kind of race-nation-Empire link posited by constructive imperialists,[90] but it raised more problems than it was ever going to solve. Many

[87] J. St Loe Strachey, 'Free Trade and the Empire', in C. S. Goldman, ed., *The Empire and the Century: A Series of Essays on Imperial Problems and Possibilities by Various Writers* (London, 1905), p. 144.

[88] *Published Proceedings and Precis of the Colonial Conference, 15th to 26th April, 1907; 30th April to 14th May, 1907*, Cd. 3406, pp. 1, 29, *PP* (1907), LV, 406–07.

[89] To Lord Minto, 2 May 1907, cited in La Nause, *Deakin*, II, p. 481.

[90] D. Cole, 'The Crimson Thread of Kinship: Ethnic Ideas in Australia, 1870–1914', *Australian Historical Studies*, XIV, 1971, pp. 511–25, and for constructive imperialist sympathy see Joseph

active supporters of the Empire found constructive imperialism wanting in terms of both its theory and its practical implications.

Constructive imperialism was handicapped from the outset. Its basic assumption, that *general* support for the Empire could be translated into enthusiasm for a *particular* concept, was wrong. Constructive imperialists sought to produce a clearly defined Imperial structure, but in so doing discovered that their vision did not find favour with all groups and interests who were still none the less supporters of Empire. The Imperial constituency in both Britain and the colonies was broad and deep but also highly stratified—an aristocratic High Commissioner did not necessarily see the Empire in the same way as a Birmingham screw manufacturer, and neither necessarily saw Imperial issues in the same light as either a farmer from Alberta or a banker from the City of London or a Lancashire cotton operative. All these groups, and many others, had 'interests' in the Empire, but they did not necessarily overlap either materially or ideologically, and when it came to the test constructive imperialists were unable to forge a coherent coalition of support. Constructive imperialism sought to reduce the complex political economy of Empire to an impossibly simple formula.

Yet the failure of the constructive imperialist vision does not imply that the British Empire had 'no theme'. It may well have been the case that in the late nineteenth and early twentieth centuries many in both Britain and the colonies were in favour of the Empire in the same way that many are against sin, that is to say, as a general position. Nevertheless, the rejection of the constructive imperialists' economically insular and racially exclusive vision of the Empire *contra mundum* was in effect an expression of preference for an open, inclusive concept of Empire which saw the Imperial relationship, especially in economic terms, as part of rather than separate from Britain's broader international position. The failure of constructive imperialism was in this sense a testimony to the ongoing strength of the arguments and interests that favoured the preservation of Britain's commitment to free trade, a liberal trading order, and a liberal Empire.

Constructive imperialism appears on the face of it to have been one of the great lost causes of the twentieth century. But its significance does not lie purely with the fact of its defeat. Although none of its goals were achieved, it represented a major attempt to redefine the Empire's role in the light of changes within the Empire itself. As an intellectual as well as political project it acknowledged the growing nationalism of the self-governing colonies, and sought to reshape the Imperial relationship to take account of this new force. Alfred Deakin has been admirably

Chamberlain's remarks at the 1897 Colonial Conference, *Proceedings*, 1897, C. 8596, p. 13, *PP* (1897) LIX, 631.

described as 'groping towards a new theory of Empire, which discarded both the traditional superior–inferior relationship between metropolitan and colonial governments and the old British race patriot dream of federation'.[91] However, Deakin's efforts must be placed in their proper, wider context, for they were part of a pan-Imperial effort to develop such a theory. In both Britain and the self-governing colonies constructive imperialists, drawing on a common framework of ideas developed largely through intra-Imperial discussion and debate, worked towards a concept of Empire based on what Robert Borden called 'co-operation and autonomy'.[92] Constructive imperialism was one of the first attempts to design a form of co-partnership or Commonwealth structure of Imperial relations, whose relevance was to become very apparent in the inter-war years. That veterans of the constructive imperialist campaigns of the early part of the century were to view the outcome of the 1932 Ottawa Conference as a belated triumph for their ideas was in many ways not unjustified. In a climate where colonial nationalism had become stronger and more widespread, the British economy weaker, and the liberal world trading order had collapsed into hostile trading blocs, elements of the constructive imperialist project were to take on renewed significance.

[91] John J. Eddy, 'Nationalism and Nation-Making From Federation to Gallipoli', in Schreuder and Eddy, *Colonial Nationalism*, p. 139.

[92] Undated remark cited in B. Holland, *The Fall of Protection* (London, 1904), p. 392.

Select Bibliography

MICHAEL BLISS, *A Living Profit: Studies in the Social History of Canadian Business, 1883–1911* (Toronto, 1974).

ROBERT CRAIG BROWN, *Robert Laird Borden: A Biography*, 2 vols. (Toronto, 1975).

—— *Canada's National Policy 1883–1900: A Study in Canadian–American Relations* (Princeton, 1964).

P. J. CAIN and A. G. HOPKINS, *British Imperialism: Innovation and Expansion, 1688–1914*, 2 vols. (Harlow, 1993).

MARCELLO DE CECCO, *Money and Empire: The International Gold Standard, 1890–1914* (Oxford, 1974).

JOHN J. EDDY and DERYCK SCHREUDER, eds., *The Rise of Colonial Nationalism: Australia, New Zealand, Canada and South Africa First Assert their Nationalities, 1880–1914* (Sydney, 1988).

MICHAEL EDELSTEIN, *Overseas Investment in the Age of High Imperialism: The United Kingdom, 1850–1914* (London, 1982).

AARON L. FRIEDBERG, *The Weary Titan: Britain and the Experience of Relative Decline, 1895–1905* (Princeton, 1988).

E. H. H. GREEN, *The Crisis of Conservatism: The Politics, Economics and Ideology of the British Conservative Party, 1880–1914* (London, 1995).

MICHAEL HAVINDEN and DAVID MEREDITH, *Colonialism and Development: Britain and its Tropical Colonies, 1850–1960* (London, 1993).

ROBERT A. HUTTENBACK and LANCE E. DAVIS with the assistance of SUSAN GRAY DAVIS, *Mammon and the Pursuit of Empire: The Political Economy of British Imperialism, 1860–1912* (Cambridge, 1986).

RONALD HYAM, *Britain's Imperial Century: 1815–1914: A Study in Empire and Expansion,* 2nd edn. (London, 1993).

WILLIAM G. HYNES, *The Economics of Empire: Britain, Africa and the New Imperialism, 1870–95* (London, 1979).

RICHARD M. KESNER, *Economic Control and Colonial Development: Crown Colony, Financial Management in the Age of Joseph Chamberlain* (London, 1981).

R. V. KUBICEK, *The Administration of Imperialism: Joseph Chamberlain at the Colonial Office* (Durham, NC, 1969).

J. A. LA NAUZE, *Alfred Deakin: A Biography*, 2 vols. (Melbourne, 1965).

H. C. G. MATTHEW, *The Liberal Imperialists* (Oxford, 1973).

A. N. PORTER, *The Origins of the South African War: Joseph Chamberlain and the Diplomacy of Imperialism, 1895–99* (Manchester, 1980).

RICHARD PRICE, *An Imperial War and the British Working Class: Working-Class Attitudes and Reactions to the Boer War, 1899–1902* (London, 1972).

JOHN CUNNINGHAM WOOD, *British Economists and the Empire* (London, 1983).

PART II

~

17

British Expansion and Rule in South-East Asia

A. J. STOCKWELL

British expansion in South-East Asia was shaped by the well-being of India, opportunities in China, and international, particularly Anglo-French, rivalry. When British authorities in Calcutta or in London sanctioned a forward policy here, it was usually in order to prevent another power from controlling a vital sea lane or threatening a sensitive frontier. Nevertheless, considerations of global strategy were frequently reinforced by prospects of profit from South-East Asia itself. From the late eighteenth century British commerce in South-East Asia became enmeshed with British commerce in India; from the late nineteenth century the development of agriculture and mining tied South-East Asian economies more closely to industrial and finance capitalism in Britain.

While business interests were not always in tune with high policy, zealous merchants and headstrong men on the spot frequently got their way in spreading British influence further than their masters might have wished. Often they took advantage of the lack of Imperial supervision; sometimes they seized chances thrown up by crises in indigenous societies. The British frequently achieved their objectives merely by rattling the sabre but, provided that intervention had been authorized, in times of trouble they could draw reinforcements from the Indian Army and Royal Navy which underpinned British power and prestige in South-East Asia.

Yet the exercise of Imperial power and the extent of colonial control were limited. Mismanagement, disease, and jungle impeded military expeditions; pirates eluded British warships in the mangroves while rebels took to the forests. Moreover, Asian rulers frequently succeeded in turning to their advantage the British propensity for negotiating and signing agreements for the purposes of protecting British subjects, nourishing commerce, securing frontiers, and foiling the ambitions of other powers. Indeed, British imperialism advanced by the pen as well as by the sword and its history is peppered with treaties—albeit unequal ones—concluded with South-East Asian monarchs, some of whom secured their thrones and dynasties through such arrangements and regarded them as a source of prestige.

Advances into 'Further India', 1786–c.1830

MARITIME SOUTH-EAST ASIA

From 1786, when Britain acquired the settlement of Penang, to about 1830 Britain's position in South-East Asia was transformed, though an empire was scarcely established. Outmatched by the Dutch in the spice trade, in the late seventeenth century the English East India Company had withdrawn from Macassar (in the Celebes) and Bantam (in Java) to Bencoolen in South-West Sumatra (Map 17.1). Although Bencoolen prospered on pepper for a time, after about 1760 it was inconveniently located to fulfil three increasingly pressing needs. The first of these was the containment of French naval power in the Bay of Bengal. Lacking a base sheltered from the north-east monsoon, the British fleet was obliged to withdraw to Bombay in order to refit. Secondly, as the economy of British India and the Company's trade with Europe became more dependent upon exports from China, a secure post was required on the maritime route between India and China. A station was sought, thirdly, to serve British 'country' (or regional) trade in South-East Asia itself. As South-East Asia was drawn into the commercial network of India, private (or non-Company) 'country' traders alleviated the imbalance of trade with China by carrying to Canton rattans, betelnut, and tin from the Malay world, in addition to cotton from Bombay, Coromandel piece-goods, and Bengal opium.[1] Late-eighteenth-century expansion in maritime South-East Asia was promoted by 'country' traders who, outnumbering all others from Europe, encroached upon Dutch preserves, and was eventually authorized by the Company, whose priorities were to counter French threats in India and improve trade with China.

After the Seven Years War (1756–63) attempts were made to establish a settlement on the eastern side of the Bay of Bengal, but they proved either abortive, as in the case of Acheh, or short-lived, as with Alexander Dalrymple's experiment (1762–75) at Balambangan in the Sulu archipelago. In 1771 and again in 1786 successive sultans of Kedah, who sought protection against the expansionist Bugis of Selangor and, later, resurgent Thai power, offered Penang to Francis Light. Light was a 'country' trader serving a Madras firm and engaged in commerce with Sumatra, the northern Malay states, and Siam. He tried to interest the Company in the island but it was unwilling to be drawn into disputes between local kingdoms; it therefore rejected Kedah's earlier offer and refused to honour the defensive clauses in the agreement by which the Sultan ceded Penang on 11 August 1786.

---

[1] Anthony Webster, 'British Expansion in South-East Asia and the Role of Robert Farquhar, Lieutenant-Governor of Penang, 1804–5', *Journal of Imperial and Commonwealth History* (hereafter *JICH*), XXIII, 1 (1995), pp. 1–3.

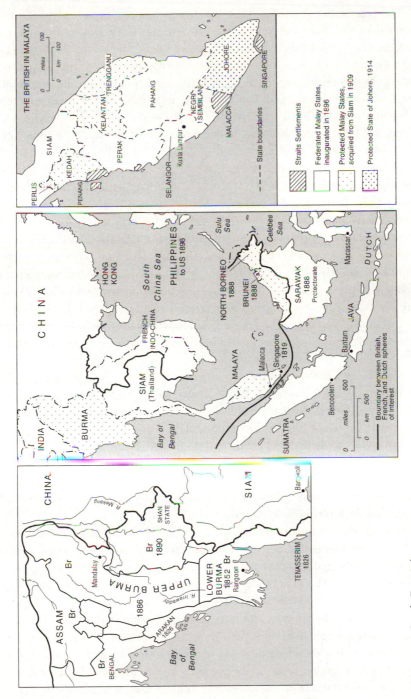

MAP 17.1. South-East Asia

THE BRITISH IN MALAYA

PERLIS
KEDAH
PENANG
PERAK
SIAM
KELANTAN
TRENGGANU
PAHANG
SELANGOR
Kuala Lumpur
NEGRI
SEMBILAN
MALACCA
JOHORE
SINGAPORE

km 100
0 100
miles
0

Straits Settlements

Federated Malay States, inaugurated in 1896

Protected Malay States, acquired from Siam in 1909

Protected State of Johore, 1914

State boundaries

CHINA
HONG KONG
FRENCH INDO-CHINA
South China Sea
Sulu Sea
PHILIPPINES to US 1898
Celebes Sea
INDIA
BURMA
SIAM (Thailand)
MALAYA
Malacca
Singapore 1819
NORTH BORNEO 1888
BRUNEI 1888
SARAWAK 1888 Protectorate
Macassar
Bay of Bengal
SUMATRA
Bencoolen
Bantam
JAVA
DUTCH

miles 500
0 500 km

Boundary between British, French, and Dutch spheres of interest

CHINA
R. Mekong
SHAN STATE
Br 1890
Mandalay
UPPER BURMA
1886 Br
R. Irrawaddi
ASSAM Br
BENGAL Br
ARAKAN 1826
LOWER BURMA 1852 Br
Rangoon
TENASSERIM 1826 Br
Bay of Bengal
SIAM
Bangkok

The French Revolutionary Wars drastically reduced the Dutch position in South-East Asia but increased the French challenge to Britain. After the French invaded the Netherlands, William V fled to England and issued the Kew Letters (1795) instructing Dutch Governors overseas to transfer their territories to British safe-keeping. Britain consequently occupied the Cape, Ceylon, Padang (Sumatra), Malacca, Ambon, and Banda. It was not until after the fall of French Mauritius in December 1810, however, that the way was clear for the Governor-General of India, Lord Minto, to mount an expedition to Java, the centrepiece of the Dutch seaborne empire. Java fell in August 1811 and Stamford Raffles was appointed Lieutenant-Governor. Raffles's desire was to spread British influence throughout the East Indies and rid them of what he condemned as the twin evils of Dutch imperialism and oriental misrule. He quashed local resistance, as in the destruction of the court of Yogyakarta, annexed land, deposed Javanese rulers, and elevated others in their place. He attempted to extirpate slavery, monopolies, tolls, and forced deliveries, and he introduced a land rent (or land tax) system adapted from Bengal. Despite his vision and energy, however, his reforms foundered on financial difficulties and lack of support from the Company. Moreover, following the defeat of Napoleon, Foreign Secretary Castlereagh wished to build up the Netherlands as part of a cordon preventing French revanchism in Europe, with the result that Java and their other East Indies interests were returned to the Dutch by 1816.

None the less, Raffles continued to urge the extension of British influence in the archipelago. He was convinced that the Dutch had a malign effect upon the area, and disappointed that Penang had not fulfilled the expectations of its founder. In its first twenty years the British settlement had prospered: its population had grown and its trade with the region had flourished. Furthermore, it had seemed eminently suitable as a naval station and in 1800 had acquired Province Wellesley, across the water in Kedah. After 1805, however, its disadvantages became clearer: the island lacked both a dockyard and supplies of timber, while it was poorly placed for ships plying between India and China.

Having won the support of the Governor-General, the Marquess of Hastings, in February 1819 Raffles took advantage of a succession dispute in Johore to conclude an agreement with one of the contestants, Sultan Hussein, by which Singapore was ceded to Britain. This bold move was of dubious legitimacy and provoked strong protests, not only from the Dutch, who laid claim to the Riau-Johore archipelago, but also from administrators and merchants in Penang, fearful that a new settlement would threaten their own. For a time the future of Singapore was uncertain but, while the British authorities were reluctant to incur Dutch wrath, they were unwilling to abandon what might prove to be a profitable commercial centre organized on free-trade principles. In 1824 Anglo-Dutch differences were settled in a treaty by which the Dutch recognized Singapore as British and exchanged Malacca for Bencoolen. Although half a century would elapse before the Dutch attempted to establish effective occupation over Sumatra or the British embarked on a forward policy in the Malay peninsula, the Anglo-Dutch Treaty of 1824 divided the Malay archipelago into two spheres of influence, splitting the kingdom of Riau-Johore and converting the Straits of Malacca from a corridor of access between kindred communities into a frontier between British and Dutch imperial zones. Two years later Penang, Malacca, and Singapore were amalgamated as the Straits Settlements under the Bengal Presidency.

BRITAIN IN MAINLAND SOUTH-EAST ASIA

Meanwhile, Penang merchants, operating in the northern Malay states and Siam, were pressing upon the closed world of the Thais, from 1782 ruled by the Chakri dynasty in Bangkok. Although the Chakri kings allowed European traders into Siam, they were anxious to restrict Western activities and maintain their authority over the northern Malay states. In 1826 Henry Burney negotiated a treaty redefining the scope of Thai suzerainty over the Malay states and the British gained some trade concessions in Siam. Penang merchants were bitterly disappointed by the meagre commercial provisions of the Burney Treaty, but the priorities of the Supreme Government of the Company lay elsewhere. So long as Asian states did not bow to French pressure or endanger the security of India, Calcutta had no wish to interfere in their affairs. For example, it refrained from intervention in Cochin-China (or southern Vietnam) once reassured by John Crawfurd (British envoy to Emperor Minh-Mang in 1821–22) that the Cochin-Chinese 'are not our immediate neighbours, but far removed from the sphere of our Indian politics'.[2] Similarly, far from hoping to prise concessions from the King of Siam, the Company wished 'to avoid contiguity of dominion or intricacy of relations with that state, and the consequent and necessary hazard of collisions and rupture'.[3] Indeed, Calcutta was anxious to reassure Bangkok that the Anglo-Burmese War of 1824–26 was not the prelude to a wave of expansionism which would threaten Siam.

Conflict between the British and Burmese arose from frontier turbulence aggravated by different perceptions of power and the state. The British settlement of Bengal was underpinned by an equation of land with power alien to Burmese concepts of authority and government. Desiring to demarcate frontiers and define power territorially, the British clashed on their eastern border with an expansive but inherently unstable regime. The fount of justice and patronage but the target

---

[2] Quoted in Nicholas Tarling, *Imperial Britain in South-East Asia* (Kuala Lumpur, 1975), p. 92.
[3] Ibid., p. 136.

of intrigue and rebellion, the Konbaung monarchy was weakened by succession contests at court and well-entrenched governors and hereditary headmen in the provinces. Boundary disputes between Arakan and Bengal, together with anxiety lest the French set up bases in Burmese ports, induced Governor-General Shore to despatch Captain Michael Symes as an envoy to the Court of Ava in 1795 (he went a second time in 1802). Although King Bodawpaya refused to treat with the representative of a mere Governor-General or to exclude the French from his harbours, he was willing to accept a British Resident who would superintend commerce. A number of short-lived attempts were made to post a British Resident in Rangoon, such as that by Captain Hiram Cox in 1796–98, and further envoys were sent to the Court of Ava to discuss frontier problems, but the upshot was only increasing mutual mistrust. In 1819 Bodawpaya was succeeded by Bagyidaw whose army commander, Maha Bandula, embarked upon expansion. Meanwhile the Company, having subdued the Marathas, turned to its eastern frontier. After a Burmese force had driven the British garrison from Shahpuri island in the disputed zone of the River Naaf, the Governor-General, Lord Amherst, declared war on Burma on 5 March 1824.

The first Anglo-Burmese War was long, mismanaged, and costly. Of the 40,000 men serving in the British force, 15,000 died, mostly from dysentery and malaria, while the Burmese, already exhausted after three-quarters of a century of military expansion, were crippled by the war and peace settlement. By the Treaty of Yandabo (24 February 1826) the Burmese were required to pay an indemnity of 10 million rupees; cede Arakan, Assam, and Tenasserim; surrender claims to Manipur and Cachar; receive a British Resident at Ava; post an envoy to Calcutta; and open negotiations for a separate commercial agreement. The British had mixed feelings about these gains; while merchants and missionaries welcomed them, administrators doubted their value. What soon became clear, however, was that, far from settling Anglo-Burmese disputes, the Treaty prepared the ground for further conflict.

British expansion into South-East Asia between 1786 and the late 1820s was part of a dramatic resurgence in British imperialism world-wide. Rocked by crises in America, India, and at home during the 1770s and 1780s, half a century later British national self-confidence rested on economic superiority, naval predominance, and recent military successes. Commercial growth and war with France had resulted in a massive expansion of British Imperial power, especially in Asia.[4] As regards South-East Asia, British intervention had been brought about by Anglo-French rivalry and fluctuating Dutch power, by the needs of India and opportunities in China, by the attractions of South-East Asian trade and the reactions of South-

---

[4] C. A. Bayly, *Imperial Meridian: The British Empire and the World, 1780–1830* (Harlow, 1989).

East Asian societies. Although in the late 1820s British formal Empire amounted to no more than two strips of coastal Burma and the Straits Settlements, British commerce had brought about significant changes in the pattern of regional trade, especially in the Straits where the focus shifted from traditional entrepôts to the Settlement ports. Moreover, local communities of British administrators, merchants, and missionaries were accumulating knowledge and interests stretching beyond the boundaries of official involvement. In the era of free trade imperialism that followed, they would vigorously demand support for their activities from frequently reluctant authorities in Calcutta and London.

Free Trade Imperialism and Turbulent Frontiers, c.1830–c.1870

MALAYA AND BORNEO

The period of so-called 'liberal non-intervention' from the Anglo-Dutch Treaty of 1824 which partitioned the Malay world into British and Dutch spheres, to the Pangkor Treaty of 1874 which laid the basis for the British Residential system in the Malay states, was in fact a half-century of immense activity. Singapore's trade soon outstripped that of Penang and Malacca and, largely because of Chinese immigration, its population rose from approximately 11,000 in 1824 to 81,000 by 1860. The island's infrastructure rapidly expanded as it attracted shipping and investment. Banking houses opened, notably the Oriental Bank 1846, Mercantile Bank 1855, and Chartered Bank 1859. Major companies, such as P&O and Jardines, established offices here. A dry dock constructed in the 1850s and Singapore became a major coaling station for steamships. Singapore profited from the liberalization of British trade with China after 1833, the British acquisition of Hong Kong in 1841–42, Dutch exploitation of Java, and French expansion in Indo-China after 1858. The opening of the Suez Canal in 1869 confirmed the Malacca Straits as the main route to East Asia and Singapore's strategic significance for the Empire. Straits merchants were also looking for opportunities in the Malayan hinterland where Straits capital was invested, especially after the discovery of rich tin deposits in Perak in 1848.

These developments placed considerable strains on the boundaries of the Straits Settlements and also on their relationship with the Government of India. Urged by merchants to intervene in the Malay states, Straits officials were also worried by Thai expansionism southwards. Several forays were made beyond the Settlements: a skirmish in 1831–32 resulted in the absorption of Naning within Malacca, and when in 1862 Siam sponsored a claimant to the Pahang throne, Governor Cavanagh bombarded Kuala Trengganu in order to warn off the Thais. The Government of India, however, frowned on exploits which threatened to incur political, military, and territorial responsibilities. When the East India Company lost the monopoly of the China trade in 1833, its interest in the Straits Settlements faded.

It retrenched on their administration, reined in those who wished to curb the Thais or conclude further agreements with Malay rulers, and even compromised the basis of their prosperity by attempting to raise revenue from their trade. Meanwhile, piracy in Malayan waters and feuds between Chinese secret societies endangered life and property; riot rocked Singapore for ten days in 1854, and again in 1857, while Penang was plagued by disturbances throughout 1857–67.[5] European and Chinese community leaders bitterly complained about the Government of India's apparent indifference to Straits interests. In the 1850s they successfully protested against Calcutta's schemes to replace the local dollar by the rupee and to end Singapore's free-port status, but calls for intervention in the Malayan hinterland went unheeded. The review of Indian government following the uprising of 1857 provided Straits leaders, such W. H. Read, with the opportunity to press for transfer of the Settlements to the Colonial Office. Largely because of Colonial Office reluctance to take on additional burdens, this was not effected for another ten years. When it did occur in 1867 it brought some significant changes, notably the introduction of the Crown Colony institutions of executive and legislative councils, but the Colonial Office appeared unmoved by mercantile pleas for intervention in the west-coast Malay states.

Meanwhile, in Borneo James Brooke had assisted the Sultan of Brunei in the subjugation of a revolt. Acting as a freelance, Brooke was rewarded by the Sultan in 1841 with the grant of Sarawak, which he and his heirs extended and ruled until 1941 as more or less autonomous rajahs. Because Sarawak lacked resources, Brooke made a virtue of necessity and, adapting the liberal imperialism of Raffles to the legacy of the Brunei regime, he founded an enlightened if impecunious despotism ostensibly committed to the conservation of the way of life of indigenous peoples. Although lionized on visiting England in 1847, James Brooke was attacked a few years later by Imperial critics, such as the radical-Liberal MP Richard Cobden, on account of the ruthlessness of his suppression of pirates. A commission of enquiry subsequently cleared him of inhumanity, but Brooke could never again call upon the Royal Navy or expect financial assistance from the British government.

BURMA

At the time when Brooke's actions were under scrutiny, Cobden also protested against the conquest of Lower Burma which, he feared, would increase taxation at home and enlarge Britain's standing army.[6] The origins of the Second Anglo-

---

[5] See chap. by Susan Bayly, p. 454.

[6] e.g. Richard Cobden, *How Wars are Got Up in India: The Origin of the Burma War* (London, 1853). See Miles Taylor, 'Imperium et Libertas? Rethinking the Radical Critique of Imperialism during the Nineteenth Century', *JICH*, XIX, 1 (1991) pp. 8–9.

Burmese War (1852) lay in the Treaty of Yandabo which was supposed to have settled the first. Resenting the loss of territory and unable to pay reparations, King Tharrawaddy (reigned 1838–46) repudiated the treaty, and in 1840 the British Resident withdrew from the Court of Ava, thereby removing the channel for peaceful settlement of outstanding problems. Under Pagan Min (reigned 1846–53) central government broke down and provincial governors were left more or less to their own devices. Eager to bring Rangoon and its hinterland into the orbit of the Indian Empire, British traders were swift to complain of ill-treatment at the hands of the Burmese but were regularly reminded, as was one Rangoon merchant in 1842, that 'A private trader who thus ventures into an unfriendly port, does so at his own risk, and cannot claim the intervention of his Government as a matter of right.'[7]

While it may not have been particularly sympathetic towards traders, the Government of India was constantly sensitive to any hint of unrest on its frontiers. Lord Dalhousie, who had annexed the Punjab after the defeat of the Sikhs in 1849, was now in a position to attend more fully to the border with Burma. In addition, there was growing support in Calcutta for merchants wishing to exploit the rich teak forests in Moulmein or open up a route through Burma to the potentially lucrative market of Southern China. Indeed, the change in Britain's relations with China in the early 1840s encouraged interest in China's traditional feudatories, Burma, Siam, and to a lesser extent Vietnam. When two British sea-captains complained about Burmese fines totalling nearly 1,000 rupees, Dalhousie despatched to Rangoon a naval force under Commodore Lambert to demand compensation and the removal of the Burmese governor, Maung Ok. Lambert's mission (November 1851–January 1852) only made things worse: he bombarded Burmese shipping but returned to Calcutta empty-handed. Consequently Dalhousie felt obliged to send a second, larger force which demanded an even greater sum in compensation for wrongs suffered by British citizens. Although British attitudes to the Burmese smacked of Palmerston's doctrine *civis Romanus sum* in the Don Pacifico affair (June 1850), Dalhousie fervently desired to avoid hostilities, largely on grounds of cost, and was furious with the 'combustible commodore' for leaving him no option but to take stronger measures. None the less, the Governor-General never contemplated retreat since it was axiomatic that 'we can't afford to be shown to the door anywhere in the East'.[8]

When negotiations failed, the British occupied Rangoon in April 1852 and war ensued. Unlike the conflict of 1824–26, the Second Anglo-Burmese War was a more

---

[7] Quoted in Oliver B. Pollak, *Empires in Collision: Anglo-Burmese Relations in the Mid-Nineteenth Century* (Westport, Conn., 1979), p. 53.

[8] Quoted in D. G. E. Hall, *A History of South-East Asia*, 4th edn. (1955; London, 1981), p. 650. For the 'Don Pacifico' affair, see above, p. 109.

clinical operation. What had started as an attempt to force concessions from the Burmese led to further annexations: first the ports of Rangoon, Martaban, and Bassein; then their hinterland, the old kingdom of Pegu; and finally, a swathe of teak forests lying north of Prome. In the wake of this Burmese disaster Pagan Min was deposed and succeeded by his half-brother, Mindon Min (reigned 1853–78). Mindon wanted peace but refused any treaty involving the cession of territory. As a result, the British unilaterally annexed Lower Burma, which they amalgamated in 1862 with Arakan and Tenasserim to form the province of British Burma, with Rangoon as its capital. In losing the fertile Irrawaddy delta, the kingdom of Burma was landlocked and the Konbaung dynasty further weakened. Some at Mindon's court urged resistance, and for a while it looked as though the frontier would erupt in war for a third time. That this did not occur was due to the Governor-General, key men on the spot, and most significantly, the King of Burma himself. Knowing the cost of territorial expansion—indeed, stubborn resistance in Lower Burma occupied Dalhousie's troops for three more years—the Governor-General wanted to avoid further fighting. In patching up differences with Mindon he was ably served by the first British Commissioner of Lower Burma, Arthur Phayre, and by Thomas Spears, who until 1861 acted as an unofficial British agent in Mindon's court. Soon Dalhousie was lauding Mindon for his 'rare sagacity, humanity and forbearance'.[9]

While hoping to regain lost land, Mindon did all he could to avoid confrontation with Britain's Indian Empire. He accepted the reality of British power which had already been proved in China as well as in Burma. Instead of succumbing to the temptation to exploit British difficulties during the Crimean War (1854–56) and the Indian rising of 1857, he strove to win British favour by administrative reforms and improving conditions for trade. Mindon concluded a commercial agreement with Phayre in 1862 by which he agreed to trade in rice from Lower Burma and the appointment of a British agent to the new capital at Mandalay. In 1867 he concluded with Colonel Albert Fytche a new treaty surrendering all his trade monopolies (save those involving rubies, oil, and timber), reducing customs dues, and granting certain extraterritorial privileges such as the right for the British to be tried in mixed courts. Mindon also introduced coinage, encouraged the mining of minerals, and set up factories with European managers for the manufacture of sugar, cotton, and silk-lace.

SIAM

Like Mindon, Mongkut of Siam (reigned 1851–68) impressed the British as an 'enlightened oriental ruler'. His predecessors had resisted Western blandishments,

---

[9] Quoted in Hall, *A History of South-East Asia*, p. 653.

so much so that in 1850, after a fruitless mission to open Siam to free trade, James Brooke had urged upon Palmerston a new, more forceful policy involving 'decisive measures to be taken without delay'.[10] Mongkut, realizing from events in Burma and China that further obstruction would be futile, pre-empted such moves by bending before the wind. In 1855 he negotiated with Sir John Bowring (Governor of Hong Kong) a treaty whereby tariffs on British imports were reduced, export duties defined, British subjects allowed to acquire land and houses in the Bangkok area, and a British Consul was to be stationed in Bangkok with extraterritorial jurisdiction over British subjects. Mongkut concluded similar treaties with France and the United States in 1856, and with other powers thereafter. Mongkut also made territorial concessions on his borders: he retreated from Pahang when opposed by the British in 1862, and in 1867 agreed to abandon all claims to Cambodia (except for Battambang and Siem Reap) in response to pressure from the French, who had advanced into Cambodia after their conquest of Cochin-China in 1859–62. In domestic affairs Mongkut embarked upon cautious reform: he employed foreign advisers to supervise government departments and modernize the army; he constructed canals and roads around Bangkok; he relaxed court ritual; and he attempted reform of the revenue system. By Victorian standards of modernization, however, these measures were limited, since at the end of his reign slavery still existed, hereditary governors held sway outside Bangkok, the infrastructure was rudimentary, and the law had yet to be codified.

Mongkut appeared to have saved Siam from colonial rule by accommodating the commercial ambitions of the West; but there was a price to pay. In addition to winning territorial and extraterritorial concessions, foreigners dominated certain sectors of Siam's economy and, notwithstanding Mongkut's strategy of balancing Western interests, the British established pre-eminence in banking, shipping, and Bangkok's import–export trade. External relations were constrained by the European presence, and during the reign of Mongkut's successor French pressure on Siam would grow. Paradoxically, Siam's survival as an independent kingdom would owe much to Britain's influence over its foreign affairs.

Imperialism and Colonialism, c.1870–1914

Although the British preferred the exercise of influence through agents, advisers, and collaborating monarchs to the annexation of territory, in the years 1870–1914 they consolidated their position in the Malayan peninsula, northern Borneo, and the rest of Burma, and tightened their hold over Siam. In so doing they reacted to three sets of circumstances: local crises, economic opportunities, and

---

[10] Quoted in Tarling, *Imperial Britain*, p. 153.

international challenges. Of course, British activities in each country had their own dynamics and were determined by factors whose significance varied with the perspective of participants and the level of decision-making. Moreover, there was no centrally directed policy from London: British interests in Burma, Malaya, and Siam were supervised by the India, Colonial, and Foreign Offices respectively. None the less, despite the absence of a coherent policy for expansion in the region, Britain completed its paramountcy there during the final phase of the European partition of South-East Asia.

MALAYA AND BORNEO

Although historians no longer accept the view that the British were 'invited, pushed, and persuaded into helping the Rulers of certain States to introduce order into their disorderly, penniless, and distracted households',[11] the evidence points to local unrest as triggering Britain's 'forward policy' in Malaya.[12] The turbulent frontier convinced the Straits government, and eventually the Secretary of State, of the need for intervention. Disturbed by decades of contact with foreign traders and by the more recent influx of Chinese tin-miners, the Straits hinterland was torn by Malay succession disputes and wars between Chinese triads. Straits officials were worried by the unruliness, which endangered shipping and from time to time washed over the frontier into the Settlements. Aggrieved merchants regularly petitioned the Colonial Office which, notwithstanding the fact that the Liberals were in office (1868–74), modified the orthodoxy of non-intervention. This change of heart was essentially the result of a keenly felt, though largely unsubstantiated, fear that another power, possibly Germany, might take advantage of Malayan unrest to move into what was a British sphere commanding a vital sea lane. Thus, while reasserting that 'Her Majesty's Government have, it need hardly be said, no desire to interfere in the internal affairs of the Malay States,' Lord Kimberley (Secretary of State for the Colonies, 1870–74) insisted that 'we could not see with indifference interference of foreign Powers in the affairs of the Peninsula'.[13]

When issued to the Governor in September 1873, Kimberley's instructions did not appear to signal a new course in British policy or a watershed in Malayan

---

[11] Sir Frank Swettenham, *British Malaya*, 3rd edn. (1906; London, 1948), pp. vi–vii.

[12] C. N. Parkinson, *British Intervention in Malaya, 1867–1877* (Singapore, 1960); C. D. Cowan, *Nineteenth-Century Malaya: The Origins of British Political Control* (London, 1961); W. David McIntyre, *The Imperial Frontier in the Tropics, 1865–75: A Study of British Colonial Policy in West Africa, Malaya and the South Pacific in the Age of Gladstone and Disraeli* (London, 1967); Emily Sadka, *The Protected Malay States, 1874–1895* (Kuala Lumpur, 1968); Eunice Thio, *British Policy in the Malay Peninsula, 1880–1910* (Kuala Lumpur, 1969); Khoo Kay Kim, *The Western Malay States, 1850–1873* (Kuala Lumpur, 1972).

[13] J. de V. Allen, A. J. Stockwell, and L. R. Wright, eds., *A Collection of Treaties and Other Documents Affecting the States of Malaysia, 1761–1963*, 2 vols. (London, 1981), II, pp. 13, 15–16.

history. He authorized Sir Andrew Clarke merely to report on conditions in the west-coast states, examine ways in which law and order might be restored, and consider the advisability of appointing British officers to reside in Malay kingdoms. Yet Clarke acted first and reported back later. In January 1874 he concluded with Perak chiefs the Pangkor Engagement whereby the accession of Sultan Abdullah and the appointment of British Residents were agreed. By the end of the year similar arrangements had been determined with Selangor and Sungei Ujong (a part of Negri Sembilan). Although the British had signed treaties with Malay rulers before, the Pangkor Engagement marked the start of a 'forward policy', becoming the model for written agreements concluded with the rest of Negri Sembilan and Pahang in the 1880s. However modest Kimberley's original intentions, intervention in 1874 began a process whereby Malay society was placed within a political and economic frame dominated by non-Malays.

These Anglo-Malay agreements proved highly ambiguous and were hotly disputed, especially in the early days of the Residential experiment. They confirmed the sovereignty of the Malay rulers yet obliged them to follow the advice of British officers. The clause, which stipulated that the sultan was bound to act upon the Resident's advice in all matters save religion and custom, left undefined both Malay sovereignty and the executive powers of British advisers. In November 1875 the first Resident in Perak, James Birch, was murdered and the state erupted in war. This reversal led neither to Perak's annexation nor to clarification of the Resident's role. Instead, Hugh Low, Frank Swettenham, and other political officers were left to work out for themselves ways of asserting power behind the throne. Gradually they secured the financial well-being of the rulers, whose authority was elevated over lesser chiefs. In so doing, Residents conserved, and in some ways even reconstructed, a set of traditional Malay kingdoms consisting of princes and peasants.

Although British policy rested on the principles of the sovereignty of the Malay rulers, the autonomy of the Malay states, and the rights of Malays as 'princes of the soil', in practice power passed to the Residents and their European staff. The need for greater uniformity in the administration of Perak, Selangor, Pahang, and Negri Sembilan, their uneven economic performance, and Pahang's insolvency, led to their incorporation within the Federated Malay States (FMS) in 1896. As a result British rule became more direct and centralized under a Resident-General and a growing number of specialist departments based in the FMS capital of Kuala Lumpur.

The British hand was felt more lightly in those Malay states remaining outside the FMS. The Foreign Office restrained officials and businessmen who in the late 1890s urged the takeover of Malay states still under Siamese suzerainty. It was unwilling to authorize expansion at the expense of Siam, whose neutrality and territorial integrity were cardinal principles of British policy in mainland South-East Asia. For reasons discussed below, it later modified this line and in 1909 Britain concluded the Treaty of Bangkok whereby Siam surrendered its rights over Kedah, Perlis, Kelantan, and Trengganu. The rulers of these states subsequently agreed to accept British Advisers rather than Residents, the different nomenclature indicating the rulers' determination not to be assimilated by the Federated Malay States. Finally, in 1914 the British lost patience with Sultan Ibrahim of Johore (reigned 1895–1959), who was turning out to be even more capricious than his flamboyant father Abu Bakar, and forced him to accept a General Adviser.

There was an element of Imperial logic, though little colonial cohesion, in this last phase of British 'forward policy'. Indeed, while various agreements concluded with Malay Rulers in 1874–1914 facilitated Imperial expansion, they also made for administrative untidiness. During the inter-war period colonial officials became preoccupied with the reform and simplification of Malayan government but, displaying a resilient capacity to survive the challenges of colonialism, the sultans frustrated further attempts to tamper with their sovereignty and the autonomy of their states.[14]

In Sarawak the Brookes lacked both the will and the means to carry out fundamental changes. Although Charles Brooke (second Rajah, 1868–1917) extended the frontier to its present-day configuration, consolidated administration, and benefited from the revenue derived from the trade and agriculture of Chinese settlers, the regime was still plagued by headhunting and poverty. To the disappointment of both Rajahs, London had refused responsibility for Sarawak, but in 1888 the Foreign Office established control over its external affairs as well as those of Brunei and the British North Borneo Company. The Company, which had won concessions from the sultans of Brunei and Sulu and received a royal charter in 1881, administered its territory loosely in 'a gambling style of government'.[15] By establishing 'protection' over these three territories, London sought to prevent border disputes between them and also with the Netherlands East Indies and the Philippines.

The prime role of the Federated Malay States government in economic development was to encourage private enterprise. Until 1900 the prosperity of the west-coast Malay states depended mainly on Chinese capital and labour. Chinese enterprise dominated retailing and pioneered the cultivation of sugar, tapioca, pepper, and gambier. Because of their command of Chinese labour and low profit-margins, Chinese entrepreneurs controlled tin-mining until, with the introduc-

[14] J. M. Gullick, *Rulers and Residents: Influence and Power in the Malay States, 1870–1920* (Singapore, 1992).

[15] Ian Black, *A Gambling Style of Government: The Establishment of Chartered Company Rule in Sabah, 1878–1915* (Kuala Lumpur, 1983).

tion of the bucket-dredge in 1912, the industry became increasingly capital-intensive. Twenty-five years later Europeans owned two-thirds of Malaya's tin mines, whose management had come under the control of international cartels, notably the London Tin Corporation and its subsidiary, Anglo-Oriental (Malaya) Ltd., which sought to control production and fix prices.

British planters experimented with sugar and coffee, but it was rubber which transformed their involvement in agriculture. Rubber cultivation took off at the end of the nineteenth century on account of a number of factors: Malaya's climate, the coffee blight, world demand, the enthusiasm of Henry Ridley (Director of the Singapore Botanical Gardens, 1888–1911), the availability of Tamil labour from South India, and European capital investment. New ventures were often under-capitalized and a number collapsed, but the booms of 1905 and 1910 prompted the formation of numerous UK plantation companies. Many of these raised capital on the London Stock Exchange, but did so under the auspices of Singapore agency houses (such as Guthries, Bousteads, Sime Darby, and Harrisons and Crosfield) which, with the benefit of local expertise, supervised their activities in Malaya. Though agency houses were answerable to shareholders in Britain, their operations were centred upon the region and to a large extent they ploughed back locally generated profits. Rubber was cultivated on estates and also Asian smallholdings along the length of west-coast Malaya, where an infrastructure had already been laid for tin. By the 1920s rubber was the main pillar of Malaya's economy and Malaya was the world's largest producer of natural rubber. Rubber was, therefore, of immense importance both for Malaya and for the Empire, but its expansion confirmed rather than revolutionized the country's role as supplier of commodities to the West.[16]

The connections between British rule and British economic interests were close yet complex. On the one hand, businessmen brought their views to bear on government through representation on the Straits Legislative Council, the Federal Council, and commercial associations in London; on the other, the colonial government secured law and order, regulated land use and labour, and financed the construction of ports, railways, and roads from revenue and loans. Nevertheless, British business interests frequently diverged and policy-makers adopted various approaches to economic development. Tin and rubber companies rivalled each other; miners and planters of the Federated Malay States were on their guard against subordination to the bankers and traders of Singapore; and whereas some administrators single-mindedly extolled the benefits of European enterprise and joined the boards of British firms on retirement, others strenuously defended peasant proprietorship.

---

[16] J. H. Drabble, *Rubber in Malaya, 1876–1922: The Genesis of the Industry* (Kuala Lumpur, 1973).

British sympathy for the Malay way of life and perceptions of the rural idyll fostered the myth of 'the lazy native'. Though Malays participated in administration and though *kampong* (village) agriculture was officially encouraged, they were neither expected nor educated to participate in the bustling 'modern Malaya' being constructed round them. By 1914 Malay élites in the Federated Malay States felt marginalized by an increasingly centralized government, which was controlled by British officials, and by the export-orientated economy dominated by Europeans and Chinese. Moreover, Malay numbers, while boosted by Indonesian immigration, had not kept pace with those coming in from China and India. Long since a minority in the Straits Settlements, Malays were now in danger of losing their majority in the west-coast states as well. Although the British persisted in the belief that non-Malays were 'birds of passage', census figures revealed a trend towards settlement and a growing proportion of second-generation immigrants amongst the Chinese and Indians. In Malaya, as in Burma, colonialism was creating a 'plural society', in which ethnic differences were reinforced by colonial attitudes, administrative practice, and the division of labour. Communal compartmentalization in turn shaped political awareness and accounted for the emergence of Malay nationalism rather than multiracial, Malayan nationalism.

Initial opposition to British intervention, such as occurred in Perak in 1875 and in Pahang in 1891–95, where Malay chiefs rose in armed resistance, was followed by more considered reactions as Malay leaders sought to articulate their community's identity in order to protect it in a rapidly changing environment. The Malay press became their principal medium. In 1906, for example, an article in the first issue of the Malay periodical *Al-Imam* declared that 'the one thing that will strengthen and realise all our desires is knowledge of the commands of our religion'.[17] The Islamic community (or *umat*) was, however, only one concept of 'Malayness'; another was ethnicity or race (*bangsa*); a third was the monarchical tradition (*kerajaan*).[18] The quest for communal identity provoked contests between Malay élites for ideological hegemony which continued to splinter the Malay nationalist movement after 1914. It also ran counter to any thought of Malayan or non-communal nationalism. Non-Malay, immigrant communities experienced the colonial impact in most direct and oppressive ways, through its labour regulations, for example, and the social repercussions of market forces. On the whole, however, their allegiances remained to their countries of origin, and it would be upheavals there, rather than those in their adopted home, which would fire their political awareness in the first half of the twentieth century.

---

[17] Quoted in William R. Roff, *The Origins of Malay Nationalism* (New Haven, 1967), p. 56.
[18] Anthony Milner, *The Invention of Politics in Colonial Malaya: Contesting Nationalism and the Expansion of the Public Sphere* (Cambridge, 1994).

SIAM

To one British visitor in the late 1880s, Bangkok appeared as 'a city made to live in watercolours, not warranted otherwise to last'. It did not bear comparison with the 'flourishing and enlightened, so advanced and well-governed' town of Singapore.[19] None the less, the reign of Chulalongkorn (1868–1910), coinciding almost exactly with the Meiji restoration (1868–1912), resembled the reformist era in Japanese history in its eclectic borrowing from the West. Chulalongkorn, himself educated by English teachers, encouraged secular education, abolished slavery, prohibited compulsory labour for government service, built hospitals, roads, and railways, and altogether behaved like a thoroughly enlightened despot. He also set up new ministries and strengthened central control over the provinces by replacing hereditary governors with civil servants. In these ways Chulalongkorn advanced along a trail blazed by his father, modernizing government while enhancing monarchical authority.

Godlike though the king remained in the eyes of his subjects, the effectiveness of his governance rested in large measure upon the guidance of advisers whom Chulalongkorn recruited from abroad. The principal areas were government finances, the legal system, and the army. Like Mongkut, he was careful to distribute favours across a range of foreigners, but the key Financial Adviser (instituted in 1898) was invariably British. Moreover, of the total Western population residing in Siam in 1889, about 40 per cent were British, whose involvement in the economy spread from Bangkok to the teak and tin areas far beyond the capital. Some have argued, consequently, that Thai needs were subordinated to the interests of British trade and investment and that Siam escaped formal colonialism only to succumb to British informal empire.[20]

Such a picture of all-pervasive British influence, however, should be qualified. First, the role of Western business was less significant than that of the Chinese, who acted both in competition with, and as vital compradores for, European firms. Secondly, although Britain was Siam's main trading partner, Siam was never one of Britain's principal economic interests in South-East Asia. The British were disappointed by the Thai market and in 1914 their investments amounted to approximately £2m compared with £16m in Burma and £25m in Malaya.[21] Finally, detailed examination of Thai administration and the activities of Financial Advisers has revealed that, while the British may have appeared to direct Siam's

---

[19] Florence Caddy, *To Siam and Malaya* (1889; Singapore, 1992), p. 227.

[20] e.g. John Gallagher and Ronald Robinson, 'The Imperialism of Free Trade', *Economic History Review*, Second Series, VI (1953), pp. 1–15; J. C. Ingram, *Economic Change in Thailand, 1850–1970* (Stanford, Calif., 1971).

[21] Malcolm Falkus, 'Early British Business in Thailand', in R. P. T. Davenport-Hines and Geoffrey Jones, eds., *British Business in Asia since 1860* (Cambridge, 1989), pp. 117–56.

financial and economic policies, in fact their advice coincided with and generally confirmed the intentions of the Thai government.[22]

Quite as significant as Chulalongkorn's domestic policies in ensuring that Thailand avoided colonial control was Anglo-French rivalry in the area. Mindful of the proverb that 'when elephants fight the grass is trampled',[23] Chulalongkorn followed a course that had characterized Siam's earlier relations with Burma and Indo-China: he made concessions to stronger neighbours in order to protect the independence and integrity of the core of his kingdom. Pressed on his eastern flank by the French, he accepted their annexation of Sipsong Chu Thai (the Twelve Thai States in the hills bordering Tongking) in 1888, surrendered all land east of the Mekong in 1893, and relinquished territory on the west bank in 1904–07. The stability of Siam was of major importance for British foreign policy in the region: were it to disintegrate or succumb to partition, a cushion between British India and French Indo-China would be lost. Another fear was that the French, Germans, or Russians might win the concession to cut a canal across the Kra isthmus, thereby circumventing Singapore, destroying its prosperity, and negating its strategic value. To prevent this, Britain first guaranteed the security of the Chao Phraya valley (that is, the heartland of Siam) through a joint Anglo-French Declaration (January 1896), and secondly, concluded a secret Anglo-Thai Convention (April 1897). By this Convention, Siam agreed not to make concessions in the Siamese Malay states and Britain offered support 'in resisting any attempt by a third Power to acquire dominion or to establish its influence or Protectorate' in that area.[24]

Subsequent events contributed to a more direct approach to Siam by the Foreign Office. The *entente cordiale* of 1904 relaxed Anglo-French tension in South-East Asia and continuing rumours of German and Russian designs on the Kra isthmus suggested that the secret Convention of 1897 was an inadequate safeguard against European interference in southern Siam. Consequently, the Foreign Office abandoned its opposition to the extension of colonial influence into the four northern Malay states. In March 1909 Ralph Paget, British Minister at Bangkok, concluded with Prince Devawongse, Foreign Minister of Siam, a treaty by which the Thais transferred to the British suzerainty over Kedah, Perlis,

---

[22] Ian Brown, 'British Financial Advisers in Siam in the Reign of King Chulalongkorn', *Modern Asian Studies* (hereafter *MAS*), XII, 2 (1978), pp. 193–215; and *The Elite and the Economy in Siam, c.1890–1920* (Singapore, 1989).

[23] Chandran Jeshuran, *The Contest for Siam, 1889–1902* (Kuala Lumpur, 1977); Patrick Tuck, *The French Wolf and the Siamese Lamb: The French Threat to Siamese Independence, 1858–1907* (Bangkok, 1995). This proverb is shared with Burma and some African societies, see John D. Hargreaves, *West Africa Partitioned: The Elephants and the Grass* (London, 1985), p. xiii.

[24] Allen, Stockwell, and Wright, eds., *A Collection of Treaties*, II, pp. 327–28.

Kelantan, and Trengganu, agreed not to admit the military presence of a third party into southern Siam, and granted the British the exclusive right to finance and supervise the construction of a railway linking Bangkok to Singapore. Britain, responding to Thai national concerns, surrendered the extraterritorial privilege of consular jurisdiction over British subjects in Siam.

BURMA

Geopolitics partly account for the contrasting fortunes of Siam and Burma in the age of European expansion. Whereas Siam's independence was underpinned by its position as a buffer between British and French empires, that of Burma was undermined owing to its location on the borders of British India. In addition, the Siamese were far more accommodating than the Burmese in responding to Western commercial ambitions and strategic concerns. While the Chakri kings avoided colonial rule by concluding unequal treaties with the British, the Konbaung dynasty ultimately failed either to resist or to meet British demands. Having lost territory to the British, the power and authority of the Burmese kings diminished, so that Mindon's strategy of co-operating with the West provoked discontent and bids for the throne. Moreover, the cloud of mutual mistrust and incomprehension overshadowing Anglo-Burmese relations, which lifted briefly during his reign, descended again in its last decade when the appetite of Rangoon merchants for further concessions seemed insatiable and the British and French competed over the route to Yunnan. Although Mindon handled this rivalry skilfully, the British were wary of his association with the French. Furthermore, in the mid-1870s disturbances involving the Red Karens of western Karenni rekindled the frontier issue. Deteriorating relations between Burmese Mandalay and British Rangoon were aggravated by the customary requirement that the British Resident remove his shoes in the presence of the king. Most significant of all for the collapse of the Anglo-Burmese *modus operandi* was Mindon's failure to secure the succession. As the Burmese saying put it, 'very difficult is the time of the changing of kings'.[25]

On the death of Mindon Min in 1878, Thibaw seized the throne in a blood bath that signalled renewed upheavals at court and elsewhere. At war with Afghan and Zulu, the British government avoided a clash with the Burmese and withdrew the Residency from Mandalay in September 1879. Non-confrontation continued during Gladstone's administration (1880–85) and the Viceroyalty of Lord Ripon (1880–84), but complaints of Rangoon merchants that the Burmese were failing to observe commercial agreements came to a head in 1885 when the *hluttaw* (council of ministers) imposed a swingeing fine on the Bombay-Burmah Trading

---

[25] Leslie Glass, *The Changing of Kings: Memories of Burma, 1934–1949* (London, 1985), p. 1.

Corporation for breaching the terms of a forestry concession. The chambers of commerce were outraged and the Government of India issued three principal demands: that the fine be suspended pending an investigation; that the British Residency in Mandalay be reopened; and that Burma place its foreign relations under British control. When Thibaw rejected this ultimatum, a force under General Prendergast invaded Upper Burma on 14 November 1885 and occupied Mandalay two weeks later (see Map 17.1).

Historians have debated the relative importance of political, economic, cultural, and strategic factors in Britain's decision to go to war with Burma a third time.[26] Lord Randolph Churchill (Secretary of State for India in Lord Salisbury's government of June 1885–January 1886) was well aware of the inherent risks. War might antagonize China, and the Conservatives could not afford a reversal like that recently experienced by the Liberal government when the Russians occupied Penjdeh in Afghanistan. Yet inaction could result in a disaster such as Gladstone had suffered in January 1885 when the British relief force reached Khartoum two days too late to save General Gordon. Victory, on the other hand, might improve Churchill's personal stock, even that of his party, while augmenting British commerce and restraining French expansion. Ultimately the Viceroy, Lord Dufferin, and the Prime Minister, Lord Salisbury, were more exercised by the prospect of a French presence on the borders of British India than by injuries to British pride or northern Burma's commercial potential. Although their understanding of French designs was obscured by rumour, the British discovered that the Franco-Burmese commercial treaty had been followed up in January 1885 with a letter promising Thibaw supplies of French arms via Tongking.

The war itself was soon over, but 'pacification' of the country tied down some 30,000 troops and Indian police until 1890. The first task being to restore order, the second was to establish a system of government. The British had promptly deposed Thibaw and, in the absence of an amenable heir and with exaggerated expectations of wealth to be derived from unimpeded access to Upper Burma, they were in no mood to cultivate a client state. Instead, having discounted a claim that Burma was a tributary of China, they annexed it on 1 January 1886. Thereafter they treated the whole of Burma as a province of British India, building on foundations laid in 1862 when Lower Burma had been annexed.

In contrast to the pragmatic sensitivity which they learned to adopt towards the customs and religion of the Malays, the British substituted forms of direct rule for

---

[26] D. P. Singhal, *The Annexation of Upper Burma* (Singapore, 1960); Dorothy Woodman, *The Making of Burma* (London, 1962), pp. 222–46; A. T. Q. Stewart, *The Pagoda War: Lord Dufferin and the Fall of the Kingdom of Ava, 1885–6* (London, 1972); E. Chew, 'The Fall of the Burmese Kingdom in 1885: Review and Reconsideration', *Journal of Southeast Asian Studies*, X, 2 (1979); Robert Vicat Turrell, 'Conquest and Concession: The Case of the Burma Ruby Mines', *MAS*, XXII, 1 (1988), pp. 141–63.

the monarchy, council of ministers, and 'circle headmen' (*myothugyis*). The new regime also dispensed with indigenous distinctions of status and disparaged the social role of Buddhism. Bereft of monarchical patronage, the authority of the *sangha* (monkhood) and *thathanabaing* (head of the monkhood) declined and monastic education languished. Central government of the colonial state was anchored in bureaucracy, lawcourts, police, and the Indian Army. As it acquired new functions, so government set up departments for forests, agriculture, public works, and so on. Local government adapted models from India; thus Burmese 'circle headmen' were replaced by an imported system of district and village administration. The colonial state has been called a leviathan,[27] but although it tore at the fabric of old Burma, its impact was uneven and its reach limited. As in the Konbaung era, the outlying Shan states and hill areas inhabited by Chin, Kachin, and Karen peoples remained semi-detached from 'Burma proper' and were administered indirectly through indigenous authorities.

As in Malaya, the government encouraged trade and created conditions in which private enterprise flourished. The colonial economy depended on the extraction, processing, and export of rice, timber, and later, oil. Migrant farmers from Upper Burma, immigrant labourers from India, and abundant cash credits provided by *chettiars* (Madras moneylenders) transformed the Irrawaddy delta into a major rice bowl exporting grain to Europe, India, and elsewhere in Asia. Of the rice exports entering the world market by 1914, mainland South-East Asia supplied 90 per cent, of which over 60 per cent came from Burma.[28] Most of the small, up-country rice mills were owned by Burmese, but Chinese and Indian merchants were prominent in rice trade with Asian ports. The larger mills and the rice trade with Europe, however, were in British hands. The government modified *laissez-faire* principles in the case of forestry, where it adopted the pre-colonial precedent of state ownership. Officials used forestry policy to control the Karens and circumscribe their shifting lifestyle, and the means to assert government's proprietary right over the rich resources of timber. Teak was exploited either by the government's own forestry department or by lessees, such as the Bombay Burma Trading Corporation and Macgregor & Company.[29]

Relationships between government and business were close, although the extent of their complicity in the exploitation of Burma is open to debate. George Orwell's Flory asserted that the 'official holds the Burman down while the businessman

[27] J. S. Furnivall, 'The Fashioning of Leviathan: The Beginnings of British Rule in Burma', *Journal of the Burma Research Society*, XXIX, 3 (1939), pp. 1–138.

[28] Paul H. Kratoska, 'The British Empire and the Southeast Asian Rice Crisis of 1919–1921', *MAS*, XIV, 1 (1990), p. 117.

[29] Raymond L. Bryant, 'Shifting the Cultivator: The Politics of Teak Regeneration in Colonial Burma', *MAS*, XXVIII, 2 (1994), pp. 225–50.

goes through his pockets', but Maurice Collis 'seldom met an English official who did not speak up for the Burmese'. Whatever their intentions, however, J. S. Furnivall argued that British administrators opened Burma to unbridled capitalism and Indian immigration. 'Under Burmese rule the Burman was a poor man in a poor country; now he is a poor man in a comparatively rich country.'[30] A 'plural society' emerged, separating ethnic communities with different social and economic roles. Whether peasants or professionals, the Burmese were vulnerable. Commercial development of rice exposed Burmese cultivators to agrarian indebtedness and expropriation by moneylenders, while the small Burmese middle class lost in the contest with the Indian bourgeoisie. By 1931 Indians, who amounted to only 7 per cent of the total population of 14,647,756, dominated internal banking and trade, were acquiring a major share of the best rice land, and competed with Burmese for skilled and unskilled jobs in Rangoon and the delta area.[31]

As with the Malays, nationalism was the means of identifying and consolidating a community challenged by Western colonialism and Asian immigration. Twenty years after Burmese princes led armed risings against the British to restore the old order, the Western-educated élite of the Young Men's Buddhist Association (1906) launched a Burmese cultural revival. After the First World War constitutional reformers, religious militants, republicans, and socialists would compete for the soul of the Burmese nation and, in so doing, clash not only with the British but also with immigrant groups and ethnic minorities.

As the British pursued their interests and extended their power in South-East Asia, the demarcation between those areas falling within Britain's formal Empire and those remaining outside it became indistinct. As the experience of Burma and Malaya showed, Britain never achieved omnipotence in those countries coloured 'British pink' on the map. Yet, as was seen in Siam or the channelling of much Netherlands East Indies trade through Singapore, Britain's influence was by no means excluded from territories which claimed to be independent or had succumbed to other colonialists. 'British pink' seeped over the whole region; nearly indelible in some areas, it merely tinged other parts and elsewhere faded fast.

Formal or informal, however, the British presence depended upon mechanisms of local collaboration. Such mechanisms fluctuated in their effectiveness, saddling each side with costs as well as benefits. Never better than rickety in Burma,

---

[30] George Orwell, *Burmese Days* (1934; London, 1967), p. 38; Maurice Collis, *Trials in Burma* (1938; London, 1945) p. 52; J. S. Furnivall in 1948, cited by R. H. Taylor, 'Disaster or Release? J. S. Furnivall and the Bankruptcy of Burma', *MAS*, XXIX, 1 (1995), p. 53. Orwell (Eric Blair) served in Burma in the Indian Imperial Police, 1922–27; Collis and Furnivall served in Burma in the Indian Civil Service in 1912–34 and 1902–23 respectively.

[31] Robert H. Taylor, *The State in Burma* (London, 1987), pp. 123–47.

collaboration contributed to overall, though fragmented, British control in Malaya, while in Siam it could inhibit as well as assist the acquisition of influence. Formal British rule depended on the active co-operation of traditional rulers, village headmen, council members, and Asian clerks, all of whom acquired vested interests in the colonial regime. Simultaneously, the new order alienated many more. Its institutions, ideas, and material demands posed a threat, as well as offering an alternative, to pre-colonial ways. Such threats provoked resistance of many kinds.[32] Before 1914, however, the British always overcame opposition in the end, if only by resorting to assistance from the Indian Army and Royal Navy.

Alongside local collaboration, the maintenance of British interests in South-East Asia necessitated compromise with other Western states. Although their power surpassed that of the French, Spanish, and gigantic Netherlands East Indies, international challenges between 1870 and 1914 forced the British into international deals. As the British and Dutch effectively occupied their respective spheres in the late nineteenth century, so they adjusted the arrangements contained in their 1824 Treaty. Similarly, in 1885 the British accommodated Spain over the frontier between British Borneo and the Philippines. Again, Britain contained French ambitions, not only by pre-emptive bids for further territory in Burma but also through diplomatic negotiations with respect to Siam. Although powerless to affect the outcome of the Spanish-American War of 1898–99, Britain somewhat grudgingly accepted US occupation of the Philippines, not least because it was preferable to that of, say, Germany. Indeed, the rise of Germany, together with the costs of global commitments, drove British governments into major agreements with Japan (1902), France (1904), and Russia (1907). By 1914 Britain's global pre-eminence may have been weakening but its position in South-East Asia was not seriously challenged. Despite shallow roots in many parts of the region, Britain's presence had yet to be shaken by nationalist protests or the international aspirations of Japan and the United States.

[32] See chap. by Susan Bayly; for twentieth-century nationalism, see Vol. IV, chap. by A. J. Stockwell.

Select Bibliography

MICHAEL ADAS, *The Burma Delta: Economic Development and Social Change on an Asian Rice Frontier, 1852–1941* (Madison, 1971).

BARBARA WATSON ANDAYA and LEONARD Y. ANDAYA, *A History of Malaysia* (London, 1982).

IAN BLACK, *A Gambling Style of Government: The Establishment of Chartered Company Rule in Sabah, 1878–1915* (Kuala Lumpur, 1983).

JOHN BUTCHER, *The British in Malaya, 1880–1941: The Social History of a European Community in Colonial Southeast Asia* (Kuala Lumpur, 1979).

JOHN F. CADY, *A History of Modern Burma* (Ithaca, NY, 1958).

C. D. COWAN, *Nineteenth-Century Malaya: The Origins of British Political Control* (London, 1961).

J. H. DRABBLE, *Rubber in Malaya, 1876–1922: The Genesis of the Industry* (Kuala Lumpur, 1973).

D. G. E. HALL, *A History of South-East Asia*, 4th edn. (London, 1981).

ROBERT HEUSSLER, *British Rule in Malaya: The Malayan Civil Service and Its Predecessors, 1867–1941* (Westport, Conn., 1981).

OLIVER B. POLLAK, *Empires in Collision: Anglo-Burmese Relations in the Mid-Nineteenth Century* (Westport, Conn., 1979).

ROBERT PRINGLE, *Rajahs and Rebels: The Ibans of Sarawak under Brooke Rule, 1841–1941* (New York, 1970).

WILLIAM R. ROFF, *The Origins of Malay Nationalism* (New Haven, 1967).

EMILY SADKA, *The Protected Malay States, 1874–1895* (Kuala Lumpur, 1968).

D. J. STEINBERG and others, *In Search of Southeast Asia: A Modern History*, 2nd edn. (Honolulu, 1987).

NICHOLAS TARLING, *Imperial Britain in South-East Asia* (Kuala Lumpur, 1975).

—— ed., *The Cambridge History of Southeast Asia*, Vol. II, *The Nineteenth and Twentieth Centuries* (Cambridge, 1992).

ROBERT H. TAYLOR, *The State in Burma* (London, 1987).

C. M. TURNBULL, *The Straits Settlements, 1826–1867: Indian Presidency to Crown Colony* (London, 1972).

DAVID K. WYATT, *Thailand: A Short History* (New Haven, 1982).

18

India, 1818–1860: The Two Faces Of Colonialism

D. A. WASHBROOK

The history of British India from the abdication of the Peshwa of Poona (1818), which secured the East India Company's supremacy, to the Great Mutiny of 1857 possesses many paradoxes. On the one hand, it can be seen as marked by a growing self-confidence among the British public and policy-makers in the 'world-destiny' of their own civilization and Imperial project. India was subjected to a battery of changes aimed at drawing it more closely under the authority of Britain and converting its culture and institutions to Western and Anglicist norms and forms. Familiarly, Parliament attempted to erode the Company's old monopoly trading privileges, utilizing the Charter Acts of 1813, 1833, and 1853 to open out the Indian economy to the forces of 'free trade' and market competition. Reforming Governors-General, such as William Bentinck (1829–35), legislated against the 'abominal' customs of *suttee* (widow suicide) and female infanticide, while innumerable lower-level officials promoted the causes of evangelical Christianity and/or Utilitarian rationality. The historian Thomas Macaulay proclaimed the transforming mission of Western education and heralded the virtues of an emergent race of 'brown Englishmen', while the colonial state steadily withdrew its patronage from the support of Hinduism and Islam. India was to become part not merely of a *Pax Britannica* but of a *Civilis Britannica* too.[1]

However, if this period is viewed less from the perspectives of British rule and more from those of the practices of Indian society, its meaning can be construed quite differently. While some Indian intellectuals, most notably around the British capital of Calcutta, may have responded positively to the new Anglicizing spirit and generated their own cultural 'renaissance',[2] elsewhere the signs of any 'beginnings of modernization' are difficult to detect. The economy hardly boomed as a result of its 'liberation': the second quarter of the nineteenth century witnessed a prolonged depression during which the growth of the colonial port-cities of

---

[1] For an interpretation following these themes, see C. H. Philips and Mary Doreen Wainwright, eds, *Indian Society and the Beginnings of Modernisation, c.1830–1850* (London, 1976).

[2] David Kopf, *British Orientalism and the Bengal Renaissance: The Dynamics of Indian Modernization, 1773–1835* (Berkeley, 1969).

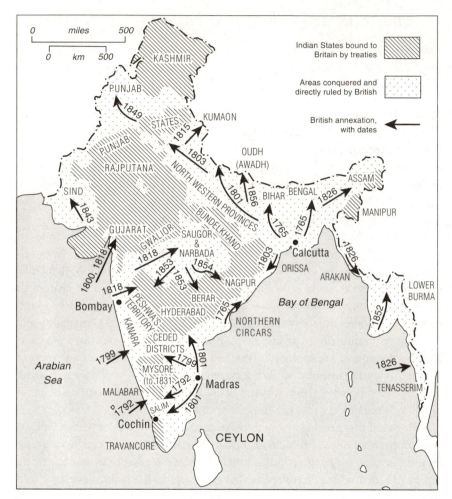

MAP 18.1. Pre-Mutiny India

Calcutta, Madras, and Bombay was more than offset by de-urbanization and de-industrialization in the hinterland.[3] India's social economy, which once had provided 'the workshop' of the early modern world, became increasingly agrarian and peasant-based. Traditional institutions, most obviously the Brahmanic caste system, were also scarcely uprooted. Rather, caste became more rigidified and spread its influence into areas—ranging from the ritual practices of South Indian temples, to the honours systems of Indian princes, to the distribution of access to land—where it had been less pervasive earlier.[4] Residual Indian kings, or maharajas, also developed royal styles which emphasized the antiquity of their origins and permanence of their authority to degrees never seen before. In other domains, the proportion of Indians pursuing Western education and, even more, converting to Christianity remained extremely small. But revivalist and fundamentalist currents in Hinduism and Islam were regularly stirred, making Indian society more overtly 'religious' and 'sectarian' than prior to British rule.[5] In the terms through which they viewed the world, Bentinck and Macaulay were preaching sermons on Westernization and progress to an Indian society which was actually becoming more 'Oriental' and 'backward'.

One way of unravelling this paradox is to see Indian society's reactions to the new colonial hegemony as dominated by resistance and reaction. It was precisely because the assault of Western modernity was so fierce that large areas of Indian society came to reject it and to promote counter-ideologies premissed on the self-conscious defence of tenaciously held 'traditions'. For many years, the responses represented in the Great Mutiny and Civil Rebellion of 1857 were interpreted in this light.[6] More recently, a new historiography of the 'subaltern' orders of society has highlighted similar imperatives.[7]

However, such an approach may not be entirely satisfactory and colonial Indian history not easily reduced to a simple dialectic of domination and resistance. In the first place, many of the 'traditions' which now were evoked appear to have been new. Several of the Islamic and Hindu religious movements emerging in this period bore the hallmarks of engagement with Christianity, frequently adopting

---

[3] C. A. Bayly, *Indian Society and the Making of the British Empire* (Cambridge, 1989), chap. 5.

[4] Arjun Appadurai, *Worship and Conflict under Colonial Rule: A South Indian Case* (Cambridge, 1981), chap. 5; Nicholas B. Dirks, *The Hollow Crown: Ethno-History of an Indian Kingdom* (Cambridge, 1987), chaps. 8, 12; Susan Bayly, *Saints, Goddesses and Kings: Muslims and Christians in South Indian Society, 1700–1900* (Cambridge, 1989), esp. part 2.

[5] Avril Powell, *Muslims and Missionaries in Pre-Mutiny India* (London, 1993); Sugata Bose, *Peasant Labour and Colonial Capital: Rural Bengal since 1770* (Cambridge, 1993), chap. 2; Kenneth W. Jones, *Socio-Religious Movements in British India* (Cambridge, 1989), chap. 2.

[6] Thomas R. Metcalf, *The Aftermath of Revolt: India, 1857–1870* (Princeton, 1964).

[7] Ranajit Guha, *Elementary Aspects of Peasant Insurgency in Colonial India* (Delhi, 1983).

its forms of discourse and weaponry of the printing-press.[8] Ideas concerning the etiquette of caste, the longevity of 'the village community', and the prerogatives of royalty also drew on an infusion of Western concepts.[9] Secondly, much of society's 'traditionalization' carried no obvious implications for anti-colonial resistance but rather reflected adaptation to new circumstances. The many members of India's once-great 'military market-place'[10] and erstwhile manufacturing economy, who now were pushed out on to the land, did not become 'traditional' peasants by choice; nor, by doing so, did they challenge the dictates of their new colonial masters. Indeed—and thirdly—in a large number of areas the traditionalization of society appears to have been promoted by the logic of colonial institutions themselves. It was the Anglo-Hindu lawcourts which enforced the rule of the Brahmanic caste system and disseminated it to deeper social levels.[11] It was the tribunals of the colonial bureaucracy which decreed agrarian society to be based on the self-sufficient village community and the privileges of royalty and aristocracy to be founded on 'ancient' prerogatives held since 'time immemorial'.[12] The assertion of India's Tradition in this context reflected as much an accommodation to the new colonial order as a rejection of it.

But why and how did British rule itself effect these imperatives towards the reconstruction of a traditional India? Here, perhaps, our received historiography has been guilty of too eclectic an approach to the discourse(s) of colonialism, and also of overemphasizing the significance of discourse (and texts) at the expense of analyses of both institutional practice and politico-economic context. Macaulay and Bentinck were not the only British statesmen to address Indian society, nor necessarily the most important. Their sojourns in India were brief and the audiences to which they spoke were largely British. Long-term Company officials—such as Thomas Munro, Charles Metcalfe, John Malcolm, and Mountstuart Elphinstone—made a far greater impact on India's effective government and held very different views.[13] Equally, current methodological obsessions with 'the word' may risk blinding history to 'the act', the unintended effects of institutional structures and the external pressures constraining the making of decisions. Even had British rulers seriously sought to Westernize Indian society they might

---

[8] Powell, *Muslims and Missions*, chaps. 5, 6; Jones, *Socio-Religious Movements*, chaps. 2, 3.

[9] Ronald Inden, *Imagining India* (Oxford, 1990); Clive Dewey, 'Images of the Village Community', *Modern Asian Studies* (hereafter *MAS*), VI, 3 (1972), pp. 291–328.

[10] See Vol. II, pp. 197–201; D. H. A. Kolff, *Naukar, Rajput and Sepoy: The Ethno-History of the Military Labour Market in Hindustan, 1450–1850* (Cambridge, 1990), chap. 1.

[11] Appadurai, *Worship*, chap. 5.

[12] Peter Robb, *Ancient Rights and Future Comfort: Bihar, The Bengal Tenancy Act of 1885, and British Rule in India* (London, 1997), chap. 5.

[13] For the differences, see Javed Majeed, *Ungoverned Imaginings: James Mill's 'History of India' and Orientalism* (Oxford, 1992).

not have been able to do so, and their failed attempts could have diverted its development in other directions.

If British rule in India in this period is approached from these angles, its character begins to take on a very different appearance. The predominant effects which it had (both intended and unintended) were less to transport British civilization to the East than to construct there a society founded on the perpetuation of 'Oriental' difference, as Edward Said has put it.[14] India became a subordinate agricultural colony under the dominance of metropolitan, industrial Britain; its basic cultural institutions were disempowered and 'fixed' in unchanging traditional forms; its 'civil society' was subjected to the suzereignty of a military despotic state. British rule before the Mutiny may be credited with having fundamentally changed Indian society. But this change moved against the anticipations of 'modernization' and left it with a vast legacy of 'backwardness' subsequently to undo.

From Conquest to . . . Conquest

If the East India Company's supremacy in India was signalled by the Treaty of Bassein (1802) and the final defeat of the Maratha Confederacy in 1818, the process leading up to it had already been long and complex and riven with many contradictions. The foundations of the Company's power in Bengal had been laid between the 1750s and 1770s by the likes of Robert Clive and Warren Hastings. Soldierly men, they had few illusions that the sources of the Company's dominance in India rested on anything other than gunpowder and musket-fire. Both also eschewed visions of a society in 'British' India founded on anything other than inherited Indian institutions—most notably those of 'Oriental despotism', which would give their state (and its rapacious officials) virtually unlimited authority.[15]

But the Clive–Hastings 'model' of Indian Empire had provoked great controversy in Britain, where it was assailed by Company shareholders concerned at its costs and parliamentarians fearful that it jeopardized 'the liberties of free-born Englishmen'. In 1786 Lord Cornwallis had been sent to India with specific instructions to curtail the rapine and bring Bengal under both British and 'civilized' government. Famously, he sought to fulfil his mandate by separating the civil and military powers of the state and bringing the latter under control of the former. He also sought to separate executive and judicial powers through a new legal system; to introduce private property rights in land through a Permanent Settlement

[14] Edward W. Said, *Orientalism* (London, 1978).
[15] In Vol. II, see chap. by Rajat Kanta Ray; P. J. Marshall, *Bengal: The British Bridgehead: Eastern India, 1740–1828* (Cambridge, 1987), chap. 4.

(1793), which would safeguard them from the revenue demands of the state; and to create a 'civil service' which depended for its income more on official salaries than the profits of private trade and the perquisites of local power.[16]

Interpretations of the nature of the colonial state after Cornwallis and through the early nineteenth century have been inclined to assume that its development continued along the lines which he set for it. And, in institutional terms, he undoubtedly set up a certain momentum. Parliament, through legislation and a Board of Control under its President (a member of the Cabinet), exercised an ever more detailed regulation of Indian affairs. The idea of 'professional' civil service was enhanced by the creation subsequently of training schools in England, at Haileybury College, and in India, at Fort William College. Lawcourts proliferated through the Company's expanding territories, notionally securing 'private' rights and property under the rule of law.

The significance of these developments cannot be denied, especially for India's long-term future. Parliament, for example, attempted to open further the Company's territories to Christian missionaries in 1813. The training colleges produced a breed of officials very different from the old, most of whom had come to India in early adolescence and grown up amidst the violence of the Company's conquests. Now the Company's servants were to spend their formative years at home receiving instruction on the scientific principles of political economy from the likes of Thomas Malthus, and imbibing the atmosphere of British evangelical revival. Their educational background has been seen as a crucial link between the Company state's expansion and the 'civilizing mission' which it is held to have adopted.[17]

However, this scenario overlooks a crucial phase in the development of British power in India: a phase which was marked by a sharp reversion to the militarism and ideology associated with the Clive–Hastings era and which, until the first Haileybury generation began to achieve senior offices in the 1840s, left the Company state in the hands of men schooled in the politics and styles of the eighteenth century. This phase arose from the dynamics of the conquest which, from 1792, saw the Company break out of its original, limited enclave in Bengal and, especially through victories over Mysore (1792 and 1799) and the Marathas (1803–05 and 1816), establish the power of its arms over the subcontinent. The conquest released imperatives which contradicted the principles on which Cornwallis had reformed the Bengal state: if his mandate was to stabilize, 'settle', and constrain, that of his immediate successors was to expand, aggrandize, and predominate. During these

---

[16] In Vol. II, see pp. 511–21; 546. P. J. Marshall, *Problems of Empire: Britain and India, 1757–1813* (London, 1968), chaps. 1, 2.

[17] Gauri Viswanathan, *Masks of Conquest: Literary Studies and British Rule in India* (New York, 1990).

years the military reasserted its effective authority over the civilian branches of government and left its own legacy not only on the state's political character, but also on the position of 'British' India in the world. For of course these conquests were but part of that much wider expansion of British power taking place during the Revolutionary and Napoleonic wars against France.[18] Out of them, Britain emerged with a newly dominant global status to which India was central, and to serve which Indian development came subsequently to be directed.

Following the defeat of Napoleonic France in 1815 Britain faced no significant international rivals (other then Russia in Central Asia) and built the framework of an Empire in the East which eventually stretched from southern Africa, through South-East Asia, to Australia. One source of the power sustaining this framework was always the Royal Navy. But the second source was the Company's forces in India, which added to Britain's Imperial position an element previously lacking— a major land-based army. The Company's army and the British navy had first come together in India during the Seven Years War (1756–63) to defeat the French and secure dominance over Bengal. Their relationship remained close and continuous during the various conquests leading up to the defeat of the Marathas, and demonstrated its extra-Indian significance as early as 1799, when the two joined forces to evict Napoleon from Egypt. Thereafter, they represented the hammer and anvil of British Imperial power in the world.

For India's own destiny, this was to be extremely consequential. Its most obvious implication was that, following the achievement of domestic supremacy, the vast war-machine that the British had built up in the course of effecting their conquest was not dismantled. Rather, it was maintained intact and utilized for further conquests and 'police' duties beyond British-Indian borders and around the world.

In a first set of manoeuvres, the machine swung eastwards following the lead that it had taken during the Napoleonic Wars when it had captured Dutch Java (1811). Singapore was acquired in 1819; the kingdom of Burma defeated and weakened (1824–26); China opened up to British trade by the First Opium War (1839–42). It then turned to the north-west. By the early 1830s Russian expansion into Central Asia was starting to cause Calcutta concern. Although the First Afghan War (1838–42) proved a disaster, it cleared the way for the conquest of Sind (1843), and eventually for the conquest of Punjab (1845–49). Ranjit Singh's great military state had held British expansionary ambitions in check for a generation. But following his death in 1839 it broke apart in turmoil—enabling the Company to extend its Indian domains right up to the 'North-West Frontier'.[19]

---

[18] C. A. Bayly, *Imperial Meridian: The British Empire and the World, 1780–1830* (London, 1989).
[19] Stanley A. Wolpert, *A New History of India*, 2nd. edn. (Oxford, 1982), chaps. 14, 15.

To sustain this continuous process of expansion, the Government of India from the mid-1820s maintained sixteen European regiments of the line as well as a permanent standing army of 170 sepoy regiments, totalling 235,000 men,[20] which represented the preponderant military force in all of Asia. Inevitably, its military institutions and purposes came to shape both state and society. Government in the newly acquired territories passed first into the hands of the soldiers who had conquered them—and often remained there for a considerable time. Munro, Malcolm, Metcalfe, and Elphinstone, who had won their spurs on fields of battle, became the dominant voices for the next generation in the provincial governments of Madras, Central India, North India, and Bombay respectively. Military influence even crept back into the government of Bengal: when, in 1824, the Bengal Army sought to mobilize for the Burma War, it was severely hampered by the number of its officers under secondment to the 'civil' service, as *de facto* Collectors and Magistrates. For Indian society too, martial qualities acquired a special premium. Those social groups who supplied loyal soldiers to the Company found themselves in receipt of special privileges and protections; and Indian princes, who contributed men and money to the Imperial effort, were treated as valuable allies—to be protected, if necessary, against the protests of their own subjects.

Military imperatives also clearly came to dictate economic policies. The army was extremely expensive and absorbed most available revenues. This made the state very reluctant to give up potential income by withdrawing from the many economic activities which it had inherited from its Indian predecessors. Parliament might attempt to prise a range of concessions for 'free' business interests— dismantling the Company's erstwhile monopolies on Indo- and Sino-British trade in 1813 and 1833—but it would be a mistake to see the Indian economy opened up to anything resembling 'free trade' in this period.

The most crucial element in the structure of the Indian economy was the land revenue system. Parliament made no move to weaken the Company's grip on this. Indeed, under the terms of the 1813 Charter Act it sanctioned procedures guaranteeing the Company increased rights of extraction. Cornwallis's Permanent Settlement had placed severe restrictions on the Company's ability to raise the revenue demand in Bengal. But the new Act sanctioned the adoption of a different *ryotwari* system of land settlement in most of the Company's newly acquired territories.[21] The *ryotwari* system permitted the direct taxation of 'individual' peasants (or *ryots*) in ways which facilitated the continuous revision and raising

---

[20] Douglas M. Peers, *Between Mars and Mammon: Colonial Armies and the Garrison State in India, 1819–1835* (London, 1995), p. 133.

[21] Burton Stein, *Thomas Munro: The Origins of the Colonial State and His Vision of Empire* (New Delhi, 1989), chaps. 3, 4.

of assessment levels.[22] The economies in these regions were then squeezed extremely hard to compensate for the revenue deficiencies of Bengal.

Parliament also made no serious effort to touch the range of monopolies which the Company now held over a wide range of the most valuable items of domestic Indian commerce. These included the production of opium, salt, saltpetre, and of high-priced woods and minerals, and the rights to retail tobacco, alcohol, and betel. The Company's military state was backed and financed by an extremely powerful state economy and the interests of the one were closely intertwined with those of the other, especially with regard to expansion to the East and North-West.

Expectations in London that the conquest of India would lead to a greatly expanded trade with Britain for a long time were only partially fulfilled—and then in ways which caused the Company problems. During the 1820s imports of British goods into India grew quickly but then levelled off for most of the 1830s at £3–4m a year.[23] However, a major difficulty arose over exports. India lost many of her textile markets to the products of Britain's industrial revolution, and by 1830 the Company had decided to abandon 'the Investment' by which it had procured large quantities of Indian-manufactured cloth for sale in Britain and as a mean of remitting funds back to Europe. The purchase and export of indigo only partially filled this vacuum, for the indigo trade to Europe was highly unstable and ultimately contracted. Europe appeared to find less and less in India worthy of purchase.

It was, instead, towards the East that the export trade now began to develop. Cotton, silver, and above all opium reached a growing number of consumers in China and South-East Asia. In several years of the 1830s and 1840s opium sales exceeded £5m and, alone, were worth over 40 per cent of the total value of India's exports.[24] Leading British-Indian spokesmen fully acknowledged this fact and demanded greater power and freedom to exploit it. In 1837 John Crawfurd argued:

Opium is an article calculated to become of vast importance to the agriculture and commerce of India...the great marts for its consumption are the Malayan islands, the countries lying between India and China, and above all, China itself...Among these customers...whose numbers cannot well be estimated at fewer than 400 million people, opium has been more or less an item of consumption ever since we knew them. During the last fifty years it has been constantly on the increase...It would be absurd, then...to sacrifice a great national advantage.[25]

---

[22] Nilmani Mukherjee, *The Ryotwari System in Madras, 1792–1827* (Calcutta, 1962).

[23] K. N. Chaudhuri, *The Economic Development of India, 1814–1858: A Selection of Contemporary Writings* (Cambridge, 1971), p. 185.

[24] Ibid., pp. 38–50.

[25] Quoted in ibid., pp. 250–51.

That Indo-British military power also, along with the export trade, should have been swinging to the East was no coincidence. In economic terms, Company India was engaged in building perhaps the world's first 'narco-military' empire, an empire in which power and profit remained as closely linked as ever they had been in the Mercantilist Age of the eighteenth century. Similar considerations were also present in the subsequent swing to the North-West, although genuine fear of 'the Russian bear' played its part in this too. Until the 1830s the strength of the Punjab state had kept British soldiers from plundering the valley of the Indus and kept British business interests out of its lucrative overland trade to West and Central Asia. The 1840s saw Lord Napier pocket a private fortune of £50,000 from his conquest of Sind, and Western commerce find a new passage to Iran and the Middle East.[26]

A Very Military State

In the post-Napoleonic era, then, the Company state veered strongly away from the course suggested by Cornwallis's administration of Bengal and back to the 'military fiscalism' practised (and enjoyed) by Clive and Hastings. With this reversion went also a reappraisal of the virtues of ruling India according to Anglicist rather than Oriental principles. The fathers of this second age of expansionary imperialism were broadly of one mind that India must be governed according to its own, and not British, precedents: they looked to 'traditional' aristocracies, 'yeoman' peasantries, and the village community 'republic' as the foundations of India's future.[27] But one aspect of supposed Oriental Tradition particularly attracted their attention, as it had done that of Clive and Hastings. This was the idea of an Oriental Despotism by which the state might exercise unitary and untrammelled authority. Whether and how far the theories of sovereignty actually informing previous Indian regimes met the criteria of this concept has, today, become a much-debated issue.[28] However, in its neo-colonial form the concept provided an incisive tool for advancing the authority of the Company state—a state whose military victories now gave it an unprecedented concentration of armed power. Appealing to the precedents of Oriental despotism, the new generation of British rulers claimed a monopoly of legitimate coercive force within society and of authority over it. They also drew back together into the same hands

---

[26] Wolpert, New History, chap. 14.

[27] Stein, Thomas Munro, chap. 2; Kenneth Ballhatchet, Social Policy and Social Change in Western India, 1817–1830 (London, 1957); Thomas R. Metcalf, Ideologies of the Raj (Cambridge, 1994), chap. 3.

[28] André Wink, Land and Sovereignty in India: Agrarian Society and Politics under the Eighteenth-Century Maratha Svarajya (Cambridge, 1986). However, Wink's theory of a weak Mughal sovereignty is widely disputed. Compare John F. Richards, The Mughal Empire (Cambridge, 1993).

the civil, military, and judicial functions which Cornwallis had sought to separate; and they posited the sovereign (i.e. the Company) as ultimate possessor of all land and resources in India.[29]

The immediate corollary to this was that, at least outside Bengal, the military asserted itself as the dominant institution within the Company state. What Cornwallis had done in Bengal could not be undone, but in the new conquest territories it was certainly not to be done again. John Malcolm proclaimed the ethic of the post-Napoleonic era thus: 'Our government of . . . [India] is essentially military and our means of preserving and improving our possessions through the operation of our civil institutions depend on our wise and politic exercise of that military power on which the whole foundation rests.'[30] The Company's military power was now to be used, not merely externally for defence against Britain's enemies, but internally to inform the institutions and ethos of its rulership.

This was accomplished in several ways. The army was made highly visible through garrison policies which dispersed it widely across the country. Pacification policies were developed which treated the slightest manifestation of civil disorder as incipient revolt and punished it accordingly. Soldiers were deputed to attend many of the functions of civil government, such as revenue collection. Non-military departments of the state adopted military-style uniforms and rituals.

Some statesmen of the epoch even thought that the process ought to go further. Elphinstone favoured extending to civil executions the extreme mode of military execution—that of 'blowing from guns'. This was not accepted, but a less severe method of military discipline, that of flogging, came to be regarded as a highly appropriate punishment for an ever-widening range of 'civil' offences. Martial force—that is, torture—was also extensively used in such tasks as the collection of land revenue.[31] By the 1820s and 1830s the ideals of Cornwallis's government were becoming but a distant memory.

Moreover, in at least one area the military offensive against civil society left a lasting impression on Cornwallis's key legacy—the rule of law—and also contributed to the changing image in Britain of India as a 'barbarous' society almost beyond the pale of civilization. After the conquests of the Napoleonic era, the Company state was left with a major problem in the detritus of the *ancien régime's* political and military economy. In the last years of the eighteenth century as many as 2 million armed men may have circulated in India's 'military market-place', looking for mercenary employment in the armies of its regional potentates.[32] The

[29] Stein, *Munro*, chaps. 3, 4.

[30] John Malcolm, *The Political History of India from 1784 to 1823*, 2 vols. (London, 1826), II, p. 245.

[31] Government of Madras, *Report of the Commissioners for the Investigation of Alleged Cases of Torture in the Madras Presidency* (Madras, 1855).

[32] Kolff, *Naukar*, pp. 110–16.

Company's victories and subsequent dismantlement of the armies of defeated princes left employment in its own forces for barely a quarter of a million. What was to be done with the rest, and how could they be 'persuaded' to beat their swords into ploughshares and to 'settle' to pacific, peasant ways of life?

But a redundant mercenary soldiery was only part of the problem. Along the main arteries of communication, large numbers of semi-armed travelling peoples had circulated, moving commodities through the interior on pack-animals and sustaining the military operations of warring states.[33] In the countryside, many peasants who did not regularly leave the land for war none the less possessed weaponry and maintained traditions of armed resistance against the encroachment of superior authorities. On the forest fringes of settled agriculture, so-called 'tribal' groups regularly raided neighbouring cultivators—or taxed them in return for not raiding them.[34] All this represented an affront and a potential threat to the despotic authority which the Company state now imputed to itself.

In response, it turned its military frontier inwards and began sustained campaigning against the society over which it ruled. Wars were launched against the *pindaris*, former soldiers who continued their 'adventuring' in Central India. The forest fringes were physically cut back and their peoples subjected to heavy military repression for pursuing their age-old livelihoods.[35] Peasants were disarmed at gunpoint and travelling peoples fixed in their tracks—not infrequently to gallows trees. One consequence of this onslaught, not least to provide justification for the Company's swelling military budget, was the representation to British audiences of India as a primitive and violent society. Most famously, perhaps, the campaign to restrict the movement of travelling peoples was attended by attempts to whip up popular hysteria against *thugee*: supposedly, a cult of ritual murder pursued on India's roads in the service of the goddess Kali. Phillip Meadows Taylor penned a popular contemporary novel on the theme, and the image which it presented fixed India in British minds ever after as definitively 'Oriental' in its fanaticism and cruelty.[36]

However, the military onslaught also had another impact. It seriously questioned the principles of Cornwallis's rule of law. As the military frontier extended into civil society, army commanders were wont to suspend civil justice and enforce the rule of martial law instead—executing offenders on the most summary of charges. This gained part-institutionalization in the cases of travelling peoples and 'tribal' groups, who often became collectively proscribed and stripped of the

---

[33] C. A. Bayly, *Rulers, Townsmen and Bazaars: Northern Indian Society in the Age of British Expansion, 1770–1870* (Cambridge, 1983), chaps. 1, 5.

[34] Eric Stokes, *The Peasant Armed: The Indian Revolt of 1857*, ed. C. A. Bayly (Oxford, 1986), chap. 3.

[35] Guha, *Elementary Aspects, passim.*

[36] Philip Meadows Taylor, *Confessions of a Thug*, 3 vols. (London, 1839).

individual rights and protections enjoyed by 'civilized' members of society.[37] It was developed further by the claim of the state to prerogatives enabling it to exile 'undesirable' or 'dangerous' people at will and in a manner scarcely different from that of the Russian Tsar.

All this put the status of the rule of law at issue. In the newly expanded presidencies of Madras and Bombay, for example, Munro and Elphinstone sought deliberately to curtail the authority of the lawcourts. They combined together the powers of taxation, magistracy, and police in the single office of the Collector; demanded that the courts be deemed incompetent in revenue matters; and insisted that executive officials be immune from legal challenges to their decisions. Admittedly, the courts were by no means willing to concede the substance of their authority, and between the 1820s and 1840s there were repeated battles between the executive and judiciary.[38] But eventually the tension began to ease, although hardly in ways which defended the spirit of a rule of law. The courts had shown greatest independence in matters where they claimed to 'discover' customary law. However, afraid to permit Indian juries or even 'learned authorities' a dominant role in the discovery process, British judges stood on their own authority and failed to establish mechanisms which could give customary law the same independent status as common law in England. This left judicial rulings vulnerable to the pressures of statutory law which, there being no constitution or representative legislature, consisted merely of the general regulations and codifications promulgated by the executive itself.[39] These reduced the scope of judicial independence and imbued executive fiat with the sanctity of law.

Here, as in the colonial Empire more generally, the idea of a rule of law became fatally confused with that of a rule by law under which 'civil society', while perhaps directed by general legal principles, is denied any part itself in formulating those principles; while the state may make law for its subjects, it posits itself as above that law and as unaccountable to it. British-Indian law became less a tool of liberty than an instrument of despotism.

While the fuller implications of this position were to become clear only later, for Indian society before 1860 its most obvious consequence was that rights to private property in land—offered by Cornwallis and subsequently talked up by Company servants as Britain's greatest gift to India—remained indistinct from the state's revenue rights and therefore equivocal, at least outside greater Bengal. The revenue demand continued to be the prime determinant of both the value and the

---

[37] William van Schendel, 'Madmen of Mymensingh', *Indian Economic and Social History Review*, XXII (1985), pp. 139–83.

[38] D. A. Washbrook, 'Law, State and Agrarian Society in Colonial India', *MAS*, XV (1981), pp. 649–721.

[39] Ibid., p. 714.

ownership of land. The Oriental despotic state lived on; indeed, given the greater power which the Company state was able to wield against civil society, it was much more potent than it had ever been before.

The Economics of Backwardness.

Another reason why, perhaps, the Company state promoted the 'rule of Oriental difference' over that of Anglicization was that, from the late 1820s, the economy in most regions of India plunged into a recession and did not recover until the early 1850s. In many ways, the effects of this broke up the more advanced indigenous institutions of commerce and investment which had sustained India during its early-modern economic heyday, and fostered an expansion of more primitive forms of petty commodity production and peasant subsistence farming.

Until the 1820s the basic structures of India's legendary manufacturing industry and commercial economy had survived war and colonial conquest more or less intact. The economies of certain sub-regions no doubt suffered, but these received compensation as labour and capital migrated and restarted elsewhere. Indeed, in the decade 1815–25 there were signs of general growth.[40] Calcutta drew on a deepening hinterland for its expanding exports; Bombay and Madras began to experiment with new forms of the China trade. However, at the end of the 1820s a rot set in. A long-term depression saw the prices of all commodities, but particularly the foodstuffs which dominated agricultural production, falling in some cases to barely half their pre-1820s levels. Many high-quality forms of artisanal production went out of commission; long-established Indian commercial families were bankrupted; outside the main colonial cities, extensive de-urbanization took place.[41]

The broad origins of the depression can be traced to changes in the international economy to which India, with its large and historic textile export trade, was peculiarly vulnerable. India's high-quality export markets were undermined by the products of Britain's industrial revolution, while the beginnings of global economic integration under British Imperial auspices reduced commodity prices world-wide. India was scarcely unique in feeling the impact of the depression, but was much more so in the depth and length of time that depression lasted. For this, distinctive features of colonial rule can be held responsible.

First, the nature of the conquest generated problems of demand. The Company set about dismantling the courts and armies of those who had resisted its expansion and been conquered. But such kings and soldiers had previously possessed purchasing power to demand a wide variety of goods and services. As this

[40] Bayly, *Rulers*, chaps. 2–5.   [41] Ibid., chap. 7.

declined, the Company-state failed to spend in ways which could fill the gap. Its resources flowed out to Europe and to China; merchants, Collectors, and officials bought Western rather than local artisan-produced goods; wealth was concentrated in the main colonial centres at the expense of up-country towns. Where the new rulers congregated or maintained large military barracks, local economies could be stimulated and might even thrive. But such places were too few in number to make up for wide stretches of the hinterland denuded of consumers and markets.[42]

The problem of demand also had a direct corollary in a growing problem of supply. Many redundant soldiers, artisans, and servants made their way on to the land to take up agriculture. In most regions cultivation expanded ahead of a population, which itself may have been expanding more rapidly than at any other time in the century. But this increased volumes of production while markets were in decline. In the 1830s and 1840s many European commentators on Company India attributed its economic troubles to the difficulty of finding sales outlets. But until the transport revolution in steamships and railways later in the century, they were at a loss to come up with a satisfactory remedy.[43]

A further depressant was the nature of Company specie policy. At least until the Opium Wars (1839–42 and 1856–60) blew China open, British merchants were unable to meet all the costs of their purchases of China goods through opium sales. Raw cotton became an important item of export, but so too did silver taken from the Indian monetary system. As India itself produced little specie metal and as its traditional sources of import were drying up with the decline of textile exports, this led to an effective contraction of the money supply.[44]

A fourth set of pressures, perhaps less quantitative than qualitative, came from revenue and fiscal policy. On the one hand, outside the Permanently Settled regions of greater Bengal, the new revenue systems were not only heavy, but operated to inhibit investment. Rates of assessment were geared to soil fertility: the more productive the land, the higher the rates that it paid. In several areas, agriculturists—faced with climatic uncertainties and declining prices—moved from good land to bad and showed little inclination to invest in improving production lest they incur rate re-evaluations.[45]

In the Permanently Settled tracts, restrictions on the state's revenue demand ought to have removed this problem, but the harnessing of landlord proprietary

[42] Bayly, *Indian Society*, chap. 4.

[43] Ibid.

[44] Asiya Siddiqi, *Agrarian Change in a Northern Indian State: Uttar Pradesh, 1819–33* (Oxford, 1973), chap. 8; A. Sarada Raju, *Economic Conditions in the Madras Presidency, 1800–1850* (Madras, 1941), parts 6, 7.

[45] Mukherjee, *Ryotwari System*, chap. 6.

rights to the new coercive powers of the Company state ensured that they did not. In Bengal and Upper India large landlords armed with eviction writs went on 'rent offensives', which increased rates of extraction from agriculture in much the same way as elsewhere.[46] Further, in the course of settling the land, both state and landed proprietors had absorbed many forms of taxation immunity (*inam*), originally intended to encourage investment, especially in irrigation. Notionally, the state or landlord held these immunities in return for providing and maintaining water supplies, but both now neglected such responsibilities. In Madras between 1825 and 1845 the amount spent on irrigation works fell to less than 0.5 per cent of the land revenue gathered.[47]

The Company state also caused havoc to indigenous commercial and banking systems by separating its own 'treasury' institutions from them. A marked feature of the eighteenth century had been the increasing interpenetration of state fiscal and 'private' commercial networks. 'Great houses' of Indian bankers had progressively taken over the revenue rights of post-Mughal regional states 'on farm' and provided finances for the latter's activities. The Company during its rise to power had made full use of these connections.[48] In many senses, it was financed to power by indigenous bankers—in Bengal in the 1740s and 1750s, by the Jagath Seth; in southern and western India later on, by a number of leading Gujarati houses. However, after achieving preponderant state power the Company then began to reconsider the nature of its fiscal strategy, viewing the profits made by tax-farmers, bill-brokers, and money-changers as notional losses of its own revenues. Under the new revenue systems of the post-conquest era, tax-farming was heavily discouraged and fiscal management taken under the prerogative of state bureaucrats. 'Private' bankers were also denied access to the facilities and cash held in government treasuries.

The effects of these changes on the economy were very considerable. Although some historians have seen the tax-farming regimes of the eighteenth century as merely exploitative, others have emphasized the benefits which they brought to investment and production.[49] Bankers advanced money to producers and often themselves invested in improved irrigation works and manufacturing facilities. Shorn of the security provided by their access to state power and revenue rights, many now ceased to do so; while the preoccupations of the Company-state with military expansion gave productive investment a low priority in its spending plans.

---

[46] Bose, *Peasant Labour*, chap. 3.

[47] D. A. Washbrook, 'Progress and Problems: South Asian Economic and Social History, 1720–1860', *MAS*, XXI (1988), pp. 57–96.

[48] Bayly, *Rulers*, chap. 6; Lakshmi Subramanian, *Indigenous Capital and Imperial Expansion: Bombay, Surat and the West Coast* (Delhi, 1996), chap. 3.

[49] Wink, *Land and Sovereignty, passim*; Bayly, *Rulers and Townsmen*, chap. 2.

In separating its own fiscal system from that of indigenous capitalist agencies, the Company appealed both to new European principles of political economy, which took the move as necessary to 'sound' financial management, and to new principles of political theory, which regarded the separation of the spheres of 'the public' and 'the private'—of the state and 'civil society'—as crucial to moral progress. Previous forms of interconnection between the two were now conceived as tantamount to 'corruption'. However, in early colonial India the definition of what exactly comprised 'the public' and 'the state' was not at all clear. The Company might be conceived variously as a commercial corporation, the armed agency of a 'foreign' power, or even a latter-day Oriental despot. But it was hardly the representative of an Indian 'body politic', as the European theory of the 'public domain' decreed.[50] In these circumstances, its eager adoption of the discourse of public and private right may have masked an ulterior purpose. Under its guise, Indian capital could be removed from the heights of the economy and from close association with the state in order to be replaced with British capital.

British business houses now came to enjoy, if sometimes informally, privileged access to loans from state treasuries and banks, to licenses from state monopolies, to contracts for government supplies, and to powers over land and agricultural production in order to found plantations. Moreover, their deepening access to state power also saw them distancing themselves from indigenous businessmen and developing a greater 'racial' exclusivity. In Calcutta, particularly after the 'indigo' crisis of the late 1820s, new British firms arose—most noticeably in the expanding import trades—which eschewed forming partnerships with Indians;[51] in Bombay, London-based companies came to dominate over Indian-based agencies.[52] Again, the benefits of this shift to the Indian economy can be seriously doubted. British businessmen were reluctant to commit themselves to heavy fixed investments and always looked to repatriate their profits home.

But the shift also raises questions about the 'moral' character of the Company state. Cornwallis had tried to restrain the private-trade interests of government officials and, subsequently, London had organized a series of campaigns aimed at converting the Company's bureaucrats into 'disinterested' civil servants. One consequence of this was that, supposedly to weaken the attractions of 'corruption', the salaries of European officials in India were raised to astronomic heights, far

[50] Majeed, *Ungoverned Imaginings, passim.*

[51] Blair B. Kling, 'Economic Foundations of the Bengal Renaissance', in Rachel M. van Baumer, ed., *Aspects of Bengali History and Society* (Hawaii, 1975), pp. 26–42.

[52] Marika Vicziany, 'Bombay Merchants and Structural Changes in the Export Community, 1850–1880', in K. N. Chaudhuri and Clive J. Dewey, eds., *Economy and Society: Essays in Indian Economic and Social History* (New Delhi, 1979), pp. 163–96.

above those to be found anywhere else in the Empire and making Company Collectors financially equivalent to Maharajas.[53]

But even this scarcely broke the nexus between state office and business activity, although it may have relocated it from individuals to families. Access to Hailey-bury School, whence the Company now drew ever more of its officials, remained patronage-based and very restricted. Many families successfully gaining entry there also sent off other sons to train in the City of London. As a result, a series of family dynasties arose represented simultaneously in the Indian bureaucracy and in companies operating in India—usually in the same local regions. In Madras, for example, the Arbuthnots provided five successive generations of leading civil servants and ran the largest agency house and private bank in the presidency. The Stokes and Sullivans were not far behind them. 'Gentlemanly' combinations of office and business remained basic to the structures of Indian Empire, as much in the nineteenth as the eighteenth century—but combinations possible now only for Englishmen.[54]

The Traditionalization of Indian Society

It is perhaps against this background of neo-Oriental despotism, economic depression, and the displacement of Indians from the leading offices of wealth and power, that Indian society's passage towards 'backwardness' and 'traditional-ization' can most clearly be seen. Their combined effects were, first, to promote forces of 'peasantization'. Peasant petty-commodity production became ever more widespread as other employments—in artisan crafts, soldiering, and 'service'—weakened. Secondly, society also tended to become noticeably more 'sedentary'. This followed both from military policies aimed at dismantling the market in mercenaries and restricting the movement of travellers, and from revenue policies aimed at tying taxpaying peasants to the land. The new *ryotwari* settlements in Madras and Bombay, for example, threatened the peasant who failed to cultivate his fields (or, at least, to pay revenue on them) for a single year with loss of his lands. And thirdly, many parts of the social structure became flattened and 'homogenized' as once-complex sets of distinctions, which had articulated net-works of status within pre-colonial Indian kingdoms and been sustained by differential tax immunities, were crushed by the weight of the Company's revenue machine.[55] In the Permanently Settled tracts, admittedly, tenurial law continued to permit greater social diversity. None the less, the rental offensives of the 1830s

---

[53] Bayly, *Imperial Meridian*, chap. 6.

[54] P. J. Cain and A. G. Hopkins, *British Imperialism: Innovation and Expansion, 1688–1914* (London, 1993).

[55] Bayly, *Indian Society*, chap. 5.

and 1840s had something of the same effect here too. The pressures of the epoch beat down the agrarian order and rendered it static and 'fixed'.

Of course, rural society did not necessarily accept its fate passively and many of its members tried to take action. Local rebellions regularly punctuated the peace which Company rulers liked to present as their gift to India, and reached their apogee during the 1857 Mutiny. But age-old methods of defending local autonomies and distinctions were becoming difficult to apply: disarmament reduced possibilities of successful revolt and growing pressure on the land curtailed opportunities for migration. Moreover, the Company state conducted a subtle ideological campaign directed at persuading rural society that its new structure of relations was based upon its 'true' past, which had been disturbed by the 'anarchy' of the war-torn eighteenth century. Particularly important in this regard was the idea (borrowed from medieval Europe) that Indian civilization was founded on the self-sufficient and unchanging 'village community'.[56] This concept regarded as 'natural' the immobilizing of Indians in their birthplaces and also offered the Company a curious form of legitimation for its new revenue practices. On the theory that village communities were self-sufficing, the state could both remove all their surplus and deny them outside investment resources without, in any way, impairing their imagined ability to self-reproduce themselves and the agrarian economy.[57]

Yet not all of Indian society was flattened and immiserated in this way. The Company state could not, in fact, function without the support and 'collaboration' of certain Indian groups. In the 1830s the number of Europeans in its territories was less than 45,000 (including soldiers) among a population of 150 million—and its efforts to stimulate greater 'white' settlement proved a failure. In order to rule, the Company needed to draw on the resources, skills, and energies of at least some of its indigenous subjects, who necessarily profited thereby. As a result, it became involved in building structures of power and hierarchies of authority within Indian society as well as over and above it. But the way that it did this marked a departure from the past and also carried strong implications for the processes of 'traditionalization'.

One set of groups who came to enjoy particular Company favour was the 'scribal gentries' who—mostly of high-caste and Brahmanic status—possessed traditions of literacy and had long served as administrators to previous regimes. Now they filled the subordinate positions in the Company's revenue bureaucracy. A second set comprised certain 'martial' communities, especially the Rajputs and Bhumihars of North India, whom the Company decided made the best soldiers for

[56] Dewey, 'Images', pp. 291–95; Robb, *Ancient Rights*, chap. 5.
[57] Eric Stokes, *The English Utilitarians and India* (Oxford, 1959), part II.

its army. A third set consisted of residual Indian princes and warrior-noblemen who had allied with the Company during the wars of the eighteenth century. They became its 'aristocracy', retaining varying degrees of independence over their domains.

Such groups, needless to say, had possessed prominent positions in society previously—but never so predominant as they were now to become. Then, all had faced competition and challenge in the fluid world of pre-colonial politics. Brahmin scribes might have possessed high status, but political power was the prerogative of warriors and wealth that of merchants. Rajputs and Bhumihars might have chased military employment, but they had constantly to prove their superior skills against warriors from other backgrounds. Princes and noblemen rose and fell with remarkable rapidity depending on the fortunes of war, imperial successions, and the tolerance of a still-armed peasantry. But under Company Raj, power and privilege—once they had been gained—became much more secure and less susceptible to challenge.

Reflecting its sense of India as a static Oriental society, Company institutional practices defined and recruited would-be collaborators largely according to criteria of caste and racial ascription and the heritage of blood. They then put the unprecedented power of the new state machine behind the maintenance of their collaborators' authority, ruling out competitors for their honours as illegitimate parvenus and challengers to their positions as contumacious rebels. Princes and noblemen who gained the Company's approval were redefined as members of an 'ancient aristocracy' to be protected against rivals, recalcitrant subjects, and even creditors for all time.[58] Rajput and Bhumihar castes benefited from privileged access to the army and also—of no small consideration—from the right to bear arms in a society whose other members were now disarmed.[59] Substantial numbers of subordinate offices in the villages—and the remaining tax-immunities and perquisites which went with them—became strictly hereditary, to be resumed by the state only if succession failed.[60] While higher bureaucratic office was notionally open to competition, *de facto* it was engorged by family dynasties of Brahmin clerks.[61] Privilege and power in Indian society became frozen in prescriptive and immutable forms, insensitive any longer to imperatives of achievement and change.

---

[58] Dirks, *Hollow Crown*, chap. 11.

[59] Seema Alavi, *The Sepoys and the Company: Tradition and Transition in Northern India, 1770–1830* (Delhi, 1995), chaps. 1, 2.

[60] Robert Eric Frykenberg, 'The Silent Settlement', in Robert Eric Frykenberg, ed., *Land Tenure and Peasant in South Asia* (Delhi, 1977), pp. 31–66.

[61] Robert Eric Frykenberg, *Guntur District, 1788–1848: A History of Local Influence and Central Authority in South India* (Oxford, 1965), chaps. 6, 7.

Under these circumstances the culture associated with privilege and power also underwent a metamorphosis, making it more arrogant and oppressive. Rajputs and Bhumihars responded to their new status by appropriating to themselves as collectivities the habits and attitudes which once were the prerogative only of kings.[62] Brahmins, especially in southern and western India where their positions had been equivocal, created greater distance between themselves and low-caste *Sudra* society.[63] It may well have been that such groups possessed aspirations in these directions before—and, indeed, that such aspirations had informed the perceptions of Indian 'tradition' held by the British, who were largely dependent on their collaborators for 'knowledge' about it.[64] But the altered colonial context changed the meaning and effect of these pretensions.

The nature of the caste system, for example, was profoundly affected by the actions of the Anglo-Hindu courts of law. Although previously effective caste status had been subject to multiple influences and flexible interpretations, the Company's lawcourts looked largely to the authority of Brahmin pundits and Sanskritic scriptural sources, which they accredited with guardianship of society's mores. The Brahmanic theory of caste (or *varna*) was extremely rigid and hierarchic, and its influence had largely been confined to élite circles before. However, now and as instrumentalized by the courts, it penetrated deeper into society, restructuring the relations of public worship, physical mobility, marriage, inheritance, and even property ownership.[65] The Anglo-Hindu law sketched out an immobile, status-bound social order perfectly in keeping with the Company state's dreams of Oriental despotism and European imaginings of a 'different' Oriental civilization.

The West Strikes Back

Yet such dreams and imaginings were not the only ones affecting the development of Indian society. The Anglicizing impulse lived on, especially in Britain, and survived the Company state's reversion to military fiscalism and 'Orientalism'. Periodically, it offered contradictory promptings: advocating the spread of Western learning, the reform of caste, the virtues of meritocracy, and the competition of the market economy. But until the later 1840s its influence remained circumscribed and many of its initiatives ended up heavily compromised. Macaulay's

---

[62] Alavi, *Sepoys*, chaps. 3, 4.

[63] Appadurai, *Worship*, chap. 4.

[64] Nicholas B. Dirks, 'Castes of Mind', *Representations*, XX (1992), pp. 126–64; Sheldon Pollock, 'Deep Orientalism?', in Carol Breckenridge and Peter van der Veer, eds., *Orientalism and the Post-Colonial Predicament: Perspectives on South Asia* (Philadelphia, 1993), pp. 84–110.

[65] Appadurai, *Worship*, chap. 4.

celebrated 1835 recommendation to promote Western education was backed by the Company's government only to the extent of £10,000 a year. Persian might have been displaced as the official language of the state but, in North India, it was replaced with Urdu, not English. Company officials were repeatedly warned that, whatever their own Christian beliefs, their government was to be strictly neutral in matters of religion.

Indeed, the tangled web of cultural meanings represented by colonialism led many attempts at Anglicizing reform to produce social consequences which actually strengthened Oriental 'tradition'. For example, the legislative attacks on 'abominal' Hindu customs, especially regarding the treatment of women, were aimed mainly at the practices of the upper castes. They served to associate those customs closely with the possession of high-caste status. In a society becoming increasingly conscious of caste hierarchy, the result was perhaps inevitable. Many lower castes, who previously had not followed such practices, now began to adopt them.[66] Suttee, female infanticide, and especially bans on the remarriage of widows showed tendencies to become more, not less, widespread. Equally, evangelical pressures to force the Company state to abandon the role which it had inherited from previous regimes in the patronage and protection of Indian religions had the effect of strengthing the latter. The state was obliged to pass the powers and properties, which it had exercised and enjoyed on their behalf, directly to authorities—priests and trustees—constituted within them. In effect, such authorities absorbed the erstwhile prerogatives of the state and became king-like in their own right: their rulings absolute, no longer subject to royal mediation, and their 'private' wealth enormous.[67]

From the 1840s, however, a sea-change began to set in and the pressures of Anglicization to become more forceful and effective. The change was partly associated with the decade-long Governor-Generalship of Lord Dalhousie (1846–56), who pronounced himself an uncompromising Westernizer. Dalhousie readdressed the issue of private property right, calling for revisions in the *ryotwari* settlement in order to reduce taxation and promote economic growth; and, in Bengal, posing the need for tenancy legislation to give productive peasants protection from rentier landlords. He also spurned India's newly 'ancient aristocracy', threatening to liquidate its landed estate-holders for bankruptcy and to reduce its 'independent' maharajas to extinction by annexing their principalities. In other domains, Dalhousie repudiated caste and sought to reform the military—in the case of the Bengal Army, both at the same time. He reduced neo-Oriental

---

[66] Rosalind O'Hanlon, 'Issues of Widowhood', in Gyan Prakash and Douglas Haynes, eds., *Contesting Power: Resistance and Everyday Social Relations in South Asia* (Delhi, 1991), pp. 62–108.

[67] Appadurai, *Worship*, chap. 4; Bayly, *Saints*, chap. 8.

privileges giving special status to Bhumihars and Rajputs, and attempted to produce a more disciplined, European-style fighting force. Finally, he reactivated the causes of both Western education and evangelical Christianity. His government committed itself to promoting mass education and laid plans for the first Indian universities (enacted in 1857); and it licensed wider missionary criticism of Hinduism and Islam.[68]

That Dalhousie should have made so deep a mark where previous Westernizers, such as Bentinck, had failed stemmed from more than just the force of his personality. Political, social, and economic circumstances also were changing. Dalhousie took office facing the increased military costs of the north-west military campaigns in the context of the deepening world economic recession of the late 1840s. It took no genius to appreciate the economically regressive nature of the Company's military-fiscalist state: stagnant levels of production and revenue had their corollary in an inability to meet government bills. The deficiencies of the Company's army were also palpable in the disasters of the First Afghan War (1838–42). The 'old system' was failing in ways which made the case for reform unanswerable.

That reforms were effective—ultimately devastatingly so—also had much to do with two novelties of the time. First, in the Company bureaucracy the generation of the Napoleonic Wars was dying out, being replaced in the higher offices of the state by the products of Haileybury and, following further service reforms in 1853, of Oxford and Cambridge. This, in turn, undid the close relationship between 'military' and 'civil' service, which had coloured the nature of Company government. The new leaders of the 1840s were long-trained in England as bureaucrats and had fewer inclinations towards Oriental despotism than their predecessors.

The success of reform, however, perhaps owed most to technological changes which brought Europe much closer to India and created broader possibilities for social transformation. Under Dalhousie, steam-shipping, telegraphs, and railways began to make a major impact. They facilitated a near-doubling in the number of Europeans working in India in the army, the bureaucracy, and the economy between 1830 and the mid-1850s.[69] They also broadened the channels of trade. British imports into India, which had stagnated in the 1830s, took off again and doubled to an annual average of £7m by the end of the 1840s. Exports, especially westwards, were also stimulated and began a rise which was to carry them well past trade to the East by the early 1850s.[70] The economic depression lifted, albeit

---

[68] Edwin Arnold, *The Marquess of Dalhousie's Administration of British India*, 2 vols. (London, 1862–65).

[69] Metcalf, *Aftermath of Revolt*, chaps. 1, 2.

[70] Chaudhuri, *Economic Development*, p. 125.

patchily and slowly at first, and prospects of growth started to pressurize economic policy. Investment, rather than simple extraction, came back into fashion as a means of raising revenues and profits. Several large irrigation schemes, long proposed but never previously funded, were now undertaken. A new attempt was made to secure property rights in land, not only by reducing taxation but also by making ownership more alienable and separating it from blood-heritage. Discussions began on converting *inams* (rent-free landholdings) and tenancy contracts into real rights of property.

The reforms so forcefully implemented under Dalhousie nevertheless had problematic consequences, which checked Westernizing initiatives in the years following his retirement in 1856. Most obviously, they were involved in provoking the Great Mutiny and Civil Rebellion of 1857, which threw not merely Company India but the entire British Empire into turmoil. The revolt of the Bengal Army neutralized British power in the central Ganges valley, the heartland of northern India, and opened the way for widespread attacks by the civil populace on the institutions and symbols of Company rule. These rebellions, no doubt, had many discrete causes. But one, indisputably, derived from the way in which Dalhousie's eager Westernizing policies rubbed up against sets of vested interests built up under the previous neo-Orientalizing Raj.

This was clearest in the case of the military mutiny, where the Bengal Army's high-caste soldiers had acquired many privileges, not least that of avoiding flogging. When these were threatened with abrogation, as a new European officer corps sought to impose British military discipline, tensions exploded.[71] Dissatisfaction was further fed by Dalhousie's annexation of the Kingdom of Oudh in 1856, which led many soldiers on detachment from the Oudh army to lose their personal perquisites.[72]

It was true also of aspects of the civil rebellion, where Hindu and Islamic priesthoods, whose authority had been enhanced by the withdrawal of state control over them, responded to more intensive goading by an expansive missionary Christianity. They utilized the moment of collapsing British military power to seek revenge on their self-avowed religious enemies. It may also explain the attacks by residual peasant communities on various institutions—especially the courts and the revenue treasuries—which had strengthened the assertion of landlord proprietary right and threatened their continued occupation of the land.[73] The contradictions of British rule—caught between inventing an Oriental

[71] J. A. B. Palmer, *The Mutiny Outbreak at Meerut in 1857* (Cambridge, 1966), chap. 2.

[72] Rudrangshu Mukherjee, *Awadh in Revolt, 1857–1858: A Study of Popular Resistance* (Delhi, 1984), chaps. 2, 3.

[73] Eric Stokes, *The Peasant and the Raj: Studies in Agrarian Society and Peasant Rebellion in Colonial India* (Cambridge, 1978), chaps. 3–5.

society and abolishing it—were manifested in many of the complex patterns of revolt witnessed in 1857.

After the Mutiny

These contradictions continued after the Mutiny, although taking on different forms. Technological transformation increased in intensity. Railways expanded greatly; new port facilities encouraged steam-shipping; factory production established itself in several urban centres. These developments enabled Indian primary products finally to find outlets on world markets. Product prices steadily rose, and occasionally, as during the American Civil War, the Indian economy enjoyed periods of 'boom'.[74] New policies of restraint on land revenue and rental demands—introduced more urgently after the terrors of the Mutiny—also permitted more resources to remain with agrarian society.[75]

Yet while material change suggested the possibilities of social change directed by market capitalism, the experiences of 1857 guaranteed that it would not be allowed to follow its most obvious logic. The army remained pivotal to British ambitions in India and continued to affect the character of the colonial state. Although military government was now more fully separated from and subordinated to civil government (not least, by the abolition of the Company in 1858 and the taking of India under the direct rule of the Crown), the presence of the army remained a dominant consideration of future Imperial policy. Further, the security problem revealed by the Mutiny created racial divisions and suspicions which were to last ever after. India was to sacrifice the prospects of both more rapid economic growth and political reform in order to be preserved as the British Empire's military barracks.[76]

This, in and of itself, ensured certain continuities with the Company's India. While, for example, the once-venerated martial prowess of the Bengal Army's Rajputs and Bhumihars now was denigrated, that of the Muslims and Sikhs of the Punjab Army, which had remained loyal in 1857, was raised and sanctified in its place. Punjab, in particular, became the Raj's favourite recruiting ground and was commanded to remain changeless, a society of peasants and feudatories, to serve the army's purposes.[77] Maintaining the 'martial races' of Punjabi society unaltered, by expending vast sums of money on irrigation projects aimed at preserving their 'traditional village communities', was to drain the Government of India's development budget for decades to come.[78]

---

[74] B. R. Tomlinson, *The Economy of Modern India, 1860–1970* (Cambridge, 1993), chap. 2.
[75] Robb, *Ancient Rights*, chap. 10.
[76] Metcalf, *Aftermath of Revolt*, chaps. 3–5; see Vol. IV.
[77] Richard G. Fox, *Lions of the Punjab: Culture in the Making* (Berkeley, 1985).
[78] Washbrook, 'Law', p. 697.

In social policy too, the Mutiny added complications. After 1857 colonial rulers regarded the overt attack of the Dalhousie years on religious traditions and customs as the primary cause of revolt. They therefore eschewed further 'interference', leaving Indian society with its neo-Orientalist ethics and social forms frozen for all eternity. They also returned to many of the traditional institutions which Dalhousie had rejected. India's 'ancient aristocracy' was rendered immutable once again and bound to the British Crown as a pillar of the new Imperial establishment.[79] Hindu and Islamic priestly authorities also regained their status of sacrosanctity.

After the Mutiny, the Westernizing and Orientalizing propensities of colonial rule thus still remained in tension, although as the century advanced a new element also began to enter their relationship. The Brahmanic scribal gentries, whose social authority had been so greatly enhanced by British rule, began to consolidate themselves as a national intelligentsia and to seek the liberation of their nation from Imperial tyranny. But, as quintessential products of the contradictory processes by which colonial India had been made, they—no less than their British opponents—remained unclear of the direction in which true liberation lay. Indian nationalism was itself to be torn between attempts to pursue a modern Western future and to evoke a glorious, unchanging, and distinctively 'Oriental' Indian past.[80]

[79] Bernard S. Cohn, 'Representing Authority in Victorian India', in Cohn, ed., *An Anthropologist Among the Historians and Other Essays* (Delhi, 1990), pp. 632–82.

[80] Partha Chatterjee, *Nationalist Thought and the Colonial World: A Derivative Discourse?* (London, 1986).

Select Bibliography

SEEMA ALAVI, *The Sepoys and the Company: Tradition and Transition in Northern India, 1770–1830* (Delhi, 1995).

ARJUN APPADURAI, *Worship and Conflict under Colonial Rule: A South Indian Case* (Cambridge, 1981).

C. A. BAYLY, *Rulers, Townsmen and Bazaars: Northern Indian Society in the Age of British Expansion, 1770–1870* (Cambridge, 1983).

—— *Indian Society and the Making of the British Empire* (Cambridge, 1988).

—— *Imperial Meridian: The British Empire and the World, 1780–1830* (London, 1989).

SUSAN BAYLY, *Saints, Goddesses and Kings: Muslims and Christians in South Indian Society, 1700–1900* (Cambridge, 1989).

SUGATA BOSE, *Peasant Labour and Colonial Capital: Rural Bengal since 1770* (Cambridge, 1993).

K. N. CHAUDHURI, *The Economic Development of India, 1814–58: A Selection of Contemporary Writings* (Cambridge, 1971).

NICHOLAS B. DIRKS, *The Hollow Crown: Ethno-History of an Indian Kingdom* (Cambridge, 1987).

ROBERT ERIC FRYKENBERG, *Guntur District, 1766–1848: A History of Local Influence and Central Authority in South India* (Oxford, 1965).

——, ed., *Land Control and Social Structure in Indian History* (Madison, 1969).

RANAJIT GUHA, *Elementary Aspects of Peasant Insurgency in Colonial India* (Delhi, 1983).

RONALD INDEN, *Imagining India* (Oxford, 1989).

DAVID KOPF, *British Orientalism and the Bengal Renaissance: The Dynamics of Indian Modernization, 1773–1835* (Berkeley, 1969).

JAVED MAJEED, *Ungoverned Imaginings: James Mill's 'History of India' and Orientalism* (Oxford, 1992).

THOMAS R. METCALF, *The Aftermath of Revolt: India, 1857–1870* (Princeton, 1964).

—— *Ideologies of the Raj* (Cambridge, 1994).

RUDRANGSHU MUKHERJEE, *Awadh in Revolt, 1857–1858: A Study of Popular Resistance* (Delhi, 1984).

DOUGLAS M. PEERS, *Between Mars and Mammon: Colonial Armies and the Garrison State in India* (London, 1995).

BURTON STEIN, *Thomas Munro: The Origins of the Colonial State and His Vision of Empire* (New Delhi, 1989).

ERIC STOKES, *The Peasant and the Raj: Studies in Agrarian Society and Peasant Rebellion in Colonial India* (Cambridge, 1978).

—— *The Peasant Armed: The Indian Revolt of 1857*, ed. C. A. Bayly (Oxford, 1986).

D. A. WASHBROOK, 'Law, State and Agrarian Society in Colonial India', *Modern Asian Studies*, XV (1981), pp. 649–721.

19

Imperial India, 1858–1914

ROBIN J. MOORE

The half-century between the crises of the Mutiny and the First World War, both of which threatened the very existence of the Indian Empire, was the long afternoon of the Raj. From 1858 India was governed in the name of the Crown. In 1876 Queen Victoria became Empress of India, the only possession to which such Imperial nomenclature was applied. The Queen's long reign seemed a symbol of Imperial stability and India was, as Benjamin Disraeli affirmed, the jewel in her Crown. There is an intrinsic and continuing interest, therefore, in pursuing some of the oldest questions in historical debate for this period. How did the Raj recover so effectively from the cataclysm of 1857–58 that India committed 1.2 million troops to the Great War? What was the rationale of the Empire in India? And what were the implications of British rule for the development of India?

The early sections of this chapter examine the post-Mutiny rehabilitation of the Raj and the relatively small adjustments to it during the late nineteenth century. On the whole, the government in London and India, as well as the military reconstruction, administrative arrangements, and financial organization, endured remarkably well, sufficiently satisfying Indian demand for participation in the regime. A later section explores the transformation that Victoria's last Viceroy, the authoritarian Lord Curzon, sought to effect in order to regenerate and remotivate an Imperial order that he found tired and complacent. Another follows the counter-revolution that, under Liberal governments from 1905 to 1914, was intended to re-establish stable relations between the Raj and Indians whom Curzon had alienated, and between Britain and rival European empires with interests in India's neighbours whom Curzon had sought to dominate. Final sections attempt to assess India's importance for the Empire, and the consequences of Empire for India.

Queen Victoria intended that her November 1858 Proclamation to the princes, chiefs, and peoples of India should be heard as the voice of 'a female Sovereign', speaking to hundreds of millions of 'Eastern people on assuming the direct Government over them after a bloody civil war'. She insisted that the Prime

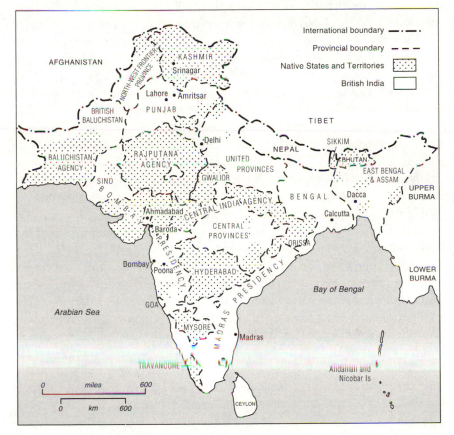

International boundary
Provincial boundary
Native States and Territories
British India

AFGHANISTAN

KASHMIR
Srinagar

NORTH-WEST FRONTIER PROVINCE

Lahore • Amritsar

BRITISH
BALUCHISTAN

PUNJAB

TIBET

Delhi

BALUCHISTAN
AGENCY

RAJPUTANA
AGENCY

SIKKIM

NEPAL

BHUTAN

SIND

GWALIOR

UNITED
PROVINCES

EAST BENGAL
& ASSAM

UPPER
BURMA

B O M B A Y

Ahmadabad

CENTRAL INDIA AGENCY

BENGAL

Dacca

Baroda

CENTRAL
PROVINCES

Calcutta

P R E S I D E N C Y

ORISSA

Bombay

Poona

HYDERABAD

M A D R A S   P R E S I D E N C Y

LOWER
BURMA

Bay of Bengal

Arabian Sea

GOA

MYSORE

Madras

TRAVANCORE

Andaman and
Nicobar Is

0   miles   600

0   km   600

CEYLON

MAP 19.1. India: Political Divisions, c.1909

Minister write the speech himself, 'giving them pledges which her future reign is to redeem, and explaining the principles of her Government'.[1] The Proclamation appointed her first Viceroy and Governor-General, who would act in her name subject to the orders issued by her through a Secretary of State. It confirmed the employees of the predecessor authority, the East India Company, in their offices and accepted responsibility for the treaties that had regulated relations between the Company and the princes of those parts of India which had not been annexed: 'We shall respect the rights, dignity and honour of native princes as our own, and we desire that they, as well as our own subjects, should enjoy that prosperity and that social advancement which can only be secured by internal peace and good government.'[2] Subjects would not be favoured or disquieted by dint of faith or race, whether at law or relative to appointments. Land rights would be protected, ancient usages and customs respected. Imperial policies for change and development must sit uneasily with such reassurances, and a tension emerges when the Proclamation espouses the stimulation of 'peaceful industry', the promotion of 'works of public utility and improvement', and the administration of government 'for the benefit of all our subjects'. It has been recognized that the Proclamation thus 'encompasses two divergent or even contradictory theories of rule: one which sought to maintain India as a feudal order, and the other looking towards changes which would inevitably lead to the destruction of this feudal order'.[3]

The Government of India Act (1858) that established the Crown's sovereign authority provided for a Secretary of State, and a Council of India with fifteen members, eight of them Crown appointees. The other seven would be elected by the directors of the East India Company in the first instance, and as their places became vacant their successors would be co-opted by the Council. Most members in each category of member must have spent at least ten years in India and not have left it more than ten years earlier. Councillors could be removed only through a petition to both Houses of Parliament. Thus would recent experience of India and the exercise of independent judgement be ensured. It was the Secretary of State who sent instructions to India but he was obliged to consult the Council before issuing them, except where they related to urgent or diplomatic matters. Each member was entitled to register his opinion on, and record his dissent from, matters that the Secretary of State laid before the Council. The minister could

---

[1] Queen Victoria to Lord Derby, 15 Aug. 1858, in C. H. Philips, ed., *The Evolution of India and Pakistan, 1858 to 1947: Select Documents* (London, 1962), p. 10.

[2] Queen Victoria's Proclamation, 1 Nov. 1858, in ibid., pp. 10–11.

[3] Bernard S. Cohn, 'Representing Authority in Victorian India', in Eric Hobsbawm and Terence Ranger, eds., *The Invention of Tradition* (Cambridge, 1983), pp. 165–209, esp. p. 166. For this tension before 1858 see chap. by D. A. Washbrook.

overrule the Council, except where expenditure was involved, in which case he had to obtain a majority vote.

The provision for a quasi-independent Council alongside the minister of the Crown and his department (the India Office) is remarkable. It conformed to the principle of 'double government', which had emerged in the eighteenth century in the form of a government Board of Control to check corrupt tendencies in the administration of India by a self-interested commercial Company. When the Company lost its commercial interests in 1833 it was preserved, as Macaulay advocated, as a 'body independent of the government . . . not a tool of the Treasury, not a tool of the opposition', but 'an efficient check on abuses practised in India'.[4] When the Company's Charter was reviewed by Parliament in 1853 its most illustrious servant, John Stuart Mill, defended the 'forms' of double government as subjecting all Indian proceedings to review by 'two separate bodies independent of one another'.[5] Mill argued in his *Representative Government* (1861) that the 'government of one people by another . . . cannot exist', that 'direct' rule would pervert every right purpose of government, and that the utmost an imperial power could do was 'to give some of their best men a commission' to rule.[6] In 1858 the roles of the India Board and the Company were, in effect, reversed in their successor authorities, with the minister of the Crown now the initiator of policy and the Council now the check on Imperial self-interest.

The adjustment of the roles of Crown, minister, and Council took time to accomplish. The Queen evinced 'an extreme jealousy of the power of the Council . . . as being a check interposed between the Sovereign and the absolute government of India'.[7] At first she required the minister to obtain her consent to all important measures before bringing them before the Council. When Sir Charles Wood (President of the Board of Control, 1853–55) began his term as Secretary of State (1859–66) he advised the Queen that she was assuming 'a false position': the minister must fully consider all measures before placing them before the Queen and that involved consulting the Council as 'a necessary part of the machinery'.[8] Wood prevailed on this aspect of procedure but had 'no slight difficulty' in overcoming the Council's assumption of 'an independence which was a hindrance to public business'.[9] His 'hardest task . . . on becoming Secretary of State was to break in the old Directors from being masters into becoming advisers'.[10] Wood's

---

[4] Cited by H. H. Dodwell, 'Imperial Leglislation and the Superior Governments, 1818–1857', *Cambridge History of India*, 6 vols. (Cambridge, 1932), VI, pp. 1–19, esp. p. 4.

[5] Cited in R. J. Moore, *Sir Charles Wood's Indian Policy, 1853–66* (Manchester, 1966), p. 30.

[6] J. S. Mill, *Representative Government* (1861; Everyman edn., London, 1944), pp. 384–86.

[7] Lord Stanley to Sir Charles Wood, 14 July 1859, in Moore, *Wood*, p. 35.

[8] Wood to Prince Consort, 30 June 1859, in ibid., p. 36.

[9] Wood to Lord Palmerston, 29 June 1861, in ibid., pp. 41–42.

[10] Wood (Lord Halifax) to Lord Ripon, 11 Jan. 1883, in ibid., p. 40.

past experience and manipulative skills enabled him to record that he won for the minister 'abundant power in one way or another of enforcing his views'.[11] He valued the Council as giving the minister 'the support requisite to resist the pressure of parties in this country—a pressure not always applied in a way conducive to the benefit of the people of India'.[12]

Wood's most eminent successor, Lord Salisbury (1866–67), resented the obstructiveness of the Council in opposing non-financial measures on the pretext that they involved expenditure. In 1869 its independence was curtailed by legislation providing for all councillors to be appointed by nomination and for their term to be ten years. For the next half-century the powers of the Council were unchanged and its influence depended largely upon the strength of particular Secretaries of State, and indeed Viceroys. However, the size of the Council was reduced—to ten in 1889 and eight in 1919–and also the period of tenure—to seven years in 1907 and five years in 1919. Two Indians were appointed in 1907. The Council did ease the difficult transition from Company to Crown, provide ongoing expertise to the minister and his department, and act as something of a watchdog, guarding against inappropriate expenditure from the revenues of India.

In India there existed in 1858 arrangements for the central government at Calcutta and the provincial governments of Bombay and Madras that resembled the 'double government' in London. At each location the Governor-General or Governor was obliged to consult, and was thus 'checked' by, councils whose members were entitled to record dissents. Decisions were taken by the 'Governor-General (or Governor) in Council'. With the mass of business swollen by the tasks of post-Mutiny reconstruction, Viceroy Canning (1856–62) found this collective or corporate procedure slow and cumbersome. He sought recourse to a portfolio system, with executive decisions to be taken by department heads in consultation with the Viceroy. By 1859 the composition of the Council suggested such specialization, for its members were the Commander-in-Chief, a military officer, a law member, a finance member, and two civil servants. The Indian Councils Act (1861) gave the Governor-General and the Governors power to conduct executive business on the portfolio system. It also provided for the expansion of the Executive Councils when they met to make laws. Up to twelve 'additional members' could be nominated by the Viceroy for two-year terms, half of them officials and half non-official Indians and British residents. The arrangements for Legislative Councils would be similar, though on a smaller scale, in the provinces. Wood emphasized that these 'Legislative Councils' had no separate existence or independence from the Executive Councils. All measures arising from

---

[11] Wood's Memorandum on Procedure, n.d. [1869], in Moore, *Wood's Indian Policy*, p. 39.
[12] Lord Halifax, 13 May 1869, *P[arliamentary] D[ebates]* (Lords) CXCVI, col. 693.

the councils required the Secretary of State's approval. The government of India was 'a despotism controlled from home'. These arrangements endured until 1892, when the Councils Act was revised as a response to Indian claims for representation.

As distinct from 'British India', the jurisdiction of the central and provincial authorities in India did not apply to the internal governance of the Princely States, where over a fifth of the population resided. Until the Mutiny states had been annexed for persistent misgovernment and, under Governor-General Dalhousie (1848–56), for lapse of heirs upon the demise of princes. During the Mutiny some disaffected or displaced rulers had risen against the Company. It became post-Mutiny policy to attach the remaining Indian 'royals' to the Crown and there were no further annexations. The princes were accorded 'sanads of adoption', assurances that on failure of natural heirs the adoption of a successor would be recognized. For cases of misgovernment the remedy was often the temporary 'attachment' of the state to British administration, or sometimes the replacement of the ruler by another member of his family, or the education of a younger prince to ascend the throne when he came of age.

The reconstruction of the military forces in India was the largest and most urgent post-Mutiny problem. The forces had included three distinct structures: the East India Company's 'native army' in Bengal, Madras, and Bombay, which numbered almost a quarter of a million troops, commanded exclusively by cadres of British commissioned officers; the Company's European army, of some 21,000 officers and men, who enlisted for a lifetime's local service; and the regiments of the Queen's Army of the Line, whose number rose during the Mutiny from 24,000 to 77,000 officers and men enlisted for general service. There was an immediate need to slash the financial burden of 100,000 European and 250,000 Indian troops to affordable yet safe levels. It was agreed that the proportion of European to Indian troops must be raised above the pre-Mutiny level and a ratio of 1 : 2 was adopted as desirable. By the mid-1860s the numbers were set at about 120,000 Indians commanded from Calcutta, Bombay, and Madras, and some 60,000 Europeans.

The most pressing problem was the constitution of the European forces. The Viceroy and his colleagues in India and the Council of India urged that at least in part the Europeans should be raised for service only in India and stationed there permanently. However, the Queen declared 'her firm determination not to sanction under any form, the construction of a British Army distinct from . . . the Army of the Crown'.[13] For a time there seemed a likelihood of a compromise whereby part of the European forces should consist of local regiments permanently

---

[13] Queen Victoria to Lord Derby, 5 Feb. 1859, in Moore, *Wood's Indian Policy*, p. 208.

stationed in India and part of the Queen's Line regiments on temporary duty there. The matter was decided by a strike or 'white mutiny' within the Company's European army, some members of which refused to accept allegiance to the Crown as required by the Act of 1858. The case for a local European force was discredited. The European regiments in the new Indian Army would be drawn from the Line and stationed temporarily in India. The 2,000-odd British officers of the Indian regiments would, on the other hand, be recruited from the ranks of subalterns of the Line army and appointed to a Staff Corps, a separate cadre serving with Indian regiments throughout a career to the age of 55.

Sir Charles Wood was at pains to 'deregularize the Native army'.[14] This meant a sharp departure from the rule-bound, rigid structure of the Company's army, with large cadres of British officers empanelled on regimental lists but frequently absent on secondment to non-military appointments. He sought more opportunities for Indians as non-commissioned officers and the improvement of their relations with their British commanders. The relationship should be that of 'a Chief and his clansmen', an attachment 'more to persons than to rules'.[15] He sought to isolate the regiments from one another to avoid them feeling 'part of a large united or connected army'.[16] They would be raised in the districts, not centrally, so that they would each be 'a community, not an Army',[17] lacking a common element such as the presence of troops from Oudh throughout the rebellious Bengal Army: 'If one regiment mutinies I should like to have the next so alien that it would fire into it.'[18] Within regiments he would have every variety of race, caste, and religion, thereby countering 'fraternising and combining among the troops'.[19] He explicitly acknowledged that 'as regards Armies and Regiments in India, I am for "Divide et impera"'.[20]

The reconstruction of the Indian Army was a remarkable success. It was effectively segregated from political movements, and the principle of paternalism prevailed as represented by the expression 'man bap' (the British officer as 'mother and father' to his Indian troops). Far greater use was made of the 'martial races', especially the Sikhs and the Gurkhas, who had not joined the Mutiny. Whereas three-quarters of the gunners had been Indians, all field artillery was transferred to the Europeans. Where possible 'native police' were used instead of soldiers. The army remained unchanged in essentials until the First World War, though in 1893

[14] Wood to Sir Hugh Rose, 3 Feb. 1862, in ibid., p. 223.
[15] Wood to Rose, 25 April 1862, and to Sir William Mansfield, 19 June 1865, in ibid., p. 222.
[16] Wood to Rose, 3 Feb. 1862, in ibid., p. 223.
[17] Wood to Sir William Denison, 8 April 1861, in ibid.
[18] Wood to Canning, 8 April, 1861, in ibid.
[19] Wood to Lord Elgin, 10 May 1862, in ibid., p. 224.
[20] Wood to Denison, 8 April 1861, in ibid.

the separate provincial commands of Bombay and Madras were abolished. Indians were not commissioned.

The selection of all officers from the same source, whether for the British army or the Indian Army, followed the principle of competitive recruitment that had already emerged for the Indian Civil Service before the Mutiny. The introduction of competitive examinations for the Indian Civil Service (ICS) anticipated by a year the adoption of the principle for the British Service pursuant to the North-cote–Trevelyan reforms (1854). The intention of the reformers, whose influence produced the abolition of the Company's civil patronage, was to recruit university graduates, 'gentlemen' of intellectual and social distinction from Oxford and Cambridge. In the first decade of competition Oxford and Cambridge men secured 181 appointments and other universities 198 out of a total of 458 places. With an expansion of employment opportunities generally, the recruitment of Oxford and Cambridge graduates became more difficult. In 1876, consistent with the original intention to appoint gentlemen scholars to India, the age limit for candidates was dropped from 21 to 19. The chosen candidates would proceed as probationers to university for two years, and by 1880 two-thirds of them were resident at Oxford colleges. While Indians were in principle accepted as candidates on an equal basis to the British, the practical difficulties they faced were substantial. The curriculum set, the location of the examinations in London, and now the lower age limit all militated against their selection. To a service of 1,021 members only thirty-three Indians had been recruited by the end of the century.

Only in the first five years, when over half of the appointments went to Oxford or Cambridge men, did the Indian Civil Service examinations fulfil the highest hopes of their advocates, including most notably Lord Macaulay, Sir Charles Trevelyan, and Benjamin Jowett of Balliol. As early as 1864 Trevelyan's son, George, was critical of 'the competition wallah'. Between 1860 and 1874 three-quarters of the recruits came from professional, middle-class backgrounds, over a quarter from the clergy, a tenth from each of government service and the medical profession, and 15 per cent from mercantile or legal families. Many did not have degrees. Most, having no Indian connections, signed on for a career of which they could know little. The ICS has been variously described as a *corps d'élite*, Platonic guardians of the Imperial mission, and a body of self-serving careerists preoccupied with their official and social status. They were the bureaucracy upon which the efficiency of the district and secretariat administration depended. They were sharply criticized as lacking capacity and commitment by an aristocratic Viceroy such as Curzon and, just before the First World War, by those peripatetic socialists, Beatrice and Sidney Webb: 'the more we learned about the Govt and the officials...the graver became our tone...Three months' acquaintance has... greatly lessened our admiration for, and our trust in, this Government of officials... Our impression is that the I.C.S. has succeeded fairly well in carrying out its ideals of Govt but its ideals are still those of 1840!'[21] In the course of their twenty-five years' expatriation, members of the ICS often lost touch with a culture of change and became unduly concerned for stability at the expense of innovation. At the pinnacle of the British community, they were also responsible for the assiduous cultivation of its racial distance from Indian society.

The conservatism observed in the Indian Civil Service appears starkly in the Indian Political Service, which was responsible for managing relations with the Princely States. It was recruited from the ICS and the Staff Corps of the Indian Army but its inferior conditions of service, in particular the poor salaries offered, made it unattractive to men of talent. No Indian was admitted before 1914. The senior appointments generally went to civilians. A recent study is somewhat iconoclastic in its correction of the self-image presented by the Indian Political Service itself: 'Prejudice against intellectual ability, emphasis on physical prowess, financial parsimony, and a lack of training in administrative skills combined to produce a service dominated by upright but slow-thinking and extremely unimaginative officers.'[22]

The Mutiny demonstrated the appalling cost in financial as well as human terms of an Imperial catastrophe. Between 1857 and 1860 India's public debt jumped by 70 per cent, imposing an additional annual interest charge of £2m upon the revenues, so that the deficits averaged £10m a year. Even before the Mutiny the balance of the Indian budget was precarious, but for almost a century there had been the option of territorial expansion as a basis for gathering additional taxes. The ongoing costs of the military reconstruction accounted for some 40 per cent of India's revenues, the whole of the yield from the major source of income, land taxes. While the cost of the enhanced British component in the army was high, so too was that of British civilian appointments generally. Before the Mutiny many large-scale works of improvement had already been launched. They were soon extended substantially and they would eventually generate additional taxable revenues. But in the short term railways, irrigation, navigation, and other projects required public investment. The budgetary problem indicated the need to economize on the cost of British administration by attracting less expensive Indians to the Imperial regime—in short, to attract Indian 'collaborators' to the service and support of the Raj.

---

[21] George Feaver, ed., *The Webbs in Asia: The 1911–12 Travel Diary* (London, 1992), 16–25 April 1912, pp. 339–40.

[22] Ian Copland, 'The Other Guardians: Ideology and Performance in the Indian Political Service', in Robin Jeffrey, ed., *People, Princes and Paramount Power: Society and Politics in the Indian Princely States* (Delhi, 1978), pp. 273–305, esp. p. 289.

There was, then, ultimately a financial calculus behind the reassurances that the Queen's Proclamation gave to the princes and the feudal order at large. Indirect rule through the princes of a quarter of India and the use of large landholders as coadjutors in judicial and revenue administration were more economical than the British bureaucracy (and, of course, the risk of alienating influential 'natural leaders' of the people would be avoided). The most remarkable example of the policy in a British province was the reinstatement as landholders and tax gatherers of the *taluqdars* of Oudh, whom the Raj had dispossessed. The most striking exemplification of the princes' association with the Empire was the Imperial Assemblage (or durbar) that Viceroy Lytton (1876–80) staged in Delhi in 1877. The emphasis of the occasion to mark the Queen's assumption in 1876 of the title 'Empress of India' was upon the role of the princes as the 'native aristocracy of the country, whose sympathy and cordial allegiance is no inconsiderable guarantee for the stability of the Indian Empire'.[23]

A more forward-looking body of collaborators emerged from British liberal policies of the 1830s. The adoption of Macaulay's famous Minute on Education (1835) gave precedence to the encouragement of Western rather than Oriental education. A largely service class of mainly high-caste Hindus fulfilled the intention of the westernizing reformers of the 1830s to create 'interpreters' between the British rulers and Indian society. Though attempts were made subsequently to reinforce vernacular education for practical ends, the Raj's dominant concern remained higher and professional learning in English, which was the basis for the recruitment of relatively inexpensive collaborators with the Imperial bureaucracy. Macaulay was also largely responsible for commencing the preparation of the Anglo-Indian law codes, which were only completed after the Mutiny. English was the language of the administrative and legal systems. The Western context of learning carried the assumption of India's advance towards constitutionalism and the enjoyment of civil rights. As a professional middle class grew in numbers, so political organizations appeared to exert claims to official employment and consultation on a representative basis.

The establishment of the universities of Calcutta, Bombay, and Madras in 1857 was a turning-point towards the modern mode of collaboration. In the thirty years following 1857, some 60,000 Indians entered the universities, overwhelmingly in Arts, but some two thousand in Law. Of the 1,712 Calcutta students to graduate by 1882 over a third entered government service and slightly more entered the legal profession. Graduates of the three universities by 1882 accounted for some 1,100 appointments to government service. But, of course, below the graduate level

---

[23] Lord Lytton to Queen Victoria, 21 April 1876, in Cohn, 'Representing Authority', p. 188.

there were required subordinate appointments. By 1887 there were 21,466 government appointments in British India paying at least Rs75 per month, of which 45 per cent were held by Hindus, 7 per cent by Muslims, 19 per cent by Eurasians, and 29 per cent by Europeans.

The national turning-point in the politicization of the middle-class, professional, and mostly high-caste Hindu collaborators was the creation of the first ongoing all-India organization, the Indian National Congress, in 1885. It built upon the foundations of provincial associations, religious and social reform movements, and more limited impermanent political organizations. Its leaders came mainly from the presidency cities, especially Calcutta, though its presidents included retired British officials. It lacked ongoing central organization, and the co-ordination of its activities amounted to little more than the passing of resolutions at annual gatherings in changing locations around Christmas time. The timing of its emergence is related to conflicts over Indian policies between British Conservatives and Liberals in the late 1870s and the 1880s. Salisbury's reduction of the ICS entrance age from 21 to 19 in 1876 was endorsed by Viceroy Lord Lytton, who thought 'the competitive system . . . wholly inapplicable to Native employment and that if it ever ceases to be a farce it will become a serious danger'.[24] He favoured closing the ICS to Indians and forming a subordinate 'close Native Service' by 'selection' from 'that class of Natives whose social position or connexions give to them a commanding influence over their own countrymen'.[25] The Secretary of State vetoed the closure as a breach of British pledges to Indians, but a new Statutory Civil Service was created in 1879 to recruit men from socially prominent families by nomination. Lytton also imposed provocative restrictions on the freedom of the press. His Vernacular Press Act (1878) discriminated against newspapers in Indian languages by extending authority to require a bond from a printer or publisher to support a pledge to refrain from disseminating matter likely to excite disaffection. Gladstone himself entered the fray, condemning the Act as affecting 'a fundamental branch of the law relating to the liberty and general condition of the country'.[26]

When the Liberals won the 1880 election Lytton resigned and Gladstone replaced him with Lord Ripon (1880–84). There would not be another Conservative Viceroy until the last year of the century. Ripon was the most doctrinaire Liberal of the late-nineteenth-century Viceroys. He repealed the Vernacular Press Act; sought, unsuccessfully, to raise the age limit for the Indian Civil Service examination in order to reopen the 'door of competition' to Indians; introduced

---

[24] Lytton to Salisbury, 10 May 1877, in Philips, *Documents*, pp. 545–46.
[25] Government of India to Secretary of State, 2 May 1878, in ibid., p. 548.
[26] W. E. Gladstone, 23 July 1878, *PD*, CCXLII (Commons), cols. 48–65.

elections and self-government at the level of local district and municipal boards; and, through a Bill associated with his Law member of Council, Sir Courtenay Ilbert, took a significant step towards civil equality by enabling Indian magistrates and judges to try Europeans charged with criminal offences in country districts. His purpose was to correct the impression conveyed by Lytton that 'in all ways...the interests of the Natives of India were to be sacrificed to those of England', to satisfy instead the 'legitimate aspirations' of Indians.[27] His radical resolution on local self-government asserted: 'It is not primarily with a view to improvement in administration that this matter is put forward and supported.'[28] Ripon did not have matters all his own way, and his success was limited by opposition within the Raj and in Britain. His policies were an encouragement to nationalism but they also drew explicit condemnation from British spokesmen for imperialism. Sir James Fitzjames Stephen spoke for the Raj in the British press in 1883. The Raj was 'founded not on consent but on conquest', implying the superiority of 'the conquering race'. Ripon's measures reflected 'principles inconsistent with the foundations on which British power rests'.[29] Britain's mission was to establish 'peace, order, the supremacy of law, the prevention of crime, the redress of wrong, the enforcement of contracts...[and] the construction of public works'.[30]

The main demands of the Congress in its early years struck at the fundamental bases of institutional reconstruction since the Mutiny. These were: the Council of India, which seemed out of touch with India's needs, and too protective of Anglo-Indian service interests; the Indian Councils, which required more Indian representatives and greater freedom of discussion; the ICS, which was too inaccessible to Indians; and the expensive, largely British, army. In 1892 Parliament amended the Indian Councils Act of 1861, which increased the Indian membership of the legislatures and widened the power of non-officials to question the executive. The Viceroy, Lord Lansdowne (1888–94), provided for a general discussion of budgets and framed rules to enable local self-governing bodies to elect provincial legislative councillors and for non-official councillors in the provinces to be elected members of the central legislature. The principles of election and representation were thus introduced, though elected legislators were still dependent upon the nomination of the Governor-General or Governor to ratify their membership. In 1893 Parliament declined to accede to the Congress demand for ICS examinations

---

[27] Ripon to Gladstone, 28 Oct. 1881, in R. J. Moore, *Liberalism and Indian Politics, 1872–1922* (London, 1966), p. 31.

[28] Resolution on local self-government, May 1882, in P. Mukherji, ed., *Indian Constitutional Documents* (Calcutta, 1918), pp. 638–51.

[29] *The Times*, 1 March 1883, in Philips, *Documents*, pp. 56–57.

[30] 'The Foundations of the Government of India', *Nineteenth Century* (Oct. 1883), in ibid., pp. 57–60.

to be held in India simultaneously with those in London, though the age limit was raised to 23. A sufficient response to the main demands of the early Congress had been made. Further concessions would not be forthcoming until George Curzon, Viceroy from 1898 to 1905, invited Congress to demand them by governing in the spirit of Fitzjames Stephen.

It is indicative of British Imperial priorities towards the end of Victoria's reign that George Curzon should have been appointed Viceroy of India. He was not yet 40 when he sailed for India and had served neither as a Proconsul nor a Cabinet minister. He had briefly been Under-Secretary of State for India (1891–92) and served as Salisbury's junior minister at the Foreign Office (1895–98). He had, in fact, written himself into the Viceroyalty, not with any book on India but with weighty works on *Russia in Central Asia* (1889), *Persia and the Persian Question* (1892), and *Problems of the Far East* (1894). The message of these volumes was the strategic necessity for an effective British defence of her Asian interests to the West and East of her pivotal Indian Empire. The danger in the West was Russia, which through the extension of transcontinental railways could, by the rapid movement of her armies, menace India's neighbours and the subcontinent itself. Curzon did not believe that Russia coveted India, but rather that the Russians wished to break into the Persian Gulf. Such access to the sea could elevate Russia as a naval power, a terrifying prospect as there was no barrier to her landward eastern advance through Central Asia. Russia was also the pre-eminent danger in the East, though the French expansion in the Pacific and Indo-China indicated the need for Siam as a buffer state. It was primarily the young Curzon who brought about Britain's occupation of Wei-hai-wei (1898) to counter Russia's presence at Port Arthur (Map 8.1). With Russia contained, Britain was secure in the Mediterranean and the Gulf, centrally placed in India to pursue prosperous relations with Persia, China, and Tibet.

Containment involved Britain's naval control of the sea-girt periphery of Europe and Asia, from Gibraltar to Hong Kong. It also involved strong frontier forces in the North-West tribal areas and friendly buffer states between them and Russian-occupied Central Asia. By study and travel Curzon had acquired an unmatched understanding of the problem of India's defence against Russia, at the very time that it became Britain's main anxiety about her Empire. Early in his Viceroyalty the South African War (1899–1902) replaced Russophobia as the central Imperial preoccupation. The risks and costs of resisting Russian expansion and advancing British interests in Afghanistan, Persia, and Tibet sorely troubled the Cabinet of A. J. Balfour. Curzon had his diplomatic successes, but his geopolitical outlook never won strong support. The members of the Cabinet were unable to subscribe emotionally or intellectually to his dictum that through 'the Empire of Hindustan ... the mastery of the world [was] ... in the possession of the British people'.[31]

Curzon had a keen sense of the implications for twentieth-century India of the completion through competitive imperialism of the partition of the world among the Great Powers. He sought no territorial expansion of the Raj but rather to maintain and enhance freedom of access and trade in Asia. The spoils of imperialism in a fully partitioned world would go to the most efficient competitor: the weapon of Empire was no longer superior force but relative efficiency. As Viceroy, Curzon at once found the administrative systems of the Raj unequal to the challenge. The Imperial mission stood in need of rehabilitation: 'The English are getting lethargic and they think only of home. Their hearts are not in this country'.[32] The 'big problems' had been 'systematically shirked by every Viceroy for 30 years'.[33] He soon identified twelve important reforms and attended to them himself during his early years. They included: frontier policy and the creation of the North-West Frontier Province; the reform of the Civil Service leave rules, which he thought undermined administrative continuity; secretariat reform, for he found the discharge of business intolerably slow; the provision of a gold standard to ensure a stable currency; railway reform and the creation of a Railway Board; irrigation reform; the relief of agricultural indebtedness; the reduction of telegraphic rates; the preservation of ancient monuments; education reform (notably in the universities), for he believed that by decentralization government had abdicated its proper authority; reform of the 'rotten' police system; and policy towards the Native States and their rulers to make them worthy partners in government. Subsequently he identified and claimed completion of a second dozen reforms: the creation of a Commerce and Industry Department, and other measures of commercial and industrial development; land revenue policy; reductions in taxation; the institution of permanent financial settlements with the provinces; the foundation of agricultural banks and of an Agricultural Department and Institute; the commemoration of historical buildings and sites; the foundation of an Imperial Library; the reform of Chiefs' Colleges and the creation of an Imperial Cadet Corps for Chiefs; Mining Acts; new famine codes; and, remarkably, the prevention of smoke nuisance in Calcutta. During his last year in office he foreshadowed a further twelve reforms: the subdivision of Bengal into two administrative units; excise reform; the creation of the Imperial Customs Service; the reorganization of the Survey Department and a new Topographical Survey of India; the extension of the Imperial Service Movement in the Princely

---

[31] George N. Curzon, *Problems of the Far East* (London, 1894), p. xv.

[32] Curzon to Alfred Lyttelton, 29 Aug. 1900, Chandos Collection, Churchill College Library, Cambridge, CHAN 1/2/4.

[33] Curzon to St. John Brodrick, 18 June 1900, Midleton Papers, B[ritish] L[ibrary] Add. MSS, 50074.

States; a game law; a technical education scheme; the reorganization of the Political Department; a Calcutta improvement scheme; a European Nursing Service; a tree-planting policy; and the encouragement of inland navigation. Curzon's reforms amounted to a revolutionary reconstruction of the administration. He complained of 'the inadequacy of our trained staff' for the task,[34] created special departments, and appointed experts: an Inspector-General of Agriculture, a Chief Inspector of Mines, an Inspector-General of Volunteers, a Government Architect, an Imperial Librarian, a Government Electrical Adviser, Directors General of Criminal Intelligence and Commercial Intelligence, a Sanitary Commissioner, a Director of a Central Research Institute, an Inspector-General of Irrigation. Where necessary, experts were brought from Britain on subjects as diverse as smoke abatement, education, railways, ancient monuments, and architecture.

Curzon significantly extended the sphere of government activity in the interests of development as well as efficiency. He assured the Bengal Chamber of Commerce that 'there is no object that is more constantly in our minds than the desire to deal both with promptitude and sympathy with every reasonable mercantile or industrial claim'.[35] He accepted the need for the Government of India 'to know everything about agriculture, commerce, emigration, labour, shipping, customs, the application of science to every form of production, the secrets of coal, iron, steel, salt, oil, tin, cotton, indigo and jute'.[36] In 1905 he observed that 'the days are gone when Government can dissociate itself from commercial enterprise'.[37] According to Curzon, it was absurd to separate government from commerce in India, where government built and worked over 26,000 miles of railways, controlled the sale of salt and opium, maintained 'gigantic' factories, manufactured its own cartridges, rifles, and guns (for it was policy to make India self-sufficient in armaments), and was the largest employer. India was 'merely at the beginning of its commercial expansion'.[38] Curzon's creation of a separate Department and Minister of Commerce and Industry in 1905 to develop the country, through Indian as well as British enterprise, symbolized his concern for commercial and industrial expansion. Other examples of this preoccupation may be found in his legislation and rules for tea planting and mining, grants for indigo research, opening new coalfields, despatch of trade missions, and new contracts with shipping companies.

---

[34] Speech to Bengal Chamber of Commerce, Calcutta, 12 Feb. 1903, in Sir Thomas Raleigh, ed., *Lord Curzon in India . . . Speeches . . . 1898–1905*, 2 vols. (London, 1906), I, p. 303.

[35] Ibid.

[36] Ibid.

[37] Budget speech to Legislative Council, 20 March 1905, in ibid., p. 173.

[38] Ibid.

While Curzon professed the objective of an 'Anglo-Indian Imperialism' in which Indians would 'share in the glory',[39] he did 'not think that the salvation of India is to be sought on the field of politics at the present stage of her development'.[40] Constitutional 'reforms or concessions' were 'premature'.[41] Curzon actually reversed the conciliatory association of professional and Western-educated nationalists with the running of such institutions as universities and municipalities. Whilst he espoused economic, social, and intellectual progress he was concerned to associate the chiefs and 'native gentry'—the traditional 'aristocracy' rather than the Congress—with public life. In 1904 he spoke of the English as 'a people who combine a love of progress and a faculty for ordered change with a most passionate attachment to our ancient institutions and a scrupulous reverence for those forms and customs whose roots are embedded in our history'.[42] In terms of the Queen's Proclamation he emphasized the feudal—'Oriental'—mode of rule at the expense of the modernist. He claimed the prince as his 'colleague and partner', an 'integral factor in the Imperial organization of India'.[43] He pictured a future society in which the princes were 'trained to all the advantages of Western culture, but yet not divorced in instinct or in mode of life from their own people'.[44] At the 'apogee' of his Viceroyalty, his durbar at Delhi to mark the coronation of King Edward VII, the princes were elevated from their role of 'spectators' at Lytton's Imperial Assemblage to leading actors, paying homage to their King-Emperor—no longer 'architectural adornments of the Imperial edifice' but 'pillars that help to sustain the main roof'.[45] Significantly, the architectural style of his durbar was Indo-Saracenic, where Lytton's had been Victorian Feudal.

The years between Curzon's departure and the War coincided with the ascendancy of the Liberals in British politics. Partly for that reason, but largely because of Curzon's own miscalculations, there were substantial shifts or reversals in the policies that he had pursued. His paternalism, insistence upon administrative efficiency, concentration upon development in public works and commerce, his vigour in foreign policy on and beyond the frontiers of India: all were moderated. In December 1905 the President of the Indian National Congress, Gopal Krishna Gokhale, summed up the legacy:

---

[39] Curzon to Brodrick, 30 June 1902, Midleton Papers, BL Add. MSS, 50074.

[40] Budget speech, 30 March 1904, Raleigh, *Speeches*, p. 156.

[41] Curzon to Arthur Balfour, 11 Dec. 1908, Curzon Papers, India Office Library, MSS, EUR. F111/409.

[42] Cited by David Cannadine, *Aspects of Aristocracy: Grandeur and Decline in Modern Britain* (New Haven, 1994), p. 78.

[43] Speech at Gwalior, 29 Nov. 1899, Raleigh, *Speeches*, p. 237.

[44] Speech at Jaipur, 28 Nov. 1902, in ibid., p. 245.

[45] Speech at Bahawalpur, 12 Nov. 1903, in ibid., p. 248.

Militarism, Service interests and the interests of English capitalists, all take precedence today of the true interests of the Indian people in the administration of the country.... Now the Congress wants that all this should change and that India should be governed, first and foremost, in the interests of the Indians themselves. This result will be achieved only in proportion as we obtain more and more voice in the government of our country.[46]

Gokhale lobbied the incoming Liberal Secretary of State, John Morley (1905–10), on the need for constitutional reform: the enlargement of the elected membership of the Legislative Councils; the subjection of budgets to the processes of discussion, amendment, and the vote; the appointment of Indian members to the Executive Councils of the Viceroy and the Governors, and to the Secretary of State's Council.

Morley was disposed to a strategy of allying the liberal nationalists with Imperial governance. There were, however, tactical difficulties, for Curzon's last major act, the partition of Bengal, had complicated the political outlook. Regarding Bengal as too large for efficient administration, Curzon divided off its eastern region. The nationalist Bengali, Surendranath Banerjea, wrote: 'We felt that the whole of our future was at stake, and that it was a deliberate blow aimed at the growing solidarity and self-consciousness of the Bengali-speaking population.'[47] The Bengal Legislature, in which the Hindu Congressmen held most of the non-official seats, disappeared. As East Bengal was predominantly Muslim, the political and economic influence of Bengali Hindus there was diminished. Curzon was accused of pursuing a policy of divide and rule. Not only were Hindu-Muslim relations affected, but Congressmen were divided between Moderates and Extremists. The latter espoused the boycott of British goods as the likeliest means of securing the reunification of the province. Acts of terrorism evoked repressive legislation that limited freedom of expression and association. When Morley began to urge the Viceroy, Lord Minto (1905–10), towards constitutional reforms, Minto agreed on the need to 'recognize' the Congress and befriend 'the best of them', but warned that there was much that was 'absolutely disloyal in the movement'.[48] He thought India 'unsuited to Western forms of government'.

Minto sought constitutional changes that would accommodate the diverse interests in Indian society, not merely the professional middle-class Hindus who dominated the Congress.[49] He thought in terms of a balance of interests, of 'counterpoise', say a Council of Princes or a Privy Council of rulers and 'a few other big men', with 'different ideas from those of the Congress'. He was not averse to appointing an Indian to his executive, but not one of 'the purely Gokhale type';

---

[46] G. K. Gokhale's speech of 27 Dec. 1905, in Philips, *Documents*, pp. 156–59.

[47] Surendranath Banerjea, *A Nation in Making* (London, 1925), p. 173.

[48] Minto to Morley, 28 May 1906, in Mary, Countess of Minto, *India, Minto and Morley, 1905–1910* (London, 1934), pp. 28–30.

[49] Ibid.

rather, a man with a stake in the country, a 'Native gentleman' such as the Maharaja of Gwalior.[50] As for the Legislatures, the Government of India recommended that to provide 'the requisite counterpoise' to the professional classes there should be a separate electorate for the monied and landed classes. Minto wanted a scheme that would 'satisfy the legitimate aspirations of the most advanced Indians, whilst at the same time enlisting the support of the conservative element of Native society'.[51] He was thus sympathetic to the wish of the Muslims to safeguard their interests, for they had been slower than Hindus to embrace Western education and enter government service or the legal profession. In response to a deputation from eminent Muslims in October 1906, he gave what he regarded as a pledge that separate Muslim electorates would be established to 'safeguard their political rights and interests as a community' (thereby encouraging 'community-consciousness').[52] That December the All-India Muslim League was formed to provide a forum for the expression of Muslim grievances.

The 'Morley–Minto reforms' took until mid-1909 to complete. While Morley appointed two Indians to his Council in 1907, only two years later were Indians appointed to the executives of the Viceroy and the Governors. The idea of a Council of Princes or notables was set aside. There was a sharp change from Curzon's policy of demanding efficient administration from the princes, who were now reassured that they might rule in conformity with their own traditional practices. The Indian Councils Act of 1909 provided for enlarged representation in the legislatures and for full discussion of budgets. A majority of officials was preserved in the central legislature but non-officials predominated in the provincial bodies. The Viceroy was empowered to regulate the electoral machinery, and he did so to ensure the balanced representation of the various interests and communities. Moderate Congressmen were disappointed that the regulations were less liberal than they had expected. The principle of responsible government was still wholly absent, with Morley denying before the House of Lords any intention to prepare India for parliamentary government. The reforms sufficed to enable the Moderates to retain control of the Congress, from which the Extremists were expelled in December 1907 at Surat. The split occurred when the session endorsed the Moderate insistence upon constitutional means of pursuing self-government. Next year B. G. Tilak, the Extremists' leader, formed a New Party of direct action and was jailed. However, by the outbreak of the First

---

[50] Minto to Morley, 5 July 1906, Philips, *Documents*, p. 75.

[51] Minto to Morley, 27 Feb. 1907, in Lady Minto, *India*, pp. 110–11.

[52] Minto's reply to Simla deputation, in ibid., pp. 46–47. On British encouragement of Muslim 'community-consciousness', see Peter Hardy, *The Muslims of British India* (Cambridge, 1972), esp. pp. 116–67.

World War even the Moderates had become disillusioned and they were losing the loyalty of the youth.

Morley maintained the partition of Bengal as 'a settled fact', the reversal of which would be seen as inconstancy of purpose. Where Minto had seen administrative and tactical advantages in the partition, his successor, Sir Charles Hardinge (1910–16), became convinced that the bitterness against it remained 'very widespread and unyielding' and that terrorism would not subside unless it was revoked.[53] In neither East nor West could the Bengalis exercise the influence to which their numbers, wealth, and education entitled them. In the reformed East Bengal and Assam Legislature the Bengali Hindus were outnumbered by the Muslims and the Assamese, in the Bengal Council by the people of Bihar and Orissa. Hardinge built a vision of India's political future upon the idea of reunifying Bengal. It was a vision of devolution, in which the Imperial capital would be moved to Delhi, leaving Calcutta as the provincial capital. The solution to the problem of political development was 'gradually to give to the Provinces a larger measure of Self-Government, until at last India would consist of a number of administrations, autonomous in all provincial affairs, with the Government of India above them all . . . ordinarily restricting their functions to matters of Imperial concern'.[54] The Liberal peer who succeeded Morley, Lord Crewe (1911–15), supported the scheme and it was announced by King-Emperor George V at a coronation durbar in Delhi. For Curzon it represented a defeat. He saw in it the end of the strong and constructive central authority that was essential to India's development. Morley and Minto had neglected the involvement of government in industrial and commercial affairs in favour of 'a mid-Victorian mixture of laissez-faire and retrenchment'.[55] It seemed more than symbolic that their successors separated the seat of Indian government from the centre of its commerce.

Yet it was probably not the Liberals' jettisoning of his internal reforms that most chagrined Lord Curzon. It was rather the formation of an alliance with Russia, which he believed compromised British interests in Afghanistan, Persia, and Tibet. In 1907 Britain embraced its major Imperial competitor as its ally as it had done with its minor rival, France, in 1902. The Triple Entente was an admission that the British Empire's defences were overextended, but of course it left Germany with little choice but to align itself with Austria-Hungary and Turkey. Thus seen, policy for the defence of India assumes a significance in the diplomacy of the European powers that resulted in the conflagration that was soon to envelop the world.

---

[53] Government of India to Secretary of State, 25 Aug. 1911, in Mukherji, *Documents*, pp. 453–66.
[54] Ibid.
[55] Stanley A. Wolpert, *Morley and India, 1906–1910* (Berkeley, 1967), p. 211.

The successful rehabilitation of British rule after the Mutiny contributed very largely to Britain's prosperity and power in the early twentieth century. The stability of India was essential to Britain's trade, investment, and security world-wide. India had become the fulcrum or pivot of the Empire in the East.[56]

Between 1870 and 1913 India rose from third to first place among Britain's export markets, as she doubled her share from 8 to 16 per cent of the whole. Some 60 per cent of India's imports came from Britain in 1913, with British textiles accounting for over a third of India's total imports. Between 1885 and 1913 India took two-fifths of Britain's total exports of cotton goods, on which low customs duties were manipulated to Lancashire's advantage. On the other hand, India's share of Britain's imports fell to about 10 per cent around the turn of the century. Whereas Britain took a third of India's total exports in 1890, twenty years later she was taking only a quarter, less than either Europe or Asia. Britain's favourable balance of trade with India was highly important, for India sustained a trading surplus with countries in Asia and Europe that enjoyed surpluses with Britain. India's export values grew fivefold between 1870 and 1914 as jute, cotton, indigo, and tea were despatched to Europe and rice to Asia. India's expanding trade nourished the wider Imperial economy. By 1907 India's aggregate exports to Asian and African ports, including Ceylon, the Straits Settlements, and Mauritius, exceeded her export trade with Europe. British merchants at Indian ports, principally Calcutta, marketed India's exports generally as well as British imports to India. One-tenth of the entire trade of the British Empire passed through India's seaports, more than a third of the total Empire trade outside Britain. The pivotal role of British merchants in India's world trade enabled them virtually to monopolize its shipping, insurance, and international banking activities. One example of the growth of banking from an Indian base is the expansion of the National Bank of India from its formation in Calcutta in 1863 into a far-flung and diversified investment enterprise with, by 1900, nineteen principal offices in India, Ceylon, Burma, and East Africa.

Britain invested heavily in the provision of the infrastructure that facilitated India's export trade. In the first eight years after the Mutiny 'the major movement of British capital was towards India, to transform the land with public works'.[57] By the 1870s some £100m had been invested in railways by 50,000-odd British holders of shares or debentures with government-guaranteed rates of interest. In 1870 £180m of a total of £785m of British overseas investment was in India. The sum ran to £270m out of a £1,300m total in 1885 and £380m out of £3,780m in 1913. Much of

---

[56] Cf. P. J. Cain and A. G. Hopkins, *British Imperialism: Innovation and Expansion, 1688–1914* (London, 1993).

[57] L. H. Jenks, *The Migration of British Capital to 1875* (London, 1938), pp. 206–07.

the investment in Indian industries and utilities was brokered by British merchant entrepreneurs through agency houses based in India's largest cities and with linkages to other Asian centres.[58] In the fifty years preceding the war some £286m was raised for India on the London stock market, 18 per cent of the total for the Empire. India became the fourth largest recipient of British investment overseas. A third of the funds flowed direct into railways, an understatement of the strength of the flow; government loans took almost half of the total and the funds went largely to railway construction. About 80 per cent of the total investment was lodged in fixed interest railway securities or public loans. The remainder supported tea and coffee plantations, mining, banking, and mercantile or managing agency enterprises. The building of the Nurski–Seistan railway was an example of government enterprise to develop Indian trade with adjoining countries.

The predominance of India in the scale of British Imperial commitments is most strikingly measured in human terms. Some 300 million people, three-quarters of the Empire's population, were concentrated in the subcontinent. The deployment of India's human resources for the development of the Empire, a great diaspora, has only recently received due attention. It has now been authoritatively established that by 1910 some 16,000 indentured Indians emigrated annually to other parts of the Empire, a total of over a million since the 1850s.[59]

The basis for the security of the Indian Empire and its outreach to East and West was the Indian Army. By 1910 it was a force of 74,000 British troops and 150,000 Indians, with 2,700 British officers. There were also 35,000 Native Reserve Troops, 33,000 Native and Eurasian Volunteers, and about 20,000 Imperial Reserve Troops. The total annual military expenditure charged to India amounted to some £20m. The British troops in the Indian Army represented a quarter of the total strength of the British army. The Indian Army, in effect, guaranteed the stability of Imperial trade and investment. In the later nineteenth century Indian troops served in China (1860), Abyssinia (1868), Perak (1875–76), Baluchistan (1876–79), Malta and Cyprus (1878), Afghanistan (1878), Egypt (1882), Burma (1886), Nyasa (1893), Mombasa and Uganda (1896), and the Sudan (1885; 1896–98). Some 13,200 British officers and men were sent from India to serve in the South African War. At one stage 30,000 British and Indian troops from the Indian Army were absent in South Africa and China (to which 1,300 British officers and men and about 20,000 Indian troops were despatched). Around the turn of the century it was agreed that India should not be charged the full cost of the Army's deployment beyond the subcontinent, but she was still to bear most of the costs of

---

[58] Stanley Chapman, *Merchant Enterprise in Britain: From the Industrial Revolution to World War I* (Cambridge, 1992), esp. pp. 107–28.

[59] See chap. by David Northrup, p. 91 esp. Table 5.2.

service in Egypt, Persia, the Persian Gulf, Afghanistan, Central Asia, and Siam, and some of the costs of service in East Africa. By 1914 there were Indian troops in colonial garrisons in Egypt, the Indian Ocean, Singapore, and China. Indians were recruited for service in the Malay State Guards, in Hong Kong, and in Singapore.

In a lecture Lord Curzon delivered on 'The Place of India in the Empire' in 1909 he presented India as 'the determining influence of every considerable movement in British power to the east and south of the Mediterranean'.[60] It was for him the key to Disraeli's purchase of shares in the Suez Canal, the occupation of Egypt, resistance to Russian expansion, the South African War, British dominance in Mesopotamia, control of the Persian Gulf, her presence in Aden, the Arabian protectorates, and the connections with the Straits Settlements, China, Japan, and Java. Five years earlier he had given another address, upon receiving the freedom of the City of London, illustrating from his own recent experience the part that India was playing in bearing 'the Imperial burden':

If you want to save your Colony of Natal from being over-run by a formidable enemy, you ask India for help, and she gives it; if you want to rescue the white men's legations from massacres at Peking, and the need is urgent, you request the Government of India to despatch an expedition, and they despatch it; if you are fighting the Mad Mullah in Somaliland, you soon discover that Indian troops and an Indian general are best qualified for the task, and you ask the Government of India to send them; if you desire to defend any of your extreme out-posts or coaling stations of the Empire, Aden, Mauritius, Singapore, Hong-Kong, even Tien-tsin or Shan-hai-kwan, it is to the Indian Army that you turn; if you want to build a railway to Uganda or in the Soudan, you apply for Indian labour. When the late Mr. Rhodes was engaged in developing your recent acquisition of Rhodesia, he came to me for assistance. It is with Indian coolie labour that you exploit the plantations equally of Demerara and Natal; with Indian trained officers that you irrigate and dam the Nile; with Indian forest officers that you tap the resources of Central Africa and Siam; with Indian surveyors that you explore all the hidden places of the earth . . . [Moreover,] India is a country where there will be much larger openings for the investment of capital in the future than has hitherto been the case, and where a great work of industrial and commercial exploitation lies before us.[61]

The great work of industrial and commercial exploitation was, of course, frustrated as the focus of Imperial concern increasingly became politics, internal and international.

The first generation of Indian nationalists alleged that the consequences of British rule for India's socio-economic development were dire. The case against imperialism was marshalled by Dadabhai Naoroji in his *Poverty and Un-British Rule in*

---

[60] George N. Curzon, *The Place of India in the Empire* (London, 1909), p. 10.
[61] Speech at the Guildhall, 20 July 1904, in Raleigh, *Speeches*, p. 38.

India (London, 1901) and R. C. Dutt in *The Economic History of India in the Victorian Age* (London, 1906). They draw upon the 'drain theory' to explain India's rural backwardness, widespread poverty, and recurrent famines. They asserted that India's wealth was being drained off to Britain, by the high costs of a foreign army and of civil administration, and in returns on British investments. It was argued that imperialism had warped and crushed the pre-colonial economy, largely as a result of British manufactures displacing Indian products. A process of de-industrialization was alleged. Modern scholarship has, while acknowledging the existence of 'the drain', been sceptical of its significance, believing it too small to explain the persistence of poverty. It has also found difficulty in testing the theory of de-industrialization: while manufacturing employment failed to rise, any fall defies accurate calculation. Some handicraft industries survived, while the emergence of factories for the manufacture of cotton goods was a success story.[62] By 1914 India had the fourth largest cotton goods industry in the world and its cotton spinning industry was three times the size of Japan's. India's cotton industry was predominantly owned and managed by Indians themselves, rather than by British agencies.

What is more certain is that under the Raj neither official nor private agencies injected sufficient funds to stimulate the economy at large. For reasons of national security fiscal policy remained conservative, leaving governments with only meagre capacity for expansive activity, although they might have directed their purchasing policies more to Indian suppliers. Concern for security and social conservatism also meant that governments were reluctant to countenance rural upheaval. In the Deccan (1879) and the Punjab (1900) there was legislative intervention to inhibit the alienation of land from agriculturists; elsewhere tenancy acts protected rights of occupancy. In 1900 almost three-quarters of male workers were employed in rural activities and the urban population was only about 10 per cent of the whole.

In 1914 as in 1858 the Raj was ultimately a despotic foreign regime dependent upon military power. The Morley–Minto reforms were consistent with the governing principle of the Indian Prince who consulted his notables in durbar while reserving his autocracy. Curzon's Viceroyalty revealed, however, that British rulers could not ignore the interests of Western-educated Indians whom their policies had encouraged. By 1914 governing India required the careful manipulation of co-operative Indians. The cultivation of support from princes, magnates, tenants, merchants, and urban notables had to be balanced by the representation of

---

[62] Neil Charlesworth, *British Rule and the Indian Economy, 1800–1914* (London, 1982); B. R. Tomlinson, *The Economy of Modern India, 1860–1970* (Cambridge, 1993); and Colin Simmons, '"De-industrialization", Industrialization and the Indian Economy, c. 1850–1947', *Modern Asian Studies*, XIX (1985), pp. 593–622.

influential professional élites. In their pursuit of collaborators the British were apt to identify and extend constitutional recognition to communities in forms that divided the incipient nation, such as separate electorates for the representation of the 60 million members of India's previously uncoordinated Muslim communities. The process exacerbated the difficulty of Congress in achieving a broad basis of support. The political consequence of British policies for India was limited advance at the price of disunity. The First World War was to place the initiative in the hands of Indians, who might now more effectively accord the support that Britain required on terms of their own. The Congress and the League would soon reach agreement on political objectives. Lord Curzon himself would draft the 1917 Declaration that promised India eventual responsible self-government within the British Empire.[63]

---

[63] Robin J. Moore, 'Curzon and Indian Reform', *Modern Asian Studies*, XXVII (1993), pp. 719–40.

Select Bibliography

KENNETH BALLHATCHET, *Race, Sex and Class under the Raj: Imperial Attitudes and Policies and their Critics, 1793–1905* (London, 1980).

JUDITH M. BROWN, *Modern India: The Origins of an Asian Democracy*, 2nd edn. (Oxford, 1994), esp. pp. 95–193.

P. J. CAIN and A. G. HOPKINS, *British Imperialism: Innovation and Expansion, 1688–1914* (London, 1993), esp. pp. 316–50.

NEIL CHARLESWORTH, *British Rule and the Indian Economy, 1800–1914* (London, 1982).

IAN COPLAND, *The British Raj and the Indian Princes: Paramountcy in Western India, 1857–1930* (London, 1982).

JOHN GALLAGHER, GORDON JOHNSON, and ANIL SEAL, eds., *Locality, Province and Nation: Essays on Indian Politics, 1870 to 1940* (Cambridge, 1973).

S. GOPAL, *British Policy in India, 1858–1905* (Cambridge, 1965).

PETER HARNETTY, *Imperialism and Free Trade: Lancashire and India in the Mid-Nineteenth Century* (Manchester, 1972).

ARNOLD P. KAMINSKY, *The India Office, 1880–1910* (London, 1986).

PHILIP MASON, *The Men Who Ruled India: The Guardians* (London, 1954).

S. R. MEHROTRA, *A History of the Indian National Congress*, Vol. I, *1885–1918* (New Delhi, 1995).

THOMAS R. METCALF, *Ideologies of the Raj* (Cambridge, 1994).

R. J. MOORE, *Liberalism and Indian Politics, 1872–1922* (London, 1966).

DAVID E. OMISSI, *The Sepoy and the Raj: The Indian Army, 1860–1940* (London, 1994).

C. H. PHILIPS, ed., *The Evolution of India and Pakistan, 1858–1947: Select Documents* (London, 1962).

SUMIT SARKAR, *Modern India, 1885–1947* (Delhi, 1983).

ANIL SEAL, *The Emergence of Indian Nationalism: Competition and Collaboration in the Later Nineteenth Century* (Cambridge, 1968).

BRADFORD SPANGENBERG, *British Bureaucracy in India: Status, Policy and the ICS in the Late 19th Century* (New Delhi, 1976).

B. R. TOMLINSON, *The Economy of Modern India, 1860–1970* (Cambridge, 1993).

20

The Evolution of Colonial Cultures: Nineteenth-Century Asia

SUSAN BAYLY

This chapter examines the phenomenon of 'invisible empire', that is, the many different encounters of the intellect and imagination which brought Asians and Britons together, often violently and contentiously, during the 'long' nineteenth century. Its aim is to ask what cultural differences British rule made to the complex societies of colonial Asia. Of course not all of these encounters were overwhelmingly important in the lives of Asians. Despite its apparent capacity to reshape minds as well as material environments in the age of the steam-powered loom, the railway, and the Gatling gun, colonialism was far from being an all-powerful agent of change in any extra-European society. Even where British power was exercised most intrusively, both through the use of military force and in the great Victorian enterprise of scientific data-collection, much of the colonial world was only lightly and unevenly touched by Western-style schools, laws, printing presses, and campaigns of missionary evangelism.[1]

These were, nevertheless, the agencies which Britons saw as bringing revolutionary transformations to their Asian subjects. Asian ways of life did change significantly in the age of high colonialism, though rarely as anticipated by Imperial social reformers and Christian evangelizers. The most far-reaching source of change for the big rural populations of South and South-East Asia was the collapse by mid-century of the many independent kingdoms which had survived the earlier phases of Britain's expansion. The destruction of such great

---

[1] On South-East Asia particular use has been made of the following: Nicholas Tarling, ed., *Cambridge History of Southeast Asia* (hereafter *CHSEA*) (Cambridge 1992), Vol. II; Anthony Milner, *The Invention of Politics in Colonial Malaya: Contesting Nationalism and the Expansion of the Public Sphere* (Cambridge, 1995); L. A. Peter Gosling and Linda Y. C. Lim, eds., *The Chinese in Southeast Asia*, Vol. 2, *Identity, Culture and Politics* (Singapore, 1983); Victor Purcell, *The Chinese in Southeast Asia*, 2nd edn. (London, 1965); and C. M. Turnbull *A History of Singapore, 1819–1975* (Kuala Lumpur, 1977); for Hong Kong: Henry Lethbridge, *Hong Kong: Stability and Change* (Hong Kong, 1978); on colonial Calcutta, Sukanta Chaudhuri, ed., *Calcutta the Living City*, Vol. I (Calcutta, 1990); and for 'syncretistic' religion in India, Susan Bayly *Saints, Goddesses and Kings, Muslims and Christians in South Indian Society, 1700–1900* (Cambridge, 1989).

armed powers as Mysore (1799), the Sikh kingdom of the Punjab (1849), and the major polities of Ceylon (1815) and upper Burma (1885), was accompanied by campaigns to disarm the land- and sea-based warrior groups which had flourished on the margins of these comparatively fluid Asian realms.

The British were particularly assertive in their dealings with these 'predator' peoples. Early in the century Britain's attempts to suppress so-called piracy had a massive impact on Asia's armed seafarers. Southern China's roving maritime populations and the archipelago's 'sea nomads' or *orang laut* communities were among the earliest such groups to be dispersed or forced into dependent livelihoods as British sea-power was consolidated. Similar effects were felt on the land, as colonial officials and their favoured intermediaries promoted the expansion of arable frontiers in the fertile interior regions of South and South-East Asia. These trends fostered the forced settlement of pastoralists and hunter-gatherers, as well as the absorption of other unsettled or semi-sedentary peoples into a world of insecure wage labour and petty commodity production. As a result, armed 'aboriginals' like India's forest- and hill-dwelling Bhils, Gonds, and Nagas, or the 'wild' Iban and *orang asli* of Sarawak and upland Malaya, were stigmatized as headhunters and dangerous 'primitives' by colonial ethnographers, and harried as rebels and criminals when they resisted the loss of their lands and livelihoods.[2]

In India this process of 'peasantization' had profound cultural effects. As increasing numbers of Indian villagers were brought into contact with moneyed townsfolk and status-conscious colonial service élites, there was a general hardening of social boundaries. These developments gave new cohesion and importance to the two elements of the Indian social order which are most commonly thought of as its defining features. The first of these was the Hindu caste system. Under British rule, more of the subcontinent's peoples than ever before found themselves drawn or coerced into the schemes of ritualized social hierarchy which are now regarded as key characteristics of caste society. The second area in which this closing of boundaries occurred was the differentiation between Hindus and Indians of other faiths, especially Muslims. During the nineteenth century the real but often ill-defined distinctions separating Hindus from non-Hindus became much more clearly demarcated. This was largely a response to the teachings of the spiritual revivalists and other proponents of stricter pious norms who became increasingly influential during the nineteenth century. The actions of colonial policy-makers and their orientalist informants further heightened these divisions of faith and community.[3]

---

[2] A. A. Yang, ed., *Crime and Criminality in British India* (Tucson, Ariz., 1985); Ranajit Guha, ed., *Subaltern Studies*, IV (New Delhi, 1985).

[3] Sandria B. Freitag, *Collective Action and Community: Public Arenas and the Emergence of Communalism in North India* (Berkeley, 1989); Seema Alavi, *The Sepoys and the Company: Tradition and*

Elsewhere too, most notably in regions which had possessed strong traditions of kingship and patrician lordliness, colonial rule brought a similar tightening of social and communal boundaries. Ceylon acquired stricter differentiations between Sinhalese Buddhists and Hindu Tamils, and an intensification of caste-like divisions proclaiming a moral difference between such people as Karava, whose caste name denoted lowly toiling origins, and the landed groups who styled themselves Goyigama, and wished to be seen as ritually superior to the island's servile populations.[4] The Malayan archipelago too became more sharply divided along boundaries which distinguished between Malay-speaking lord and peasant and Chinese entrepreneur and immigrant labourer groups. Almost everywhere British rule acted as a catalyst to changes which redrew and often strengthened the distinction between the public and the private, and tended to highlight issues affecting the status and conduct of women.[5]

Of course Asians were already experiencing profound intellectual and social upheavals long before the age of Victorian high colonialism. The cosmopolitan and culturally diverse peoples of the Empire assimilated influences from their colonial rulers and their fellow Asians at different rates and in different ways. Furthermore, the Empire's so-called collaborating élites often interpreted Western faiths and intellectual traditions in ways which astonished and discomfited their rulers and proselytizers.

Even so, in order to grasp the full complexity of Empire it is important to assess the interactions between Britons and their Asian subjects in the realms of religion, law, science, education, and modernizing social activism. This chapter therefore focuses on three main aspects of 'invisible empire'. The first of these is setting and context, that is, the basic facts of urbanization, literacy, and other forces shaping local cultural encounters. The second is religion, since it was in the arena of worship that the peoples of East and West had many of their most far-reaching confrontations. The third is the intersection of culture and politics, with the political defined to include public debates on the status of women as well as other 'modern' issues touching the definition of collective and individual rights and moral standards.

Transition in Northern India, 1770–1830 (Delhi, 1995), chaps. 1–2; Rosalind O'Hanlon, 'Historical Approaches to Communalism', in Peter Robb, ed., *Society and Ideology, Essays in South Asian History* (Delhi, 1993), pp. 247–66; for 'peasantization' see Lim Teck Ghee, *Peasants and their Agricultural Economy in Colonial Malaya, 1874–1941* (Kuala Lumpur, 1977).

[4] John D. Rogers, 'Post-Orientalism and the Interpretation of Pre-modern and Modern Political Identities: The Case of Sri Lanka', *Journal of Asian Studies*, LIII, 1 (1994) pp. 10–23.

[5] For the emergence of a colonial 'bourgeois' public sphere, Sandria Freitag, ed., *Culture and Power in Banaras* (Berkeley, 1989); and C. A. Bayly, *Empire and Information, Intelligence Gathering and Social Communication in India, 1780–1870* (Cambridge, 1996).

Setting and Context: New Élites in the Colonial Milieu

Colonialism left its most visible imprint on Asian minds through the building of certain distinctive institutions and environments. There were the widespread economic changes, which were both predicated on and brought in their train a body of laws and public pronouncements proclaiming the virtues of public probity, free trade, and uniform contractual obligations. There were the great towns with their industrial workplaces, universities, and military cantonments; these were the milieux in which Asians most commonly met unfamiliar definitions of public and private space, as well as new standards of gentility, morality, and social refinement.

So what were the basic structural features of Anglo-Asian 'culture contact'? The British made English the language of law and upper-level bureaucracy in their most important Asian dependencies, but they were never systematic Anglicizers. For all their claims about the supposed backwardness of the 'Orient', Imperial officials were reluctant spenders, ever fearful that tampering with native laws, faiths, or learned traditions might undermine their fragile authority over large, and often turbulent subject populations. Indeed, by selecting certain indigenous languages for lower-level official use—Urdu and Hindi in much of India, Malay in maritime South-East Asia, Cantonese in the South China seas—the British helped to standardize both written and spoken forms of these Asian 'mother tongues'.[6] At the same time, the remarkable Victorian glossary *Hobson Jobson* records the lively circulation of neologisms and loan-words throughout the Asian Empire. These contacts brought the Indian caste name Koli to China, where it became 'coolie', and introduced the Malay term *kampong* to India, where it emerged as 'compound', an enclosure in which a house stands. Outside the Empire too, English became seeded with such terms as 'tycoon', a borrowing from Chinese through Japanese, and innumerable Indian loanwords, including 'mogul', 'pajama', 'thug', 'loot', 'juggernaut', 'shampoo', and 'tank', together with a rich vocabulary of Urdu-derived soldier's slang: 'bint' for girl, 'bundook' for firearm; and 'Blighty' (England), from *vilayat*, homeland.[7]

None of this added up to a shared sense of cultural purpose either within or beyond Asia. Britons did not subscribe to an ideal of French-style 'civilizing mission'.[8] Also few Britons made permanent homes outside Europe, unlike their Ibero-American and Afrikaner counterparts. But while there was no cultural

---

[6] e.g. C. M. Naim, 'Prize-Winning Adab', in B. D. Metcalf, ed., *Moral Conduct and Authority: The Place of Adab in South Asian Islam* (Berkeley, 1984), pp. 290–314.

[7] Arthur Coke Burnell and Henry Yule, *Hobson Jobson* (1883; Wordsworth Edns, Ware, 1996).

[8] Michael Adas, *Machines as the Measure of Men: Science, Technology, and Ideologies of Western Dominance* (Ithaca, NY, 1989).

master plan for the Empire, the great commercial and administrative centres, most notably Calcutta and Bombay, together with Singapore, Hong Kong, Rangoon, and other East Asian ports, were crucial arenas of the colonial experience. The most obvious signs of a common Asian colonial culture can be discerned in these populous cities with their Anglophone bureaucracies, Western business firms, and polyglot migrant populations. It was Asians themselves, particularly those advancing themselves in the newer commercial or professional callings, who gave this special vigour and volatility to the Empire's great towns.

Nothing in the French and Dutch colonies, or Russia's central Asian dominions, quite matched the mobile and assertive intelligentsias whose descendants still play a disproportionate role in the public life of Britain's former dependencies. Everywhere in British-ruled Asia there were people from modest trading and service backgrounds who made the risky leap into a 'modern' livelihood. The most successful of these 'respectable native gentlemen' pursued careers as lawyers, teachers, journalists, and doctors, as well as technical specialists and government functionaries. They included migrant Armenians and Baghdadi Jews whose forebears had made modest gains in trade and office-holding under Asian rulers, or as clients of the Portuguese and Dutch. Equally important were the Ceylon Burghers and other élite Eurasian groups whose ancestors had been patronized by earlier colonial powers, and the Malacca-based Chinese known as Christangs, after the local name for their modified Portuguese trading language. Many of these people's descendants learned English and became prominent in British-ruled colonial territories.

Other arbiters of the new colonial cultures were Bengal's rentier-descended urban service and professional population, the high-caste Hindus known as *bhadralok* ('good' or refined people) and their many regional counterparts elsewhere. These included India's Parsis, originally Persian-speaking Zoroastrian migrants who became prominent in both commerce and the professions in Bombay and the Far East. In the East Asian Empire, the most important 'native gentlemen' were the richer Hokkiens, Hakkas, and Cantonese-speakers, many of whose forebears had emigrated from southern China long before 1800. These people, who came to be known as Straits Chinese, achieved dominant positions in South-East Asia's major cities; most were of modest peasant origin despite their leading families' economic successes. There were also India's Bohras and Memons, together with the Hadrahmauti Saiyyids and other Arabic-speaking traders who operated everywhere from the Red Sea to the South-East Asian entrepôts, and other wide-ranging groups such as the Tamil Muslim *maraikkayars* who founded notable fortunes in Singapore and Penang.[9]

---

[9] L. W. C. Van den Berg, *Le Hadhramout et les colonies Arabes dans l'archipel Indien* (Batavia, 1886).

In both India and Malaya, rentier groups and descendants of regional rulers formed the other important subdivision of this gentleman class. British attitudes to these 'traditional' élites were always ambivalent. The more conservative scholar-officials wanted such people to be conciliated and honoured on the grounds that 'Orientals' were culturally predisposed to revere the lordly grandees of their native land. More puritanical Britons condemned patrician rent-receivers as decadent and seditious. Indeed, as early as the 1820s such groups as Malacca's superior Eurasian and Malay rent-receivers, deemed 'useless' and unenterprising, were summarily deprived of their proprietary rights.[10] Elsewhere too, attempts to introduce uniform legal codes tended to bear heavily on these gentry lineages, suppressing their rights of ancestral or corporate land tenure in favour of simplified conceptions of private property and individual ownership.[11]

The Tensions of Respectability

The culture of Asia's new colonial environments forged connections between the world of the 'native gentlemen' and less exalted rural and urban peoples. Whether one looks at the material facts of architecture, language, and livelihoods, or the more elusive features of perceptions and mentalities, the great cities where most of these migrants were concentrated had more in common with one another than with the older court and market towns and their rural hinterlands. This was in part because of their newness, their great size compared to other Asian cities, and their remarkably rapid growth. India's two largest cities, Calcutta and Bombay, grew by nearly 300 per cent from the 1820s to the end of the nineteenth century, each having a population of nearly 800,000 in 1881. The colonial centres of East Asia, including China's treaty ports, also expanded dramatically: Shanghai, a small town in 1843, had over 400,000 residents in 1895.

Of course many older Indian towns had grown very rapidly in the centuries preceding the consolidation of British power. Those like Benares (Banaras) which had long combined commercial and pilgrimage functions retained much of their importance throughout the colonial era. But the newer ports and industrial centres grew to even greater size and often swamped their hinterlands. Calcutta's population was ten times that of any other town in nineteenth-century Bengal. Despite its social diversity, this city became the idealized focus for a new sense of regional ethno-linguistic identity. Even in the early nineteenth century it had become axiomatic among those who would once have looked for cultural reference points to a more diverse array of older market towns and Islamized courts,

---

[10] Brian Harrison *Holding the Fort: Melaka under Two Flags, 1795–1845* (Kuala Lumpur, 1986), p. 109.
[11] David S. Y. Wong, *Tenure and Land Dealings in the Malay States* (Singapore, 1977); Thomas R. Metcalf, *Land, Landlords and the British Raj: Northern India in the Nineteenth Century* (Berkeley, 1979).

that to be truly 'Bengali' was to partake of the forms of modernity to be found in Calcutta. Colombo, Rangoon, Hong Kong, and Singapore all played similar regional roles.[12]

These colonial towns were especially important to urbanizing commodity producers such as the Gujarati cotton-growers who were known by the caste name Patidar. These and other 'peasantized' smallholders became increasingly inclined to adapt their ideals of faith and morality to those which they observed in the lives of town-based traders and service people. The more influential of these urban groups had come in past centuries to follow traditions of Hindu spirituality which exalted the values of sobriety, thrift, and pious respectability. There had been comparable new syntheses in Buddhism and Islam in both South and South-East Asia, and here too it was traders and other townsfolk who often responded most enthusiastically to such teachings.[13] Well before the nineteenth century, these forms of religion had come to define the standards by which people with vulnerable livelihoods to protect could try to impress those who had reason to judge their worth and substance. Despite local variations, almost invariably the purity of dependent women was a critical test of this kind of respectability. And, in so far as there really were certain shared cultural traits within the Asian Empire, these ideas mattered particularly because they forged links between so many different kinds of urban and rural people under the anxious scrutiny of the colonial state.

British observers were ambivalent about these interactions between socially conservative city-dwellers, and the growing populations of industrious upper peasants who were coming to emulate them. Colonial officials generally preferred these people's notions of propriety to the licentiousness which they ascribed both to landed patrician groups and to the 'wild' martial peoples of the forests and remoter plains. But they knew too that these changes involved initiatives emanating from Asians themselves, and that such moves could provide a focus for anti-colonial 'resistance', as well as provoking unrest between their subjects. They particularly had in mind cases where people such as south India's newly commercialized Nadar cultivators placed themselves under the 'civilizing' sponsorship of evangelical missionaries, and then proclaimed their new-found respectability in ways which aroused opposition from insecure local élites. Many Nadars did this by adopting a form of modest female dress, the breast-cloth, which their higher-caste neighbours were seeking to reserve as a marker of their own superior status.[14]

---

[12] D. K. Basu, ed., *The Rise and Growth of the Colonial Port City in Asia* (Santa Cruz and Berkeley, 1979).

[13] S. P. Sen, ed., *Social and Religious Reform Movements* (Calcutta, 1979).

[14] Robert Hardgrave, *The Nadars of Tamilnad* (Berkeley, 1969); David Ludden *Peasant History in South India* (Princeton, 1985), pp. 192–95.

These tensions of the urbanizing colonial milieu were also apparent in the Far East. Here the key cultural fact in Britain's colonial cities was the growing size and wealth of the Chinese immigrant populations. Hong Kong had a population of 300,000 Chinese and 20,000 Europeans at the end of the nineteenth century. In 1821 Singapore contained a mere 5,000 Malay, Chinese, and other migrants, and had grown into a metropolis of 185,000 in 1911. Rates of growth were spectacular: Singapore's population rose by 40 per cent between 1871 and 1881. In most Chinese-dominated South-East Asian towns, men greatly outnumbered women: the proportions were 8 to 1 in Singapore in 1911. The flow of transients was also enormous: over 200,000 Chinese indentured labourers landed in Singapore in 1900, and 250,000 in 1912.

These then were towns full of insecure newcomers which had grown haphazardly, without serious urban planning or significant expenditures on monuments and heroic adornments. They had in common the rigid separation between the airy suburbs or civil lines where the white expatriates lived, often adjoining the local military cantonments, and the densely populated 'native' quarters. These so-called 'Blacktowns' were subdivided by custom and sometimes by official ordinance into separate enclaves inhabited by different 'races' or 'communities'.

The non-white populations of these colonial cities were highly diverse and generally poor, though there were instances of spectacular wealth amongst such people as the great compradors and trader-bankers of maritime South-East Asia. There were hugely wealthy corporate institutions too, notably the Hong Kong and Singapore clan and service associations (*huis* and *kongsis*), to which many Chinese emigrants were affiliated. Many of these guild-like confraternities had occult membership rituals, and came to be known in English as triads or secret societies. Such covert networks came to be regarded by Western orientalists as a dark and mysterious force pervading the overseas Chinese communities both within and beyond the British-ruled territories. In 1857 both the abortive uprising in Singapore, and the attempted coup against Rajah Brooke's rule in Sarawak, were reportedly led by fanatical anti-Christian triads. This view of the secret society as an ineradicable fact of Chinese culture generated much orientalist writing. There were also numerous attempts to control triad activity through the imposition of curfews, pass laws, and other measures, including the Suppression of Dangerous Societies Ordinances in the Straits Settlements, Singapore (1869, 1885, and 1890) and Hong Kong (1872).[15]

---

[15] On other possibly mythical forms of Asian criminality, cf. Carl A. Trocki, *Opium and Empire, Chinese Society in Colonial Singapore, 1800–1910* (Ithaca, NY, 1990); John M. Chin, *The Sarawak Chinese* (Kuala Lumpur, 1981), p. 34; Gustave Schlegel, *Thian Ti Hwui: The Hung-league or Heaven-earth-league* (1866; Thornhill, 1991); Wilfred Blythe, *The Impact of Chinese Secret Societies in Malaya* (London, 1969); Mak Lau Fong, *The Sociology of Secret Societies* (Kuala Lumpur, 1981).

Asian Responses: Women and 'Oriental Vices' in the Colonial City

The big colonial cities were often turbulent, though the major insurrections, most notably India's 1857 Mutiny-Rebellion, originated amongst the hard-pressed peasantries, forest-dwellers, and townsfolk of the remoter hinterlands. Furthermore the greatest of this period's Asian upheavals, China's Taiping Rebellion (1850–64), and the Boxer Rising (1900), occurred outside the regions of formal Western rule. At the same time, the turmoil created by these mainland Chinese rebellions was important in prompting millions of distress migrants to seek new livelihoods in the docks, mines, and plantations of the Asian colonial centres. This powerfully affected South-East Asia's more established Chinese populations, whose richer families sought to adjust to this influx by claiming the status of cultural exemplars to 'backward' newcomers. Migration to these labour-hungry centres aroused contradictory reactions amongst Asians, even in localities where the migrants came from areas familiar with long-distance trade and pilgrimage. As early as the 1830s, Calcutta's celebrated Kalighat watercolourists were disseminating trenchant social comments on the experience of urban modernity, portraying this city of migrants and new experiences as a place of vulgar new wealth and corrupting temptations. Their stock images were of rootless young office-workers in awkward, semi-Europeanized clothes, and of young women depraved through exposure to the city's indecorous freedoms. Such women were shown emasculating and impoverishing their menfolk, making them neglect their righteous mothers in favour of demanding wives and grasping courtesans, and provoking them to acts of unholy violence, as in a famous Calcutta murder case which was widely depicted in these popular art-forms.[16]

Other colonial cities too acquired a rich popular culture which was closely linked to the spread of vernacular and English-language newspapers and other ephemeral media. This world of print and pictures made much of crime and sex scandals, both as a source of entertainment and as a means of promoting moralistic messages on behalf of an extraordinarily heterogeneous range of public commentators and would-be social reformers. These contributors to the debates about faith and morals which preoccupied so many of Britain's Asian subjects played a crucial role in creating a distinctive new political culture within the Empire. Its habits of speech and argument were forged by self-styled 'public men' (and significant numbers of women) who adapted Western concepts of

---

[16] Tapati Guha-Thakurta, *The Making of a New Indian Art: Artists, Aesthetics and Nationalism in Bengal, c.1850–1920* (Cambridge, 1992), pp. 18–32. A painting of the case in question *c.*1880 in which an outraged husband brutally murdered his unfaithful wife, is reproduced in P. J. Marshall, ed., *The Cambridge Illustrated History of the British Empire* (Cambridge, 1996), p. 251.

citizens' rights and philanthropy to the new civic arenas of the Asian colonies. This culture was nourished on public platforms, in the press, and in the transactions of innumerable educational trusts, social uplift organizations, and other 'modernizing' voluntary associations. It drew too on conceptions of revived or rediscovered spiritual and political tradition, and therefore, as it acquired a capacity to express ideals of nationhood and patriotic mission, it had an impact far beyond the world of the anglophone colonial intelligentsias.[17]

Even outside areas of formal British control, the colonial societies loomed large, especially in the thinking of cultural élites in uncolonized kingdoms—Japan and Siam, Burma before annexation, and above all China. Thus, in the early nineteenth century China's Manchu authorities sought in vain to restrain migration to South-East Asia. In orthodox Confucian thought, emigration from mainland China to Nanyang (the southern Ocean), especially by women, had been represented for centuries as a disturbance of the social and environmental harmonies which both the Emperor and the Confucian mandarinate had a sacred duty to preserve.

These fears emphasizing the special dangers surrounding women in the corrupting colonial milieu came to loom large in the thinking of early Chinese nationalists and social reformers both within and beyond the imperial mainland. Of particular concern was the traffic in young girls, reportedly enticed in large numbers from South China to the vice dens of Shanghai and Hong Kong. The plight of these so-called brothel slaves, and of purchased Chinese household concubines, had originally been highlighted by such key Victorian philanthropic organizations as the Aborigines' Protection Society. Western social reformers saw these trades, like the forms of racketeering which prevailed in the recruitment of Chinese 'coolie' labourers, as products of age-old Chinese 'vices'. These they regarded as being reinforced by the secret societies whose agents were held to control all illicit enterprises in the Far East, including gambling, prostitution, and the opium trade.

To Chinese commentators, on the other hand, colonialism and modernity were to blame for these proliferating evils, the coolie and brothel recruiters being represented as kidnappers whisking innocent rustics from their villages by rail and steamer. The question, though, was whether Western moralists should be praised or resisted in their attacks on the supposed social failings of the overseas Chinese communities. Thus, there was much debate about whether concubinage was an old and benign custom of respectable households, or a new and vicious form of slavery which had been generated in the unsettled environment of the colonial

[17] Douglas Haynes, *Rhetoric and Ritual in Colonial India: The Shaping of a Public Culture in Surat City, 1852–1928* (Berkeley, 1991); W. R. Roff, *The Origins of Malay Nationalism* (Kuala Lumpur, 1967); Khoo Kay Kim, *Malay Society: Transformation and Democratisation* (Petaling Jaya, 1991); Partha Chatterjee, *Nationalist Thought and the Colonial World* (New York, 1986).

cities. The debate about female foot-binding aroused equally strong emotions amongst Hong Kong and Straits-based pamphleteers and philanthropists.

Chinese thinkers who struggled with these issues had much in common with the educated Indians who were under pressure to pronounce on sensitive matters in their own societies. For the many Hindus who contributed to learned societies and press debates on matters of faith, morals, and science, the most painful controversies were about whether the high-status practices of female infanticide, pre-pubescent female marriage, and suttee (sati—the ritualized burning of Hindu widows) were as 'uncivilized' as the missionaries and other Western critics claimed.[18] If so, then Asian contributors to these debates felt it necessary to decide who was to blame, and how their culture should be purged of these defects. Some participants in these controversies opted for socially conservative solutions, focusing on organizations and causes which emphasized a rediscovery of past cultural glories and the preservation of established norms and values. In other cases one can see the first steps being taken towards the positions adopted by radical twentieth-century 'modernizers' and secularizers, most notably by socialists and revolutionary nationalists whose vision of the future involved a complete break with traditions which they perceived as bad, 'backward' and unprogressive.

These debates in the Anglophone and vernacular press, and in the new representative Assemblies which came into being in the Asian Empire, had an impact far beyond the colonial milieu. By the 1890s China's rulers were beginning to fear the potentially seditious influence of self-professed social reformers and anti-Manchu nationalists amongst the overseas Chinese populations, especially in areas of British control. The Manchus' response to this was to try to woo the 'modernity'-minded Straits Chinese élites, especially prominent Babas or Peranakans, Malay-speaking Chinese with a distinctive tradition of acculturation to Malay life. The richer Baba traders and professional men represented themselves as fervent Empire loyalists; some even preferred to be known as 'King's Chinese', to distinguish themselves from the mass of 'coolie' migrants. Nevertheless, from the 1890s the Straits Settlements' Baba activists campaigned to foster the learning of Mandarin as a means of discovering what they considered a lost bond of Confucian cultural values. In 1907 the Manchu government founded a Mandarin-medium school in Nanking for Chinese from the South-East Asian migrant communities, hoping to lessen threats of an alliance between home-grown anti-Manchu nationalists and influential Straits Chinese who were pressing Malaya's Babas to 'uplift' themselves through education and the abandonment of 'backward' practices (opium-smoking, foot-binding, and the wearing of the pigtail).[19]

---

[18] L. Mani, 'Official Discourse on Sati in Early Nineteenth-Century Bengal', in K. Sangari and S. Vaid, eds., *Recasting Women: Essays in Colonial History* (New Delhi, 1989).

[19] Turnbull, *History of Singapore*, p. 107.

Capturing Western Skills and Knowledge

Since the British built their rule in Asia around the use of indigenous clerical and professional skill, those who aspired to advantage themselves in the colonial milieu responded eagerly to this demand for 'modern' educational qualifications. It was through literacy and particularly knowledge of English that Asians could aspire to the most lucrative opportunities. The big Indian and South-East Asian towns acquired larger concentrations of schools, colleges, libraries, learned societies, and other points of contact with Western learning and science than anywhere else in Asia. Between 1818 and 1867, 219 English and Bengali periodicals were published in Calcutta; Benares became an expanding centre of Hindi publishing, and printing in dozens of other Asian languages including Arabic and Chinese became a great feature of the British-ruled colonial societies.[20]

With the expansion of professional and clerical employment, education itself became a major industry. In the subcontinent English education was initially provided by missionaries, but in the 1860s the governments of India and Ceylon created Departments of Public Instruction with authority over a growing network of English-medium schools. Most of Hong Kong's seventy government-supported schools taught English by 1900. State-sponsored universities were established in Calcutta, Bombay, and Madras in 1857; new universities were founded in the Punjab and Allahabad in 1882 and 1887, and Rangoon's Government College (founded in 1873) was upgraded to a university in 1920.[21]

At the same time Asians took important initiatives of their own. The establishment of Muslim educational foundations (*madrasas*) with 'modernized' Koranic (Quranic) curricula was one of the chief expressions of Islamic reformism among such groups as colonial South-East Asia's élite 'new generation' Malays. Equally widespread was the endowment of Asian-run institutions with Western-style curricula: these were intended to counter the dominance of missionary-run schools and colleges as providers of English education to the aspiring colonial intelligentsias.[22]

Steady expansion in the size and influence of the Empire's English-educated classes fostered the large-scale migration of Anglophone clerks and professional men to distant parts of the Empire. Even the many Indian, Chinese, and Arabic-speaking Muslim traders who preserved the techniques of the 'traditional' Asian

---

[20] Chaudhuri, ed., *Calcutta the Living City*, I, pp. 128–36.

[21] In 1901 there were over 23,000 Indian college students, and 634,000 secondary school pupils: H. H. Dodwell, ed., *The Cambridge History of India*, VI (Cambridge, 1932), p. 348; also Marshall, ed., *Cambridge Illustrated History of the British Empire*, p. 187; Philip Loh Fook Seng, *Seeds of Separatism: Educational Policy in Malaya, 1874–1940* (Kuala Lumpur, 1975).

[22] Kenneth W. Jones, *Socio-Religious Reform Movements in British India* (Cambridge, 1989), pp. 28–29.

family firm needed literate English-speaking clerks for their dealings with Western officials and merchants. Many Asian commercial men also invested in English education for their younger kinsmen so that they could represent themselves more directly in dealings with colonial courts and bureaucracies.

For most Asians, learning English was initially a matter of narrow occupational skill. But the results of such schooling were often unexpected and troubling, and not just for those with firsthand experience of Chinese mission schools or Western-style university curricula. Even the non-literate took an anxious interest in the big nineteenth-century controversies about whether or in what ways the colonial authorities should seek to educate the 'Oriental mind'. In the subcontinent the most influential of these debates concerned the value of 'Anglicist' learning as opposed to a socially conservative vision of Indian élites schooled in a 'traditional' manner. This meant an emphasis on the sacred scriptural works which many scholar-officials continued to defend as the core of true knowledge and culture. The debate was keenly followed by the many Indians with a personal stake in the status of Benares and other established centres of pious learning.

There were many important Asians whose cultural encounters with the West were positive and creative. The remarkable Calcutta polymath Raja Ram Mohan Roy (d. 1833) was proficient in Greek, Latin, Hebrew, and English, as well as Bengali, Sanskrit, and Persian. He debated the concept of Christ's incarnation with Christian missionaries, and berated British officials in 1823 for being slow to instruct their Indian subjects in the 'useful sciences'.[23] The so-called Young Bengal radicals of the 1830s and 1840s went even further in embracing novel ideologies imbibed from their Western-style schooling, denouncing the Hindu scriptures in favour of Tom Paine and the French positivists, and shocking their cow-revering teetotal elders by publicly consuming beef and brandy. In contrast, however, even Singapore's richest Chinese trader, the famous 'Whampoa' (Hoo Ah Kay, d. 1880), who associated closely with the British and became the first Asian member of the Singapore Legislative Council, was incensed when his son returned from school in England in 1847 calling himself a Presbyterian and with his pigtail cut off.[24]

Throughout British-ruled Asia, such inter-generational battles were a notable feature of colonial 'culture contact'. But something approximating to Hoo Ah Kay's stance, a kind of negotiated arms-length encounter which both absorbed and contained the effects of 'modernity', was far more common than the radicalism of small groups like Young Bengal. Much more representative of the literate Indian's world-view in the later nineteenth century were the pious Hindu activists who formed associations for the preservation of orthodox faith (*sanatan dharm*

---

[23] Chaudhuri, ed., *Calcutta: The Living City*, I, pp. 101–02.
[24] Turnbull, *History of Singapore*, pp. 55, 105.

sabhas). These groups' adherents preached revived orthodox Hinduism in a form which was at least partly shaped by Western conceptions of transcendent divinity, though these were synthesized with indigenous Hindu ideals of the transcendent. At the same time, these activists told believers to assert their Hinduness in the face of Christian teaching, and to recognize that adoption of the white man's ways and language could result in dangerous spiritual and moral contamination.

Nevertheless, knowledge of English spread very widely across the Asian Empire, especially among those who moved ever further afield in search of commercial and service posts. Furthermore, after mid-century members of Asia's 'respectable' élites were increasingly incorporated into the limited forms of local self-government introduced by such measures as the Municipalities Acts for India, Malaya, and Burma (1856–74), and the formation of quasi-representative bodies, including the Hong Kong District Watch Committee (1866) and the State Councils of the Federated Malay States.[25] These developments had far-reaching cultural importance. By mastering the committee procedures and other forms of institutional life which these measures introduced, men of wealth and education found new ways to achieve power and status within the colonial milieu. By the 1890s the prime expressions of this new political culture were to be found in the proceedings of organizations which were founded or taken over by Asians themselves. Among the most influential were those in which concepts of nationhood were forged and debated, most notably the Indian Social Conference, the Indian National Congress, and their 'modernizing' counterparts in Burma, Malaya, and Ceylon.[26]

These moves towards representative government forced Britons to debate how precisely to deal with such people as Parsi High Court judges, Chinese justices of the peace, Ceylon Burgher degree-holders, and other 'native gentlemen' who were held to be highly sensitive about social contacts with whites. Civil servants' manuals were detailed on these points, proclaiming it safe for British officials to offer non-alcoholic 'aerated waters' to educated 'modern' visitors, but warning that by 'tradition' Muslims were dog-haters who had to be protected from being fawned on by the British officer's pets. Above all, the well-meaning Briton should refrain from making polite enquiries about the 'gentlemen's' womenfolk.[27]

Those Asians deemed politically reliable were encouraged to perform 'modern' political tasks in a 'traditional' cultural idiom. In Victorian Hong Kong, the powerful Chinese notables who amassed fortunes as compradors for Western businesses acquired status by endowing large-scale philanthropic ventures. These charitable trusts became the colony's most important 'modern' institutions. The largest of these, the Tung Wah Hospital, was founded in 1870 at a time when

---

[25] Tinker, *Foundations of Local Self-Government in India, Pakistan and Burma* (London, 1954). p. 32.
[26] See e.g. Haynes, *Rhetoric and Ritual*.
[27] *The Indian Civil Service Manual (Madras)* (Madras, 1931), pp. 40–47.

the colony's Anglophone press had been campaigning against one of the city's ancestor-tablet shrines, where indigents were allegedly left to die unattended and in great squalour. This press campaign was similar to India's colonial panics about the evils of *suttee* and so-called bathing-ghat deaths, this being the practice, supposedly common amongst pious Hindus, of taking ailing relatives to die on the banks of the sacred River Ganges. Hong Kong's new hospital was therefore a 'modern' venture funded by subscriptions from rich Chinese as a means of declaring their leadership in campaigns to eradicate 'backwardness' among their fellow 'Orientals'.

Although these ideas about the 'Orient's' supposed depravities were initially derived from missionaries and other Western commentators, many Asians reshaped them to fit their own definitions of morality or public conduct, and their needs for status and credibility in the eyes of colonial authorities. From the early 1880s, membership of the controlling bodies of these powerful associations, and especially a seat on Hong Kong's District Watch Committee, became critical marks of power and status for the city's Chinese grandees. All these organizations emphasized the duty of 'public men' to impose moral and physical controls on the turbulent lower orders. Although Hong Kong was a 'modern' city with Western-style civic government, the Chinese businessmen who became trustees of the Tung Wah and similar foundations were encouraged by successive British administrations to dress and conduct themselves like Confucian mandarins. Hong Kong's British-run Secretariat for Chinese affairs modelled its official documents on those of imperial China's Confucian bureaucracy. So while no official mandarinate existed in the British-ruled dependencies, here too there was an attempt to 'indigenize' colonialism by exalting what were supposed to be the 'essences' of a traditional Asian culture.

Religion and Modernity in the 'Invisible Empire'

As key informants in this quest for cultural knowledge, 'native' intelligentsias had a disproportionate effect on the formalizing of colonial thought about Asia's belief systems. It was largely from educated Asian 'gentlemen' that Western scholars derived their view of Eastern faiths as textually-based 'religions', defined both in the colonial law codes and electoral categories which they helped to frame, and by their own self-aware communities of believers on the basis of scriptural or moral codes. Thus, many of colonial Asia's most significant interactions between ruler and ruled occurred in the domain of religion. These involved many misperceptions on the part of the colonizer and Western theorizer, but also instances of creative adaptation of the white outsider's beliefs, languages, institutions, and value systems.

This can be seen particularly in the decidedly uneven impact of Christianity in Britain's Asian colonies. 'Responses' to the presence of evangelizing Christians in Asia were largely a matter of indirect and unintended influences.[28] Nevertheless, it was through interactions with missionaries and British scholar-officials that the idea of religion itself entered Asia, if by religion we mean a separate sphere of experience, requiring, for example, a distinction between the 'religious' and 'secular' aspects of a Hindu royal procession in which kings and gods are honoured by an assembled populace.

Even when the intention was to refute the so-called untruths of Asian faiths, from the 1830s onwards it was generally missionaries and evangelical scholar-officials who collected and published both vernacular and English editions of such important texts as the Ramcharitmanas, the Vedas, the Koran (Quran), and the texts of the Buddhist canon.[29] The irony was that Western orientalists made these scriptures far more accessible to Asians than had previously been the case. Indeed, it was largely through them that these texts became revered in virtually every Asian culture as the cornerstones of a standardized or 'modern' Hindu, Muslim, Buddhist, or Confucian faith. This process involved much conflict between different schools of 'modernists' and 'traditionalists'. But from this period onward, large numbers of Asians actively spread a vision of their ancestral faiths as modern, revitalized bodies of truth deriving authority from revealed written texts. These were forms of belief which Asians themselves came increasingly to exalt, proclaiming them superior to the many pre-existing forms of theistic cult religion hitherto practised in India and South-East Asia.

In those relatively rare cases where Christianity took root, this almost always occurred through synthesis and accommodation. China's great Taiping revolt originated in an area of long-standing contact with Western power, and had its roots in a 'crisis cult' which amalgamated Protestant missionary accounts of Jesus as redeemer with an indigenous prophetic tradition proclaiming the imminent coming of the next Buddha, the Maitreya. In India too, most people whom missionaries claimed as converts retained a pluralistic vision of the divine, creating pantheons which amalgamated Hindu gods and Muslim cult saints with the saints and martyrs of Christianity.

On the other hand, Christianity did not remain harmoniously 'syncretized' with other Asian faiths. The religion of the British conqueror came to be widely perceived as depraved, subversive, and decidedly 'other'. In many different settings, for example, amongst China's Confucian élites at the time of the Boxer

---

[28] A. N. Porter, *Atlas of British Overseas Expansion* (London, 1994), pp. 124–37.

[29] R. S. McGregor, *Hindi Literature of the Nineteenth and Early Twentieth Centuries* (Weisbaden, 1974).

Rebellion, Christianity was written and spoken about as a seditious, socially destabilizing heterodoxy, just as it was at the court of the Nguyen dynasty in present-day Vietnam in the face of nineteenth-century French expansion. By the end of the century the combative preaching of many Western evangelicals, their dissemination of Christian polemic in print, and their association with the expanding frontier of British power had evoked militant counter-polemics from educated Muslims and Hindus in India, from neo-Buddhist purifiers in Ceylon, and from pan-Islamist thinkers in virtually every Muslim locality from Egypt to Malaya. Whatever their theologies and linguistic traditions, pamphleteers and orators from very disparate backgrounds were uttering similar messages, reviling the Christian's faith as false and degenerate, and calling on fellow believers to embrace a new and formalized sense of union binding Muslims, Hindus, and Buddhists as members of separate, self-aware 'communities'.

Spirituality and Anti-Colonial 'Resistance'

By the end of the century missionaries and colonial officials were increasingly preoccupied with the organized cults and movements of self-proclaimed spiritual 'revival', which were widely held to be a potent and dangerous force throughout the Asian Empire. In Burma the British occupation in 1885 of Mandalay, seat of the Buddhist Konbaung dynasty which claimed the status of *cakkavartin*, the world-conqueror whose task in Buddhist cosmology is to deliver the world from unright-eousness, was followed by waves of armed millenialism. These risings were led by Burmese monks and occult adepts, *sayas*, whose preachings about the imminent end of unrighteous British rule prefigured Burma's great anti-colonial Saya San revolt of the 1930s.[30] British observers saw equally alarming messages in the teaching of other purist revitalizers and sectarian prophets. This can be seen in reports on the Taipings and Boxers, as well as accounts of the Hindu and Buddhist puritan revivalisms of Ceylon and India. The same fearful note marked descriptions of Islamic insurgencies such as the Pahang War in Malaya, the Mat Salleh rebellion in North Borneo, and more broadly, discussion of the dynamic pan-Islamic movements which spread along the trade routes and devotional networks of maritime Asia from the later nineteenth century.

This side of the purist revitalization movements coexisted uneasily with the more self-consciously respectable forms of conspicuous piety pursued by members of the colonial intelligentsias and other native gentleman élites. Their munificence embellished maritime Asia's Hindu shrines, expanded the Buddhist

---

[30] Michael Adas, *Prophets of Rebellion: Millenarian Protest Movements Against the European Colonial Order* (Chapel Hill, NC, 1979).

pilgrimage sites, and founded or re-endowed Islamic teaching institutions, thus contributing significantly to the new vigour and competitiveness of these faiths both within and beyond the British-ruled colonies. From the sophisticated intellectual environments of the Anglophone élites emerged a tremendous outpouring of theorizing and campaigning on spiritual matters. Only rarely did these people convert to Christianity; instead, they involved themselves in large and assertive movements of religious revival and purification.

The most important of these were the Arya Samaj or 'Society for the revival of Hindu Aryanism', and for Muslims, the pan-Islamizing organizations of South and South-East Asia. Ceylon's closest equivalent was the so-called Protestant Buddhist movement which rejected otherworldly detachment and exhorted lay believers to seek salvation in a life of active social engagement which placed particular emphasis on the education and moral uplift of women. Despite their manifold differences, these groups and their numerous rivals and allies told believers, in a language which many found convincing, that they lived in an age of decadent impiety. It was, they said, through knowledge of scripture, and the purging from everyday life and worship of so-called 'superstition' and moral laxity, that they could equip themselves to regain lost glories, and to thrive in a challenging and unpredictable 'modern' milieu.[31]

Some British missionaries, and the many colonial officials who perceived Empire as a providential achievement of Protestant Christian truth, looked approvingly at this so-called 'modernist' activity. But by about 1900 Western commentators realized that most activists who talked about spiritual purification and reinvigoration of their faith as Hindus, Sikhs, Muslims, and Buddhists were ardently anti-Christian. Over the next two decades they also became closely tied to emerging anti-colonial nationalist organizations, most notably the Indian National Congress. Elsewhere similar links were forged with Burma's twentieth-century Congress-equivalent, the General Council of Burmese Associations; with the Ceylon National Congress; and with the militant pan-Islamists and Khilafatist campaigners of India and Malaya.[32]

For many educated South Asians, the central source of these militant formulations was Theosophy, the American-born cultural revivalist organization which claimed to offer humankind a path to spiritual liberation through the mystical insights of the East. Theosophy strongly influenced Ceylon's most important revivalist, Anagarika Dharmapala (1864–1933). This ascetic Buddhist teacher and polemicist sought to turn his vision of religious reform into a supra-national

---

[31] David Kopf, *The Brahmo Samaj and the Shaping of the Modern Indian Mind* (Princeton, 1979); Steven Kemper, *The Presence of the Past: Chronicles, Politics, and Culture in Sinhala Life* (Ithaca, NY, 1991).

[32] On the GCBA, see Tarling, ed., *CHSEA*, II, p. 286.

regenerative force. From the 1890s he toured both hemispheres extolling purified Buddhism as a source of unlimited power for Asians, and promising his hearers that they too could learn the secret of self-aware spirituality which, he said, had enabled the base materialistic Europeans to advance themselves in the sphere of culture and morality.[33] Dharmapala had much in common with Burma's most celebrated activist monk, U Ottama, and with India's Hindu sage-polemicists, especially Swami Dayananda Saraswati (1824–83), founder of the Arya Samaj, and the Bengali seer Swami Vivekananda (1863–1902), whose advocacy of a spiritually informed path to national uplift anticipated much of Gandhi's philosophy.[34]

The vision of Asians invigorated and on the march through an exercise of spiritually inspired will-power fascinated and appalled the many British scholar-officials who had embraced the influential science of race–ethnology, and its related doctrines of eugenics and social Darwinism. What such commentators thought they were hearing from the prophets of revived Hindu nationhood, as well as from Malay and Egyptian pan-Islamists and Buddhist revitalizers in Burma and Ceylon, was an echo of key themes in the writings of Western race theorists. Of particular note was the view of global empire as the fulfilment of Aryan racial essences. To those who subscribed to these views, it was deeply unsettling to find Asians applying European ideas of nationhood and global struggles for mastery to their own expansive conceptions of faith, race, and nation.[35]

At the end of the 'long' nineteenth century Asians were beginning to act on these visions of assertive nationality. By the 1890s the major colonial towns had become a focus for complex new forms of social and political activism. These included constitutional nationalist organizations, as well as underground terrorist networks like those of western India's Poona-based paramilitary society the Chapekars, whose initial protests involved nothing more sinister than the vandalizing of cricket pitches. But in 1897 two of its members assassinated the region's British Plague Commissioner, a deeply hated figure during India's 1896–97 plague outbreak because of his power to send sanitary inspectors into the *purdah* quarters (secluded women's areas) of high-status urban households.[36] Elsewhere too, most notably in Burma, where the Young Men's Buddhist Association appropriated the propaganda techniques of the Anglo-American YMCA (Young Men's Christian Association) to mount a vigorous moral critique of colonialism, new forms of

---

[33] Kemper, *Presence of the Past.*

[34] William Radice, ed., *Swami Vivekananda and the Modernization of Hinduism* (Delhi, 1998).

[35] Charles Morris, *The Aryan Race: Its Origins and its Achievements* (London, 1888); L. Poliakov, *The Aryan Myth* (New York, 1974); Frank Dikötter, *The Discourse of Race in Modern China* (London, 1992); Thomas R. Trautmann, *Aryans and British India* (Berkeley, 1997).

[36] I. Catanach, 'Plague and the Tensions of Empire', in David Arnold, ed., *Imperial Medicine and Indigenous Societies* (Manchester, 1988); John R. McLane, *Indian Nationalism and the Early Congress* (Princeton, 1977), pp. 332–57.

anti-colonial militancy were nourished by views of European rule as an assault on customary faith and morality.[37]

Faced with all this, few of the professionally trained specialists who had come to dominate the fields of soldiering, administration, medicine, engineering, and missionary work could see themselves as presiding over an Empire of safely domesticated subject peoples. Britons pursuing these colonial careers were ever conscious of being surrounded by dangerous frontiers. Even at the end of the century, British scholar-officials continued to make much of the regions just beyond the heartlands of colonial hegemony where unsettled upland and forest peoples might suddenly erupt in revolts and murderous occultisms, born out of a memory of what British ethnographers conceptualized as the lost nationhood of the casteless tribesman.

More disturbing still was the vision of an inner frontier which was also constantly written and spoken about in colonial reportage. Underlying the intermittent colonial panics about *thuggee*, the famous but possibly imagined blood-cult of the goddess-worshipping Indian stranglers, or the supposed threat of fanatical Islamic *wahhabism*, was the fear that one could never know when another rebellion might erupt from within the colonial soldiery. Apparently safe, domesticated peasants and town-dwellers were also widely held to be easily 'aroused' by the teachings of prophets and other messengers of irrational or seditious spirituality.[38]

'Modernity' in education and culture was therefore not widely thought to have brought stability and social harmony to the Empire. By 1914 many Britons had realized that the more their Asian subjects travelled, prospered, and educated themselves, the less they were inclined to see themselves as living in a self-contained or uncontested world of British power and influence. Increasing numbers of Eastern peoples were known to be following a disquieting path that had brought the Empire's intelligentsias and cosmopolitan commercial intermediaries into new and dangerous company. Many Muslims in colonial India were known to be looking to pan-Islamists in Singapore and Dutch-ruled Sumatra and Java, or even further afield to the Ottoman caliphate, as symbols of Islamizing anti-colonialism.[39] There were even Malay Muslim purists who praised the Japanese for their love of *watan* (nation), and celebrated Japan's victory over Russia in 1905. Indeed, the industrial and military expansion of Japan was the other key stimulus to uneasiness about Britain's Asian subjects in an age when both East and West were apparently experiencing the force of so-called 'modernist' faith in a form

---

[37] Robert H. Taylor, *The State in Burma* (London, 1987), p. 177.

[38] For a comparison with French views, Oscar Salemink, 'The Return of the Python God', in *History and Anthropology*, VIII, 4 (1994).

[39] P. M. Holt, Ann K. A. Lambton, Bernard Lewis, eds., *The Cambridge History of Islam*, 2 vols. (Cambridge, 1970), II. 6, pp. 170–81.

which was increasingly bound up with ideologies of racial awakening, and national self-assertion.[40]

'Orientalist' Encounters

In the early nineteenth century British plans for the Asian Empire had come temporarily to be rooted in a broadly modernizing premise. Until mid-century increasing numbers of British scholar-officials dismissed the orientalizing views of eighteenth-century 'nabobs' who had admired Asia's faiths, arts, and mores. With their insistence on ideals of individuality, westernizing social 'uplift', and modern citizenship, the most influential policy-makers of the early Victorian Empire were equally hostile to the Rajah Brooke tradition of colonial rule, with its attempt to build on indigenous South-East Asian princely culture.[41]

By the end of the century, however, the threatening new religious and political trends discerned in so many regions of Asia had radically changed British thinking about law, faith, and morality in their eastern dominions. The great paradox of colonial rule was that these fears and vulnerabilities ultimately made the British notably more conservative in cultural matters than their Asian subjects. Thus, at a time when many Asians were beginning to embrace socialism and other radically materialist ideologies, the British defended the validity of economic and strategic policies built on a conception of 'oriental' norms and 'essences'.[42] Martial race theory became the dominant principle in colonial military recruitment: later-nineteenth-century innovations in law and policing stressed collective racial and moral essences rather than individual rights. Thus, India's Criminal Tribes Acts of 1871 (revised and extended in 1911) empowered the state to define entire castes or communities as criminals by blood and genetic inheritance. In Malaya too, as northern Kedah and other frontier zones were opened up to mining, colonial officials became preoccupied with fears of 'dacoity' (organized brigandage) and a belief in the inherent criminality of certain so-called tribes or 'gypsy-like' racial groups.[43] Paradoxically, however, British officials also decided that in the more established colonial centres their surveillance techniques had successfully domesticated the secret societies, which could therefore be safely left to regulate the Chinese 'coolie' traffic.[44]

[40] Milner, *Invention of Politics*, p. 168.

[41] R. H. W. Reece, *The Name of Brooke: The End of White Rajah Rule in Sarawak* (Kuala Lumpur, 1982).

[42] For an ultra-conservative view, Sir Michael O'Dwyer: *India as I Knew It* (London, 1925), esp. chap. 21, 'Is India a "lost Dominion"?'

[43] David E. Omissi, *The Sepoy and the Raj: The Indian Army, 1860–1940* (Basingstoke, 1994); for Burma, see Tarling, ed., *CHSEA*, II, p. 92. On policing: Cheah Boon Kheng, *The Peasant Robbers of Kedah* (Singapore, 1988), p. 16; Yang, *Crime and Criminality*.

[44] Trocki, *Opium and Empire*, p. 158.

In constitutional politics too, the Empire's ostensibly modern institutions were designed to reflect this same idea of the tribe, caste, or religious 'community' as the central element in Asian culture. Like governing bodies in many other colonial cities, the Rangoon Municipality became a predominantly elected body in 1882, but its members were elected as representatives of one of the city's specified ethno-linguistic populations—Burmese, Armenian, European, Chinese, Hindu, Muslim—much like the *kapitans* (designated community headmen) in the old East India Company trading enclaves. In India too the new electoral constituencies, created under the 1882 Resolution on Local Self-Government and the 1909 Morley–Minto reforms, were defined on the basis of collective interest or 'community', rather than any Western notion of one-person, one vote.[45]

Paradoxically, many of these constitutional measures coincided with moves towards the system of so-called indirect rule as devised for Fiji and colonial Africa. Ceylon's colonial Governor, Sir A. Hamilton-Gordon (1883–90), tried to do this by treating members of the island's Goyigama caste as a 'traditional' native aristocracy who could be vested with power like the 'paramount chiefs' of Lugard's Nigeria.[46] Even where landed patrician groups had lost materially and politically to more adaptable 'modern' élites, Britain, like other Western colonial powers, looked for ways to adopt the symbolic trappings of Asia's dynastic lordships. Like the French, the British sought to achieve this by means of the spectacular public rituals which they called 'durbars', and also through the creation of a colonial military culture which dressed white officers in the kind of archaic Oriental splendour which had become unthinkable for European civilians.

Archaeological research and the study of indigenous arts and literature were applied to the same purpose. By the mid-nineteenth century influential scholar-officials had deemed that India's most 'virile' cultural inheritance was the architectural style which they dubbed Indo-Saracenic. To create modern buildings which echoed the creations of pre-colonial Muslim conquerors was thus to assert both the permanence and the authenticity of British rule. From the 1870s, in the building of everything from new schools to railway stations, a 'nativized' pastiche was adopted, neo-Mughal in India, and quasi-Abbasid for the new town mosques and other public buildings of colonial Malaya. These conventions rapidly supplanted the neo-Georgian forms used by previous generations of Imperial architects.[47] The authorities' atavistic preoccupation with princely culture was also expressed in their commitment of scarce revenues to the support of schools and

[45] Tinker, *Foundations of Local Self- Government*.

[46] Patrick Peebles, 'Governor Arthur Gordon and the Administration of Sri Lanka', in N. G. Barrier, ed., *British Imperial Policy in India and Sri Lanka, 1858–1932* (New Delhi, 1981).

[47] Thomas R. Metcalf, 'Imperial Towns and Cities', in Marshall, ed., *Cambridge Illustrated History*, pp. 224–53.

colleges catering to the sons of Indian and Malay patrician households. In such establishments as the so-called 'Malay Eton' at Kuala Kangsar, the sons of lordly rent-receivers were supposed to learn 'manliness' and enlightened moral principles in imitation English public schools stressing team sports and 'modern' deportment, while simultaneously deferring to their pupils' supposedly inextinguishable religious and cultural 'essences'.[48]

These encounters between Western and Asian modes of thought were therefore not truly 'colonial'. Throughout the nineteenth century there was much debate, exchange, and 'resistance' across the realm of culture, rather than any one-sided transfer of values or institutions. Indeed, it was Asians as much as Britons who shaped these developments in faith, knowledge, and perception. In the twentieth century it was Asians again who took the lead in dismantling the 'invisible empire', even though its influence can still be traced in the ideologies of so-called Asian values which may well establish themselves across the world as the twenty-first century's most potent cultural force.

[48] Metcalf, *Land, Landlords and the Raj*, pp. 321–27; Milner, *Invention of Politics*, pp. 73, 241.

Select Bibliography

NICHOLAS DIRKS, 'The Invention of Caste: Civil Society in Colonial India', *Social Analysis*, XXV (1989).

RICHARD GOMBRICH and GANANATH OBEYESEKERE, *Buddhism Transformed: Religious Change in Sri Lanka* (Princeton, 1988).

RONALD INDEN, *Imagining India* (Oxford, 1990).

KENNETH JONES, ed., *Religious Controversy in British India* (Albany, NY, 1992).

BARBARA DALY METCALF, *Islamic Revival in British India: Deoband, 1860–1900* (Princeton, 1982).

ANDREW PORTER, 'Cultural Imperialism and Protestant Missionary Enterprise, 1780–1914', *Journal of Imperial and Commonwealth History*, XXV, 3 (1997), pp. 367–91.

FRANCIS ROBINSON, *Atlas of the Islamic World Since 1500* (Oxford, 1982).

THOMAS R. TRAUTMANN, *Aryans and British India* (Berkeley, 1997).

D. A. WASHBROOK, 'Economic Depression and the Making of "Traditional" Society in Colonial India, 1820–1855', *Transactions of the Royal Historical Society*, VI, 3 (1993), pp. 237–63.

21

The British West Indies

GAD HEUMAN

The British West Indies in 1815 consisted of a large number of islands and territories acquired over two centuries. The original colonies established in the seventeenth century, Barbados, Jamaica, and the Leeward Islands, were still the most important British possessions in the region. During the eighteenth century Dominica, St Vincent, Grenada, and Tobago were added to this group as a result of the Seven Years War (1756–63). In the early nineteenth century the British gained St Lucia, Trinidad, and British Guiana. The British were also present in the Bahamas, in parts of the Virgin Islands, and in British Honduras.

These colonies were characterized by different forms of colonial government. The older colonies had their own legislatures, with elected Assemblies and nominated Legislative Councils. Although a Governor represented the Crown, the local Assemblies had significant powers of legislation and taxation. There were very different constitutional arrangements in the most recently acquired territories, St Lucia, Trinidad, and British Guiana. These became Crown Colonies, controlled directly from London, with much less local participation in their political affairs.

The levels of economic development of the British colonies also differed significantly. While all produced sugar, some of the early colonies had been doing so continuously for almost 200 years. Nearly all the land in Barbados, for example, was devoted to sugar; yet in Trinidad and British Guiana the large-scale production of sugar was a relatively new development. These differences would become more marked during the nineteenth century, especially as a result of emancipation and its aftermath.

The economies of the British West Indies in this period have been the source of considerable debate. In *Capitalism and Slavery*, Eric Williams argued that the declining economies of the British West Indies led to the abolition of the slave trade and of slavery. More recent research has rejected this conclusion; it is now clear that the colonies of the British Caribbean profited considerably during the Revolutionary and Napoleonic Wars. The collapse of the largest sugar producer in the Caribbean, Saint-Domingue, led to an increased output of sugar and

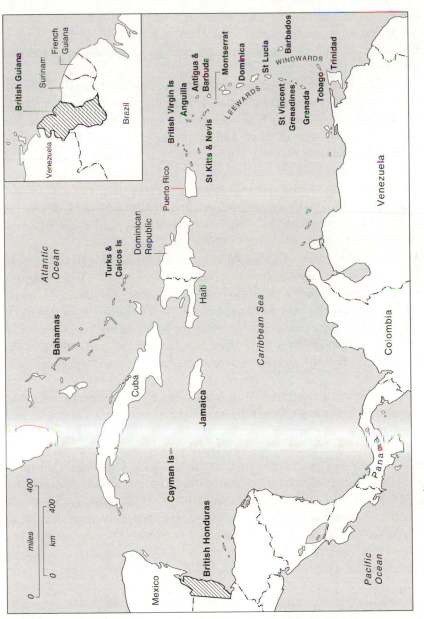

MAP 21.1. The West Indies

Atlantic Ocean

Bahamas

Turks &
Caicos Is

Dominican
Republic

Puerto Rico

British Virgin Is

Anguilla

Antigua &
Barbuda

Montserrat

St Kitts & Nevis

LEEWARDS

Dominica

St Lucia

WINDWARDS

Barbados

St Vincent
Grenadines

Grenada

Tobago

Trinidad

Haiti

Cuba

Jamaica

Cayman Is

British Honduras

Mexico

Caribbean Sea

Colombia

Venezuela

Pacific Ocean

Panama

British Guiana

Surinam

French Guiana

Venezuela

Brazil

miles

km

0   400

0   400

other staples throughout the British West Indies. Yet this boom proved temporary. With the end of the Napoleonic Wars, British colonies in the Caribbean faced difficult economic times: post-war deflation by 1820 led to a slump in the sugar market. Some of the older West Indian colonies had more difficulty coping with these problems than Britain's newer and less developed acquisitions.[1]

Although different in their economies and their political structures, all British West Indian colonies were slave societies. The institution of slavery is crucial to understanding the nature of these colonies. In general, a small planter class controlled a large number of slaves. The figures are revealing: at one end of the scale, British Guiana in 1823, the ratio of blacks to whites was 20:1. On the plantations of the colony, the numbers were even higher, often reaching figures of 60:1.[2] In the more settled colony of Jamaica, the preponderance of slaves was still significant, the ratio closer to ten slaves for every white. The exception in the British West Indies was Barbados, where a largely resident planter class remained in the island. Yet even there, the ratio of blacks to whites was 4:1.

Another general characteristic of West Indian society was a marked degree of absentee ownership of the sugar estates. Many whites regarded the West Indies as a place to make money; their hope was to make their fortunes and return to England to live off their estates. Most whites did not achieve this aim, but a significant proportion of the sugar plantations, generally the largest and richest, were owned by absentees. Although there were often significant white populations in the British West Indies, the absentee *mentalité* had an important effect on these societies.[3]

By 1815 another class in British West Indian society, the free people of colour, had grown in importance. Originally the offspring of whites and blacks, free coloureds in the early nineteenth century consisted of manumitted (freed) slaves as well as men and women born free. Largely mixed in colour and predominantly female, they suffered a number of political and economic disabilities. They could not vote, partake in political life, or testify in court against whites; they were also barred from certain occupations, including supervisory posts on the plantations. Yet the free coloureds were an increasingly important class numerically: in many of the West Indian colonies they outnumbered the whites. During the first few decades of the century the free people of colour sought to improve their legal condition in these societies. While many whites were still prejudiced against them,

---

[1] Eric Williams, *Capitalism and Slavery* (Chapel Hill, NC, 1944); Seymour Drescher, *Econocide: British Slavery in the Era of Abolition* (Pittsburgh, 1977).

[2] Michael Craton, *Testing the Chains: Resistance to Slavery in the British West Indies* (Ithaca, NY, 1982), p. 269.

[3] J. R. Ward, *British West Indian Slavery, 1750–1834: The Process of Amelioration* (Oxford, 1988), p. 13.

others believed it important to respond to their demands, especially in the face of attacks on the slave system itself.[4]

Unlike the free coloureds, the slave population in the British West Indies generally continued to decline in the early nineteenth century. This was a considerable disappointment to the humanitarians, who believed that the abolition of the slave trade in 1807 would lead to an improvement in the condition of slaves. The humanitarians argued that slaves would no longer be expendable as they had previously been, and consequently planters would look after them more carefully. Indeed, slavery itself might disappear as planters realized that free labour was cheaper and more efficient than slave labour.[5]

The reality was very different. All British West Indian colonies, apart from Barbados and the Bahamas, failed to maintain a positive natural increase in the slave population in the period 1816 to 1834. While there were some significant variations from colony to colony, the heaviest decreases occurred in those areas dominated by sugar plantations.[6] Barbados was an exception to this rule. There, the slave population was more creole (locally born) than elsewhere in the British West Indies. While 44 per cent of Trinidad's slave population consisted of Africans in 1817, only 7 per cent of the Barbadian slaves had been born in Africa. By the turn of the nineteenth century Barbadian planters were secure in the knowledge that their slave population was self-reproducing. Some Barbadian planters even supported abolition of the trade, seeing African slaves as more problematical than creoles and more likely to rebel.[7]

Notwithstanding their success in abolishing the slave trade, British humanitarians continued to monitor developments in the West Indies. Since they feared the possibility of illegal slave trading, the humanitarians succeeded in obtaining a system of public registration in the slave colonies. Beginning in 1817 and usually repeated every three years, the registration of slaves revealed that conditions for the slaves had not improved after 1808. As low birth rates and high mortality rates continued, abolitionists concluded that the planters were still mistreating their slaves and working them to death.[8]

The abolitionists therefore decided to establish a new organization and a new policy to deal with the problem of colonial slavery. In the spring of 1823, they

---

[4] Gad J. Heuman, *Between Black and White: Race, Politics, and the Free Coloreds in Jamaica, 1792–1865* (Westport, Conn., 1981), pp. 3–51.

[5] Howard Temperley, *British Antislavery, 1833–1870* (London, 1972), p. 7.

[6] B. W. Higman, *Slave Populations of the British Caribbean, 1807–1834* (Baltimore, 1984), pp. 72–76.

[7] Hilary McD. Beckles, 'Emancipation by Law or War? Wilberforce and the 1816 Barbados Slave Rebellion', in David Richardson, ed., *Abolition and its Aftermath: The Historical Context, 1790–1916* (London, 1985), p. 86; Hilary McD. Beckles, *A History of Barbados: From Amerindian Settlement to Nation-State* (Cambridge, 1990), pp. 77–78.

[8] Temperley, *British Antislavery*, p. 7. On mortality rates see Vol. II, chap. by Philip D. Morgan.

founded the Anti-Slavery Society; its leading members included prominent humanitarians such as William Wilberforce, Thomas Clarkson, and Zachary Macaulay. Thomas Fowell Buxton replaced Wilberforce in 1824 as leader and parliamentary spokesman. Although the Anti-Slavery Society sought to develop a gradual plan for the ultimate abolition of slavery, it also favoured an immediate improvement in the condition of the slaves.[9]

Accordingly, Buxton presented proposals to Parliament in May 1823 which included the emancipation at birth of all children as well as measures to ameliorate slave conditions. In response, the government submitted an alternate set of proposals agreed with representatives of the West India planters. These were designed to provide the slaves with more opportunity for religious instruction, prevent the break-up of slave families, end the flogging of women, and make possible compulsory manumission. Most importantly, the measures did not involve emancipation, and were to be formulated and implemented in the legislative colonies by the colonists themselves. The government was seeking to move slowly, being anxious to retain the constitutional relationship between the older colonies and Britain rather than exercise its authority over them.[10]

Yet even this moderate stance was too much for the colonists in the West Indies. In Jamaica the response was particularly defiant. A committee of the House of Assembly accused the government of accepting 'principles laid down by the enemies of the colonies'. The reaction in Barbados was more direct; a mob destroyed the Methodist chapel of the missionary William Shrewsbury, believing that he sympathized with the government's proposals. This resistance set the pattern for several years: the British government provided suggestions for amelioration which were met by strong opposition in the colonies.[11]

Angered by these delays, more radical members of the Anti-Slavery Society decided in 1831 to seek immediate emancipation. They established the Agency Committee, which was designed to mobilize popular support for their cause. The Committee also sought pledges from parliamentary candidates to back emancipation and urged voters to support only those candidates who supported the abolition of slavery. In the face of this renewed pressure, the government revived an earlier Order-in-Council which recognized slaves as legal witnesses. To ensure compliance in the legislative colonies, the government promised a considerable reduction in sugar duties if the order was adopted in its entirety.[12]

---

[9] Ibid., pp. 9–10. See above, p. 203.

[10] D. J. Murray, *The West Indies and the Development of Colonial Government* (Oxford, 1965), p. 107; Temperley, *British Antislavery*, p. 11.

[11] Temperley, *British Antislavery*, p. 12; Beckles, *History of Barbados*, p. 86.

[12] Murray, *The West Indies*, p. 188; Heuman, *Between Black and White*, p. 83.

When news of the renewed anti-slavery drive and the Imperial government's intentions reached the West Indies in the late spring and summer in 1831, the whites immediately protested. As in 1823, the protests in Jamaica were especially vehement. Colonists were not just objecting to the Order-in-Council; because of the actions of the abolitionists, whites now feared a slave rebellion. Seeing the government prepared to expose whites to this risk, colonists even threatened to reconsider their allegiance to the Crown.[13]

The problem for the whites was that slaves were aware of the activities of the Anti-Slavery Society and the local resistance to it. This had already led to serious outbreaks elsewhere in the British West Indies. In 1816 Barbadian slaves had become agitated about the Assembly's resistance to Imperial legislation concerning slave registration. Reports at the time equated the Registration Act with a plan for emancipation, and some slaves believed that freedom was being withheld from them. One literate domestic slave, Nanny Grigg, claimed that slaves were to be freed on Easter Monday 1816, but 'the only way to get it was to fight for it, otherwise they would not get it; and the way they were to do, was to set fire, as that was the way they did in Saint Domingo'.[14] When the slave rebellion did break out on Easter Sunday, it spread to a third of the island. Its leader, Bussa, an African head ranger on a plantation in south-east Barbados, timed the rebellion to coincide with the peak of the harvest season. The slaves made use of arson in an attempt to obtain their freedom; however, the rebellion proved short-lived and the repression was savage.[15]

There was a similar backdrop to the Demerara slave rebellion in 1823. Again, slaves believed that the local whites were withholding their freedom; in this case, the Imperial context of the rebellion was the formation of the Anti-Slavery Society and the beginning of the abolitionists' campaign in Britain. The rebellion broke out in August, involving thousands of slaves. Like the Barbados uprising it was repressed severely, with the death of about 250 slaves. The planters linked the rebellion to the work of the humanitarians and, more specifically, to the chapel in Demerara of the Revd John Smith, a missionary for the London Missionary Society. Found guilty of complicity in the rebellion, he died in prison while awaiting a reprieve from the Crown.[16]

As in Barbados and Demerara, slaves in Jamaica in 1831 concluded that they too had been freed, in part because of the whites' resistance to the 1831 Order-in-Council. When the rebellion broke out just after Christmas it was the largest

---

[13] Heuman, *Between Black and White*, pp. 83–84.

[14] Craton, *Testing the Chains*, p. 261.

[15] Beckles, *History of Barbados*, pp. 79–81.

[16] Craton, *Testing the Chains*, chap. 21, but see also Emilia Viotti da Costa, *Crowns of Glory, Tears of Blood: The Demerara Slave Rebellion of 1823* (New York, 1994).

outbreak Jamaica had seen. One report claimed that 20,000 slaves were involved; the uprising spread throughout western Jamaica and 226 estates sustained damages involving more than £1 million sterling. As in Demerara, missionaries were implicated; the rebel, Sam Sharpe, was a leader in the Baptist Church as well as a 'Daddy' in the Native Baptist Church. After the rebellion, which the authorities suppressed ferociously, whites attacked missionaries and tore down their chapels, blaming them for the upheaval. Indeed, the rebellion was called 'The Baptist War'.[17]

Jamaica's slave rebellion made it clear to many in Britain that slavery could not continue. The abolitionists were now seeking immediate emancipation, and after 1832 the reformed House of Commons was more responsive to popular pressure. One of the Baptist missionaries attacked in Jamaica after the rebellion, William Knibb, toured England, recounting the horrors of slavery and seeking its abolition. Since emancipation was now in the forefront of political concerns, ministers and officials began to think seriously about how to achieve it.

Officials in the Colonial Office were struck by the need to free the slaves while still retaining the basic structure of plantation society in the West Indies. In their minds, one of the potential dangers for the slaves was a reversion to 'barbarism' once they became free. Henry Taylor, senior clerk in the West India Department of the Colonial Office, therefore devised a plan based on the Spanish model of *coartación*. Under this system, the British government would declare the slaves free for one day; thereafter, slaves could use the proceeds of working on that day to buy further days of freedom. Taylor's superior, Lord Howick, the Under-Secretary of State for the Colonies, sought to solve the problem of labour in a different manner. His solution was to impose a tax on ex-slaves' provision grounds, which would force the freedmen to work for wages on the estates to pay the tax. Although neither scheme was eventually adopted, the rationale in each case was clear: freedom and continued sugar cultivation on the plantations were inextricably linked.[18]

The final act to emancipate the slaves was a compromise, worked out by the government with representatives of the Anti-Slavery Society and the West Indian planters. At its heart was the establishment of an apprenticeship system: slaves would be freed but become apprentices, working for their former masters for up to forty-five hours a week, and less for those who maintained themselves by provi-

---

[17] Gad Heuman, 'A Tale of Two Jamaican Rebellions', in Wim Hoogbergen, ed., *Born Out of Resistance: On Caribbean Cultural Creativity* (Utrecht, 1995), pp. 196–204. See also Mary Turner, *Slaves and Missionaries: The Disintegration of Jamaican Slave Society, 1787–1834* (Urbana, Ill., 1982), chap. 6; Craton, *Testing the Chains*, chap. 22; Thomas C. Holt, *The Problem of Freedom: Race, Labor, and Politics in Jamaica and Britain, 1832–1938* (Baltimore, 1992), pp. 14–15.

[18] Holt, *The Problem of Freedom*, pp. 45–47; Murray, *The West Indies*, p. 195.

sion grounds. The legislation separated field and skilled slaves, with skilled slaves ending their apprenticeship after four years while field slaves would do so after six. Children under the age of 6 were to be freed immediately, and special magistrates were to be appointed to oversee the workings of the system. Most important from the planters' point of view was a grant of £20 million compensation for the loss of their slaves. Although the legislative colonies were given the responsibility of passing the specific emancipation legislation, they did so readily since compensation payments were dependent on it. Two colonies, Antigua and Bermuda, decided to opt for full freedom immediately. In Antigua planters believed they could control their freedmen without the intervening apprenticeship; in Bermuda slaves worked in maritime occupations and apprenticeship was therefore less applicable.[19]

At midnight on 31 July 1834, 750,000 former slaves in the British West Indies celebrated their freedom. In general, observers reported calm; missionaries described full churches and peaceful celebrations to mark the end of slavery. But there were problems. In St Kitts the labourers on the plantations had resolved not to return to work without pay. Some of the apprentices said that 'they would give their souls to hell and their bodies to the sharks rather than be bound to work as apprentices'. The authorities declared martial law, rounded up the striking apprentices who had fled, and forced them all back to work.[20]

There were also longer-term difficulties. One immediate problem was an insufficient number of special magistrates established by London to monitor the apprenticeship system. Some islands, such as Nevis, Montserrat, and Tobago did not have any special magistrates at the outset of the system; St Kitts had one, and there were two for the whole of Trinidad. Yet one of these was too ill to work and the other died only six weeks after arrival. The special magistrates, many of them former military officers sent from Britain, were insufficiently paid; and apprentices often regarded them as biased towards the planters, even when that was not the case.[21]

The planters' perception of the apprenticeship system caused further difficulties. Some planters took a very exacting approach towards the apprentices, being no longer prepared to grant apprentices the allowances they had enjoyed during slavery. In certain instances planters withdrew food allowances formerly given to

---

[19] William A. Green, *British Slave Emancipation: The Sugar Colonies and the Great Experiment, 1830–1865* (Oxford, 1976), chap. 5.

[20] Richard Frucht, 'From Slavery to Unfreedom in the Plantation Society of St. Kitts, W.I.', in Vera Rubin and Arthur Tuden, *Comparative Perspectives on Slavery in New World Plantation Societies* (New York, 1977), p. 384. See also Robert S. Shelton, 'A Modified Crime: The Apprenticeship System in St. Kitts', *Slavery and Abolition*, XVI, 3 (1995), pp. 331–45.

[21] Green, *British Slave Emancipation*, pp. 137–40.

slaves; in others, women who had given birth to six children and were therefore exempted from field labour during slavery were sent back to the field. Since all non-agricultural workers were to be freed in four years rather than six for agricultural workers, many planters sought to classify more slaves as working solely in agriculture. In Grenada planters persisted in classifying all apprentices as agricultural labourers, despite Crown rulings to the contrary.[22]

Abolitionists in Britain, who had opposed the establishment of the apprenticeship system, were aware of these problems and began an anti-apprenticeship campaign. Led by a wealthy merchant, Joseph Sturge, it gathered momentum after Sturge and one of his associates, Thomas Harvey, published an attack on the system, *The West Indies in 1837*, and continued despite government attempts to improve the workings of the system in early 1838. Bowing to this pressure, the West Indian Assemblies ended the system prematurely on 1 August 1838. Even in its abbreviated form the apprenticeship system was not successful; it did not establish a useful basis for a free society. Instead, it frequently brought bitterness and controversy and made the working out of freedom that much more difficult.

By ending the apprenticeship system early, planters in the British West Indies believed they would no longer be subject to further Imperial legislation. For the planters, it was important that they control local legislation; they did not envisage emancipation altering either the hierarchical nature of society or their political dominance. In the colonies with Assembly governments, this meant that whites sought to enact legislation limiting the rights of the ex-slaves, including vagrancy and police acts designed to restrict their mobility.

The Colonial Office, however, continued to see itself as the protector of the ex-slave population. Through the work of James Stephen, who was Permanent Under-Secretary for the Colonies between 1836 and 1847, the Colonial Office continued to monitor closely the legislation of the Assembly governments in the immediate post-emancipation period. As a result, the British government disallowed many of the Acts passed in 1838. Instead, Lord Glenelg, the Colonial Secretary, drafted a series of Orders-in-Council as well as specific instructions for colonial legislatures on a wide range of issues. The Orders-in-Council became law in the Crown Colonies; in the legislative colonies the instructions were models for legislation to be passed locally. Governors were to withhold consent from any measures which did not conform to these models.[23]

The Assemblymen in the British West Indies were indignant at this interference in their legislative autonomy. As so often, the Jamaican Assembly was especially

---

[22] Green, *British Slave Emancipation*, pp. 132–33.
[23] Ibid., pp. 164–65.

vehement in its denunciation. It had seen the home government disallow many of its laws during apprenticeship, and it had vigorously protested against the premature ending of the system. When Parliament legislated further in August 1838, providing a blueprint for reform and regulation of the local prisons in the West Indies, the Jamaican Assembly took strong action. It went on strike, declaring a moratorium on public business until the Prisons Act was withdrawn.

The issue was much wider than the Prisons Act itself. At stake was whether the British government or the local Assemblies would legislate for the freed population. In October 1838 Henry Taylor wrote an important memorandum attacking the West Indian legislatures and arguing for the adoption everywhere of Crown Colony government. In Taylor's view, the Assemblies were unfit to govern a free people; moreover, it was useless to attempt a great social experiment, emancipation, with a political system designed for a slave society. Taylor was arguing for a form of trusteeship, since the British government would look after the interests of the majority of the population.

Taylor's proposal met considerable opposition when presented to the Cabinet, and it was significantly watered down. Rather than suspend all the Assemblies, the measure was to apply only to Jamaica, for a period of five years. Given the weak state of the Whig government, even that proposal did not command sufficient support in Parliament. In the end the Jamaican Assembly survived intact, with the planter class remaining in power.[24]

Yet the planter class did face challenges to its political domination, especially from black and brown representatives to the Assemblies. As free coloureds and free blacks, they had achieved full civil rights in the early 1830s, in part because of the support of British abolitionists and the Colonial Office. Although not a single political bloc, black and brown Assemblymen generally supported Imperial government policies. Moreover, they could carry weight: in Dominica, for example, coloured representatives formed a majority in the Assembly. Their presence prevented the passage of harsh legislation against the ex-slaves which characterized many other West Indian colonies.[25]

In Jamaica the coloured and black members of the Assembly united to form the Town Party, a faction which opposed the planter-dominated Country Party. The coloureds favoured funds being spent on education, resisted expensive immigration schemes, and sought to counter planter attempts to restrict the franchise. Moreover, the coloureds also voted against measures to shift the burden of taxation almost entirely on to small settlers. Brown and black representatives

[24] Holt, *The Problem of Freedom*, pp. 108–12.

[25] Russell Chace, Jr, 'Protest in Post-Emancipation Dominica: The "Guerre Negre" of 1844', *Journal of Caribbean History*, XXIII, 2 (1989), p. 119.

remained a minority in the Jamaican House of Assembly, but as their numbers grew, the planters became increasingly alarmed about the possibility of being outnumbered.[26]

Coloured and black politicians were not the planters' only opponents. European missionaries, notably the Baptists, were especially concerned about the plight of the ex-slaves. They attacked the harsh legislation emanating from the Jamaican Assembly and also wished to sever the connection between church and state in the colony. Led by William Knibb, the Baptists sought to organize the small settler vote. Wanting to elect Assemblymen committed to their programme, they therefore attempted to register large numbers of freeholders who would return suitable candidates. In the early 1840s, they were becoming a potentially important political force: Governor Charles Metcalfe regarded them as a political party with great influence over the ex-slave population. However, when his successor, Lord Elgin, called a surprise election in 1844, the Baptists were unable to affect the results significantly and declined thereafter as a political force in Jamaica.[27]

Baptist missionaries acted on behalf of the freed people in other ways, serving, for example, as advisers to ex-slaves over wages. In the aftermath of emancipation this was a highly fraught issue; consequently, Baptist missionaries supported ex-slaves in their strikes for higher wages and for better working conditions.[28] Ex-slaves also had to contend with a related problem: the development of the rent-wage system. Although as slaves they had enjoyed the use of provision grounds and their homes without any charge, after emancipation planters charged rents for these facilities. The rents were linked to work on the estates; if the work was unsatisfactory, the planters could threaten their labourers with eviction. For the planters, this system meant lower wage costs and a captive labour force; for the freed people, it meant a severe restriction on their freedom.

The rent-wage system differed from colony to colony. In Barbados, for example, work on an estate for five days a week entitled the tenant to live rent free. Those who worked less were subject to a fine, effectively a payment of rent deducted from the estate wages. This compelled the ex-slave to work on the estate. Elsewhere, as in Jamaica, rents were sometimes exorbitant; although they averaged 2s. a week, the rents could be as high as 6s.8d. per household, with each family member being charged. There was wide variation among the colonies when examining rents as a

---

[26] Heuman, *Between Black and White*, chap. 10.

[27] Robert J. Stewart, *Religion and Society in Post-Emancipation Jamaica* (Knoxville, Tenn., 1992), pp. 19–20.

[28] Swithin Wilmot, 'From Falmouth to Morant Bay: Religion and Politics in Jamaica, 1838–1865', unpublished paper presented at the Association of Caribbean Historians' Conference, Havana, April 1985, p. 1.

percentage of wages: in Barbados and Tobago rents were about 20 per cent of wages, in Grenada 35 per cent, and in Jamaica they were as high as 48 per cent.[29]

High rents and threats of eviction alienated many freed people. Where land was available and where planters could not restrict its sale, ex-slaves frequently left the estates to establish their own freeholds. The movement of freed people off the estates was therefore not an instinctive reaction to the horrors of slavery. Instead, 'it was a protest against the inequities of early "freedom"'.[30] It also had significant economic effects: freed people contributed to the growth of both export and local markets.

Missionaries aided the process of setting up villages. Often helped by British philanthropists, missionaries bought land from the planters for the purpose. Some of Jamaica's free villages were established during the apprenticeship period: the first such, Sligoville, was founded in 1835. During the next six years Baptist missionaries settled more than 3,000 people in Baptist villages, some with evocative names such as Buxton, Wilberforce, and Victoria.[31]

Not only missionaries but ex-slaves also organized free villages. In British Guiana former plantation headmen bought up estates on behalf of a larger group of freed people. For example, in November 1839, sixty-three people, many of whom were headmen, bought Northbrook Estate for $10,000; this was subsequently subdivided. A few years later four headmen purchased Den Amstel estate on behalf of seventy field workers. Villages were also established in some of the smaller colonies: in Antigua, by 1842, there were twenty-seven independent villages containing over 1,000 homes and 3,600 people.[32]

The establishment of free villages highlighted the problem of labour for the planters. Yet it was not just the flight from the estates which deprived plantations of their labour. Many freed people preferred to work on their own land or for themselves rather than on the estates. This was especially the case for women, many of whom ceased to work on the estates after emancipation. As women had made up more than half the field labourers during slavery, their withdrawal from the plantations inevitably affected the planters. Although less important as labourers, children also left the plantations in the wake of emancipation. Reflecting on the shortage of labour before a Select Committee of Parliament in 1842, an

---

[29] O. Nigel Bolland, 'Systems of Domination after Slavery: The Control of Land and Labour in the British West Indies after 1838', *Comparative Studies in Society and History*, XXIII, 4 (1981), p. 596.

[30] Douglas Hall, 'The Flight from the Estates Reconsidered: The British West Indies, 1838–1842', *Journal of Caribbean History*, X/XI, (1978), p. 23.

[31] Philip D. Curtin, *Two Jamaicas: The Role of Ideas in a Tropical Colony, 1830–1865* (Cambridge, Mass., 1955), p. 115.

[32] Green, *British Slave Emancipation*, p. 302; Douglas Hall, *Five of the Leewards, 1834–1870: The Major Problems of the Post-Emancipation Period in Antigua, Barbuda, Montserrat, Nevis and St. Kitts* (Barbados, 1971), p. 53.

estate owner in St Kitts maintained that there was a sufficient number of
labourers in the island, but not 'labour enough'. Ex-slaves were unwilling to
provide the continuous labour which the planters sought, especially during
the harvest.[33]

With fewer labourers, planters in some colonies sought to improve the technology of sugar-making. Throughout the West Indies agricultural societies were
established to exchange information on sugar production and improve methods.
The Governor of Jamaica, Lord Elgin, founded a Royal Agricultural Society, and
agricultural shows became a feature of plantation life in the island. Planters made
more use of the plough and harrow as well as of a new type of vacuum pan in
the production of sugar. They also introduced steam engines in their sugar
factories in place of cattle or windmills. In Trinidad and British Guiana, nearly
all the plantations adopted steam, but it was important elsewhere. St Kitts had
thirty-three steam mills by 1846, and a third of the mills in Tobago by 1849 were
steam driven.[34]

These new signs of relative optimism among the West Indian plantocracy were
accompanied by a shift in Colonial Office thinking. During the 1830s the emphasis
in the Colonial Office had been on the emancipated population. Henry Taylor and
James Stephen had scrutinized the legislation of the colonies to protect the ex-
slaves. With the development of free villages and the significant increase in the
number of small freeholders, Colonial Office officials became more concerned
about survival of the plantations. Fearing that they might even collapse, officials
adopted measures designed to preserve the estates. The new Colonial Secretary in
1841, Lord Stanley, embodied this change of policy. Unlike his immediate predecessor, Stanley responded more favourably to the arguments of the West Indian
planters than to the complaints of the humanitarians.[35]

As a consequence, the Colonial Office was prepared to allow legislation which
previously would have been regarded as inimical to the interests of ex-slaves.
Taxation was one such area. During the 1840s Assemblies in the West Indies shifted
the tax burden away from the planters on to the majority of the population by
raising import duties, often on necessities. The franchise was another contentious
issue. Most Assemblies in the 1830s sought to raise franchise qualifications, and
deny blacks and coloureds the vote. Although the Colonial Office disallowed this
legislation, it was prepared in the following decades to countenance a more
restrictive franchise. The Barbados Assembly, for example, passed franchise legislation preserving a predominantly white legislature during this period. The

[33] Hall, *Five of the Leewards*, p. 32.

[34] Douglas Hall, *Free Jamaica, 1838–1865: An Economic History* (New Haven, 1959), p. 27; Green,
British Slave Emancipation, p. 212.

[35] Heuman, *Between Black and White*, pp. 137–38.

number of voters also remained small in the other West Indian colonies: for example, in 1854 Grenada had 191 electors, St Vincent 273, and Tobago 135.[36]

However, the planters' optimism did not last. In 1846 Lord Russell's Whig government passed the Sugar Duties Act, which was designed to equalize the duties on all sugar by 1851. Until then, the West Indies had enjoyed preferential tariffs on their sugar, and this protected market was crucial to the survival of many West Indian plantations. Since British West Indian sugar now had to compete with the slave-grown sugar of Cuba and Brazil, planters claimed that they would be ruined.

There is little doubt about the depth of the economic crisis caused by the move to end preferential tariffs. Coming at the same time as severe depression in Britain and Europe and a steep fall in sugar prices, the British government's actions led to the collapse of a large number of West India merchant houses. Estate values plummeted. In British Guiana an estate worth £50,000 in 1822 and £24,000 in 1842 was sold for £625 in 1849. Similarly, in Jamaica a plantation valued at about £80,000 during slavery sold for just £500 in 1849. The West Indian Bank, based in Barbados, suspended payments in December 1847, and the Planters' Bank in Jamaica found itself in a similar position a month later.[37]

The response of the planter class to the equalization of sugar duties was to put pressure on the British government to retain protection. In Jamaica and British Guiana legislators sought to reduce the costly colonial establishment and, specifically, to revise the salaries of the leading officials. The government resisted these attempts at retrenchment, but as in 1838–39, the Jamaican Assemblymen were again prepared to stop the revenues and to create a constitutional crisis. From their point of view, the planters had little to lose. On the one hand, many faced economic ruin; on the other, they were concerned about the increase in black and brown representatives to the House of Assembly. The planters were therefore willing to risk the survival of their Assembly to ensure their continued economic and political dominance.[38]

In the end, the British government responded by postponing the date of the equalization of duties until 1854. It also offered to guarantee the interest on loans up to £500,000, which the colonists could use for capital projects such as the railroad construction and the importation of labour. Although initially reluctant to accept the offer of guaranteed loans, the planters in Trinidad and British Guiana eventually took advantage of them. Immigrant labour proved to be an important element in the survival of many West Indian plantations in the years ahead.

[36] Green, *British Slave Emancipation*, pp. 176–77.
[37] Ibid., pp. 234–35.
[38] Heuman, *Between Black and White*, pp. 142–43.

The planters had sought to attract labour as early as the 1830s and were particularly interested in Europeans. Some of the early immigrants were Germans, who settled in western Jamaica. The planters expected European immigrants to do more than replace slave labour on the plantations: they were to offset the racial imbalance of West Indian society. Moreover, the planters envisaged European labourers occupying the highlands of islands such as Jamaica and providing a model for black workers.

However, the European migrants were badly chosen; many came from seaports and were unaccustomed to agricultural work. The preparations for their arrival were often haphazard, and many of the migrants did not remain on the estates. This was also the case for immigrants from Madeira in the 1840s, most of whom went to Trinidad and British Guiana. But they suffered very high mortality, and many survivors quickly moved off the estates to become shopkeepers and merchants. In general, European immigration proved to be a failure.[39]

The planters therefore turned to other sources of labour. Trinidadian and British Guianese planters tried to attract workers from the heavily populated eastern Caribbean, especially the Leewards and Barbados, much to the consternation of the local plantocracy. They also sought labour from Africa, especially among liberated Africans who been rescued from slave ships and sent to Sierra Leone. Planters even hoped for free blacks from the United States. Yet these schemes were dwarfed by those tapping the source of most of the nineteenth-century migrants to the West Indies, India.

Immigration from India began in 1838, with several hundred Indians attracted to British Guiana. Concerned about the conditions of the Indians on the plantations, British humanitarians succeeded in having the immigration stopped. However, with the Colonial Office thinking about the survival of the plantations and the great demand for labour, Indian immigration was revived in 1845 and continued until 1917. Initially immigrants were indentured for one year, although the British government regarded this as a concession in the light of the larger number of Indians who deserted their employers. Continued planter pressure led to the introduction of three-year contracts for indentured labourers in 1850, which were increased to five-year contracts in 1862. To qualify for a return passage to India, the immigrant was obliged to reside in the colony for ten years.[40]

There were serious problems associated with Indian immigration. It was difficult to attract female emigrants, despite efforts to increase their numbers, and the gender imbalance among Indians in the West Indies remained a significant

[39] Douglas Hall, 'Bountied European Immigration with Special Reference to the German Settlement at Seaford Town up to 1850', *Jamaica Journal*, IX, 1 (1975), pp. 2–9.

[40] K. O. Laurence, *Immigration into the West Indies in the 19th Century* (Kingston, 1971), p. 24. See above, pp. 90–93.

problem, often leading to violence in the Indian community. The high cost of importing Indians, much of which was paid by the ex-slaves themselves through general taxation, was a strain on the revenues of the West Indian colonies. Moreover, the presence of the indentured Indians reduced the wages of free labour throughout the West Indies. It was perhaps inevitable that free labourers and Indians would compete for work on the plantations; in the case of British Guiana, this resulted in racial confrontation. Generally, however, Indian immigrants remained physically and culturally separate from the blacks.[41]

Yet the Indian immigrants also had a significant effect on the sugar production. In the 1850s and 1860s immigration from India stopped the economic decline of British Guiana and Trinidad; by 1870 the immigrants had helped to sustain a substantial degree of prosperity in these colonies. Their numbers were considerable: nearly 250,000 went to British Guiana, almost 150,000 to Trinidad, and over 36,000 to Jamaica. In each of these colonies more than two-thirds of the Indians chose to remain rather than return to India.[42] Although Indian immigration benefited the West Indian sugar industry, it did little to improve the condition of the ex-slave population. Instead, the planters' focus on importing labour meant that the problems of the freed people were often ignored, with serious results. For example, in the aftermath of emancipation there was a lack of doctors available for the ex-slave population, planters were no longer obliged, as during slavery, to provide doctors for their labourers. Moreover, epidemics swept through the West Indies, often causing terrible loss of life. A cholera epidemic in Jamaica in 1850 cost 30,000 lives; it was followed by an outbreak of influenza as well as smallpox, and then a return of cholera. The disease also spread through the Lesser Antilles and Barbados; in 1854 upwards of 15,000 people died from its effects.[43]

Ex-slaves did not passively accept their condition. After emancipation, riots and protests throughout the region were not uncommon. In 1844 freed people protested violently in Dominica against the taking of a census. At first enumerators were assaulted, but then followed attacks on estate property and managers. A conspiracy four years later in western Jamaica was accompanied by a series of protests and riots in other parts of the island. Jamaica was also the scene of two riots in 1859, one directed against toll-gates in parts of western Jamaica. In 1862 a labour strike in St Vincent degenerated into a riot. Freed people assaulted estate managers and plundered planters' houses and shops over a wide area; the

---

[41] Laurence, *Immigration into the West Indies*, p. 46; Brian L. Moore, *Race, Power and Social Segmentation in Colonial Society: Guyana After Slavery, 1838–1891* (New York, 1987). pp. 195, 210. See also Walter Rodney, *A History of the Guyanese Working People, 1881–1905* (Kingston, 1981).

[42] Laurence, *Immigration into the West Indies*, pp. 66, 26.

[43] Green, *British Slave Emancipation*, pp. 311–12.

authorities killed four people and wounded at least seven others in putting down the riot. There were two important riots in 1876, one in Tobago, the other in Barbados. The Barbados riots were the more serious: the issue was whether Barbados would be joined politically to the Windward colonies, and the disturbances resulted in the death of eight people.[44]

There were common grievances in many of these riots. One was low pay, made worse by irregular payments and arbitrary work stoppages. When linked to the truck system, in which estates had their own shops and created a type of debt peonage among their workers, the situation could become tense. Another serious grievance centred around the fear of re-enslavement; this was the motivating force behind the Dominica riots, and a factor in several others. In addition, the ex-slaves' desire for land was often an element in these disturbances. Freed people in Dominica believed that freedom implied more than a change in legal status; it also meant a grant of land.[45]

Several of these factors were prominent in the Morant Bay Rebellion in Jamaica, the most important post-emancipation outbreak before 1914. On 11 October 1865 several hundred blacks marched into Morant Bay, the principal town in the sugar parish of St Thomas in the East. Led by Paul Bogle, a native Baptist deacon, the crowd attacked the police station before confronting the militia and the parish authorities. In the subsequent mêlée the crowd killed eighteen people. Over the next few days local people killed two planters and attacked many plantations in the parish.

The government's response was swift and brutal. The Governor, Edward John Eyre, declared martial law in the eastern part of Jamaica, despatched British troops to the parish, and organized the Maroons to deal with the outbreak.[46] The month-long period of martial law resulted in the deaths of over 400 blacks. Because of the severity of the repression, the case became a *cause célèbre* in England. John Stuart Mill was among a group of radicals and Nonconformists who organized a campaign to try the Governor for his part in the suppression of the rebellion. In response, Thomas Carlyle, Charles Kingsley, and Charles Dickens helped to establish an Eyre Defence Committee. Although Eyre was never tried, the controversy surrounding his case raised important issues about the nature of colonial rule, martial law, and governmental accountability.[47]

---

[44] Gad Heuman, 'Post-Emancipation Resistance in the Caribbean: An Overview', in Karen Fog Olwig, *Small Islands, Large Questions: Society, Culture and Resistance in the Post-Emancipation Caribbean* (London, 1995), pp. 123–34.

[45] Ibid.

[46] Maroons, formerly a community of runaway slaves, were an irregular and effective army of the colony.

[47] Gad Heuman, *'The Killing Time': The Morant Bay Rebellion in Jamaica* (London, 1994).

In Jamaica, Eyre made use of the rebellion to push for constitutional change. Since the Colonial Office had wanted for some time to abolish the House of Assembly, Eyre convinced a frightened House that they should opt for Crown Colony government. Despite some opposition to this change, the legislators ultimately accepted a nominated Council, consisting of six officials and three unofficial members, and the abolition of the 200-year-old House of Assembly. Apart from Barbados, the other legislative colonies in the West Indies followed suit, although colonies such as Grenada and Tobago were slow to change. By the mid-1870s, and with the continuing exception of Barbados, Crown Colony government was fully established in the British West Indies.[48]

Crown Colony government brought certain advantages. Unlike the system of representative government, with its often fractious Assemblies, there was less scope for serious political divisions in the legislature. Administration was smoother; there was effectively no opposition to the Governor. It was therefore possible to inaugurate long-overdue administrative changes.

Jamaica serves as an important example. There, the new Governor in 1866, Sir John Grant, was a retired Indian civil servant whose last appointment was as Lieutenant-Governor of Bengal. Used to strong executive powers, Grant initiated a significant number of administrative reforms. Among these were a new system of district courts, the creation of a more modern police force, and the disestablishment of the Church of England in the colony. Grant also encouraged the immigration of East Indian labourers; roads were improved, new irrigation schemes developed, and more money devoted to education. Many of these projects had been debated by the House of Assembly but had been shelved because of cost or the lack of political will to carry them out.[49]

There were, nevertheless, also problems with Crown Colony government. Grant's reforms were expensive and taxes had to be increased. This was done without the involvement of the people or their representatives; one local newspaper described the system as one of 'paternal despotism'. In theory, the Crown was acting on behalf of the mass of the population, until the people became sufficiently educated for the exercise of representative government. In practice, the Colonial Office was not always well placed to act in this capacity. Its knowledge of local conditions was often fragmentary, and its distance from the West Indies frequently led to delays and misunderstandings. Because of the nature of work in

[48] Ibid., p. 190; H. A. Will, *Constitutional Change in the British West Indies, 1880–1903* (Oxford, 1970), p. 11.

[49] Heuman, '*The Killing Time*', p. 177; Vincent John Marsala, *Sir John Peter Grant: Governor of Jamaica, 1866–1874* (Kingston, 1972).

the Colonial Office, its officials generally reacted to developments in the colonies rather than initiated new policies.[50]

During the 1870s hostility to Crown Colony government increased in Jamaica. Since the system excluded Jamaicans generally and was dominated by expatriate white officials, blacks, people of colour, and local whites all felt the loss of political offices previously open to them. Agitation against the system brought some modifications: in 1884 the Legislative Council was altered. Thereafter, it consisted of equal numbers of official and unofficial members; the unofficial, elected on a restricted franchise, could only be outvoted if the Governor declared the issue one of paramount importance. Similar changes took place in British Guiana. After 1891 members of the Court of Policy (effectively, the legislature apart from financial matters) were chosen by direct election. In general, however, Crown Colony government remained largely unmodified until after the First World War. It was this political system which had to deal with the economic crisis of the late nineteenth century.[51]

At the time of the Morant Bay Rebellion the sugar industry in the British West Indies, apart from Jamaica, was reasonably profitable. This was partly a function of improved technology; on many of the estates of British Guiana and Trinidad vacuum pans had been introduced in the production of sugar, increasing its quality as well its quantity. Output was undoubtedly aided by the continuing importation of Indian indentured labourers. It is also possible that the passage of the Encumbered Estates Act in 1854, facilitating the sale of insolvent estates, helped to expand production (see Table 21.1). As a result of this legislation, many estates were purchased by British merchant houses who specialized in sugar and had a highly commercial approach to estate production.[52]

Not only British Guiana and Trinidad did well. In the other colonies, where the traditional production of muscovado sugar was continuing, profits were also good. Between 1861 and 1871 sugar exports from St Vincent increased by 5,000 hogsheads. A planter in St Kitts claimed in 1872 that the colony's plantations were at the height of their prosperity. In the same period, Barbados was regarded as the most prosperous of the sugar colonies, with all of its 608 estates functioning and a plentiful supply of labour.[53]

---

[50] Will, *Constitutional Change*, p. 3.

[51] Heuman, '*The Killing Time*', pp. 177–78; J. H. Parry and Philip Sherlock, *A Short History of the West Indies* (1956; 3rd edn., London, 1976), pp. 216–17.

[52] R. W. Beachey, *The British West Indies Sugar Industry in the Late 19th Century* (Oxford, 1957), pp. 41–42; Richard A. Lobdell, 'Patterns of Investment and Sources of Credit in the British West Indian Sugar Industry, 1838–1897', *Journal of Caribbean History*, IV (1972), pp. 44–45.

[53] Beachey, *British West Indies Sugar Industry*, p. 42.

TABLE 21.1. *Exports of sugar from the British West Indies, 1820–1899* (tons per year)

	Barbados	Leeward Islands	Jamaica	Windward Islands	Trinidad, British Guiana	Total
1820–29	11,946	16,910	72,051	32,495	50,846	184,248
1830–39	18,696	15,794	58,841	26,405	66,356	186,092
1840–49	17,353	15,789	32,158	17,061	50,606	132,967
1850–59	31,261	17,187	24,447	17,604	68,828	159,327
1860–69	38,216	19,776	25,766	17,842	101,910	203,510
1870–79	41,108	22,074	24,281	21,558	134,489	243,510
1880–89	54,789	29,048	19,974	16,067	164,911	284,789
1890–99	50,451	28,858	20,546	8,485	151,808	260,148

Source: Ward, *British West Indian Slavery*, p. 242.

In terms of sugar production, Jamaica was the exception in the West Indies: its sugar industry was declining in relation to other products. By 1865 about half of the 600 estates in the island at the time of emancipation had been abandoned. As a result, sugar comprised just over 40 per cent of Jamaica's total exports. Other commodities, such as logwood, cattle, and increasingly after 1870, bananas made up the remainder of Jamaica's output. But like the rest of the British West Indies, Jamaica's economy suffered considerably from competition with beet sugar.[54]

European beet sugar producers increased their production substantially during the second half of the century. By 1870 they produced nearly one-third of the total world sugar output. When Germany, the world's major producer of beet sugar, doubled bounties on its sugar exports in 1883–84, the effect on the British market was dramatic. There was a massive increase in beet sugar imports into Britain and, consequently, a collapse in the sugar price. During the 1870s and early 1880s the price of sugar had remained relatively steady at around 20 shillings per hundred-weight; in 1884, however, it fell to just over 13 shillings per hundredweight. Since this was less than the cost of production on many West Indian estates, the distress there was immediately visible.[55]

As in the crises of the late 1840s, a number of West Indian merchant houses collapsed, especially those involved in the smaller islands. The production of West Indian sugar was drastically affected. For example, Grenada's output immediately dropped by more than half; two-thirds of the sugar cultivation in St Vincent had

[54] Ibid., p. 43.
[55] Lobdell, 'Patterns of Investment', p. 325; Beachey, *British West Indies Sugar Industry*, p. 59.

been abandoned by 1886. Jamaica's production was affected by the simultaneous exodus of thousands of labourers to work on the Panama Canal.[56]

A further consequence of the late-century economic crisis was the amalgamation of sugar plantations. Of the 150 estates in British Guiana in 1865, for instance, only fifty remained by the turn of the century. In Trinidad, where the first central factories were established in the West Indies, there was also a reduction in the number of estates, from 110 in 1865 to half that number by 1900. Numbers in Jamaica continued to decline, with only about 140 remaining in 1896. Overall in the British West Indies, estates declined in numbers by about a third between the time of emancipation and 1900. Yet this decline did not inevitably mean decreased production, since the larger units proved to be more efficient and often more favourably located. The economic crisis also had the effect of radically shifting the market for sugar. Since beet sugar was dumped into Britain's market, the West Indies turned elsewhere. By 1900 over two-thirds of British West Indian sugar was sent to the United States.[57]

The position of West Indian sugar worsened further when the French and Germans doubled their bounties on beet sugar in 1896, leading to a further drop in sugar prices the following year. West Indian producers claimed that they were threatened with extinction. The Secretary of State for the Colonies, Joseph Chamberlain, responded by despatching a Royal Commission to investigate the economic crisis in the West Indies. As a result of the Commission's report and the continuing economic difficulties, the Imperial government decided to confront the problem of sugar beet bounties. Although the Europeans agreed to cease bounties on their sugar from 1903, this did not immediately revive the West Indian sugar industry. The United States market dwindled, as Cuba now enjoyed a highly preferential tariff there, but Canada proved to be the one growth area for West Indian sugar in the early twentieth century. Other Imperial economic initiatives met with only limited success.[58]

The prolonged economic depression had repercussions for the working population in the West Indies. In response to the crisis planters reduced wages, which created considerable hardship for sugar-cane workers. There were reports of widespread destitution and malnutrition after 1884, as well as an increasing incidence of disease. As in the years following emancipation, the economic and social difficulties of the period were reflected in a large number of riots and disturbances.[59]

[56] Beachey, *British West Indies Sugar Industry*, p. 59.

[57] Ibid., pp. 121–27.

[58] Ibid., chap. 8.

[59] Bonham C. Richardson, 'Prelude to Nationalism? Riots and Land Use Changes in the Lesser Antilles in the 1890s', in Hoogbergen, *Born Out of Resistance*, p. 206.

Violence erupted in Grenada in 1895, St Vincent in 1891, and Dominica in 1893. In 1896 strikes and demonstrations over the issue of lowered wages marked the beginning of the harvest season in St Kitts; during the subsequent riots two people were killed and many others wounded. A plantation riot among Indian indentured workers in British Guiana later the same year also led to five Indian workers killed and another fifty-nine injured when the police opened fire on the crowd. In addition to smaller outbreaks in Montserrat and Dominica, there were serious riots in Montego Bay, Jamaica, in 1902, difficult economic conditions being exacerbated by high taxes. Montego Bay was the target of the rioters for two days, and it took British forces from across the island to restore order. The 1905 riots in British Guiana linked urban workers and sugar estate labourers and were also a response to workers' declining living standards at the end of the century. As with many of these outbreaks, women in British Guiana played a significant role in the riots.[60]

The 1890s also witnessed the first organized workingmen's association in the West Indies. In Jamaica, skilled tradesmen created separate unions, beginning in 1898 with the establishment of the Artisans' Union. A decade later two others, made up of cigar-makers and printers, were also formed. Elsewhere, the Trinidad Workingmen's Association sought to bring together various trades within one organization. Unlike the unions in Jamaica, the Trinidad union had political objectives, such as the reduction of taxes and constitutional reform. But these unions either foundered after unsuccessful strikes or simply ceased to function; it was not until after the First World War that more permanent bodies were established.[61]

This period saw another important development: a reaction to the pseudo-scientific racism in British thought. One strand of British thinking in the mid-nineteenth century was reflected in the work of Thomas Carlyle, who regarded blacks as an inferior race and emancipation as the ruin of the West Indies. The Morant Bay Rebellion in Jamaica helped to strengthen these views, and the emergence of Social Darwinian ideas reinforced belief in white domination as well as the subordination of blacks. But not all blacks accepted these notions, any more than they did the Crown Colony government they seemed to justify. A Trinidadian, J. J. Thomas, in a book entitled *Froudacity* published in 1888, called for united action to uplift blacks and for a recognition of the links between the New World and Africa. Although some middle-class blacks in Trinidad undoubt-

---

[60] Ibid., pp. 208–09; Patrick Bryan, *The Jamaican People, 1880–1900* (London, 1991), pp. 271–74; Rodney, *The Guyanese Working People*, chap. 8.

[61] Richard Hart, 'Origin and Development of the Working Class in the English-Speaking Caribbean Area, 1897–1937', in Malcolm Cross and Gad Heuman, eds., *Labour in the Caribbean: From Emancipation to Independence* (London, 1988), pp. 43–50. In Vol. IV, see chap. by Howard Johnson.

edly rejected their racial heritage, a significant number were strong proponents of race consciousness. In Jamaica such views were reflected in a black colonizing scheme. In 1899 Dr Albert Thorne, a Barbadian, held a meeting in which he proposed to settle West Indian settlers in Africa, with the intention of improving the status of the African race. Thorne had some influence on Marcus Garvey, a black Jamaican whose ideas about black capability and self-worth became highly popular just after the First World War.[62]

As with these black challenges to racism, many of the changes in the nineteenth and early twentieth centuries laid the groundwork for future developments. Politically, representative government gave way to Crown Colony administration, but there were already modifications to the system which would lead to a wider electorate. Attempts to maintain control of labour in the aftermath of emancipation met with considerable resistance; this not only led to riots and disturbances but also to the growth of a significant peasantry. Moreover, by the end of the nineteenth century Colonial Office officials and policy-makers had changed their views about the importance of the peasantry: sugar was no longer king and the idea of progress was not tied solely to sugar cultivation.[63] Much had changed by 1914, but more fundamental political and social developments in the West Indies would have to wait until the labour disturbances of the 1930s and the coming of political independence later in the century.

[62] Bridget Brereton, 'The Development of an Identity: The Black Middle Class of Trinidad in the Later Nineteenth Century', in Hilary McD. Beckles and Verene Shepherd, *Caribbean Freedom: Society and Economy to the Present* (Kingston, 1993), pp. 281–82; Bryan, *Jamaican People*, p. 258.

[63] Richard A. Lobdell, 'British Officials and the West Indian Peasantry, 1842–1938', in Cross and Heuman, *Labour in the Caribbean*, pp. 199–202.

Select Bibliography

R. W. BEACHEY, *The British West Indies Sugar Industry in the Late 19th Century* (Oxford, 1957).

BRIDGET BRERETON, *Race Relations in Colonial Trinidad, 1870–1900* (Cambridge, 1979).

PATRICK BRYAN, *The Jamaican People, 1880–1900* (London, 1991).

MICHAEL CRATON, *Testing the Chains: Resistance to Slavery in the British West Indies* (Ithaca, NY, 1982).

PHILIP D. CURTIN, *Two Jamaicas: The Role of Ideas in a Tropical Colony, 1830–1865* (Cambridge, Mass., 1955).

EMILIA VIOTTI DA COSTA, *Crowns of Glory, Tears of Blood: The Demerara Slave Rebellion of 1823* (New York, 1994).

WILLIAM A. GREEN, *British Slave Emancipation: The Sugar Colonies and the Great Experiment, 1830–1865* (Oxford, 1976).

DOUGLAS HALL, *Free Jamaica, 1838–1865: An Economic History* (New Haven, 1959).

GAD HEUMAN, *Between Black and White: Race, Politics, and the Free Coloreds in Jamaica, 1792–1865* (Westport, Conn., 1981).

——'*The Killing Time': The Morant Bay Rebellion in Jamaica* (London, 1994).

B. W. HIGMAN, *Slave Population and Economy in Jamaica, 1807–1834* (Cambridge, 1976).

——*Slave Populations of the British Caribbean, 1807–1834* (Baltimore, 1984).

THOMAS C. HOLT, *The Problem of Freedom: Race, Labor, and Politics in Jamaica and Britain, 1832–1938* (Baltimore, 1992).

K. O. LAURENCE, *A Question of Labour: Indentured Immigration into Trinidad and British Guiana, 1875–1917* (Kingston, 1994).

D. J. MURRAY, *The West Indies and the Development of Colonial Government, 1801–1834* (Oxford, 1965).

WALTER RODNEY, *A History of the Guyanese Working People, 1881–1905* (Kingston, 1981).

HOWARD TEMPERLEY, *British Antislavery, 1833–1870* (London, 1972).

MARY TURNER, *Slaves and Missionaries: The Disintegration of Jamaican Slave Society, 1787–1834* (Urbana, Ill., 1982).

H. A. WILL, *Constitutional Change in the British West Indies, 1880–1903* (Oxford, 1970).

DONALD WOOD, *Trinidad in Transition: The Years after Slavery* (London, 1968).

22

Ireland and the Empire

DAVID FITZPATRICK

The formal Union of the kingdoms of Ireland and Great Britain (1801–1922) masked a hybrid administration with manifest colonial elements, allowing variant interpretations of the character of Ireland's dependency. Was Ireland an integral part of the United Kingdom, a peripheral, backward sub-region, or a colony in all but name? These were the conflicting assumptions of unionists, devolutionists, and separatists respectively. The manner in which the contending parties specified Ireland's current status reflected, yet also restricted, their visions of its future condition. Underpinning these perceptions of the present and future were incompatible beliefs about the Irish past, reinforced and mobilized by historians and polemicists. Yet the sense of destiny associated with historical mythology, whether unionist or nationalist, was repeatedly challenged by external influences such as legislative reform and changing economic opportunities. Even unionists, pledged to defend the liberties conferred by the Glorious Revolution and incorporated in the Imperial Parliament, might contemplate rebellion against a 'radical' government should it tamper with the Empire. Even those who viewed Ireland as a vassal colony within the Empire might hope to benefit from employment in the Empire's service. Thus changes in the practical operation of the Union were capable of transforming Imperialists into rebels, and separatists into colonists. This chapter explores the involvement in the Empire of both Ireland and the Irish. Is it appropriate to depict Ireland under the Union as a colony? Why have historians found Ireland so difficult to place in their constructions of the Empire and Imperialism? In what ways did political conflict concerning Ireland's future intersect with broader issues of Imperial development? How important were the Irish themselves as colonists? And in what ways did Ireland and the Irish influence the Empire?

The Act of Union terminated Ireland's formal status as a 'Dominion' or dependent kingdom, a condition of colonial subjection inadequately ameliorated by the spurious independence granted to the Irish Parliament in 1782–83. The Union, though eventually accepted by that body, was universally interpreted as annexation in response to the bloody conflicts of 1798. The formal amalgamation of the two kingdoms allowed Ireland substantial representation in both Houses of Parliament, with occasional opportunities to influence legislation when the major parties were closely balanced. The hundred-odd Irish members comprised about a seventh of the House of Commons, a proportion initially mean but eventually generous. In addition to twenty-eight 'Irish representative peers', some of them beneficiaries of the bribes which had secured the Act of Union, the House of Lords included many with English titles but Irish property. The spiritual lords also included a few Irish representatives until the religious Union was shattered by the disestablishment of the Protestant Church of Ireland (effected in 1871).

The parliamentary Union was not accompanied by economic or administrative integration. Free trade between Ireland and Britain was enacted only in 1824, separate currencies persisted for another two years, and excise duties and taxation remained sharply at variance until 1853. The systems of central and local taxation were never fully reconciled; and Ireland's 'Imperial contribution' to maintaining the armed forces and servicing the national debt was inequitable with respect to both its population and its wealth. The economic inequity was not invariably to Ireland's disadvantage. Until 1853 Irish taxation and excise duties were relatively light. For a few years after 1908, when the introduction of the old-age pension led to disproportionate Irish expenditure, the Imperial contribution became negative and, by some calculations, Ireland was 'under-taxed'. In most years, however, Ireland paid dearly for its incomplete Union. In addition to maintaining a large paramilitary police force under the guise of 'Irish services', Irish taxes often contributed several millions per annum to Imperial burdens—such as the upkeep even in peacetime of a sizeable military and naval establishment.[1] By the late nineteenth century Ireland was clearly disadvantaged by comparison with the formal colonies, which regulated their own taxes and duties, and were exempt from responsibility for Imperial services and the National Debt. In fiscal terms, colonial rule would have been less disadvantageous to Ireland than integration.

The Irish administration remained distinctively colonial in both form and function, despite the legislative Union. As in India after 1858, annexation was followed by direct rule under a 'Lord-Lieutenant' or 'Viceroy' (properly the Lord Lieutenant-General and General Governor of Ireland), whose powers remained ill-defined in the absence of a Parliament over which to preside. The preservation of this office, though largely ceremonial, was a perpetual irritant to virtually every faction: in 1871 Earl Spencer's own private secretary is identified as having declared

---

[1] W. E. Vaughan, 'Ireland c.1870', in Vaughan, ed., *A New History of Ireland* (Oxford, 1989), V, pp. 784–94.

that 'the Lord Lieutenancy ought to be abolished as a mark of national inferiority and colonial dependence'.[2] The Viceroy's 'Chief Secretary' was the effective head of government, being usually, but not by entitlement, in Cabinet. An Under-Secretary supervised the Irish administration centred in Dublin Castle, without exercising any control over the armed services or the numerous Whitehall departments with Irish branches. By 1914 there were eleven of these, together with seven Irish departments controlled by the Treasury or Whitehall, and twenty-two boards or bodies under the formal direction of the Chief Secretary. The Lord-Lieutenant retained powers of patronage or veto over appointments to only twenty of these institutions.[3] The administration, in short, was a mess, with limitless opportunities for misunderstanding and collision between the Chief Secretary and the Lord-Lieutenant, the civil and military authorities, or the Castle, the Irish Office, and the Treasury. Despite reiterated demands for assimilating Irish and English laws and institutions, no government could bring itself to accept the full implications of the Union.[4]

In practice, the hybrid Irish administration differed significantly from those of England and Scotland: 'Irish government was remarkable for the extent to which centralization, uniformity, inspection and professionalism spread throughout the system before 1850.'[5] These attributes were evident in the training, arming, and central direction of the Irish Constabulary ('Royal' from 1867), the increasing subjection of local government and the magistracy to the Castle, the creation of a surprisingly successful system of National Education, and the staggering achievement of the Board of Works and the Poor Law Commissioners in mobilizing thousands of officials for famine relief (inadequate though it was) in 1846–47. Irish unrest provoked measures of repression and coercion unthinkable in Britain; Irish poverty justified welfare experiments and state intervention to a degree shocking to orthodox political economists. In these respects, Ireland was not only exceptional within the United Kingdom but akin to a colony, efficiency in government being valued above the liberty of the subject and the sanctity of property.

Pursuit of efficiency demanded active participation from a widening range of Irishmen hitherto excluded from public employment. Initially this was accomplished mainly through official patronage, whereby the Castle functioned as a

---

[2] Alan J. Ward, *The Irish Constitutional Tradition: Responsible Government and Modern Ireland, 1782–1992* (Washington, 1994), p. 36.

[3] R. B. McDowell, *The Irish Administration, 1801–1914* (London, 1964), esp. p. 29.

[4] Henry L. Jephson, 'Irish Statute Law Reform', *Journal of the Statistical and Social Inquiry Society of Ireland*, VII, pt. 55 (1879), p. 376; cf. Thomas A. Boylan and Timothy P. Foley, eds., *Political Economy and Colonial Ireland* (London, 1992), p. 136. Though Ireland, unlike Scotland, had no distinct legal code, its statute law differed sharply from England's as a result of innumerable acts excluding or restricted to Ireland.

[5] Oliver MacDonagh, *Ireland* (Englewood Cliffs, NJ, 1968), p. 31.

'proconsular despotism' in creating a bureaucracy unrestrained by the 'créole élite' (as Bayly pertly characterizes Ireland's Protestant 'Ascendancy').[6] Over the period of the Union, the Irish civil service was progressively opened to meritorious candidates without patrons, to Catholics as well as Protestants. This process was accelerated by the introduction of routine competitive examinations in 1871, although forty years later these accounted for only three-fifths of civil appointments. At least two-thirds of ordinary recruits to the Irish Constabulary were Catholics from its foundation in 1836; three-fifths of prison officers were Catholics in the census of 1901; and Protestants were barely in the majority among magistrates by 1912.[7] As in the shifting preference from Hindu to Muslim officials in inter-war India, the Irish administration gradually encouraged a burgeoning colonial élite (the Catholic bourgeoisie) to displace an established ally (the Ascendancy) as its chief mediator between government and people.

Yet the 'democratization' of the Irish administration and its sporadically benevolent conduct scarcely mitigated its colonial character. Even Augustine Birrell, most 'Irish-minded' of Chief Secretaries, acted the part of a District Commissioner when discussing an appointment to the Board of National Education: 'He *must* be a Catholic, & *ought* to be a Layman—I want a good sound sensible sympathetic Irish Educationist, not a representative of any *body* in particular—on the *Irish Language* Question he *should* be sympathetic—but no more than Reason and Patriotism demand.'[8] The Indian approach was made overt by Sir Antony MacDonnell, an Irish Catholic member of the Council of India who became Under-Secretary in Wyndham's Conservative executive in 1902. MacDonnell, who affirmed his 'strong Irish sympathies' when specifying conditions for his appointment, reminded Wyndham that 'for many years I directed administration on a large scale; and I know if you send me to Ireland the opportunity of a mere secretarial criticism would fall far short of my requirements'. As a prominent nationalist later complained: 'We are much oppressed by a gentleman of whom you know who moves in an Indian atmosphere, quite aloof from the fact of the situation in Ireland. . . . His idea appears to me to be to break up the Irish party machine and dominance in Irish politics and get a kind of Indian Council composed of . . . non-political businessmen.'[9] MacDonnell, humane though he

[6] C. A. Bayly, *Imperial Meridian: The British Empire and the World, 1780–1830* (London, 1989), pp. 195–97.

[7] W. J. Lowe and E. L. Malcolm, 'The Domestication of the Royal Irish Constabulary, 1836–1922', *Irish Economic and Social History*, XIX (1992), pp. 27–48; R. Barry O'Brien, *Dublin Castle and the Irish People* (Dublin, 1909), p. 62; McDowell, *Irish Administration*, p. 116.

[8] Birrell to W. J. M. Starkie, 23 April 1909, Trinity College Dublin, MSS 9209, f. 30.

[9] MacDonnell to Wyndham, 22 Sept. 1902, quoted in Earl of Dunraven, *The Outlook in Ireland: The Case for Devolution and Conciliation* (Dublin, 1907), pp. 288–89; Dillon to Morley, 19 Dec. 1906, in F. S. L. Lyons, *John Dillon: A Biography* (London, 1968), p. 291.

was, had much in common with Sir Charles Edward Trevelyan, Assistant Secretary to the Treasury and ruthless regulator of relief during the Great Famine, before his return to India to apply similar fiscal precepts with equal severity. Ireland's rulers, whether grim or benevolent, tended to regard the Irish as a separate and subject native population rather than an integral element of a united people.

The colonial spirit was evident in what nationalists saw as a substantial 'army of occupation', in which the police performed paramilitary functions while the army offered vigorous 'aid to the civil power' in suppressing riots, affrays, illegal assemblies, and rebellions. In 1881 the Irish garrison of over 25,000 soldiers vastly exceeded that in any dependency except India, amounting to twice the size of the police establishment.[10] The police were largely Irish in origin until the massive enlistment of British ex-servicemen as temporary constables ('Black and Tans') in 1920–21. Their officers, however, included a sprinkling of British gentlemen (as well as Irish Protestants) who might otherwise have joined colonial forces. As Robert Baden-Powell told a succession of English audiences in 1907, the ideal type of the scout 'was to be found... above all in the Canadian North-West Mounted Police, the South African Constabulary, Royal Irish Constabulary, British South African and numerous other police forces'.[11] English and Scottish soldiers were predominant within the Irish Command, especially after Fenian infiltration of the forces in the 1860s had reinforced the War Office's preference for stationing Irish units out of temptation's way, in Britain or beyond. Even in 1861 53 per cent of officers and men (excluding the militia) had been natives of Britain. Tommy's accent made 'occupation' manifest in the numerous garrison towns, though the occupying forces were popular enough with shopkeepers, publicans, and prostitutes.

Apart from Britishness visible in uniform, the evidence of physical 'colonization' was thinly scattered throughout the country. Ireland's British-born population trebled between 1841 and 1911, yet even by 1911 it amounted to only 55,000 women and 74,000 men (2.9 per cent of the ever-declining Irish population). Of these nearly half were clustered in the vicinities of Dublin and Belfast, reflecting the prominence of British immigrants in professional, clerical, and certain skilled employments.[12] The ancient dream of resettling Ireland with thrifty Scots and

---

[10] Andrew Porter, *European Imperialism, 1860–1914* (London, 1994), p. 115.

[11] 'A New Scheme to Develop Good Citizens', in Robert H. MacDonald, *Sons of the Empire: The Frontier and the Boy Scout Movement, 1890–1918* (Toronto, 1993), p. 245.

[12] The occupational census for 1861 shows that the sectors in which British men were most over-represented were (in declining order) hatters, revenue officers, sailors, civil engineers, coastguards, engineers, army officers, merchants, land stewards, commercial travellers, and gentlemen. The most over-represented groups of British women were governesses, teachers, ladies, milliners, annuitants, and factory workers.

enterprising Saxons briefly revived after the Great Famine, when massive emigration rendered land temporarily accessible and the opportunities for capital investment seemed alluring. Otherwise, Anglicization was pursued through education in the English language (sometimes associated with campaigns for religious conversion in a 'Second Reformation'), rather than through renewed plantation by a superior race.

The prevalence and political consequences of racial 'stereotypes' are notoriously tricky to demonstrate, and clearly not all British administrators regarded 'the Irish' as a distinct and inferior race, intermediate between barbarism and civilization. Moreover, the assumption of Celtic inferiority was consistent with conflicting methods of government, depending on the relative weight ascribed to heredity and environment. If Celtic barbarism was inherent and therefore incorrigible, its menace could only be held in check by discipline, firmness, and recurrent coercion. If it resulted from poverty, ignorance, or religious delusion, then it might be eliminated through education and enlightenment.[13] This duality in British perceptions of Irishness was closely paralleled in Imperial attitudes towards the native peoples of Asia, Australasia, and Africa. However, explicit comparisons between coloured races and the Irish were usually insulting to both, and Salisbury was not alone in likening the Irish to the Hottentots (being likewise incapable of self-government). In 1892 Sydney and Beatrice Webb honeymooned in Dublin, reporting that 'the people are charming but we detest them, as we should the Hottentots—for their very virtues'.[14] At the nadir of the Anglo-Irish conflict in 1921, the army commander (General Sir Nevil Macready) denounced his republican opponents for 'acts of provocation such as would not be indulged in by the wildest savages of Central Africa'.[15] In the racial vision of British politicians and administrators, the Irish veered unpredictably between savagery and childlike dependency.

Most studies of Ireland under the Union have neglected its colonial elements.[16] This may be attributed partly to the scholarly practice of allowing formal constitutions rather than practical relationships to circumscribe political analysis.

---

[13] L. P. Curtis, *Anglo-Saxons and Celts: A Study of Anti-Irish Prejudice in Victorian England* (Bridgeport, Conn., 1968); Curtis, *Apes and Angels: The Irishman in Victorian Caricature* (Newton Abbot, 1971).

[14] Curtis, *Anglo-Saxons and Celts*, pp. 102–03, 63.

[15] David Fitzpatrick, 'The Overflow of the Deluge: Anglo-Irish Relationships, 1914–1922', in Oliver MacDonagh and W. F. Mandle, eds., *Ireland and Irish-Australia: Studies in Cultural and Political History* (London, 1986), p. 89.

[16] Joseph Ruane, 'Colonialism and the Interpretation of Irish Historical Development', in Marilyn Silverman and P. H. Gulliver, eds., *Approaching the Past: Historical Anthropology through Irish Case Studies* (New York, 1992), pp. 292–323. Ruane's strictures against historians of Ireland are undermined by his neglect of Mansergh, O'Farrell, and MacDonagh (discussed below).

Furthermore, the confusing amalgam of colonial and integrative processes in the British government of Ireland has discouraged most scholars from defining Ireland's place in the nineteenth-century Empire, although recent publications are likely to provoke further analysis from both Irish and Imperial specialists.[17]

The available analyses highlight the difficulty of incorporating Ireland within any colonial model of general application. Notwithstanding comparisons drawn between Ireland's experience and that of the white settler colonies, few historians have detected the germ of Dominion Status within the shell of the Union.[18] However, several have noted Britain's enduring disposition to govern Ireland like a Crown Colony. The Union itself had been largely prompted by fear of French invasion, and Ireland's proximity to Britain conferred it with a strategic import-ance comparable with that of Gibraltar or Aden. Governments became gradually less preoccupied with Ireland's strategic role 'as the Bonapartist threat receded'; and by the 1880s it was sometimes suggested that the Empire's strategic interests could be defended without military occupation of the western island.[19] Never-theless, the imposition of martial law in response to the 1916 Rising, that 'stab in the back' of the British Empire, demonstrated that in wartime strategic calcula-tions still outweighted political common sense in determining the government of Ireland.

It has been suggested that Irish and Indian administrators were equally ready in moments of crisis to apply coercion and suspend civil liberties, but less inclined in the Irish case to initiate 'radical departures from English norms' in matters such as land reform.[20] There is perhaps a parallel to be drawn between Ireland after 1801 and India after 1858, the imposition of direct control being followed in each case by economic spoliation.[21] A variety of 'Irish lessons' may have helped Indian and other colonial administrators 'to tighten the grip of the colonizers or to engender economic growth or social harmony by governing more or less in apparent conformity with established indigenous customs'.[22] There is, however, a subtler parallel between ambiguities in the management of Ireland and the non-European

---

[17] Bayly, *Imperial Meridian*, p. 12; Keith Jeffery, ed., *An Irish Empire? Aspects of Ireland and the British Empire* (Cambridge, 1996).

[18] Tom Garvin, *The Evolution of Irish Nationalist Politics* (Dublin, 1981), pp. 4, 213, 2; Nicholas Mansergh, *The Commonwealth Experience*, 2 vols., 2nd edn. (London, 1982), I, p. 225; Ward, *Irish Constitutional Tradition*, pp. 29, 30; Patrick O'Farrell, *England and Ireland since 1800* (Oxford, 1975), p. 37.

[19] Oliver MacDonagh, 'Introduction', in Vaughan, *New History*, pp. liii–liv; Vaughan, 'Ireland c.1870', pp. 791–92.

[20] O'Farrell, *England and Ireland*, p. 37.

[21] V. G. Kiernan, *Imperialism and its Contradictions* (New York, 1995), pp. 56–57.

[22] Scott B. Cook, *Imperial Affinities: Nineteenth-Century Analogies and Exchanges between India and Ireland* (New Delhi, 1993), pp. 29, 26.

colonies: 'The need to treat Ireland as a subordinate collided constantly with the policy of converting her into a component of an integrated society in the British Isles. It also vitiated the policy of converting Irishmen into outer Britons. These cross-purposes, strikingly manifested in Anglo-Irish relations, also characterized, more or less, Britain's relations with all her other dependencies at that time.'[23] Within the Empire, the government of Ireland was not unique in its confusion.

The problem of specifying Ireland's place in the British Imperial system remains unresolved, partly because of continuing disagreement over the character and rationale of that system. If, as John Gallagher and Ronald Robinson maintain, the Imperial impulse was served better by informal than formal annexation, it might also be served by formal absorption into the metropolitan power. Though Gallagher and Robinson make no attempt to incorporate Ireland within their taxonomy of Imperial forms, the Act of Union might be interpreted as a still more reluctant 'last resort' than colonial annexation in the pursuit of 'security for British enterprise (whether commercial, philanthropic or merely strategic)'.[24] Ireland, after all, was one of Britain's major trading partners, a fact obscured for most of the period of the Union by the predictable absence of statistics for movement of goods within a formally United Kingdom. When Irish industrial revivalism led to the publication of trade returns for Irish ports during the pre-war decade, it became apparent that the value of British trade with Ireland exceeded that between the United Kingdom and Australasia, rivalling commerce with British India. Britain's balance of visible trade with Ireland, as with most countries except India, was unfavourable.[25] By one interpretation, Ireland's 'colonial status' under the Union entailed its decline into 'a feudal agricultural slum in the immediate neighbourhood of modern middle-class England'.[26] Yet free access to the rapidly expanding British market encouraged marked if unspectacular growth in Irish agricultural output and productivity after the Famine, while industrial production in the Belfast region (mainly for export) expanded rapidly from the 1870s. Ireland's economic importance for British consumers was to be underlined

[23] MacDonagh, *Ireland*, p. 22.

[24] John Gallagher and Ronald Robinson, 'The Imperialism of Free Trade', reprinted in Gallagher, *The Decline, Revival and Fall of the British Empire: The Ford Lectures and Other Essays*, ed. Anil Seal (Cambridge, 1982), p. 16. In a more recent essay in that volume, Gallagher treats Irish unrest as a domestic problem, distinct from colonial conflicts: 'We have no Dublin Post Offices in our story' (p. 79).

[25] In 1911 the estimated value of British imports from Ireland was £63.5m, and that of exports £51.7m. Corresponding figures for Australasia (whose population considerably exceeded Ireland's by 1911) were £57.0m and £45.1m, and for British India £45.4m and £53.9m. The Irish statistics exclude exports to foreign and colonial countries (worth £1.6m in 1911) and Ireland's share of imports from outside Britain (worth £15.0m): *Thom's Official Directory* (Dublin, 1915), pp. 682–89, 776.

[26] E. Strauss, *Irish Nationalism and British Democracy* (London, 1951), p. 135. This passage refers to the mid-nineteenth century.

during the First World War, when Irish farmers filled much of the gap caused by the dislocation of transoceanic trade.

Little is known about the Anglo-Irish movement of capital, by some accounts a more significant motive for Imperial expansion than the exchange of goods. Calculations for the period 1883–1907 indicate that Irish-based stockholders played conspicuously little part in capitalizing firms registered in the United Kingdom but located in the Empire. The Irish, by this index, were insignificant as economic imperialists. Irish investors were scarcely more prominent in British-based firms,[27] and the net flow of capital was undoubtedly from Britain to Ireland. Though few attempts have been made to apply Marxian materialism to the Irish case, one has depicted Ireland as 'Europe's only capitalist colony' (serving the interests of the metropolis rather than the settlers); whereas another has chronicled 'the diminishing returns of Imperialism' as the rents, labour, and also taxes extracted under the Union steadily declined.[28]

It remains to be shown that nineteenth-century Ireland ever provided a major field for British capital investment. As the statistician Robert Giffen observed in 1886, British investment in Ireland was negligible compared with that in India or Australia.[29] Most of the rental income from Irish landed estates, though the distant outcome of massive past investment by English and Scottish settlers, was paid to landlords or rentiers usually resident in Ireland. Furthermore, the cumulative effect of the Great Famine and of subsequent land agitation and legislation was to reduce rents as a proportion of output, and eventually to induce the government to lend sufficient money to enable most occupiers to buy out their landlords. The extent and profitability of non-agricultural investments are even less well documented. Most insurance companies operating in Ireland in 1844 were London-based, while British investors were prominent in the formation of several major Irish banks and railway companies. Although 'the capital markets of Ireland and Britain were closely integrated', there was a substantial net movement of gilt-edged stocks from London to Dublin between 1818 and 1863 which subsequently petered out.[30] Another analysis of Ireland's 'provinciality or colonyhood' under the Union

---

[27] Lance E. Davis and Robert A. Huttenback, with the assistance of Susan Gray Davis, *Mammon and the Pursuit of Empire: The Political Economy of British Imperialism, 1860–1912* (Cambridge, 1986), pp. 196, 209. The analysis refers to 126 Imperial firms (listed in the *Stock Exchange Official Yearbook*) with 39,680 stockholders, of whom 0.9 % were resident in Ireland compared with 7.6 % in Scotland and 8.5 % in the colonies.

[28] Raymond Crotty, *Ireland in Crisis: A Study in Capitalist Colonial Undevelopment* (Dingle, Co. Kerry, 1986), p. 62; Strauss, *Irish Nationalism*, pp. 196–205.

[29] Vaughan, 'Ireland, *c*.1870', p. 791.

[30] P. J. Cain and A. G. Hopkins, *British Imperialism: Innovation and Expansion, 1688–1914* (London, 1993); Oliver MacDonagh, 'The Economy and Society, 1830–45', in Vaughan, *New History*, p. 231; Cormac Ó Gráda, *Ireland: A New Economic History, 1780–1939* (Oxford, 1994), p. 350.

also casts doubt on the usefulness of Ireland as an economic possession: 'If... economic "exploitation" is conceived of as a necessary element in colonialism, it is difficult to see what Britain gained from her Irish "possession" in the nineteenth century.... No matter what kind of balance-sheet we contrive, it would hardly show Ireland to have been profitable.'[31] It seems unlikely that Ireland under the Union was a significant asset to Britain, whether as a trading partner, a site for capital investment, or even a source of revenue from taxes and duties (except, perhaps, for a few decades after 1853). If so, Ireland probably shared its unprofitability with the Empire at large.[32]

The development of the National Education system after 1831 has justifiably been depicted as a classic example of 'cultural imperialism', directed towards the moral and intellectual advancement of a hitherto backward people. As the last (and only Catholic) Resident Commissioner observed of his predecessors: 'Archbishop Whately and his friends treated the Irish as the Kaffirs are not treated now. His real ambition, as was divulged after his death, was to destroy "the gigantic fabric of the Catholic Church", not by a frontal attack, but by discouraging the Irish language and national feeling, and by the dissemination of snippets of political economy and science, in the form of reading books.'[33] Until the turn of the century the Irish reading books paid little attention to Irish geography or history, instead giving detailed information on Britain's overseas colonies and their picturesque peoples. Australia's Aborigines were 'more like brutes than men', but even they might become civilized: 'What makes the difference between any of us Europeans and those poor creatures? ... Evidently it is education.'[34] The inclusion of Irish pupils among 'us Europeans' was implicitly contingent upon continued school attendance. The preoccupation with Imperial rather than domestic geography (British as well as Irish) was deplored by P. W. Joyce, whose history readers were largely responsible for restoring Ireland to the schoolroom after the 1890s: 'It is strange to find a class of children acquainted with the minute features of the map of Asia or of Africa, and yet ignorant of the course of the Shannon or the Thames.'[35] Despite their disregard for local particulars, the lesson of the

[31] Oliver MacDonagh, *States of Mind: A Study of Anglo-Irish Conflict, 1780–1980* (London, 1983), p. 52; MacDonagh, 'Introduction', p. liii.

[32] Patrick K. O'Brien, 'The Costs and Benefits of British Imperialism, 1846–1914', *Past and Present*, CXX (1988), pp. 163–200.

[33] W. J. M. Starkie, *The History of Irish Primary and Secondary Education during the Last Decade* (Dublin, 1911), p. 1.

[34] John Coolahan, 'The Irish and Others in Irish Nineteenth-Century Textbooks', in J. A. Mangan, ed., *The Imperial Curriculum: Racial Images and Education in British Colonial Experience* (London, 1993), p. 59.

[35] P. W. Joyce, *A Handbook of School Management and Methods of Teaching*, 15th edn. (Dublin, 1892), p. 255.

readers, even in Whately's vision, was that Irish children had the potential to become metropolitans and colonists instead of colonials.

The broader question of colonial qualities in Irish thought and imagination, which has recently provoked vigorous if opaque debate among literary critics and 'cultural theorists', lies beyond the range of this chapter. Said's specification of 'Ireland's colonial status, which it shares with a host of non-European regions: cultural dependence and antagonism together', is based upon a premiss incapable of historical verification. Said assumes that 'Irish people can never be English any more than Cambodians or Algerians can be French', finding confirmation in the record of Irish protest against British government.[36] As argued in the next section, the political expression of Irish attitudes towards the Empire was far more various and discordant than this allows. Ireland had its rebels, its 'mediators' and 'collaborators' or 'shoneens', its Imperialists, and its unselfconscious metropolitans. The battlegrounds of Anglo-Irish and intra-Irish conflict are littered with the ghoulish shards of incompatible images representing the Empire, and Ireland's place within it.

For republicans and separatists, Ireland's colonial subjection to a foreign force of occupation was an article of faith. Republicanism rested on the belief that the Irish nation had remained essentially intact through centuries of oppression, requiring only reawakening to cast off its veneer of Anglicization. Not only did republicans long for the destruction of the British Empire in war, but they also viewed Imperial conflicts as providing an opportunity for rebellion. The spirit of 1798 was re-invoked in 1916, despite powerful evidence that war had argumented the oppressor's coercive capacity rather than weakening it. Just as the Fenians had prayed for war with America or Russia, so their successors saw Germany as a potential saviour. As Maeve Cavanagh wrote in 'Ireland to Germany':

> I watch the red flame fiercer grow,
> The tide of war, its ebb and flow,
> And see the nations writhe and strain—
> I, who my freedom strive to gain,
> The while I pray 'swift fall the blow
> That lays the tyrant England low'.[37]

Even nationalists hopeful of a constitutional settlement were inclined to relish the alternative path of Imperial collapse, as in the case of a Cork emigrant writing from Australia in 1887: 'Myself and Pat often come to the conclusion that nothing will

---

[36] Edward W. Said, *Culture and Imperialism* (London, 1993), pp. 266, 275.
[37] Copy, with music by Cathal Mac Dubhghaill, in National Library of Ireland, Ir 780p23.

save Ireland but a home legislature or otherwise a war that will rake Ingland from one of her dominions to the other, May God send either of the two.'[38] For a few Irish nationalists all of the time, and for many occasionally, the Union was tantamount to colonial annexation and the promise of freedom lay in its destruction. This interpretation shaped the behaviour not only of Irish rebels, but of many subsequent 'anti-colonial' movements for which the Irish experience provided a 'pathfinder'.[39]

The manifest failure of successive rebellions and conspiracies between 1798 and 1916 fostered various less adventurous and more tactical programmes of nationalism. The movements for dual monarchy, repeal of the Act of Union, Home Rule, federation, and devolution all stopped short of demanding full separation, while deploring the economic, social, and moral consequences of the Union. One of the curiosities of Edwardian nationalism is Arthur Griffith's pre-revolutionary Sinn Fein programme, with its demand for restoration of an idealized version of the Irish constitution of 1782, under a system of dual monarchy modelled on Hungary's supposed autonomy in the Austro-Hungarian Empire.[40] Despite its formal adherence to monarchy, Griffith's nationalism was bitterly anti-Imperialist in its assault upon the Anglicization of Irish culture. This qualification did not apply, in general, to the Repeal or Home Rule movements. Daniel O'Connell was a powerful advocate of the application of English liberties, enlightenment, and culture to backward Ireland. Isaac Butt, founder of the Home Rule League in 1873, demanded metropolitan status for Ireland within a federation which would 'consolidate the strength and maintain the integrity of the Empire'. The Irish, having 'paid dearly enough' for the acquisition of Imperial possessions since the Act of Union, were 'entitled to our share in them'.[41] In 1880 J. L. Finegan, Parnellite representative for Ennis, could refer in the same speech to 'the present unjust and tyrannous system of government in Ireland' and the 'great and noble Empire', to which Ireland had contributed so much blood and muscle. Parnell's party included several members with close Indian links, who variously campaigned for fairer Irish representation in the Indian Civil Service or for self-government in both countries.[42] Frank Hugh O'Donnell, whose brother Charles James became a Commissioner in the Indian

---

[38] Phil Mahoney (Footscray, Victoria) to Lar Shanahan (Lurrig, Co. Cork), 18 Aug. 1887: David Fitzpatrick, *Oceans of Consolation: Personal Accounts of Irish Migration to Australia* (Cork, 1995), p. 264.

[39] MacDonagh, *Ireland*, p. 95.

[40] [Arthur Griffith], *The Resurrection of Hungary: A Parallel for Ireland* (Dublin, 1904), concerning the *Ausgleich* of 1867.

[41] H. V. Brasted, 'Irish Nationalism and the British Empire in the Late Nineteenth Century', in MacDonagh and Mandle, *Ireland and Irish-Australia*, pp. 85–86.

[42] Alan O'Day, *The English Face of Irish Nationalism: Parnellite Involvement in British Politics, 1880–86* (Dublin, 1977), pp. 161–65.

Civil Service, regarded Irish nationalists as the 'natural representatives and spokes-men of the unrepresented nationalities of the Empire'. He himself attended the Indian Constitutional Reform Association's inaugural meeting at Tagore's London house in 1883, and campaigned unavailingly for the nomination of Naoroji for an Irish constituency.[43] Like many nationalists, O'Donnell viewed the struggle for Home Rule as part of the broader demand for devolution of power throughout the Empire.

John Redmond, nationalist leader between 1900 and 1918, looked forward to 'a measure of legislative autonomy similar to that enjoyed by any of your self-governing Colonies or Dependencies. If you want an illustration look at Canada, look even to the Transvaal.'[44] Redmond's admiration for the forms of colonial self-government was perfectly consistent with his own and his party's indignant denunciation of the war against the Boers, drawing upon what the police termed 'a seditious and treasonable spirit towards England which, in its extent and intensity, has surprised many who believed they had the fullest knowledge of the people'.[45] Recurrent Imperial wars reminded the Irish of their own history of coercion and annexation; yet in its more benign aspect, evolving towards a 'Commonwealth', the Empire seemed to many nationalists to offer the prospect of an acceptable condition of self-government sheltered by Britannia's protective shield. The relevance to Ireland of the Canadian precedent was repeatedly affirmed by advocates of Home Rule, recurring in the Anglo-Irish agreement of 1921–22. Gladstone presented Home Rule as being 'strictly and substantially analogous' to Canada's status in the Empire, a comparison vigorously denied by unionists.[46] Viscount Milner, when privately discussing the possibility of future unionist acceptance of some form of Home Rule, insisted that Ireland's autonomy should be restricted to that of Quebec within Canada rather than of Canada within the Empire.[47] In reality, the scope of the three Home Rule Bills fell far short of the Canadian settlement of 1867, and responsible government on colonial lines was never a serious option before the First World War.

The compatibility of autonomy and participation in the Empire was central to the many proposals for federal devolution, within either the British Isles or the Empire as a whole, which won adherents in all parties from the 1840s onwards.

---

[43] Mary Cumpston, 'Some Early Indian Nationalists and their Allies in the British Parliament, 1851–1906', *English Historical Review*, LXXVI, 299 (1961), pp. 281–85.

[44] O'Brien, *Dublin Castle*, pp. 420–21.

[45] Inspector-General, R[oyal] I[rish] C[onstabulary], Monthly Confidential Report for Oct. 1899, in National Archives, Dublin.

[46] Ward, *Irish Constitutional Tradition*, pp. 62–63, 79–84.

[47] Milner to Balfour, 17 April 1910, in John Kendle, *Ireland and the Federal Solution: The Debate over the United Kingdom Constitution, 1870–1921* (Kingston, Ontario, 1988), p. 112.

O'Connell toyed with Sharman Crawford's proposal in 1843 for subsidiary Irish, English, and Scottish parliaments; Butt considered that under a 'Federal Union' Ireland might 'enjoy all of self-government and distinct nationality which would be necessary for the full development of her national life'; Earl Grey and the Earl of Selborne, former Governors-General of Canada and South Africa respectively, advocated a modest devolution of powers to parliaments in Ireland, Scotland, England, and Wales.[48] The Earl of Dunraven, whose programme of conciliation had been briefly but spectacularly effective in facilitating the purchase of farms by tenant occupiers, also advocated federal devolution as a means of strengthening rather than disintegrating the Empire. Dunraven maintained that the attempt in Ireland 'to obliterate distinctive characteristics and usages, and to produce absolute homogeneity by force', was a negation of the principles which had rendered the Empire successful. Though 'Ireland cannot be anglicised', its well-being required 'the force and backing of a great Empire'.[49] No scheme for an Irish settlement based on federal devolution aroused substantial popular or political interest, partly because the broader design of Imperial federation never became practicable. Nevertheless, the underlying aspiration to find a place for a free Ireland in a reformed Empire appealed to a surprising range of nationalist thinkers, as well as Imperial visionaries.

If nationalist attitudes towards the Empire were diverse and responsive to changes in its organization, 'loyalist' opposition to any form of devolution became ever more uncompromising. Though the abolition of the Irish Parliament had been deplored by many Irish Protestants as subverting the Ascendancy and opening the way to Catholic Emancipation (belatedly enacted in 1829), the Union once established was promptly redescribed as the most effective bulwark against further unwelcome reforms. More significantly, adherence to the Union was widely perceived as offering commercial advantages to both capitalists and their employees, and as protecting Protestant tenant farmers from predatory Catholic neighbours. For a large minority of the Irish people, liberty resided in the reinforcement of the Union rather than its dismemberment. Despite Joseph Chamberlain's early support for a devolved Irish administration and the federalist dreams of many Tory grandees, it became extremely hazardous after 1886 for Conservative politicians or Irish Protestants to question in public the desirability of perpetual integration in the United Kingdom. The expedient alliance between Conservatism and 'Ulster' in the campaigns against Home Rule reinforced the

[48] Ibid., pp. 9, 12–13, 107–09, 180–82. Grey advocated federal devolution in the United Kingdom as a necessary prelude to Imperial federation.

[49] Dunraven urged devolution along the lines of Quebec within Canada, the provinces within India, and the Channel Islands, Canada, and Australia within the Empire: Dunraven, *Outlook in Ireland*, pp. 195, 201–02, 264–65.

conviction of Irish loyalists that they were metropolitans rather than fringe-dwellers, let alone colonial subjects.

Nor did most Irish Protestants accept the nationalist innuendo that they were mere 'colonists' or settlers, proud though they were of the doughtiness of their distant ancestors who had admittedly performed those roles.[50] Instead, they pictured themselves as full citizens and redoubtable defenders of the Empire. Like the Marquess of Salisbury, they believed that 'to maintain the integrity of the Empire must undoubtedly be our first policy with respect to Ireland': the survival of the Union and the Empire were inseparable.[51] Though it has been claimed that the Imperial element in Ulster unionism was a fabrication of the Diamond Jubilee and the South African War, its imprint was obvious from 1867 in the triennial meetings of the Imperial Grand Orange Council.[52] Orangeism, the fraternity at the heart of Ulster unionism, provided a microcosm of Ulster's Protestant diaspora through its interlocking networks of lodges in Ireland, Britain, North America, and Australasia. The ceremonious conferences of the Imperial Grand Orange Council symbolized the Ulsterman's dual role as metropolitan and empire-builder.

Irish Protestantism produced several outstanding exponents of poetic imperialism, including the Munster clergyman Richard Sargint Sadleir Ross-Lewin. In a scruffy volume published in 1907, he affirmed 'our' metropolitan status:

> But our little western island
> Could never stand alone,
> And we share in the greatest Empire
> That the world has ever known.
> To Celt and Scot and Saxon
> That Empire was decreed,
> Twas won by Irish soldiers
> Of the grand old fighting breed.

Ross-Lewin had only contempt for 'the Little England Pygmies', who 'left the empire making to men like Cecil Rhodes', while idly watching 'the Tottenham Hotspur wipe out some rival team'—an arresting repudiation of the games ethic as a foundation of imperialism.[53] The Irish Imperial vision was further amplified

---

[50] The tag 'settler (unionist) population' recurs in Gretchen M. MacMillan, *State, Society and Authority in Ireland* (Dublin, 1993), p. 147.

[51] L. P. Curtis, Jr., *Coercion and Conciliation in Ireland, 1880–1892: A Study in Conservative Unionism* (Princeton, 1963), pp. 59, 355.

[52] Alvin Jackson, 'Irish Unionists and Empire, 1880–1920', in Jeffery, *An Irish Empire?*, p. 135.

[53] *Poems by a County of Clare West Briton* (Limerick, 1907), pp. 8, 86–87. Ross-Lewin called upon the loafers to forego football and 'attend at rifle practice, like men of martial mien'. Ross-Lewin echoed (or

in rhyme by Edward Coyle, a Belfast doctor, in 1905. Though devoting stanzas to each of the overseas colonies, Coyle alluded to Ireland only once, when reflecting that:

> Erin's moon would shine afar
> O'er west'ring seas to distant lands
> Where fair Columbia folds her hands.

Coyle's 'Homeland' was 'these British Isles', for which 'England' was the most suitable equivalent term ('for poetic purposes'). Like J. R. Seeley's, his vision transcended the formal possessions: 'The term "The Empire"... is used to connote all the English-speaking nations, and thus we include the United States, which, although having an independent and different form of government is really one with us in race, in language, in religion, and in laws.'[54] For Irish unionists, belonging to the Empire signified attachment to English civilization, not subjection to an external authority.

Irish responses to the Empire were modified through the nineteenth century by changing perceptions of its character and likely future evolution. The possibility of movement towards a devolved Commonwealth made many nationalists optimistic that membership might eventually be reconcilable with freedom. Yet the recurrence of punitive wars against subject peoples simultaneously reinforced the separatist conviction that the Empire was intrinsically oppressive. For unionists, the extension of the Imperial quest from strategic domination to cultural proselytism gave even greater force to their sense of being metropolitan participants. Interpretations of Ireland's status, whether metropolitan or colonial, were also influenced by the practical consequences of Imperial legislation for various sectors of the Irish population. Altered perceptions of the relative benefits and costs of continued attachment were reflected in seeming inconsistencies of rhetoric, whether on the part of ex-Fenians becoming Home Rulers or devolutionists becoming intransigent unionists. Irish thinking about the Empire thus mirrored the broader complexities and uncertainties of the Anglo-Irish connection.

Among the attractions of the Empire were the associated opportunities for employment. Colonial services provided a significant outlet for educated Irishmen, Catholic as well as Protestant. The introduction of competitive examinations for the Indian Civil Service met with a vigorous Irish response—Trinity College,

---

perhaps anticipated) Kipling's contemptuous reference in 'The Islanders' (1902) to 'the flannelled fools at the wicket or the muddied oafs at the goals': *A Choice of Kipling's Verse: Selected with an Essay on Rudyard Kipling by T. S. Eliot* [1963] (London, 1990), p. 130.

[54] Dr Edward Coyle, *The Empire: A Poem* (London, 1905), pp. 10, 5–6; W. J. Reader, *At Duty's Call: A Study in Obsolete Patriotism* (Manchester, 1988), pp. 46–47.

Dublin, being uncharacteristically alert in immediately offering crash-courses. Trinity College alone provided 180 recruits between 1855 and 1912, by contrast with its futile attempts to prepare candidates for the Royal Engineers and the Royal Artillery. Other Irish colleges soon followed suit, and a quarter of entrants between 1855 and 1863 were Irish-born. This proportion declined sharply thereafter, but Irish recruits remained prominent in the Indian medical service. Although Protestants with professional fathers were predominant, about a fifth of the Irish recruits to Indian posts seem to have been Catholics.[55] Prominent among these were James McNeill from Antrim, a Commissioner in the Bombay Presidency until 1914 and subsequently Governor-General of the Irish Free State; and Sir Michael O'Dwyer from Tipperary, who as Lieutenant-Governor of the Punjab after 1913 secured half a million recruits for the wartime forces. O'Dwyer had two brothers in the Society of Jesus, while McNeill's brother Eoin was the titular Chief of Staff of the Irish Volunteers who attempted to abort the Easter Rising in 1916.[56] Irish candidates were less successful in penetrating the Sudanese political service after 1899, and shrill complaints of discrimination by the Provost of Trinity 'only confirmed' the administrators 'in the wisdom of preferring Oxford and Cambridge'.[57] At a lower level of administration, Irish Catholic emigrants became prominent in the public service in both Australia and Canada. In 1867 the Conservative Prime Minister, Sir John A. Macdonald, claimed credit for that achievement in Canada: 'What Irish Catholic ever held office above the rank of a Tide Waiter or Messenger, until I did them justice?'[58] Among senior colonial administrators, however, Catholics failed to disturb the dominance of Protestant Englishmen, Scots, and Irishmen.

The armed services provided a still more important Imperial outlet for Irishmen of all religions and classes. For Irish as for Scottish university graduates, openings in the Indian Army offered them 'a stake in defending national, that is to say British, interests'.[59] Protestant Ireland was over-represented among officers in the Bengal Army between 1758 and 1834,[60] as also in the British army. Census returns indicate that in 1851 Irishmen accounted for over a quarter of all regular

---

[55] Scott B. Cook, 'The Irish Raj: Social Origins and Careers of Irishmen in the Indian Civil Service, 1855–1914', *Journal of Social History* (hereafter *JSH*), XX, 3 (1987), pp. 507–29; R. B. McDowell and D. A. Webb, *Trinity College Dublin, 1592–1952: An Academic History* (Cambridge, 1982), p. 538, n. 38.

[56] T. G. Fraser, 'Ireland and India', in Jeffery, *An Irish Empire?*, pp. 88–89; Sir Michael O'Dwyer, *India as I Knew It, 1885–1925* (London, 1925), pp. 1–15.

[57] J. A. Mangan, *The Games Ethic and Imperialism: Aspects of the Diffusion of an Ideal* (London, 1986), pp. 83, 205, n. 33.

[58] MacDonald to J. G. Moylan, 4 July 1867, in Public Archives of Canada, Ottawa, MG/29/D15.

[59] Cain and Hopkins, *British Imperialism*, p. 330.

[60] P. E. Razzell, 'Social Origins of Officers in the Indian and British Home Army, 1758–1962', *British Journal of Sociology*, XIV, 3 (1963), p. 250.

army officers born in the British Isles, a proportion falling to a seventh by 1901 but usually exceeding the Irish component of the population at large. Military commissions provided employment for members of most families of Irish gentry, the pool of officers remaining virtually closed to the middle classes and to Catholics until the First World War. The feats of Irish generals and heroes provided the basis for numerous affirmations of racial superiority in war. As Ross-Lewin boasted:

> Nor shall we now relinquish the prize of field and flood,
> Our share in glorious Empire won by our fathers' blood.
> Nor lack we still of heroes with Saxons to compete
> While Roberts rules our Armies, and Beresford our fleet.[61],

Both Roberts and Beresford chose Irish as well as colonial designations when accepting peerages; but in other cases Irish birth was incidental or even embarrassing to the heroes of Britain's colonial wars. Horatio Herbert Kitchener, 1st Earl of Khartoum and of Broome in Kent, may have been born near Ballylongford in Co. Kerry; yet he cared as little for his nativity as had the Duke of Wellington. As Birrell observed, 'Lord Kitchener was not a real Irishman, only an accidental one'.[62] Only occasionally did Irishness intrude upon military professionalism, as in the case of Sir William Francis Butler, son of a Tipperary landowner and Commander-in-Chief in South Africa on the eve of the South African War. Butler was a Catholic Home Ruler, whose sympathy (according to Milner) was 'wholly with the other side'.[63] In general, Ireland's military heroes were drawn from a stock equally alien to ordinary nationalists and unionists, and the Irish deeds that won the Empire were those of a caste rather than a people.

Natives of Ireland were slightly over-represented among 'other ranks' in the regular army, though notably deficient in the Royal Navy, Royal Marines, and merchant service.[64] Irishmen were only just outnumbered by Britons among soldiers enlisted in the Bengal Army between 1825 and 1850.[65] After the official admission of Catholics to the British army in 1799, natives of Ireland quickly became a sizeable component, reaching about two-fifths in 1830 and 1840, but falling to a quarter by 1872 and less than a tenth by 1911. This decline was mainly attributable to Ireland's rapidly diminishing share of the United Kingdom's

---

[61] Ross-Lewin, *Poems*, p. 29.

[62] Augustine Birrell, *Things Past Redress* (London, 1937), p. 218.

[63] John Springhall, 'Up Guards and at Them!', in John M. MacKenzie, ed., *Popular Imperialism and the Military* (Manchester, 1992), p. 64.

[64] Census returns giving the birthplaces of men in the various services were tabulated between 1851 and 1921.

[65] Bayly, *Imperial Meridian*, p. 127.

population.[66] Though more than 150,000 men were raised in Ireland between 1865 and 1913, the Irish Command invariably provided less than its expected share of recruits; but this deficiency was outweighed by heavy enlistment of Irish emigrants in Britain.[67] The prominence of Irish servicemen in Imperial wars, particularly in South Africa, could produce strange juxtapositions, as at Ladysmith where two brothers from Co. Longford apparently lost their lives, one fighting for the Boers with Blake's Irish Brigade and the other for the Royal Inniskilling Fusiliers.[68] It could also lead to the bitterness expressed in a letter sent home to Newry by a private in the Royal Dublin Fusiliers: 'I was reading in the papers where the Irish people were subscribing for the Boers, and are backing them up; but the Irish people will want to be careful of themselves, or we will do the same with them as we are doing with the Boers.'[69] In addition to service in the Imperial forces, Catholics (mainly of Irish descent) were fully represented in colonial units such as the Australian Commonwealth Horse in South Africa.[70] Nationality did not effectively discourage unemployed Irishmen, mostly Catholics, from volunteering to fight the Empire's wars.

The most far-reaching contribution of the Irish to the development of the Empire was through emigration. Although most Irish emigrants made for the United States or Britain, there were nearly 300,000 natives of Ireland living in Canada in 1861 and close to a quarter of a million in the Australian colonies by 1891. As a proportion of the entire overseas-born population, the Irish were as prominent in Australasia and Canada as in the United States itself. In about 1870, for example, a third of immigrants in the United States were Irish, a slightly smaller proportion than in Canada. In Australia the Irish component exceeded a quarter, compared with less than a fifth in New Zealand. Even in the quieter period between 1876 and 1914, Canada and Australia each attracted over 90,000 emigrants from Irish ports. In the course of the century Irish emigrants scattered throughout the Empire. Census returns testify that in 1911 there were about 14,600 Irish natives in the Union of South Africa, 12,200 in the Indian Empire, 1,000 in the Maltese

---

[66] Peter Karsten, 'Irish Soldiers in the British Army, 1792–1922: Suborned or Subordinate?', *JSH*, XVII, 1 (1983), pp. 31–64; H. J. Hanham, 'Religion and Nationality in the Mid-Victorian Army', in M. R. D. Foot, ed., *War and Society: Historical Essays in Honour and Memory of J. R. Western, 1928–1971* (London, 1973), pp. 57–69.

[67] David Fitzpatrick, '"A Peculiar Tramping People": The Irish in Britain, 1801–70', in Vaughan, *New History*, p. 641; Fitzpatrick, '"A Curious Middle Place": The Irish in Britain, 1871–1921', in Roger Swift and Sheridan Gilley, eds., *The Irish in Britain, 1815–1939* (London, 1989), p. 23.

[68] RIC, Crime Special Branch, file 21831S (carton 16), in National Archives, Dublin. Irish army casualties during the South Africans War amounted to 133 officers and 2,961 men, about a tenth of the total: Donal P. McCracken, *The Irish Pro-Boers, 1877–1902* (Johannesburg, 1989), pp. 123–24.

[69] Ibid., p. 126.

[70] W. N. Chamberlain, 'The Characteristics of Australia's Boer War Volunteers', *Historical Studies* (Melbourne), XX, 78 (1982), pp. 48–52.

islands, 400 in Ceylon, 250 in the Straits Settlements, and 160 in the Federated Malay States. In almost every Imperial possession, Irish colonists had become a significant element of the settler population.

Irish emigration to the more distant colonies was facilitated by state subventions, without which the much cheaper British or American options would have seemed irresistible. About half of all emigrants from the United Kingdom to the Australian colonies up to 1900, and the large majority of Irish settlers, received some public assistance. For the 160,000 convicts transported there between 1788 and 1867, of whom over a quarter were Irish-born, settlement at public expense was involuntary though not always unwelcome—during the Great Famine, the impulse to escape Ireland was sufficient to induce paupers to petty crime in the hope of being sentenced to transportation. Until the 1830s the system of convict labour was surprisingly efficient in satisfying colonial demand for domestic and outdoor service, compensating for Australia's lack of slaves.[71] Voluntary emigration was encouraged by a variety of schemes, mostly funded from colonial land revenues with supplementary contributions from the emigrants or from private sponsors already in the colonies. Nearly a quarter of a million Irish settlers were assisted to Australia between 1836 and 1919 (a third of the total from the British Isles), and 30,000 were shipped to Vogel's New Zealand during the 1870s. The most lavish scheme involved the removal to Australia of 4,000 female 'orphans' from Irish workhouses between 1848 and 1850, outfit and passage to Plymouth being provided by the Boards of Guardians while the full cost of shipping was paid from colonial funds. Most subsequent assistance was contingent on the nomination of emigrants by colonial sponsors, creating a form of subsidized chain migration which the Irish exploited far more methodically than did the English, Welsh, or Scots.

Irish movement to Canada and sometimes southern Africa was accelerated by promises of land grants, though seldom by direct payment of transportation costs. Despite recurrent demands for systematic colonization of Canadian or other wastelands by the 'surplus' population of rural Ireland, the vast cost of Peter Robinson's pilot scheme of 1823–25 discouraged further experiments. With support from Wilmot Horton in the Colonial Office, Robinson had shipped 2,300 people in family groups from a dozen densely populated and restive Munster estates to Upper Canada (Ontario), at a cost of no less than £20 per capita. Subsequent official assistance to North America was largely restricted to supplements, worth about £5, which enabled some 45,000 paupers to leave Ireland (mostly for Canada) between 1849 and 1906. Local Boards of Guardians again provided outfit and transportation within the British Isles for paupers whose

---

[71] Stephen Nicholas, ed., *Convict Workers: Reinterpreting Australia's Past* (Cambridge, 1988).

passages had been funded by previous settlers. The bulk of Irish emigrants to Canada received no official subsidy, many proceeding to the United States after taking cut-price passages to Quebec or New Brunswick. This applied particularly in 1847, when nearly 100,000 passengers, many already emaciated and feverish, were shipped to Quebec from Irish ports and Liverpool (often at the expense of their landlords). About one in six died aboard or shortly after arrival, prompting understandable Irish aversion to vessels bound for Canada, and eventually generating more rigorous regulation of passenger shipping. The reduced flow from post-Famine Ireland to Canada was once again dominated by Ulster Protestants, already a tight-knit and powerful element of rural society in Ontario. Whereas state subsidies and therefore quality controls shaped Irish colonization of the most distant dominions, the drift to Canada was fitful and mainly governed by private decisions.

Despite colonial objections to the shovelling out and dumping of Irish paupers and papists, often at colonial expense, only Ireland proved capable of supplying the required blend of agricultural workers and domestic servants. Ireland's greatest comparative advantage as a source of colonists was the absence of effective restraint upon female emigration. The dearth of non-agricultural employment in Ireland pushed out men and women with roughly equal force, while the Famine emergency had overwhelmed parental resistance to exposing young girls to the moral and physical perils of transoceanic travel. Whereas men vastly outnumbered women in British emigration, the sexes were evenly balanced in movement from Ireland after the 1840s. Though young unmarried women were usually offered preferential assistance to the woman-starved Australasian colonies, the official agencies had great difficulty in enticing English or Scottish girls with prospects of domestic service and marriage in rude colonial surroundings. Only the Irish fulfilled Wakefield's requirement for a successful colonization: 'an equal emigration of the sexes'.[72] By about 1870 Australia (like Britain and probably the United States) had an almost equal number of Irish-born men and women. Whereas the majority of Irish emigrants to Canada were Protestants, the proportion was less than a quarter in Australia, despite energetic official attempts to encourage settlement by Ulster Protestants. New Zealand had a larger component of northern Protestants, exemplified by the Tyrone Orangemen and their families who colonized Kati-Kati or 'New Ulster' in 1875, under the leadership of George Vesey Stewart. Initially concentrated in the menial sectors of service and labour, Irish settlers in Australasia and Canada rapidly colonized a broad range of occupations such as farming, mining, shopkeeping, policing, and the civil service. By contrast with the American Irish, they showed no marked propensity to cluster in urban

---

[72] Fitzpatrick, 'Emigration, 1801–70', in Vaughan, *New History*, p. 573.

enclaves or indeed to settle in cities.[73] As 'human capital', Irish voluntary colonists proved no less sound an investment than their convict brethren.

Irish colonization of the Empire had the further effect of stimulating a substantial reverse migration. Admittedly, only about 8,000 natives of the British possessions and the Indian Empire (in roughly equal numbers) were enumerated in the Irish census for 1901. Yet between 1895 and 1913 some 18,400 Irish nationals 'immigrated' to the United Kingdom from British North America, 11,300 from Australasia, and 14,900 from British South Africa.[74] Though some of these were doubtless tourists or business travellers rather than returning emigrants, their colonial experience brought the realities of the Empire closer to many Irish homes. Their presence reinforced the already extensive coverage of Imperial affairs and conditions of life in the Irish provincial press, popular novels, and (above all) personal letters from emigrant friends and relatives.[75] Migration in both directions, mainly voluntary and often undertaken with enthusiasm, gradually entangled the Irish with all the nationalities of the Empire. If most of Ireland eventually wriggled out of the Imperial embrace, many of its people did not.

Ireland's influence on the Empire cannot be precisely assessed, since the impact of particular Irish men and women was only partly and dubiously attributable to their ethnicity. Journalistic attempts to chronicle the achievements and 'contribution' of the expatriate Irish were commonplace in the later nineteenth century, serving to defend Irish and often Catholic prestige against British and colonial sniping.[76] The following sketch is confined to institutional, legislative, political, and religious echoes or imitations of Irish models. Ireland's importance as a colonial model was enhanced by its own ambiguous status as a 'colonial' element within the United Kingdom, which generated many exportable experiments in social and political control. Moreover, Irish techniques of resistance to British authority were occasionally appropriated by colonial nationalist movements. Though to some extent reciprocal, the balance of trade in colonial structures and techniques was overwhelmingly favourable to Ireland.

The centralization of Irish elementary schooling and policing, introduced in 1831 and 1836 respectively, had obvious implications for colonial administrators.

---

[73] See Donald Harman Akenson, *The Irish Diaspora: A Primer* (Toronto, 1993); David Fitzpatrick, *Irish Emigration, 1801–1921* (Dublin, 1984).

[74] Board of Trade, annual *Statistics and Tables of Emigration and Immigration*, in House of Commons Papers, *passim*.

[75] See Fitzpatrick, *Oceans of Consolation*; Cecil J. Houston and William J. Smyth, *Irish Emigration and Canadian Settlement: Patterns, Links, and Letters* (Toronto, 1990), pt. 3.

[76] James Francis Hogan, *The Irish in Australia* (Melbourne, 1888); Nicholas Flood Davin, *The Irishman in Canada* (London, 1877).

The English model, in which local interests controlled both services, was un-appealing to governments attempting to harness or break the power of local élites. In territories with large native populations, centralized education and policing provided twin means for Anglicizing and subduing subject peoples. Even in the Australian colonies, the rapid expansion of white settlement, and the proliferation of 'currency lads' and lasses born in the colonies, created an unruly and scarcely civilized population which generated similar administrative challenges and responses. The Irish system of National Education, designed to inculcate universal literacy and numeracy through a vast network of elementary schools funded by the state, became a significant model for primary education in the Australasian colonies. As in Ireland, a common curriculum and system of inspection was applied to state primary schools. The impassioned debates over state funding of denominational education in Ireland had powerful echoes in the Empire, although colonial governments often proved less willing to support schools under clerical management. The exemplary function of the Irish system was also evident in the export of millions of Irish National readers and textbooks (amply studded with information about the overseas Empire) to colonial schools. They carried the appealing message that education could redeem the ignorance and incompetence of even the Irish people, providing a pathway towards metropolitan culture and status for those not resident in Britain itself.

Colonial administrators were besotted with the Irish Constabulary, an armed force under semi-military discipline but civilian control which occupied 'barracks' throughout Ireland (outside Dublin). The successful management by mainly Protestant officers of 12,000 'native' constables of humble origin, mostly Catholics, heartened Imperialists everywhere. In order to restrict entanglement with local interests, constables were regularly relocated and marriages discouraged. Initially a paramilitary force alienated from a lawless population, the Irish Constabulary gradually secured a more comfortable social niche, despite the intimidating effect of its uniforms and weaponry. It remained responsible for the suppression of occasional riots and rebellions, sometimes in combination with military detachments acting 'in aid of the civil power'. It used to be generally accepted that the Irish Constabulary was the model for almost all colonial police forces, during what Jeffries termed the 'second phase' of militarization (following initial improvisation and preceding the creation of civilian forces). Jeffries identified direct Irish influences in the nomenclature, training, and paramilitary functions of forces ranging from Ceylon and India to the West Indies and Palestine. After 1907 all cadets for colonial forces were trained at the Irish depot in Phoenix Park, Dublin. These influences were reinforced by the numerous former officers and members of the Irish Constabulary who became colonial policemen, and also by the legion of

Irish-inspired Indian officers who helped establish forces elsewhere.[77] Though Jeffries confined his account of the 'Irish model' to the policing of colonies with large native populations, other studies have detected Irish influence in the centralized forces serving the Australasian and Canadian administrations.[78] Despite recent demonstrations that the diversity of colonial policing defies reduction to a single model, that the London Metropolitan Police was also imitated, and that many aspects of Irish practice were ignored, the strength of Irish influence in Imperial policing remains incontestable.[79] The Irish case had shown the Empire that a relatively small and dispersed armed force could subdue a large and recalcitrant population over a long period.

Imperial attempts to regulate and modernize peasant societies also drew from Irish experience. Before 1870 state interference in the Irish land market had been designed to reinforce the rights of landlords by facilitating eviction, restricting subletting, promoting the sale of heavily encumbered estates to solvent purchasers, and replacing ill-defined entitlements by explicit contracts. As in India, where confirmation of the property rights of the *zamindars* aroused growing resentment from insecure peasant holders, Britain's attempt to create a free market in Irish land collapsed in the face of collective tenant resistance. Gladstone's recognition of customary entitlements in 1870 signified the state's acceptance that the principles of English land law were not universally exportable. This discovery had already affected Indian administration, and the reform campaign preceding the Irish Act of 1870 was strongly influenced by Indian recognition of the customary entitlements of the *ryots* (peasant cultivators). In turn, Indian legislators were influenced by subsequent Irish legislation providing for controlled rents or 'dual ownership' (1881–82), which set in motion the gradual collapse of landlord power. The Bengal Land Tenancy Act of 1885 drew heavily on the Irish reforms, following a campaign involving Irish officials such as Charles James O'Donnell and Sir Antony MacDonnell. Yet the *zamindars* also had their influential Irish supporters, including the Viceroy (the Marquess of Dufferin).[80] Of all Irish exports, conflict was the most ubiquitous.

Echoes of Irish struggles between landlord and tenant also reached the Australian colonies, where the equivalent battle involved 'squatters' against 'selectors'. Most colonies implemented 'Selection Acts' whereby industrious farmers with

---

[77] Sir Charles Jeffries, *The Colonial Police* (London, 1952). For Indian echoes of the Irish Constabulary in Sind (1843), Bombay (1847), Madras (1855), Oudh (1858), and the entire subcontinent (1861), see Cook, *Imperial Affinities*, pp. 31–32.

[78] David M. Anderson and David Killingray, eds., *Policing the Empire: Government, Authority and Control, 1830–1940* (Manchester, 1991), pp. 3, 39, 56–57.

[79] Richard Hawkins, 'The "Irish Model" for the Empire: A Case for Reassessment', in ibid., pp. 18–32; editors' Introduction, pp. 3–4.

[80] Boylan and Foley, *Political Economy*, p. 156; Cook, *Imperial Affinities*, pp. 85–89, 111, 130–31.

little capital were given smallholdings of uncleared land, formerly claimed by the
'squattocracy' (Australia's ramshackle Ascendancy). Like Irish tenant purchasers,
the selectors were required to repay their debt to the state through annuities.
Despite the obvious disparities, the campaign for better terms of selection drew
heavily from Irish rhetoric, skilfully adapted to Australian conditions by Irish
emigrant politicians such as Sir Charles Gavan Duffy (the former Young Irelander
and agitator for tenant rights who became Her Majesty's impeccably loyal Premier
of Victoria). As in India and Ireland itself, the attempt to create a class of small
farmers with secure tenure betokened a broader vision of the colonial future, in
which civic virtue and patriotism would be reinforced by benevolent social
engineering. By restraining the arbitrary power of the filthy rich, colonial administrations would acquire popular legitimacy and so secure the fragile bonds of
Empire.

The broader political consequences of Irish colonization, expressed through the
actions and attitudes of countless settlers and their descendants, defy easy encap-
sulation. To many British and Protestant colonists, Irish Catholics seemed a
potentially subversive and disloyal underclass, always inclined to reapply their
Irish grievances to colonial agitation. Such apprehensions were strongest among
Ulster Protestant settlers, who used the international fraternal network of the
Loyal Orange Institution to proclaim their own loyalty and defend the colonies
against papist aggression. In South Africa, Australia, New Zealand, and Canada
the Orange lodges were rapidly assimilated into Conservative politics, the sons of
Ulster soon being outnumbered by local activists exploiting the efficiency and
popular appeal of Ireland's most sophisticated fraternity. Among the leading
Orangemen of New South Wales in the 1870s, for example, less than a third were
natives of Ireland.[81] The Canadian Orange Institution was particularly influential
in Conservatism, drawing prestige from its prominent role in resisting the feeble
Fenian 'invasions' of Canada in 1870 and 1871. Irish emigrants were also active in
the development of colonial Freemasonry, forming networks of lodges with
warrants from the Grand Lodge of Ireland rather than England or Scotland. The
'loyal institutions' provided a superb vehicle for Irish Protestant settlers sloughing
off the unwanted connotations of 'Paddy' and 'Mick', stereotypes applied indiscriminately to Irish emigrants of all origins.

Irish fraternal expertise was also exhibited by Catholic emigrants, who protected their collective interests through friendly societies such as the Hibernian
Benefit Associations in Australasia, and the related Ancient Order of Hibernians in

---

[81] Mark Lyons, 'Aspects of Sectarianism in New South Wales, *circa* 1865 to 1880', unpublished Ph.D.
thesis, Australian National University, 1972, pp. 423–30. For comparable Canadian findings, see Cecil J.
Houston and William J. Smyth, *The Sash Canada Wore: A Historical Geography of the Orange Order in
Canada* (Toronto, 1980), pp. 91–95.

North America. Though not primarily political in function, the Hibernian divisions helped mobilize lay Catholics as a social and potentially a political force. Irish nationalist organizations supporting Repeal and Home Rule received essential moral and financial support from equivalent colonial networks, drawing upon Australian Catholics as well as Irish emigrants. Yet colonial support for Fenianism and other movements favouring 'physical force' was minuscule by comparison with response in the United States. The former Young Irelander Thomas D'Arcy McGee, three years before his assassination in Ottawa in 1868, described Fenianism as 'the worst obstacle, the Devil has ever invented for the Irish, an *irreligious revolutionary society*, in which patriotism takes the garb of indifferentism, or hostility to religion'.[82] In Sydney, the demented Irishman who almost murdered the Duke of Edinburgh in March 1868 evidently acted without accomplices, despite the ingenious attempts of Conservative politicians to fabricate an Irish-Australian conspiracy.[83] The 'Catholic' (otherwise 'Irish') vote became a major factor in mainstream colonial politics, being generally aligned, as in Britain, with parties favouring liberal reform, and subsequently with parties representing the interests of trades unions. Labor Party candidates in pre-war New South Wales were disproportionately successful in constituencies with large Catholic components, although Catholics did not predominate in the federal Labor Party until the 1930s.[84] Careful to avoid challenging the legitimacy of the Imperial affiliation, Irish colonists and their Catholic descendants nevertheless made a distinctive contribution to the terms of democratic debate.

The Imperial influence of Irish institutions extended to the churches, which provided a surplus of highly trained spiritual managers for deployment throughout the Empire. This was most evident in the proliferation of Catholic priests ordained in Ireland, and in the rapid colonial extension of Irish-based religious orders providing educational and medical services. Irish Catholicism, though thoroughly 'Romanized' by the 1850s, was often at loggerheads with the established networks of French or English priests who had typically initiated diocesan organization in the colonies. Though Irish emigrants were at first their central concern, the army of Irish clergy rapidly extended their ministrations to the conversion of aboriginal peoples, the reclamation of godless colonials, and the care of Catholic emigrants from Britain and Europe as well as Ireland. Often ignored in studies of missionary Imperialism, the Catholic clerical diaspora was

---

[82] McGee to J. G. Moylan, 27 Oct. 1865, in Public Archives of Canada, Ottawa, MG/29/D15.

[83] Phillip M. Cowburn, 'The Attempted Assassination of the Duke of Edinburgh, 1868', *Royal Australian Historical Society Journal*, LV, 1 (1969), pp. 19–42.

[84] Celia Hamilton, 'Irish Catholics of New South Wales and the Labor Party, 1890–1910', *Historical Studies of Australia and New Zealand*, VIII, 31 (1958), p. 265; Declan O'Connell and John Warhurst, 'Church and Class', *Saothar*, VIII (1982), p. 49.

scarcely distinguishable in its aims and ideology from its Protestant counterpart.[85] In every colony the Catholic church worked assiduously to overcome its baneful Irish reputation and to affirm its Imperial patriotism. Though never ceasing to bemoan past Irish wrongs, the Irish-trained priests and nuns conveyed little hint of alienation from British rule when indulgently applied through the mediation of representative government.

Colonial Protestantism also had unmistakably Irish elements, though these were easily assimilated with the dominant English and Scottish strains. Trinity College, Dublin, was a major source of Anglican missionaries in India and elsewhere, producing doctors who could hold their 'own at tennis with the best in Bengal'. One such muscular Irish Christian would enlighten the heathen by 'getting the patients to squat down on the ground at the daily dispensary, and giving them a fifteen or twenty minutes' talk before the medicine was dispensed'.[86] Irish Protestants were also prominent in the Canadian and Australasian clergy, whether Anglican, Methodist, or Presbyterian. Among Presbyterian ministers recruited in the various eastern Australian colonies between 1823 and 1900, for example the Irish-born proportion ranged between a ninth and a quarter.[87]

The imprint of Ireland may thus be detected in virtually every colonial institution, ranging from schools and police forces to land law, fraternities, political parties, and the churches. Likewise, the imprint of Britain may be found in every Irish institution, signifying the ambiguity of Ireland's location in the Empire. Through the exercise of imagination, the nineteenth-century Irish might elect to play the parts of colonials (whether deferential or resentful), metropolitans, or colonizers. To be 'Irish' was, among other things, to face that unsettling choice.

[85] Edmund M. Hogan, *The Irish Missionary Movement: A Historical Survey, 1870–1980* (Dublin, 1990).
[86] K. W. S. Kennedy, *Fifty Years in Chota Nagpur: An Account of the Dublin University Mission* (Dublin, 1939), pp. 40–41.
[87] Malcolm D. Prentis, *The Scots in Australia* (Sydney, 1983), p. 136.

Select Bibliography

DONALD HARMAN AKENSON, *The Irish Diaspora: A Primer* (Toronto, 1993).

RAYMOND CROTTY, *Ireland in Crisis: A Study in Capitalist Colonial Undevelopment* (Dingle, Co. Kerry, 1986).

L. P. CURTIS, *Anglo-Saxons and Celts: A Study of Anti-Irish Prejudice in Victorian England* (Bridgeport, Conn., 1968).

DAVID FITZPATRICK, *Irish Emigration, 1801–1921* (Dublin, 1984).

MICHAEL HECHTER, *Internal Colonialism: The Celtic Fringe in British National Development, 1536–1966* (London, 1975).

KEITH JEFFERY, ed., *An Irish Empire? Aspects of Ireland and the British Empire* (Cambridge, 1996).

JOHN KENDLE, *Ireland and the Federal Solution: The Debate over the United Kingdom Constitution, 1870–1921* (Kingston, Ontario, 1988).

OLIVER MACDONAGH, *States of Mind: A Study of Anglo-Irish Conflict, 1780–1980* (London, 1983).

R. B. McDOWELL, *The Irish Administration, 1801–1914* (London, 1964).

PATRICK O'FARRELL, *England and Ireland Since 1800* (Oxford, 1975).

E. STRAUSS, *Irish Nationalism and British Democracy* (London, 1951).

W. E. VAUGHAN, ed., *A New History of Ireland*, Vols. V and VI (Oxford, 1989, 1996).

ALAN J. WARD, *The Irish Constitutional Tradition: Responsible Government and Modern Ireland, 1782–1992* (Washington, 1994).

23

Canada from 1815

GED MARTIN

In March 1815 news reached Canada that the war between the United States and the British Empire had ended with a peace treaty, signed at Ghent in modern Belgium. The War of 1812 had been fought and ended by the British. Indeed, Wellington's forces at Waterloo—only 24,000 of them British regulars—were dangerously weakened by the diversion of experienced troops to defend Canada. Colonial resistance to American incursions had been enough to found a patriotic myth, but only the British could effectively protect the northern half of North America. The small, scattered population could neither defend nor govern itself. Almost all administration was in British hands, subject to inefficient controls from London, and London was the sole source of minimal co-ordinating policy.

When Britain's security was again menaced by an invasion of Belgium in 1914, Canada proved not a liability but an asset. Population had grown tenfold to just over 8 million, including the separate colony of Newfoundland. With that sole exception, all the Imperial territories had coalesced into the transcontinental Dominion of Canada, a self-governing entity within the Empire. Canada promptly offered to send 25,000 men to Europe, and in October 1914 actually despatched over 30,000, probably the largest military contingent ever to cross the Atlantic. The preceding century had seen a remarkable political transformation, and well before 1914 the Canadian example was naturally studied for solutions of other Imperial problems. Yet the story seems incomplete, one of union and self-government achieved within a framework of arrested development. White settlers had served a seventy-year apprenticeship as 'ideal prefabricated collaborators',[1] but there was no indication that Canada was moving towards decolonization and full nationhood. The Dominion was presided over by a Governor-General (in 1914 a son of Queen Victoria). It had no foreign embassies, and was barely even agreed upon a local flag. Not surprisingly, those appealing to Canadian precedents elsewhere in the Empire often cited them in support of conflicting solutions.

---

[1] Ronald Robinson, 'Non-European Foundations of European Imperialism: Sketch for a Theory of Collaboration', in Roger Owen and Bob Sutcliffe, eds., *Studies in the Theory of Imperialism* (London, 1972), pp. 124–25.

The simplest summary of the country's past might suggest that between 1815 and 1914 British North America had become Canada. Yet this would impose an unjustified coherence upon the British territories north of the United States: Imperial actions crucially shaped the fitful development of their east–west alignment. Major external boundaries remained in dispute with the Americans until 1846. Paradoxically, British territorial surrenders in Minnesota (1818) and Oregon (1846) reduced the likelihood of an alternative colonial nucleus developing west of the Great Lakes. Only as the Red River and British Columbia were shorn of potential hinterland did their future role emerge within an east–west system. The most notable British diplomatic success in 1842 was also vital to the formation of east–west links: had Americans claims been conceded in the Maine boundary dispute, United States territory would almost have reached the St Lawrence, leaving an impossibly narrow corridor between Canada and New Brunswick. Newfoundland apart, there thus emerged no Australia–New Zealand or South Africa–Rhodesia divide in British North America.

Although the Protestant Irishmen's Orange Order was using the term by 1830, the all-embracing label 'British North America' appealed mainly to outsiders, such as Lord Durham and J. A. Roebuck. In 1851 Sir Edmund Head could discern 'no enlarged view of the interests of New Brunswick as a part of British North America'. Indeed, another Governor reported that their only common element of identity as 'New Brunswickers' was that 'they all unite in hating & abusing Halifax'.[2] When existing provinces were federated in 1867, 'British North America' was rejected, notwithstanding the protest of one British minister that it was 'in the large language of the age', in favour of the 'familiar and important' name of Canada.[3] Certainly no sense of shared interests brought the colonies together. The province of Canada carried on less than 2 per cent of its external trade with the Maritimes, while the provinces most dependent in 1865 upon intercolonial trade—Prince Edward Island and Nova Scotia—were the most reluctant to join a British North American union.

Science did more than commerce to create a British American identity, and extend it across the continent: London cartographer John Arrowsmith used 'British North America' in this sense in 1850. The absorption of California by the United States probably encouraged a mirror-image to the north. By the 1850s geologists and botanists were laying a scientific foundation for a transcontinental identity, one which appealed to the Victorian passion for undigested statistics

[2] 9 Dec. 1851, cited in D. G. G. Kerr, *Sir Edmund Head: A Scholarly Governor* (Toronto, 1954), p. 94; Gordon to Monck, copy, 8 May 1862, University of New Brunswick, Harriet Irving Library, Stanmore Papers, Reel 3.

[3] Minute by C. B. Adderley, 28 Sept. 1866, C[olonial] O[ffice] 42/656, f. 370; G. E. Buckle, ed., *Letters of Queen Victoria: Second Series . . ., 1862–1878*, 2 vols. (London, 1926), I, p. 392.

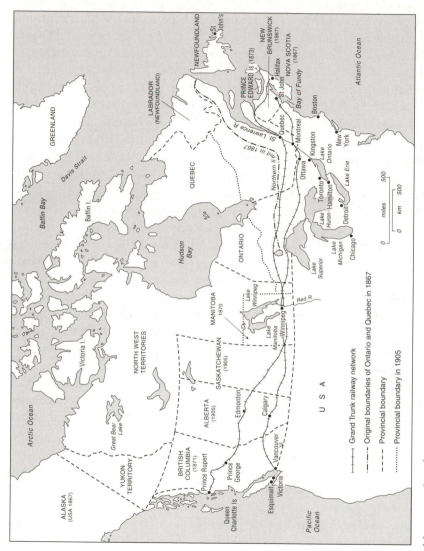

MAP 23.1. Canada, to 1905

Legend:
- Grand Trunk railway network
- Original boundaries of Ontario and Quebec in 1867
- Provincial boundary
- Provincial boundary in 1905

GREENLAND

Davis Strait

Baffin Bay

Baffin I.

Arctic Ocean

Victoria I.

Great Bear Lake

ALASKA (USA 1867)

YUKON TERRITORY

BRITISH COLUMBIA (1871)

Prince Rupert

Prince George

Queen Charlotte Is

Esquimalt
Victoria

Vancouver

Pacific Ocean

NORTH WEST TERRITORIES

ALBERTA (1905)

SASKATCHEWAN (1905)

Edmonton

Calgary

Hudson Bay

MANITOBA 1870

Lake Winnipeg

Lake Manitoba

Winnipeg

Red R.

QUEBEC

ONTARIO

LABRADOR (NEWFOUNDLAND)

NEWFOUNDLAND

St John's

St Lawrence R.

Still in 1867

Northern Lt

Quebec

Montreal

Ottawa

Kingston

Lake Ontario

Toronto

Hamilton

Lake Erie

Detroit

Lake Huron

Lake Michigan

Chicago

Lake Superior

PRINCE EDWARD Is (1873)

NEW BRUNSWICK (1867)

NOVA SCOTIA (1867)

St John Halifax

Bay of Fundy

Boston

New York

Atlantic Ocean

U S A

0   500
miles

0   500
km

MAP 23.1. Canada, to 1905

indicating a vast potential heritage which the provinces might claim. Political union did little to overcome incoherent diversity. Even in 1891, six years after completion of the transcontinental railway, Goldwin Smith could dismiss the Dominion as 'four separate projections of the cultivable and habitable part of the Continent into arctic waste...divided from each other by great barriers of nature, wide and irreclaimable wildernesses or manifold chains of mountains'.[4]

In 1815 the disparate nature of the British territories was particularly striking. On the Atlantic seaboard, the Maritime colonies—Nova Scotia, New Brunswick, Prince Edward Island, and Cape Breton (subsequently absorbed into Nova Scotia)—were geographically extensions of New England, from which the two mainland colonies had derived many of their inhabitants. Newfoundland was shaped by its origins as the outpost of England's west-country fishery. About 200,000 people lived in this region. Although usually grouped together, the colonies had different economies: the timber trade was beginning to dominate New Brunswick, agriculture was important in Prince Edward Island, while Nova Scotia had a more mixed economy, with an emphasis on Atlantic trade.

Their common feature was an orientation towards Britain and an almost total absence of commercial or cultural links with the St Lawrence valley–Great Lakes region, popularly known as 'the Canadas'. About 350,000 people lived in Lower Canada, at least 80 per cent of them descendants of the 55,000 French settlers absorbed into the Empire in 1763. The interior province of Upper Canada was growing rapidly and probably numbered 90,000 inhabitants. Gladstone later described Canada as a 'long and comparatively thin strip of occupied territory... between the States on one side, and the sterility of pinching winter on the other'.[5] He was wrong about winter: it engulfed all the colonies, but fortunately heavy loads moved more easily over frozen snow than colonial mud roads. What pinched Canada to the north-west was the Canadian Shield, a combination of rock and swamp stretching 800 miles from the backcountry settlements of Upper Canada to the vast interior plains which were not British colonies at all, but the Hudson's Bay Company's domain. Montreal fur-traders had challenged the Company's commercial control, providing a shadowy transcontinental outline much cherished by later historians as evidence of the 'Laurentian' inevitability of east–west political integration. Unfortunately it was short-lived. In 1821 the overextended Montreal fur-trade was swallowed by the London-based Hudson's Bay Company, and it was thirty years before an expanding Toronto revived Canadian westward ambitions.

[4] Goldwin Smith, *Canada and the Canadian Question* [1891], ed. Carl Berger (Toronto, 1971), p. 4.
[5] Memorandum, 12 July 1865, in Paul Knaplund, *Gladstone and Britain's Imperial Policy* (London, 1966), p. 235.

A few thousand Europeans occupied trading posts across the West, and the only real settlement, at the Red River, faced an uncertain future: colonists sent by Lord Selkirk were attacked in 1816 by the Métis, an early indication that their mixed descent from native people and fur-traders would not make them enthusiastic intermediaries between old and new. Indigenous people were hardly more numerous: one estimate calculates 34,000 native people ('Indians') on the interior plains in 1809. While some, such as the Plains Cree, successfully adapted to change, native people overall were dangerously dependent on the buffalo. Further west, in a 'sea of mountains' 400 miles wide, lay the area which in 1858 became British Columbia, with a population of perhaps 80,000. Of the Inuit ('Eskimo') population in the far north, we can only guess.

Very little of this vastness was suitable for farming. Newfoundland had almost no agriculture. The Maritimes had pockets capable of supplying local demand. In the St Lawrence valley, soil exhaustion was a developing problem, and historians speak of 'agricultural crisis' in Lower Canada by 1815. Much land in eastern Upper Canada was poor, thanks to an outlying finger of the Shield which also created a series of rapids on the St Lawrence between Kingston and Montreal. Only in the peninsula between Lakes Ontario and Erie did settlers find truly prosperous farmlands. On the Plains in the 1850s explorers identified another strip, the 'fertile belt', running west-north-west from the Red River. Identifying fertile land was one thing; learning to farm it was another. Not until the early twentieth century did populations grow rapidly on the Canadian prairies. The sparsity of land fit for farming paradoxically helps explain why Canada grew in such jumps to become by 1914 second in land area only to Russia. In the first half of the nineteenth century the rush to strip British North America of its tree cover obscured the minimal utility of much of the land beneath, except in the fertile area of south-west Upper Canada. There is little truth in the stereotype that loggers cleared the way for farmers. The two activities were carried on in parallel, often by the same labour force in seasonal rhythms, and many areas were unsuitable for farming. Canada nevertheless remained predominantly agricultural. While almost 0.5 million people worked in manufacturing in 1910, one-third of these were in timber and food processing. Canada had only two cities with over 200,000 people, but even on their modest canvas, Montreal and Toronto were reproducing the horrors of old-world disease and slums.

Changes in the distribution of population reflected the unequal spread of fertile land. Upper Canada had barely counted 10 per cent of the British North American total in 1815. Renamed Ontario in 1867, it was by 1911 home to more than one-third of the Canadian total, with a population of 2.5 million. Immigration plus a high birth rate had pushed Lower Canada (Quebec since 1867) to 2 million. The three prairie provinces contained 1.3 million people in place of the virtual emptiness of fifty years earlier. As the demographic centre of gravity moved west, the Maritimes' declining share pointed to political marginalization. However, even though the combined populations of Nova Scotia, New Brunswick, and Prince Edward Island remained short of 1 million people, the Maritimes (so often condemned as sleepy) still had more than twice as many people as British Columbia.

One explanation of the paradox of a predominantly rural population in an overwhelmingly infertile landscape lies in the slow development of Canadian mining. For instance, transcontinental railways faced the problem that there was virtually no coal between Nova Scotia and Alberta. The absence of large-scale mineral resources explains some key differences between Canada's experience and that of settler colonies in the southern hemisphere. Copper and nickel were discovered north of Lake Superior, but with a population of 12,500 by 1911, the Sudbury Basin was hardly Canada's Rand. The mainland colony of British Columbia in 1858 was created in response to a gold rush but, unlike Victoria or Otago, the influx of miners had little lasting impact. In the Yukon gold rush and the related Alaska boundary dispute the British displayed nothing of the aggressive expansionism seen in South Africa. Only two British North American politicians could be regarded as mining tycoons: newspaperman George Brown made money from shale oil, while Charles Fox Bennett of Newfoundland owned a copper mine. There was no Canadian Cecil Rhodes.

The tenfold increase in population in the century to 1914 was scarcely impressive on an Imperial scale. Although Canada contained the majority of the Empire's overseas white settler population, it was dwarfed by India's 300 million. It was hardly more important on the transatlantic stage. With a population just equal to that of Greater London by 1914, Canada sustained ten parliamentary systems, one each for Ottawa and the nine provinces. More positively, politics was brought close to the people thanks to a vigorous press: in 1856 Toronto's 35,000 people had a choice of fourteen newspapers, including two dailies. Unfortunately, bringing politics to the people did not necessarily produce just or effective government. Lord Dufferin deplored the treatment of Indians in British Columbia, where the provincial government simply ignored Native title to the land: 'the truth is British Columbia is hardly a large enough Community to have as yet developed a conscience.'[6] Legislatures were small and unstable: a few defections could unseat a ministry. Hence politics focused on the foreground of local interests, rather than the horizons of statesmanship. Healthy parliamentary government depended on the prospect of turning out one set of ministers and installing another, 'but in a small community there is difficulty enough in finding the materials even for a

---

[6] To Carnarvon, private, 21 Dec. 1874, in C. W. de Kiewiet and F. H. Underhill, eds., *Dufferin–Carnarvon Correspondence, 1874–1878* (Toronto, 1955), p. 125.

Ministry—much less can we expect to find the materials of a government and an opposition also'.[7]

The provinces did generate impressive political talent, but rarely in depth. The management skills of John A. Macdonald dominated Canadian politics throughout thirty crucial years, but his death in office in 1891 left a leadership vacuum at a time when the Dominion was under structural strain. In smaller political pits leadership choices were far more circumscribed, producing personalities such as the erratic William Lyon Mackenzie in Upper Canada or the bizarre Amor de Cosmos (born William A. Smith) in British Columbia. The Red River Métis barely numbered 5,000 in 1869 when they accepted the leadership of the 25-year old Louis Riel. Riel blundered in killing an obstreperous Orangeman, but otherwise led his people effectively, securing provincial status for Manitoba. When he returned to head a second uprising, in the Saskatchewan country in 1885, he had become deranged and led the Métis into millenarian disaster.

Small populations and unimpressive leadership underlined the social and political insignificance of the provinces in British eyes. In the 1840s emigration to Canada was 'a last resource to people who have ruined themselves at home'. The provinces contained 'three or four millions of labourers and small farmers, with scarcely a gentleman or a good income among them'.[8] Seventy years later, when the Irish nationalist Kevin O'Higgins was expelled from a seminary, his irate father told him he was 'only fit for the Canadian police'.[9] In contrast to the two returned Australian colonists in Gladstone's first Cabinet, British North Americans made no impact at Westminster. J. A. Roebuck, who spent his teenage years in Canada, was a maverick. T. C. Haliburton (MP, 1859–65) and Edward Blake (MP, 1892–1907) were ineffective. Andrew Bonar Law and Max Aitken (Lord Beaverbrook) were late exceptions, both products of the diaspora of the Presbyterian manse. No serving British Prime Minister visited Canada until 1927 and few Imperial statesmen had transatlantic experience. The British governing élite knew little of Canada, less of the Maritimes, and generally behaved with patronizing superiority towards the colonials. Hence Sir Edmund Head's belief that 'the presence of an English gentleman acting as Governor' could provide 'a wholesome check' on the corrupt tendencies of colonial politicians.[10]

Faced with such evidence, historians have had difficulty in explaining both why many people thought British dominance in Canada desirable, and how it was

---

[7] Alice R. Stewart, 'Sir Edmund Head's Memorandum of 1857 on Maritime Union: A Lost Confederation Document', *Canadian Historical Review*, XXVI (1945), p. 415.

[8] Gordon to Aberdeen, 28 July 1845, in J. K. Chapman, *The Career of Arthur Hamilton Gordon First Lord Stanmore, 1829–1912* (Toronto, 1964), p. 6; *The Times*, 22 Oct. 1844.

[9] Terence de Vere White, *Kevin O'Higgins* (Dublin, 1986), p. 7.

[10] Stewart, 'Sir Edmund Head's Memorandum', p. 414.

maintained. Some have sought the answer in economic ties. In 1900 Britain provided 85 per cent of all external capital invested in the Dominion. However, this was hardly surprising, Britain being a major exporter of capital both within and notably beyond the Empire. More specifically, the carrot of a guaranteed (and therefore cheap) loan for canal-building helped secure Upper Canadian acquiescence in union with Lower Canada in 1840. A British offer in 1862 to underwrite the Halifax–Quebec railway provided the context rather than cause of the union of the provinces five years later: certainly, the British did not make cash conditional on Confederation. Loan guarantees were not simple tools of Imperial manipulation. Macdonald forced the British to guarantee a loan for the transcontinental railway in 1871 by threatening to block American access to Canadian inshore waters, and so sabotage the Treaty of Washington.

Government-endorsed loans probably encouraged Canada to embark on over-ambitious projects. However, such loans were exceptional. Much British investment came from individuals, such as Charles Stewart Parnell's widow, who unwisely entrusted her savings to the Grand Trunk Railway, and historians arguing for the manipulative power of investment capital have yet to identify the mechanisms by which such disparate private interests influenced Imperial policy. Nor was Canada entirely reliant on imported capital; even in the boom years after 1901 domestic savings were almost double external investment.

It is difficult to locate Canada clearly in either the formal or informal spheres of Empire.[11] Ambiguity is understandable since commercial ties, no less than financial, had varying consequences. In 1815 British North America formed part of an Imperial trading unit, and political subordination was justified by essentially mercantilist arguments. After 1846 the colonies were allowed to set their own tariffs, provided they did not discriminate against British manufactures. That restriction apart, there was much to justify Cobden's view that, under free trade, 'Canada is not a whit more ours than is the great Republic'.[12] However, there was an undercurrent of belief in Britain that an effective American tariff would be 'a dream—an utter impossibility, so long as England possesses Upper Canada', thanks to cross-border smuggling.[13] The process was briefly encouraged by the Reciprocity Treaty, which gave the provinces free access to American markets for natural products. However, Canada's politicians were not content to be hewers of wood for Americans. In 1859 the Canadian tariff was raised to encourage local industry. The smuggling argument was now inverted. British manufacturers

[11] John Gallagher and Ronald Robinson, 'The Imperialism of Free Trade', *Economic History Review*, Second Series, VI (1953), pp. 1–15.

[12] Cobden to Combe, 8 Feb. 1849, in John Morley, *The Life of Richard Cobden* (London, 1905), pp. 506–07.

[13] 19 June 1849 *Parliamentary Debates* (Commons), CVI, col. 481.

protested that their goods were taxed at entry ports, while American goods evaded tariffs along the inadequately policed border. Canada's finance minister, Alexander Galt, ingeniously argued that the tariff would effectively make British imports cheaper since the revenue was applied to improving internal communications. Any pretence of Imperial control over colonial tariffs had thus been abandoned prior to Confederation. The first Dominion tariff was set to accommodate free-trading Nova Scotia, but duties crept upwards to maintain revenue, and in 1879 protection was explicitly adopted. Aimed at creating an east–west Canada as an Imperial keystone, this 'National Policy' was directed mainly against the United States. Thus, in 1897 the French-Canadian Liberal Prime Minister, Wilfrid Laurier, simultaneously asserted his free-trading credentials and appeased imperialist critics by reducing duties on British goods without seriously denting the overall policy of protection.

Overall, to invoke investment or trade as devices to explain Imperial hegemony over Canada is to provoke more questions than answers. At most, such explanations may help to explain *how* Imperial influence was exercised over Canada. With the partial exception of the strategic importance of colonial timber until perhaps the 1830s, these arguments hardly tell us *why* British North America was important to the Empire. The answer lies in the essential non-Imperial context of British North America, that of its southern neighbour, the United States.

The 7 million Americans of 1810 had not merely doubled the area of their republic a century later but had rocketed to a population of 92 million. Moreover, rapid territorial growth was accompanied by political centralization, making the United States into a potential Imperial state. The unsuccessful war for Southern independence between 1861 and 1865 saw the Northern States emerge as the first modern fully mobilized and mechanized war machine, adding massive economic strength to the American ideological challenge to British monarchical institutions.

Why did British North America escape the 'event...which we all know must happen', as a Nova Scotian described absorption by the United States in 1824? 'Annexation' was 'an ugly word' that implied a destiny that would engulf the provinces whether they liked it or not.[14] Fortunately, there were only two periods when British North America lay athwart the westward movement of the American frontier. For two decades after 1815, south-western Upper Canada was a natural extension of Upper New York. Hunger for Canadian land fuelled border raids in 1837–38. Thereafter the main thrust of United States expansion bypassed the

---

[14] T. C. Haliburton to P. Wiswall, 7 Jan. 1824, in Richard A. Davies, ed., *The Letters of Thomas Chandler Haliburton* (Toronto, 1988), p. 16; Smith, *Canada and the Canadian Question*, ed. Berger, p. 212.

limited pickings of Canada until the early twentieth century, when American settlement turned north into the prairies. Except perhaps in British Columbia, there were never significant fifth columns of Americans ready to subvert Canada as they had seized Texas, although instability at the Red River in 1869–70 aroused some American hopes. The slow spread of the quintessential American game of baseball from its original footholds in Ontario is one index of the relative weakness of US influences within Canada.

Only rarely was annexation seriously proposed. The best-known episode, the Annexation Manifesto of 1849, was largely a protest by Montreal merchants. Forty years later one signatory felt it necessary to deny that they 'had any more serious idea of seeking annexation with the United States than a petulant child who strikes his nurse had of deliberately murdering her'.[15] In provinces where expressions of loyalty to Britain dominated political discourse, it was dangerous to flirt with the Americans. William McDougall's veiled threat that discontented Upper Canadians would turn to the United States for support was used against Reformers in the 1861 election. Proposals for closer trade relations were rejected at the elections of 1891 and 1911, the cry of Imperial loyalty mingling with protectionist self-interest. Etienne Taché's warning that if they failed to unite, the provinces 'would be placed upon an inclined plane' towards annexation, tells more about the strength of anti-American feeling than the reasons for Confederation.[16] Ambitious or discontented Canadians found it far simpler to emigrate to the United States than campaign for annexation. By 1900 over a million of them lived south of the border, one in five of all the Canadian-born in North America. When the fictional mayor of Stephen Leacock's Mariposa announced that he would soon journey 'towards that goal from which no traveller returns', the townsfolk assumed he was moving to the United States.[17]

For their part, boastful orations apart, Americans made few efforts to absorb their neighbours. Unlike the earlier Articles of Confederation, the Constitution of 1787 contained no provision for the admission of Canada. A bill offering statehood, introduced into Congress in 1866, disappeared in committee. Perhaps wooing the provinces would have been tantamount to doubting the inevitability of 'Manifest Destiny'. Perhaps, too, American politicians did not think the Canadian prize worth British antagonism—unlike the easier pickings of Alaska and Hawaii. The Montreal annexationists also made Britain's agreement a precondition, but the British Prime Minister, Russell, wrote that 'I never could give my

[15] Joseph Pope, *Memoirs of the Right Honourable Sir John Alexander Macdonald* (Toronto, 1930), p. 74.

[16] *Parliamentary Debates on the Subject of the Confederation of the British North American Provinces* (Quebec, 1865), p. 6.

[17] Stephen Leacock, *Sunshine Sketches of a Little Town* (1912; Toronto, 1982), p. 138.

assent'.[18] As Trollope's Phineas Finn put it, British public opinion was determined 'that Canada should not go to the States, because,—though they don't love the Canadians, they do hate the Americans.'[19]

The diversity of British North America and the nature of change may be seen in the experience of five groups of people through the century: women, Native people, French Canadians, immigrants, and the locally born English-speaking population.

Given the contribution of women to pioneer life, it might be expected that they would throw off subordinate roles in a 'new' society: in 1875 Mount Allison College produced the first woman graduate in the British Empire. Moreover, in the formative years women were scarce: in early Vancouver there were almost two males for every female. In fact, women actually lost ground. Not being explicitly debarred, propertied women took part in elections in Lower Canada, 199 voting in Montreal West in 1832. The radical *Patriotes* deprived women of the franchise in 1834 to protect their 'natural modesty'. By 1851 the Maritimes had followed, and the only amendment Westminster made in passing the British North America Act was the insertion of the word 'male' in the definition of the right to vote. As late as 1908, New Brunswick's Premier promised that women would be given the vote 'when they wanted it'. Campaigns against drink and prostitution led some, mainly middle-class, women to seek the vote, but the members of a Halifax campaigning group were described, by a female journalist, in 1912 as 'essentially womanly women'.[20] Nor were Canadian women notably nationalist. Perhaps their most prominent organization, the Imperial Order of the Daughters of Empire was founded in 1900 to harness 'women's influence to the bettering of all things connected with our great Empire'.[21]

Limited economic opportunities opened in the later nineteenth century. Women established a foothold in office work: the twenty-four female Dominion civil servants of 1886 grew to 700 in the next twenty years, prompting the complaint 'women clerks claim the rights of men and the privileges of their own sex as well'.[22] Women, however, rarely received equal pay. The 'feminization' of the teaching profession probably tells much about the low status of schoolteaching. In his 1885 painting *The Meeting of the School Trustees*, Robert Harris caught the imploring body language of the female teacher pleading her case to a resistant

[18] To Grey, 6 Aug. 1849, University of Durham, Grey Papers.
[19] Anthony Trollope, *Phineas Finn: The Irish Member* (1869; London, 1968), p. 464, chap. 56.
[20] E. R. Forbes and D. A. Muise, eds., *The Atlantic Provinces in Confederation* (Toronto, 1993), pp. 189, 202.
[21] Robert Craig Brown and Ramsay Cook, *Canada, 1896–1921: A Nation Transformed* (Toronto, 1974), pp. 42–43.
[22] John Hilliker, *Canada's Department of External Affairs*, Vol. I, *The Early Years, 1909–1946* (Montreal, 1990), p. 48.

group of homespun farmers. For rural communities, appointing a teacher was a way of importing 'a prime matrimonial prospect' into the district.[23] Overall, the most striking fact was the extent to which women were confirmed in Old-World roles. In rural Quebec, birth rates were as high in the early twentieth century as they had been in the eighteenth: 'nowhere else in the world was the Catholic ideal of a large family realized as effectively.'[24] Yet in 1871 the fertility rate among women of child-bearing age had actually been higher in Ontario. To quote an earlier observer, the immigrant father could expect that within a year of arriving in Upper Canada, 'all his sons will be *free* and all his daughters *confined*'.[25]

For Canada's indigenous peoples, the nineteenth century was a disaster. They had constituted at least one-fifth of the population in 1815 but by 1911 their total numbers halved to just over 100,000, barely 1 per cent of Canada's total. In Newfoundland, the Beothuk were extinct by 1829. A few groups, such as the Six Nations, remained important in Upper Canada at least until 1837, but most were brushed aside. The Mississauga, who had sold most of their lands north of Lake Ontario in 1805, were still seeking payment in 1905. With no organization to provide Native groups with a common front, only the white man's government could determine overall policy. The titles of legislation, such as the Gradual Civilization Act (1857) or the Indian Advancement Act (1884), are memorials to failure. Indians east of the Great Lakes were offered the vote in 1885. Few had accepted before the privilege was withdrawn in 1898.

West of the Great Lakes there were no Canadian frontier wars like those of the southern hemisphere colonies. Over-hunting of buffalo combined with alcohol and disease to render Indian resistance unlikely, if not impossible. One incentive in Treaties Number Six and Seven which extinguished native title across the southern prairies in 1871–77 was the provision of a medical chest on each reservation. Canada could at least guarantee order, thanks to the North-West Mounted Police, founded in 1873 and significantly modelled on the Royal Irish Constabulary. Few indigenous people were tempted to support Riel in 1885.

By contrast, French Canadians flourished. The 1911 census counted over 2 million, although for the first time their share of the total dipped below 30 per cent. Four-fifths of French Canadians lived in the province of Quebec, where they also constituted four-fifths of the province's population. Quebec's English-speaking enclaves were shrinking, but the province's largest city, Montreal, remained a stronghold of English power. Although French Canadians might see all of Canada as their homeland, their retreat into the Quebec provincial fortress was

[23] John Kenneth Galbraith, *The Scotch* (Toronto, 1964), p. 88.
[24] Paul-André Linteau and others, *Quebec: A History, 1867–1929* [1979], trans. R. Chodos (Toronto, 1983), p. 22.
[25] Ronald Hyam, *Empire and Sexuality: The British Experience* (Manchester, 1990), p. 106.

a by-product of the creation of a French-majority province in 1867. Out-migration from Quebec went mainly to the nearby United States. Consequently, Manitoba failed to develop into a second French-speaking province, and in 1890 began to dismantle the legal protection enjoyed by the French language. In the Maritimes, the Acadians formed their own cultural organization in 1881, and also looked more to exiled kin in New England than to Quebec.

Religion was almost as much a key as language to understanding Canada's French fact. Largely cut off from metropolitan France, French Canadians rallied around the Catholic church, whose distaste for the Revolution of 1789 further distanced them from their secular European cousins. However, while the church was undoubtedly a force for social control and Imperial accommodation, it is possible to overestimate its conservative role, as the rebellions of 1837–38 demonstrated. Excesses such as the Guibord affair, in which the ultramontane Bishop Bourget blocked the burial of a political opponent, were atypical. Laurier opened an ingenious route to compromise in 1877 by defining himself as a Gladstonian Liberal rather than a continental anticlerical. Outside Quebec, the church was a less reliable protector of French identity, especially where the Irish challenged for control: Bishop Michael Fallon was prominent in the attack on French schools in Ontario after 1910. The Vatican was usually anxious to defuse church–state clashes, notably forcing Catholics to accept substantial defeat over Manitoba Schools in 1897.

In public life the French language was barely audible: even the Quebec Conference of 1864, which designed Confederation, was conducted entirely in English. Francophone parliamentarians often spoke in English, and it was not until 1910 that the Quebec legislature required utilities to provide customer services in French. In 1914 Canadian stamps and banknotes—indeed, even the cheques issued by the Government of Quebec itself—were entirely in English. Yet language remained the core of French Canadian identity. Durham's dismissal of them as 'destitute of all that can invigorate and elevate a people'[26] goaded F.-X. Garneau into writing a four-volume history of French Canada. Anglicization was not simply a process of linguistic change. The use of French in the Canadian Assembly was legalized in 1848, but probably more significant was codification of Lower Canada's civil law, completed in 1866, which added to the attractions for the French-Canadian professional classes of re-creating their own province in Confederation.

Both the fact and the failure of armed revolt against British rule in 1837–38 enabled French Canadians to see collaboration with the Imperial power as a policy

---

[26] C. P. Lucas, ed., *Lord Durham's Report on the Affairs of British North America*, 3 vols. (Oxford, 1912), II, p. 294.

of accommodation rather than surrender. The real threat to a French and Catholic identity came from American democracy, which was threatening and close at hand. As early as 1846, the former rebel Taché proclaimed their allegiance to the Empire 'till the last cannon . . . shot on this continent in defence of Great Britain is fired by the hand of a French Canadian'.[27] However, talk of Britain as 'la Mère Patrie' was shallow. French Canadians showed little enthusiasm for Britain's other Imperial ventures, notably the Second Anglo-Boer War, and it was fortunate that the two European motherlands remained at peace throughout the century.

Studies of 'colonial nationalism' and new identities encourage the assumption that British North America's inhabitants became more 'Canadian' throughout the century. In fact, in demographic terms the people of Canada became steadily more British. Newfoundland excepted, in 1815 the dominant population groups were of French and American origin. Immigration thereafter came overwhelmingly from the United Kingdom. Well-known examples of non-British groups were statistically unimportant. Canadians were proud that blacks could find freedom, if not practical equality, on British soil, but by 1911 there were fewer than 17,000 black people in Canada, a total regularly surpassed by annual immigration from Britain. The Doukhobors, encouraged to move to Canada by the Russian writer Tolstoy, numbered barely 7,000. More significant were the 100,000 Ukrainians entering Canada between 1896 and 1914—but 150,000 people came from the United Kingdom in 1913 alone.

Although until 1910 the vast majority of British migrants headed for the United States, there were phases when Canada—with its relatively small host population—was overwhelmed. A third of a million came between 1826 and 1837, contributing to the dislocation underlying the rebellions. Two-thirds of a million followed between 1840 and 1857, fuelling Upper Canadian demands for 'representation by population' that challenged the artificial equality with Lower Canada in the Canadian Union. The fact that many migrants were young adults maximized their impact: the British-born constituted about one-quarter of the population of Upper Canada on the eve of Confederation, but made up 40 per cent of Upper Canadian legislators. Crossing the border in 1862, a correspondent of *The Times* noted that Canadians looked 'stouter and ruddier of hue' than Americans and many had Scots or Irish accents.[28] Immigration surged again in the 1880s, and from 1903. One and a half million immigrants entered between 1910 and 1914, almost half from the British Isles. In 1901 7 per cent of the population of Canada was British-born; by 1911 almost 11 per cent. Canada was becoming more British, not less.

---

[27] Jacques Monet, *The Last Cannon Shot: A Study of French-Canadian Nationalism, 1837–1850* (Toronto, 1969), p. 3.

[28] W. H. Russell, *Canada: Its Defences, Condition, and Resources* (London, 1865), p. 57.

Of course, British immigrants were neither socially nor culturally homogeneous. Scots were often divided by language—Lowlanders regarded Gaelic as 'gibberish'—and their predominant Presbyterian faith was quarrelsomely fissile. Toronto Scots were organizing in support of the Free Kirk within four months of the Disruption of the Church of Scotland in Edinburgh in 1843, although Canadian Presbyterians reunited in 1875, half a century before ecclesiastical peace returned to Scotland.

Irish divisions proved longer-lasting. The largest immigrant group until the 1850s came from Ireland. Unlike the more visible Irish of the United States, they were rural rather than urban, Protestant rather than Catholic, and the Famine of 1845–49 was far less significant in explaining their migration. In fact, Irish migration virtually ceased after 1855 as Upper Canada began to run out of land for settlement. The Newfoundland Irish were overwhelmingly Catholic, heavily drawn from the hinterland of Waterford; Ulster Catholics were common in New Brunswick, rare in Halifax. The Protestants who predominated among the Upper Canadian Irish were by no means all from Ulster. The Baldwins in Upper Canada and Uniackes in Nova Scotia, Cork Protestant families, led the demand for colonial self-government, inspired by memories of Grattan's parliament rather than any vision of future Commonwealth partnership.

The Orange Order, whose members were pledged 'to resist all attempts to ... dismember the British Empire',[29] was the most widespread social institution in British North America: Ontario had 900 Lodges in 1870. Despite official hopes that Orangeism would die out, the Order became Canadianized through resistance to Catholic demands for publicly funded separate schools. Riel's murder of an Orangeman brought the conflicts of seventeenth-century Ireland to the green grassy slopes of the Assiniboine. Canadian Orangeism in turn fuelled Ulster resistance. A disapproving Manchester Liberal regarded Bonar Law's 'Orange fanaticism' as something he had 'brought ... with him from Canada'.[30]

Orangemen had no monopoly on loyalty. Unlike Australia, Canada offered an easy alternative for Irish Catholics who rejected the British flag: they could go to the United States. American Fenians, seeking to liberate Ireland by attacking Canada, only underlined that choice. D'Arcy McGee, a self-styled traitor in 1848, was assassinated twenty years later because he had come to prefer colonial freedom to republican democracy.

The colonial-born were the Empire's second-class citizens, part of a world focused somewhere else. 'The Boston boy may become President of the United States,' complained Joseph Howe, but 'the young native of Halifax or Quebec'

[29] Cecil J. Houston and William J. Smyth, *The Sash Canada Wore: A Historical Geography of the Orange Order in Canada* (Toronto, 1980), p. 120.

[30] Trevor Wilson, ed., *The Political Diaries of C. P. Scott, 1911–1928* (London, 1970), p. 403.

could hope only for 'some paltry office' in a local ministry.[31] Inspired by McGee's vision, in 1868 five Canadian-born government clerks formed Canada First, a pale equivalent of assertive nativism in Australia. Despite some indirect influence, the movement fizzled out within a decade. A handful of writers solemnly debated the nature of Canadian literature, but there was no answer to McGee's challenge: 'Who reads a Canadian book?'[32] Even twentieth-century Canadian Liberals such as Mackenzie King and Paul Martin were inspired by Morley's *Life of Gladstone*. By 1914 there were signs of the distinctive school of art that later emerged in the Group of Seven (two of whom were English migrants who had arrived in 1911), which drew inspiration from Canada's northern landscapes. Significantly, these rarely included any sign of Canada's peoples.

Although there were French words to 'O Canada' when Lavallée composed the stirring tune in 1880, it was twenty years before an English version hymned 'our home and native land', replacing the original land of altars. Many English Canadians preferred 'The Maple Leaf for Ever', which defined Canadianism as a British entwining of thistle, shamrock, and rose, and praised Wolfe's heroism. The composer was an Orangeman born in Scotland. In 1872 Lady Dufferin assumed that a Canadian flag must include a beaver and a maple leaf, but there was no such distinctive symbol in the Canadian version of the Red Ensign sanctioned in 1892 merely for use by merchant ships. As late as 1911, a Liberal politician declared that the Union Jack would fly over Canada until the end of time.

Evidently nineteenth-century Canada did not conform to a decolonization model of progression through stages of self-government to full independence. Its constitutional evolution is better seen in terms of three levels of government: Imperial at the top and colonial or (after 1867) provincial at the bottom, with an intermediate tier gradually forming in between. Rather than adopt the conventional divide of 'pre-' and 'post-Confederation', it is more helpful to consider the century in three phases, demarcated by divides around 1840 and 1880.

The Canadian rebellions of 1837–38 did not prove that the system of government was unworkable. They were rather incidents in the confrontation between the negative leadership of Papineau and Mackenzie and irresolute Imperial responses hinting at reforms the existing system could not deliver. Although worsened by economic depression, insurrection was localized. The colonial yoke may have seemed intolerable in Deux Montagnes but it did not provoke rebellion at Trois Rivières. Fighting broke out as much by accident as revolutionary design. There

---

[31] J. A. Chisholm, ed., *The Speeches and Public Letters of Joseph Howe*, 2 vols. (Halifax, 1908), I, p. 623.

[32] Francess G. Halpenny, ed., *Dictionary of Canadian Biography*, 13 vols. to date (Toronto, 1976), IX, p. 492.

was no revolt against the colonial system in Nova Scotia, where opposition rhetoric rivalled that of the Canadas.

The rebellions were suppressed by military force in Lower Canada, and snuffed out by a momentary local civil war in Upper Canada. Easy suppression misled the British into thinking they could impose their own solutions, but they were at least forced to focus on underlying issues of colonial autonomy and interprovincial co-operation. Generally, military Governors were replaced in the larger colonies by civilians who combined social status with political or administrative experience, albeit rarely at the highest levels of British government. The habit of command was replaced by an appreciation that in some form the Imperial factor must coexist with the people, not least because their Assemblies voted revenue needed for efficient administration. Until 1837 controversy over sharing political power between Imperial centre and colonial periphery had concentrated on demands to change structures, such as pressure for locally elected Legislative Councils. From the 1840s both Imperial policy-makers and colonial politicians adopted the more successful strategies of seeking their ends by subtle manipulation of existing institutions.

Although the Governor-General based in Lower Canada was technically supreme over all the provinces except Newfoundland, in practice there were no intercolonial co-ordinating structures. Some British policy-makers, Durham included, considered inserting a mezzanine level of government, between metropolis and colonies, to create a British North American buffer against the United States and conscript English-speaking colonists to control the discontented French. However, a union of all the provinces seemed impracticable; the British took the lesser but important step in 1840 of uniting Upper and Lower Canada into a bi-valved province, with an Assembly in which Upper Canada was given equal representation, despite its smaller population, in order to check the still-suspect French.

Historians have conventionally explained that colonial self-government was impractical in 1840 because free trade had not yet provided the necessary space for autonomy within the Empire. Another explanation may be suggested by considering the slow growth of state structures. The Governor of Upper Canada pleaded in 1836 that it was 'impossible' for him to consult his Executive Council 'on all subjects . . . unless they were to live with me at Government House and be morning, noon, and night at my elbow'.[33] The quasi-presidential rule attempted by Governors from Durham to Metcalfe only worsened the problem—and overwork helped kill two of them. Colonial government, in other words, was a form of

---

[33] Sir Francis Bond Head to Glenelg, Private and Confidential, 27 April 1836, C[olonial] O[ffice] 42/ 429, ff. 451–52.

household administration, but the provinces needed a modern Civil Service. In 1842 the province of Canada employed a central administrative staff of ninety-five, with a further 342 employees scattered around the province. By 1867 the numbers had risen to 354 and 2,300. While Confederation was probably not caused by the need for administrative integration, it did make centralization possible. Nova Scotia, for instance, reduced its own civil service in 1867, recognizing that the real authority had passed to Ottawa.

The other requirement for self-government was the emergence of a cadre of professional politicians. Presiding over the new system in New Brunswick in 1848, Sir Edmund Head refused routine administrative work himself and insisted that if colonists desired effective responsible government, 'they must ... pay the men who give up their time to the public service'.[34] Indeed, the last formal Imperial attempt to resist responsible government, Sir Charles Metcalfe's victory over the Reformers in 1843–44, was only possible because in W. H. Draper, the Governor-General had an alternative Premier able to manage the Assembly.

The advent of responsible government during the 1840s can be largely identified through two linked processes: decisions by the British to allow a larger measure of local autonomy, and the changing role of Governors from executive presidents to constitutional monarchs. The defining moment in the first was Gladstone's failure in 1849 to persuade the House of Commons to challenge the Rebellion Losses Act for Lower Canada. The principle of non-intervention was confirmed by this political test case rather than the constitutional division of spheres proposed by Durham ten years earlier. As Lord Elgin showed in Canada between 1847 and 1854, a Governor acting as constitutional monarch provided the basis for effective power-sharing between Empire and periphery.

Responsible government presupposed party politics, so that ministries might be sustained in the division lobbies but replaced at the polls. Unfortunately, early party alliances proved unstable: the 'Great Ministry' of 1848 fragmented within six years. Many of its French-Canadian supporters became 'Bleus' in alliance with moderate English-speaking Conservatives. The Reformers were perhaps victims of their own success: since secularization of the clergy reserves and modernization of land tenure, both carried in 1854, discharged key pledges in their programme of government. Conversely, defeat on these issues enabled Conservatives to abandon outdated ideological baggage and some, like Macdonald, proved effective at regrouping around practical issues, such as railway construction. Mid-century Canadian politics were therefore based on constant manœuvring for coalitions. However sordid the politics of railways, kaleidoscopic factionalism at least some-times forced competing groups to co-operate. The only alternative means of

---

[34] Kerr, *Sir Edmund Head*, p. 77.

building majorities—the politics of religion—entailed long-term divisions. Party polarization around a major issue only returned in the late 1870s with tariff protection.

Unstable party politics gave Governors-General scope to act on their own initiative. Sir Edmund Head secured the choice of Ottawa as the seat of government in 1857. His refusal to call a general election in 1858 barred the divisive Upper Canadian Reformer, George Brown, from office. A similar refusal by Head's successor, Lord Monck, in 1864 helped force Brown into coalition with his opponents in order to tackle the constitutional issue. In 1867 Monck insisted on commissioning John A. Macdonald as sole Prime Minister of the new Dominion, thereby ending the system of dual ministries which had prevailed in the province of Canada. Lord Dufferin played an independent hand in placating secessionist tendencies in British Columbia. 'You said last night you are not a Crown Colony,' Dufferin wrote to his aggrieved Prime Minister Alexander Mackenzie after a 'stormy meeting' on the subject in 1876, 'but neither are you a Republic.'[35]

Canada by 1876 was not a republic but a Dominion. Visionary elements notwithstanding, practical considerations rather than revolutionary nationalism explained why Canada, New Brunswick, and Nova Scotia united to form a British North American core in 1867. For Maritimers, Confederation meant that Canadian money would subsidize the interest payments on the British capital available since 1862 for a railway from Halifax to Quebec. That railway offered little to Canadians, and union with small colonies to the east was not a precondition for Canadian westward expansion. Rather, Confederation offered a painless transfer of additional political power to Upper Canada's growing population, within a framework guaranteeing the Catholic identity of French Canada. Above all, it was acceptable to the British Parliament, which passed the necessary legislation.

Essentially, Confederation in 1867 was the extension of the union of the Canadas over a larger area. The particularism of Maritimers and French Canadians required the trappings of local Assemblies and ministries, although the main agent for the government of the provinces envisaged at the Quebec Conference had been the centrally appointed Lieutenant-Governor. Since Ottawa would also appoint the Senators who were supposed to defend provincial interests in the central legislature, it was clear the Dominion was to be the master. Not only did the British North America Act allow the Dominion 'to make Laws for the Peace, Order, and good Government of Canada', but Macdonald revived the Imperial power of disallowance to strike down provincial legislation even in fields entrusted to the lowest tier of government. In 1865 he privately hoped to see the provinces

---

[35] Dufferin to Mackenzie, Private and Confidential, 19 Nov. 1876, in de Kiewiet and F. H. Underhill, eds., *Dufferin–Carnarvon Correspondence*, p. 319.

'absorbed in the general power',[36] and his creation in 1870 of the 'postage-stamp province' of Manitoba, with its small area and limited powers, is suggestive. 'Confederation is only yet in the gristle,' Macdonald wrote in 1872, 'and it will require five years more before it hardens into bone.'[37] Had he not lost office in a scandal in 1873, he might even have emulated New Zealand, where the provinces were abolished altogether in 1875. Even the unhappy and divided Liberal administration of 1873–78 actually strengthened Dominion power by creating a Canadian Supreme Court. Indeed, the rise of the tariff issue promised to create both firmer party alliances and a more integrated Canadian state. 'Never since the settlement of the great questions of the Clergy Reserves and Seignorial Tenure', said the *Montreal Gazette* in 1876, 'have party lines been so distinctly drawn upon a clear and easily understood principle.'[38] The protectionist National Policy of 1879, carried by Macdonald after the Conservatives' return to office, and the completion of the transcontinental railway and the crushing of the 1885 rebellion seemed to set the seal on the physical unity of Canada.

It seems ironic that this centralist ascendancy was now challenged by a counter-attack from the provinces. Perhaps Macdonald's greatest mistake in the design of Confederation was to re-create Upper Canada as the fully fledged province of Ontario, thereby giving the Dominion's powerhouse an alternative political focus, an inconvenience which became evident after he lost control of it in 1871. Yet it may be that the provincial counter-campaign was a necessary corrective in so large and diverse a country. Canada's constitutional umpire, the London-based Judicial Committee of the Privy Council, certainly thought so, for from 1883 onwards it generally supported the view of Ontario's Liberal Premier, Oliver Mowat, that the provinces were supreme in their own sphere.

The provinces sought to extend their boundaries as well as their jurisdiction. Manitoba ceased to be a postage stamp in 1881. Ontario pushed its large claims west of Lake Superior, securing additional territory in 1884, and Crown rights over natural resources in 1888. Macdonald came to fear that Ontario and Quebec would acquire a 'vast preponderance . . . over the other provinces in the Dominion'.[39] 'Old Canada', as Goldwin Smith still called the core region in 1891, now felt it had regional interests contrary to those of the Dominion it had created.

In 1887 the Premiers of five of the seven provinces, all Liberals, held a symbolic conference at Quebec to argue that Confederation was the creation of the

---

[36] John A. Macdonald to M. C. Cameron (copy), 19 Dec. 1864, National Archives of Canada, Macdonald Papers, vol. 510.

[37] To Rose, Private, 5 March 1872, in D. G. Creighton, *John A. Macdonald: The Old Chieftain* (Toronto, 1955), p. 130.

[38] *Montreal Gazette*, 18 March 1876.

[39] Creighton, *John A. Macdonald: The Old Chieftain*, p. 484.

provinces, and to demand the abolition of disallowance. The attractions of a provincialist stance were underlined by the failure of Liberal assaults on the National Policy at the elections of 1887 and 1891. The party's opportunity came with the slow-burning fuse of the Manitoba Schools dispute. It mattered little that it was a provincial Liberal government that withdrew public funding from Manitoba's Catholic schools in 1890. Manitoba Schools revealed the inadequacy of Macdonald's attempt to square the sectarian circle in 1867, and his Conservative successors—four in the five years after his death in 1891—were unable to reconstruct the balance. Section 92 of the British North America Act had made education a provincial responsibility, but the Dominion was compelled by Section 93 to intervene to defend the rights of a threatened minority. The provision, designed to safeguard Quebec's Protestants, was successfully appealed to by Manitoba's Catholics. In 1895 the Judicial Committee ruled that Section 93 applied and so required the Conservative Prime Minister, Sir Mackenzie Bowell, Grand Master of the Orange Order, to impose a Catholic victory on the Protestant Manitobans. In the cross-currents of the 1896 election, Quebec voters apparently preferred the principle of provincial autonomy to Dominion intervention in support of the threatened Manitoba minority, and helped make Laurier Canada's first francophone Prime Minister. Three former Premiers joined his Liberal Cabinet: the provinces had captured Ottawa.

Thus, by 1896 the establishment of a middle tier of government at British North American level had not eroded the nether millstone of provincialism. Nor had the Dominion gone far in enlarging its powers at the Imperial centre's expense. When Dufferin departed, two books were written about his 'administration' of Canada. None of his successors played such a pervasive role in domestic politics, although Lord Aberdeen's hyperactive wife tried. It is revealing that while Dufferin (1872–78) and Lorne (1878–83) were adopted as names for Canadian boys, Stanley (1888–93) and Grey (1904–11) were remembered for their gifts of sporting trophies. However, the Governor-General continued to be the channel of communication with the British government. A Canadian High Commission, established in London from 1880, dealt largely with immigration and trade. The second High Commissioner, Donald A. Smith (Lord Strathcona), was appointed when 75 and remained in office for eighteen years. There was little pressure for independent representation in any other capital. Canadians were angered when the British failed to back them against the United States in the Alaska boundary dispute, but on balance preferred unreliable Imperial support to facing the Americans totally alone. A Department of External Affairs was established in 1909, with its tiny staff located in an office over an Ottawa barber's shop, but it represented little threat to Imperial diplomatic unity.

The withdrawal of British garrisons in 1870—except from Halifax and Esqui-malt, where troops remained until 1906 to protect the naval bases—was a recognition that Canada could not be defended against American attack. The Dominion's 'Permanent Force' did little to fill the gap: in 1891, with Canada's population approaching 5 million, its establishment of 966 men was poorly trained and undisciplined. Whereas in 1870 Canada had relied on British redcoats to subdue the Red River, in 1885 volunteer militia smothered the Saskatchewan rebellion. Macdonald dismissed pressures to send troops to the Sudan in 1884, but Laurier was unable to resist in 1899. Even without a provocative appeal from Joseph Chamberlain, English-Canadian enthusiasm would probably have forced Laurier to prove his loyalty to the Imperial cause in South Africa, despite French-Canadian sympathy for the Boers. Whereas for Australia South Africa provided something of a surrogate war of national independence, Canada had to resort to hole-in-the-corner support. Laurier authorized the despatch of 1,000 men who would become the responsibility of the British once they reached Cape Town. His insistence that the compromise was not a precedent was rightly dismissed by Henri Bourassa.

Although the Dominion had established an officer-training college in 1876, Canada's soldiers continued to be commanded by British generals, some of whom chafed at such a career backwater. Like many Imperial enthusiasts, General the Earl of Dundonald equated disagreement with treason. Dismissed in 1904 for resisting the possible appointment of a Canadian as his successor, Dundonald's parting shot was an appeal to Canadians to 'keep both hands on the Union Jack!'[40] The appeal was hardly necessary. Canadian politicians rebuffed occasional demands for contributions to Imperial defence costs by pointing out that they had built the Canadian Pacific Railway. This argument, luckily never tested, assumed that transcontinental Canada was the capstone of Empire, linking the British naval bases of Halifax and Esquimalt.

Despite an initial bipartisan façade, Canada's political system did not respond effectively to the realization after 1909 that it was no longer possible to shelter under the world-wide protection of the Union Jack and the British fleet. Laurier's plan for a fleet of eleven warships, an auxiliary navy for an auxiliary state, was too little for Ontario and too much for Quebec, contributing to his defeat at the 1911 election. His Conservative successors were equally unable to carry through their policy of giving three Dreadnoughts to the Royal Navy. By 1914 Canada's 'tin-pot' navy consisted of two superannuated British cruisers, one at each end of the country.

[40] Desmond Morton, *Ministers and Generals: The Politics of the Canadian Militia* (Toronto, 1970), p. 181.

Continental as well as Imperial pressures contributed to Laurier's defeat in 1911. Unexpectedly, the Americans offered an attractive free-trade agreement—so attractive that critics alleged that Canadian prosperity, even its membership of the Empire, would be at the mercy of the American Congress. The intersection of the naval issue with protectionist fears of American competition prevented Laurier from repeating the balancing act of 1899. The Liberals were engulfed on the crucial battleground of Ontario, winning only thirteen of the eighty-six constituencies. Yet in 1900 an identical popular vote had won them three times as many. Four-hundred thousand migrants had poured into Ontario in the interval, and recently arrived British migrants rallying to the flag figured largely in Laurier's defeat.

It is unlikely that the British Cabinet gave much thought to Canada as Europe moved towards war in July 1914. The Prime Minister, Sir Robert Borden, was urged by his secretary to abandon his holiday and return to Ottawa. As war approached, Borden assured London, through the correct channel of the Governor-General, that 'the Canadian people will be united ... to ensure the integrity and maintain the honour of our Empire'.[41] Only ten days earlier Canada had shown a different attitude to the integrity of the Empire when HMCS *Rainbow* had turned back to India a shipload of would-be Sikh immigrants.

Late on 4 August 1914 a telegram from London informed the Governor-General that war had broken out with Germany. Few were troubled that Canada had been committed without consultation: Laurier, leader of the Opposition, said Canadians had always known 'that when Great Britain is at war we are at war'.[42] 'England has always protected our liberties', Archbishop Bruchési told French-Canadian volunteers, urging them 'to do your utmost to keep the Union Jack flying'.[43] Laurier insisted—in language embarrassing to subsequent generations—that Canada, 'a daughter of old England', could only respond 'in the classical language of the British answer to the call to duty: "Ready, aye, ready"'. More remarkable still was the peroration, in which the French-Canadian statesman hailed a 'union of hearts' in Ireland, Australia, New Zealand, and South Africa. Nineteenth-century Canada was coming to a close, not with a vision of national independence but with 'the hope that from this painful war the British Empire will emerge with a new bond of union, the pride of all its citizens, and a living light to all other nations'.[44]

[41] *Documents on Canadian External Relations*, 20 vols. (Ottawa, 1967), I, p. 37.

[42] Arthur Berriedale Keith, ed., *Speeches and Documents on British Colonial Policy, 1763–1917* (Oxford, 1961), p. 358.

[43] Brown and Cook, *Canada 1896–1921: A Nation Transformed*, p. 251.

[44] Keith, ed., *Speeches and Documents on British Colonial Policy, 1763–1917*, pp. 362–63, 366–67.

Select Bibliography

ROBERT CRAIG BROWN and RAMSAY COOK, *Canada, 1896–1921: A Nation Transformed* (Toronto, 1974).

PHILLIP A. BUCKNER, *The Transition to Responsible Government: British Policy in British North America, 1815–1850* (Westport, Conn., 1985).

—— and JOHN G. REID, eds., *The Atlantic Region to Confederation: A History* (Toronto, 1994).

J. M. S. CARELESS, *The Union of the Canadas: The Growth of Canadian Institutions, 1841–1857* (Toronto, 1968).

D. G. CREIGHTON, *The Road to Confederation: The Emergence of Canada, 1863–1867* (Toronto, 1964).

OLIVE PATRICIA DICKASON, *Canada's First Nations: A History of Founding Peoples from Earliest Times* (Toronto, 1992).

E. R. FORBES and D. A. MUISE, eds., *The Atlantic Provinces in Confederation* (Toronto, 1993).

PAUL-ANDRÉ LINTEAU, RENÉ DUROCHER, and JEAN-CLAUDE ROBERT, *Quebec: A History, 1867–1929*, trans. R. Chodos (Toronto, 1983).

DOUGLAS MCCALLA, *Planting the Province: The Economic History of Upper Canada, 1784–1870* (Toronto, 1993).

GED MARTIN, *Britain and the Origins of Canadian Confederation, 1837–1867* (Basingstoke, 1995).

W. L. MORTON, *The Critical Years: The Union of British North America, 1857–1873* (Toronto, 1964).

FERNAND OUELLET, *Lower Canada, 1791–1840: Social Change and Nationalism*, trans. P. Claxton (Toronto, 1980).

DOUG OWRAM, ed., *Reader's Guide to Canadian History*, Vol. II, *Confederation to the Present* (Toronto, 1994).

COLIN READ and RONALD J. STAGG, eds., *The Rebellion of 1837 in Upper Canada* (Toronto, 1985).

C. P. STACEY, *Canada and the Age of Conflict*, Vol. I, *A History of Canadian External Policies* (Toronto, 1977).

GARTH STEVENSON, *Ex Uno Plures: Federal–Provincial Relations in Canada, 1867–1896* (Montreal, 1993).

M. BROOK TAYLOR, ed., *Reader's Guide to Canadian History*, Vol. I, *Beginnings to Confederation* (Toronto, 1994).

P. B. WAITE, *The Life and Times of Confederation, 1864–1867: Politics, Newspapers, and the Union of British North America* (Toronto, 1962).

—— *Canada, 1874–1896: Arduous Destiny* (Toronto, 1971).

SUZANNE ZELLER, *Inventing Canada: Early Victorian Science and the Idea of a Transcontinental Nation* (Toronto, 1987).

24

Australia and the Western Pacific

DONALD DENOON WITH MARIVIC WYNDHAM

After 1770 Captain James Cook and his publicists revealed to politicians, entrepreneurs, and missionaries a new oceanic world to conquer. The slow beginnings
of that process have been sketched in the previous volume.[1] Even by 1815, while
Britannia might claim to rule the Pacific waves, Imperial authority was still frail,
especially on land. Few Western Pacific islanders and fewer indigenous Australians
were yet aware of Britain, and most of the few British settlers had arrived
involuntarily, as transportees. In every respect, however, the nineteenth century
witnessed the complete overturning of this picture. By the 1860s, both in the
islands and on the mainland, indigenous peoples were decimated and outnumbered by new, expanding societies of free British migrants; colonial authority, and
Imperial naval power were firmly anchored in continental Australia (Map 24.1).

This transformation involved settlers' adaptation to the pastoral and farming
opportunities of a dry continent. Their original beach settlements gradually
became thriving entrepôts, sending wheat and wool from the countryside to
Britain, and handling the migrants and the capital attracted by this new production. Gold and base metals, then railways, intensified the social and economic
pattern whereby each hinterland was served by its port and each was largely
independent of the others. Sydney (for New South Wales) and Hobart (for
Tasmania) were the templates for parallel developments in Melbourne (for Victoria), Brisbane (for Queensland), Perth (for Western Australia), and Adelaide (for
South Australia). Uniform culture and settlement experience failed to arrest the
fragmentation of a continent into six distinct colonies.

The evolution of settler societies everywhere generated internal tensions, such
as those between workers and employers, or in gender relations, irresolvable by
simple application of metropolitan models. Political innovation was therefore
essential. From the 1850s, in Australia as elsewhere, the major colonies enjoyed
Responsible Government, which conferred great autonomy on recently created
Assemblies elected by a broad manhood suffrage. The colonies subsequently

---

[1] In Vol. III, see chap. by Glyndwr Williams.

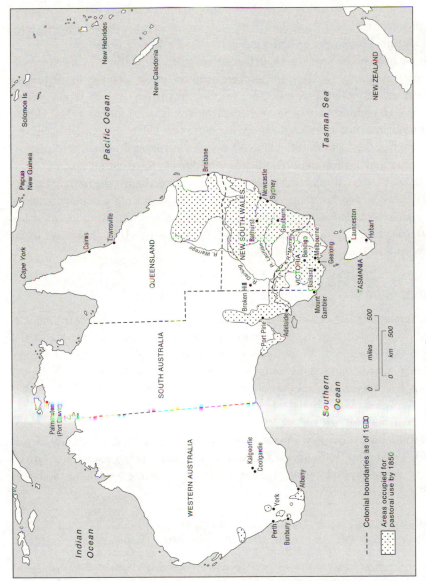

MAP 24.1. Australia: Colonies and Pastoral Settlement

agreed to delegate some of their powers to a new federal government, which was created in 1901 and addressed the related problems of defence, race, class, gender, and work. Its prescriptions—white Australia, racial hierarchy, the domestication of women, and the taming of trade unions—were bound up with continuing dependence on Britain. Australia's participation in Britain's wars between 1885 and 1918 measured the impressive strength of its Imperial connections.

These inversions have long lent themselves to triumphalism, in the form of historical accounts stressing the achievements of political integration, liberal democracy, economic progress, and cultural emancipation.[2] In recent years, however, as demonstrated below, other voices have become increasingly audible, compelling the modification of that master narrative. The mid-twentieth-century liberation of the region's colonial dependencies introduced limited critiques of Australian and British colonial practice; Aboriginal, Torres Strait Islander, and South Sea Islander struggles to remedy historic injustices now throw light on the nineteenth century; historians' recent discovery that women have always lived in the region is undermining some shibboleths; and new attempts to integrate Australia's economy with 'Asia' are encouraging the search for historical links other than the obvious British umbilical cord.[3]

Demographics

This dramatic transformation hinged on a demographic revolution, strikingly if roughly illustrated in population figures. In 1815 Sydney and Hobart were garrisons on the beaches of an unexplored continent and a scarcely charted ocean. Convicts, guards, and settlers comprised a mere 15,000 people. Indigenous populations, by comparison, were overwhelming and concentrated elsewhere. Since the First Fleet, Australia's Aboriginal population had declined by at least a third, but still stood at about half a million. Fiji's population, already in decline, may have been still about 135,000 in the 1870s. At least 90,000 people lived in the main island of New Caledonia. The Solomon and New Hebrides archipelagoes each supported at least 100,000 people, while at least 3 million lived in New Guinea and the Bismarck Archipelago.[4]

---

[2] Donald Denoon, *Settler Capitalism: The Dynamics of Dependent Development in the Southern Hemisphere* (Oxford, 1983). For an earlier example, see Russel Ward, *The Australian Legend* (Oxford, 1958).

[3] A. D. Gilbert, K. S. Inglis, F. Crowley, and P. Spearitt, eds., *Australians: A Historical Library*, 10 vols. (Broadway, NSW, 1987). For the Western Pacific, see Donald Denoon, Stewart G. Firth, and others, eds., *Cambridge History of the Pacific Islanders* (Cambridge, 1997).

[4] Norma McArthur, *Island Populations of the Pacific* (Canberra, 1967); for Australia, J. Peter White and D. J. Mulvaney, 'How Many People?', in Mulvaney and White, eds., *Australians* (Broadway, NSW, 1987). pp. 115–17.

These proportions and geographical distribution were swiftly reversed. The 1861 census counted over a million colonists, while Aboriginals had dwindled to perhaps 250,000 and many islands were ravaged. Natural increase made the colonies less dependent on immigration, and immigration became steadily less reliant on British magistrates with the ending of transportation between 1840 (Queensland) and 1868 (Western Australia). By 1911 4.5 million colonists outnumbered not only the 100,000 surviving Aboriginal Australians but everyone else in the region. Smallpox outran the people who introduced it, killing perhaps 60 per cent of Aboriginal people, destroying tradition and order along with their bearers.[5] Indigenous Australians declined to a nadir of 70,000 in the 1930s. In the Solomons and New Hebrides some societies were driven close to extinction: the New Hebrides as a whole lost half their people as venereal diseases and crowd infections devastated non-immune populations. Measles in Fiji in 1875 killed a quarter of the people.[6]

Local peoples, however, were affected in different ways. Although epidemics were fateful in 'virgin fields' unaccustomed to European diseases, some societies recovered quickly. Population increased in Fiji for several years following the measles epidemic; numbers then declined for twenty years, more slowly—but no less inexorably. Those who were dispossessed of their land suffered most.[7] In the labour trade which brought islanders to plantations in Fiji and Queensland the annual death rate declined from about eighty per thousand to about thirty-five, as workers became inured,[8] but some risks increased. Concentration itself was a hazard, whether on estates or in village congregations promoted by missionaries. Tuberculosis, dysentery, and pulmonary infections flourished in plantations, thence to be taken home when workers' contracts expired. Mission schools were so lethal that Kanaks called tuberculosis *christiano*, the disease of the Christians.[9]

New Guinea's people suffered less than Australia's, a million or more highlanders being untouched by the outside world until the 1930s. Europeans found Melanesia sickening and steered clear. Missionaries mainly sent Polynesian converts there as evangelists, where they often died as martyrs to malaria, and commercial frontiers reached Papua only in the 1870s. There colonial authority

---

[5] Noel Butlin, *Our Original Aggression* (Sydney, 1983).

[6] For fuller figures, see Donald Denoon, 'Pacific Island Depopulation: Natural or Unnatural Causes' in Linda Bryder and Derek A. Dow, eds., *New Countries and Old Medicine* (Auckland, 1995).

[7] Stephen Kunitz, *Disease and Social Diversity: The European Impact on the Health of Non-Europeans* (Oxford, 1994).

[8] Ralph Shlomowitz, 'Mortality and Workers', in Clive Moore, Jacqueline Leckie, and Doug Munro, eds., *Labour in the South Pacific* (Townsville, Queensland, 1990), pp. 124–27.

[9] Bronwen Douglas, 'Discourses of Death in a Melanesian World', in Donna Merwick, ed., *Dangerous Liaisons: Essays in Honour of Greg Dening* (Melbourne, 1994).

was asserted in 1884, but physical restraints persisted, and only a few Europeans tried to wrest a living from gold or coconuts.[10]

The immigrant population concentrated itself in the temperate south-east, whence settlement flowed south into Victoria in the 1840s, west across the dividing range, and north into Queensland and the tropics, especially after 1860. This pattern was replicated on a smaller scale from Perth in the west (from 1829) and Adelaide in South Australia (from 1836). Though based economically on farming and pastoralism, the new societies were from their inception highly urbanized. By federation in 1901, two-thirds of the immigrants lived in New South Wales and Victoria, and the same proportion in towns, especially Sydney and Melbourne which accounted for a quarter of all colonists.[11] The region's ancient pattern of dense tropical populations and sparse Australian settlement was thus overthrown.

Material Triumphs

Throughout the region settlers necessarily, even eagerly, enmeshed themselves in the evolving global market.[12] They herded sheep and cattle, grew wheat, sugar, and coconuts, dug ores, and raided marine resources, exporting and importing everything that could be shipped. Their regional neighbours were only marginally committed to exports, but colonists exported and imported goods to the value of £17m in 1861, and by 1913 exports and imports each topped £90m. Britain accounted for half of this trade, and capital investment also reflected the colonies' dependence on British markets. Significant agricultural capital began to arrive in the 1820s, but from about 1860 governments and companies courted capital assiduously; by 1891 their borrowings from abroad stood at £155m, or over £50 per head. Ebbs and flows in this tide spelt boom or bust. The 1880s were boom years, followed by deep depression in the 1890s when investors lost faith. As the tide turned again, £10m were invested in 1902, but twice as much was disinvested between 1904 and 1911.

Patterns of settlement and economic development depended on control of the land. Notwithstanding early experiments with land grants, Imperial policy aimed to secure almost all land for the Crown, preventing large-scale alienation to a few pastoralists until closer settlement became feasible, and making some rhetorical provision for Aboriginal access.[13] Settler response took the form of 'squatting', at first illegal but always uncontrollable; colonial authorities ultimately had to

---

[10] Donald Denoon, with K. Dugan and L. Marshall, *Public Health in Papua New Guinea, 1884–1984: Medical Possibility and Social Constraint* (Cambridge, 1989).

[11] Wray Vampew, ed., *Australians: Historical Statistics* (Broadway, NSW, 1987), chaps. 1–2.

[12] See above, pp. 32–36, 43–45, 48–50; 56, 63.

[13] Henry Reynolds, *The Law of the Land* (Ringwood, Victoria, 1987).

recognize and licence their occupation. After 1836 there emerged a system whereby settlers and pastoralists either bought or leased land. Exotic merino sheep multiplied to 17 million in the 1820s, and to over 100 million by the end of the century, their increase interrupted only by drought. Selective breeding, fencing, and improved handling increased their value. Wool was the first and most enduring staple, providing between 20 and 40 per cent of exports throughout the century. A frontier of cattle complemented sheep, notably in Queensland and what became the Northern Territory, and from 1880 refrigerated ships began to carry butter and meat to London. However, they were equally vulnerable to climatic catastrophes, as pastoralists discovered during eight years of drought which descended in 1895, killing two-fifths of the national herd which exceeded 12 million at its peak in that year.

The coastal climates did not favour grain, but the 'opening up' of the inland plains by mining and railways provoked a massive increase in acreage under wheat after 1860. By 1913 more than 100 million bushels of wheat were produced on 9 million acres, and half was exported. New techniques (the stump-jumping plough, for example, and the combine harvester) made this possible, but European methods could trigger alarming declines in productivity, since irregular rain and thin soils often demanded greater care than farmers could afford. Their predicament also flowed from public policy which, from the 1860s, aspired to widen access to land and to settle a dense, white rural population. Land legislation enabled men, and single women, with little capital to select land, farm it, and purchase freehold title as their incomes grew.

Industry long meant little more than mining. By 1815 coal was already being mined at Newcastle, New South Wales, and South Australian copper followed in the 1840s; but the most dramatic development was alluvial gold, provoking a rush which swamped Victoria and New South Wales in the 1850s, offering to energetic and lucky white men a rare opportunity for opulence.[14] Victoria, uncolonized in 1815, sustained 500,000 settlers by 1861 (compared with 330,000 in New South Wales). Ballarat was the richest-ever alluvial gold-field, and news of gold had a magnetic effect—during the 1850s one-third of a million migrants landed in the colonies. Throughout the 1860s gold out-weighed wool in export values, and remained significant thereafter. Silver, lead, and zinc in western New South Wales was the base on which arose Broken Hill Proprietary Company (BHP) in the 1880s. South Australian ports were the nearest outlet and Port Pirie became the smelting site. In 1911 when these ores were exhausted, the Company turned to iron and steel, concentrating on Newcastle rather than South Australia, and creating at last the possibility of heavy industry and industrialization.

[14] Geoffrey Blainey, *The Rush that Never Ended: A History of Australian Mining*, 3rd edn. (Melbourne, 1978).

Colonial entrepreneurs regarded not only the continent but the ocean and islands as fields of opportunity. From the early nineteenth century whalers loaded victuals and crews at island anchorages. Island traders, mainly from Sydney, began carrying smoked bêche-de-mer (sea slugs) to China. Divers collected shell, while sandalwood provided other cargoes during the 1840s. As islanders' knowledge of the newcomers grew, so did the quantity and quality of trade goods they demanded, until profits were squeezed between declining prices in China and increasing rewards for chiefs. To secure islanders' co-operation, they were introduced to tobacco, alcohol, and firearms. An evolving triangular trade meant that islanders learned to smoke tobacco, exchanged for sandalwood so that Chinese could burn incense, so that Australians in turn could drink tea.[15]

From south-east Australia prospectors pursued the rainbow far and fast. Armed parties reached the tropical North in the 1870s and crossed the Coral Sea to Papua.[16] They concentrated on small islands until a state structure could offer protection against Papuans—if not malaria or dysentery. Investment was inhibited until the British New Guinea government, established in 1884, offered security. Then Sydney promoters exploited the convenient provision for 'No Liability' companies which tolerated stock market manipulation, insider trading, exaggerated assays, and generous rewards to promoters and vendors.[17] Gold became Papua's main export. Australians also discovered gold in New Caledonia in 1870, but the most significant discovery there was nickel: Rothschild, the London bankers, put nickel mining on a sound footing during the 1890s. There, as elsewhere in the islands, most white men were squeezed out except as artisans and supervisors of unskilled men.

When the American Civil War disrupted cotton production, Australians took up Fijian land under the patronage of chiefs who also mobilized labour. When Fiji's cotton bubble burst in the 1870s, coconuts stood alone as the crop requiring the least labour.[18] Copra (dried coconut flesh) became by far the largest export from islands under European influence. To ensure cargoes, traders bent their minds to acquiring land, instead of relying on independent production. As planters they then wanted cheap, regular, and plentiful labour. With islanders disappearing, the late nineteenth century was the heyday of Asian indentured

---

[15] Dorothy Shineberg, *They Came for Sandalwood: A Study of the Sandalwood Trade in the Southwest Pacific, 1830–1865* (Melbourne, 1967).

[16] Hank Nelson, *Black, White and Gold: Gold Mining in Papua New Guinea, 1878–1930* (Canberra, 1976).

[17] W. A. McGee and G. R. Henning, 'Investment in Lode Mining, Papua, 1878–1920', *Journal of Pacific History*, XXV (1990), pp. 244–66.

[18] Doug Munro and Stewart G. Firth, 'Company Strategies—Colonial Policies', in Moore and others, *Labour in the South Pacific*, pp. 3–29. For more details see Brij V. Lal, *Girmitiyas: The Origin of the Fiji Indians* (Canberra, 1983).

labour. For example, over 60,000 Indians were introduced to Fiji between 1879 and 1916, mainly to work for the Australian Colonial Sugar Refining Company (CRS).[19] Perversely, since all employers preferred workers from elsewhere, islanders themselves embarked for plantations in Queensland, Fiji, Samoa, and New Caledonia precisely when Indians were arriving in the Islands (Map 24.2).

The western Pacific was itself transformed into a 'labour reserve' in the perception of planters once sugar became an export staple in tropical North Queensland during the 1860s. From 1863 until 1904 over 62,000 islanders worked in Queensland, most recruited from Vanuatu and the Solomons.[20] The first recruits were ill-informed, and often kidnapped. Kidnapping became rare after 1872, when Britain passed the Pacific Islanders Protection Act and Queensland enacted complementary legislation. The Royal Navy policed minimum standards, and Queensland vessels carried agents to ensure some measure of consent by recruits. The proliferation of missionaries reinforced these restrictions, although the refusal of French authorities to act in concert enabled French recruiters to perpetuate coercion. In any event, coercion became redundant: returning workers were persuasive, and so were tobacco and alcohol. In Queensland the islanders worked as field labourers until the turn of the century. By then the Colonial Sugar Refining Company had taken control of sugar production. While their Fijian enterprises rested on cheap Indian labour, their Australian profits were generated by capital-intensive technology which ultimately allowed growers to dispense with islanders altogether.[21]

Several islands produced fertilizers to compensate for the poor fertility of Australian soils.[22] The Pacific Islands Company, incorporated in 1897, gained access to phosphates on Banaba (Ocean Island) in 1900, through a 999-year concession, and a vital injection of capital when the British businessman William Lever bought out the Company's Solomon Island land claims for copra production. On the strength of the Banaban concession the company was restructured in 1902 as the Pacific Phosphate Company, and achieved market leverage in 1907 by securing similar rights in the German dependency of Nauru. In 1908 a deal with the Compagnie Française des phosphates de l'Océanie, involving Makatea, northeast of Tahiti, created a *de facto* regional monopsony.[23] Of all the catastrophes which befell islanders, phosphates were the worst. Rights were cheaply alienated;

---

[19] See above, p. 91.

[20] Clive Moore, *Kanaka: A History of Melanesian Mackay* (Boroko, 1985).

[21] A. G. Lowndes, *South Pacific Enterprise* (Sydney, 1956).

[22] Maslyn Williams and Barrie Macdonald, *The Phosphateers: A History of the British Phosphate Commissioners and the Christmas Island Phosphate Commission* (Melbourne, 1985).

[23] Colin Newbury, 'The Makatea Phosphate Concession', in R. G. Ward, ed., *Man in the Pacific Islands* (Oxford, 1972), p. 185.

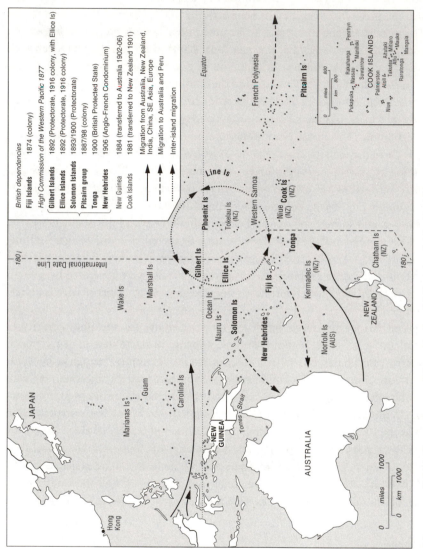

MAP 24.2. British Possessions and Inter-Regional Migration in the Pacific

and there was no need to involve islanders in production, nor even to provide space for them.

Leviathans

The colonists' political progress matched their economic successes. Until the 1840s Australia's colonies were known to the world as penal settlements. By the 1860s most were self-governing democracies. That transformation reflected the end of transportation to New South Wales (1840) and Tasmania (1853), assisted immigration and the founding of non-convict colonies in Victoria (1835) and South Australia (1836), and the 1850s gold rushes. Beginning in the 1820s, power was transferred from autocratic Governors, 'first to appointed councils, then to councils elected on a property franchise, and finally to parliaments whose lower houses were elected by all men who were neither mad nor bad enough to be incarcerated'.[24] The Imperial government offered responsible government on the Canadian model through the Australian Colonies Government Act (1850), responding to colonists' growing wealth and numbers before their desire for local control became too importunate. Although Crown Lands and their revenues were temporarily withheld from the Assemblies in a vain bid to retain Imperial influence, most other powers were delegated, including the right to amend their electoral systems.

In the absence of widespread opposition, these new institutions and procedures developed smoothly. Governors learnt to limit themselves to advisory roles, civil servants reinforced continuity of policy, and a core of conservative politicians organized factions to ensure passage of legislation.[25] Commitment to the free-market economy had implied the replication of European social relations. Local distinctions emerged between 'sterling' (British-born) and 'currency' (locally born), and, deeply, between both and Aboriginal Australians. These crossed with the caste conflicts between convicts, emancipists (time-expired transportees), and free settlers. None the less, the settlers rapidly divided themselves into landholders, labourers, merchants, and administrators on a distinctly British pattern, with predictable political consequences. The structural opposition between pastoral squatters and farming selectors fuelled much of the colonial politics of the later nineteenth century. Catholics and Irish Home-Rulers resented the Protestant ascendancy and Imperial connection, but that passion was subsumed in mundane

---

[24] P. Grimshaw, S. Janson, and M. Quartly, eds., *Freedom Bound, I, Documents on Women in Colonial Australia* (Sydney, 1995), p. 36.

[25] T. H. Irving, '1850–1870', in F. Crowley, ed., *A New History of Australia* (Melbourne, 1974), pp. 124–64; P. Loveday and A. W. Martin, *Parliament, Factions and Parties: The First Thirty Years of Responsible Government in New South Wales, 1856–1889* (Melbourne, 1966).

debates about free trade and tariff protection, the accommodation of trade unions, and ingenious devices for attracting further British investment.[26]

In the Western Pacific islands, by contrast, British governments until the 1870s avoided responsibility, relying for influence instead on the navy informed by missionaries and consuls.[27] Missionaries from the London Society (especially in the Cook Islands and Samoa) and Wesleyan Methodist Society (notably in Tonga and Fiji), saw themselves representing British and Protestant civilization in the area, especially after the 1840s, when French intervention in Tahiti disrupted their activities. Other missions expanded from Polynesia into the Western Pacific in mid-century. Consuls were often one-time Protestant missionaries or their sons (W. T. Pritchard and John C. Williams, for instance), who exercised great influence in island affairs.

After severe discouragements, and largely through the agency of Polynesian teachers and evangelists, Christianity made massive advances.[28] The sandalwood rush had reached its climax here in the 1840s, followed quickly by the labour trade. Evangelization thus coincided with depopulation and other mounting pressures, such that Islanders could imagine the extinction of their cultural traditions, and even of their societies. Their willingness to embrace radical change is perhaps largely explained by this circumstance. The nexus between commerce and Christianity was most explicit among Protestant missionaries, supporting large families on small stipends, collecting and selling copra with mission boats. Through their responses to missionaries, and to beachcombers and traders, some island communities 'pre-adapted' themselves to commerce, and might, in happier circumstances, have enjoyed equal participation in the new economies and polities.

In 1861, for example, Consul Pritchard, one of a dynasty of missionary-trader-diplomats and latest in a line of foreign advisers to the chief of Bau (Fiji), described him as 'the most powerful, the most influential, the most dignified Chieftain of his race—the only Chieftain whose words and acts are circulated with any appearance of authority, and heard with any degree of authority and respect'.[29] On Pritchard's advice, Cakobau requested a British Protectorate. This was denied, and in 1871 he declared himself King of a united Fiji, co-opting other chiefs and traders as ministers. When British officials changed their strategy and demanded the cession

---

[26] G. L. Buxton, '1850–1890', in Loveday and Martin, *Parliament, Factions and Parties*, pp. 165–215.

[27] Deryck Scarr, *Fragments of Empire: A History of the Western Pacific High Commission, 1877–1914* (Canberra, 1967).

[28] Joel Bonnemaison, *The Tree and the Canoe: History and Ethnogeography of Tanna* (Honolulu, 1994); Douglas, 'Discourses on Death'; M. J. T. Spriggs, 'Vegetable Kingdoms, Toro Irrigation and Pacific Prehistory', unpublished Ph.D. thesis, Australian National University, 1981; Oscar Spate, *The Pacific Since Magellan*, Vol. III, *Paradise Found and Lost* (Canberra, 1988).

[29] Consul W. T. Pritchard to Commissioner Smythe, 14 Jan. 1861, cited in Deryck Scarr, *The Majesty of Colour: A Life of Sir John Bates Thurston*, 2 vols. (Canberra, 1973) I, pp. 23–24.

of Fiji, Cakobau could only acquiesce. Cession, in 1875, occurred on relatively favourable terms. Fijian lands were largely protected, the islands were brought under one government, and an aristocracy was entrenched. Governor Sir Arthur Gordon was determined to avoid the dispossession characteristic of the Australian colonies, and devised a paternalist policy whereby chiefly authority was codified.

Imperial supervision was further formalized by the Western Pacific High Commission, created in 1877 to oversee British interests in the Islands but still reliant on co-operation from Islanders or the Royal Navy.[30] This device collapsed once the Berlin Congress in 1884–85 prescribed effective occupation as a criterion for recognizing colonies. The Protectorate of British New Guinea (i.e. Papua) was declared in 1884 in reaction to the abrupt announcement of German New Guinea (to the north), and on condition that the settler colonies covered its costs. The Protectorate over the Solomons (in 1893) was also conceived as a holding operation pending Australian federation.[31]

As it happened, however, most colonial administrators expected islanders to become extinct, and colonial policies were dilatory, unfunded, and repressive of islander initiatives. Unlike the settled mainland colonies, island governments had no capacity to borrow and relied, perforce, on private investors. Almost any concession would be made to attract them. The Colonial Sugar Refining Company in Fiji and Burns Philp in the Australian sphere both enjoyed political patronage and economic privilege.[32] Colonial governments were poorly equipped to regulate big corporations, even when so inclined. Fiji had promised well in 1875 and had a better-developed bureaucracy than most colonies, yet—as the merchant Morris Hedstrom explained in 1911—'the people who profit by the prosperity of the colony are the landowners and the merchants and capitalists, and these are the people who escape almost scot free under our present [taxation] system'.[33] In the Solomons, Commissioner Woodford expected islanders to die out, and adopted a strategy of plantation development rather than peasant production.[34] Deep-seated habits of consumption encouraged some islanders to sell land, yielding money faster than wage labour or copra. Woodford was delighted to see planters take up land, and in 1898 the Pacific Islands Company began to negotiate for Chartered Company rights and 'unoccupied' land. As matters turned out, Lever stepped in and accumulated 400,000 acres. Burns Philp and other Australians were also

---

[30] Ibid.; see above, pp. 192–93.

[31] Stewart G. Firth, *New Guinea Under the Germans* (Melbourne, 1983); Judith Bennett, *The Wealth of the Solomons: A History of a Pacific Archipelago, 1800–1978* (Honolulu, 1987).

[32] Munro and Firth, 'Company Strategies', p. 25.

[33] Fiji, *Legislative Council Debates*, 1911, quoted by Bruce Knapman, 'Capitalism's Economic Impact in Colonial Fiji, 1874–1939: Development or Underdevelopment?', *Journal of Pacific History*, XX (1985), pp. 66–83.

[34] Bennett, *Wealth of the Solomons*, pp. 125–49.

attracted by freehold and 999-year leaseholds. Only in Papua did government decree that non-indigenous people could only obtain land under lease. Everywhere revenue was raised mainly by head taxes, income and import taxes, and was never enough to transform living standards. Changes from new technologies, crops, and animals sometimes reduced islanders' workloads, but the common requirement to enter wage labour in order to pay poll taxes had the opposite effect.

External Affairs, Cultural Change, and Australian Federation

The interplay of colonial authority and Imperial interests was also shaped by the changing international environment. Before the penal colony, the only regular regional links were Western New Guinea's exports to Tidore; trade across Torres Strait; and annual visits by Makassans for bêche-de-mer. The first settlers were awed by a silent continent and an empty ocean: by the end of the century the ocean teemed with seemingly rapacious rivals. As settlers flourished, shipping became more frequent: British trade and an Australian connection with China was consolidated by the cession of Hong Kong in 1842. Trade then brought other foreign powers closer to Australia where, acutely aware of their isolation, colonists took alarm by turns against France, Germany, and Japan.[35]

Inspired by British example, French colonization was worrying even if markedly less successful. The navy annexed the Marquesas in 1841, Tahiti the next year, and New Caledonia ten years later.[36] Although the colonies depended on Australian supplies, Australian and French settlers began to compete for resources and each became anxious about the others' ambitions. Recruiting labour for the nickel mines in New Caledonia's New Hebridean labour reserve, the naturalized French entrepreneur John Higginson observed with dismay that Protestant missionaries were well established, and that Australians were urging the British government to annex. To forestall that outcome Higginson encouraged Catholic evangelization, created the Caledonian Company of the New Hebrides for plantation development, and in 1882 set out to buy the archipelago. By 1886 the Company had paper claims to half the land, and had begun to plant French settlers. Although when Higginson died in 1904 his Caledonian Company and much else had failed, interdenominational rivalry and the conflicting aims of Australian and New Caledonian settlers none the less required resolution. The metropolitan powers sought a minimalist solution, creating an Anglo-French Condominium in 1906 and hoping to hear no more from the islands and their turbulent missionaries.[37]

---

[35] T. B. Millar, *Australia in Peace and War: External Relations, 1788–1977* (Canberra, 1978).

[36] John Connell, *New Caledonia or Kanaky? The Political History of a French Colony* (Canberra, 1987).

[37] Bonnemaison, *The Tree and the Canoe*, pp. 81–96.

Australian colonists also feared the expansion of German commerce based in Samoa. Few material interests were at stake in New Guinea, but German and Australian trading firms both recruited labour there, and local imperialist urges had manifested themselves by the 1860s. The Queensland government's 'annexation' of eastern New Guinea in 1883 failed only when Whitehall repudiated the action on the grounds that 'Our responsibilities are already heavy enough'.[38] Such restraint, however, was short-lived. When the next year Bismarck determined to 'protect' New Guinea, the British government itself stepped in to 'protect' Papua.

The emergence of Japan caused dismay even before Japan's comprehensive defeat of Russia in 1905. Most alarming to racially sensitive Australians was the arrival of Japanese entrepreneurs in Australia's north. Prostitution was the earliest industry, followed by pearl-diving from the 1880s. To the dismay of legislators, Japanese bought or built their own pearling luggers. Only racially restrictive licensing laws prevented them from outright ownership of the whole fleet.[39] Japan's alliance with Britain (from 1902), and the crystallization of alliances between European powers demonstrated that British and colonial priorities might not always coincide.

Such events constantly reminded colonists of their small numbers, their isolation, and dependence on the Royal Navy. In these anxious circumstances it is hardly surprising that Australians volunteered to assist the British Empire whenever it was threatened: in New Zealand during the Maori Wars of the 1860s; and even the remote Sudan in the 1880s.[40] The South African War provoked excitement and intense competition between the colonies to send the first and the most troops.[41] By 1914 there was already a vigorous tradition of fighting in Britain's campaigns. These diplomatic and defensive preoccupations formed the shifting background to processes of cultural change and, at the turn of the century, closer association of the colonies with each other.

On the other side of the world from 'home' and with a shoreline thousands of vulnerable-miles long to protect, Australians felt as keenly the tyranny of proximity to regional neighbours as the 'tyranny of distance' from the mother country. One nineteenth-century visitor from Europe noted that it was 'necessary to have been in Oceania to realise to what an extent neighbours seven to nine hundred miles away can be thought annoying'.[42] Fear of invasion and a siege mentality

---

[38] Brian Fitzpatrick, *The British Empire in Australia* (Melbourne, 1949), pp. 186–87.

[39] Regina Gantner, *The Pearl-Shellers of Torres Strait: Development and Decline, 1860s–1960s* (Melbourne, 1994).

[40] K. S. Inglis, *The Rehearsal: Australians at War in the Sudan, 1885* (Adelaide, 1985).

[41] Laurie Field, *The Forgotten War: Australia and the Boer War* (Victoria, 1995).

[42] The visitor was an André Siegfried, quoted in W. K. Hancock, *Australia*, 2nd edn. (Brisbane, 1964), p. 49.

permeated an emergent brand of popular culture and nationalism which, by the 1890s, bore distinctively xenophobic characteristics. More than 'love of country', it was 'pride of race' that held Australians, and in part the Empire, together. Their sense of insecurity served the interests of Empire well, helping to keep this most distant colony from straying too far towards independence. Australians sparred only gently with the mother country, reserving the sharp edge of their nationalism for their Asian neighbours, China and Japan in particular. The illusion that only the Royal Navy stood between themselves and the 'yellow hordes' stilled republican stirrings, even if the rhetoric often suggested otherwise.

That distinctive popular rhetoric was most vociferously expressed in the Sydney *Bulletin*, whose contributors favoured republicanism, a democratic franchise, land taxation, state education, and 'A United Australia and Protection Against the World'.[43] Banjo Paterson's ballads and Henry Lawson's short stories attracted a large, passionate readership, helping to make the *Bulletin* 'the Bushman's Bible'. Such was its force that a legend eventually grew of the 1890s as a pivotal decade in relations between Empire and colonists: the crystallizing 'moment' of the Australian as a type, separate and distinct from the old British stock, and the first blossoming of an Australian—radical—nationalism. The construction of Left historians mostly, this legend endowed Australians on the eve of Federation with a degree of political consciousness and a commitment to national self-definition that belonged in reality to a minute—intellectual—proportion of the population.

It was not intellectual but physical activity which above all marked the emerging popular culture, half-borrowed, half-new. Sport was critical in maintaining links with the Old World and lending familiarity to the new. Boxing and horse-racing were favourite spectator sports, and the leisure hours of boys and working men were occupied by cricket in summer and three codes of football in winter: only Australian Rules was a distinctly colonial code. The year 1861 saw the arrival of yet another British cultural icon, the Melbourne Cup, Australia's version of Royal Ascot. Sporting competitions, in boxing matches and on the cricket field, also provided local lads with a friendly context in which to pit new against old British stock. Pride in their sporting prowess early on emboldened the 'currency lads'. 'The young Australians', wrote one observer in the 1840s, 'think themselves unrivalled...and wish Lord's players would come out and be stumped out.'[44] Their wishes were eventually fulfilled in 1861, when the first English cricket team visited. Although the *Bulletin* thundered 'Australia for the Australians', the com-

---

[43] 'Bulletin' entry, *Oxford Companion to Australian Literature* (Oxford, 1991), p. 123.

[44] Ward, *Australian Legend* (Oxford, 1983), p. 67; W. F. Mandle: 'Games People Played: Cricket and Football in England and Victoria in the Late Nineteenth Century', *Historical Studies*, XV (1973), pp. 511–35. 'Cricket and Australian Nationalism in the Nineteenth Century', *Journal of the Royal Australian Historical Society*, LIX (1973), pp. 225–46. D. H. Borchardt, ed., *Australians: A Guide to Sources* (Broadway, NSW, 1987), chap. 48.

mon threads of Australian identity were Imperial rather than republican. The real birth of a 'national sentiment' lay some years away in the exploits of the ANZAC troops in the Dardanelles.

Political federation of the Australian colonies in 1901 seems inevitable only in retrospect, because the pressures contributing to it at the time were for most colonists frequently weak and fitful. It did not, of itself, make Australia a nation; it only facilitated it. Each colony was more tightly integrated into British commerce than with each other, so that (for example) railway systems still linked hinterlands to entrepôts, but isolated each catchment area from the others. (A standard gauge was achieved only in 1995.) No powerful 'national sentiment' transcended loyalties to colony, city, or faction. Potent emotional ties to Britain remained. State loyalties in particular were strong and abiding, and led delegates at constitutional conventions in 1891, 1895, and 1898 to press constantly for protective measures against the Australian federal—not the British—government. The emerging popular culture and nationalism had minimal influence on federation or the process which led to it.

Conceived and executed from above, the drafting of the federal constitution, and the passage of the Commonwealth Constitution Bill through the Imperial Parliament in 1900 were the activities of a narrow élite of mainly urban, professional, liberal politicians. Labour politicians were distinctly under-represented in the process. The political campaign took its lead from men such as Sir Henry Parkes, Prime Minister of New South Wales, or the Victorian politician Alfred Deakin, and propaganda by enthusiasts such as those in the Australian Natives' Association. Even so, the colonies' delegates debated federation for ten years before conceding limited powers to a federal Commonwealth in 1901. Such momentum as the movement had was sustained by the economic difficulties of the 1890s, and discreet encouragement from Imperial politicians such as Joseph Chamberlain, who welcomed the Federal Parliament's early attention to national defence within an Imperial framework.

The Federal Inheritance: Landscape and Race

Although settlement, economic expansion, and federation were widely regarded as at least modestly successful, they also embodied a past as well as an agenda for the future which prompted rather different interpretations. The Commonwealth's agenda was not merely to resolve intercolonial tensions, equalize regulations and opportunities, and provide for national defence; it was to create a national identity distinct from 'Asia', clarify borders, and foster economic development through the 'New Protection', whereby high tariffs would protect organized labour's wages and conditions.

Historians, turning their gaze from gross domestic product and economic statistics towards the localities, can discover another picture. The triumphalist mode finds its apogee in histories of Australian exploration, where tales of intrepid, fearless explorers and their 'brave assaults upon the interior' of 'the last-found and least-favoured of continents' abound. Recently, however, not only have the reputations of individual travellers such as Matthew Flinders, Thomas Mitchell, or Charles Sturt been re-evaluated; increasingly, the 'advent of the white man with his ready-made civilisation' has also emerged problematically.[45] Although it was less obvious, the resource-raiding of the ocean had its continental counterpart, and farmers and pastoralists were less willing, or able, to move on when they had transformed the landscape. Yet the introduction of millions of sheep and cattle (not to mention rabbits, foxes, pigs, goats, rats, and cats) was bound to have an impact on an environment which had never sustained sharp-hoofed creatures. The compulsive 'clearing' of bush to create pasture and appropriation of water for commercial agriculture were equally consequential.

One shire in New South Wales has been studied with sufficient care to reveal some of the immediate effects and further consequences of treating the Australian environment like a cut-rate, temperate British landscape. Settlers in the 1840s were delighted by the pastoral paradise of Narrandera, on the Murrumbidgee River of south-central New South Wales. Turning the grasslands to pasture, however, inflicted serious damage. Cattle ate out the most succulent grasses, exposing the earth to erosion by wind and rain. Herded animals trampled the ground, preventing it from absorbing rain, drying up swamps and waterholes, and creating watercourses instead. The Wiradjuri had controlled scrub by firing the grasses; when they were prevented from doing so, the grasslands were rapidly displaced by pine. As native flora were eradicated, the landscape was transformed in ways radically reducing its value, even to the pastoralists who initiated the changes. Native fauna were equally threatened. A bounty was introduced to finance extermination of the dingo, and in the 1880s settlers declared noxious the emu, bilby, and wedge-tailed eagle. They followed up by anathematizing kangaroo, wallaby, kangaroo rat, and raven. Unintended victims included koala, echidna, bandicoot, platypus, innumerable species of birds, and fish. Their places were taken by exotic animals representing a much more serious threat to pastoral profits: not only the obvious rabbits, but mice, feral cattle, goats, pigs, and horses. 'In short, an economic and social attachment to civilization and progress led Europeans to make war on the land', and then compelled them to make 'strenuous and expensive attempts to rescue the land from the consequences of their own improving'.[46]

[45] e.g. Hancock, *Australia*, chap. 1, 'The Invasion of Australia', pp. 1–23; for exploration, Paul Carter, *The Road to Botany Bay: An Essay in Spatial History* (London, 1987).

[46] Bill Gammage, *Narrandera Shire* (Narrandera, 1986), chap. 13, quotation from p. 229.

Questions of race were no less persistent than problems of the physical environment, confronting Australia's colonists from within as much as, and for longer than, those from without. Although each prompted distinct responses, they shared two major features. Responses were led from above and were underpinned by an unquestioned assumption that to British invaders and their race belonged the sole right to own and occupy the island continent.

In the conquest of this continent, no treaties were made: colonists elaborated a doctrine of *terra nullius* which asserted that British settlement extinguished native rights to land. In the opinion of governments, courts, and colonists, land was also bought and sold without incurring social obligations.

The frontier settlers [were] revolutionaries, and the landscape reflects the success of revolutionary violence. It shows that settlement proceeded without concessions to traditional culture, settlement patterns or land use. The survey lines and the fences could run straight for hundreds of miles as though they crossed vast sheets of blank paper... Settled Australia has a landscape reflecting sudden and dramatic change, the complete and violent overthrow of one social and economic system, one mode of production, by another. [The landscape reflected] the success of the bourgeois revolution in Australia—one of the most prolonged, complete and successful in the world.[47]

Sweeping across the continent, pastoralists shattered Aboriginal communities; survivors became domestic workers and stockmen, or Native Police. White brutality carried special dimensions for native women, submitted to violent sexual encounters with white men on the frontier and to domestic abuse by white mistresses in the home.[48] Federation did not affect race relations directly, since Aboriginal affairs remained with the states, and Aboriginal Australians were neither accepted as citizens nor even enumerated in census returns. Queensland, therefore, empowered by the Aboriginal Protection and Restriction of the Sale of Opium Act of 1897, segregated the races and created reserves. As its title implies, the law was intended to segregate black from white Australians—and both from 'Asia'. Aborigines and their property rights, like Melanesians, were expected to disappear.

The strategy adopted by the Commonwealth Parliament is commonly summed up in the slogan 'White Australia'. Most immigrants were British, but in the 1850s one in ten was Chinese, until the hostility of white miners led to physical violence on the gold-fields and immigration restrictions. By the end of the century the separate colonies had legislated against further Chinese immigration. With the

---

[47] Henry Reynolds, *Frontier: Aborigines, Settlers and Land* (Sydney, 1987), pp. 192–93.

[48] Recent feminist histories of Australian convict and colonial society emphasize the fact that it was a European—rather than European male—dispossession of Aboriginal peoples; P. Grimshaw, M. Lake, A. McGrath, and M. Quartly, *Creating a Nation* (Victoria, 1994); Introduction, pp. 1–5.

endorsement of all three major parties, this approach was consolidated and extended through a dictation test, explicitly designed to bar all non-Europeans. That strategy might be expected to yield a European—and overwhelmingly 'British'—population in short order.

Obstructing this vision stood an anomalous Melanesian frontier of sugar workers, whose presence offended the Commonwealth, although Queensland's legislature was divided on the issue, and had veered between migration and exclusion for a generation. The Commonwealth's Pacific Island Labourers Act (8 November 1907) determined, retrospectively, that islanders be repatriated by 1906. Sugar producers were forewarned. During the 1890s plantations yielded to family farms, while the Colonial Sugar Refining Company processed cane in central mills. The Commonwealth paid a bounty on sugar produced by white workers, so that the industry not only survived but flourished. Islanders did not: nearly 10,000 in 1901, by 1906 they numbered fewer than 5,000. Those whose long residence entitled them to stay found most jobs closed by the preference for white labour. They were largely excluded from white society, and with lower standards of living and less education, pressed always closer to the even more marginal Aboriginal population.[49]

The Commonwealth also turned its attention to Torres Strait and Cape York, meeting-points for Aborigines, Papuans, and Makassans, whalers, pearlers, and sandalwood-getters. European goods were carried beyond Torres Strait along trade routes encircling New Guinea, and more goods were scavenged from shipwrecks. Polyglot Thursday Island was the 'sink of the Pacific'. Some order was imposed by the pearl-shell and bêche-de-mer industries. Trading companies advanced the money with which captains bought luggers. The masters brought crews and shore parties already employed in Pacific pearling, and luggers relied on 'dress-divers' at the end of air pumps. Japanese divers demanded trusted tenders—preferably their kin. The Queensland government, 2,000 kilometres away in Brisbane, merely codified these conventions into regulations. More surprising was the tolerance of the Commonwealth, which exempted Japanese pearlers from the provisions of White Australia, thus preserving an enclave of nineteenth-century colonial labour practices.

Torres Strait islanders' knowledge of luggers and bêche-de-mer expanded when sailors settled among them, and again when they embraced Christianity. At the turn of the century missionaries and Queensland officials resolved to transform them into entrepreneurs, exempting them from the Aboriginal Protection Act, and conferring a civil status like that of the Kanakas—neither white nor Aboriginal. Officials imposed increasingly onerous obligations, partly to promote work-

---

[49] Moore, *Kanaka*, pp. 200–73.

ing habits, partly to raise revenue, and relations became vexed. Islanders who might have managed resources on a sustainable basis were excluded, in favour of captains who merely ransacked pearl and bêche-de-mer.[50] The regional economy entered a slow decline, but the islanders' legal status survived, and their lands were not expropriated.

From the perspective of the new Commonwealth, order was thus achieved on a remote frontier, and the circle of colonial authority, which included the British Protectorate over Papua and a Dutch administrative centre at Merauke (1893), finally closed. The white Australia immigration policy restricted Japanese to prescribed jobs, and brought Chinese immigration to a halt. With the repatriation of Kanakas, these measures amounted to gradual ethnic cleansing and tidying.

The Federal Inheritance: White Labour and Gender

White working men began forming trades societies in the cities as early as the 1850s. During the 1860s the failure of their industrial actions sharpened interest in the political process and especially in campaigns for an eight-hour day. Not until the deep depression of the 1890s, however, did these forms of organization move beyond urban artisans into the mass of the labour force. The new, militant unionism was exceptional in deriving its strength from unskilled and semi-skilled workers. Miners and transport workers were crucial, but even more influential were shearers and other pastoral workers. Bush-workers, organized by the Australian Workers' Union, were the largest groups 'in the great industrial disputes, amounting at times almost to civil war, between 1890 and 1894. It was they who bore the brunt of the battle, stood as symbols of its ideology, and renewed the struggle single-handed in 1894, when the transport workers and miners had admitted temporary defeat.'[51]

In the countryside, trade unions immediately attracted huge memberships, for reasons some of which were articulated by W. G. Spence:

Unionism came to the Australian bushmen as a religion. It came bringing salvation from years of tyranny. It had in it that feeling of mateship which he understood already, and which always characterized the action of one 'white man' to another. Unionism extended the idea, so a man's character was gauged by whether he stood true to Union rules or 'scabbed' it on his fellows . . . The lowest term of reproach is to call a man a 'scab'.[52]

Spence's career is as revealing as his analysis. His family brought him from Scotland during the 1850s gold rushes, and he educated himself largely by studying the

---

[50] Ganter, *Pearl-Shellers*, passim.
[51] Ward, *Australian Legend*, pp. 212–13.
[52] Quoted in ibid., p. 215.

Bible. As a miner he rose to become General Secretary of the Amalgamated Miners' Association, and President of the Shearers' Union founded in gold-mining Ballarat in 1886. His enthusiasm for unionism led him often to exaggerate its powers, so that the Maritime Strike of 1890 was a catastrophic failure. Despite that setback, he became the first Secretary (and later President) of the Australian Workers' Union in 1894, bringing together shearers and other rural workers.

Like the Maritime Strike, those involving shearers and miners in the same era were eventually crushed. Thwarted in industrial actions, thoughtful leaders turned to politics, creating Labor parties which contested elections with increasing success during the 1890s, introducing the idea (and sometimes the practice) of party discipline to Assemblies hitherto notable for fluid loyalties and parochial enthusiasms.[53] At the turn of the century a Labor party even, albeit briefly, formed a government in Queensland, and non-Labor parties were gradually induced to incorporate the interests of working men into their own programmes. Once again Spence's career is exemplary, entering the new Commonwealth Parliament as a Labor member, becoming a minister in the first Labor ministry—and being forced to resign from the Australian Workers' Union during the war owing to his support for conscription, and for the Nationalist ministry of Billy Hughes, by then *bête-noire* of the Labor movement.

The fruits of political power included labour legislation in most territories, enacting compulsory conciliation and arbitration, protecting workers from the worst excesses of arbitrary employers in lean times, and constraining their ambitions when conditions were buoyant. These institutions were capped by the creation of a Commonwealth Arbitration Court, and especially by the judgments of Henry Bourne Higgins, its President from 1907. The Harvester Judgment of that year became the benchmark for industrial policy thereafter. Higgins determined that the basic wage for unskilled men must provide for an average family of five, and satisfy 'the normal needs of the average employee regarded as a human being living in a civilized community'.[54] These criteria led to a daily wage of seven shillings, little more than the rate already prevailing, but it was the criteria which mattered. Minimum wages were laid down which would apply across the continent. They were available only through complex mechanisms of conciliation and arbitration which conferred broad power and influence on organized trade unions, since they were an indispensable element of industrial bargaining. To sustain these wage levels, tariff protection was absolutely essential—and tariff protection rested on a concept of civilization which in practice prohibited the

---

[53] Brian Galligan, ed., *Australian Federalism* (Melbourne, 1989).

[54] Humphrey McQueen, 'Higgins and Arbitration', in E. Wheelwright and K. Buckley, eds., *Essays in the Political Economy of Australian Capitalism* (Sydney, 1983).

employment of coloured workers. The catch-cry of 'a workingman's paradise' thus glossed many inequities, but had some substance both in law and in reality by 1914.

Labor's emphasis on the 'mateship' of white men was not merely rhetorical. Early colonial Australia was literally a white man's country in that men greatly outnumbered women until the end of the convict era and the gold rushes. Women also concentrated more in urban areas than the bush, heartland of the white man's dreamtime.

Convictism branded the Australian colonial experience as unique, and its raw brutalities scarred society. Women convicts constituted the bulk of the female population of convict society, and bore extra burdens peculiar to their sex. Few had many options but to yield to the sexual advances of their masters, and for their troubles, few escaped the brand of loose women or 'damned whores'. With the end of transportation, conditions slowly began to improve. Transition from a convict to a colonial society called for dramatic changes in women's roles, and for cleaning up the image of womanhood. Marriage was a help. Rare in the early period, it became by mid-century a feasible goal for a majority of colonists. Yesterday's 'damned whores' were now called upon to be God's and the Empire's moral police in their new twin functions as wives and mothers.[55] Migration schemes ensured a steady supply of respectable girls from the mother country to feed a growing demand for governesses and brides. Among the most successful was Caroline Chisholm's Immigrants Home in Sydney; operating from 1841 to 1846, it placed hundreds of young unmarried women in good homes.

State and church authorities focused narrowly on the colonial woman's reproductive role, proclaiming it her primary duty to bear children. From government, pulpit, and press alike, voices urged 'populate or perish': Australia's wide open spaces were beckoning the 'yellow hordes'. That anxiety was inflamed by the sharp decline in birth rate towards the end of the century. In 1903 a Royal Commission on this decline was established in New South Wales, inquiring into the reasons why women were ignoring official instructions. The commission found selfishness at the root of the problem, 'driving . . . the women to contraception and abortion in order to avoid the joys and delights of childbearing and the raising of children'.[56] Ultimately, there was little authorities could do to arrest the trend towards smaller families. Contraceptive technology was becoming available, although for financial, religious or moral reasons, few could afford it. For some time 'stratagems of desperation', such as the ghastly, illegal practices of abortion, infanticide, and

[55] For an elaboration of this view, see Anne Summers, *Damned Whores and God's Police: The Colonization of Women in Australia* (Ringwood, Victoria, 1975).

[56] Judith Allen, 'Octavius Beale Reconsidered: Infanticide, Babyfarming and Abortion in NSW, 1880–1939', in Sydney Labour History Group, *What Rough Beast?* (Sydney, 1982).

baby-farming remained widespread. Even so, the advent of artificial birth control had profound implications in recognizing women's need to control their reproductive lives. Payment of a maternity allowance or a 'baby bonus' was introduced in 1912 as an enticement, but proved futile.

Women's domain was the domestic sphere, but it was an increasingly contested one. They were early and thoroughly enlisted in the work-force, informally as wives or formally as employees, but lacked organization. They worked largely in areas where there was no union activity, and little will to accommodate them. However, the argument often advanced to explain the lack of trade-union support for females, namely, that women were not largely employed as skilled labourers, does not altogether hold true. By mid-century women were engaged in a wide range of jobs well beyond the stereotypes of teachers, nurses, and dressmakers. In the 1861 census the women of Castlemaine, Victoria—a new but 'flourishing, well-built city' with its own mayor and town council—appear also as 'merchants, printers and bookbinders, cattle dealers and saleyard keepers, quarry men and brickmakers, blacksmiths and whitesmiths, carriers and bullock drivers, shepherds and overseers, miners and puddlers'.[57] Their exclusion from trade unions meant working women lacked the collective muscle to represent their own interests. Nevertheless, progressive politicians' concern about conditions of women's work eventually led in 1891 to the establishment of a parliamentary Royal Commission.[58]

Women had virtually no input into public constructions of popular culture and nationalism, which essentially reflected the perspectives of one discrete segment of the population: white, male, urban working-class and of the Left. Women's contributions remained mostly hidden from the public, and their experience and perspective have been eclipsed, rather than encompassed, by the traditional 'universal' histories. Women painters, fiction and non-fiction writers, poets, and dramatists, it now emerges, had all along been helping to piece together the wider picture, and not always from a 'feminine' perspective. Barbara Baynton's *Bush Stories* (1902) tell a rawer tale of life in the Australian outback than do Henry Lawson's sketches in his celebrated collection *While the Billy Boils* (1896). But the time was then not yet ripe for recognition of women's contribution to the arts, literature, and public debate on Australian national identity. Public distinction was reserved for women of the respectable, educated middle classes, and mostly through charitable work.

[57] P. Grimshaw, C. McConville, and E. McEwen, *Families in Colonial Australia* (Sydney, 1985), pp. 83–104, esp. p. 101.

[58] For women not members of trade unions, see Grimshaw, Janson, and Quartely, *Freedom Bound*, I, pp. 150–54.

The enfranchisement of women far ahead of Imperial Britain may seem anomalous in these circumstances. But in the Australian context, the impulse and the will to achieve female suffrage stemmed from a complex blend of conservative and radical forces, ranging from propertied males to leading feminists. South Australian women began to vote in 1894, and the last colony, Victoria, followed suit in 1908. Leading the campaign were temperance associations, the chief public focus of women's reformist enthusiasms. There was remarkably little resistance to female suffrage, which could be seen as entrenching and reinforcing women's civilizing role rather than foreshadowing new roles for women in the public domain. A leading feminist of the time, Rose Scott, welcomed the vote as an instrument of 'women's mission' which was 'to inspire man and to help him build up our young nation upon all that is righteous'.[59] Whereas the Labor parties' entries into parliamentary politics led directly to industrial legislation, the entry of women into the electorates led neither to their arrival in parliaments, nor to significant changes in their political and economic conditions. The Arbitration court not only implied in the Harvester Judgment a subordinate economic and social role for women: it determined quite explicitly that women's work was worth two-thirds of that of their brothers and husbands.

Recognition of such gender-based inequities was, by the turn of the century, tempering the triumphalist narrative. Side-by-side with celebrations of 'those brave pioneer mothers!' who toiled 'from morn till night, turning hands to anything, living in tents', performing 'splendid work in the development of Britain's Australian dependencies' were lamentations that, despite their toils, women in Australia were not getting their just rewards. Such sentiments even found their way into a volume of 'The British Empire Series' in 1900, where the chapter on 'Women of Australasia' argued forthrightly for the principle of equal pay for equal work, and claims were made of a national identity for Australian women.[60]

Dominion and Colonies

In formal terms British influence grew after 1815 from minimal to overwhelming, coming to rest upon the enthusiastic, but essentially voluntary, commitment of the settlers in Australia. By 1914 they were prosperous but still acutely conscious of isolation, aloof from both Asia and the Pacific, and dependent not only on British naval power, capital, and markets, but equally on English, Irish, and Scots cultural traditions. White Australia was British not only in the obvious senses of British

[59] Grimshaw and others, *Creating a Nation*, p. 185. For Rose Scott's comment, see *The Australian Woman's Sphere* (Dec. 1903), p. 379.

[60] Grimshaw and others, *Freedom Bound*, I, pp. 169–73. Mrs Hirst Alexander, 'Women of Australia', in *Australia, The British Empire Series*, IV (London, 1900), pp. 280–309.

descent, the aspiration of successful colonists to careers in London, and their yearning for Imperial honours or to take their retirement at 'Home'. Many programmes aimed to replicate British norms and procedures (through high and popular culture, schools and the new universities, selective immigration, and the affiliation of professional bodies and unions to metropolitan counterparts) or to improve upon them. Female suffrage and industrial arbitration were clearly advances on British practice, but were compatible with British traditions and progressive tendencies. The achievement of a prosperous, domesticated settler society entailed a highly defensive posture against the rest of the region. The 'New Liberalism' inspiring the makers of the Commonwealth and its first ministries was inexorably committed to the Imperial government for defence, to London for capital and trading partners, and to 'New Protection' with immigration controls to defend working men and their families from 'unfair' (that is 'coloured') competition. Governments and their constituents, in other words, welcomed foreign capital as ever but had come to reject a free market in labour and the free movement of people. There was a role for women, as almost-equal citizens, and for organized working people. But the rhetoric of mateship explicitly denied room in the future for 'Asians' (even for most Japanese, although they rejected Asia with equal vehemence); and there was no room at all for the original Australians, whose demise was anticipated with mixed regret and satisfaction.

King Stork in Australia behaved like King Log in the islands. Australian policy in Papua espoused plantations, but the ban on Asian labour, the requirement that vessels be manned by white crews, and shortage of funds, spelt few planters and small crops. Neighbouring German New Guinea, with Chinese indentured labour and subsidized shipping, sustained much more prosperous plantations. Australian interests in the islands preferred stability to the hazards of change. The colonial states were at best rudimentary. The British Solomon Island Police had to beg transport from planters and missionaries to fulfil their duties.[61] Even with two colonial governments, New Hebrideans were more likely to encounter missionaries, and to work in New Caledonia, than to deal with colonial officers.[62] All islanders became subject to Native Regulations which denied them the civil rights, training, and employment prospects of settlers. Policy and practice divided the region absolutely into settler and native realms, separate and unequal. Australian workers were unionized and politicized, while islanders were subject to indenture. Primary education was becoming compulsory for white Australians, whereas a very few islanders had to be content with mission schools.

Australia also served as an exemplar for French policy in New Caledonia, a convict settlement enriched by minerals and impoverished by the appropriation of

---

[61] Bennett, *Wealth of the Solomons*, pp. 103–24.
[62] Bonnemaison, *The Tree and the Canoe*, pp. 52–80.

land for pastoralists, creating a colonial economy which did not rest on the labour of the Kanaks but excluded them and penned them into reserves.[63] Islanders themselves made rather different judgements of Australia, as is evident in the code of behaviour devised by New Hebrideans returning to Aoba from the Queensland plantations. Australia also served as a negative model. Although the Fijian colonial economy was underpinned by Australian capital, it was also the only British dependency in the region resting on a treaty of cession with islanders. Gordon and his successors created a structure of indirect rule and immigrant labour explicitly to save Fijians from the fate of Aboriginal Australians and native Hawaiians. The practices and traditions of the British Empire in Australia were mediated and modified by the settlers. In the Western Pacific more generally they were refracted through an Australian lens.

[63] Connell, *New Caledonia or Kanaky?*, *passim*.

Select Bibliography

PETER BEILHARZ, *Imagining the Antipodes: Culture, Theory and the Visual in the Work of Bernard Smith* (Cambridge, 1997).

GEOFFREY BOLTON, *Spoils and Spoilers: Australians Make Their Environment, 1788–1980* (Sydney, 1988).

PAUL CARTER, *The Road to Botany Bay: An Essay in Spatial History* (London, 1987).

A. CURTHOYS and A. MARKUS, eds., *Who Are Our Enemies? Racism and the Working Class in Australia* (Sydney, 1978).

ELEANOR DARK, *The Timeless Land* (Sydney, 1941).

GREG DENING, *Performances* (Melbourne, 1996).

PHILIP DREW, *The Coast Dwellers: A Radical Reappraisal of Australian Identity* (Melbourne, 1994).

TIM FLANNERY, *The Future Eaters: An Ecological History of the Australasian Lands and People* (Melbourne, 1994).

RICHARD P. GILSON, *Samoa, 1830–1900: The Politics of a Multi-Cultural Community* (Melbourne, 1970).

ROBERT HUGHES, *The Fatal Shore: A History of the Transportation of Convicts to Australia, 1787–1868* (London, 1987).

CLAUDIA KNAPMAN, *White Women in Fiji, 1835–1930: The Ruin of Empire* (Sydney, 1986).

BRIJ V. LAL, DOUG MUNRO, and Ed BEECHERT, eds., *Plantation Works: Resistance and Accommodation* (Honolulu, 1994).

ANN MCGRATH, ed., *Contested Ground: Australian Aborigines Under the British Crown* (Sydney, 1995).

GANANATH OBEYESEKERE, *The Apotheosis of Captain Cook: European Mythmaking in the Pacific* (Honolulu, 1992).

HENRY REYNOLDS, *The Other Side of the Frontier: Aboriginal Resistance to the European Invasion of Australia* (North Townsville, 1981).

K. SAUNDERS and R. EVANS, eds., *Gender Relations in Australia: Domination and Negotiation* (Sydney, 1992).

GEOFFREY SERLE, *From Deserts the Prophets Come: The Creative Spirit in Australia, 1788–1972* (Melbourne, 1973).

R. GERARD WARD and ELIZABETH KINGDON, eds., *Land, Custom and Practice in the South Pacific* (Melbourne, 1995).

GEOFFREY WHITE, *Identity Through History: Living Stories in a Solomons Island Society* (Cambridge, 1991).

RICHARD WHITE, *Inventing Australia: Images and Identity, 1688–1980* (Sydney, 1981).

25

Southern Islands: New Zealand and Polynesia

RAEWYN DALZIEL

In the mid-nineteenth century New Zealand became the furthest frontier of the British Empire. It was not uncommon for writers to use the colony as a metaphor for distance; the New Zealander as an analogue for the stranger, the outsider with the puzzled gaze. Yet, as with all colonies of settlement, the purpose was to shrink distance, to eliminate strangeness, imposing British civilization and control on a land viewed as a wilderness and on an indigenous people seen as barbarous. Coming within the Empire at a moment of liberal humanitarianism, New Zealand experienced a colonialism and colonization less brutal than some. Maori, a tribal people who had occupied the country for over a thousand years, were settled agriculturalists with powers to resist, negotiate, and adapt. For years British control was fragile as the migrant aspiration for material prosperity and control conflicted with the Maori desire to retain land and autonomy. Nevertheless, annexation and colonization were acts of possession and dispossession, settlement and unsettlement. By 1914 New Zealand's humpbacked, mountainous, but fertile land had been traversed by Europeans, renamed, and domesticated. The radical transfer of ownership and control over land and resources, the creation of a grassland, exporting economy and a state system modelled on that of Britain seemed to prove the success of the colonial experiment. Their cost to Maori and race relations had been enormous.

New Zealand was annexed by Great Britain in 1840, at a time of supposed low interest in Empire. Direct rule followed some fifty years of contact by sailors, traders, missionaries, and officials, the advance guard of an Empire being fatally led, as Lord Melbourne said, 'step by step over the whole globe'.[1] While the violence of some early encounters and British antipathy to formal expansion in the late eighteenth century meant that the claims to parts of New Zealand made by Captain James Cook in 1769 were never validated, the British foothold in Australia ensured that New Zealand and its people would be incorporated into Imperial strategic and economic designs. By the 1790s British naval vessels were visiting

---

[1] Melbourne to Howick, 16 Dec. 1837, cited in Peter Adams, *Fatal Necessity: British Intervention in New Zealand, 1830–1847* (Auckland, 1977), p. 110.

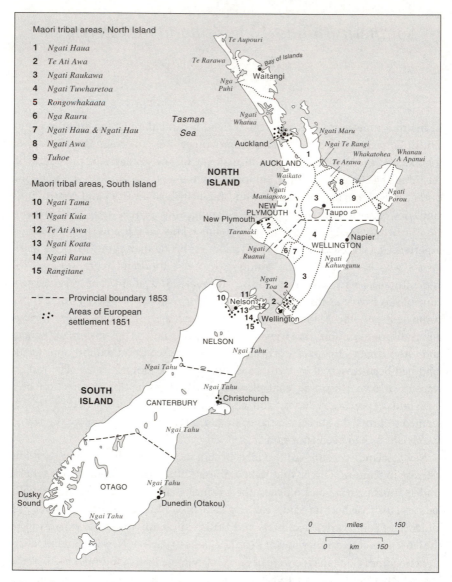

Maori tribal areas, North Island

1 *Ngati Haua*
2 *Te Ati Awa*
3 *Ngati Raukawa*
4 *Ngati Tuwharetoa*
5 *Rongowhakaata*
6 *Nga Rauru*
7 *Ngati Haua & Ngati Hau*
8 *Ngati Awa*
9 *Tuhoe*

Maori tribal areas, South Island

10 *Ngati Tama*
11 *Ngati Kuia*
12 *Te Ati Awa*
13 *Ngati Koata*
14 *Ngati Rarua*
15 *Rangitane*

- - - - Provincial boundary 1853

∴∴   Areas of European
       settlement 1851

Te Aupouri
Te Rarawa
Bay of Islands
Nga Puhi
Waitangi

Tasman
Sea

Ngati Whatua
Auckland
Ngati Maru
Ngai Te Rangi
Whakatohea
Whanau A Apanui

NORTH
ISLAND

AUCKLAND
1
Te Arawa
Waikato
Ngati Maniapoto
8
NEW
PLYMOUTH
3   9
Ngati Porou
New Plymouth
2   Taupo
Taranaki   4
Ngati Ruanui   6 7   Napier
WELLINGTON
2
3
Ngati Kahungunu

Ngati Toa
2
10 11
Nelson 12
13
14
15 Wellington

NELSON
Ngai Tahu

Ngai Tahu
Ngai Tahu
SOUTH
ISLAND
CANTERBURY
Christchurch

Ngai Tahu

OTAGO
Ngai Tahu
Dusky
Sound
Dunedin (Otakou)
Ngai Tahu

0   miles   150

0   km   150

MAP 25.1. New Zealand: Native Peoples and White Settlers

northern harbours and taking cargoes of flax and timber. In 1792 two young Maori men of chiefly families were kidnapped and taken to Norfolk Island to teach flax-dressing to convicts. Mortified to learn that they knew nothing of the work, which, in Maori society, was a woman's skill, Lieutenant-Governor King sent the men, Tuki and Huru, home in November 1793 with pigs, maize, and potatoes. The indigenous agriculture was able to expand into a lucrative trade. Sealing and whaling also drew foreign economic interests to New Zealand. In 1792 crew from the *Britannia* sited at Dusky Bay on the south-west coast of the South Island killed 4,500 seals in nine months. However, regular expeditions to New Zealand, financed by Australian businessmen, did not occur until after the depletion of Australia's sealeries and the growth of a market for sealskins in the British hatting trade. Declining seal numbers from the late 1820s gradually ended the slaughter. The southern whaling grounds, long monopolized by the East India Company, were opened to independent American and British whalers at the end of the 1790s, and whales were hunted in the seas around New Zealand from just after the turn of the century. Australian firms became active from the 1820s. Whalers also stopped over in New Zealand for supplies and repairs and traded extensively with Maori. The first shore whaling station was set up at Te Awaiti in the Marlborough Sounds in 1827 and within a decade eighty shore stations had been established.

As a society which rapidly incorporated new technologies, trading practices, literacy, and religion into its own culture and proved a formidable fighting force, Maori commanded considerable respect from foreign visitors. They were themselves travellers, chiefs visiting Sydney and London, and younger men joining the crews of whaling and sealing vessels. Europeans were valued mainly for advantages they could confer in pre-existing tribal political and economic contests, and for the most part this meant providing access to literacy, tools, and guns. On a visit to England in 1820 Hongi Hika not only instructed Professor Lee in the Maori language but also collected together a small arsenal of weapons. Guns gave inter-tribal warfare a new and more deadly power.

Trading exchanges were well established by the time the church arrived in the Bay of Islands. Samuel Marsden, senior chaplain at the convict settlement in Sydney, was so impressed by his perception of Maori potential for civilization and conversion that in 1809 he brought Church Missionary Society (CMS) lay missionaries, William Hall, John King, and their families, to Sydney, bound for New Zealand. Racial tensions in the north delayed the work and when the missionaries were eventually located, along with schoolteacher William Kendall, at Rangihoua in 1814, they quarrelled, and lapsed into despair, jealousy, and doubt. Despite the establishment of a second station at Kerikeri in 1819, missionaries had little success in converting Maori until the Revd Henry and Marianne Williams began to reorganize the mission and to focus on the teachings of the church and

Bible in 1823. The Wesleyans established a mission in 1823 and Roman Catholics in 1838.

Until the late 1820s mission stations survived on Maori terms and under Maori domination. Even nominal conversions were rare, although missionaries became significant agents of change through their integration into Maori trading, agricultural, and economic life. Literacy also conferred a privileged status. The mission breakthrough came as European technology and disease made an increasing impact on Maori society. Throughout the 1820s tribes with guns went to war to avenge old defeats and insults. Peace returned when the balance of arms neutralized early advantages, but in some cases the loss of life and disruption to the traditional patterns of landholding and authority caused tribes to turn to missionaries as peacemakers. European treatments and prayers were also sought as possible cures for the diseases caused by rampant foreign viruses. Religion had a greater impact as the mission stations expanded: by 1839 the Anglicans had eleven stations and the Wesleyans six, located as far south as Kawhia and Rotorua. As inter-tribal fighting subsided, freed captives and slaves spread Christian teachings. Missionaries often found that both the gospel and literacy had preceded them.

During this period British control over its nationals in New Zealand was exercised spasmodically from Sydney, usually in response to complaints by Maori or to a beachhead disruption. In 1805, acting on a complaint from the chief, Te Pahi, about the behaviour of whalers at the Bay of Islands, Governor King proclaimed that his permission would be needed before Maori could be taken off shore. Serious incidents, such as the 1809 massacre of the crew of the *Boyd* and the revenge sacking of Te Pahi's settlement, caused an outcry but the authorities of Sydney could do little. In 1813 Macquarie issued an order extending British protection over Maori and requiring ships calling at New Zealand to post a bond for good behaviour. The next year he appointed Kendall a Justice of the Peace and empowered northern chiefs, Hongi Hika, Korokoro, and Ruatara, to enforce his orders.

With the establishment of the missions, calls for law and order became more insistent. The missionaries considered that unruly seamen, escaped convicts, and traders endangered their lives and work. Acting on reports of violence and disorder, the Church Missionary Society petitioned the Secretary of State for the Colonies for effective punishment of crimes committed in New Zealand and an 1817 Act empowered the courts to try cases of murder and manslaughter committed by British subjects outside British territory. In 1823 New South Wales courts were authorized to try offences committed in New Zealand.

This legislation explicitly recognized New Zealand's independence and British responsibility for the growing number of its offshore nationals. The power to exercise this responsibility was limited. In 1830 the Ngati Toa warrior leader, Te

Rauparaha, negotiated the transport of a war party to Akaroa on the *Elizabeth* in return for a cargo of flax. Te Rauparaha's Ngai Tahu enemies paid a fearsome price for the deal while an outraged Governor Bourke failed in his attempt to try the ship's captain. New Zealand had also attracted the interest of France. In October 1831 a French naval vessel called at the Bay of Islands, preceded by rumours that France intended to annex New Zealand. Unfounded though the rumours were, a missionary-inspired meeting of northern chiefs made a pre-emptive strike, petitioning the King to become 'a friend and guardian of these islands'. Concerned by these and other events, in 1832 the Colonial Office decided to appoint James Busby British Resident at the Bay of Islands. Busby's instructions were to prevent, as best he could, European violence towards Maori, to protect 'well-disposed settlers and traders', to apprehend escaped convicts, and to 'conciliate the good-will of native chiefs'.[2]

Such aspirations now seem bizarre, for Busby had neither police nor troops and the infrequent visits of a naval vessel to the Bay provided little support. He tried to enforce order by occasionally gathering together posses of local residents to pursue offenders, and hoped to persuade local chiefs to exercise a collective authority. In 1834 a meeting of chiefs established a ships' register and selected a national flag to fly over ships built in the embryonic shipyards of the Hokianga. Northern chiefs met again in October 1835 when it was claimed that a French adventurer, Baron de Thierry, planned to set up a state in New Zealand. This meeting led to a Declaration of Independence asserting the sovereign power and authority of the chiefs, while appealing to the King to be the 'parent of their infant State and ... its Protector from all attempts upon its independence'.[3] Busby collected signatures to the Declaration for several years, but the intention to hold an annual congress of chiefs came to nothing.

Busby's official presence significantly increased the information on New Zealand reaching Sydney and London. The news was often alarming. Early in 1837 a series of despatches warned Bourke that inter-tribal fighting was imminent and he ordered William Hobson, captain of HMS *Rattlesnake*, to the Bay to protect British subjects and shipping and report on the state of the country. Although Hobson discovered little danger, he proposed British authority be enhanced by factories (trading stations) headed by magistrates located wherever there was a sizeable British population, and by the appointment of a chief factor accredited to the united chiefs as a political agent or consul. British subjects would be required to register and the chiefs should be asked to sign a treaty recognizing the factories and protecting British subjects and property.[4]

[2] Bourke to Busby, 13 April 1833, C[olonial] O[ffice] 209/1.
[3] A Declaration of the Independence of New Zealand, Facsimile (Wellington, 1976).
[4] Hobson to Bourke, 8 Aug. 1837, CO 209/2.

Reports of discord and conflict contrasted with accounts of a mild climate, fertile land for the taking, and almost certain mineral wealth which created a picture of a southern utopia, inevitably attracting the attention of British promoters of emigration and colonization. The first attempt at a planned settlement, sponsored by a group of politicians and businessmen in 1825–26, was unsuccessful, but a number of the men involved later joined Edward Gibbon Wakefield's colonization scheme. Wakefield entered the emigration debate in the late 1820s and rapidly became one of its key figures. A creative thinker, articulate, and with influential patrons, he advocated 'systematic colonization' to solve the contemporary problems of wealth creation, surplus capital, and surplus labour. New Zealand, as Wakefield informed the Parliamentary Committee on the disposal of land in British colonies in 1836, was 'the fittest country in the world for colonisation'. Flanked by a bevy of politicians, financiers, and businessmen he launched the New Zealand Association, later floated as the New Zealand Company, at a public meeting on 22 May 1837. The Association proposed to promote legislation authorizing the annexation of New Zealand and empowering the 'Founders of Settlements in New Zealand' to purchase land cheaply from Maori, send out migrants, and rule the colony. A powerful vested interest in New Zealand had been created.

The Colonial Office was now listening to several competing voices on New Zealand. The missionaries and humanitarians wanted law and order but, consistent with contemporary views on the impact of culture contact, they feared a more formal British presence would bring settlement fatal to Maori. The New Zealand Association sought approval and protection for its colonizing venture. Officials in Sydney wanted peace. The Maori voice was interpreted in the main by missionaries, working within the framework of their own goals. By December 1837 the British government had decided that a policy of minimal intervention was no longer viable. During 1838 it decided to appoint a Consul and in December offered Hobson the position. As Consul-Designate, Hobson was told that he would be negotiating for the establishment of British sovereignty in areas where British interests were concentrated, offering protection over the rest of the country. These plans were later changed to extend sovereignty over part or all of the country, and Hobson's instructions made clear his role as a buffer between Maori and future settlers. Another decision, that future land purchases would require a Crown title to be valid, so concerned the New Zealand Company that it rapidly despatched a survey party to purchase land, and then a shipload of settlers.

The crucial event in negotiating the future of New Zealand was the signing of the Treaty of Waitangi. The Treaty, eventually signed by between 530 and 540 high-ranking men and women and Hobson, became the founding document of New Zealand as a bi-cultural society. Although it was repudiated by some British politicians, easily slipped from the consciousness of most settlers, and was ignored by the courts, it has always been regarded by Maori as a living document, a covenant of paramount importance in recognizing Maori rights and establishing a relationship with the Crown.

The Treaty has recently been the subject of extensive historical research. Whereas in the past it was seen as the product of the particular New Zealand situation conjoined with the humanitarian ethos expressed in the 1837 Report of the Committee on Aborigines, it is now clear that it had precedents in other parts of the Empire and that it drew on British constitutional and legal history.[5] The Treaty covered three essential conditions for the future relationship: the chiefs would accede to British sovereignty; the Crown would guarantee Maori possession of their land, forests, and according to the Maori text, treasures, and the English, fisheries, and become the exclusive purchaser of any land that Maori wished to sell; Maori would receive all the rights and privileges of British subjects. Unlike most earlier treaties, the Treaty of Waitangi was translated into the indigenous language, for many Maori had learned to read in their own language. Most chiefs signed the Maori version, which is now regarded as authoritative. There were significant differences between the two versions of the Treaty, causing much speculation as to the meaning intended by the translator, Henry Williams, and the understandings of the Maori signatories. Whether it will ever be possible to assign these meanings with absolute certainty is problematic, and the debate is now in the hands of linguists and lawyers rather than historians. It does, however, seem clear that Maori signatories expected that *tino rangatiratanga* or the powers of full chief-tainship, guaranteed to them by the second clause of the Maori version, would enable them to exercise customary law and authority within tribal areas and over their land. This expectation was not seen by them, or necessarily by the other parties, as incompatible with the sovereignty or, as the Maori version stated, the *kawanatanga* (government) ceded to the Crown.[6]

The Treaty was debated vigorously at Waitangi. The initial opposition rising from fear of losing land, authority, and government control of commerce, was offset by the support of three powerful chiefs, Hone Heke, Patuone, and Tamati Waka Nene. They argued that European contact made the accommodation envisioned in the Treaty inevitable and that access to European technology, control over British subjects and friendship with Britain were positive steps forward. Reassembling on 6 February, the chiefs signed the Treaty, each signature

[5] M. P. K. Sorrenson, 'Treaties in British Colonial Policy: Precedents for Waitangi', in William Renwick, ed., *Sovereignty and Indigenous Rights: The Treaty of Waitangi in International Contexts* (Wellington, 1991), pp. 15–29.

[6] P. G. McHugh, 'The Lawyer's Concept of Sovereignty, the Treaty of Waitangi, and a Legal History of New Zealand', in ibid., p. 182.

accompanied by Hobson's optimistic remark, 'He iwi tahi tatou': we are now one people. Copies of the Treaty were subsequently taken to Maori tribes around the country for negotiation and signatures. Some tribes readily assented; others, such as Tuwharetoa, were never Treaty signatories. In the end the Treaty facilitated annexation, but control over the South Island was declared on the basis of discovery and the definitive step was taken by the gazetting of annexation in London on 2 October 1840.

The Treaty made promises and gave guarantees to Maori which the Colonial Office neither fully understood nor was strong enough to honour. James Stephen, Permanent Under-Secretary at the Colonial Office, soon came to believe that whatever safeguards he tried to ensure or whatever benefits colonization might bring, the end result would be disastrous to Maori. By December 1846 Earl Grey was stating that, although injustices must be avoided, any acknowledgement of Maori right to ownership of uncultivated land must be regarded 'as a vain and unfounded scruple'.[7] Maori were rapidly disillusioned with British observance of the Treaty, Hone Heke expressing his frustration and anger by axing the flagpole at Kororareka twice and sacking the small town. Actions of non-signatories raised the issue of whether they were bound by annexation and British law. In 1842 Taraia, a non-signatory chief of Ngati Tama-Te-Ra in the Coromandel, attacked enemies on the east coast, killed and reportedly ate some, and took others captive. When Hobson sent officers to investigate and negotiate a settlement, Taraia challenged their right to interfere, sparking a debate over the parameters of government authority. The Colonial Office considered that all Maori were British subjects, although a blind eye could be turned to the practice of most traditional customs in inter-tribal relations.

At this stage Maori were in a majority and had military superiority, shown dramatically in the Wairau valley in 1843. Twenty-two Europeans, attempting to arrest Maori resisting the survey of disputed land, were killed. Robert FitzRoy, Governor 1843–45, with few forces at his command, decided that the settlers were wrong and refused to retaliate. When military action was attempted, as at Ohaea-wai in the north in 1845, it was a débâcle. Both Hobson and FitzRoy tried to assert authority instead by a policy of moral suasion, exercised through a Native Pro-tector, who was also a land-purchase officer. A Commissioner, William Spain, was appointed to investigate the pre-Waitangi land purchases and much of the land, especially in New Zealand Company claims, was returned to Maori. FitzRoy, critically short of funds, then tried to placate Maori, discontented at restrictions on land dealings, and settlers by waiving the Crown right of pre-emption.

---

[7] Minute, 23 Dec. 1846, cited in W. P. Morrell, *British Colonial Policy in the Age of Peel and Russell* (Oxford, 1930), pp. 315–16.

Reviled by the settlers for his policy of conciliation with Maori and humiliated by the contempt with which Maori treated him, FitzRoy was recalled to England in September 1845. He was replaced by the young, ambitious George Grey. Grey's aim was 'Anglicization', bringing Maori within the settler social and political system, replacing the customs of 'barbarism' with those of 'civilization'. Maori men were to be integrated into the European economy as farmers, traders, and labourers; women were to become useful housewives. Chiefs were to be courted and made the instruments of British authority and children taught to read and write. First, however, Grey, who had an increased military force, had to establish his control. Although it now appears that the victory he claimed in the northern war after Imperial troops captured Ruapekapeka *pa* (fortified settlement), already strategic-ally evacuated by its defenders, was spurious, resistance in the north weakened and Grey gained credit with the Colonial Office and settlers. He had similar propaganda successes in southern North Island in 1846 and 1847. Grey then used the injudicious personal land dealing of the Protector to destroy the Native Protectorate and bring Maori policy, administered by a Native Secretary, under his own control. In pursuit of the amalgamation of the two races, he attempted to introduce British law into Maori tribal areas through the 1846 Resident Magistrates' Courts Ordinance. This provided for the appointment of resident magistrates in tribal districts with powers of summary jurisdiction in cases between Maori and Europeans. In cases between Maori, the resident magistrate and two chiefs constituted a court of arbitration. The success of the system depended on the preceding consultation with local people and the role taken by the chiefs.[8] The courts were backed by an armed police force in which Maori men served under Pakeha officers.

Grey acknowledged Maori claims to tribal land, restored the Crown right of pre-emption, and resumed land purchases. Travelling extensively, he personally negotiated a number of land purchases, often alienating sellers by his manipulative methods. Reserves set aside for Maori, as in the South Island, were usually totally inadequate to their needs.

At the time of the Treaty-signing the European population of New Zealand was not much more than 2,000. The most recent estimates of the 1840 Maori popula-tion are between 70,000 and 90,000.[9] Musket warfare, increasing mortality rates, and declining fertility had taken a heavy toll. The Treaty then became a licence for settlement on a scale undreamt of by Maori. By 1858 the European population, at

---

[8] Alan Ward, *A Show of Justice: Racial 'Amalgamation' in Nineteenth-Century New Zealand* (Auck-land, 1973), pp. 74–86.

[9] Ian Pool, *Te Iwi Maori: A New Zealand Population Past, Present and Projected* (Auckland, 1991), p. 55.

over 59,000 exceeded the Maori population, estimated at about 56,000. The census of 1896 recorded 701,000 Europeans and just over 42,000 Maori. Thus colonialism marginalized Maori and ensured European dominance.

Until 1886 the European population grew mainly from a migration of epic proportions. Powerful motives and a massive logistic effort were needed to overcome the barriers of distance, expense, and uncertainty. Only the gold discoveries of the 1860s attracted a mass of unsponsored migrants. Immigration had to be organized and subsidized, migrants enticed by cheap passages, reduced-price land, and promises of employment and high wages. The New Zealand Company was the first to apply these techniques, later adopted by provincial and central governments.

Wakefield considered that the colonial social structure should reflect that of Britain, with a balanced ratio of men and women and a vertical slice of the home society minus the aristocracy and the lumpenproletariat. The success of his Company in persuading members of gentry families and university-educated lawyers, doctors, and clergymen to purchase land in New Zealand imposed an air of gentility on the colony. One later Governor was fond of describing it as the 'gentleman's colony', indicating his perception of its class and gender composition.[10] Such views masked the rural and working-class origins of the vast majority of migrants who were seeking work, decent wages, security, and an independency for their families. The European settlement of New Zealand was essentially a labour migration from the British Isles, with lesser numbers from Germany, Scandinavia, and other parts of western and southern Europe.

The gendered nature of migration meant that European men outnumbered women until the 1920s. However, New Zealand was always promoted as a colony for women. European settlement coincided with the full flowering of the domestic ideology that emphasized woman's role within the home and community, and her moral influence. No one was more aware of the power of this ideology than Wakefield, who proclaimed that 'A Colony that is not attractive to women, is an unattractive colony'.[11] Propaganda was designed to attract women migrants and women were offered cheap and free passages and domestic work on arrival. Women saw themselves as partners in the colonial enterprise.

The nature of migration and migration flows were determined primarily by economic and secondarily by social factors. Cash-strapped provincial councils tried to recruit migrants in the 1850s and 1860s, but only Otago and Canterbury were successful. Much of their effort was directed at single women to supply the market for domestic servants created by expanding pastoral and gold-mining

---

[10] Fergusson to Carnarvon, 12 March 1874, Carnarvon Papers, Public Record Office, 30/6/39.
[11] E. G. Wakefield, *A View of the Art of Colonization* (London, 1849), p. 156.

communities. In the 1870s central government sponsored large-scale migration of agricultural, construction, and domestic workers as the labour force for railway building, urban, and rural development. But behind the economic considerations there was a perception of the ideal society. Single male migrants were notoriously transient, moving in search of work. They served colonial labour needs but caused deep anxiety about instability and disorder. Government policy favoured the immigration of small family groups and women who would ensure the stability and respectability of the population. Assisted migrants required proof of their good character from employers and clergymen. The unfit, the unstable, and the idle were unwelcome. Stocking the country with sober and thrifty men and women able to work and breed were the priorities.

In 1840 the new settler colony was set up with a system of Crown Colony government, excluding all but an inner circle of male settlers from positions of power and influence in the public arena. Maori, occupied with tribal concerns, land alienation, and economic change, soon recognized their exclusion from this ruling structure and opted for their own institutions. But middle-class male settlers, who saw rule by a Governor and placemen as an affront to their nationality and their manhood, campaigned for inclusion in a familiar system of Westminster-style government.

With British policy moving towards self-government for colonies of settlement, it seemed that British men need not wait long for their rights. Stephen had noted in March 1839 that self-government should be introduced if it could be reconciled 'with allegiance to the Crown, and with the Colony moving in the same political orbit with the parent state—participating that is, in the Commercial, Diplomatic, Belligerant [sic] or Pacific relations of the Parent State'.[12] However, given Maori dominance, the Colonial Office hesitated, reluctant to risk government by a settler minority that might ignore the responsibilities of the Treaty and would certainly be unable to defend itself against any consequences of its policy. Self-government was denied until 1846 when a Liberal government divided the colony into two provinces, each with a Lieutenant-Governor and a bicameral Assembly, sending representatives to a General Assembly with responsibility for matters of common interest. Adult males who could read and write English gained the vote, leaving Maori men, whose literacy was restricted to their own language, unenfranchised. The constitution established a complex form of minority rule. Receiving Grey's advice that it was impractical and would endanger race relations, a more nervous British government suspended its introduction for five years.

Suspension cost Grey the co-operation of many leading settlers. They boycotted his nominated councils and formed Constitutional Associations to agitate for self-

---

[12] Memorandum, 15 March 1839, CO 209/4.

government. A succession of colonial delegates lobbied in London for immediate action but the Imperial government, having bought time to devise a more appropriate structure and to allow Grey and the settlers to consolidate their hold on the country, refused to be pressured.

Between 1846 and 1852 the settler population doubled. Communities sponsored by associations inspired by Wakefield and based on religious affiliation were established in Otago and Canterbury. Their leaders included able advocates of self-government. Grey's increasingly optimistic despatches on race relations also implied that self-government could safely be introduced in 1852. The new Constitution Act, building on the 1846 proposals and adopting suggestions from Grey and the colonists, created six provinces based on the settler towns, each administered by an elected superintendent and a council, and a bicameral General Assembly. A liberal franchise gave the vote to adult males who owned or rented property. There were no racial distinctions, but only Maori holding land according to English tenurial conditions could vote. Although the General Assembly controlled most internal matters, including disposal of wasteland, legislation required the Crown's assent, and external and Maori policy and land purchase were reserved to the British government and the Governor. In 1857 an Amending Act made it clear that the colony had the power to change the constitution.

The colony had a quasi-federal system—'a most Brobdingnagian Government for a series of Lilliputian States', as one British politician complained—but the weight of power was intended to lie with the central government. Regional strength and needs ensured a contest. Provincial councils, meeting before the General Assembly, adopted extensive powers over land and development. A couple of years later the land revenue was localized, giving a strong financial base to the South Island provinces, where the government had rapidly and ruthlessly purchased huge blocks of land. The North Island provinces struggled on with a growing sense of grievance and an increasing reliance on central government for support.

The Constitution Act did not provide any clear indication of responsibility in the new order. Grey left the colony in December 1853 and an inexperienced administrator, Wynyard, opened the first session of Parliament and confronted demands for a ministry. Wynyard's creation, a hybrid of officials and elected members, caused a political storm, quietened only by Colonial Office instructions that the leader with a majority in the House should form the government. In 1856 the member for Christchurch, Henry Sewell, led the first responsible ministry. Defeated in the House within a month, he was followed even more briefly by William Fox, then by the centralist Nelson landowner, Edward Stafford. Fox and Stafford dominated politics for the next fifteen years.

From 1854 the high ground of politics was occupied by the men in Parliament and the male voters who elected them. They saw their responsibility as the creation of an environment in which settler society could develop and prosper. The preconditions for the fulfilment of this aim were the displacement of Maori from land viewed as unproductive, its clearing and cultivation by European farming families, the development of internal transport and communication with the outside world, and a stable social order. The tenuous European hold on the country was to be converted into a permanent occupancy.

In 1851 Grey expressed the view that the 'process of the incorporation of the native population into the European settlements has . . . for the last few years been taking place with a rapidity unexampled in history'.[13] However, although Maori agriculture was thriving, Grey had not advanced genuine understanding between Maori and *Pakeha* (foreigner, expecially white settlers), nor brought Maori into government. Resentment against increased European settlement and loss of land was about to take an organized, supra-tribal form. In 1853 and 1854 *hui* (meetings) round the North Island discussed land sales, a union of tribes, and a Maori Assembly similar to the European Assembly. At Taupo in 1856 it was proposed that Potatau Te Wherowhero, a leading Waikato chief, become the Maori King. Two years later he was installed at Ngaruawahia.

The King Movement was an attempt by Maori tribes—mostly from the central North Island—to reassert chiefly mana, control over their lands and people, and to unite in resistance to further land sales. Although not all the tribes joined the federation, most shared its aims. As a forum expressing Maori claims to auto-nomy, the King Movement was seen by many Europeans as a fundamental challenge to the assumption that sovereignty over the country had passed into British hands. What to do about the King Movement became a major question for the Governor and ministers.

Before this issue was confronted a crisis was reached in Taranaki, where, although the context was sovereignty and control, the immediate cause was land. Visiting Taranaki in 1859, Governor Thomas Gore Browne was offered land at Waitara, an area coveted by settlers, by a minor chief. After a cursory investiga-tion of the ownership and overriding the objections of the important chief, Wiremu Kingi, Browne ordered payment for the land and a survey. When the survey pegs were removed by Kingi's people, Browne declared martial law, and on 5 March 1860 troops occupied the Waitara. For nearly a year Taranaki was a war zone. Neither side emerged with a clear victory, but a sort of truce existed in which the British held Waitara and Maori regained Tataraimaka, previously in European possession.

---

[13] Grey to Colonial Office, 30 Aug. 1851, CO 209/93.

Maori resistance in Taranaki indicated the strength of the challenge to settler and British authority. It is possible that if Browne had remained in office he would have immediately moved against the Kingites. But his fate was similar to FitzRoy's. Failure brought dismissal and Grey was reappointed to resolve the situation.

Grey was an austere, rigid man, determined to control a deteriorating situation. At first he responded to a call from an assembly of chiefs at Kohimarama in 1860 for involvement in lawmaking and administration. He supported the establishment of local *runanga* (councils) with powers to make by-laws and special mixed courts to enforce the law. Given a stable situation the *runanga* might have worked, but the situation was far from stable. A bungled attempt to exchange the Waitara for Tataraimaka led to renewed fighting, although another lengthy Taranaki war was averted. And the King Movement was gathering strength and feeding settler paranoia. Grey visited the Waikato in January 1863 and tried to persuade moderate factions to give up the King; by mid-1863 rumours of imminent attacks kept Auckland in a state of perpetual excitement. Grey secured extra Imperial troops, improved the roads into the Waikato, and on 9 July 1863 Maori living between the Waikato and Auckland were asked to swear an oath of allegiance to the Queen and to surrender their arms. Three days later troops entered the King's territory and within a week had fought the first action of the Waikato war. Fighting continued into the next year, with a series of battles in which Maori defended from near-impregnable *pa* sites in the Waikato and on the east coast. Finally the numerically stronger Imperial and colonial forces, in some cases aided by *kupapa* (friendly Maori), achieved a limited victory. The Kingites, severely weakened by losses of fighting men and declining stocks of food and ammunition, ended armed resistance and retreated behind an *aukati* (boundary) line.

During the wars the Imperial and colonial governments clashed over responsibility and the participation of British troops. As long as the Governor was responsible for Maori policy, the British government accepted a duty to defend the settlers and pay for the war. Yet the wars coincided with the withdrawal of British troops from around the Empire and attempts to shift internal defence and policy-making to colonial governments. New Zealand governments vacillated, wanting control yet afraid of it; eager to avoid paying for war but anxious to exploit any gains. Finally, in 1864 a ministry led by Frederick Weld accepted the necessity for self-reliance.

Except for one regiment, Imperial troops were withdrawn from New Zealand in 1865–66, but the fighting was not over. On the east and west coasts of the North Island, Te Kooti and Titokowaru, combining spiritual with military leadership, mounted guerilla struggles. They used tiny forces and an intimate knowledge of the land and bush to devastating effect, thwarting the colonial militia time after time. Eventually, in 1869 Titokowaru lost his support, his leadership undermined by breaches of Maori propriety, and Te Kooti evaded capture by moving into the King Country which remained closed to Europeans.

The wars of the 1860s determined the question of sovereignty for the settlers, but not for Maori. The settler Parliament saw Maori in arms as rebels, justifying the confiscation of some 3.25 million acres of land in the Waikato, Taranaki, and on the east coast. This land-grab, eagerly advocated by Auckland speculator-politicians, has been described as the 'worst injustice ever perpetrated by a New Zealand government'.[14] Although about half the land was subsequently returned or paid for, the loss remained a major grievance to the tribes, to be addressed by periodic commissions, the latest being the Waitangi Tribunal in the 1990s. Thousands more acres passed into European ownership through the agency of the Maori Land Court established in the 1860s. The Court provided a process for certifying titles to Maori land, thus making it easier to sell and purchase. The 1865 Land Act stipulated a maximum of ten names on a title deed but in 1873 this was amended to require the listing and consent of all owners to the sale or lease of land. By 1892 Maori retained under 11 million acres as communal property, mostly in isolated areas of the North Island and nearly a quarter of it leased to Europeans.

In the aftermath of the wars Maori followed strategies of resistance, separation, and accommodation. Resistance often centred on a spiritual leader or prophet such as Te Kooti, Te Whiti, or later Rua Kenana, all figures in a tradition of visionary Maori leaders. Both Te Kooti, the spiritual founder of Ringatu, and Tawhiao, the second Maori King, who started the Tariao sect in 1875, borrowed from Pai Marire, a scriptural religion founded by Te Ua Haumene Tuwhakaro in Taranaki in 1862, with adaptations to the post-war situation of their people. Te Whiti founded the village of Parihaka on confiscated land in South Taranaki and preached passive resistance. Parihaka became a well-organized centre for Maori from a number of tribes and Te Whiti's monthly meetings attracted large crowds. However, eventually the government determined to take possession of the land, countered the resistance with arrests, and in 1881 imprisoned the Parihaka leaders and destroyed most of the village. The followers of Hipa Te Maiharoa who reoccupied ancestral lands in North Otago were also forcibly removed. After the wars the Kingite Maori organized their own political and social life behind the aukati line. Pakeha needed permission to cross the aukati until 1883, although Maori living near the boundary traded freely over it.

Some Maori participated in settler politics. In 1867 Parliament created four Maori seats in the Lower House. Donald McLean, former land-purchase Commis-

---

[14] Keith Sinclair, *A History of New Zealand* (Harmondsworth, 1959), p. 140.

sioner and later Native Minister, argued that the seats would help Maori 'feel they have a voice in the management of public affairs'.[15] Maori members, and those appointed to the Upper House, must often have doubted this as they became pawns in political games and failed to prevent legislation contrary to Maori interests. Repeated requests for extra seats, based either on population or tribal affiliation, were ignored. An alternative political strategy kept alive the spirit of the Treaty of Waitangi. Through *hui* and *komiti* Maori developed the idea of a separate Maori Parliament and a special relationship with the Crown. In the 1880s two Maori delegations, from Ngapuhi in 1882 and from Waikato, including the Maori King, in 1884, visited England to appeal to the Crown to investigate grievances under the Treaty and recognize a Maori Parliament. The Aborigines' Protection Society was friendly, but officially Britain refused to interfere in the colony's internal affairs. Disappointed with these responses, Maori leaders promoted a unity movement. A commitment to *kotahitanga* (unity) was forged at meetings in the late 1880s and the first full session of the Maori Parliament was held at Waipatu in June 1892. It continued to meet, without the Kingites who had their own council, for eleven years. A few younger Maori formed the Young Maori Party to reform social and economic conditions. The census of 1896 was the last to record a declining Maori population.

The last Imperial troops left New Zealand in 1870, after years of recriminatory negotiations between the two governments. The settler Parliament was split over the significance of withdrawal for future relations with Britain. Was this the beginning of separation from the Empire? Was it the ultimate triumph for Little England? Should New Zealand focus on becoming an independent nation state? Would it be better off joining the United States? Independence, separation, nationalism, Imperial federation, as immediate options and future policy, were discussed intensely. The settlers' need to extend and consolidate their territorial gains and to develop a sustainable economy, largely determined the outcome.

The New Zealand economy in 1870 was small-scale, regional, geared to the export of primary produce and importing most manufactured goods. Colonization had been premissed on the development of an agricultural economy. Wakefield rejected the large-scale pastoral farming of New South Wales and mapped out a future in arable farming. Intensive farming worked in some places—Nelson, for instance—but the domestic market was so small and labour so limited that whenever land and capital were available, pastoral farming was preferred. James FitzGerald stated this baldly in 1851 when he wrote, 'the only way to make money here is by sheep farming. Money may be literally coined in that trade. And it is eminently the profession of a gentleman. The sheep farmer may have his comfort-

---

[15] *New Zealand Parliamentary Debates*, I, pt. 1, 1867, p. 457.

able house and gardens and a little farm producing all he requires, but his personal task is to ride about the country inspecting his vast flocks and giving directions for their management.'[16] While he understated the effort required to build a successful sheep station, FitzGerald was right about the potential profits from the industry. Wool was the major export throughout the nineteenth century, rivalled only by gold in the 1860s.

New Zealand's gold rushes followed those of California and Victoria and boosted incomes and population. Most of the gold was in the South Island, also the main pastoral region. The South, consequently, had a very different history from the North Island. Southern politicians, irritated by the way northern problems dominated the political agenda and drained the economy, occasionally floated the idea of separation. But despite the greater European population of the South and their access to resources, a separate destiny would have been difficult.

In 1870, facing the prospect of standing alone, fully responsible for domestic policy, the government decided to take decisive steps to shape the economic future. The 'sacred fires of colonization' as William Fox, Premier from 1869 to 1872, referred to European settlement, were to be rekindled through the agency of the state as the sponsor of migration, land purchaser, railway promoter, and road-builder. New Zealand would take advantage of new sea routes and technologies such as the telegraph to improve communications with Australia, the United States, and Great Britain. Farming families would be assisted to take up land and markets would be sought for New Zealand products. In 1870 Julius Vogel, the Treasurer, announced that the country would borrow overseas to finance this policy.

Between 1870 and 1914 central government policy was designed to create a modern state, with a balanced population structure, the infrastructure for a primary producing and trading economy, a streamlined political system, and the administrative and social institutions necessary for a maturing society. Such a state, it was believed, would fulfil the vision for a European polity in the South Pacific. It would enable settlers and their children to put conflict behind them and validate the experience of colonization. Maori figured little in these policies.

In 1874 Parliament agreed to abolish the old provincial councils and governments in the North Island. By 1876 they had gone throughout the country. The councils had effectively sustained regional rivalries at a national level and interfered with central government planning. The old institutions, weakened by the intrusions of central government into settlement and economic development,

---

[16] Quoted in G. C. Hensley, 'Land Policy and the Runholders, 1853–7', in W. J. Gardner, ed., *A History of Canterbury*, 2 vols. (Christchurch, 1971), II, p. 32.

nevertheless resisted and regionalism remained a factor in politics. Borough, city, and county councils; road, education, and hospital and charitable aid boards were eventually established to carry out the specialized functions of local government. Politics became more democratic. In 1879 manhood suffrage was added to the existing property qualifications for voting and triennial Parliaments were introduced. During these debates Parliament considered a proposal to enfranchise women. Women's suffrage had been raised, pseudonymously, by Mary Anne Müller in *An Appeal to the Men of New Zealand* in 1869. Her call was taken up by political reformers, influenced by John Stuart Mill, but although legislation could occasionally command a majority in the House, a conservative adherence to the dogma of separate spheres sapped the will of government to pass this reform.

Government sponsored and prosperity-driven immigration helped double the European population in the 1870s. Surveyors, contractors, and labourers cut and dug their way across the countryside, removing the primeval forest and covering the land with roads and railways. The government was itself a contractor and promoter and encouraged business and enterprise, in some cases bailing out companies that failed.

The colony began to look to its relationships with offshore states. Links with the Australian colonies became important in the 1870s and 1880s as joint interests in shipping, cables, and defence emerged. There had always been an interchange of labour across the Tasman; politicians now participated in intergovernment negotiations and conferences. Preferential tariffs among the colonies were finally agreed to by a reluctant British government. An attempt to establish trade and diplomatic links with the United States, however, encountered American protectionism and British disapproval.

The British outreach of the first half of the century had encompassed the islands of Polynesia in addition to New Zealand. Missionaries from the London Missionary Society, the Church Missionary Society, and the Wesleyan Methodist Missionary Society were working in Tahiti, Tonga, and Samoa by the 1830s and in the Cook Islands (Map 24.2) from the 1840s. Complex political arrangements in the Hawaiian, Tahitian, and Tongan groups resolved themselves over time into kingdoms, often with successful rulers using Christianity as one of the mechanisms for consolidating their power. The Samoan Islands, where there was a strong tradition of local village control, did not produce a monarchy, but powerful families disputed dominance. Trade was well established by the 1840s with European exploitation of sandalwood, bêche-de-mer (sea-slug), coconut oil, pearls, and pearl shell.

British policy, established in 1845, was to ensure that its influence in the region was as great as any other foreign power and to strengthen the authority of indigenous rulers. Consuls were appointed in most Island groups to protect

British interests and cultivate local leaders. But the settlement of New Zealand created a new frontier with territorial ambitions of its own. From the 1840s a succession of political leaders and church- and businessmen saw the islands of the Pacific as their empire.

New Zealand interest in the Pacific grew from Bishop Selwyn's Melanesian mission in the 1840s and Grey's attempts to keep the French out of the region. For three decades the Pacific mission, although low-key in practice, was a marked feature of the rhetoric about the nation's future. Then from the 1870s, as French, German, and American interest in the Pacific escalated, politicians such as Vogel, Grey, Robert Stout, and Richard Seddon intensified pressure on Great Britain to annex Island groups.

Few of the islands of Polynesia were exempt from imperialistic New Zealanders. Persistent requests were made for Britain to annex Samoa, the Kermadecs, Tonga, the Cook Islands, and Rapa. In Melanesia offers were out on Fiji and concern was expressed over French interest in New Caledonia and the New Hebrides. Constrained by colonial status from acting on their own behalf, the annexationists attempted to influence British policy. In the early 1870s Vogel supported Auckland financiers and businessmen who dominated trade with the Islands. He believed that the flag would follow trade and hoped that government-guaranteed companies and steamer lines would be profitable to New Zealand and force British action. He offered to administer Fiji on Britain's behalf and to take over Samoa. An irritated Lord Kimberley supposed that the 'N. Zealand Govt. would have thought it as well first to get possession of the whole of *New Zealand* before undertaking to govern other territories. They will have enough to do in New Zealand for years to come without embarking on these Quixotic schemes.'[17] Grey, when Premier in 1879, told an eager audience that they were 'the proper future rulers and governors' of the Pacific.[18] In 1883 he shepherded through Parliament a Confederation and Annexation Act inviting Island requests to federate with the colony. Vogel argued in 1880 that New Zealand could not escape 'the responsibilities entailed upon [it] by geographical and natural laws'.[19] Pacific trade and defence should be in British hands, administered through New Zealand. He argued, less convincingly, that affinity between Maori and Pacific islanders and the New Zealand government's experience with Polynesians fitted it to rule. In 1884 and 1885, when rival dynastic factions began to war in Samoa, the Stout government instructed a steamer to stand by to intervene until warned off by the Colonial Office. When Britain finally decided to declare a Protectorate over the

---

[17] Minute, 28 Dec. 1873 on Fergusson to Colonial Secretary, 22 Oct. 1873, CO 209/230.

[18] *Otago Daily Times*, 1 Sept. 1879, cited in Angus Ross, *New Zealand Aspirations in the Pacific in the Nineteenth Century* (Oxford, 1964), p. 131.

[19] Vogel to Hall, 27 Jan. 1880, *Appendices to the Journals of the House of Representatives* (1880), A–8.

Cook Islands in 1888 New Zealand promptly found the salary for a Resident. And in 1899, when Samoan factions were again embattled, Seddon offered both troops and the government steamer.

On occasion Australia and New Zealand co-operated over Pacific issues at home and through their representatives in London. Their constant lobbying had some impact on Britain's freedom of action. In 1886 New Zealand and Australian defence of their mission interests in the New Hebrides forced Britain to compromise with the French. Settlement colonies with imperial ambitions could prove to be inconvenient. They could not, however, prevent the European powers and the United States from carving up the Pacific according to their own strategic agendas, although before the First World War British acquisitions in Polynesia were limited.

During the 1870s New Zealand strengthened its economic relations with Britain. Development was largely financed by British investment. The Vogel migrants were recruited mainly from the villages and cities of Britain. British manufacturers supplied the tracks and rolling stock for the railways, machinery for the farming sector, and most requirements of the expanding consumer market. Whereas in the 1860s imports came almost equally from Australia and Britain, by the mid-1870s two-thirds came from Britain. Exports increasingly went directly to Britain: in 1877 84 per cent of exports, in the main wool, were destined for the United Kingdom. Business, land companies, and farmers relied on funds channelled through banks, stock and station agents, and finance companies with British connections, some, such as the National Bank, being entirely owned in Britain.

The linkages between the two economies came under strain from the mid-1870s when the government, nervous about growing public debt, started to retrench. Private investors and developers responded with a frenzy of land buying. In 1879 the collapse of the Bank of Glasgow heralded a withdrawal from colonial investment and falling prices for agricultural exports. New Zealand, so dependent on the depressed British economy, faced a long period of low returns, declining investment, and unemployment. Treasurers, notably Harry Atkinson from 1879 to 1884 and 1887 to 1891, were driven in search of new policies to ease the financial pressures. Atkinson tried a property tax and protective tariffs, but basically the country had to await the return of prosperity to its overseas markets.

The hard times of the 1880s thwarted hopes for economic progress and revealed social problems of a kind and on a scale that settlers had thought New Zealand would avoid. These were the structural problems of a developing society, exacerbated by recession—the elderly unable to support themselves, single women bringing up families in poverty, unemployed men tramping the countryside, deteriorating work conditions, neglected children, and rebellious youths taking over the streets. They were largely urban problems in a society that still placed a premium on rural virtues. Divisions from within combined with economic difficulties to fracture the hope of creating a southern utopia.

When the men of the country cast their votes in the general election at the end of 1890 they registered a shift in public opinion, not obvious at the time, but which in retrospect marked a new political era. The ascendancy of the Liberals, who won a majority in the election and took office under the leadership of John Ballance in January 1891, lasted until 1912. More than anything else the Liberals were characterized by a will to respond to the demands of a wider constituency than their predecessors had listened to. Populist and progressive, the Liberals had a vision of New Zealand as the most advanced nation of the Empire, able, because of its newness, size, and natural advantages, to move ahead of the Old World. Their goal was to restore faith in the original migrant dream. It was supported by the return of higher agricultural prices from 1895 and capitalization on refrigeration which enabled frozen meat and dairy produce to be shipped to an apparently limitless market in Britain. The Liberals, who came to power on a policy opposed to overseas borrowing, soon returned to the money markets to raise funds for government investment in land and agriculture.

A major part of the Liberal vision related to land ownership and distribution. The notion that there was a 'land-hunger' in the towns and cities had become a staple of reform rhetoric in the 1880s. Large pastoral farms were portrayed as blocking economic progress and access to the land by new generations of aspiring farmers. Earlier governments had experimented with village settlements, various forms of leasehold, and cheap money for land purchase. Ballance, a prominent land reformer and a strong supporter of taxing the unearned increment, and other Liberals were determined to deal with land issues more effectively. During the 1890 election they had repeatedly referred to 'bursting up the great estates'; achieving a more equitable pattern of landholding among Europeans became a major policy through to the First World War. Under Ballance and the Minister of Lands, John McKenzie, a graduated land tax was imposed, the Land Act of 1892 introduced a variety of leases on Crown land, and under the Lands for Settlement Act 1.3 million acres previously held in large estates were bought by the government. McKenzie also resumed purchase of Maori land in the North Island, the government buying 3.1 million acres between 1891 and 1911.

The problems of labour were tackled by William Pember Reeves, first Minister of Labour, whose legislation governed working conditions in factories and shops and, most significantly, set up a system of industrial conciliation and arbitration. Reeves aimed to harmonize labour and capital by empowering the labour movement whose weakness had been demonstrated in the 1890 maritime strike. Industrial conciliation and arbitration were initially effective, expanding a union movement of about 20,000 members in 1889–90, but which had plummeted after the strike, to about 50,000 by 1908. The conciliation and arbitration framework also contained strike action until 1908 when miners, waterside workers, and seamen moved outside its constraints to form the Federation of Labour. Industrial conflict returned to the country.

Democracy made further advances. In 1893, after an eight-year campaign directed by Kate Sheppard, the suffrage superintendent of the Women's Christian Temperance Union, women's suffrage easily passed the House of Representatives but was expected to be lost in the Legislative Council. The majority of two in favour of the bill was something of a surprise to the government, led, since the recent death of Ballance, by Richard Seddon. It meant that both men and women were to vote in the forthcoming election, a prospect Seddon, needlessly as it turned out, feared. The legislation enfranchised Maori and European women on the same basis as men of their own race. The suffragists had argued from the enlightenment view that a just society could not deny the vote on the grounds of sex and from the reform tradition that women's suffrage would bring political and social progress. Women were not given the right to enter Parliament (this came in 1919), but, on the grounds that women's status was an indicator of social progress, women's suffrage played a powerful role in the construction of the country as a progressive and civilized nation. The actual changes were less obvious: some social legislation and an increase in the political power of women's organizations, rather than a major shift in gender relations.

Whereas before 1891 politics had been largely parliamentary, political leaders stitching together coalitions of regional factions, interest groups, and individuals whose fads and ambitions could be indulged, the Liberals created a modern political party, linked to the electorate and with a cohesive organization. The Opposition, which did not even take a party name until it became Reform in 1911, was almost annihilated. This undoubtedly helped the Liberals remain in power, but their legislation attracted the most attention. In addition to the measures already mentioned, they introduced old-age pensions in 1898 and enacted legislation for child protection and equal divorce. Politicians prided themselves on having outstripped the Old World in their reforming zeal, a feeling reinforced by the enthusiastic verdicts of 'progressive' overseas visitors.

The Liberal period consolidated several trends in New Zealand development. It was a period when many implicit and explicit decisions about the future were made. A growing conviction about the country's uniqueness meant that it did not join the Australian colonies when they federated in 1901. The maturing of a native-born generation led to self-conscious attempts to express a new identity in Native Associations, nationalistic literary journals, and through competition in sport. Few seemed to see this nationalism as in any way contradictory to a continued dependence on British markets and British naval forces or an eager involvement in the South African (Anglo-Boer) War. If asked, most settlers would have seen their exports as helping Britain rather than as creating a dependency. Protection was regarded as a right, although from the Russian scares of the late 1870s and the Australasian Naval Agreement of 1887, New Zealand had contributed to its defence. Nor was the notion of a distinct New Zealand people seen as contradicting support for Imperial federation, which was perceived as a way of New Zealand influencing foreign policy not at all at odds with the emergence of a nation state at home. A strident Imperialism and the presentation of New Zealand as a social laboratory for the new century were both attempts by a settler society to convince themselves and others that they had secured a home and an identity yet remained part of an important global community. Dissenting voices, among Maori who were still resistant to the process of assimilation, the labour movement, and to a lesser degree among women, were as yet low murmurs, heard but rarely listened to.

Select Bibliography

PETER ADAMS, *Fatal Necessity: British Intervention in New Zealand, 1830–1847* (Auckland, 1977).

ROLLO ARNOLD, *The Farthest Promised Land: English Villagers, New Zealand Immigrants of the 1870s* (Wellington, 1981).

JAMES BELICH, *The New Zealand Wars and the Victorian Interpretation of Racial Conflict* (Auckland, 1986).

—— *Making Peoples: A History of the New Zealanders: From Polynesian Settlement to the End of the Nineteenth Century* (Auckland, 1996).

RAEWYN DALZIEL, *Julius Vogel, Business Politician* (Auckland, 1986).

MILES FAIRBURN, *The Ideal Society and its Enemies: The Foundations of Modern New Zealand Society, 1850–1900* (Auckland, 1989).

PATRICIA GRIMSHAW, *Women's Suffrage in New Zealand* (Auckland, 1972).

DAVID HAMER, *The New Zealand Liberals: The Years of Power, 1891–1912* (Auckland, 1988).

K. R. HOWE, *Where the Waves Fall: A New South Sea Islands History from First Settlement to Colonial Rule* (Sydney, 1984).

CHARLOTTE MACDONALD, *A Woman of Good Character: Single Women as Immigrant Settlers in Nineteenth-Century New Zealand* (Wellington, 1990).

TIMOTHY McIVOR, *The Rainmaker: A Biography of John Ballance, Journalist and Politician, 1839–1893* (Auckland, 1989).

A. H. McLINTOCK, *Crown Colony Government in New Zealand* (Wellington, 1958).

W. H. OLIVER with B. R. WILLIAMS, *The Oxford History of New Zealand* (Oxford and Wellington, 1981); 2nd edn., ed. Geoffrey W. Rice (Auckland, 1992).

CLAUDIA ORANGE, *The Treaty of Waitangi* (Wellington, 1987).

ANGUS ROSS, *New Zealand Aspirations in the Pacific in the Nineteenth Century* (Oxford, 1964).

J. RUTHERFORD, *Sir George Grey K.C.B., 1812–1898: A Study in Colonial Government* (London, 1961).

KEITH SINCLAIR, *A History of New Zealand* (Harmondsworth, 1959).

—— *A Destiny Apart: New Zealand's Search for National Identity* (Wellington, 1986).

R. C. J. STONE, *Makers of Fortune: A Colonial Business Community and its Fall* (Auckland, 1973).

ALAN WARD, *A Show of Justice: Racial 'Amalgamation' in Nineteenth-Century New Zealand* (Auckland, 1973).

26

Southern Africa, 1795–1910

CHRISTOPHER SAUNDERS AND IAIN R. SMITH

During the course of the nineteenth century the growing British presence profoundly shaped South Africa. At the beginning of the century there was no certainty that British rule would continue; by 1900 all of modern South Africa had come under British rule, and British influence had spread far beyond the borders of what, in 1910, became the Union of South Africa. But the extension of British power and influence in the region, although pervasive, was not straightforward. It occurred on many different levels and by no means only as a result of the decisions of policy-makers in London.

Seizing the Cape from the Dutch in 1795, for strategic reasons during the French Revolutionary wars, Britain acquired a vast new possession in which a Dutch-Afrikaans-speaking white minority, of some 20,000, dominated a much larger black population, made up of over 25,000 slaves, 15,000 Khoikhoi, and in the extreme east, a few thousand Bantu-speaking Africans, part of an African population beyond the colony many times larger than the entire colonial population.[1] The processes of colonization and dispossession, which by 1795 had been under way for a century and a half and had decimated the Khoikhoi, were continued and intensified when British rule replaced that of the Dutch East India Company. For Britain not only established a strong military and naval presence on the Cape Peninsula, as the pivot of its South African interests; it also became involved in keeping the peace on the colony's porous and expanding frontiers of white settlement far inland. The struggle between white settlers and African populations for control of the limited well-watered land was marked by recurrent warfare, in which British troops repeatedly intervened to play a crucial role in supporting settlers who were unable on their own to displace African farmers. In the east, British forces helped to clear Ndlambe's Xhosa people from the Zuurveld, west of the Fish River, as early as 1811–12.[2] Throughout the nineteenth century the frontier

---

[1] Cf. Richard Elphick and Hermann Giliomee, eds., *The Shaping of South African Society, 1652–1820* (Cape Town, 1979), p. 360, Table 10.1.

[2] Ben Maclennan, *A Proper Degree of Terror: John Graham and the Cape's Eastern Frontier* (Johannesburg, 1986); Noel Mostert, *Frontiers: The Epic of South Africa's Creation and the Tragedy of the Xhosa*

of white settlement expanded rapidly and forcefully into the South African hinter-land, as the settler population grew and African societies were conquered or incorporated and their land expropriated. Within a few years of the arrival of British rule at the Cape, British missionaries, traders, and travellers were also to be found far beyond, as well as within, the colonial borders. Their presence often paved the way for the future extension of those borders, sometimes decades later.[3]

Only gradually did the full impact of the British presence make itself felt, although the relative efficiency of British administration soon made it more intrusive than Dutch East India Company rule had ever been. The new British rulers began by making few changes to the system of government at the Cape, and used Dutch-Afrikaans collaborators, some of whom gradually became Anglicized. For two decades there was doubt whether Britain would retain the Cape when the Napoleonic Wars in Europe came to an end. In 1803 the Cape was returned to the Dutch, and therefore had to be captured again in 1806, when war resumed in Europe. Finally, however, as a result of the peace settlement in Europe (1814–15), it was decided that the Cape Colony would remain in British hands. Thus, it was not until 1820 that large-scale British settlement began. In that year almost 5,000 British immigrants were settled in the eastern Cape, on land from which the Xhosa had been ejected, to help stabilize and defend that frontier. Immigration from Britain to South Africa during the first half of the nineteenth century lagged behind that to other parts of the Empire, however, and English-speaking whites at the Cape continued to be outnumbered by those who spoke Dutch or Afrikaans.[4] Various attempts were made at mid-century and after to establish a separate, English-dominated, Eastern Cape colony, but they failed, largely because such a colony would not have been able to defend itself in the continuing wars for control of the land with dense African populations along the colonial frontier.[5]

Having decided to retain the Cape, the British began to shape the colony to their own designs. The autocratic rule of Governor Lord Charles Somerset (1814–26) and the arrival of the 1820 settlers intensified that process, which was also assisted

---

People (London, 1992); Clifton C. Crais, *The Making of the Colonial Order: White Supremacy and Black Resistance in the Eastern Cape* (Cambridge, 1992).

[3] In the Tswana case, the first British expedition from the Cape arrived in 1801, missionaries of the London Missionary Society followed a decade later, but British rule was not extended, in part thanks to missionary pressure, until 1885. The role of the missionaries has been well covered, e.g. in Jane Sales, *Mission Stations and the Coloured Communities of the Eastern Cape* (Cape Town, 1975); the work of the traders has been little explored, but cf. R. Beck, 'The Legalisation and Development of Trade on the Cape Frontier, 1817–1830', unpublished Ph.D. dissertation, Indiana 1987.

[4] In 1891 some 35% of whites in the Cape colony were of British origin. Of those, between 25% and 30% lived on the Cape Peninsula: A. Keppel-Jones, *South Africa: A Short History*, 3rd edn. (London, 1963), p. 85. On emigration figures from Britain see p. 47, Table 2.5.

[5] Basil A. le Cordeur, *The Politics of Eastern Cape Separatism, 1820–1854* (Cape Town, 1981).

by the presence of activist missionaries, most notably John Philip of the London Missionary Society. From the mid-1820s the colonial order, inherited from the Dutch East India Company, began to be reshaped in fundamental ways. Reforms in the system of administration, and in social and economic policy, were introduced in part for humanitarian reasons, but also to promote economic development. These reforms both gave the colony an increasingly British character and began to transform what had been essentially a slave-based, white settler society into one in which wage labour was increasingly important.[6] There was never any large-scale plantation slavery at the Cape and the total slave population was small compared to that of, say, Jamaica. During the eighteenth century most white-owned farms had had some slaves, but most had only a handful. In the rural areas, the indigenous Khoikhoi had become part of an underclass of labour, alongside the slaves, as land was appropriated by white farmers. Between 1806 and 1834 the institution of slavery was eroded as the size of the free labour force grew and the Cape became integrated into the world-wide trading system of the British Empire.

Formal discrimination against the Khoikhoi and 'other free persons of colour' was removed by Ordinance 50 of 1828, and in 1834 the slaves at the Cape, along with those elsewhere in the Empire, gained their freedom, but no great change in their socio-economic status.[7] In South Africa the abolition of slavery was thus directly linked to the expansion of British colonial rule and to the more effective and intrusive nature of the government which came with the British takeover. In this case, emancipation stabilized rather than disrupted the rural economy and resulted in some increase in economic production.

From the beginning the British experienced difficulties in ruling so large and complex a colony. Most Cape Dutch-Afrikaners disliked British rule, though only a minority disliked it enough to resist it actively, as at Slagtersnek in the eastern Cape in 1815. Throughout the nineteenth century, however, British immigrants did not assimilate into the Afrikaner population, as earlier French Huguenot and German arrivals had done. They came mostly from urban backgrounds in Britain and, in South Africa, they soon settled in the towns, many of which soon became predominantly English-speaking. They looked to Britain as their mother country and were proud to be part of the British Empire. Cape Dutch-Afrikaners, meanwhile, were descendants of an earlier pattern of emigration from Europe and were mostly farmers. There was little social mixing or intermarriage between

---

[6] Cf. esp. J. B. Peires, 'The British and the Cape, 1814–1834', in Elphick and Giliomee, eds., *The Shaping of South African Society*, 2nd edn. (Middletown, Conn., 1989), pp. 472–511.

[7] Nigel Worden and Clifton C. Crais, eds., *Breaking the Chains: Slavery and its Legacy in the Nineteenth-Century Cape Colony* (Johannesburg, 1994). As elsewhere, the ex-slaves had to serve a four-year period of 'apprenticeship'.

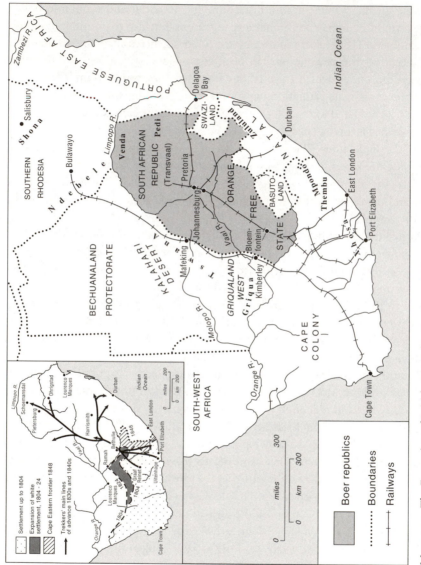

MAP 26.1. The Expansion of British Control in Southern Africa

Map labels

Zambezi R.

Salisbury

Shona

SOUTHERN
RHODESIA

PORTUGUESE EAST AFRICA

Bulawayo

Ndebele

Limpopo R.

Delagoa
Bay

Venda

Pedi

SWAZI-
LAND

Zululand

Durban

SOUTH AFRICAN
REPUBLIC
(Transvaal)

Pretoria

ORANGE

BASUTO-
LAND

NATAL

Mpondo

East London

Johannesburg

FREE

Thembu

Vaal R.

Bloem-
fontein

STATE

Xhosa

Port Elizabeth

BECHUANALAND
PROTECTORATE

KALAHARI DESERT

Mafeking

Tswana

GRIQUALAND
WEST

Griqua

Kimberley

Molopo R.

CAPE
COLONY

SOUTH-WEST
AFRICA

Orange R.

Cape Town

Indian Ocean

Legend

Boer republics

.... Boundaries

+—+—+ Railways

Inset map

Limpopo R.

Schoemansdal

Pietersburg

Ohrigstad

Lourenço
Marques

Vaal R.

Harrismith

Durban

Ramah

Bethulie

1848

Indian
Ocean

East London

Port Elizabeth

Graaf Reinet

Lourenço
Marques

Uitenhage

Orange R.

1804

Cape Town

Settlement up to 1804

Expansion of white
settlement, 1804 - 24

Cape Eastern frontier 1848

Trekkers' main lines
of advance 1830s and 1840s

0   200
0 km 200

0   300
0   km   300

0 miles 300
0   km   300

the two groups, outside Cape Town and a few other towns. The European population in South Africa thus became ethnically divided between Afrikaner and British during the nineteenth century, as happened between French and British in Canada. But whereas in Canada the British settlers soon outnumbered the French, in South Africa the Dutch-Afrikaners always predominated. By the end of the nineteenth century the Dutch-Afrikaner population in the Cape Colony still outnumbered the British by about three to two.

The Expansion of European Settlement

In response to the reforms of the 1820s and 1830s, some 15,000 Afrikaners, mostly from the frontier districts of the eastern Cape, trekked inland away from British rule and in search of new land between 1834 and 1840, on what became known as the Great Trek.[8] Individual pastoral farmers (*trekboers*) had long formed a continuously moving frontier of white settlement into the interior, where they retained no more than a vague allegiance to the Cape Colony. Now, with the mass migration of the Great Trek, the *voortrekkers* sought to break with Britain altogether and to establish their own republics. While there were those in London who wished to wash their hands of these 'emigrants', British governments found it difficult to do so. They acknowledged that instability and warfare in the interior, resulting from the seizure of African land and livestock by the *voortrekkers*, was likely to have repercussions on the Cape Colony itself.

It was with extreme reluctance, however, that British governments followed the Boer trekkers into the interior; and British rule was advanced there only by fits and starts. Imperial Proconsuls, the men on the spot, were often keener to extend British rule in South Africa than were their governments in London; but they did not always get their way. In May 1835, in the course of yet another frontier war, Governor Benjamin D'Urban annexed, as Queen Adelaide Province, the land beyond the existing colonial boundary, between the Fish and the Kei Rivers, the home of the Western Xhosa. When news of this reached London he was instructed to give up the territory: for both humanitarian and financial reasons, the British government did not welcome ruling large numbers of Xhosa. It feared that the area might have to be pacified and held by force.[9]

In 1847 D'Urban's successor, the swashbuckling Sir Harry Smith, used the new powers given him under the vaguely worded High Commission, to act again

---

[8] It was known at the time as the 'emigration' of the frontier farmers. The classic account, not entirely superseded to this day, is Eric Walker, *The Great Trek* (London, 1934). Cf. Timothy Keegan, *Colonial South Africa and the Origins of the Racial Order* (Cape Town, 1996), esp. chap. 6.

[9] John S. Galbraith, *Reluctant Empire: British Policy on the South African Frontier, 1834–54* (Berkeley, 1963), pp. 128–54.

without prior approval from London.[10] In the aftermath of the War of the Axe, another expensive frontier war brought on largely by land-hungry settlers in the eastern Cape, he annexed more land and then succeeded in persuading the government in London that this would help to prevent future wars.[11] By the end of 1850, however, Britain was more deeply involved in war with the Xhosa than ever. When Sir George Grey, Governor and High Commissioner from 1854, wished, in the aftermath of the mass cattle-killing by the Xhosa (1857), to annex more territory, he was strictly forbidden to do so.

Meanwhile, Sir Harry Smith had also acted to extend British rule northwards, from the Orange to the Vaal rivers, through the establishment of the short-lived Orange River Sovereignty (1848–54). Here again, the British government ordered a retreat. By the Sand River (1852) and Bloemfontein (1854) Conventions, Britain recognized the independence of the *voortrekkers* north of the Vaal and Orange rivers respectively, and new Boer republics—the South African Republic (Transvaal) and the Orange Free State—were established beyond British rule. Until the 1880s Britain was the only European power with an interest in the region, and British paramountcy over it did not seem to require the extension of formal British rule in the interior, with all its accompanying costs and liabilities, especially if Britain controlled the coasts.

In 1843 Britain had acquired a second coastal colony in Natal. This had come into being as a short-lived Boer republic, and was annexed by Britain in order to secure Port Natal (Durban) and the coast for British interests and stabilize the area south of the Zulu kingdom. Its previous Boer settlers then moved on, into the Boer republics, and a further 5,000 British immigrants arrived in Natal in the late 1840s and early 1850s to form a new, 'very English' settler élite which dominated a very much larger African population. As in the case of the eastern Cape, their settlement on the land was not a success, and most soon moved into Pietermaritzburg and other urban centres, where they engaged in trade. When a system of representative government was inaugurated in Natal in 1856, the colonists there arranged that it would, in fact, be confined to whites; and the British government failed to block this. Although responsible government was not granted until 1893, the Natal colonists exercised an effective control over their own affairs long before that. Until the end of the 1870s, however, they remained dependent on the British for defence, especially against their powerful northern neighbours, the Zulu.[12]

---

[10] John Benyon, *Proconsul and Paramountcy in South Africa: The High Commission, British Supremacy and the Sub-Continent, 1806–1910* (Pietermaritzburg, 1980); A. Harrington, *Sir Harry Smith: Bungling Hero* (Cape Town, 1980).

[11] Basil le Cordeur and C. C. Saunders, eds., *The War of the Axe, 1847* (Johannesburg, 1981).

[12] A. Duminy and W. Guest, eds., *Natal and Zululand: From Earliest Times to 1910: A New History* (Pietermaritzburg, 1989).

The area of South Africa under European settlement and control doubled between the mid-1830s and the mid-1850s. This greatly expanded territory was now divided between two Afrikaner republics in the interior and two British colonies dominating the coasts. Direct or indirect British influence usually preceded the extension of formal British rule, and continued even when it was removed. The land-locked Boer republics remained dependent on ports in Natal and the Cape Colony and were linked to the British colonies by trade and a network of cultural ties. As elsewhere in those parts of the British Empire where British immigrants had settled, the extension of British rule was accompanied by the practice of devolving administrative responsibilities on to local agents and by the aspiration to unite as much of the region as possible. Ironically, attempts to bring about unification in South Africa would lead British governments into increased involvement in the interior in the last quarter of the nineteenth century. At mid-century, however, the concern to limit formal responsibilities won the day, although British power was exercised repeatedly beyond the formal boundaries of its colonies in South Africa. By the time the British army left the Cape frontier in 1878, it had played a decisive role in defeating both major groups of Xhosa, west and east of the Kei River.[13] The following year it was to play an equally decisive role in Natal in defeating the Zulu.

Within the Cape Colony, liberal ideas introduced from England found a small local constituency among key officials, and it was with such local support that Britain granted a non-racial parliamentary franchise, with a relatively low qualification, in 1853. By the late 1860s the Secretary of State for the Colonies was keen that the Cape become fully self-governing, and take over its own internal defence, but High Commissioner Philip Wodehouse thought responsible government was premature for so relatively poor a colony. By 1872 the new prosperity brought by the expansion of agricultural production and the discovery of diamonds encouraged the British to grant, and the Cape colonists to accept, responsible government. This meant that here too the British government had in effect conceded to the colony's white minority the right to rule as it wished.

Britain's reluctance to acquire new responsibilities in southern Africa was again thwarted in 1868. To prevent the Boers of the Orange Free State absorbing all Moshoeshoe's territory and pushing thousands of Sotho over the Drakensberg on to the Cape frontier, Wodehouse claimed that it was necessary for him to annex Moshoeshoe's largely mountainous kingdom. Moshoeshoe himself was eager to bring his territory and his people under the protection of the British.[14] Once again

[13] Christopher Saunders, 'The Annexation of the Transkeian Territories', *Archives Yearbook for South African History, 1976* (Pretoria, 1978).

[14] Leonard Thompson, *Survival in Two Worlds: Moshoeshoe of Lesotho, 1786–1870* (Oxford, 1975), pp. 297, 301.

the British government was persuaded that British annexation of this territory, which came to be called Basutoland, was but a prelude to its incorporation within an enlarged Cape Colony. When the boundaries of the new acquisition were demarcated in 1869, the map showed that British rule now linked the Cape and Natal, which suggested that the territory between the Drakensberg and the sea, which remained under independent African rule, would in time likewise be brought under British rule and be included in one or other British colony, as Basutoland was in the Cape in 1871. The only possible port on that coast, St John's, was annexed for Britain in 1878, in the aftermath of the last frontier war, but the rest of the Transkeian territories were left for the Cape Colony to take over when it wished to do so. Not all Cape colonists welcomed the prospect of ruling the Transkei's large African population, however, and there was always the risk that the establishment of colonial control would mean further warfare, which the Cape forces would now have to handle on their own. The process of Cape expansion and annexation in this area, therefore, took until 1894 to be completed.[15]

Strategic considerations, concerning the coastal littoral of South Africa, remained of major importance to British governments throughout the nineteenth century, for the Cape sea-route retained its significance long after the opening of the Suez Canal in 1869. The British navy ruled the South African waters, and Britain dominated the external trade of the region in which wool was, until the 1870s, the main export commodity (Fig. 26.1). But compared with the other 'white dominions', South Africa's economic prospects seemed poor and it therefore failed to attract many British immigrants. With the discovery of first diamonds and then gold, South Africa's prospects were to change dramatically, so too would its importance in the minds of those who shaped Imperial policy.

Diamonds and the Failed Attempt at Confederation

Diamonds were found near the confluence of the Orange and Vaal Rivers in 1867. Once it realized the scale of the discovery, the British government was concerned to take over the area in the interests of stability and control. Outmanœuvring the Orange Free State, which also claimed the land, Britain stepped in and annexed Griqualand West (1871).

In the nine years before the Cape agreed to take over this territory, the economy of much of the region was transformed. Almost 25,000 new immigrants, most of them British, arrived from Europe between 1873 and 1883. Tens of thousands of migrant labourers travelled to Kimberley over great distances from the north and east. White and black farmers responded to the demand for increased food

---

[15] Saunders, 'The Annexation of the Transkeian Terrikories', *passim.*

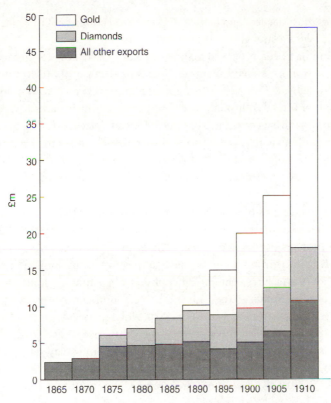

FIGURE 26.1. Exports of South African produce, 1861–1910 (average for five-year period)

Source: Monica Wilson and Leonard Thompson, eds., The *Oxford History of South Africa* (Oxford, 1971), II, p. 18.

production by developing a more commercial agriculture. Imports through Cape Town more than doubled between 1871 and 1875. By 1886 the Cape had spent £14m on the construction of 1,000 miles of railways between its main coastal ports and the interior. Donald Currie's Castle Line joined the older Union Line in 1872 to provide a weekly steamship service from the Cape to England, and telegraph communication was established in 1880.

In the early 1870s the Cape was the largest, richest, and most populous settler state in Southern Africa, with 237,000 whites (more than twice the number in the three other states together) and half a million blacks. The British government looked to the Cape to take the lead in initiating a movement towards uniting South Africa into a British Dominion able to rule and defend itself, on the Canadian model. A unified economy and communications system would encourage foreign investment and development, facilitate the flow of African labour to where it was most needed, and help to dissolve local conflicts of interest. A united South Africa would strengthen Britain's position in the world.

Federation had been proposed before, but Lord Carnarvon, Secretary of State from 1874, was more forceful than his Liberal predecessor, Lord Kimberley, and impatient to achieve in South Africa a confederation similar to the one he had inaugurated in Canada, through direct Imperial action if necessary. When his attempts to organize a conference of South African delegates to discuss a federation were rebuffed, he resolved to bring the Transvaal within the Empire. In Fiji, Malaya, and the Gold Coast of West Africa Britain had intervened to settle local crises in internal government and external relations; in South Africa, British intervention was primarily to further a federal cause.

After the rival claims of Britain and Portugal to the east-coast port at Delagoa Bay (Maputo) were settled in favour of Portugal in 1875, the Transvaal's dream of access to a nearby port outside British control suddenly became a reality. Whilst President T. F. Burgers attempted to raise money for the building of a railway to Delagoa Bay, Carnarvon sent Sir Theophilus Shepstone, a long-time Native Administrator in Natal, to the Transvaal. He found the government there in disarray. An inconclusive war against the Pedi, who retained *de facto* independence in the eastern Transvaal, had bankrupted the Treasury and the government had lost the support of many of the 30,000 burghers. Shepstone played upon their fear of the Zulu, claimed that the Transvaal would not survive as a state without the assistance of the British government, and annexed the country by Proclamation on 12 April 1877.

By then Carnarvon had appointed Sir Bartle Frere as High Commissioner at the Cape. A determined imperialist, who viewed South Africa narrowly in terms of what he conceived to be the interests of the British Empire, Frere sought quick results. Convinced that the power of the Zulu had to be broken, he demanded the disbandment of the Zulu army and then launched the British army, fresh from its success over the Xhosa, into an invasion of Zululand (January 1879). The result was the opposite of what he intended, for the destruction of a British regiment at Isandhlwana ruled out an early confederation. With the despatch of new forces, the British defeated the Zulu at Ulundi and divided Zululand into thirteen separate chiefdoms, and the British army then turned on the Pedi, who were also defeated (1879). Secured for the present from African threats, through the intervention of British troops, the Transvaal Boers were able to take up arms to regain their independence from Britain.

The series of African defeats in the late 1870s may not have brought confederation nearer, but they did mark the end of effective African resistance to the imposition of European rule throughout South Africa. Although many African polities remained independent for a while longer, British troops had ensured that European supremacy in the region was firmly established in the region as a whole.

The Transvaal War (1880–81) and the German Challenge

In the last twenty years of the century conflict between the British and the Boers for supremacy grew in intensity. Far from advancing the cause of federation, the British annexation of the Transvaal provoked an anti-Imperial reaction which helped to destroy it. The British administration established in the Transvaal was tactless, authoritarian, and inadequately funded. Opposition to it was led by the Boer leader Paul Kruger, whose determination to recover and then maintain the independence of his country was the dominating purpose of his life. When he visited London—first to demand a plebiscite and then to deliver petitions which showed that a large majority of Transvaalers opposed the British annexation—he was told that the Transvaal could be self-governing, but only under the sovereignty of the Queen and as part of a South African confederation.

Open rebellion against British rule was postponed pending the result of the British general election in 1880, for in his Midlothian speeches Gladstone had denounced Disraeli's South African policy as contrary to the wishes of the people concerned and the product of a Conservative Party 'drunk with imperialism'. Once in office, however, Gladstone sought to achieve the South African confederation that had eluded Disraeli; and Kimberley, his Secretary of State for the Colonies, was eager to succeed where he had failed previously. Despite warnings from President Brand of the Orange Free State of the growing likelihood of a Transvaal rebellion, and the defeat of a motion proposing federation in the Cape Assembly, Gladstone insisted on the retention of British sovereignty over the Transvaal, thereby provoking the *coup de grâce* to the project of federation. By December 1880 a British Cabinet preoccupied with the Irish question found itself facing a Boer revolt against British rule in the Transvaal.

Having blundered into a war in the Transvaal, Gladstone's government sought to extricate itself through negotiations brokered by Brand, Sir Henry de Villiers (Chief Justice of the Cape Colony), and Sir Hercules Robinson (who had replaced Frere as British High Commissioner in South Africa). Kimberley told the House of Lords that he feared that Britain was in danger of creating another Irish Question in the Transvaal, and of uniting Afrikaners throughout South Africa against Britain. Peace negotiations were already under way when the self-willed Sir George Colley, acting against the spirit of his instructions, made a series of military blunders which culminated in a British defeat at Majuba Hill (27 February 1881). Like the failure to relieve Gordon at Khartoum, this battle came to be regarded as a blot upon the British Imperial record, which Conservatives pointed to as an example of Liberal mismanagement. 'Remember Majuba' was to be the rallying cry when British soldiers again went into action against the Transvaal Boers in 1899. Yet, this humiliating defeat did not deflect Gladstone's government from the negotiated peace on which it was already set. An armistice was declared and peace was agreed by the Convention of Pretoria (March 1881).

This 'second yielding' by the British to Boer separatism was more limited than that of the 1850s, for now the Transvaal was given self-government under British suzerainty with continued British rights of over-rule in specific areas, which included foreign relations and the conduct of 'native affairs'. After his election to the first of four successive terms of office as President, Kruger returned to London and there persuaded Gladstone's government to replace the Pretoria Convention with the London Convention (1884). This restored the name of the South African Republic to the Transvaal, reduced the debt, removed the assertion of British suzerainty, retained British control over foreign relations, and allowed any future expansion of the state only to the north. This Convention was an attempt by the British government to return to a policy of minimal control over what was still a poor, land-locked, and ramshackle republic. It was also a conciliatory move by a British government preoccupied with Egypt, the Sudan, and Ireland, and determined to limit its liabilities in an area of the South African interior of no obvious interest to Britain, at a time when Britain was the only Great Power on the South African scene.

The weakening of the British hold over the Transvaal did not mean that Britain had withdrawn from asserting her paramountcy over South Africa as a whole, or was less concerned to keep other Great Powers out. In 1884, mainly for domestic reasons, Bismarck challenged the 'sort of Munro [sic] doctrine' which Britain had assumed over South Africa.[16] Bismarck's sudden annexation of the coast from the Orange River to the border with Angola as a German protectorate in August 1884 struck at Britain's complacent supremacy, and aroused fears that it might be followed by German claims to areas of the east coast which might give the Transvaal a route to the sea. Further British annexations, including that of Zululand in 1887, were made to prevent that happening. Bechuanaland, which had previously been dismissed as worthless, suddenly took on a new importance as the wedge of territory between German South West Africa and the Transvaal Republic. In January 1885 Sir Charles Warren was despatched with a strong force to establish British control over the region. The area south of the Molopo River was eventually incorporated within the Cape Colony in 1895; the area to the north became a High Commission Territory (Bechuanaland), like Basutoland, which had reverted to

[16] J. Butler, 'The German Factor in Anglo-Transvaal Relations', in Prosser Gifford and Wm. Roger Louis, eds., *Britain and Germany in Africa: Imperial Policy and Colonial Rule* (New Haven, 1967), p. 185.

direct Imperial control in 1884, after the Cape had been unable to suppress a Sotho rebellion there without calling for Imperial assistance.

While the German factor remained important in British considerations to the end of the century, British fears that Germany might exploit her position to become a potential patron of the Transvaal Republic were exaggerated. Considerable German capital was invested in the Transvaal, the concession to develop its railways was granted to a German-Dutch syndicate, and the Kaiser sent a provocative telegram at the time of the Jameson Raid; but although Kruger played the German 'card' from time to time, he had no intention of putting his burghers under German colonial rule. Britain made it clear to the German government that she would not tolerate a German challenge to her supremacy in an area of the world which she regarded as a British sphere of influence. Germany accepted this and, in August 1898, an Anglo-German Agreement was signed by which Germany effectively left to Britain the whole of South Africa.

The Impact of Gold-Mining

The discovery of gold on the Witwatersrand in 1886 dwarfed earlier gold finds in the Transvaal, and by 1898 the Transvaal was the largest single producer of gold in the world, accounting for 27 per cent of total production; by 1914 this had risen to 40 per cent. The development of the Witwatersrand gold-fields was one of the most dramatic examples of late-nineteenth-century capitalist enterprise. Much more capital was invested—£75m by 1899, £125m by 1914—and the technical challenges were greater than had been the case with the gold-mines of Australia or the United States. With the additional discovery of large deposits of coal in the Transvaal and Natal, a 'mineral revolution' occurred which transformed relations between the various South African states and led to the development of by far the most industrialized economy on the African continent. South Africa took on a far greater importance in the eyes of the world as its gold supplies contributed to the underpinning of currencies and international trade during the heyday of the Gold Standard.

Gold-mining depended upon huge numbers of African workers, who came from many different parts of southern Africa, though during the 1890s nearly half of them came from Mozambique. By 1899 the total number of African mine-workers on the Rand had reached 100,000. A large influx of European immigrants (Uitlanders), many of them British, were also attracted to the Rand, which acted as the new magnet for immigrants to South Africa. The total Afrikaner population of the Transvaal still outnumbered the Uitlanders by 1899, though there may have been more Uitlander than Afrikaner male adults. The Uitlanders were no monolithic group but a motley collection of individuals of diverse nationalities, divided by class. Most were birds of passage, drawn to the Transvaal for a few years to make money before returning home, and few were eager to renounce their existing citizenship and take on that of the South African Republic. Most of them lived in and around Johannesburg which, as one of them put it, 'although a town in a foreign state, was enthusiastically British in its sentiments'.[17]

The cultural gap separating the materialistic Uitlanders from the poor, rural, God-fearing Boer population of the Transvaal was immense. Whilst many burghers regarded the Rand as a Sodom and Gomorrah in their midst, Kruger recognized the gold-mining industry as both an asset, able to rescue the Transvaal from its chronic poverty, and a liability, for the sudden influx of so many Uitlanders might threaten not only the Boer way of life but also the political basis of the state. Steps were soon taken to extend the period of residence required for naturalization and eligibility for the franchise from the two years required in 1881; by 1890 it was fixed at fourteen years. The Uitlanders complained about their exclusion from political power, the cost of living, the high rates of taxation, the poor provision of schools, and the inefficiency and corruption of the Transvaal administration. But until 1896 the British government deliberately avoided being drawn into supporting their grievances or those of a mining industry preoccupied with reducing its costs. The mine-owners were particularly critical of the Transvaal government's policy of granting concessions or monopolies in key areas such as dynamite, alcohol, and the railways.

Rhodes, Rhodesia, and the Raid

For a decade Cecil Rhodes played a crucial role in extending British influence in southern Africa. He had long seen immense possibilities in the north, where the acquisition of new territory for Britain might open up a second Rand, provide land for white settlement, and hem in Kruger's Transvaal. Prepared to use the vast wealth he had accumulated on the diamond fields for political ends, Rhodes was eager to promote British interests as local agent of the Crown. In this he had the support of successive British governments and of the Afrikaner Bond which, under Jan Hofmeyr, was able to make or break Cape governments through the giving or withholding of its support. Though sympathetic to the Afrikaners in the interior, the Bond remained loyal to Britain and, with its support, Rhodes became Prime Minister of the Cape Colony in 1890.

Rhodes's drive to open up and establish European settlement north of the Limpopo River was premised on the hope, shared by the British government, that the area which became Southern Rhodesia would join the other white-ruled

---

[17] Maryna Fraser, ed., *Johannesburg Pioneer Journals, 1888–1909* (Cape Town, 1985), p. 58.

states in a united South Africa and ensure a British predominance over the two Boer republics. Rhodes's British South Africa Company (BSAC) was, however, granted a royal charter in 1889 to secure for British and Cape interests not only the area north of the Limpopo, but that north of the Zambezi as well. In 1890–91 a series of conventions demarcated British from German and Portuguese territory in Central Africa.[18] Because of opposition to the BSAC by both missionaries and the African Lakes Company, what became known as Nyasaland (later Malawi) became a separate Protectorate in 1891, not under the BSAC, and what became Northern Rhodesia (later Zambia) was only slowly brought under Company control in the 1890s.

The Pioneer Column, which set out in 1890 from the Cape Colony to occupy what was to become Southern Rhodesia (later Zimbabwe) was a risky enterprise, poorly prepared but well armed, expecting to fight its way into the country of the Ndebele and Shona. An invasion force of latter-day conquistadores in search of land and gold, it expropriated land and cattle wholesale from the African population, whose resistance, when it came (by the Ndebele in 1893–94; by both Ndebele and Shona in 1896–97), was put down with great severity. Rhodes's hope that a 'second Rand' would be discovered north of the Limpopo proved ill-founded, and his venture there consumed rather than added to his wealth. By 1894 it was clear that the future of gold-mining lay in the 'deep levels' of the Witwatersrand then coming into operation. The Transvaal was clearly the key to the future of the entire region.

Rhodes was convinced that the future prosperity and development of South Africa required a political federation of self-governing South African states, under British leadership, within the British Empire. As a first step towards this goal he sought a railway and customs union. This would end the rivalry which had developed between the various states (and especially between Natal and the Cape Colony) as railways were built between the coastal ports and the Rand, and a sizeable portion of state revenues came to depend on customs and freight charges. The Cape controlled 85 per cent of the Rand traffic. The Transvaal Boers, now surrounded by British territory, feared that, between the ambitions of Rhodes and the designs of the British government, even the qualified independence of their country under the London Convention was under threat. When the railway to Delagoa Bay was finally opened in 1895, Kruger attempted to challenge the Transvaal's dependence on the Cape line. The result was the Drifts Crisis, in which the British government backed the Cape government and threatened to use force if Kruger did not give way. When he did, British convictions that he would always back down if firmly challenged were reinforced, and Rhodes was

---

[18] See below, pp. 639–41.

encouraged to proceed with the reckless gamble which was to ruin his career and set Britain and the Transvaal on a collision course.

In 1894 Sir Henry Loch, the High Commissioner, had proposed that an Uitlander uprising on the Rand might be assisted by an armed British expedition from the railhead at Mafeking. This was at once rejected by the Colonial Office, and Loch was recalled, but Rhodes adapted the idea and thereby secured the connivance of Joseph Chamberlain, the forceful and openly imperialist Secretary of State, who came into office under Lord Salisbury's Conservative government in July 1895. The external armed intervention from the Bechuanaland border would not be by British troops operating from British territory but by border police in the employment of the British South Africa Company, operating from a strip of territory along the border which the British government transferred to the Company for the purpose of extending the railway north from Mafeking to Bulawayo. Towards the end of 1895 it was common knowledge that an Uitlander revolt against Kruger's government was being planned in Johannesburg. But those plans began to fall apart before Jameson entered the Transvaal with his raiders, intent on stimulating a revolt there.

The fiasco of the Raid—for both raiders and Uitlander leaders were quickly arrested and imprisoned—shattered the alliance which Rhodes had constructed with the Afrikaner Bond, and polarized opinion throughout South Africa. Many Afrikaners outside the Transvaal felt a new surge of sympathy towards their kinsfolk within it. Rhodes, who had been at the heart of the conspiracy, was forced to resign as Prime Minister of the Cape Colony and, for a while, as a Director of the BSAC (the majority of whose Directors had been ignorant of what he had been up to). Official enquiries in Cape Town and London cleared Chamberlain and other British officials of any complicity in 'Rhodes's plot'. Rhodes accepted responsibility in return for the preservation of the BSAC's charter.

Kruger acted with skill and forbearance, releasing Jameson and his raiders into British custody, and commuting the sentences imposed on the Uitlander conspirators into fines. But Kruger and the Transvaal burghers never doubted that the British government, and Chamberlain in particular, had been behind the plot to overthrow their independence, and their suspicions were confirmed by the rapid rehabilitation of those who had taken part. From 1896, therefore, Kruger's government expected and began to prepare for further assaults on the independence of the Transvaal from 'British' interests within and without the country. The Uitlanders had demonstrated their disloyalty, so political control of the Transvaal state had to be kept out of their hands. The weakness and vulnerability of the Transvaal's defences had been revealed, and so a massive programme of defence works and arms' importation was undertaken in the next three years. By 1899 Boer commandos were equipped with the latest weapons imported from Europe.

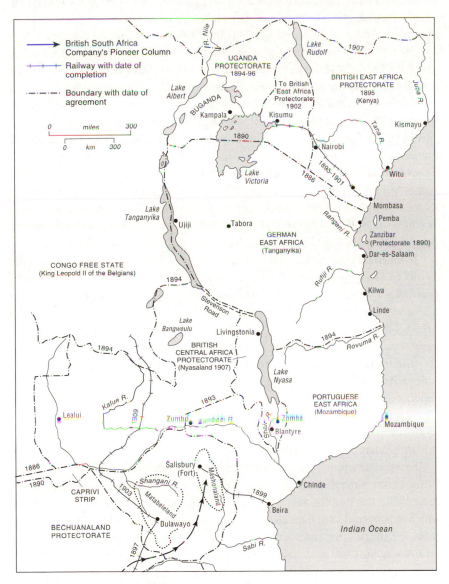

MAP 26.2. The Partition of East and Central Africa

Believing that the Uitlanders outnumbered the Boers in the Transvaal, and produced nine-tenths of its revenue, the British government hoped that their enfranchisement might still enable a peaceful takeover of its government to occur. Kruger was old, and after him a more progressive coalition of forces might come into power and preside over a peaceful transition to a reformed administration and the rectification of Uitlander grievances. This presented the last best means by which the British government could hope to attain its ends without a resort to war; it might also win the support of the British public. From January 1896 Uitlander grievances joined the strict observance of the London Convention as the basis on which the British government asserted its right to intervene in the Transvaal. This encouraged the politically active minority amongst the Uitlanders to unite behind the issue of their grievances and to look to the British government and its representatives in South Africa to press their case for them. During 1896–97 the South African League established itself in the Transvaal as a mouthpiece for the reborn Uitlander political movement. It also became an effective propaganda organization in Britain for educating British public opinion about South African issues and supporting Chamberlain's 'tough' policy towards the Transvaal.

Chamberlain believed that a reassertion of what Rhodes had called 'the imperial factor' in South Africa was necessary if British interests there were to be safe-guarded. In March 1896 his right-hand man, Lord Selborne, raised the question of whether South Africa was going to develop into another United States, outside the British Empire, or into another Canada within it. He saw the Transvaal as 'the natural capital state and centre of South African commercial, social and political life', and the danger to be that, under its republican leadership and dominance, a United States of South Africa might emerge outside the Empire.[19] To prevent this, Britain could no longer rely merely upon intermediaries like Rhodes, the loyalty of the Cape Afrikaners, the reliability of Natal, and the passage of time. The British government itself would have to act to ensure that South Africa did not drift out of British 'guidance' and out of the Empire.

Chamberlain approached the problem posed by the Transvaal with the larger issues of the Empire ever in mind. He saw it as his task to strengthen and consolidate the Empire as a network of trade, influence, and defence without which Britain could not hope to compete with Germany or the United States in the coming century. Since the Suez Canal route to the East could not be guaranteed in time of war, the Cape route remained important, and the docking facilities at Cape Town and the British naval base at Simonstown were used more intensively as the century wore on. The wealth of the Transvaal could benefit the whole region.

---

[19] Selborne Memorandum, 26 March 1896, quoted in Ronald Robinson and John Gallagher with Alice Denny, *Africa and the Victorians: The Official Mind of Imperialism* (London, 1961), pp. 434–37.

Between 1896 and 1898 the British government was preoccupied elsewhere, but a government which was to commit itself to the military reconquest of the Sudan, and to face down the French at Fashoda (1897–98), was not going to see its supremacy challenged in South Africa without a fight. Chamberlain was determined to unite the region and establish British supremacy there on a firmer basis.

The Road to War

The appointment of Sir Alfred Milner as the new High Commissioner in 1897 strengthened the hand of Chamberlain and brought South Africa into new prominence in Imperial considerations. In Milner, Chamberlain found a single-minded imperialist and able collaborator, who saw South Africa as 'the weakest link in the Imperial chain' which he had to prevent snapping by uniting it under white minority rule and British predominance. The re-election of Kruger as President for a fourth term early in 1898, and the failure of the Transvaal government to act on the reforms recommended by its own Industrial Commission for the mining industry, convinced him that a confrontation with Kruger's government was inevitable and that this would result in either a further capitulation to British demands or a resort to war. Since he thought that a war would be short and an annexation of the Transvaal difficult to achieve otherwise, Milner faced the possibility of a war with equanimity. He therefore sought to 'work up to a crisis' utilizing the Uitlander franchise as the issue which would best unite not only the Uitlanders but also British public opinion behind a British intervention. War would provide the opportunity for the Transvaal to be reconstructed and integrated with the rest of South Africa, under British auspices. This would settle the South African problem once and for all.

The British government, however, did not set out in 1897 to conquer and annex the Transvaal as a British colony. Although Milner argued strongly for the strengthening of the British garrison in South Africa, he was at first told to play a waiting game. The Anglo-German Agreement, and the easing of Britain's situation internationally, encouraged Chamberlain to reassert Britain's claim to suzerainty over the Transvaal and support the mining industry in a challenge to Kruger's government over the dynamite monopoly at the beginning of 1899. The mine-magnates, like the majority of the British Cabinet, believed that Kruger would capitulate rather than fight, but by mid-1899 Kruger was convinced that Uitlander grievances, including the franchise, were not the real issue and that the British government would always find further grounds for a quarrel since it was a take-over of the Transvaal itself which it was after. Belated Colonial Office calculations suggested that, even under a generous provision, a continued Afrikaner predominance in the Transvaal Volksraad was likely. When Kruger and Milner finally met, at the Bloemfontein Conference in June, Kruger moved some way to meet Milner's demands, but the conference failed. Chamberlain and the British Cabinet continued to believe that Kruger would capitulate at the eleventh hour. They therefore repeatedly refused to agree to the military preparations urged by the War Office, for fear of jeopardizing a peaceful settlement. Having abandoned hope of a peaceful resolution, Kruger's government prepared for war and hurried to declare it in October whilst the combined forces of the republics outnumbered the British forces in South Africa by four to one.

At least half of the £75 million invested in the Rand gold-fields in 1899 was British capital, and two-thirds of South Africa's trade was with Britain, making the region by far the most important area of economic interest for Britain in Africa. Yet Britain did not go to war because of its existing or future economic stake in the Transvaal, which was not thought to be at risk, but because it feared the political consequences of the growing economic power of the Transvaal for the region as a whole. The Transvaal, in turn, was dependent on the City of London, and this dependency extended into that whole network of financial, shipping, insurance, and technical services (including the refining of South African gold) which London was uniquely well equipped to provide. The difficulty encountered by Kruger's government when it attempted to escape the London network only emphasized the Transvaal's economic dependency. By 1899 German capitalists and traders—like their French, Dutch, and American counterparts—supported the reforms which Britain was determined to impose on the Transvaal. For them, Kruger's control of 'the richest spot on earth' was an anomaly, and they assumed that if Britain took it over a strong, free-trading, and effective administration would be established which would create better conditions for the expansion of trade and increased profits on foreign investment, and unite the region into a more effective whole.

So the British government did not go to war in 1899 to protect British trade or the profits of capitalists in the Transvaal. It was not only there that capitalists suffered at the hands of an inefficient and corrupt government. Political control of the Transvaal was not sought in order to control the gold-mines, nor to secure access to the supply of gold which would continue to flow to London, as the bullion and financial capital of the world, and underpin the Gold Standard whether the Transvaal remained a republic or became a British colony. There is no evidence that anxiety about the gold supply to London was ever a major consideration as war approached. The war was expected to be short and its outcome certain. Transvaal gold formed only a small proportion of the low level of gold reserves which was a deliberate feature of Bank of England policy before, during, and after the war—testimony to the still-awesome strength of the British economy and to the fact that sterling operated as an international currency alongside gold. It was not gold that Britain was after in 1899, but the establishment of British power and influence over the Transvaal on a firmer basis, to advance the unification of the region within the British Empire.[20]

The South African War, 1899–1902

The South African War was the greatest test of British Imperial power since the Indian Mutiny and turned into the most extensive and costly war fought by Britain between the defeat of Napoleon (1815) and the First World War. It cost three times as much as the Crimean War and involved four times as many troops. What the British government expected in 1899 was a short campaign which might involve 75,000 troops, result in—at worst—a few hundred casualties, cost about £10m, and be successfully completed within three to four months. In the event, the war lasted for two years and eight months, cost £230m, involved a total of 450,000 British and Empire troops, and resulted in the deaths of some 22,000 soldiers on the British side, about 34,000 Boer civilians and combatants, and an unknown number of the African population which has been estimated at not less than 14,000. By March 1900 some 200,000 British and Empire troops were involved in a prolonged struggle with Boer commandos who never fielded more than 45,000.

At the outset of the conflict the Boer leaders hoped that, if their forces could advance deep into Natal and the Cape Colony, inflict decisive defeats on the 20,000 or so British troops already in South Africa, and raise a rebellion amongst the Cape Afrikaners against British rule, the British government might choose to negotiate a settlement, as in 1881, rather than despatch a massive expeditionary force—with all the complications this might involve elsewhere in the Empire. But Lord Salisbury's strong government was in no mood to follow in Gladstone's liberal footsteps and was determined that 'the real point to be made good to South Africa is that we, not the Dutch, are Boss'.[21] Despite its belated and inadequate military preparations, once battle was joined the British government became determined on a British victory and the annexation of the republics.

Mahdist, Zulu, Asante, and Afghan wars were no preparation for the sort of war which the British faced in South Africa. The Boers were mobile, resourceful, crack shots, used to life in the saddle, with an intimate knowledge of the country, and equipped with the latest Mauser and Martini-Henry rifles and some heavy artillery imported from Germany. During the first three months of the war they were able to inflict heavy reverses on the British forces, culminating in the Battles of Magersfontein, Stormberg, and Colenso during 'Black Week' in December 1899.

---

[20] Iain R. Smith, *The Origins of the South African War, 1899–1902* (London, 1996), pp. 404–23.

[21] Selborne to Milner, 27 July 1899, in D. George Boyce, ed., *The Crisis of British Power: The Imperial and Naval Papers of the Second Earl of Selborne, 1895–1900* (London, 1990), p. 92.

The British then developed a military operation of quite new dimensions under the fresh command of Lord Roberts. This British 'steam-roller' then advanced, the sieges of Ladysmith and Kimberley were relieved during February 1900, and after a major Boer defeat at Paardeberg, the way was open for the British occupation of Bloemfontein (13 March). After a serious typhoid epidemic, in which far more British soldiers died than were killed in the whole war, British forces advanced on the Transvaal and occupied Johannesburg (31 May) and Pretoria (5 June). Mafeking was relieved in a separate operation, and by September 1900 both the Orange Free State and the Transvaal had been annexed as colonies of the British Crown.

The war then continued as the first of the twentieth century's anti-colonial guerrilla wars. This involved the British army in a scorched-earth policy, the wholesale destruction of Boer farms and livestock (some 30,000 farms were burnt down), and the incarceration of Boer civilians in 'concentration camps' in which some 28,000 died from epidemics amidst overcrowding and maladministration. Since most of these were women and children, these civilian deaths—which far outnumbered the Boer combatants killed in the war and amounted to about 10 per cent of the Boer population of the two republics—cast a long shadow over Boer–British relations after the war was over. In its guerrilla phase the South African War revealed the difficulty and cost to a great power of bringing such a war to an end despite its possession of an army ten times the size of the commandos it was fighting. Only with the development, after March 1901, of Kitchener's gigantic grid of some 8,000 blockhouses and 3,700 miles of wire fencing, guarded by 50,000 troops, were the Boer forces gradually squeezed into increasingly restricted areas. By the beginning of 1902 the war was costing the British government £1.5m a week. This increased its readiness to contemplate a negotiated peace settlement rather than the 'unconditional surrender' which it had demanded in June 1900.

The South African War was an Imperial war in which thousands of volunteers from Canada, Australia, and New Zealand joined British forces in a common Imperial enterprise to conquer and incorporate two of the then world's smallest states as colonies within the British Empire. Although some Irish and other foreigners joined the Boer commandos—and 'pro-Boers' conducted a vociferous campaign in Britain—the war was initially widely supported in Britain itself and the government was returned with a convincing majority at the 'khaki' election in 1900. From the outset it was decided not to include 'coloured' troops from other parts of the Empire in what was regarded as 'a white man's war'. But both sides to the conflict depended upon the African population. Over 100,000 Africans acted as scouts, spies, patrols, transport drivers, messengers, and labourers on the British side. Lord Kitchener (Commander-in-Chief of the British forces, 1900–02) admitted arming over 10,000 but the total was probably closer to the 30,000 which Lloyd George estimated at the time. At the siege of Mafeking Africans fought on the British side, and they died in large numbers in separate 'concentration' and labour camps established for them by the British. For many Africans in Natal and the Cape Colony the war meant a boom in employment opportunities, with better pay and prices paid for agricultural produce, cattle, horses, and services of all kinds by the huge British army at a time when drought, rinderpest, and the closure of the mines had seriously affected the rural areas. In several parts of South Africa, Africans were armed by the British and encouraged to turn their territories into 'no go areas' against the Boers. In other areas, Africans took advantage of the war to extend the areas under their control—the Kgatla and Pedi were notably successful in taking over Boer land and cattle. Unlike the Boers, the British enjoyed widespread support amongst the African population, many of whom looked to a British victory to result in the extension to other parts of South Africa of the civil and franchise rights already existing in the Cape Colony.

Peace-feelers, extended by Kitchener at Middelburg early in 1901, had been refused but in April 1902, after preliminary discussions at Klerksdorp, the Boers agreed to open peace talks and, with British assistance, an assembly of sixty Boer representatives eventually met at Vereeniging in May. After two weeks of discussions, a peace settlement was signed in Pretoria. By fifty-four votes to six, the Boer representatives agreed to the surrender of the independence of the two republics and recognition of the British Crown in return for the promise of eventual self-government and an undertaking, by Article 8 of the Treaty of Vereeniging, that the question of extending the franchise to Africans in the ex-republics would not be decided until after the reintroduction of self-government there. British undertakings with regard to other matters—including an amnesty and economic settlement—were generous by the standards of the time.

Reconstruction and Unification

Now based in the Transvaal, Milner embarked upon the post-war reconstruction of a devastated country, assisted by a group of young Oxford graduates known as his 'Kindergarten'. Since he had always viewed the South African situation in terms of a struggle for supremacy between two rival imperialisms, Boer versus British, Milner brought to bear on his task a racial imperialism which led him to believe that South Africa would never be 'safe' for Britain and her Empire unless the Boer population was outnumbered by white people of British descent, brought about by extensive immigration and settlement—in the rural areas as well as in the towns. He also looked to the introduction of the English language and an English education system in combination with economic growth and modernization to denationalize the Afrikaners and remove the republican threat.

When he left South Africa in 1905 Milner considered that he had failed. His administration, however, helped to establish the infrastructure for the development of the modern South African state, with an effective administration, a commercial agriculture, and an environment favourable to the development of the gold-mining industry. After a slow start gold-mining developed rapidly, assisted by the introduction of Chinese indentured labourers (1904–07) to rectify the chronic shortage of African labour. Although some British soldiers remained behind after the war, Milner's state-sponsored settlement schemes failed to attract extensive European immigration: most British emigrants preferred to go to the better land and more settled conditions in Canada, the United States, or Australia, and few of those who did go to South Africa settled in rural areas. Afrikaner predominance therefore continued in the Transvaal, and both there and in the Orange Free State Milner's Anglicization policy only served to stimulate a new degree of Afrikaner national consciousness and self-assertion which resulted in an Afrikaner political revival after 1904.

The black élite had expected a British victory in the war to usher in a more liberal age, and were now bitterly disappointed. Given the racism of the dominant white minority in the Transvaal and Orange River Colony, the provision in the Treaty of Vereeniging that the question of extending the franchise to blacks there would not be decided until after the reintroduction of self-government in the ex-republics ensured that there would be no such extension. After the war the Boer landlords were encouraged to return to their farms in the ex-republics, and African hopes of land redistribution were dashed. Most blacks now found themselves living under ever harsher rules, more strictly enforced. Even in relatively liberal Cape Town, Africans were forced to live in a location set aside for them in 1901. The 1905 report of the South African Native Affairs Commission, which Milner appointed to set out a 'native policy' for a united South Africa, laid the foundations for the development of South Africa into a racially segregated society during the twentieth century. The basis of this was thus established during the British 'moment' of supreme power in South Africa between 1900 and 1910.[22]

The Liberal Party, which took office in Britain in December 1905, was critical of the way the war had been fought, and soon granted the Transvaal and Orange River Colony not merely representative government, as the preceding Unionist government proposed, but full self-government, only five years after the end of the war. In the elections held in the Transvaal (1907) and Orange River Colony (1908) Afrikaner parties triumphed, and an Afrikaner Bond-led government was returned in the Cape Colony in 1908.

---

[22] See Martin Legassick, 'British Hegemony and the Origins of Segregation in South Africa, 1901–14', in William Beinart and Saul Dubow, eds., *Segregation and Apartheid in Twentieth Century South Africa* (London, 1995).

The Liberals had hoped that a pro-British majority might win the Transvaal election, but the result was not disastrous, for the Generals Louis Botha and Jan Smuts now argued for conciliation between English and Afrikaners, supported the development of the mining industry, and believed in unification as 'the only alternative to Downing Street',[23] and the means to achieve the maximum self-determination within the Empire.

In the making of Union there were two thrusts, one Imperial, the other local to South Africa. Milner arranged a common railway tariff and customs union (1903), and the Kindergarten came to believe that in working for 'Closer Union' in South Africa they were establishing a model for the wider federation of the British Empire. The merits of Union were clearly set out in a document by Lionel Curtis (issued under the name of Lord Selborne, Milner's successor) sent to the various governments of the South African colonies and Southern Rhodesia in January 1907. But the Imperial role in the creation of Union was necessarily a secondary one, for otherwise the Afrikaner politicians would not have gone along with it.

In 1908 the four colonies sent delegates to an all-white National Convention to discuss the terms of Union. The talk by some white Natalians of remaining out of Union came to nothing, when the likely economic implications were realized. In 1909 the draft constitution hammered out at the Convention was sent to Britain to be approved by the British Parliament. The draft provided for a unitary rather than a federal state, for reasons of cost and because Smuts believed the federal system in the United States had encouraged disunity and civil war there, and for a racially exclusive parliamentary system. In a series of meetings in South Africa blacks had rejected the draft constitution, and in particular its colour-bar clauses and its failure to extend the non-racial, class-based franchise to the whole of the proposed Union. In 1909 a delegation of black leaders, led by W. P. Schreiner, former Premier of the Cape, went to London to try to persuade the British Parliament to reject the South Africa Bill in its existing form, but met with no success. The fact that the existing Cape franchise arrangements were to continue and be entrenched in the new constitution against easy repeal was enough for some supporters of the South Africa Bill. The British government regarded the new constitution as a South African product which could not be altered without jeopardizing the entire project for a united South Africa, which had for so long been a goal of British policy. A Union of South Africa within the British Empire, it was believed, represented reconciliation between Boers and British; it would promote economic development, and be in Britain's long-term strategic and economic interests. Increasingly preoccupied with the growing German threat in

---

[23] J. Smuts to J. X. Merriman, 1 August 1907, quoted in W. K. Hancock and Jean van der Poel, *Selections from the Smuts Papers*, 7 vols. (Cambridge, 1966), II, p. 354.

Europe, the British congratulated themselves on what they regarded as a timely and successful solution to the South African problem.

In Britain it was widely anticipated that a united, confident, white-ruled South Africa would be more just in ruling its large African population than individual states acting on their own. Natal's brutal suppression of the Bambatha rebellion (1906–07) was often cited in this regard. The conditions laid down for the future incorporation in the Union of the High Commission territories—Basutoland, Bechuanaland, and from 1902 Swaziland—were also designed to help ensure that the Union government ruled its subordinate populations justly. It was assumed that in time these three territories and Southern Rhodesia would join an enlarged Union, but in the event British southern Africa was to remain divided into a relatively strong Union of South Africa and other much less powerful countries.

In 1909 the British government hurried to approve the South Africa Bill and welcome the inauguration of a Union of South Africa within the British Empire in which power was devolved to South Africa's white minority in a Union which was Boer-dominated. As Milner had foreseen in 1897, such a Union inevitably meant 'The abandonment of the black races . . .'[24] France had acted similarly in Algeria in 1905 and Britain was to do so again in Southern Rhodesia in 1923. In South Africa Britain followed the course already set in Canada, Australia, and New Zealand, transferring power to the dominant ruling élite in order to preserve British interests in the area. The government of the new Union would be Afrikaner-led, but British interests were maintained and gold-mining was to boom in the new dominion, which was to remain in the British Empire-Commonwealth until 1961 and to return to it, after the collapse of apartheid, in 1994.

---

[24] Milner to Asquith, 18 November 1897, quoted in G. H. Le May, *British Supremacy in South Africa, 1899–1907* (Oxford, 1965), pp. 11–12.

Select Bibliography

A. ATMORE and S. MARKS, 'The Imperial Factor in South Africa in the Nineteenth Century: Towards a Reassessment', *Journal of Imperial and Commonwealth History*, III, 1 (1974), pp. 105–39.

JOHN BENYON, *Proconsul and Paramountcy in South Africa: The High Commission, British Supremacy and the Sub-Continent, 1806–1910* (Pietermaritzburg, 1980).

T. R. H. DAVENPORT, *South Africa: A Modern History*, 4th edn. (London, 1991).

RICHARD ELPHICK and HERMANN GILIOMEE, eds., *The Shaping of South African Society, 1652–1840*, 2nd revised edn. (Middletown, Conn., 1989).

C. F. GOODFELLOW, *Britain and South African Confederation, 1871–81* (Cape Town, 1966).

TIMOTHY KEEGAN, *Colonial South Africa and the Origins of the Racial Order* (Cape Town, 1996).

ARTHUR KEPPEL-JONES, *Rhodes and Rhodesia: The White Conquest of Zimbabwe, 1884–1902* (Kingston and Montreal, 1983).

J. S. MARAIS, *The Fall of Kruger's Republic* (Oxford, 1961).

G. H. L. LE MAY, *British Supremacy in South Africa, 1899–1907* (Oxford, 1965).

P. MAYLAM, *Rhodes, the Tswana, and the British: Colonialism, Collaboration, and Conflict in the Bechuanaland Protectorate, 1885–1899* (Westport, 1980).

SHULA MARKS, 'Southern Africa, 1867–1886' and 'Southern and Central Africa, 1886–1910', in Roland Oliver and G. N. Sanderson, eds., *The Cambridge History of Africa*, Vol. VI, *From 1870–1905* (Cambridge, 1985).

—— and STANLEY TRAPIDO, 'Lord Milner and the South African State', *History Workshop*, VIII (1979), pp. 50–80, and 'Lord Milner and the South African State Reconsidered', in Michael Twaddle, ed., *Imperialism, the State and the Third World* (London, 1992), pp. 80–94.

W. P. MORRELL, *British Colonial Policy in the Mid-Victorian Age* (Oxford, 1969).

A. N. PORTER, *The Origins of the South African War: Joseph Chamberlain and the Diplomacy of Imperialism, 1895–99* (Manchester, 1980); also, 'The South African War (1899–1902): Context and Motive Reconsidered', *Journal of African History*, XXXI (1990), pp. 43–57.

D. M. SCHREUDER, *Gladstone and Kruger: Liberal Government and Colonial 'Home Rule', 1880–85* (London, 1969).

—— *The Scramble for Southern Africa, 1877–1895: The Politics of Partition Reappraised* (Cambridge, 1980).

IAIN R. SMITH, *The Origins of the South African War, 1899–1902* (London, 1996).

LEONARD THOMPSON, *A History of South Africa* (New Haven, 1991).

L. M. THOMPSON, *The Unification of South Africa, 1902–1910* (Oxford, 1960).

JEAN VAN DER POEL, *The Jameson Raid* (Cape Town, 1951).

PETER WARWICK, ed., *The South African War: The Anglo-Boer War, 1899–1902* (Harlow, 1980).

27

Great Britain and the Partition of Africa, 1870–1914

COLIN NEWBURY

Priorities

Africa's resources, of course, had been partitioned for millennia by dispersal, incorporation, and conquest among regional societies; and there were precedents for foreign empire in Algeria and at the Cape. This chapter, however, focuses on the meanings of 'partition' in the variety of techniques used to protect the interests of one power.[1] British politicians and officials had no clear territorial agenda for the continent as a whole by the 1870s; when speaking of Africa they used the language of Viscount Palmerston or Thomas Buxton on 'access' and 'reform' in specific regions. These were seen as components of Imperial strategies for the maintenance of a network of overseas markets and defence commitments. Africa was a base for action against the slave trade, an entrepôt for resources, a staging post to India and the East.

Differences between Liberals and Conservatives were matters of emphasis on methods of access and control at public or private cost. Annexations or abandonment were risky and unpopular. Before 1880 the details of regional policies were left to Secretaries of State and their officials, while Prime Ministers Gladstone and Disraeli concentrated on the power politics of Turkey's decline as a buffer against Russia. In Egypt, where Turkey's international weakness had African repercussions, Britain applied the diplomatic techniques used to minimize European conflict over the Ottoman Empire by internationalization of its financial problems.

Elsewhere, Britain applied two other techniques evolved from Imperial experience. One was the plan taken over from Lord Kimberley by Carnarvon, as Secretary of State for the Colonies, to consolidate the fractious colonies, republics, and African societies south of the Zambezi into a 'confederation' ruled from a self-

---

[1] For general surveys, see Select Bibliography and E. Hertslet, *The Map of Africa by Treaty*, 3rd edn., 3 vols. (London, 1909). For other international factors and the politics and xenophobia of late-nineteenth-century British Imperialism, see Introduction and chaps. by Christopher Saunders and Iain R. Smith, and Afaf Lutfi al-Sayyid-Marsot.

governing Cape Colony. The other was simply to continue public or private support for the work of British administrators, missionaries, merchants, and Consuls, carried on from enclaves in tropical Africa. Such an African Empire might not be cheap, as the expenditure of West African settlements demonstrated (Fig. 27.1). But in the coastal enclaves low taxes on imports and the practice of stipending chiefs and reformed slavers were all that was necessary. And costs

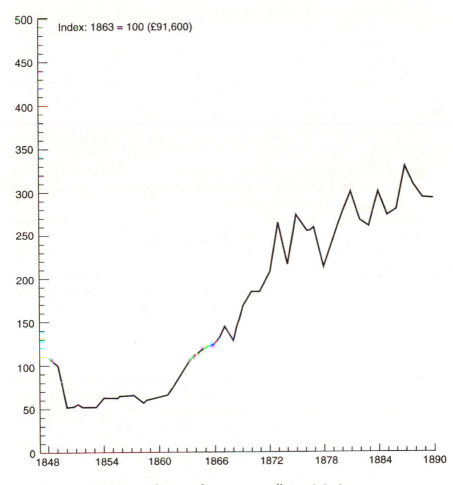

FIGURE 27.1. British West African settlements: expenditure, 1848–1890

SOURCE: C. W. Newbury, ed., *British Policy Towards West Africa. Select Documents, 1875–1914, with Statistical Appendices, 1800–1914* (Oxford, 1971), Table VII, pp. 621–25

Note: Excluding military expenditure, but including courts and Consuls under Foreign Office for Sierra Leone, Luanda, and Lagos, and special Parliamentary grants. In addition, the West Africa Squadron cost about £170,000 a year in the late 1850s.

elsewhere could be shared between settlers and the Imperial patron, as a 'regional power system' developed in South Africa.[2]

All three policies were flawed—the South African one seriously—because of assumptions about the stability of African states over a period of increasing external contacts. But taken together they reflected British priorities in protecting a world-wide trading system through regional defence and British subjects through treaties and consuls.

Those priorities were based squarely on an evaluation of Africa's importance for British overseas trade worked out in the late 1870s by the War Office, which took into account local exchanges and transit values through the Suez Canal and round the Cape.[3] The two poles of British commerce emerged clearly, then and subsequently, as Egypt and the Maghrib, and Southern Africa (Fig. 27.2). In addition, most of Egypt's bonded debt was held in Britain by 1878, serviced from earnings on trade predominantly with Britain and France.[4] In Southern Africa the Cape had a public debt of £1.5m raised in London as early as 1872 and heavy military expenditure at the end of the decade funded from loans. Direct private investment rapidly followed the diamond discoveries and the British colonies' adoption of joint-stock systems of company promotion. British trade easily survived a recession to expand again in the mining-led boom of the later 1880s.[5]

Elsewhere, British interests relied on public subsidies for posts in West Africa and the private enterprise of miscellaneous British subjects—missionaries, liberated Africans, traders, and merchants—justified publicly by humanitarian and commercial motives. To support these ends the four West African enclaves—the Gambia, Sierra Leone, the Gold Coast, and Lagos Colony—incurred rising expenditure over the period 1860 to 1890. This was steepest in the 1860s and 1870s, when their merchants faced foreign competition, falls in commodity prices, expensive credit to African suppliers, and political conflict in African markets.

But at the outset of the accelerated partition of the 1880s considerations about trade and transit at Suez and the Cape most influenced decisions to administer Egypt's debt and to create a 'supremacy' in South Africa. The formula devised by the War Office for assessing defence costs and priorities was applied to Africa by

[2] C. F. Goodfellow, *Great Britain and South African Confederation (1870–1881)* (Cape Town, 1966); John Benyon, 'Overlords of Empire? British "Proconsular Imperialism" in Comparative Perspective', *Journal of Imperial and Commonwealth History* (hereafter *JICH*), XIX, 2 (1991), p. 172.

[3] Donald M. Schurman, 'Cape Defence in the Eighteen Seventies and Eighties: A Study in the Fractured Nature of an Imperial Problem', in G. A. Wood and P. S. O'Connor, eds., *W. P. Morrell: A Tribute* (Dunedin, 1973), pp. 37–49.

[4] *British Documents on Foreign Affairs: Reports and Papers from the Foreign Office Confidential Prints*, ed. David Gillard, Series B, Vols. VIII, IX (New York, 1984); Roger Owen, *The Middle East in the World Economy, 1800–1914* (London, 1981), pp. 136–38.

[5] S. Herbert Frankel, *Capital Investment in Africa: Its Course and Effects* (Oxford, 1938), pp. 50–59.

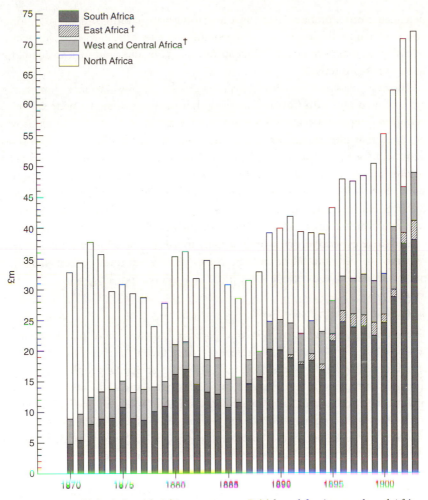

FIGURE 27.2 British trade with Africa, 1870–1903. British and foreign goods and African products [1]

Source: Statistical Abstracts for the United Kingdom (London, 1869–1879, 1879–1903).

[1] Total trade in current values, including imports of gold and diamonds, but excluding imports and exports of specie.

[†] Including British and foreign possessions and independent markets.

Carnarvon's Royal Commission in 1881. With an estimated £91m of British trade goods transported round the Cape and £65.6m through the Suez Canal in mind, the Commission found little comfort in any future possession of Port Said. Drawing on a confidential report on Egyptian defences, it concluded that if the eastern Mediterranean were lost to British sea-power, the Canal could only be defended from Bombay.[6] For the Cape, however, a thousand or so colonial volunteers, plus the navy, were judged sufficient to safeguard harbour works, releasing the main Imperial contingents of some 3,000 men and African auxiliaries to secure the hinterland.

This, too, was in line with British experience of how 'defence' forces were actually used and with Carnarvon's view that Britain assumed a wide sphere of action in Egypt and the Cape interior 'as far as the Zambesi'.[7] The truth was, however, that after three committees and one Royal Commission the costs of paramountcy in the south could not be resolved, as Cape ministers and Natal colonists proved unreliable and impecunious clients. With no confederation in sight, the South African colonies were 'under large and indefinite obligations' to the Imperial treasury, after a series of wars, costing some £2.5m.[8] By 1880 it was well established that in British spheres of interest the politics of influence and control were expensive, and would become more so unless Egypt's finances were reformed to bear the burden of the country's defence under a consortium of powers, and the Cape became a key piece in a regional power system.

SOUTHERN AFRICA TO 1890

The economic, social, and political aspects of partition were manifest earliest south of the Zambezi. Access to resources since the late eighteenth century was conditioned by the huge displacement of Nguni-speaking peoples and by the intrusive settlement of Europeans in competition for land and water. Annexation of Natal and recognition of two Afrikaner states in mid-century had applied a form of territorial demarcation to the politics of southern Africa along the Vaal and the Orange Rivers, but left other marches open to contest, as the brief gold discovery at Tati and the more momentous discovery of diamonds in Griqualand West in the late 1860s amply demonstrated.[9] Partition of mineral resources was decided at first by British annexation of Griqualand West and a boundary adjustment to the detriment of the Griquas and Free State. An award by Lieutenant-Governor Keate of Natal in 1871 held back the western Transvaal frontier from lands disputed with the Tswana, leaving open a major trade route from the Cape to territory north-west of the Limpopo River (Map 26.1).

---

[6] 'First Report of the Royal Commission Appointed to Enquire into the Defence of British Possessions and Commerce Abroad', in *Proceedings of the Colonial Conference, 1887*, 2 vols. (London, 1887), II (Appendix), p. 299 (also *PP*); *Report* by Major-General Macdougal, 1876, in *British Documents*, VIII, p. 221.

[7] Goodfellow, *Great Britain and South African Confederation*, p. 117.

[8] *Colonial Office Confidential Print African* (hereafter *CPA*), No. 183 A, p. 14; and Nos. 174, 227, 228, for costs of warfare in South Africa.

[9] A. E. Atmore, 'Africa on the Eve of Partition', in *Cambridge History of Africa*, VI, pp. 83–92; Leonard Thompson, 'The Subjection of the African Chiefdoms', in Monica Wilson and Leonard Thompson, eds., *The Oxford History of South Africa*, Vol. II, *South Africa, 1870–1966* (Oxford, 1971), chap. 5.

But Crown rule was only resorted to when other methods failed. These were of two kinds by the late 1870s: subordination and incorporation into an existing colony, used extensively in the eastern Cape; and, secondly, forms of clientage relationship under the authority of the Cape High Commissioner, used in 1868 when Basutoland came under British protection and was partitioned with the Free State. Annexed to the Cape in 1871, the Sotho retained a High Commissioner's agent, loyally fought in the Phuti rising in 1879, but rebelled against the Cape's disarmament policy. Unaware 'that they had ceased to be under the personal control of the High Commissioner',[10] the Sotho came once more under Crown patronage in 1884, as an example of political and economic adaptation and missionary lobbying which Gladstone was forced to accept as the first South African Protectorate.

Within the two British colonies and the republics other forms of partition of resources continued relentlessly. At stake was something more than demographic demarcation, namely, a fundamental innovation in exclusive 'proprietorship rights' for settlers backed by political sovereignty.[11] Where the lines were drawn on the map was a matter of diplomacy and force. One of the arguments for annexing the Transvaal in 1877 was the failure of a bankrupt settler state to exercise such sovereignty over a frontier of 1,200 miles without the backing of the Cape and Natal and the authority of the High Commissioner. A second argument, recognized in the Colonial Office, was that economic change had upset the political balance between settler and African societies through the development of agricultural and mineral resources, the spread of cash earnings, and a market in firearms.[12]

To deal with this 'danger', the Cape Governor, Sir Bartle Frere, plunged into boundary investigations in 1878 and decided to 'force the fighting', if his demands on Cetshwayo's political sovereignty in Zululand were not met by acceptance of a Resident with jurisdiction over British subjects. This plan collapsed with British defeat at Isandhlwana; to regain the upper hand Sir Garnet Wolseley was sent in with civil and military authority over the Transvaal and Natal, and the Zulu kingdom was dismembered. Zulu alliance with Natal in the mid-1870s, cemented by arms and labour brokers, turned into a partition with beacons and boundaries 'absolutely fixed' in ways that left Cetshwayo 'speechless' during his interviews with Lord Kimberley in London in August 1882.[13]

By then, too, the Transvaal had inflicted severe defeats on the would-be patron's forces, ending in the compromise of the 1881 Pretoria Convention which defined

[10] Fairfield, 'Memorandum' [1880], CPA, No. 227.

[11] Fairfield, 'Memorandum on the Zulu Question', 20 March 1879, CPA, No. 164.

[12] Ibid.

[13] CPA, No. 247; and 'Report of the Zululand Boundary Commission' [1878], in Frere to CO, 16 Feb. 1880, in ibid.

the boundaries of an autonomous state, subject to a vague British 'suzerainty' and control of external affairs. A British Resident in Pretoria without jurisdiction or sanctions signalled influence without power.

The new High Commissioner who arrived to oversee this settlement was better versed in the art of patronage politics.[14] A Gladstonian in proconsular dress, Sir Hercules Robinson was at his best in Bechuanaland settling problems of territoriality by 'protectorate or wardship'.[15] In the face of Liberal indecisiveness and Cape ministerial opposition, the continuing need to save the Tswana from the establishment of 'robber republics' along the strategic route to the north brought about constructive co-operation between the 'imperial factor' and Cecil Rhodes as businessman and Cape politician. Collaboration was further encouraged by German imperial intervention at Angra Pequena from May 1883, which made Tswana territorial problems important in Cape and Transvaal competition for external support.

One solution was to make the High Commissioner a patron-administrator in February 1884, when southern Bechuanaland became a Protectorate and John Mackenzie was sent in as Robinson's deputy. Secondly, the Secretary of State for the Colonies, Lord Derby, struck a deal with President Kruger in the London Convention, lifting an Imperial veto on native legislation, dropping talk of suzerainty, but keeping a vestigial control on foreign relations. Police action by Sir Charles Warren, authorized by a divided Cabinet, cleared out Boer freebooters from Tswana territory and in 1885 established a Protectorate for Bechuanaland north of the Molopo and a Crown Colony to the south. The Tswana were thus partitioned between two Imperial agencies and partly incorporated into a settler state. The boundary with the Transvaal was confirmed, and an Order-in-Council for the administration of justice in Bechuanaland Protectorate set a precedent for similar extensions of Imperial authority in other British spheres of interest in Africa.

From the mid-1880s the struggle for Imperial influence turned on the same combination of official and private agencies from the Cape, as the balance of economic growth began to favour the Transvaal. In the east, when Swazi concessions to Transvaalers threatened partition of an African kingdom with access to the sea, the Colonial Office came round to Rhodes's view that the Swazi could be surrendered to the Boers, once Tongaland had been taken under British protection in 1887. High Commissioner Loch took a tougher line, demanding Transvaal accession to a customs agreement in return for a railway link to Kosi Bay. As a

---

[14] Kenneth O. Hall, *Imperial Proconsul: Sir Hercules Robinson and South Africa, 1881–1889* (Kingston, Ontario), p. 19.

[15] D. Chanaiwa, 'African Initiatives and Resistance in Southern Africa' in A. Adu Boahen, ed., *General History of Africa*, Vol. VII: *Africa under Colonial Domination, 1880–1935* (Paris, 1985), pp. 207–13.

temporary bargain Kruger agreed to a convention, ratified in August 1890, for joint rule over Europeans in Swaziland, but postponed the customs union.

Gradually, Rhodes's colonial and business priorities to extend British influence prevailed over Imperial reservations. While the Bechuanaland solution might seem fitting to the Liberals and the humanitarian lobby, to Cape politicians rule over the Tswana was simply a means of access to other resources, as well as a buffer zone between Germans and Transvaalers. On this point Sir Hercules agreed with the colonials, and his policy of imperialism through colonialism matched Rhodes's plans for expansion on a grand scale by a chartered company.

The joint venture of concessionaires under High Commission patronage from July 1888 in Lobengulas's sphere in Ndebeleland proved irresistible to the British government, if carried out by 'capitalists in good standing'. The duplicity of the British South Africa Company's (BSAC) application for a charter on the basis of a concession it did not own was beside the main point, for at issue was not a clash between 'imperialism' and 'colonialism', but simply a common search for an effective agency.[16] Salisbury's government decided to admit Rhodes's monopoly into the vague sphere proclaimed by Britain in April 1888 from Bechuanaland to the Zambezi and 20 degrees East longitude, as a pre-emptive move against the Transvaal, the Germans, and the Portuguese.

Another partition of resources turned on the allocation of revenue from trade between the colonies and the republics. A complex system of railway tariffs and rebates changed from 1886 into a search for fiscal co-operation as an alternative to the Transvaal's policy of seeking an outlet through Delagoa Bay. While Pretoria rejected all customs harmonization, the Cape and the Free State moved into a customs and railway union in 1889 as the battle for railway extensions continued, and Rhodes enlisted local support for a Cape Bechuanaland Railway Agreement which the BSAC would finance and build.

By the late 1880s, then, the main territorial lines of British influence and control in Southern Africa had been laid down in a series of contests, alliances, and incorporations (Map 26.2).[17] Where not absorbed into the territories of the Eastern Cape or Natal, the resources of African states and societies were defined in terms of administrative control, or circumscribed as independent polities. The techniques of alliance and clientage, as alternatives to conquest, were widespread and provided the basis of more legalistic forms of Crown Colony and Protectorate. They owed much to the expansive use of the authority of the Cape Governor, as

[16] Hall, *Imperial Proconsul*, p. 166; cf. Ronald Robinson and John Gallagher, with Alice Denny, *Africa and the Victorians: The Official Mind of Imperialism* (London, 1961), p. 239.

[17] John Benyon, *Proconsul and Paramountcy in South Africa: The High Commission, British Supremacy and the Sub-Continent, 1806–1910*. (Pietermaritzburg, 1980).

formal head of two British colonies with representative and responsible governments, or as a judicial authority and negotiator in the frontier zones of British
influence. The Transvaal resisted both occupation and informal control, though
the Free State was more susceptible to the mixture of financial and economic co-
operation offered by the Afrikaans and English-speaking Cape. The northern
republic was, therefore, contained rather than absorbed, although British and
Afrikaner boundaries with Ndebeleland, Damaraland, and Portuguese territory
were still provisional.

German and Portuguese factors were contingent to this basic competition in
settler and African societies for partition of resources. That process left the
Cape, Natal, and the two republics commanding land, minerals, and communications, the major ports, and sources of labour by the 1880s, though they had
not agreed how to share out revenue from trade and tariffs. That the small
German settlement at Angra Pequena became a 'factor' at all for the Cape is
testimony to Britain's reluctance to commit Imperial resources simply to control
of territory, without colonial willingness to share costs. Confrontation with
Portugal was another matter, as Rhodes's pioneers moved into Mashonaland
and the colonial agent threatened to become more belligerent by 1890 than the
Imperial power.

EGYPT AND THE SUDAN TO 1890

Britain's demarcation of Egypt in 1882 as a British sphere by unilateral naval
and military action has its origins in both the internationalization of the khedivate's insolvency and the methods pursued by foreign agencies to cure that
condition (Map 28.1). At one level the Khedive was right to look on his country
'as part of Europe',[18] and therefore part of the more general problem of Ottoman
decline and naval strategy in the eastern Mediterranean. But at another level
Egypt's weakness stemmed from the ease of access for European commerce and
finance into a state with a patrimonial system of offices legitimized by the Turkish
sultanate, and extensive judicial privileges reserved for foreigners in consular
courts.

Although 'dual control' through financial officers was of more concern to
French investors, the Conservatives before 1880 took a close interest because of
the vulnerability of the Suez Canal. Britain's stake in Egypt, as Lord Salisbury
emphasized, was 'largely commercial', with 'political considerations' which
required intervention in partnership with France to the exclusion of other

---

[18] Frederick Madden, ed., with David Fieldhouse, *The Dependent Empire and Ireland, 1840–1900:
Advance and Retreat in Representative Self-Government. Select Documents on the Constitutional History
of the British Empire and Commonwealth* (New York, 1991), V, p. 713 and note.

powers.[19] France could not be left to act alone; and Khedive Ismail could not be trusted to manage. Indeed, the Conservatives might well have gone further towards armed intervention in 1879, but for the military crisis in South Africa.

However, the more the controllers-general enforced debt-servicing, the more they interfered with local patronage exercised through the khedive's control of the Civil List, and offended sections of the Egyptian state's civil and military personnel. A rising, educated bureaucracy, owing appointments to the Khedive's family and court or to Turco-Circassian and Egyptian notables, resented importation of foreign officials; the corps of army officers was alienated by economies and became a focus for more general resentment; a third threat to European outsiders' regulation of the state debt lay in an indigenous movement for constitutional reform.

Through the late 1870s agents' reports accumulated on the operation of Egyptian administration as a gigantic tax farm, emphasizing the difficulty of influencing change in a system where public office 'from the Pashas downwards...is a tenancy at will' held by intrigue.[20] When Ismail chose to defend this system in 1879, by siding with the army corps and dismissing European controllers, he was deposed by Britain and France in favour of the more malleable Tawfiq, with the Sultan's compliance.

Dual control was reinforced in 1880 by the Law of Liquidation, which eased the situation for French investors and gave London finance a stake in the probity of the regime. From then on, with the Liberals in office, British policy was sharply divided between the necessity for a continued mandate from the powers and pressure for unilateral action from within the Foreign Office and the Cabinet. By the end of 1881 Britain and France were committed to support the new Khedive. As the protest movement headed by the Egyptian Colonel Ahmad Urabi threatened to unite reformers, army, and bureaucracy against the foreign-controlled executive, they issued their warning Note of January 1882 followed by a demand for dismissal of officers. Talk of anarchy by British agents on the spot aggravated the Liberals' desperation, and the Alexandria riots in June 1882 were used to justify the despatch of the fleet, sending tremors through the London stock market. French withdrawal from the naval demonstration left Admiral Seymour free to bombard Alexandria's forts and land 40,000 men under Wolseley, in July–August 1882. In a wave of Gladstonian justification and City satisfaction, Parliament approved the official underwriting of a 'special interest' in trade through the Canal, investment

---

[19] Lord Tenterden, Memorandum, 10 Oct. 1881, *British Documents*, IX, pp. 13–14; Richard A. Atkins, 'The Conservatives and Egypt, 1875–1880', *JICH*, II, 2 (1974), pp. 190–205; Marvin Swartz, *The Politics of British Foreign Policy in the Era of Disraeli and Gladstone* (London, 1985), p. 130.

[20] Stephen Cave, n.d., *British Documents*, VIII, pp. 202; P. Currie, Memorandum, 17 Sept. 1881, *British Documents*, IX, pp. 22–25; Anouar Abdel-Malek, *Idéologie et renaissance nationale: l'Egypte moderne* (Paris, 1969); H. A. Ibrahim, 'African Initiatives and Resistance in North-East Africa', in Boahen, ed., *General History*, VII, p. 70.

of 'capital and industry', and protection of British nationals. These motives for the defeat of Urabi's forces at Tel-el-Kebir in September left Britain the task of patching up 'the great disintegration'.[21]

The dual watch on Egypt's accounts thus became a British watch on the Nile. The immediate problem for the self-appointed guarantor was to find a constitutional framework which allowed a measure of reform but kept control of finance with a supervised executive. Lord Dufferin's reports on Egypt supplied a blueprint, enacted 1 May 1883 by Tawfiq, setting up a limited representative system and a Council of State responsible to the Khedive.[22] Dufferin justified this dispensation by his analysis of the channels of authority in a patrimonial society. Egypt would have to be ruled more lightly than an Indian princely state, because Britain had no executive or judicial powers; but by nominating loyal Turco-Circassians, Copts, and imported Englishmen, efficient cadres might be built up and courts reformed. Indeed, British access to the levers of power and financial resources already operated in key departments where European officials numbered some 1,300 in 1882.[23]

International approval was, however, withheld, although further loans were guaranteed and a mandate was provided by Turkey in the Convention of October 1885 which, in effect, partitioned authority over the khedivate. Assurances of withdrawal within five years, in any case, divided the Liberal Cabinet on the problem of timing and Canal security. The Mahdist revolt in the Sudan and the destruction of the Egyptian army at El Obeid in 1883 removed whole provinces from Egyptian control and opened Red Sea ports to attack. A respite was secured by a British campaign up the Nile, too late to save Gordon at Khartoum, but sufficient to keep the Mahdists at bay, before Wolseley was ordered to retire from the Sudan in May 1885. Thereafter, the methods of India were applied in the field as in the secretariat: a Nile Frontier Force of retrained Egyptian troops and British regulars was formed by Sir Evelyn Wood, as Sirdar or commander-in-chief. In Drummond-Wolff's phrase, the British stayed on to exercise authority through 'management supported by material force'.[24]

By 1888–89 the Egyptian budget was managed into surplus; a plan for the issue of bonds for loans raised on public lands opened a new field for speculation, patronage, and influence by control of khedival family tenures and the Civil List.[25] Withdrawal became less likely than ever when the Conservatives returned to

---

[21] Granville to Dufferin, 11 July 1882, *British Documents*, IX, p. 64; Gladstone to Granville, 3 Oct. 1882, in Madden, ed., *Dependent Empire*, V, p. 720.

[22] Dufferin to Granville, 18 Nov. 1882, in ibid., V, p. 721.

[23] Lord Tenterden, 'Egyptian Civil Service', *British Documents*, IX, pp. 279–83; Owen, *The Middle East*, p. 135.

[24] Drummond-Wolff, Memorandum, 17 Aug. 1886, in Madden, ed., *Dependent Empire*, V, p. 746.

[25] *British Documents*, XV, p. 225.

power under Salisbury, especially after the failure of the Drummond-Wolff negotiations at Constantinople in 1887. By then, the watch on the Nile had consequences for British partition elsewhere on the continent.

EAST, WEST, AND CENTRAL AFRICA TO 1890

The resources and peoples of the rest of the sub-Saharan continent were also
subject to division well before European agencies began to accelerate the pace of
change. But south of the Ethiopian highlands, no African state emerged as a
contender for regional power over the vast area from the White Nile and the
interlacustrine kingdoms of the Great Lakes region to the Limpopo.[26] Britain
herself had few interests to defend. On the Somali coast, Egypt was used as a sub-
imperial agent until 1884, and the supervision of British treaty relations with
Somali clans was left to a consulate. She sought no patronage of Menelik,
recognized as Emperor of Ethiopia in 1882, and the Italians were encouraged to
occupy the strategic centre of Massawa in 1885 to exclude France.

South of the Gulf of Aden the sultanate of Zanzibar, and the commercial
networks created by shipping companies in the Indian Ocean and by Swahili
Arabs on land, became the mechanisms for European agencies. The sultanate
exercised commercial and financial influence over the region's slave trade and
staple exports, but had little administrative control. This weakness made it an easy
client state for Britain under treaties which outlawed the slave trade and initiated a
rapid change in the credit structure of commerce in cloves and ivory. However
superficial the authority of Sultan Bargash (and the influence of Sir John Kirk's
Consulate, 1873–87), there was a large measure of commercial cohesion throughout East Africa imposed by the Swahili trading system. The general result for
British enterprise—exploring, commercial, and philanthropic—was to create
trading alliances, sources of mercenaries, and routes to the interior for Livingstone's successors.

There was potential for conflict in this mixture of philanthropy and concession-
hunting, as the internal slave trade expanded to meet the need for armed expeditions throughout the interlacustrine region and along the trading networks
between the east coast and the Congo basin. Farther south, the Portuguese were
seen in the late 1870s as another possible client state, possessing historic influence
in Angola and Mozambique but little territorial consolidation. Important to
Britain's southern African strategies as possessor of Delagoa Bay, Portugal was
an unpredictable factor in the Zambezi basin and at the Congo mouth.[27]

[26] Ake Holmberg, *Tribes and European Agencies: Colonialism and Humanitarianism in British South
and East Africa, 1870–1895* (Göteborg, 1966).
[27] E. Axelson, *Portugal and the Scramble for Africa* (Johannesburg, 1967).

In western Africa the major trade routes from the Hausa-Fulani emirates to the Dyula and Mandinka markets of Upper Guinea and the Senegambia rivers were known but little penetrated, although disputed at the coast between French and British exporters. The second primary location of resources lay south of the savannah in the forest belt from the Gambia and Casamance along the coastal region to the Niger Delta and the Congo basin. In this region of specialist investment and very limited control, European factors depended on African middlemen for the movement of goods between forest and savannah, until British investigation of the Niger–Benue rivers, backed by naval protection from 1876.

Thus, British interests were identified with anti-slave trade measures, steam communications, and open access to primary resources in the coastal markets. The methods for promoting these interests were: retention of existing colonial posts; treaties of friendship with interior chiefdoms, backed by 'moderate (continual) bribery';[28] and, more hesitantly, the extension of jurisdiction in the vicinity of British Settlements and in consular courts to both protect and control British subjects.

From 1879 such methods were called in question by friction between French and British enclaves north of Sierra Leone and west of Lagos over expansion of customs for revenues and by indications that the commercial and political system which required merchants to work through African brokers in the Delta and Congo markets, but excluded Africans from the export trade, was under strain. British concepts of 'free trade' were threatened by French protectionism, just when capital restructuring of Niger and Congo firms increased competition in conditions of temporary recession. If the French military advance from the Upper Senegal swept eastward, could commercial treaties with chiefs in the interior of Sierra Leone, the Futa Jalon, or the Niger–Benue confluence provide a political defence? Treaty-making by de Brazza on the Congo in September 1880 also indicated an expansion of French Gabon, in competition with Leopold II of the Belgians' International African Association, the vehicle since September 1876 of the king's territorial ambitions. Doors kept open by naval action or by official and unofficial activities were beginning to close.

Britain responded with diplomacy and a search for additional clients. Negotiations with France in 1879–81 revealed that colonial tariffs were mutually discriminatory but were settled temporarily by territorial demarcation in the rivers north of Sierra Leone, leaving internal boundaries open, under the unratified Convention of 28 June 1882. Treaties and stipends were renewed in the interior of Sierra Leone, the Upper Gambia, and the Futa Jalon to keep trade routes open. Thought was given to using the newly formed National African Company as a political

[28] Herbert, Minute, 1 Dec. 1871 C[olonial] O[ffice] 96/89; for collections of treaties, *CPA*, No. 332.

agent on the Lower Niger to counter French companies.[29] French claims to the navigable Congo, north of Stanley Pool in November 1882, aroused further misgivings in the Foreign Office's African department. Accordingly, negotiations to flatter Portugal's pretensions to territory north of Angola, in return for reform of discriminatory tariffs in East and Central Africa, were revived and completed in the Anglo-Portuguese Treaty, 26 February 1884, to block both France and Leopold at the Congo mouth.[30] In only four years the British government was driven to an unwelcome revision of techniques required to defend the concept of open access in tropical Africa.

The change is detectable in the policy formulations of permanent officials in the Colonial and Foreign Offices who stiffened the resolve of successive Secretaries of State and prepared papers on African expansion which Salisbury made a Cabinet responsibility from 1880. By 1883 French pressures at Porto Novo, on the Niger, and the Congo, and the likely failure of any negotiation for a general exchange of West African posts, set the Foreign Office in search of a refurbished treaty system leading to Protectorates. The Cabinet approved on 22 November 1883, and the Consul to the Bight of Benin, E. H. Hewett, set about gathering pre-emptive agreements with chiefs as far as the Cameroons, in parallel with the National African Company's agent, David McIntosh, as far as the Benue confluence.[31]

A second challenge came from German colonial interventions at Angra Pequena, in South Togo, and Cameroon, and from an attempted cession at St Lucia Bay, north of Durban. Bismarck's irritation at British procrastination in negotiating on South-West Africa was matched by British irritation at the reception given Afrikaner delegates in Berlin on June 1884.[32] A treaty of trade and friendship with the Transvaal smacked of German patronage in the most sensitive of British spheres. St Lucia was snatched back by raising the British flag at the end of the year, in the same month as Warren's expedition was sent to close off the hinterland in Bechuanaland.

Despite anxiety that Germany might become 'a South African Power',[33] the Cabinet concluded in July 1884 that Britain had no grounds to protest over South-West Africa, and was aware that Bismarck's annoyance was linked with the Congo and his objections to the Anglo-Portuguese Treaty. The chorus of international disapproval of that device was amplified by French opposition to the occupation

---

[29] John E. Flint, *Sir George Goldie and the Making of Nigeria* (London, 1960).

[30] Roger Anstey, *Britain and the Congo in the Nineteenth Century* (Oxford, 1962); Wm. Roger Louis, 'Sir Percy Anderson's Grand African Strategy, 1883–1893', *English Historical Review* (1966), LXXXI, pp. 292–314.

[31] *Foreign Office Confidential Print*, Nos. 4825, 5064.

[32] *CPA*, No. 274.

[33] Ampthill to Granville, 25 June 1884, *British Documents*, VIII, p. 195; Bramston to Currie, 12 Sept. 1884, in ibid.

of Egypt; by a temporary German entente with France; and by a general mistrust of Portuguese administration of trade and taxes. Britain miscalculated in seeking a bilateral solution to the problem of international access to the Congo, leaving the way open for Leopold's intricate diplomacy which gained him the recognition of France in return for right of pre-emption over the Association's territories in April 1884, and Bismarck's acceptance of his sweeping territorial claims in August 1884. But if British tactics were questionable, her objectives remained the same: defence of preponderant commerce in Africa by the use of surrogates, with or without formal control through extended jurisdiction. Appreciating the larger danger implied by the Congo–French agreement, the Foreign Office accepted Bismarck's mediation, but reserved Britain's position 'as *the Niger Power*' through treaties and a chartered company, when agreeing to the Berlin West Africa Conference in October 1884.[34]

In the event, the conference conceded this claim, and Bismarck moved closer to the British representatives on the second question of a free trade zone across Central Africa including the lower Zambezi, in the teeth of French and Portuguese reservations. The price was British recognition of Leopold's Association, extracted by Bismarck for co-operation over Egypt (and the failure of the Foreign Office to question Leopold's self-proclaimed boundaries). On the final basis for the Conference protocols, Britain agreed to notification procedures for occupation of coastal territory, and went further than Bismarck required in the exercise of jurisdiction on behalf of foreigners in Protectorates. This was reviewed at length by Crown Law Officers, and provided a basis for an expanded system of consular courts in West Africa from 1885, administration of justice by chartered companies, and consolidation of the British Foreign Jurisdiction Acts in 1890.[35] There was less enthusiasm for the Brussels Conference and its humanitarian aims, 1889–90, when Salisbury's support for international controls was restricted to the maritime slave trade and spirits traffic.[36]

For the rest of the initial phase of the 'scramble' in West and East Africa, Britain relied on the agency of travelling commissioners, consular authority in the Niger Coast Protectorate from 1885, the commercial and political monopoly of the Royal Niger Company (RNC), from 1886, the expanded Political Agency and Consulate-General at Zanzibar, and Mackinnon's Imperial British East Africa Company (IBEA), from 1887.

---

[34] H. P. Anderson, Memorandum, 14 Oct. 1884, in C. Newbury, ed., *British Policy Towards West Africa. Select Documents*, 2 vols., Vol. II, *1875–1914* (reprint, Aldershot, 1992), pp. 185–86.

[35] Colin Newbury, '"Treaty, Grant, Usage and Sufferance": The Origins of British Colonial Protectorates', in Wood and O'Connor, eds., *W. P. Morrell*, pp. 69–84; Madden, ed., *Dependent Empire*, V, pp. 5–39.

[36] Suzanne Miers, *Britain and the Ending of the Slave Trade* (London, 1975), chap. 6.

None of this provided defence against the activities of Carl Peters on the Zanzibari mainland or French military advance in the western Sudan. At best, an Anglo-German agreement in November 1886 demarcated spheres in German and British East Africa, leaving the interior open and reducing Zanzibari claims on the coast. Similarly, in West Africa a boundary between Togo and the Gold Coast was arranged in 1887 as far as 'neutral ground' at ten degrees north; and a provisional agreement of 1888 settled the Lagos and Porto Novo boundary at the coast. Within that sphere behind Lagos Colony officials arranged treaties excluding other powers from Yoruba states, and arbitrated in local wars. But treaties with Mende and Temne and contact with the Almamy Samori Ture in the Guinea interior counted for little in Anglo-French negotiations during 1889; these confirmed the Gambia Protectorate's boundaries, the Dahomey boundary short of the Niger, ratified Gold Coast and Ivory Coast boundaries, and agreed some equalization of tariffs between Assinie and the Gold Coast and at Porto Novo. Foreign Office and French attention was focused on wider issues of revision of the Anglo-Tunisian Convention, Zanzibar, Madagascar, and the emerging French ambition for a zone from the Mediterranean to Lake Chad.

That expansive aim brought to a head Britain's relations with Germany on African issues. With Salisbury back in office, the period after the Berlin Conference witnessed Anglo-German accommodation at the highest level and hostility among officials in the Foreign Office and agents in the field. But by 1888 Salisbury's view of the importance of the interlacustrine region began to change, as the Congo State and the Germans launched expeditions to 'rescue' Emin Pasha from Equatoria, and the Italians moved into Ethiopia. The possibility that some power might control the Nile sources seemed to threaten Egypt's agricultural surplus, finances, and debt servicing.[37] Moreover, the alliance of Leopold, Stanley, and Mackinnon to carve out a concession in the guise of a rescue operation brought to a head the need for a territorial settlement in the marches south of the Sudan and in Uganda. 'Equatoria' took on a strategic significance for Salisbury, made more acute by his reliance on Liberal Unionists at home and the fall of Bismarck abroad. The relief of Emin in 1888 by Stanley and Peter's continued activity in Uganda in March 1890 in competition with the IBEA, therefore, precipitated a more general diplomatic settlement.

This was prefaced by informal partition between Leopold, Mackinnon, Stanley, and Salisbury in April–May 1890 (the Mackinnon Agreement, 24 May 1890), which gave Leopold access to the Nile valley in return for a strip of territory from Uganda to Lake Tanganyika. But in the bargain with Germany made in 1890, Salisbury sacrificed the corridor and the dream of 'Cape to Cairo' that went with it, and

[37] William L. Langer, *The Diplomacy of Imperialism, 1890–1902*, 2nd edn. (New York, 1951), pp. 105–06.

ceded Heligoland in return for recognition of a British sphere from the coast to the Congo State and to Italian Somaliland. Conceding German access through Damaraland to the headwaters of the Zambezi settled problems over Togo–Gold Coast and Rio del Rey boundaries and transit rights on the Benue. Britain's Zanzibar Protectorate was recognized, the German protectorate over Witu withdrawn. The effect was to eliminate challenges to British influence, according to Salisbury, from the Equator to the borders of Egypt.[38]

There was, however, a Portuguese claim to be fended off in Nyasaland, where the humanitarian and commercial work of Scottish and Universities missions and the African Lakes Company had come into conflict with Swahili Arabs along the Zambezi, Shiré, Nyasa trade routes leading to Livingstonia and Karonga. An anti-slavery campaign led by Captain F. D. Lugard rallied the missions and attracted the speculative attention of Cecil Rhodes and the Imperial initiative of Consul H. H. Johnston at Blantyre. Treaty-making (funded by Rhodes's BSAC) among the Shiré and Nyasa chiefs preserved for Britain the highlands to the west of the lake by the Anglo-Portuguese Convention of August 1890.

French reactions to these settlements were sharpened by differences over conversion of the Egyptian debt which brought evacuation no nearer, by British commercial advantage in Tunisia, residual rights in Zanzibar, and an accumulation of objections to the monopoly exercised by the Royal Niger Company. Of these however, only Zanzibar influenced Niger–Chad negotiations.[39] Salisbury agreed in July 1890 to the Say–Barruwa line, leaving Sokoto within the RNC sphere, and recognized French Madagascar in return for recognition of the British Zanzibar Protectorate.

Control and Conquest, 1890–1914

The 1890s thus opened with spheres of influence on the African continent outlined but imperfectly occupied. The Upper Nile was hardly demarcated at all outside the Mahdist Sudan. In East Africa, as in the West, Consuls, Commissioners, and unofficial agencies were still the principal pathfinders for British influence. If pre-emptive claims meant anything, then contested 'hinterlands' would have to be administered, so as to safeguard the interests of other nationals. From 1890 both the Foreign Office and the Colonial Office, secure in the legal basis provided by the Foreign Jurisdiction Acts, took a more relaxed attitude to exercising 'power to protect'.[40]

[38] Langer, Diplomacy of Imperialism, p. 119.
[39] A. S. Kanya-Forstner, 'French African Policy and the Anglo-French Agreement of 5 August 1890', Historical Journal, XII, 4 (1969), pp. 628–50; Newbury, ed., British Policy Towards West Africa, II, p. 205.
[40] Hemming, 'Minute', 10 Nov. 1890, in Newbury, ed., British Policy Towards West Africa, II, p. 206.

The cartography of control, as recognized by European states, therefore, implied a measure of government, as well as access to resources; and both these aspects of partition provoked African resistance. From the early 1890s there was greater use of locally raised militias, 'frontier' forces, and Imperial troops, on the South African pattern, both as a response to French military expeditions and as a major commitment to securing territory and communications.

The assumption, then, that territory could be held by means of clients and informal agencies was steadily revised, to remedy the exposed position of Anglo-Egyptian administration, to repair the damage left by Rhodes's attempted coup against the Transvaal in 1895, and to rescue the Royal Niger Company and the Imperial British East African Company. Thereafter, revolts in West Africa, Company conquest of the Ndebele, occupation of the Sudan, and a civil war in South Africa put diplomatic partition in the shade. Compared with the results of contests for power over African states, Anglo-French 'confrontations' at Fashoda or on the Upper Niger diminish in significance. In the end, the problems of keeping a European peace through diplomacy were overtaken by the problems of Imperial control of African subjects.

SOUTHERN AFRICA

In 1890, with the Transvaal contained and Rhodes in office as Premier of the Cape, British interests looked secure, as Company pioneers moved into Mashonaland and the great 'amalgamator' worked to extend the Cape–Free State Customs Union of 1889. Railways from the south and patronage of Afrikaner Bondsmen in Parliament through shares and land grants would enable the Cape to undermine Kruger, restore the balance upset by the precocious development of the Rand, and leave the British South Africa Company free to expand into 'Zambesia' and beyond.

To the extent that the chartered agency was able to finance territorial imperialism, this strategy had a measure of success. A preliminary partition with Portugal along the line of the Zambezi and Sabi Rivers divided Barotseland, but drove Rhodes to buccaneering.[41] In this way most of Manicaland in Mozambique was taken over under an Anglo-Portuguese Convention of 1891. A concession of Barotseland in the same year created a sphere with land and mineral rights. Rhodes's patronage of Consul Johnston and purchase of African Lakes Company interests turned the Nyasa Districts into a Company protectorate. When this arrangement broke down in 1894 over the costs of Johnston's conquests and failure to endorse BSAC claims, there was a partition into the Central African Protectorate of Nyasaland and a Company sphere north of the Zambezi—Northern

[41] Robert I. Rotberg, *The Founder: Cecil Rhodes and the Pursuit of Power* (Oxford, 1988), pp. 311–13.

Rhodesia. Revolt and conquest in Ndebeleland led to a further division of authority in 1898 with the Cape High Commissioner, Alfred Milner, which subordinated Company administration in Southern Rhodesia to a Deputy-Commissioner, in return for settler control of a legislature and all resources.

By then, Imperial confrontation with the Transvaal had reached breaking-point. As in other Imperial and African contests, the origins of that conflict can be understood in terms of the Republic's refusal of political subordination and economic integration. The difference lies in the scale of the interests contested by the British settler colonies and the republics, and in divisions between both Dutch and British at the Cape and Afrikaners, foreign workers (Uitlanders), and foreign companies on the Rand. At stake were the commercial and fiscal returns from trade, customs, and railways in a gold-dominated economy; and secondly, the rights of Uitlanders to representation. For both economic and political reasons, then, the game involved, first, accommodating the Transvaal with partition agreements in the early 1890s, followed later by intimidation and the deployment of force.

In 1890 and 1893 Swaziland became a pawn in this game, and was offered to the Transvaal in return for a customs union which did not eventuate. Cape annexation of territories between Swaziland and the sea, accordingly, cut off independent outlets except through Delagoa Bay. At the same time, railway strategies and provision of a loan in 1891 enabled the Cape to operate lines to Johannesburg and fix rates until 1894. A line through Bechuanaland reached Bulawayo in 1897. But the termination of the 1891 Agreement led to a tariff war in 1894, as German trade with the Transvaal and diplomatic support increased.[42]

The fiasco of Jameson's Raid (a result of Rhodes's scheme to remove the uncooperative Transvaal government), therefore, not merely polarized politics in ways that aligned Chamberlain, Selborne, and Milner with the partisans of political representation in the Transvaal, but aggravated the strain on Cape and Natal finances from loss of railway receipts. Trade and investment were diverted to Free State lines and to Delagoa Bay, which gained some 40 per cent of Transvaal's transit trade. This change lay behind the exaggerated prediction of the Selborne Memorandum in 1896 that the self-governing colonies would become satellites of the Transvaal, and raised doubts about the political loyalty of the Cape under Schreiner's pro-Bond ministry in 1898. If no agreement on the partition of political power and fiscal resources could be reached, deployment of military power became the final option.

[42] J. J. Van-Helten, 'German Capital, the Netherlands Railway Company and the Political Economy of the Transvaal, 1886–1900', *JAH*, IX, 3 (1978), pp. 369–90; Kenneth E. Wilburn, 'The Climax of Railway Competition in South Africa, 1886–1899', unpublished D. Phil. thesis, Oxford, 1982.

In preparation, Salisbury was obliged by Chamberlain and Balfour to take advantage of German insistence on a future share-out of Portuguese territories, in return for abstention from interference in Transvaal affairs, under an Agreement of 30 August 1898.[43] Diplomatic isolation of the Transvaal coincided with German mining capital's misgivings over Kruger's policies in a British 'sphere' about to be reclaimed by force.

EGYPT, THE SUDAN, AND EAST AFRICA

British policy in Cairo after 1890 presented the two dominant trends of the 1880s and 1890s: reliance on methods of clientage in the relationship between the Consul-General and the khedivate; and an acceptance by 1895 that the defence of this position required military and diplomatic action in the Sudan and neighbouring territory. Both policies stemmed from Salisbury's conviction that security in the eastern Mediterranean depended as much on Cairo as on Constantinople, which made Egypt and the Nile prime factors in British African diplomacy for reasons of prestige and power.

Under Baring (Lord Cromer), reserves were built up, taxes were restrained, and Britons, Armenians, and Syrians replaced Egyptians. True, there was resistance in 1892 by the new Khedive Abbas, better educated and with a following from within a nationalist movement. But displays of pride and French competition for khedival loyalty were not a threat. Power lay with Sir Edwin Palmer, as financial adviser, and in Cromer's command of the civil service and the Egyptian Frontier Force. The Khedive ruled, but Cromer controlled the state 'as a sort of unrecognised Prime Minister'.[44]

Although this position came to be tolerated by European powers except France, the stalemate with the Mahdist Sudan and creation of a British sphere between the Congo state and East Africa entailed a partition of interests around the Upper Nile. The hollowness of the claim to the 'western Nile Basin—as a British interpretation of the Anglo-German Agreement of 1890—was exposed when Rosebery and Anderson in the Foreign Office tried to use Leopold's Congo state as a buffer on the western Nile under the Agreement of April–May 1894, and were frustrated by France and Germany. What could not be achieved in bilateral negotiation was claimed unilaterally in the Grey Declaration of March 1895, as French pre-emptive rights to the Congo state were renewed and reinforced by military missions.

Two other precautions were taken to defend the Upper Nile, by agency work in Uganda, and diplomatic work in Somaliland and Ethiopia. Profiting from the Anglo-German Agreement, the Imperial British East Africa Company sent in F. D.

---

[43] J. A. S. Grenville, *Lord Salisbury and Foreign Policy* (London, 1964), pp. 186–98.

[44] Cromer, 'Memorandum', 22 Aug. 1892, *British Documents*, XV, p. 278.

Lugard to hoist the Company flag at Kampala and make a treaty with Kabaka
Mwanga in December 1890, in order to collect revenue and campaign against
Muslims in north-west Buganda. In fact, the Company was too weak for such a
programme, and the position was saved only by missionary propaganda at home
and religious partition in the field to avoid civil war in 1892, when a new Agreement divided territory between Catholics and Protestants. Gladstone and Harcourt favoured evacuation; Rosebery inherited Salisbury's view of the strategic
importance of Buganda, reprieved the IBEA temporarily, and arranged in 1893 for
a suitable report from the Consul-General at Zanzibar, recommending retention.
As the Company moved out, a deputy for the administrator of British East Africa
moved in and used a new treaty as a basis for a colonial Protectorate. As a final
security, Salisbury's railway from Mombasa to Kisumu, rejected by Parliament in
1891, was begun in 1895.

On the eastern flank in Somaliland, British encouragement of Italian aspirations in Africa, in return for the Mediterranean Agreement of 1887 and support in
Egypt, was confirmed by demarcation of spheres from the mouth of the Juba to the
Blue Nile and between Eritrea and the Sudan. This left military use of Kassala open
to Italy; and Rosebery countered French moves inland from Jibouti by delimita-
tion of Somaliland, 5 May 1894, opening Harar to Italian occupation. This co-
operation survived Italian defeat by Ethiopia at Adowa, 1 March 1896. But twelve
days after Adowa Salisbury set in motion a British reconquest of the northern
Sudan, while actively contesting French influence with Menelik and arranging a
treaty, of 14 May 1897, to divide Ethiopians from Mahdists in the coming struggle
between Abdallahi and Sir Herbert Kitchener, Sirdar of Egypt's army since 1889.

Behind that initiative, which sent Kitchener's army to Dongola and Berber, lay
Salisbury's concern at French penetration of a British 'sphere' by Marchand's
expedition from the Congo; and behind that episode and others in West Africa
was 'the relative status of Britain and France as Powers'.[45] Destruction of the
Mahdists at Omdurman in 1898 enabled Kitchener to face down Marchand at
Fashoda and obtain his withdrawal. More importantly, Salisbury was able from
June 1898 to assert a claim to the Sudan as a joint Anglo-Egyptian sphere of
occupation and lift the incubus of international intervention under a Condominium Agreement of January 1899. Thus, both the deployment of force, including
naval mobilization, and the use of a client state put an end to French claims to the
Bahr al-Ghazal and Darfur by the Agreement of 21 March 1899 and saved Salisbury's political reputation, before a greater conflagration absorbed British Imperial energies in South Africa.

[45] G. N. Sanderson, 'The Origins and Significance of the Anglo-French Confrontation at Fashoda,
1898', in Prosser Gifford and Wm. Roger Louis, eds., *France and Britain in Africa: Imperial Policy and
Colonial Rule* (New Haven, 1971), p. 289.

WESTERN AFRICA

From 1890 the practice of extending British influence and control north of the coastal enclaves by treaties and jurisdiction worked well enough, as long as claims were not challenged by African resistance or by French expansion. In Gambia and Sierra Leone, administrative patronage of chieftaincies in the interior was formalized by Protectorates in 1893 and 1895 on the models of Bechuanaland and Zululand. In the Gold Coast, Asante refused such patronage and was taken under a Resident at Kumasi.[46] In the Lagos hinterland administrators extended clientage by treaty with Yoruba states, after minor annexations and a display of force against Ijebu in 1892. To the north-east, Lagos Colony contested influence with the Royal Niger Company in Ilorin; and to the east the Niger Coast Protectorate was forced into a boundary demarcation at Forcados, in return for assurances the Company would not operate in the Lagos hinterland (Map 27.1).[47]

The African challenge to this elementary partition for jurisdiction and control arose from changes in the credit structure and the monopolies of trading systems in the Niger Delta markets under consular authority and Company rule, or from taxation and legislation for concessions in Sierra Leone and the Gold Coast. Eviction of prominent African merchants, suppression of a rising by middlemen at Akassa in 1894, and reform of the Oil Rivers' courts at Old Calabar, removed political leaders and turned more pliant Igbo, Ibibio, and Efik traders into 'consul men'.[48] While European firms declined to move inland, these agents operated networks which rivalled German trade at the Cross River, and challenged the RNC, prompting a formal enquiry into its methods in 1895. For the rest of the decade the Company was on trial, as it tried to extend its control by armed intervention in Nupe and Ilorin and contested the French advance to Bussa. In Sierra Leone the Hut Tax revolt of 1898 warned against imposing the costs of administrative partition on to chieftaincies; and Gold Coast resistance to the Lands Bill, 1894–97, warned that concessions in West Africa might have to be treated on a different basis from those in East Africa.

While treaties and use of force could be adapted to deal with problems of control, the unresolved contest with France over tariffs and frontiers left vague in the 1890 Agreement sharpened after French conquest of Dahomey. Protectionism in French treaties worried British exporters and was taken sufficiently seriously by Salisbury and Rosebery to obtain informal concessions to British trade in

---

[46] Newbury, ed., *British Policy Towards West Africa*, II, pp. 270, 292–95.

[47] Flint, *Goldie*, chap. 11; W. I. Ofonogoro, 'The Opening up of Southern Nigeria to British Trade and its Consequences: Economic and Social History, 1881–1916', unpublished Ph.D. dissertation, Columbia University, 1971.

[48] Kannan K. Nair, *Politics and Society in South Eastern Nigeria, 1841–1906: A Study of Power, Diplomacy and Commerce in Old Calabar* (London, 1972), pp. 203–04.

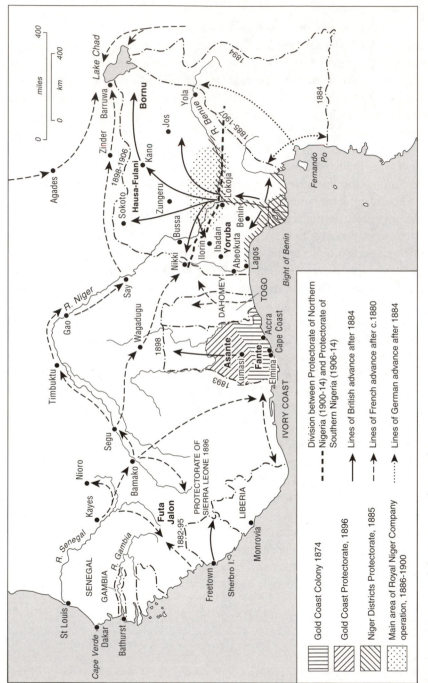

Gold Coast Colony 1874

Gold Coast Protectorate, 1896

Niger Districts Protectorate, 1885

Main area of Royal Niger Company
operation, 1886–1900

Division between Protectorate of Northern
Nigeria (1900–14) and Protectorate of
Southern Nigeria (1906–14)

Lines of British advance after 1884

Lines of French advance after c.1880

Lines of German advance after 1884

MAP 27.1. Britain and the Partition of West Africa

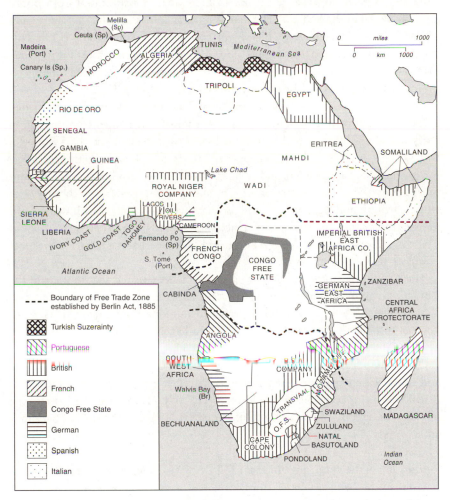

Melilla
(Sp)
Ceuta (Sp)
Madeira
(Port)
Canary Is (Sp.)
MOROCCO
ALGERIA
TUNIS
Mediterranean Sea
TRIPOLI
EGYPT
RIO DE ORO
SENEGAL
GAMBIA
GUINEA
ERITREA
SOMALILAND
MAHDI
Lake Chad
ROYAL NIGER
COMPANY
WADI
ETHIOPIA
SIERRA
LEONE
LIBERIA
IVORY COAST
GOLD COAST
TOGO
DAHOMEY
LAGOS
OIL
RIVERS
CAMEROON
Fernando Po
(Sp)
S. Tomé
(Port)
FRENCH
CONGO
IMPERIAL BRITISH
EAST
AFRICA CO.
Atlantic Ocean
CONGO
FREE
STATE
ZANZIBAR
CABINDA
GERMAN
EAST
AFRICA
CENTRAL
AFRICA
PROTECTORATE
ANGOLA
SOUTH
WEST
AFRICA
COMPANY
Walvis Bay
(Br)
MADAGASCAR
TRANSVAAL
SWAZILAND
BECHUANALAND
O.F.S.
ZULULAND
NATAL
CAPE
COLONY
BASUTOLAND
PONDOLAND
Indian
Ocean

miles   1000
km   1000

Boundary of Free Trade Zone
established by Berlin Act, 1885

Turkish Suzerainty

Portuguese

British

French

Congo Free State

German

Spanish

Italian

MAP 27.2. Britain and the Partition of Africa, *c.*1891: International Boundaries and Areas
of Effective Occupation

Guinea and the French Sudan in Anglo-French boundary negotiations for Sierra Leone, 22 January 1895. But trade rights remained an issue for both sides as diplomacy concentrated on reconciling territorial claims in Gwandu and Borgu with French claims to a port on the Niger.

Behind this contest in the west lay, too, the problem of Egypt. Kimberley might well have linked Niger territory to the Nile, after the collapse of the Anglo-Congolese agreement in 1894, but not to the extent of withdrawal from Borgu and self-denial in the Sudan.[49] The march on Dongola ruled out any such trade-off; and the evidence is that while Egypt continued to sour relations, the Nile provinces were excluded from negotiations over West Africa. At most the impending crisis over Marchand's advance to Fashoda served to concentrate diplomatic minds, before public rhetoric became too strident.

On the British side Joseph Chamberlain's arrival at the Colonial Office stiffened Salisbury and British representatives on the Anglo-French Niger Commission in Paris and allowed time to build up 'a small West African army' and back doubtful treaty claims by force.[50] Use of force against French patrols was sanctioned in 1897 for the region west of Sokoto, and advances from Lagos into Borgu were military precautions against diplomatic failure. The stakes were raised from February 1898, when partition and freedom of trade on the Niger were linked with wider tariff harmonization. Once this bargain was accepted in Paris, the last arguments about a port of access and the division of Borgu and Mossi were settled, leaving the most populous emirates to the British sphere.

The Anglo-French Convention of 14 June 1898 demarcated the frontiers of the Gold Coast and Northern Nigeria contiguous to French territories, and was complemented by an agreement on the neutral zone boundary with German Togo. It spelled the end of the RNC as a political agency; its tortuous background negotiations over a region of exaggerated worth risked political reputations and national prestige. As such, the Convention marked a climax in British official and unofficial chauvinism represented by Chamberlain and Goldie, as much as British moves to consolidate a hold on Egypt and advance on the Upper Nile marked the high point of a more subtle Imperial resolve in the style of Salisbury and Cromer.

Ratification of the 1898 Convention the following year and agreement by France to stay out of the Bahr-al-Ghazal and Darfur had a significance beyond Africa. In combination with increasing naval and industrial competition with Germany,

---

[49] Anderson, Memorandum, 13 Oct. 1894, cited in Claire Hirshfield, *The Diplomacy of Partition: Britain, France and the Creation of Nigeria, 1890–1898* (The Hague, 1979), p. 65.

[50] Chamberlain to Maxwell, 4 June 1897, in Newbury, ed., *British Policy Towards West Africa*, II, p. 224.

these settlements unblocked the way to an accommodation with France and an approach to Russia to settle contests in Asia.

Before that could happen British policy survived international vulnerability during the South African War, because of naval command of the approaches to South Africa. By 1900 the isolation which Salisbury had used to advantage was recognized as dangerous in terms of continental naval combinations. Chamberlain and Balfour were willing to seek an approach to Russia through France, rejecting further overtures to Germany. The occasion for a rapproachement offered in North Africa, where France still refused recognition of the occupation of Egypt, exercising a veto over funds administered by the Debt Commission, and where both powers sought patronage over the sultan of Morocco. British influence weakened in Rabat and French leverage weakened in Cairo as Egypt's finances improved, resulting in Agreements (1903–04), which included toleration of British occupation in return for withdrawal from Moroccan customs control.[51] Diplomatically the Anglo-French Entente of 1904 led to support for France against Germany during the two Moroccan crises of 1904–06 and 1911. Acceptance of the Anglo-Egyptian Condominium by Menelik in 1902, and abandonment of claims to the Sudan provinces by Leopold in 1906, rounded off two decades of British intervention by diplomacy and force on the Nile.

Partition did not stop there with lines on maps. The map was redrawn, of course, for some German territories after 1914. But cartography was only one aspect of the partition of peoples and resources. Reallocation of territory continued as access to land and minerals featured in provincial and district demarcations and concessions.[52] African revolts, 1900–06, in Asante and Zululand, and the conquest of Northern Nigeria, resulted in division of authority in both hierarchical and geopolitical terms, as major ethnic units were incorporated into colonial units. The clearest cases of resource allocation through internal partition were those favouring white settlers, which took place in Rhodesia in the 1890s, in Kenya's highlands from 1902, and continuously in South Africa over a longer period. Everywhere in British Africa partition 'changed the cultural landscape',[53] and left boundaries which testify to the results of conflict resolution between European powers and between the British and their successors.

---

[51] Pierre Guillen, 'The Entente of 1904 as a Colonial Settlement', in Gifford and Louis, eds., *France and Britain*, pp. 333–68.

[52] *CPA*, Nos. 537, 772, 869, 929, for partition of resources in East and Central Africa; Newbury, ed., *British Policy Towards West Africa*, II, pp. 519–93, for concessions in British West Africa; and for boundaries, A. I. Asiwaju and P. O. Adeniyi, eds., *Borderlands in Africa: A Multidisciplinary and Comparative Focus on Nigeria and West Africa* (Lagos, 1989).

[53] Antoine Jean Bullier, *Partition et répartition: Afrique du Sud, histoire d'une stratégie ethnique (1880–1980)* (Paris, 1988).

Select Bibliography

J. D. FAGE, *An Atlas of African History* (London, 1966).

STIG FÖRSTER, WOLFGANG J. MOMMSEN, and RONALD ROBINSON, eds., *Bismarck, Europe and Africa: The Berlin Africa Conference, 1884–1885, and the Onset of Partition* (Oxford, 1988).

PROSSER GIFFORD and WM. ROGER LOUIS, eds., *Britain and Germany in Africa: Imperial Rivalry and Colonial Rule* (New Haven, 1967).

—— *France and Britain in Africa: Imperial Rivalry and Colonial Rule* (New Haven, 1971).

VINCENT T. HARLOW and E. M. CHILVER, eds., *History of East Africa*, Vol. II (Oxford, 1965).

JOHN D. HARGREAVES, *Prelude to the Partition of West Africa* (London, 1966).

—— *West Africa Partitioned*, I: *The Loaded Pause, 1885–89.* (London, 1974); II: *The Elephants and the Grass* (London, 1985).

WILLIAM L. LANGER, *European Alliances and Alignments, 1871–1890*, 2nd. edn. (New York, 1950).

—— *The Diplomacy of Imperialism, 1890–1902*, 2nd edn. (New York, 1951).

ROLAND OLIVER and G. N. SANDERSON, eds., *The Cambridge History of Africa*, Vol. VI: *From 1870–1905* (Cambridge, 1985).

RONALD ROBINSON and JOHN GALLAGHER, with ALICE DENNY, *Africa and the Victorians: The Official Mind of Imperialism*, 2nd. edn. (London, 1981).

G. N. SANDERSON, *England, Europe and the Upper Nile, 1882–1899* (Edinburgh, 1965).

ALEXANDER SCHÖLCH, *Egypt for the Egyptians: The Socio-Political Crisis in Egypt, 1878–1882* (London, 1981).

D. M. SCHREUDER, *The Scramble for Southern Africa, 1877–1895: The Politics of Partition Reappraised* (Cambridge, 1980).

MONICA WILSON and LEONARD THOMPSON, eds., *The Oxford History of South Africa*, Vol. II, *South Africa, 1870–1966* (Oxford, 1971).

28

The British Occupation of Egypt from 1882

AFAF LUTFI AL-SAYYID-MARSOT

Many contemporaries doubted neither the necessity nor the ultimate success of Britain's intervention in Egypt, designed to overcome the economic and political crisis of 1875–82. According to Sir Alfred Milner:

Here was a country... which during the last half-century had been becoming ever more and more an appanage of Europe, in which thousands of European lives and millions of European capital were at stake, and in which of all European nations Great Britain was, by virtue of its enormous direct trade and still more enormous transit trade, the most deeply interested. And this country, which the common efforts and sacrifices of all the Powers had just dragged from the verge of bankruptcy, was now threatened, not with bankruptcy merely, but with a reign of blank barbarism... And when at last we had overcome our conscientious, if ill-timed hesitancy, our action was beyond all anticipation prompt and effective. Let it always be remembered that Great Britain did save Egypt from anarchy, and all European nations interested in Egypt from incalculable losses in blood and treasure, to say nothing of the deep dishonour which those losses... would have brought on civilized mankind.[1]

Milner's account, published in 1892 immediately after his three years at the Egyptian Finance Ministry, was constantly reprinted to reiterate contemporary wisdom. Its thirteenth edition appeared in 1920, timed to remind politicians of Britain's achievement as they contemplated a new, post-war settlement of Anglo-Egyptian relations. It was, nevertheless, a study revealing more of the official class to which Milner belonged and the audience for which he wrote, than of Britain's interest in and impact upon the country which it virtually ruled.

That there was some truth in Milner's description of Egypt's position on the eve of Britain's invasion is clear from the broad outlines of Britain's nineteenth-century involvement with Egypt. Napoleon's Egyptian campaign in July 1798, his conquest of Alexandria and Cairo, and his advance into Syria, may now seem ill-calculated,

---

[1] Viscount Milner, *England in Egypt*, 11th edn. (London, 1904), pp. 13–14.

short-lived ventures. Napoleon himself returned to France in August 1799, and the French were finally driven out of Egypt by British arms in 1801. British officials, however, remained conscious of French ambitions to dominate the Mediterranean, their search for influence or territory in North Africa and the Levant, and the potential threat these posed, to Britain's own Mediterranean commerce which grew rapidly after 1840, and to the far greater interests which she was accumulating in India. During the nineteenth century nothing happened to calm these worries; if anything, they grew more serious.[2]

In Egypt itself, two sustained processes were at work. Under both Muhammad Ali and later khedives government policy aimed in various ways to exploit European resources—capital, communications, technical skills, and education—to establish Egypt's effective independence of Constantinople. This state-building exercise became entangled with the associated transformation of Egypt's economy, which took a direction contrary to khedival ambitions. Well before 1880 modernization, diversification, and industrial growth were being moulded by incorporation into a global economy, principally as a supplier to Europe of raw materials, notably cotton, and consumer of its manufactured goods.

Economic change had significant social and political consequences. Not only overseas connections but the numbers of resident 'foreigners' grew considerably, from $c.8,000–10,000$ in 1838 to some 90,000 by 1881. This polyglot capitalist community embraced not only Armenians, Jews, Greeks, and others from the eastern Mediterranean, but British, French, and Italians, newcomers as well as old. Indigenous élites also thrived: surviving members of the traditional Turco-Circassian ruling class increasingly integrated into Egyptian society; landed proprietors, from highly placed members of the extended royal and official families down to local village notables; and administrators with Western educations absorbed into the enlarged state machine. Blurring distinctions between 'foreign' and 'indigenous', 'European' and 'Egyptian', these groups lived together in uneasy relationships, at once co-operative and intensely competitive, participants in a kaleidoscopic medley of economic ambition and social, ethnic, or occupational bonds.

The careers of Muhammad Ali's successors after 1848 demonstrated how inadequate Egypt's own institutions were to the management of this rapidly expanding economy with its attendant social change and domestic political challenges. They also revealed that external impositions, in the shape of ever-freer trade and extraterritorial privileges for Europeans, while designed to remedy local 'deficiencies', tended simultaneously to unleash a tide of commercial rapacity which seriously exacerbated local problems, hindering the development of local indus-

---

[2] See above, pp. 10–12.

tries and destroying the trust, confidence, and sense of proportion essential to sound exchange.[3]

Matters came to a head under the Khedive Ismail (1863–79). Fresh attempts at industrialization faltered without adequate local powers of trade protection, and financial problems arose from his involvement in construction of the Suez Canal. Constant borrowing, unchecked by internal government restraints, much of which was spent on public works and economic improvements but with some waste on unproductive investments, finally brought bankruptcy in 1875–76.[4] With commercial confidence temporarily shattered, the livelihoods of firms, business groups, and individuals of many nationalities were also threatened. External intervention therefore followed, led by private financial interests in Britain and France. A body known as the Caisse de la Dette Publique, organized by the four chief bondholding European powers, was set up to supervise the Egyptian budget and economy, and to make sure the bondholders were paid. A Dual Control (whereby two controllers, an Englishman and a Frenchman, came to control the Egyptian economy) was imposed in 1876. Stringent financial controls and economies provoked great discontent and disputes with the Khedive, which led the Powers to engineer his deposition by the Ottoman Sultan in 1879.

With European governments still anxious to limit their direct involvement, a full financial settlement, the Law of Liquidation, was devised and imposed on Ismail's weak son and successor, Tawfiq (1879–92). A Commission dominated by the British and French but also including Germany, Austria, and Italy, was established to manage the two-thirds of Egypt's revenues assigned to Debt repayment, but also with considerable influence over the revenues left in Egyptian government hands. More than 1,300 foreign officials were brought in at highly inflated salaries to do work previously done more cheaply by Egyptians. Resentment at such actions not only fuelled anti-European feeling but undermined the remaining prestige of the Khedive's government. This resulted in the Urabi Rebellion of September 1881, a military revolt led by the only four native Egyptian colonels in the army; with its nationalist slogan of 'Egypt for the Egyptians' directed at their Turco-Circassian rulers, it was broadly supported among élite groups, intellectuals, and the rural population.

This marked the final phase of the crisis, prompting British fears for the security of the Suez Canal and worry among Europeans that the Egyptian nationalists might renege on repayment of the Debt. The Khedive dreaded deposition by his army, which, with considerable civilian support, was demanding a constitution.

---

[3] David S. Landes, *Bankers and Pashas: International Finance and Economic Imperialism in Egypt* (London, 1958); see above, pp. 149–53.

[4] Roger Owen, *The Middle East in the World Economy, 1800–1914* (London, 1981), pp. 127–28.

When an Anglo-French Joint Note was presented in January 1882 and a naval force was sent to Egypt in May, as gestures of support for the ruler, they only provoked yet more unrest and further weakened the Khedive. Riots in Alexandria in June, involving Europeans fearing massacre and Egyptians afraid of imminent occupation, resulted in the killing of about fifty Europeans and 170 Egyptians. Panic, arrogance, desperate concern for British strategic and economic interests, partial information, and biased reportage blended in a final confusion of thought and intention which has generated debate ever since about British motives.[5] Alexandria was bombarded by the Royal Navy. When the Ottoman Sultan refused to intervene, a military expedition was planned which the French also refused to join. With the Khedive's backing, British troops landed on 16 August and defeated Egyptian nationalist forces in the Battle of Tel-el-Kebir (13 September). Thus began the occupation of Egypt.

British government pronouncements suggested that Britain's occupation was temporary, its intention being to 'rescue' Egypt from 'disorder' and the Egyptian throne from a nationalist movement, dubbed a 'military mutiny', and then to 'retire'. There was in reality neither general agreement nor clearly conceived policy. While liberals anticipated rapid restoration of Egyptian political control, hardliners in Whitehall and men on the spot, notably Sir Evelyn Baring (British Consul-General from September 1883, later Lord Cromer), reasoned otherwise. The fundamental incompatibility between desire for rapid withdrawal and the time required to create the stability which was its precondition became ever more apparent, especially after Britain's forced evacuation of the Sudan in 1885 and her failure to secure the Convention negotiated with the Ottoman Sultan in 1887. Ever more strongly supported by the Foreign Office, Baring persuaded successive Imperial governments of the need to remain and reform not only Egyptian finances, which he returned to solvency by 1889, but a wide range of other institutions.[6]

Prominent in arguments for prolonging the occupation was the Suez Canal. British Military and Naval Intelligence became steadily more convinced that the security of Imperial routes required direct control; and a naval base like Alexandria, added to Malta and Cyprus, strengthened Britain's regional position. There were beneficial economic interests, evident before 1875 but growing steadily in importance after 1882 as a consequence of the measures to restore Egyptian solvency: Egyptian long-staple cotton for the mills of Lancashire, valuable markets

---

[5] A. G. Hopkins, 'The Victorians and Africa: A Reconsideration of the Occupation of Egypt, 1882', *Journal of African History*, XXVII (1986), pp. 363–91.

[6] Afaf Lutfi al-Sayyid, *Egypt and Cromer* (London, 1968); Alexander Schölch, *Egypt for the Egyptians* (Ithaca, NY, 1981).

for British goods, and opportunities for overseas investment.[7] Interwoven with other private preoccupations like careers and pensions, as well as genuine belief that Egyptians could not run their own country effectively, these interests came to seem increasingly vulnerable to a British withdrawal.

Politically, the occupation profoundly influenced Egypt's development. Local attempts between 1879 and 1882 to limit the Khedive's autocracy through constitutional reform were ignored. 'Good government' was exalted above 'self government', and British advisers were gradually placed in all departments to guide the Egyptian ministers. Their association with Baring as no more than 'British Agent and Consul-General' sustained the fiction of Cairo's subordination to Constantinople, but in practice Egyptian ministers who disagreed with advisers on what they designated 'important questions' were forced to resign. The Khedive, Tawfiq, accepted British rule to safeguard his throne, and appointed a series of Cabinet ministers likely to defer to British advice. The Egyptian army was temporarily disbanded before being refashioned under British officers, and British forces, financed from the Egyptian treasury, were stationed permanently in Egypt. This system, whereby the Egyptians supposedly ruled their own country, but were manipulated by British advisers responsible to no one save Baring, came to be known as the 'Veiled Protectorate'. As a form of Imperial political control, although evoking striking parallels with British administration in India, it remained *sui generis*.[8]

British contempt for Egyptians was perhaps most starkly illustrated in their handling of the Sudan. Conquered in 1822 by Muhammad Ali, it had revolted against Egyptian rule in 1880 under the aegis of a religious leader, known as the Mahdi (see Map 28.1). In 1883–84, after humiliating defeats by Mahdist troops, the Egyptians were prevented from further attempts at reconquest, and Gladstone's ministry accepted Baring's arguments that cost and security necessitated complete withdrawal. Reconquest of the Sudan only took place in 1896–98, and then according to Imperial diplomatic and military calculations with no intention of rebuilding Egypt's empire. From 1899 the Sudan was put under a condominium government in which ostensibly Egypt and Britain ruled jointly, but where in practice Britain ruled and Egypt paid.[9]

Cowed by a failed nationalist revolt, Urabi's court-martial and exile to Ceylon, and a foreign occupation, the bulk of the population followed the Khedive's lead, and for a decade remained more or less politically quiescent. In the early 1890s, however, a nationalist movement revived at the hands of young men who were, at

---

[7] See Table 28.1.

[8] E. R. J. Owen, 'The Influence of Lord Cromer's Indian Experience on British Policy in Egypt, 1883–1907', *St Antony's Papers*, XVII (1965), pp. 109–39.

[9] See above, pp. 643–44.

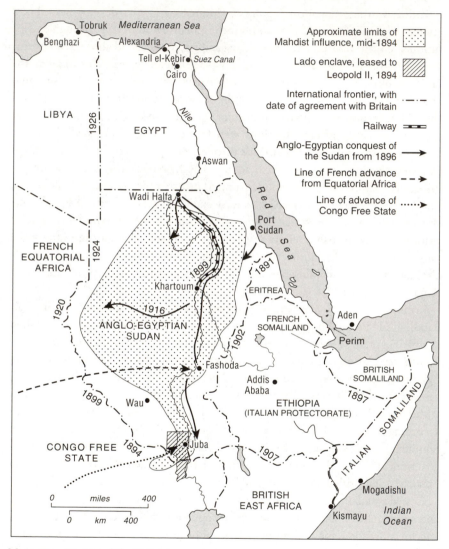

Map 28.1. Egypt and the Sudan

first, aided and abetted by Tawfiq's successor, the Khedive Abbas II (1892–1914). When Abbas tried to rid himself of the restraints of British rule, in confrontations with Baring during 1893–94 over his choice of ministers and army issues, he was threatened with dethronement and exile, and his popularity rose markedly. The movement tried to rouse nationalist feelings among the wider population and so generate a groundswell of opposition to the occupation that would force an evacuation. It had variable success among the literate and educated young, particularly after 1900 under two very different leaders, the gifted orator journalist Mustafa Kamil, and the scholarly liberal constitutionalist Ahmad Lutfi al-Sayyid.

When Lord Cromer retired in 1907, his successor Sir Eldon Gorst was instructed by the Foreign Office to pursue a different policy, one of friendship with the Khedive in order to stem the rising nationalist current. However, the nationalists, after 1904 no longer hopeful of French support, had by then parted company with the Khedive. While apparently open to nationalist approaches, Gorst died in 1911 and was replaced by Lord Kitchener. Kitchener disliked and continued to alienate the Khedive, but his talks with the nationalists regarding independence from the Ottomans also produced no progress towards self rule before the outbreak of war in 1914. Britain's occupation thus deferred self-government, turning Egyptian authorities and officials into cogs in the wheel of a British-directed administration.

This process of tying Egypt more closely to the Empire was reinforced by international circumstances. The Ottoman suzerain, always needing British support against Russian infringement of his territories, acquiesced in the arrangement. The responsibilities of the Caisse de la Dette, which continued to oversee Egyptian revenues and secure interest repayments, allowed member Powers the possibility of vetoing measures touching economic matters. French and German opposition to British actions in many parts of the world was expressed through the Caisse by limiting access to funds, but this only intensified Britain's feeling that she should stay. After 1882 British officials—like their Egyptian predecessors and others elsewhere, such as the Chinese—found foreign nationals endlessly vexatious. Again according to Milner: 'the foreign residents, and especially the Greeks ...are obstreperous and exacting. The Capitulations remove them, to a great extent, from the control of the authorities, and their consuls are disposed to push foreign privilege to its extremest limits.'[10] Following Turkey's support for Germany in November 1914, the British at last unilaterally declared Egypt a Protectorate and imposed a new ruler.

British rule in Egypt was as authoritarian as that of the Khedives. One alien power, Britain, replaced another, the Ottoman suzerain, both intent on using the equally

[10] Milner, England in Egypt, p. 318.

alien Egyptian royal family as their tool. British rule was more orderly and efficient, but no new institutions were established. The administrative arts of census-taking, statistical measurement, and policing were the system's forte, areas of responsibility such as education its Achilles' heel. Baring's reforms and administration concentrated above all on the technical and financial measures necessary to restore long-term solvency, and to minimize European intervention while cultivating local support. This involved stimulating agricultural exports, supporting essential public works, raising government revenues, and attracting foreign capital. These measures inevitably extended the occupation, produced drastic economic changes in both the agricultural and industrial sectors, created stronger bonds with British production, and gave a new direction to Egyptian society.

Well before 1882 Egypt had became a major exporter of cotton to England and a substantial importer of British finished goods. As the result of expanded irrigation works and an increase in the area devoted to cotton production to between 750,000 and 875,000 faddans, cotton provided 76 per cent of all exports by 1880. From the mid-1890s, under the British administration, growth recommenced still more rapidly; cotton farms occupied 1,700,000 faddans from a total cultivated area of 7.5 million between 1909 and 1912, and cotton exports reached 93 per cent.[11]

Symbolic of the link between this transformation and the new balance of political power were the Anglo-Indian irrigation engineers brought in by the new administration. Unlike their predecessors, in Milner's words, 'They do not sit at headquarters, but traverse the country from end to end. And they have a power behind them, which ensures their advice being followed... That is the root of the whole matter... European skill is useless without European authority.'[12] Agriculture the year round and over far wider areas followed completion of the Aswan Dam (1902) and other lesser works by 1908.

Trade with Britain reached 63 per cent of total exports and 38 per cent of imports in the late 1890s, and while trade with other countries also increased significantly, it did so in different proportions. Thus, in 1909, while the total trade with Britain reached £E13m, doubling that of 1885–89, that with France had also doubled, but only from £E1m to £E2m; trade with Turkey, which a century earlier had formed the bulk of Egyptian trade, increased by barely £E1,000. Because the cotton crop was so lucrative, the area devoted to other major food export crops (onions, rice, beans, barley, sugar) declined between 1886 and 1909. By then Egypt was in serious danger of becoming a single-crop economy. Eventually, even basic foods—cereals, peas, and lentils—had to be imported to meet the shortfall in local supplies.[13]

[11] One faddan is slightly larger than an acre. A. E. Crouchley, *The Economic Development of Modern Egypt* (London, 1938), pp. 153, 259, 263–64.

[12] Milner, *England in Egypt*, p. 233.

[13] Crouchley, *Economic Development*, p. 169; Owen, *The Middle East*, pp. 110–16, 136, 218.

Agricultural lands owned by the khedivial family, known as the Daira Saniyya (Domain lands) and used as collateral on its various loans, were also sold off. With sales organized in parcels of over 50 faddans, the equivalent of a comparatively large estate, only the affluent—usually existing large landowners—could afford to buy them. Sometimes the buyers were foreigners, as in 1898 when unsold Daira Saniyya lands, some 108,122 faddans, were sold off to just four French and British nationals. By 1907 foreigners controlled roughly 12 per cent of the land. However, most went to existing local landowners, thus strengthening the notables on whom the British relied to keep order in the countryside. Such sales complemented the insistence on free trade, helping to ensure that cotton remained the favoured crop, and so guaranteeing the support of the landowners who sold their cotton crop to England (Table 28.1).[14]

These developments pressed hard on the peasants (fellahin). Although population grew from 7.6 to 12.3 million (1880–1914), peasant-produced food crops remained less financially rewarding than either cotton or rice, which were grown mainly by the medium and large landowners. This perpetuated a trend, evident shortly after 1821 when long-staple cotton was first discovered in Egypt, and paralleled in many parts of British India, whereby small landowners were slowly squeezed out of their holdings and obliged to sell to the large. Rising demand for land, which had become the major source of wealth in the country for Egyptians, brought increased land prices and rents and a marked decline in the average size of peasant holdings, thus bankrupting many of the less wealthy. Large estates, latifundia, grew at the expense of the middling and small owners and occupiers.

TABLE 28.1. *Egypt's foreign trade, 1885–1913* (annual averages, £E000)

	Imports				Exports	
	Textiles: cloth and thread	Cereals, flour and vegetables	Coffee, sugar	Total all imports	Cotton and cotton seed	Total all exports
1885–89	2,586	720	309	7,947	9,874	12,548
1890–94	2,981	736	323	8,872	11,322	14,494
1895–99	3,161	1,112	257	10,249	12,338	14,963
1900–04	4,898	1,672	318	16,297	17,779	20,583
1905–09	6,296	3,260	765	23,805	24,412	27,161
1910–13	7,178	3,321	838	26,238	29,675	32,652

Source: Roger Owen, *The Middle East in the World Economy, 1800–1914* (London, 1981), p. 241

[14] Asim Disuqi, *Kibar mullak al-aradi al-ziraiyya wa dawruhum fi-l mujtama al-Misri* [Large Landowners and their Role in Egyptian Society] (Cairo, 1975); Ali Barakat, *Tatawwur al-milkiyya al-ziraiyya fi Misr wa atharuh ala-l-haraka al-siyasiyya* [The Development of Agricultural Landownership in Egypt and its Effect on the Political Movement] (Cairo, 1977).

Growing numbers of poor or landless peasants then became part of a large reservoir of cheap labour for the cotton fields of the wealthy landowners. As the population grew, peasants relied more on cheaper but less nutritious staples such as maize. Furthermore, the turnover of the land from basin to perennial irrigation encouraged the growth of parasites in the irrigation canals, which infected more and more peasants, causing the debilitating diseases bilharzia and schistomiasis. The physical output of the peasant diminished, and the diseases eventually often killed him.

Changes in industry were just as drastic and were closely related to those in agriculture. Baring frowned on the establishment of local industries, especially any requiring economic protection, which was persistently refused. Only those relating to the processing of cotton or to those with 'natural advantages' (soap, sugar, bakeries) were allowed.[15] Whatever industries arose were often financed and owned by foreigners who benefited from the Capitulations by not being subject to Egyptian laws, and could avoid taxes paid by Egyptian nationals. Furthermore, all state enterprises set up by the Khedive Ismail were sold, many to new European immigrants, to pay off Egypt's loans. Entrepreneurs brave enough to set up industries linked to cotton-weaving were made to pay an 8 per cent tax on textiles produced locally, making them little cheaper than textiles imported from Britain that also paid an 8 per cent duty. Egyptians seeking to invest in industries found themselves battling against excess taxes and unrestrained international competition. There nevertheless emerged after 1890 a highly complex pattern of rival coalitions of local investors and business groups, a 'business oligarchy' of old residents and newcomers, nationals, resident and non-resident foreigners, whose investments spanned industry, trade, transport, and landed property. United not by simple ethnic or 'international capitalist' identities, but by substantial local interests and an entrepreneurial ethic, their members had increasingly to be cultivated by Cromer and his successors.[16]

In his two-volume work *Modern Egypt*, Baring justified his economic programme in Egypt by contrasting his fiscal rectitude with Ismail's 'spendthrift ways'.[17] Yet Egypt's foreign debt increased to £E116.6m over the two decades following the occupation, spent mainly on irrigation works and other improvements to the infrastructure similar to Ismail's expenditures. While 30 per cent of the country's exports went to pay the Public Debt, the remainder was spent on consumption, expatriated or reinvested in the export sector, leaving little for

---

[15] Robert Mabro and Samir Radwan, *The Industrialization of Egypt, 1939–73* (Oxford, 1976), pp. 19–20.

[16] Robert Vitalis, *When Capitalists Collide: Business Conflict and the End of Empire in Egypt* (Berkeley, 1995), chaps. 1–2.

[17] Earl of Cromer, *Modern Egypt*, 2 vols. (London, 1908).

domestic investment (Table 28.2).[18] Egypt's evident economic well-being was the justification most frequently given for the continued British occupation of the country. Yet when financial solvency was pursued at the cost of destroying local industries, allowing trade and commerce to fall into British or other foreign hands, and denuding the majority of their country's wealth in favour of foreigners, the programme alienated Egyptians of all classes. Indeed, ending the transfer of Egyptian wealth into foreign pockets became a justification for ridding Egypt of the occupation. Baring only exacerbated Egyptian animosity when he claimed that there was no Egyptian nationality, as most of the country's wealth lay in foreign hands, and that all the nationalists meant to do was exploit their fellow countrymen. It was clear to Egyptian political and social élites that that was precisely what Britain was doing while claiming to protect the Egyptian peasant.

Egyptian society under the occupation was also to change in a number of ways. Past Egyptian rulers had tried to bring in European codes, such as the Code Napoléon, to replace the Sharia (law based in part on the teachings of the Koran, the sayings of the Prophet Muhammad, and on analogy and consensus). According to Ottoman regulations non-Muslims were judged by their own religious sects, under the *millet* system. Ismail and his minister, Nubar Pasha, had tried to create a legal system that would allow commercial litigation between Egyptians and foreigners. This produced a new hybrid, the Mixed Courts, but the judges were mostly Europeans with but few Egyptians, and lawyers licensed to plead before these courts had to be Western-trained and cognizant of a foreign language. Baring, who was contemptuous of Islam and the Islamic laws of the Sharia, continued the process of Europeanizing the law. This resulted in the rise of a school for judges and a school for law, mostly taught in French since the legal system was based on the Code Napoléon.

TABLE 28.2. *Egypt's balance of trade and movements of capital, 1884–1914* (£E)

Period	Adverse balance of trade	Inflow of capital
1884–92	419,000	12,000
1893–97	1,268,000	1,065,000
1898–1902	2,723,000	2,144,000
1903–07	9,072,000	8,616,000
1908–14	2,550,000	3,150,000

Source: A. E. Crouchley, *The Investment of Foreign Capital in Egyptian Companies and Public Debt* (Cairo, 1936), p. 196.

[18] Mabro and Radwan, *Industrialization of Egypt*, pp. 19–20.

Knowledge of a foreign language increased the popularity of foreign institutions of learning which served not only to educate a new élite but also to distance or alienate them from their own language and culture. While Baring bemoaned the lack of education, he nevertheless refused government money for public schools, and the increasing limitation of Muslim establishments to purely religious learning evident before 1882, continued. The administration became crowded with Englishmen, Maltese, and Levantines, hired because they spoke English or French. Young Egyptians, educated either abroad or among the 60,000 or so in Egypt's private 'western' schools by 1910, were made subservient to equally young Englishmen. The latter, imported in growing numbers, helped to exacerbate nationalist feelings. The new taxes and legal system were totally incomprehensible to the workers and the peasants. When the latter lost their land for failure to pay taxes, they resorted to social brigandage—a phenomenon Cromer, like the often alien and absentee landowners, failed to grasp. Society thus became divided between the Europeanized administration and élites, and the masses whose culture remained Islamic and Arabic.[19]

The increasing numbers of foreign residents encouraged altered patterns of consumption. Changes in fashion and consumption already begun under Ismail accelerated under the occupation. In major cities, traditional artisanal workshops made way for new-style department stores, owned and run by wealthy outsiders. These sold European goods, encouraging fashionable changes in lifestyle for the affluent Egyptian who built new Italianate-style villas, apartments, and government buildings, designed by Italian and Greek architects. Furniture changed from *a la turca* to European, as did *objets d'art*. In brief, everything European from food to musical instruments was adopted by élites desperate to show their occupiers how westernized they had become. This displaced numerous local workers in favour of Greek, Italian, Armenian, and Maltese immigrants, who took over significant areas of production, only occasionally using Egyptians as their apprentices.[20]

Lastly, many women also experienced further changes in their position. Women in the eighteenth century had had considerable opportunities. According to Islamic law they were free to own property, invest widely, and sue in the courts over financial or personal matters, supported by the *ulama* (clerics). Under a more centralized regime beginning with Muhammad Ali, they were isolated and pushed out of professions they had previously practised. Muhammad Ali had monopolized all money-making venues and allowed only males who served him to benefit

[19] Robert L. Tignor, *Modernization and British Colonial Rule in Egypt, 1882–1914* (Princeton, 1966), pp. 319–30.

[20] J. Beinin and Z. Lockman, *Workers on the Nile* (Princeton, 1987), pp. 33–35.

from them.[21] The development of new interest groups in the course of the nineteenth century had eroded their position still further, but in the 1880s and 1890s women were encouraged to become educated in the European fashion and consequently became avid consumers of European goods.[22] Cromer, like many others, pointed to the position of women as an indication of the backwardness of Egypt and hence its unfitness for self-rule. To belie this accusation, élites hurried to educate women in foreign-language schools, most opened by missionaries and religious orders. Where in the past élite women, a whole strata of whom were alien, spoke Turkish, using Arabic only for religious activities, now an entire generation of indigenous élite women arose who spoke better French than Turkish or Arabic, and were better acquainted with European culture than their own. This reduced still further the possibility of managing their own economic affairs, and kept them just as dependent as before on males.

The immediate outcome of the occupation was to limit the income-generating possibilities of the average Egyptian, and to displace many by non-Egyptians. It entrenched a new class system, composed of large landowners, a business oligarchy, and small middle class of government bureaucrats, and a large class of workers and peasants. It exacerbated the chasm between the élites and the masses by encouraging foreign elements in the administration, and created groups with totally different world outlooks as a consequence of different kinds of education and cultural upbringing. Last, but not least, it inhibited industrialization and the search for alternative sources of wealth while entrenching a large landowning class depending for its income on the sale of cotton to Britain. For Imperial Britain, the occupation provided a naval base and strengthened control of an indispensable passage to Asia. It provided a market for British goods and a guaranteed source of raw materials for British industries. Lastly, it acted as a safety valve for surplus youth, allowing young men to find positions overseas that they could not have found at home.

Colonial occupations have invariably prompted the rise of nationalist movements underlining the economic, legal, and political discrimination inseparable from foreign rule. Egypt was no exception either in this or in the willingness of its people after 1914 to overturn 'efficient' government in favour of a less 'efficient' one, to escape colonial subordination and conscious alienation. Nationalist movements, however, are born not only of resentment and resistance, much as events such as the shocking British retribution for the Danishway (Dinshawai) incident

[21] Afaf Lutfi al-Sayyid Marsot, *Women and Men in Eighteenth-Century Egypt* (Austin, Tex., 1995), p. 140.

[22] Timothy Mitchell, *Colonising Egypt* (Cambridge, 1988), p. 113.

of 1906 lived on in Egyptian memories.[23] They are also the creation of Imperial rulers' never-ending search for collaborators, of the cultural and political adaptation found necessary by rulers and ruled to sustain government and promote social and economic improvement. Cromer's caution, his capable but unimaginative administration, his inflexibility, and genuflection towards Indian precedents, often caused offence. But they also embodied values akin to those important to Ahmad Lutfi's People's Party in the years immediately before 1914, the civic virtues, Western education, rule of law, and the reformation of Islamic society, appropriate to the independent Egypt which emerged after 1918.

[23] al-Sayyid, *Egypt and Cromer*, p. 173. In a confrontation between local villages and British officers out shooting at Danishway, one officer was killed and several injured. A special tribunal summarily sentenced four Egyptians to be hanged and fourteen to be flogged, in public.

Select Bibliography

JACQUES BERQUE, *Imperialism and Revolution*, trans. Jean Stewart (London, 1972).

JUAN COLE, *Colonialism and Revolution in the Middle East* (Princeton, 1993).

ALBERT HOURANI, *Arabic Thought in the Liberal Age* (Cambridge, 1962).

ROBERT HUNTER, *Egypt under the Khedives* (Pittsburgh, 1984).

DAVID S. LANDES, *Bankers and Pashas: International Finance and Economic Imperialism in Egypt* (London, 1958).

ROBERT MABRO and SAMIR RADWAN, *The Industrialization of Egypt, 1939–73* (Oxford, 1973).

PETER MANSFIELD, *The British in Egypt* (New York, 1971).

BILLIE MELMAN, *Women's Orients: English Women and the Middle East, 1718–1918, Sexuality, Religion and Work*, 2nd edn. (London, 1995).

VISCOUNT MILNER, *England in Egypt* (London, 1920).

TIMOTHY MITCHELL, *Colonising Egypt* (Cambridge, 1988).

E. R. J. OWEN, *Cotton and the Egyptian Economy* (Oxford, 1969).

—— *The Middle East in the World Economy, 1800–1914* (London, 1981).

SAMIR RADWAN, *Capital Formation in Egyptian Industry and Agriculture, 1882–1967* (London, 1974).

ALAN RICHARDS, *Egypt's Agricultural Development, 1800–1980* (Boulder, Colo., 1982).

AFAF LUTFI AL-SAYYID, *Egypt and Cromer* (London, 1968).

AFAF LUTFI AL-SAYYID-MARSOT, *Egypt in the Reign of Muhammad Ali* (Cambridge, 1984).

—— *Women and Men in Eighteenth-Century Egypt* (Austin, Tex., 1995).

ALEXANDER SCHÖLCH, *Egypt for the Egyptians* (Ithaca, NY, 1981).

ROBERT L. TIGNOR, *Modernization and British Colonial Rule in Egypt, 1882–1914* (Princeton, 1966).

29

Cultural Encounters: Britain and Africa in the Nineteenth Century

T. C. MCCASKIE

Encounters between cultures are complex, ambiguous, and unstable transactions, simultaneously events in time and works of the imagination. Their leitmotif is a tangled knot of realities and representations. This is difficult to untie, for it clothes issues of cause and effect in projections and fantasies. Motive and purpose then become hard to tease out of an already complex factual record that reveals the process of encounter between cultures as a constantly shifting kaleidoscope of give and take. Tension is implicit in this quotidian incommensurability between cultures. Thus, imperatives to imposition and acculturation by one side invoke strategies of negotiation and inculturation by the other. The historical result is an ever evolving cultural hybrid in which imagined, willed, and contingent acts are densely interwoven.[1]

Irrespective of disparities in power, cultural encounters between Britain and Africa in the nineteenth century conformed to the model just described. It is important to acknowledge this, for it is all too easy—but profoundly misleading—to equate the achieved territorial substance of the British Empire in Africa with a hegemony in areas other than the geographical. The image conjured up by this misreading supposes a nineteenth-century retrospect in which an ascendant Britain stamped its cultural imprint ever more forcefully upon passive or other-wise cowed Africans. Leaving aside the issue of Britain's purposes and her own understanding of them, this is simply untrue. The British encounter with African cultures in the nineteenth century—as indeed in the twentieth—was never a direct, one-way road leading from London. This is not to deny the potency of British influence. But it is to situate it in a dialogue. On both sides of this conversation, cultural encounters commonly led to unforeseen or unintended

---

[1] Compare Gananath Obeyesekere, *The Apotheosis of Captain Cook: European Mythmaking in the Pacific* (Princeton, 1992), with Marshall Sahlins, *How 'Natives' Think: About Captain Cook, For Example* (Chicago, 1995). For the early history of the British in West Africa, see Vol. I, chap. by P. E. H. Hair and Robin Law, and Vol. II, chap. by David Richardson.

consequences. Britain assimilated readings and misreadings of Africa to her own concerns with the continent. Africa reciprocated, interpreting the historical substance of the encounter to its own purposes. Even when one partner in the dialogue raised its voice to an Imperial shout, no earlier than the mid-1870s, this changed the tone rather than the fact of conversation.[2]

This latitude of response on both sides needs to be seen in the light of a simple fact. Until the last quarter of the nineteenth century Britain encountered very few African cultures, because the British presence in tropical Africa was perfunctory and equivocal. For much of the century the British presence was confined to small coastal enclaves, to intermittent expeditions or embassies into an unknown interior, or to the offshore influence of the Royal Navy. Britain was a power only of the littoral, with an often precarious tenure and a limited commitment in—and to— Africa. The rest was imagination. In this dispensation the West African coast between the Senegambia in the west and the Niger delta in the east was of singular importance. Here, in West unlike East Africa, the British had an established physical presence—notably on the Gold Coast—going back to the seventeenth century. It was along this West African coast, the hub of British activity in the transatlantic slave trade, that interests were concentrated at the beginning of the nineteenth century. It is here, in what is now Sierra Leone, Ghana, and Nigeria, that we must start with the history of cultural encounter in the nineteenth century. The account given is necessarily complex, and involves much toing and froing between actions and ideas.[3]

The ideas and ideologies that were in play between the epochal Mansfield decision in the Somerset case of 1772 (which prohibited the restitution of former slaves in Britain to their masters) and the emancipation of slaves in Britain's colonies in 1834, were of prime importance in redefining British attitudes and policies towards Africa. In the aftermath of the Mansfield decision the abolitionist Granville Sharp took the lead in organizing the repatriation to Africa of ex-slaves and black refugees from the War of American Independence. Sharp's impulse was evangelical and moral. It was also prescriptive. It presumed that Britain, having unilaterally liquidated slaving, knew what was best for the improvement of Africa. Sharp wanted a Christian colony in Africa, and to this end he and his associates

---

[2] A readable overview is J. D. Fage, *A History of Africa*, 3rd edn. (London, 1995). On key aspects, John Lonsdale, 'States and Social Processes in Africa: A Historiographical Survey', *African Studies Review*, XXIV, 2/3 (1981), 139–225.

[3] For western African societies in the era of the slave trade, Philip D. Curtin, *Economic Change in Precolonial Africa: Senegambia in the Era of the Slave Trade* (Madison, 1975); B. Barry, *La Sénégambie du XVᵉ au XIXᵉ siècle: traite négriere, Islam et conquête coloniale* (Paris, 1988); Robin Law, *The Slave Coast of West Africa, 1550–1750: The Impact of the Atlantic Slave Trade on African Society* (Oxford, 1991); J. C. Miller, *Way of Death: Merchant Capitalism and the Angolan Slave Trade, 1730–1830* (London, 1988).

drew up a constitution for a self-governing community of yeoman farmers. This 'Province of Freedom' was to be planted in Africa, a donation from the morally enlightened to the spiritually impoverished. It would act as beacon and inspiration, casting its Christian light and self-improving example over the surrounding darkness. Britain had abolished the slave trade but still knew best. The 'Province of Freedom' was to be sited in the Sierra Leone estuary (where the British had traded since the sixteenth century). Government fell in with this plan to export an undesirable black community from Britain, and in 1787 some 400 settlers reached Sierra Leone. Land was secured from the uncomprehending Temne of Koya by an agreement rich in irony. Britain's attempt to improve Africa had as its foundational act the first instance, in West Africa, in which sovereign rather than tenant rights were transferred by treaty.

The 'Province of Freedom' foundered. It was unable to sustain itself economically by farming, and mortality rates were high. Interested idealism had to compromise with harsh reality. The venture was taken over and refinanced by a shareholding company (1791–1808) and thereafter by government. In the process it lost its autonomous status and was administered by London bankers and then by the Secretary of State. Despite these vicissitudes numbers grew. In 1792 the company recruited 'Nova Scotians' (escaped American slaves), numbers of whom were already literate Christians, and in 1800 these were joined by Jamaican Maroons (runaway slaves, predominantly of Gold Coast Akan origin). All these repatriated communities joined together in forming a distinctive culture (sometimes termed Euro-African), albeit not exactly on the model formulated by Sharp. They were enterprising traders rather than subsistence or export farmers, urban rather than rural dwellers, but imbued with ideologies of Christian improvement and material advancement. Their settlement—Freetown—was laid out on the North American colonial grid model, with substantial European-style dwellings sited on large plots. This town became the fount and hub of an emergent culture that was to be replicated elsewhere in West Africa. Its citizens were certainly Christians who placed a premium on literacy and education, but they also modelled their consumption patterns after those of the British middle classes and saw their future in terms of commercial profits and reinvestment in urban property.

The Freetown population was much increased by British measures to implement the abolition of the transatlantic slave trade. After 1808 the Royal Navy patrolled West Africa in order to intercept slave ships under the provisions of a series of bilateral treaties. Captured slavers were arraigned before a Court of Mixed Commission in Freetown and their cargoes, known as Recaptives or Liberated Africans, were settled in Freetown and its peninsular hinterland. By 1820 these freed slaves greatly outnumbered the original settlers, and they continued to arrive until mid-century with a peak in the 1830s to 1840s. By birth Recaptives originated from the entire West African coast, from Senegambia down to the Congo and Angola. But the majority were Yoruba speakers (from present South-West Nigeria), enslaved as a result of the political anarchy, population movement, and endemic warfare that accompanied the protracted collapse (from the 1790s to the 1830s) of the Oyo empire. Recaptives were initially integrated into Sierra Leone's settler society as servants, soldiers, or smallholders. But Governor MacCarthy (1814–24) saw in their numbers an opportunity to revive something of Sharp's original vision of an exemplary Christian community that would cast its civilizing light over African peoples. In short, he proposed to Christianize them and then send them 'home' to serve as models for their countrymen. The Recaptives were settled in villages around Freetown and there exposed to missionary instruction from Anglicans (the Church Missionary Society, arrived 1804) or Methodists (the Wesleyan-Methodists, arrived 1811). Missionaries, always few in number, were joined in this enterprise by already established Freetown settlers.

The Christianizing of Yoruba Recaptives in Freetown was a decisive moment in the cultural encounter between Britain and Africa. Cast up on an alien shore and with a functioning model of a new society placed before them, the Recaptives adopted Christian salvation as a spiritual counterpart to their secular emancipation. Trauma and disorientation must have played a part in this, but so too did the willing embrace of a new life furnished by providence. Recaptives learned English, and took on European names, dress, habits, and tastes. They prized Christian education, the redemptive cornerstone of their own second chance in life, and insisted upon it for their children. But Recaptive Christianity and westernization had specifically African cultural initiatives and components. Yoruba veneration of and identification with ancestors (as in the masked spirits of *egungun*), the spatialized notion of religion in the community (as in the sacred centre—*akata*—of a town quarter), the hierarchies of seniority and authority (as in the institution of the king—*oba*—and the mass of subordinate title-holders), and a host of other cultural signifiers were all assigned reformulated significance in the light of Christian belief. It is a moot point as to what extent Recaptive Yoruba were born again into a new life or familiarly encountered themselves in another guise in the pages of the Bible. Be that as it may, Recaptive cultural norms were syncretically fused together with evangelical precepts and the British understanding of the achieving individual. Important in this syncretism was the widespread concept of the 'big man'—found among Yoruba speakers, but also among the Igbo and the Akan—by which understanding a successful Christian was also required to manifest traditional, if modified, norms of attainment: the public accumulation, display, enjoyment, and conspicuous consumption of wealth; the possession of a following of clients, conferring esteem, prestige, and weight in the community; the scrupulous provision of goods in exchange for services from lineage kin and other dependants; and the fitting conclusion to the well-lived life in the form of elaborate funeral obsequies and fervent commemorations. To variable degrees all these customary norms shaped and informed Recaptive life. Some, such as competitive pieties in adherence and giving, chimed in with evangelical sensibilities. Others, such as the lavishing of money on big houses or on imports to furnish ostentatious weddings, offended them deeply. Recaptive Christianity was a mobile dialogue between cultures, an equipoise by turns sustained, interrogated, or overturned.[4]

Like their settler predecessors the Freetown Recaptives took to trade, forsaking farming. This disappointed British evangelicals and industrialists alike, for each interest hoped for an export agriculture, either to sustain settlement or to provide raw materials. But trade offered high returns and surpluses for reinvestment. In 1842, for example, the Nupe Recaptive and Methodist John Ezzidio visited Britain, established trading contacts there, and returned to Freetown to create an import–export business that eclipsed all of the British firms in the town. Money from trade was certainly spent on consumption and property, but *rentiers* also invested in Christian education. In 1827 the Church Missionary Society (CMS) established Fourah Bay College east of Freetown, intended to train missionary teachers for the purpose of spreading the Gospel throughout West Africa. Eventually supported by Society grammar schools, Fourah Bay College became the Christian educational forcing-ground of Freetown society. It had a particular impact on Recaptives and their children. In 1839 a group of Yoruba Recaptives, inculcated with the idea of proselytizing among their own people and wishing to see home again, sailed to Badagry, a major slaving port for the illicit Yoruba trade. Government refused their petition to establish a British colony there, but their example had important consequences. Other Yoruba Recaptives and Creoles, the term that came into use to identify the Freetown community, followed these pioneers. Returned Yoruba were known as Saro (a local corruption of Sierra Leone). They induced the CMS and Methodists to establish among them and they were at the cutting edge of bearing the Christian message—and their culture—into the Yoruba country. Outstanding among them was Samuel Ajayi Crowther, born at the Yoruba town of Osogun about 1806, enslaved in the war that destroyed his home, recaptured

---

[4] John Peterson, *Province of Freedom: A History of Sierra Leone, 1787–1870* (London, 1969); Arthur T. Porter, *Creoledom: A Study of the Development of Freetown Society* (London, 1963); A. Wyse, *The Krio of Sierra Leone: An Interpretive History* (London, 1989). On Yoruba cultural history, J. D. Y. Peel, *Ijeshas and Nigerians: The Incorporation of a Yoruba Kingdom, 1890s–1970s* (Cambridge, 1983); Karin Barber, *I Could Speak Until Tomorrow: Oriki, Women and the Past in a Yoruba Town* (Edinburgh, 1991). On Asante, greatest of the Akan states, Ivor Wilks, *Asante in the Nineteenth Century: The Structure and Evolution of a Political Order* (Cambridge, 1975; reprinted with a new 'Preamble', 1989); T. C. McCaskie, *State and Society in Precolonial Asante* (Cambridge, 1995). On Igbo, Richard N. Henderson, *The King in Every Man* (New Haven, 1972); Elizabeth Isichei, *A History of the Igbo People* (London, 1976).

and landed at Freetown by the Royal Navy, and the first pupil of Fourah Bay College. In 1864 he was created Bishop in the Church of England, and thereafter headed a CMS Mission to the Niger peoples.

Freetown Saro opened the first Christian church in Lagos, and it was that coastal settlement that became the centre of Victorian Yoruba Christian life after intervention (1851) and annexation (1861) by the British. By 1870 approximately 1,500 Saro had made their homes in Lagos, involving themselves in the palm-oil trade and contributing to the building and governance of the town. The Saro impact on Yoruba culture generally was profound, but it is difficult to give a succinct evaluation. This is because, apart from their transplantation of Freetown cultural syncretism to the Niger, and their role in spreading Christianity, the Saro and those who followed them played a fundamental role in the (re)construction of a usable Yoruba 'national' identity in the second half of the tumultuous nineteenth century. If they are memorialized in the churches and dwellings of Victorian Lagos, then their devotion to a specifically Yoruba identity inclusive of Christianity and education is commemorated in their writings. Supreme among these, and indispensable to historians, is the monumental, late-nineteenth-century history by the Yoruba divine and 'nationalist' the Revd Samuel Johnson.[5]

As Creole society became embedded in Freetown its goals extended beyond the worlds of missionary Christianity and trade to encompass middle-class, professional education. In time Fourah Bay College came to accept students for general higher education; eventually it was affiliated to Durham University in 1876 so that it might confer British degrees. Secular education in Freetown, and increasingly in Britain herself for the wealthy, opened the doors to law, medicine, journalism, scholarship, and other professional opportunities. Thus, in 1859 the Creoles J. A. B. Horton and W. B. Davies qualified as doctors in Britain. Both served in the army in West Africa as medical officers, and Horton published books on scientific and political topics. The Freetown lawyer and politician Samuel Lewis was knighted for services to the colony. Behind these leading figures stood a host of others. Like their evangelizing counterparts they sought employment along the West African coast in towns where their skills were esteemed and remunerated. The flourishing of later-nineteenth-century Gold Coast and Nigerian newspapers had a significant Freetown Creole input. So too did the legal and medical professions in British West Africa. By the second half of the nineteenth century Freetown was at the centre of a diaspora extending from the Gambia to the Bight of Benin and to Britain herself.

[5] S. Johnson, *The History of the Yorubas: From the Earliest Times to the Beginning of the British Protectorate* (London, 1921); J. F. Ade Ajayi, *Christian Missions in Nigeria, 1841–1891: The Making of a New Elite* (London, 1965); E. A. Ayandele, *The Missionary Impact on Modern Nigeria, 1842–1914: A Political and Social Analysis* (London, 1966); Kristen Mann, *Marrying Well: Marriage, Status and Social Change among the Educated Elite in Colonial Lagos* (Cambridge, 1985).

This linked together expatriate Sierra Leoneans in a network that also included the emergent Victorian middle classes of the Gold Coast and Nigeria.[6]

Developments on the Gold Coast paralleled but were distinct from those in Freetown and in the Yoruba country. Here the British presence was stronger than anywhere else in tropical Africa. Competition over the slaves and other resources of the Gold Coast led to the building of over thirty European castles and fortified posts between the fifteenth and eighteenth centuries. By the beginning of the nineteenth century the British, Dutch, and Danes were the only remaining European powers. The British headquarters at Cape Coast Castle was situated among the small trading polities created by the Fante, a Twi-speaking Akan people. The British were historically embroiled in local politics, and from 1807 onward this brought them into repeated conflict with the powerful inland Akan state of Asante. The British presence here, whether under trading-company or government authority, was configured in such a way that, despite equivocation, London found itself inexorably drawn ever deeper into local political affairs. The Anglo-Asante Treaty (1831) and the so-called Bond (1844) locked Britain into a vague Protectorate over, and rights of judicial interference in, the Fante states. This was extended to the eastern Gold Coast when the Danes quit (1850). The departure of the Dutch (1872) prefigured a British expedition against Asante (1873–74), following which British colonial control over an enlarged southern Gold Coast was formalized by direct annexation.

In the 1830s Methodist missionaries were invited to Cape Coast. This initiative came from the nominally Christianized urban mulatto élite that had originally risen to prominence under the aegis of the slave trade and that had then turned to other types of commerce. Under the dynamic leadership of the Revd T. B. Freeman, himself a West Indian mulatto, the Methodists proselytized among the Fante. As in Freetown and among the Yoruba, there swiftly emerged an evangelized, trading, property-owning, Victorian middle class. First confined to the British posts at Cape Coast and Anomabo, Christianity carried by British missionaries and a growing network of indigenous catechists then made inroads into the Fante hinterland. This was not without its problems. Resistance was offered by the *akomfo* ('priests') of Fante religion, but on the Gold Coast missionaries enjoyed the direct, if sometimes reluctantly given, sanction of British law. The world of the Fante Christian bourgeoisie is portrayed at length in the pages of the

---

[6] An overview is Akintola Wyse, 'The Place of Sierra Leone in African Diaspora Studies', in J. F. Ade Ajayi and J. D. Y. Peel, eds., *People and Empires in African History: Essays in Memory of Michael Crowder* (London, 1992), 107–20. Also Johnson U. Asiegbu, *Sierra Leone Creoles in British Nigeria Revisited, 1857–1920* (Oxford, 1984). A pioneering biography is John D. Hargreaves, *A Life of Sir Samuel Lewis* (London, 1958). The best overall guide to the Gold Coast is R. Jenkins, 'Gold Coast Historians and Their Pursuit of the Gold Coast Pasts, 1882–1917', unpublished Ph.D. thesis, Birmingham, 1985, 2 vols.

British official Brodie Cruickshank's *Eighteen Years on the Gold Coast of Africa* (1853). The picture that emerges from Cruickshank, as from many other texts, is one that resonates with the experiences of Freetown or Lagos.

Fante Christianity was resolutely aspirational in terms of salvation, but also in the worldly spheres of status, wealth, education, and consumer modernity. The Fante conception of the Akan 'big man' (*obirempon*) laid emphasis on instrumental strategies of seeking advantage in status competition among peers. In a sense, trading wealth, Western education, the building of imposing houses, and the rest were simply added to the existing repertoire of Fante norms and values. In this environment Christianity itself, whatever the strength of personal belief invested in it, was a further token of individual attainment in its own right within this intensely competitive milieu. Broadly speaking, mission education among the Fante followed the path already described (although there was no equivalent of Fourah Bay College in the Gold Coast). Schools turned out catechists and government employees. The latter were much in demand, for British administration and commerce had more need for clerkly skills on the Gold Coast than in any other part of tropical Africa. After mid-century the Fante urban élite produced a notable intelligentsia of writers, journalists, and pamphleteers. These were bound together by Christianity, education, and modernity, but also by older patterns of proximity and intermarriage, given a new fillip by an increasingly self-conscious sense of belonging to an élite.[7]

Mid-nineteenth-century Sierra Leone, Nigeria, and the Gold Coast, with their confident élites, is a useful point to pause and take stock. The background to the developments just described was the quickening pulse of British industrial and financial power. This manifested itself in numerous ways. For present purposes we must look first to the growing capacity and desire—religious, economic, scientific—to replace the tropical Africa of the imagination, virtually a *terra incognita*, with a continent explored, explained, and domesticated to British ideals of Christian culture. However, caution is required, for it is only with hindsight that this impulse can be cast in the role of preamble to colonial overrule.

In 1841 a mission was despatched to the confluence of the Niger and Benue rivers in the interior of what is now southern Nigeria. Its purpose was to explore West Africa's greatest river, to root out slave-trading at source, to assess Christian prospects, and to establish cash-crop plantation agriculture. Grandiose plans,

[7] G. E. Metcalfe, *Maclean of the Gold Coast: The Life and Times of George Maclean, 1801–1847* (London, 1962); Edward Reynolds, *Trade and Economic Change on the Gold Coast, 1807–1874* (London, 1974); Mary McCarthy, *Social Change and the Growth of British Power in the Gold Coast, 1807–1874* (Lanham, 1983); and the important K. Arhin, 'Rank and Class among the Asante and Fante in the Nineteenth Century', *Africa*, LIII, 1 (1983), pp. 2–22.

however, did not prevent its failure. This sounded the death-knell of the original abolitionist dream of African farmers organized and mobilized to support themselves by producing for the British market. West African exports—notably palm-oil—became the province of indigenous entrepreneurs rather than Christianized communities of yeomen. But if the Niger expedition was a failure, it was one with heroic resonances.[8] Anti-slavery and Christianization were inspired to a new urgency in tandem with the growing wish to explore and to cast light on the 'dark continent'. Sometimes these imperatives were joined together, sometimes they operated independently. The objective was the interior of tropical Africa. The greatest unknown of all was East and Central Africa, and it was there that the legacy of the Niger expedition found its fullest expression.

In the eighteenth century Europeans, including the British, rarely visited East Africa. The western end of the Indian Ocean trading network was an Omani Arab domain. An Islamic Swahili coastal élite brokered commerce between Gulf seafarers and the trading networks of East and Central Africa. The Yao and later the Nyamwezi traded ivory, slaves, and gold from the interior into Portuguese Mozambique and such long-established coastal entrepôts as Kilwa and Mombasa; until the 1850s cloth, beads, and copper were the most prized imports. A complex of developments drew Britain into this world in the nineteenth century. First, slaving in this area greatly increased after British abolition. Demand from the Gulf, Cuba, and Brazil, and from intensified sugar production on the Mascarenes (Réunion and Île de France) all contributed to anti-slavery outrage in Britain. The East African slave trade became a moral crusade. Secondly, although the Royal Navy's anti-slavery presence in the Indian Ocean was limited by comparison with the Atlantic, Britain felt able to fix upon Zanzibar as the key to increased slaving. For economic reasons Sayyid Said ibn Sultan, ruler of Oman, transferred his court to Zanzibar in 1840, and when he died in 1856 the island became independent. In addition to slaving wealth Zanzibar possessed an enticingly valuable export industry in cloves. Abolitionist and commercial interests saw a British Consul appointed to Zanzibar in the 1840s. Thirdly, although Britain lacked details it seemed clear that the East African slave trade was conducted with particular brutality. Zanzibari merchants, Indian financiers, Arab-Swahili caravans, and their predatory African partners extended the destabilizing trade far inland to the Bemba and beyond to the Lozi and Lunda of Central Africa. Accounts of savage cruelty reinforced British anti-slavery with an urgent wish to carry the saving grace of Christianity into the heart of Africa.[9]

[8] Most recently, Howard Temperley, *White Dreams, Black Africa: The Antislavery Expedition to the River Niger, 1841–1842* (New Haven, 1991).

[9] E. A. Alpers, *Ivory and Slaves in East Central Africa: Changing Patterns of International Trade to the Later Nineteenth Century* (London, 1975); Frederick Cooper, *Plantation Slavery on the East Coast of*

The totemic figure in the Christian fight against the East and Central African slave trade was David Livingstone. An ambiguous and complicated individual, Livingstone traversed the continent (1853–56) and then sought to reach Central Africa via the Zambezi River (1858–64). He achieved heroic stature in Britain, and did more than anyone else to expose and keep before the public the horrors of slavery. To him belongs a deal of the credit for the British decision to impose an end to the Zanzibari slave trade in 1873, but his impact on African cultures themselves was less than was claimed by later Imperial hagiographers. In addition to his Christian mission against slavery, his significance lay in his contribution to the collective British enterprise of exploring eastern Africa.[10] Here the prize—the Niger writ large—was the source of the Nile. The Royal Geographical Society presided over intense public interest in this question. The expeditions of Burton and Speke (1857–58), from East Africa to Lakes Tanganyika and Victoria, of Speke and Grant (1860–63) from East Africa via Lake Victoria, Buganda, and Bunyoro down the Nile to Cairo, and of Baker (1862–65), from Cairo via Khartoum, Lake Victoria, and Bunyoro to Lake Albert, explored vast, previously unknown areas but failed to resolve the Nile question. In 1866 the Society recruited Livingstone to settle the matter. His five-year journey, until his celebrated 'rescue' by Stanley in 1871, became an iconic representation of Victorian England's view of herself. But Livingstone died in 1873 and it was left to Henry Morton Stanley (1874–77) to conclude the quest for the source of the Nile. In the course of his journey he linked the Indian and Atlantic oceans, travelling from the interlacustrine region of eastern Africa down the Lualaba–Congo river system to its mouth on the coast of western Africa.[11]

The explorers Burton and Stanley were unusual individuals, but in their views and writings both gave pointed expression to shifting attitudes towards Africa and Africans. European ideas of African cultures were increasingly informed by new ideological currents against which Britain assessed herself and her experience of Africa. These included a burgeoning power and concomitant sense of a superior British destiny, reinforced by Imperial gains elsewhere and underpinned by the sedulous rise of pseudo-scientific racism; a growing confidence that Africa might be civilized in its own interest, not simply by missionary enterprise and free trade,

Africa (New Haven, 1977); Thomas Q. Reefe, *The Rainbow and the Kings: A History of the Luba Empire to 1891* (Berkeley, 1981); Abdul Sheriff, *Slaves, Spices and Ivory in Zanzibar: Integration of an East African Commercial Empire into the World Economy, 1770–1873* (London, 1987); Charles H. Ambler, *Kenyan Communities in the Age of Imperialism: The Central Region in the Late Nineteenth Century* (New Haven, 1988).

[10] Consult now Adrian Hastings, *The Church in Africa, 1450–1950* (Oxford, 1994).

[11] Clements R. Markham, *The First Fifty Years' Work of the Royal Geographical Society* (London, 1881); and see above, chap. by Robert A. Stafford.

but also by exposing its peoples to all of the many ordering technologies and secular disciplines of modern bourgeois life. As corollaries, the failure to effect wholesale Christian conversion despite the expenditure of money, effort, and lives, the lack of success in fostering an export-oriented plantation economy, the continuing stain of the slave trade, despite abolition (now combined with more information—and misinformation—about the extent and nature of African domestic slavery), and the presumed barbarism of great African states and cultures (Asante, Dahomey, Buganda, the Congo) were all intimations that, perhaps, Africans were irredeemable if left to govern themselves. Such ideas were the prelude to the Imperial Age in Africa. They were first articulated and acted upon in West Africa.[12]

First, some indicative straws in the wind. The explorer Richard Burton served as Consul in the Bight of Benin (1861–64) and travelled again in West Africa in 1881. In his writings on West Africa he expressed (predictably enough) a prurient fascination with the barbaric splendour, as he saw it, of the Dahomean court. But he abhorred West African Creole culture, regarding it as no more than an inauthentic, offensive, comic mimicry of its British counterpart. As ever, Burton's opinions were highly coloured, but there is much evidence that by the 1860s many British commentators and officials shared his dismissive view of the ultimate outcome of early abolitionist hopes and policies.[13] Increasingly, this rejection assumed racial forms. Educated or westernized West Africans of whatever sort came to be widely viewed as mimic-men, legatees of a false, pre-colonial start in civilizing Africa. Racial tensions developed, even in mission circles. Thus, indigenous Africans complained of the rise of patronizing, racist attitudes within the Methodist mission to the Gold Coast, and looked back with longing to the more egalitarian ethos that had prevailed before mid-century. In 1879 the finances of the Church Missionary Society's Niger mission were entrusted to a European. Africans resigned or were dismissed in an atmosphere of racial division. When the celebrated Bishop Crowther died in 1891 he was replaced by a European.[14]

Policy mirrored these shifts. In 1868 J. A. B. Horton, the Freetown Creole army doctor long resident on the Gold Coast, published his *West African Countries and Peoples*. This distilled the widespread educated African aspiration for a part in government and offered blueprints for political participation. Horton directly

---

[12] Philip D. Curtin, *The Image of Africa: British Ideas and Action, 1750–1850* (Madison, 1964).

[13] Richard Burton, *Wanderings in West Africa: From Liverpool to Fernando Po*, 2 vols. (London, 1863), *Abeokuta and the Camaroons Mountains. An Exploration*, 2 vols. (London, 1863), and *A Mission to Gelele King of Dahome*, 2 vols. (London, 1864); Richard F. Burton and Verney Lovett Cameron, *To the Gold Coast for Gold*, 2 vols. (London, 1883). Cf. W. Reade, *Savage Africa* (London, 1863) and *The African Sketch-book*, 2 vols. (London, 1873).

[14] These changes can be traced in detail in Wesleyan-Methodist Missionary Society Archives (School of Oriental and African Studies, London) and in Church Missionary Society Archives (Birmingham University).

inspired the creation of the Fante Confederation and its (second) 1871 Constitution, providing for a King or President and representative and national Assemblies, was based on his proposals. A Great Seal was struck and a Supreme Court convened. The Fante, historically disunited, banded together in confederacy around the issues of British impositions and high-handedness. Taxes, the lack of a right of consultation or voice in policy-making, and uncertainty over Britain's commitment to defend them against Asante were key concerns. Confederation failed, in part because of internal disagreements, but also because Britain was opposed to it. Ideas of governmental modernization along Western lines spread inland beyond the sphere of British jurisdiction. As early as 1865 the Abeokuta Egba on the western fringe of Yorubaland set up a United Board of Management with a President, a High Sheriff, a Supreme Court, and a postal system. The Sierra Leonian G. W. Johnson played a leading role in this experiment, but the Egba modernizers enjoyed only limited success. The larger significance of events among the Fante and Egba is that, just as British attitudes were hardening in the manner described, westernized Africans—both under British jurisdiction and beyond it— were taking tentative first steps towards modern forms of political participation and autonomy.[15]

In 1865 a Parliamentary Select Committee recommended that Britain reduce her commitments in West Africa wherever possible. The Colonial Office favoured retrenchment on the grounds of expense and the vagueness of British jurisdiction. This last consideration, it was felt, had the potential to involve Britain in unwanted future conflicts and obligations.[16] In essence, and despite much equivocating argument, nothing was done. Eight years later in 1873–74 Britain found herself confronting an Asante invasion of Fante and then committing troops to advance 150 miles inland to burn the Asante capital of Kumasi. The politics of this first serious British military venture into the tropical African interior need not detain us here. More germane is the fact that this Anglo-Asante War was the first conflict to be fought in the aftermath of the Cardwell reforms. It was commanded by Sir Garnet Wolseley and officered by members of his 'ring'. These men rose to dominate British military thinking about Africa until the South African (Anglo-Boer) War (1899–1902), and directed military policy at the height of the colonial conquest. Famously self-promoting, the Wolseley 'ring' deluged the British public with accounts of its first success as a team. These writings concerned a sophistic-

---

[15] Francis Agbodeka, *African Politics and British Policy in the Gold Coast, 1868–1900: A Study in the Forms and Force of Protest* (London, 1971); Saburi O. Biobaku, *The Egba and Their Neighbours, 1842–1872* (Oxford, 1957); A. Pallinder, 'Adegboyega Edun: Black Englishman and Yoruba Cultural Patriot', in P. F. de Moraes Farias and Karin Barber, eds., *Self-Assertion and Brokerage: Early Cultural Nationalism in West Africa* (Birmingham, 1990), pp. 11–34.

[16] *Report from the Select Committee on Africa (Western Coast), PP* (1865) 412, V.

ated culture and great state in the interior of West Africa, and because of the later importance of the authors their views formed a powerful template for subsequent readings of other polities during—and beyond—the conquest.[17]

Several broad, complementary interpretations of Asante culture prevailed in the writings of the Wolseley 'ring', and were endorsed by journalists (including Stanley) who accompanied the expedition.[18] The first view was a graphic enlargement of earlier missionary presumptions concerning an Asante—and African—predilection for 'human sacrifice'. Wesleyans such as T. B. Freeman in the 1840s condemned such practices but believed they would disappear with the advent of Christianity. The Wolseley 'ring' termed Kumasi 'the city of blood', and argued that 'human sacrifice' was a mode of government. That is, Asante needed humbling and conquest rather than empathy and conversion before it would change its ways. The second view was a crystallization of emergent British racial attitudes. As members of an inferior race the Asante required discipline rather than understanding in order to function as a culture. The current dispensation of blood-letting and 'human sacrifice' was inhumane, but any future British administration would have to adopt Draconian measures for Asante's own good. The equation of Africans 'in a savage state of nature' with wilful children underpinned this brisk recommendation. The third view was that, as all Africans were damned to an inferior place within the human family, then the 'natural' Asante, provided he was strictly ruled, was to be preferred to the abomination that was westernized Fante Creole culture. In extension of Burton's strictures the Wolseley 'ring' urged the sheer unnaturalness of any sort of hybridity. Cultures were fixed in rank, and any attempt to assimilate an African to Anglo-Saxon ideas and practices could only result in a displaced, pathetic caricature. The final view, much enlarged upon by Wolseley in later life, combined pseudo-scientific racism with fashionable canards about the influence of climate and ecology upon cultural history.[19] The Asante were manly and warlike because they lived under iron discipline in an invigorating environment. The Fante were weak and cowardly because they were creolized residents of a debilitating milieu. Forests, deserts, and highlands were good; coasts, swamps, and lowlands were bad. These were all extreme, formalized versions of opinions in general circulation on the eve of Britain's subjugation of its African

[17] From a large choice, Henry Brackenbury, *The Ashanti War: A Narrative: Prepared from the Official Documents by Permission of Major-General Sir Garnet Wolseley*, 2 vols. (London, 1874); William Francis Butler, *Akim-Foo: The History of a Failure* (London, 1875); E. Wood, *The Ashanti Expedition of 1873–4* (London, 1874).

[18] Henry M. Stanley, *Coomassie and Magdala: The Story of Two British Campaigns in Africa* (London, 1874).

[19] General Viscount Wolseley, 'The Negro as a Soldier', *The Fortnightly Review*, New Series, CCLXIV (1888), 689–703.

Empire. Repetitions, traces, or echoes of all of them are to be found in the literature of colonial conquest concerning Benin, Yorubaland, Igboland, and Sokoto in West Africa, or Zululand and the Sudan elsewhere on the continent.[20] They testify *inter alia* to the continuing potency of an imagined Africa in an era of greatly increased factual knowledge.

The colonial conquest of East Africa was preceded by a period around and after mid-century when the informal advance of traders, missionaries, explorers, and the rest not only augmented Europe's store of information about Africa, but also exposed African cultures to an indiscriminate, eclectic barrage of new ideas, practices, and technologies. Nowhere did this development call forth a more complex response than in Buganda, most powerful of the interlacustrine kingdoms. By the early nineteenth century the *kabaka* (king) of Buganda controlled the western side of Lake Victoria. From there Buganda was linked into the long-distance trade network of eastern Africa, including the route that ran nearly 800 miles via Nyamwezi to the coast facing Zanzibar. Early in his reign the *kabaka* Mutesa (late 1850s–84) developed a strong interest in the culture, religion, and technology of the Zanzibari traders who visited his court. Advanced guns and consumer goods were his initial concern. These were conventional trade items, but Mutesa also had a consuming interest in theology. He became fascinated with the precepts of Zanzibari Islam, introduced the Koran, and rewarded youthful royal pages who learned Arabic. However, when Zanzibar failed to assist Buganda against threats from the Sudan, devout pages argued that this was because Mutesa's Zanzibari Islam was too lax. In 1876 the *kabaka* executed the most critical of his Muslim subjects. But having opened the door to foreign trade and ideas Mutesa found that he could not close it again. Protestant and Catholic missionaries were invited into Buganda to check Islam, and one another. When Mutesa died he had lost control of the situation. In 1886 his desperate successor martyred Christians in the name of the local spirit cults. But a Muslim, Protestant, and Catholic alliance deposed and then reinstated him on their own terms. Thus far these developments had been matters of court politics, barely affecting the countryside. But in the 1890s British troops arrived, Protestantism triumphed with their support, and religious fervour—exacerbated by the chaotic uncertainties of foreign conquest—spread to embrace all Buganda. As the world of the Ganda people was turned upside down many thousands embraced Christianity, looking to the Bible to explain what had happened.[21]

---

[20] For one aspect, C. Madge and R. Cline-Cole, 'The West African Forest Zone in the European Geographical Imagination', *Geography*, no. CCCLIII, 81 (1996), pp. 24–31.

[21] M. S. M. Kiwanuka, *A History of Buganda* (London, 1971); M. Wright, *Buganda in the Heroic Age* (Nairobi, 1971); D. A. Low, *Religion and Society in Buganda, 1875–1900* (Kampala, n.d. [1957?]). Sir Apolo

The European 'scramble' for Africa was breathtaking in its rapidity.[22] As a result Britain and a host of African cultures and peoples suddenly found themselves confronting each other. The ostensible arrangement was one of rulers and ruled, but this simple equation in theory turned out to be subtly complex in practice. British conquest was accomplished with no clear idea of how particular areas should be governed nor any substantive knowledge of many subject cultures. The choice of responses open to Africans was bewilderingly complex, both between and—importantly—within cultures. They might 'collaborate' in an effort to secure British favour; they might 'resist' to the point of defeat or disintegration; they might submit in a process of bargaining the conditions of their subjection; they might equivocate, dissemble, change their minds, or simply await develop-ments. Choices with longer-term implications surrounded the issue of European culture. Nowhere did Africans resolve this by polar responses of outright rejection or acceptance. Everything was shaded; thus, for example, Africans might embrace education but be sceptical about the mission Christianity of its bearers. In truth, cultural encounters between Briton and African during the late-nineteenth-century conquest, even where violence was involved, were on both sides matters of probing negotiation towards the equilibrium of a changed order rather than permanently binding choices between strategies of outright collaboration or resistance.[23]

Example rather than comprehensiveness must suffice to illustrate the theme of negotiated cultural contact during the colonial conquest. The object is to show something of the range and complexity of an encounter that was misleadingly assumed to be simple (even one-sided) before the development of modern African historiography. The examples of Asante and Sokoto in West Africa and the Ndebele in Central Africa serve to make the point.

The British invasion of Asante in 1873–74 was a punitive expedition, Asante retained its political autonomy, but was subject to increasing British pressure and influence thereafter. The British finally deposed the *asantehene* Agyeman Prempe in 1896, suppressed an uprising against them in 1900, and formally annexed Asante as a Crown Colony in 1901. Pre-colonial Asante was a culture in which the state exercised formidable controls over political office, access to wealth, and ingress or egress from the country. Weakened and laid open after 1874, Asante experienced a series of crises including a protracted dynastic conflict (1883–88). In the course of this numbers of Asante became alienated from a polity that monopolized wealth

Kaggwa, *The Kings of Buganda*, English translation (Nairobi, 1971) is an insider account from the early colonial period.

[22] See chap. by Colin Newbury.

[23] See the chaps. by John D. Hargreaves and Terence Ranger in L. H. Gann and Peter Duignan, eds., *Colonialism in Africa*, 5 vols. (Cambridge, 1969–75), I.

but no longer reciprocated with security. They voted with their feet and fled into the British Gold Coast. Once there, they were exposed to the acquisitive individualism of *laissez-faire* capitalism, the dispositionary rights of the person under English common law, and the gamut of Western cultural influences. They supported British subversion and conquest of Asante, but in a particular way that sought to combine their acquisitive individualism with access to the prestigious chiefships of historic Asante culture. After 1901 the British relied on these people to implement colonial rule and supported and favoured them. Their example, and the unchecked access of European norms and values, swiftly fused historic Asante identity with an untrammelled capitalism. The uprising of the old order in 1900 was not repeated. It was capitalism—expressed in the rapid spread of cocoa as a cash crop—that reconciled Asante to British colonial overrule. Official records from the early colonial era show the significant extent to which administrators relied for support upon Asante who were ideologically reconciled to the new order. Nor was there a realistic alternative, for British personnel were few and their knowledge of Asante was very limited. Earlier British stereotypes of savage, warlike Asante survived into the colonial period but were soon replaced by admiration for a 'progressive' people devoted to making money.[24]

Sokoto (in present-day northern Nigeria) reveals another set of variations on the theme of cultural encounter during the conquest. Created by jihad (holy war) in the first decade of the nineteenth century, the Sokoto Caliphate was the largest West African Muslim polity annexed by the British. Due to its geographical remoteness from the coast it was little known by the British prior to the conquest of 1903. Extensive and presumed to be formidable, Sokoto puzzled the British by offering little concerted resistance. The immediate British explanation relied on the late-nineteenth-century European commonplace about the corruption, decadence, and weakness of Islamic polities. The truth was much more complex. Sokoto was constructed out of potentially volatile and conflicting components— Hausa, Fulani, and smaller ethnic groups, core and periphery, town and countryside, orthodox and popular Islam (syncretically fused with non-Islamic beliefs)— and the shock of British conquest brought latent cleavages between the ruling élite and its subjects into the open.

First, the urban, orthodox Islamic élite around the Caliph consulted Muslim precedents for guidance in dealing with infidels. A choice was made to practise canonically sanctioned dissembling; that is, to submit in body but not thought. The state's autonomy (a thing of this world) was surrendered so as preserve the

---

[24] Apart from works already cited, Thomas J. Lewin, *Asante Before the British: The Prempean Years, 1875–1900* (Lawrence, Kan., 1978); William Tordoff, *Ashanti Under the Prempehs, 1888–1935* (Oxford, 1965); and Jean Marie Allman, *The Quills of the Porcupine: Asante Nationalism in an Emergent Ghana* (Madison, 1993).

integrity of Islam against any excess of British destructiveness provoked by military resistance. Secondly, the arrival of the British coincided with a rising tide of
popular Islamic Mahdist expectation and acted to confirm the belief that the end
of the material world was imminent. Accordingly, numbers of commoners began
to move eastward to meet 'the expected one' (the Mahdi) and prepare for the last
battle between good and evil. Throughout the nineteenth century the Sokoto élite
had discouraged such radical views among its subjects. It was now alarmed by
wholesale defections to the east, and particularly so as in the prevailing confusion
the Caliph (willingly or not) was with his migrating subjects. British forces caught
up with the Mahdists and the Caliph was killed in the fighting. Mahdist expectation survived, and in 1906 became centred on the insurrectionary village of Satiru
near Sokoto. The British were caught unprepared. However, the Sokoto élite allied
itself with its infidel rulers and suppressed its own rebel subjects on their behalf.
This was a calculated act. The British administration had already guaranteed the
survival of Islam and the precolonial emirate system. Indeed, Sokoto's conqueror
Sir Frederick Lugard developed his concept of 'indirect rule' through historically
sanctioned native rulers—*the* theory of British colonial rule in Africa—out of his
experience governing these very emirates. The Sokoto élite for its part had opted
for British support in maintaining its sway over its own historically disaffected
subjects.[25]

The Ndebele were a creation of the *mfecane* or 'time of troubles', the revolutionary changes that convulsed southern Africa in the late-eighteenth and early-
nineteenth centuries.[26] Fleeing before Shaka's Zulu, the Ndebele settled in the late
1830s as overlords among a part of the decentralized Shona people (in present-day
Zimbabwe). The Ndebele kingdom preserved its own language and military
arrangements, but it adopted the Shona territorial cult of *mwari* and other rituals.
British missionaries arrived in 1859 but entirely failed to gain converts. In 1889 the
British South Africa Company occupied Shona territory with little difficulty.
Initially, the Ndebele opted for a policy of coexistence. But in 1893 a mix of British
high-handedness and chafing resentment on the part of youthful Ndebele warriors
provoked a limited war. Three years later, in 1896–97, a full-scale revolt occurred as
the Ndebele came to realize, with the advice of their spirit cults, that pioneer
British South Africa Company officials and gold-seekers were the advance guard of

[25] D. Murray Last, *The Sokoto Caliphate* (London, 1967); R. A. Adeleye, *Power and Diplomacy in Northern Nigeria, 1804–1906: The Sokoto Caliphate and its Enemies* (London, 1972); Robert W. Shenton, *The Development of Capitalism in Northern Nigeria* (London, 1986); Paul E. Lovejoy and Jan S. Hogendorn, *Slow Death for Slavery: The Course of Abolition in Northern Nigeria, 1897–1936* (Cambridge, 1993); and in Vol. IV, see the chap. by John W. Cell.
[26] Carolyn Hamilton, ed., *The Mfecane Aftermath: Reconstructive Debates in Southern African History* (Johannesburg, 1995).

a wave of whites who planned to settle. Fearing massive land seizures, loss of cattle, and extinction as a culture, the Ndebele and their Shona clients conducted guerrilla warfare and besieged the nascent settlement of Bulawayo. The revolt, which the Ndebele were now convinced was a matter of national survival, was bitterly fought and bloodily suppressed. Defeat led to the dissolution of the Ndebele polity, to landlessness, to cultural disorientation, and personal anomie. The barrier to unrestricted white inroads into this part of Central Africa was removed and farmers flooded in after the gold-prospectors. The Ndebele were left to negotiate their place in the colonial order from a position of virtual power-lessness. Under the new dispensation they were reduced to labouring on white grain and tobacco farms.[27]

The cultures of Asante, Sokoto, and the Ndebele were organized around and arbitrated by complex state structures. But very many of the African peoples that succumbed to British conquest lived in acephalous, decentralized, small-scale societies. Statelessness posed special problems for the British conquerors. Often, and quite literally, there was no one with the authority to make formal submission. The imposition of colonial rule over such peoples was a slow osmotic process rather than a finite political event. Thus, in the occupation of south-east and central Nigeria the British sent military columns into Igboland and among the Tiv of the Benue river valley. Other than as a declaration of intent these were some-what futile exercises. Resolving the cultural encounter between the British and such decentralized peoples was something that took time. In the first stages of conquest British administrators were as much persuaders as conquerors. The Igbo or Tiv had to be won over to an understanding of the advantages and obligations of British rule. Tax-gathering by diktat in the absence of an indigenous chain of command would have required manpower resources that the British did not possess. Igbo or Tiv people responded to the perceived benefits and drawbacks of colonial rule on an individual and sectoral basis, a point complexly illustrated in the Igbo novelist Chinua Achebe's celebrated *Things Fall Apart*. In the cultural encounter with the Igbo the British ran the risk of subverting negotiation by radical innovation in the interests of a more structured, hierarchical, transparent administration. Thus, the eventual introduction among the Igbo of 'Native Administration' chiefs, a variant of Lugard's 'indirect rule', was a greatly resented mistake and acknowledged as such by experienced officials on the spot.[28]

Among the issues that preoccupied the British immediately following conquest none was of wider concern than that termed 'domestic slavery' by officialdom.

---

[27] The classic account is T. O. Ranger, *Revolt in Southern Rhodesia, 1896–7*, 2nd edn. (London, 1979).

[28] Sir F. D. Lugard, *The Dual Mandate in British Tropical Africa* (London, 1922); A. E. Afigbo, *The Warrant Chiefs: Indirect Rule in South Eastern Nigeria* (London, 1972). In Vol. IV, see chap. by John Cell.

This phenomenon was held to be endemic to Africa's cultures; certainly, very diverse forms of indigenous servitude and clientage existed on the continent together with other sorts of dependency barely understood but disapproved of by the British. Nineteenth-century abolitionists and missionaries deplored 'domestic slavery' but recognized its fundamental place in societies they could do little to change. Commercial interests took the sanguine view that 'domestic slavery' was functionally necessary to African economic production. In theory the moral responsibilities of colonial rule precluded the continuation of such indulgent attitudes. In practice matters were not so simple. The British abolished 'domestic slavery' by fiat in cultures where they wished to quash opposition or punish intransigence. In 1897 a British mission to the Edo kingdom of Benin (in present-day Nigeria) was virtually annihilated.[29] A punitive expedition then occupied Benin, but the capital had been abandoned. The British declared emancipation for any slave coming back to the town, and then freed the royal slaves to teach the Edo king a lesson. But the Edo experience was unusual. In most cultures the British swiftly learned the accuracy of nineteenth-century perception. 'Domestic slavery' was the existing mechanism for mobilizing labour, and British officials needed it as much as had African rulers. Practice diverged from theory. The British continued to abhor 'domestic slavery' but permitted its continued existence under one or another fictive legalism. Sometimes this caused conflict with zealous missionaries.[30] But 'domestic slavery' survived in parts of British Africa into the 1920s until such time as labour needs could be fully met from within the developed cash economy.

Slavery of another kind produced the first crisis in Britain's nineteenth-century involvement in another, quite distinct part of Africa. South Africa was a special case and needs to be treated as such.[31] Britain occupied the Cape in 1795 and established a permanent presence at the end of the Napoleonic Wars in 1815. Here, uniquely, Britain encountered after 1795 earlier European settlers of Dutch, German, or French Huguenot stock who first settled in 1652. These Boers (or Afrikaners) evolved their own, fiercely independent religion, language, and culture, based upon crop and livestock farming supported by indentured and African slave labour. In the century-long clash which developed between Briton and Boer, culminating in the protracted, bitterly fought war of 1899–1902 and the compromise of the Union of South Africa in 1910, the ultimate victims were the African peoples.

---

[29] P. A. Igbafe, *Benin Under British Administration: The Impact of Colonial Rule on an African Kingdom, 1897–1938* (London, 1979).

[30] e.g. in Asante between British officials and Basel missionaries in Kumase.

[31] See chap. by Christopher Saunders and Iain R. Smith.

The Xhosa, borrowing from Christian missionary eschatology, killed their cattle in 1857 in an other-worldly attempt to expel Europeans once and for all. This extreme measure precipitated the destruction of Xhosa society by the British Cape government and Boer farmers. The Zulu kingdom—greatest of the states to emerge from the upheavals of the 1790s to 1830s among the Bantu societies of eastern South Africa (the *mfecane*)—finally went down to military defeat in 1879 after a victory over British forces at Isandhlwana. African 'resistance', whether cultural or military, was ultimately unable to stand against Boer and British imperialism.

Once drawn into the orbit of the white colonial societies, many Africans were confronted by new and difficult problems of adjustment. Others, however, initially adapted very successfully to the opportunities presented by change. In the early phases of mining development paid African labour was needed and offered better wages than those available on white farms. From mission stations like Lovedale in the eastern Cape numbers of Africans took away an education that held out prospects of employment in the cash economy. African farmers and transport drivers took advantage of the commercial openings offered by colonial urban expansion; their output was vital, for instance, in feeding the Rand. However, African economic independence was no more acceptable than political. From the 1890s, and ever more rapidly after 1902 and 1910, the colonial government cut back African prospects to fit the demands of white enterprise, using the mechanisms of land control, labour legislation, and taxation. Thus, in the second half of the nineteenth century and beyond the African peoples of South Africa experienced political annexation, societal breakdown, and cultural anomie. Africanized Christianity with its numerically small, emergent middle class offered one of the few means of sustaining the seeds of a new African politics which was gradually to find its voice in the twentieth century.[32]

Deposited in all British—and European—archival records of the colonial conquest are maps, ranging from the nearly blank to the elaborately detailed. Maps are perhaps the most potent of all symbolic representations of the partition of Africa. Indeed, a familiar image of the Berlin Conference of 1884–85, at which Britain and the other imperial powers delimited their future African possessions, is of intent

---

[32] From a huge literature, Richard Elphick and Hermann Giliomee, eds., *The Shaping of South African Society, 1652–1840*, 2nd revised edn. (Middletown, Conn., 1989); J. B. Peires, *The House of Phalo: A History of the Xhosa People in the Days of their Independence* (Johannesburg, 1981), and *The Dead Will Arise: Nongqawuse and the Great Xhosa Cattle Killing Movement of 1856–7* (Johannesburg, 1989); Jeff Guy, *The Destruction of the Zulu Kingdom: The Civil War in Zululand, 1879–1884* (London, 1979); Philip Bonner, *Kings, Commoners and Concessionaires: The Evolution and Dissolution of the Nineteenth Century Swazi State* (Cambridge, 1983); Peter Delius, *The Land Belongs to Us: The Pedi Polity, the Boers and the British in the Nineteenth-Century Transvaal* (London, 1984); Elizabeth A. Eldredge, *A South African Kingdom: The Pursuit of Security in Nineteenth-Century Lesotho* (Cambridge, 1993).

statesmen poring over a map of the continent.[33] The cartographic enterprise was pivotal to implementing conquest and embedding colonial rule—the siting of boundaries, ports, railways, roads, or towns and the labelling of forests, rivers, lakes, mountains, or plains were all referenced to map-making and sprang from it. Maps also symbolized the reconfiguration of cultural encounter. By 'filling in' Britain's map of Africa cartographical knowledge enabled the recasting of the continent's cultures in terms of colonial concepts of bounded spatial identities and rigid territorial attachments. Much evidence exists to suggest that the majority of pre-colonial African societies annexed by the British construed themselves in terms of cultural indicators of belonging rather than geographical delimitations of territory. The 'great states' of pre-colonial Africa themselves operated with fluid notions of core, periphery, and influence rather than fixed ideas of demarcation, frontier, and foreignness. By labelling and fixing African cultures in space to define possession and expedite overrule the British—like other imperial powers—opened a Pandora's box. In particular, issues of ethnicity and identity referenced to spatial boundaries became contentious urgencies of the colonial era. The construction, content and nature of 'Yorubaness' within Nigeria, say, or 'Kikuyu-ness' within Kenya, or 'Gandaness' within Uganda, or 'Asanteness' within the Gold Coast, became pointed, contested questions that continue to trouble Africans in the post-colonial era.[34]

Some attempt at retrospect and prospect is offered here. At the start of the nineteenth century Britain's presence in tropical Africa was narrowly confined to the—mainly West African—coast. Systematic exploration of the interior occupied the entire nineteenth century (and extended in remoter areas into the twentieth), dating, perhaps, from the 1788 foundation of the African Association by the savant Joseph Banks and others.[35] The ideological grounding of this effort shifted over time. At its outset the British cultural encounter with African societies was dominated by inquiries dedicated to accumulating knowledge, to bridging the gap between imagination and reality. That this reconciliation might be reconfig-ured but never achieved is apparent in all nineteenth-century British reporting of Africa. The most generalized indication of this is the way in which—around and after mid-century—the imagined Africa of pseudo-scientific racial thinking became the optic through which an ever increasing factual knowledge was viewed. Bowdich's first eyewitness account of Kumasi (1817) is characterized by scientific

---

[33] See T. Bassett, 'Cartography and Empire Building in Nineteenth-Century West Africa', *Geographical Review*, LXXXIV, 3 (1994), pp. 316–35.

[34] The best treatment (on Kenya) is Bruce Berman and John Lonsdale, *Unhappy Valley: Conflict in Kenya and Africa*, 2 vols. (London, 1991).

[35] See chap. by Robert A. Stafford, and in Vol. II, chap. by Richard Drayton.

curiosity, but none the less treats Asante culture as a complex achievement in its
own right and on its own terms. Robert Baden-Powell's participation in the British
occupation of Kumasi (1896) resulted in an account of Asante that enlarges on the
views of the Wolseley 'ring'. In this, Asante is a blood-soaked despotism condemned to its fate by racial inferiority. Only Anglo-Saxon rule can redeem it from
the excesses of its birthright.[36] This is an extreme distillation of a widespread
climate of opinion. Even those dedicated to a humane tutelage of Africans by
colonial overlordship shared implicitly in ideas of superiority and inferiority that
were grounded in assumptions about race and destiny.[37]

It needs to be restated that the British missionary enterprise in Africa arose from
a complex of ideas. Principled abolitionism and anti-slavery were accompanied by
paternalist ideas of social improvement to be rooted in economic production for
British markets. This is not to question the Christian sincerity of British missionaries. Africa was remote and unhealthy; many missionaries died but the supply of
replacements never dried up. But missionary work, like exploration, requires
ideological contextualization. Missionaries were products of British society and
to a degree shared in its evolving values. Thus, it is scarcely surprising that the later
decades of the nineteenth century saw an increasing racial awareness being added
to early Victorian paternalism. Ironically, this development was greatly sharpened
by the very real, if localized, success of missionaries among peoples such as the
Fante and Yoruba. A latent contradiction existed between the ongoing Christianizing of Africans and the point at which an established African Christianity might
be deemed ripe for emancipation from stewardship. Missionary writings of the
later nineteenth century are replete with vexed—and vexing—discussions about
autonomy and independence for African congregations. Issues of race certainly
played their part in British reluctance to relinquish control, in African alienation
from mission churches, and in the rise of the independent African church movement in the 1880s and 1890s.[38]

By then one of the guiding suppositions of the early abolitionists had long since
proved false. The foundation of Freetown led to the emergence of a property-
owning middle class and not a community of industrious agriculturalists. This
pattern was repeated wherever urbanized societies emerged on the Sierra Leone
model or out of the conditions of trade. Like their Creole counterparts, indigenous
West or East African entrepreneurs (in palm-oil, timber, ivory, gum, etc.) who
achieved economic success as individuals also came to take many of their cultural

---

[36] T. E. Bowdich, *Mission From Cape Coast Castle to Ashantee* (London, 1819); R. S. S. Baden-Powell,
The Downfall of Prempeh: A Diary of Life with the Native Levy in Ashanti, 1895–96 (London, 1896).

[37] For some of the resonances, Thomas Richards, *The Imperial Archive: Knowledge and the Fantasy of
Empire* (London, 1993).

[38] Hastings, *Church in Africa*, chap. 7.

cues from bourgeois Victorianism. This westernized African society, fostered by abolitionists, missionaries, and a whole panorama of economic possibilities in commerce had a complex nineteenth-century history. Evolving racial attitudes again played an instrumental role. The 1850s and 1860s are sometimes spoken of as being an 'Indian summer' for this community. It was in these decades that it realized the British were opposed to granting it due political participation and that the source of this denial lay in shifting metropolitan attitudes towards the very idea of civilized, Anglicized Africans. In the second half of the century this community suffered a cultural ambivalence. On the one hand British civilization was an admirable thing; but on the other its representatives in Africa were increasingly rejectionist and contemptuous towards westernized Africans. Members of this community took to separating out the message from the messenger. Constitutionalism, the rule of law and a concern with asserting (and defending) juridical rights came to occupy a central place in their thinking and discourse. Britain was often said to be failing her own ideals. Obversely, the rhetoric and terms of encroaching British colonialism fed a reactive interest in the specificity of African cultures and history. Late-nineteenth and early-twentieth-century writing by Africans is shot through with these often contradictory impulses.[39]

In 1800 most Africans had seen few if any Europeans. In 1900 nearly all of Africa was ruled by Europe. The sheer number and diversity of African cultures that encountered the British in the course of the nineteenth century is bewildering. Exemplary cases have been discussed throughout, for generalization about such a range of societies risks relapse to levels of analysis that obtained before the emergence of a modern African historiography. Having entered that caveat, it remains important to draw attention to a theme that applies to African cultures generally in their encounter with the British, whatever the historical specifics of place and time. That theme is the conditions of the cultural encounter seen with hindsight from the perspective of African peoples. Early-nineteenth-century British sojourners in African cultures were supplicants of one kind or another. They *asked* for audience, consideration, protection, information, trade, diplomatic relations, converts, and the rest. By corollary, African cultures maintained the capacity not only to accede to or deny such requests but also to control or expel British visitors. A vital element in the same configuration was that African cultures had considerable powers of arbitration in rejecting or accepting British ideas and artefacts. The record overall shows African cultures to have been aware of the notion of *caveat emptor*.

---

[39] e.g. J. E. Casely Hayford, *Gold Coast Native Institutions, with Thoughts upon a Healthy Imperial Policy for the Gold Coast and Ashanti* (London, 1903).

These conditions shifted after mid-century, and from the 1870s on African cultures found themselves increasingly unable to resist British penetration. By this reading colonialism can be contextualized as the culmination of a century-long shift from a Britain that *asked* to one that *demanded* and at last *commanded*. The reasons for this change are to be sought in the politics of Europe, in Britain's evolving strategic view of herself, and—perhaps most directly for Africa's peoples—in the 'speeding up' of British cultural capacity; in the period from the 1860s to the 1890s a series of revolutions in bureaucratization, technology, weaponry, communications, medicine, and the rest conferred upon Britain (and Europe) a hugely augmented capacity for cultural transmission and imposition in the broadest sense. African cultures succumbed to the onslaught of a Britain (and Europe) now organized, translated, and mobilized through the ever accelerating pace of modernity. Max Weber is as trustworthy a guide, as ever Marx was presumed to be, to the British overcoming of African cultures. This is not at all to argue that African cultures lay supine and inert before Europe's insertions and subversions. In the final quarter of the nineteenth century numbers of African societies braced themselves against change, engaged with it, and even tried to bend aspects of it to their own purposes. But the conditions of the cultural encounter were running against them, and whatever negotiation they managed to achieve within the new dispensation must be seen against the background of a single, blunt fact. British and other European colonialisms incorporated African peoples into the ideological and materialist worlds of Western modernity. All African cultures are still negotiating dialogue with—and within—the implications of that fact.

Select Bibliography

J. F. ADE AJAYI and MICHAEL CROWDER, eds., *Historical Atlas of Africa* (London, 1985).

——eds., *History of West Africa*, Vol. I, 3rd edn. (London, 1985), and Vol. II, 2nd edn. (London, 1987).

RALPH A. AUSTEN, *African Economic History: Internal Development and External Dependency* (London, 1987).

P. J. CAIN and A. G. HOPKINS, *British Imperialism: Innovation and Expansion, 1688–1914* (London, 1993).

JEAN and JOHN COMAROFF, *Of Revelation and Revolution: Christianity, Colonialism and Consciousness in South Africa* (Chicago, 1991).

T. R. H. DAVENPORT, *South Africa: A Modern History*, 4th edn. (London, 1991).

CHRISTOPHER FYFE, *A History of Sierra Leone* (London, 1962).

——*Africanus Horton: West African Scientist and Patriot* (Oxford, 1972).

JONATHAN GLASSMAN, *Feasts and Riot: Revelry, Rebellion and Popular Consciousness on the Swahili Coast, 1856–1888* (London, 1995).

ROBIN HALLETT, ed., *Records of the African Association, 1788–1831* (London, 1964).

JOHN ILIFFE, *Africans: The History of a Continent* (Cambridge, 1995).

ELIZABETH ISICHEI, *A History of African Societies to 1870* (Cambridge, 1997).

DAVID KIMBLE, *A Political History of Ghana: The Rise of Gold Coast Nationalism, 1850–1928* (Oxford, 1963).

MARTIN LYNN, *Commerce and Economic Change in West Africa: The Palm Oil Trade in the Nineteenth Century* (Cambridge, 1997).

PHYLLIS MARTIN and PATRICK O'MEARA, eds., *Africa*, 3rd edn. (London, 1995).

ROLAND OLIVER and others, eds., *History of East Africa*, 3 vols. (Oxford, 1963–76).

RONALD ROBINSON and JOHN GALLAGHER, with ALICE DENNY, *Africa and the Victorians: The Official Mind of Imperialism*, 2nd edn. (London, 1981).

NIGEL WORDEN, *The Making of Modern South Africa: Conquest, Segregation and Apartheid* (Oxford, 1994).

C. C. WRIGLEY, *Kingship and State: The Buganda Dynasty* (Cambridge, 1996).

30

Costs and Benefits, Prosperity, and Security, 1870–1914

AVNER OFFER

Empire for what? A benefit or a cost? Agent of peace or engine of war? To ask these questions about the late-Victorian Empire necessarily involves contemplating imaginary alternatives, 'counter-factual' worlds, in which the Empire did not exist or existed in a different form; imaginary worlds in which the First World War was avoided, or perhaps had been lost. There is no end to counter-factuals, but only one past. Counter-factuals nevertheless help us to define which aspects of the past are significant, and what questions to ask. To evaluate the past, as opposed to merely describing it, history must be compared with what did not happen.

To begin with, the questions of cost and benefit will apply to Britain alone. The experience of scores of societies overseas is beyond our scope. What benefits should we value? Intangibles such as 'well-being', or 'virtue' (e.g. in the form of 'the white man's burden')? These may be rewards of Empire, but they are difficult to measure, and it is necessary to fall back on other proxies for success. Two predominate: one is prosperity, or economic performance, using the measuring-rod of money. Another is security: preserving the peace or prevailing in war. To be sure, prosperity and security do not capture the full range of rewards or address important non-economic and non-political motives for Empire.[1] But prosperity and security, while only parts of the picture, are large and important ones. This chapter therefore surveys economic thinking about the theory of Empire, and goes on to evaluate the impact of trade, emigration, investment, governance, and defence on some British balance sheets.

Theory

The economics of Empire are informed by a few simple ideas, stated by Adam Smith and further developed by subsequent writers. Smith encompassed trade,

I am grateful to Michael Edelstein and James Foreman-Peck for valuable comments and corrections.

[1] Ronald Hyam, *Empire and Sexuality: The British Experience* (Manchester, 1990); Avner Offer, *The First World War: An Agrarian Interpretation* (Oxford, 1989), chaps. 9, 21.

investment, settlement, governance, and conquest into one comprehensive system of analysis. His fundamental insight was that Empire opened access to new economic opportunities, thus increasing the scope for the division of labour which is the main source of productivity and growth. Pursuing these opportunities was bound to alter the structure and pace of development at home, for the better under free trade, possibly for the worse under monopoly. Furthermore, colonies cost money to govern and defend, and these costs could wipe out the gains. If colonies were necessary at all, they should be self-governed, and commercial relations should correspond as much as possible to those of a voluntary trading partner.[2]

Subsequent thinking about the costs and benefits of Empire developed these insights. David Ricardo and John Stuart Mill analysed precisely the benefits of specialization and trade, and endorsed free trade as the policy to maximize economic welfare. Both Ricardo and Mill worried that diminishing returns to investment in natural resources (primarily in agriculture) might curb the rate of growth and could bring it to a halt eventually. Reaching out for new reserves of natural resources through trade and overseas development could keep the rate of return at a higher level, and could stave off the onset of stagnation.[3]

Edward Gibbon Wakefield, writing in the 1830s and the 1840s, shifted the emphasis from trade to emigration. Colonial settlement and investment provided an escape from cyclical slump and stagnation in Britain. A glut of savings and discouraged entrepreneurs in Britain could be mobilized to colonize the virgin lands of the Empire, where settlers could gain a better living and capital much higher returns.[4]

Karl Marx, an avid reader of both Smith and Wakefield, adopted their ideas and gave them an additional twist: competition was driving down the rate of profit at home, but this decline of the rate of profit could be postponed by investing overseas, where exploitation was easier and rates of return higher. Since the world was finite, colonization could not go on forever, and once the last frontier was reached, the crisis of capitalism could not be long in coming.[5]

Round about 1900 J. A. Hobson applied a similar approach to the most salient Imperial problem of his time: the war in South Africa. His original diagnosis

---

[2] Adam Smith, *An Inquiry into the Nature and Causes of the Wealth of Nations*, ed. E. Cannan (New York, 1937), Book I, chap. 3. Also Book IV, chap. 7, parts ii–iii, esp. pt. iii, pp. 563–79.

[3] Ricardo's model is diffused throughout his writings; see Mark Blaug, *Ricardian Economics: A Historical Study* (New Haven, 1958), chaps. 2 and 9, sect. ii; John Stuart Mill, *Principles of Political Economy with Some of their Applications to Social Philosophy*, ed. W. J. Ashley, new edn. (London, 1909), Book IV, chaps. 1–6.

[4] e.g. Edward Gibbon Wakefield, *A View of the Art of Colonization in Letters Between a Statesman and a Colonist* [1849], Introduction by James Collier (Oxford, 1914), letters 12–16.

[5] Karl Marx, *Capital: A Critical Analysis of Capitalist Production*, 2 vols. (1867; Moscow, 1954), I, chap. 33.

(echoing Wakefield) was one of over-saving, in which the accumulated wealth of the rich found no worthwhile domestic investments, because of workers' lack of purchasing power. Instead, these savings sought an outlet in the Empire, especially in speculative gold-mining: aggressive mineral magnates in Africa provoked international conflict and war. This analysis reflected the circumstances of the period c.1893–1904 in Britain, when deflation had pushed down domestic interest rates. The most attractive overseas investment was gold in South Africa. A wave of speculative investment generated tensions which eventually culminated in the South African (Boer) War. However, Hobson also noted that Britain's overseas investment had gone largely to the settler colonies (Australia, New Zealand, South Africa, Canada) to the United States, and to South America. He believed that most of this investment was productive, and a benefit to domestic consumers, but thought it even better for these savings to have been invested or consumed at home.[6]

Hobson set out a broad statistical framework to support his argument. By the eve of the First World War G. Paish and C. K. Hobson had provided a detailed quantitative account of Britain's assets overseas. Several scholars have developed these estimates, including (chronologically) Feis, Imlah, Hall, Simon, Feinstein, Davis and Huttenback, and Pollard.[7] Edelstein's recent investigation is used extensively below.[8] In assessing these figures, it is useful to examine their several components, namely, investment, trade, and emigration.

Investment

Adam Smith predicted that overseas investment would pay more than investment at home, and would also bias the course of domestic development, possibly to its detriment. These prognoses are still at the core of investigation and debate. Investment in Empire conforms with the temporal pattern of British overseas investment in general (see chap. 2 above). The serious outflow of British investment began in the 1800s, and tended to move in cycles, pouring into one region after another in response to local development opportunities. In Britain, the Low Countries, and Germany urban growth and industrialization created a large appetite for food and raw materials. For the settler societies, this need created an opportunity to develop and export the harvest of farms, forests, and mineral

---

[6] J. A. Hobson, *Imperialism: A Study* [1902], 3rd edn. (London, 1938), chaps. 2, 4, 6.

[7] Listed in the Select Bibliography, except for Simon, whose article is printed in Hall.

[8] Michael Edelstein, *Overseas Investment in the Age of High Imperialism* (New York, 1982); 'Foreign Investment and Accumulation', and 'Imperialism: Cost and Benefit', chaps. 7 and 8, in Roderick Floud and Donald McCloskey, eds., *The Economic History of Britain since 1700*, 2nd edn., 3 vols. (Cambridge, 1994), II, pp. 173–216.

deposits. Investment went mostly (about 70 per cent) into extractive infrastructure: predominantly railways, but also urban utilities (gas, electricity, public works). Much of this was lent to governments and local authorities. A smaller fraction (about 12 per cent) was sunk directly in agriculture and mining.[9] British funds also supported local financial institutions (banks, insurance, mortgage and land companies) which financed urban and rural housing, agricultural construction, and merchant inventories.

In composition, about 70–80 per cent of these assets constituted 'portfolio investment', that is, tradeable financial assets such as overseas government bonds or the securities (bonds and shares) of foreign companies. The rest was made up of 'direct investment', that is, the material and financial assets of British companies and entrepreneurs operating directly overseas.[10] About 38 per cent of British investment overseas went to the Empire, and about 62 per cent outside it, while more than two-thirds of British investment raised in financial markets was destined for overseas. Within the Empire, more than two-thirds of all investment went to the areas of recent settlement, occupied almost entirely (apart from South Africa) by British and other European migrants, and their descendants (Table 2.6 above).[11] At the end of the period the income from overseas assets contributed about 8 per cent of British national income, and these assets, valued at about £4.2 billion, made up about 37 per cent of all British capital assets (including such domestic assets as buildings and land, not traded in financial markets).[12] Given that only the wealthy normally invested in bonds and shares, and that about two-thirds of financial assets were invested overseas, it is clear that the professional, managerial, and rentier classes had a strong preference for overseas assets.

Overseas income grew faster than overseas investment. In principle, overseas investment did not have to draw on domestic resources at all: it could be financed entirely from reinvesting the returns on earlier investments, and would still have left a considerable surplus. Property income from abroad exceeded net foreign investment for the whole period after 1865 except for a few years around 1870.[13] Of

---

[9] Edelstein, 'Foreign Investment', p. 179.

[10] Edelstein fixes the boundary between the two at 30% British ownership.

[11] Calculated from Lance E. Davis and Robert A. Huttenback, with the assistance of Susan Gray Davis, *Mammon and the Pursuit of Empire: The Political Economy of British Imperialism, 1860–1912* (Cambridge, 1986), Table 2.1, pp. 40–41. Minimal estimate.

[12] Edelstein, 'Foreign Investment', Table 7.1, p. 175; value of domestic and overseas capital: land was 21% and reproducible capital 41%; C. H. Feinstein, *National Income, Expenditure and Output of the United Kingdom, 1855–1965* (Cambridge, 1972), Table 46, col. 9, p. T104; Table 50, p. T110; C. H. Feinstein, 'National Statistics, 1760–1920', in C. H. Feinstein and Sidney Pollard, eds., *Studies in Capital Formation in the United Kingdom, 1750–1920* (Oxford, 1988), Table 18.5, p. 400.

[13] Edelstein, 'Foreign Investment', Table 7.1, p. 175.

course as interest flowed in and capital was repaid, investors had a choice between consumption and reinvestment, at home or abroad; since most investment came from the wealthy, who earned much more than they consumed, the choice of consumption would rarely arise. Investment could be and was withdrawn from one region and diverted to another. This gradual accumulation of assets over decades, across the globe, meant there was little overlap between the flash-points of political and military expansion, and the geographical configuration of economic imperialism, concentrated in the temperate countries, the 'informal empire', and the United States.

Effect of Investment on Trade

Adam Smith insisted on no discrimination in favour of Imperial trade and investment, and his doctrine informed Britain's nineteenth-century commitment to free trade. British trade and investment were not channelled by policy into British territories, and British defence, in the form of the Royal Navy, extended equally to traders with Imperial and non-Empire territories.

Not all property income from abroad was reinvested. Enough of it remained (together with earnings from shipping and financial services, other arms of Britain's overseas orientation) to finance a permanent trade deficit of enormous magnitude. On average, Britain imported 46 per cent more merchandise (by value) than she exported during the period from 1871 to 1914.[14] Not only could Britain import far more goods than she exported for decades on end, she did so at falling prices. Between the 1870s and 1914 the terms of trade, the price relation between British exports and imports, improved about 10 per cent in Britain's favour. These price improvements were facilitated by Britain's nvestments in railways, in steamships, in trading services, and in urban and rural development overseas. More than two-thirds of these imports took the form of natural resource products, mostly food, fodder, and industrial raw materials.[15]

Those imports caused Britain to run down its own domestic agriculture. The imports of cheap food into Britain acted to depress the value of agricultural land, to depopulate the countryside, and to diminish the influence of the landed aristocracy, the gentry, and the farmers; they barely harmed the farm labourers, who migrated increasingly to the towns. Cheap food imports thus had a progress-

[14] Re-exports deducted from imports. Calculated from B. R. Mitchell, *British Historical Statistics*, 2nd edn. (Cambridge, 1988), Table 'External trade 3', p. 453.

[15] Offer, *The First World War*, Table 6.1, p. 82; terms of trade, Mitchell, *British Historical Statistics* 'External trade 23', pp. 526–27.

ive effect (in the economic sense, of reducing inequality, and also arguably in the social and political ones), redistributing income from landowners and farmers to the rest of society. In particular, British investment overseas made food cheaper for manual workers. Food still accounted for more than half of working-class expenditure, so this was a substantial benefit.[16] Some gains in quantity were offset by losses in quality. Much of this imported food (and the bulk of working-class imported food consumption) was taken in the form of mechanically processed staples, of white flour, frozen meat, and white sugar, that neither nutritionists nor chefs would hold in high regard today. Unlike continental European countries Britain did not develop a rich indigenous food culture with distinctive cheeses, breads, and preserved meats, based on rural and small-town traditions and skills.

As the classical economists had predicted, an overseas trade orientation acted to restructure the British economy. A quantitative measure of this commitment can be derived from the scale of British overseas earnings as a proportion of GNP.[17] Over the period 1871–1913 as a whole, Britain derived an average 31.5 per cent of its income from overseas. Broken down, an average 15.9 per cent came from visible exports, 6.5 per cent from the export of services, 3.8 per cent was earned by shipping, and 5.3 per cent as property income from abroad.[18]

Visible exports relied on a set of successful industries inherited from the industrial revolution. Pride of place belonged to textile industries, cotton and wool, and their ancillary machine-building industries, which also exported widely. Both cotton and wool imported the bulk of their raw materials, while cotton exported more than three-quarters of its output, and wool almost half. Engineering, iron and steel, and shipbuilding remained strong throughout the nineteenth century. Coal, which powered Britain's own development, also found growing markets abroad.

Exported services were mostly commercial and financial. London banks financed commodity inventories and goods in transit. Insurance companies took on marine and commercial risks. Shipping and cargo brokers provided one intermediary service, while commodity exchanges provided another. Merchants moved everything from sugar and tea to wheat and zinc. The City of London formed a financial hub that brought overseas borrowers into contact with British

[16] Kevin H. O'Rourke, 'The European Grain Invasion, 1870–1913', *Journal of Economic History* (hereafter *JEcH*), LVII (1997), pp. 775–801.

[17] GNP (gross national product) is GDP (gross domestic product) plus property income from abroad.

[18] Derived from Feinstein, *National Income*, Table 3, pp. T10–T11; Mitchell, *British Historical Statistics*, Table 'External trade 3', p. 453; Albert H. Imlah, *Economic Elements in the Pax Britannica: Studies in British Foreign Trade in the Nineteenth Century* (Cambridge, Mass., 1958), Table 4, p. 39.

wealth. The great majority of Britain's great and middling non-landed fortunes were made in this metropolitan cluster of finance and trade. This nexus has been christened 'gentlemanly capitalism', to distinguish it from 'manufacturing capitalism'. Indeed, it has been claimed that this service industry was the real source of Britain's comparative advantage, not its industrial skills.[19] It is questionable, however, whether a financial and mercantile capitalism on this scale could have flourished for so long, and to such an extent, without a successful manufacturing industry, with its large export earnings and its large demand for imports. Perhaps the peculiar talent of 'gentlemanly capitalism' was its ability to appropriate such a large share of the returns to industrial enterprise in Britain; perhaps financial success acted to cramp industrial development. To anticipate, if 'gentlemanly capitalists' had been a little less prosperous, and business capitalists a little more so, the British economy might have developed along more enterprising and dynamic lines.

Shipbuilding and shipping, among the largest of domestic industries, were devoted to servicing this trade. British shipbuilding was the largest such industry by far, producing about 60 per cent of the world's tonnage. Britain's merchant fleet was also by far the largest in the world, with about 35 per cent of world tonnage throughout the period (and another 5–9 per cent in British possessions), way ahead of the runner-up (Germany) with 6 per cent growing to 9 per cent in 1911.[20] British trade and investment built up the demand for ships, and provided them with cargoes. The Royal Navy, another pillar of trade and Empire, gave rise to an export industry of warships, guns, and armour.

This process of industrial and mercantile specialization made British society into the most urbanized in the world. Come the First World War, more than 60 per cent of its food (by calories) was imported. Britain, as it were, had sent her grain-fields overseas. The surge of overseas development financed by British wealth stimulated a large emigration from Britain to the American and Australasian frontier (Table 3.6 above). Emigration coincided, on the whole, with the cyclical pulses of overseas investment. It highlights a crucial difficulty in assessing the consequences of Empire. British migrants mostly left with some equipment of education and training, but with the bulk of their working lives still ahead of them. It is reasonable to think that migrants as a group had ambition, initiative, and drive. The loss of human capital to Britain was a gain to the immigrants concerned. By permitting, through free trade, the emergence of such a specialized global economy, Britain created large opportunities across the seas for her own

[19] W. D. Rubinstein, *Capitalism, Culture and Decline in Britain, 1750–1990* (London, 1993), chap. 1.
[20] Derek H. Aldcroft, 'The Mercantile Marine', in Aldcroft, ed., *The Development of British Industry and Foreign Competition, 1875–1914* (London, 1968), Table 1, p. 327.

citizens. It is only the conventions of national accounting that prevent us from adding these opportunities to the benefits of Empire.

For most permanent immigrants (in the Edwardian period as many as one-third came back), conditions overseas were at least as good as at home. Real wages were much higher, and the rise in status even greater: Australia and Canada were much more equal societies than Britain, and a much smaller share of their income went to property-owners.[21] Farmers, however, often accepted very low incomes in expectation of economic independence and future gains from land appreciation. In social indicators like infant mortality and home ownership, migrants fared considerably better than the wage-worker at home. For those going to Australia and New Zealand, the climate was also better. By leaving, they took some pressure off the labour markets at home, allowing more opportunities for those who stayed behind, and improving the distribution of income. There is a category of persons, colonial administrators, policemen, soldiers, and experts in hundreds of localities world-wide, for which Empire opened up the scope for official careers which Britain alone could not afford. But in another Britain, less colonial and mercantile, their abilities might have contributed to a more dynamic economy. Emigration presented private opportunities for farmers, workers, businessmen, and professionals. In more subtle ways, the intermingling of cultures and the wide Imperial spaces opened up new horizons for imagination, aspiration, and experience, enriched the culture, and made it less insular than it would have been otherwise. Without Empire, no Conrad, no Kipling, no *King Solomon's Mines*.

Costs and Benefits of Trade

Estimates of costs and benefits depend crucially on the imaginary alternative or counter-factual chosen as a benchmark for comparison. In estimating gains from trade, Edelstein chose two plausible counter-factuals: In (a) the territories of Empire are independent or colonized by other powers. The main loss to Britain is the Empire as a free trade area, kept open (forcibly or by persuasion) to British exports. Britain now faces tariffs (of 20 per cent) comparable to those imposed by independent countries at the time. Counter-factual (b), a more radical one, assumes that in the absence of Empire, British trade with the Empire would have been lower; more precisely, a 75 per cent reduction in trade with the non-Dominion colonies (placing them on a level with British trade with, for example, China or Turkey); and a 30 per cent reduction in exports to the Dominions (comparable with, for example, Argentina). These 'facts' are highly stylized, but

---

[21] Robert C. Allen, 'Real Incomes in the English-speaking World, 1879–1913', in George Grantham and Mary MacKinnon, eds., *Labour Market Evolution* (London, 1994).

convey a sense of the magnitudes involved. Using counter-factual (a) (higher tariffs), the benefits of Empire to British trade are estimated as rising from 1.6 to 3.8 per cent of GNP between 1870 and 1913. Under counter-factual (b) (less trade), they rise from 4.3 to 6.5 per cent of GNP during the same period. Edelstein implicitly regards trade as by far the largest economic benefit conferred by Empire on Britain.[22] Even counter-factual (b) appears to be small, but for such a mature and diversified economy, it is actually a substantial benefit to come from a single source, comparable in size to the more conservative estimates of benefits of the railways (7–11 per cent of GNP) or of free trade (about 6 per cent).[23] On the other hand, trade theory suggests that a protectionist Britain, as a dominant buyer of many goods, could have off-loaded the cost of a tariff on to its trading partners, perhaps sufficiently to compensate for losing the benefits of free trade.[24] Intuitions of this kind haunted the Edwardian protectionist movement.

Did the Imperial connection provide Britain with the right trading mix? On the face of it, the answer would seem to be 'yes'. Britain imported primary and semi-fabricated commodities, and exported manufactures. Closer in, the answer is less clear-cut. Towards the end of the nineteenth century, and despite some successes, Britain failed to achieve the same standing in the new emerging technologies of electricity, chemicals, and internal combustion as she had in the technologies of the first industrial revolution, for example, in textile manufacture and machinery, in iron and steel, engineering, steam engines, and shipbuilding. One study suggests that British exports were only intensive in low-skilled labour.[25] Many writers detect a failure to upgrade the human-capital base. Was that a failure bred of complacency caused by the success of the large import-export economy in sustaining 'gentlemanly capitalism'? If so, it did not disappear with Empire, and the same problems of under-training continued to dog the post-Imperial economy as well.

The Balance Sheet of Foreign Investment

Investment in Empire can be approached in a similar way. Was it to Britain's advantage to invest so much of its savings overseas, rather than at home? It is investment rather than trade which has tended to dominate discussions of the

---

[22] Edelstein, 'Imperialism: Cost and Benefit', Table 8.1, p. 205.

[23] C. Knick Harley, 'Foreign Trade: Comparative Advantage and Performance', in Floud and McCloskey, eds., *Economic History of Britain*, I, p. 306.

[24] Donald N. McCloskey, 'Magnanimous Albion: Free Trade and British National Income, 1841–1881', *Explorations in Economic History*, XVII (1980), pp. 303–20.

[25] N. F. R. Crafts and Mark Thomas, 'Comparative Advantage in UK Manufacturing Trade, 1910–1935', *Economic Journal*, LXXXXVI (1986), pp. 629–45.

benefit of Empire. Estimating the benefits (or possibly the costs) of investment in Empire depends, once again, on the benchmark chosen for comparison.

One simple counter-factual is to assume no investment overseas. The procedure is then simply to compare the rate of return on overseas investments with comparable domestic ones. Investment in Empire paid better than comparable domestic investments, and investment overseas outside the Empire paid even more. Railway bonds in Britain apparently returned 3.8 per cent, colonial railways 4.5 per cent, and foreign railways 5.7 per cent between 1870 and 1914.[26] A sample of 566 domestic and overseas securities between 1870 and 1913 has produced a realized rate of return (i.e. including capital appreciation/depreciation) of 5.72 per cent a year for overseas investments, and 4.6 per cent for domestic ones. This difference of 1.1 percentage points was not trivial. Projected on to the magnitude of Edwardian property income from abroad, this advantage represents about 1.6 per cent of national income.[27]

So far we have assumed that Empire boosted the rate of return. From a different angle (but with the same data), Empire can be seen to depress the rates of return. Investments in Empire may have paid more than investments at home, but the rate of return outside the Empire was even higher. In another counter-factual, no overseas investment goes into the Empire, and other things are kept equal. Under these assumptions, the Empire actually depressed the potential returns from overseas investment. The counter-factuals are similar to the trade ones and assume (a) no special relationship between Britain and the colonies, or (b) a lower level of overseas investment. Consequent estimates of the benefits from investment in Empire range (depending on the counter-factual used) between −0.9 and +0.4 per cent of national income at its peak in 1913, in other words, as negligible if not actually negative.[28]

What, then, do the different rates of return signify? Why were rates of return higher in the Empire than at home, and higher still beyond the formal Empire? This was not due to greater market risks of loss and default abroad. If anything, market volatility was greater at home. If investors required a higher return on overseas investments, it was not due to adverse experience with such investments. Edelstein argues that the difference is due entirely to the higher economic productivity of overseas investment. That explains, perhaps, why the bulk of British portfolio investment was placed there. But it does not entirely explain why the efficient capital market of late-Victorian Britain was unable to transfer capital

[26] Davis and Huttenback, *Mammon and the Pursuit of Empire*, p. 81.

[27] Edelstein, 'Foreign Investment', p. 183. In contrast to Avner Offer, 'The British Empire, 1870–1914: A Waste of Money?', *Economic History Review* (hereafter *EcHR*), XLVI (1993), p. 221, based on Edelstein's much higher risk-adjusted differential.

[28] Edelstein, 'Imperialism: Cost and Benefit', Table 8.1, p. 205.

from low-return to high-return investments, and to equalize the rate of return, as economic theory would suggest. Why would anyone accept a low return when a higher one was available, at a lower risk, consistently, over decades?

The difference must lie in investors' *perception* of risk; not in the actual market risk of gain and loss, captured by measures of volatility. On the evidence of rates of return, British investors regarded their investments as being more secure at home, somewhat less so in Australia and Canada, and least secure in territories outside British jurisdiction. This does not seem to be a reflection of the *systemic* risk of political upheaval and war.[29] Britain's position near the cockpits of Europe, threatened by maritime blockade, would not seem to make it more secure than the main destinations of Imperial and overseas investment, but knowledge and ignorance may be more relevant. British investors understood domestic business conditions and institutions, knew less about Dominion and colonial ones, and least of all about foreign ones. Resolving disputes would be cheaper under British jurisdiction at home and in the Empire, the 'rules of the game' more familiar. Hence, to borrow in London, Imperial and foreign enterprises had to bid higher than comparable British ones. On the whole, however, wealthy British savers were willing to put up with additional uncertainty if it offered a higher rate of return. They may not have been so poorly informed after all. What determined the actual rates of return, then, was the distribution of risk preferences among British investors, who were willing to place more than two-thirds of their portfolio funds in overseas baskets.

Does it follow that overseas portfolio investment, with its higher rates of return, was also economically better for Britain? There are two conflicting perspectives on this crucial issue.

The first perspective, assuming diminishing returns to domestic investment, and hence a priority for overseas investment, is rooted in the classical theories already discussed. It regards the stock of investment opportunities as limited. As capital accumulates, the opportunities for high-return investments at home are gradually exhausted and the yield begins to fall. One method of keeping up the rate of return is to shift investment into underdeveloped territories overseas, where opportunities still abound. When Britain had constructed one railway system, there was little room for a second. Hence, for a capital-rich country like Britain, investment overseas was the natural progression.[30]

The other view, which assumes the possibility of increasing returns, and hence priority for investment at home, echoes Hobson's concern about 'overinvestment'

[29] Offer, 'British Empire', p. 221. If that had been the case, the home–overseas differential would narrow as dangers to Britain mounted after 1900. This does not seem to have happened.

[30] e.g. Donald N. McCloskey, 'Did Victorian Britain Fail?', *EcHR*, Second Series, XXIII (1970), pp. 446–59.

overseas. It regards the allocation of such a large proportion of Britain's savings to portfolio investment overseas as depriving the domestic economy of vital resources and as a source of lasting damage. Britain invested a much smaller proportion of her national income than the United States and Germany, and sent about one-third of this investment overseas. A moderate version argues that a somewhat higher rate of domestic investment (comparable with, for example, the United States or Germany) would have delivered a much higher level of consumption, as much as 25 per cent more, even on diminishing-returns assumptions.[31] Even a sceptic can concede that with capital-market imperfections the extra returns to domestic investment could have amounted to as much as 7 per cent of GNP.[32] A more radical critique points out that it was only in large, hands-off investments typically sold in financial markets that overseas investment had any advantage: 'The yield on the [UK] gross domestic capital stock for the years 1910–14 can be shown to be 10.6 per cent . . . British domestic investments as a group yielded a higher private return than did the assets which comprised the bulk of the British foreign portfolio.'[33]

If domestic returns were better, why then did savings flow overseas? The costs of floating a loan or issuing shares in London was high. To tap the financial markets, investments had to be substantial; that is the main reason why the railways and other large public works, with their large capital requirements, were the typical City investments. Smaller projects and public goods of various kinds found it more difficult to gain access to financial markets. The bulk of British savings were held by a small fraction of the population. These investors were, on the whole, passive. They were *rentiers*, who had no desire to 'get their hands dirty' with enterprise and management. Given the particular risk aversion of these investors, the Empire (and overseas in general) was a good place for them to invest. According to this view, the unequal distribution of wealth ensured a mismatch between the preferred private rate of return to savers, and the optimal rate of return for society, which could have been much higher. Financial markets failed to allocate investment funds to their best social uses.

The loss to Britain went beyond the funding itself. Investment embodies new knowledge and stimulates change, its benefits spill over beyond their specific locus; more domestic investment could have led to higher returns, by stimulating positive changes in the structure of the British economy. This perspective

---

[31] N. F. R. Crafts, 'Victorian Britain Did Fail', *EcHR*, Second Series, XXII (1979), pp. 533–37.

[32] McCloskey, 'Did Victorian Britain Fail?', p. 455.

[33] William P. Kennedy, *Industrial Structure, Capital Markets, and the Origins of British Economic Decline* (Cambridge, 1987), p. 152–53.

currently enjoys some popularity, both theoretical and empirical. Investment at home would have raised the rate of growth and the level of consumption.[34] Conversely, diversion of investment to safe and undemanding projects overseas undermined the urban fabric, and deprived Britain of the technological and institutional dynamism which would have delivered greater economic growth.

From this point of view overseas investment was not an economic priority for Britain; the lower rate of return at home did not indicate exhaustion of investment opportunities. A clear-cut superiority of overseas investment was only in evidence over a narrow range of assets, those securities (mostly bonds) traded on the Stock Exchange. These financially liquid assets excluded the bulk of domestic physical capital, such as the value of land, housing stock, and business premises, as well as most public capital: roads, schools, civic facilities, hospitals. They excluded most equipment and buildings of manufacturing industry. They left out the educational facilities of Britain's schools and universities, as well as the knowledge and skills embodied in her population.

With a more equal distribution of income, domestic demand would have been higher, and would have shifted away from food and raw materials towards consumer durables, better housing, and education. This could have provided higher returns to investment at home. It has been argued that capital could not find its way into more productive investments at home due to the inflexibility of capital markets: that the City of London found it easier to lend at lower rates of return for projects that it knew and understood, than to make difficult decisions about industrial creditworthiness at home. Government support for overseas investment seriously undermined public investment at home, especially in education.[35] In the process of urbanization, Britain's cities 'became ugly, crowded and polluted', and this may have held back productive investment as well.[36] The argument that there were no more useful investments to be made at home can be dismissed. The development of the telephone system in Britain, and of urban electric public transport, lagged far behind the United States. Britain also lagged considerably in the production and application of electricity and of motor transport. Some

---

[34] For a survey of endogenous growth theory, Jonathan Temple, 'New Growth Theory and New Growth Evidence', *Nuffield College Working Papers in Economics* (Oxford, Sept. 1995); more specifically, e.g. J. Bradford de Long, 'Productivity Growth and Machinery Investment: A Long-Run Look, 1870–1980', *Journal of Economic History*, LII (1992), pp. 307–24. Previous research, Sidney Pollard, 'Capital Exports, 1870–1914: Harmful or Beneficial?', *EcHR*, Second Series, XXXVIII (1985), p. 513, n. 103.

[35] Kennedy, *Industrial Structure*; Avner Offer, 'Empire and Social Reform—British Overseas Investment and Domestic Politics, 1908–1914', *Historical Journal*, XXVI, 1 (1983), p. 138.

[36] Jeffrey Williamson, 'Coping with City Growth', in Floud and McCloskey, eds., *Economic History of Britain*, I, pp. 353–55.

estimates suggest that the rise of investment and the consequent structural shifts could have delivered dramatically higher standards of living in Britain.[37]

For a different use of the wealth that went overseas, we have to envisage a different kind of society: either a more equal society, with lower levels of accumulation and higher levels of domestic demand, consuming more and investing more in technologically advanced enterprise at home, or possibly a society still unequal, but with fewer outlets for overseas investment, which might then have taken a longer view of both its industrial opportunities and of its social and educational needs, in both respects rather like Sweden or Germany. Both of these visions bring out how closely the structure of British economy and society were bound up (as the theorists of Empire had predicted) with its overseas orientation.

Some caution is in order. It is easy to get carried away by radical counter-factuals, and well to remember that they are counter-factual. Although the world has seen large shifts and international differences in growth rates, it nevertheless seems rash to attempt to pin Britain's relative stagnation in the late-Victorian period on one variable alone, important as that variable may be. Moreover, the relation between investment and growth remains opaque. Were Britain's industrial and investment weaknesses a result of excessive overseas investment, or were they maybe its causes? It is not clear that higher investment in Britain would have had the same effect as high investment elsewhere. Investment does not occur in a vacuum, and British industrial culture was resistant to change. Did Britain have the 'social capacity' to be an industrially dynamic society? Total Factor Productivity, a measure of the efficiency of capital and labour jointly, was considerably lower in Britain than in the United States. What is clear is that the counter-factual of no overseas investments suggests a society quite radically different from the one that actually existed. In this respect, British overseas investment made a real difference to the British experience, so much that it is hard to visualize an alternative.

Governance and Security

Benefits of Empire must be set off against the cost of its governance. Adam Smith considered that it was folly to cling to Empire by force, but that the benefits of Imperial trade, even monopolistic trade, still exceeded the cost of governing and defending it. This is the other key debate about the benefits of Empire. Given the existence of benefits in trade, employment, and investment, did they exceed the

---

[37] Kennedy, *Industrial Structure*, Table D4, p. 168. These particular calculations have been criticized, e.g. by C. Knick Harley, in a review in *American Historical Review*, LXLIV, 4 (1989), p. 1380.

costs of Empire? And what were those costs? The first of these was the cost of Imperial administration and defence; the second was exposure to the risks of war.

How much did trade and investment rely on the territorial presence and naval protection provided by Empire? No other large country before or since, not even the United States after 1945, has placed so much of its assets overseas. Other economic powers—France, Germany, the United States—committed far smaller shares of their resources to overseas investment. Perhaps that was prudent: France and Germany eventually lost the bulk of their overseas assets in the First World War. When the United States embarked on massive investment overseas after 1945, it had acquired its own 'free trade empire', underpinned by earth-straddling military, naval, and air forces. The overseas orientation of the British economy certainly exposed it to the risks of international conflict, and justified construction of a large navy. This national commitment to naval power aligned the interests of overseas investors with the security interests of society as a whole, and provided a further incentive for affluent British savers to accept overseas uncertainties This is a crucial link between Empire and overseas investment.

Its position as an island off the continental mass, with open access to the ocean, allowed late-Victorian Britain to dispense with a conscript army. Naval power conferred a technological advantage. Steam power provided excellent mobility at sea in comparison with marching, horse-drawn transport, and even railways. Continental powers had to give priority to their land forces. The United States was so remote from any threat that it could almost ignore defence altogether. Australia, New Zealand, and Canada also neglected their defences, secure in the knowledge that their sea routes were as valuable to Britain as to them. While potential rivals were preoccupied with military threats on land, Britain was free to maintain by far the largest navy. This asymmetry remained in place throughout most of the nineteenth century.

For all the Empire's expanse, its military cost was not excessive even by low contemporary standards. Between 1870 and 1913 Britain spent an average of about 3 per cent of her national income on defence. This was hardly crippling, compared with, for example, 5 or 6 per cent of a much larger economy after 1945. This level of expenditure was either in line with or actually lower than European Great Power norms, depending on the assumptions used.[38] France and Germany each kept more than 600,000 men under arms after 1895, Russia about 900,000 (rising fast), and all of the Great Powers (including Austria, Italy, and Turkey) had millions of men ready for wartime mobilization. Indeed, if the economic idling of conscripts

---

[38] Offer, 'British Empire: A Waste of Money?', pp. 222–26; John M. Hobson, 'The Military-Extraction Gap and the Wary Titan: The Fiscal Sociology of British Defence Policy, 1870–1914', *European Economic History Review*, XXII, 3 (1993) pp. 461–507.

is taken into account, French and German defence costs were substantially higher than Britain's. British defence manpower was smaller, but not insubstantial. On the eve of the South African War, in 1898, there were 99,000 regular soldiers in regiments at home, 75,000 in India, and 41,000 in the other colonies. The navy had another 100,000 officers and men. Britain kept a total of some 315,000 men permanently under arms, and also a 'native army' in India of about 148,000.[39] Naval spending rose from one-half of defence outlays in 1895 to almost two-thirds in 1913. Britain's defence effort, like her economy, was based on skilled and specialized wage labour, her long-service officers, soldiers, seamen, stokers, and mechanics, and on large lumps of capital in the form of armoured ships.

Naval command reduced the need for land forces. It was unnecessary to maintain a large garrison at every potential trouble spot; forces could be carried by sea wherever needed. During the South African War Britain supported a large military effort 6,000 miles from home. The Indian garrison, the largest standing army in the Empire, was more than half native, and was financed entirely from local sources. Apart from South Africa, no other component of the Empire faced any serious threats on land.

By the 1890s sea-power was no longer a matter of cheap gunboats and cruisers, but of expensive battleships and their large flotillas of smaller vessels. Technological change eroded British dominance. Cheaper weapons, the mine, the torpedo, and the submarine, enabled small powers to mount a real threat, while each cohort of capital ships became obsolete in little more than a decade. Other industrializing nations all grew faster than Britain, and were thus able to compete in naval construction. No single power aspired to match the Royal Navy before the First World War, but several of them outclassed or threatened it in their home waters during the Edwardian period. Britain gave way to Japan in the Far East, to France, Italy, Austria, and Russia in the Mediterranean, to Germany and Russia in the Baltic, and to the United States in North America; she needed the bulk of her firepower simply to match the German threat in the North Sea. This sudden eclipse of British dominance undercut the viability of the free-trade Empire. Hence, during the Edwardian period, the anxious attempts to recast the arrangements for Imperial defence, such as Chamberlain's Tariff Reform campaign, the Imperial conferences, and an implicit reliance on American resources in British defence strategy.[40]

What was the relation between economic and military strength? Mercantilist writers regarded power and plenty as inseparable. In India, Britain continued to run an Empire held by military forces, and governed directly. India dominated the

---

[39] *Hazel's Annual for 1899* (London, 1899).
[40] Offer, *The First World War*, pp. 253–56; see above, chap. by E. H. H. Green.

Empire in terms of numbers, with some 85 per cent of its population in 1911. It also ran a permanent payments deficit with Britain, which helped the metropolis to balance its transactions elsewhere. In 1910 India paid a net £60m to Britain, at a time when the overall British deficit on visible trade was £144m.[41] There is some controversy as to whether any part of this payments surplus should be regarded as exploitative: in economic terms, British investment did not receive exorbitant returns, and the cost of British administration may be regarded as moderate.[42] But the gratifications of governance remained British, and there is also a question whether the combination of unilateral transfers to Britain, and the British management of a silver monetary base, did not have a harmful effect on India's terms of trade.[43] There is also a question whether British goods would have been so successful in India without British rule. But India did not dominate British trade. Together with all the other dependent colonies, it only took between 15 and 21 per cent of British exports during this period. The vast bulk of British overseas economic activity was not mercantilist in nature: it had no direct reliance on military force or commercial privilege, but depended instead on the free flow of trade.

A commercial policy of free trade, and the relative openness of the Empire to foreign trade, had the advantage of reducing friction with the other powers. In the context of free trade, it was less important to dominate a territory than to keep it open. That was the meaning of the 'imperialism of free trade'. But the Raj in India and expansion in Egypt and Africa were not entirely consistent with this doctrine. Freedoms of governance and of trade were reserved for the dominant race of the Empire.

Lenin called the Great War an 'imperialist war'. Britain had the largest of Empires. Can its Empire be implicated in the collapse of peace in Europe in 1914? There is such a link, in which the pursuit of prosperity eventually acted to undermine security. By opting for free trade, Britain gave up self-sufficiency in food and raw materials, and came to depend on unmolested passage for its world-ranging merchant marine. British naval supremacy was an implicit premiss of economic specialization. The Royal Navy kept a watch in distant waters, and was relied upon to safeguard food supplies in time of war. The rapid growth of other industrial countries, however, eroded British naval supremacy, and gave rise to a serious concern about security around the turn of the century.

Simultaneously, Britain's trading Empire, more particularly its English-speaking components in Canada, Australasia, and South Africa, was emerging as a

---

[41] S. B. Saul, *Studies in British Overseas Trade, 1870–1914* (Liverpool, 1960), p. 58 and chap. 8; Mitchell, *British Historical Statistics*, Table 'external trade 3', p. 453.

[42] James Foreman-Peck, 'Foreign Investment and Imperial Exploitation: Balance of Payments Reconstruction for Nineteenth-Century Britain and India', *EcHR*, XLII (1989), pp. 365–72.

[43] Ibid., pp. 371–72.

strategic asset for Britain. The main purpose of Chamberlain's tariff reform campaign was to bind these societies into a British *Kriegsverein* (i.e. military alliance) by means of a *Zollverein* (customs union). The perceived menace of the German naval build-up pushed Britain into defensive alliances with France and Russia. Between 1906 and 1908 British naval planners investigated the new geo-strategic alignment, and concluded that Germany was also reliant on maritime trade, and similarly exposed to blockade. In 1908 the Committee of Imperial Defence decided on a hybrid strategy for a possible war with Germany. A small expeditionary force would be despatched to stiffen French resistance, and this would provide a naval blockade, the decisive weapon, with the time required for its work.[44] In Germany, a similar analysis inclined the leaders towards a desperate strategy of pre-emptive attack.[45] International economic specialization, and especially the British division of labour which relied on food from overseas, thus helped to dislocate the balance of power in Europe and impelled Britain into continental alliances; the naval arms race was one of the precipitating causes of war. Some writers have suggested that the Empire might have given Britain a false sense of security; that Britain was not assertive enough; that by merely raising its spending to European levels it could have helped to deter Germany from launching the First World War.[46]

What had failed was the system of 'hegemonic stability'.[47] According to this interpretation, peace and plenty depend on the presence of a Great Power with military superiority, willing to act as arbiter and enforcer of the peace. From this standpoint, British military and naval efforts should not be viewed as merely a contribution to British defence. The Royal Navy extended protection to the Dominions and their trade, to Britain's informal empire in Asia and South America, as well as to its trading partners, especially the United States. In deterring war, it extended the benefits of peace to Britain's adversaries as well, to France and later to Germany. Indeed, this benefited these countries economically more than it benefited Britain, since the rest of the developed world was growing faster at the end of the nineteenth century than was Britain. If the international division of labour underpinned by Britain's free trade did increase growth, and if growth occurred faster in other countries, then the system of hegemonic stability was redistributing economic and military power away from Britain and making a challenge to its hegemony more likely.

[44] Offer, *The First World War*, part 3.

[45] Ibid., chaps. 22–23.

[46] Hobson, 'The Military-Extraction Gap', pp. 493–500.

[47] Associated with Robert Gilpin, Robert O. Keohane, and Charles P. Kindelberger; a critical survey in Isabelle Grunberg, 'Exploring the "Myth" of Hegemonic Stability', *International Organization*, XLIV, 4 (1990), pp. 431–77.

When Britain decided to enter the war, she was able to draw on the resources of its Empire and its great informal trading web. Some of the best assets of British security turned out to be the bonds of the English-speaking world overseas: economic, social, political, sentimental, forming a complex but effective system of practical kinship. Australia, New Zealand, and Canada added some 30 per cent to the population of the British Isles, and almost 40 per cent to their income.[48] By extending British resources, the Empire made Britain more prone to take military action. It created resources, which stood ready for dissipation by statesmen, admirals, and generals. The military effort of the Dominions was formidable. Canada, Australia, and New Zealand mobilized 1.2 million men, almost one-fifth of the numbers enlisted in the British Isles. India mobilized almost another million. In addition, the Empire provided money, as well as vast resources of food, raw materials, and industrial capacity. In 1917 the allied margin of superiority was very small, and Britain might have had to settle on difficult terms without this Imperial support. The 'informal empire' also made a crucial economic contribution, and the United States, part of the British overseas web of trade, migration, and finance, proved decisive economically even before its formal intervention in the war guaranteed the military outcome.

Conclusion

Any balance sheet of Empire depends on the counter-factual chosen. In comparison with a world that had not been colonized by Britain, other things being equal, the benefits of Imperial trade alone contributed at most 5–6 per cent to British national income at the end of the period, and perhaps even less. Imperial investment, compared with a world without Empire, added very little, while a world with no overseas investment, and other things kept equal, is not a realistic counterfactual. In total, then, the direct contribution of Empire to Britain was not entirely negligible, but in its absence British average incomes would still have been ahead of such contemporary first-rank economies as France and Germany, Sweden and Switzerland.

If one assumes constant or increasing rather than diminishing returns on domestic investment, the Empire can be seen as a diversion from a more productive development path in which more equipment and talent had been allocated to the domestic economy. Such counter-factuals throw up dramatic improvements in British welfare, but are they to be believed? Periods when the option of overseas investment was not so readily available (during the 1890s, 1930s, and the 1950s)

---

[48] At prevailing exchange rates, though only about 27% at Purchasing Power Parity, as calculated from Allen, 'Incomes in the English-speaking World', Table 6A, p. 128.

were indeed times of more dynamic domestic development and growth by British standards, though still lacklustre by the standards of other countries. This suggests that the problem was as much the productivity of domestic investment as the domestic share of overall investment. The link between investment and growth (indeed, all the determinants of growth) is poorly understood, and appears to involve social, cultural, and institutional factors as well. High investment in Britain might not have been so productive as elsewhere, due to such inhibitions and constraints: the traditions and adversarial attitudes of workers and employers, the parsimony of local government, the low level of education and training—all militate against the assumption of increasing returns to domestic investment. High estimates of growth forgone should be qualified accordingly. Other things would have had to change as well; given the strong trade orientation of the British economy, and the Imperial share in its trade (about one-third), there is a real question whether existing output levels could have been maintained without the Empire. At any rate, the radical counter-factual of increasing-return investment at home takes us a long way from reality. One has to go very far back in history, to the outcomes of the Revolutionary and French wars, to find the historical crossroads which would have made a different world possible.

The real welfare impact of Empire lies elsewhere, and it requires shifting one's gaze away from the British Isles. The attractions of Imperial and overseas investment and trade were not merely matters of clever finance, but reflected a unique economic opportunity. This was embodied in the vast potential of natural resources in thinly occupied countries in temperate climates: minerals, timber, but mostly agricultural land and its products: grain, wool, cheese, meat, hides. What opened it up was the demand of metropolitan urban societies, and their capacity to pay in cheap manufactures. Given the large cost advantages of these newly productive areas, opening them up with railways and export facilities provided straightforward economic benefits.

The establishment of overseas English-speaking societies was by far the largest permanent benefit created by Britain and her Empire. In doing so, it inflicted an appalling cost on the aboriginal peoples of Canada, Australia, New Zealand, and South Africa. Most of the benefits did not accrue directly to Britain, but were reaped on the spot. Some of these countries, the Dominions, were politically integrated in the Empire. The United States had been so in the past, and was bound to Britain by strong ties of language, kinship, and commerce. These communities were among the richest in the world. Britain planted the seed, and nourished it with infusions of migrants, talent, and money. She also transferred a set of mature institutions, a legal system, property rights, and the management of diplomacy and defence. Take Australia, the richest society in the world between the 1860s and the 1890s, settled almost entirely by British migrants and their descendants, financed (over and above local accumulation) from Britain, subject to British jurisdiction, and accepting British sovereignty. While these self-governing societies only received about a tenth of British exports, the Antipodes at least depended absolutely on Britain for their markets. At the end of the period, overseas 'New Britannias' added, as we have seen, almost 40 per cent to British GNP, dwarfing any other actual contribution of Empire to welfare in the British Isles alone. Their inhabitants may not have been more wealthy than Britons on the average, but manual workers (the majority) were much better off in terms of wages and status, and lived in more equal societies. The overseas, English-speaking, natural resource economy absorbed millions of migrants from Britain. In reality, at the end of the nineteenth century the Dominions were extensions of the British Isles, tied to Britain by a web of kinship, investment, and trade, and by the political institutions of Empire which still had a binding force. Had there been no Empire, these territories would not have remained undeveloped. Settlers would have come from elsewhere in Europe, North America, or even Asia. This would have been a loss to the people of Britain, and perhaps (given these countries' democratic instincts and their internal stability), a loss to global welfare. These societies became British instead, and were still substantially so in 1914.

Selected Bibliography

MICHAEL BARRATT BROWN, *Economics of Imperialism* (Harmondsworth, 1974).

LANCE E. DAVIS and ROBERT A. HUTTENBACK, with the assistance of SUSAN GRAY DAVIS, *Mammon and the Pursuit of Empire: The Political Economy of British Imperialism, 1860–1912* (Cambridge, 1986).

MICHAEL EDELSTEIN, *Overseas Investment in the Age of High Imperialism* (New York, 1982).

C. H. FEINSTEIN, *National Income, Expenditure and Output of the United Kingdom, 1855–1965* (Cambridge, 1972).

HERBERT FEIS, *Europe: The World's Banker, 1870–1914* (New Haven, 1930).

D. K. FIELDHOUSE, *Economics and the Empire* (London, 1973).

JAMES FOREMAN-PECK, 'Foreign Investment and Imperial Exploitation: Balance of Payments Reconstruction for Nineteenth-Century Britain and India', *Economic History Review*, XLII (1989), pp. 365–72.

A. R. HALL, ed., *The Export of Capital from Britain, 1870–1914* (London, 1968).

C. K. HOBSON, *The Export of Capital* (London, 1914).

JOHN A. HOBSON, *Imperialism: A Study* (1902; 3rd edn., London, 1938).

J. M. HOBSON, 'The Military-Extraction Gap and the Wary Titan: The Fiscal Sociology of British Defence Policy, 1870–1914', *European Economic History Review*, XXII, 3 (1993), pp. 461–507.

ALBERT H. IMLAH, *Economic Elements in the Pax Britannica: Studies in British Foreign Trade in the Nineteenth Century* (Cambridge, Mass., 1958).

A. OFFER, 'The British Empire, 1870–1914: A Waste of Money?', *Economic History Review*, XLVI (1993).

—— *The First World War: An Agrarian Interpretation* (Oxford, 1989).

G. PAISH, 'Great Britain's Capital Investment in Other Lands', *Journal of the Royal Statistical Society* LXXII (1909), pp. 465–95.

—— 'Great Britain's Investments in Individual Colonial and Foreign Countries', *Journal of the Royal Statistical Society*, LXXIV (1911), pp. 167–200.

SIDNEY POLLARD, 'Capital Exports, 1870–1914: Harmful or Beneficial?', *Economic History Review*, Second Series, XXXVIII (1985), pp. 489–514.

A. G. L. SHAW, ed., *Great Britain and the Colonies* (London, 1970).

S. B. SAUL, *Studies in British Overseas Trade, 1870–1914* (Liverpool, 1960).

ADAM SMITH, *An Inquiry into the Nature and Causes of the Wealth of Nations,* ed. E. Cannan (New York, 1937).

BRINLEY THOMAS, *Migration and Economic Growth*, 2nd edn. (Cambridge, 1973).

EDWARD GIBBON WAKEFIELD, *A View of the Art of Colonization in Letters between a Statesman and a Colonist* (1849; Introduction by J. Collier, Oxford, 1914).

JOHN CUNNINGHAM WOOD, *British Economists and the Empire* (London, 1983).

CHRONOLOGY

Year	Great Britain and General	South, South-East, and East Asia
1783	Peace of Versailles	
1784	Pitt's India Act	Foundation of Asiatick Society of Bengal
		Peace with Mysore
1785		Warren Hastings leaves India
1786		Cornwallis Governor-General of Bengal
		First British settlement on Malay coast at Penang for the East India Company
		1786–93 artists Thomas and William Daniell visit India
1787	London Committee for the Abolition of the slave trade formed	
	Sierra Leone established as settlement for freed slaves	
1788	African Association founded	Trial of Warren Hastings begins (1788–95)
1789	Outbreak of French Revolution	
1790		Start of the war with Tipu Sultan of Mysore
1791		
1792	House of Commons votes for gradual abolition of slave trade	Defeat of Tipu and end of Mysore War
	Baptist Missionary Society founded	
	FRENCH REVOLUTIONARY WAR	
1793	War with France	Macartney's mission to the Chinese Emperor in Peking
		Renewal of East India Company Charter

Africa and Middle East	Americas, Caribbean, Australasia, and the Pacific	Year
Peace of Versailles, Britain loses Senegal	Samuel Seabury consecrated Bishop of Connecticut	1783
		1784
		1785
		1786
First settlers reach Sierra Leone	US Constitution Charles Inglis consecrated Bishop of Nova Scotia	1787
	Captain Arthur Phillip, first Governor of New South Wales, founds Port Jackson settlement (Sydney)	1788
		1789
		1790
	Canada Act establishes colonies of Upper and Lower Canada	1791
Commons votes for abolition of slave trade		1792
	Jacob Mountain consecrated Bishop of Quebec	1793

Year	Great Britain and General	South, South-East, and East Asia
1794		William Carey, Baptist missionary, arrives in Bengal
1795	Foundation of London Missionary Society	William IV of the Netherlands issues Kew Letters
		Michael Symes's first mission to the court of Ava (Burma)
1796	Glasgow and Scottish Missionary Societies founded	Hiram Cox posted as Resident to Court of Ava (Burma)
		East India Company conquer Dutch coastal area of Ceylon
1797		
1798	Irish rebellion	Wellesley Governor-General of Bengal
		Napoleon's expedition to Egypt
1799	Foundation of the Society for Missions to Africa and the East (the Church Missionary Society)	Death of Tipu and conquest of Mysore
1800	Malta occupied	
	Muzzle-loading, smooth-bore musket	
1801	Irish Act of Union	
1802	Peace of Amiens	Peace of Amiens: Britain retains coastal Ceylon, as a Crown Colony
		Michael Symes's second mission to the court of Ava (Burma)

NAPOLEONIC WARS

Year	Great Britain and General	South, South-East, and East Asia
1803	Renewed war with France	
	First Passenger Act (others in 1823, 1825, 1835, 1842, 1852, 1855)	
1804		
1805	Destruction of French and Spanish fleets at Trafalgar	Wellesley recalled from India
1806		
1807	Act abolishing the British slave trade from 1 May	
1808	Start of Peninsular War to eject French from Spain	

Africa and Middle East	Americas, Caribbean, Australasia, and the Pacific	Year
	Jay Treaty adjusting territory and trade with USA	1794
First British occupation of the Cape of Good Hope, South Africa		1795
		1796
	LMS missionaries arrive at Tahiti	1797
		1798
First LMS mission to South Africa under Dr J. T. Van der Kemp		1799
		1800
		1801
Peace of Amiens: Cape of Good Hope returned to the Dutch	Peace of Amiens: Britain gains Trinidad	1802
	British settlement in Van Diemen's Land (Tasmania)	1803
		1804
		1805
Second British occupation of the Cape of Good Hope	Commodore Popham seizes Buenos Aires	1806
British abolition of the Atlantic slave trade		1807
The African Institution formed		
Sierra Leone becomes a British Crown colony	Braganza royal family quits Portugal for Brazil	1808

Year	Great Britain and General	South, South-East, and East Asia
1809		
1810		French island of Mauritius conquered
1811		British conquest of Java
1812		
1813		East India Company Charter Act opens India trade and eases restriction on missionaries' access to India
1814		First Bishop of Calcutta arrives in India
1815	Battle of Waterloo, Vienna Peace Settlement: Britain retains Malta, and Ionian Isles	Vienna Settlement: Britain retains Mauritius, and Ceylon, Java and other territories returned to Dutch
1816		Abortive Amherst mission to China
1817		James Mill's *History of India*
1818	Wesleyan Methodist Missionary Society established	Abdication of Baji Rao II (Peshwa of Poona), and absorption of Maharashtra into Bombay Presidency
1819		Stamford Raffles acquires Singapore; Batavia returned to Dutch
1820		
1821		
1822	Death of Sir Joseph Banks	
1823	Anti-Slavery Society formed: campaign begins	First Anglo-Burmese War begins

Africa and Middle East	Americas, Caribbean, Australasia, and the Pacific	Year
		1809
	1810–21 Spanish–American Wars of Independence	1810
Expulsion of Xhosa from the Zuurveld begins	Selkirk's Red River grant	1811
		1812
	First crossing of the Blue Mountains (NSW) by Blaxland, Lawson, and W. C. Wentworth	1813
	CMS mission established at Rangihoua	1814
Vienna Settlement: Britain retains Cape Colony	Vienna Settlement: Britain retains Tobago, St Lucia, and Guiana	1815
Slachtersnek Rebellion, Cape Colony	Louis-Joseph Papineau elected speaker of the Lower Canadian Assembly	
	Governor Macquarie (NSW) establishes first native institution in Paramatta for education of Aborigines of both sexes	
	(April) Barbados slave rebellion (May) Imperial government recommends Slave Registration Act	1816
	Bank of New South Wales established	1817
	49th parallel adopted as boundary between United States and British territory from Lake of the Woods to the Rocky Mountains	1818
		1819
British settlers arrive at Algoa Bay		1820
British government take control of Gold Coast trading forts	Merger of Hudson's Bay Company and North-West Company ends Montreal fur-trade	1821
	Brazil becomes an independent republic under Pedro I	1822
British merchants establish post at Natal	Monroe doctrine enunciated (Aug.) Demerara slave rebellion	1823

Year	Great Britain and General	South, South-East, and East Asia
1824		Anglo-Dutch Treaty: Britain cedes Bencoolen and acquires Malacca First Anglo-Burmese War ends
1825		
1826	Select Committee of Enquiry on the Expediency of Encouraging Emigration from the UK	Treaty of Yandabo: Burma cedes Arakan and Tenasserim to Britain Henry Burney concludes treaty with Siam Formation of the Straits Settlements
1827		
1828		William Bentinck appointed Governor-General of India
1829	E. G. Wakefield's *A Letter from Sydney*	Suttee abolished
1830	From 1830s diffusion of steam trains and river steamers underway Ripon Regulations inaugurate sales of Australian lands by auction Royal Geographical Society founded	Drive launched against thugee
1831		
1832		

Africa and Middle East	Americas, Caribbean, Australasia, and the Pacific	Year
First Anglo-Asante War	The *Australian*, first in a mushrooming of newspapers in convict NSW	1824
British government rejects Protectorate over Mombasa	Britain recognizes independent republics of Latin America	
	1824–25 Brief boom in British trade and investment with Latin America	
	Anglo-Brazilian commercial treaty renewed	1825
	Argentine-Brazil War begins	
	Britain assists in the creation of Uruguay	
	First British settlements established in Western Australia	1826
Fourah Bay College, Sierra Leone, founded		1827
Control of Gold Coast forts restored to merchants	Argentine-Brazilian War ends	1828
Cape Colony Ordinance 50 removes legal discrimination against the Khoikhoi		
	Death of Shawnadithit, last Newfoundland Beothuk	1829
	Entire Australian continent declared British	
	Swan River Colonization Association settlement established at Perth, Western Australia	
		1830
Anglo-Asante Treaty	(Dec.) Jamaica slave rebellion	1831
	Representative government introduced into Newfoundland	1832

Year	Great Britain and General	South, South-East, and East Asia
1833	Emancipation Act, abolishes slavery as from 1 Aug. 1834	Charter Act abolishes East India Company monopoly of the China trade
	First steamer crosses the Atlantic	Death of Rammohun Roy, father of the Bengal renaissance
1834	Seven agents appointed at British ports to ensure protection of migrants	
1835	Foundation of the Geological Survey of the United Kingdom	T. B. Macaulay's Minute on Education in India
		Chesney's Euphrates expedition (1835–37)
1836	Report of Select Committee on the Disposal of Land in British Colonies 1836–37 Famine in Scottish Highlands coincides with extension of government bounty emigration	
1837	T. F. Elliot appointed Agent-General for Emigration	
	Report of the Select Committee on Aborigines	
	Aborigines' Protection Society formed	
1838		Sir David Wilkie's painting *Sir David Baird discovering the body of Tipu Sultan*
1839	British and Foreign Anti-Slavery Society formed	East India Company seizes Aden Anglo-Chinese Opium War begins
		First Afghan War begins
1840	Colonial Land and Emigration Commission appointed	

Africa and Middle East	Americas, Caribbean, Australasia, and the Pacific	Year
	James Busby takes up appointment as British Resident, New Zealand	1833
	Britain seizes the Falkland Islands	
Emancipation of slaves in British colonies	British colonial slavery abolished; period of Apprenticeship begins	1834
Cape Colony Eastern Frontier War Afrikaners' Great Trek begins	92 Resolutions passed by Lower Canadian Assembly	
	7th Report on Grievances adopted by Upper Canadian Assembly	
Annexation of Queen Adelaide Province, Cape Colony	Port Phillip Association settlement at Melbourne (Victoria)	1835
	New Zealand chiefs sign the Declaration of Independence	
	Arrival of Methodist missionaries in Fiji	
Retrocession of Queen Adelaide Province	South Australian Association settlement at Adelaide (South Australia)	1836
Cape of Good Hope Punishment Act		
	Formation of the New Zealand Association	1837
	1837–38 Rebellions in Upper and Lower Canada	
	(Aug.) Beginning of full freedom for slaves	1838
	Lord Durham's Report on the Affairs of British North America	1839
Anglo-Zanzibar anti-slave trade treaty	(Jan.) First New Zealand Company settlers arrive at Port Nicholson	1840
	(6 Feb.) First signing of the Treaty of Waitangi	
	(May) Hobson proclaims sovereignty over all New Zealand	

Year	Great Britain and General	South, South-East, and East Asia
1841	Select Committee on Emigration from Scotland	James Brooke becomes Rajah of Sarawak
	Colonial Bishoprics Fund set up The Niger Expedition	*De facto* beginning of the British administration of Hong Kong
1842		Treaty of Nanking ends the Opium War First Afghan War ends
1843	British Settlements Act Foreign Jurisdiction Act	Annexation of Sind Slavery abolished in British India
1844	Founding of the Ethnological Society of London by Thomas Hodgkin	
1845	Retirement of Sir John Barrow, Second Secretary of the Admiralty	First Sikh War First 'Land Regulations' inaugurate the International Settlement at Shanghai
1846	Earl Grey's colonial defence review	Sultan of Brunei cedes island of Labuan to Britain
	Repeal of the Corn Laws Sugar Duties Act 1846–47 French invasion scare	
1847		
1848		Marquess of Dalhousie appointed Governor-General of India Second Sikh War
1849	Repeal of the Navigation Acts	Annexation of Punjab

Africa and Middle East	Americas, Caribbean, Australasia, and the Pacific	Year
British Consul stationed at Zanzibar	Inauguration of the united province of Canada: equal representation in Assembly for Upper and Lower Canada	1841
	Ashburton-Webster Treaty fixes boundary of N. Brunswick and Maine	
1841–42 The Niger Expedition	French annexation of Marquesas	
	Murray memorandum on policy to Latin America	
	Constitution Act granted representative government to New South Wales	1842
	French annexation of Tahiti	
British annexation of Natal		1843
Resumption of Imperial control over West African settlements	Electoral defeat of Reformers in Canada by Sir Charles Metcalfe and W. H. Draper	1844
The 'Bond', establishes British protection over southern Gold Coast		
	1845–47 Franklin Expedition in search of North-west Passage	1845
	Anglo-French blockade of Buenos Aires (1845–48) begins	
War of the Axe, Cape Colony, begins	Sugar Duties Act	1846
	Settlement of the Oregon boundary dispute with United States	
Annexation of land between Fish and Kei Rivers, Cape Colony	First local responsible ministry formed in Nova Scotia	1847
War of the Axe ends	Order-in-Council grants Australian squatters security of tenure	
Annexation of the Orange River Sovereignty	La Fontaine–Baldwin 'Great Ministry' formed in Canada	1848
	Canadian self-government confirmed when British Parliament declines to intervene in Lower Canadian Rebellion Losses Bill after riots in Montreal	1849

Year	Great Britain and General	South, South-East, and East Asia
1850	Shipping companies obtain mail subsidies and introduce time-reducing long-distance steamers	Railway construction begins in India
	British Association reorganized to recognize geography as an independent science	
	Robert Knox, *The Races of Man*	
1851	Emigration Advances Act	First Indian telegraph line laid
	Great Exhibition at the Crystal Palace	
	Sir Roderick Murchison elected to second term as RGS President, and assumed effective control	
1852	French invasion scare	Udaipur lapses to East India Company
	Highland and Island Emigration Society sends almost 5,000 migrants to Australia (1852–58)	Second Anglo-Burmese War leads to annexation of Lower Burma
1853	Nationalities of migrants distinguished for the first time	Parliament renews East India Company Charter
		Competitive entry to Company service introduced
		First Indian railway line opened
1854	Outbreak of Crimean War	Nagpur lapses to East India Company
		Sir Charles Wood's Education Despatch
		Great Ganges Canal opened
		Beginning of British involvement with the Chinese customs administration
1855	Sir Roderick Murchison appointed Director-General of the Geological Survey	*Ryotwari* system in Madras revised
		John Bowring concludes treaty with King Mongkut (1851–68) of Siam
1856	End of Crimean War	Oudh annexed

Africa and Middle East	Americas, Caribbean, Australasia, and the Pacific	Year
	Vancouver Island colony established	1849
Heinrich Barth's Sahara and Sudan expedition	Gold discovered in Bathurst district, NSW	1850
	Australian Colonies Government Act	
	Transportation to Australia ends (except Tasmania 1852, and W. Australia 1868) Sydney University founded	
	Britain steps up pressure on the Brazilian slave trade	
Bombardment of Lagos		1851
Sand River Convention recognizes the Transvaal republic	Britain permits Australian colonial legislatures to draft new constitutions	1852
	New Zealand constitution enacted by British Parliament	
	Fall of Rosas, Argentine dictator	
British Consul appointed at Lagos	French annex New Caledonia	1853
David Livingstone traverses the African continent		
Representative government constitution for Cape Colony		
Bloemfontein Convention recognizes the Orange Free State	Reciprocity Treaty establishes partial free trade between USA and Britain	1854
	Abolition of seigneurial tenure in Lower Canada	
	Secularization of the Canadian Clergy Reserves	
	1st meeting of NZ General Assembly, Auckland	
		1855
	1856–57 Canadian legislation disestablishes the Anglican Church	1856

Year	Great Britain and General	South, South-East, and East Asia
1856		Hindu Widows Remarriage Act passed
		1856–60, the 'Arrow War' between China and an Anglo-French coalition
1857		First Indian Universities founded
		Outbreak of the Indian Mutiny/ Rebellion
1858	David Livingstone's missionary appeal in Cambridge to the universities	Government of India Act abolishes the East India Company
		Straits Settlements transferred from East India Company to the new India Office
1859	Universities' Mission to Central Africa formed	First Bengal Rent Act
	French invasion scare	
	Canadian information office opens in Liverpool	
	Charles Darwin's *The Origin of Species*	
1860	Machine-made single-shot breech-loading rifles proliferate	Treaty of Peking marks end of the 'Arrow War'
	Rotary presses and newsprint increase newspaper circulation	Acquisition of Kowloon (Jiulong) opposite Hong Kong Island
		1860–61 Hankou and Tientsin opened as 'treaty ports', including British concessionary areas
1861	Select (Mills) Committee on Colonial Military Expenditure	Indian Councils Act
1862		Amalgamation of Lower Burma, Arakan, and Tenasserim
		Arthur Phayre's commercial treaty with King Mindon Min of Burma
		British naval intervention against China's Taiping rebels
1863	The Anthropological Society of London founded	(Sir) Robert Hart becomes head of the Chinese Imperial Maritime Customs
1864		

Africa and Middle East	Americas, Caribbean, Australasia, and the Pacific	Year
		1856
Xhosa cattle-killing on eastern Cape Colony frontier	1857–58 A. C. Gregory North Australian Exploring Expedition	1857
1857–59 Richard Burton and John Speke expedition to discover sources of Nile	1857–60 Palliser Expedition across western British North America	
1857–64 W. B. Baikie Niger expedition		
1858–64 David Livingstone's appeal to the universities, followed by his Zambezi expedition	Alexander T. Galt joins Cartier-Macdonald ministry pledged to work for inter-colonial union	1858
	Potatau Te Wherowhero installed as Maori king	
	Canadian tariff raised to levels considered as protectionist by British manufacturers	1859
	Canada's Grand Trunk Railway completed	
1860–63 John Speke and James Grant locate source of Nile in Lake Victoria	Imperial troops occupy Waitara	1860
	1860–62 Sturt Expeditions transversing Australia south to north	
	US Civil War (1860–65)	
British annexation of Lagos	1861–62 Allied intervention in Mexico	1861
Anglo-French agreement over Zanzibar		1862
1862–65 Samuel Baker's expedition to discover Nile's Abyssinian tributaries and Lake Albert		
	Imperial troops invade Waikato	1863
	1863–66 French intervention in Mexico	
The Yoruba 'recaptive' and Anglican, Samuel Adjai Crowther, consecrated Bishop of the Niger	Outline plans for union of British North America adopted at Charlottestown and Quebec Conferences	1864

Year	Great Britain and General	South, South-East, and East Asia
1865	Colonial Naval Defence Act	
	Colonial Laws Validity Act	
	Parliamentary Select Committee on Britain's West African Settlements	
	China Inland Mission established by J. Hudson Taylor	
1866		
1867	First Lambeth Conference	Straits Settlements transferred to Colonial Office supervision
1868	The Colonial Society founded in London, becoming the Royal Colonial Society (1869) and finally the Royal Colonial Institute (1870)	
	Charles Dilke's *Greater Britain* W. E. Gladstone Prime Minister	
1869	Maria Rye and Annie Macpherson inaugurate mass juvenile migration schemes	
1870	Introduction of compound steam engines reduces fuel consumption and operating costs of iron-hulled steamers	India has 5,000 miles of railway track
	Undersea cable laying proliferates, connecting with overland telegraphs and creating a world-wide network	

Africa and Middle East	Americas, Caribbean, Australasia, and the Pacific	Year
Parliamentary Select Committee on the West African Settlements	Morant Bay rebellion in Jamaica 1865–70 War of Triple Alliance (Argentina, Brazil, Uruguay against Paraguay)	1865
1866–71 David Livingstone's expedition in search of the source of the Nile ends with his 'discovery' by H. M. Stanley	Abrogation of Reciprocity Treaty with British N. America by USA	1866
	Nova Scotia and New Brunswick agree to negotiate a British North America Union under British auspices	
	Vancouver Island annexed to British Columbia	
	Fenian raids on Canada and N. Brunswick	
Discovery of diamonds in Griqualand West	Passage of British North America Act	1867
	Creation of Maori seats in the New Zealand General Assembly	
Britain's Abyssinian Expedition Annexation of Basutoland	Foundation of Canada First, nationalist and imperial-minded ginger group	1868
	Queensland's Act to Regulate and Control the Introduction and Treatment of Polynesian Labourers	
Suez Canal opened	Red River crisis delays transfer of Hudson's Bay Company's territories to Canada	1869
	Confederation decisively rejected in Newfoundland general election	
	Manitoba created as Canada's fifth province	1870
	Withdrawal of last Imperial troops from New Zealand	
	Introduction of New Zealand's immigration and public works policies	

Year	Great Britain and General	South, South-East, and East Asia
1870	British troops withdrawn from New Zealand, Australia, and Canada John Ruskin's inaugural lecture as Slade Professor of Art at Oxford, with strong Imperial content	
1871	Death of Sir Roderick Murchison Charles Darwin's *The Descent of Man* Ethnographical and Anthropological Societies combine as Anthropological Institute	
1872	Board of Trade assumes responsibility for collecting migration statistics and administering Passenger Acts	
1873	Death of David Livingstone	
1874	Benjamin Disraeli Prime Minister	Treaty of Pangkor: Andrew Clarke concludes agreements with Malay States of Perak, Selangor, and Sunjei Ujong which accept British Residents
1875	1875–80 Shipping tonnage through Suez Canal increases sharply to 3.5 million tons p.a.	Murder of James Birch, first Resident of Perak
1876		Royal Titles Act: Queen Victoria becomes Empress of India
1877	The word 'jingoism' coined from songs by G. W. Hunt during the Russo-Turkish War	Lord Lytton's Delhi durbar

Africa and Middle East	Americas, Caribbean, Australasia, and the Pacific	Year
		1870
(Oct.) Annexation of Griqualand West to Cape Colony	British Columbia joins Confederation with promise of transcontinental railway	1871
	Sir John Macdonald member of Imperial delegation to negotiate Treaty of Washington with USA	
	Murder of Bishop John Patteson in Melanesia	
Cape Colony granted responsible government	British government concedes financial guarantee for Canada's Pacific railway	1872
	Victoria Education Act, first to introduce free, compulsory, secular education	
	Pacific Islanders' Protection Act	
Death of David Livingstone at Chitambo's (Zambia)	Creation of Canada's North West Mounted Police	1873
Anglo-Zanzibar Treaty ending the slave trade	Missionary activity begins in New Guinea	
Anglo-Asante War begins		
1874–77 H. M. Stanley concludes search for source of Nile	British annexation of Fiji	1874
End of Anglo-Asante War		
(Nov.) Britain purchases 44% of Suez Canal shares	Creation of Supreme Court of Canada	1875
Egypt bankrupt: Anglo-French 'Dual Control' of finances established	(April) Confederation riots in Barbados	1876
	Completion of Canada's Inter-colonial Railway	
	South Australia pioneers legal recognition of trade unions	
British annexation of the Transvaal	Western Pacific High Commission set up	1877
Sir Bartle Frere appointed High Commissioner for South Africa		

Year	Great Britain and General	South, South-East, and East Asia
1878	British occupation of Cyprus	India's Vernacular Press Act Second Afghan War (1878–80)
1879	First publication of *Boys' Own Paper* Carnarvon Commission on the Defence of British Possessions and Commerce abroad (1879–82)	
1880	Repeating rifles, machine-guns, and mobile artillery spread widely Europe linked to East and West Africa by telegraph cables	Lord Ripon Viceroy of India
1881	Death of Benjamin Disraeli, Lord Beaconsfield	British North Borneo Company granted Royal Charter
1882		
1883	J. R. Seeley, *The Expansion of England* Formation of National Association for Promoting State-Directed Emigration and Colonization Boys' Brigade formed	The Ilbert Bill
1884	Foundation of the Imperial Federation League, and the Manchester Geographical Society established	

Africa and Middle East	Americas, Caribbean, Australasia, and the Pacific	Year
Annexation of Port St John's and British Protectorate over Walvis Bay, South Africa		1878
Khedive Ismail deposed and replaced by son Tawfiq	Adoption of 'National Policy' of tariff protection in Canada	1879
Anglo-French 'Dual Control' of Egyptian finances confirmed	War of the Pacific begins in which Chile defeats Peru	
(Jan.–Sept.) Anglo-Zulu War, British defeat at Isandhlwana and final victory at Ulundi		
Anglo-Pedi War		
First South African (Anglo-Boer) War, with British defeat at Majuba Hill	Appointment of first Canadian High Commissioner in London	1880
	Native-born Australians outnumber migrants	
	Protectorate over Cook Islands	
The Urabi Revolution, Egypt	End of War of the Pacific	1881
Pretoria Convention restores independence to Transvaal subject to British 'suzerainty'		
British bombardment of Alexandria and occupation of Egypt after victory at Tel el-Kebir		1882
Evelyn Baring arrives in Egypt as Agent and Consul General	Privy Council decision in *Hodge* v. *The Queen* strengthens Canadian provinces against Dominion government	1883
Civil war in Asante begins		
Evacuation of Egyptian forces from Sudan	Increased bounties on European beet sugar brings collapse of sugar prices and sugar economies	1884
London Convention relaxes conditions on Transvaal independence	German actions prompt declaration of Protectorate of British New Guinea	
Anglo-Portuguese treaty to control Congo mouth		
German protectorate over South-West Africa		
Berlin West Africa Conference		

Year	Great Britain and General	South, South-East, and East Asia
1885	Final Act of the Berlin West Africa Conference	Formation of the Indian National Congress
	Colonial Defence Committee established	The 'Penjdeh incident'
	Royal Scottish Geographical Society founded	Third Anglo-Burmese War
1886	Liberal Party splits over Home Rule for Ireland	Annexation of Burma
	Emigrants' Information Office opens	
	Lord Salisbury Prime Minister	
	Keltie Report on the state of geographical education in Britain published	
	Colonial and Indian Exhibition in South Kensington, London	
1887	June: First Colonial Conference held in London	Agreements with Pahang (Malaya) leading to appointment of British Resident
1888	Imperial Exhibition, Glasgow	Sarawak, North Borneo, and Brunei become British Protectorates
1889	Naval Defence Act Hartington Commission on army administration (1889–90)	
	Brussels Conference on the Slave Trade Select Committee on Emigration (1881–91)	
1890	Steel-hulled ships with triple expansion engines into regular commercial use; purpose-built refrigrated versions	
	Medicines alleviate tropical diseases Chemical and metallurgical advances permit profitable mining of low grade ores	
1891		The Pahang rising (Malaya)

Africa and Middle East	Americas, Caribbean, Australasia, and the Pacific	Year
Death of General Gordon and fall of Khartoum to Mahdists	North-West Rebellion in Canada Canadian Pacific Railway completes trans-Canadian link	1885
British Protectorates over Niger Coast and Bechuanaland		
Transvaal gold rush and foundation of Johannesburg		1886
African Christians 'martyred' in Buganda		
Royal Niger Company granted charter Anglo-German agreement on spheres of influence in East Africa		
Annexation of Zululand	Anglo-French Condominium over the New Hebrides Australian Naval Agreement	1887
Imperial British East Africa Company granted charter	Abolition of slavery in Brazil	1888
End of Asante civil war		
British Protectorate over Shire districts of Nyasaland	Anglo-German-USA supervision of Samoa	1889
British South Africa Company granted charter	Fall of the Brazilian monarchy	
	Berlin Conference guarantees independence of Samoa and preserves rights of Britain, USA, and Germany	
Anglo-German Heligoland Treaty (for Zanzibar, Uganda, and Witu) Anglo-French Declaration on West Africa	Manitoba rescinds official recognition of French language and abolishes public funding of Church schools Baring crisis, Argentina	1890
Cecil Rhodes Prime Minister of Cape colony	1890–93 severe Australian economic depression and industrial unrest	
Death of Bishop Crowther	Death of Sir John A. Macdonald	1891
Anglo-Portuguese Treaty delineates spheres of influence in South-East Africa	Liberal government takes power in New Zealand under John Ballance Chilean civil war	

Year	Great Britain and General	South, South-East, and East Asia
1892		Indian Councils Act amended
1893	Break-up of the Imperial Federation League	
1894		
1895	Joseph Chamberlain becomes Secretary of State for the Colonies Navy League founded Beginning of sequence of Imperial Exhibitions mounted by Imre Kiralfy	Treaty of Shimonoseki inaugurates new phase of imperialism in China
1896		Anglo-French declaration on Siam Formation of the Federated Malay States (Perak, Selangor, Negri Sembilan, and Pahang)
1897	Queen Victoria's Diamond Jubilee Second Colonial Conference held in London	Anglo-Thai secret convention Large-scale railway building begins in China
1898	Death of W. E. Gladstone	99-year lease of the New Territories as an extension of Hong Kong Lease of Wei-hai-wei Lord Curzon Viceroy of India
1899	(Oct.) Outbreak of Second South African War	

Africa and Middle East	Americas, Caribbean, Australasia, and the Pacific	Year
Abbas II succeeds his father, Tawfiq, as Khedive of Egypt Portal sent to report on Uganda after chartered company failed	First sitting of the Maori Parliament British Protectorate over Gilbert and Ellice Islands	1892
British South Africa Company War with Ndebele	Enactment of women's suffrage in New Zealand British Protectorate of Solomon Islands	1893
British secret Congo Treaty with King Leopold II Cape Colony annexation of Pondoland completes takeover of Transkei territories	South Australian women first to get the vote	1894
(29 Dec.) Jameson 'Raid' on the Transvaal East African Protectorate established	US intervention in Anglo-Venezuelan border dispute	1895
Ndebele–Shona revolt against British South Africa Company rule begins 1896–98 Reconquest of the Sudan, with railways and armed gunboats prominent in the campaign	Election of Wilfred Laurier, first French-Canadian Prime Minister Henry Lawson's famous bush sketches, *While the Billy Boils*, published	1896
Sir Alfred Milner appointed High Commissioner for South Africa Ndebele–Shona revolt ends	Royal Commission investigates economic crisis in West Indies Canada announces tariff preferences for British goods at the Colonial Conference Beginning of Klondike gold rush	1897
Sierra Leone Hut Tax War Anglo-French Agreement on West Africa Battle of Omdurman The Fashoda Crisis Anglo-German Agreement on future of Portuguese colonies	Introduction of Old Age Pensions in New Zealand Spanish-American War	1898
Anglo-Egyptian Condominium over Sudan Anglo-French Agreement over Sudan Bloemfontein Conference Outbreak of Second South African War	Britain relinquishes Samoa Islands to Germany and the United States German–British convention establishes rights in Samoa, Tonga, Niue, and the Solomon Islands	1899

Year	Great Britain and General	South, South-East, and East Asia
1900	(Oct.) Conservative victory in general ('Khaki') election	Punjab Land Alienation Act
	Relief of Mafeking occasions great excitement	1900–01 British participation in the Western suppression of the Boxer Rebellion
		1900–04 India's 25,000 miles of railways carry 188 million passengers
1901	(Jan.) Death of Queen Victoria	
1902	Committee of Imperial Defence established	Curzon's Delhi durbar Anglo-Japanese Alliance
	South African War ends Third Colonial Conference held in London	1902–11 Moderate Chinese nationalism manifested in the 'Rights Recovery Movement'
1903	Tariff Reform campaign begins	British military-diplomatic mission to Lhasa (Tibet)
1904	Anglo-French Entente Congo Reform Association formed Controversy begins over importation of Chinese labour to South Africa	
1905	Richard Jebb's *Studies in Colonial Nationalism*	Partition of Bengal First large-scale Chinese boycott of western (American) trade
1906	Liberal victory in general election	Formation of the All-India Muslim League
		British Resident posted to Brunei British recognize Chinese suzerainty in Tibet
1907	4th Colonial Conference held in London: favours promotion of Empire settlement over foreign emigration	The Anglo-Russian Convention eases the defence of India Afghanistan a British Protectorate

Africa and Middle East	Americas, Caribbean, Australasia, and the Pacific	Year
British Protectorate over Northern Nigeria, succeeds Royal Niger Company	Annexation of Cook Islands by New Zealand	1900
British annexation of Asante	Political federation of the six colonies into the Commonwealth of Australia	1901
Treaty of Vereeniging concludes South African War	International sugar convention ends bounties on European beet	1902
Aswan Dam built	Pacific Cable laid, providing 'all-red' route around the globe	
	Canada, Australia, and New Zealand announce tariff preferences on British goods	
	1902–03 Anglo-German coercion of Venezuela	
British conquest of Sokoto, Northern Nigeria	Canadian case rejected in the Alaska boundary award	1903
	New South Wales Royal Commission to investigate declining birth rate	
	Batlle becomes President of Uruguay	
Anglo-French Entente settles Egyptian and Moroccan Issues		1904
South African Native Affairs Commission Report	Creation of the provinces of Alberta and Saskatchewan	1905
First Moroccan crisis		
Sir Eldon Gorst succeeds Cromer as Consul-General in Egypt	Australia takes over British New Guinea, renamed Papua	1906
Satiru uprising in Northern Nigeria		
1906–07 Transvaal and Orange River Colony granted responsible government	Brazilian coffee support programme starts	
Selborne Memorandum advocates Union of South Africa	Commonwealth of Australia introduces federal tariffs and passes Pacific Islanders Act retrospectively repatriating islanders by 1906	1907

Year	Great Britain and General	South, South-East, and East Asia
1907	Founding of Boy Scout movement	Indian National Congress splits at Surat 1907–09 Morley–Minto reforms of India's government
1908	Pan-Anglican Congress held	B. G. Tilak convicted of sedition
1909	Imperial Defence Conference Merger of Anti-Slavery and Aborigines' Protection Societies	Treaty of Bangkok: Siam cedes to Britain rights over Malay States of Kedah, Perlis, Kelantan, and Trengganu
1910	(Jan. and Dec.) Conservatives defeated in two general elections World Missionary Conference, Edinburgh Death of King Edward VII	
1911	First Imperial Conference held in London	Delhi Coronation durbar Revocation of the partition of Bengal Revolution in China and the establishment of a Republic
1912		'Custodian Bank System' strengthens foreign grip on Chinese state revenues
1913	Conservative leader announces that his party will not introduce Imperial Tariff Preference without a specific electoral mandate	'Reorganization Loan' to Chinese Republic by British-led banking consortium India's Tata Iron and Steel Company produces steel rails

FIRST WORLD WAR

Year	Great Britain and General	South, South-East, and East Asia
1914	(Aug.) Outbreak of war	(Aug.) Outbreak of war Johore state (Malaya) accepts British General Adviser

Africa and Middle East	Americas, Caribbean, Australasia, and the Pacific	Year
	Australia's Arbitration Court hands down Harvester Judgement determining minimum wage for unskilled men	1907
		1908
Passage of South Africa Act, providing for Union	Department of External Affairs established in Canada	1909
Northern Nigeria Land and Native Rights Proclamation	Naval Service Act passed by Canadian Parliament	1910
Union of South Africa	Mexican Revolution begins	
Death of Sir Eldon Gorst, and Lord Kitchener named Consul-General in Egypt	Defeat of Laurier's government Canada's new Conservative government rejects reciprocity agreement with United States	1911
	Reform Government takes power in New Zealand under William Massey	1912
		1913
Egypt declared a British Protectorate and Khedive Abbas II deposed	Australia takes German New Guinea	1914
	New Zealand takes German (Western) Samoa	
	Opening of the Panama Canal	

INDEX

Abbas II, Khedive of Egypt 643, 657
Aberdeen, George James Gordon, Fourth Earl of
 (Foreign Secretary and Prime Minister) 130,
 131, 211
Aberdeen, Lady 542
Abolition Society (London) 202, 275
Aborigines' Protection Society 209, 210, 212,
 215–20, 456, 588
Abyssinia (Ethiopia) 106, 108, 109, 113
Acadians 534
Achebe, Chinua (writer) 682
Acts of Parliament, see Statutes
Adam, James (emigration agent) 83
Addington, Henry, First Viscount Sidmouth
 (Prime Minister) 203
Adelaide, South Australia 255, 550
Aden 18, 108, 114, 255, 635
Admiralty 18, 215, 332, 333, 337, 340
 Hydrographic Department 295, 296–7
 Instructions for Hydrographic Surveyors
  309
 Manual of Scientific Enquiry 309
 role in exploration 295, 296–7, 300, 306
Adowa, Battle of (1896) 644
Afghanistan, Afghans 12, 13–14, 177, 262, 278, 341,
 434, 440
 First Afghan War (1838–42) 250, 401, 417
 Second Afghan War (1878–79) 334
Africa, Africans 13–15, 18, 24, 42, 65, 102, 113–4,
 118, 140, 217, 244, 259, 267, 342
 exploration in 296, 301, 302, 304, 306–7, 311,
  312, 313, 674–5
 partition of 6, 14–15, 17, 118, 140–4, 216, 218,
  287, 624–50
 partition by:
  annexation 628, 629, 637, 643; diplomacy
   624, 629, 633, 636–40, 641, 643, 648–9;
   European conquest 640–49; frontier
   demarcation 628, 629–30, 632, 639, 640,
   644; Protectorates 629, 630, 637, 638, 641,
   644
  responses to conquest 679–88
Africa, Central 637, 638, 673, 674, 682
Africa, East 15, 92, 118, 194, 265, 206, 313, 351, 352,
 666, 673–5, 678
 partition of 635, 637, 638, 639, 640, 643–4,
Africa, North 11, 626, 649, 652
Africa, South 24, 56, 135, 512, 597–623, 626,
 629–30, 649, 683–4, 693, 706–7
 annexations 601, 602, 603–4, 608
colonial self-government in 602, 603, 608, 610,
 614, 615, 619, 620–2
Drifts Crisis 611
economy and trade 44, 45, 48, 598, 599, 601,
 602, 603, 604–5, 616, 619, 620, 630–1, 632, 642
federation of 22, 605–6, 607, 610–11, 614,
 619–22, 624–5, 628
frontiers of white settlement 192, 597–8, 601–3,
 609, 611
gold 604, 609–10, 611, 616–17, 619–20, 621, 622
High Commission for 601, 606, 607, 608, 615,
 629, 631–2
migration to 36, 46–7, 78, 81, 598, 599–601, 602,
 604–5, 609–10, 619–20
partition of 624–5, 628–32, 641–3
population 598, 601, 604, 605, 609
Union of 6, 18, 22, 234, 614, 620–22
and western technology 257–8, 261–2, 263,
 264–5
see also Cape Colony; Natal; Orange Free
 State; railways; South African
 War; Transvaal
Africa, South-West 608, 637
Africa, Southern 5, 24, 172, 207, 304, 326, 353, 365,
 626, 628–32, 635, 641–3
Africa, West 179, 182, 210, 211, 306, 342, 666–73,
 675–7, 679–81
 extension of British authority in 191–4
 partition of 625, 636–7, 638, 639, 641, 644,
  645–9
 trade 14–15, 35, 43, 118, 636–7, 645–8
 and western technology 250, 252, 259, 261, 263,
  265
African Association 206, 295, 296, 300, 685
African Civilization Society 210, 216
African Lakes Company 611, 640, 641
Afrikaners 4, 20, 23, 180, 186, 189, 209, 265, 304,
 342, 597–623, 628, 630, 683
 Dutch Reformed Church 225
 Great Trek 601
 see also Africa, South; Cape Colony; Orange
  Free State; Transvaal
Agency Committee 203
agriculture 20, 40, 56, 61, 65–7, 112–13, 115, 138,
 482, 501–2, 504, 526, 550, 564, 575, 588–9,
 658–60, 669, 694–5
 machinery 248, 252, 264, 267, 482, 551
 in South Africa 599, 601, 603, 619, 620
 see also plantations
Ainsworth, William (explorer) 296

Akan people, West Africa 667, 668, 671
Akassa, West Africa 645
Al-Imam (Malay periodical) 386
Alaska 527, 531, 542
Albert, Lake, East Africa 674
Alcock, Sir Rutherford (British Consul in China)
    155
alcohol 138, 230, 552, 553, 610
Alexandria, Egypt 255, 633, 651, 654
Algeria 622, 624
All-India Muslim League 439
Allahabad, India 458
Amazon, River, South America 141
America, British North *see* Canada
America, Central 122, 132, 140
America, Latin 9, 13, 19, 58, 102, 109–10, 115–16,
    122–45, 257
    Britain and economic development in 118–20,
        134–6
    British position in (1914) 142–4
    'Scramble' for 139–42
    War of the Pacific (1879–81) 140
    see also individual countries
America, North:
    thirteen colonies 5, 31, 35–6, 38, 129, 178
    trade 32–3, 35, 36, 42, 50
American Civil War 331, 332, 552
Amery, Leopold C. M. S. (journalist and
    Conservative MP) 356
Amherst, William Pitt, Earl Amherst of Arracan,
    1826 (Governor-General of India) 376
Anderson, Sir H. Percy (Permanent Secretary,
    Foreign Office) 643
Anderson, Rufus (American missionary society
    secretary) 236
Anglican Church, Anglicanism, Anglicans, *see*
    also Church of England; Church Missionary
    Society; Evangelicals
anglicization:
    in Canada 534
    in Cape Colony 598–9, 605, 610
    in Ireland 498–9, 504, 505
    see also westernization
Angola, central Africa 635
Angostura, British consul at 125
Angra Pequena 630, 632, 637; *see also* Africa,
    South-West
Anomabo, Gold Coast 671
Anthropological Institute, London 286
Anthropological Society of London 286
anthropology 219, 241, 283, 285–6
    see also ethnology; race
Anti-Corn Law League 275
anti-imperialism 104, 153, 196, 350, 355, 364–5, 508
    in China 146–69
anti-slavery 125, 130–1, 181, 198, 201, 292, 299, 304,
    306, 636, 666, 672, 673

movement 202, 206, 209–20, 473–7, 673
Anti-Slavery Reporter 203
Anti-Slavery Society 203, 209–10, 474–7
    see also British and Foreign Anti-Slavery
        Society
Antigua, Leeward Islands 477, 481
Aoba, New Hebrides 571
Arab peoples 265
    Arabia 106
    Swahili 635, 640, 673
architecture 29, 468, 662
Argentina 45, 56, 58, 59, 63, 110, 115, 123–5, 130, 143,
    265
    trade with Britain 127, 132, 135–8
Armenia, Armenians 296, 451, 643, 662
arms trade 126, 220, 552, 575–6, 629, 678
    see also weaponry
Army, British 323–32, 334, 341–3, 344, 429, 522,
    586, 588, 633, 704, 705
    Canadian 543
    colonial garrisons 323–4, 327–8, 330, 332, 427,
        428
    colonial manpower 342–3
    Egyptian 633–4, 653–4, 655
    Irish in 510–12
    in South Africa 603, 606, 617–19, 626, 629
Army, Indian 6, 20, 326, 371, 390, 391, 393, 402,
    404, 413–14, 433, 510, 705
    Bengal army 416, 418, 419, 427, 428, 510, 511
    Imperial use of abroad 16, 322, 401, 442–3,
        708
    number of troops 405–6, 413, 427, 442
    Punjab army 419
    reform and costs of 322, 416–7, 419–20, 427–9,
        430
Army, Irish 498
Arthington, Robert (financial supporter of
    missions) 243
Arya Samaj (Society for the Revival of Hindu
    Aryanism) 464, 465
Asante (Ashanti), West Africa 238, 260, 342, 617,
    645, 649, 671, 676
    Anglo-Asante Treaty (1831) 671
    Anglo-Asante War (1873–4) 215, 676, 677
    British images of 677, 686
    uprising (1900) 679–80,
Ashley, Sir William James (economic
    historian) 350 n. 21
Asia 9–10, 24, 42, 53–74 *passim*, 447–69
    Central 11–14
    East 9, 60–1, 451, 452; *see also* China, Japan
    South 447, 453, 464; *see also* Ceylon, India
Asia, South–East 60–1, 93–6, 102, 371–94, 447–8,
    451, 453, 454, 455, 457, 458, 464, 467
    Britain and China in 375, 378, 379, 380
    British authority in 371, 374, 376, 377–81,
        382–93

British Residents in 376, 377, 379, 383, 389
economy and trade 372, 376–7, 378, 379, 380, 381, 384–5, 387, 389–90, 391, 392
European rivalry in 372, 374, 375–6, 381, 382, 384, 388, 389, 393
links with India 371–81, 388, 389–90
migration 377, 382, 384–5, 387, 392
see also Malay peninsula
Asiatic Society of Bengal 305
Assam 60, 92
assimilation *see* westernization
Assiniboine, River, Canada 536
Associated Chambers of Commerce (Britain) 358
Aswan Dam, Egypt 658
Atkinson, Harry Albert (New Zealand social reformer, colonial Treasurer and Prime Minister) 592
Auckland, New Zealand 591
Australasia 264, 322, 336–7, 516
Australasian Naval Agreement (1887) 337–8, 339, 340, 595
Australia, Australians 10, 20, 21–3, 42, 56, 67, 72, 119, 135, 172, 176, 232, 517–18, 546–71
  Aborigines of 22, 174, 207, 304, 503, 548, 549, 550, 555, 562, 563, 564, 571
  Amalgamated Miners' Association 566
  Commonwealth Parliament 563–4, 566
  defence 325–6, 333, 336–8, 339, 340, 342, 559, 561, 570, 704
  economics and trade 32–6, 43–5, 48, 49, 50, 63, 69, 550–5, 558, 559, 561, 566–7, 569, 570, 575, 697, 700, 708, 709–10
  environment 562
  exploration 302–4, 562
  federation of 21, 22, 548, 557, 561
  gold rushes 34, 46, 49, 555, 565
  and Imperial Preference 353, 355, 359, 360, 364, 365
  Inter-Colonial Conferences 336, 337
  Irish in 512, 513, 514, 516, 518, 519, 520
  migration to 36–7, 46–7, 76–9, 81, 82, 84, 93, 563
  political parties 519, 555, 561, 566, 569
  popular culture 559–61, 565, 568, 569–70
  responsible government 187, 189, 546–8, 555
  settlement of 548–51
  technology 252, 257, 263
  wartime contributions 343, 708, 709–10
  'White Australia' 24, 95, 559, 563, 564, 570
  see also entries for separate colonies; convicts; migration
Australian Commonwealth Horse 512
Australian Natives' Association 561
Australian Workers' Union 565–6
Austria 63
Austro-Hungarian Empire, Austria 505, 653, 705
Axe, War of the (Cape Colony, 1846–7) 602

Babas (Malay-speaking Chinese) 457
Baden-Powell, Sir Robert Stephenson (soldier, founder of scout movement) 282, 498, 686
Bahamas, West Indies 473
Bahr al-Ghazal, Sudan 644, 648
Baikie, William Balfour (trader and explorer) 306, 308, 309, 311
Baker, Sir Herbert (architect) 27
Baker, Sir Samuel White (explorer) 674
Baldwin family (Upper Canada) 536
Balfour, Arthur James, First Earl of (Prime Minister) 649
Balfour Williamson (merchants) 19
Ballance, John (New Zealand politician, first Liberal Premier) 593, 594
Ballarat goldfield, Victoria, Australia 20, 551, 566
Balta Liman, Convention of (1838) 112
Baltic Sea 34, 705
Bambatha rebellion (Natal, 1906–7) 622
Banaba (Ocean Island), western Pacific 553
Banda Oriental, South America 130
Banerjea, Surendranath (Bengali nationalist) 438
Bangkok, Siam 381, 387, 389
Bangkok, Treaty of (1909) 384
Bangor, North Wales 84
Bangweulu, Lake (Central Africa) 214
Bank of England 616
Bank of Glasgow 592
banking 112, 123, 125, 165, 483, 502, 626, 695
  in Australasia 552, 556, 589, 592–3
  in China 150, 152–3, 157, 159, 164–6
  in India 410, 441–2
  in Latin America 127, 135, 137, 138
  in South Africa 609, 616
  in South-East Asia 377, 381, 392,
  see also entries for individual banks; overseas investment
Banks, Sir Joseph (botanist, President of the Royal Society) 295, 296, 297, 300, 685
Baptists:
  Baptist Missionary Society 228
  missionaries 210, 218–9, 476, 480, 486
Barbados, West Indies 190, 225, 470, 485, 486, 487
  demography 472, 473
  maintains prosperity 488, 489
  planters' resistance to change 474, 482–3
  rent-wage system 480, 481
  slave rebellion (1816) 475
Barclay, family of (Quakers) 212
Barghash, Sultan (of Zanzibar) 635
Baring Bros. (bankers) 134, 137
Baring, Sir Evelyn, *see* Cromer, Evelyn Baring, First Earl
Barlow, Sir George Hilaro (Governor-General of Bengal) 230
Barnado, Thomas (philanthropist and migration promoter) 82

Barotseland, southern Africa 641
Barra, Hebrides 81
Barrons, family (Mexico) 136
Barrow, Sir John (Second Secretary of the
    Admiralty) 295, 296–7, 300, 316
Basel Mission 229
Bassein, Treaty of (1802) 399
Basutoland, South Africa 604, 608, 622, 629
Batlle y Ordóñez, José (President of Uruguay)
    143
Bau, see Fiji
Bay of Islands, New Zealand 576, 577
Baynton, Barbara (writer) 568
beachcombers 556
Beaufort, Francis (hydrographer) 296
Beaverbrook, Max Aitken, First Baron
    (Canadian-born British politician, press
    baron) 528
bêche-de-mer 552, 558, 564, 565, 590
Bechuanaland, southern Africa 4, 194, 195, 217,
    608–9, 612, 622, 630, 631, 637
bee, bumble 55 n. 4
Beecroft, John (Consul, Bights of Benin and
    Biafra, West Africa) 15, 109
beef 135, 138
beer, see alcohol
Belfast, Ireland 501
Belgium 63, 70, 218, 522, 692
    Anglo-Belgian Agreement (1894) 643
    interests in China 152, 159, 167
Beloff, Max, Baron Beloff of Wolvercote (political
    scientist and historian) 270, 271, 292
Bemba people, central Africa 673
Benares, India 452, 458
Bencoolen, Sumatra 372, 375
Bengal, India 266, 372, 375, 376, 399, 400, 401, 402,
    403, 404, 405, 410, 416, 435, 436, 438, 440, 451,
    517
Bengal, Bay of 372
Bengal Army, see Army, Indian
Benin, West Africa 637, 670, 675, 683
Bennett, Charles James Fox (Canadian merchant,
    politician) 527
Bentham, Jeremy (philosopher) 177
Bentinck, Lord William Cavendish
    (Governor-General of India) 200, 231, 396,
    397, 398, 417
Benue, River, West Africa 636, 637, 640, 682
Beothuk people (Native Americans) 533
Berber, Sudan 644
Berlin West Africa Conference (1884–85) 191, 193,
    217, 218, 557, 638, 684–5
Bermuda, Atlantic 325, 334, 477
bhadralok 451
Bhumihars 413, 414, 415, 417, 419
Bible, The 565–6, 575–6, 678
biology 299

Birch, James (British Resident in Perak) 383
Birmingham, England 358
Birrell, Augustine (Chief Secretary for Ireland)
    497, 511
birth-control 567–8
Bismarck, Otto Edward Leopold von (Chancellor
    of Germany) 608, 637, 638, 639
Bismarck Archipelago, western Pacific 548
'Black and Tans' (Auxiliary Division, Royal Irish
    Constabulary) 498
Black Sea 11
Blackburn, England 358
Blair, Eric Arthur, see Orwell, George
Blake, Edward (Canadian, Premier of Ontario,
    later Irish Nationalist MP) 528
Blantyre, Nyasaland 640
Bloemfontein, Orange Free State, South Africa
    618
Bloemfontein Conference (1899) 616
Bloemfontein Convention (1854) 602
Blomfield, Charles James (Bishop of London) 233
Blue Nile, River 644
Bly, Nellie (journalist) 257
Boer Wars, see South African War (1899);
    Transvaal War (1880)
Boers, see Afrikaners
Bogle, Paul (Baptist deacon) 486
Bogotá, Colombia 128
Bohras 451
Bolivarians 132
Bolivia 132
Bombay, India 232, 236, 251, 254, 255, 260, 266,
    305, 372, 397, 407, 408, 411, 412, 426, 451, 452
    University of 431, 458
Bombay–Burmah Trading Corporation 389–90,
    391
Bond, Afrikaner (political party, Cape
    Colony) 610, 612, 620, 641, 642
'Bond' (Anglo-Fante agreement, 1844) 671
Booth, William (founder, Salvation Army) 82
Borden, Sir Robert Laird (Canadian Prime
    Minister) 363, 364, 367, 544
Borgu, West Africa 648
Borneo 378, 381, 384, 393, 463
Bornu Mission 309
Bose, Paramatha Nath (geologist) 266
botany, botanical gardens 298, 299, 302, 304, 305,
    310, 385, 523
Botha, Louis (Prime Minister of the Transvaal)
    621
Boultons, family (Venezuela) 136
Bourget, Ignace, Bishop (French Canadian
    churchman) 534
Bourke, Sir Richard (Governor of New South
    Wales) 20, 577
Bowdich, Thomas Edward (traveller, writer on
    West Africa) 685

Bowell, Sir Mackenzie (Canadian Prime Minister) 542
Bowring, Sir John (Governor of Hong Kong) 109, 163, 381
Boxer Movement (1900–1), *see under* China
Boy Scouts 282
Boyd (whaling ship) 576
Boys' Brigade 282
Boys' Life Brigade 282
Boy's Own Paper 289
Bradford, England 358
Braganza, royal family of 127, 130
Brahmins 413, 414, 415, 420
Bramston, John (Colonial Office official) 194
Brand, Sir Johannes Henricus (President of Orange Free State) 607
Brassey, Thomas (railway entrepreneur) 256, 257
Brazil 70, 107, 110, 123, 126, 127, 128, 130–3, 137, 140, 673
Brazza, Pierre Savorgnan de (French explorer) 636
Breadalbane 80
Bright, Charles (telegraphy expert) 260
Bright, John (Liberal MP and Cabinet Minister) 104
Brisbane, Queensland 546
Britannia (sealers' ship) 575
British African Colonization Society 206
British–American Tobacco Corporation 160
British Association for the Advancement of Science 297, 298, 315
British Central Africa Protectorate 194
  see also Nyasaland
British Columbia, Canada 523, 526, 527, 528, 531, 540
British East Africa Protectorate 194, 195
British and Foreign Anti-Slavery Society 210, 211–12, 214, 215, 216, 220
British and Foreign Bible Society 231
British Guiana (Guyana), South America 5, 88, 91, 96, 122, 212, 259, 296, 351, 470, 472, 481, 482, 483, 484, 485, 488, 489, 490, 491; *see also* Demerara
British Honduras (Belize), Central America 122
British North America, *see* Canada
British North Borneo Company 193, 384
British South Africa Company 18, 194, 217, 352, 498, 611, 612, 631, 640, 641–2, 681–2
  Constabulary 498
British Women's Emigration Association 81
Broken Hill Proprietary Company 551
Brooke, Sir Charles (formerly Charles Johnson) (Rajah of Sarawak, 1868–1917) 384
Brooke, Graham Wilmot (missionary) 243
Brooke, James (Rajah of Sarawak, 1841–68) 378, 381, 384, 454

Brown, David (East India Company chaplain) 228
Brown, George (Canadian newspaperman and politician) 527, 540
Browne, Thomas R. Gore (Governor of New Zealand) 585, 586
Bruce, Sir Frederick William Adolphus (first British envoy to China, 1858) 157
Bruchési, Paul (Archbishop of Montreal, Canada) 544
Brunei, sultans of 378, 384
Brussels Slave Trade Conference (1889–90) 217, 218, 638
BSAC, *see* British South Africa Company
Buchanan, Claudius (East India Company chaplain) 230
Buddhism, Buddhists 183, 391, 392, 453, 463–5
Buenos Aires, Argentina 114, 123, 126, 127–30, 135, 257
Buenos Aires Herald 136
Buganda, East Africa 644, 674, 678
Bulawayo, Ndebeleland, central Africa 642, 682
Bunge, Alejandro (Argentine polemicist) 143
Bunyoro, East Africa 674
Burgers, Thomas F. (President of the Transvaal republic) 606
Burke, Edmund (statesman and political philosopher) 198–9, 201, 220, 223
Burma 16, 61, 92, 375, 381, 382, 387, 389–92, 401, 402, 448, 460, 463, 464, 465
  Anglo-Burmese Treaties (1862, 1867) 380
  Anglo-Burmese War, First (1824–26) 375–6
  Anglo-Burmese War, Second (1852) 378–80
  Anglo-Burmese War, Third (1885) 389–90
  Franco-Burmese Treaty (1885) 390
Burney, Henry (British envoy to Siam) 375
Burns Philp and Co. (Australian company) 557–8
Burroughs, Wellcome & Co. 262–3
Burton, Richard (explorer) 307, 318, 674, 675, 677
Busby, James (British Resident at the Bay of Islands, New Zealand) 577
Bush Stories (Baynton) 568
Bushire, Persian Gulf 16
Bussa (slave) 475
Butler, Lady Elizabeth (artist) 274
Butler, Sir William Francis (General Officer Commanding in South Africa) 511
Butt, Isaac (founder of Irish Home Rule League) 505, 507
Butterfield and Swire (merchants) 160
Buxton, Thomas Fowell (anti-slavery campaigner) 203, 204, 209–10, 211, 212, 216, 474, 624

Cabul, *see* Kabul

Cairnes, John Elliot (economist) 350
Cairo, Egypt 651
Caisse de la Dette Publique, Egypt 653, 657
Cakobau (chief of Bau, Fiji) 556–7
Calcutta, India 7, 92, 200, 225, 254, 255, 396, 397,
    400, 408, 411, 426, 432, 435, 436, 440, 441,
    452–3, 455, 458
  Botanical Garden 305
  St Andrew's Church 20
  University of 431, 458
Caledonian Company of the New Hebrides
    558
California, United States 67
Callao, Peru 110
Cambodia 381
Cambridge, George William Frederick Charles,
    Second Duke of (military commander) 332
Cameroon, West Africa 637
Campbell, James (Scottish merchant in China) 11
Canada (formerly British North America) 5,
    21–2, 56, 174, 522–44
  Annexation Manifesto (1849) 531
  arts in 532–3, 537
  'clergy reserves' 186, 224, 226, 233, 540
  constitutional development 180, 185–7, 537–42
  defence 322, 324, 326, 330–2, 336, 340, 342, 343,
    543, 704, 706–8
  economy and trade 32, 34–6, 38–9, 41, 44–6,
    48–9, 63, 83, 186, 490, 523, 525–6, 528 529–30,
    541, 544, 697, 700, 708
  exploration 304, 309
  external relations 523, 530–2, 538, 540–1, 542
  and federation 21, 84, 359, 540–1, 606
  French Canadians 4, 20, 175, 180, 185, 525,
    533–5, 537, 538, 539, 540, 544
  Imperial Preference 354, 363–4, 365
  Irish in 326, 510, 512, 513–14, 518, 520, 523, 536–7
  migration to 36, 46–7, 77, 79–82, 96, 186, 528,
    535–7, 697
  as model for Ireland 506
  'National Policy' 353, 530, 541, 542
  nationalism 535–7
  native peoples of 526, 527, 533
  party politics 186, 359, 363, 364, 527–8, 532,
    539–40, 544
  popular culture 226, 518, 523–5, 535–7, 540
  population 526–7, 533–4, 535–6
  rebellions:
    (1837) 77, 84, 178, 187, 534, 537–8
    (1870) 528, 543
    (1885) 528, 541
  Scots in 536
  technology 252, 257, 263, 264, 265
  wartime contributions 343, 522, 544, 708
  see also migration; newspaper press; police
    forces; railways; Roman
    Catholicism; United States of

America; women; and entries for separate
    colonies and provinces
Canada, Lower 180, 186, 525, 526, 532, 534, 538
  Union of 1840 529
  see also Quebec (from 1867)
Canada, Upper 186, 224, 525, 526, 528, 533, 535,
    536, 538, 540, 541
  Union of 1840 529
  and United States of America 530, 531
  see also Ontario (from 1867)
Canadian High Commission 542
Canadian Shield 525, 526
canals 249, 263–4, 267, 529
Canning, Charles, Viscount (Governor-General
    and Viceroy of India) 426
Canning, George (Foreign Secretary and Prime
    Minister) 102, 115, 126–7, 205
Canning, Stratford (Ambassador at
    Constantinople) 112
Canterbury, Archbishop of 224, 232, 234
Canterbury, New Zealand 79, 582, 584
Canton (Guangzhou), China 150
Cape Breton Island, Canada 525
Cape Coast Castle, Gold Coast, West Africa 671
Cape Colony Bechuanaland Railway Agreement
    631
Cape Colony, South Africa 6, 18, 23, 129, 212–3,
    217, 229, 304, 340, 359, 597–622, 624–32, 642
  '1820 settlers' 598–9
  Afrikaner Bond 610, 612, 620, 641, 642
  'Cape liberal tradition' 603, 620, 622
  defence of 326, 340, 602, 604, 628; see also
    under Army, British
  eastern Cape 597, 598, 599, 601, 602, 629, 683
  'road to the north' 628, 630
  self-government, development of 175, 185,
    187–9
  see also Africa, South; Rhodes
Cape-Orange Free State Customs Union (1889)
    641
Cape of Good Hope, see Cape Colony
'Cape to Cairo' 639
Cape Town, South Africa 225, 230, 254, 259, 260,
    601, 605, 614, 620
  naval base 597, 604, 614
  strategic importance of 14, 189, 604, 614, 621,
    626, 628
capital exports see overseas investment
capitalism 5, 55–64, 204, 371, 684
  British 101–9, 125
  and Empire 1, 8–10, 53, 56, 61, 70–4, 140–4, 680
  and immiseration 93, 413, 659–60
Carden, Lionel (British Minister in Mexico) 140
Cardwell, Edward (Secretary of State for War)
    332, 342, 676
Carey, William (missionary and translator) 231,
    239

Caribbean, *see* West Indies

Carlyle, Thomas (writer) 137, 486, 491

Carnarvon, Henry Howard Molyneux Herbert,
Fourth Earl of (Secretary of State for the
Colonies) 22, 606, 624, 628

'Carnarvon Commission' 334–5, 339, 627–8
see also Royal Commissions

cartography 258, 268, 295, 297, 302, 305, 314, 523,
684–5

Casamance, River, West Africa 636

Casement, Sir Roger David (British Consul and
humanitarian) 141, 218

Cassel, Sir Ernest Joseph (banker and
philanthropist) 14

Castlemaine, Victoria, Australia 568

Castlereagh, Robert Stewart, Viscount, and
Second Marquis of Londonderry (Foreign
Secretary) 109, 123, 127, 129, 130, 323, 374

Castro, Cipriano (Venezuelan dictator) 139

Cathcart, Lady Emily Gordon (Scottish
landowner) 81

Cavanagh, Maeve (poet) 504

Cavanagh, Orfeur (Governor of the Straits
Settlements) 377

Cetshwayo (Zulu king) 629

Ceylon 92, 183, 185, 188, 259, 448, 449, 458, 460,
463, 464, 468, 513
Burghers 451, 460

Chakri dynasty, Bangkok 375, 389

Chalmers, James (missionary) 239, 240–1

Chamberlain (Joseph) Austen (Chancellor of the
Exchequer) 348

Chamberlain, Joseph (Secretary of State for the
Colonies) 16, 217–8, 261, 346, 490, 507, 543,
561
and colonial development 51, 195–6, 264, 351–3
critics of 364–5
and Imperial defence 339–40
and Imperial federation 349, 350, 360–1,
and Imperial Preference 347, 355, 356, 362, 705,
707
and race 357
and South Africa 22, 361–2, 543, 612, 614, 615,
616, 642
and West Africa 648, 649

Changsha, China 154

Chapekars 465

Chartered Bank 377

chartered companies 18, 39, 217, 218, 230, 352, 557,
638, 641
see also British North Borneo Company;
British South Africa Company; East India
Company; Imperial British East Africa
Company; Royal Niger Company

Chartism 275

Chatfield, Frederick (British Consul in
Guatemala) 123, 130, 140

chemistry 247, 263

Cherbourg, France 325

Chesney, Francis, Captain (explorer) 305–6, 311

Chesson, F. W. (Secretary of Aborigines'
Protection Society) 215

Childers, Hugh C. E. (First Lord of the
Admiralty) 333

Chile, South America 45, 56, 59, 110, 126, 128, 129,
132, 135, 138, 140

China, Chinese 1, 9, 11, 12, 60, 109, 146–69, 455,
456–7, 552, 560
Arrow War (1856–60) 104, 108, 146, 409
Boxer Movement and Rebellion (1900–1) 13,
152, 158, 159, 164, 165, 237, 244, 455, 462–3
British ambitions and impact in 102, 110–11,
116–17, 118–20, 155, 157–8, 161–2, 166–7
economy and trade 6, 39, 60, 106, 110–11,
116–17, 160, 161, 164–7, 372, 377, 379, 401, 409,
552, 558
foreign loans to 166–7
Imperial (Chinese) Maritime Customs 111,
156–7, 164–5
migrants 454, 456, 457, 563–4, 620
Opium War (1839–42) 110, 131, 146, 149, 157,
161, 249, 401, 409
religion 462–3
Revolution (1911) 163, 164, 167–8
secret societies 378, 454
Sino-French War (1884–5) 157
Sino-Japanese War (1895) 164, 166
Taiping Rebellion (1850–64) 148, 154, 155, 157,
455, 462, 463
'Treaty Ports' 110–11, 116, 146, 149–50
'Unequal Treaties' 152–4, 165, 168
weapons 265
Zongli Yamen 154, 156

Ch'ing dynasty 111, 148, 157, 168

China Inland Mission 242

China Merchants' Steam Navigation Company
266

China Sea 12

China Station 332

Chisholm, Caroline 567

Christangs 451

Christianity 179, 200, 207–8, 222–46, 311, 397, 400,
417, 418, 462–3, 464, 543, 555–6, 564, 575–6,
590, 666–73, 678, 679, 684, 686
church-state relations 21, 186, 222–8, 232–5,
237–8, 243–4, 487, 495, 534, 540
and civilization 236, 242–4, 556, 575
and commerce 231, 235–7, 556, 669, 672
Protestant–Catholic rivalry 215, 540, 542,
555–6
Protestantism 125, 128, 158, 204, 215, 219, 227,
232–3, 243, 395, 555–6, 558
'Providence' 39, 102, 207–8, 232
and religions in India 398, 416, 424, 461–5

Christianity (*cont.*):
    Roman Catholic Emancipation 507
    Roman Catholicism 158, 183, 210, 215, 226, 227,
        232, 233, 534, 558, 678
    see also Evangelicals; Ireland; missions;
        Scotland; *and separate churches or*
        denominations
Chulalongkorn, King of Siam 387–8
Church and Schools Corporation (New South
    Wales) 225, 233
Church Lads' Brigade 282
Church Missionary Society 200, 214, 228–30, 231,
    236, 237, 238, 242, 243, 575, 576, 590, 668, 669,
    670, 675
Church of England 223–7, 230, 232–5, 237, 668
Church of Ireland 495
Church of Scotland 536
church-state relations, *see under* Christianity
Churchill, Lord Randolph (Secretary of State for
    India) 390
Churchill, Winston Leonard Spencer (Under-
    Secretary of State for the Colonies,
    later Prime Minister) 365
CIM, *see* China Inland Mission
cities:
    colonial culture of 450, 451, 453–4, 667–72
    unrest in 455
    urban élites 451, 460–3, 465–7, 667–72
    women in 455–7
Civilistas (political party, Peru) 139
Clapham Sect 200, 202, 229
Clapperton, Hugh (explorer) 301, 302, 308, 312
Clarendon, George William Frederick Villiers,
    Fourth Earl of (Foreign Secretary) 112
Clarke, Sir Andrew (Governor of the Straits
    Settlements) 383
Clarkson, Thomas (anti-slavery
    campaigner) 202, 218
Clayton–Bulwer Treaty (1850) 140
Clergy Reserves Corporation, Upper Canada 226
Clive, Robert, Baron (1762) (commander in
    India) 274, 399, 404
clocks and timekeeping 249–50, 254–5, 257
cloves 635
coal 143, 551, 609
Cobden, Richard (Liberal MP and free trader) 41,
    103–4, 105, 378, 529
Cobdenites 106, 109, 129, 237
Cochin-China, *see* Indo-China
Cochrane, Thomas, Tenth Earl of Dundonald
    (commander of Chilean and Brazilian
    navies) 126
cocoa 60, 680
coconuts, copra 550, 552, 556, 557
coffee 33, 135, 138, 143
Colenso, Battle of (1899) 617
Colenso, John William (Bishop of Natal) 241

Colley, Sir George (military commander) 607
Collis, Maurice (Burma civil servant) 392
Colomb, John C. R. (British naval officer) 333–4
Colombia, South America 135, 138
Colombo, Ceylon 254, 453
colonial administration 17, 18, 19, 23, 286, 323,
    557, 570, 653, 662, 681, 682–3
    attitudes to other cultures 179–84, 452, 453,
        463–9, 557, 563
    Colonial Service 176–7, 697
    see also Indian Civil Service
Colonial Bishoprics Fund 233
Colonial and Imperial Conferences 17, 347
    (1887) 335, 337, 347, 349, 359
    (1894) 359
    (1897) 339–40, 358, 359, 360–1
    (1907) 365
    (1911) 29
    see also Australia: Inter-Colonial Conferences
Colonial Defence Committee (1885) 18, 335, 336,
    342
colonial development policy 51, 195, 351–3
    in India 424, 430, 435–7
    see also Chamberlain, Joseph
Colonial Institute (London) 215
colonial knowledge 18, 24, 46, 149, 184–5, 297–8,
    302, 310–14, 317, 658, 670, 677–8, 684–5
    see also cartography; exploration
Colonial Land and Emigration Commission 79,
    98
Colonial Office 16–17, 215, 234, 260–1, 378, 382,
    612, 615, 629, 630, 637, 640, 676
    and colonial defence 326, 327, 330
    and colonial governors 176–7
    and colonial institutions 171, 173, 175, 180,
        188–9, 195–6, 378
    established 205
    and exploration 296, 300, 304, 306
    and lobbyists 215, 234, 378, 382
    and migration 75, 77–8, 96
    and New Zealand 577, 578, 580, 583, 591
    relations with other departments 191, 194
    and trusteeship 219–20
    and West Indies 476, 478, 482, 484, 487–8,
        492
'Colonial Reformers' 104, 327
Colonial Sugar Refining Company (Australia)
    89, 553, 557, 564
commercial policy 7, 26, 38–42, 45, 50–1, 105–14,
    129–32, 189, 353–4, 359–61, 402
    free trade 7, 26, 38–42, 43, 101–5, 148, 149, 153,
        157, 190, 209–11, 220, 283, 360, 362–5, 529–30,
        554, 556, 636, 659–60, 690–711
    free trade, obstacles to 107, 109, 115–20, 127–8,
        131–3, 141, 149, 363, 611
    free trade treaties 105, 107–8, 110, 112, 130, 132,
        150–3, 210, 360

Imperial Preference 7, 50, 291, 347, 350–1, 354–6, 359–60, 362–4, 483, 705, 707; *see also* Chamberlain, Joseph
Navigation Acts 36, 37, 38, 39–41
'Old Colonial System' 33, 38, 39, 50, 103
'Open Door' *see* free trade *above*
protection 7, 20, 26, 39–40, 50, 108–9, 128, 541, 556, 566, 570, 592, 645, 698
tariffs 33–4, 37, 39–41, 105, 474, 490, 630, 631, 636–7, 642
see also under individual territories economy and trade
Committee of Imperial Defence 707
Commonwealth Arbitration Court, Australia 566, 569
communications 8–9, 42, 46, 60, 97–8, 127–8, 134, 176
see also railways; shipping; telegraphs
Compagnie Française des Phosphates de l'Océanie 553
Compatriots' Club 347, 348
compradors 111, 116, 163, 460
Congo, River, central Africa 141, 635, 674
Congo Balolo Mission 218
Congo Basin, central Africa 265, 636, 638
Congo Free State 218, 639, 643
Congo Reform Association 218–20
Congregationalists 243 *see also* London Missionary Society
Conrad, Joseph (writer) 697
Conservative and Unionist Party 358, 362, 365, 432
Constantinople (Istanbul) 14–15, 17
consuls 17–18, 92, 113–14, 124, 149, 192–3, 381, 625, 632, 635, 638, 657, 673
in China 151, 154–6
in Latin America 127, 132
in West Africa 17, 191–2, 637, 675
consumption 62, 160, 662
convicts:
settlement 548, 575
transportation 78–9
Cook, James, Captain (navigator) 274, 276, 292, 302, 546, 573
Cook Islands, western Pacific 556, 590, 591, 592
copper 138
Coral Sea 552
Córdoba, Argentina 128
Cork, Ireland 536
Corn Laws, repeal of 40
Cornwallis, Charles, First Marquis and Second Earl (Governor-General of India) 200, 399–400, 402, 404, 405, 407, 411
Coromandel, New Zealand 580
Corrie, Daniel (East India Company chaplain, later Bishop of Madras) 228
Cosmos, Amor de (Canadian politician) 528

cotton, raw 32–6, 42–6, 57, 62, 112, 126, 150, 403, 409, 552, 654, 658–60, 663
cotton textile trade 32, 34, 44, 60, 112, 127, 128, 135, 138, 161–2
Council of India 424–6, 427, 433
courts, *see under* law
Coyle, Edward (Belfast doctor) 509
Cox, Hiram, Captain (Resident at Rangoon) 376
Craig, Sir James (Governor of Lower Canada) 226
Crawford, Sharman 507
Crawfurd, John (envoy to Emperor Minh-Mang) 375, 403
Creoles, Africa 669, 670, 677
Latin America 160
Crimean War (1854–6) 10, 111, 326, 327
Cromer, Evelyn Baring, First Earl of (Consul-General in Egypt) 177, 178–9, 643, 648, 654, 655, 657, 658, 660, 661, 662, 663, 664
Cropper, James (anti-slavery campaigner) 203
Cross River (West Africa) 645
Crown Agents for the Colonies 17
Crown Colony government 4, 17, 18, 22, 173, 378, 540, 583, 630, 631
evolution of 185, 188
Hong Kong 163–4
and Ireland 494–502
West Indies 471, 487–8, 491–2
Crowther, Samuel Ajayi (Yoruba recaptive, Bishop of the Niger) 237, 238, 669–70, 675
Cruickshank, Brodie 672
CSR, *see* Colonial Sugar Refining Company
Cuba, Caribbean 93, 135, 138, 140, 673
Cunard, Samuel (shipping magnate) 257
Cunningham, William (economist) 350 n. 21
Currie, Sir Donald (Scottish shipping magnate) 257, 605
Curtis, Lionel George (public servant, crusader for Commonwealth) 621
Curzon, George Nathaniel, Marquis Curzon of Kedleston (Viceroy of India) 23, 177, 202, 422, 429, 434–8, 440, 443, 444, 445
Cyprus 12, 351, 654

Dahomey, West Africa 113, 639, 645, 675
Daily News 339
Dalhousie, James Andrew Broun-Ramsay, Tenth Marquis of (Governor-General of India) 5, 6, 251, 379, 380, 416–17, 418, 420, 427
Damaraland, South-West Africa 640
dams, *see* irrigation
Daniell, Thomas and William (artists) 274
Danishway (Dinshawai) incident, Egypt 663–4
Darfur, Sudan 644, 648
Darwin, Charles (naturalist) 137, 285, 295, 298
Darwinism 286, 348
see also race

Davies, W. B. (Creole doctor) 670
Deakin, Alfred (Australian statesman and Prime
    Minister of Victoria) 359, 366–7, 561
Deccan, India 444
defence 7–8, 10–11, 16, 21, 189, 320–45, 442–3,
    543–4, 627–8, 649, 700
    colonial and dominion contributions to
        325–31, 334, 335, 336–7, 338–40, 343, 543, 559,
        595
    costs 324–9, 330, 332–3, 337, 339–40, 430, 626–8,
        703–8
    garrisons overseas 189, 213, 230, 326, 543, 705
    reform and strategic reassessment of 325–7,
        328–9, 330, 333–6, 338, 586, 705
    strategy 12, 16, 117, 118, 371, 372, 389
    see also Army; 'Carnarvon
        Commission'; Colonial Defence
        Committee; Committee of Imperial
        Defence; Navy
De la Beche, Sir Henry (geologist) 298
Delagoa Bay (Maputo), Mozambique 606, 611,
    631, 635, 642
Delhi, India 440
Demerara, British Guiana 203, 225, 230, 475
Denham, Dixon (explorer) 301, 302, 309
Denison, George Taylor (Canadian advocate of
    imperial federation) 364
Denmark 15, 63, 123, 671
Denny, William (shipbuilder) 256–7
Derby, Edward George Geoffrey Stanley,
    Fourteenth Earl of (1851) (Secretary of State
    for War and Colonies, 1841) 482
Derby, Edward Henry Stanley, Fifteenth Earl of
    (1869) (Secretary of State for the Colonies,
    1882) 630
Descent of Man, The (Darwin) 285
Devawongse, Prince (Foreign Minister of Siam)
    388
Devonport, England 254
Devonshire Commission 318
Dharmapala, Anagarika (Buddhist teacher)
    464–5
diamonds 44, 604, 626, 628
Dilke, Sir Charles (Liberal MP) 6, 22, 23, 75,
    216
Dinshawai, see Danishway incident
disease 94, 98, 306, 307–8, 485, 490–1, 526, 533,
    549, 552, 576, 660; see also medicine
Disraeli, Benjamin, First Earl of Beaconsfield
    (Prime Minister) 112, 127, 215, 327, 331, 333,
    341, 422, 443, 607, 624
Dolben, Sir William (MP and abolitionist) 202
Dominica, West Indies 479, 485, 486, 491
Dominions 21, 26–7, 44, 50–1, 278, 335, 339, 342,
    500, 604, 697, 709–10
    compared with Latin American states 135, 138,
        142

relations with Britain 346–7, 353, 359–66, 704,
    706–8
Dongola, Sudan 644, 648
Doukhobors 535
Drifts Crisis, South Africa (1895) 611
Drummond Wolff, Sir Henry, see Wolff
Dublin:
    'Dublin Castle' (Irish administration) 496–7
    Phoenix Park 516
    Trinity College, Dublin 509–10, 520
Duff, Alexander (Scottish missionary) 231
Dufferin, Frederick Temple Blackwood, First
    Marquis of (Governor-General of Canada,
    Ambassador at Constantinople, Viceroy of
    India) 390, 517, 527, 540, 542, 634
Dufferin, Lady Helen Selina (song writer) 537
Duffy, Sir Charles Gavan (Prime Minister of
    Victoria) 518
Dundas, Henry, First Viscount Melville (1802)
    (President of the Board of Control) 146
Dundonald, Douglas Mackinnon Baillie
    Hamilton Cochrane, Twelfth Earl of,
    General (military commander in
    Canada) 543
Dunraven, Windham Thomas Wyndham-Quin,
    Fourth Earl of (Irish politician) 507
D'Urban, Sir Benjamin (Governor of Cape
    Colony) 207, 601
durbars 431, 437, 440, 468
Durham, John George Lambton, Earl of
    (Governor-General of Canada) 187, 523, 534,
    538, 539
Dutch-Afrikaners, see Afrikaners
Dutch East India Company 597, 598, 599
Dutch Guiana 92
Dutch Republic, United Provinces of the
    Netherlands 692
    Anglo-Dutch Treaty (1824) 374–5, 377
    and South-East Asia 372, 374–5, 376, 377, 393,
        565
    and West Africa 671
Dutt, Romesh Chunder (Indian writer, civil
    servant and politician) 444
Du Yueshang (gangster) 155
Dyula people, West Africa 636

East India Company 16, 19, 198–9, 206, 225, 228,
    249, 305, 322, 395–419, 424, 425, 427
    impact on Indian societies 412–19
    interest in South-East Asia 372, 375, 376, 377–8
    trade of 39, 60, 403–4, 408–12, 575
Easter Rising (1916), Dublin 510
Eastern Telegraph Company 257, 260, 262
Economist, The 103
Edelstein, Michael (economic historian) 692,
    697, 698, 699
Edinburgh, Scotland 35

Edinburgh Missionary Society 228
Edinburgh Review, The 228
Edo people, West Africa 683
education 158, 179, 183, 201, 224–6, 272, 288, 447,
  560, 570, 657, 662, 663, 667, 670, 672, 675,
  702
  English language 231, 458–9, 619, 663
  and empire in Britain 272, 281–2, 285, 288, 318
  in India 200, 395, 400, 417, 458–9
  in Ireland 497, 503–4, 516
  schools and colleges 137, 200, 224, 226, 236,
    288, 400, 412, 417, 457, 458–9, 468–9, 532, 669,
    670
  see also language; Manitoba Schools; missions;
    universities
Edwardes, Major-General Sir Herbert Benjamin
  (military commander in India) 281
Edwards, family (Chile) 136
Efik people, West Africa 645
Egba people, West Africa 676
Egremont, Earl of (landowner) 80
Egypt 177, 263, 264, 266, 279, 401, 651–64
  Anglo-Egyptian Condominum Agreement
    (1899) 644
  British interests in 11, 12, 73, 112–13, 194, 341–2
  British occupation of 12, 108, 113, 120, 140,
    653–4
  British withdrawal considered 634–5, 649, 654,
    658
  declared a Protectorate 657
  defence of 627–8
  economy and trade 652–3, 654–5, 657–61
  Egyptian Frontier Force 643
  finances 113, 117–18, 165, 626, 632–5, 639, 643,
    649, 653, 657, 659–61
  Indian administrative models for 634, 654, 664
  nationalist movement in 28, 653–4, 655–7, 661
  and partition of Africa 624, 626, 632–9, 638,
    639, 640, 641, 643, 644, 648, 649
  see also cotton; Cromer; Danishway
    incident; Muhammad Ali
*Eighteen Years on the Gold Coast of
  Africa* (Cruickshank) 672
El Obeid, Battle of (1883) 634
Elder, John (shipbuilder) 256–7
Elgin, James Bruce, Eighth Earl of (Governor of
  Jamaica, Governor-General of Canada,
  British envoy to China) 111, 116–17, 480, 482,
  539
Elizabeth (ship) 577
Ellenborough, Edward Law, First Earl of
  (Governor-General of India) 14
Ellice, Edward (British MP, banker and
  businessman in North America) 175
Elliot, Sir Gilbert, Baron Minto (1798), First Earl
  of Minto (1813) (Governor-General of
  India) 374

Elliot, Sir Gilbert John, Fourth Earl of Minto
  (1847) (Governor-General of Canada,
  Viceroy of India, 1905–10) 438–9, 440
Elliot, T. F. (Agent-General for Emigration) 78,
  328
Ellis, Henry (Cape Colony official) 175
Elphinstone, Hon. Mountstuart (Governor of
  Bombay) 398, 402, 405, 407
emigration, *see* migration
Emin Pasha 639
Empire, British
  and the arts 274–80, 282–4, 288–9, 455, 468,
    537, 662, 697
  and 'Britishness' 22, 25, 85–6, 97, 156, 175, 232,
    273–5, 365–6
  and citizenship 23, 173, 186
  and 'civilization' 102, 107, 172, 217, 280–6, 311,
    400, 450, 467–9
  and class 21, 22, 151, 163, 315, 316, 668–72, 684,
    686–7
  and collaborating élites 18, 55 n. 3, 133, 168,
    179–84, 196, 266–7, 430–4, 437, 438–40, 522,
    534–5, 557, 581, 634:
      in Africa 629, 631, 632–3, 635, 640, 643–4,
        667–71, 675–6, 680; in Egypt 660, 662,
        663–4; in Latin America 124, 125, 132–7,
        139–42
  costs and benefits of, 27–9, 31–52, 138, 202,
    501–3, 522, 626–7, 628, 632, 690–711; *see also*
    India, value to Britain
  and 'dependency' 124, 125, 128, 134, 137–44
  and economic theorists 348–51, 443–4,
    690–2
  and heroism 274, 275, 277, 280–1, 314, 317–18
  and identity 22, 24–6, 28, 29, 75, 85–6, 97, 109,
    136, 186, 198, 232, 289–92, 356, 507–9, 670,
    685
  and invented traditions 383, 467–9, 672–8
  types of 6, 10–12, 38, 51–6, 65–6, 70–4, 101,
    122–6, 128–34, 137–42, 163, 191, 291, 504, 559
  'imperialism of free trade' 10–12, 38, 119–20,
    350, 377–81, 706
  'informal control' beyond formal boundaries
    10–12, 15–16, 38, 51, 60, 70–4, 101–21, 708:
      in Africa 624–5, 630, 631, 634, 636, 640,
        645; in China 148–9, 150–3, 157, 159–62;
        in Egypt 626, 628, 632–5, 651–64; in Latin
        America 122–6, 129–34, 137
  and the 'official mind' 129–32, 170–7
  see also capitalism; race
Empire Day 183
Encina, Francisco (Chilean polemicist) 143
England in Egypt (Milner) 651, 657, 658
Equatoria, East Africa 639
Erie, Lake, Canada 80
Eskimo, *see* Inuit
Esquimalt, Canada 332, 543

ETC, *see* Eastern Telegraph Company
Ethiopia, *see* Abyssinia
Ethnological Society of London 286
ethnology, ethnography 212, 241, 284, 299, 302, 448, 465
Eton College, Berkshire 137, 469
eugenics 81
Euphrates, River, Middle East 249–50, 305–6
Evangelicals 200, 204, 209, 242–4, 281, 418
'Ewo', *see* Jardine Matheson
exhibitions 282–4
   South Kensington (1862) 282
   see also Great Exhibition
Expansion of England, The (Seeley) 285, 336, 346, 348–9
exploration 16, 25, 286, 294–319, 635
   explorers 307–9
   literature of 310–14, 316
   naming 315–16
Eyre, Edward John (explorer, Governor of Jamaica) 214, 280, 302–4, 307, 486–7
Ezzidio, John (Nupe Methodist) 669

Fabians 292
Fairfield, Edward (Colonial Office official) 193
Falkland Islands, South Atlantic 122
Fallon, Michael Francis (Canadian bishop) 534
famine 81, 82, 85, 93, 97, 496
Fante people, West Africa 671–2, 676, 677, 686
Farquhar, John Nicol (missionary) 241
Fashoda, Sudan 644, 648
Federal Council of Australasia 336
Federated Malay States 383–6, 513
   State Councils 460
Female Middle Class Emigration Society 81
Fenians 86, 498, 504, 518, 519, 536
Fernando Po, West Africa 14
Fiji, western Pacific 89, 92, 93–4, 95, 96, 99, 190–1, 193, 215, 548, 549, 552, 556–7, 571, 591, 606
finance 6, 12, 13, 35–6, 49–50, 60, 616–7, 673
   see also banking; *entries for individual banks*; overseas investment
Finegan, J. L. (Parnellite politician) 505
Finland 63
Finney, Charles (American revivalist) 242
First World War (1914–18) 422, 440, 445, 502, 522, 544, 704, 706, 707–8
FitzGerald, James Edward (New Zealand politician) 588–9
FitzRoy, Robert (Governor of New Zealand) 580–1
flax 575
Flinders, Matthew (explorer) 562
FMS, *see* Federated Malay States
Foreign Office 15–16, 105, 215, 261, 296, 300, 306, 637, 638, 654, 657

expansion in China and Latin America 124, 131, 155, 156
expansion in South-East Asia 382, 383–4, 388
   see also consuls; Protectorates
forestry 290, 305, 391
Fort William College, Calcutta 200, 400
Fourah Bay College, Sierra Leone 669, 670
Fox, Charles James (Joint Secretary of State) 199, 230
Fox, William (New Zealand Prime Minister) 584, 589
Fox-Bourne, Henry Richard (Secretary of the Anti-Slavery Society) 209, 216, 219
France 1, 11, 22, 38, 170, 320, 333, 334, 336, 348, 401, 440, 500, 622, 652, 704, 705, 707
   and African partition 635–39, 640, 641, 643, 644, 645–9
   Anglo-French Agreement (1899) 644; (1890) 645
   Anglo-French Convention (1898) 648
   Anglo-French Declaration (1896) 388
   Anglo-French Entente (1904) 388, 649, 707
   Anglo-French Shipping conventions (1860, 1861) 98
   and Britain in China 110–11, 166, 167
   colonial rivalry with Britain 10–15, 112–13, 126, 127, 210
   and Egypt 632–3, 651–2, 653–4, 657, 658
   and Pacific 553, 558, 591, 592
   and South-East Asia 372, 374, 376, 377, 381, 388, 389, 390, 393, 434
Franklin, Sir John (explorer) 296
Frazer, James George (anthropologist) 241
Freeman, Thomas Birch (missionary) 671, 677
Freemasonry 518
Freetown, Sierra Leone, West Africa 667–71, 686
Frere, Sir Bartle (High Commissioner in South Africa) 606, 629
Fulani people, western Sudan 636, 680
Furnivall, J. S. (Burma civil servant and historian) 392
Futa Jalon, western Africa 636
Fytche, Albert, Colonel (Burma official) 380

Gabon, French West Africa 636
Gairdner, Gordon (Colonial Office official) 189
Gallagher, John A. (historian) 119, 129 n. 29, 134
Galt, Alexander T. (Canadian businessman and finance minister) 530
Galt, John (land company promoter, Canada) 80
Gambia, West Africa 12, 194, 215, 626, 636, 639, 645, 670
Ganda people, East Africa 678
Ganges, River, India 96, 305
Garneau, François-Xavier (French Canadian notary and historian) 534
Garvey, Marcus (Jamaican political activist) 492

Garvin, James Louis (editor of the *Observer*) 357
geography 285, 286–8, 295–304, 318, 503
  see also Royal Geographical Society
geology 297–9, 302, 305, 310, 314, 523
  Geological Survey of Great Britain 298–9
  Geological Survey of India 305
George IV, King of Great Britain and Ireland 126
Germany 11, 13, 166, 393, 440, 489–90, 559, 591
  Anglo-German Agreement (1886) 193, 194, 639
  Anglo-German Agreement (1890) 194, 639–40, 643
  Anglo-German Agreement (1898) 609, 615, 643
  and Britain in Africa 608–9, 621–2, 632, 637–8, 639, 640, 642, 643, 648, 649, 653, 657
  colonial expansion of 13, 22, 194, 336, 608
  competition with Britain 138–42, 159, 348
  expansion compared with Britain 692, 701, 703, 704, 705, 707
Ghekiang, China 161
Ghent, Low Countries 522
Gibraltar, Iberian pensinsula 334
Giffen, Robert (civil servant and statistician) 502
Gilbert and Ellice Islands, western Pacific 193
Girl Guides 282
Girl's Own Paper 289
Gladstone, William Ewart (Prime Minister) 16, 23, 213, 215, 233, 234, 300, 318, 389, 390, 432, 506, 517, 525, 539
  and Britain in Africa 215, 607, 608, 624, 629, 644, 655
  and defence 327, 329, 330–1, 332, 333
Glasgow, Scotland 84, 257, 275
Glasgow Missionary Society 228
Glenelg, Charles Grant (son of Charles Grant q.v.), Lord (Secretary of State for War and Colonies) 205, 478
Godley, John Robert (War Office official) 327, 378
Gokhale, Gopal Krishna (President of the Indian National Congress) 437–8
gold 34, 57, 58, 66, 77, 90, 94, 126, 298, 305, 527, 582, 589, 692
  in Australia 42, 49, 305, 550, 551, 552
  gold standard 609, 616
  in South Africa 44, 604, 609–10, 611, 616, 620, 628
Gold Coast 14, 192, 195, 209, 215, 261, 263, 351, 606
  and African partition 626, 639, 640, 645, 648
  colonial impact on 666, 670, 671–2, 675, 680
Goldie, Sir George Taubmann (merchant in West Africa) 194, 196, 648
Goodall, Frederick (artist) 274, 281
Gordon, Sir Arthur *see* Hamilton-Gordon, Sir Arthur
Gordon, Charles George, General (military commander) 266, 274, 275, 277, 281, 607, 634
Gordon, John (Scottish landowner) 81

Gordon Memorial College, Khartoum 244
Gore, Robert, Captain (Chargé d'Affaires in Buenos Aires) 133
Gorst, Sir (John) Eldon (Consul-General in Egypt) 657
Goschen, George Joachim, First Viscount (First Lord of the Admiralty) 340
Goshawk, HMS (gun vessel) 258
Grahame, Thomas (emigration agent) 84
Grant, Anthony (Anglican clergyman) 233, 234
Grant, Bishop of Victoria 236
Grant, Charles (East India Company director) 200, 231
Grant, James Augustus (explorer) 674
Grant, Sir John (Governor of Jamaica) 487
Granville, George Leveson-Gower, Second Earl (Colonial Secretary, Foreign Secretary) 330
Great Exhibition (1851) 250, 282
Great Lakes (North America) 523, 525
Great Trek 601
Greater Britain, concept of 22, 509
Gregory, Sir Augustus Charles (explorer and Assistant Surveyor-General, Western Australia; Surveyor-General, Queensland) 304
Grenada, West Indies 478, 481, 483, 487, 489, 491
Grey Declaration (1895) 643
Grey, Sir George (Governor of New Zealand, and of Cape Colony) 177, 212, 213, 581, 583–4, 585, 586, 591, 602
Grey, Henry George, Third Earl (Secretary of State of War and Colonies) 18, 177, 213, 325–7, 507, 580; *see also* Howick, Lord
Griffith, Arthur (founder of Sinn Fein) 505
Griffith, W. L. (emigration agent) 84
Grigg, Nanny (slave) 475
Griqualand West, South Africa 604, 628
Group of Seven (Canadian artists) 537
guano 113, 133, 137
Guatemala, Central America 122, 135
Guiana, British *see* British Guiana
Guiana, Dutch *see* Dutch Guiana
Guibord affair 534
Guinea, West Africa 636, 639, 648
Guinness, Dr Harry (missionary) 218
Gurkhas 428
Gurney, family of (Quakers) 212

Haddon, Alfred Court (anthropologist) 241
Hadrahmauti Saiyyids 451
Haggard, Sir (Henry) Rider (novelist) 289, 312
Haileybury College 400, 412, 417
Haliburton, Thomas Chandler (Nova Scotian politician and British MP) 528
Halifax, Nova Scotia, Canada 332, 334, 523, 532, 536, 543
Halifax, Viscount, *see* Wood, Sir Charles

Hall, William (missionary) 575

Halsbury, Giffard, Hardinge Stanley, First Earl (Lord Chancellor) 194

Hamilton, George (Treasury official) 328

Hamilton, Lord George (First Lord of the Admiralty) 337

Hamilton-Gordon, Sir Arthur Charles, First Baron Stanmore (colonial governor) 468, 557, 571

Hankow (Hankou), China 150, 151

Hannington, James (Bishop of Eastern Equatorial Africa) 239

Harar, Abyssinia 644

Harcourt, Sir William Vernon (Liberal MP and Cabinet minister) 644

Hardinge, Charles, Baron Hardinge of Penshurst (Viceroy of India) 440

Harris, John and Alice (missionaries) 218

Harris, Robert (artist) 532–3

Hart, Sir Robert (Inspector-General, Imperial (Chinese) Maritime Customs) 11, 111, 156–7, 165

'Hartington Commission' 342
see also Royal Commissions

Harvester Judgement (1907) 566, 569

Harvey, Thomas (anti-apprenticeship campaigner) 478

Hastings, Francis Rawdon-Hastings, First Marquess of (Governor-General of Bengal) 6

Hastings, Warren (Governor-General of Bengal) 399, 404

Hausa people, western Sudan 636, 680

Havelock, Sir Henry (military commander) 281

Hawaii, Pacific 531, 590

Haweis, Thomas (missionary society organizer) 242

Hay, R. W. (Permanent Under-Secretary, Colonial Office) 205

Head, Sir Edmund Walker, Eighth Baronet (Lieutenant-Governor of New Brunswick, Governor-General of Canada) 523, 528, 539, 540

Heart of Darkness (Conrad) 313

Hector, James (geologist) 309

Hedstrom, Morris (Western Pacific merchant) 557

Heligoland 639

Hemming, Augustus W. L. (Colonial Office official) 182

Herbert, Sir Robert George Wyndham (Colonial Office Permanent Secretary) 213

Hewett, E. H. (Consul in West Africa) 637

Hewins, W. A .S. (economist, tariff reformer) 347, 348, 349–50, 355–6

Hibernian associations 518–19

Higgins, Henry Bourne (President of Arbitration Court, Australia) 566

Higginson, John (Western Pacific entrepreneur) 558

Himalayas 305

Hinduism, Hindus 396, 397–8, 416, 417, 418, 420, 431, 432, 438, 439, 448, 453, 457, 459–65
Aryanism 464, 465

Hints to Travellers (Royal Geographical Society) 309

Hipa Te Maiharoa (Maori chief) 587

historiography 1–2, 131, 133–4, 146, 148, 270–3, 503, 548, 670, 692–703
'orientalism' 184, 467–9
see also Volume V

Hobart, Tasmania 546, 548

Hobson, C. K. (economist and statistician) 692

Hobson Jobson (glossary of Indian terms) 450

Hobson, John A. (economist and journalist) 28, 219, 272, 362, 691–2, 700–1

Hobson, William (naval officer, first Governor of New Zealand) 577, 578, 580

Hodgkin, Thomas (ethnologist and humanitarian) 209, 212, 215, 286

Hofmeyr, Jan Hendrik (South African politician) 610

Holland, Sir Henry, First Lord Knutsford (Secretary of State for the Colonies) 16, 338

Holt, Alfred (shipping magnate) 257

Hone Heke (Maori chief) 579, 580

Hong Kong 6, 11, 93, 98, 110, 114, 149, 236, 252, 377, 558
as Crown Colony 163–4, 177, 558
District Watch Committee 460, 461
trade of 35, 149–50, 157, 159, 160, 161, 163
Tung Wah Hospital 460–1
urban society of 453, 454, 456, 457, 458

Hongkong and Shanghai Banking Corporation 159, 165–6

Hongi Hika (Maori chief) 575, 576

Hoo Ah Kay ('Whampoa') 459

Hooker, Sir Joseph (botanist) 295, 298

Hooker, Sir William (botanist, father of Joseph) 298

Horton, J. Africanus B. (Creole doctor) 670, 675–6

Horton, R. J. Wilmot (Parliamentary Under-Secretary, Colonial Office) 175, 513

Howe, Joseph (Premier of Nova Scotia) 536–7

Howick, Lord, later Third Earl Grey q.v., (Under-Secretary of State for the Colonies) 204, 476

Hudson's Bay Company 525

Hughes, William Morris, 'Billy' (Prime Minister of Australia) 566

humanitarianism 23, 173, 195, 274–5, 482, 601, 631, 635, 638, 640, 683, 686–7

and Imperial government 204–20
  roots of 198–204
  and self-government 212–13
Humboldt, Alexander von (naturalist) 294, 297
Hunt, G. W. (song-writer) 278
hunting 309
Huntington, Ellsworth (geographer) 66
Huskisson, William (President of the Board of
  Trade, Secretary for War and Colonies) 39,
  40, 104, 175, 178
Hut Tax War (Sierra Leone, 1898) 18, 196, 645
Hutton, J. F. (merchant) 287
Huxley, Thomas (biologist) 295, 298

IBEAC, see Imperial British East Africa
  Company
Ibibio people, West Africa 645
Ibrahim of Johore, Sultan 384
ICS, see Indian Civil Service
IFL, see Imperial Federation League
Igbo, Igboland, West Africa 645, 682
Ijebu people, West Africa 645
Île de France 673
Ilorin, West Africa 645
immigration, see migration
Imperial British East Africa Company 194, 352,
  638, 639, 641, 643–4
Imperial Defence League 336
imperial federation 291, 336, 338, 343, 614, 621
  'constructive imperialism' 347–57
  failure of 357–67
  neglects India 365
  race as basis for 356–7
Imperial Federation League 347–8, 349, 350, 358,
  359, 360, 362
Imperial Grand Orange Council 508
Imperial Order of the Daughters of the Empire
  532
Imperial Ottoman Bank 112
incense 552
indentured labour, see under labour
India 4, 5–6, 10, 18, 22, 24, 26, 112, 129, 157, 443
  (1818–60) 396–420
  (1858–1914) 422–45
  Anglo-Indian society 23, 182–3, 430, 433
  British images of 184–5, 276, 277, 279, 280, 281,
    406
  caste in 184–5, 397, 398, 414–5, 432, 448
  cultural change in 395, 397–9, 408, 415–20,
    431–2, 435–7, 447–69
  defence of 11–14, 171, 322, 326, 341, 705–6
  economic development of 58–61, 65–6, 70–2,
    395, 397, 403, 408–12, 417–8, 441–2, 443–4
  economy and trade 5–6, 19, 32–5, 42, 43, 44, 60,
    106, 161, 365, 372, 403–4, 408, 419, 430–1, 435,
    436, 441–2, 444, 706
  education 431–2, 458, 459, 468–9

government, character of 174–5, 181–4,
  199–201, 183, 397–9, 400–2, 404–8, 411,
  412–15, 416–20, 430–4, 437–9, 443–4, 448
government, revenues of 6, 399–400, 402–3,
  407–8, 409–10, 414, 430
government, structure of 16, 177, 419, 422–7,
  433, 437, 438–9
government of, as colonial model 196, 199,
  497–8, 500, 505, 634, 654, 664
Great Trigonometrical Survey 305
Irish in 512
nationalism 420, 432–4, 437–40, 444–5, 462,
  465, 466, 467
new élites 431–2, 451, 452, 453
North-West Frontier 322, 324, 341, 401, 404,
  434, 435
'oriental despotism' 399, 404–5, 408, 411, 412,
  417, 444
'peasantization' 412–3, 448
princes, princely states 181, 194, 414, 416, 420,
  424, 427, 430, 435–6
representative government 426–7, 433, 438–9,
  445, 468
social issues 457, 461, 517
and South-East Asia 375, 377, 378, 379, 382, 390
transport and communications 250–1, 252,
  257, 259, 262, 264, 266, 279, 417, 419, 436, 442
value to Britain 6, 50, 72, 104, 401, 434–5,
  440–3, 705–6, 708
see also Army, Indian; banking; Christianity;
  East India Company; Hinduism; Islam;
  labour; land; law; migration;
  missions; overseas investment; race
India Office 16, 296, 322, 425
Indian Civil Service 124, 156, 177, 182, 400, 402,
  411–12, 417, 429–30, 432, 433–4, 435, 505–6,
  509–10
Indian Constitutional Reform Association 506
Indian Mutiny and Civil Rebellion (1857) 18, 90,
  174, 178, 213, 280–2, 322, 326, 397, 413, 418–20,
  422, 427, 430, 455
Indian National Congress 432, 433–4, 437–8,
  439–40, 445, 460, 464
Indian Ocean 36, 635, 673
Indian Political Service 430
Indian Social Conference 460
indigo 33
indirect rule 196, 431, 468, 681, 682
Indo-China 375, 381, 388, 463
Indonesia 60
Indus, River 106, 305
industrialization:
  colonial 27, 113, 138, 150, 168, 380, 551, 609,
    652–3, 660, 705
  European 31–2, 40, 53–74, 103, 114, 138–44, 692,
    695, 698, 702–3
  see also entries for individual countries

Influence of Sea Power upon History, The (Mahan) 338–9
'informal empire', *see* empire, 'informal control'; imperialism, types of
Inglis, Charles (Bishop of Nova Scotia) 224–5
Intelligence Services, British 654
International African Association 636, 638
Inuit people, Canada 526
Ireland, Irish 4, 38, 129, 271, 289, 494–520
  economy and trade 63, 495, 501–2, 507
  empire as opportunity for 509–12
  empire, influence on 515–20
  government, character of 499–504, 506, 515
  government, structure of 495–9, 505–7
  Great Famine 40, 496, 499, 502, 513
  Home Rule movement 505–7, 511, 519, 555–6, 607
  migration from 20, 63, 78, 81, 85, 510, 512–15, 536
  nationalism 504–7, 512, 528
  religion 503, 510, 511–20, 536
  unionism 507–9, 510, 536
  see also language; race
Irigoyen, Hipólito (President of Argentina) 143
Irish Brigade 512
Irish Constabulary (Royal, from 1867) 496, 497, 498, 516–17, 533 *see also* 'Black and Tans'
Irish Volunteers 510
Irrawaddy, River, Burma 259, 266, 380, 391
irrigation 249, 263, 264, 418, 562, 658, 660
Isaiah (prophet) 231–2
Isandhlwana, Battle of (1879) 606, 629, 684
Islam, Muslims 386, 458
  in Africa 196, 661, 673, 678, 680
  and Christianity 238, 244, 397–8, 417
  in India 395, 418, 419, 420
  and partition of Bengal 438
  revitalization of 453, 459–66
  see also India
Ismail, Khedive of Egypt 632–3, 653, 660, 661, 662
Italy 348, 635, 639, 644, 653, 662
ivory 635
Ivory Coast, West Africa 639

Jack Tar (fictitious character) 277
Jaja of Opobo 258
Jamaica, West Indies 189, 205, 225, 472, 474, 486–8, 492
  economic difficulties after 1865 489, 490, 491
  emancipation in 205, 478–80, 481, 483, 484, 485
  Rebellion (1831) 204, 231, 475–6
  see also Morant Bay Rebellion
Jameson Raid, South Africa 261, 609, 612, 642
Japan, Japanese 191, 393, 466, 559, 560, 564, 570, 705
  Anglo-Japanese Alliance (1902) 393
  and Britain 22, 393, 705

in China 149, 152, 159, 164, 166
  economic development of 60, 71–2, 73, 162
Jardine Matheson and Co. 19, 111, 160, 161, 162, 377
Java, Indonesia 374, 377, 401
Jay Treaty (1794) 39
Jeffries, Sir Charles Joseph (Joint Deputy Under-Secretary of State, Colonial Office) 516–17
Jervois, Colonel Sir William (Royal Engineer and colonial defence expert) 330
Jevons, William Stanley (economist and logician) 114, 115
Jews 20, 451
Jibouti, Somaliland 644
jingoism 278–9, 362
Johannesburg, South Africa 610, 612, 618, 642
  Caledonian Society of 20
Johnson, Charles, *see* Brooke, Charles
Johnson, G. W. (Sierra Leonian) 676
Johnson, Samuel (Yoruba clergyman) 670
Johnston, Sir Harry (Hamilton) (administrator, British Central Africa) 238, 244, 640, 641
Johore, *see* Riau-Johore
Joyce, P. W. (educationalist) 503–4
Juba, River, East Africa 644
Jukes, Joseph Beete (geologist) 295
jute 43, 62

Kabul, Afghanistan 12
Kailan Mining Adminstration 152
Kaiping, China 152
Kamil, Mustafa (Egyptian journalist) 657
Kampala, Buganda 644
'Kanakas', Queensland 564
Kanaks, New Caledonia 549, 571
Karens, *see* Red Karens
Kassala, East Africa 644
Kati Kati, New Zealand 514
Keate, Robert William (Lt.-Governor of Natal) 628
Kedah, Malay peninsula 372, 374, 384, 388, 467
Kelantan, Malay peninsula 384, 389
Kelvin, William Thomson, First Baron (scientist) 256
Kendall, William (schoolteacher) 575
Kennaway, Sir John (MP and President of the Church Missionary Society) 216
Kenya, East Africa 60, 243, 649
Kerikeri, New Zealand 575
Kermadec Islands 591
Kew, Royal Botanical Gardens 298, 302
Kew Letters 374
Key, Sir Astley Cooper (First Sea Lord) 337
Kgatla people, southern Africa 619
Khartoum, Sudan 244, 266, 634
Khoikhoi people, South Africa 207, 597, 599

Kidd, Benjamin (civil servant and sociologist) 24
Kikuyu Conference (1913) 243
Kilwa, East Africa 673
Kimberley, John Wodehouse, First Earl of
    (Secretary of State for the Colonies) 182,
    216, 382–3, 591, 607, 624, 629, 648
Kimberley, South Africa 263, 604
    Siege of 618
King, John (missionary) 575
King, Philip Gidley (Lt-Governor of New South
    Wales and Norfolk Island) 575, 576
King, Philip Parker (naval captain) 302
King, William Lyon Mackenzie (Canadian Prime
    Minister) 537
King Movement, New Zealand 585–7, 588
King Solomon's Mines (Rider Haggard) 312
King's College (at Fredericton, and Windsor) 226
Kingsley, Mary (traveller and anthropologist)
    219, 306
Kinnaird, Arthur (MP and humanitarian) 216
Kipling, (Joseph) Rudyard (writer) 24, 697
Kiralfy, Imre (exhibition organizer) 283
Kirk, Sir John (Consul-General at Zanzibar) 635
Kisumu, East Africa 644
Kitchener, Horatio Herbert, First Earl Kitchener
    of Khartoum and Broome (military
    commander) 341, 511, 618, 619, 644, 657
Kiukiang, China 149
Klerksdorp, South Africa 619
Knatchbull-Hugessen, Edward, First Baron
    Brabourne (Parliamentary Under-Secretary,
    Colonial Office) 191
Knibb, William (missionary) 476, 480
Knox, Robert (anthropologist) 286
Knox, William (Under-Secretary of State,
    American Department) 223
Knutsford, *see* Holland, Sir Henry
Kohimarama, New Zealand 586
Konbaung dynasty, Burma 376, 379, 380, 389,
    463
Korokoro (Maori chief) 576
Kororareka, New Zealand 580
Kosi Bay, South Africa 630
Kra Isthmus, Siam 388
Kruger, S. J. Paul (President of the South African
    Republic) 607, 608, 609, 611, 612, 614,
    615–16, 630, 631, 641, 643
'Kruger Telegram' 609
Kuala Kangsar, Malaya 469
Kuala Lumpur, Federated Malay States 383
Kumasi (Kumase), Gold Coast, West Africa 645,
    676, 677, 685–6
Kurdistan 296

labour (non-European) 61, 63, 88, 92–3, 95, 127,
    266, 392, 514, 549, 563–5, 660, 684, 709–10
    compared with British migration 95–9

'free labour' 203, 208, 211, 219–20, 480–2
    government regulation of 88–100, 196, 212–13,
        386, 563–5, 566–7, 599
    indentured labour 88, 91–9, 212, 484–5
    kidnapping 94, 553, 575
    liberated Africans ('recaptives') 90, 212, 667–8
    numbers 88–96
    protest 142–3, 163, 203, 204, 225, 230, 231, 456,
        475, 485–7
    recruitment from: China 88, 89, 90, 93–9, 217,
        563, 565, 620; India 89–93, 95–9, 385, 442,
        484–5, 552–3; Pacific 88, 89, 93, 94–5, 215,
        549, 556, 563–5; other sources 88, 484
    repatriation 95, 564
    wages 65, 69, 88, 90, 96, 476–7, 480–1, 485,
        490–1, 557, 599, 605–6
    see also slavery; *for British and European
        labour, see* migration
Labour Party 292
    Australian Labor 519, 566, 567
Labuan, South-East Asia 6, 177
Ladysmith, Siege of (1899–1900) 512, 618
Lagos, Nigeria, West Africa 6, 17, 114, 190, 259,
    261, 351, 639, 645, 670
Lagos Colony 20, 108, 626, 639, 645
Laing, Alexander Gordon (explorer) 301, 302
Laird, Macgregor (merchant and explorer) 108,
    249, 256, 306, 313
Lambert, Commodore (British naval
    commander) 379
Lambeth Conference 234
Lancashire 47, 57
land 150, 578, 684
    colonial policies 41, 42, 151, 172, 189, 195–6, 208,
        212, 213, 517–18, 533, 550–1, 557–8, 580, 583,
        587, 645
    dispossession 527, 548, 587, 597–8, 599, 601
    empty 56, 563, 557, 580
    property rights 61, 65, 106, 173, 186, 201, 216–17,
        219–20, 486, 563, 587, 662–3, 697, 709
    property rights in India 217, 399–400, 416, 418,
        424, 444, 517
    purchase of 557, 580, 581, 584, 587, 593, 659–60
    titles to 195, 208, 481, 482, 495, 533, 558, 563, 565,
        578, 580, 587, 593
Lander, Richard and John (explorers) 301, 302,
    306, 312, 318
language 27, 156, 163, 450, 452, 497, 534, 661–3
    English 7, 25, 27, 431, 450, 458–60, 619 *see also*
        education
Lansdowne, Henry Petty-Fitzmaurice, Fifth
    Marquis of (Viceroy of India) 433
Laurier, Sir Wilfrid (Prime Minister of
    Canada) 340, 530, 534, 542, 543, 544
law 17, 45, 148, 193, 203, 207, 232, 380–1, 389, 447,
    454, 661–2, 683
    administration of 153–5, 164–5, 173, 181, 201

law (*cont.*):
  codification of 184–5, 435, 534
  courts 164, 192, 398, 407, 487, 566, 569, 576, 581,
    587, 638, 645, 667
  'effective occupation' 193
  European law 175, 193, 661
  extension of British law and jurisdiction
    191–6, 576, 577, 630, 636, 640, 645, 671, 676,
    700, 709
  extraterritoriality 110, 112, 148, 149–53, 155, 164,
    165, 191–6, 632, 652, 657, 660
  India 398, 405, 407, 415, 431, 432, 435
  Judicial Committee of the Privy Council 232,
    541, 542
  Law Officers of the Crown 17, 191, 194, 638
  lawyers 153, 164, 661, 670
  'Mansfield Judgement' 666
  martial law 477, 486, 500, 585
  review and disallowance of 205, 213, 478–9,
    482, 540–1
  see also land
Law, Andrew Bonar (Canadian-born British
  Prime Minister) 528, 536
Lawrence, Sir Henry Montgomery (soldier and
  Indian administrator) 281
Lawson, Henry (Australian writer) 568
lead 551
Lee, Samuel (Regius Professor of Hebrew,
  Cambridge University) 575
Leopold II, King of the Belgians 215, 218–9, 636,
  637, 638, 639, 649
Lesser Antilles, Caribbean Sea 190
Levant, Middle East 14, 652, 662
Lever, William Hesketh, later Viscount
  Leverhulme (entrepreneur and
  philanthropist) 553, 557
Lewanika (ruler of the Lozi) 267
Lewis, Sir Samuel (Freetown lawyer) 670
Leys, Norman (colonial adminstrator) 220
Liberal Party 187, 292, 331, 432, 437, 570, 624,
  633
  and South Africa 607–8, 617, 620–1, 630, 631
  and Tariff Reform 359, 364–6
Life of Gladstone (Morley) 537
Light, Francis (trader) 372
Lima, Peru 126, 128
Limpopo, River, South Africa 611, 628
literacy 576, 583, 667
  see also education
Liverpool, England 7, 35, 77, 84, 127, 196, 358
Liverpool, Robert Banks Jenkinson, Second Earl
  of (Prime Minister) 205
Livingstone, David (missionary and
  explorer) 107, 214, 215, 236, 237, 239, 256, 257,
  275, 281, 290, 296, 301, 304, 635, 674
Loch, Sir Henry B. (High Commissioner for
  South Africa) 612, 630

Lockhart, James Stewart (colonial
  administrator) 149
London, England 7, 35, 79, 81, 84, 224, 358, 616
  City of 47–8, 49–50, 137, 616, 633
London Convention (1884) 608, 611, 614, 630
London Female Emigration Society 81
London Missionary Society 228, 556, 590, 598 n.3,
  599
London Tin Corporation 385
Lovedale school, eastern Cape 236, 684
Lozi people, central Africa 673
Lugard, Sir Frederick John Dealtry (soldier and
  colonial administrator) 196, 259, 640,
  643–4, 681
Lunda people, central Africa 673
Lutfi al-Sayyid, Ahmad 657, 664
Lutyens, Edwin (architect) 27
Lytton, Edward Robert Bulwer, First Earl of
  (Viceroy of India) 177, 183, 431, 432, 433,
  437

MacArthur Forrest cyanide process 263–4
Macartney, Sir George, Baron (1776), Earl (1792)
  (Ambassador to China) 146
Macaulay, Thomas Babington, First Baron
  (historian, legal member of Supreme
  Council of India) 181, 231, 396, 397, 398,
  415–16, 425, 431
MacCarthy, Lt.-Colonel Sir Charles (Governor of
  Sierra Leone) 668
Macdonald, Sir John A. (Canadian Prime
  Minister) 353, 359, 510, 528, 539, 540–1, 542,
  543
MacDonnell, Sir Antony (Under-Secretary for
  Ireland) 497–8, 517
McDougall, William (Lt.-Governor of the North
  West Territory, Canada) 531
MacFarlane, William (missionary) 236
McGee, Thomas D'Arcy (former Young
  Irelander) 519, 536, 537
MacGregor, Sir William (Governor of Lagos) 20,
  220
McIntosh, David (National African Company
  agent) 637
Mackenzie, Alexander (Canadian Prime
  Minister) 540
Mackenzie, Charles Frederick (Anglican
  missionary bishop) 237
MacKenzie, John (missionary and Resident
  Commissioner, Bechuanaland) 217, 237,
  630
McKenzie, John (New Zealand Minister of Lands)
  593
Mackenzie, William Lyon (Canadian politician)
  528, 537
Mackinnon, Sir William (Scottish shipping
  magnate) 215, 257

Mackinnon Agreement (1890) 639
Mackinnon Mackenzie (trading company) 19
McLean, Donald (native and defence minister, New Zealand) 587–8
Maclennan, John (emigration agent) 84
McNeill, Eoin (Irish scholar, Chief of Staff of Irish Volunteers) 510
McNeill, James (Commissioner in Bombay Presidency) 510
Macpherson, Annie (emigration promoter) 82
Macquarie, Lachlan (Governor of New South Wales) 177, 576
Macready, General Sir (Cecil Frederick) Nevil (British military commander) 499
Madagascar, Indian Ocean 11, 639, 640
Madeira, Atlantic 97
Madras, India 92, 96, 179, 232, 397, 407, 408, 410, 412, 426
  University of 431, 458
Mafeking, Siege of (1899–1900) 282, 362, 612, 618, 619
Magersfontein, Battle of (1899) 617
Maghrib, The, North Africa 626
Mahan, Alfred Thayer (naval historian) 338–9
Maharajas 397, 416
Mahdists, Mahdist state 18, 634, 644, 681
  see also Sudan
mails 7, 250, 266, 279
Maine, United States 523
Maitland, Sir Peregrine (Lt. Governor of Upper Canada) 226
Majuba Hill, Battle of (1881) 607–8
Makassan people, Pacific 558, 564
Makatea, Pacific French Polynesia 553
Malacca, Malay peninsula 375, 377, 451, 452
Malacca, Straits of 375, 377
Malay archipelago 375
Malay peninsula, Malaya 6, 13, 15, 190, 263, 375, 377–8, 381, 382–6, 387, 393, 448, 449, 452, 457, 460, 463, 467, 468–9, 606
  see also Federated Malay States; Straits Settlements
Malcolm, Sir John (Governor of Bombay) 398, 402, 405
Malta, Mediterranean 175, 183, 185, 325, 334, 512–13, 654, 662
Malthusianism 76–7
Manchester, England 162, 287, 288
Manchu dynasty 456, 457
Manchuria, China 152, 160, 166
Mandalay, Burma 389, 390, 463
Mandeville, John (Minister Plenipotentiary at Buenos Aires) 123
Mandinka people, West Africa 636
Manicaland, Portuguese East Africa 641
Manitoba, Canada 84, 528, 534, 541
Manitoba Schools dispute 542

Maori Land Court 587
Maori people, New Zealand 22, 180, 192, 233, 250, 252, 329, 573, 575–7, 578–82, 583, 584, 593, 594, 595
  and annexation 578–80, 581, 585
  and humanitarians 207, 212, 213, 216
  and representative government 584–5, 587–8, 594, 595
  Declaration of Independence (1835) 577
  King Movement 585–6, 587
  Maori Parliament 588
  Young Maori Party 588
  see also New Zealand; Waitangi, Treaty of
'Maple Leaf for Ever, The' (song) 537
maraikkayars 451
Marathas 400, 401
Marchand, Colonel Jean Baptiste (French military officer) 644, 648
Maritime Provinces, Canada 34, 185, 187, 223, 224, 525, 526, 527, 528, 532, 534, 540
  see also New Brunswick; Nova Scotia; Prince Edward Island; Cape Breton Island
Maritime Strike (Australia, 1890) 566
Maroons 486, 667
Marquesas Islands, Pacific 558
Marsden, Samuel (colonial chaplain, New South Wales) 225, 229, 575
Martin, Paul (Canadian Liberal politician) 537
Marx, Karl (political theorist) 247, 691
Masai Land, East Africa 311, 312
Mashonaland, southern Africa 632, 641
Massawa, Eritrea, East Africa 114, 635
Matabele people, see Ndebele people
Mauritius, Indian Ocean 88, 91, 96, 98, 177, 185, 188, 212, 374
Meath, Reginald Brabazon, Twelfth Earl of (diplomat, 'Empire Day' promoter) 183
medicine 14, 92–3, 98, 151, 158, 212, 262–3, 266, 306, 460–1, 533, 670
Mediterranean Agreement (1887) 644
Mediterranean Sea 11, 12, 14
Melanesia, Melanesians, Pacific 94, 549, 563, 564, 591
Melanesian Mission 215, 233
Melbourne Cup 560
Melbourne, Victoria, Australia 546, 550
Melbourne, William Lamb, Second Viscount (British Prime Minister) 205
Memons 451
Menelik, Emperor of Ethiopia 635, 644, 649
Merauke, western Pacific 565
Mercantile Bank 377
Merivale, Herman (economist, colonial reformer, and historian) 114, 177
metallurgy 247, 258, 264
Metcalfe, Sir Charles Theophilus, First Baron (East India Company official) 398, 402

Metcalfe, (*cont.*):
  (Governor of Jamaica) 480
  (Governor-General of Canada) 538, 539
Methodists 202, 210, 215, 217, 226, 556, 576, 590,
  668, 671
  missionaries 19–20, 228, 231, 671, 677
Métis (mixed-descent Canadians) 526, 528
Mexico, Central America 110, 123, 126, 128, 131,
  135, 138, 140, 143, 263
Middelburg, Transvaal 619
Middle East 15, 102, 404
  see also Afghanistan; Arab peoples; Egypt;
    Levant; Ottoman empire; Persia
migration 7, 19, 20, 36–7, 41, 51, 53, 56, 61, 63, 72,
  75–100, 279–80, 283, 314, 454–7, 546, 582, 583,
  598–9, 696–7, 708, 709–10
  assisted 37, 41, 46–7, 51, 78–83, 97, 172, 513–14,
    555, 582, 589–90, 620
  continental European 20, 64, 97, 136, 484, 535,
    599
  destinations 36–7, 46–7, 58, 75–86, 93, 136, 484,
    512–15, 548–50, 592
  emigration agents 77, 78, 79, 83–4, 85
  English 36, 46, 498–9, 513
  female migration 78, 81–2, 513, 514, 567–8,
    582
  Irish 19, 20, 36, 72, 77, 78–9, 81–2, 85–6, 499,
    504–5, 509–15, 535
  migrants, character of 37, 47, 78–9, 80–5, 93,
    95–6, 513–14, 582–3, 696
  numbers 36–7, 46–7, 75, 78, 80–3, 85–8, 512–14
  return migration 46, 515, 697
  Scottish 19, 20, 36–7, 46, 72, 78–82, 85–6,
    498–9, 513, 535–6, 565
  Welsh 20, 37, 46, 84–6, 513
Mill, James (East India Company
  employee; father of John Stuart Mill) 181,
  200
Mill, John Stuart (economist and
  philosopher) 137, 350, 425, 486, 590, 691
Mills, Arthur (MP and colonial reformer) 328
Milner, Sir Alfred, First Viscount
  (Under-Secretary of Finance in Egypt, High
  Commissioner for South Africa) 22, 23, 171,
  175, 261–2, 349, 357, 361, 615–16, 619–20, 621,
  622, 642
  'Kindergarten' 619, 621
Mindon Min, King of Burma 380, 389
mining, miners 20, 65–6, 78, 88, 90, 94, 97, 127,
  138, 220, 565
  in Australia 551–2
  in China 152
  in Latin America 127, 138
  in South Africa 604, 609–10, 611, 615, 616–22,
    626
  in South-East Asia 380, 384–5
  machinery 249, 263–4

Minnesota, United States 523
Minto, Lord (Governor-General of India), *see*
  Elliot, Sir Gilbert, Baron Minto (1798), First
  Earl of Minto (1813)
Minto, Lord (Viceroy of India), *see* Elliot, Sir
  Gilbert John, Fourth Earl of Minto (1847)
missions 19, 20, 155, 158, 170, 183, 198, 201–2, 204,
  214, 218, 219, 222–46, 289–90, 315, 447, 463,
  519–20, 564, 624–5, 683
  and converts 235–8, 243, 549, 576, 666–73
  and education 231, 236, 549, 570
  relations with governments 155, 208, 218,
    228–32, 237–8, 244–5, 417, 668, 671
  translation and scholarship 231, 240–2, 286,
    459, 462
  World Missionary Conference (1910) 22
  in Africa (East) 640, 644, 674–5, 678
  in Africa (South) 237, 240, 275, 290, 598, 611,
    629, 630, 681
  in Africa (West) 229, 231, 235, 238, 243–4,
    666–73, 677, 683, 686
  in Asia 457, 460–4
  in China 155, 158, 235, 236, 237, 242, 244
  in India 229, 236, 239, 241, 243, 397, 400, 417,
    418, 459
  in New Zealand 229, 233, 573, 575–6, 577, 578
  in Pacific 215, 229, 233, 239, 244, 549, 556, 558,
    570, 590, 591
  in South-East Asia 376–7
  in West Indies 228, 229, 475–7, 480–1
  see also entries under *individual
    societies*; Christianity; Livingstone; Scots
Mississauga people (Native Americans) 533
Mitchell, Sir Thomas Livingstone (Surveyor-
  General, New South Wales, and explorer)
  302, 303, 562
Modern Egypt (Cromer) 660
Moffat, Robert (missionary) 240, 275, 290
Molopo, River, South Africa 608, 630
Mombasa, East Africa 214, 351, 352, 644, 673
monarchy 111, 116, 125, 183, 289, 290, 431, 437, 440,
  468
  powers of the Crown 4, 170, 205, 424–6,
    578–80, 583, 608
  see also Victoria, Queen
Monck, Sir Charles Stanley, Fourth Viscount
  (Governor-General of Canada) 540
Mongkut, King of Siam 380–1
Montevideo, South America 126, 129
Montreal, Canada 525, 526, 531, 532, 533
Montreal Gazette 541
Montserrat, Leeward Islands 477, 491
Morant Bay Rebellion, Jamaica (1865) 20, 213,
  214, 280, 486–7, 488, 491
Moravian missionaries 228, 229
Morel, Edmund Dene (humanitarian activist)
  218–20

Morley, John (Secretary of State for India) 365, 438, 439, 440, 537
Moroccan Crises (1904, 1911) North Africa 649
Moshoeshoe (King of the Sotho) 603
Mosquito Coast, Central America 131
Mossi, West Africa 648
Mott, John R. (American religious leader) 242
Mount Allison College, Canada 532
Mountain, Jacob (Anglican Bishop of Quebec) 224, 226
mountaineering 314
Mowat, Sir Oliver (Canadian Prime Minister) 541
Mozambique, East Africa 609, 635, 641, 673
Muhammad Ali, Khedive of Egypt 12, 112–3, 652, 655, 662
Müller, Mary Anne, *pseudonym* (writer) 590
Munro, Sir Thomas (Governor of Madras) 200, 231, 398, 402, 407
Munster, Ireland 513
Murchison, Sir Roderick (geographer) 256, 257, 297–9, 306
Murray, John (publisher) 316
Murrumbidgee, River (New South Wales) 562
museums 298, 299, 309
Muslims, *see* Islam
Mutesa, Kabaka of Buganda 678
Mwanga, Kabaka of Buganda 644
Mysore, India 230, 274, 400, 448

Nadars 453
Naning, Malay peninsula 377
Nanking, Treaty of (1842) 110
Naoroji, Dadabhai (British MP, President of the Indian National Congress) 443–4, 506
Napier, Sir Charles James (soldier, conqueror of Sind) 404
Napier Commission (on emigration) 89
Napoleon Bonaparte 127, 651–2
Napoleonic Wars 16, 31, 126, 131, 203, 232, 401, 405, 471–2, 598
Narrandera, New South Wales 562
Natal, southern Africa 11, 217, 359, 603, 604, 609, 611, 614, 619, 622, 629, 632, 642
annexation of 209, 628
and Indian labour 88, 92, 96, 98, 212
and self-government 187, 602, 621
National African Company 194, 636–7
National Bank of India 441
National Colonization Society 76
National Fair Trade League 350
National Review 361–2
National Union of Conservative Associations 358
nationalism 23–4, 26–7, 28, 151, 153, 289–90, 356–7, 457, 465–7, 560, 619, 633, 641, 670
see also entries under individual territories
Native Americans (Canada) 526, 527, 533

Nauru, western Pacific 553
Navy, Canadian 543
Navy, Indian 305–6
Navy, Royal 34, 41, 113–14, 124, 295, 298, 372, 511, 604, 627–8, 633, 649, 654
bases 322, 327, 328, 334–5, 543, 654, 663
and Britain's global power 7–8, 109, 172, 192, 249, 371, 393, 401, 434, 696, 705, 706
costs 332–3, 337–8, 340, 704–5
role in colonial/imperial defence 320, 322, 323, 324, 332–5, 336–41, 343–4
slave trade suppression 203, 211, 667
in China 151, 154, 164, 323
in East Africa 15, 114, 215, 673
in Latin America 110, 123, 131, 132, 133, 139, 323
in Pacific 553, 557, 559, 560, 573–5
in South-East Asia 371, 372, 378
in West Africa 14, 90, 114, 206, 323, 666
Navy League 339
Ndebele people, central Africa 342, 611, 631, 632, 641, 642, 681–2
Ndebeleland 631, 642
Negri Sembilan, Malay peninsula 383
Nemesis (steamer) 249
Nepean, Sir Evan, First Baronet (Governor of Bombay) 231
Nevis, Leeward Islands 477
New Brunswick, Canada 185, 187, 523, 525, 527, 532, 536, 539, 540
New Caledonia, western Pacific 548, 552, 553, 558, 570–1, 591
New Guinea, western Pacific 194, 548, 549, 552, 558, 559, 564, 565, 570
German New Guinea 557, 570
Protectorate of 557
New Hebrides (Vanuatu), western Pacific 548, 549, 558, 570, 571, 591, 592
New South Wales, Australia 20, 78–9, 185, 212, 225, 433, 519, 546, 550, 551, 555, 562, 567, 576
New Territories, *see* Hong Kong
New Ulster, New Zealand 514
New York, United States 7
State of 530
New Zealand 5, 10, 11, 21, 36, 56, 174, 177, 573–95, 708
annexation of 190, 209, 573, 578–80
defence 324, 326, 329–30, 337, 338, 340, 343, 353, 359, 559, 704
early British contacts 575–8
economy and trade 43–5, 69, 575, 577, 588–90, 592, 593
exploration 304–5
external relations: with Australia 573–5, 576–8, 588–90, 592; with Britain 586, 588–90, 591–2, 594–5; sub-imperialism 590–2
government, structure of 185, 187, 189, 213, 583–4, 589–90, 594

New Zealand (*cont.*):
  Irish in 512, 513, 514
  migration to 46, 76–9
  nationalism 594–5
  party politics in 584–5, 587–8, 589, 593, 594,
    595
  social policy 581, 592–5
  technology 250, 252
  Wars 25, 213–14, 559, 581, 585–7
  see also land; law; Maori; migration;
    missions; New Ulster; North Island; South
    Island; Waitangi, Treaty of
New Zealand Association 578
New Zealand Company 578, 580, 582
Newbolt, Sir Henry (poet) 265–6
Newcastle, Henry Pelham Fiennes Pelham
    Clinton, Fifth Duke of (Secretary of State for
    War and Colonies) 173, 188
Newcastle, New South Wales 551
Newfoundland, Canada 522, 523, 525, 526, 533,
    535, 536
newspaper press 173, 288–9, 309, 460–1, 527, 670
NFTL, *see* National Fair Trade League
Ngaruawahia, New Zealand 585
Ngati Tama-Te-ra, New Zealand 580
Ngidi, William (Zulu) 241
Nicaragua, Central America, *see* Mosquito Coast
nickel 552, 558
Niger, River, West Africa 10, 15, 109, 113, 249, 259,
    296, 636, 637, 638, 648
  and exploration 300, 302, 306, 309, 311
  focus of humanitarian and missionary
    attention 230, 237, 238, 243, 672–3
Niger Coast Protectorate 193–4, 638, 645
Niger Expedition (1841) 210, 672–3
Nigeria, Northern, West Africa 196, 648, 649
Nigeria, West Africa 351, 352, 671, 682
Nile, River, Africa 191, 259, 306, 634–5, 639–40,
    643–4, 648, 649, 674
Ningpo, China 161
nitrates 143
Norfolk Island, western Pacific 575
North Borneo 6
North Borneo Company 384
North Island, New Zealand 584, 585, 586, 587, 589,
    593
North-West American Boundary
    Commission 304
Northern Territory, Australia 551
Nova Scotia, Canada 185, 187, 523, 525, 527, 530,
    536, 538, 539, 540
'Nova Scotians' 667
Nubar Pasha (Egyptian minister) 661
Nupe, West Africa 645
Nyamwezi people, east-central Africa 673
Nyasa, Lake, Africa 214
Nyasaland 611, 640, 641

'O Canada' (song by Lavallée) 537
Observer 357
O'Connell, Daniel (Irish political leader) 505, 507
O'Donnell, Charles James (Commissioner in the
    Indian Civil Service) 505–6, 517
O'Donnell, Frank Hugh (Irish nationalist)
    505–6
O'Dwyer, Sir Michael Francis (Lieutenant-
    Governor of the Punjab) 510
O'Higgins, Kevin Christopher (Irish nationalist)
    528
oil, *see* petroleum
Oil Rivers, Niger Delta 194, 645
Old Calabar, West Africa 645
Oliver, Frederick Scott (businessman and
    publicist) 171
Omai (native of Tahiti) 275–6
Oman, Middle East 673
Omdurman, Battle of (1898) 265, 279, 644
O'Neill, Henry Nelson (painter) 274, 281
Ontario, Canada 513, 514, 533, 534, 536, 541, 543,
    544
  see also Canada, Upper (pre-1867)
Ontario, Lake 526
opium 161, 220, 403, 409
Opium Wars, *see* China: Arrow War; Opium War
Orange Free State, South Africa 602, 603, 604,
    618, 620, 629, 631, 632
Orange Order 507–9, 514, 518, 523, 536, 542
Orange, River 628
Orange River Sovereignty, South Africa 602
Oregon, United States 523
Oriental Bank 377
'orientalism', *see* historiography; Said, Edward
    W.
Origin of Species, The (Darwin) 285
Orwell, George, *pseudonym for* Eric Blair (writer,
    member of Indian Imperial Police in
    Burma) 391–2
Osborne House, Isle of Wight, England 284
Otago, New Zealand 79, 83, 582, 584, 587
Ottama, U (Burmese monk) 465
Ottawa, Canada 540, 542
Ottawa Conference (1932) 367
Ottoman empire 1, 12, 13, 104, 111–12, 117–20, 191,
    216, 624, 632
  see also Egypt
Oudh (Awadh), Kingdom of, India 418, 428, 431
Oudney, Walter (explorer) 301, 302, 309
Outram, General Sir James (commander in
    India) 281
overseas investment 37, 45, 47–50, 102, 179
  and British trade 694–8
  destination of 48–9, 56–7, 72, 110, 112, 113, 117,
    135, 166, 377, 385, 387, 410, 441–2, 483, 502–3,
    626, 693, 698–700
  empire share of 48, 693

profitability of 47–50, 692–4, 698–703

sources of 47, 59, 72, 609, 626

statistics for 135, 150

see also banking; colonial development policy; railways

Oxley, John W. M. (Surveyor-General, New South Wales, and explorer) 302

P&O, *see* Peninsular and Oriental Steamship Navigation Company

Paardeberg, Battle of (1900) 618

Pacific Cable 259, 262

Pacific islands 546, 548–50, 552–5, 556–9, 564–5, 570–1

Pacific Islands Company 553, 557

Pacific Ocean 13, 17, 36, 89, 131, 140, 192–3, 195, 216, 232–3

High Commissioner for the Western Pacific 193

Pacific Phosphate Company 553

Paget, Ralph (British Minister at Bangkok) 388

Pahang, Malay peninsula 383, 386, 463

Pai Marire (Maori religion) 587

painting 274, 281, 284, 532–3, 537

Paish, George (economist and statistician) 692

Pall Mall Gazette 338

Palliser, Captain John (Canadian prairie explorer) 309

Palliser Expedition 304, 309

palm-oil 14, 35, 43, 60

Palmer, Sir Edwin (financial adviser in Egypt) 643

Palmerston, Henry John Temple, Third Viscount (Prime Minister) 102, 105, 106, 107–13, 116–17, 127, 210, 332, 624

Pamirs 14

Panama Canal, Central America 490

Pangkor Engagement (Treaty) (1874) 377, 383

Papineau, Louis-Joseph (French Canadian politician) 537

Papua, Western Pacific 549–50, 552, 557, 558, 559, 564, 565, 570

Paraguay, Paraguayan War (1865–70) 140

Paraná, River, Paraguay 130

Parihaka, New Zealand 587

Park, Mungo (explorer) 296

Parke, Thomas Heazle (medical officer) 263

Parkes, Sir Henry (Prime Minister of New South Wales) 561

Parkin, Sir George Robert (Canadian supporter of imperial federation) 358

Parliament, British 4, 203–4, 215, 396, 400, 476, 495, 539, 633–4

authority over colonies 18, 174–5, 178, 204–6, 224–7

and defence 325, 327, 328–9

Select Committees: Aborigines (British Settlements) (1837) 207–9, 212, 213; Africa (Western Coast) (1865) 17, 676; Colonial

Military Expenditure (1861) 328; Finance (1818) 324

see also self-government

Parnell, Charles Stewart (MP and Irish Nationalist leader) 505

Parnell, Katherine (widow of Charles) 529

Parsis 451, 460

Paterson, 'Banjo' (Australian entertainer) 560

Patidar caste (Gujarat) 453

Patteson, John Coleridge (Anglican missionary Bishop of Melanesia) 215, 244

Patuone (Maori chief) 579

pearling 559, 564–5

Pearson & Son, Samuel 263

Pedi people, southern Africa 606, 619

Pedro I, Emperor of Brazil 127

Sir Robert Peel, Second Baronet (Prime Minister) 40, 178

Peking (Beijing), China 157, 158, 164

Peking, Sino-French Treaty of (1860) 158

Pellegrini, Carlos (President of Argentina) 137, 139

Penang, Malay peninsula 372, 374, 375, 377, 378

Penang, Treaty of (1786) 372

Pender, Sir John (telegraphy entrepreneur and MP) 257, 260

Peninsular and Oriental Steam Navigation Company 258, 279, 377

Penjdeh Crisis (1885), Afghanistan 14, 341, 390

Perak, Malay peninsula 377, 383, 386

Peranakans (Malay-speaking Chinese) 457

Perlis, Malay peninsula 384, 388

Persia 11, 12, 14, 41, 434, 440

Persian Gulf 214, 673

Perth, Western Australia 546, 550

Peru 93, 110, 115, 127, 128, 132

petroleum 138, 391

Peshwa of Poona 395

Peters, Carl (German colonialist) 639

Phayre, Arthur (Commissioner of Lower Burma) 380

Philip, Dr John (missionary) 229, 237, 290, 599

Philippines, Pacific 13, 393

Phoenix Park, Dublin 516

phosphates 553

Phuti rising (1871) 629

Pierson, Arthur Tappan (American revivalist) 242

Pietermaritzburg, Natal 602

Pioneer Column 611

pirates 154, 156, 161, 378, 448

Pitt, William, the Younger (Prime Minister) 38, 199

plantations 65, 83, 88, 89, 92, 94, 96–7, 220, 549, 552–3, 557–8, 564, 570, 672

see also rubber; sugar; tea

Planters' Bank, Jamaica 483

Plate, River, Argentina 110, 130, 139
Platt, D. C. M. (historian) 119 n. 48, 134
Plowden, William (British political agent, Abyssinia) 109
police forces 151, 178, 185, 189, 428, 487, 496, 498, 516, 528, 533, 570, 581, 697
Polynesia, western Pacific 11, 556, 590–2
Pope-Hennessy, Sir John (Colonial governor) 177
Popham, Rear-Admiral Sir Home (British naval commander) 129–30, 131
population 5, 6, 22, 36–7, 53, 68, 93, 485, 567, 581–2
    of Canada 527, 533, 535
    depopulation 548–50, 556
    of Hong Kong 149, 163–4
Porfiriato, Porfiristas (Mexico) 135, 139
Port Arthur, Manchuria 434
Port Natal (Durban), South Africa 602
Port Pirie, South Australia 551
Port Said, Egypt 627
'Porteño' 127 n. 30
Porteous, Beilby (Bishop of London) 228
Porto Novo, western Africa 637, 639
Portugal 15, 108, 109, 125, 155, 211, 220, 606
    and African partition 632, 635, 637, 638, 640, 641, 643
    Anglo-Portuguese Convention (1890) 640, (1891) 641
    Anglo-Portuguese Treaty (1884) 220, 637
Potatau Te Wherowhero (Maori king) 585
Presbyterians 243, 289, 520, 528, 536
Pretoria, South Africa 618, 630
Pretoria Convention (1881) 608, 617, 629–30
Prince Edward Island, Canada 80, 185, 187, 523, 525, 527
printing 256, 257, 398, 458
Pritchard, W. T. (British Consul, western Pacific) 556
Privy Council, Judicial Committee of, see under law
Protection of our Commerce and Distribution of our Naval Forces, The (Colomb) 333–4
Protectorates 18, 118, 637, 638, 640, 644, 657, 671
    development of 190–6, 215, 217
    in Polynesia 591–2
    in Southern Africa 629, 630, 631, 641
    in Western Pacific 556–7, 559, 565
Protestantism, see Christianity
Province of Freedom, see Sierra Leone
Puebla 128
Punjab, India 7, 181, 322, 379, 401, 404, 444, 448, 458
    army 419
Purvis, Commodore John (naval commander, Brazil Station) 123

Qianlong, Emperor of China 146

Quakers 202, 210, 212, 219
Quarrier, William (juvenile migration promoter) 82
Quarterly Review 316
Quebec, Canada 81, 185, 223, 226, 533–4, 541, 542, 543
Quebec Conference (1864) 534, 540
Queen Adelaide Province, South Africa 207, 601
Queensland, Australia 24, 79, 88, 94–6, 215, 549, 550, 551, 553, 559, 563, 564, 566
quinine 306

race 10, 17, 21, 22–5, 97, 164, 198, 276–7, 280–1, 499, 509, 559, 619, 677, 685–6
    Anglo-Saxon 22, 24, 509, 686
    challenges to the idea of 24, 174, 491–2
    and class 182–3, 272–7, 564
    and culture 24, 174, 181–3, 213–14, 216–17, 284, 452, 560, 674–5
    and evolutionary biology 216, 285, 465
    extinction anticipated 22–3, 557, 563
    'Hottentots' 22, 499
    and Imperial unity 24–6, 356–7, 365–6, 509, 560, 619
    and India 402, 414, 419, 428
    and Ireland 499, 503, 511
    'Kaffirs' 503
    'martial races' 402, 414, 419, 428, 453, 467, 677
    'Orientals' 12, 459–61
    racism 125, 284, 491, 620, 675
    segregation 563, 570, 571, 581, 620
    and self-government 482, 491, 602, 603, 619, 620, 621, 655
    'social Darwinism' 24, 164, 285, 292, 491
    'white man's burden' 24, 217, 690
    'yellow peril' 146, 560, 567
    see also colonial administration; exploration; labour; land; law; migration
Races of Man (Knox) 286
railways 12, 38, 42, 48, 60, 80, 88, 117, 152, 250–1, 256–66, 268, 351, 389, 502, 561, 589, 694, 699, 701
    in Canada 38, 96, 529, 539, 540, 541, 543
    in China 166–7
    in India 38, 167, 417, 419, 441–2
    in Latin America 115, 135, 138, 143
    in South Africa 610, 611, 612, 630, 631, 642
Raffles, Sir (Thomas) Stamford (zoologist and Lieutenant-Governor of Java) 374
Rainbow, HMCS 544
Rajputs 413, 414, 415, 417, 419
Raleigh Club 295
Ram Mohan Roy, Raja (Indian scholar) 459
Rangihoua, New Zealand 575
Rangoon, Burma 389, 453, 458
Rangoon Municipality 468
Rapa, Polynesia 591

Rattlesnake, HMS 577
Recife, Brazil 135, 136
Reciprocity Treaty 529
Red Karens 389, 391
Red River, Canada 80, 523, 526, 528, 531, 543
Redmond, John Edward (MP and Irish
    Nationalist leader) 506
Reeves, William Pember (New Zealand Minister
    of Labour) 593–4
refrigeration 593
Religious Tract Society 289
representative government 20, 185–90, 487, 520,
    555
Representative Government (Mill) 425
republicanism 86, 290, 504–7, 512, 528, 540, 560,
    614, 619
responsible government 33, 41–2, 185, 187–9,
    212–13, 218, 232, 506, 538, 539, 546, 584
Réunion, Island, Indian Ocean 11, 92, 673
RGS, *see* Royal Geographical Society
Rhodes, Cecil John (entrepreneur, Cape Colony
    Prime Minister) 22, 194, 261, 263, 508, 527,
    610–12, 614, 630, 631, 640, 641, 642
Rhodesia 649
    'Pioneer Column' 611
Rhodesia, Northern 611
Rhodesia, Southern 194, 610–11, 621, 622, 642
Riau-Johore, South-East Asia 374, 375
Ricardo, David (economist) 106, 691
rice 56, 60, 61, 89, 391
Ridley, Henry (Director of the Singapore
    Botanical Gardens) 385
Riel, Louis (Canadian Métis leader) 528, 533, 536
Rio de Janeiro, Brazil 128, 130, 135
Rio del Rey, Africa 640
Ripon, George Frederick Samuel Robinson, First
    Marquis of (Secretary of State for the
    Colonies) 16
    (Viceroy of India) 432–3
RNC, *see* Royal Niger Company
Roberts, Frederick Sleigh, Lord Roberts of
    Kandahar and Waterford (1892)
    (Commander-in-Chief in India, Ireland and
    South Africa) 179, 341, 618
Robinson, Sir Hercules (High Commissioner in
    South Africa) 607, 630, 631
Robinson, Peter (promoter of Irish
    emigration) 513
Robinson, Ronald E. (historian) 119, 129 n. 29,
    134
Roebuck, John Arthur (British MP and Agent for
    Lower Canada) 523, 528
Rogers, Sir Frederick (Permanent
    Under-Secretary, Colonial Office) 191
Rolph, Thomas (emigration agent) 84
Roman Catholicism, *see* Christianity
romanticism 312–13

Rosas, Juan Manuel (President of Argentina)
    124 n. 10, 125, 130, 133
Roscoe, John (missionary) 241
Rosebery, Archibald Philip Primrose, Fifth Earl of
    (Foreign Secretary, Prime Minister) 358,
    643, 644, 645
Ross-Lewin, Richard Sargint Sadleir (Irish cleric,
    poet) 508, 511
Rothschild (bank) 552
Royal Colonial Institute 288
Royal Commission on the Civil and Professional
    Administration of the Naval and Military
    Departments (1888–90), *see* 'Hartington
    Commission'
Royal Commission on the Defence of British
    Possessions and Commerce Abroad
    (1879–81), *see* 'Carnarvon Commission'
Royal Commission on the Depression of Trade
    and Industry (1885) 358
Royal Commission on the West Indies (1898) 490
Royal Dublin Fusiliers 512
Royal Geographical Society 214–15, 216, 287,
    295–6, 297–302, 304, 306, 309, 310, 315, 316,
    674
    Keltie Report 318
Royal Inniskilling Fusiliers 512
Royal Niger Company 194, 230, 352, 638, 640, 641,
    645, 648
Royal Scottish Geographical Society 287, 288
Royal Society (London) 298, 300
Royal Society of Victoria 304
Ruakenana (Maori leader) 587
Ruapekapeka, New Zealand 581
Ruatara (Maori chief) 576
rubber 43, 60, 61, 62, 137, 138, 385
Ruskin, John (writer) 280, 281–2
Russell, John, First Earl (Secretary for War and
    Colonies) 91
    (Prime Minister) 41, 531–2
Russia 1, 10–14, 22, 166, 333, 334, 348, 404, 595, 657,
    704
    Anglo-Russian agreement (1907) 16, 393, 440,
    649, 707
    in Central Asia 262, 305, 322, 341, 401, 404, 434
Russo-Japanese War (1905) 466, 559
Ryder, Henry (Anglican Bishop of Gloucester)
    228
Rye, Maria (feminist, migration promoter) 81, 82

Sabi, River, central Africa 641
Sabine, Sir Edward (scientist) 302
Said, Edward W. (literary scholar and writer)
    270–1, 292, 310, 312, 399, 504
    see also historiography
St Augustine's College, Canterbury 233
Saint-Domingue (later Haiti), West Indies 470
St Helena, Atlantic 90

St John d'El Rey, Brazil 138
St John's, South Africa 604
St Kitts, Leeward Islands 477, 482, 488, 491
St Lawrence River, Canada 40, 523, 525, 526
St Lucia, West Indies 188
St Lucia Bay, southern Africa 637
St Vincent, Windward Islands 483, 485–6, 488, 489–90, 491
Salisbury, Robert Cecil, Third Marquis of (Secretary of State for India, Foreign Secretary and Prime Minister) 123, 137, 322, 341, 362, 390, 426, 432, 508
  and African partition 118, 352, 637, 638, 645, 648
  and Nile Valley 12, 632, 635, 639–40, 644
  and race 23, 182, 499
  and South Africa 262, 617, 631, 643, 649
Salvation Army 82, 282
Samoa, western Pacific 553, 556, 559, 590, 591, 592
Samori 639
San Francisco, California 131, 140
San Martin, José de (South American liberator) 124 n. 10
San Paulo Railway Company 138
Sand River Convention (1852) 602
sandalwood 552, 556, 564, 590
Saraswati, Swami Dayananda (Hindu sage) 465
Sarawak, Borneo 6, 378, 384, 448, 454
Sarmiento, Domingo Faustino (Argentinian liberal) 137
Saro (returned Yoruba people) 669–70
Schomburgk, Sir Robert Hermann (explorer) 296
schools, see education
Schreiner, William Philip (Prime Minister, Cape Colony) 621, 642
science, imperial role of, see anthropology; botany; cartography; colonial knowledge; exploration; geography; technology
Scotland, Scots 19, 20, 81, 84, 85, 271, 273–4, 287, 289–90
  Free Church of 79
  Protestantism 210, 225, 227, 510, 536
  see also Church of Scotland
Scott, Rose (Australian feminist) 569
sealing 575
Seddon, Richard John (Prime Minister, New Zealand) 591, 592, 594
Seeley, Sir John Robert (historian) 247–8, 285, 336, 346, 348–9
Selangor, Malay peninsula 383
Selborne, William Palmer, Second Earl of (First Lord of the Admiralty, High Commissioner in South Africa) 349, 507, 614, 642
  'Selborne Memorandum' 642

self-government 10, 17, 18, 21, 26, 104, 136, 185, 203, 205, 212–13, 467–8, 506, 583, 676, 709–10
  in West Indies 470, 474, 476–9
  see also representative government; responsible government
Selkirk, Thomas Douglas, Fifth Earl of (promoter of Canadian settlement) 80
Selwyn, George Augustus (Bishop of New Zealand and Melanesia) 233, 234, 591
Selwyn College, Cambridge 244
Senegal, Upper, West Africa 11, 636
Senegambia, West Africa 636
Seringapatam, Mysore, India 279
Service, Robert (poet) 75
settlement (white) 4, 5, 17, 20–1, 26, 45, 46, 51, 56, 84, 170–4, 190, 207–9
  limits to 61, 237, 525–6
  'neo-Europes' 55, 56–8, 61, 68–74, 311
  see also entries for individual territories
Seven Years War (1756–63) 323, 401, 470
Sewell, Henry (New Zealand politician) 584
Shanghai, China 149, 150–2, 155, 158, 163, 164, 165, 452, 456
  British role in 150–2, 159, 160, 161
Shannon, River, Ireland 503
Shantung, see Wei-hai-wei
Sharp, Granville (anti-slavery campaigner) 202, 218, 666–7
Sharpe, Sam (Baptist missionary) 476
Shearers' Union, Australia 566
sheep 551, 562–3, 588–9
shell 552
Sheppard, Kate (New Zealand suffragist) 594
Shepstone, Sir Theophilus (Secretary for Native Affairs, Natal) 606
Shimonoseki, Sino-Japanese Treaty of (1895) 150
shipbuilding 41, 695–6
shipping 36, 39, 41, 42, 46, 49, 83–4, 93, 97–8, 127, 155, 157, 167, 574–5, 577, 590, 695–6
  companies: British India Steam Navigation Co. 21, 98; Castle Line 21, 605; China Merchants Steam Navigation Co. 160; City Line 21; Clan Line 21; Irrawaddy Flotilla Co. 266; Peninsular and Oriental Steam Navigation Co. 258, 279, 377; Union Steam Ship Co. 605
  steamshipping 160–1, 249–50, 252, 256–66, 296, 305–6, 417, 636
Shiré, River, East Africa 640
Shona people, central Africa 611, 681, 682
Shore, Sir John, First Baron Teignmouth (Governor-General of Bengal) 200, 376
Shrewsbury, William (missionary) 474
Siam 9, 11, 91, 375, 377, 380–1, 382, 383–4, 387–9, 393, 434
  Anglo-Siamese Convention (1897) 388

Anglo-Siamese Treaties (1826) 375, (1855) 381, (1909) 384, 388
Siegfried, André (traveller, writer) 559 n. 42
Sierra Leone, West Africa 14–15, 90, 192, 194, 195, 207, 313, 626, 636, 648, 667–71, 686
 Hut Tax War (1898) 18, 196, 645
 Sierra Leone Company 207, 229
Sikhs 250, 419, 428, 544
silk 32, 35, 60
silver 58, 127, 403, 551
Simonstown, South Africa 614
Sind, India 5, 322, 401, 404
Singapore, Malay peninsula 6, 35, 93, 149, 374–5, 377, 378, 385, 388, 389, 401, 453, 454, 459
 ceded to Britain (1819) 374
Singh, Ranjit (Sikh leader) 401
Sinn Fein (Irish Republican movement) 505
Sipsong Chu Thai, Siam 388
Six Nations (Native Americans) 533
Slagtersnek rebellion (1815), Cape Colony 599
slave trade 15, 90, 95, 107–8, 126, 198, 201, 202, 209–11
 abolition of Atlantic 16, 91, 107, 109, 110, 113, 130–1, 203–4, 306, 638
 in East/Central Africa 214, 304, 309, 635, 638, 673–4
 treaties 107, 130, 206, 210–11, 215
slavery 17, 40, 88, 133, 172, 198, 201, 202, 216, 470–92, 675, 682–3
 see also anti-slavery; humanitarianism
slaves 7, 90, 203, 204, 231, 472–5, 513, 576, 599, 667
 emancipation of 204, 206, 474–8, 666
Slessor, Mary (missionary) 275
Small Sword Society 156
Smiles, Samuel (social reformer) 137, 281
Smith, Adam (economist) 16, 103, 106, 137, 171, 690–1, 692, 694, 703
Smith, Goldwin (Professor of Political Economy, Oxford University) 525, 541
Smith, John (missionary) 230
Smith, Sir (Henry George Wakelyn) Harry (Governor of Cape Colony) 177, 601–2
Smith, Sydney (Anglican clergyman and essayist) 232, 238
Smith, William A., see Cosmos, Amor de
smuggling 123, 126, 132, 154
Smuts, Jan Christian (Transvaal State Attorney, later Prime Minister of South Africa) 621
Social Democratic Federation 292
Society for Effecting the Abolition of the Slave Trade, see Abolition Society
Society for the Oversea Settlement of British Women 81
Society for the Promotion of Christian Knowledge 228, 289

Society for the Propagation of the Gospel 223, 224, 228
Society of Jesus (Jesuits) 510
Sokoto, West Africa 312, 640, 680
Solomon Islands, western Pacific 48, 193, 215, 549, 553, 557, 570
Somaliland, East Africa 635, 643, 644
Somerset, Lord Charles (Governor of Cape Colony) 177, 598–9
Somerset, James, case of 666
Sotho people, southern Africa 265, 603, 629
South Africa, see Africa, South
South African College (Cape Town) 226
South African League 614
South African Native Affairs Commission 620
South African Republic, see Transvaal
South African War (1899–1902) 10, 18, 26, 78, 90, 175, 266, 272, 343–4, 361–2, 434, 506, 512, 543, 559, 595, 615–19, 649, 676, 691–2, 705
 Africans and 618–19
 colonial contributions to 343, 512, 543, 559, 618–19
 concentration camps 178, 216, 618
 cost of 617
South Australia 171, 546, 551, 555, 569
South Island, New Zealand 585, 589
South Uist, Hebrides 81
soya beans 117
Spain, empire of 13, 102, 108, 109, 126, 393
Spain, William (Land Claims Commissioner in New Zealand) 580
SPCK, see Society for the Promotion of Christian Knowledge
Spears, Thomas (British agent in Burma) 380
Speke, John Hanning (explorer) 674
Spence, W. G. (Australian trade unionist) 565–6
Spencer, Herbert (philosopher and sociologist) 137, 285
SPG, see Society for the Propagation of the Gospel
sport 125, 136–7, 508–9 and n. 53, 531, 560
Stafford, Edward W. (Prime Minister of New Zealand) 330, 584
Stanley, see Derby, Edward George Geoffrey Smith, Fourteenth Earl of
Stanley, see Derby, Edward Henry, Fifteenth Earl of
Stanley, Henry Morton (explorer, journalist) 263, 287, 639, 674, 677
statutes:
 Quebec Act (1774) 6
 Pitt's India Act (1784) 199
 Navigation Act (1786) 38
 Constitutional Act for Canada (1791) 6, 224
 Act of Union (1801) 494–5, 501, 505
 Passenger Acts (1803–55) 77, 98, 514

statutes: (*cont.*):
  Corn Laws (1804, 1815, 1822, 1828) 38, 39, 103,
    106
  Slave Trade Abolition Act (1806) 203
  East India Co. Charter Renewal Act (1813) 39,
    395, 402
  East India Co. Charter Renewal Act (1833) 206,
    395
  (Emancipation) Abolition of Slavery Act
    (1833) 204, 205, 206
  Cape Colony Vagrancy Act (1834) 212
  Cape of Good Hope Punishment Act
    (1836) 192
  Bishops in Foreign Countries Act (1841) 233
  Coast of Africa and Falklands Act (1843) 192
  Foreign Jurisdiction Act (1843) 191, 209, 233
  Navigation (Consolidating) Act (1845) 40 n.
    44
  Sugar Duties Act (1846) 483
  Navigation Acts, repeal of (1849) 40
  Rebellion Losses Act (1849), Canada 326, 539
  Australian Colonies Government Act (1850)
    555
  New Zealand Representative Constitution Act
    (1852, amended 1857) 584
  Act to provide for the Government of India
    (1853) 395
  West Indies Incumbered Estates Act (1854) 488
  Municipalities Acts (1856–74) 460
  Gradual Civilization Act (1857), Canada 533
  Act for the Better Government of India
    (1858) 424
  Indian Councils Act (1861) 426–7
  Colonial Laws Validity Act (1865) 19, 189
  Colonial Naval Defence Act (1865) 333
  New Zealand Land Acts (1865, 1892) 587, 593
  British North America Act (1867) 532, 540, 542
  Elementary Education Act (1870) 285
  Landlord and Tenant (Ireland) Act (1870) 517
  Criminal Tribes Act (1871), India 467
  West African Settlements Jurisdiction Act
    (1871) 192
  The Kidnapping (Pacific Islanders Protection)
    Act (1872) 215, 533
  Pacific Islanders Protection Act (1875) 193
  Vernacular Press Act (1878), India 432
  Confederation and Annexation Act (1883),
    New Zealand 591
  Indian Advancement Act (1884), Canada 533
  Bengal Land Tenancy Act (1885), India 517
  Naval Defence Act (1889) 338
  Foreign Jurisdiction Act (1890) 195, 638, 640
  Indian Councils Act (1892) 433
  Aboriginal Protection and Restriction of the
    Sale of Opium Act (1897), Queensland 563,
    564
  Colonial Loans Act (1899) 351
  Colonial Stock Act (1900) 351
  Commonwealth of Australia Constitution Act
    (1900) 561
  Pacific Island Labourers Act (1907),
    Australia 564
  Indian Councils Act (1909) 439
  South Africa Act (1909) 621–2
  Empire Settlement Act (1922) 76
Steel-Maitland, Arthur (MP and Tariff Reformer)
  350 n. 21
Steere, Edward (missionary Bishop of Central
  Africa) 214
Stephen, Sir James (Under-Secretary for the
  Colonies) 17, 175, 177, 205, 478, 482, 580, 583
Stephen, Sir James Fitzjames, First Baronet (son
  of Sir James) (jurist) 433, 434
Stewart, George Vesey (Orangeman) 514
Stewart, James (explorer) 316
Stokes (merchant family) 412
Stokes, John Lort (naval captain) 302
Stormberg, Battle of (1899) 617
Stout, Robert (New Zealand lawyer and Prime
  Minister) 591
Strachan, John (Archdeacon, and first Bishop of
  Toronto) 226, 227
Strangford, Percy Clinton Sydney Smythe, Sixth
  Viscount (British minister in Lisbon and
  Brazil) 123
Straits Chinese 451
Straits Settlements, South-East Asia 16, 90, 92,
  94, 375, 377–8, 382, 386, 454, 457, 513
Strathcona, Donald Alexander Smith, First Baron
  (Canadian High Commissioner) 542
Stuart, John McDouall (explorer) 309, 313
Student Volunteer Movement 242–3
Sturge, Joseph (anti-slavery campaigner) 203,
  204, 210, 211, 214–15, 218, 478
Sturt, Charles (Australian soldier and
  explorer) 302, 303, 307, 309, 562
Sudan 11, 18, 265, 266, 279, 342, 343, 543, 559, 634,
  640, 641, 643, 644, 648, 649, 654
  Anglo-Egyptian Condominium 655
  reconquest of 617, 655
Sudbury Basin, Canada 527
Suez Canal 9, 14, 112, 252, 258, 322, 341, 377, 443,
  604, 614
  strategic importance of 626–8, 632–3, 634, 653,
    654
Suez Canal Company 112
suffrage:
  Australia 555, 560, 569, 570
  Canada 532
  New Zealand 583–4, 590, 594
  West Indies 482
sugar 32, 33, 36, 40, 42, 60, 62, 88, 92, 94, 135, 190,
  211, 470–93, 553, 564
Sullivan (merchant family) 412

Sunshine Sketches of a Little Town (Leacock) 531
Suppression of Dangerous Societies
    Ordinances 454
Surat, India 230
suttee (sati) 395, 457, 461
suzerainty 608, 630
Swahili-speaking peoples, East Africa 635, 640
Swan, River, Western Australia 171
Swaziland, southern Africa 261, 622, 630–1, 642
Sweden 703
Swoboda, Rudolf (artist) 284
Sydney, New South Wales 7, 225, 519, 546, 548,
    550, 552, 576
    Bulletin (newspaper) 560
Symes, Michael, Captain (envoy to Burma) 376
Syria, Syrians 643, 651
'systematic colonization' 172, 513, 514, 578, 582
    see also Wakefield
Szechwan, China 161

Taché, Etienne (French Canadian politician) 531,
    535
Tagore, Rabindranath (Indian writer and
    philosopher) 506
Tahiti, Pacific 556, 558, 590
'Taikoo', *see* Butterfield and Swire
Taiping Rebellion, *see* China
Talbot, Colonel Thomas (Canadian settlement
    promoter) 80
Tamati Waka Nene (Maori chief) 579
Taraia (Maori chief) 580
Taranaki, New Zealand 585–6, 587
Taranaki War 329
Tariff Commission 355
Tasmania, Australia 78, 185, 188, 546, 555
Tata family (industrialists, India) 266
Tataraimaka, New Zealand 585, 586
Taupo, New Zealand 585
Tawfiq, Khedive of Egypt 633, 634, 653–4, 655
Tawhiao (Maori king) 587
taxation 18, 151, 157, 165, 172, 181, 482, 487, 491,
    495, 557–8, 560, 565, 584, 592–3, 625, 676, 682,
    684
    in Egypt 633, 653, 660, 662
    in India 399–400, 402–3, 407–8, 409–11, 416,
    430–1
    see also commercial policy
Taylor, Henry (Colonial Office senior clerk) 205,
    476, 479, 482
Taylor, Phillip Meadows (writer) 406
Te Kooti (Maori chief) 586–7
Te Pahi (Maori chief) 576
Te Ruaparaha (Maori chief) 576–7
Te Ua Haumene Tuwhakaro (Maori religious
    leader) 587
Te Whiti (Maori chief) 587
tea 32, 43, 60, 62, 552

technology 16, 27, 56, 179, 247–69, 277, 311, 314–17,
    523–4, 702–3, 705
    and imperial control 248, 252, 257, 260–4, 266,
    267–8, 316, 435–7, 466, 687–8
    norms and values 247, 256, 257, 267–8, 286, 311,
    316–18, 456
    transfer 249, 251, 256, 262, 264–8, 482, 488, 551,
    553, 558, 575–6, 579, 612, 617, 652
    see also exploration; medicine; railways;
    shipping; telegraphs
telegraphs 247, 251–2, 257, 259–62, 268, 417, 589,
    605, 694
    'All Red [Cable] Route' 336, 347
Tel-el-Kebir, Battle of (1882) 279, 634, 654
Temne people, of Koya 667
Texas, United States 531
Thailand, Thais, *see* Siam
Thames, River, England 503
Theosophy 464–5
Thibaw, King of Burma 389, 390
Thierry, Baron de (French adventurer) 577
Things Fall Apart (Achebe) 682
Thomas, J. J. (Trinidadian activist) 491
Thomason, Thomas (East India Company
    chaplain) 230
Thomson, Joseph (explorer) 308, 309, 311, 312,
    313, 316, 318
Thorne, Dr Albert (Barbadian activist) 492
Thornton, Henry (evangelical reformer) 200,
    228
Thursday Island, western Pacific 564
Tibet 434, 440
Tidore, Moluccas, East Indies 558
Tientsin (Tianjin), China 149–50, 151, 152, 161
Tigris, River, Middle East 305–6
Tilak, Bal Gangadhar (radical Indian nationalist)
    439
Tilsit, Treaty of (1807) 13
timber 33, 4, 36, 38, 42, 62, 83, 379, 391, 575
Times, The 129, 535
tin 43
Tipu Sultan (ruler of Mysore) 274, 276
Titokowaru (Maori chief) 586–7
Tiv people, West Africa 682
tobacco 60, 552, 553
Tobago, West Indies 477, 481, 482, 483, 486,
    487
Togo, West Africa 637, 639, 640, 648
Tolstoy, Leo Nikolayevich, Count (writer) 535
Tommy Atkins (fictitious character) 278
Tonga, western Pacific 556, 590, 591, 630
Tongaland, South Africa 630
Toronto, Canada 81, 525, 526, 527, 536
Torres Strait 548, 558, 564–5
Tottenham Hotspur, football team 508
Tozer, William George (missionary Bishop of
    Central Africa) 214

trade 5, 6–7, 9–10, 16, 19, 20, 31–74, 101–69, 626,
  627, 694–8
  Empire and balance-of-payments 49–50, 62–3
  Empire share of British 32–6, 42–5
  18th and 19th centuries compared 53–55, 58–9,
    62–3
  Napoleonic Wars and 34, 35, 38, 39
  statistics 31–74, 110–13, 116–17, 119, 127, 135,
    161–2, 335, 417, 605, 627, 659, 661
  see also entries for separate commodities,
    commercial policy, *and* economy and trade
    under individual territories
trade unions 22, 491, 548, 556, 565–7, 568, 593–4
Trafalgar, Battle of (1805) 203
Transkei, South Africa 604
transportation 172, 513, 549, 555
  see also railways; shipping
Transvaal, South Africa 6, 22, 23, 90, 94, 95, 265,
  602, 606, 607–21, 628–32, 637, 641,
  642–3
Transvaal War (1880–81) 607–8, 617
treaties 13, 15, 38, 146, 148, 150–3, 208–9, 636–40,
  645
  see also individual entries; slave trade
Trengganu, Malay peninsula 384, 389
Trevelyan, Sir Charles Edward (Assistant
  Secretary to the Treasury) 498
Trinidad, West Indies 122, 175, 470, 473, 482, 488,
  489, 490, 491–2
  government of 185, 188, 205, 477
  indentured labour in 88, 96, 212, 483, 484,
    485
Trinity College, *see under* Dublin
Triple Entente 440
Tripolitania, Africa 15
trusteeship 151, 173–5, 198–9, 201, 216–17, 219–20
Tryon, George, Rear-Admiral (Commander of
  the Australian Station) 337
Tswana people, southern Africa 20, 240, 628, 630,
  631
Tucker, Alfred (Anglican Bishop of Uganda) 238
Tunisia, North Africa 640
  Anglo-Tunisian Convention 639
Turco-Circassians 633, 634, 652
Turkey, *see* Ottoman empire
Tuwharetoa 580
Twi language 671

Uganda, East Africa 177, 194, 639, 643–4, 685
  missions and Christianity in 220, 237, 238, 239
  Uganda railway 258, 351, 644
Uitlanders 609–10, 612, 614, 615, 642
Ukrainians 535
Ulster 156, 536
Uniacke family, Nova Scotia 536
Union Jack (Union flag) 537
United Church of South India 243

United States of America 13, 15, 20, 21–2, 24,
  45, 56, 57, 158, 291, 353, 490, 529, 621, 701,
  702
  and Canada 171, 178, 187, 331, 364, 523, 530–2,
    538, 542
  Civil War (1860–65) 41, 57, 214, 530
  Constitution of 531
  expansionism 131, 140, 158, 233, 348, 393
  migration to 36–7, 46–7, 58, 77, 84
  and the Pacific 589–90, 591–2
  relations with Britain 127, 138–42, 171, 187, 393,
    523, 703–8, 709
  trade with Britain 32, 34, 38–9, 45, 50, 57,
    62–3
  War of 1812 39, 522
universities 158, 226, 288, 299, 431–2, 458, 509–10,
  520, 575, 670
Universities' Mission to Central Africa 214, 237,
  241
Urabi, Ahmad, Colonel (leader of nationalist
  revolt in Egypt) 633, 634, 653, 655
urbanization 22, 27, 62, 150–2, 290, 452–4, 550,
  696, 702
  see also cities
Uruguay 56, 110, 123, 130, 131, 143

Vaal, River, South Africa 628
Van Diemen's Land, *see* Tasmania
Vancouver, Canada 532
Vancouver, George (explorer) 307
Vanuatu, western Pacific 553
Vellore, India 230
Venezuela 13, 123, 125, 130, 131–2, 135
Venn, Henry (cleric and Church Missionary
  Society secretary) 236–7, 238
Vereeniging, Treaty of (1902) 619, 620
Verne, Jules (writer) 257
Victoria, Australia 79, 234, 304, 337, 546, 550, 551,
  555, 569
Victoria, Lake (East Africa) 674
Victoria, Queen of Great Britain and Ireland
  (1837–1901), 18, 290, 422–4, 431
  Empress of India (1876) 431
  and Indian Army 427–8
  see also monarchy
Vienna, Treaty of (1815) 374
Vietnam, *see* Indo-China
Villiers (Johan Hendrik) Sir Henry de (Chief
  Justice of Cape Colony and politician)
  607
Viti Levu, *see* Fiji
Vivekananda, Swami (Bengali seer) 465
Vogel, Julius (New Zealand politician and Prime
  Minister) 589, 591

Waikato, New Zealand 586, 587, 588
Wairau Valley, New Zealand 580

Waitangi, Treaty of (1840) 192, 578–80, 581–2, 583, 588
Waitara, New Zealand 585, 586
Wakefield, Edward Gibbon (New Zealand colonizer) 76–7, 84, 104, 172, 514
and later economists 691, 692
and New Zealand 578, 582, 584, 588
see also migration; systematic colonization
Wales 22, 84, 271
Wallace, Alfred Russel (scientist) 298, 300
Waller, Reverend Horace (humanitarian campaigner) 214–15
War Office 327–8, 342, 616, 626
Warren, Sir Charles (Royal Engineer and military commander) 608, 630
Washington, John (hydrographer) 296
Washington, Treaty of (1871) 529
Waterloo, Battle of (1815) 522
weaponry 247, 250, 252, 265–6, 612, 617, 705
Weber, Max (sociologist) 688
Webb, Beatrice and Sidney (social reformers) 429–30, 499
Wei-hai-wei, China 149, 434
Weld, Frederick A. (New Zealand colonist and Prime Minister) 329, 586
Wellesley, Richard Colley, Marquis (Governor-General of India) 200
Wellington, Arthur Wellesley, First Duke of (soldier and Prime Minister) 12
Wesleyan Methodist Missionary Society 556, 590, 675
Wesleyans, *see* Methodists
West Africa Frontier Force 342
West African Countries and Peoples (Horton) 675
West Indian Bank 483
West Indies 5, 10, 13, 42, 83, 88, 90, 140, 180, 204, 206, 211, 324, 326, 359, 470–92
'amelioration' 203, 212, 225
economy and trade 32, 34, 36, 40–1, 470–2, 476, 482–4, 488–92
free coloureds 190, 472–3, 479–80
government, structure of 189–90, 487–8, 491
migration to 90–3, 96, 98, 212, 484
planters and technology 482, 488
politics of 474–5, 478–9, 482–3
see also individual territories; labour; migration; slavery
Western Australia 78, 171, 188, 212, 546
westernization 107, 174–5, 181–3, 387
in Asia 435–6, 455–7, 458–61
whaling 552, 564, 575
'Whampoa', *see* Hoo Ah Kay
Whately, Richard (Archbishop of Dublin) 503, 504
wheat 40, 43, 46, 48, 62, 112, 135, 138, 551
Whig Party 203, 204, 210, 232

While the Billy Boils (Lawson) 568
Wilberforce, Samuel, son of William (Anglican Bishop of Oxford) 233
Wilberforce, William (MP and anti-slavery campaigner) 200, 202, 203, 204, 209, 218, 233, 275, 474
Wilkie, Sir David (artist) 274
Williams, Eric (West Indian historian and politician) 470
Williams, Henry and Marianne (missionaries) 575–6, 579
Williams, John (missionary) 239
Williams, John C. (consul, son of John) 556
Wilson, Daniel (Anglican Bishop of Calcutta) 231
Wilson's High School and College, Bombay 236
windmills 482
Wiradjuri people, Australia 562
Wiremu Kingi (Maori chief) 585
Witu, East Africa 640
Witwatersrand, Transvaal 609, 611
Wodehouse, Sir Philip (Governor of the Cape Colony) 603
Wolfe, General James 537
Wolff, Sir Henry Charles Drummond (British diplomat) 634, 635
Wolseley, Sir Garnet, later Viscount (military commander) 629, 633, 634, 676–7, 686
women 23, 24, 25, 198, 203, 271, 275, 277, 287–8, 306, 309, 453, 464, 570, 582–3, 590, 594
convicts 78, 567
employment 90, 484, 514, 563, 567, 568, 575, 662–3
migration of 81–2, 514, 567–8, 582–3
prostitution 456, 559
status of 449, 453, 455–7, 464, 567–9, 581, 662–3
in Australia 563, 567–9, 570
in Canada 532–3
Wood, Sir Charles (President of the Board of Control, and Secretary of State for India) 174–5, 425–6, 428
Wood, Sir (Henry) Evelyn (Commander-in-Chief, Egyptian Army, and field marshal) 634
Woodford, Commissioner (western Pacific official) 557
wool 33, 35, 42, 43, 62, 135, 589, 592, 551
World Missionary Conferences (1900; 1910) 243
World War (1914–18) 21, 27, 162, 706–8
Wyndham, George (Chief Secretary for Ireland) 350 n. 21, 356–7
Wynyard, Colonel R. H. (Administrator of New Zealand) 584

Xhosa people, southern Africa 597, 598, 601, 602, 603, 684

Yandabo, Treaty of (1826) 376, 379
Yangtze (Yangtzi), River and region 114, 149, 150, 159–60
Yao people, East Africa 673
Yihetuan, *see* China, Boxer Rebellion
Yoruba people, West Africa 645, 668–71, 686
Young Bengal radicals 459
Young Men's Buddhist Association 392, 465
Yuan Shih K'ai (Chinese leader) 165, 168
Yukon gold rush 527

Zambezi, River, central Africa 237, 256, 267, 296, 304, 611, 635, 638, 640, 674
zamindars 517

Zanzibar, East Africa 11, 214, 635, 638, 639, 644, 673, 674, 678
  Anglo-Zanzibar Treaty (1845) 211
  Anglo-Zanzibar Treaty (1873) 215
  Britain's early presence at 15, 16, 113–14
  British modes of influence in 190, 191
  British Protectorate recognized 640
Zapatistas 143
zinc 551
Zulu people, South Africa 265, 342, 602, 603, 681
Zulu War (1879) 606, 617
Zululand, South Africa 606, 608, 629, 649, 684

8/03

Robotic Explorations

A Hands-On Introduction to Engineering

Robotic Explorations

A Hands-On Introduction to Engineering

Fred G. Martin

PRENTICE HALL
Upper Saddle River, New Jersey 07458

Library of Congress Cataloging-in-Publication Data

Martin, Fred G.
    Robotic explorations: a hands-on introduction to engineering/Fred G. Martin.
        p. cm.
    Includes bibliographical references and index.
    ISBN 0-13-089568-7
     1. Robotics. 2. Engineering design. I. Title.
    TJ211 .M36645 2001
    629.8′92–dc 21   00-058013

Publisher: Tom Robbins
Editorial Assistant: Jessica Power
Vice President and Editorial Director, ECS: Marcia J. Horton
Vice President and Director of Production and Manufacturing, ESM: David W. Riccardi
Production Supervision: Barbara A. Till
Managing Editor: David A. George
Executive Managing Editor: Vince O'Brien
Manufacturing Buyer: Pat Brown
Manufacturing Manager: Trudy Pisciotti
Marketing Manager: Holly Stark
Marketing Assistant: Karen Moon
Creative Director: Paul Belfanti
Art Director: Jayne Conte
Cover Designer: Bruce Kenselaar
Art Editor: Adam Velthaus

Printed in the United States of America
10 9 8 7 6 5 4 3

ISBN 0-13-089568-7

Prentice-Hall International (UK) Limited, *London*
Prentice-Hall of Australia Pty. Limited, *Sydney*
Prentice-Hall Canada Inc., *Toronto*
Prentice-Hall Hispanoamericana, S.A., *Mexico*
Prentice-Hall of India Private Limited, *New Delhi*
Prentice-Hall of Japan, Inc., *Tokyo*
Pearson Education Asia Pte. Ltd. *Singapore*
Editora Prentice-Hall do Brasil, Ltda., *Rio de Janeiro*

Contents

Acknowledgments ix

1 Introduction 1

1.1 Feedback Control, Cybernetics, and Robotics **1**
1.2 Toys to Think With **4**
  1.2.1 LEGO/Logo 9
  1.2.2 The Programmable Brick 10
  1.2.3 The MIT 6.270 Robot Design
        Competition 11
1.3 About the Technology **12**
  1.3.1 The Handy Board 12
  1.3.2 Interactive C 15
  1.3.3 LEGO® Technic® 16
1.4 An Overview of the Book **17**

2 A First Robot 20

2.1 Interactive C and the Handy Board **20**
  2.1.1 Interactive C Prompt 21
  2.1.2 Motors 22
  2.1.3 Sensors 23
  2.1.4 Files and Functions 25
  2.1.5 The Main Function 26
2.2 The HandyBug **28**
  2.2.1 HandyBug 9645 28
  2.2.2 HandyBug 9719 50
2.3 A First Program **71**
  2.3.1 Plugging in Motors and Sensors 72
  2.3.2 Obstacle Avoidance 72
  2.3.3 Obstacle-Avoidance Exercises 73
  2.3.4 Turtle Movements 74
  2.3.5 Turtle Movement Exercises 74
2.4 Braitenberg Vehicles **75**
  2.4.1 One Motor and One Sensor 76
  2.4.2 Two Motors and Two Sensors 76

  2.4.3 Multisensor Vehicles 78
  2.4.4 Light Sensors 80
  2.4.5 Coding Braitenberg Vehicles 80
2.5 Light and Touch Sensitivity **86**
  2.5.1 Light and Touch Exercises 87
2.6 Randomness **87**
  2.6.1 Random Exercises 89
2.7 Emergence and Meta-Sensing **89**
  2.7.1 Emergence 90
  2.7.2 Meta-Sensing 91
  2.7.3 Emergence and Meta-Sensing
        Exercises 92
2.8 Conclusion **94**

3 Sensors 96

3.1 Sensor Interfacing **96**
  3.1.1 Digital Inputs 96
  3.1.2 Analog Inputs 98
  3.1.3 Ohm's Law 99
  3.1.4 Ohm's Law Exercise 101
3.2 Building Sensors **101**
  3.2.1 Connector Wiring 101
  3.2.2 Sensor Mounting 103
3.3 Switch Sensors **104**
  3.3.1 Switch Sensor Construction 105
  3.3.2 Switch Sensor Applications
        Examples 107
3.4 Light Sensor Circuits **108**
  3.4.1 The Single-Photocell Circuit 108
  3.4.2 The Differential Photocell
        Sensor 111
  3.4.3 Polarized Light Seeking 114
3.5 Resistive Position Sensors **115**
  3.5.1 Bend Sensors 115
  3.5.2 Potentiometers 116
3.6 Reflective Optosensors **118**
  3.6.1 Applications 120
  3.6.2 Interfacing 121

3.6.3   Building It   123
3.6.4   Correcting for Ambient Light   125
3.6.5   Exercises and Projects   126
3.7   Break-Beam Sensors   **127**
3.7.1   Interfacing   129
3.7.2   Building the Break-Beam Sensor   129
3.7.3   Object Detection   130
3.7.4   Break-Beam Exercises   130
3.8   Shaft Encoding   **130**
3.8.1   Counting Encoder Clicks   131
3.8.2   Driver Software   134
3.8.3   Measuring Velocity   136

4 *Motors, Gears, and Mechanism* 139

4.1   DC Motors   **139**
4.1.1   Exercises   140
4.2   Gearing   **143**
4.2.1   Meshing Gears   145
4.2.2   Exercise   146
4.3   Electronic Control   **146**
4.3.1   The H-Bridge Motor Driver Circuit   146
4.3.2   Enable and Direction Logic   147
4.3.3   Active Braking   147
4.3.4   Speed Control   149
4.3.5   Handy Board Implementation   150
4.3.6   Exercises   151
4.4   The Servo Motor   **152**
4.4.1   The Servo Control Signal   152
4.4.2   Generating the Control Waveform   155
4.4.3   Continuous Rotation   156
4.4.4   Exercises   157
4.5   LEGO Design   **157**
4.5.1   Structure   157
4.5.2   Gearing   159
4.5.3   Mechanism   167
4.5.4   Exercises   172

5 *Control* 174

5.1   Simple Feedback Control   **174**
5.1.1   Wall Following   175
5.1.2   Gentle Turning Algorithm   179
5.1.3   Exercises   179
5.2   Proportional-Derivative Control   **179**
5.2.1   Proportional Control   182
5.2.2   The Derivative Term   188
5.2.3   Exercises   189

5.3   Sequential Control   **190**
5.3.1   The Robo-Pong Contest   190
5.3.2   Sequential Strategies   194
5.3.3   Exercise: Groucho's Program   198
5.3.4   Exit Conditions   199
5.3.5   Exercise: Groucho with Timeouts   206
5.4   Reactive Control   **206**
5.4.1   A Priority-Based Control Program   208
5.4.2   How the Prioritization Algorithm
          Works   214
5.4.3   Using Reactive Control   219
5.4.4   Exercises: Reactive Control   221
5.5   Conclusion   **223**

6 *Advanced Sensing* 224

6.1   Quadrature Shaft Encoding   **224**
6.1.1   Construction Notes   226
6.1.2   Driver Code   228
6.1.3   Using the Driver   232
6.1.4   Quadrature Encoder Exercises   232
6.2   Infrared Sensing   **233**
6.2.1   Modulation and Demodulation   234
6.2.2   Proximity Sensing   237
6.2.3   Using Proximity Sensors   238
6.2.4   IR LED Exercises   239
6.2.5   Advanced IR Proximity Sensing   240
6.2.6   Infrared Communications   251
6.3   Ultrasonic Distance Sensing with the
       Polaroid 6500   **271**
6.3.1   Connection Diagram   275
6.3.2   Basic Driver Code   276
6.3.3   Driver with Close-Up Capability   278
6.3.4   A Test Routine   279
6.3.5   Converting Time Measurements to
          Actual Distance   279
6.3.6   Sonar Exercises   279
6.4   Optical Distance Sensing with the Sharp
       GP2D02   **280**
6.4.1   Connection Diagram   281
6.4.2   Construction Notes   281
6.4.3   Sensor Communications Timing   282
6.4.4   Driver Code   283
6.4.5   Optical Ranging Exercises   285
6.5   Sensor Data Processing   **286**
6.5.1   Line Following as a Reference
          Activity   286
6.5.2   Fixed Thresholding   287
6.5.3   Parameterized Fixed Thresholding   287
6.5.4   Thresholding with Hysteresis   288

6.5.5   Calibration by Demonstration   289
6.5.6   Persistent Calibration   291
6.5.7   Sensor Histories   291

A Inside the Handy Board Design   308

A.1   Introduction to Microprocessors and the
68HC11   **308**
  A.1.1   Bits, Bytes, and Characters   308
  A.1.2   Memory Map   310
  A.1.3   Registers   312
  A.1.4   Evaluation Sequence   313
  A.1.5   Machine Code Versus Assembly
          Language   313
  A.1.6   Addressing Modes   314
  A.1.7   Data Types   316
  A.1.8   Arithmetic Operations   316
  A.1.9   Signed and Unsigned Binary Numbers   317
  A.1.10 Condition Code Register and Conditional
          Branching   318
  A.1.11 Stack Pointer and Subroutine Calls   319
  A.1.12 Interrupts and Interrupt Routines   320
A.2   Introduction to Assembly Language
Programming   **321**
  A.2.1   Development Cycle   322
  A.2.2   Write the Source Code   322
  A.2.3   Assemble the Source Code   324
  A.2.4   Download the Object File   326
  A.2.5   Run the Program   327
  A.2.6   Delay Loops and Subroutines   327
  A.2.7   Digital Sensors and the User Buttons   329
A.3   The 68HC11 with the Handy Board Hardware   **330**
  A.3.1   Architecture of the 68HC11   331
  A.3.2   Microprocessor and Memory   332
  A.3.3   Peripherals   336
  A.3.4   Analog Inputs   346
  A.3.5   The Serial Line Circuit   347
  A.3.6   The Infrared Transmission
          Circuit   353
  A.3.7   The LCD Display   355
  A.3.8   Piezo Beeper and Interrupt
          Routines   360
  A.3.9   Power and Battery Charging   368
A.4   The AS11 Assembler   **372**
  A.4.1   Labels   372
  A.4.2   Arithmetic Expressions   372
  A.4.3   Assembler Pseudo-Operations   372
  A.4.4   Comments   373
A.5   Differences Between A and E Series 68HC11
CPUs   **375**

B Construction Techniques   376

B.1   DC Motor   **376**
  B.1.1   Motor Compatibility   376
  B.1.2   Motor Wiring   377
  B.1.3   Interfacing Hobby Motors to the
          LEGO Technic System   377
B.2   Servo Motors   **379**
  B.2.1   Electrical Interface   379
  B.2.2   Continuous Rotation   379
B.3   Infrared Sensor and Transmitter   **381**
B.4   LEGO Adapter Cables   **382**

C Serial Communications and Data Collection   384

C.1   Serial Line Interaction   **384**
C.2   Connecting to a Terminal Program   **386**
C.3   Printing to the Serial Line   **387**
  C.3.1   Exercises   389
C.4   Capturing Data   **389**
  C.4.1   Exercises   389

D Handy Board Specification   391

D.1   Specifications   **391**
D.2   Ports and Connectors   **392**
D.3   Battery Maintenance   **394**
  D.3.1   Battery Charging   394
  D.3.2   Adapter Specifications   394
D.4   Part Listing   **395**
D.5   Printed Circuit Board Layouts   **396**
  D.5.1   Handy Board Component Side   396
  D.5.2   Handy Board Solder Side   397
  D.5.3   Handy Board Silkscreen   398
  D.5.4   Interface/Charger Board Component
          Side   399
  D.5.5   Interface/Charger Board Solder
          Side   399
  D.5.6   Interface/Charger Board Silkscreen   400

E Interactive C Reference   401

E.1   Quick Start   **401**
E.2   6811 Downloaders   **401**
  E.2.1   Overview   401
  E.2.2   Putting the Handy Board into
          Bootstrap Download Mode   402

E.2.3   MS-DOS   402
E.2.4   Windows 3.1 and Windows 95   402
E.2.5   Macintosh   402
E.2.6   Unix   403
E.3   Interactive C   **403**
E.3.1   Using IC   404
E.3.2   A Quick C Tutorial   405
E.3.3   Data Types, Operations, and
        Expressions   407
E.3.4   Control Flow   410
E.3.5   LCD Screen Printing   411
E.3.6   Arrays and Pointers   413
E.3.7   Library Functions   415
E.3.8   Multitasking   419
E.3.9   Floating Point Functions   421
E.3.10 Memory Access Functions   422
E.3.11 Error Handling   422
E.3.12 Binary Programs   423
E.3.13 IC File Formats and Management   428
E.3.14 Configuring IC   429

F   *Robot Contests   430*

F.1   Introduction   **430**
F.1.1   Why Robot Contests?   430
F.1.2   Why Not Contests?   430
F.1.3   Types of Contests   431
F.1.4   Social Message   432

F.2   Sample Contests   **432**
F.2.1   Kick the Can   432
F.2.2   Robo-Golf   434
F.2.3   Robo-Pong   436
F.2.4   Egg Hunt   438
F.3   Contest Rule Analysis   **441**
F.3.1   Materials   441
F.3.2   Design   442
F.3.3   Robot Size   443
F.3.4   Multiple-Robot Entries   443
F.3.5   Creativity Rule   444
F.3.6   Starting the Round   444
F.3.7   Robot Beaconing   444
F.3.8   Playing Field Features   445
F.3.9   Practical Concerns   446
F.4   Conclusion   **446**

G   *Resources   447*

References   449

Index   451

Acknowledgments

The roots of this work can be traced back to the "6.270" MIT Robot Design course, begun by Mike Parker. After two years of software-only competitions, with his contagious enthusiasm, Mike recruited Randy Sargent and myself to create hardware for the third year of the project.

Randy and I worked together developing a series of controller boards and software for our students. Pankaj Oberoi joined the project, contributing a great love of learning and working with students, along with strong organizational skills.

During this time I was a graduate student in Seymour Papert's research group at the MIT Media Laboratory. I owe a great debt to Seymour for many things: his inspiring and controversial ideas about learning, his specific vision of computation as a learning toy, and his wonderful way.

As a Ph.D. student I had the great fortune to work with two other fantastic individuals. Edith Ackermann was my advisor, and as I said in my dissertation, she was able to find and connect the strands of meaning in what initially seemed to me as only a mess of interesting issues.

I also had the opportunity to work with Don Schön. Don was extraordinarily generous with his time, and his insight that "design is a conversation with the materials of a situation" continues to guide my thinking.

The LEGO company has always supported my work, as a sponsor of the Media Laboratory, contributing directly to the Robot Design project, and in many other ways. I'd like to thank Allan Toft, a LEGO engineer with whom I worked on our first "programmable brick" when he was stationed at MIT for a year in 1987.

I first met Steve Ocko when he was a researcher at MIT; he later worked for LEGO for a number of years. Steve's love of play and his childlike creativity always inspires me. Probably without realizing it, he also taught me how to design with LEGO Technic.

Robert Rasmussen, head of LEGO's educational Dacta division in the United States, has been a close colleague and supporter of my work for many years. In his group I'd like to also thank Cathy Fett, who generously proofread this book, and Allen Demers, who contributed to the *HandyBug* design presented herein.

This book has had many caretakers on its way to print. It began when Tim Cox, then an acquisitions editor at Benjamin-Cummings, saw a copy of my course notes for the Robot Design class and realized that this robot stuff was going to become popular. Thanks Tim, for believing in me and these ideas.

Benjamin-Cummings was then in the process of being acquired by Addison-Wesley, which shortly thereafter became Addison Wesley Longman. Paul Becker helped move things along during that time.

At last, Prentice Hall acquired portions of AWL, and Tom Robbins and Barbara Till took over management of my project. Tom saw that the book was essentially done and set in motion actual publication, thereby forcing me to finish it off. Barbara helped me through the final stages of editing and proofing. My thanks to both of you.

I'd like to thank the reviewers organized by my editorial team. In addition, I'd like to thank Maja Mataric for her perspective and her contributed sidebar, and Rich Drushel for his contribution in the contest design section.

Finally, I'd like to thank my wife Wanda, whose constant support and encouragement has kept me happy in so many ways.

Robotic Explorations

A Hands-On Introduction to Engineering

1 *Introduction*

Welcome to *Robotic Explorations: A Hands-On Introduction to Engineering*. On the surface, this text is about the practice, technique, and theory behind mobile robotic systems, but it is different from most texts because you have to build a robot to learn about how they work. In doing so, you learn not only about robots, but about technological systems of all kinds—electrical, mechanical, and computational. More important, you engage in engineering design and problem solving as you work on activities and projects inspired by your own ideas.

Soon enough, we'll have the soldering irons, motors, gears, and chips out to play with, but to get started, let's take a quick tour through years of thinking about *feedback control*—a way of understanding systems that is of central importance to our explorations of robotics.

Next in this introduction, we examine an entirely different sort of history—a collection of toys. These toys are of strong personal meaning because they are toys I owned as a child. But they are unusual toys, and relevant to our discussion, because they were designed to let young learners explore key ideas in technology like process, program, and algorithm.

The "toy stories" lead into a discussion of some more advanced toys, including some designed at the Massachusetts Institute of Technology (MIT) beginning in the 1960s. Like the toys I played with as a child, these MIT toys were designed to help kids learn.

That is what this book is about: a yet more sophisticated set of toys (call it educational technology if you like) that is specifically designed to lead students into thought-provoking and challenging engineering situations. In other words, while the set of toys you will be using alongside this text will let you build mobile robots, the real work is in your hands, thinking hard about issues and problems in the design of *your* robot.

Thus, this text is part reference, part project guide, part philosophy, and part theory. You will design and build a mobile robot, but, more important, you will learn about engineering design and the process of invention because, although all of the pieces are presented here, it's up to you to put them together in original ways.

1.1 Feedback Control, Cybernetics, and Robotics

The central idea of a robotic system—that of a device that can measure its own state and take action based on it—has a long and interesting history. In Otto Mayr's *The Origins of Feedback Control*, the use of feedback in engineered systems is traced from ancient times to the modern world [May70].

Originally conceived in ancient Greece and built into time-measuring devices, the idea of feedback control was forgotten and had to be rediscovered in Renaissance Europe. By way of introduction to the idea of feedback, let's briefly examine its progression from these ancient origins to the present day.

Some of the earliest inventions that incorporated feedback control were water clocks. To produce a constant flow of water, a float valve regulated the amount of water in a large holding tank. This body of water applied a constant pressure through a precise orifice, resulting in an even flow of water. Various mechanisms measured this water flow, which translated into a measure of elapsed time.

The float valve worked by detecting the level of water in a tank and controlling the amount of water that would flow into the tank. When the water fell below a certain level, a valve was opened, allowing water to fill the holding tank. Essentially, these early water clocks—ingenious devices of their time—employed the same mechanism now commonly found in the household toilet.

Float valves were then likely the first instance of a self-regulating device: that is, a mechanism that senses the quantity to be regulated and then takes an action that controls that same quantity. Without the float valve, there would have been no way of providing a steady flow of water, and the clocks would not have been able to keep accurate enough time to be of any use.

The feedback concept embedded in the early water clocks progressed into water clocks built in Arabic cultures until about 1200 A.D., but it did not spread to Europe. Instead, the idea of feedback control had to be rediscovered by Western inventors much later.

The first feedback system developed in modern Europe was a temperature-regulating oven invented by Cornelis Drebbel in the early 1600s. Drebbel was a prolific inventor; his other inventions included telescopes, microscopes, and a submarine. He worked on the regulated oven to help in his chemical experiments (which included pyrotechnic materials and a scarlet dye). Drebbel's son-in-law, the physician Johan Sibertus Kuffler, attempted to commercialize the heat-regulated furnace, but was largely unsuccessful.

Drebbel's furnace worked on a similar principle as the float valve water regulators. A chamber inside the furnace held a quantity of mercury; as the mercury expanded due to increasing heat inside the furnace, it rose in the chamber and caused a damper to close off the flow of air to the coals, reducing the amount of heat being generated.

Although Drebbel's work was unpublished, others wrote about his invention and spread the concept to other engineers. In the mid-1700s, the physicist Réaumur revived the heat-regulated furnace for the purpose of incubating chickens. Interestingly, much of the subsequent work done on heat regulation over the next 50 years was based on the problem of hatching chickens.

The turning point for temperature-regulation devices came with the work of the French engineer Bonnemain in the late 1700s. Bonnemain vastly improved on the mechanism by which the oven temperature was sensed and then controlled the subsequent heating of the oven. Bonnemain's regulation mechanism was described in the leading French, English, and German journals and became widely known. He built a chicken farm on the outskirts of Paris and, using his incubators, raised large numbers of chickens for the royal court (until the time of the French Revolution, after which demand for the poultry substantially lessened). Bonnemain's heat-regulated incubators were the first such devices that were true industrial equipment and not just laboratory demonstrations.

After the incubators/ovens, feedback control was designed into windmills and boilers. In windmills, the fan tail pointed the main wheel into the wind and regulated the pressure of the grindstones on the grain; in steam boilers, a feedback system controlled the pressure in the boiler unit. But it was as a speed regulator in the steam engine that feedback control achieved its breakthrough in terms of engineering effectiveness and public recognition.

At Boulton & Watt, a steam mill firm in London, James Watt, the chief engineer, adopted a centrifugal control mechanism (which he had seen on windmills) for the purpose of controlling the output engine speed of his firm's steam engines. The "governor," as he called it, accomplished this by measuring the actual speed of the engine and throttling the steam inlet valve of the engine, allowing more steam to enter if the speed had slowed down and less steam if the engine was going too fast. Figure 1.1 represents Watt's early drawings of the invention.

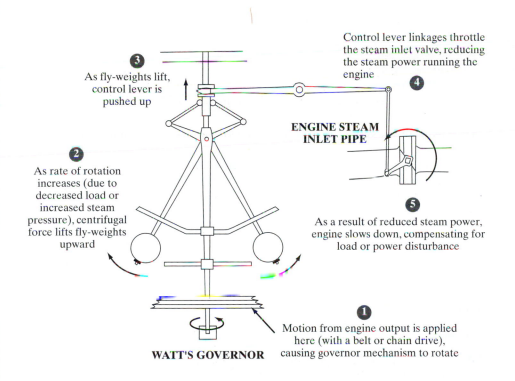

FIGURE 1.1 James Watt's Governor for Feedback Control of Steam Engine Speed

At the time, Watt thought he was applying a known principle to a new application; he did not take credit for having invented a new idea. Rather, he wrote that the governor principle had been previously applied in the regulation of water and windmills.

By the early 1800s, the Watt governor was well known and the subject of discussion in engineering textbooks of the day. The idea of feedback and the specific mechanism of the Watt governor spread through public consciousness as the Industrial Revolution gained momentum; Watt's governor became iconified as the symbol of our collective ability to harness the power of technology.

Up until the 20th century, the technology of automatic control was a specialty of mechanical engineering. By the turn of the century, classical mathematics theory—i.e., differential equations—formalized the understanding of speed control. In the early 1900s, spurred by new applications in electrical engineering, new theory was developed. Scientists such as Laplace and Nyquist helped to create techniques that are still used today in the analysis of automatic control systems.

The next big surge in control engineering came during World War II, with research and development in munitions such as radar, guided missiles, and automatic pilots. After the war ended, the research became generally available to the larger scientific community. One of the leading war scientists, Norbert Wiener, turned his attention from using feedback controls in weaponry to thinking about its larger implications—specifically, the role of feedback in biological systems. Wiener's 1948 book, *Cybernetics: Control and Communication in the Animal and the Machine*, was a seminal contribution to modern thinking; fields of inquiry such as social sciences, psychology, biology, and engineering were affected by Wiener's work [Wie48].

Wiener coined the term *cybernetics*, representing the entire field of control and communication theory, from the Greek word $\chi\upsilon\beta\epsilon\rho\nu\acute{\eta}\tau\eta\varsigma$, meaning "steersman." This was to recognize the central importance of the centrifugal governor popularized in Watt's steam engines.

Wiener's work was part of a larger societal recognition of the role of feedback in social, economic, and biological systems in our world. In the late 1940s and early 1950s, W. Grey Walter, a British neurophysiologist, developed the first true "robotic animals"—mobile electronic robots specifically designed to mimic the behavior of living creatures [Wal51]. Walter's robots, built before the invention of the transistor, were powered by batteries and used vacuum tubes for control. With just six vacuum tubes, Walter's robots were able to perform behaviors like light-seeking (i.e., "tropism"), wandering about randomly, and finding their hutch to recharge their batteries.

To emphasize the creature-like characteristics of his robots, Walter called them "turtles" and gave them playful, pseudoscientific names like *Machina docilis* and *Machina speculatrix*. Walter's turtles later inspired Seymour Papert to call his programmable robots—designed for use by children—"turtles" and influenced Valentino Braitenberg's robot-like "vehicles." (The work of both of these people is discussed shortly.)

1.2 Toys to Think With

My childhood was in the 1960s and 1970s. During that time, there was great popular recognition of the importance of science and technology in the United States, and there were many initiatives to improve science education for young students. During that time, many engineers created computer learning toys—simple plastic, wood, or pen-and-paper kits that revealed some aspect of programming or computation as part of a toy or game. One of the earliest toys I remember, when I was about 8 years old, was a battery-powered car that looked a lot like one of today's radio control cars—it could drive forward and backward and steer like a regular car. The difference was that this car was not directly controlled, but rather was *programmed* by placing pegs on a control wheel.

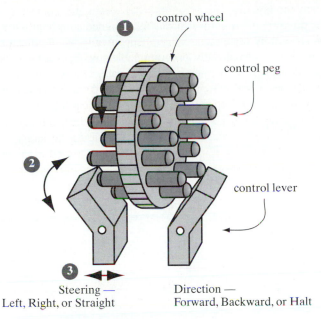

control wheel

①

control peg

②

control lever

③

Steering —
Left, Right, or Straight

Direction —
Forward, Backward, or Halt

FIGURE 1.2 Control Mechanism from Mechanically Programmable Toy Car

The mechanism "under the hood" of the programmable toy car. The control wheel was turned (indicated by arrow 1) by a pinion gear (not shown). Control pegs, of varying lengths, sequentially pressed against control levers open (2), which were mechanically connected to steering and direction mechanisms (3).

The central control wheel was driven by a gear and slowly turned at a fixed rate. To program the car control pegs of three different lengths were placed onto the control wheel. As the wheel turned, the pegs would successively press against control levers. One control lever connected mechanically to the car's steering system, and by choice of peg the car would go straight, to the left, or to the right. The other control lever controlled the car's movement as either forward, backward, or halted. By coordinating the choice of steering and direction pegs, the car could be programmed to drive in a specific path (see Figure 1.2).

For very young children, the typical radio control car is a level of abstraction beyond direct body motion. The child manipulates a steering wheel that guides the movement of an artifact external to the child. But my programmable car encouraged thinking about movement in a yet more abstract way. Rather than directly controlling the car's movement, I programmed a series of actions in advance. This program had a tangible, physical instantiation in the pegs on the control wheel.

The mechanical car was not a big commercial success, but 10 years later an electronic version of the same idea—the Big Trak by Milton-Bradley—was immensely popular. The Big Trak, one of the first microprocessor-based toys, was a tank-like vehicle with a keypad for entering movement sequences. It was fundamentally the same concept as the mechanical car I had owned, with the programming done electronically rather than mechanically. The Big Trak is no longer manufactured, but the Roamer, an egg-shaped robot designed by Valiant Technology,[1] has similar programmable movement capabilities. The Roamer is part of an elementary school curriculum for learning about angles and motion in the United Kingdom. These devices continue to be popular because they make

---

[1] The Roamer is distributed in the United States by Harvard Associates. See the *Resources* appendix for contact information for both Valiant Technology and Harvard Associates.

a powerful idea—that of constructing a series of actions into a program—immediate and accessible.

The mechanically programmed car is my first recollection of a programmable toy, but it is by no means the last.

Whereas the programmable car was probably designed simply as a toy, the Digi-Comp Computer was created by computer scientists specifically as an educational device. The Digi-Comp was also a mechanically programmable toy, but rather than controlling the state of another device (like the steering of the car), Digi-Comp operated on its own internal state—as does a real computer. As proclaimed on the cover of its manual, the Digi-Comp was "the first real operating digital computer in plastic."

FIGURE 1.3 The Digi-Comp Computer

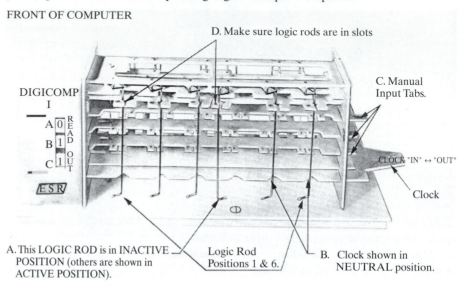

FRONT OF COMPUTER

D. Make sure logic rods are in slots

C. Manual Input Tabs.

DIGICOMP I

A 0
B 1
C 1

READ OUT

ESR

CLOCK "IN" ↔ "OUT"

Clock

A. This LOGIC ROD is in INACTIVE POSITION (others are shown in ACTIVE POSITION).

Logic Rod Positions 1 & 6.

B. Clock shown in NEUTRAL position.

Figure 1.3 shows a photograph of the Digi-Comp device. The computer consisted of three sliding plates, each of which could be in one of two different positions (representing the "0" state and the "1" state). The user placed plastic tubes (not shown) onto tabs that jutted out from the plates. A clocking mechanism, activated by the user, caused a set of vertical bars to swing back and forth. When Digi-Comp was clocked, these bars knocked into the tubes and caused the plates to move.

The Digi-Comp was programmed by judicious placement of the tubes. As a child playing with it, I did not really understand how precisely the tubes caused the Digi-Comp to perform different functions, although it was clear to me that they were central. Looking over the instruction manual as a computer scientist, the mechanism is less mysterious, although it is still quite clever. Fundamentally, the tubes cause each plate of the Digi-Comp to act as a set-reset flip-flop.

Despite its humble plastic construction and arcane programming method, the Digi-Comp really was a computer. The examples in the manual, which I worked through as a 10-year-old, included Boolean operations like "and" and "or," binary counting, bit-shift operations, and other such classics.

The Digi-Comp was of course limited, but it was remarkable in what it accomplished with just plastic and a few metal rods. For me personally, it certainly served its designers' goal of introducing binary numbers, logical operations, and simple computational mechanisms. These helped prepare me for the ultimate toy of my childhood, the Radio Shack TRS-80 computer.

The TRS-80 computer was in the first generation of machines sold as "home computers," although of course they were really hobbyist playthings. I was fortunate to have owned the model with "Level II BASIC," which supported features like floating point numerics and an interface to assembly language routines. The machine came with only 4K of memory, which I later expanded to a generous 16K.

A big difference between these early computers and contemporary machines was that commercial productivity software, as it were, did not yet exist, so the main application of the early home computers was for their owners to explore how they worked. Essentially, every computer owner was also a computer programmer.

Another important difference was that these early computers were simple enough that a dedicated hobbyist could completely understand every layer of functionality that was built into them, from the CPU instruction set, to memory-mapped hardware and video display, to system software built into the machine's permanent memory. Today's machines, in terms of both their hardware and software designs, are far too complex to be thoroughly understood. As a pedagogical tool, the early computers had a distinct advantage.

When I first got the TRS-80, I began by learning the BASIC language; I then progressed to programming in the Z-80 machine language of the computer, learning about its hardware subsystems, and finally learning how to patch the operating system and various ways and directly call subroutines located in the computer's built-in operating program.

The set of projects I always wanted to work on, but did not have the expertise to do so at the time, was to interface the computer to the real world. That would have to wait until college. I knew that I wanted to do work in the field of robotics; as a sophomore, I was fortunate enough to join the research group of Warren Seering, who as a member of the Mechanical Engineering faculty had a research group located at MIT's Artificial Intelligence (AI) Laboratory.

Seering's research group was working on an experimental robot arm, a "Cartesian" manipulator with linear X, Y, and Z axes. It was a large, powerful robot arm designed for exploring new robotic manufacturing techniques. The robot was strong enough to be dangerous; it could easily crush a person's hand if it came between the robot's body and its limit stops.

My work involved writing assembly language code that served as the low-level feedback positioning controller. While I was working on this project, my coursework included the formal study of feedback control. It was a remarkable experience to be learning the theory behind feedback control while my code was controlling a large and potentially dangerous piece of equipment. The robot was bolted down to the concrete ninth floor of the building that housed the AI Lab; legend had it that when previous students' control code caused unstable oscillations of the arm, it literally shook the whole building. I soon discovered these stories to be accurate. Fortunately, the robot came with a large, red emergency stop button.

The reason for telling all of these personal learning stories is to give a sense of the type of learning experience I instinctively sought out as a young learner. The exercises and projects proposed in this book are ideally done in the same spirit of hands-on, engaged experimentation. When I became a master's student, I began working with Seymour Papert, a pioneer in the area of what he calls "constructionist learning"—the development and study of technology to foster this kind of learning. I now take a step back from this personal history to the direct heritage of the work on which this book is based.

Seymour Papert is a mathematician, computer scientist, and, in the 1960s, was co-director of MIT's AI Laboratory. Papert was a leader of the community of AI researchers during a period of intense creativity and intellectual excitement. AI researchers had developed the Lisp programming language and were engaged in writing programs to test, explore, and embody their ideas about the nature of human intelligence.

Papert wanted to bring this spirit of inquiry to the world of children. He believed that children weren't fluent with mathematics because of a lack of challenging and engaging "mathematical stuff" in the world of a child. In the late 1960s and early 1970s, Papert led the development of Logo, a programming language designed for children. Logo shared many ideas with the Lisp programming language used in the MIT research laboratories, like an interactive interface, but had a simplified syntax to make it easy to learn.

In *Mindstorms*, his seminal book on the experiences of children programming with Logo, Papert made an analogy between trying to learn a foreign language (say French) in the classroom versus learning it in a place where it is spoken (France). It's easy to learn to speak French while living in France because speaking the language is a natural, contextualized activity with real-life relevance. If you want to eat an ice cream cone, you must ask for it in French! In contrast, speaking in a classroom is based on role-play conversation, which cannot have the same personal relevance. Papert hoped to create an environment—the Logo programming language—where children could work with mathematical ideas that have the same personal meaning as does speaking French in France.

As the Logo language was developed, it came to have at least two characteristics that distinguished it from other contemporary computer programming environments. The first was its interactivity, which it shared with Lisp, the language on which Logo was based. When children were sitting in front of a Logo console, they could type a Logo command and the computer would execute it immediately. This was a completely different sort of interface to a computer than what was typical in those days, namely, batch mode programming. With the Logo approach, a budding programmer could immediately see the result of an interaction with the computer. This encouraged a whole different style of work on the computer, one that was more oriented to exploration and play—children's natural ways of thinking—than abstract symbolic thought.

The other feature of Logo projects was that they expanded the realm of the computer beyond data manipulation. Most computer interactions, including early Logo projects, were based on some sort of data transformation. Numeric or textual data would be processed by the computer and the result would be displayed for the programmer. For example, a Logo program might take lists of English nouns, verbs, and adjectives and string them together into nonsense sentences—a word play experiment.

Papert and his colleagues began experimenting with robots connected to computers running Logo. Rather than being fixed arms or XY-tables with Cartesian geometries, these robots were mobile robots that could be understood with a relative, robot-centric geometry. Children would first play with robot movement using button-boxes to control the robot's motion. Then they would use Logo primitives to control the robots, typing statements like `FORWARD 50` to make the robot move forward 50 "steps" or `RIGHT 90` to make the robot turn in place 90 degrees. By making sequences of these movement commands, children could cause the robot to move around in specific ways or even to draw geometric patterns on the floor, as a robot would carry a pen to mark the path it traveled. This was a similar sort of programming as I had experienced using the mechanical car, only with computer statements instead of plastic pegs.

Papert noticed that children's interactions with the Logo robots had a quality that was different from the other projects based on data manipulations. The children were able to *relate* to the robots in a way that they hadn't with the data projects: They could imagine themselves as the robot and literally walk themselves through a Logo program by moving about as the robot would. Papert felt strongly that the way children were able to think about the robot by using their bodies, what he called a "body syntonicity," was key to making Logo accessible to children with a broader range of intellectual styles. More children would become engaged in projects based on robot control than data manipulation because they were able to "think with their bodies" in doing so.

The Logo robot became a defining feature of the Logo environment. Inspired by Walter's vacuum tube robot turtles, the Logo robot was dubbed the "turtle" because early robots were shaped vaguely like turtles, because they moved sort of like a turtle would, and to give children (and adult researchers for that matter) a playful and familiar object to hold in their mind when thinking about how the device would behave.

As computers developed video display technology that replaced line printer interfaces, the Logo turtle moved "off the floor" and "onto the screen." This is to say that the physical electromechanical Logo robots were supplanted by iconic images of turtles on the video display screen. When a child gave a command to a screen turtle, it would move about and draw on the display screen rather than on the floor.

The screen turtles had certain advantages and drawbacks with respect to the floor turtles. Perhaps the most important advantage of the screen turtles was that they could be used on any computer with a video display so they could reach many more children. Also, screen turtles could move very precisely and rapidly—there were no mechanical slippage problems—so children could easily create complex geometric displays.

On the other hand, screen turtles were more conceptually abstract than their floor turtle ancestors. Children had more difficulty understanding rotations from screen turtles—in some implementations of Logo, the turtle would snap immediately to its new position rather than step through a series of rotations to accomplish a movement. A child could not get up and walk around a screen turtle. When the turtle was facing downward on the screen, children would often become confused about the meaning of "turning left" (counter-clockwise rotation) versus "turning right" (clockwise rotation).

Still, the screen turtles were a valuable invention that greatly accelerated children's ability to relate to computer programming activities. It was much easier for children to understand how to program a turtle to make a drawing than to use cartesian geometry, the "native" language of the computer hardware, as was typically available in early microcomputer versions of the BASIC language.

1.2.1 LEGO/Logo

In 1971, Papert and colleague Cynthia Solomon published a short memo entitled "Twenty Things to Do with a Computer" [PS71]. When this paper was written, the contemporary interface to a computer was the TeleType—a line-oriented typewriter-like system, in which the user and computer alternately typed information onto a continuous scroll of paper.

Papert and Solomon's paper suggested 20 computer-based activities that assumed that many different kinds of electromechanical devices—similar in spirit to the Logo floor turtles—could be attached to the computer. Several of the activities involved the Logo turtles, but several others imagined more sophisticated and versatile possibilities of the computer controlling other more fanciful mechanical devices that ideally would be constructed by the children themselves. For the sake of practicality, the paper even provided technical suggestions on how these devices could be connected to the mainframe computer via the standard TeleType interface!

In the mid-1980s, Stephen Ocko and Mitchel Resnick, two researchers working in Papert's group, began experimenting with electronic interfaces that would allow children to hook motors and sensors up to a computer running Logo. But there was an important

difference between this work and the early Logo floor turtle experiments: With the newer work, children were able to not only write the programs to control electromechanical devices, but could actually build those devices as well. The vision laid out by Papert and Solomon's memo of 15 years ago was being realized.

The LEGO/Logo project, as it became called, used a recently developed set of LEGO parts called *LEGO Technic*. The LEGO Technic set included not only the familiar plastic LEGO building blocks, but newer pieces like gears, beams, wheels, and motors, which enabled a LEGO builder to create animated and exciting mechanical projects. The range of devices that could be constructed with LEGO Technic was as wide as the imagination: Children created ferris wheels, toasters, elevators, walking robots, and animated sculptures, to name just a few.

Coincidentally, as the MIT researchers were building prototype interfaces that allowed the Logo language to control LEGO devices, the president of the LEGO company read *Mindstorms*, Papert's book. Sensing a shared set of ideals about the role of children's play in learning and the value of constructive materials in children's hands and minds— whether they be the grammatic building blocks of the Logo language or the physical building blocks of a LEGO set—Papert's group and principals at the LEGO company arranged a meeting. A sponsored research project resulted, and Resnick and Ocko performed research and development that led to the commercialization of the LEGO/Logo system as a product for the educational market. The LEGO company named the first generation of the product *LEGO TC logo* ("tc" for Technic Control) and has been selling it since the late 1980s. Around 1990, an updated version, *LEGO DACTA*™ *Control Lab*™, was introduced; currently, it is estimated that 20,000 schools in the United States have the materials and more than 1 million children have used them.

1.2.2 The Programmable Brick

Shortly after Ocko and Resnick had finished their work on what became the *LEGO TC logo* product, they began looking for new directions to extend the LEGO/Logo concept. One limitation of the commercial product was that LEGO constructions needed to be tethered with wire to the electronic interface sitting aside the controlling desktop computer. The system tended to encourage the construction of stationary machines like a merry-go-round, rather than mobile machines like a LEGO floor turtle. Researchers in Papert's group were also interested in exploring children's work with mobile creature-like robots that exhibited cybernetic characteristics.

Resnick and Ocko experimented with remote control technology in which the controlling computer broadcasted commands to a LEGO machine that carried an infrared- or radio-based receiver. The system was functional, but it too had its limitations: Reliable, bidirectional communications (needed so the LEGO machine could report sensor data back to the host computer) were difficult to implement, and a system that would be suitable for classroom use, in which there might be a dozen or more simultaneous projects, would make the communications technology unwieldy. Additionally, it seemed like poor aesthetics for a big desktop computer to be controlling a little LEGO machine. Why not build a miniature computer that could be embedded into the LEGO machine itself?

In 1987, I joined Papert's team to assist in the development of the concept, which we called the "programmable brick"—a hand-held plastic box that contained an entire computer capable of running Logo. Two additional people joined the development team: LEGO engineer Allan Toft, who visited at our MIT lab for a year-long period, and Brian Silverman, chief scientist at Logo Computer Systems, Inc. (LCSI), who had done the software development of the Logo implementation of many versions of Logo, including the one used in the commercial *LEGO TC logo* product.

In about a year's time, we created a prototype Programmable Brick and manufactured about a half-dozen copies of them. The "Brick" had outputs to control four LEGO motors and inputs to receive data from four sensors. Existing LEGO sensors—a touch switch and light sensors—as well as custom sensors could be used. The Brick was based on a version of the 6502 microprocessor—the same device as was used in the Apple II series of computers, which were prevalent at the time. Brian Silverman ported the commercial version of Logo, written for the Apple II computer, to run on our Programmable Brick.

To program the Brick, it would be hooked up to a host computer using a serial line connection. Then the user could type commands to the brick or download Logo procedures to it. After downloading, Logo procedures could be invoked by giving commands through a "command center" on the computer screen or by pressing a button on the Programmable Brick, which would run a specially named Logo procedure.

This work on the MIT Programmable Brick has now come full circle. In 1998, the LEGO Group announced *LEGO Mindstorms*™, a new brand, and its flagship product, Robotics Invention System and the RCX Programmable LEGO Brick. The LEGO Mind-Storms brand represents the company's belief in the entertainment and educational value of robotics and its commitment in bringing it to children. The RCX Brick, inspired by the line of work at MIT beginning with our first Programmable Bricks in the late 1980s, is part of the first robotics system truly designed for children ever to reach the mass market.

1.2.3 The MIT 6.270 Robot Design Competition

Our work on the Programmable Brick for children led to the creation of the MIT Robot Design course and competition, through the intervention of an MIT undergraduate, Michael Parker, who worked in our LEGO/Logo lab at the time that the Programmable Brick was being developed.

Parker, a computer science student, had just taken MIT's Introduction to Mechanical Design class. In this class, created in the 1960s by Woodie Flowers, students are given an assorted kit of mechanical parts, including metal, plastic, wood, and cardboard, and the specification for a contest challenge. Over the duration of the term, students use the materials in their kit to design and build a machine that will satisfy the contest game. The course culminates in a contest in which the students' machines play against one another in an elimination-style event.

Parker had participated in the course and was excited by the concept. Having seen the Programmable Brick technology, Parker recruited me and Randy Sargent, another computer science student, to develop a version of the Brick for use in a class with MIT students.

It took several years to develop the format and technology for the project, including several revisions of the hardware and software provided to the students. Taking inspiration from Flowers' design course, we gave students a complete robot-building package, which included LEGO Technics elements for mechanical construction, various electronic sensors, and a controller board that could be programmed to operate autonomously. Like the mechanical design course, our project culminated in a final contest challenge. The big difference was that our project, which we called the LEGO Robot Design Competition, included electronics and software as part of the design space and required students to embed their control ideas in a program, rather than being able to control their machines directly.

The technology and approach presented in this book are based on similar materials and ideas developed for the MIT 6.270 Robot Design project.[2] Readers who are interested

---

[2]   Within MIT, all classes are known by their course number. We named our project "6.270" in honor of the Mechanical Engineering design course 2.70, by adding a "6," the number for the Electrical Engineering and Computer Science Department. The class number of the Mechanical Engineering course has since changed,

in more details about the evolution of the MIT course, including a study of students'
learning, are referred to my Ph.D. dissertation, *Circuits to Control: Learning Engineering
by Designing LEGO Robots* [Mar94].

Now let's look at the technology we use in this book. Much of it grew directly out
of work done for the MIT LEGO Robot Design project.

1.3 About the Technology

In developing the projects for this book, I chose to base them around a particular set of
hardware and software. This should make it much easier for those who do adopt these
materials, while providing concrete examples that should also serve to illuminate the
issues for any choice of technology. At the same time, I attempted to create examples
and projects that would be applicable to being implemented with a variety of robotic
technologies.

These materials were originally developed for the MIT Robot Design project and since
have been further refined and also tested by an extended community of users who have
adopted them for similar purposes. Although the materials obviously cannot satisfy all
needs, they are very well suited as robot-design technology for students at a variety of
levels of advancement.

The technology has three different components: hardware, software, and mechanism.

Hardware. For the electrical and computational hardware, we use the *Handy Board*, a
hand-held, microprocessor-based robot control board. The Handy Board includes a
variety of features that make it suited for controlling small robots, including outputs
for DC motors, inputs for numerous sensors, an LCD screen, and an integrated
battery pack.

Software. A custom software environment for the Handy Board, called *Interactive
C*, has been developed. Interactive C is a multitasking implementation of the C
programming language that is designed to run on a small, 8-bit microprocessor
like the one that the Handy Board uses. Interactive C also has a console window
that allows the user to interact with the robot while it is executing programs. This
latter feature distinguishes Interactive C from other versions of the C language that
are available for typical small microprocessor systems.

Mechanism. For the body of the robot, the LEGO Technic system is the basis of
the examples and exercises presented in this book. LEGO Technic is an extension
of the widely known and popular LEGO building brick system. Technic includes
axles, gears, wheels, motors, and other parts to facilitate the construction of intricate
and functional mechanical systems, including robot movement drivetrains and other
effectors.

Following is a brief introduction to each of these materials; as we come to each of
them in the main course of the text, much additional detail is presented. Also discussed
here are some suggestions for alternatives.

1.3.1 The Handy Board

The Handy Board was especially designed to be the controller of small, mobile robots.
At the heart of the Handy Board (Figure 1.4) is the Motorola 68HC11, an 8-bit micro-processor that includes a collection of features that make it ideally suited for robot control
applications.

---

but the "name" of the LEGO Robot Design Competition has not.

FIGURE 1.4 The Handy Board

Overview

The Handy Board's primary features include:

- *32K of main system memory.* The Handy Board has 32K of static RAM memory. This may not sound like a lot with today's desktop computers with tens of megabytes of memory, but remember that the Handy Board does not need to support a graphical user interface or a modern operating system. Further, the approach used by the Interactive C compiler uses the memory in an efficient manner.

    The Handy Board's memory is battery-protected, meaning that its contents are preserved even when power is switched off. This allows you to download a program to the robot, disconnect it from the computer, and carry it over to a play environment without worrying about losing the contents of the robot's memory.

- *Output drivers for four DC motors.* Up to four standard DC motors can be driven directly from the Handy Board. The drivers provide nine volts and about one ampere of current; this is ideal for powering many small motors.

    Under software control, the power provided to the motors can be varied in strength, providing a rudimentary speed control.

- *Inputs for analog and digital sensors.* Using a compact sensor connector, the Handy Board will accept up to seven analog (continuously varying) sensors and nine digital (switch type) sensors. The standard sensor connector is a three-wire circuit that can provide a five-volt power source to the sensor. This allows easy connection of active sensors, such as infrared reflectance sensors, that require power to operate.

- *Internal, rechargeable battery pack.* A battery pack consisting of eight nickel cadmium AA cells is built into the Handy Board case allowing projects to be constructed without worrying about separate batteries to operate the motors. The internal battery pack recharges whenever the Handy Board is plugged into the interface board that connects it to its host computer.

- *LCD screen.* The Handy Board comes with a 16-character, two-line liquid crystal display screen, which can display textual and numeric information under user control. The LCD screen greatly facilitates debugging of robot programs because sensor values and internal program state can be readily displayed on the screen.

For more information about the Handy Board design, see Appendix A.

Alternatives

The main features that the Handy Board provides that make it ideal for robotics projects are the integrated motor driver circuits, the 32K bytes of memory (which allows the use of Interactive C), its small size, and the sensor connector that allows the easy attachment of multiple, individually wired sensors. Most commercial microprocessor boards for embedded control applications do not allow easy attachment of individual motors and sensors.

Its limitations include the 32K bytes of memory (for some kinds of projects, this is not enough) and the fact that it is based on an 8–bit microprocessor (some applications will require more CPU horsepower). These concerns are discussed shortly.

For some applications, a board with even less capability than the Handy Board may be acceptable. This would be true if the intent were to support robot projects of limited complexity or if it were desired to program primarily in assembly language for pedagogical reasons. In this case, a controller board like the Mini Board, which has only 2K bytes of memory and no display screen, would be suitable (see Appendix G, *Resources*, for more information on the Mini Board). The Mini Board cannot support Interactive C, so it is typically programmed either with a traditional C compiler or in assembly language.

Most people will find the 2K byte memory limitation of a board like the Mini Board to be too constraining for open-ended, experimental work. Alternatively, there are dozens of inexpensive controller boards available, based on the 68HC11 or other embedded control microprocessors, that include 32K, 64K, or more memory. These designs are not typically targeted for robotic applications, however, and do not include circuitry for powering DC motors, convenient connectors for sensors, or a collection of software drivers for useful robotic peripherals. This is where the Handy Board is especially valuable.

There are applications for which the power of the Handy Board will not be adequate. For example, sophisticated programming languages like Lisp or other interpreted environments cannot be implemented with the limited memory and CPU power. Robot tasks that involve the collection of large amounts of data will exhaust the 32K bytes of memory. Finally, some sensory processing tasks, like visual recognition, require newer and more powerful microprocessors.

This should not be seen as selling short the versatility of the Handy Board, however. For a wide range of projects, including beginning through intermediate robotics work, C-language and assembly language programming, and electronic design and interfacing, the Handy Board is an ideal solution.

Indeed, the 8–bit microprocessor is far from having outlived its usefulness, despite the barrage of information to the contrary coming from the chip industry. Certainly on the desktop, faster and faster processors continue to make radical changes in the nature of the computing experience. Yet do we really need a 32–bit microprocessor running our toasters? Probably not. In recent years in the embedded controls field, there actually has been a popular uprising against more and more complex chips and toward particular chips that are simpler than the average 8–bit micro—for example, the Microchip PIC series of devices.

No doubt there will soon be a time that a 32–bit microprocessor is the right choice for a system like the Handy Board, but presently there still are complexity and cost versus performance trade-offs to be made. The Handy Board errs on the side of simplicity, which has certain pedagogical advantages.

1.3.2 Interactive C

The Handy Board can be programmed using a variety of standard 68HC11 development tools, including C-language compilers and assemblers for writing directly in 68HC11 code. The standard software environment used in this book, however, is *Interactive C*, a special kind of C-language compiler developed for educational robotics applications.

Interactive C was created by Randy Sargent and the author originally for use in the MIT Robot Design project. There were several considerations in the design of Interactive C that make it ideal for robotics projects:

Interactivity. With a conventional C-language compiler, it is difficult to interact with one's program while it is running. The typical development sequence consists of writing code, compiling it, and then running it. Such programs are difficult to debug because it is hard to test the various subprograms independently.

Interactive C instead provides a command-line console that allows the user to type expressions and function calls interactively, even while other programs are running. This capability, the hallmark of interpreted computer language environments, makes it much easier to try out ideas as they are hatched.

Stability. In the traditional C-language system, the compiler does not protect the programmer from making mistakes that will crash the computer. For example, if the programmer references an array element that is out of bounds of the predetermined size of the array, the computer will gladly oblige and allow errant data to corrupt system memory (leading to a crash).

In working with our students in the MIT Robot Design project, we found that debugging was especially difficult when not only software errors but also electronic hardware failures could cause a system crash. Therefore, we designed Interactive C to report a runtime error for common programming problems (e.g., divide-by-zero, out-of-bounds array reference) rather than crashing the system.

Multitasking. For many of the ideas we wished students to explore with their robotics projects, the capability to have multiple programs running simultaneously was important. Interactive C has built in the ability to multitask up to about a dozen user programs.

There are two versions of Interactive C: a free version that is based on the original MIT source code, and a commercial version that is a product of Newton Labs, a robotics firm that Sargent has since founded. The projects and examples prepared in this book can all be completed with the free version. The commercial version provides additional features, as well as an improved user interface that would be of interest to the advanced user. Both the free and commercial versions are available for a number of popular computer operating systems, including MS-DOS, Windows, Macintosh, and Unix.

Alternatives

Some users may wish to program their Handy Board directly in 68HC11 machine language. This is generally a prerequisite when writing drivers for new devices, but also has great pedagogical value as a way to deeply understand the interactions between the microprocessor and the hardware of the Handy Board. Generally, it is more difficult to write larger and more complex programs in assembly language than in a language like C, but for smaller projects there is much to be learned by working "close to the machine."

Motorola, the company that designed the 68HC11 chip, provides a free assembler program. Source code (written in portable C) for Motorola's 68HC11 assembler, along with ready-to-go versions for the Macintosh and MS-DOS operating systems, are available from Motorola's web site. Code downloader programs, which take the output of the assembler program and load it onto the Handy Board, are also freely available. See the *Resources* appendix.

For programming in C, there are a number of high-quality conventional C-language compilers available for the 68HC11 chip. Some of these are targeted at industrial users and cost USD$1000 or more. These tend to be complex and difficult to use, and it is not necessary to spend anywhere near that amount to purchase a reliable product.

One of the best of the inexpensive C-language compilers for the 68HC11 is ICC11 by ImageCraft, Inc. MS-DOS and Windows versions are available, and a Macintosh version is planned. ICC11 is officially supported as a compiler for use with the Handy Board. Another good compiler product is Micro-C by Dunfield Development Systems. Micro-C is available in MS-DOS and Windows versions only.

1.3.3 LEGO Technic

For the structural and mechanical aspects of robot design, this book is based on the use of LEGO Technic. *Technic* is the brand name for the mechanized portion of the LEGO product line. LEGO Technic includes axles, gears, motors, and other parts that allow the construction of complex and functional mechanical systems.

LEGO Technic is a wonderful material because it combines the playful appeal of the basic LEGO brick with a sophisticated and powerful set of mechanical design components. LEGO Technic allows rapid idea generation, prototyping, and evaluation. For many projects, Technic is satisfactory as a final building material, meaning that the robot built as a prototype from Technic can also serve as a valid experimental platform.

Technic is ideal for both structural purposes—building the frame or other support elements of a project—as well as the gear reduction and power transmission mechanism. Because of this, LEGO Technic can be used to create a huge variety of different mechanisms and mechanical systems that are designed from the ground up. It can be a profoundly satisfying feeling to design, build, and debug a mechanical device that performs as intended. With LEGO Technic, this can be done without knowing how to use the tools in a machine shop, greatly accelerating the creative process.

Most of the examples in this book are demonstrated using the LEGO Technic system. Although some of these ideas are particular to the Technic product, most of the mechanical design principles apply to any type of mechanical design. Because of this versatility and expressive power, the LEGO Technic system is adopted as the standard building material for this book.

Considerations

LEGO Technic sometimes has a reputation for being expensive and not structurally sound.

Cost. Although it is certainly true that LEGO Technic is not inexpensive, it is comparable in price to other high-quality building systems, such as *Fischertechnik*. Compared with products on a retail toy shelf, LEGO Technic is more expensive, but the quality of the LEGO manufacturing process—which uses only the best plastics and precision molding techniques—far surpasses copycat products. In short, if compared to products of similar quality, LEGO materials are not overpriced, and LEGO materials are in a far higher quality class than the typical toy.

Stability. Projects built with LEGO elements have a reputation for easily falling apart. Certainly, it is the case that the "clutching power" of the LEGO stud is not immensely strong, and projects that are held together only by the stud force are liable to break apart easily. Astute LEGO designers, however, have learned the secret LEGO dimensional relationship and know how to brace their structures with cross-beams that will lock their designs in place. These secrets are (of course) revealed in this book and change perceptions of LEGO materials as not being capable of building sturdy structures.

Alternatives

Fischertechnik, manufactured by the German company of the same name, is a precision building system that shares many qualities with the LEGO Technic product.[3] While LEGO Technic evolved from the famous rectangular building brick, *Fischertechnik* started out as a system for engineers to prototype factory layout designs. As such, *Fischertechnik* excels at constructing rectilinear structures; it has a locking joint that allows these frame-like structures to be built with great rigidity.

Fischertechnik now includes elements for mechanized structures, such as gears, axles, and other such parts. Projects designed with *Fischertechnik* tend to be larger than their LEGO Technic counterparts and have a more industrial appearance.

Although this author prefers LEGO Technic for its play value and greater versatility, both LEGO Technic and *Fischertechnik* are very high-quality, powerful building systems. For those who have prior experience with *Fischertechnik* or otherwise find it appealing, it is an excellent choice.

Fischertechnik and LEGO Technic cost approximately the same, so neither are solutions if cost is the issue. For building robots on a budget, several possibilities exist:

Modified Radio Control Cars. Inexpensive toy radio control (RC) cars can make excellent robot platforms because they are durable and well designed for basic locomotion. There are some challenges involved in using them, centering around the problem of interfacing to their high-current motors, but once these are solved, the RC car is a good alternative.

Scrap Materials. For those who are comfortable working with basic construction stock like wood, metal, and plastic, robot building can be a very rewarding endeavor. It is certainly the case that building a robot from these "raw" materials is much less expensive than using the commercial building systems. For the mechanized aspect of the designs, several companies sell gears, chain link, and other such components, or such parts can be removed from junk devices like portable cassette stereos and RC cars.

Teaching how to design from scrap materials is beyond the scope of this book, but many of the design principles that are discussed in this book are relevant to builders who are working in the machine shop.

1.4 An Overview of the Book

The text has been organized with a set of chapters and appendices to encourage nonlinear use. That is, the progression of ideas from the first chapter to the last appendix does not follow a sequential progression, and readers are encouraged to skip around and pursue their own path through the material.

The book is filled with various exercises and examples to help illustrate the ideas presented. Although it is certainly possible to be an "armchair roboticist" and enjoy the material just by reading it, the idea is that the project work goes hand in hand with the flow of the text.

---

[3] *Fischertechnik* is distributed in the United States by Model A Technology. See the *Resources* appendix for contact information.

Following is a synopsis of each of the chapters and appendices.

Chapter 1: Introduction. The introductory chapter, which you are reading now, includes a history of the ideas that led to contemporary robotics, along with a history of the work that led to this book being created.

Chapter 2: A First Robot. Chapter 2 is a set of experiments in which an entire working robot is constructed and programmed to exhibit various behaviors. Chapter 2 is a microcosm of the entire book because it introduces all of the aspects involved in building a robot: mechanism, sensors, electronics, programming, and control.

Chapter 3: Sensors. Chapter 3 explains how simple sensors function and introduces a variety of common and useful robotic sensors, including touch switches, resistive position sensors, photocell light sensors, photo-transistor light sensors, and shaft encoders. Along with an explanation of the principles of each sensor, sample robotic behaviors based on each sensor are presented.

Chapter 4: Motors, Gears, and Mechanism. Chapter 4 is about a robot's body and drivetrain. It discusses motors and the electronics used to operate motors. Use of the LEGO Technic system, geartrains, and gear reduction are presented. Also, the servo motor and its uses are discussed, along with general principles of mechanical design using the LEGO Technic system.

Chapter 5: Control. In chapter 5, we examine the various ways that a robot control system can be constructed. The discussion begins with simple feedback control and then introduces proportional-derivative control, which is commonly used in systems design everywhere. Next, two different approaches to robot control—algorithmic and reactive—are presented, along with exercises and examples of their use.

Chapter 6: Advanced Sensing. Chapter 6 discusses techniques in processing sensor data, including calibration, filtering, and averaging. Additionally, several more advanced sensor devices are presented, including infrared distance sensing and communication, ultrasonic ranging, and quadrature shaft encoding.

The chapter on control brings together many ideas presented throughout the book; in a sense, after that chapter, the core of the work has been presented. Additionally, a project-based class that concludes in a robotic contest will want to make use of the appendix on robot contests.

The appendices provide additional information and resources to support in-depth project work:

Appendix A: Inside the Handy Board Design. This appendix presents the architecture of the Handy Board design, and explains how to program the 68HC11 Microprocessor in assembly language.

Appendix B: Construction Techniques. This appendix provides construction notes for building sensors, motors, and in adapter cables.

Appendix C: Serial Communications and Data Collection. This appendix explains how to use the Handy Board to capture data and transmit it to a host computer at a later time.

Appendix D: Handy Board Specification. This appendix provides additional documentation for the Handy Board.

Appendix E: Interactive C Reference. This appendix documents the Interactive C language, including library features customized for the Handy Board.

Appendix F: Robot Contests. This appendix describes a selection of robot contests, including the MIT 6.270 Robot Design competitions.

Appendix G: Resources. This appendix is a list of helpful resources.

OK, let's start building some robots!

2 A First Robot

In this chapter we build a robot. A simple robot, but a complete one nonetheless.

What kind of robot? That is the question. And what do we mean exactly, "robot"? Rather than giving a definition, let's dive in and start building a robot. There is no better way to know what something is than by having built it yourself.

Here is a map of this chapter. The first section, "Interactive C and the Handy Board," introduces the electronic hardware and software system we start using in this chapter and continue using throughout the rest of the book.

In the second section, "The HandyBug," we construct a two-motor vehicle named *HandyBug*. This simple but reliable robot serves as the platform for all of the experiments in this chapter and many subsequent projects as well.

Next, in "A First Program," we put together these first two sections and create a basic touch-sensor obstacle-avoidance program.

In the fourth section, "Braitenberg Vehicles," we explore virtual sensorimotor "creatures" invented by Valentino Braitenberg. Using *HandyBug*, we build a few of these hypothetical creatures, instantiating them with LEGO bricks, electronics, and a program.

The last several sections propose various extensions to robot behaviors, including randomness and meta-sensing, the ability for a robot to monitor its own performance.

Now, how to proceed? Despite the fact that just after this paragraph ends, you will be presented with an introduction to Interactive C, you should not feel obligated to start there. Many may prefer to first play with LEGO bricks, building the *HandyBug*. If you'd prefer to build the robot body before programming the robot brain, go ahead and skip forward to page 28.

In either case, we'll come together for "A First Program."

2.1 Interactive C and the Handy Board

Interactive C is a version of the popular "C" programming language that was especially designed for running on a small, 8-bit microprocessor—like the Handy Board's 68HC11. Let's boot up the Handy Board with Interactive C and get to work. Appendix E.1, "Quick Start," explains how to connect the Handy Board to a desktop/laptop computer (henceforth, the workstation), initialize the Handy Board with Interactive C's runtime system (the "pcode" program), and then boot Interactive C. Go ahead and perform those steps as described.

Now we can assume that the Handy Board is successfully plugged into the workstation, and Interactive C booted and displaying its prompt, "C>".

At this point, commands may be typed, which are immediately compiled, downloaded, and executed on the Handy Board. For example, try typing

```
beep();
```

followed by the Return key. (All subsequent examples to be typed at the Interactive C prompt will assume that the Return key is pressed.) After just a brief delay, the Handy Board should emit a short beep.

Despite this seemingly simple action, a lot of activity goes on "behind the scenes" to make the Handy Board actually emit a beep. When the Return key is pressed, here is what happens in detail:

1. Interactive C compiles the line of code just entered;
2. The compiled code is downloaded via the serial line into the Handy Board;
3. Interactive C tells the Handy Board to execute the code it has just received;
4. The Handy Board beeps.

This interactive capability of the Interactive C/Handy Board system is an extremely powerful feature when developing, testing, and debugging robot programs. After getting used to it, it may be difficult to go back to traditional software development environments, which do not provide this capability.

Upload or Download?

The question sometimes arises, should the process of sending data from the workstation computer to the Handy Board be called downloading or uploading? After all, it is generally agreed on that when data are transferred from the Internet to a workstation, this is called *downloading*, and when data are transferred from a workstation to the Internet, this is *uploading*. Why, then, should it not be called uploading when data are sent from the workstation to the Handy Board?

Partly, this is a matter of personal preference—an aesthetic judgment. The argument for download has to do with which is the "bigger computer" in the system. In the case of the Internet and the personal workstation, clearly "the Internet" is the bigger computer, so when data move from the bigger computer to the smaller one, it is downloading. In the workstation/Handy Board system, the workstation is the bigger computer, and again moving data from the bigger to the smaller is called downloading.

Besides, the Handy Board is usually mounted on a robot sitting on the floor, and it sounds silly to 'upload' data to something that's sitting down at your feet.

2.1.1 Interactive C Prompt

Everything typed at the Interactive C prompt must be either a valid C statement or a command to the Interactive C application itself. Let's examine what it means to be a "valid C statement."

Previously, the phrase "`beep();`" was typed at the Interactive C prompt. This is an example of a call to the C function named `beep`. The open and closed parentheses contain the arguments, or parameters, to the function call; in this case, there are none. Yet for C to understand `beep` as a function call, the empty set of parentheses is required.

The trailing semicolon is the required end-of-statement marker. Putting it together, the entire sequence of the function call, the parenthetical arguments, and the trailing semicolon comprises a single C statement.

Statements can also be arithmetic expressions. For example, try typing

```
2 + 2;
```

at the Interactive C prompt. After pressing the Return key, Interactive C prompt compiles the expression and downloads it to the Handy Board. The Handy Board then calculates the sum, and the answer is returned back to Interactive C, where it is displayed in the Interactive C console window on the workstation computer's screen. Note that it *is* the Handy Board, not the workstation computer, that is doing the arithmetic!

It is also possible to evaluate multiple statements on one line by using the C-language's curly-braces "{...}" to enclose any number of semicolon-terminated statements. For example:

```
{beep(); sleep(2.0); beep();}
```

When this line is executed, the Handy Board will beep, wait 2 seconds (the `sleep` function), and then beep again.

2.1.2 Motors

When Interactive C starts up, it loads library files for controlling the specific hardware features—motors and sensors—of the Handy Board. These library files include functions for controlling the motor outputs and monitoring the sensor inputs.

FIGURE 2.1 Plugging into Motor Port 0

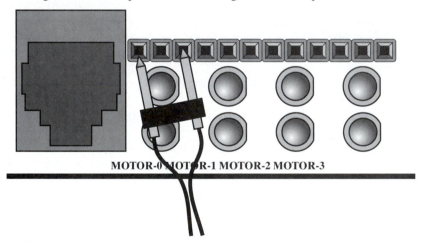

MOTOR-0 MOTOR-1 MOTOR-2 MOTOR-3

Let's experiment with the motor output functions. Plug a motor into the Motor 0 output connector (see Figure 2.1). Now, from the Interactive C command line, type

```
fd(0);
```

and the Motor 0 output port should turn on, lighting the associated green LED, and the motor should start spinning.

Next, try the command

```
bk(0);
```

and the motor should spin in the opposite direction with the red LED lit. Now try

```
off(0);
```

and the motor should turn off.

The power level of the motor output ports can be controlled using the `motor` function, which takes two arguments: a motor port number and a power level. As with the `fd`, `bk`, and `off` functions, the port numbers range from 0 to 3. Power levels range from −100 to +100, where −100 is full on in the "bk" direction, 0 is off, and +100 is full on in the "fd" direction. So, for example:

```
motor(0, 50);
```

turns motor port 0 on in the "fd" direction with a power level of 50%. Try it!

It's worth noting the difference between speed and power. The Handy Board controls motor performance using a technique called *pulse width modulation* (PWM), which is a fancy term for turning something on and off very quickly. (Pulse width modulation is discussed in detail in chapter 4.) When a motor output is set at the 50% point (e.g., `motor(0, 50);`), the Handy Board is alternately applying power and then turning power off to the motor, making sure that the *duty cycle*—the "on time" versus the "off time"—is 50%. This process happens so rapidly that it appears simply that the motor is running more slowly.

The important thing to keep in mind is that speed does not equal power. In other words, the Handy Board's `motor` function allows control of the amount of *power* delivered to a motor, but this does not necessarily translate in an obvious fashion to the motor's resulting *speed*.

The effect is particularly pronounced on a well-geared motor drive, where the motor is not working too hard. Even at a 50% or less power level, a motor may run at speeds near to its 100% power level.

Motor Direction

Question: How many different ways are there to get a robot's wheels to turn the opposite direction? Answer: a lot.

The direction that a motor's shaft turns depends not only on which motor command is used (i.e., `bk()`, `fd()`, or + and − arguments to `motor()`), but also the polarity with which it is plugged in. That is, if the motor plug is pulled from the port connector, rotated 180 degrees, and plugged back, the motor will spin in the opposite direction.

The direction a robot will ultimately move further depends on the design of the gear system—each successive gear introduces a reversal of direction into the rotational movement.

Consider a one-motor robot that can simply move forward or backward. From a practical standpoint, it would be nice if the `fd` function actually made the robot move forward. Turn the motor port on using the `fd` function and then just try both ways of plugging in the motor until the robot goes forward.

Now the `fd()` function will indeed make the robot move forward, the `bk()` function will make it move backward, and programming the robot will be a lot easier.

2.1.3 Sensors

The Handy Board has inputs for nine digital (switch-type) sensors and seven analog (continuously varying) sensors. Let's briefly introduce how switch sensors may be used.

FIGURE 2.2 Plugging into the Sensor Inputs

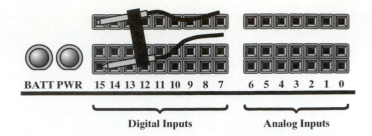

The Handy Board's digital inputs are numbered from 7 to 15, as labeled directly on the printed circuit board. Figure 2.2 shows how a sensor connector is plugged into the Handy Board's digital input 15. For the following experiments, obtain a simple switch sensor and plug it into digital input 15. Please see Section 3.3 for instructions on building a switch sensor if one is not already constructed.

The state of the switch can be tested using the Handy Board library function `digital()`, which takes as its argument the sensor port number. The function returns "true" (numerically, a one) if the switch is closed and "false" (a zero) if it is open.

To try this out, type the following statement at the Interactive C prompt:

```
digital(15);
```

Press Return, and Interactive C should display `<int> 0`, indicating that the value of the switch sensor is zero or false.

Try it again, this time holding the switch lever or button closed when the Return key is pressed. Now, Interactive C should display `<int> 1`, indicating the switch value is true.

Next, let's make the Handy Board perform an action based on the value of the sensor. Try the following:

```
if (digital(15)) {beep();}
```

When pressing Return for the first time, leave switch contact open. Nothing should happen—although the Handy Board should accept the statement without generating any errors! Run the statement again, this time holding the switch closed. The Handy Board should now beep.

Notice that the `if` statement runs only one time each time the Return key is pressed. To continuously test the state of the sensor, it is necessary to put the `if` statement inside of a loop so that the sensor state is repeatedly checked. For example, try the following:

```
while (1) {if (digital(15)) {beep();}}
```

Press Return and first notice that the Interactive C prompt disappears. This means that Interactive C is waiting for the Handy Board to finish executing the statement that has just been downloaded. Meanwhile, the Handy Board is in an infinite loop—the `while (1) {...}` statement!

The `while` construct is a C language control structure that repeatedly executes a statement—or a block of statements, as contained by the curly-braces {...} symbols—while its condition is true. In this case, the condition is simply the number 1, which is always true. So, `while (1) {...}` is C-programmer shorthand for an infinite loop.

Let's check the operation of the `while` statement. Close the switch contact and the Handy Board should beep. If the switch is held closed, the Handy Board should repeatedly beep, with each note immediately following the previous one. After each time the `if` statement is run, the `while` loop recycles and runs it again.

Debugging

What if it didn't work? Maybe the switch is plugged into a port other than 15, or maybe the switch sensor is improperly wired or broken.

Try loading the Handy Board test program `hbtest.c`. At the Interactive C prompt, type "`load hbtest.c`"; Interactive C should compile and download the file. Now type "`testdigitals();`" at the prompt to run the digital sensor test function.

Looking at the Handy Board's LCD screen, the Handy Board will ask you to first press its Start button and then its Stop button. Then it will display a continuous readout of the digital sensor values, like this:

```
Digital inputs:
000000000
```

Remember, this display is on the Handy Board's LCD screen. Try closing the test switch sensor now and see whether any of the zeroes changes to a one on the screen. The left-most zero represents digital input 15, and the right-most is digital input 7.

To regain control of the Handy Board, simply press the Return key. Interactive C will then force the Handy Board to stop what it's doing and get ready to accept another statement from the command line. In an actual program, the programmer would typically use the `break` statement, which forces an exit from a loop.

2.1.4 Files and Functions

Let's continue the introduction to the Handy Board/Interactive C system by learning how to define new functions, save them in files, and load them into Interactive C.

First, create a new document using any text editor or word processing program. A programmer's text editor is preferable because it will automatically save the file in the necessary plain ASCII text format, but a word processing program may also be used.

In the new document, type the following example program:

```
void test() {
    fd(0);
    sleep(1.0);
    bk(0);
    sleep(1.0);
    off(0);
    beep();
}
```

Let's take this code apart one bit at a time. The keyword `void`, just before the function name, indicates that the function has no return value. Functions may have return values, such an integer numeric value; if they have no return value, however, the `void` keyword must be used.

Next comes the function name, followed by open and closed parentheses, which enclose any arguments that the function may have. In this case, our `test` function has no arguments, and it is acceptable to put nothing between the parentheses.

Next is the open brace, followed by the definition of the function, followed by a closed brace. The actual contents of the function should be familiar—motor on and off function calls, a beep, and use of the `sleep` function, which creates a delay.

In the specification of the C language, spacing, indentation, and new lines—collectively, termed *whitespace*—are not significant. For instance, it would be legitimate, although considered "poor form," to put an entire function definition on a single line:

```
void test(){fd(0);sleep(1.0);bk(0);sleep(1.0);beep();off(0);}
```

The above is perfectly legal C code, if very difficult to read. Indeed, there are "obfuscated C" contests to see who can code up certain functions in the most obscure way. Getting rid of spaces, new lines, and indentation is a good way to make a program hard to read.

Thus, for C programmers, the appearance of code, including indentation and related conventions, is a matter of aesthetic judgment and community agreement, not something forced by the specification of the language.

As demonstrated in our example, the syntactic features of the language that *are* necessary include:

- the keyword at the beginning of a function definition to indicate its return value (`void`, in the example `test` function);
- the function name (of course);
- the open and closed parentheses delimiting the functions arguments (which may be empty, as in our example case);
- the open and closed braces delimiting the function definition, and;
- a semicolon at the end of each statement.

Let's save the file defining the `test` function and load it into the Handy Board. Save the document containing the `test` function, giving it a file name that ends in ".`c`"—for example, `test.c`. If using a word processor rather than a programmer's text editor, make sure to save the file using the "text only," "ASCII," "raw text," or similar such format. For convenience, save the file in the Interactive C folder on the workstation computer's hard drive; this is the place that the Interactive C application first looks for user files.

Now switch back into Interactive C and, at its command-line prompt, type "`load test.c`". There should be no semicolon at the end of the line to let Interactive C know that the line is a command to the application and not a bit of C code to be compiled and downloaded.

Interactive C should load the file, compile it, and download the resulting code to the Handy Board. After the download finishes, type

```
test();
```

at the command line to run the `test` function. The motor 0 port should turn on in the forward direction for one second, switch to the backward direction for one second, and turn off, and finally the Handy Board should beep. This is not terribly exciting in and of itself, but now the pieces of programming the Handy Board in Interactive C should be falling into place.

2.1.5 The Main Function

As the final example for this introduction, let's create a function that causes the Handy Board to react to a sensor stimulus (i.e., a switch press) by running its motor backward for a while. We introduce three new features: the syntax for comments in C code, the capability for the Handy Board to automatically run a program when it is turned on, and printing a message to the Handy Board's LCD screen.

In a new blank document, type in the following code:

```
/* sample robot program */
void main() {
    while (1)  {
        printf("Going forward...\n");
        fd(0);
        if (digital(15)) {
            printf("Backing up!\n");
            bk(0);
            beep();
            sleep(2.0);
        }
    }
}
```

and save it in a new file named `robot.c`.

Most of this example should already be familiar: the definition of a function, an infinite loop created by `while (1) {...}`, and an `if` statement to test the state of the sensor.

Notice two new C-language features. At the top of the example is a comment line enclosed by the "`/* ...*/`" syntax. Anything between the open-comment "`/*`" and the closed-comment "`*/`" sequences is ignored. Please note that in some implementations of C, comments embedded within comment (e.g., `/* /* please ignore this? */ */`) are not allowed.

The other new language feature is the `printf` statement. The name `printf` stands for *formatted print*. In the two instances in the example, there's the special sequence `\n` at the end of the text to print. This `\n` means *newline*, which causes the Handy Board to clear the screen before printing the next time it gets to a `printf` statement.

The other hidden special feature is the name of the function : `main`. In traditional C systems, `main` is the function that is called when an application is launched. Similarly, for the Handy Board, if there is a function named `main` loaded into its memory, when it is turned on, the Handy Board will automatically run the `main` function.

From Interactive C, go ahead and download our example `main` function, as saved in the file `robot.c`. After it loads, turn the Handy Board off and then back on. It should start running the program automatically. Try pressing the touch sensor lever plugged into sensor input 15, and the motor should reverse for two seconds, displaying the message `Backing up!` on the Handy Board's LCD screen.

There is one additional detail necessary to work with the `main` function auto-start feature: how to *prevent* the Handy Board from running `main`. Although Interactive C can interrupt the Handy Board while it's running a program, there are occasions when the Handy Board is connected to a robot, and one would like to turn on the Handy Board and not have it drive away!

The answer is to *hold down the Handy Board's Start button* while turning on the power switch. Then the Handy Board will boot up without running `main`.

This concludes the beginning introduction to Interactive C and the Handy Board. In this section, we have seen how to:

- Connect the Handy Board to a workstation computer and use Interactive C's command line to type C statements, which the Handy Board executes immediately;

- Define new C functions, save them in files, and download them to the Handy Board; and

- Turn motors on and off, react to sensor information, and print messages and values to the Handy Board's LCD screen.

Throughout the course of the book, when a new aspect of programming is first used, it is accompanied by an introduction to the associated concepts. For additional information about using Interactive C with the Handy Board, please see Appendix E, the *Interactive C Reference*.

If you began with *HandyBug*, please continue with *A First Program*, on page 71. Otherwise, continue immediately next with building *HandyBug*.

2.2 The HandyBug

Let's continue by building *HandyBug*, a two-motor, two-sensor robotic vehicle that was designed to carry the Handy Board.

Two sets of plans are provided. The first model, called the *HandyBug 9645*, is built primarily from parts in the LEGO DACTA 9645 kit. It is based on the rectangular LEGO Technic motor, for which a standard DC motor can readily be substituted.

The second model, called the *HandyBug 9719*, is built entirely from parts in the LEGO Mindstorms Robotics Invention System. It uses the newer LEGO Technic gear reduction motor. A standard DC motor cannot be substituted here, because the model's gear train relies on the gear reduction provided in this LEGO motor.

Depending on which LEGO materials you have readily available, please construct one of the models from the plans. Or, adapt the plans and customize the design, or design a robot of your own. For the examples that follow in the book, it would be best to use a vehicle that shares the basic "turtle" configuration of separate left-side and right-side motor drive.

The *HandyBugs* were designed to satisfy a number of design considerations. Most important, they are a simple and functional vehicle for carrying out the experiments and projects presented in the book. Additionally, they serve as an example of good LEGO design, use commonly available LEGO parts, and are reliable.

The *HandyBugs* were designed with strong gear reduction, so they move powerfully and somewhat slowly. They work best on a smooth floor, such as linoleum tile or wood, but can drive on a carpet as long as the pile is short. On a plush carpet, a *HandyBug* cannot turn.

2.2.1 HandyBug 9645

The following pictures provide step-by-step instructions for building the *HandyBug 9645*. This *HandyBug* uses two 9v LEGO motors for power and two LEGO touch sensors. Figure 2.3 is a schematic drawing of *HandyBug 9645*; Figure 2.8 shows the completed assembly.

FIGURE 2.3 Schematic Drawing of LEGO Turtle Robot

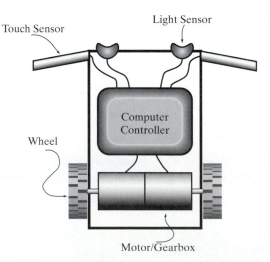

To begin, procure the parts listed in Figures 2.4, 2.5, and 2.6. *HandyBug* can be built from LEGO DACTA kit 9645, supplemented with one worm gear (part number 779854, a small gear assortment that includes 10 worm gears) and one 9v motor (part number 775114).

It's also possible to build *HandyBug* from DACTA's *Technology Resource Set* (part number 9609) supplemented with one additional 9v motor. This is a much larger kit of materials that would allow substantial building projects beyond *HandyBug*. Figure 2.7 lists some parts substitutions for working from the *Technology Resource Set*.

Custom cables must be made to connect the LEGO touch sensor and LEGO motor to the Handy Board. Please see directions in Appendix B.4 regarding these modifications.

Using Non-LEGO Motors and Sensors

The building plans presented here show how to build *HandyBug 9645* using off-the-shelf LEGO motors and sensors. However, it is possible to use non-LEGO motors and touch switches instead. In Appendix B there are construction techniques for "LEGOizing" a standard DC motor so it may be mounted as part of a LEGO Technic model and wiring instructions for a standard microswitch.

Now, here are step-by-step plans for building *HandyBug 9645*.[1] Let's begin.

Step 1. Start by getting one 1×16 Technic beam, one 24–tooth gear, one medium pulley wheel, one 8–tooth gear, one bevel gear, and one 6–stud long axle:

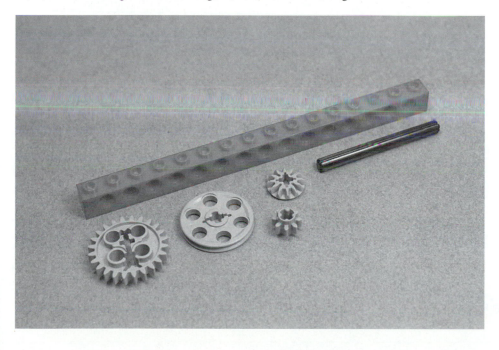

---

[1] Allen Demers of LEGO DACTA graciously contributed to the design of the HandyBug 9645.

FIGURE 2.4 *HandyBug 9645*
Parts Listing (1 of 3)

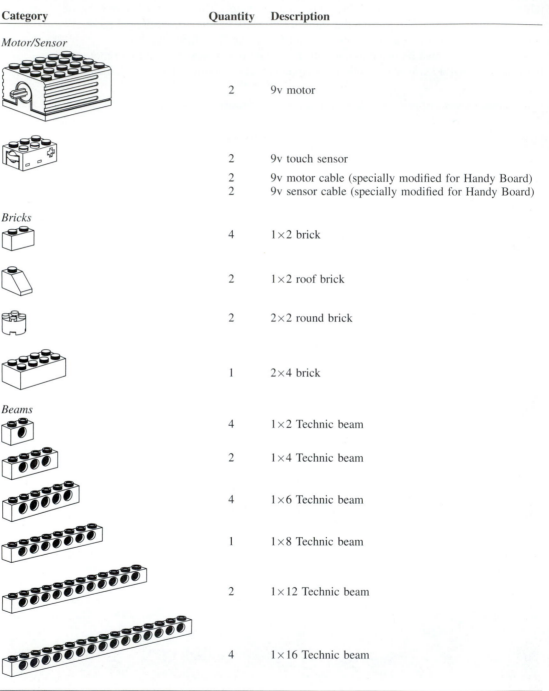

Category	Quantity	Description
Motor/Sensor		
	2	9v motor
	2	9v touch sensor
	2	9v motor cable (specially modified for Handy Board)
	2	9v sensor cable (specially modified for Handy Board)
Bricks		
	4	1×2 brick
	2	1×2 roof brick
	2	2×2 round brick
	1	2×4 brick
Beams		
	4	1×2 Technic beam
	2	1×4 Technic beam
	4	1×6 Technic beam
	1	1×8 Technic beam
	2	1×12 Technic beam
	4	1×16 Technic beam

FIGURE 2.5 *HandyBug 9645*
Parts Listing (2 of 3)

Category	Quantity	Description
Plates		
	2	1×2 plate
	2	1×8 plate
	2	1×10 plate
	3	2×4 plate
	1	2×6 Technic plate (with holes)
	4	2×8 Technic plate (with holes)
	1	6×8 plate
Gears		
	2	8–tooth gear
	2	16–tooth gear
	2	24–tooth gear
	2	24–tooth crown gear
	2	40–tooth gear
	2	worm gear
	2	bevel gear

FIGURE 2.6 *HandyBug 9645*
Parts Listing (3 of 3)

Category	Quantity	Description
Axles		
	2	4–stud long axle
	2	6–stud long axle
	2	8–stud long axle
	2	10–stud long axle
Wheels/Tires		
	2	medium pulley wheel (23 mm)
	6	full-width stop bush
	8	tire hub
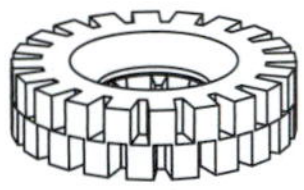	2	tire (42 mm)
Miscellaneous		
	6	connector peg, black
	4	connector peg with axle
	4	piston rod
	2	counter (yellow)
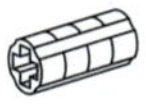	1	axle extender
	2	crank
	2	red belt

FIGURE 2.7 Alternate Parts from
Technic Resource Set

Original Part	Substituted Part
1×2 angled brick	1×2 brick
2×2 round brick	2×2 brick
bevel gear	half bushing
medium pulley wheel	half bushing
crank	half bushing

Step 2. Assemble these as illustrated. Note that the axle is one back from the end hole of the beam:

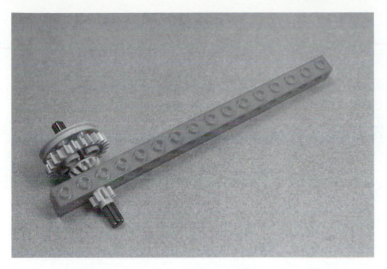

Step 3. Get three full-size stop bushes, one 24–tooth crown gear, one 40–tooth gear, one tire hub, one tire, and one 8–stud long axle:

Step 4. Assemble these onto the prior mechanism as shown:

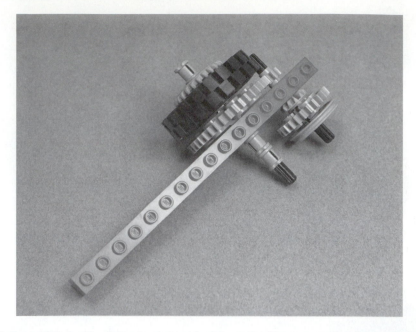

This assembly is *HandyBug*'s right-side drivetrain. Next we make the left-side drive by following the same steps, resulting in a mirror image of the just-completed assembly.

Step 5. Get one 1×16 Techic beam, one 24–tooth gear, one medium pulley wheel, one 8–tooth gear, one bevel gear, and one 6–stud long axle:

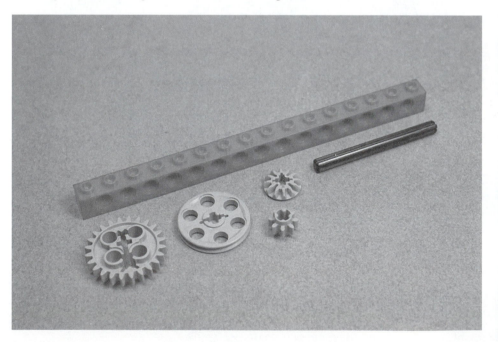

Step 6. Assemble these as shown:

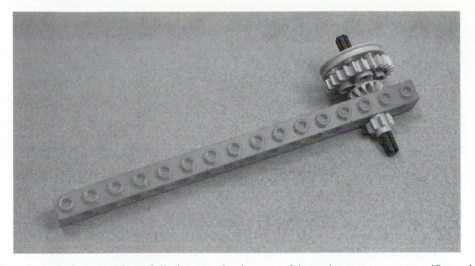

Step 7. As before, get three full-size stop bushes, one 24–tooth crown gear, one 40–tooth gear, one tire hub, one tire, and one 8–stud long axle:

Step 8. Assemble onto the prior mechanism:

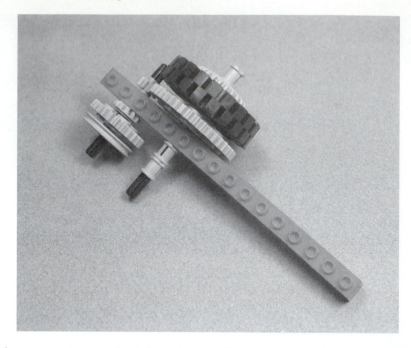

In the next two steps, the left- and right-side gear trains are brought together and *HandyBug*'s chassis begins to take shape.

Step 9. Get two 16–long beams and three 2×8 plates:

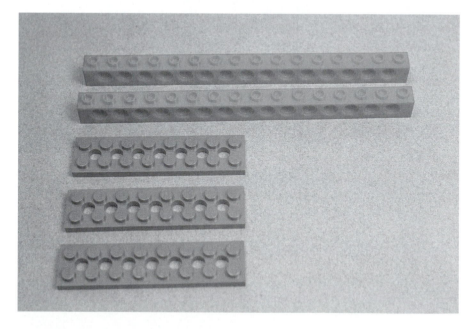

Step 10. Now bring the two gear trains together, with the new beams in the middle, using the plates to brace from underneath:

In the next steps, the chassis is prepared for motor mounting.

Step 11. Get one 2×4 brick, two 1×2 angled bricks, two 1×2 plates, and three 2×4 plates:

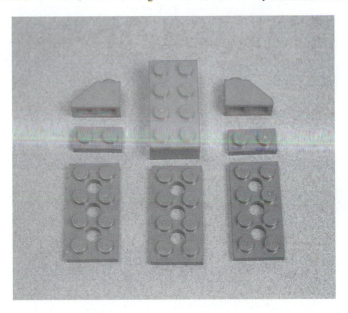

Step 12. Two of the 2×4 plates are mounted in the middle of the chassis, and the other parts mount near the back end (by the tires):

Step 13. Get the two modified motor cables:

Step 14. Install in the center of the chassis above the 2×4 plates just mounted:

Step 15. Get the two 9v motors:

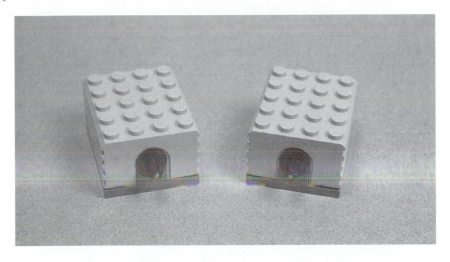

Step 16. Mount directly on top of the motor cables as shown:

Step 17. To complete the gear train, we install the worm gears onto the motor shafts and hold them in place with a beam. Also, a 2×8 plate is used to strengthen the chassis. Get the 2×8 plate, two worm gears, and a 1×8 beam:

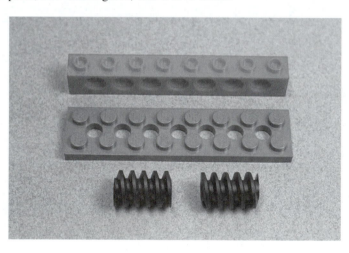

Step 18. Install as illustrated:

In the next two steps, *HandyBug*'s front slip wheels are installed.

Step 19. Get two 1×6 beams, two tire hubs, two connector peg with axle parts, and one 1×10 plate:

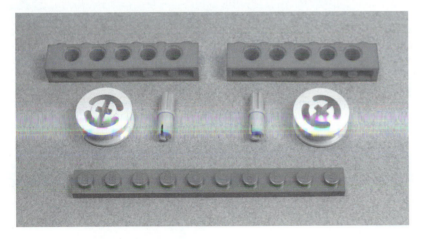

Step 20. The 1×10 plate mounts underneath *HandyBug* in the very front, with the 1×6 beams holding it in place. The wheel hubs mount in the center of the 1×6 beams:

Step 21. Next, *HandyBug*'s touch sensors are installed. Get the two touch sensors, two 2×2 round bricks, and one 2×6 plate:

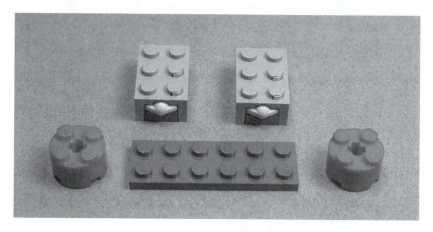

Step 22. Mount as illustrated:

Step 23. Continuing with the touch sensor mounting, get one 1×10 plate, four 1×2 Technic beams, and two 1×2 bricks:

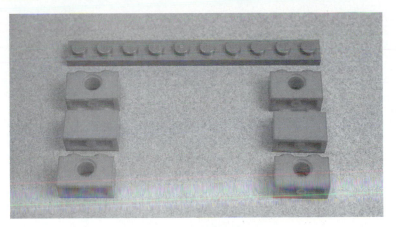

Step 24. Mount the two modified LEGO sensor cables:

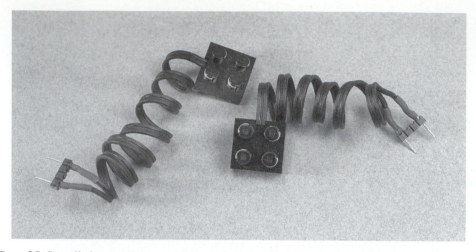

Step 25. Install these parts on and around the touch sensors as shown:

Step 26. In the next several steps, *HandyBug*'s chassis is completed. Get two 1×12 beams, two 1×4 beams, and two 1×2 bricks:

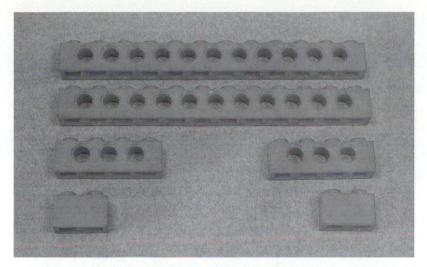

Step 27. Install as shown. Make sure to thread the motor and sensor cables out the opening that is created near the motors when these parts are installed:

Step 28. Continuing, get the 6×8 plate, four black connector pegs, and two 1×6 beams:

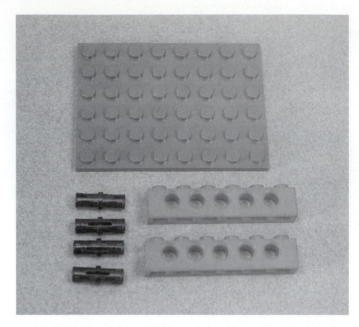

Step 29. Mount the 6×8 plate across the motors as shown, and use the black connector pegs to lock the 1×6 beams in a cross-configuration:

Step 30. At this point, the chassis is complete, and the remaining work constructs the touch sensor bumper. Get two 16–tooth gears, two connector peg with axle parts, four piston rods, and two 4–stud long axles:

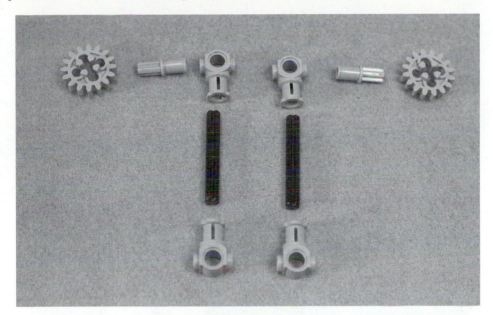

Step 31. These parts form two identical assemblies that are used to hold the bumper. Install the assemblies on either side of the front of *HandyBug*:

Step 32. Get the two red belts and two black connector pegs:

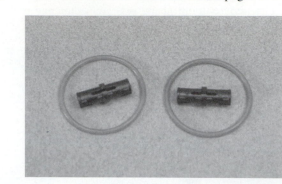

Step 33. Install these parts to push the touch bumper holders forward:

Step 34. Next the bumper is constructed. Get four tire hubs, two 10–stud long axles, two yellow "counters," and one axle extender:

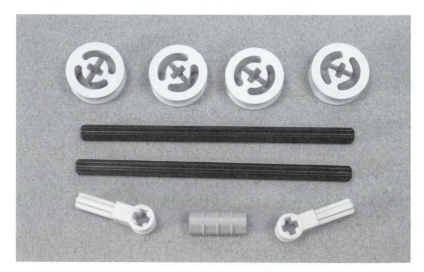

Step 35. Assemble as shown:

Step 36. The touch bumper can now be mounted onto *HandyBug*. The axle rods of the yellow "counter" part drop down into the piston rod holders already installed on *HandyBug*:

Step 37. The two crank parts, shown below, are used to hold the touch bumper in place.

Step 38. *HandyBug* is almost done! The last step is to mount the Handy Board. Get two 1×8 plates:

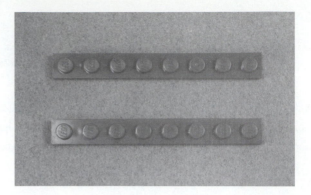

Step 39. Place on top of the upper chassis beams:

The Handy Board can then be glued to these 1×8 plates. A cyanoacrylate instant glue (e.g., Krazy Glue) is recommended; be sure not to use so much that the 1×8 plates are glued to the chassis!

The Handy Board should be positioned so that its back edge is aligned almost to the back edge of the *HandyBug*, so that the weight of the Handy Board is just forward of the rear drive wheels. Figure 2.8 shows the final assembly.

HandyBug 9645 is now done! If you started with *HandyBug* before the introduction to Interactive C and the Handy Board, please continue at page 20 to learn about the robot "brain."

Otherwise, please continue with "A First Program."

2.2.2 HandyBug 9719

In this section, step-by-step directions are given for building a *HandyBug* robot from the *LEGO 9719* kit (the kit that is included with the LEGO Mindstorms Robotics Invention System). This kit includes two 9v gear-reduction drive motors along with a wealth of over 700 Technic parts.

FIGURE 2.8 The Completed *HandyBug 9645* Robot

In the following three tables all of the parts required are shown. With the exception of custom cables to plug into the Handy Board's motor ports (for the two motors) and sensor ports (for the two touch switches), all of the parts are included in the 9719 kit. To see an image of the final result, turn to Figure 2.12 on page 71.

Now, here are step-by-step plans for building *HandyBug 9719*. Let's begin.

Step 1. Begin by getting two 1×2 plates with motor mount tabs and two 1×8 Technic beams:

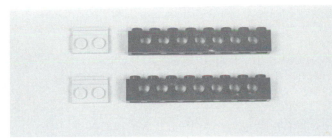

Step 2. Place the beams side by side, and attach the 1×2 plates so that the mounting tabs protrude outward:

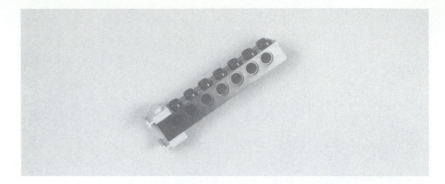

Step 3. Get two more 1×2 plates with motor tabs and two 1×6 Technic beams:

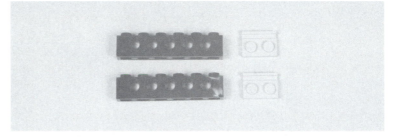

Step 4. Connect these parts as with the previous beam assembly, as shown:

Step 5. Next, get a gear reduction Technic motor, and insert the two beam assemblies into the motor:

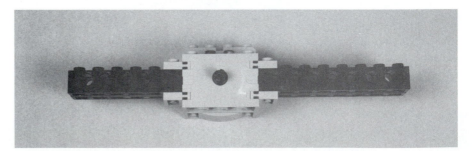

Step 6. Get two 1× plates and one 2×6 Technic plate:

Step 7. Mount on the underside of the motor/beam assembly:

Step 8. Get two more 1×2 plates and two 2×2 plates:

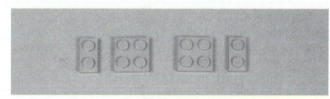

Step 9. Mount these on the top of the motor/beam assembly:

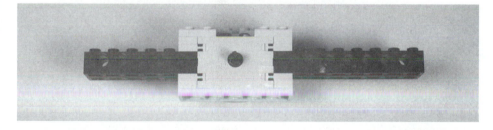

You have just completed the right-side drive of the *HandyBug* robot. Over steps 10 through 18, a mirror copy of this assembly will be constructed (for the left-side drive).

Step 10. Get two 1×2 plates with motor mount tabs and two 1×8 Technic beams:

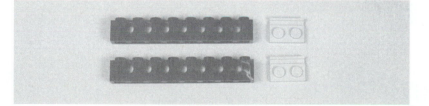

FIGURE 2.9 *HandyBug 9719*
Parts Listing (1 of 3)

Category	Quantity	Description
Motor/Sensor		
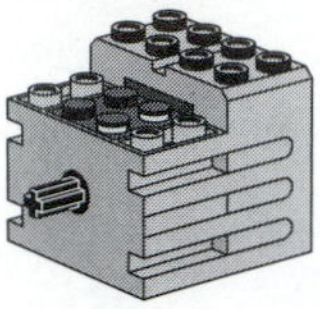	2	9v gear reduction motor
	2	9v touch sensor
	2	9v motor cable (specially modified for Handy Board)
	2	9v sensor cable (specially modified for Handy Board)
Bricks		
	4	1×2 brick
	2	2×3 brick with arch, green
	2	2×2 round brick
	4	2×4 brick
Beams		
	8	1×6 Technic beam
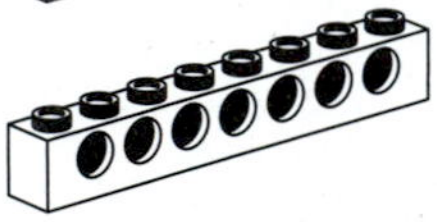	6	1×8 Technic beam
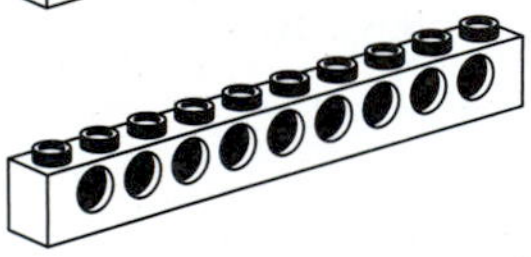	1	1×10 Technic beam
	4	1×12 Technic beam
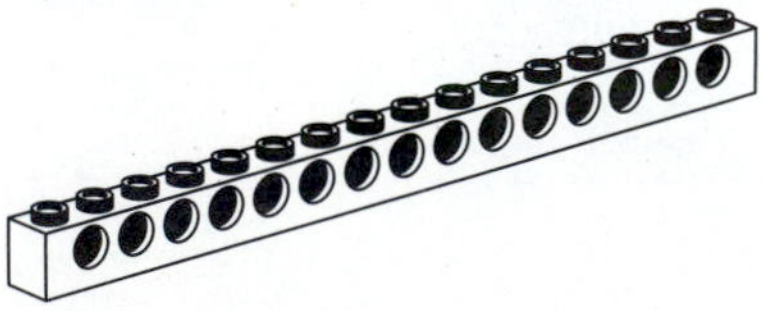	2	1×16 Technic beam

Category	Quantity	Description
Plates		
	8	1×2 plate
	2	1×6 plate
	2	1×10 plate
	4	2×2 plate
	2	2×4 plate (yellow)
	2	2×4 Technic plate (with holes)
	2	2×6 Technic plate (with holes)
	2	2×8 Technic plate (with holes)
Gears		
	2	8–tooth gear
	2	40–tooth gear
Axles		
	2	3–stud long axle
	2	6–stud long axle
	2	10–stud long axle

FIGURE 2.10 *HandyBug 9719*
Parts Listing (2 of 3)

FIGURE 2.11 *HandyBug 9719*
Parts Listing (3 of 3)

Category	Quantity	Description
Wheels/Tires		
	2	small pulley wheel
	2	full-width stop bush
	6	tire hub
	2	tire (large)
	2	tire (small)
Miscellaneous		
	2	connector peg, gray
	6	connector peg, black
	2	long connector peg, black
	2	cross axle with stop
	4	axle connector #1, blue
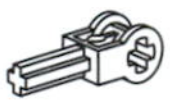	2	catch, gray
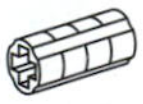	1	axle extender
	8	1×2 plate with slide (for motor mount)
	2	2×2 skid plate
	2	rubber band, black

Step 11. Place the beams side by side, and attach the 1×2 plates so that the mounting tabs protrude outward:

Step 12. Get two more 1×2 plates with motor tabs and two 1×6 Technic beams:

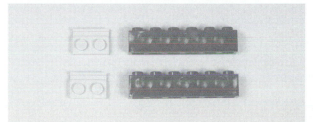

Step 13. Connect these parts as with the previous beam assembly, as shown:

Step 14. Next, get a gear reduction Technic motor, and insert the two beam assemblies into the motor:

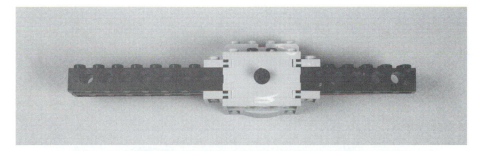

Step 15. Get two 1× plates and one 2×6 Technic plate:

Step 16. Mount on the underside of the motor/beam assembly:

Step 17. Get two more 1×2 plates and two 2×2 plates:

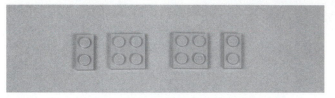

Step 18. Mount these on the top of the motor/beam assembly:

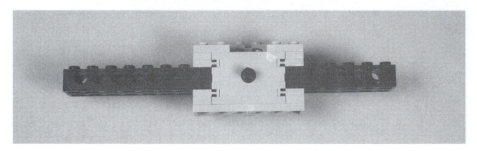

The left-side drive of *HandyBug* is now done. Next, the two drives will be attached.

Step 19. Get four 1×12 Technic beams:

Step 20. With these four beams, attach the two sides of *HandyBug*, using two beams on either side of the motor mounts:

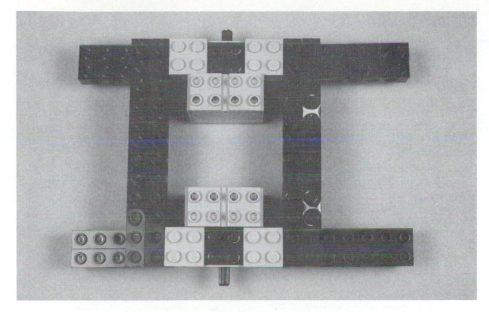

Step 21. Get two 2×4 plates, and two 2×4 bricks:

Step 22. Attach these on top of the beams as shown. The bricks are snapped down first, followed by the plates:

Step 23. Get two 2×4 bricks, and two 1×10 plates:

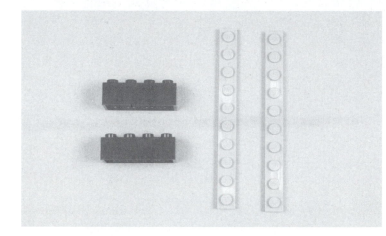

Step 24. Attach the bricks on top of the cross-beams to hold the motors, and attach the plates across the front of *HandyBug*:

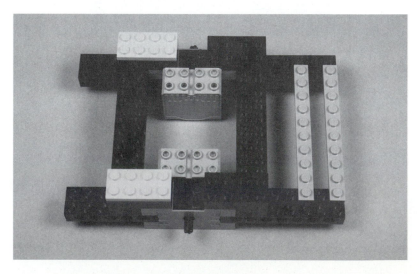

Step 25. Get two LEGO touch sensors and four 1×2 bricks:

Step 26. Attach the touch sensors on top of the 1×10 plates, with a stack of two 1×2 bricks next to each:

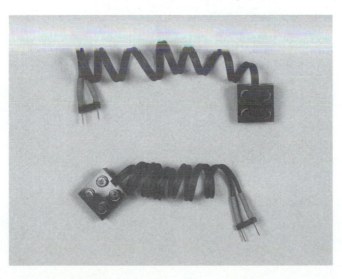

Step 27. Get two cables for the touch sensors. These should have the standard 2×2 LEGO electrical connector at one end, and a connector for Handy Board sensors at the other end:

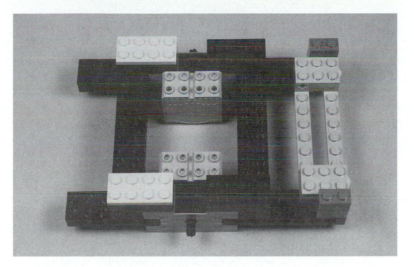

Step 28. Attach these onto the front part of the touch sensors as shown:

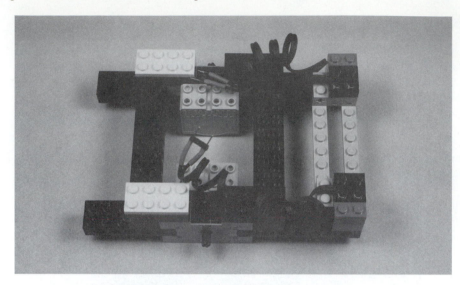

Step 29. Get two 2×8 plates:

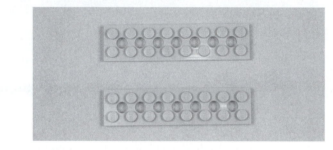

Step 30. Attach these over the touch sensors, as shown:

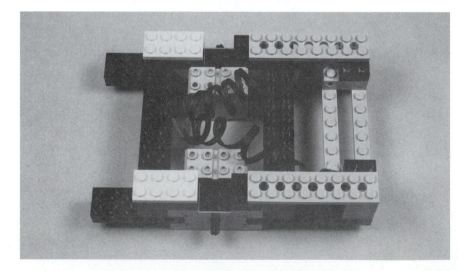

Step 31. Get two motor cables, and two 2×3 bricks with arch. The motor cables have the standard 2×2 LEGO electrical connector at one end, and a connector for Handy Board motors at the other end:

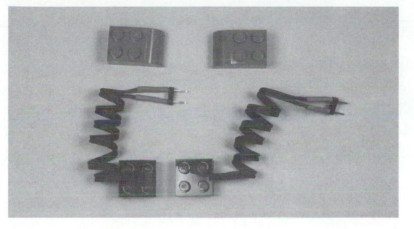

Step 32. Plug the motor cables on top of the motors' power connectors, with the arched bricks to hold them down:

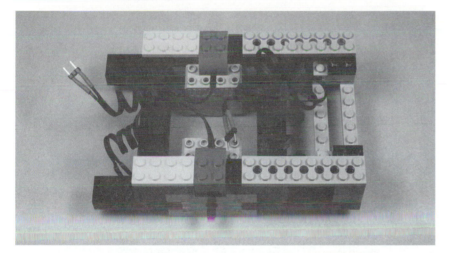

Step 33. Get two 1×16 Technic beams:

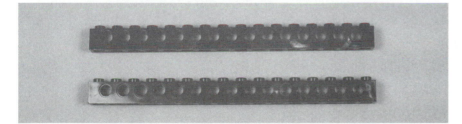

Step 34. Attach these lengthwise, from the back of *HandyBug*:

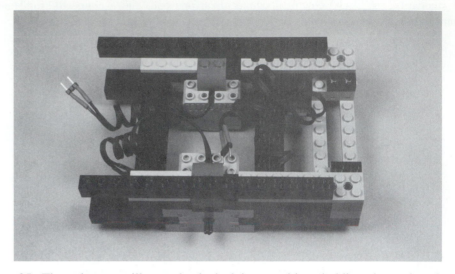

Step 35. These beams will now be locked into position, holding the entire chassis together firmly. Get four 1×6 Technic beams, two 3–long black connector pegs, and six 2–long black connector pegs:

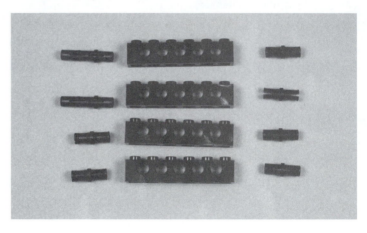

Step 36. Insert the connector pegs into the end holes of the 6–long beams, and lock the 16–long beams to the chassis. Note that the 3–long pegs stick out through the long beams in the top back:

The core of the chassis is now completed. The design is solid enough that it should be able to survive even a waist-high drop! In the next steps, the touch sensor bumper is constructed.

Step 37. Get two gray cross-axles with stop, and one 1×8 Technic beam:

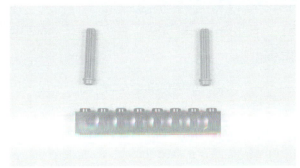

Step 38. Turn the *HandyBug* chassis upside-down, and mount the three parts in the front underside as shown:

Step 39. Get one 1×8 Technic beam, the blue #1 axle connector, a 3–stud long axle, and a gray connector peg:

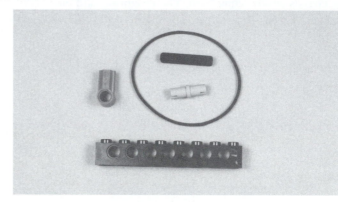

Step 40. Assemble these parts as shown. The 3–stud long axle is inserted into the blue connector. The rubber band is pushed through the axle connector's hole and then through the adjacent hole of the 8–long beam:

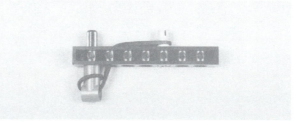

Step 41. Get another collection of the same pieces, less the beam:

Step 42. Mount these into the other side of the beam, as shown:

Step 43. Now, mount this assembly underside *HandyBug*. The cross-axles sticking out from *HandyBug* should now be spring-loaded by the rubber bands of the assembly:

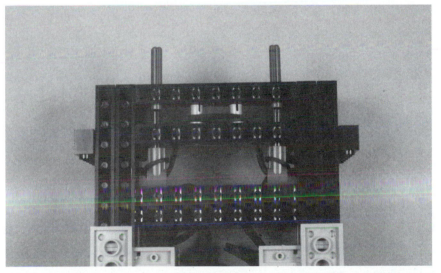

Step 44. Get two 1×6 plates, two 2×4 plates, two 2×2 round bricks, and two 2×2 skid plates:

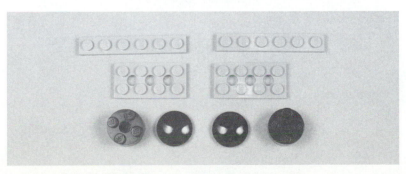

Step 45. Mount these underside *HandyBug*, holding the touch sensor assembly together:

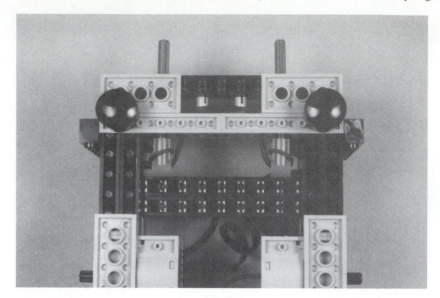

Next, the touch bumper assembly is constructed.

Step 46. Get one axle connector, two gray catch pieces, two small tires, four tire hubs, and two 10–stud long axles:

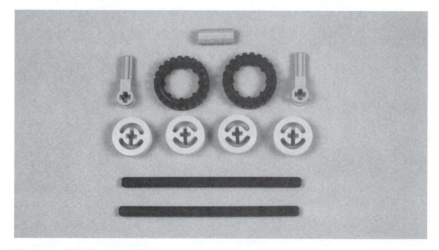

Step 47. Assemble these as shown:

Step 48. Get two blue #1 axle connectors and two small pulley wheels:

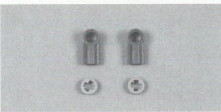

Step 49. Turn *HandyBug* right side up, and drop the bumper assembly into bumper posts that are extending forward. Use the small pulley wheels to hold the bumper in place, inserting them from underneath the bumper:

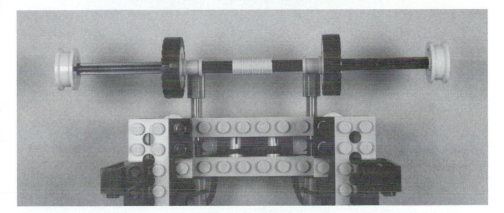

HandyBug is almost complete. In the remaining steps, the rear drive wheels and gears are installed.

Step 50. Get one large tire, one tire hub, one 40–tooth gear, one 8–tooth gear, and one 6–stud long axle:

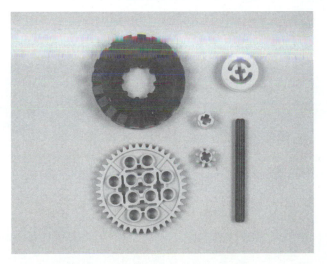

Step 51. Mount these onto *HandyBug*. The 8–tooth gear goes directly on the motor shaft, and the other parts mount as shown:

Step 52. Get another collection of the same parts, and mount onto the other side of *HandyBug*:

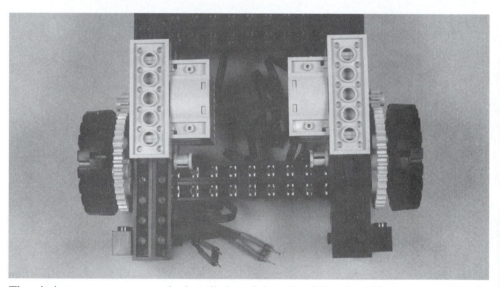

There's just one more part to be installed, and then *HandyBug* is ready to accept a Handy Board.

Step 53. Get a 1×10 Technic beam:

FIGURE 2.12 The Completed
HandyBug 9719

Step 54. Turn *HandyBug* right side up, and mount the beam across the front.

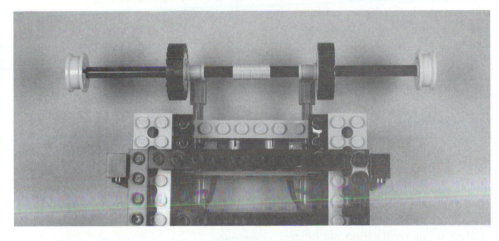

The Handy Board can now be simply dropped into the *HandyBug*. At the rear, the 3–long black pegs should hold the Handy Board in place. Figure 2.12 shows the final model, with Handy Board installed.

HandyBug 9719 is now done! If you started with *HandyBug* before the introduction to Interactive C and the Handy Board, please continue at page 20 to learn about the robot "brain."

Otherwise, please continue with "A First Program."

2.3 A First Program

All right! At this point, you have already built *HandyBug* and played with the Handy Board and Interactive C—in whichever order you chose—and now you are ready to put a first purposeful program into the *HandyBug* creature. We assume that you're already comfortable booting up Interactive C and typing statements at its command line, and that you've seen the basics of how to create a new C function.

2.3.1 Plugging in Motors and Sensors

After getting the Handy Board mounted on *HandyBug* as illustrated in Figure 2.8, plug one of the motors into motor port 0 and the other into port 3. For the two touch sensors, plug them into ports 10 and 11. (See the sidebar, "Not All Ports Are Created Equal" to explain this choice of port numbering.)

Let's make sure that the `fd()` command actually makes *HandyBug* drive forward. From the Interactive C command line, type

```
{fd(0); fd(3);}
```

Both motors should turn on. If *HandyBug* is not driving straight ahead, unplug any motor that is running backward, turn its plug around 180 degrees, and plug it back in.

Not All Ports Are Created Equal

Motors. Why ports 0 and 3 to run the two motors? The Handy Board has two motor driver chips, and each chip is capable of operating two motors. The upper chip runs motor ports 0 and 1, while the lower chip runs motor ports 2 and 3.

During normal motor operation, these chips will get warm or even mildly hot as a result of the power being dissipated in the chips. When only powering two motors, as is the case with the stock *HandyBug*, it's best to share the load between the two chips. This means that one motor should be plugged into port 0 or 1, and the other into port 2 or 3. Then each chip only works half as hard as if it were operating both motors.

Sensors. Why ports 10 and 11 for touch sensors? The Handy Board's digital inputs—which are ideal for touch sensors—are numbered from 7 to 15, but all of these are not alike. Digital inputs 7, 8, and 9 are connected directly to the 68HC11 microprocessor, while ports 10 through 15 are interfaced through a separate latch chip. The three ports connected directly to the 68HC11 have additional capabilities than just indicating true/false levels, such as timing the precise wavelength of a signal.

For simple switches, it makes sense to use the ports 10 through 15 first, leaving the "special" ports 7, 8, and 9 free for more sophisticated applications. Also, in case of a wiring problem with a sensor, it would be better to potentially cause the external latch chip to fail, rather than the 68HC11 processor.

Of course, if it is desired to connect more than six switches to the Handy Board, there is no reason ports 7 through 9 should not be used. It just makes sense to leave them for last.

2.3.2 Obstacle Avoidance

Now let's create a program for *HandyBug* to avoid obstacles. Well, more precisely, *HandyBug* will still run into things, but at least it should back up and turn after doing so:

```
/* sample touch sensor program */
void main() {
```

```
while (1) {
    /* go forward */
    fd(0);
    fd(3);
    /* test for touch */
    if (digital(10)) {
        /* go backward */
        bk(0);
        bk(3);
        sleep(0.5);
        /* turn */
        fd(0);
        sleep(0.5);
    }
}
}
```

As we have seen before, the program builds an infinite loop using the `while (1)` {...} construct. Inside the loop, the two motors are set to drive *HandyBug* forward. Then the touch sensor is checked. If it is true, then a sequence of actions is taken:

- the motors are set to the backward direction;
- a half-second delay is executed, allowing *HandyBug* to drive backward for that period of time;
- one motor is set to the forward direction, causing *HandyBug* to spin in place while the other motor is still going backward;
- another half-second delay is executed, meaning *HandyBug* will do the spin for one-half second.

After the touch sensor sequence finishes, the `while` loop restarts, making *HandyBug* go forward again. So the overall result is that *HandyBug* should start up and drive straight ahead. If it hits something on its touch sensor plugged into port 10, it should back up for a half-second, spin for a half-second, and then start going forward again.

Try it—does it work?

2.3.3 Obstacle-Avoidance Exercises

1. *Turn direction.* Does *HandyBug* turn to get away from obstacles or does it turn toward them? For instance, suppose the left-side touch sensor is the active one. After bumping the sensor, does *HandyBug* turn to the left (toward the obstacle) or to the right (away from it)?
   Make sure that *HandyBug* turns away from the obstacles. If it's turning toward them, fix it.
2. Name at least four different ways this problem can be fixed. Hint: Not all of these require reprogramming.
3. *Both touch sensors.* Extend the sample program so that both touch sensors are active. Make sure *HandyBug* turns away from obstacles regardless of which touch sensor is hit.
4. *Performance.* Let *HandyBug* run around without human assistance for a while. How well does it do—does it manage to "survive" without getting stuck?
   Obtain one of those toy balls with an asymmetric internal motor mechanism, one that manages to turn itself around when it drives itself into a corner. Compare the performance of the microprocessor-controlled *HandyBug* to the $10 toy ball. Are there instances where *HandyBug* gets stuck and the toy ball gets free? Vice versa?

2.3.4 Turtle Movements

Before going much further, it is helpful to create a set of *movement abstractions* for controlling the overall motion of *HandyBug*—for example, telling it to go forward, backward, or make a turn. This way, we won't have to always remember "for a left turn, set motor 0 forward and motor 3 backward," or whatever the case may be, when writing code. Also, it will make programs a lot more readable.

Given *HandyBug*'s geometry, a set of basic movements might include:

- forward—both motors on driving forward.
- backward—both motors on driving backward.
- spin left—left motor on backward; right motor on forward.
- spin right—left motor on forward; right motor on backward.

Additional movements are possible with just one motor turned on at a time (e.g., left motor on forward to make *HandyBug* advance while turning to the right), but these four are a useful starting point. Sample code to implement these movements, as well as stopping, is shown in Figure 2.13.

From the Interactive C prompt, load the `turtle.c` file and try out the movement commands.

A Tale of Turtles

W. Grey Walter, a British cybernetician, was probably the first to refer to small mobile robots as "turtles." In the 1950s, Walter built a series of battery-powered mobile robots to explore ideas in sensing, control, and feedback. Walter's turtles' "intelligence" was based on clever designs using just one or a few vacuum tubes to perform a variety of functions. His turtles were able to demonstrate fairly sophisticated behaviors, including using sources of light as beacons for docking maneuvers to connect to battery recharge stations. Walter tried to give his turtles creature-like abilities, such as the ability to perform for extended periods without human attention.

In the 1960s, Seymour Papert and his Logo Research group at MIT's AI Lab created tethered mobile robots that they connected to Logo, a programming language designed for children. Using a relativist geometry (e.g., "forward 50 turtle steps" and "right 90 degrees"), children could program the turtle to move around. The turtle was then equipped with a pen, and children were able to write programs to cause the turtle to make drawings on the floor.

Later, Papert's "floor turtles" transformed into CRT-based "screen turtles" as vector- and raster-computer displays became common. But the core idea of the turtle as an "object to think with" has become part of the Logo programming environment ever since the early floor turtles hooked up to mainframes with TeleType interfaces.

2.3.5 Turtle Movement Exercises

1. Make sure that the functions in `turtle.c` work properly; in particular, the `left()` and `right()` functions, which should have only a 50/50 chance of working the first time.

FIGURE 2.13 Listing of
`turtle.c`

```
/*
    turtle.c

    basic movement commands:
    forward, backward, right, left, and stop
*/

int LEFT_MOTOR=     0;
int RIGHT_MOTOR=    3;

void forward()
{
    fd(LEFT_MOTOR);
    fd(RIGHT_MOTOR);
}

void backward()
{
    bk(LEFT_MOTOR);
    bk(RIGHT_MOTOR);
}

void right()
{
    fd(LEFT_MOTOR);
    bk(RIGHT_MOTOR);
}

void left()
{
    fd(RIGHT_MOTOR);
    bk(LEFT_MOTOR);
}

void stop()
{
    off(LEFT_MOTOR),
    off(RIGHT_MOTOR);
}
```

How did you choose to fix the problem if the code did not work right?

2. Rewrite the earlier dual touch sensor program to use the new movement abstractions.

2.4 Braitenberg Vehicles

Let's step back and take a broader look at what it means to be a robot. Clearly a robot must have sensors, actuators, and some kind of control relationship among these components. But what exactly does this mean? As a lens for focusing our look, let us examine the work of Valentino Braitenberg.

A neurobiologist by profession, Braitenberg wrote a short book, *Vehicles: Experiments into Synthetic Psychology* [Bra84], as a thought experiment into how sentient creatures might have evolved from simpler organisms. The book presents a series of hypothetical creature-like "vehicles," beginning with *Vehicle 1*, a one-motor, one-sensor device (Figure 2.14).

FIGURE 2.14 Braitenberg's *Vehicle 1*, a One-Motor, One-Sensor Creature

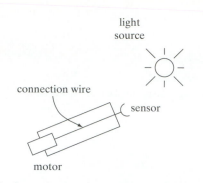

In Braitenberg's *Vehicle 1*, a wire connects the vehicle's sensor to its motor, and the sensor generates a signal proportional to the strength of the quality that the sensor detects. Imagine that the sensor detects light: The more light *Vehicle 1*'s sensor receives, the stronger a signal it sends, and the faster the motor turns. This stimulatory relationship—the sensor's signal "stimulates" the motor to turn—is indicated by a + symbol near the motor.

2.4.1 One Motor and One Sensor

What does *Vehicle 1* do? When it "sees" a light source, it starts moving. If it happens to be pointed toward the light, as it gets closer it will speed up because the light is brighter. Eventually it will overshoot the light because it has no way of steering or slowing down when it reaches it.

Sensors can also be wired with an inhibitory relationship to the motor. If *Vehicle 1* were wired in such a way, it would drive full speed in the dark, slowing down when it reached light sources. It might even appear to be "feeding on light," seeking out sources of light and slowing down when it found them. Of course, we would know it had just one sensor and a simple control law determining its motor performance based on the sensed quality, but it might not be so obvious to the casual observer.

Robot or Creature?

People's reactions to little robots scurrying around the floor are striking. People of all ages tend to anthropomorphize the robots—to attribute human- or animal-like intentionality to them, such as desire, dismay, persistence, and so on. All it takes is a little bit of "intelligent" behavior—backing up when hitting something, turning away from a light—and a robot appears to know what it's doing.

2.4.2 Two Motors and Two Sensors

Vehicle 1 is fun, but it has a limited repertoire of behaviors because it can only move in a straight line. Braitenberg's *Vehicle 2b*, a more interesting vehicle, is built with two motors and two sensors (Figure 2.15).

The diagram shows one of several possible configurations *Vehicle 2b* can take. The sensors are cross-wired—each to the motor on the opposite side—and with stimulatory effect. How does *Vehicle 2b* behave?

When *Vehicle 2b*'s left-side sensor is closer than the right-side one to the light source, it drives the right-side motor faster than the left-side one, and *Vehicle 2b* veers to the left (Figure 2.16).

FIGURE 2.16 Braitenberg's
Vehicle 2b Moves Toward Light

Vehicle 2b's left-side sensor
(indicated by the thicker lines)
is closer to the light, so it
receives a greater stimulus than
the right-side sensor. The
left-side sensor then drives the
right-side wheel at a faster rate,
and *Vehicle 2b* steers to the
left—thereby aiming it toward
the light. By continually turning
toward sources of greater
stimulation, *Vehicle 2b* seeks out
such sources.

By continuously turning toward light in this fashion, *Vehicle 2b* hunts down and
finds light sources—much more effectively than *Vehicle 1*, which can only slow down
when it accidentally runs by one. *Vehicle 2*'s corrective control system is an instance
of *feedback*—a goal-seeking behavior accomplished by continually making corrective
actions. *Vehicle 2b* always *reduces the difference* between its heading and the brightest
source of light. This type of correction is called *negative feedback* because it is continually
reducing an error or difference.

Negative feedback tends to bring a system toward a goal state (in *Vehicle 2b*'s case,
the resultant goal is to be pointed directly at a light source). *Positive feedback* occurs
when a system's actions repeatedly push it away from a stable state—especially when
greater errors cause even greater "away from the goal" corrections.

For example, suppose *Vehicle 2b* is rewired so that the sensor-to-motor connections
no longer cross over, creating *Vehicle 2b* (Figure 2.17). How does this creature perform?

Instead of turning toward light sources, *Vehicle 2a* is driven away from them because
a brighter left-side light will make it turn to the right. Positive feedback drives it away
from light and toward dark spots. So *Vehicle 2a* is drawn to the dark as a result of it
being driven away from the light.

FIGURE 2.17 Braitenberg's
Vehicle 2a

"I'd Like Some FeedBack"

As a technical term, *positive feedback* has an opposite meaning from its colloquial usage. From an engineer's point of view, a positive feedback system is one that's inherently unstable, just waiting for a trigger to knock it out of control. Imagine a ball sitting on the top of a hill. It's a stable configuration, but as soon as the ball is perturbed, gravity pulls it off the top and it runs away.

On the other hand, if someone gives you "positive feedback" on your activities, it means "keep doing what you're doing." This is more like the engineer's *negative feedback* system—a system that takes corrective actions to reduce errors, bringing the system always closer to a goal state, which is the state when the error is zero.

But if a friend gave you negative feedback on your behavior, that would probably discourage you from pursuing your activities.

2.4.3 Multisensor Vehicles

Vehicles need not be limited to just one kind of sensor. Braitenberg's *Vehicle 3* (Figure 2.18) illustrates the idea of having multiple, independent sensors on one creature. *Vehicle 3*'s "round sensors" detect the hypothetical quality emitted from circular source, whereas its "rectangular sensors" detect the emissions of the square source. The two qualities are assumed to be entirely independent of one another—imagine the "round quality" is light, whereas the "square quality" is sound.

The sensors are wired to the motors in different ways: The round sensors are cross-wired with a stimulatory effect, whereas the rectangular sensors are wired straight through with an inhibitory effect. The sensors' connections could additionally be weighted with different amounts, so, for example, the effect of the round sensors could be twice as strong as that of the rectangular sensors.

How does *Vehicle 3* perform? Remember that the effects of the "round quality" and the "square quality" are independently detected and then combine at the motors. Given

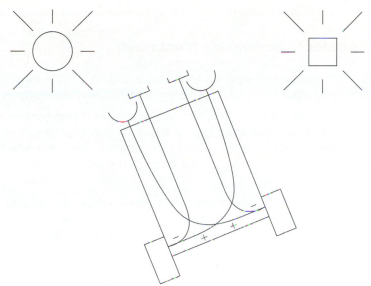

FIGURE 2.18 *Vehicle 3*

Vehicle 3 has two different kinds of sensor: "rounded sensors," which detect emissions from the circular source, and "rectangular sensors," which detect emissions from the square source. These are independently wired to control the motors: the rounded sensors are cross-wired with a stimulatory effect, while the rectangular sensors are straight-through-wired with an inhibitory effect.

only stimulus of the round quality, *Vehicle 3* is attracted to it because of the cross-wired stimulous (just like the original *Vehicle 2b*).

Because *Vehicle 3*'s square-quality sensors can only inhibit, let's assume a constant level of motor drive, so in the absence of the square quality, the vehicle will move. When encountering a source of square-quality on its left-hand side, *Vehicle 3*'s left sensor will fire more strongly, inhibiting the left-side motor more than the right side. Hence, *Vehicle 3* will turn toward the source of stimulation—but slow down as it does so. Neglecting friction and other real-world concerns, *Vehicle 3* will head toward sources of square quality, slowing down to a crawl as it draws very near.

Taking both pairs of sensors together, *Vehicle 3* is attracted to everything, speeding up in the presence of round quality and slowing down in the presence of square quality. Depending on the relative strengths of the two types of sensors, nearby round-quality sources may be able to overpower square-quality ones, the opposite may be true, or nearby sources might cause *Vehicle 3* to stop altogether—paralyzed in a state of perfect equilibruim.

Advanced Braitenberg

The additive wiring metaphor is only the beginning of Braitenberg's control ideas. Some of the extensions to the basic vehicle concept that Braitenberg proposed are:

Nonlinear Connections. Wires could have other functions than linear scaling to connect their inputs to their outputs. If a wire produced no output until its input reached a certain threshold, the vehicle might appear to be "making a decision" to take an action at a certain point.

Memory Wires. Braitenberg's *Mnemotrix* wire made a better connection each time it was used, simulating the learning that occurs in a neural network. By replacing the normal wires with Mnemotrix wires, simple vehicles could be transformed into learning vehicles.

Advanced Braitenberg (Continued)

Eye-like Sensor Grids. With an array of light sensors and a lens, a vehicle could use simple networks to perform functions like edge detection and motion detection.

In addition to these features, Braitenberg presented an amusing and provocative way to think about evolution. Suppose there were lots of these vehicle creatures running about on a table top. You, the agent of change, watch over them, entertained with their derrings-do. Whoops! One of them just drove off the edge of the table and crashed to its demise.

You arbitrarily pick up one of the others and make a copy of it, putting the original and the copy onto the table-top world. Perhaps the copy isn't identical to the original—you made a little mistake in the reproduction job. The new vehicle will likely still mostly work—maybe it's better at surviving on the table top or maybe it's worse and drives off the edge. Whichever way it occurs, evolution is in progress.

2.4.4 Light Sensors

To model Braitenberg's ideas of attraction and repulsion, we use simple *cadmium sulfide photocells* as light sensors. These devices (also known as *CdS photocells* or *photo resistors*) are resistors whose resistance varies in proportion to the amount of light striking the surface of the device.

Figure 2.19 shows a light sensor built from the CdS photocell. CdS photocells are easy to work with because electrically they are simple resistors. Also they are inexpensive and robust components. Other light-sensitive devices, such as photo transistors and photo diodes, have advantages in certain applications, but photocells are ideal for sensing ambient or room lighting.

2.4.5 Coding Braitenberg Vehicles

Braitenberg's light-seeking *Vehicle 2b* can be used as a model for programming *Handy-Bug*'s. To do so, the signal from each of two light sensors must be programmed to

FIGURE 2.19 Cadmium-Sulfide Photocell Sensor

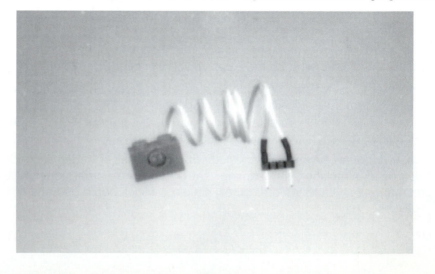

determine the power of the opposing motors. This simulates Braitenberg's wiring model of sensors controlling motor speed.

To begin, let's explore the performance of light sensors we use. Light sensors plug into the Handy Board's analog inputs, numbered from 0 to 6. Figure 2.2 shows the location and numbering of the analog input header on the Handy Board.

Obtain two wired photocell light sensors and mount them on either side of *HandyBug*'s front end above the touch sensors. Plug the light sensors into analog inputs 0 and 1. Next, type in the following quick test program, save it in a file, and download it to the Handy Board:

```
void main() {
    while (1)  {
        printf("sensor 0=%d     sensor 1=%d\n",
          analog(0), analog(1));
        sleep(0.1);
    }
}
```

BEAM Robotics

Using a microprocessor and a computer program to model Braitenberg's ideas is a bit of a mismatch because the wiring metaphor is so evocative in his work. How about building robots that really have a control structure like Braitenberg proposes?

Mark Tilden, a researcher at the Los Alamos National Laboratory, is doing just that with what he calls *BEAM Robotics* for biology, electronics, aesthetics, and mechanics. Tilden has created a veritable world of robots, each with different capabilities and survival skills. Many of Tilden's robots are powered by solar cells and use transistor circuits as their control "program," so they are always ready to move around—unlike many laboratory robots, which spend most of their lives sitting in a corner, waiting to be turned on.

Tilden is not only a brilliant roboticist, but also an artist in the true sense of the word. His robotic creations are animated, beautiful sculptures, each one different from the next. Built from scavenged parts from defunct consumer electronic devices, Tilden's BEAM robots suggest that we may soon be sharing our world with new mechanical forms of life.

This program continuously prints the value of analog inputs 0 and 1 to the Handy Board's LCD screen (see the sidebar, *LCD Printing*). Power cycle the Handy Board to run the new `main` function. The Handy Board should now show a continuously updated display of the values of the two light sensors on its LCD screen.

Now experiment with the response of the light sensors. Rotate *HandyBug* to different orientations with respect to ambient sources of light. Carry *HandyBug* to different places in the room, noticing the sensor readings. Get a flashlight or table lamp and shine it on *HandyBug*.

Light Sensor Exercises

1. How do the light sensor readings change as the amount of light increases?
2. Do the two light sensors typically give the same reading, or do they vary by the angle toward the nearest light source?

3. What are the maximum and minimum readings you can obtain? What are typical readings from just ambient light sources?
4. Do both sensors seem to provide the same reading for the same amount of light, or are the readings from one shifted with respect to the other?

LCD Printing

The `printf` function is a good example of why the C language has a bad reputation as a programming language for beginners. Here is how to understand it, looking at the example from the test routine just presented:

```
printf("sensor 0=%d sensor 1=%d\n", analog(0), analog(0));
```

The "f" in `printf` stands for "formatted." The first argument of `printf` is the format string, which may just be simple message. Thus, "`printf("hello!");`" is a valid C statement.

The format string also may contain formatting symbols. For example, the "`%d`" stands for a number printed out in decimal notation. "`%x`" formats a number in hexadecimal notation, and "`%f`" formats a number in floating point notation.

For each format symbol embedded in the format string, there must be a corresponding item that is to be formatted. In the example, there are two `%d` format commands and two corresponding values to be printed—the calls to the `analog` function.

The "`\n`" at the end of the example's format string is a special character meaning *newline*. In most implementations of C, this inserts a carriage return in the display, but when printing to the LCD screen, Interactive C uses the newline function to mean "clear the screen before the next print."

Finally, the `sleep(0.1)` statement provides a delay in between successive prints. This gives the LCD screen a chance to display each line before it is cleared for the next and minimizes flashing.

Shielding Light Sensors

Often unshielded photocell sensors do not provide a useful range of response. They may flood in normal room lighting and not provide a variable response until the light levels fall dramatically.

A solution to this problem is to put optical shields in front of the sensors. This may be as simple as an opaque tube of construction paper; black heat-shrink tubing also works quite well. A dab of glue from a hot-glue gun is ideal for holding the tube in place.

Figure 2.20 illustrates several ways that a light sensor may be shielded. If a photocell is fitted with a long, narrow tube, it will only respond to a source of light directly in its aim. If a photocell has a short, squat tube, it will reduce the amount of ambient light, putting normal room light levels into a more active portion of the photocell's range. A tube with one side open will let the photocell have better "side vision," which can be

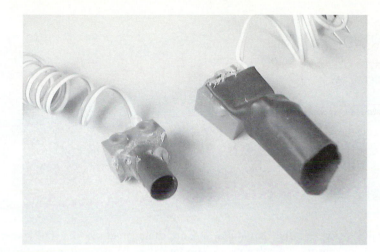

FIGURE 2.20 Optically Shielded Photocell Light Sensors

helpful if the goal is to have a vehicle perform light-seeking activities. It's often a good idea to shield from light directly above because ceiling light is usually not relevant to a robot's desired behavior.

The key is experimentation. Depending on the specific properties of the photocells being used and the amount and type of ambient light, a different shape and size of shield is desirable. Fortunately, because the shields are just made of paper or heat-shrink tubing, it's easy to cut them to size with scissors and remove them and start over if they are cut too small.

Light-Shielding Exercise

Design shields for *HandyBug*'s light sensors that will be suitable for it to perform a light-seeking operation.

As an experimental set-up, identify a source of light in the room (e.g., a table lamp placed on the floor) that will serve as *HandyBug*'s goal.

After being shielded, the light sensors should yield approximately equal values when *HandyBug* is directly facing the light source and distinctly different levels when *Handy-Bug* is rotated in place.

Normalizing Light Readings to Motor Commands

To accomplish the Braitenberg vehicle behavior, a signal from the light sensors must be used to control the performance of a motor. The next step is to convert the light sensor readings to values that can be used in the motor functions.

As we've seen, the `motor()` functions take two arguments: The first is the motor to control and the second is its power level, in the range of −100 (full on backward) to +100 (full on forward). Because we don't want *HandyBug* to drive backward, we use the range from 0 to 100.

Thus, the task is to convert the light sensor reading to a value from 0 to 100, where the brightest light reading yields 100 and the darkest yields 0.

Figure 2.21 shows the function `normalize`, which converts photocell readings into this 0 to 100 range. Let's go through the function line by line to see how it works.

First, notice that `normalize` is declared with an integer return value—`int`—rather than the `void` functions we have used until now. This means that the function will produce an integer value when it returns.

`normalize` takes one argument, which is the light sensor reading to be converted. It begins by declaring two integer variables, `MAX_LIGHT` and `MIN_LIGHT`, which it sets to 10 and 200, respectively.

FIGURE 2.21 Light Sensor
Conversion Function

```
/* normal.c */
/* converts light sensor readings to 0-to-100 motor power levels */
int normalize(int light) {
    int MAX_LIGHT= 10;
    int MIN_LIGHT= 200;

    int output= 100 - ((light - MAX_LIGHT) * 100) / (MIN_LIGHT -
MAX_LIGHT);

    if (output < 0) output= 0;
    if (output > 100) output= 100;

    return output;
}
```

These values represent the maximum and minimum readings that one expects from *HandyBug*'s light sensors. Note that the maximum value, 10, is *smaller* than the minimum value, 200. This answers the earlier question about the characteristic performance of photocell light sensors: Brighter light yields smaller readings. But you already know this.

In the next line, a variable named output is declared, and the conversion is performed. All the real work is done right here, so let's look at it in detail.

At the top level, the calculation is output = 100 - *some-big-expression*. The expression is going to result in a number from 0 to 100, where 0 is very bright and 100 is very dark. But we want "very bright" to result in "motors fully on," so we must take 100 minus that expression to give the correct sense of the answer. This need for 100 - *the-expression* is the consequence of light sensors performing "backward" and giving smaller numbers with brighter light.

Now let's look at the expression. The first part, (light - MAX_LIGHT), offsets the input light reading into a range from 0 (very bright) to the highest dark reading, less the MAX_LIGHT offset. Next, the value is multiplied by 100 and then divided by the magnitude of the whole light sensor range—(MIN_LIGHT - MAX_LIGHT). Thus, the light sensor reading is scaled by 100 (divided by the light sensor range), yielding a result from 0 to 100—the desired range for powering the motors.

Let's work through this expression with a concrete light sensor value. Suppose the light sensor reading is 100. This should give a motor power result pretty much in the middle of the power range—50—but a little closer to full power (because a light sensor reading of 100 is closer to 20 than 200).

Plug the light sensor reading of 100 into the formula:

$$\texttt{output} = 100 - \frac{(100 - 20) * 100}{(200 - 20)}$$

$$= 100 - \frac{80 * 100}{180}$$

$$= 100 - 44$$

$$= 56$$

The result, 56, is just about what we expected: close to the middle of the motor power range, with a bias toward the full-on 100 value.

The next two lines of the normalize function check if we inadvertently computed a value of less than 0 or greater than 100, making sure that the result is within the bounds of the desired motor power argument.

Finally, the function terminates using the `return` keyword, which provides `normal-ize`'s return value. The computed result, `output`, is returned.

Normalizing Exercises

In this exercise, we experiment with the `normalize` function.

1. Type in the `normalize` function and save it in the file `normal.c`, replacing the `MAX_LIGHT` and `MIN_LIGHT` constants with values determined from your prior experimentation with *HandyBug*'s light sensors. What values will you use for the maximum and minimum light readings?

2. From the Interactive C command line, load the `normal.c` function and experiment with the `normalize` function. For example, if the light sensor is plugged into analog input 0, try:
   ```
   while (1) {printf("normal=%d\n", normalize(analog(0))); msleep(.1);}
   ```
   Does `normalize` operate as advertised? What is the range of values that you are able to get it to produce?

3. In the `normalize` function, there are checks to test whether the computed `output` value is less than zero or greater than 100. How is it possible that either of these cases may occur?

Putting it Together

From here, finally programming the Braitenberg light-seeking behavior into *HandyBug* is easy. All we need is an infinite loop to continually set left and right motor powers based the normalized value of the opposing light sensor:

```
void main() {
    while (1)   {
        motor(LEFT_MOTOR, normalize(analog(RIGHT_EYE)));
        motor(RIGHT_MOTOR, normalize(analog(LEFT_EYE)));
    }
}
```

Of course, the port numbers for `LEFT_MOTOR`, `RIGHT_MOTOR`, `LEFT_EYE`, and `RIGHT_EYE` must be defined in a similar fashion as the motor ports in the `turtle.c` example (see page 75).

Light-Seeking Exercises

1. *Light seeking.* Type in the six-line Braitenberg light-seeking program, adding assignment statements for the two motor port and two light sensor port variables. Load your program along with the `normalize` function in the file `normal.c`, and let *HandyBug* loose. Does it work? Does *HandyBug* seek out light sources?

2. *Light avoidance.* Rewrite *HandyBug*'s program so that it avoids sources of light. Describe its actual performance when presented with a variety of stimuli.

3. *Improvements.* *HandyBug*'s speed is directly proportional to ambient lighting conditions. When there's not much light, it hardly moves at all. Also, *HandyBug* may not turn very well; it may be necessary to shine a flashlight deliberately in one of its sensors and not the other, or to shield one of its sensors from ambient light to get it to turn sharply.

Here are some ways to make *HandyBug*'s performance more dramatic:

- Adding a third light sensor, which faces upward and measures ambient light conditions. By correcting for ambient light, the overall speed of the vehicle could remain relatively constant.

- Making sure the two photocells are equally balanced in their response to light. A good way to change their performance is by placing and calibrating optical shields on the photocells.
- Rewriting the control function to accentuate differences between the two eye sensors.

2.5 Light and Touch Sensitivity

Now that *HandyBug* has both light and touch sensors, it is possible to write a program that causes it to react to both sorts of stimuli. Figure 2.22 shows a modified version of a basic light-follower program that allows *HandyBug* to react when its touch sensors are triggered.

The program simply inserts tests for the two touch sensors in the main loop. If a touch sensor is pressed, the test fires, and a sequence of code causes *HandyBug* to back up and turn.

The `li-touch.c` program introduces a distinction between two types of control. Before the touch sensor code, the program could be said to operate in a *stateless* fashion. The program had virtual wires that connected sensor readings to motor output values.

FIGURE 2.22 Listing of Main Routine from `li-touch.c`

```
/*
    main routine from li-touch.c
*/

void main()
{
    while (1) {

        /* set speed of left motor based on right eye */
        motor(LEFT_MOTOR, normalize(analog(RIGHT_EYE)));

        /* set speed of right motor based on left eye */
        motor(RIGHT_MOTOR, normalize(analog(LEFT_EYE)));

        /* check for touch sensors */
        if (digital(LEFT_TOUCH)) {
            backward();
            sleep(.25);
            right();
            sleep(.4);
        }

        if (digital(RIGHT_TOUCH)) {
            backward();
            sleep(.25);
            left();
            sleep(.4);
        }
    }
}
```

With the touch sensor code, however, the internal state of program execution matters. Specifically, the delays after the movement commands are required to accomplish the desired motions. This breaks the metaphor of wiring-based control. As long as the touch sensors are not pressed, the program executes as before, but when the touch sensor code runs, the program ignores information from the light sensors and performs a specific set of movements.

2.5.1 Light and Touch Exercises

1. Describe the performance of *HandyBug* with a light and touch sensor code. Does the touch sensor code accomplish the goal of getting *HandyBug* to work its way around obstacles? Explain why or why not.
2. Modify the sample program so that *HandyBug* does a better job of dealing with obstacles while seeking light sources.

2.6 Randomness

In the natural world, living things often have a fair bit of randomness in their behavior. Consider bugs flying around in a jar while attracted to the light of a candle flame (Figure 2.24).

As long as the bugs obey their instinct to be attracted toward the light, they become trapped inside the jar even though the lid of the jar is open. If a bug has enough randomness in its performance, however, it will "accidentally" stray close enough to the lip of the jar to escape. This bug is not any smarter than its compatriots; indeed, it is doing a poorer job of finding the light than the others! The sloppiness of its behavior, however, is exactly what gives it the advantage here.

It is possible to add this same randomness to *HandyBug*, with the same advantages. Interactive C provides a random number generation function that may be used to generate unpredictable behaviors.

Figure 2.23 shows a modification of the `li-touch.c` program that includes a randomized response to the touch sensor reaction. The `random()` function takes a number as input and returns a value from 0 to that number minus 1. This is used to occasionally cause *HandyBug* to do something strange—which might cause it to "get out of the jar."

There are a couple of tricks in the way that `random` is used that are worth explaining. In the two touch sensor code blocks, `random` is used to determine whether a randomized turn will be performed and, if so, for how long.

To decide whether to perform the randomized turn, the following code is used:

```
if (random(4) == 0) {...}
```

Here's how it works. `random(4)` returns either 0, 1, 2, or 3; if this result is 0, then the target of the `if` statement fires and the random turn is taken. Thus, on one out of every four touch-bumps, *HandyBug* takes a random turn.

Inside the random turn, the `sleep` function is called with a randomized argument:

```
sleep((float)random(100)/100. + .5);
```

Remember that `sleep` requires a floating point argument, whereas `random` returns an integer value. The fragment "`(float)random(100)`" calls the `random` function and converts its return value into a floating point number. This technique is known as *type coercion* and is the standard way to convert across different numeric representations.

FIGURE 2.23 Listing of Main Routine from bugcand.c

```
/*
      main routine from bugcand.c
*/

void main()
{
    while (1) {

        /* set speed of left motor based on right eye */
        motor(LEFT_MOTOR, normalize(analog(RIGHT_EYE)));

        /* set speed of right motor based on left eye */
        motor(RIGHT_MOTOR, normalize(analog(LEFT_EYE)));

        /* check for touch sensors */
        if (digital(LEFT_TOUCH)) {
            backward();
            sleep(.25);
            right();
            if (random(4) == 0) {
                set_beeper_pitch(1000.);
                beeper_on();
                sleep((float)random(100)/100. + .5);
                beeper_off();
            } else {
                sleep(.4);
            }
        }

        if (digital(RIGHT_TOUCH)) {
            backward();
            sleep(.25);
            left();
            if (random(4) == 0) {
                set_beeper_pitch(1000.);
                beeper_on();
                sleep((float)random(100)/100. + .5);
                beeper_off();
            } else {
                sleep(.4);
            }
        }
    }
}
```

FIGURE 2.24 Bugs Trapped in a Jar

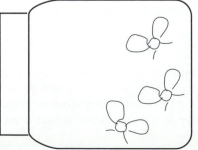

This result is divided by a floating point `100.` (notice the decimal point), yielding a value of 0 to 0.99. To this, a constant delay of 0.5 seconds is added, making the final delay a value between 0.5 and 1.49 seconds.

A new way to use the Handy Board's piezo beeper is also demonstrated. The `set_-beeper_pitch` function sets the frequency of the beeper; `beeper_on` turns it on for the duration of the randomized turn. This audio feedback lets you know that the random turn is occurring. When the random turn is complete, `beeper_off` turns the beeper off.

2.6.1 Random Exercises

1. Characterize the performance of *HandyBug* with the randomized turn procedure. Is it able to "get out of the jar"?
2. Modify the `bugcand.c` program so that randomness is added to *HandyBug*'s light-seeking behavior. How does this affect *HandyBug*'s ability to locate and move toward light sources?

Weird Creatures

For her doctoral research, Nira Granott observed people's interactions with a series of different small LEGO robots or "weird creatures." Some robots reacted to light stimulus, others to sound, touch, or a combination of stimuli. Granott put the robots in a custom environment with objects like flashlights and noisemakers, and then invited her subjects to come and play with them.

For the participants, the task was to ascertain how each robot behaved and why. They could do this by presenting the robots with various stimuli and observing their response—forming and testing their hypotheses. They also were allowed to take the robots apart and put them together in new ways.

Granott's research focused on her subjects' process of exploration and discovery. To summarize, Granott found that her subjects (adult learners) went through several distinct phases during investigations:

> The actual phase revolved around understanding the "behavior" of the robots through actual actions and perceptions. In the representational phase, the participants understood the causality underlying that "behavior" and could represent it. . . . In the abstract phase, these representations were established; having understood the relationship between structure and function, the participants started to explore why the functional bricks made the robot do what it did. They focused on issues of signal transmission, trying to understand the operation of specific sensors and logic bricks. (p. 414)

Granott's work reveals in detail how experimental play can lead to important learning [Gra93].

2.7 Emergence and Meta-Sensing

One of the failure modes that *HandyBug* may experience is the situation of *getting stuck in a loop*, rather than simply getting stuck altogether. That is, *HandyBug* may find its

FIGURE 2.25 *HandyBug* Stuck in a Loop

HandyBug starts at Diagram 1, heading into a corner. After hitting its left touch sensor, it backs up (Diagram 2). Then it turns to the right (Diagram 3). It goes forward and strikes its right touch sensor (Diagram 4). Then *HandyBug* backs up (Diagram 5) and turns left (Diagram 6). At this point, *HandyBug* is back where it started ready to perform this dance all over again!

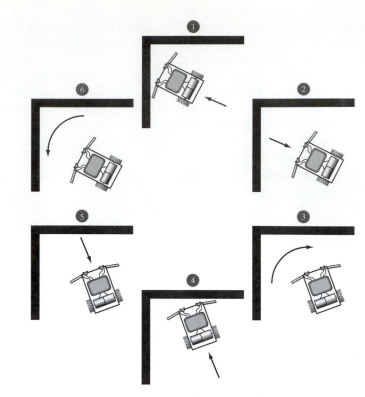

way into a corner, hit one wall, back up and turn, hit the other wall, back up and turn toward the first wall, and then repeat. Depending on the timed parameters for backing up and turning, this might be a quite common occurrence, leading to frequent and fairly stable bump-and-turn loops (see Figure 2.25).

Reload your touch sensor program from Section 2.3 and experiment with *HandyBug*'s behavior. When it encounters a corner, does it easily back out of it, or does it oscillate back and forth for a while before it gets away?

2.7.1 Emergence

For the purposes of experimentation, let's assume that *HandyBug* does have a problem getting stuck in corners and back-and-forth loops. If this is not the case, take it as an exercise to modify *HandyBug*'s backup and turn-timing parameters so that it does exhibit the back-and-forth loop behavior.

If *HandyBug* required hand-tuning to get it to demonstrate the cyclic behavior, the pedagogic point is somewhat less clear, but nevertheless this back-and-forth loop behavior can be seen as an *emergent* phenomenon. That is, nowhere in *HandyBug*'s program does it say that *HandyBug* should get stuck in a corner going back and forth. This response emerges from the interaction of *HandyBug*'s basic rules—back up and turn left when the right-hand sensor is pressed, back up and turn right when the left-hand sensor is pressed—with a particular environment (i.e., the corner).

Emergent phenomena occur more often than one would expect. Particularly as systems grow more complex, interactions between different pieces of the system are hard to predict and sometimes hard to understand. In this touch sensor example, the back-and-forth loop response is easy to understand; it might even have been necessary to coax into occurring. This is not always true of robotic systems and systems in general.

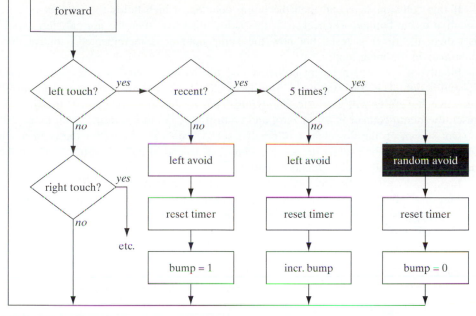

2.7.2 Meta-Sensing

We have already seen one way to cope with the touch sensor loop problem: adding a bit of randomness to the system's behavior. The bug-in-a-jar example suggested that creatures (insects, or *HandyBug*) with randomness in their actions might have a functional advantage.

There is a more subtle way to handle the loop problem, however. What if *HandyBug* could sense that it was in a behavior loop? Its "lower level" behavior of dealing with touch sensor stimulus would remain unchanged, but *HandyBug* would monitor its own performance, looking for unproductive loop states.

This concept might be called *meta-sensing*, because it refers to sensing of a condition that is a result of other sensor-action rules. It presents a significant challenge from a programming standpoint. Indeed, some robot control languages have been developed specifically to make tasks like this easy to do (e.g., Rodney Brooks' layered control work).

To explore this idea, let's modify the simple touch sensor avoidance program to monitor its own performance. Two new items will be added: a bump counter, to keep track of successive collisions, and a timer, to determine whether the collisions are happening one after the next. When five collisions happen in rapid succession, the program will take a special "random avoid" action, rather than the stock left- or right-avoidance maneuvers.

Figure 2.26 presents a flowchart to describe this new behavior precisely. Let's look at the approach in detail to see how it works.

The main loop is similar to what we've seen before: The robot is commanded to go forward, the left touch sensor is checked, and then the right touch sensor is checked.

Suppose the left touch sensor is pressed. Next, the amount of time since the last collision is checked. If this collision is not recent—it has been a while since the last bump—then the normal "left avoid" routine is called. Both the collision timer and bump counter are reset, and control flow continues back at the main loop.

If this collision *is* recent, then the bump counter—which holds the number of consecutive recent bumps—is checked. If this is less than five, then the normal "left avoid" is called, the timer is reset, but now the bump counter is incremented. Control flow continues in the main loop.

Finally, if we have a recent collision and the bump counter is five, then we take special action. The "random avoid" routine is called, which will perform a randomized turn that hopefully will extricate *HandyBug* from its situation. After that, the timer is reset, the bump counter is set to zero, and control flow continues in the main loop.

Not shown on the flowchart is a parallel set of tests and actions for the right touch bumper. It would be exactly the same except that instead of calling "left avoid" for the normal cases, "right avoid" would be called.

Figure 2.27 shows an Interactive C program to implement this strategy. There is nothing particularly fancy about the program other than getting the nestedness of the `if else` statements to match our intentions of the flowchart.

One new C-language feature is the manner in which the `recent_bumps` variable is incremented:

```
recent_bumps++;
```

The `++` operator means "add 1 to this variable."

The timer functions are implemented in a separate program, `timer.c`. The function `reset_timer` resets the timer to zero, and the function `timer` reports the elapsed time since the reset in floating point seconds. As shown in Figure 2.28, these functions make use of an Interactive C library function, `seconds`, which reports elapsed time since Handy Board reset in seconds. When `reset_timer` is called, it stores system time in the `_timer` global; the elapsed time function, `timer`, is then just the difference between current time and the saved reset time.

Figure 2.29 shows possible definitions for the avoidance functions.

2.7.3 Emergence and Meta-Sensing Exercises

1. Run the `metasens.c` program on *HandyBug*. Compare its performance to the unmodified touch sensor program from Section 2.3 and the randomized avoid program from Section 2.6. Which one performs the best? Describe your experimental procedure.
2. Add light-seeking capability to the `metasens.c` program and describe the resulting behavior.
3. *Advanced.* Logically, the `metasens.c` program can be broken apart into two functional units: the core obstacle-avoidance behavior and a monitoring routine that checks for multiple, repetitive bumps.

Interactive C includes the capability for *multitasking*—running multiple programs at once as if there were a processor dedicated to each program. Read Appendix Section E.3.8 on multitasking with Interactive C and reimplement `metasens.c` as two processes: one for performing the basic obstacle-avoidance maneuvers, and a second to detect repetitive bump-loops.

FIGURE 2.27 Listing of
metasens.c

```
/* metasens.c */
/* requires turtle.c, timer.c, avoid.c */

int LEFT_TOUCH= 10;
int RIGHT_TOUCH= 11;

void main() {
  int recent_bumps= 0;
  reset_timer();

  while (1)  {
    forward();
    if (digital(LEFT_TOUCH)) {
      if (timer() < 2.) {          /* last bump recent? */
        if (recent_bumps == 5) { /* yes; many recent? */
          random_avoid();          /* yes; perform avoid */
          reset_timer();
          recent_bumps= 0;
        } else { /* normal avoid, increment, and reset */
          left_avoid();
          reset_timer();
          recent_bumps++;
        }
      } else {              /* haven't bumped for a while */
        left_avoid();
        reset_timer();
        recent_bumps= 1;
      }
    }
    if (digital(RIGHT_TOUCH)) {
      if (timer() < 2.) {          /* last bump recent? */
        if (recent_bumps == 5) { /* yes; many recent? */
          random_avoid();          /* yes; perform avoid */
          reset_timer();
          recent_bumps= 0;
        } else { /* normal avoid, increment, and reset */
          right_avoid();
          reset_timer();
          recent_bumps++;
        }
      } else {              /* haven't bumped for a while */
        right_avoid();
        reset_timer();
        recent_bumps= 1;
      }
    }
  }
}
```

FIGURE 2.28 Listing of
`timer.c`

```
/* timer.c */
float _timer;

void reset_timer() {
    _timer= seconds();
}

float timer() {
    return seconds() - _timer;
}   return seconds() - _timer;
```

FIGURE 2.29 Listing of
`avoid.c`

```
/* avoid.c */
void random_avoid() {
    backward(); sleep(.4);
    set_beeper_pitch(1000.); beeper_on();
    if (random(2) == 0) left();
    else right();
    sleep((float)random(100)/100. + .5);
    beeper_off();
}

void left_avoid() {
    backward(); sleep(.4);
    right(); sleep(.4);
}

void right_avoid() {
    backward(); sleep(.4);
    left(); sleep(.4);
}   left(); sleep(.4);
```

2.8 Conclusion

This chapter was the first working introduction to robotics. Now robots are not just the-oretical entities but actual moving creatures. Using the Handy Board, Interactive C, and *HandyBug*, a two-motor LEGO robot, we explored a variety of approaches to conceptu-alizing and programming robot behaviors.

Braitenberg's *Vehicles* suggested that robots can be as simple as devices with a sensor and a motor and a wire that connects them. With two sensors and two motors, it is possible to make a robot that demonstrates goal-seeking behaviors, like light-following and light avoidance. Using a C program, we simulated Braitenberg's wiring metaphor for robot control.

With touch sensors, we saw an example of emergent behavior: *HandyBug* could get trapped in a corner by repeatedly turning back into it. This result, which was easy to understand in retrospect, was never directly "programmed in" to *HandyBug*'s behavior. In the last section, we looked at ways of programming meta-sensing into our robot: letting it detect and react to loops in its own behavior.

Looking ahead to the rest of the book, chapter 3 introduces a collection of valuable robotic sensors and what one might do with them. Chapter 4 explores the world of mechanics and designing with LEGO Technic materials. Chapter 5 presents a number of different approaches, beyond the ones in this chapter, for controlling robots with software.

Any of these chapters may be approached next; they are not sequentially dependent on one other. Just as we invited you to choose whether to play with the robotic "brain" or "body" first in this chapter, you are free to proceed in whichever area you find most interesting.

3

Sensors

Without sensors, a robot is just a machine, capable only of moving through a predetermined sequence of action. With sensors, robots can react and respond to changes in their environment in ways that can appear intelligent or life-like.

This chapter introduces a variety of common sensors used in robotic applications, including touch switches, ambient light sensors, reflected light sensor, break-beam light sensors, and shaft encoders. All of these sensing technologies are used in industrial settings and consumer electronics as well as mobile robotics.

The chapter combines the theory behind how sensors work with practical information about how to build and use them. Here is an overview of this chapter's contents:

- We begin with an introduction to the Handy Board's sensor inputs and an explanation of Ohm's Law, the basic electrical relationship that explains the performance of most of the sensor applications.

- Next, general construction techniques for building sensors are presented.

- Each sensor technology is then described in turn, with information about how it is interfaced to the Handy Board, its applications, examples, exercises, and projects.

3.1 Sensor Interfacing

It is easy to connect individual sensors to the Handy Board. Figure 3.1 shows where sensors plug into the Handy Board. There are separate banks for nine digital sensors, numbered 7 to 15, and seven analog sensors, numbered 0 to 6.

Each sensor port is a three-wire connection consisting of power, ground, and signal. Figure 3.2 illustrates how a sensor plugs into a Handy Board's sensor port. Not all sensors require +5v power; for example, switches and photocells may be wired between the sensor signal and ground lines.

Electrically, the circuitry looks as shown in Figure 3.3. The Handy Board provides +5 volt and ground to the sensor and expects the sensor's signal to be provided on the "sensor signal" line. This signal line is "pulled up" to the +5 volt level with a 47K resistor as shown. The effect of the resistor is to give the signal line a default value when nothing is plugged in, and also to provide one half of the common *voltage divider* circuit as discussed in the following. The resulting signal of the circuit, V_{sens}, connects to either digital input circuitry (for the nine digital inputs) or analog input circuitry (for the seven analog inputs).

3.1.1 Digital Inputs

The nine digital sensor ports connect to circuitry on the Handy Board that interprets each sensor's V_{sens} voltage as a digital, or true/false, value. Electrically, this circuitry compares the V_{sens} signal to the 2.5 volt midpoint value. If the V_{sens} signal is greater

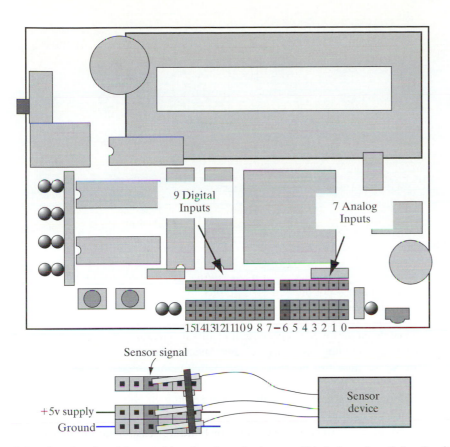

FIGURE 3.1 The Handy Board's Analog and Digital Sensor Banks

The Handy Board provides two banks for sensors: digital inputs, numbered from 15 to 7 on the left, and analog inputs, numbered from 6 to 0 on the right. Analog input 6 is highlighted.

9 Digital Inputs

7 Analog Inputs

1514131211109 8 7—6 5 4 3 2 1 0

Sensor signal

Sensor device

+5v supply
Ground

FIGURE 3.2 Generic Sensor Device Connection

Each of the Handy Board's sensor ports provides three signals to the sensor: +5v power, ground, and the sensor signal line. The lower row of the sensor bank pins are ground, the middle row are +5v, and the upper row are the individual sensor signal connections. The diagram shows a generic "sensor device" plugging into a sensor port.

than 2.5 volts, the signal is considered to be a logic one; if it is less than 2.5 volts, it is interpreted as a logic zero.

To connect a switch to the digital input circuit, it is wired between the sensor signal line and ground (Figure 3.4). The diagram shows a "normally open" switch, meaning that the switch provides an open circuit, or no connection, when it is released and a closed circuit when it is depressed. This is the typical switch used in a sensing application.

When the switch is released, it is open, so there is no connection between the V_{sens} sensor line and ground. The 47K pull-up resistor on the Handy Board then provides the default value of +5v or logic one to the sensor input circuitry. When the switch is pressed, it connects the V_{sens} sensor line to ground, the zero volt level. Then the sensor input circuitry detects a logic zero reading.

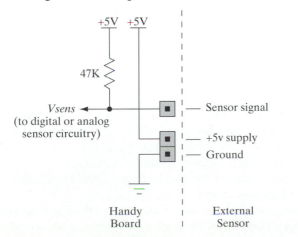

+5V   +5V

47K

$Vsens$
(to digital or analog sensor circuitry)

Sensor signal

+5v supply

Ground

Handy Board

External Sensor

FIGURE 3.3 Handy Board Sensor Input Circuitry

The 47K Ω resistor, wired between the +5v supply and the sensor signal, provides a default level of +5v to the V_{sens} sensor line. Resistive sensors can connect between the signal line and ground. Sensors can also make use of the +5v power source provided at the sensor connector.

FIGURE 3.4 Switch Sensor Circuit

A switch is wired to the Handy Board simply by connecting it between the sensor signal line and ground. When the switch is not pressed, its circuit is open, and the 47K resistor provides +5v or logic one level to the V_{sens} signal line. Pressing the switch causes its circuit to close, connecting V_{sens} to ground (zero volts), which results in a logic zero. In software, these two states are inverted so that a switch sensor is considered "true" when it is closed (the zero volt reading).

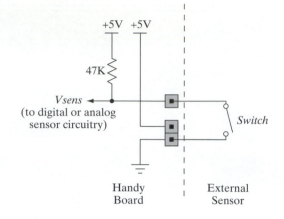

Thus, the switch performs as:

switch state	V_{sens} voltage	hardware reading
open – not pressed	5 volts	1
closed – pressed	0 volts	0

Notice that when the switch is pressed, it results in a reading of zero. In most programming languages, including Interactive C, zero means false. This is the opposite of what one would like because the question "is the switch being pressed?" should be answered with "true."

The solution to this is to invert the switch reading in software. Indeed, Interactive C's function for reporting the value of a switch, `digital()`, returns one, or true, when it sees a *zero* on the hardware level, and returns false when it sees a one on the hardware:

switch state	V_{sens} voltage	hardware reading	digital() result
open – not pressed	5 volts	1	0 – false
closed – pressed	0 volts	0	1 – true

Note that this logical inversion of the hardware reading is based on the use of normally open switches, and the interface design questions whether a pressed switch is "true" or "false." In the intended application, with a normally open switch, the `digital()` function makes the choice that a switch reading is true when pressed and false when open.

3.1.2 Analog Inputs

In addition to the input bank for digital sensors, the Handy Board has seven analog inputs for measuring the value of continuously varying sensors. The analog inputs connect to special pins on the 68HC11 microprocessor that have the capability of converting a voltage into a number. Input voltages from 0 to 5 volts are converted into 8-bit numbers from 0 to 255 (decimal). This process is known as *analog-to-digital conversion*, or simply *A to D*.

Figure 3.5 shows how a resistive device like a photocell element is typically wired into the analog sensor circuit. The photocell, R_{photo}, connects between the sensor signal line and ground (just like the switch did in the digital sensor case). The difference is that the photocell provides a variable resistance, which is balanced against the fixed 47K pull-up resistor that is part of the Handy Board circuitry. These two resistors form a circuit known as a *voltage divider*.

The V_{sens} voltage, at the center tap of the two resistors, is proportional to the ratio of the two resistances. One end of the fixed 47K resistor is connected to the +5v supply;

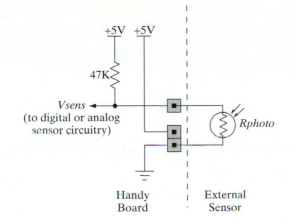

FIGURE 3.5 Attaching the Photocell Sensor to the Handy Board

Resistive sensors, like the R_{photo} photocell, connect between the sensor signal line and ground. Thus, the sensor forms a voltage divider with the 47K pull-up resistor. This circuit is explained in detail in the subsequent section.

one end of the variable R_{photo} resistor is connected to ground (zero volts). If both of these resistors are equal in value (i.e., if R_{photo} is 47K), then V_{sens} is exactly midway between 0 volts and 5 volts—2.5 volts. If R_{photo} is small compared to the fixed resistor, then the V_{sens} signal will be closer to ground. If R_{photo} is large compared to the fixed resistor, then V_{sens} will be closer to +5 volts.

Any kind of resistive sensor can be connected to the Handy Board with this method, but it is also possible to connect circuits that generate a voltage (as long as it is between the 0 to 5 volt range of the 6811's A-to-D converters).

Next, we look at the performance of these resistive arrangements in detail.

3.1.3 Ohm's Law

Ohm's Law explains the relationship among the three basic quantities of interest in electrical systems—*voltage*, *current*, and *resistance*. Ohm's Law states that the difference in voltage between two points in a circuit (V) is equal to the product of the resistance (R) between those points and the amount of current (I) flowing through them, i.e.:

$$V = IR$$

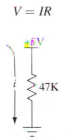

FIGURE 3.6 Single Resistor Ohm's Law Example

How much current (i) flows through the resistor?

Using Ohm's Law, we know that $I = V/R$, which in this case becomes:

$$i = \frac{5V}{47000\Omega} \simeq 0.0001A$$
$$= 0.1mA \text{ (milliamperes)}$$

In this equation, the voltage V is measured in volts (V), the current I is measured in amperes (A), and the resistance R is measured in ohms (Ω).

As an example of Ohm's Law at work, let's figure out how much current flows through a resistor connected between a 5V supply and ground (Figure 3.6). The voltage across the resistor is 5V because ground is defined as the zero voltage point. So the current that flows through the resistor is simply $I = V/R$, an inversion of the Ohm's Law relation $V = IR$.

In this case, we get $i = 5V/47000\Omega$, which is approximately 0.0001A, or 0.1 mA (milliamps).

Series Resistance

When two resistors are connected in series (Figure 3.7), how do their resistances combine? The current flowing through each of them (i) must be equal because the

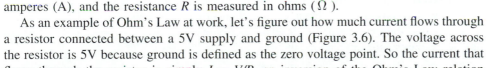

FIGURE 3.7 Series Resistance
Circuit

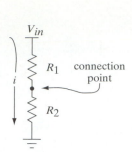

current has nowhere else to go. Then we can calculate the voltage drop across each resistor.

The voltage drop across R_2 is iR_2, and the voltage drop across R_1 is iR_1. This is just another way of saying that if we were to measure the voltage between ground (one side of R_2) and the connection point between the two resistors (the other side of R_2), we would see a voltage of iR_2 volts. Similarly, the voltage between the connection point and the V_{in} point is iR_1 volts.

Voltages in a circuit must add up; that is, the voltage drop across R_1 and R_2 must equal V_{in}. In other words,

$$V_{in} = iR_1 + iR_2$$
$$= i(R_1 + R_2)$$

Because series voltages add, series resistances add too.

The Voltage Divider

This discussion now explains the *voltage divider* circuit (Figure 3.8), which is used in the photocell—and many other—sensor applications. In the voltage divider circuit, an input voltage V_{in} is dropped across two resistors (R_1 and R_2), with an output voltage V_{sens} tapped between the resistors.

The V_{sens} voltage is a function of the ratio of the two resistances and the V_{in} voltage. We can calculate the current running through the resistors as

$$i = \frac{V_{in}}{R_1 + R_2}$$

because the two series resistances add. Then the voltage drop across R_2—the output voltage—is the product of this current and R_2:

$$V_{sens} = V_{in}\frac{R_2}{R_1 + R_2}$$

This relation shows how the voltage divider works. For example, if R_1 and R_2 are equal, the output formula reduces to $V_{sens} = \frac{1}{2}V_{in}$.

Intuitively, if R_1 is smaller than R_2—it provides less resistance—then the output voltage will be closer to the input voltage than to the zero volt ground. Conversely, if R_2 is smaller, the output will be closer to zero volts. This way of thinking can be born out by examining the analytic result.

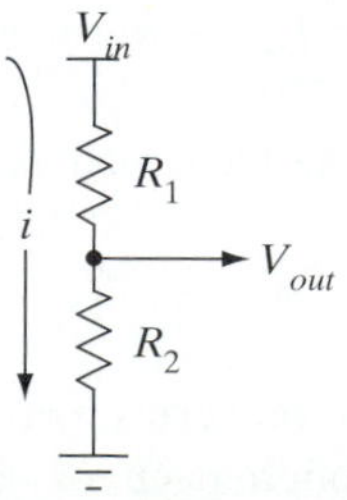

FIGURE 3.8 Voltage Divider
Circuit

3.1.4 Ohm's Law Exercise

Taking the circuit shown in Figure 3.5, write a formula that expresses the voltage V_{sens} as a function of R_{photo}.

3.2 Building Sensors

This section provides general construction advice for building sensors that are compatible with the Handy Board.

The Handy Board uses 0.1-inch male header as the standardized plug for both motors and sensors. Figure 3.9 shows the sensor plug pin-out.

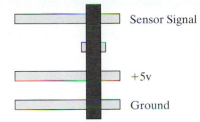

Sensor Signal

+5v

Ground

FIGURE 3.9 Handy Board Sensor Plug Pin-Out

Following are instructions for wiring to this plug and suggestions for adapting sensors to work with the LEGO Technic building system.

3.2.1 Connector Wiring

Connectors are the bane of existence of all electronics. If there is one weak link in the reliable performance of any electronic system, it is its connectors. With this in mind, the importance of patiently and neatly built robot connectors cannot be overemphasized. Particularly because a robot is a mobile system subjected to various jolts and shocks, care taken in the construction of the robot's connectors will always pay off in the long run.

The Handy Board 0.1-inch male header connectors are not the easiest connectors to work with, but have a very compact footprint, allowing a large number of devices to be individually connected to the Handy Board.

The technique presented here demonstrates how to wire to these 0.1-inch plugs. This method has been time-tested to yield reliable results. There are four basic steps in the process:

1. Stripping and tinning wire ends.
2. Inserting heat-shrink tubing on the individual wires.
3. Soldering wire ends to male header connector.
4. Shrinking tubing around the joints.

The remainder of this section explains the technique, showing diagrams for building a switch sensor connector.

Wire Type

It is important to use stranded, not solid, wire cable. Each length of stranded wire consists of a twisted bundle of very thin thread-like wires. Solid wire, on the other hand, is a single thick wire segment.

The advantage of stranded wire is that it is much more flexible than solid wire and also less susceptible to breakage. One thread of a stranded wire length can break without affecting the performance of the connection, but if a solid wire breaks the connection is lost.

An ideal wire for building sensor and motor cables is 28-gauge ribbon cable. Ribbon cable is stranded, and the 28 gauge is the right weight to carry the current required to

drive motors while still providing excellent flexibility. Ribbon cable also "zips" apart easily, so that sets of two or three wires can easily be made. Finally, rainbow ribbon cable is brightly colored in a 10-color sequence, making it easy to keep track of which wire connects where.

Stripping and Tinning Wire Ends

The first step is to strip insulation from the wire cable and *tin* the wire ends. "Tinning" is the process of infusing the stranded wire end with solder.

Referring to Figure 3.10, remove between 1/8 and 1/4 of an inch of insulation from the end of each wire. With your fingertips, individually twist the threads of each wire end tightly (follow the existing weave of the stranded wire bundle). Then put a dab of solder onto the soldering iron, hold it to the wire end, and add some solder to the wire end. Draw the iron tip along the wire end to evenly distribute solder into the wire end.

FIGURE 3.10 Tinning the Wire Ends

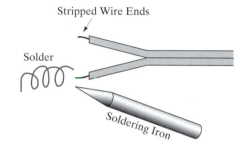

Installing Heat-Shrink Tubing

Cut a 1/4-inch length of heat-shrink tubing for each connection and feed a tubing segment onto each wire.

In preparation for soldering, align the wires with the male header pins as indicated in Figure 3.11. If necessary, zip back the individual wires so that the tubing does not get in the way of the connection. (The use of a "helping hands" tool is helpful here—a tool with two alligator clips on flexible arms.)

Soldering to Male Header

Referring to Figure 3.12, line up the wire ends with the male header pins and solder. Make sure that the heat-shrink tubing is far enough away from the joint that the tubing does not shrink prematurely.

Shrinking the Tubing

Referring to Figure 3.13, slide the heat-shrink tubing over the joints and apply heat from a heat gun. Hold the joint so the heat-shrink tubing is at least 1 inch above the tip of the flame.

FIGURE 3.11 Installing Heat Shrink Tubing

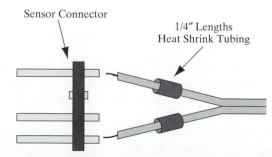

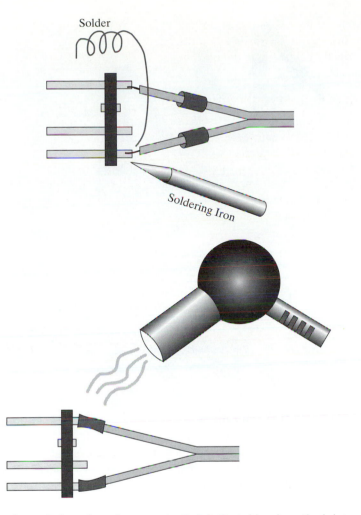

FIGURE 3.12 Soldering to Male Header

Solder

Soldering Iron

FIGURE 3.13 Shrinking the Tubing

Gently apply heat from heat gun to shrink the tubing over the joints.

That's it! The connector end that plugs into the Handy Board is now complete. Figure 3.14 is a photograph of the completed sensor plug connector, enlarged for clarity.

3.2.2 Sensor Mounting

Experimenting with sensor placement on a robot is often necessary to optimize performance. Also, it is typically the case that sensor components need to be reused from robot to robot. For both of these reasons, it is desirable to construct sensors so that they are modular components that can be easily mounted anywhere on a robot.

Assuming the use of LEGO Technic materials, sensors elements can readily be glued to LEGO bricks and thereby become "full-fledged members" of the LEGO building system.

For instance, one of the standard microswitch sizes has its contact spacing such that the switch pins can neatly fit into the holes of a Technic beam (see Figure 3.15). To build this, it is necessary to do just a little planning—inserting the wires through the LEGO beam holes before soldering to the switch pins. Then the switch can be pushed into the Technic beam, and hot glue can be squeezed into the beam holes to make a secure bond.

FIGURE 3.14 Photograph of
Completed Switch Sensor Plug

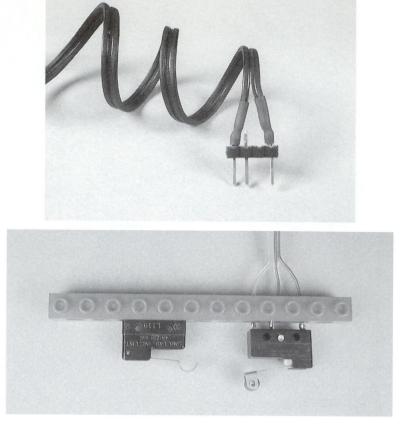

FIGURE 3.15 Mounting
Microswitch into LEGO
Technic Beam

Photocells and other sensor devices often fit nicely into standard LEGO parts. Use your imagination, with the goal being to build modular sensors that can be easily snapped into position, tried in different orientations and shared across projects.

3.3 Switch Sensors

The switch sensor is perhaps the most common sensor used in robotic applications. Switch sensors are used for a variety of purposes, including:

- *Contact (touch) sensing.* Switch sensors can be used to indicate when a mechanism has made physical contact with another object. For example, a switch sensor can trigger when a robot's body runs into a wall or when a robot's gripper closes around a cube.

- *Limit sensing.* Related to simple contact sensing, a limit sensor detects when a mechanism has moved to the end of its range of travel, signaling to the control program that the motor should be turned off.

- *Shaft encoding.* As with past instances of shaft encoding, an axle may be fitted with a contact switch that clicks once per revolution. Software that counts the clicks can then determine the amount and speed of the axle's rotation.

Figure 3.16 shows a number of common switches useful for touch sensing applications. Two basic kinds of switches are illustrated: the microswitch, which is encased in a rectangular housing and often has an attached lever, and a pushbutton switch.

Microswitches typically have three terminals: "NO" (normally open), "NC" (normally closed), and "C" (common). Figure 3.17 illustrates the internal wiring of such a

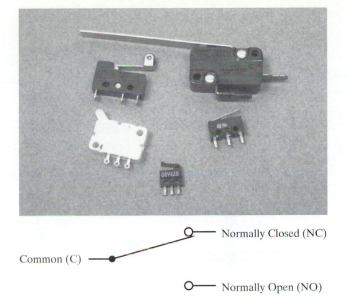

FIGURE 3.16 Various Switches

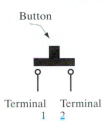

Normally Closed (NC)

Common (C)

Normally Open (NO)

FIGURE 3.17 Three-Terminal Switch Schematic

microswitch. As shown in the figure, the common terminal may connect to either of the other two terminals depending on whether the switch is pressed. In the relaxed, unpressed state, the common terminal is connected to the normally closed contact; when pressed, the common terminal moves to the normally open contact.

A pushbutton switch is simpler. Figure 3.18 shows a normally open pushbutton; when the switch is pressed, the two contacts are connected. Normally closed pushbuttons also exist, but these are less common.

Button

Terminal 1   Terminal 2

FIGURE 3.18 Normally Open Pushbutton Schematic

3.3.1 Switch Sensor Construction

Figure 3.19 shows how to wire a microswitch-style sensor to the Handy Board. As indicated in the diagram, the switch terminals labeled "C" (common) and "NO" (normally open) should be connected to the sensor plug.

This wiring creates a switch sensor that is normally open or disconnected except when the switch is pressed. The normally open case means that the sensor line is pulled high by the 47K resistor on the Handy Board. The standard software for reading the state of a switch interprets this logic high value as "not pressed" or false. When the switch is closed, the sensor line is connected to ground, and the software reads a logic low value, which is interpreted as "pressed" or true.

A normally open pushbutton switch, with two electrical contacts, would be wired in the same fashion, as shown in Figure 3.21.

Figure 3.20 illustrates a simple hinged bumper design that makes use of a normally open pushbutton or microswitch. The bumper lever is hinged at one end, and the body of the lever presses against the switch button. The force of the switch spring pushes the bumper outward; when the bumper makes contact with an object, the switch is pressed in.

FIGURE 3.19 Microswitch Wiring
Diagram, Normally Open
Configuration

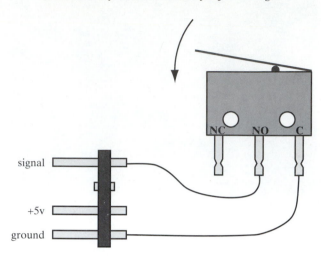

Microswitch–style Sensor, Normally-Open Wiring

Wire to switch terminals labeled
C (common) and **NO** (normally open)

FIGURE 3.20 Design for a Simple
Touch Bumper

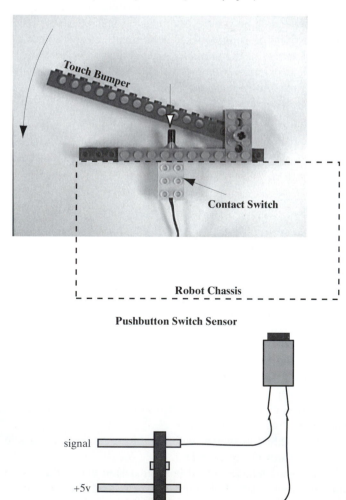

FIGURE 3.21 Pushbutton Switch
Wiring Diagram

Pushbutton Switch Sensor

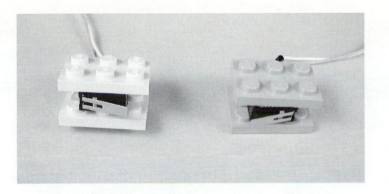

FIGURE 3.22 Left- and
Right-Hand Switch Construction

Microswitch–style Sensor, Normally-Closed Wiring

FIGURE 3.23 Microswitch Wiring
Diagram, Normally Closed
Configuration

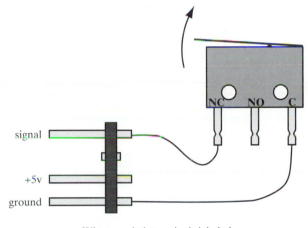

Wire to switch terminals labeled
C (common) and **NC** (normally open)

When building sensors from microswitches, it often makes sense to build left-handed
and right-handed versions for mounting symmetrically on a robot. Figure 3.22 illustrates
this idea and shows a suggested method for mounting microswitches on LEGO plates.

3.3.2 Switch Sensor Applications Examples

Figure 3.23 shows how to wire the microswitch in a normally closed fashion. When the
switch sensor is wired in this manner, the sensor will normally read true (in the relaxed
state); when it is depressed, it will read false.

This arrangement makes sense when the switch is to be used in an application where
it is normally depressed. Figure 3.24 illustrates a touch bumper that can detect pressure
from the front or behind: Movement in either direction will push the levered arm *away*
from the contact sensor, releasing the switch into the open position. Rubber bands pull
the arm back onto the switch when pressure is released.

Designing effective touch bumpers can be a valuable contribution to a robot's performance. Figure 3.25 illustrates the design of *HandyBug*'s bumper. Rotational and sliding
pivot points allow the bumper to react to pressure from any forward direction. In the case
of the LEGO switch sensor, which has only a small spring action of its own, rubber bands
are used to hold the bumper forward, providing the resistive force against triggering. The
overall design is quite effective in reacting to contact from any direction, assuming that
the overall robot is driving forward!

FIGURE 3.24 Design for Bidirectional Touch Bumper

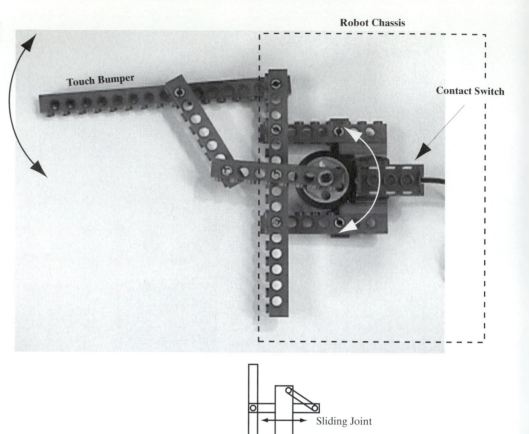

FIGURE 3.25 *HandyBug* Bumper Design

3.4 Light Sensor Circuits

There are many ways to assemble light sensor elements into sensor devices that can be employed on a robot. Let's begin with the simplest—the single photocell circuit.

3.4.1 The Single-Photocell Circuit

Photocells are interfaced to the Handy Board using the voltage divider circuit presented earlier in Section 3.1.3. Figure 3.26, the single-photocell circuit that uses this voltage divider, is labeled operating voltages and component resistor values. As indicated in the circuit, a 47K pull-up resistor, present on the Handy Board, is used in conjunction with the photocell device. The output voltage V_{sens} in the circuit is the resulting sensor voltage.

As per the voltage divider relationship, V_{sens} varies as to the ratio between the two resistances—the fixed 47K resistance and the varying R_{photo} resistance. When the photocell resistance is small (as when brightly illuminated), the V_{sens} signal is close to

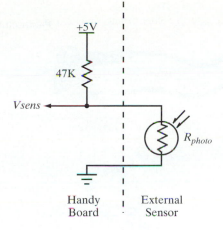

+5V

47K

Vsens

R_{photo}

Handy Board   External Sensor

FIGURE 3.26 Photocell Voltage Divider Circuit

zero volts; when the photocell resistance is large (as in the dark), V_{sens} is close to $+5$ volts, with a continuously varying range between the extremes.

This means that the sensor will report small values when brightly illuminated and large values in the dark. In this regard, the photocell may be thought of as a "dark sensor": Increasing darkness yields bigger readings.

If it seems too counterintuitive to use the photocell in dark-is-bigger fashion, a simple routine may be used to invert the sense of the readings from the Handy Board's analog ports:

```
int light(int port)
{
    return 255 - analog(port);
}
```

Because the range of the Handy Board's analog sensor ports is 0 to 255, returning 255 minus the raw reading yields the same 0 to 255 range, but with the sense of the values inverted. Now the `light()` function will give bigger values with increasing amounts of light.

Building It

Figure 3.27 shows the wiring diagram for constructing a photocell sensor based on this design. The wiring is quite simple: The photocell element is connected to the circuit ground and the Handy Board's sensor input line.

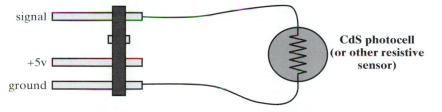

signal

+5v

ground

CdS photocell
(or other resistive
sensor)

FIGURE 3.27 Single-Photocell Sensor Wiring Diagram

Figure 3.28 shows a close-up of the assembly process at the photocell. Before soldering, heat-shrink tubing is placed on the wire ends so that individual joints may be insulated with the tubing afterward. When soldering, do not apply too much heat; the photocell can be damaged if overheated.

The photocell has only two wires, so it is not strictly necessary to use heat shrink on both wires: If one is well insulated, the other has nothing to short up against. Still it is better practice to use the heat shrink on both wires, which provides more mechanical support and redundancy against shorting.

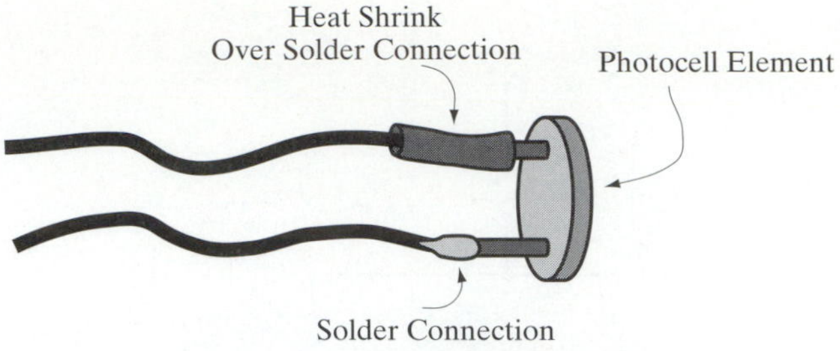

FIGURE 3.28 Photocell Wiring Detail

Heat Shrink
Over Solder Connection

Photocell Element

Solder Connection

FIGURE 3.29 Photocell Sensor Mounted on LEGO Technic Beam

If using the LEGO Technic system to build robots, it is helpful to mount the photocell's leads through holes of a LEGO Technic beam, making a sensor device that can easily be positioned anywhere on the robot and subsequently reused. If the photocell is small enough—about the size of the axle holes of a Technic beam—it may be mounted with both wires passing through a single LEGO beam hole. Alternatively, a larger photocell may be installed such that each of its two leads passes through adjacent beam holes (Figure 3.29). Use hot glue to hold the assembled photocell in place after inserting through the LEGO beam.

After building the photocell, test that it works with a simple command-line print statement loop from Interactive C. For example, if plugging the sensor into port 0:

```
while (1) {printf("%d\n", analog(0)); msleep(100L);}
```

Now experiment with the sensor's performance. In typical room lighting, one must almost completely shield the sensor with one's hand to get the reading to back off from the flooded, full brightness level. (This depends on the specifications of the photocell and the value of the biasing resistor, which is fixed at 47K in our case.) If your photocell easily floods from ambient room light, then the next order of business is to build an optical shield to limit the amount of ambient light that is able to fall on the sensor.

Optical shields are just black tubes, typically constructed out of construction paper or heat-shrink tubing, that mount in front of the photocell element. There is no hard-and-fast rule as to the optimal size and shape of the shields; it depends on the application for which the light sensor is being used, the typical amount of ambient light, and other factors.

For example, if a photocell were being used in a break-beam configuration, pointed at a source of light and detecting when an object comes between the light source and a sensor, then a long, narrow tube would be called for to minimize the amount of ambient light reaching the sensor.

However, if a light sensor is to be used for detecting a source of light at floor level in the room, it might make sense to shield mostly light from the ceiling and fan out the shield horizontally to allow floor level light in easily.

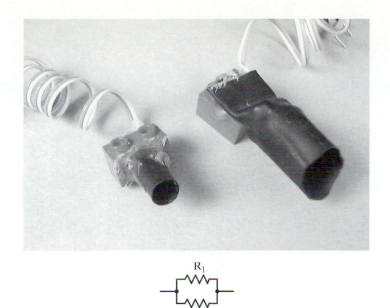

FIGURE 3.30 Photocell Sensors with Light Shields

FIGURE 3.31 Parallel Resistor Circuit

Figure 3.30 depicts a couple different shielding styles. Hot glue is an ideal method for attaching the base of the shield to the LEGO brick holding the sensor. It's often a good strategy to deliberately make the shields too long and snip away at the ends until the desired performance is achieved.

Photocell Exercises

1. Given Ohm's Law and the understanding of voltage drop and current flow presented in the previous section, prove that the effective resistance of two parallel resistors (R_{eff}) is $1/(1/R_1 + 1/R_2)$ (Figure 3.31).
2. Simplify the formula for R_{eff} to facilitate ease of computation.
3. Generalize the relationship for parallel networks of an arbitrary number of resistors.
4. Simplify the general relationship for the case where all resistors are equal in value.

3.4.2 The Differential Photocell Sensor

The *HandyBug* robot presented in the "First Robot" chapter used two individual photocell sensors to perform tasks like light seeking and light avoiding. In the robot's program, the photocells were wired by software to control the speed of motors (in the Braitenberg vehicle simulation) or compared by software to determine in which direction the robot should move.

Another way of performing this comparison function is to wire a pair of photocells to produce a voltage that represents the difference in value between the two. The circuit used to do this is the same voltage divider circuit we used to connect the single photocell; instead of comparing the single photocell to a fixed resistor value, the values of two photocells are compared to each other. Figure 3.33 illustrates the differential sensor circuit, and Figure 3.36 shows how to wire two photocells to the standard Handy Board sensor connector.

According to the voltage divider relationship, the output voltage of the differential photocell circuit, V_{sens}, is proportional to the ratio of the two photocell resistors, R_{photo1} and R_{photo2}, multiplied by the input voltage, 5 volts. Expressed as a formula, this is

$$V_{sens} = 5 \frac{R_{photo1}}{R_{photo1} + R_{photo2}}$$

FIGURE 3.32 The Differential Photocell Sensor

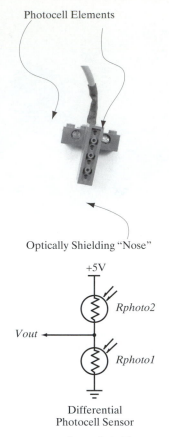

Photocell Elements

Optically Shielding "Nose"

FIGURE 3.33 Ideal Differential Photocell Sensor Schematic

The differential photocell sensor is constructed by wiring two like photocells in the voltage divider configuration. The resulting output voltage is then:

$$V_{sens} = 5 \frac{R_{photo1}}{R_{photo1} + R_{photo2}}$$

+5V

R_{photo2}

V_{out}

R_{photo1}

Differential
Photocell Sensor

Even without the formula, one can gain an intuitive sense for the performance of the circuit. If both photocells are receiving equal amounts of light (i.e., $R_{photo1} = R_{photo2}$), then the voltage divider outputs exactly half of its input voltage, and V_{sens} is 2.5 volts. If the upper photocell is receiving more light, then R_{photo2} will be smaller than R_{photo1}, and the output voltage will be closer to the input voltage—that is, it will be greater than 2.5 volts. Conversely, if the lower photocell receives more light, then R_{photo1} is smaller than R_{photo2}, and the output voltage is closer to ground (zero volts), so it is less than 2.5 volts.

The result of all this is that the differential sensor provides a signal that can be directly interpreted to indicate which side of the sensor is receiving more light and by how much. Because the Handy Board converts an input voltage to a number from 0 to 255, a value around the midpoint, 128, indicates both photocells receiving approximately an equal amount of light, whereas swings to high and low values indicate one photocell receiving lots more light than the other.

A Light-Seeking Program

It is then straightforward to construct a light-seeking or light-avoiding program using the differential light sensor. One example, `stepdiff.c`, is shown in Figure 3.34. Inside a main loop, the program compares the differential sensor reading to the midpoint value (128) and moves *HandyBug* to the left or right depending on whether the sensor reading is greater or less than the midpoint value.

Effects of the Sensor Input Circuit

An additional complicating factor to consider when using the differential sensor is the effect of the Handy Board's sensor input circuit. The Handy Board's sensor input circuit

```
/*
    stepdiff.c
*/

int      LEFT_MOTOR=      0;
int      RIGHT_MOTOR=     3;

int      DIFF_EYE=       0;

void main()
{
    while (1) {
        if (analog(DIFF_EYE) < 128) {
            /* turn to left  */
            motor(RIGHT_MOTOR, 100); sleep(0.1); off(RIGHT_MOTOR);
        } else {
            /* turn to right */
            motor(LEFT_MOTOR, 100); sleep(0.1); off(LEFT_MOTOR);
        }
    }
}
```

FIGURE 3.34 Listing of `stepdiff.c`

The `stepdiff.c` program tests the value of the differential light sensor to decide which way to turn. If the value is less than 128, the program causes *HandyBug* to take a step to the left; otherwise, *HandyBug* takes a step to the right. Depending on how the sensor is wired, this will implement either a light-seeking or light-avoiding behavior; changing the comparison from "less than 128" to "greater than 128" will reverse the seek or avoid characteristic.

contains a 47K Ω pull-up resistor from the $+5v$ supply to the sensor input. Thus, the performance of the sensor is biased because the R_{photo2} sensor has a 47K Ω resistor effectively in parallel with it, making its value artificially smaller (see Figure 3.35).

In practice, this problem is not as bad as it might seem, because most photocells, under typical ambient lighting conditions, have a value between 100 Ω (bright) and 10K Ω (dark). In the bright case, a 47K Ω resistor in parallel with a 100 Ω resistor makes less than a 1% difference to the effective resistance value. (This can be verified by thinking about the Ohm's Law equation for two parallel resistances, $R_{eff} = (R_1 \times R_2)/(R_1 + R_2)$.)

The effect of the 47K Ω pull-up resistor is more pronounced when the photocells' values are in the 10K Ω range—a 47K Ω resistance in parallel with a 10K Ω resistance is about 8.25K Ω—but in most applications this will not create too adverse an effect on the sensor's performance. It is advisable, however, to use photocells with dark resistance values that top out around 10K Ω; otherwise, the differential sensor will exhibit a persistant bias when in the dark.

It is worth noting that the differential sensor has no way of determining the absolute magnitude of light (i.e., how much light is there). All it can do is detect differences between the left and right sides. For many applications, such as light seeking, this may

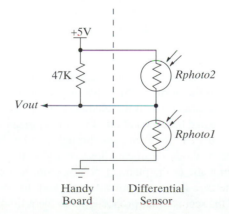

FIGURE 3.35 Actual Differential Photocell Sensor Schematic

FIGURE 3.36 Differential Photocell Wiring Diagram

When building the differential photocell, it is a good idea to decide on a standard physical configuration—for example, always mounting the photocell wired between the sensor terminal and ground (R_{photo1}) on the left. This way, all copies of the sensor will perform with the same characteristic. With R_{photo1} on the left, the sensor will return values less than 128 when receiving more light from the left and values greater than 128 when receiving more light from the right.

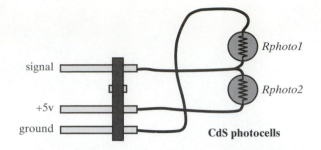

not pose any problem, but for others, knowing the amount of light may be important, and two discrete photocells should be used.

Building the Dual Photocell Sensor

The dual photocell sensor is constructed from two photocell elements wired in a voltage divider configuration. Figure 3.36 shows the sensor's wiring diagram.

In order to get good performance, it is best to use photocells that have a relatively small dark resistance (i.e., about 10K). Otherwise the 47K pull-up resistor present on the Handy Board will bias the sensor reading when in the dark.

It is also helpful to mount a "nose" between the two sensor elements—an opaque shield that casts a shadow on one element if there is a distinct source of light off to the side. Experiment with different materials to find what works best.

Differential Photocell Exercises

1. Rewrite the `stepdiff.c` light-seeking program to distinguish three states: light brighter on the left, light brighter on the right, and light approximately equal. Make *HandyBug* drive straight forward when the light is approximately equal. Describe the performance of this new program.
2. Compare the capabilities of the differential photocell device to two discrete photocells. What information is lost and what information is gained?
3. Compare the differential photocell plus a discrete photocell to two discrete photocells.
4. Brainstorm other sensors that could be effective in the differential configuration.
5. Build the polarized beacons and the corresponding polarized differential sensor, and experiment with the set-up. Write a program to make *HandyBug* perform light seeking for either of the two beacons.

3.4.3 Polarized Light Seeking

Some robot design contests have employed *polarized light beacons* to mark two opposing goal positions. Each of these goals consists of a light box with a Polaroid light filter in the front; one has the polarization filter aligned vertically, whereas the other has it aligned horizontally (Figure 3.37).

The principle of Polaroid's polarizing light filters is the following. Light emanating from most sources is nonpolarized in nature, meaning that the light waves travel at all orientations with respect to the horizon. After passing through the polarizing filter, only those light waves that were aligned with the characteristic plane of the filter are allowed through. The light is attenuated because not all of the unpolarized light "makes it through" the filter, but the polarized light can then pass through another layer of the filter, at the same polarization angle, without significant loss of light. If polarized light is passed through a filter at a right angle to the plane of polarization, it is completely blocked out. At angles in between the zero degree alignment angle and the 90 degree blocking angle, the light passes through the second filter proportional to the ratio of the polarization angle.

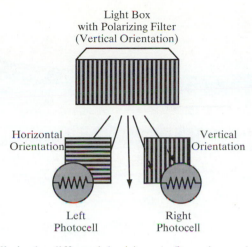

Light Box
with Polarizing Filter
(Vertical Orientation)

Horizontal
Orientation

Vertical
Orientation

Left
Photocell

Right
Photocell

FIGURE 3.37 Light Box with Polarizing Filter and Photocells

In the contest application, each of two robot's goal areas is marked with a light box that emits visible light through a polarizing filter, rotated at a + or − 45 degree angle. Robot employ a pair of photocells, one with a +45° rotation (the right-hand photocell) and one with a −45° rotation (the left-hand photocell). Depending on the polarization of the light source, either the light will pass equally through both photocells' filters (no polarization), be blocked in the left and transmitted in the right (+45° polarization, as per the diagram), or blocked in the right and transmitted in the left (−45° polarization). Using the differential photocell configuration, a robot can easily tell which of these conditions is true.

A pair of photocells in the differential wiring configuration makes an ideal sensor for detecting the polarized light from the beacons. One photocell is shielded with a piece of the same polarizing filter rotated to the vertical orientation, whereas the second uses the horizontal one. Thus, when aimed at one of the light beacons, one photocell's filter will align with the polarization of the beacon, whereas the other photocell will be off by ninety degrees. The photocell in line will receive maximal transmission, whereas the other will be completely opaque.

The performance of the differential sensor with polarized shields makes it easy to tell if the robot is pointed at a light beacon. In the absence of polarized light, both photocells receive equal amounts of light because unpolarized light passes through both filters equally. This results in a sensor reading in the middle of the scale (128). When the device is facing a beacon, one photocell receives ambient light plus the beacon's polarized light, whereas the other receives just ambient light. The sensor's reading then swings in the direction of the photocell that is receiving the light of the beacon.

Sensor readings above the midpoint indicate readings from one beacon and readings below the midpoint indicate readings from the other. If the sensor reading is far away from the midpoint, it indicates that the sensor is receiving strong polarized light from a beacon.

3.5 Resistive Position Sensors

There are a variety of resistive devices that may be easily interfaced to the Handy Board in the same manner as the single photocell.

3.5.1 Bend Sensors

Figure 3.38 shows a device known as a *bend sensor*. These were originally developed to detect finger flexing in the Nintendo® PowerGlove™, a videogame control device that fit over one's hand, but can be useful in robotic applications like contact sensing and wall tracking.

Electrically, the bend sensor is a simple resistance. As the plastic strip is bent (with the silver rectangles facing outward), the resistance increases.

To interface the bend sensor with the Handy Board, wire it just as a single photocell (between the signal line and ground). The 47K pull-up resistor forms a voltage divider with the resistance of the bend sensor.

Mechanically, the bend sensor is not terribly robust and requires strong protection at its base near the electrical contacts. Unless the sensor is well protected from direct forces, it will fail over time.

FIGURE 3.38 The Resistive Bend Sensor

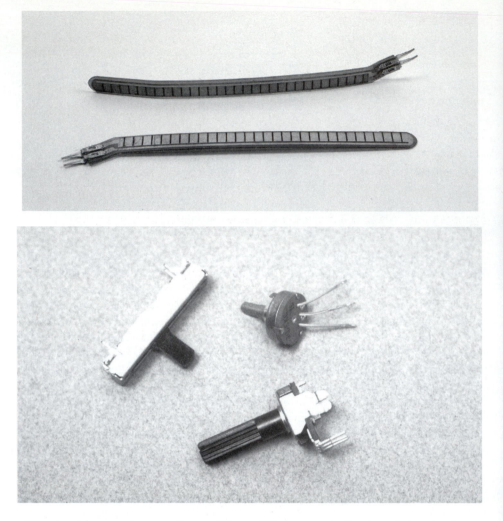

FIGURE 3.39 Linear and Rotational Potentiometers

The bend sensor is manufactured by AGE, Inc. and distributed by the Images Company and Jameco (see Appendix G, *Resources*). The device is now fairly expensive (about $10). This is unfortunate because the bend sensor is quite easy to use, and if it were inexpensive would be an obvious choice for robotic applications.

3.5.2 Potentiometers

The *potentiometer* is a manually controlled variable resistor commonly found in consumer electronics as the volume and tone controls of stereo systems. Potentiometers come in both linear and rotational styles (see Figure 3.39); in robotic applications, these devices make easy-to-use position sensors for both sliding mechanisms and rotating shafts.

Most potentiometers (or just *pots*, for short) are three-terminal electrical devices consisting of a resistive element with end taps and an adjustable, center swipe tap. The resistance between the end taps is fixed, but the resistance between either end tap and the center swipe varies based on the position of the swipe.

Figure 3.40 shows the electrical schematic symbol of the potentiometer, which is representative of its physical construction. The two end taps are connected to the resistor, while the center tap drops down into the middle of the resistor. Effectively, there is one

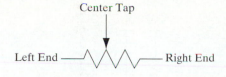

Center Tap

Left End —/\/\/\— Right End

FIGURE 3.40 Potentiometer
Schematic Symbol

resistance between the left end and the center tap, and another resistance between the center tap and the right end. The sum of these two resistances is the left-end-to-right-end resistance.

Linear Taper Versus Audio Taper

In addition to the form factor varieties (i.e., rotational or linear slide), potentiometers come in two electrical varieties: *linear taper* and *audio taper*. These terms refer to the relationship between position and resistance along the resistive element within the potentiometer.

Linear taper means that there is a linear relationship between position and resistance. Turn the pot one quarter of the way and the resistance between the nearer end and the center is one quarter of the end-to-end resistance. Turn the pot halfway and the resistance between either end and the center is exactly half of the end-to-end resistance.

Audio taper means that there is a logarithmic relationship between position and resistance. At one end of the scale, a quarter turn would swipe over a small bit of total resistance range, whereas at the other end, a quarter turn would be most of the range.

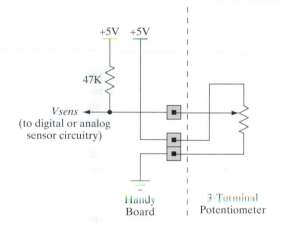

+5V   +5V

47K

Vsens ◄
(to digital or analog
sensor circuitry)

Handy
Board

3-Terminal
Potentiometer

FIGURE 3.41 Potentiometer Wiring Diagram, Three-Terminal Connection

The three-terminal potentiometer wiring works best when the effect of the Handy Board's 47K pull-up resistor is negligible (i.e., when the potentiometer resistance is small enough such that a 47K resistance in parallel with the pot's resistance has only a small effect).

Audio taper potentiometers are typically used in volume control circuits (hence the name), where great sensitivity is required at low volumes, but the difference between the final steps approaching full volume is miniscule. Because of the logarithmic relationship between amount turned and resistances, they generally are to be avoided for robotic position-sensing applications.

Interfacing

There are two ways to interface potentiometers to the Handy Board, illustrated in Figures 3.41 and 3.42. If there were no pull-up resistor on the Handy Board, all pots would be interfaced using the three-wire connection of Figure 3.41. This wiring method gives the best response, yielding a perfectly linear relationship between position and output reading.

For pots that have an end-to-end resistance of less than about 10K, the 47K pull-up resistor on the Handy Board has a negligible effect, and the three-terminal wiring may be used. For pots with a resistance of greater than about 10K, the two-terminal wiring of Figure 3.42 should be used.

FIGURE 3.42 Potentiometer Wiring Diagram, Two-Terminal Connection

The two-terminal potentiometer works best when the pot's value is large and the 47K pull-up resistor would be problematic in the three-terminal wiring.

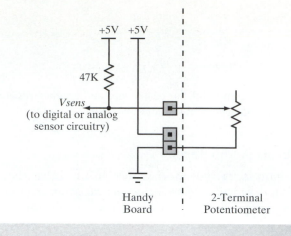

FIGURE 3.43 LEGO Mounting Ideas for Potentiometers

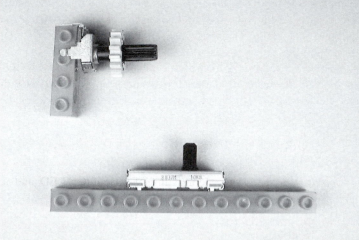

Potentiometers of less than 1K resistance should not be used with the Handy Board. If used in the two-terminal wiring configuration, there is not enough range to get a good response; if used in the three-terminal configuration, too much current will be drained by the pot's resistor, which has +5v wired across it.

Figure 3.43 illustrates some ideas for mounting potentiometers to the LEGO Technic system. For rotary pots, glue a bushing to the end of the shaft (using a permanent glue-like twin-tube epoxy); then a LEGO axle mounted into the bushing can turn the pot. If the pot is small enough, the shaft can fit through an axle hole, allowing easy alignment with other mechanisms.

Linear pots can simply be glued to a LEGO beam for ease of positioning.

Exercise

Assuming a linear potentiometer taper with a resistance of 10K, make a graph of pot center tap position versus output voltage for each of the two wiring options. Which of these would be preferable and why?

3.6 Reflective Optosensors

The previous sections discussed sensors that are essentially passive in nature; the stimulus that provides for the sensors' functioning comes directly from the environment. It's also possible to build sensors that include their own source of energy. This and the

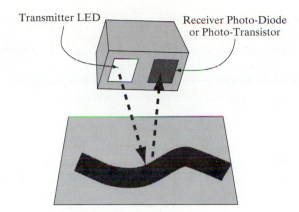

Transmitter LED   Receiver Photo-Diode or Photo-Transistor

FIGURE 3.44 Reflective Optosensor Aimed at Black Line

The *reflective optosensor* includes a source of light (the emitter LED) and a light detector (the photodiode or phototransistor). These are arranged in a package so that the light from the emitter LED bounces off an external object (e.g., the black line on a surface) and is reflected into the detector. Depending on the reflectivity of the surface, more or less of the transmitted light is reflected into the detector.

following section discuss two types of light-sensing devices that include their own light source:

Reflectance sensors In this mode, light is reflected off a surface into a detector element.

Break-beam sensors In this mode, light is shined directly into a detector element, and the device detects when an opaque object interrupts the beam of light.

These light sensors are an instance of the more general category of *active sensors*—devices that include their own source of the quantity being detected.

This section introduces several common applications for reflectance sensors, including surface feature detection and object detection.

The *reflective optosensor* is a device consisting of an emitter LED and a detector photodiode/phototransistor. These two devices are typically encased in a single plastic package, holding them in the ideal alignment for their application. The emitter LED generates a beam of light that is reflected off a surface and into the detector device.

Figure 3.44 illustrates the typical optosensor device. Housed in a rectangular package are the emitter LED (indicated by the light square on the left) and the detector device (on the right). The dashed lines indicate light from the emitter LED that is reflected into the detector device. Depending on the reflectivity of the surface, more or less light is reflected back into the detector; this is the quantity that is reported by the sensor.

Figure 3.45 is a photograph showing several styles of reflective optosensor devices. In some of these, the individual circular LED emitter/detector components are clearly

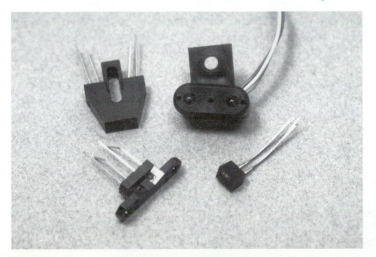

FIGURE 3.45 Several Reflective Optosensor Devices

distinguishable. In others, these components are rectangular and are formed into the overall device case packaging.

Most commercial reflective optosensors use infrared light. This is because the typical semiconductor junction used in LEDs is most efficient at an infrared wavelength. Also, reflectance sensors often include a filter in front of the detector device; these filters can easily be made to pass infrared wavelengths while trapping visible ones, thereby reducing interference from visible light.

3.6.1 Applications

In industrial applications, reflective optosensors are used mostly for object detection—determining whether an object is located in front of the sensor. Of course, this only works if the object's surface coloring reflects at least some of the infrared light beam; objects that are completely black to infrared light cannot be detected.

In mobile robotics, there is a wide range of applications:

Object detection. As in the industrial application, reflectance sensors may be used to measure the presence of an object in the sensor's field of view. In addition to simply detecting the presence of the object, the data from a reflectance sensor may be used to indicate the object's distance from the sensor. These readings are dependent on the reflectivity of the object, among other things—a highly reflective object that is farther away may yield a signal as strong as a less reflective object that is closer.

Surface feature detection. Reflective optosensors are great for detecting features painted, taped, or otherwise marked onto the floor. Line following using a reflective sensor is a typical robot activity.

Wall tracking. Related to the object-detection category, this application treats the wall as a continuous obstacle and uses the reflective sensor to indicate distance from the wall.

Rotational shaft encoding. Using a pie-shaped encoder wheel, the reflectance sensor can measure the rotation of a shaft (angular position and velocity).

Barcode decoding. Reflectance sensors can be used to decode information from barcode markers placed in the robot's environment.

Of the applications in this list, the first three are presented in this section. An example of shaft encoding is done with break-beam optosensor technology, discussed in Section 3.7. The barcode application is not further discussed, and is left as an advanced project for readers looking for a fun engineering challenge.

It is often tricky to get reflectance sensors to perform as desired. Like any sensor, they work best in highly controlled environments. Sensor calibration is necessary for nearly all sensor devices, but especially for reflectance situations in which readings may vary based on fluctuations in ambient lighting, distances between the sensor and the object being sensed, the reflectivity of the sensed object, and other factors.

Ambient light is always a problem unless the sensor and sensed object are both inside an opaque box. At a start, it is necessary to position the sensor so that ambient light does not directly reach the detector element. In many applications, it is necessary to provide some kind of sheath to further insulate the device from outside lighting. In some applications, active control of the reflectance sensor's own illumination source may be required. This is discussed shortly in Section 3.6.4.

Photocells Versus Phototransistors

The previous section of this chapter introduced photocells as light-sensitive devices. This section uses phototransistors and photodiodes as light-detecting components. How do you choose one type of device rather than the other?

Photocells are easy to work with because electrically they are just resistors, but their response time is slow compared to the photodiode or phototransistor's semiconductor junction. This means photocells are suitable for detecting levels of ambient light or acting as break-beam sensors in low-frequency appliations (like detecting when an object is between two fingers of a robot gripper).

For applications like shaft encoding, the rapid response time of the photodiode or phototransistor is required. Also, these devices are more sensitive to small levels of light, which allow the illumination source to be a simple LED element.

3.6.2 Interfacing

The reflectance sensor connects to the Handy Board as shown in Figure 3.46. The two components of the sensor, the emitter and detector, have logically separate circuits, although they are wired to the same connector plug.

The emitter LED (LED_1) is wired to the Handy Board's +5v power supply through R_1, the current-limiting resistor. R_1's value can vary from about 220 to 470 Ω depending on how much brightness is desired from the emitter LED.

Q_1 is the detector, shown as a phototransistor, and is wired between ground and the sensor signal line—just like a photocell might be wired. It would be improper, however, to think about the transistor as a resistive device. Instead, imagine it as a light-sensitive current source. The more light reaching the phototransistor, the more current passes through it.

All of this current is supplied through the 47K pull-up resistor on the Handy Board; the more current going through this resistor, the greater the voltage drop across it, and the smaller the voltage on V_{sens}, which is presented to the Handy Board's sensor input circuit. This is illustrated in Figure 3.47.

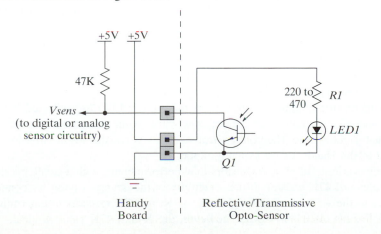

FIGURE 3.46 Reflectance Sensor Interface Diagram

FIGURE 3.47 Phototransistor Current Flow Diagram

The current, i, flowing through the Q_1 phototransistor is indicated by the dashed line. The more light received by the phototransistor, the more current flows. This creates a voltage drop in the 47K pull-up resistor on the Handy Board. This voltage drop is reflected in a smaller voltage on the V_{sens} sensor signal line, which has a level that is equal to 5 volts minus the 47K resistor's voltage drop.

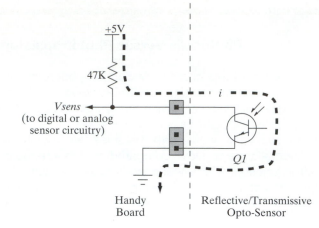

As an example of the circuit's performance, suppose that under a certain lighting situation, the current i is 0.01 mA, or 0.00001 amperes. Then by Ohm's Law, the voltage drop through the 47K pull-up resistor is

$$V = I \times R$$

$$= 0.00001 \, A \times 47000\Omega$$

$$= 0.47v,$$

about a half of a volt. Then V_{sens} is about 4.5v—half a volt drop from the +5v supply.

Depending on the specific properties of the phototransistor, smaller values than 47K may be required to obtain good performance from the circuit. In particular, if the transistor can typically generate currents of 0.1 mA or more, then the voltage drop across the pull-up resistor will be so high as to reduce V_{sens} to zero. The solution is to wire a smaller pull-up resistor with the sensor itself; because the Handy Board supplies the +5v power out each sensor connector, this is not a problem.

3.6.3 Building It

The reflective optosensor consists of two elements: an LED emitter and a detector phototransistor or photodiode. The detector and emitter are matched so that the peak sensitivity of the detector is at the same wavelength of the emissions of the emitter. Usually these components are based in the infrared spectrum, making it a little difficult to ascertain that things are hooked up properly because the emitter's light is invisible.

Figure 3.48 illustrates the wiring for a sample infrared reflectance sensor. The device depicted in the diagram is the *Quality Technologies QRB1114*; the emitter LED is on the left and the detector is on the right.

The wiring for the reflectance sensor is straightforward. The emitter LED is powered by the Handy Board's +5v supply, with a 330 Ω resistor in series to limit the current through the LED to an appropriate value. The detector transistor is pulled high with the Handy Board's internal 47K resistor.

When increasing amounts of light from the emitter LED are reflected back into the detector, increasing amounts of current flow through the detector transistor and hence the internal 47K resistor. The voltage drop across this resistor results in a lower voltage presented to the Handy Board's analog input.

Different varieties of phototransistors may perform better with a smaller resistor value than the onboard 47K resistor. If the sensitivity of the device is poor, try connecting the signal line to the +5v supply through 10K, 4.7K, or 2.2K resistors to determine the best response. For the QRB1114 device, however, the default 47K value is ideal.

Seeing (Infra) Red

Working with infrared devices can be frustrating because infrared light is indeed invisible—making it hard to tell if a given infrared LED is emitting light. The CCD "retinas" of consumer video cameras are sensitive to infrared emissions, however. When looking at an IR LED through a camera with a video display of the image, if it appears lit up, then it is emitting infrared light. This is most easily demonstrated with household TV/VCR remotes; their IR LEDs are driven with brief but intense current bursts, making their light output quite powerful.

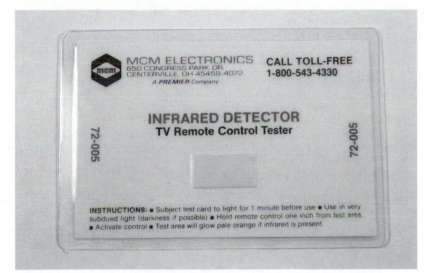

Another method is to purchase an *infrared detector card*, shown above, from an electronics supplier like *Radio Shack*, catalog number 276–099, or *MCM Electronics*, catalog number 72–003 and 72–005 (see Appendix G, *Resources*). These credit-card size devices contain a phosphorescent panel that glows visibly under infrared illumination. Aim the infrared LED at the sensitive portion of the card and a faint orange glow will be visible when the IR LED is turned on. It's necessary to provide subdued ambient light to see the glow, but it is quite definitive once you know what it looks like.

When working from an unknown reflective optosensor, the first order of business is to figure out which element is the transmitter and which is the detector. Some devices have an opaque visible light filter in front of the detector component; others mark the emitter with the letter "E" and/or the detector with a "D." Unfortunately, for most reflective assemblies it is not possible to visually determine which is which.

If the device comes with component leads, rather than an integral wiring harness, then one can generally tell the polarity of the emitter and detector by the lengths of the leads: The longer leads are positive, and the shorter leads are negative. This reduces the number of wiring permutations to two; the two shorter leads go to ground, and the two remaining leads connect either to the sensor signal line (for the detector) or the +5v power supply, *after* the 330 Ω resistor (for the emitter). Take a guess as to which is the emitter and which is the detector; if you guess wrong, nothing bad will happen to the device. If you guess right, then the device's emitter will light up (invisibly, however),

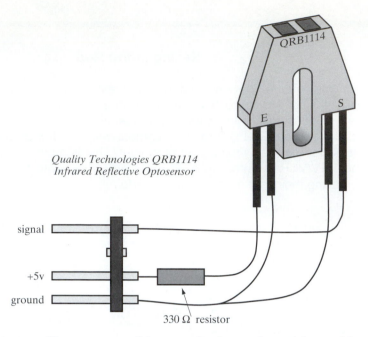

*Quality Technologies QRB1114
Infrared Reflective Optosensor*

and the detector will generate a valid range of voltages that can be read by the Handy
Board.

Optosensors that come with wire bundles are the hardest to figure out, and an infrared
detector card can be invaluable here. These credit-card size devices contain a phosphorescent panel that glows visibly under infrared illumination. Get one from *Radio Shack*
(catalog number 276–099) or *MCM Electronics* (catalog numbers 72–003 and 72–005).
Apply +5v through the 330 Ω resistor until the emitter device lights up. Make sure to
use the 330 Ω current-limiting resistor when poking around for the emitter LED because
if you apply +5 volts directly to the LED it will burn visibly, quite brightly indeed, for
about 1 second before expiring. If you don't have a detector card and you have enough
optosensors to spare that you don't mind destructively testing them, it could be a way to
figure out which component is the emitter!

After figuring out the emitter, the other device is the detector, and there are only two
ways it can be wired, so the rest of the job is easy. Just try both polarities; the diode
or transistor won't be damaged if it is wired backward—the 47K resistor on the Handy
Board limits how much current can flow.

Figure 3.49 illustrates a readily available infrared optosensor (see *Digi-Key*) that was
deciphered using this method. The detector component is marked with a dot (the upper left-hand corner), but this was readily observable because of the dark filter plastic.

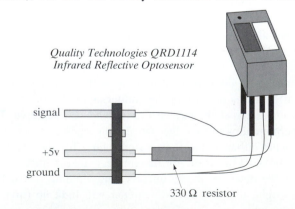

*Quality Technologies QRD1114
Infrared Reflective Optosensor*

Both the emitter and the detector have length-coded leads (this is not represented in the diagram, however); the short leads go to ground.

3.6.4 Correcting for Ambient Light

Compensating for the effects of ambient light is always an issue when using reflectance sensors. How can a robot tell the difference between a stronger reflection (more light) and simply an increase in light in the robot's environment? The answer is to switch a reflectance sensor's emitter light source on and off under program control. By taking two light level readings—one with the emitter on, and one with the emitter off—a program can subtract away the ambient light levels, yielding a much more accurate reflectance measurement.

The circuit drawings presented so far for using reflectance sensors have the emitters wired so that they're constantly on (and, as an aside, continuously drawing power). To implement this idea, we must provide separate wiring for the emitter LEDs, which can be switched on or off under program control.

The LEDs used in reflectance sensors are actually fairly high-powered devices from the point of view of the digital electronics on the Handy Board: a typical LED draws between 5 and 20 mA of current (depending on how efficient and how bright it is), and a typical digital out (e.g., from the 68HC11 processor) is capable of supplying only 20 to 25 mA. Thus, depending on the current draw of the LEDs, a 68HC11 pin can drive from one to a maximum of five LEDs.

Figure 3.50 shows a circuit for operating an LED from one of the unused 68HC11 pins on the Handy Board design—the Port D SPI (serial peripheral interface) pins. These four pins can be used to form a high-speed communication link between the 68HC11 and other microprocessors, but these pins may also be used as general-purpose digital inputs and outputs. Here we use a Port D pin as a mundane LED driver.

To gain control of the Port D pins, values are written to particular 68HC11 registers. One register controls which pins are outputs (they default to inputs); a second register controls the state of the pins selected as outputs (1 being +5v and 0 being 0 volts). As per Figure 3.50, we use Bit 2 of Port D to control the LED.

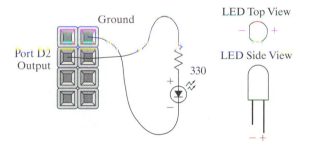

Ground

Port D2 Output

330

LED Top View

LED Side View

FIGURE 3.50 Wiring an LED to a Port D Pin

The 68HC11's Port D pins are available at the 2×4 header located midway down the right edge of the Handy Board. Wire an LED with a 330 ohm current-limiting resistor between the Bit 2 pin and ground.

To enable Bit 2 as an output, we must write a 1 into the corresponding bit position of the Port D Data Direction Register (DDRD), which is located at address 0x1009 (hexadecimal) in the 68HC11's memory. Then to set the output high (it defaults to a logic low), we can write a 1 into the proper bit in the Port D Data Register (PORTD), located at address 0x1008.

Before trying this out, build the resistor-LED circuit shown in Figure 3.50 using a *visible* LED! Get it working with an LED you can see; then trust that it will still work when you switch to an invisible infrared LED.

With the resistor-LED pair plugged into the Port D pins, type the following at the Interactive C prompt:

```
bit_set(0x1009, 0b00000100);
```

This sets Bit 2 of the DDRD, making the Bit 2 pin an output. Now type:

```
bit_set(0x1008, 0b00000100);
```

This sets Bit 2 of PORTD, actually setting the bit high. The LED should turn on—did it? If not, check the polarity of the LED; it might be inserted backward.

To turn the LED off again, clear the bit in the PORTD register:

```
bit_clear(0x1008, 0b00000100);
```

Next, wire one of the emitter LEDs from a reflectance sensor to the same pair of pins on Port D. The following code demonstrates how to use the reflectance sensor, correcting for ambient illumination. Because brighter readings yield smaller numbers, we subtract the reading with the illumination on from the reading with the illumination off:

```
int active_read(int port)
{
  int dark, light;                    /* local variables */
  dark= analog(port);                 /* reading with light off */
  bit_set(0x1009, 0b00000100);        /* turn light on */
  light= analog(port);                /* reading with light on */
  bit_clear(0x1009, 0b00000100);      /* turn light off */
  return dark - light;
}
```

(Elsewhere in the code, the statement to establish the Bit 2 pin as an output must be executed.)

This active sensing method can go a long way toward making reflectance sensing more reliable.

3.6.5 Exercises and Projects

1. *Best load resistance for phototransistor.*

   As discussed, the Handy Board provides a standard 47K pull-up resistance from the sensor signal line to +5v. Depending on the sensitivity of a particular phototransistor, a smaller resistance might be necessary to yield good performance.

   Referring to Figure 3.51, experimentally determine the ideal value of an additional resistor, R_{load}, to be placed in parallel with the Handy Board's built-in 47K resistance. Describe your experimental procedure.

FIGURE 3.51 Determining the Best Loading Resistor for a Phototransistor

The phototransistor Q_1 draws current through the parallel resistance of R_{sens}, the 47K resistor on the Handy Board, and R_{load}, an additional resistor. For the phototransistors you are working with, find the value of R_{load} that yields the best results.

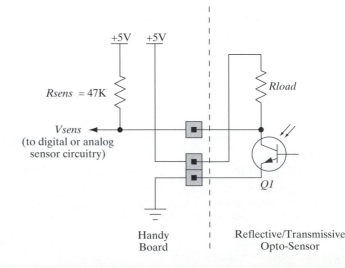

2. *Extending the active sensing approach.*

   (a) *Current consumption of LEDs.* Assuming that the emitter LED has a voltage drop of 2 volts, calculate how much current would be drawn by the LED-resistor circuit assuming the Handy Board's +5v power supply and a 330 ohm resistor.

   (b) *Multiple sensors.* To operate multiple reflectance sensors, at least two approaches are possible: (1) provide a separate control line for each LED emitter, or (2) gang multiple emitters on a single control line. Because spare 68HC11 pins for control purposes are limited, the latter approach makes more sense. Figure 6.16 illustrates the proper method for operating multiple LEDs from a single voltage source. Given your calculation from the prior exercise, how many LEDs may connected using this method? The transistor circuit shown in Figure 6.27 shows how to use a driver transistor, which can readily supply 100 mA or more, controlled from a 68HC11 output. Also, a Handy Board motor output can be used to operate LEDs—as long as the current limiting resistors are appropriately scaled up to compensate for the +9v level provided by the motor drivers.

3. *Line following.* Lay down a path on the floor using black electrical tape. Equip your *HandyBug* robot with one or more reflectance sensors aimed at the floor and write a program to follow the line.

   (a) How many sensors does your solution use? Why did you choose this number?

   (b) Does your program follow along the *edge of the line*, or does it drive *down the middle of the line*? Why?

   (c) What happens when *HandyBug* drives off the end of the line? How do you explain this?

   (d) Create a fork in the black line road. Does *HandyBug* always take the same direction when it reaches the fork? Can you rewrite the program to deliberately choose one of the two paths?

4. *Wall following.* Configure a reflectance sensor so that it is suitable for measuring a wall (it will probably be necessary to construct an opaque tube to block ambient light from shining in the sensor). Mount it on the *HandyBug*, and write to drive a constant distance from a wall.

   (a) One approach is to threshold the sensor value to indicate two states: too close to the wall, in which case *HandyBug* should take a step away from the wall, and too far from the wall, in which case *HandyBug* should drive toward the wall. Implement this solution and then modify it to distinguish a third state—at the ideal distance from the wall—which results in driving straight. Compare these two solutions, and experiment with the width of the "just right" state. What works best, and why?

   (b) Experiment with sensor placement. What is the best place to locate the sensor, and why?

   (c) Rewrite the control program to use a Braitenberg vehicle approach, in which sensor values are wired to motor speeds. Compare this approach to the earlier ones.

3.7 Break-Beam Sensors

In addition to the reflective configuration, pairs of light-emitting and light-detecting components may be used in the break-beam configuration. The break-beam device consists of the light-emitting component aimed at a light-detecting component. When an opaque object comes between the emitter and detector, the beam of light is occluded, and the output of the detector changes (Figure 3.52).

FIGURE 3.52 Break-Beam
Sensing Diagram

In the break-beam sensing
application, an emitter device
shines light at a detector device.
When an opaque object passes
between the emitter and the
detector, the beam is broken and
the signal from the detector
changes.

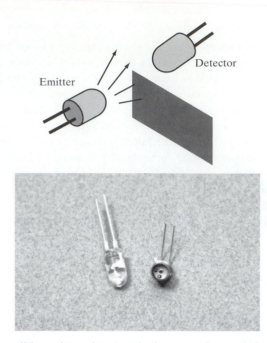

FIGURE 3.53 Discrete Infrared
LED and Phototransistor

Any pair of compatible emitter–detector devices may be used: incandescent flashlight
bulbs and photocells, red LEDs and visible-light-sensitive phototransistors, or infrared
emitters and detectors. The applications discussed in this section are based on infrared devices because of their ease of use and fast response time. Figure 3.53 shows an individual
infrared LED emitter and phototransistor detector.

Industrial break-beam optosensors typically consist of an infrared emitter and infrared
detector housed in a U-shaped plastic assembly. The gap between the vertical beams
of the "U" is typically less than a half of an inch. Figure 3.54 shows several styles of
commercial optosensor devices.

For sensing objects between larger gaps, simply use discrete emitters and detectors.
Figure 3.55 shows an industrial solution using a discrete emitter and detector. When
covering larger distances, it may be necessary to use higher-powered or multiple emitters,
lenses, or light shields to get good performance. Also, the light source can be switched
on and off to determine the validity of the detector reading and minimize errors caused
by ambient light.

FIGURE 3.54 Various
Break-Beam Optosensors

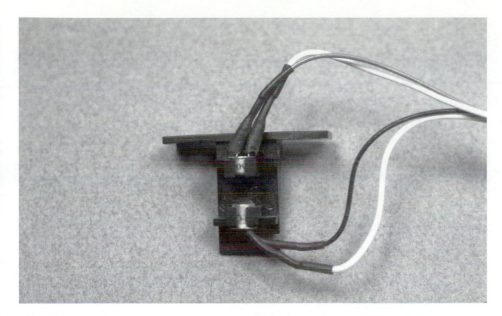

FIGURE 3.55 Break-Beam Sensor Built From Discrete Components

This photograph shows a subassembly from a commercial product. The engineers apparently chose to use a pair of discrete IR emitters and detectors in lieu of a packaged solution—perhaps for cost savings or perhaps because their application required a custom fit.

3.7.1 Interfacing

The circuitry of break-beam sensors is the same as for the reflective optosensors. Section 3.6.2 discusses how common infrared emitters and detectors are interfaced to the Handy Board.

3.7.2 Building the Break-Beam Sensor

Electrically, the break-beam sensor is identical to the reflective optosensor. An emitter LED is powered from the Handy Board's +5v supply through a dropping resistor. A detector phototransistor is connected between the sensor signal line and ground, using the Handy Board's internal 47K pull-up resistor to measure the current drain through the transistor.

Figure 3.56 illustrates how to wire an example break-beam optosensor, the Motorola MOC70V1, to the Handy Board. This is an excellent model because of the width and depth of gap between the emitter and detector.

On the top face of the sensor are markings that indicate which component is the emitter and which is the detector, as well as their polarity. The emitter is marked with the symbols "E" and "+"; the detector is marked with "D" and "+." On this device, the polarity is *not* indicated by the length of the device leads, so the imprinting of the + lead

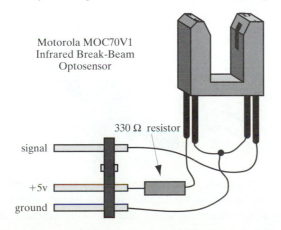

Motorola MOC70V1
Infrared Break-Beam
Optosensor

330 Ω resistor

signal

+5v

ground

FIGURE 3.56 Break-Beam Optosensor Construction Diagram

on the package case is helpful. For unknown break-beam devices, follow the instructions for reflective optosensors to determine the emitter, the detector, and their polarity.

When using the break-beam sensor for shaft encoding applications, experimentation is the best way to align the counter wheel within the sensor. First wire the sensor and ascertain that it is working electrically, and use the Handy Board to dynamically display sensor values while playing with the alignment of the counter wheel.

3.7.3 Object Detection

Break-beam sensors are excellent for detecting the presence of an object between two points that may be aimed at each other—for example, detecting something between the fingers of a robotic gripper.

3.7.4 Break-Beam Exercises

- Brainstorm robotic applications for break-beam sensing.
- Experiment with the break-beam sensor configuration to determine its efficacy at various distances and environmental lighting conditions. Vary optical shielding on the receiver element and/or the optical technology employed (phototransistors and LEDs vs. photocells and light bulbs). Try the active sensing method presented in the reflectance sensor section—is this relevant to break-beam sensing? Describe your results.

3.8 Shaft Encoding

One of the predominant uses of break-beam sensors is in the service of a device called a *shaft encoder*. The shaft encoder measures the angular rotation of an axle, reporting position and/or velocity information. An everyday example of shaft encoding is the speedometer on an automobile, which reports how fast the wheels are turning, and its odometer, which keeps track of the number of total rotations.

Figure 3.57 illustrates the concept. An opaque circular disk with notches cut into its circumference is mounted on the shaft to be monitored. The disk is positioned so that as it rotates, the notches chop the light beam from the emitter to the detector. Hardware or software circuit is connected to the detector signal to decode and count the light pulses.

Figure 3.58 is a photograph of a shaft encoder built from a LEGO Technics pulley wheel and a Motorola break-beam sensor. The pulley wheel is positioned in the sensor so that the holes in the wheel and the plastic between the holes chop the light beam.

FIGURE 3.57 Single-Disk Shaft Encoder Diagram

To use the break-beam sensor as a shaft encoder, a perforated disk is mounted on the shaft and placed between the emitter–detector pair. As the shaft rotates, the holes in the disk chop the light beam. Hardware and software connected to the detector keeps track of these light pulses, thereby monitoring the rotation of the shaft.

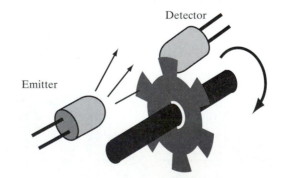

Figure 3.59 is a graph of data collected from a shaft encoder (built from the Motorola MOV70V1 break-beam sensor and a LEGO Technic pulley wheel). As the shaft was rotated continuously in one direction, sensor readings were sampled, stored on the Handy

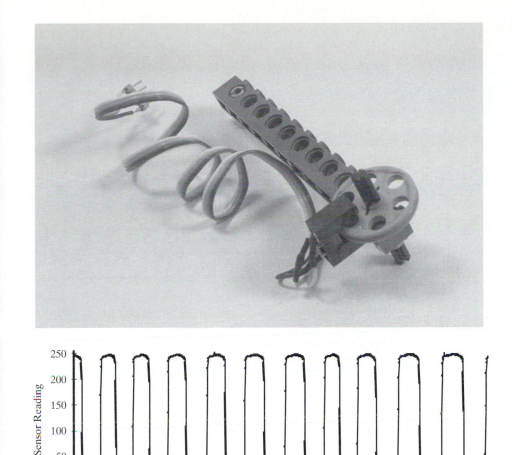

FIGURE 3.58 A Shaft Encoder Built from LEGO Parts

This assembly uses the Motorola break-beam sensor discussed in the text with the LEGO Technic medium pulley wheel as a photo-interrupter. After determining a position of the break-beam sensor that yielded good break and make transitions, the sensor was hot-glued into position along the LEGO beam.

FIGURE 3.59 Sample Shaft Encoder Data

Board, uploaded to the host computer, and graphed. (See Appendix C for information on how to collect and upload sensor data.)

The sensor data graph is a nearly ideal square wave. Using the standard Handy Board analog input, which reports a sensor reading between 0 and 255 (corresponding to sensor voltages between 0 and 5 volts), the sensor's output varies from a low of about 9 (about 0.18 volts) to a high of about 250 (4.9 volts) with a sharp edge between the transitions. This is just about a perfect square wave response; other break-beam sensors yield a time graph that looks more like a sine wave.

3.8.1 Counting Encoder Clicks

The trick to making sense of the data from a shaft encoder is to install a routine that repetitously checks the sensor value, looking for rising or falling edges that indicate the counter wheel has turned one "click." The more often this routine checks the sensor value, the better it can keep up with the encoder wheel's transitions. If the encoder wheel turns faster than the routine checks the sensor state, it will start missing transitions and lose track of the shaft's rotation.

A simple way to look for transitions is to threshold the sensor data at some midrange point. With the response in the sample graph, the value in the middle of the analog

FIGURE 3.60 Flowchart for Basic Encoder Counting Algorithm

Variables:

encoder_state   Keeps track of last encoder reading.
1 if high, 0 if low.

encoder_counter Keeps running total of encoder "clicks."

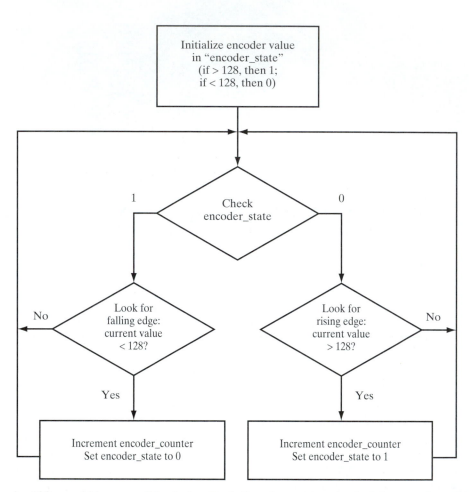

scale, 128, would be a sensible choice. Each time the routine checked the encoder value, it would determine whether the value had changed from above 128 to below 128 (the falling edge) or from below 128 to above 128 (the rising edge).

Figure 3.60 depicts this algorithm in a flowchart format. Two state variables are required: encoder_state, which keeps track of whether the last reading was "high" (above 128) or "low" (below 128), and encoder_counter, which counts the "encoder clicks."

The encoder_state variable is necessary so that the routine can tell whether the encoder sensor reading has changed from the high portion of the square wave to the low portion. The first step is to initialize this variable with a reading sample. The routine uses the arbitrary convention that the value "1" means that the encoder reading is in the high portion of the square wave (i.e., it is greater than the midrange 128 value) and that "0" means it is in the low portion.

Then the routine enters its main loop, checking the `encoder_state` value. If it is 1, then it means that the last time through the loop, the encoder was high, so now we should be looking for a low value if the shaft has turned. This is represented by the left-hand path. If `encoder_state` was 0, then the algorithm should look for a rising edge transition, indicated by the current encoder value being greater than 128.

Opto-Electronic Computer Mice

The common desktop mouse uses shaft encoder technology to figure out how the mouse ball is turned. As shown in the photograph above, two slotted encoder wheels are mounted on shafts that are turned by the ball's movement. On either side of each encoder wheel are the infrared emitter and detector pair.

Mice use *quadrature shaft encoding*, a technique that provides information about which way the shaft is turned (in addition to the total "encoder clicks"). The IR detector on each shaft actually has two elements, aligned so that as one element is being covered up by the leaf between the slots, the other is being exposed. This method is described in detail in chapter 6.

After checking for the falling or rising edge transition, as appropriate, the algorithm either goes back to the main loop (no transition) or increments the `encoder_counter` variable and resets `encoder_state` to reflect the new state.

Exercises

1. Build a shaft encoder using a break-beam optosensor and a perforated disk or LEGO pulley wheel. Verify the raw sensor performance—what values represent the light beam being broken versus not broken?

2. Follow the method presented in Appendix C for collecting sensor data, and capture raw data from the encoder sensor as the shaft is spun. Graph the data, and compare it to the encoder data graph presented in the text.

3. Based on either or both of the previous exercises, choose a suitable midpoint value for determining encoder transitions. Write a program in Interactive C to implement the simple encoder counting algorithm presented in the flowchart and text. Use Interactive C's multitasking capability to display the `encoder_counter` variable while the counting routine is running, and experiment with the encoder. Can you determine the performance limit of the algorithm in your implementation in terms of counts per second? What is a fundamental problem with this implementation method?

3.8.2 Driver Software

The software task of monitoring the shaft encoder values and calculating encoder steps and velocity needs to run fast, and in the case of the velocity measurement, needs to run at regular intervals in order to be accurate. This task is best done by a machine language *software driver*—a routine that gets loaded into Interactive C's underlying layer of direct 68HC11 code and provides an interface to the user C level.

Interactive C includes a capability for loading *IC binary* (ICB) files, which run directly as 68HC11 code. These binary programs also have the capability install themselves in the interrupt structure of the 68HC11 so they can trigger directly on particular hardware conditions or repeatedly at regular invervals.

The software libraries provided with the Handy Board include a set of routines for supporting the shaft encoders discussed in this chapter, for both position counting and velocity measurement. For each analog input on the Handy Board, a pair of shaft encoder routines is provided. For each pair, there is a high-speed version and a low-speed version. The high-speed version checks for transitions on the encoder sensor 1000 times per second (1000 Hz), whenever the low-speed version checks 250 times per second. Both versions calculate the velocity (position difference) measurement at about 16 Hz. For most applications, the low-speed routines are functional and preferable because they impose less of a processing load on the system.

The high-speed routines are named `fencdr?.icb`, where the "?" is replaced by the number of the analog input that the routine uses (e.g., `fencdr0.icb` is the encoder driver for analog port 0). The low-speed routines are named by the same convention using file names `sencdr?.icb`. The driver routines may be loaded for any or all of the seven analog inputs, but only one of the pair should be loaded for a given input. For example, if `fencdr0.icb` is loaded, then `sencdr0.icb` should *not* be loaded.

When a given encoder routine is loaded, two new variables become declared as globals within the Interactive C environment:

`int encoder?_counts` This variable keeps a running total of transitions on the encoder sensor.

`int encoder?_velocity` This variable keeps a velocity measurement calculated by successive position differences.

As with the file naming convention, the "?" is replaced by the single-digit encoder number.

Once loaded into Interactive C, the encoder routines are automatically active; no additional commands are needed to turn them on. Each `encoder?_counts` variable will automatically increment every time it senses a transition on its corresponding encoder sensor, and the `encoder?_velocity` value is continously updated.

If it is desired to reset a `encoder?_counts` variable to zero, this may be done simply with an assignment statement; e.g.,

```
C> encoder3_counts= 0;
```

will reset the encoder 3 counter to zero.

Hysteresis

Rather than thresholding a single sensor value to determine an encoder "click," the library routines use two thresholds to track changes in the raw encoder reading. The reading must rise above a high threshold value to be considered high and then fall below a low threshold to be considered low.

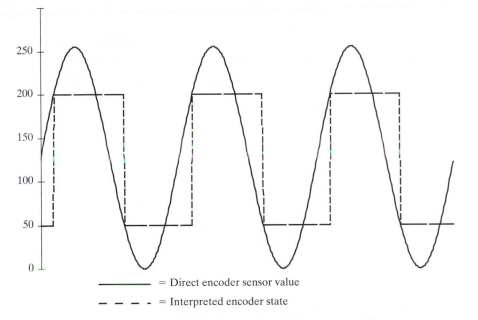

= Direct encoder sensor value

= Interpreted encoder state

FIGURE 3.61 Graph of Direct Encoder Reading and Intepreted Encoder State

The sine wave illustrates the direct analog encoder reading, which is shown as varying between the full-scale analog input range of 0 to 255. The dashed square wave illustrates how this signal is interpreted by the encoder routine. For the interpreted signal to be considered "high," the direct signal must rise above 200. For the interpreted signal to be low, the direct signal must fall below 50. In the range in between 50 and 200, the value of the interpreted signal depends on the last transition about the high or low thresholds.

Figure 3.61 illustrates this idea. The sine wave represents the raw encoder value. The dashed square wave represents the encoder state of the driver routine—each transition on the square wave corresponds to an encoder count. The square wave changes state either when the encoder reading *rises above 200* or *falls below 50*. When the encoder value is

between these two thresholds, the square wave "waits" for the value to reach a threshold before changing state.

This algorithm implements a property known as *hysteresis*, in which an output signal depends on the input signal and its recent history. It can be a very robust way of interpreting sensor data because any fluctuations in the middle range of the sensor values are ignored until they become significant by rising above a high threshold or falling below a low threshold.

The encoder library routines for implementing shaft encoders use this method of counting encoder transitions. In addition to defining the `encoder?_counts` and `encoder?-_velocity` variables, each encoder routine defines variables for the two threshold points: `encoder?_high_threshold` and `encoder?_low_threshold`. These variables are initialized to the values 200 and 50, respectively, but they may be adjusted depending on the actual readings of a given encoder sensor. It is best to define them such that the width of the positive and negative portions of the resulting encoder state square wave are approximately equal.

3.8.3 Measuring Velocity

The supplied driver routines measure rotational velocity as well as position. This is done simply by subtracting differences in the position readings after an interval of time has elapsed.

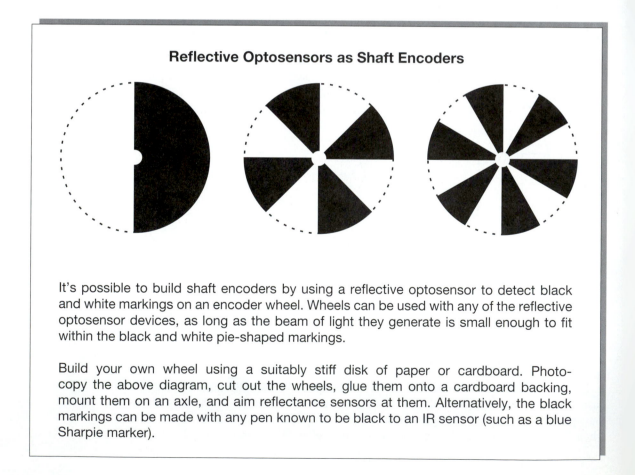

Reflective Optosensors as Shaft Encoders

It's possible to build shaft encoders by using a reflective optosensor to detect black and white markings on an encoder wheel. Wheels can be used with any of the reflective optosensor devices, as long as the beam of light they generate is small enough to fit within the black and white pie-shaped markings.

Build your own wheel using a suitably stiff disk of paper or cardboard. Photocopy the above diagram, cut out the wheels, glue them onto a cardboard backing, mount them on an axle, and aim reflectance sensors at them. Alternatively, the black markings can be made with any pen known to be black to an IR sensor (such as a blue Sharpie marker).

Velocity readings can be useful for a variety of purposes. A robot that has an unpowered trailer wheel with a shaft encoder can easily tell whether it is moving by looking at encoder activity on the trailer wheel. If the robot is moving, the trailer wheel will be dragged along and will have a nonzero velocity. If the robot is stuck, regardless of whether its main drive wheels are turning, the trailer wheel will be still. There is no surer way to tell that a robot is stuck than to notice that a trailer wheel isn't moving.

Velocity information can be combined with position information to perform tasks like causing a robot to drive in the straight line or rotate a certain number of degrees. These tasks are inherently unreliable because of mechanical factors like slippage of robot wheels on the floor and backlash in geartrains, but to a limited extent they can be performed with appropriate feedback from shaft encoders.

Exercises and Projects

1. Load a library shaft encoder routine and experiment with its performance. Based on the graph of raw encoder performance obtained in a previous exercise, choose suitable high- and low-threshold values. Explain your choices.

2. One limitation of current encoder routines, both the Interactive C and library versions, is that they cannot determine which *direction* the shaft is rotating. A solution called *quadrature encoder* is presented in a later chapter (also see the sidebar on computer mice on page 133). Can you think of a different approach for determining the direction of rotation? If it is easily implemented, try it.

3. Implement the trailer wheel idea discussed in the text on your *HandyBug*. Write a program to make *HandyBug* drive around and stop, back up, and turn when the trailer wheel's velocity is 0. Can you think of other applications for knowing the robot's velocity other than as a nonzero/zero (i.e., moving/not moving) quantity?

4. Instrument one of *HandyBug*'s drive wheels with an encoder, and write a program at attempts to maintain constant velocity on the drive wheel by varying the power level delivery to the motor. Experiment with the system by holding *HandyBug* in the air and applying pressure to the drive wheel. Is the system able to maintain the velocity? What happens if you suddenly remove the pressure?

This concludes the presentation of the basic robotic sensors. In many regards, this chapter has simply presented the technology of these devices and left it up to the reader to design the creative applications, either as suggested in the Exercises or left unsaid. For example, it is fairly obvious that a switch may be used to build a contact sensor, but the mechanical implementation of such a device remains a challenge. Some of these aspects of sensing are presented in chapter "Motors, Gears, and Mechanism."

Similarly, the treatment of shaft encoders only pointed in general directions to their applications. It is difficult to discuss such a sensor out of the context of a particular mechanism being monitored and the overall control intent of monitoring the mechanism. Some of the higher level strategies used in conjunction with shaft encoding are discussed in chapter 5, " Control."

As a final pointer forward, chapter 6, "Advanced Sensing", presents a variety of sensor technologies based on the principle of broadcasting information into the world and measuring how it is "reflected" back in the broad sense. The reflective and break-beam optosensor technologies are basic instances of this approach; a more provocative one, which is discussed in a later chapter, is the use of ultrasonic radar, such as that used by bats to see.

Keep in mind that, although the number of sensors discussed thus far may seem small, the possibilities given their creative application are large. A robot with just a handful of sensors can exhibit quite complex behaviors and can be quite a challenge to debug—as any reader who has been building robots along the way surely already knows!

4 Motors, Gears, and Mechanism

This chapter is about getting robots to move. Engineered systems use a variety of methods to generate physical motion, including pneumatics (air pressure) and hydraulics (fluid pressure), but we focus on direct-current (DC) motors here. DC motors are small, cheap, reasonably efficient, and easy to use. Other methods and other electrical motors have their applications strengths, but for our purpose of building small robotic systems, DC motors are ideal.

Here is a roadmap of this chapter. First we examine the basic DC motor, including its properties and performance. Next, we study how gears can be used to convert the output of the DC motor into a usable drive source.

Electronic control of DC motors, including speed control, is then discussed, followed by an explanation of servo motors, which incorporate a DC motor, gear reduction, and control circuitry into a single device.

In the final section, which explores gearing and mechanism, we use the LEGO Technics building system to exemplify the ideas presented. Although not all readers will necessarily use these parts, they are excellent pedagogical tools and practical building materials, and are ideal for illustrating a variety of mechanical concepts.

4.1 DC Motors

The DC motor is a device that converts electrical energy into mechanical energy. DC motors come in various sizes and configurations. Figure 4.1 illustrates some common miniature DC motors suitable for small mobile robot applications.

DC motors work by running electrical current through loops of wire mounted on a rotating shaft (called the *armature*). When current is flowing, the loops of wire generate a magnetic field, which react against the magnetic fields of permanent magnets positioned around the wire loops. These magnetic fields push against one another and the armature turns.

As with any real-world device, no DC motor is perfectly efficient; various limitations of motors (including mechanical friction) cause some electrical energy to be wasted as heat. Inexpensive toy motors typically have efficiencies as low at 50%, whereas industrial grade motors can be as good as 90%.

There are a number of properties that describe a motor's power requirements and performance. One of the most fundamental is its *operating voltage*. This is the recommended voltage for powering the motor. Most motors run fine at lower voltages, although they are less powerful. Also most manufacturers are somewhat conservative in their voltage ratings, so motors can be operated at higher voltages than the rated specification, delivering increased power output at the expense of operating life.

The next electrical property of motors to consider is their operating current. When provided with a constant voltage, a motor draws current proportional to how much work it is doing. When there is no resistance to its motion, the motor draws the least amount

FIGURE 4.1 Photograph of Various DC Motors

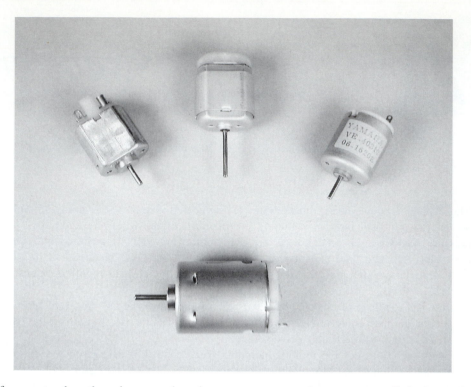

of current; when there is so much resistance as to cause the motor to stall, it draws the maximal amount of current. This is referred to as the motor's *stall current*—the maximum amount of operating current that a motor can draw at its specified voltage.

The more current going through a motor, the more rotational force or *torque* is produced at the motor's shaft. This is a direct consequence of the electromagnetic reaction between the loops of wire in the motor's armature and the permanent magnets surrounding them. The strength of the magnetic field generated in the loops of wire is directly proportional to the amount of current flowing through them; the torque produced on the motor's shaft is a result of the interaction between these two magnetic fields.

Often a motor will be rated by its *stall torque*. This is the amount of rotation force produced when the motor is stalled at its recommended operating voltage, drawing the maximal stall current at this voltage. For small motors, torque is measured in units like ounce-inches (i.e., the amount of linear force produced at a lever arm of 1 inch away from the center of the motor shaft).

The amount of *power* supplied by a motor is the product of the output shaft's *rotational velocity* and torque. When a motor is spinning freely, with no load on the shaft, the rotational velocity is at its highest, but the torque is zero—it's not driving any mechanism—so the output power is zero. (Actually, the motor is doing some work to overcome internal friction, but that work is of no value as output power.) When a motor is stalled, it is producing its maximal torque, but the rotational velocity is zero, so again, it is producing zero power. In between these two extremes, the output power has a characteristic parabolic relationship, as illustrated in Figure 4.2. A motor produces the most power in the middle of this performance range.

4.1.1 Exercises

1. *Measuring motor torque.* Figure 4.3 illustrates an experimental set-up for measuring a motor's torque. In the experiment, a motor winds a nylon thread carrying a known

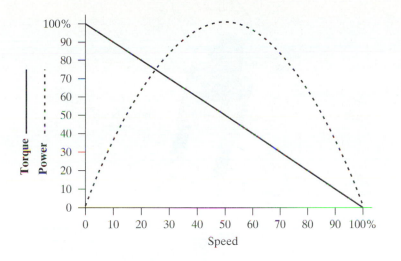

Motor Speed, Torque, and Power

FIGURE 4.2 Idealized Graph of Motor Speed, Torque, and Power Output

The solid line shows the relationship between motor speed and torque. At the right of the graph, the speed is greatest (100%) and the torque is zero; this represents the case where the motor shaft is spinning freely but doing no actual work. At the left of the graph, the speed is zero but the torque is at its maximum; this represents the case where the shaft is stalled because of too much load. The dashed line shows the power output, which is the product of speed and torque. It is the highest in the middle of the motor's performance range, when both speed and torque are produced.

weight around the motor shaft. As the thread winds up around the shaft, like a bobbin, the effective radius of the shaft increases. This process will continue until the radius of the spool of thread increases to a point where the motor can no longer lift the weight.

When the motor stops turning, measure the radius of the bobbin. The motor's stall torque is the product of this radius and the weight of mass (e.g., if the radius is $\frac{1}{2}$ an inch and the mass weighs 2 ounces, then the torque is 1 ounce-inch).

2. *Measuring motor speed in revolutions per minute (RPM).* Figure 4.4 illustrates an experimental set-up for measuring a motor's top speed. An opaque disk is mounted directly on the motor shaft. A break-beam optosensor is positioned such that, as the disk rotates, it interrupts the sensor's light beam once per revolution.

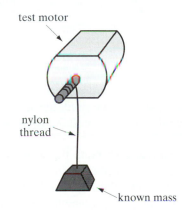

test motor

nylon thread

known mass

FIGURE 4.3 Experiment to Measure Motor Torque

To measure a motor's stall torque, attach a weight to the motor's shaft using nylon thread. Apply power to the motor, and the thread will begin to wind around the motor shaft. As the amount of thread wound around the shaft increases, forming a bobbin, the effective radius of the shaft increases. Thus, the lever arm lifting the weight increases, and the torque required to lift it increases. At the point where the required torque is greater than the torque delivered by the motor, the shaft will stop turning.

Figure 4.5 is a photograph of a motor with this instrumentation. It is important to use a light-weight material for the disk so that it puts as little load on the motor as possible and thereby reduces the unloaded speed as little as possible. Aluminum foil is suitable for this application.

For counting the transitions on the sensor, there is a hardware feature of the 68HC11 processor, known as the *pulse accumulator input* (PAI), that is ideal. This input circuit counts pulses on a particular digital input pin with hardware ancillary to the 6811 core. This allows it to operate at a very fast rate, transparently to the rest of the processor's functioning.

FIGURE 4.4 Experiment to Measure Motor Speed

To measure a motor's maximum speed, use a break-beam sensor and an opaque disk mounted on the motor shaft. When the shaft turns, the disk breaks the beam of light in the sensor; the speed is determined by measuring the number of interruptions in a given time period.

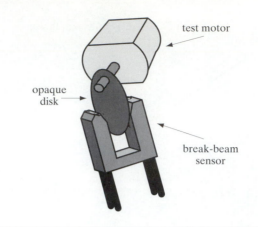

FIGURE 4.5 Photograph of Motor Speed Measurement Experiment

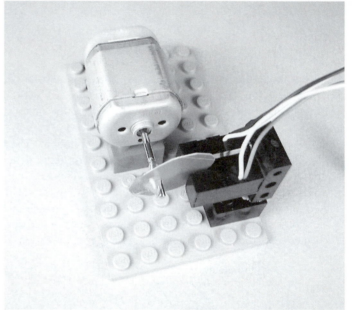

Most DC motors have unloaded speeds in the range of 3,000 to 9,000 RPMs which translates to between 50 and 150 revolutions per second. This is slow enough that a regular 68HC11 analog input could be used, but it is possible that Interactive C would not be able to keep up with this rate. It is therefore convenient to demonstrate usage of the PAI input.

Figure 4.6 is a listing of `rpm.c`, a program that may be used for measuring the motor's speed. Using the `poke`, `bit_set`, and `bit_clear` operations, the program manipulates two 68HC11 registers, the PACTL (Port A ConTroL) and PACNT (Port A CouNT), to perform the pulse-accumulation function. The main loop of the program runs for 6 seconds, incrementing a `hi_count` variable when the PACNT register overflows (it is only one byte long, and thus can only count from 0 to 255). The total number of counts is multiplied by 10 to yield a measurement of RPMs. Using the `rpm.c` program and this method, measure the speed of various DC motors.

3. *Symmetry.* Some motors are designed to operate more efficiently turning in one direction and then the other. Using the torque and/or RPM tests, determine if your experimental motor is symmetric in both directions.

FIGURE 4.6 Listing of `rpm.c`

```
/*
  rpm.c

  uses 6811's pulse accumulator input (PAI)
  to facilitate high-speed counting of transitions

  the PAI is sensor input 9 on the Handy Board
*/

int     PACTL=  0x1026; /* pulse accumulator control */
int     PACNT=  0x1027; /* pulse accumulator count */
int     PAEN=   0x40;   /* bit to enable counting */

int rpm()
{
  long end_time;
  int hi_count= 0;
  int last_count= 0;

  bit_set(PACTL, PAEN);         /* enable counting */
  poke(PACNT, 0);               /* reset to 0 */
  end_time= mseconds() + 6000L; /* 6 sec */

  while (mseconds() < end_time) {
    if (peek(PACNT) < last_count) hi_count++;
    last_count= peek(PACNT);
  }

  bit_clear(PACTL, PAEN);       /* disable counting */

  /* report result in revolutions per minute */
  return 10 * (hi_count * 256 + last_count);
}
```

4.2 Gearing

DC motors are inherently high-speed, low-torque devices. Very few applications can make use of the power delivered directly from the output shaft; a desktop fan is one example. But nearly all of the mechanisms in robots, including drive trains and actuators, require more torque and less speed.

Gears are the common way to address this problem. Using gears, the high speed of the motor is traded off into torque. Let's examine how gears are used to achieve this goal.

The common playground seesaw demonstrates lever action, an important principle of basic mechanics that is relevant to the discussion of gearing. As shown in Figure 4.7, people sitting on the seesaw generate a downward force F equal the product of their mass and their distance from the seesaw's fulcrum. This allows lighter people (as the person drawn on the left) to displace heavier people simply by increasing their distance from the fulcrum.

In a similar fashion, the rotational force, or torque, generated at the center of a gear is equal to the product of the gear's radius and the force applied at its circumference. Figure 4.8 illustrates a gear of radius r, with applied force F, rotating with torque $T = F \times r$.

When two gears of unequal sizes are meshed together, their respective radii determine the translation of torque from the driving gear to the driven one. This mechanical

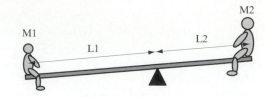

FIGURE 4.7 Seesaw Physics

On a seesaw, people exert a downward force equal to their weight times their distance from the fulcrum. The person on the left, with mass M_1, is a distance of L_1 from the fulcrum, while the person on the right has mass M_2 at distance L_2. Even though the left-hand person may be lighter than the right-hand person, both can play on the seesaw because of the multiplying effect of distance.

advantage is easiest understood from a "conservation of work" point of view. From basic physics, work is defined as force times distance. In the case of rotation and gears, this translates as work equals torque times amount of angle movement. Neglecting losses due to friction, no work is lost or gained when one gear turns another.

For example, in Figure 4.9, suppose gear 1's radius is one-third that of gear 2. Because gears are circles, their circumferences are also in a three to one ratio, so it take three turns of the small gear to produce one turn of the larger gear.

FIGURE 4.8 Radius, Force, and Torque on a Gear

The torque T—or, turning force—is defined as the product of a force F applied perpendicularly at a radius r.

F = rt

Suppose in a given amount of time, gear 1 turns three times (for a angular movement of 1080 degrees). Then gear 2 will turn once (360 degrees). The work done by the smaller gear 1 is some torque $T_{small} \times 1080$, and the work done by the large gear 2 is $T_{large} \times 360$. Since no work is lost or gained, these two values must be equal:

$$T_{large} \times 360 = T_{small} \times 1080$$

$$\frac{T_{large}}{T_{small}} = \frac{1080}{360}$$

$$\frac{T_{large}}{T_{small}} = 3$$

Thus, because the ratio of the gear radii is 3:1, the ratio of the resulting torques is 3:1. More generally, the ratio of gear sizes determines the ratios of the resulting torques; *if the output gear is larger than the input gear, then the torque increases.*

In addition to the change of torque, there is a corresponding change of speed. The larger gear will rotate more slowly than the smaller gear, again at a rate proportional to their radii.

FIGURE 4.9 Gear Physics

Gear 1 with radius $r1$ turns an angular distance of $\theta1$ while gear 2 with radius $r2$ turns an angular distance of $\theta2$.

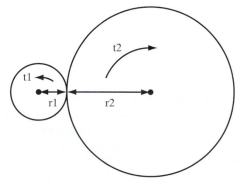

Gear 1   Gear 2

These two parameters—speed and torque—are the key to understanding gearing. When a small gear drives a larger one, torque increases and speed decreases. When gearing is used with DC motors, the excess speed of the motor is "traded" for torque.

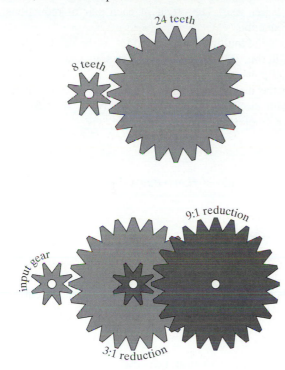

FIGURE 4.10 3 to 1 Gear Reduction

It requires three turns of the gear on the left, with 8 teeth, to cause one turn on the gear on the right, with 24 teeth.

FIGURE 4.11 Ganged 3 to 1 Gear Reductions

By ganging—putting in series—two 3:1 gear reductions, a 9:1 reduction is obtained between the 8-tooth input gear on the left and the darker 24-tooth gear on the right.

Designing Gear Teeth

The task of designing the shape of gear teeth is an art and a science unto itself. The goal is to get the teeth to push against one another as perpendicularly as possible as they rotate in and out of position. Additionally, it is desirable to minimize *backlash*—the unproductive play between adjacent gears in a geartrain. But this latter goal runs counter to another important property—minimal friction.

To get the teeth to mesh properly at all, gears must be proportionally sized; that is, a 24-tooth gear must have a radius three times the size of an 8-tooth one. This is so that the basic lever arm properties discussed earlier conform with the properties inferred by counting gear teeth.

4.2.1 Meshing Gears

Figure 4.10 illustrates an 8-tooth gear and a 24-tooth gear meshed together. By simple arithmetic, it's easy enough to see that three turns of the 8-tooth gear are required to get one turn of the 24-tooth gear. If power is applied to the 8-tooth gear, the result is a 1/3 reduction in speed at the 24-tooth gear, and a corresponding 3 times increase in torque. This is typically referred to as a "3 to 1 gear reduction."

By putting two 3:1 gear reductions in series—or "ganging" them—a 9:1 gear reduction is created. Figure 4.11 illustrates this concept. The trick is the co-axial placement of a large gear, which is driven by a smaller gear, and a small gear, which acts as the driver of a the subsequent larger gear. The effect of each pair of reductions is multiplied to achieve the overall reduction.

This method, of ganging multiple gear reductions, is the key to achieving useful power from a DC motor. With this gear reduction, the high speed and low torque is transformed into usable speeds and powerful torques.

We will return to the matter of gearing later in this chapter, in Section 4.5, which delves into design with the LEGO Technic system. Next, we examine how electronics are used to control DC motors.

4.2.2 Exercise

Calculate the effective gear ratio of *HandyBug*'s drivetrain.

4.3 Electronic Control

Compared with other electronic parts, motors require a great deal of operating current. For example, a typical small DC motor may need between 100 milliamps and an ampere to operate (and this is for a small motor!), whereas the operating current of the 68HC11, one of the most power-hungry chips on the Handy Board, is only 5 milliamps. Therefore, special circuitry for powering motors is required.

4.3.1 The H-Bridge Motor Driver Circuit

Figure 4.12 illustrates a typical circuit used to control DC motors. The circuit is known as an *H-bridge driver* because of its resemblance to the letter H. Four transistors form the vertical legs of the H, while the motor forms the crossbar. (Please note, Figure 4.12 and the subsequent two diagrams are representational rather than complete. Among other things, the circuitry driving the transistors is not drawn.)

To operate the motor, a diagonally opposite pair of transistors must be enabled. For example, Figure 4.13 shows transistors Q_1 and Q_4 enabled. Starting with the positive power terminal, current flows down through Q_1, through the motor from left to right, down Q_4, and to the negative power terminal. As illustrated by the circular arrows, this causes the motor to rotate in a clockwise direction.

FIGURE 4.12 H-Bridge Motor Driver Circuit

The H-bridge motor driver circuit consists of four transistors and a motor in the configuration shown. To turn on the motor, a pair of diagonally opposite transistors is enabled. Depending on which pair is active, the current flows through the motor either left to right or right to left, allowing control of the motor direction.

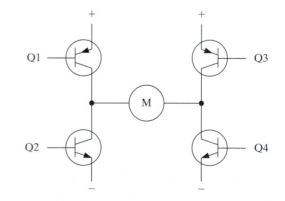

Figure 4.14 shows the other pair of transistors, Q_2 and Q_3, enabled, which results in current flowing through the motor from right to left.

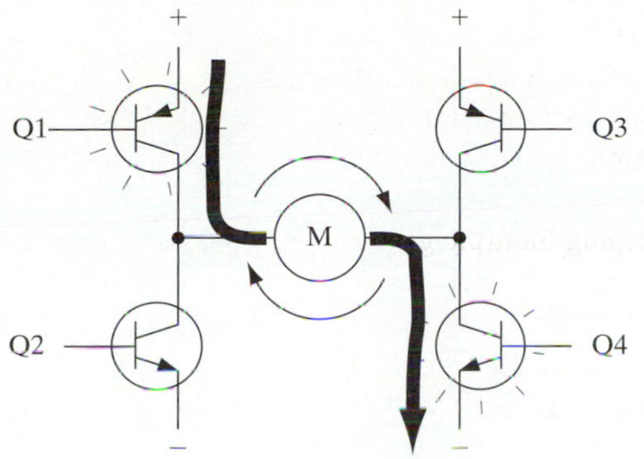

FIGURE 4.13 H-Bridge Operating
Motor in Clockwise Direction

By enabling transistors Q_1 and
Q_4, current flows through the
motor from left to right and the
motor spins a particular
direction (indicated as clockwise
by the circular arrows around
the motor).

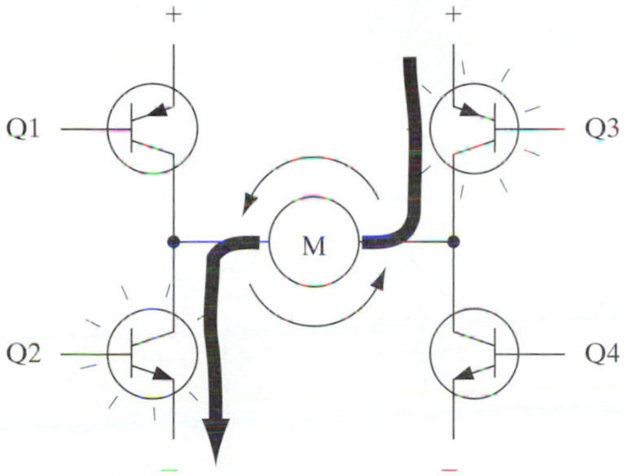

FIGURE 4.14 H-Bridge Operating
Motor in Counterclockwise
Direction

In the opposite case, transistors
Q_2 and Q_3 are enabled. Current
flows through the motor from
right to left and the motor spins
the other way (indicated by the
counterclockwise arrows around
the motor).

4.3.2 Enable and Direction Logic

It is critical that the pair of transistors in either of the vertical legs of the "H" are
never turned on at the same time. If transistors Q_1 and Q_2 were turned on together,
then current would flow from the positive supply source to the negative supply terminal
through the two transistors. There would be no load in this circuit other than the transistors
themselves, so the maximal amount of current possible for the circuit would flow, limited
only by the power supply or when the transistors self-destruct.

For this reason, it is typical in an actual circuit to have hardware to facilitate control
of the transistor switches.

Figure 4.15 illustrates this idea. The basic transistor "H" is augmented with four AND
gates and two inverters. The AND gates accept an enable signal that allows one signal to
turn the whole circuit on and off. The inverters ensure that only one transistor in each
vertical leg of the H is enabled at any one time, providing a direction input. (As with the
previous schematics in this section, Figure 4.15 is not electrically correct; in particular,
the wiring between the AND gates and the transistors would not work.)

With this method, a motor can be controlled with just three signals: two direction bits
and one enable bit. If the DIR—L signal is zero, the DIR—R signal is one, and the enable
signal is one, then transistors Q_1 and Q_4 turn on and current flows through the motor
from left to right. This is illustrated in Figure 4.16. If the two direction bits are flipped,
then transistors Q_2 and Q_3 are active and current flows in the reverse direction.

4.3.3 Active Braking

What happens if both direction bits are the same state (either both are one or both are
zero) and the enable bit is turned on?

Figure 4.17 illustrates this possibility. Both direction bits are one and the enable bit
is turned on, causing transistors Q_2 and Q_4 to be activated. This causes both terminals

FIGURE 4.15 H-Bridge Circuit
with Enable and Direction Logic

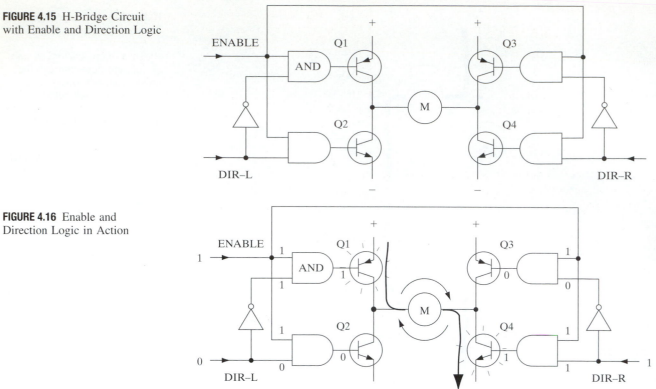

FIGURE 4.16 Enable and
Direction Logic in Action

of the motor to be tied to the negative (−) voltage supply (usually the zero volt ground), less the voltage drop of the transistor (0.6v).

Thus, there is a 0.6v potential at both terminals of the motor. *Effectively, both terminals of the motor are connected together.*

This is significant because a motor can also act as a generator, creating electricity. That is, when a motor shaft is driven from an external impetus, the motor generates electricity. If there is a load connected to the motor, then the motor resists being turned proportional to the amount of the load. If the load increases, the motor's resistance to turning increases.

When the motor terminals are grounded through the transistors, as in Figure 4.17, it is as if the motor were driving an infinite load. The transistors in the H-bridge act as a wire connecting the motor terminals—the infinite load. The final result of all this is that the circuit acts to actively brake the motor's spin. The transistors absorb the energy generated by the motor and cause it to stop.

FIGURE 4.17 Active Braking
Using the H-Bridge

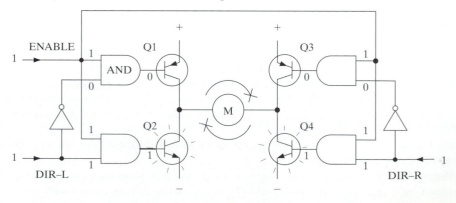

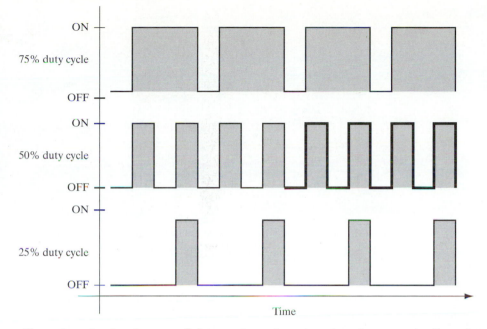

Time

FIGURE 4.18 Three Pulse Width Modulation Waveforms

Pulse width modulation works by rapidly turning the motor drive power on and off. The proportion of "on time" to "off time" is the duty cycle, which determines the fractional amount of full power delivered to the motor.

If, on the other hand, none of the transistors is active, then the motor is allowed to spin freely (i.e., to coast).

4.3.4 Speed Control

The H-bridge circuit also allows control of a motor's speed simply by turning the drive transistor pair on and off rapidly. The duty cycle—the proportion between the "on time" and the "off time"—determines the fractional amount of full power delivered to the motor.

This technique is known as *pulse width modulation* (PWM). Figure 4.18 illustrates the idea. Three sample duty cycles are shown: a 75%, a 50%, and a 25% rate. Given the example H-bridge control circuitry we have been using, waveforms shown would be connected directly to the enable input.

The frequency used in PWM control is generally not critical. Over a fairly wide range, from between 50 Hz and 1000 Hz, the motor acts to average the power that is applied to it.

Active Braking in Action

In small robots with lots of friction in their geartrains, there isn't much energy to be recovered from a robot's inertia. But in other systems, like electric cars, active braking can recover a significant amount of energy.

Contemporary electric car designs incorporate circuitry to convert the drive motor into a generator for recharging the main batteries when braking. This way, the power stored in the car's motion is recovered back into electrical energy. The active braking doesn't apply enough force to replace conventional brakes, but it can significantly extend the electrical car's operating range.

Note that PWM is not the only way to control a motor's speed. Reducing the voltage applied to the motor would also work. PWM is more commonly used in

FIGURE 4.19 One Half of L293D/SN754410 Motor Driver Chip

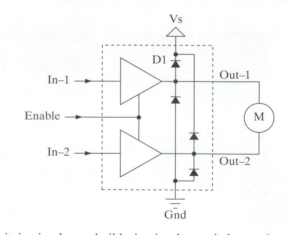

Each L293D/SN754410 motor driver chip contains circuitry for powering two motors; one motor's worth is depicted here. The components inside of the dashed line are contained with the chip package.

Each triangular driver replaces one "leg," or two transistors, in the H-bridge circuits shown earlier. Each driver may be either driven high (enabled and input is high), driven low (enabled and input is low), or turned off (disabled and input doesn't matter).

To make the motor spin, the enable input must be high, and one driver input must be high and the other low. If the enable is high and both driver inputs are high or both are low, then the circuit actively brakes the motor. If the enable is low, then the motor is allowed to coast. The function of the four diodes is explained in the sidebar, "Spike-Cancelling Diodes."

practice because it is simpler to build circuits that switch transistors on and off than to supply varying voltages at the currents necessary to drive motors. Also, PWM tends to be fairly linear (i.e., a 25% duty cycle yields pretty close to one quarter of full power). Giving a motor 1/4 of its normal operating voltage typically would result in much less than 1/4 of nominal power because the power increases approximately as the square of the voltage (simplifying the motor model to a fixed resistance).

4.3.5 Handy Board Implementation

To operate up to four DC motors, the Handy Board uses two copies of an integrated H-bridge driver, either the SGS-Thomson L293D or the Texas Instruments SN754410.[1] These chips abstract away many of the details involved in designing an H-bridge circuit; the chips accept digital logic signals as input and drive motors directly on their outputs.

The L293D/SN754410 driver is illustrated in Figure 4.19. Two such drivers, each capable of operating one motor, are contained in each chip package.

There are some differences between the integrated chip drivers and the schematics shown earlier. Each leg of the "H," which contains two transistors, is indicated as a simple triangle driver circuit. Each driver has its own input line and a shared enable line. These drivers can be either high, low, or off depending on the state of the input line and the enable line.

To run the motor, one driver must be high and the other low, as with the transistor H-bridge. To actively brake the motor, both drivers must be high or both must be low. To allow the motor to coast, the enable line is taken low, which disables both drivers.

Figure 4.20 shows how the Handy Board uses the L293D/SN754410 motor driver chips. Rather than individually control each of the two direction inputs (In–1 and In–2), the Handy Board adds an inverter so that a single bit may be used to determine motor direction. When the direction input is high, then In–2 is high and In–1 is low. When the direction is low, In–2 is low and In–1 is high. Thus, this bit determines direction, and the enable bit turns the motor on and off.

---

[1]   These two chips are work-alikes, with the difference that the SGS-Thomson chip can supply 600 mA per channel, whereas the TI chip can supply 1,000 mA.

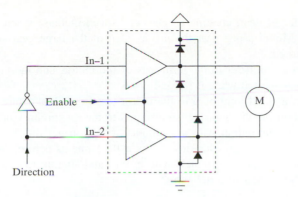

FIGURE 4.20 Handy Board
H-Bridge Circuit

The Handy Board adds an
inverter to allow just two bits, a
direction line and an enable
line, to control each motor. The
direction line ensures that when
one leg of the H-bridge is high,
the other is low. The enable line
connects directly to the
L293D/SN754410 chip's enable
input.

Note that with this circuit active
braking is not possible, but
PWM speed control may be
done by modulating the enable
line.

The full Handy Board circuit uses an 8-bit latch, the 74HC374 chip, which provides
the eight bits necessary to control four motors.

Spike-Canceling Diodes

Also part of the motor driver chips, and not mentioned in previous motor driver circuits,
are four diodes connecting from each driver output to either V_s, the motor voltage supply,
or ground. These diodes perform the important function of trapping and shunting away
inductive voltage spikes that naturally occur as part of any motor's operation.

Diodes allow current to flow in one direction only. If there is a higher voltage on the
anode than on the cathode, then current flows through the diode (see below).

Anode (+)

Cathode (−)

Current flows from higher voltages on the anode to lower
voltages on the cathode, in the direction of the diode's
arrowhead.

The diodes in the motor driver chip may appear to be connected backward, but
they are drawn correctly. When a motor is running, the coil of wire in its armature
acts as an inductor, and when the electricity in this coil changes, voltage spikes are
generated that might be of *higher voltage than the V_s power supply* or *lower voltage than
ground*.

For example, suppose a voltage greater than V_s is generated by the motor on the OUT−I
line. Then the diode labeled D_1 conducts, shunting this voltage to the V_s power supply.
If the diodes were not present, these inductive voltage spikes would enter the voltage
supply of the rest of the project circuitry, possibly doing damage to more sensitive
components.

4.3.6 Exercises

1. *Motor as generator.*

   (a) Build a hand-crank apparatus for driving a motor so that it can act as a generator.
   A good way to do this is to put a small gear on the motor shaft and mesh it

with a larger gear, creating a "gear up" speed increase when the larger gear is turned. Mount a peg near the inside edge of the large gear so that it may be hand turned.

(b) Connect a voltmeter to the terminals of the motor, and measure the amount of voltage generated when it is hand cranked.

(c) Connect a small light bulb to the motor terminals. Make sure the voltage rating of the light bulb is greater than or equal to the maximum voltage you saw when measuring the output with a voltmeter. Can you get the light bulb to light? Measure the voltage when it is lit; is it the same as before? Why?

(d) Short out the motor terminals with a wire and attempt to crank the motor. Is it noticeably harder to turn? Why?

2. *Limits of L293D/SN754410 Driver Chip.*

(a) With the Handy Board turned on, measure the motor voltage supply on the L293D/SN754410 chip. The positive V_s terminal is Pin 8 and the ground Pins are pins 4, 5, 12, and 13.

(b) With no motor plugged in, turn a motor output on at full power (e.g., use `fd(0)`, `bk(0)`, or `motor(100, 0)` to turn on motor 0). Measure the voltage at the motor outputs—e.g., for motor 0, that would be Pins 11 and 14 of the upper motor driver chip, U10. Is it different from the motor power supply voltage? Why or why not?

(c) Now plug a motor into the powered output and let it run freely (with no load). Measure the voltage again—any change? Why?

(d) Finally, stall the motor and measure the voltage. You will need an assistant for this experiment or a mechanism to keep the motor shaft from turning. How has the voltage changed? Why? Note: the motor chip will probably get hot if you leave the motor stalled for more than a few seconds—does the output voltage change over a 30-second period? Why?

4.4 The Servo Motor

The servo motor is a specialized motor that may be commanded to turn to a specific position. The servo motor consists of a DC motor, a gear reduction unit, a shaft position sensor, and an electronic circuit that controls the motor's operation. The word *servo* refers to the system's capability to self-regulate its behavior; that is, to measure its own position and compensate for external loads when responding to a control signal.

Servo motors are widely used in hobby radio control applications: On RC cars, they position the front wheel rack-and-pinion steering; on RC airplanes, they control the orientation of the wing flaps and rudders. Because of the size of this consumer hobby market, a wide selection of small servo motors are available at low prices (USD$15 to $40, typically). Figure 4.21 shows the *Futaba S148*, a widely available workhorse model.

Most hobby servo motors (or servos, for short) are made for positioning applications, and hence their shaft travel is restricted to about 180 degrees. The input to the servo is a waveform that specifies the desired angular position of the output shaft. The servo electronics provide the function of measuring the current position and determining whether it is different from the desired position. If there is a difference, the electronics turn on the servo motor to drive the shaft to the desired position.

4.4.1 The Servo Control Signal

Most hobby servo motors use a standard three-wire interface consisting of a power, ground, and control line. The power supply is typically 5 to 6 volts.

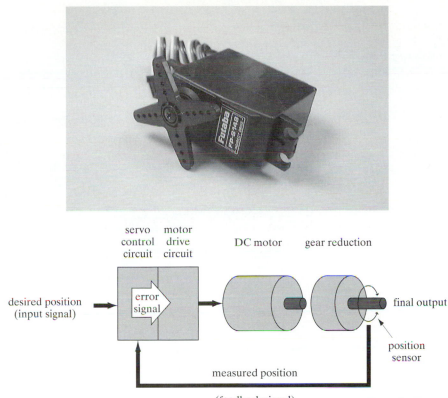

FIGURE 4.21 Futaba S148 Servo Motor with Mounting Horns

FIGURE 4.22 Schematic Diagram of Servo Motor

The servo motor accepts an input signal that represents the desired position of the output shaft. This signal is compared with a feedback signal indicating the actual position of the shaft (by the servo control circuit), and an "error signal" is generated that directs the motor drive circuit to power the motor. The servo includes a built-in gear reduction, which drives the final output. The position sensor returns the feedback signal of the actual position.

The control line uses a PWM scheme for encoding the position signal. The servo PWM method is different from the speed control PWM discussed earlier in this chapter. In the speed control PWM method, the overall duty cycle (i.e., percentage of ontime) determines the speed of the motor. In the servo PWM method, the *length of the pulse* is interpreted to signify a specific control value.

Figure 4.23 shows three sample waveforms for controlling a servo motor. The waveforms range from 920 μs to 2120 μs in length. Each length-in-time of the pulses corresponds to a specific angular position that the servo will take; the middle pulse length, 1520 μs, represents the center position of the servo's range travel. (See the sidebar "Tiny Time" for a discussion of units of time.)

To complete the servo control, one must periodically repeat the individual control pulses. For Futaba servo motors, the recommended interval between control pulses is 14 to 20 ms. Figure 4.24 illustrates the complete waveform.

There are a few other useful details related to the servo timing signal:

When microseconds matter. The positive-going pulse determining desired servo position is very sensitive to variations as small as a few microseconds. If the timing widths are not stable across consecutive pulses in the waveform, the servo will exhibit noticeable "jitter" as it tries to match the slightly different position values. So it's very important to be able to generate pulse widths accurate to just a couple microseconds.

When milliseconds don't matter. On the other hand, the interval *between* the control pulses is surprisingly noncritical. Any value in the recommended range between 14 and 20 ms is fine, and if the interval between successive pulses is not exactly the same there are no dire consequences. Basically, the repeated pulses tell the servo control circuit to stay "on the job," attempting to drive the output shaft to the

FIGURE 4.23 Servo Motor Pulse Width Positioning Waveforms

The length of the positive-going control pulse determines the desired position of the servo motor. For Futuba servos, valid pulse lengths range from 920 μs to 2120 μs with the center "dead" position at 1520 μs.

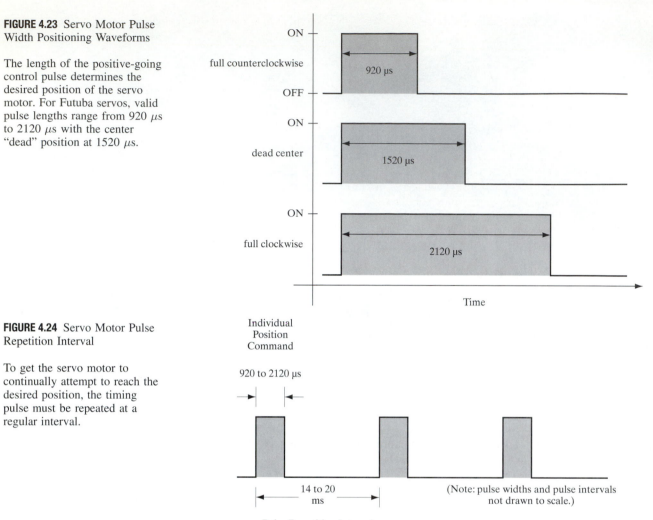

FIGURE 4.24 Servo Motor Pulse Repetition Interval

To get the servo motor to continually attempt to reach the desired position, the timing pulse must be repeated at a regular interval.

commanded position. When the pulses stop coming, the servo circuit automatically turns off.

Limits are first mechanical, then electrical. What happens if you tell a servo to go to the position corresponding to just shorter than 920 μs or just longer than 2120 μs? The electronics are able to handle these signals, and the result is that the servo attempts to drive the output shaft to a point beyond its mechanical limits. In other words, the electronics don't realize that anything is wrong; they just blindly try to get the motor to turn to a position that it's physically prevented from reaching.

When using each different model of servo, it's a good idea to experiment to find its particular range of motion. The timing figures that have been discussed here are a good place to start; not all models of servo motor will have exactly the same range, but they all should be in the neighborhood.

Don't plug it in backward. Most current electrical components (including many ICs, transistors, etc.) can withstand brief intervals of a reverse-polarity voltage, but servo motors cannot. If the power and ground wires to the servo are plugged in backward, the servo electronics will self-destruct nearly instantaneously. Be careful.

Tiny Time

It's important to have the units straight when thinking about the servo control signal. We've been using two different units to talk about the pulse length and pulse interval:

- *milliseconds*, which are thousands-of-a-second, abbreviated ms or msec, and
- *microseconds*, which are millionths-of-a-second, abbreviated μs or μsec.

Thus, there are 1000 microseconds in a millisecond. The servo pulse widths are (approximately) between 1 and 2 milliseconds long—exactly, from 920 μs to 2120 μs. The interval between the pulses is relatively long—14 to 20 milliseconds.

4.4.2 Generating the Control Waveform

Because of the critical nature of the timing of the positive-going servo positioning pulse, it is necessary to use special timer circuitry built into the 6811 chip to generate the control waveform.

For a thorough discussion of how to use the 6811's timer hardware, please see Appendix A; here we discuss usage of the standard servo motor driver software distributed with the Handy Board.

Driver Routines

Two driver routines are provided, named `servo_a5.icb` and `servo_a7.icb`. Each of these routines is capable of generating the waveform to control one servo motor; thus, the basic Handy Board can operate two servo motors simultaneously.

Driver Pins

The `servo_a5.icb` routine generates its signal on the 6811's Port A bit 5 (Pin 29 of the chip), which is timer output #3. This signal is available on a connector header of the Expansion Bus, labeled "TO3."

The `servo_a7.icb` routine generates its signal on the 6811's Port A bit 7 (Pin 27 of the chip), which is one of the timer #1 outputs. This signal is available on a connector header of the Digital Input Bank, labeled as input 9. (Although it is on the digital input bank, this particular pin may be configured as an output for driving the servo motor.)

Software Interface

The routines provide a primitive but functional interface for controlling the position of the servo. For each servo, a global variable is set, generating the pulse train that acts as a desired position input to the servo.

The value of the control global should be set to twice the length of the desired control pulse when measured in microseconds. For example, to generate the 1520-microsecond centering pulse, the control global should be set to 3040.

The routines do not provide a "sanity check" to validate the value of the global being in a usable portion of the servo's range. Values outside of the workable portion of the range will cause the servo to overtax itself as it tries to reach a position that is not mechanically possible.

Usage

The two drivers (`servo_a7.icb` and `servo_a5.icb`) must be loaded into IC, either at the command line or via a `.lis` file. The drivers may be loaded individually or together.

Each driver declares a global variable for setting the servo position and an initialization routine for turning the servo on and off.

servo_a7.icb   This driver replaces the `servo.*` drivers from the standard IC library distribution. *Do not load* `servo.icb` *and* `servo_a7.icb` *at the same time.*

The servo control signal is generated on Port A bit 7, which is brought out as digital "input" 9 on the HB connector bank (this input line is converted to an output when driving the servo).

int `servo_a7_pulse` Integer global variable determining value of servo control signal. Units are 0.5 microsecond counts (e.g., a value of 3040 yields a pulse length of 1.52 milliseconds, which is just in the middle of a typical servo's range). The default value of this global is 2560, which is reestablished on board reset.

int `servo_a7_init(int enable)` Function to enable and disable the servo output. Call with argument equal to one to enable, and zero to disable.

servo_a5.icb   The servo control signal is generated on Port A bit 5 (aka Timer Output 3), which is brought out on the HB expansion bus (labeled "TO3").

int `servo_a5_pulse` Integer global variable determining value of servo control signal. Units are 0.5 microsecond counts (e.g., a value of 3040 yields a pulse length of 1.52 milliseconds, which is just in the middle of a typical servo's range). The default value of this global is 2560, which is reestablished on board reset.

int `servo_a5_init(int enable)` Function to enable and disable the servo output. Call with argument equal to one to enable, and zero to disable.

4.4.3 Continuous Rotation

Most off-the-shelf hobby servo motors are intended for actuating specific devices like the steering mechanism of a radio-controlled car or the wing flaps of a model airplane. For these purposes, the limited range of rotation and positioning capability of the servo is desirable.

For other applications—like the main drive of a robot—it is desirable to have a servo that rotates freely. Such a device would integrate the functionality of a DC motor, the H-bridge drive electronics, and the gear train into a single device.

Fortunately, it is a relatively straightforward task to modify most hobby servos, like the Futaba S148, for continuous rotation. Then the input signal acts as a combined speed/direction control.

The steps are as follows:

1. Remove the mechanical limit stops that prevent the output gear from continuous rotation.
2. Remove the potentiometer position sensor (which also cannot rotate continuously).
3. Replace the potentiometer with a pair of equal resistors, thereby "fooling" the servo's electronics to thinking the output shaft is centered.

The last of these steps is the key to the conversion trick. With the servo's positioning sensor removed and replaced with a pair of resistors, the servo acts as if the shaft were fixed in its center position.

Then a control signal telling it to move to a point clockwise of the center position causes the electronics to make the motor move clockwise. The shaft, which has had its limit stops removed, begins continuous clockwise rotation. The position sensor continues to indicate that the servo is centered, so the control electronics continue to generate the clockwise movement. Hence, the motor simply spins toward the direction of the control signal.

This method allows both speed and direction control because the strength of the motor's turning is proportional to the difference between the desired position and the "actual" position.[2] Thus, the farther the control signal is away from the center position, the faster the motor turns.

See Appendix B.2 for detailed building plans on how to modify servo motors for continuous operation.

4.4.4 Exercises

1. Calculate the duty cycle of the servo control pulse, assuming dead center positioning and pulse intervals of 18 ms.
2. For each variety of servo motor that you have on hand, experimentally determine the control pulse values corresponding to the limits of rotary travel.
3. Write wrapper functions for setting the servo control globals and protecting the servo motors from out-of-bounds values.
4. Write a function to cause the servo motor to "sweep" its position back and forth.
5. With a servo that has been modified for continuous rotation, determine how far away from the center position the control signal needs to be to get the motor to run at its maximum speed. What does this tell you about the control function mapping the error signal into motor power?

4.5 LEGO Design

The final section of this chapter presents a set of ideas about mechanical design using the LEGO Technic building system. Although much of the material is specific to these LEGO parts, there are also general principles that apply to any sort of mechanical construction.

The first section, "Structure," reveals hidden properties of the LEGO system and how to exploit them in your designs. The second section, "Gearing," discusses a variety of gears and how to build effective geartrains. The third section, "Mechanism," presents design technique and several "macro" assemblies as jumping-off points for your designs.

4.5.1 Structure

Let's begin by examining the LEGO brick in detail. Most people realize that the LEGO brick is not based on a cubic form. The height of the brick is a larger measure than the length and width (assuming the normal viewpoint of studs on the top). There is a specific relationship between these dimensions, however—the vertical unit is precisely 6/5 times the horizontal one.

Figure 4.25 illustrates the unit LEGO brick. It is $5i$ units long (and deep, although this dimension is not shown) and $6i$ units tall. The "i" represents a conversion factor between "LEGO lengths" and standard international units like the meter or the foot. Measured by

FIGURE 4.25 Unit LEGO Brick

The unit LEGO brick measures $5i$ long by $6i$ tall, where i is a conversion factor between "LEGO lengths" and standard units like inches or millimeters.

---

[2] This is true to a first approximation; for more about the servo control function, see chapter 5.

hand, the unit LEGO length is approximately 8 mm or 5/16 inches, making i equal to 1.6 mm or 1/16 inch, but the exact conversion factor is a trade secret.

Because of this 6/5 relationship, a stack of five LEGO bricks, measured by height, is equal to the length of a six-stud LEGO beam (Figure 4.26).

Cross-Bracing

The origin of this obscure relationship is unknown, but this knowledge may be put to real practical value. By building structures with vertical heights equal to integral horizontal measures, it is possible to use beams to cross-brace LEGO constructions. This is the key to building sturdy and reliable LEGO designs.

In addition, there exists thin LEGO plates (Figure 4.27). Three of these plates stack to be equal in height to the unit brick. Each LEGO plate, therefore, is $\frac{1}{3}$ of the $\frac{6}{5}$ vertical unit, making a plate $\frac{2}{5}$ of the horizontal unit in height.

FIGURE 4.26 Stack of Five LEGO Blocks and Six-Long LEGO Beam

A stack of LEGO blocks five units high (on the left) is equal in height to a six-long LEGO beam (right).

FIGURE 4.27 One-Third Height LEGO Plates

Three of the thin LEGO plates are equal in height to the unit brick. Thus, each LEGO plate is $\frac{6}{5} \times \frac{1}{3} = \frac{2}{5}$ of a horizontal unit in height.

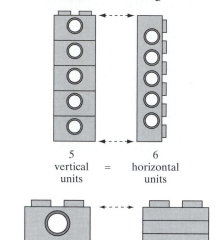

5
vertical   =   horizontal
units   units

Thus, we have $\frac{6}{5}$ height full-size bricks and $\frac{2}{5}$ height thin plates. By combining these, there is an assortment of *integral horizontal measures that can be built in the vertical dimension.* For example, one full-size brick and two plates yields a measure of $\frac{6}{5} + (2 \times \frac{2}{5}) = \frac{10}{5} = 2$ horizontal units!

Figure 4.28 illustrates this configuration, along with the 4–unit long measure created by $3\frac{1}{3}$ vertical units. Figure 4.29 is a photograph of two LEGO beams locked at the $1\frac{2}{3}$ vertical spacing using cross-beams and connector pegs.

The following table shows several common combinations of full- and one-third-height bricks to make integral horizontal lengths.

Full Height Bricks	One-Third Height Plates	Horizontal Units
1	2	2
3	1	4
5	0	6
6	2	8

Connector Pegs

For connecting beams together, the connector peg component is employed. There are two kinds of pegs, however: the black peg and the gray peg (Figure 4.30).

Although the two pegs appear the same (other than color), there is a difference. The black peg is slightly larger, making a snug fit when inserted into a beam hole. The black

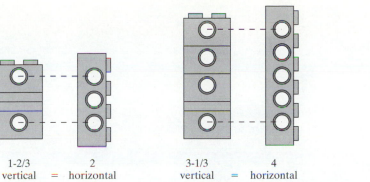

FIGURE 4.28 Two-Unit and
Four-Unit Vertical LEGO
Spacings

1-2/3
vertical
units
=
2
horizontal
units

3-1/3
vertical
units
=
4
horizontal
units

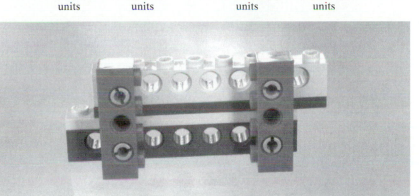

FIGURE 4.29 Two Beams Locked
Using $1\frac{2}{3}$ Vertical Spacing
Relation

Two beams are separated by
two $\frac{1}{3}$-height LEGO plates
creating a vertical interval of $1\frac{2}{3}$
units, which is equal to two
horizontal units. The beams are
locked into place using
cross-beams and connector pegs.
This is the method for making a
sturdy LEGO construction.

peg is good for locking beams together, as in the cross-bracing arrangement illustrated
earlier.[3]

The gray peg is smaller and rotates freely within the beam hole. It's best for forming
a hinge between two beams (Figure 4.31).

FIGURE 4.30 Black and Gray
Connector Pegs

Squareness

It's somewhat of an obvious point, but worth stating nonetheless: To build structures
with square corners, using the $2\times$ plates to connect beams provides the desired result.
If four beams are connected in a rectangular arrangement, the corners are free to sway,
turning the structure into a parallelogram (Figure 4.32).

It is especially important to have genuinely square corners when building geartrains,
as we will see in the following section.

4.5.2 Gearing

Earlier in this chapter, we discussed the premise of gears and using gear reduction to
transform a DC motor's fast, weak energy into a slower, stronger drive for doing real
work. In this section, we explore practical issues of using the gears in the LEGO Technic
system.

First, we cover the collection of different gears available; then we study how to build
them into geartrains.

---

[3] Devoted LEGO observers know that there actually has been a series of designs for the black peg. Early
black pegs made a very stiff connection, which was great for binding structures together, but made the peg
quite difficult to remove once inserted. An intermediate design overcompensated and the peg was too loose.
The current model strikes a good compromise, although there are some who prefer the early design.

FIGURE 4.31 Connector Pegs in Action

The black connector peg vs. the gray connector peg: what is the difference? The answer is that the black peg is *slightly larger*, so it fits quite snugly in the beam hole, while the smaller gray peg rotates freely. Use the black pegs to bind structures together, as suggested by the discussion on locking cross-beams, and use the gray peg when making hinged joints.

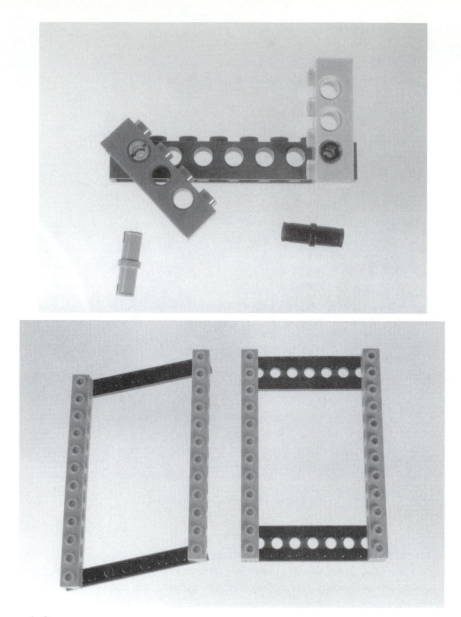

FIGURE 4.32 Locking Parallel Beams Together with 2× Parts

To make rigid structures with square corners, brace beams with the 2× plates rather than the 1× ones. The 2× plates will lock the corners at right angles.

Round Gears

The round gear, or *spur gear* as it is known more formally, is the building block of geartrains. Figure 4.33 shows the four basic LEGO round gears—the 8-tooth, 16-tooth, 24-tooth, and 40-tooth sizes.

All of these gears mesh interchangeably with one another, with the caveat that they must be spaced properly. Each gear's diameter is exactly proportional to the number of teeth that it has; thus, the diameter of the 40-tooth gear is five times the diameter of the 8-tooth. The following table compares gear tooth count to gear radius:

Number of Teeth	Radius in Horizontal Units
8	1/2
16	1
24	1–1/2
40	2–1/2

8–tooth   16–tooth   24–tooth   40–tooth

FIGURE 4.33 Four Basic LEGO Round Gears

FIGURE 4.34 Half-Radius Round Gears

The 8-tooth, 24-tooth, and 40-tooth round gears all mesh properly along a horizontal beam because they have "half unit" radii. For example, the 8-tooth gear has a radius of $\frac{1}{2}$ LEGO units, and the 24-tooth gear, $1\frac{1}{2}$ units, so they mesh at a spacing of two horizontal LEGO units.

The example shows the 8- and 24-tooth gears meshed horizontally at two units and, using the $1\frac{2}{3}$ vertical spacing trick, vertically as well (a common and useful configuration).

Notice that, of the four sizes, three of them (the 8-, 24-, and 40-tooth) have radii equal to an integral measure plus one half of a unit. When these gears are meshed together, the intergear spacing (from the gear centers) then becomes an integral horizontal LEGO unit. Thus, these gears may readily be spaced along a LEGO beam or in the vertical dimension when using the perfect LEGO spacing technique discussed earlier.

Figure 4.34 shows these "half-radii" gears meshed to one another. The 8-, 24-, and 40-tooth gears are meshed along a single LEGO beam, and an additional 8-tooth gear is meshed to the 24-tooth using the $1\frac{2}{3}$ vertical = 2 horizontal spacing technique.

The 16-tooth gear, on the other hand, has a radius of one LEGO unit, so it meshes properly only with itself (at the standard horizontal unit spacing). A pair of two 16-tooth gears thus requires a space of two LEGO units, which happens to be the same interval as the pair of an 8-tooth and a 24-tooth gear. Thus, these respective pairs of gears may be easily interchanged—a useful trick for adjusting the performance of an existing geartrain without performing a major overhaul (Figure 4.35).

Geartrains

As discussed earlier in this chapter, the basic purpose of a geartrain is to transform the motor's fast but weak rotation into a slower but stronger rotation for doing actual work. The technique is to mesh small gears to drive larger gears; the gears act as levers to increase the torque on the output gear (see Figures 4.10 and 4.11).

The gear ganging concept is the foundation of geartrains. Figure 4.36 shows a model LEGO geartrain that produces a 243-to-1 reduction from the motor shaft to the output wheel. The example is a bit of overkill—this much reduction will produce too

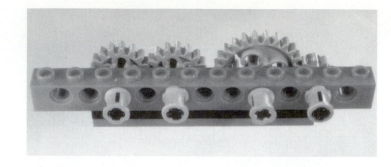

FIGURE 4.35 Gears Meshed at a Spacing of Two Units

The 16-tooth gear has a radius of 1 LEGO unit, so two of them mesh properly together at a spacing of two units (left side of diagram). Because 8- and 24-tooth gears also mesh at two-unit spacing, these respective pairs of gears can be swapped for one another in an existing geartrain—a handy way to change the performance of a geartrain without rebuilding it from scratch.

slow a final rotation for the typical robot drive train—but it serves to illustrate the point.

Supporting Axles

It is important to keep axles well supported in a geartrain. Practically, this means using at least two beams to carry the axles. More important, all beams with common axles running through them must be held together squarely. If the beams are not held together, the axles will bind and lock up inside the beam-hole bearing mounts.

Figure 4.32 demonstrated the idea of using the $2 \times$ plates to lock beams at right angles, and the example geartrain, Figure 4.36, uses 2×3 plates liberally for this purpose.

Stop Bushes

The stop bushes, or axle holders, are to keep axles from sliding back and forth in their mounts. In addition to the standard full-width stop bush, the small pulley wheel and the bevel gear may be put into service (Figure 4.37).

FIGURE 4.36 Sample LEGO Geartrain

A five-stage reduction using 8- and 24-tooth gears creates a 243-to-1 reduction in this sample LEGO geartrain. Note the need for three parallel planes of motion to prevent the gears from interfering with one another. Four 2×3 LEGO plates are used to hold the beams square and keep the axles from binding.

FIGURE 4.37 Stop Bushes and Other Parts

The standard 1-LEGO-long stop bush (upper axle, front) is not the only part that can act as a bushing (axle holder). Use the small pulley wheel (middle axle) to act as a half-sized spacer—it also grabs tighter than the full bush. In a pinch, the bevel gear (upper axle, back) makes a great bushing. Finally, the nut-and-bolt parts (lower axle) can be used to make a tight connection (if you can find them).

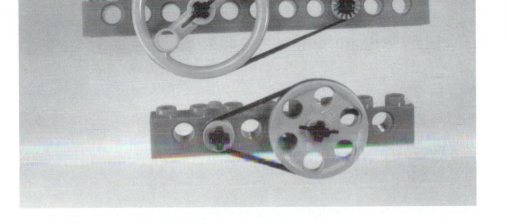

FIGURE 4.38 Using Pulley Wheels

There are three sizes of pulley wheel: the tiny one, which doubles as a stop bush, the medium-sized one, which doubles as a tire hub, and the large-sized one, which is sometimes used as a steering wheel in official LEGO plans.

Pulley Wheels

Sometimes a geartrain is quite noisy. Usually most of the noise is generated by the very first meshing of gears from the motor. Here is the ideal place to use a pulley wheel drive (Figure 4.38).

Use the small pulley wheel on the motor shaft and the medium or large pulley wheel on the driven shaft. The ratio of the circumferences of two pulleys creates a reduction just like the ratio of the gear teeth of a pair of meshed gears. (Figure 4.39 shows the three LEGO pulley wheels.)

LEGO pulley drive belts—thin rubber bands—are best when used in high-speed, low-torque situations because they can't transmit a lot of force. So the first stage is really the best place to use a pulley drive.

Be careful, however, about using pulleys in a competitive situation. They have a penchant for breaking or falling off at the most inopportune moment.

FIGURE 4.39 Small, Medium, and Large Pulley Wheels

small pulley   medium pulley   large pulley

Chain Link Drive

Chain link drives are best suited for the final stage of a geartrain—transmitting power down to the axles holding the wheels (Figure 4.40). This is because they can easily deliver the necessary torques, and they impose frictional losses that are minimized when rotational speeds are low.

FIGURE 4.40 Chain Link Drive
Chain link can be an effective way to deliver large amounts of torque to a final drive while providing a gear reduction if needed.
Chain link works best at the slower stages of gearing and with a somewhat slack linkage. Use the larger gears—the 8-tooth one won't work very well.

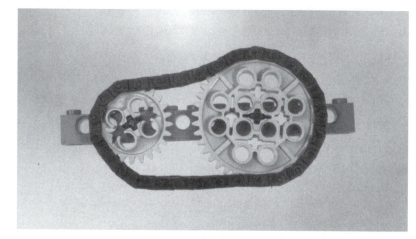

Getting the right amount of chain links can be tricky. Generally a looser chain works better—chains that are too tight will bind up. If the chain is too loose, however, it may skip when there is a lot of resistance.

The Crown and Bevel Gears

In a geartrain with only round gears, all of the axles must be mutually parallel. With the worm gear, the output round gear's axis of rotation is at right angles to the worm's. Two other kinds of gears, the *crown gear* and *bevel gear*, are available in the LEGO kit for changing the axis of rotation within a geartrain.

The crown gear is a round gear that is specially designed to mesh at right angles to the standard round gear.

Figure 4.41 shows the gear alone; Figure 4.42 shows the crown gear meshing with the 8-tooth gear. Meshing the crown to the round 24-tooth and 40-tooth gear is also possible,

FIGURE 4.41 Crown and Bevel Gears

24–tooth
crown gear   bevel gear

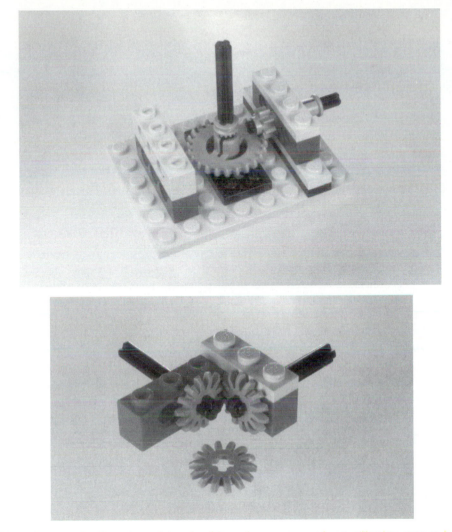

FIGURE 4.42 8–Tooth Gear Meshing with Crown Gear
The 8-tooth gear, in conjunction with the 24-tooth *crown gear*, is used to change the axis of rotation in a gear train.

In this instance, the configuration provides for a vertical shaft output. Horizontal output is also possible.

FIGURE 4.43 Meshed Bevel Gears

The bevel gears are used to change the angle of rotation of shafts in a gear train with a 1:1 ratio. In this case, they are used to effect a change in the horizontal plane.
This picture shows the older-style bevel gears, which have limited usefulness due to their relatively high friction and lack of strength. The newer bevel gears are thicker and perform much better.

although using the 8-tooth to drive the 24-tooth crown gear is an effective way to build in a gear reduction while changing the rotation axis.

The 24-tooth crown gear is the same size as the standard 24-tooth round gear, so it can be used as a replacement for that gear when a parts shortage occurs.

The bevel gear is used in pairs to provide a similar function to the crown gear, although without the capability for gear reduction. LEGO bevel gears only mesh to each other; Figure 4.43 shows how two bevel gears mesh together.

There are two styles of bevel gear: the older style (shown in Figures 4.41 and 4.43), which is fairly flat, and a newer style, which is the same diameter but thicker. The old style bevel gear is somewhat flimsy and lossy and is not suitable for delivering larger torques. The new bevel gear is a significant improvement.

Old style bevel gears can be put to good use by serving as stop bushes (Figure 4.37).

The Worm Gear

The worm gear is a fascinating invention, sort of a Mobius strip in the world of gears. When meshed with a conventional round gear, the worm creates an *n*-to-1 reduction: Each revolution of the worm gear advances the opposing gear by just one tooth. So, for example, it takes 24 rotations of the worm gear to revolve the 24-tooth round gear once. This forms quite a compact gear reduction—it would take about three gangs of

FIGURE 4.44 Using the Worm Gear

The worm gear is valuable because it acts as a gear with one tooth: Each revolution of the worm gear advances the round gear it's driving by just one tooth. So the worm gear meshed with a 24-tooth gear (as pictured) yields a whopping 24 to 1 reduction. The worm gear, however, loses a lot of power to friction, so it may not be suitable for high-performance, main-drive applications.

the 3-to-1 reduction, forming a 27-to-1 relation, to do the same work as a single worm meshed with a 24-tooth round gear.

There is a drawback, however. The worm gear uses predominantly sliding friction when advancing the teeth of the round gear. The teeth of round gears are generally designed to minimize sliding effects when they are meshed with each other, but there is no getting around the problem with worm gears.

Thus, worm gears create more frictional losses than round gears. At higher torques they have a tendency to cause a geartrain to stall. For instance, if a worm gear is used in the main drive of a robot, it may stall if the robot is heavy and is driving uphill.

Worm gears have another interesting property: They cannot be back-driven. If one attempts to turn the shaft through the round gear meshed with a worm, all that will happen is that the worm gear will slide forward and back along its axle, but it will not turn. It is possible to take advantage of this property—for example, if a worm gear is used to raise an arm lifting a weight, then the arm will not fall down when power is removed from the motor.

Figure 4.44 shows how to mesh a worm gear to a round gear, and Figure 4.45 illustrates putting two LEGO worm gears onto the same shaft.

The Gear Rack

The gear rack is like a round gear unrolled and laid out flat. When driven by a round gear (the 8-tooth usually works best), it traverses back and forth in a linear motion (Figure 4.46).

FIGURE 4.45 Multiple Worm Gears on One Shaft

This diagram shows an arrangement of worm gears. At the bottom is the basic worm gear, two horizontal LEGO units in length. At the top is an unsuccessful attempt to put two worm gears on the same shaft. In the middle is the successful attempt. When placing multiple worm gears on a shaft, the trick is to try all four possible orientations to find the one that works.

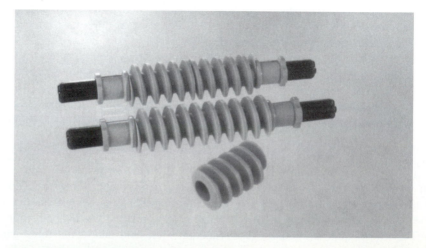

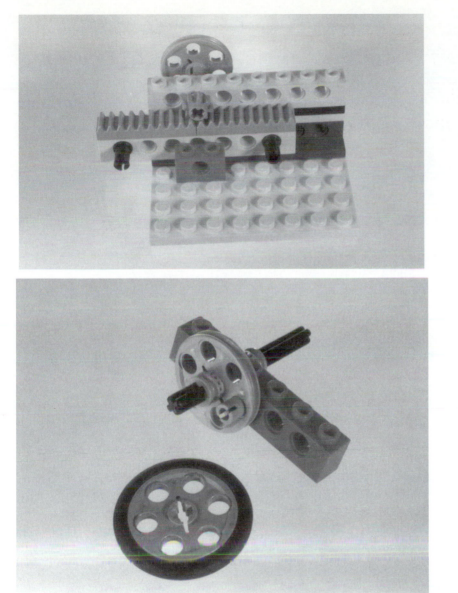

FIGURE 4.46 Using the Gear Rack

The gear driving the gear rack is often referred to as the "pinion," as in "rack-and-pinion steering," which uses the transverse motion of the gear rack to orient wheels. The 8-tooth gear is a good candidate to drive the rack because of the gear reduction it achieves—one revolution of the gear moves the rack by eight teeth.

FIGURE 4.47 Axle Locked Through Beam Using Pulley Wheel

On occasion it is necessary to lock a beam to an axle. This figure shows how to use a medium pulley wheel, which rigidly locks to an axle to hold the beam in place.

Gear racks can be laid end to end to make longer stretches of motion. Underneath a beam driven by gear racks, use the smooth-topped LEGO plates as a surface for the beam to slide on.

4.5.3 Mechanism

This section presents assorted design tips when working with the LEGO Technic system, as well as some partially completed modules that may be adopted into larger designs.

Geartrain Design

When designing a new geartrain into a model, it is often easier to work *backward from the final drive*, rather than forward from the motor. This makes sense because usually there is a fair bit of flexibility about where the motor is ultimately mounted, but much less in the placement of drive wheels or leg joints (for example).

FIGURE 4.48 The Gear Mounter Part

The special "gear mounter" piece is an axle on one side and a loose connector peg on the other. It can be used to mount gears used as idlers in a gear train—used simply to transmit motion or reverse the direction of rotation.

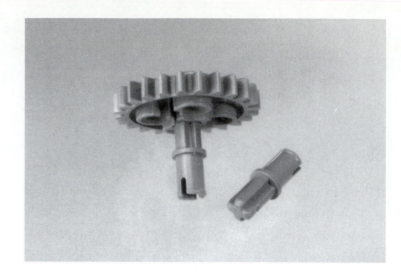

FIGURE 4.49 An Axle Joiner

This configuration of parts can be used as a compact axle joiner. LEGO now produces a part designed for this purpose; but in lieu of that part, this is a useful trick.

FIGURE 4.50 One Method of Building Outward from a Vertical Wall

To build outward from a vertical wall of axle holes, a smaller beam may be mounted with its top studs in the holes of the beam wall.
You will not see this configuration in LEGO's model plans because the top studs are *slightly* too big for the axle holes, and a model left in this state will gradually experience solid flow as the stressed plastic expands. The official LEGO solution is to use the "connector peg with stud" parts (see Figure 4.51), but this method is actually stronger (or at least until the LEGO parts deform).

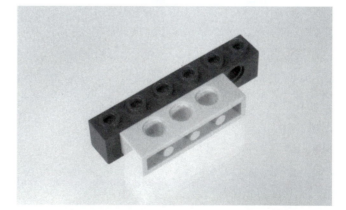

FIGURE 4.51 Connector-Peg-With-Stud Part

The recommended way to build outward from a beam wall is to use the connector-peg-with-stud piece, which is a loose-style connector peg on one end and a top stud on the other.
This method is somewhat weaker than the method of simply plugging top studs into axle holes (Figure 4.50), but will not deform the plastic.

FIGURE 4.52 Using a Stop Bush to Retain an Axle

The full-size stop bush can be used in one orientation to hold an axle through a plate hole so that the axle can freely rotate. In Figure 4.53, an additional plate is used to trap the axle, but allow it to rotate freely.

FIGURE 4.53 Trapping an Axle Between Two Plates Using Stop Bush

By using the stop bush to hold an axle in place between two plates, a vertical axle mount can easily be created. Depending on the orientation of the stop bush, it can be made to either lock the axle in place or allow it to rotate freely. In this diagram, the axle is allowed to rotate.

FIGURE 4.54 Using a Stop Bush to Lock an Axle to a Plate

In the other orientation, the stop bush locks between four top studs, perfectly centered over the axle holes in flat plates. This allows the stop bush to lock a plate to an axle.

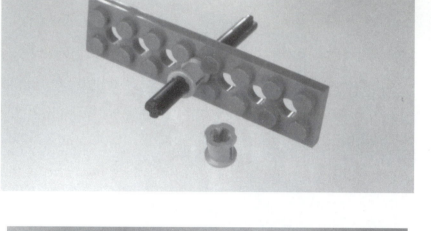

FIGURE 4.55 Toggle Joint

The "toggle joint" can be used to lock two axles at a variety of odd angles. The short axle running through the two toggle joints is equipped with stop bushes on either end to hold the joint together. LEGO now produces a set of parts to hold two axles at several pre-configured angles.

FIGURE 4.56 Toggle Joint With Free or Locked Axle

Here the toggle joint is used to connect two axles at right angles. The small pulley wheel is deployed on the axle htat runs through the toggle joint to either lock the axle or allow it to rotate.

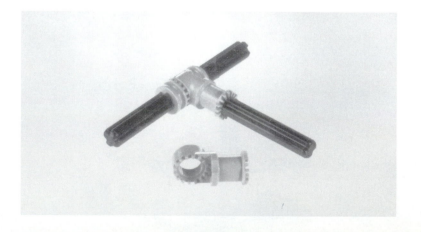

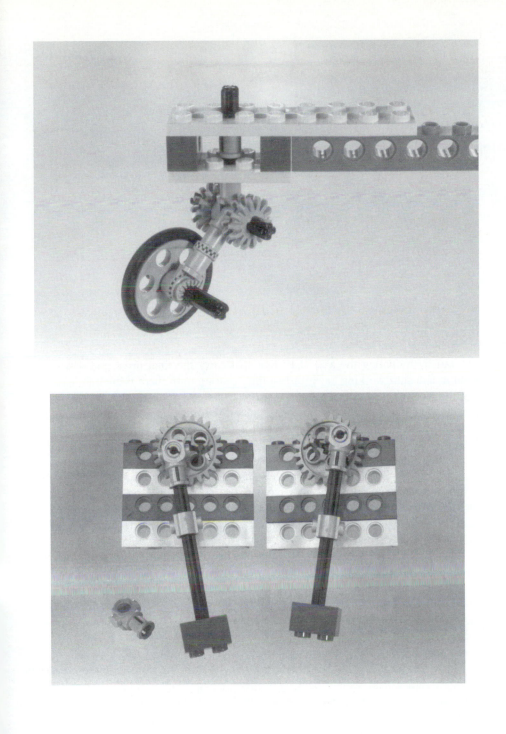

FIGURE 4.57 A Caster Design

Several clichés are used to construct this caster wheel. The vertical axle is trapped between two plates, but allowed to rotate using the trick shown in Figure 4.53. The angled joint down to the wheel is done using toggle joints in the configuration suggested in Figure 4.55, and the final mounting of the wheel is done using the toggle joint per Figure 4.56.

FIGURE 4.58 LEGO Legs

The "piston rod" part (shown in the left foreground) is used twice in each mechanism to create a LEGO leg. By using a chain drive or gear linkage to lock legs in sync, a multi-legged creature can be designed.

FIGURE 4.59 Robot Gripper
Using Gear Rack

So start by mounting the axle shaft that will carry the final drive, put a wheel and gear on it, and start working backward, adding gearing until there is enough, and finally mount the motor in a convenient spot.

When designing a vehicle, do not forget about the role of the tire in determining the relationship between the rotational speed of the final drive axle and the linear speed that is achieved. Small tires act as gear reductions with respect to large tires, and this may have an effect on how much gear reduction is necessary. Experiment.

If a geartrain seems to be performing badly, there are a few things to check. Make sure the stop bushes are not squeezing too hard—there should be some room for the axles to shift back and forth in their mounts. Check that all beams holding the axles are squarely locked together. The most common cause of poorly performing geartrains is beam mounts that are not square.

To test a geartrain, try driving it backward. Remove the motor and gently but firmly turn the final drive wheel or shaft. If there is not too much friction, all of the gears in the train will start moving, with the motor's gear spinning around rapidly. If your geartrain can be readily back-driven, it is a sure sign that the geartrain is performing well.

LEGO Design Clichés

This section presents a miscellaneous assortment of ideas in a visual fashion. I've come to call these LEGO ideas "clichés" because I hope that they become common, everyday knowledge, rather than secrets held by some small group of LEGO experts. Browse through this collection and perhaps you will find one or more of these techniques useful in your own LEGO designs.

4.5.4 Exercises

1. *Diagonal LEGO spacings.*

   (a) Using a combination of the 6/5 height full-size bricks and the 2/5 height thin plates, it is possible to create various integral spacings in the vertical LEGO dimension.

   It's also possible to create diagonal spacings that are an integral number of horizontal units. For example, a horizontal spacing of 3 coupled with a vertical

FIGURE 4.60 Robot Gripper
Using Worm Gear

spacing of $3\frac{1}{3}$ (equals 4 horizontal units) yields a diagonal of 5 horizontal units, by the Pythagoran relationship for right triangles.

Using spreadsheet software, construct a table that calculates various diagonal measures that are attainable using standard LEGO measures. Which of these, in addition to perfect fits like the 3–4–5 right triangle, are close enough to work in practice?

(b) Use the prior methodology to determine workable diagonal spacings for meshing the 8- and 40-tooth gears, and the 16- and 24-tooth gears.

2. *Sturdy structures.* Using the cross-bracing method, build a three-dimensional LEGO frame that measures at least 8 LEGO studs in two dimensions and 12 in the third. Design it so that it will not break apart when dropped first from waist-high and then shoulder-high levels.

3. *Chasses.* Using the geartrain examples presented, build at least two substantively different chasses that are capable of carrying the Handy Board. Remove the Handy Board and perform the drop test on your designs.

5 Control

This chapter is about control, the heart of a robot's functioning. We begin the chapter with classical models of control, used widely in a variety of industrial settings, and then examine larger frameworks for control of robotic devices, including sequential and reactive control. Along the way, we develop an extended example based on an actual robot contest event.

5.1 Simple Feedback Control

Classical control, also known as feedback control, is a set of techniques intended to bring a system to a goal state and keep it there over time as external conditions vary.

For example, consider a household with central heating. A thermostat located in the living quarters measures the temperature and determines whether the air temperature is "too cold," in which case the furnace turns on, or "warm enough," in which case the furnace turns off. The thermostat setting—threshold between these two conditions—is, of course, adjusted by the household's occupants.

The standard household heat control is a simple system, yet it exhibits some interesting properties. The furnace is a "binary" heat source—either it is on or it is off. But air takes a while to heat, so there is a delay between the time when the furnace turns on and when the room hosting the thermostat warms up. Then when the furnace turns off, it takes some time for the air to cool off and for the thermostat to prompt the furnace to turn on again. Hence, we see that the room air temperature oscillates around the thermostat's setpoint in a continuous process of temperature measurement and correction.

The diagram of Figure 5.1 is a "canonical" representation of the classic feedback system. Let's interpret the diagram with the thermostat-based heating system in mind.

As indicated in the diagram, an input signal, which represents the desired state, is combined with the feedback signal, representing the actual state of the system. In the heating system example, this represents comparing the actual temperature of the room with the desired temperature established by the thermostat.

FIGURE 5.1 Block Diagram of Canonic Feedback System

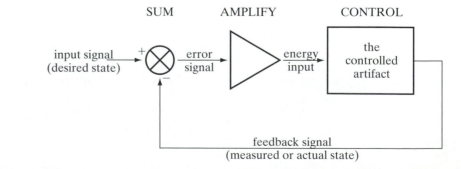

174

An error signal is produced, which corresponds to how far away the actual state of the system is from the desired state. In the diagram, this error signal is fed into an amplifier, which turns it from a control signal—pure information—into a physical action. For the heating system, the furnace is the amplifier: If the control signal indicates the room is colder than the thermostat's setpoint, the furnace turns on.

The output of the amplifier becomes the energy input to "the controlled artifact." In the heating system case, the artifact is the house, which receives the heat energy from the furnace.

Finally, a feedback signal—the temperature measurement on the thermostat—closes the feedback loop, joining the beginning of the control cycle again.

All kinds of feedback systems are based on this configuration of elements: sensing, comparison, control, and sensing again. Let's do some experimentation with *HandyBug* to explore the characteristics of basic feedback control.

5.1.1 Wall Following

The wall-following experiments described in this section require a *HandyBug*-style robot equipped with a bend sensor to measure the distance to the wall (Figure 5.2). Alternatively, a reflective infrared sensor can be used as a wall-distance sensor.

The first experiment is much like the heating system thermostat example. *HandyBug* runs a program to make it turn toward the wall if the distance sensor indicates it is too far from the wall and away from the wall if it is too close. As with the thermostat, a single threshold determines the transition between the "too close" and "too far" states.

Figures 5.3 and 5.4 show the listing of `wallfoll.c`, a demonstration program for the *HandyBug* wall-following behavior. The `wallfoll.c` includes not just for creating the feedback behavior, but also for code for keeping track of the 'bug's distance from the wall while it's doing its task, and for later writing the data to the serial line. There are several tricks and techniques, so let's look at the code in detail.

Feedback Systems and Intentionality

There is an interesting literature that explores the relationship between psychological language and engineering terms for describing feedback control.

For example, I've been calling the input signal to the feedback system the "desired state." This, of course, refers to *our* intentions as system designers. The thermostat doesn't *desire* that the room temperature match the value set on its dial—although it does make the furnace behave in a way to reach that goal.

Yet *goal* is a rather loaded term in itself. Can an inanimate system have a goal? When a light-following robot heads toward a light or when a wall-following robot tracks the wall, it appears to behave in an intentional manner, but we know it's just wires and a program.

Here's an attempt to describe the feedback control system without resorting to psychological terms: It acts in a way to make the error signal equal to zero.

The intriguing part of this matter is that it's often lots easier to get an intuitive understanding of feedback control when human behavioral language is allowed to spice up our descriptions.

FIGURE 5.2 *HandyBug* with Bend Sensor Outrigger

The stock *HandyBug* design is equipped with a bend sensor "outrigger," enabling it to detect its distance from the wall. The closer to the wall, the more the sensor is flexed. This increases its resistance, and a greater value is detected by *HandyBug*'s sensor circuitry.

At the beginning are declarations for the left-side motor port, right-side motor port, and wall sensor, which is assumed to be mounted on the left-hand side (as illustrated in Figure 5.2).

Next, the `goal` variable is declared as a program global, with the special keyword `persistent`. This is a custom Interactive C feature that allows global variables to retain their values *even when the Handy Board is switched off*. The `goal` variable is used to hold the threshold point between the "too close" and "too far" from-the-wall states.

Following this are declarations for the data capture variables: a 1,000-element array named `data` and an index pointer into this array named `ix`. These globals are also declared as `persistent` so they will retain their values when the board is power-cycled.

Next is the `calibrate` routine, which allows you to manually set the wall-sensor threshold by physically placing *HandyBug* up against the wall and capturing the actual sensor value. The `calibrate` routine is called by `main` every time the robot is turned on; to capture a new goal point, press the Handy Board's START button. To exit the `calibrate` routine, press the STOP button. This technique—of capturing actual sensor values as calibration points and storing them in persistent globals—has great general applicability in robot programming.

Now we come to the `main` routine. It starts off by calling the `calibrate` routine just described. Remember, you can always press the STOP button to continue without changing the previously captured threshold value.

After returning from the `calibrate` routine, the data array pointer `ix` is reset to zero, so new performance run data are entered from the beginning of the data array.

Then the `main` routine enters the heart of the program: the infinite loop that makes *HandyBug* track the wall. The current wall value is captured into a local variable named `wall`; this value and the threshold `goal` value are printed on the Handy Board's LCD display for monitoring.

Next the `if -- else` statement causes *HandyBug* to turn left—that is, toward the wall—if the current wall reading is less than the threshold point. This is correct, when the bend sensor is used, because the wall reading decreases when *HandyBug* gets farther away from the wall. If *HandyBug* is too close to the wall—the reading is larger than the setpoint—then *HandyBug* turns right, away from the wall.

Before the loop repeats, two more things must be done. The current wall reading is captured into the data storage array while incrementing the `ix` array index pointer for the next time. Also, a delay of 100 milliseconds is inserted so that the main loop will run approximately 10 times per second. This prevents the data from being captured too

FIGURE 5.3 Listing of
`wallfo1a.c` (1 of 2)

```c
/*
    wallfol1.c: simple threshold-based wall follower
    with data collection
*/

/* motor and sensor ports  */
int     LEFT_MOTOR=    0;
int     RIGHT_MOTOR=   3;
int     LEFT_WALL=     0;

/* wall conditions  */
persistent int goal;

/* data capture */
persistent int data[1000];
persistent int ix;

void calibrate()
{
  while (1) {
    int wall= analog(LEFT_WALL);
    printf("goal is %d; wall is %d\n", goal, wall);

    if (start_button()) {
      goal= wall; beep();
    }

    if (stop_button()) {
      printf("Set goal to %d\n", goal);
      beep(); sleep(0.5); break;
    }

    msleep(50L); /* give a pause for the display */
  }
}

void main()
{
  calibrate();

  ix= 0;

  while (1) {
    int wall= analog(LEFT_WALL);
    printf("goal is %d; wall is %d\n", goal, wall);

    if (wall < goal) left();  /* too far from wall -- turn in */
    else right();             /* turn away from wall */

    data[ix++]= wall;         /* take data sample */

    msleep(100L);             /* 10 iterations per second */
  }
}
```

FIGURE 5.4 Listing of
wallfo1b.c (2 of 2)

```
void left()
{
  motor(RIGHT_MOTOR, 100);
  motor(LEFT_MOTOR, 0);
}

void right()
{
  motor(LEFT_MOTOR, 100);
  motor(RIGHT_MOTOR, 0);
}

void dump_data()
{
  int i;

  disable_pcode_serial();

  printf("Press START to send data...\n");
  start_press();

  for (i=0; i< ix; i++) {
    printdec(data[i]);
    serial_putchar(10); serial_putchar(13);
  }

  printf("Done sending data.\n");
  beep();
}
```

rapidly and overrunning the 1,000-element array (at 10 samples per second, the array is good for 100 seconds of performance data), and more generally makes the experiment more repeatable.

Continuing on with the program listing are the `left` and `right` routines, which cause *HandyBug* to take hard turns, enabling one motor at full power and turning the other motor off.

Last is the `dump_data` routine, which writes the data from the global `data[]` array to the serial line. This routine makes use of several tricks—which are explained in Appendix C—for allowing Interactive C to write data to the serial port.

Running the Wall-Following Experiment

Because of the serial line data reporting features, the `wallfol1.c` program requires two drivers described in Appendix C: `serialio.c` and `printdec.c`. From the Interactive C command line, type

```
C> load wallfol1.c serialio.c printdec.c
```

to run the `wallfol1.c` program.

Results

Figure 5.5 shows the result of following a straight wall with the bend sensor threshold set to 138, 150, and 160 (corresponding to bend sensor values progressively closer to the wall). What can we ascertain from these graphs about how *HandyBug* performs the wall-following task?

First, it's easy to see *HandyBug*'s oscillations around the setpoint "goal" value of the algorithm. Indeed, *HandyBug* is continuously oscillating—it's never going straight.

Each of the graphs is labeled with the goal setpoint, the arithmetic average of the data samples, and the standard deviation of the sample. In all cases, the average is quite close to the goal; the goal can essentially be induced as the average.

In the last graph, the data set's standard deviation is smaller than the first two. Visually, on the graph, it can be seen that the oscillations are smaller and more frequent. In this case, it appears that *HandyBug* works better when it's closer to the wall (assuming one wants to minimize the size of the oscillatory swings).

5.1.2 Gentle Turning Algorithm

In the `wallfol1.c` program, *HandyBug*'s turning commands cause abrupt movement (e.g., when turning right, the left motor is on at full power and the right motor is completely off). Suppose we modify the turning routines so that *HandyBug* makes smoother turns—what will the resulting performance graph look like?

Figure 5.6 shows the turning routines in our second demonstration program, `wallfol2.c`. When turning left, the left motor is on at a 50% power level; when turning right, the right motor is on for the same power level. Other than this change, `wallfol2.c` is identical to `wallfol1.c`.

Figure 5.7 illustrates the result of running *HandyBug* with the modified turning routines. As can be easily seen from the graph, there are fewer oscillations over the run, and in general the swings are less abrupt. This is confirmed by the calculation of the standard deviation, which is less than in any of the three earlier runs.

Also, *HandyBug* completed the run in about 16 seconds, versus 19 seconds for the same length in the earlier runs. This is easily explained by the fact that the gentle turns inherently make *HandyBug* spend more of its time advancing along the wall rather than turning into it.

5.1.3 Exercises

1. Figure 5.8 shows a performance run using a three-state algorithm. Two thresholds are used, allowing *HandyBug* to either turn left, go straight, or turn right.
   Implement your own version of this idea and compare your result to the graph.
2. The graphs of Figure 5.5 and 5.7 compare the performance of the wall-following algorithm when *HandyBug* is following along a straight wall. Compare the hard-turn and gentle-turn methods when *HandyBug* has to make inside or outside cornering maneuvers. Which works better? Why?
3. Test the three-state algorithm for cornering ability, comparing it to the gentle and abrupt turning methods. Which works the best?
4. Generalize the three-state method to an algorithm that makes progressively stronger turns as the wall sensor indicates that *HandyBug* is farther away from the goal distance.
5. Set up an obstacle course with straight runs, inside turns, and outside turns, and race your *HandyBug* algorithm against those of your classmates. Given a standardized mechanical platform, which is the fastest algorithm?

5.2 Proportional-Derivative Control

The wall-following algorithm described in the previous section had the same response to being too far away or too close to the wall, no matter how large the error was. Suppose, instead, that the control algorithm generated a stronger response the farther away the

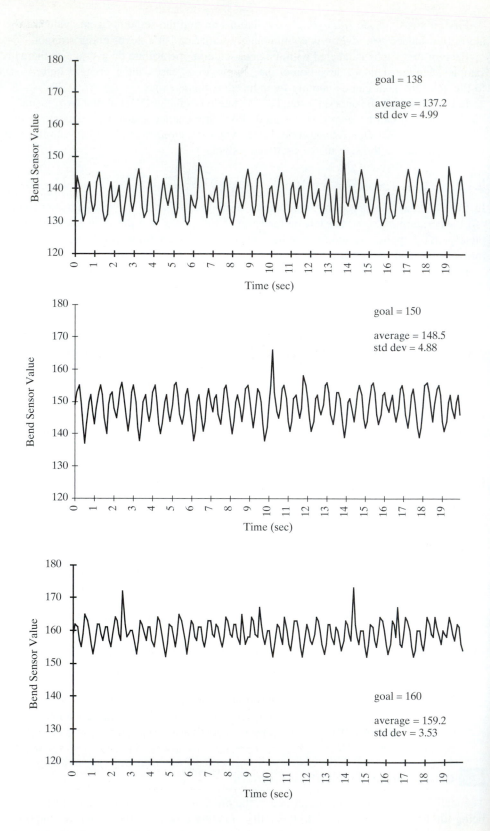

FIGURE 5.5 Performance Graphs of Simple Wall-Following Algorithm

```
void left()
{
  motor(RIGHT_MOTOR, 100);
  motor(LEFT_MOTOR, 50);
}

void right()
{
  motor(LEFT_MOTOR, 100);
  motor(RIGHT_MOTOR, 50);
} motor(RIGHT_MOTOR, 50);
```

FIGURE 5.6 Turning Routines in
`wallfol2.c`

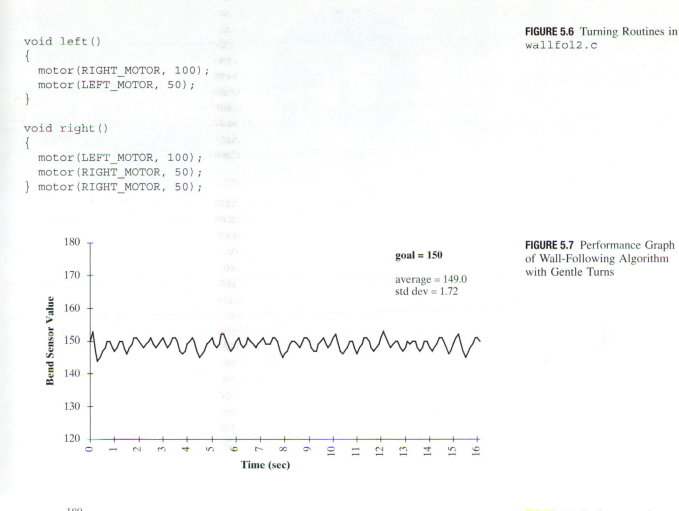

goal = 150

average = 149.0
std dev = 1.72

FIGURE 5.7 Performance Graph
of Wall-Following Algorithm
with Gentle Turns

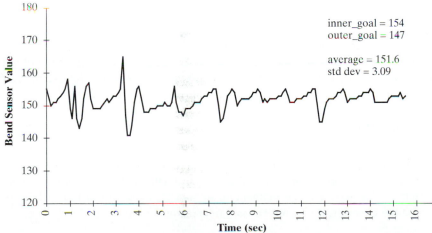

inner_goal = 154
outer_goal = 147

average = 151.6
std dev = 3.09

FIGURE 5.8 Performance Graph
of Three-State Wall-Following
Algorithm

FIGURE 5.9 Photograph of System for Testing PD Control

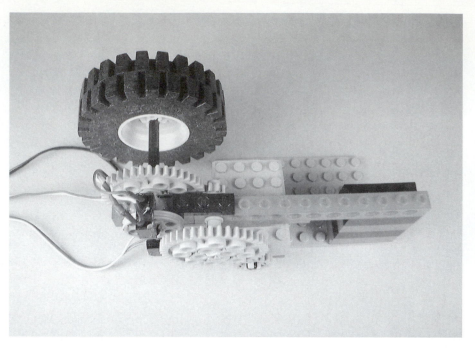

system was from the goal state. This is known as *proportional control*—the response of the control algorithm is proportional to the amount of the error.

In this section, we experiment with proportional control and an extension of it called *proportional-derivative control*. To perform these experiments, a test system is needed. The contraption illustrated in Figure 5.9 is suggested.

The device shown in the photograph consists of a DC motor driving a two-stage geartrain reduction. At the end of the geartrain are a shaft encoder to measure the rotation of the shaft and a large LEGO wheel, which acts as a load.

For the experiments to work properly, the shaft encoder is a quadrature type. This type of encoder (which is discussed thoroughly in Section 6.1) measures not only the amount of rotation, but also the direction in which the shaft turns. That is, the quadrature encoder counts up in one direction and down in the other. This allows the sensor to determine the precise position of the shaft even after it changes directions.

The artifact being controlled is the rotational position of the LEGO wheel. This isn't too exciting; who cares about the position of a wheel that's not doing any work? Think of the wheel not as a disembodied rotating disk, but as representing the position of a more interesting system—say, the angle of a jointed robot arm or the position of a linear actuator (like a print head moving on its carriage).[1] In our example, the rotating mass of the wheel represents the momentum of an actual (more practical) system.

5.2.1 Proportional Control

Let's put together the pieces needed to play with the Figure 5.9 test system. Build a two-stage geartrain as indicated in the photograph. It's important that the motor speed is not slowed down so much that frictional forces dominate. When the motor is turned off, the system should have enough momentum to spin the wheel for a little while longer. Otherwise the experiment will not be very interesting.

---

[1] Actual printers typically use stepper motors to control the movement of the print head. A stepper motor moves through discrete positions as it rotates; as long as there is not too much resistance to its movement, it can keep track of exactly where it is with no further sensing, simply by moving from one discrete position to the next.

Toaster Control

When I was a child, I thought all sorts of devices must have (what's officially called) proportional control. That is, when you slide the lever on the toaster toward dark, it must cook hotter. (Never mind that darker toast took longer, it must have also been cooking hotter, too.)

When you turned up the thermostat to 90 degrees, it must heat hotter than if you set it to 80. And when you turn on the oven to 500 degrees, it must heat faster than if you set it to 350.

It turns out that all of these systems work perfectly well with simple threshold-based, on-off control, as we say in the last section. But my childhood notions weren't so far off base—many systems in the world are run by proportional controllers.

Section 6.1 explains how to build the required quadrature shaft encoder. Mount the shaft encoder at the final stage of the geartrain (the axle carrying the wheel). This is necessary so that the shaft isn't turning too fast for the sensor.

After building the mechanism and mounting the encoder, it's ready for testing. Boot up Interactive C and load the driver for the shaft encoder. Here we'll load qencdr10.icb, the driver that assumes the two break-beam sensors are plugged into digital inputs 10 and 11:

```
C> load qencdr10.icb
```

Test the shaft encoder by resetting the counter variable to zero and then writing a one-liner to display its value on the Handy Board's LCD screen:

```
C> encoder10_counts= 0;
Downloading 7 bytes (addresses C200-C206): 7 loaded
Returned <int> 0
C> while (1) {printf("%d\n", encoder10_counts); msleep(50L);}
```

Now manually turn the geartrain and observe the counter values on the LCD screen. When using the LEGO pulley wheel with six holes, the encoder should register 24 counts per complete revolution of the shaft. Try turning the gears both ways to demonstrate that the system counts up one direction and down the other.

Next, enter a test statement that turns on the motor, waits a little while, turns it off, and then prints out the encoder reading. For example:

```
C> {encoder10_counts=0; motor(0, 100); msleep(100L); off(0);
msleep(500L); printf("%d\n", encoder10_counts);}
```

Notice that there is an extra delay after the motor is turned off but before the encoder reading is printed. This is to allow the system to settle before taking and printing the encoder reading.

Experiment with the first, motor on-time delay to get the final wheel to spin about one complete revolution. It might be helpful to put a piece of tape on the wheel, marking a point so it's easier to see it turn. After one full turn, does the encoder reading yield a measurement of 24? If not, it might mean that the shaft is spinning too fast for the encoder to keep up. Use additional gearing to slow down the final shaft speed.

For the purpose of this experiment, make sure that the encoder is counting up with positive motor speeds. That is, the previous statement should yield positive encoder values. If you are getting negative encoder readings when the motor is turned on in the positive speed direction, simply reverse the control polarity by giving the motor plug a half-turn where it connects to the Handy Board.

Now we're ready to write a quick-and-dirty proportional error controller. It's so easy that it's just a one-liner at the IC prompt. Just set the encoder counter to 0 and then write an infinite loop to repeatedly set the motor speed to the difference between a desired position (say, 100) and the actual position:

```
C> {encoder10_counts= 0;
while (1) {motor(0, 100 - encoder10_counts);}}
```

When the program starts to run, the difference between the desired position (100) and the actual position (0) is 100, so the motor turns on full speed, driving the wheel toward the desired position. As it starts going, the error becomes progressively smaller. When it's halfway, at position 50, the error is only 50, so at that point the motor goes at 50% of full power. When it arrives at the intended position of 100, the error is zero, and the motor is off.

While the loop is still running—but after the controller has brought the wheel to the "100" position—manually turn the wheel. At some point you should feel resistance as the error gets large enough for the motor to overcome friction and try to drive the wheel back. With the current ratio between error count and motor speed, it requires an error of 100 counts—just over four turns of the wheel at 24 counts per turn—to generate the full force of the motor (the 100% speed level). As you turn the wheel, it may feel something like a spring being coiled up as the motor power resisting your turns increases up to the full-power level. Release the wheel and the "coil" unwinds as the motor drives the wheel back to its 100 counts setpoint.

Now let's increase the rate at which the motor power reacts to error. Instead of a one-to-one ratio between error counts and motor power percentage, we'll modify the controller so it multiplies the error value by 5:

```
C> {encoder10_counts= 0; while (1) {motor(0, 5 * (100 -
encoder10_counts));}}
```

With this 5 to 1 ratio between error counts and power percentage, the response should feel much "snappier." The wheel should reach the setpoint position faster, and it should resist being turned away from it much more aggressively.

In the terminology of the control discipline, this ratio between error and power is known as a *gain*. In our current example, the power correction is directly proportional to the error, so it is known as a *proportional gain*—that is, the amount of gain applied to the proportional error.

With the above control function, experiment with the gain factor. Notice that as the gain becomes larger, two things start to occur: *overshoot* and *oscillation*. Overshoot is when the system goes beyond its setpoint and has to change direction before stabilizing on it. For the test system of a LEGO wheel turning in space, overshoot doesn't seem to be much of a problem, but imagine if the system were a robot arm moving to a particular position. If it went beyond the position on its way getting there, it could have collided with some object just beyond the setpoint position—not a good thing.

Oscillations are related to overshoot. After the system goes beyond its setpoint, when it corrects and drives the other way it can "overshoot" in the other direction as well. Then the phenomenon repeats and one sees the system going back and forth around the setpoint in a nervous or jittery manner.

Both of these properties, along with others, are of serious concern to system designers. One wants to minimize both overshoot and oscillation, but provide adequate system response to changes in setpoints.

Experimental Measurement

To better understand the properties of the proportionally controlled position controller, it is a good idea to run the proportional controller while taking measurements of the position and power function generated by the control law. In this section, we examine results from such data-taking experiments, as we did in the previous section with the wall-follower example.

The basic strategy for data collection is the same. Within the core loop that runs the proportional control function, the data are also collected. Here is the central piece of the code.

```
void collect_data()
{
  int i, power, counts;

  for (i= 0; i< SAMPLES;) {
    counts= encoder10_counts;

    power= pgain * (0 - counts);
    motor(0, power);

    data[i++]= counts;
    data[i++]= power;
  }
}
```

In the `for` loop, the controller generates the power function as the product of the global `pgain` variable and the position error (the difference between the setpoint of zero and the `counts` reading). The instantaneous `counts` and `power` values are then stored in the global `data[]` array for later upload.

Figures 5.10 to 5.13 show the result of running the position control system with proportional error gains of 10, 20, 30, and 50. The "units" of the gain factor are somewhat arbitrary; for this example, it's a conversion between error counts and percentage of full power. A gain of 10 means that a 10-count error results in a full-power (100%) action. But the meaning of this gain depends on how much rotary motion is necessary per encoder count.

Nevertheless, the gain units have relative meaning, and there are distinctly different characteristics to the performance in the four example runs. Before we analyze the specifics of each graph, here are some general comments about the data presentation.

The vertical scale has different meanings for the two data sets plotted (position and power), although they are conveniently both on a scale from −100 to +100. For the position graph, this indicates actual encoder counts beginning at 100 and heading toward zero as a setpoint.

For the power graph, this represents the percentage of full power as calculated by the control function. These power commands are thresholded at +100 and −100 by the `motor()` function call and by the spreadsheet software used in making the graphs. This is a little tricky because the data captured by the control program shown above will allow power values as high as might be computed by the proportional control function. Nevertheless, if the control function generates a value above 100% power, either in the positive or negative direction, it is simply cut off at the 100% level.

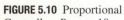

FIGURE 5.10 Proportional
Controller, $P_{gain} = 10$

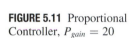

FIGURE 5.11 Proportional
Controller, $P_{gain} = 20$

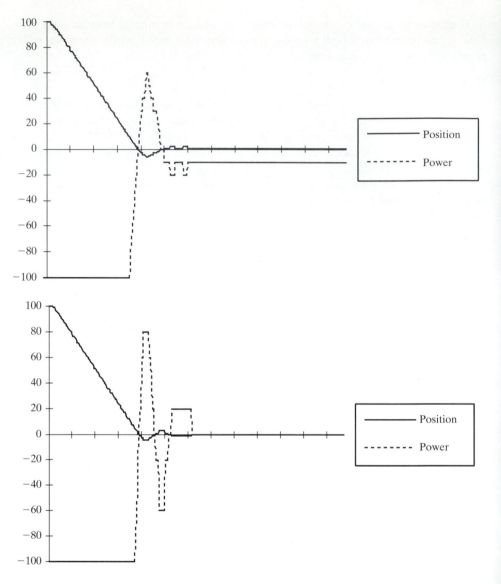

The horizontal axis is time. Each hash mark represents approximately 0.2 seconds of real time. In actuality the full graph is 333 data points, which was reported by the software as having taken a bit under 2.5 seconds (on average) to sample. The graphs are drawn with a hash mark every 26 data samples, which is just about 0.2 seconds per hash mark.

Interpreting the Graphs

In all of the performance runs, the system started at a position of 100 counts and headed toward the 0 count position.

In the first graph, Figure 5.10, the proportional gain is set to 10. This generated a full-power command as the wheel headed toward the zero position. When the position got to within 10 counts of zero, the power command began to fall off. Nevertheless, the system overshot the zero point and had to turn around (this is between 0.8 and 1.0 seconds of the run).

Notice that the system did not stabilize at the goal. From around the 1.2-second mark onward, the position was fixed at a count of 1. This generated a power command of

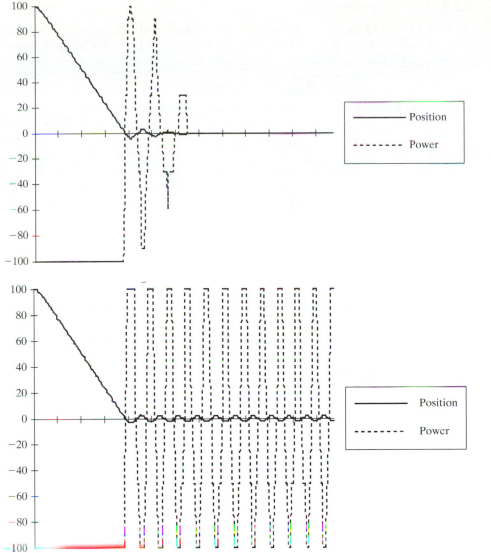

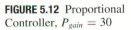

FIGURE 5.12 Proportional Controller, $P_{gain} = 30$

FIGURE 5.13 Proportional Controller, $P_{gain} = 50$

10%, which was too small to activate the motor. This phenomenon, sometimes called *offset error*, is a common occurrence. With a mechanical system like the experimental position controller, the static friction is higher than the dynamic or moving friction, and the system can get "stuck" in a state near to but not at its setpoint.

Suppose the gain is increased—this should ameliorate the offset problem, because the same static error will result in a higher power command. Figure 5.11 shows the system response with a gain of 20. Sure enough, the offset error is solved, but there is another problem: the beginnings of an oscillation. Now the system overshoots three times—twice beyond the setpoint and once before it.

Figure 5.12 illustrates the case when the gain is set to 30. The oscillation problem is more pronounced; there are five oscillatory swings.

In Figure 5.13, with the gain set to 50, the oscillation behavior has taken over. The system moves to within a slight distance from the setpoint, but cannot stabilize at the setpoint. Even a small error generates a power command that moves the system across the setpoint, resulting in a power command in the opposite direction. Although the position error is small on the graph, the power command swings are quite evident.

5.2.2 The Derivative Term

As demonstrated by the set of performance graphs, simply cranking up the proportional gain does not get the system to perform better. With higher gains, the motor does drive the output wheel to its position faster, but it still overshoots and oscillates at higher gains.

The problem is that driving at full power is appropriate when the system is far away from its setpoint; however, it does not make sense as the system gets close. When the proportional gain is high, then even a slight deviation from the setpoint causes a large power command. Further, the momentum of the system causes it to carry beyond the setpoint even when the power input is removed (as when the proportional error is small or zero).

The solution is an additional term in the power control equation that corrects for the momentum of the system as it moves toward the setpoint. From basic physics, we know that momentum is mass times velocity; therefore, momentum is directly proportional to velocity. Double the velocity, double the momentum. We can correct for the velocity when the system nears its setpoint by *subtracting* an amount from the power equation based on the velocity of the system.

Here is the revised control loop:

```
void collect_data()
{
  int i, power, counts, velocity;

  for (i= 0; i< SAMPLES;) {
    counts= encoder10_counts;
    velocity= encoder10_velocity;

    power= pgain * (0 - counts) - dgain * velocity;
    motor(0, power);

    data[i++]= counts;
    data[i++]= velocity;
    data[i++]= power;
  }
}
```

The power command is now the combination between a term due to the proportion of the error (`pgain * (0 - counts)`) and the velocity of the system (`- dgain * velocity`). The velocity correction is commonly known as the *derivative term* in control parlance (because velocity is the derivative of position in calculus); hence the names *proportional-derivative control* and *PD loop* describe this methodology.

Figure 5.14 shows the result of driving the test LEGO wheel system with a proportional gain of 4 and a derivative gain of 1. (The derivative gain is assumed to be negative, so it's customary to just talk about its magnitude.) The overshoot is minimized, and there is no oscillatory behavior at all.

Note the discrete nature of the velocity graph. This is due to the fact that the encoder software calculates the velocity measure rather infrequently—about every 0.15 seconds, as indicated by the steps in the velocity curve. (The encoder driver simply takes the difference between the last encoder reading and the current one to determine the velocity.) Because the testbed LEGO geartrain is overall a rather low-performance system, this is probably inconsequential, but this "discrete sampling error" is endemic to digital control systems and is a topic of much concern in control theory.

It's easy to create instabilities if the derivative gain is too large. Figure 5.15 shows the performance curve when the proportional gain is set to 10 and the derivative gain is

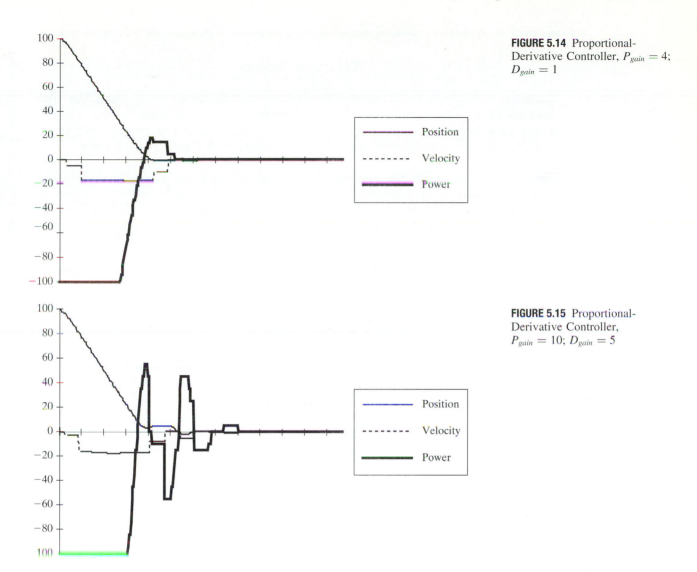

FIGURE 5.14 Proportional-Derivative Controller, $P_{gain} = 4$; $D_{gain} = 1$

FIGURE 5.15 Proportional-Derivative Controller, $P_{gain} = 10$; $D_{gain} = 5$

set to 5. As can be seen in the position graph, the controller "puts on the brakes" too hard and the system stops moving before the destination setpoint (this is between the 0.8- and 1.0-second mark). When the velocity hits zero, the proportional gain kicks in again and the system corrects. Overall it makes for a pretty ugly response.

Proportional-derivative control is used extensively in industrial process control. For just about anything more serious than a toaster, it is quite effective to vary the power input when the system is far away from the setpoint and correct for the momentum of the system as it approaches the setpoint.

5.2.3 Exercises

1. Experiment with the proportional-derivative control concept on your testbed system. Find a pair of gains that achieves a response similar to Figure 5.14. What are the gains? What process did you use to determine them?
2. Replace the LEGO tire on your test system with a larger mass. Are the gains you chose still ideal? If not, find better ones.
3. Name three systems in the world that you would expect to be operated by a PD controller. Why?

Classical Control

Classical control theory is all about analyzing the response of systems like the testbed LEGO wheel controller. By modeling factors like the mass of the system being controlled, the power flow into the system, the load on the system, and other characteristics, it is possible to determine the optimal values for the gain factors.

Techniques also exist for creating *self-tuning* or *adaptive controllers* that dynamically adjust the gain parameters while the system is in operation. This allows a controller to compensate for changing factors external to the system, like the amount of load on the system. A standard P-D controller does a good job even when external conditions change, but an adaptive controller can do better.

You may run across the term *PID control* in control literature. The "I" stands for integral; an integral term can correct for steady-state errors like in the first example, where the system came to rest a few counts away from the setpoint. By integrating this error over time, the controller can deliver a "kick" to drive the system to the setpoint.

4. Equip the *HandyBug* robot with shaft encoders on each of its two wheels. Write a program that uses PD control techniques to coordinate the movement of the two wheels so that you can give a distance command and *HandyBug* will drive in a straight line to that distance. What kinds of problems do you encounter?

5.3 Sequential Control

This section introduces some ideas about how to design an overall control strategy for operating a robot. The past two sections discussed feedback controls appropriate for one piece of a robot's behavior—tracking a wall, for instance. But how should a robot coordinate a bunch of these lower level feedback behaviors? That is the question explored in this section.

We examine two differing approaches to this problem: *Sequential* control and *reactive* control. Sequential control refers to a procedural series of steps or phases that a robot's program moves through in service of accomplishing some task. Reactive control refers to a collection of stimulus–response behaviors that dynamically trigger and retire as the robot moves through the physical environment. These approaches represent endpoints along a continuum of possibilities; this "control space" becomes more clear as we work through some examples.

Also this section introduces the *Robo-Pong* robot contest, which was run in the 1991 MIT Robot Design competition. This is the first of the actual contest examples we use to illustrate ideas in robot control.

5.3.1 The Robo-Pong Contest

The MIT *Robo-Pong* contest was played in January 1991. The contest involved two robots and 15 plastic practice golf balls (similar to ping-pong balls, but slightly larger, heavier, and less bouncy). The goal of the game was to have your robot transport balls from its side of the table to the opponent's—when the 60-second round ended, the robot with fewer balls on its side was the winner.

Approaches to Robot Control

by Maja J. Mataric

Robot control refers to the way in which the sensing and action of a robot are coordinated. There are infinitely many possible robot programs, but they all fall along a well-defined spectrum of control. Along this spectrum, there are four basic practical approaches being used today: 1) deliberative control, 2) reactive control, 3) hybrid control, and 4) behavior-based control. A good way to think about these alternatives is as follows:

Deliberative Control: Think hard, then act.
Reactive Control: Don't think, (re)act.
Hybrid Control: Think and act independently, in parallel.
Behavior-Based Control: Think the way you act.

No single approach is "the best" for all robots; each has its strengths and weaknesses. Control requires some unavoidable trade-offs:

Thinking is slow.
Reaction must be fast.
Thinking allows looking ahead (planning) to avoid bad actions.
Thinking too long can be dangerous (e.g., falling off a cliff, being run over).
To think, the robot needs (a lot of) accurate information.
The world keeps changing as the robot is thinking, so the slower it thinks, the more inaccurate its solutions.

As a result of these trade-offs, some robots don't think at all, while others mostly think and act very little. It all depends on the robot's task and its environment. If the task and environment require the robot to move and react very quickly, there is usually no time for thinking, such as in automated fast-moving cars, or in soccer playing robots. On the other hand, if the environment does not change much and the robot has enough time, it can plan far ahead to find the best action, such as in playing chess, monitoring a warehouse at night, or assembling a complicated object.

Figure 5.16 illustrates the *Robo-Pong* playing table, which was approximately four by six feet in size. As shown in the diagram, the table consisted of two inclined surfaces with a small plateau area in the center. Robots started the round in diagonally opposite corners of the table (indicated as the large circled starting areas). Six balls rested at the base of each ramp (the *ball troughs*), and three balls were placed on the plateau. The two sides of the table were painted in solid contrasting colors so that robots could use reflectance sensors to determine which side of the table they were on.

By placing the three balls on the center plateau, we hoped to encourage a diversity of robot strategies.[2] We predicted that some robots would opt to play the center balls first, whereas others would begin with the balls at the base of the ramps. The center balls also made it possible for a simple robot—one that just climbed uphill—to be

---

[2] *Robo-Pong* and the other MIT robot contests were designed by a group of people, including myself and other founding organizers of the MIT Robot Design project, Randy Sargent and Pankaj Oberoi.

The Four Types of Control

We will now briefly review how each of the four different approaches to robot control addresses these trade-offs.

"Don't think, react!" Reactive control is a technique for tightly coupling sensory inputs and effector outputs, to allow the robot to respond very quickly to changing and unstructured environments. Think of reactive control as "stimulus-response." This is a powerful control method; many animals are largely reactive. Limitations to this approach are that such robots, because they only look up actions for any sensory input, do not usually keep much information around, have no memory, no internal representations of the world around them, and no ability to learn over time.

"Think hard, then act." In deliberative control, the robot takes all of the available sensory information, and all of the internally stored knowledge it has, and it creates a plan of action. The robot searches through potentially all possible plans until it finds one that will do the job. This requires the robot to look ahead and think in terms of: "If I do this next, and then this happens, then what if I do this next, then this happens, . . . " and so on. This can take a long time, which is why if the robot must react quickly, it may not be practical. However, if there is time, this allows the robot to act strategically.

"Think and act independently, in parallel." In hybrid control, the goal is to combine the best of both reactive and deliberative control. In it, one part of the robot's "brain" plans, while another deals with immediate reaction, such as avoiding obstacles and staying on the road. The challenge of this approach is bringing the two parts of the brain together, and allowing them to talk to each other, and resolve conflicts between the two. This requires a third part of the robot brain, and as a result these systems are often called "three-layer systems."

"Think the way you act." Behavior-Based control is inspired from biology, and tries to model how animal brains may deal with hard problems of both thinking and acting. Behavior-based systems, like hybrid systems, also have different parts or layers, but unlike hybrid systems, they are not as different from each other. All of them are encoded as behaviors, processes that take inputs and send outputs to each other, quite quickly. So if a robot needs to plan ahead, it does so in a network of behaviors which talk to each other and send information around, rather than a single planner, as with hybrid systems. Behavior-based systems are an alternative to hybrid systems; these days, they are equally powerful and equally popular. However, they are not the same and thus are used for different types of robot applications.

How time—or the lack of it—is handled really distinguishes different approaches to robot control. Reactive systems respond to the immediate requirements of the environment, and do not look into the past or the future. Deliberative system look into the future (plan) before deciding how to act. Hybrid systems respond to some of the urgent requirements, while taking time to think about some others. This requires waiting for the thinking to finish, or interrupting the reaction based on new information. Behavior-based systems also think and act at the same time, but spread out

The Four Types of Control (Continued)

the thinking over multiple distributed computation modules (behaviors). Thus they think the way they act, as quickly as possible.

In many cases, just by observing a robot's behavior, it is impossible to tell what control approach it is using. This is similar to not knowing in what language some program is implemented, what somebody is thinking, or what exactly makes an animal do what it does. New robot control "architectures" for structuring robot control are being invented all the time, as novel applications for robotics are found. Sometimes, they become specialized robot programming languages. However novel they are, they can still fit into the fundamental control spectrum just described. Thus, once you can program a robot in all of the four approaches above, you know all possibilities at your disposal.

To learn more about approaches to robot control, see:

Maja J. Matarić, "Behavior-Based Control: Examples from Navigation, Learning, and Group Behavior," *Journal of Experimental and Theoretical Artificial Intelligence*, 9(2–3), 1997, 323–336.

Behavior-Based Robotics by R. Arkin, MIT Press, 1998.

MIT Encyclopedia of Cognitive Sciences, Robert A. Wilson and Frank C. Keil, eds., MIT Press, 1999.

able to win a contest round, thus allowing the contest to be satisfied without great difficulty.

Successful *Robo-Pong* robots needed to be able to go uphill and downhill, maneuver in the trough area, and coordinate activities of collecting and delivering balls. Overall, ball-collecting robots were the most popular design choice. This was not surprising in that they were also the mechanically least complex design. There were two basic types of the ball-collectors: *harvester robots* and *eater robots*.[3]

In the harvester approach, chosen by 18 teams, robots scooped the balls into some sort of open arms and then pushed them onto the opponent's side of the playing field. Eater robots, constructed by 11 teams, were similar in principle to the harvester approach with the exception that the eaters collected balls "inside their bodies" before driving over to the opponent's side. Students believed the eater robots to be a safer design than the harvesters, because balls couldn't be returned to the robot's own side by the opponent. On the other hand, the eaters were more mechanically complex and hence more prone to failure.

Four teams successfully deployed *shooter robots*, which catapulted balls onto the opponent's side of the table. We had placed a clause in the contest rules that we hoped would encourage shooter designs: If a ball went over the playing field wall on the opponent's territory, the ball would be permanently scored against the opponent—it couldn't bring the ball back to your robot's side.

---

[3] Prof. David Chen, Head of the Institute for Science and Technological Education at Tel Aviv University in Israel, was a Visiting Professor at the MIT Media Lab during the 1991 academic year and contributed his insights to the Robot Design project, including this analysis of the *Robo-Pong* design strategies.

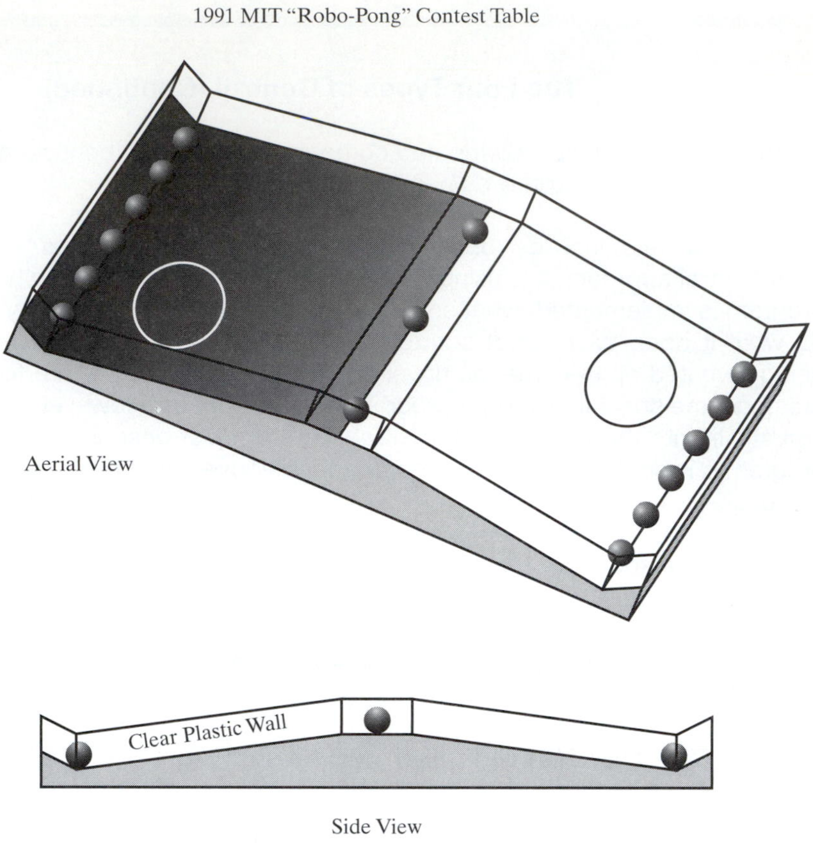

FIGURE 5.16 The 1991 *Robo-Pong* Contest Table

1991 MIT "Robo-Pong" Contest Table

Aerial View

Clear Plastic Wall

Side View

Building a shooter design required a fair bit of mechanical ingenuity, both in the shooting mechanism and a device to load balls into the shooter; a number of teams started work on shooter designs and then abandoned them. The four shooters that were finally fielded were sophisticated and pleasing to watch, but ultimately lost against aggressor designs, which could trap them easily, and effective collector designs, which delivered balls back after they had been shot across the table.

5.3.2 Sequential Strategies

The *Robo-Pong* contest lent itself to sequential solutions, especially if the robot was a harvester or eater variety. A typical solution was to drive in a square path pattern, up along a wall, across the black/white field divider, down along the wall, and back across the ball trough area (scooping up balls along the way).

The following discussion is based on *Groucho*, an actual robot in the *Robo-Pong* contest, which performed the exact pattern presented here. However all of the collectors were based on a variation of this approach. (*Groucho* was designed by Matthew Domsch, Adam Skwersky, and Ed Tobin.)

Figure 5.17 illustrates *Groucho*'s strategy. As indicated by the numbered robot positions, the robot performed a looping strategy of scooping up balls along the bottom trough, driving up the ramp and dumping the balls onto the opponent's side (Position 3), driving across the center plateau and dumping those balls (Position 6), driving back down it own ramp, turning back along its ball trough, and repeating. There is some complexity in the 5–6–7 step sequence required to dump the center plateau balls.

Thus, *Groucho* perfectly exemplifies the sequential approach: a series of actions that are performed to accomplish the desired task—as a mathematical algorithm prescribes a

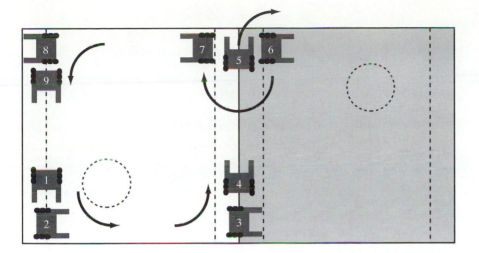

FIGURE 5.17 *Groucho*'s Sequential Ball Harvester Strategy in *Robo-Pong*

The strategy pattern of *Groucho*, a sequential ball harvester. From the start circle, the robot drives to Position 1. It drives forward until striking the wall and then rotates to Position 2. From there, it climbs up the ramp until crossing the black/white divider (Position 3)—at which point any balls it has collected are dumped onto the opponent's side. Then it rotates to Position 4 and drives across the center plateau until striking the opposing wall (Position 5). Next it turns to face down the opponent's slope (Position 6), dumping any balls it may have collected along the center plateau. Then it performs a 180-degree turn, lining itself up to drive down its own slope (Position 7), and it drives downward until striking the back wall (Position 8). Finally it rotates to Position 9 and scoops up balls in the trough, continuing the loop at Position 1.

series of operations to perform on data. Figure 5.18 is a "pseudocode" listing of a program to perform *Groucho*'s activity. As suggested by the listing, the sequential approach is based on a linear series of actions, which are performed in a repetitive loop. Sensing may be used in the service of these actions, but it does not change the order in which they will be performed.

Subloops in an Sequential Program

For the sequential approach, it's necessary that each piece of the program, each substrategy, does its job. Suppose that the `forward()` routine in the Figure 5.18 listing didn't go exactly straight—then the robot would veer off course. Or suppose that the `rotate_left_ninety()` routine turned more than 90 degrees—then *Groucho* would be headed off into the center of the playing field, rather than following along its square path pattern. In practice, robots rarely go precisely straight or turn a precise number of degrees (unless they have very high performance mechanics, high traction wheels, and a control system dedicated to this ability), so it's safe to assume that some kind of feedback based on the surrounding environment will be necessary.

Let's explore how the actual *Groucho* robot solved the *Robo-Pong* tasks and then look at some alternatives and extensions to its behavior. Figure 5.19 illustrates the design of *Groucho*. It used a basic turtle drive system with a pair of driven wheels on each side.

We discuss the way *Groucho* used sensors in a moment, but first notice a useful mechanical device: a pair of free-spinning rider wheels mounted parallel to the floor, jutting out from the front "arms." These rider wheels allowed *Groucho* to drive along a wall with no sensing or feedback required: *Groucho* would simply drive straight ahead, and a rider wheel would be pressed to the wall, guiding the robot along. It was an effective trick that made *Groucho*'s design a lot easier to complete. The wheels also helped the robot when turning out of a corner; even if *Groucho* were aimed slightly into the wall, a rider wheel would "catch" and guide the robot into a position parallel to the wall.

Groucho used two kinds of sensors: a touch sensor at the end each of its "arms," and a pair of light sensors facing downward located near its geometric center. *Groucho* used the touch sensors for cornering, and the light sensors determined when it had crossed onto the other side of the table and tracked the light/dark boundary across the center plateau.

Referring to the strategy diagram (Figure 5.17), the actual *Groucho* did not make a 90-degree turn from Position 1 to Position 2, strictly speaking. *Groucho* instead was

FIGURE 5.18 Pseudocoding of *Groucho*'s Strategy

```
void groucho() {

    while (1) {                     /* loop indefinitely */

        /* for simplicity, assume robot starts at position 1 */
        forward();
        waituntil_hit_wall();
        rotate_left_ninety();    /* now at position 2 */

        forward();
        waituntil_see_black();   /* position 3 */

        rotate_left_ninety();    /* position 4 */

        forward();
        waituntil_hit_wall();    /* position 5 */

        rotate_left_ninety();    /* position 6 */

        rotate_onehundred_eighty();  /* position 7 */

        forward();
        waituntil_hit_wall();    /* position 8 */

        rotate_left_ninety();    /* position 9 */
    }
}
```

FIGURE 5.19 Schematic of *Groucho* Robot, Top View

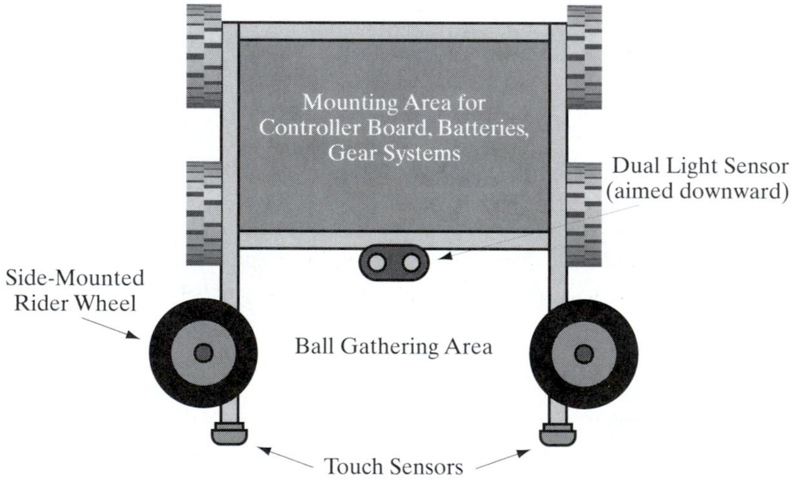

designed to take corners with a repetitive series of little turns and collisions back into the wall. Each time *Groucho* hit the wall, it would back up, turn a little, and then start driving forward again. After about four or five of these iterations, *Groucho* would have turned the required amount, and it would be able to continue along its path (Figure 5.20).

This turning method was fairly reliable because even if the wheels slipped a little on one turn, *Groucho* kept turning until the touch sensor no longer struck the wall—in which case it would have completed its turn. Note that this method works for a wide range of corners—ones less than and greater than the right angles on the *Robo-Pong* playing field. This adaptability is the great strength of feedback methods. Also, feedback can correct for variances in a robot's performance, not just variance in the environment.

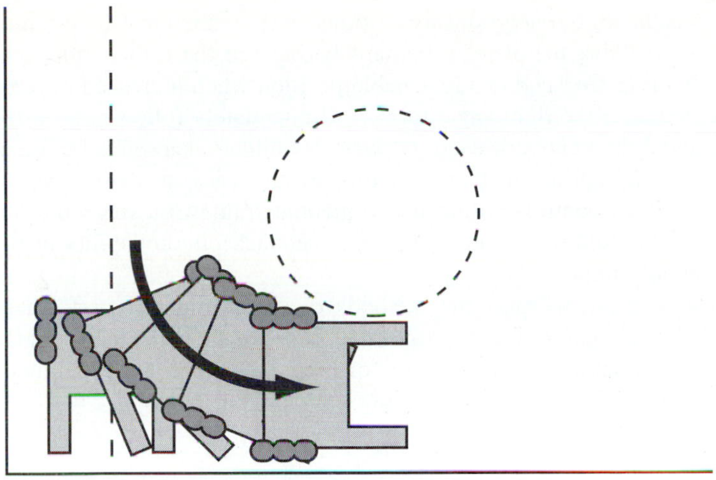

FIGURE 5.20 *Groucho*'s Cornering Algorithm

Groucho negotiated corners by making a series of bumps, back-ups, and turns. This is an example of using feedback to accomplish a particular action within a larger strategy.

In performing the 90-degree turn from Position 3 to Position 4 (on the plateau at the top of the hill), *Groucho* did things differently—it simply executed a single timed turn movement. The students who built *Groucho* attempted to use feedback to ensure that the robot would turn the proper amount, but found it difficult to get reliable results (lacking the wall as a reference point, as they had done with the inside-corner turns). Instead, a timed turn (with the duration determined experimentally) performed satisfactorily to them.

The students did not expect *Groucho* to be able to cross the center plateau without feedback sensing, however. This is where the dual light sensor, aimed downward at the playing surface, was used. As *Groucho* drove across the table, it made sure that one sensor was kept on the dark side of the table and the other on the light side. The sensor and a feedback program thus compensated for any variances in the mechanical performance of *Groucho*'s geartrain, and *Groucho* would reliably reach the opposite side of the plateau, triggering a touch sensor.

To summarize, the sequential strategy method is relatively simple and can be effective when a straightforward algorithm can be devised. The *Groucho* robot for *Robo-Pong* is a good example of such an approach.

The strengths of the sequential approach are its simplicity, directness, and predictability when things go according to plan. Its weaknesses include an inability to detect or correct for problems or unexpected circumstances and the serial dependencies required for proper functioning.

A sequential solution is like a chain, in that if any one step fails, the whole solution typically fails. The adage "a chain is only as strong as its weakest link" applies in spades: Each link step of a sequential solution has a chance of failing, and this chance *multiplies* throughout the set of steps. For example, suppose in a sequential solution, each step has a 90% chance of functioning properly on any given trial, and there are six such steps in the solution. Then the likelihood of the overall program working is the likelihood that each step functions properly: $0.9 \times 0.9 \times 0.9 \times 0.9 \times 0.9 \times 0.9$, which equals about a 53% chance. Thus, the overall program has only a slightly better than half chance of working on any given run!

A sequential process can be bolstered by having separable steps along the way performed by feedback loops. With *Groucho*, an example of this is the way that it handled the inside corners. Rather than just turning by a timed amount, *Groucho* used a series of little turns and bumps to negotiate the corners. This method implicitly acknowledged that *Groucho* would not reliably hit the wall at a perfect perpendicular angle, from which a timed turn could be based. The feedback used at the corners thereby compensated for variances in the playing field, the performance of the robot, and real-world unpredictability.

On the other hand, *Groucho* did use a timed turn at the crest of the hill, turning in preparation for crossing the plateau. Perhaps because of the rolling rider wheels (which would reliably bring *Groucho* to a repeatable position when it crossed over the light/dark boundary) or because the right-angle turn was immediately followed by a feedback program that tracked the light/dark edge, *Groucho*'s builders determined that an open-loop, timed turn was appropriate in that situation. In any case, it should be clear that, by embedding feedback controls within the sequential framework (e.g., the inside cornering feedback or the follow-the-light/dark-edge feedback), the reliability of the sequential approach is greatly improved.

In the next section, we examine methods of monitoring the performance of these embedded feedback controls as a way to further improve the performance of the sequential method, and also pointing in the direction of more reactive control methodologies.

5.3.3 Exercise: *Groucho's* Program

In this exercise, we construct a program to control *Groucho* through the sequential strategy as discussed in the text. It would be ideal to have a physical mock-up of the *Groucho* robot and the *Robo-Pong* playing field for testing your code, but if this is not possible, you may adapt *HandyBug* to the task and build pieces of the playing field (e.g., walls, corners, and a light/dark edge) to help debug your programs.

For the purposes of the code written for this exercise, assume that the following functions are already defined and available for your use. If you are testing your solutions with an actual robot, you will need to write these simple movement and sensor functions before getting started:

- Movement functions, assuming *Groucho* is a standard "turtle" style robot: `forward()`, `backward()`, `spin_left()` and `spin_right()` (rotate in place), and `veer_left()` and `veer_right()` (turn while moving forward by operating one motor and leaving the other motor off).

- Sensor functions: `left_touch()` and `right_touch()` for the two touch sensors, which return 0 if not pressed and 1 if pressed, and `left_eye()` and `right_eye()` for the dual light sensors, which return 0 if positioned above the dark surface and 1 if above the light surface.

The control program is based on the following "main" program, which is revised from the earlier example presented in the text:

```
/* grchmain.c */

void groucho()
{
  while (1) {
    inside_corner();          /* position 1 to 2 */
    drive_to_top();           /* 2 to 3 */
    align_with_edge();        /* 3 to 4 */
    follow_edge_to_wall();    /* 4 to 5 */
    dump_ball_shuffle();      /* 5 to 6 to 7 */
    drive_to_bottom();        /* 7 to 8 */
    inside_corner();          /* 8 to 9 */
  }
}
```

In the program segments that follow, please refer to the *Groucho* strategy diagram, Figure 5.17.

1. Write a subroutine to negotiate the inside corner represented by the transition from Step 1 to Step 2. Name the subroutine `inside_corner()`; on entry, it should assume that the *Groucho* has just struck the wall with either or both of its touch sensors. The subroutine should exit after *Groucho* has turned the corner and has been following along the wall on its right side for at least 2 seconds (see Figure 5.20).

2. Write `drive_to_top()`, a subroutine that takes control after `inside_corner()` (Position 2) and drives *Groucho* until it senses the light/dark boundary (Position 3). At this point, the routine should stop *Groucho* from moving and return.

3. Write `align_with_edge()`, which should drive *Groucho* forward for a second or two (dumping any collected balls over to the opponent's side), drive back, and then rotate to parallel to the light/dark edge (Position 4). Use the light sensor to determine when the robot has rotated back to cross over the light/dark edge, and open-loop timing for the forward and backward motions. Return when the robot has crossed over the light/dark edge and is ready to follow the edge across the table.

4. Write `follow_edge_to_wall()`, which uses the dual light sensor to follow the light/dark edge across the playing field. The routine should attempt to keep one light sensor on the dark side and the other on the light side, thereby tracking the edge and traversing the table. Terminate when either of the touch sensors is pressed, signaling that the robot has reached the far wall of the playing field (Position 5).

5. Write `dump_ball_shuffle()`, which takes *Groucho* from having contacted the far wall head on (Position 5), to facing down the opponent's side (Position 6), to turning around 180 degrees heading down its own side with the wall to its right (Position 7). This function is difficult to accomplish using feedback; this exercise should best be done with an actual robot. Alternatively, this function may be replaced with another call to `inside_corner`.

6. Write `drive_to_bottom()`, which drives *Groucho* straight ahead and terminates when a touch sensor is pressed (Position 8).

7. The final cornering action (Positions 8 and 9) may be done with another call to `inside_corner()`.

8. At this point it should be possible to test the `groucho()` program loop presented at the beginning of this exercise. If you are working with an actual robot, attempt the unified program and describe the results.

5.3.4 Exit Conditions

The main trouble with the basic sequential approach is that there is no provision for detecting, no less correcting for, problem situations. Consider *Groucho*'s program: Most of the time, it is waiting for a touch sensor to trigger the next phase of action. If something were to impede its travel, without striking a touch sensor, *Groucho* would just sit there, unable to take corrective action. Many a robot has failed in this way in contest situations.

There are a variety of other ways *Groucho* could fail. Suppose it is crossing the top plateau, weaving its way back and forth across the light/dark boundary, and the opponent robot gets in the way and *does* trigger a touch sensor. Then *Groucho* would begin its behavior that is normally activated when it reaches the opposing wall. Depending on the interaction between *Groucho* and the opponent robot, this might or might not be a sensible thing to do.

Instead, suppose it were possible for *Groucho* to "know" that it had struck the opponent and not the opposite wall. Then it might be possible for *Groucho* to take an action that would have a better likelihood of a desirable result, rather than just blindly proceeding with the sequential plan. This section presents a number of techniques for error detection and discusses recovery within a sequential framework.

Timeouts

Consider the stage of *Groucho*'s program in which it traverses the light/dark edge across the playing field, taking it from Position 4 to Position 5 in the strategy diagram (Figure 5.17). In the earlier exercise, we named this subroutine `follow_edge_to_wall()`; the core loop of this function is feedback based on the dual light sensors, with an exit check from the touch sensors:

```
/* "eye" sensors return 1 if above light, 0 if above dark */
/* try to keep left on light, right on dark */

while (1)  {
  /* if left eye sees black, turn left */
  if (left_eye() == 0) veer_left();

  /* if right eye sees white, turn right */
  else if (right_eye() == 1) veer_right();

  /* otherwise, go straight */
  else forward();

  /* check for touch sensors */
  if (left_touch() || right_touch()) break;
}
```

The only way this loop can exit is if one of the touch sensors is pressed; if *Groucho* were to hit something without the touch sensors being pressed, the loop simply would never end (and *Groucho* would look pretty dumb).

A simple solution to this problem is to allow the subroutine to *timeout*. After a predetermined period of time has elapsed, the subroutine exits even if a touch sensor was not pressed.

Interactive C includes built-in functions for measuring elapsed time. The `seconds()` function reports the number of seconds since the last system reset as a floating point number; the `mseconds()` function reports the same quantity as the number of *milliseconds* since reset as a long integer (see sidebar). Using either of these functions, it is easy to keep track of how much time has elapsed since a subroutine began execution and take action at some point in time.

The following code fragment illustrates how this may be done. A long integer variable, `timeout`, is declared and initialized with the value of the current time plus four seconds (4,000 milliseconds, or `4000L`). Inside the body of the feedback loop, the current time is compared with the timeout point; if the current time is later than the timeout value, the loop exits:

```
/* declare and initialize timeout variable */
long timeout= mseconds() + 4000L;

while (1)  {
  if (left_eye() == 0) veer_left();
  else if (right_eye() == 1) veer_right();
  else forward();

  if (left_touch() || right_touch()) break;
```

```
  /* check for timeout */
  if (mseconds() > timeout) break;
}
```

The last statement performs the elapsed time check and breaks the loop if too much time has elapsed. (It would also be possible to put the timeout check as the condition of the `while` loop.)

In most cases, the higher level control program should take a special action when a subroutine exits because of a timeout rather than the normal conclusion of its duties. The

---

Seconds Versus Mseconds

When Interactive C reports the elapsed time, the last system reset is the zero point for all time measurements. System reset occurs whenever the board is turned on.

There are two functions for reporting the time: `seconds()`, which reports the number of seconds since reset as a floating point number, and `mseconds()`, which reports the number of *milliseconds* (thousandths of a second) since reset as a long integer. So, for example, if 23 seconds had elapsed, `seconds()` would report `23.0` and `mseconds()` would report `23000`. Why should you use one function over the other?

The `seconds()` function can be easier to use because it uses the more intuitive units of seconds rather than milliseconds. It reports its value as a floating point number, so you must use a floating point variable to store the result. For example, "`float time= seconds();`" defines a floating point variable named `time` and initializes it with the current system time.

On the other hand, all floating point (FP) operations on the Handy Board are quite slow. Each FP operation takes between 1 and 5 milliseconds of real time to compute. That can add up, especially if you are running multiple processes. So it's best to avoid floating point operations except where they're really needed, and use `mseconds()` for timing functions.

`mseconds()` uses long integers to represent the time value because long integers—which are 32 bits long, rather than Interactive C's normal 16–bit integers—can hold a large enough number for most timing purposes. The positive limit with a long integer in milliseconds is a reasonably long time (for a robot): nearly 25 days.

Here is an example of declaring a long integer variable and setting it to the current system time reported by `mseconds()`: "`long time= mseconds();`" To specify a time period constant, remember that 1,000 "mseconds" is one second, and that the letter "L" must follow the number to make it a long integer (e.g., "`if (mseconds() > 4000L) {...}`" would evaluate the expression in braces if more than 4 seconds had elapsed since reset).

For the efficiency reasons mentioned, the examples in the book use `mseconds()`.

---

following code sample turns the previous code fragment into a full-fledged function. The function has a return value that indicates whether the routine terminated normally (with

a touch sensor press) or abnormally (because of a timeout):

```
/* define exit codes */
int NORMAL= 0;
int TIMEOUT= 1;

int follow_edge_to_wall()  {

  long timeout= mseconds() + 4000L;

  while (1)  {
    if (left_eye() == 0) veer_left();
    else if (right_eye() == 1) veer_right();
    else forward();

    if (left_touch() || right_touch()) return NORMAL;

    if (mseconds() > timeout) return TIMEOUT;
  }
}
```

Of course, the robot's main program would need to be modified to take action based on the success or lack thereof of the program's subroutines. However, at least the timeout technique allows the master program to have the opportunity to take corrective action. We examine this matter shortly, but first, let us look at other timeout techniques.

Premature Exits

In a similar fashion as one concludes that something has gone wrong if a subroutine takes too *long* to conclude, one can postulate there is a problem if a routine finishes in too *little* time. For example, suppose *Groucho* is happily traversing that center median and the opposing robot is in the way. If circumstances are fortunate, one of *Groucho*'s touch sensors will be triggered. With the right software, *Groucho* could "realize" that something unusual has happened because from past empirical observation there is no way that *Groucho* could already have reached the far wall.

The following code sample illustrates how this may be done. The "too-long" timeout has been made into a program constant (TOO_LONG), along with a new parameter, the "too-short" timeout (TOO_SHORT). When the touch sensors are hit, the elapsed time is checked; if it is less than the TOO_SHORT amount, it returns with the EARLY error result rather than the NORMAL exit result:

```
/* define exit codes */
int NORMAL= 0;
int TIMEOUT= 1;
int EARLY= 2;

/* sample timing parameters */
long TOO_LONG= 4000L;
long TOO_SHORT= 1500L;

int follow_edge_to_wall()  {

  long start= mseconds();
  long timeout= start + TOO_LONG;

  while (1)  {
    if (left_eye() == 0) veer_left();
    else if (right_eye() == 1) veer_right();
```

```
    else forward();

    if (left_touch() || right_touch())
      if (mseconds() < (start + TOO_SHORT))
        return EARLY;
      else return NORMAL;

    if (mseconds() > timeout) return TIMEOUT;
  }
}
```

Again, it remains to be considered what the master program should do with this new information.

Monitoring the Inner Loop

There is a final piece of the timeout puzzle. While a robot is performing a feedback process like following the light/dark edge, it is typically shuttling back and forth between the various modes. That is to say, when *Groucho* is traversing the edge, it is continuously correcting its movements, one moment veering left, then going straight, then going right, then another way. In the edge-following algorithm, *Groucho* may stay in the "go straight" mode for a fair while, but it shouldn't stay in the "veer left" or "veer right" modes for very long.

These transitions between the *different modes of the feedback loop* can be monitored along with the overall performance as discussed earlier. The code to do this is somewhat more complicated than the previous examples, but not complicated in principle.

Three new timeout parameters are necessary: VL_TIME (veer left timeout), VR_TIME (veer right timeout), and GS_TIME (go straight timeout). These parameters represent the longest time that *Groucho* may spend *continuously* in any given movement state.

In the core of the program, two new state variables are necessary: last_mode, to keep track of the loop's state the last time through, and last_time, to keep track of the time the last state began. Three new return codes, VL_STUCK, VR_STUCK, and GS_STUCK, are reused as codes to represent the states.

Here is the new function listing:

```
/* define exit codes */
int NORMAL= 0;
int TIMEOUT= 1;
int EARLY= 2;
int VL_STUCK= 3;
int VR_STUCK= 4;
int GS_STUCK= 5;

/* sample timing parameters */
long TOO_LONG= 4000L;
long TOO_SHORT= 1500L;
long VL_TIME= 2000L;
long VR_TIME= 2000L;
long GS_TIME= 3000L;

int follow_edge_to_wall() {

  long start= mseconds();
  long timeout= start + TOO_LONG;
  int last_mode= 0;
  long last_time= 0;
```

```
while (1)  {
  if (left_eye() == 0)  {
    veer_left();
    if (last_mode == VL_STUCK)
      if ((mseconds() - last_time) > VL_TIME)
        return VL_STUCK;
    else  {
      last_mode= VL_STUCK;
      last_time= mseconds();
    }
  }

  else if (right_eye() == 1) {
    veer_right();
    if (last_mode == VR_STUCK)
      if ((mseconds() - last_time) > VR_TIME)
        return VR_STUCK;
    else  {
      last_mode= VR_STUCK;
      last_time= mseconds();
    }
  }

  else {
    forward();
    if (last_mode == GS_STUCK)
      if ((mseconds() - last_time) > GS_TIME)
        return GS_STUCK;
    else  {
      last_mode= GS_STUCK;
      last_time= mseconds();
    }
  }

  if (left_touch() || right_touch())
    if (mseconds() < (start + TOO_SHORT))
      return EARLY;
    else return NORMAL;

  if (mseconds() > timeout) return TIMEOUT;
}
}
```

The routine has three copies of similar code for keeping track of the last state and elapsed time for each of the three driving states (veering left, veering right, and going straight). Consider, for the purposes of explanation, the code associated with veering left. After deciding to veer_left(), the code checks whether the mode the last time through the loop (stored in the last_mode variable) was the veer left mode. If so, then the amount of elapsed time is checked; if it's greater then the VL_TIME timeout constant, then the routine exits with the VL_STUCK error code.

If the last_mode was *not* the VL_STUCK mode, then it sets the two state variables for the next time through the control loop. The last_mode variable is set to VL_STUCK, and the entry time is recorded in last_time.

The previous two timeouts, for early conclusion or delayed conclusion, are still active. At the beginning of the routine, notice that the sample values for the timeout durations

VL_TIME are VR_TIME different than the value of GS_TIME. This is to point toward one potential problem with this approach: What if the robot tracks the line *too well*? Although it's safe to assume that the robot should not stay in either of the turning states (veer left and veer right) for too long, it's entirely possible that it might stay in the "go straight" state for a long uninterrupted period. If a given robot seems to perform very well when it's directly centered and going straight, one would not want the going-straight timeout to interrupt it from the fine job it's doing. These sort of cases must be determined experimentally; if necessary, the GS_TIME value can be increased to as large as the EARLY timeout value to ensure that the robot is allowed to go straight without being disturbed by the monitoring software.

Taking Action

The next question, of course, is how to take advantage of all of this new knowledge about the performance of feedback loops while they are running. There lies the rub: It is very difficult for most sequential controls to know what action to take on learning that a problem has occurred.

Consider our case of *Groucho* crossing the center median once again. Suppose it is running the latest version of the follow_edge_to_wall() function, and the function exits with the VL_STUCK error code. What has occurred? Perhaps *Groucho* has run into the opponent robot part of the way across the playing field, or perhaps *Groucho* has mistracked the median edge and driven itself into a playing field wall, or perhaps something else has gone wrong—there is simply no way to determine exactly what the situation is. So it is quite difficult for the sequential control program to take the "appropriate" course of action based on the error result.

One possibility is that an error condition from a feedback routine could prompt a reexamination of all other sensors to make sense of the situation. If *Groucho*'s touch

Proprioceptive Sensing

The term *proprioceptive* (from the Latin root *proprius*, meaning "own") is typically used to describe biological mechanisms for self-monitoring in an organism (e.g., a creature's ability to detect when it is hungry, tired, too hot, etc.).

In a similar fashion, proprioceptive refers to sensors that report various aspects of a robot's internal state—e.g., its battery level, how much force it's applying to its motor outputs, whether it's moving and how fast.

The feedback loop monitoring we're discussing in this section is yet another form of proprioception—monitoring not simple qualities like battery strength, but the performance of algorithms in action.

Much can be learned just by observing the performance of a simple interaction loop between the robot and its environment.

sensors went off only part way across the playing field, in the context of a contest situation, it could be because the opponent robot got in the way. If *Groucho* had any other sensors that could be used to detect the opponent robot, now would be the time to check them.

Even if it is difficult to design an appropriate reaction to each various situation that might be detected by the timeout methods, it is often possible to figure out a single recovery behavior that would suffice for many circumstances. In *Groucho*'s case, heading downhill until hitting the bottom wall and then proceeding with the cornering routine should allow *Groucho* to recover from a variety of problems.

5.3.5 Exercise: Groucho with Timeouts

In this exercise, we rewrite *Groucho*'s program to incorporate a variety of timeout-detecting and error-correcting mechanisms.

As in the earlier exercise, it is best if a working model of the *Groucho* robot design and the playing field is available, but if not, this exercise may be completed theoretically rather than practically.

1. *Timeout detection.* For each of the following *Groucho* subroutines, decide on suitable methods for determining timeout conditions and rewrite the functions to implement them. Which one or which combination of the techniques—simple timeout, premature timeout, or feedback loop monitoring—are most appropriate for each subroutine, and why?

   - `inside_corner()`
   - `drive_to_top()`
   - `align_with_edge()`
   - `drive_to_bottom()`

2. *Corrective action.* For each of the previous four subroutines, postulate reasons that the routine could fail with a timeout, how your routines would detect the failures, and possible corrective actions.

3. *Putting it together.* Rewrite the main *Groucho* program, which previously was just a loop running the subroutines, to choose the appropriate corrective action based on the error codes reported by the modified subroutines.

5.4 Reactive Control

In the previous section, the sequential model of robot control was explored. In this model, the robot's program is fundamentally a series of steps or actions to be taken in a predetermined order. This method is most effective when the robot's world and its interactions with it are well structured; manipulator arms in factories typically use sequential control with great success.

The sequential method loses its appeal when the robot must deal with unexpected situations, however. When it is extended to deal with error situations, the sequential method becomes a complicated tree of branching decisions that is hard to design and debug.

Suppose instead that the robot's program were organized around a collection of separate miniprograms all running at once and able to take control of the robot as they saw fit. For a very simple, minimal *HandyBug* program, there might be a touch sensor process that monitored the robot's touch sensors and caused the robot to back up and turn when it hit something, a periodic turn process that caused the robot to take a turn every now and then, and a wander process that caused the robot simply to move.

Sensor Fusion

In the field of robotics, *sensor fusion* is a technique for interpreting data from disparate robot sensors to form a unified "picture" of what is happening in the robot's world.

Sensor fusion is based on models of human cognition with our senses. When we experience something in the world—say, a waterfall—our visual interpretation of the churning water and our auditory interpretation of the rushing sound combine to form our sense of "the waterfall." Virtual motion theaters, which combine a movie with hydraulically actuated chairs moving in sync with the imagery, work because our brains are so good at performing this "fusion" of different sensory inputs, creating the powerful illusion of being in motion even if we are just being shaken around.

In a similar fashion, sensor fusion researchers devise methods of processing robotic sensor data so that they feed into a coherent worldview. This is challenging because sensor data are typically ambiguous or even conflicting.

Figure 5.21 illustrates this idea. The three separate processes, Touch, Turn, and Wander, all are active and checking their conditions continuously. For the Touch process, if a touch sensor is pressed, then its action will run and it will back up the robot and turn a little. The Turn process activates every 10 seconds, causing the robot to make a small turn. The Wander process is always active and causes the robot to drive straight ahead.

For this to work out, there has to be a way of deciding which process gets priority over the others at any given point in time. Although all processes can be active at once—in that they can be checking their conditions to determine whether they should do something—only one process can have control of the robot's outputs at a time.

One way of arbitrating among processes is a simple, fixed priority system. In this method, each process is assigned a priority level; at any given point in time, the process with the highest priority gets control of the robot.

In Figure 5.21, the arrows indicate a path of priority among the three processes. Touch has the highest priority, followed by Turn and then Wander. This ordering makes sense because while the robot is wandering about, if it hits something, the obstacle avoidance should take precedence over the wandering.

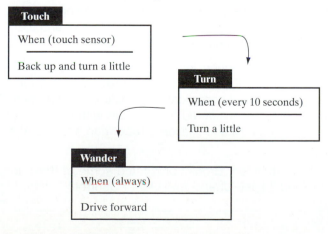

FIGURE 5.21 Simple Reactive Robot Program Diagram

In this simple reactive robot program, a touch sensor process, Touch, has highest priority, followed by a periodic turn process, Turn, and, last, a wander process, Wander.

5.4.1 A Priority-Based Control Program

In this section, we describe a framework program written using Interactive C for creating priority-based, multitasking robot programs like those suggested by Figure 5.21 (the simple, three-behavior robot program). We build up the program one behavior at a time, and then delve into the details of how the prioritization method is implemented.

The example program consists of three files, which must be loaded together:

- `priority.c`, which contains the prioritization code.
- `plegobug.c`, which contains standard movement and touch sensor routines for the *HandyBug* robot; that is, `forward()`, `backward()`, `left()`, `right()`, `left_touch()`, and `right_touch()`.
- `lb1task.c`, which contains one robot behavior. (As we add behaviors to the robot, this module expands and is renamed `lb2task.c` and `lb3task.c`.)

In a moment, we look at the code of `lb1task.c`, which contains a version of a touch sensor avoidance program implemented within the framework of the prioritization method. But first consider the following generic touch sensor program:

```
/* generic touch sensor program */
void touch () {
  while (1) {
    if (left_touch()) {
      backward(); msleep(500L);
      right(); msleep(500L);
    } else if (right_touch()) {
      backward(); msleep(500L);
      left(); msleep(500L);
    }
  }
}
```

"Fast, Cheap, and Out of Control"

Professor Rodney Brooks of the MIT Artificial Intelligence Laboratory is considered the father of the reactive robotics approach. The central idea is that more sophisticated robot competences should be built on top of simpler ones—an approach called the *subsumption architecture*.

Instead of all robot inputs feeding into a sensory perception unit, which creates a "world model" of the robot's environment, that feeds into a planning module, Brooks has argued that robot perception and action should be closely linked, and that complex behaviors can be built from the interactions of simple ones.

Brooks has proposed that future unmanned interplanetary missions should be performed by hundreds—or thousands—of simple, insect-like robots that act in teams to accomplish work, rather than a large and complicated monolithic device. With Brooks' approach, individual robots could be considered expendable without jeopardizing the success of the entire mission, whereas if a single large robot had a failure, the mission would be over.

In a paper that garnered much attention, Brooks presented some of these ideas. The paper was provocatively entitled, "Fast, Cheap, and Out of Control."

Introduction to Multitasking

Interactive C comes with the ability to *multitask* or run several programs at once. This is ideal for reactive robot programming, where the robot has several "behaviors" running at the same time.

For example, consider the following two functions and `main()` routine. The two functions are `back_and_forth()`, which turns on motor 0 forward and then backward repeatedly, and `sensor_beep()`, which repeatedly checks analog sensor 0 and beeps if it is less than 100. The `main()` routine calls the other two functions in order:

```
void back_and_forth () {          void main () {
  while (1) {                       back_and_forth();
    fd(0); msleep(500L);            sensor_beep();
    bk(0); msleep(500L);          }
  }
}

void sensor_beep () {
  while (1) {
    if (analog(0) < 100) beep();
  }
}
```

As it stands, the `sensor_beep()` function in `main()` will never run because the computer would be stuck in an infinite loop performing `back_and_forth()`. Interactive C's `start_process()` function, however, allows multiple programs to execute in tandem. All that is required is to rewrite the `main()` function to use `start_process()` to "launch" the subroutines as separate processes:

```
void main () {
  start_process(back_and_forth());
  start_process(sensor_beep());
}
```

Now both subroutines will execute at once; motor 0 will flash back and forth, and the beeper will trigger whenever analog sensor 0 falls below 100. Note that `start_process()` can also be used from Interactive C's command line on the host computer.

IC's multitasking capability makes it easy to implement reactive control for robot programming.

This program consists of an infinite loop that contains one if–else statement. The first part of the if–else checks the left touch sensor; if it is pressed, the robot is made to move backward for 0.5 seconds and then right for 0.5 seconds. If the left touch sensor is not pressed, then the right touch sensor is checked. If it is true, then the robot backs up and turns to the left. Then the loop repeats.

The generic touch sensor program is a good example of how one would like to write a robot task: It is simple and clear, and it only deals with issues that concern the task. Of course, if other tasks like the generic touch sensor one are running in parallel, their respective motor commands will conflict.

Robot Control Vocabulary

In much of the discussion that follows, we use several words more or less inter-changeably to describe a robot's activity. The terms *task*, *behavior*, and *process* mean essentially the same thing: a self-contained piece of code that causes a robot to perform a particular activity.

Key to this concept is that multiple tasks, behaviors, or processes can be active at once. This is what distinguishes the following discussion of robot control from the previous.

The term *process* is sometimes used to mean an Interactive C process (see sidebar on multitasking), but it may also simply suggest the more general idea of some code that causes the robot to perform an activity in parallel with other processes.

Hence the need for the prioritization structure. In the algorithm, each task is assigned a *process number* and a *priority level*. The task uses its process numbers to identify itself when issuing motor commands; this allows the prioritization routine to identify the motor commands of each different task. The priority level allows tasks with higher priority to supercede tasks with lower priority.

Figure 5.22 shows how the touch sensor routine can be rewritten using the priority algorithm, along with a `main()` routine that installs the touch sensor task into the priority algorithm. In this first example, there's only the touch sensor task, so the need for the priority algorithm is academic, but this example builds the framework for adding in multiple, prioritized tasks.

Let's examine the touch sensor routine and then the `main()` routine that launches it. Notice that the touch sensor task takes the argument `pid`, which stands for *process ID* (process identifier). Then this argument is used in movement commands (e.g., `backward[pid]`). The special movement commands accept the process ID argument as indicating which *process is requesting which motor commands*. Also, there is a pair of commands used to enable and disable a process' functioning.

Separately (and in parallel), the prioritization routine determines which process is enabled and has the highest priority and then issues the movement commands selected by that process to the motors. Essentially, one can think of the process' movement commands as requests; if a process has enabled itself (using the `enable()` function with its process ID) and it has the highest priority of all enabled processes, then its movement commands get to run.

Notice that after issuing each set of movement commands that react to a touch sensor press, the touch sensor routine issues a `disable(pid)` command. It's necessary that a process disable itself after having "done its thing" so that other processes that have lower priority get a chance to operate. If the touch sensor process did not disable itself, then it would have control of the robot even if it were not issuing any movement commands (unless a process with higher priority were active, of course).

Now consider the `main()` routine. This performs two pieces of housekeeping: setting up the touch sensor task itself, and launching the prioritization program.

There are three steps to setting up the touch sensor task. First, a process priority is assigned. The touch sensor process is given the priority level of 3 (zero priority is off; higher numbers are higher priority) because there will be two more tasks of lower priority

FIGURE 5.22 Listing of
`lb1task.c`

```
/*
  lb1task.c:  main program for LEGObug and priority.c
              one task:  touch
*/

void main () {
  int pid= 0;

  /* touch sensor */
  process_priority[pid]= 3;
  process_name[pid]= "Touch";
  start_process(touch(pid++));

  /* motor arbitration process */
  num_processes= pid;
  start_process(prioritize());
}

/* touch sensor process */
void touch (int pid) {
  while (1) {
    if (left_touch()) {
      enable(pid);
      backward(pid); msleep(500L);
      right(pid); msleep(500L);
      disable(pid);
    } else if (right_touch()) {
      enable(pid);
      backward(pid); msleep(500L);
      left(pid); msleep(500L);
      disable(pid);
    }
  }
}
```

as we continue developing this example. Next, a process name is assigned; this name is displayed by the prioritization program when the process is made active. Last, the process itself is launched, and the process counter variable, pid, is incremented for the next process set-up. (There are no more processes set up in this example, but there will be soon.)

Then the prioritization program, named `prioritize()`, is launched. Before doing so, the process counter variable is stored in the program global num_processes; this is an efficiency measure for the *prioritize()* program.

Are you ready to try out the code? With a stock *HandyBug*, the example program is ready to run by loading the file `lb1task.lis`, which loads the files `lb1task.c`, `plegobug.c`, and `priority.c`. In `plegobug.c`, the motor and sensor wiring connections are defined: left motor in motor port 0, right motor in motor port 3, left touch sensor in digital port 7, and right touch sensor in digital port 8. (Make sure that the motors are plugged in so that the direct motor control `fd(0)` and `fd(3)` functions cause *HandyBug* to move forward.)

With the full program running, notice that *HandyBug* just sits there unless a touch sensor is pressed. That's because when the touch sensors are not pressed, the `touch()` process is disabled, and because it's the only control task, no control tasks are active. The `prioritize()` routine realizes that no tasks are active, and it shuts the motors off and displays the message "No tasks enabled."

When a touch sensor *is* pressed, then the touch sensor task enables itself and issues motor commands to back up and turn away from the direction of contact. While the touch sensor task is active, `prioritize()` issues its motor commands to the motors and displays the message "`Running touch.`"

Considering this *HandyBug* as an artificial creature, one might say that it has a certain minimum competence: It can get out of the way if something hits it. *HandyBug* doesn't go anywhere on its own; however, if something comes and bothers it, it will move. Later behaviors can "exploit" earlier ones: A task that causes *HandyBug* to move can make use of the knowledge embedded in the behavior that allows *HandyBug* to get out of the way.

The prioritization scheme we have been using thus far does not support one task taking advantage of another's capabilities; it only allows one task to override (or *suppress*) another. But it provides a good start in working with the ideas of behavior-based control.

Looking Around

Let's add another behavior to *HandyBug*: the capability to make a quick turn every 10 seconds. From the "*HandyBug* as creature" perspective, this is as if *HandyBug* were to "glance around" periodically. Now that we've learned how to use the prioritization scheme, adding new behaviors is easy.

Figure 5.23 shows the listing of `lb2task.c`, which includes the code for `periodic_turn()`, the new behavior. First, look at the revised `main()` routine. The `periodic_turn()` task is set up in exactly the same fashion as the touch sensor task is. Nothing new to learn here!

The `periodic_turn()` routine is basically simple, with a tricky conditional expression in the `if` statement (see sidebar). Every 10 seconds, the conditional fires and runs the code to make *HandyBug* turn: First it enables itself, then it turns right for a half a second, then it disables itself (allowing other processes to take over), and then it waits another half second. That last delay is necessary because the conditional expression will be true for an entire second every 10 seconds. Without the trailing delay, the `if` statement would fire again immediately, and *HandyBug* would end up turning for a whole second.

Try out *HandyBug*'s dual behavior code—load `lb2task.lis`, which loads the new `lb2task.c` along with unchanged versions of `plegobug.c` and `priority.c`. (Please note: If you still have Interactive C open after loading `lb1task.lis`, you will have to type "`unload lb1task.c`" to unload the previous versions of `main()` and `touch()`, avoiding conflict.)

Now *HandyBug* not only just sits there waiting to be bothered, but every 10 seconds takes a little turn. It's still a bit shy, but it's investigating its surroundings!

Wandering

Now let's add a super-simple wandering algorithm: simply driving straight ahead! "Wandering," as it were, happens because `periodic_turn()` will kick in every 10 seconds, causing *HandyBug* to veer from a straight-line path.

Compared with either the touch sensor or the periodic turn behaviors, the wandering behavior we add now is all but trivial. Here it is:

```
/* wander process: just go forward */
void wander (int pid) {
  enable(pid);
  forward(pid);
}
```

The one thing to notice about the `wander()` process is that it doesn't even need a loop to work. It simply enables itself and sets its movement command as drive forward. Because it is installed as the lowest priority task, having it run as always enabled is

```
/*
  lb2task.c:  main program for LEGObug and priority.c
              two tasks:  periodic_turn and touch
*/

void main () {
  int pid= 0;

  /* touch sensor */
  process_priority[pid]= 3;
  process_name[pid]= "Touch";
  start_process(touch(pid++));

  /* periodic turn */
  process_priority[pid]= 2;
  process_name[pid]= "Turn";
  start_process(periodic_turn(pid++));

  /* motor arbitration process */
  num_processes= pid;
  start_process(prioritize());
}

/* periodic turn:  every 10 secs, turn a bit */
void periodic_turn (int pid) {
  while (1) {
    if (((int)seconds() % 10) == 9) {
      enable(pid);
      right(pid); msleep(500L);
      disable(pid);
      msleep(500L);
    }
  }
}

/* touch sensor process */
void touch (int pid) {
  while (1) {
    if (left_touch()) {
      enable(pid);
      backward(pid); msleep(500L);
      right(pid); msleep(500L);
      disable(pid);
    } else if (right_touch()) {
      enable(pid);
      backward(pid); msleep(500L);
      left(pid); msleep(500L);
      disable(pid);
    }
  }
}
```

FIGURE 5.23 Listing of lb2task.c

acceptable. If no other task wants control of *HandyBug*, then `wander()` is happy to tell the robot to simply drive straight ahead.

One Second Every Ten Seconds

There are a couple C-language shortcuts and a mathematical trick embedded in the conditional expression of the `periodic_turn()` routine. We dissect it piece by piece; first, the code in question:

```
if (((int)seconds() % 10) == 9) { ... }
```

As we have seen, the `seconds()` routine reports the elapsed time as a floating point number (e.g., 53.374 seconds). By prefacing the functional call with "`(int)`," this floating point value is converted to an integer value (e.g., 53). In computer science parlance, this is called *type coercion*.

The type coercion is necessary so that we may use the "%" operator, which is the arithmetic *modulus* function—that is, "the remainder when divided by." Putting it together, "`(int)seconds() % 10`" means, "take the elapsed system time, convert it to an integer, and report the remainder after dividing by 10."

This provides a number from 0 to 9; the rest of the `if` statement simply compares this value with 9 (using the "`==`" equality operator). Thus, in the final second of every 10-second period, the full expression yields a true, and the clause of the `if` statement runs.

One final note. The reason that the type coercion from floating point number to integer is used is that Interactive C does not have a modulus operator that works on floating point numbers. It does support floating point division, but not remainder. So the conversion to integer is used to circumvent this limitation.

Figure 5.24 shows the revised `main()` routine from the file `lb3task.c`. The `wander()` task is installed in the standard way with a priority of 1, the least among the three processes now installed.

Load `lb3task.lis` to give it a try. Now *HandyBug* is a full-fledged explorer robot able to roam about a room and back up and turn away from any obstacles in its way—after hitting into them, of course!

5.4.2 How the Prioritization Algorithm Works

Now let us delve into the internal workings of the prioritization algorithm. The basic concept is that each process has a priority level, a pair of output values representing its left and right motor commands, and an enable/disabled state indicator. There also is a process name character string associated with each process for display to the user.

The `prioritize()` process, which runs alongside all of the behavior processes, is fairly simple. All it does is cycle through the list of enabled processes, find the one with the highest priority, and copy its motor output commands to the actual motors.

The Data Structures

Five global arrays are used to store the behavior process state variables as follows:

- `process_priority[]`. Stores each process' priority level.

```
void main () {
  int pid= 0;

  /* touch sensor */
  process_priority[pid]= 3;
  process_name[pid]= "Touch";
  start_process(touch(pid++));

  /* periodic turn */
  process_priority[pid]= 2;
  process_name[pid]= "Turn";
  start_process(periodic_turn(pid++));

  /* wander */
  process_priority[pid]= 1;
  process_name[pid]= "Wander";
  start_process(wander(pid++));

  /* motor arbitration process */
  num_processes= pid;
  start_process(prioritize());
}
```

FIGURE 5.24 Revised `main()` Function from `lb3task.c`

- `process_enable[]`. Indicates whether a process is enabled or disabled at any given point in time. When a process is enabled, its priority level is stored here; when a process is disabled, a zero is stored.

- `left_motor[]`. Holds a process' current left motor command.

- `right_motor[]`. Holds a process' current right motor command.

- `process_name[]`. Stores the process name.

Additionally, there are two global variables used along with two global variables used by the prioritization method: `num_processes`, which holds the number of processes (to simply search for the one with the highest priority), and `active_process`, which is dynamically set by the `prioritize()` process each time it chooses a behavior task to run.

Figure 5.25 shows these data structures and system globals. The diagram illustrates actual values that might be in the data arrays while running the example program presented earlier:

- The `process_name[]` array holds the process names as set up by the `main()` routine.

- The `process_priority[]` array holds the fixed priority values as assigned to the processes in `main()`.

- The `process_enable[]` array holds dynamic enable values. In the diagram, the touch sensor process is enabled because its priority level has been copied into the `process_enable[]` array. The periodic turn process is disabled, and the wander process (which is always enabled in our example) is indeed enabled.

- The `left_motor[]` and `right_motor[]` arrays hold values assigned by the behavior tasks. Although the periodic turn process is disabled, its entries are still present in the motor arrays from a previous time that it became active. There is no need to clear them out because, when a process is disabled, the `prioritize()` process ignores its motor commands anyway.

- The `active_process` variable, assigned by `prioritize()`, is zero, indicating that the process with an index 0—the touch sensor process—is active.

FIGURE 5.25 Data Structures of the Prioritization Algorithm

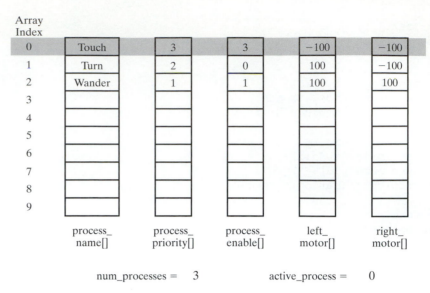

Array Index	process_name[]	process_priority[]	process_enable[]	left_motor[]	right_motor[]
0	Touch	3	3	−100	−100
1	Turn	2	0	100	−100
2	Wander	1	1	100	100
3					
4					
5					
6					
7					
8					
9					

num_processes = 3   active_process = 0

The Prioritization Code

Now let's look at the code that makes use of these data structures to perform the task prioritization. Figure 5.26 is a listing of the `priority.c` file, which contains the central `prioritize()` function and two supporing functions, `enable()` and `disable()`.

Enabling and disabling processes is easy. To enable a process, all that is necessary is to copy its priority level, stored in the `process_priority[]` array, into the "enabled" array:

```
/* set process_enable entry to process's priority level */
void enable (int pid) {
    process_enable[pid] = process_priority[pid];
}
```

To disable a process, a zero is stored in its position in the `process_enable[]` array:

```
/* set process_enable entry to 0 */
void disable (int pid) {
    process_enable[pid] = 0;
}
```

Finally, the heart of the operation is the `prioritize()` function. The first order of business is to scan the `process_enable[]` array, looking for the process with the highest priority level. The local variable `max` is initialized to zero and then the array is scanned.

If `max` is still zero after looking through all of the installed processes, then none of them is enabled. In this case, both motors are turned off, and the message "No tasks enabled" is displayed on the LCD screen.

If `max` is greater than zero, then at least one process is enabled. The next step is to again search through the list of processes and find one with a priority that matches the maximum value. If there is a "tie," with more than one process at the maximum priority, the current implementation simply selects the first one it encounters. This could be rewritten to randomly choose a process from the set of highest priority processes, for example.

The global variable `active_process` is set to hold the index of the highest priority process, and then the motor commands of this process are written out to the motor ports. Finally, the name of the active process is printed on the LCD display.

At this point the loop repeats, and the process-selection activity begins anew.

FIGURE 5.26 Listing of priority.c

```
/* priority.c:  arbitration program for multi-behavior robot con-
trol */

/* define process tables */
int process_priority[10];
int process_enable[10];
char process_name[0][10];

/* define motor output tables */
int left_motor[10];
int right_motor[10];

/* globals */
int num_processes= 0;
int active_process= 0;

/* set process_enable entry to process's priority level */
void enable (int pid) {
  process_enable[pid]= process_priority[pid];
}

/* set process_enable entry to 0 */
void disable (int pid) {
  process_enable[pid]= 0;
}

void prioritize () {
  int max, i;

  while (1)  {
    /* find process with maximum priority */
    max= 0;
    for (i=0; i< num_processes; i++)
      if (process_enable[i] > max) max= process_enable[i];

    /* if no processes enabled, turn off motors */
    if (max == 0)  {
      motor(LEFT_MOTOR_PORT, 0); motor(RIGHT_MOTOR_PORT, 0);
      printf("No tasks enabled\n");
    } else {
      /* get pid of active process */
      /* if more than one at highest level, get the first one */
      for (i=0; i< num_processes; i++)
        if (process_enable[i] == max) break;
      active_process= i;

      /* set the motors based on the commands of this process */
      motor(LEFT_MOTOR_PORT, left_motor[active_process]);
      motor(RIGHT_MOTOR_PORT, right_motor[active_process]);

      /* display name of active process */
      printf("Running %s\n", process_name[active_process]);
    }
  }
}
```

FIGURE 5.27 Listing of plegobug.c

```
/*
  plegobug.c:  movement and touch sensor commands
                  for LEGObug with priority.c
*/

/* motor and sensor ports */
int LEFT_MOTOR_PORT= 0;
int RIGHT_MOTOR_PORT= 3;
int LEFT_TOUCH_PORT= 7;
int RIGHT_TOUCH_PORT= 8;

/* movement commands */
void forward (int pid) {
  left_motor[pid]= 100;
  right_motor[pid]= 100;
}

void backward (int pid) {
  left_motor[pid]= -100;
  right_motor[pid]= -100;
}

void right (int pid) {
  left_motor[pid]= 100;
  right_motor[pid]= -100;
}

void left (int pid) {
  left_motor[pid]= -100;
  right_motor[pid]= 100;
}

void halt (int pid) {
  left_motor[pid]= 0;
  right_motor[pid]= 0;
}

/* sensor functions */
int left_touch () {
  return digital(LEFT_TOUCH_PORT);
}

int right_touch () {
  return digital(RIGHT_TOUCH_PORT);
}
```

The *HandyBug* Movement Routines

The file plegobug.c, listed in Figure 5.27, contains support routines for *HandyBug*'s movement and touch sensing.

Each of the movement routines—forward(), backward(), right(), left(), and halt()—take the process index as an argument and store the appropriate motor commands into the left_motor[] and right_motor[] arrays.

The left_touch() and right_touch() routines simply report the values of the left and right touch sensors, respectively. These routines do not interact with the prioritization framework at all.

5.4.3 Using Reactive Control

Reactive control excels in complex situations with many unpredictable interactions.

The 1995 MIT Robot Design contest was called "Robo-Miners" and was played on a table as shown in Figure 5.28. The table was a rectangular area with a central, raised square platform. Embedded underneath the platform were air hoses; at the beginning of each round, one ball was placed in each of the four air streams emanating from the hoses. Additional balls were placed at various other points on the table surface and on the ledges formed by the enclosing walls, as illustrated.

The scoring scheme for manipulating balls was somewhat arcane. Simplifying, points were awarded (in geometrically increasing units) for collecting balls, depositing balls into one's goal area, and successfully placing collected balls into the streams of air.

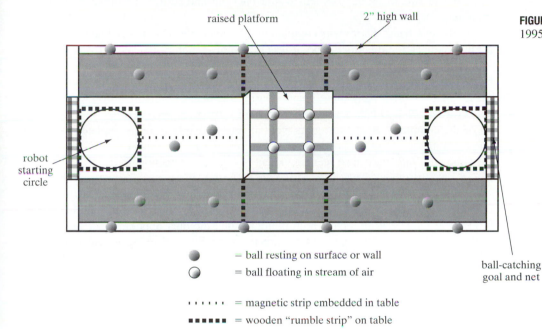

FIGURE 5.28 Table Design for the 1995 MIT *Robo-Miners* Contest

raised platform

2" high wall

robot starting circle

ball-catching goal and net

●   = ball resting on surface or wall
◐   = ball floating in stream of air

······· = magnetic strip embedded in table
■■■■■■ = wooden "rumble strip" on table

Various features were designed into the table for robots to use when navigating. For example, white and black areas were painted onto the main surface of the table and in a cross-hatched pattern on the raised platform (indicated by the shaded portions of the diagram); these could be detected by downward-facing reflective light sensors. A magnetic striping embedded in the table led from the robot starting circles to the raised platform, detectable by hall effect sensors. Also, wooden molding "rumble strips," originally intended to impede robot motion, could be detected by robots (using simple touch switches) and used for navigational purposes.

Typical robots designed to solve the contest were large, complex machines. Most had multiple mechanisms for manipulating balls; several had one or more arms with claws and several degrees of freedom.

An unusual robot, aptly named *The Arm*, is a good example of the sequential design. *The Arm* consisted of a small car at the end of a lazy tongs arm. The car would drive out of a nest, scoop up one ball, and drive backward into the nest while the lazy tongs held it straight. The nest would then rotate the car-arm assembly into position to grab the next ball, using shaft encoding to turn to predetermined "correct" angles. The designers tackled multiple problems to get the machine to perform as per their plan, including one in which the nest's base would rotate with respect to the playing surface, thus rendering subsequent rotations incorrect. This was solved by stretching LEGO tires as big rubber bands, but other serious problems remained: The robot was highly sensitive to correct initial placement, the ball-grabbing mechanism at the end of the car-arm extension didn't perform well, and the overall mechanism was not terribly reliable. Ultimately, the robot did quite poorly in the contest because what seemed like an easy win ("just reach out and grab the balls; we know where they are") turned out to be difficult to perform in practice.

The final contest event revealed one surprise robot, mockingly named *Fluffy the Sunshine Robot* by its creators. *Fluffy*, designed in 2 or 3 *days* before the contest, was the result of a team of students discarding 3 weeks of effort trying to get their sequential robot to work with any degree of reliability. *Fluffy*'s strategy was absurdly simple. It just wandered around the playing field, scooping up balls that it happened to run over. It had two touch sensors and would back up and turn when either of them was triggered.

On the one hand, *Fluffy* was completely unpredictable: One never knew which balls it might collect. On the other hand, it was incredibly reliable—because it was so simple, it *always* got at least a few balls. By the scoring method of the contest, simply collecting balls scored the least number of points; returning them to your goal or placing them in the airstream scored many more points. During the contest, although all it could do was collect a few balls, *Fluffy* surprised everyone by *tying for second place* overall. Nearly all of the complex, sequential robots were at least as likely to fail completely and score no points as they were to score a sizable bounty, and *Fluffy* almost carried the day.

Although *Fluffy* may have seemed like an isolated phenomenon to the casual observer, it was not. Just about every year of the MIT contest, there are one or two robots with a similar story behind them as *Fluffy*: Students who became frustrated with repeated failures during the progress of their sequential robot design decided to rebuild a simple robot from scratch. With almost no time remaining, the only approach that seems viable is the reactive one (although students are not consciously making a decision between sequential and reactive).

Collecting Soda Cans with Reactive Control

While a graduate student at the Artificial Intelligence Laboratory at MIT, Jonathan Connell created a robotic arm that collected soda cans using the behavioral control principles of Prof. Rodney Brooks, his supervisor.

Connell's arm controller was based on a collection of 15 independent behaviors that operated with six levels of priority. The behaviors had names like Grab (which closed the hand anytime something broke a light sensor beam between two fingers), Excess (which prevented the hand from squeezing too hard), Extend and Over (which helped the arm move out and above a soda can), and Home (which brought the arm near to the robot's body).

Designed in the early 1980s, when today's advanced microprocessors were prohibitively expensive and complex, Connell's robot used a collection of simple 8-bit microprocessors—indeed, the same one used in the Handy Board—wired into a local network. Each microprocessor ran a couple of the behavior tasks, and if the robot needed computational power for new behaviors, Connell simply plugged in a new microprocessor board.

The surprise fact is that a last-ditch reactive machine comes in second or third place nearly every year of the MIT contest. The culture of the MIT contest is heavily weighted toward sequential machines, so the successes of the reactive machines are typically blamed on luck—people don't remember that in previous years, reactive machines have also done well.

Students in the MIT class tend to blame performance failures on particular component failures or unexpected circumstances, rather than reevaluating their overall control strategies. It requires a new way to think about design a system that works properly only as the result of many small interactions rather than a master plan.

5.4.4 Exercises: Reactive Control

1. *Reactive Groucho.* Based on the ideas of reactive robot control, reconsider the algorithmic *Groucho* program presented earlier. Would it be possible to devise an effective reactive control program for *Groucho*'s task?

   Figure 5.29 takes a stab at this challenge. There are eight separate behaviors at five priority levels. The main behaviors for getting work done are Search, Scoop, Deliver, Dump, and Return.

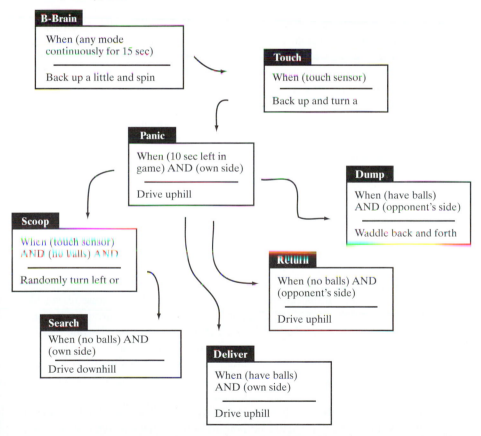

FIGURE 5.29 Priority Diagram of Possible Reactive *Groucho* Program

Here is how they work. Search activates when *Groucho* is on its own side and isn't carrying any balls, and drives the robot downhill—toward the ball trough, where balls should be waiting.

Scoop is intended to run after Search when *Groucho* reaches the far wall on its side. Then Scoop triggers and turns *Groucho* so that it can pick up some balls.

Deliver should trigger next, causing *Groucho* to drive uphill. When the robot drives over to the opponent's side, Dump activates, releasing the balls. Then Return can

become active when *Groucho* notices it is on the opponent's side and has no balls. Three supervisory processes help make sure *Groucho* doesn't get stuck as it performs its task. Panic will drive the robot onto the opponent's side (if it isn't already there) when the contest round is about to expire, as a safety measure. Touch makes sure that *Groucho* does not get wedged if it runs into a wall unexpectedly. Finally, B-Brain (see more about this in the later exercise) monitors all of the other behaviors and executes an emergency "get unstuck" action if it notices that *Groucho* has been lodged in the same task for too long.

(a) This collection of behaviors for getting *Groucho* to perform its job has not been tested. Do you think it would work? Why or why not? What are some problems with the approach? How can they be remedied?

(b) If you are not confident that the solution presented is viable, invent a different collection of behaviors that would be effective in getting *Groucho* to perform the ball collection and transportation task.

(c) With a *Groucho*-style robot and a *Robo-Pong* playing field, implement your choice of the solution presented, the solution with your modifications, or your approach (whichever you have the most confidence in). What surprised you as you tested the solution?

2. *Extending the Prioritization Framework.* The earlier in-depth discussion of the prioritization program is meant to (1) encourage use of the framework as it stands, and (2) serve as the basis for a variety of extensions to the idea. In this exercise, we implement two different extensions to the approach.

(a) *Dynamic Priorities.* The framework presented uses static robot task priorities that are established at start-up time and do not change. But there is no reason that a task's priority level could not be a dynamic quantity that varied depending on various internal and external factors.

Consider an example based on the *Groucho* robot task. Suppose that *Groucho* had several different strategies for searching for balls, some more conservative and others more aggressive and risky. At the start of the round, it would make sense to try the conservative approaches first, but, if these failed, to switch to the more aggressive search modes. A supervisory task could monitor the *Groucho*'s performance and elapsed time and then adjust other tasks' priority levels as it saw fit.

Describe other ways that *Groucho* could be improved with a dynamic task priority structure.

(b) *A-Brain, B-Brain.* In his famous book, *The Society of Mind*, one of the ideas that Marvin Minsky presented is a particular model of cognitive operation that he terms *A-Brain and B-Brain*. The idea is as follows: Suppose one part of the brain is directly connected to a creature's sensor and motor apparatus and is responsible for performing sensorimotor tasks such as hand–eye coordination. Call this part of the brain the "A-Brain." Other parts of the brain have no direct connection to the sensorimotor apparatus and are only connected to various A-Brains. These B-Brains then are perfectly situated to monitor how well the A-Brains are doing and should be able to notice unproductive loops or other failure modes that the A-Brains may have without them realizing it. Thus, the B-Brains are responsible for stimulating and suppressing A-Brain function to achieve maximum benefit for the organism.

This idea fits wonderfully into the reactive model of robot control. The earlier exercise presented a reactive program for *Groucho* that includes a simple B-Brain component that would notice if *Groucho* were stuck in a single behavior for too long.

Based on Minsky's concept, generalize this approach. For example, write a B-Brain function that notices if *Groucho* were to go back and forth between a pair of behaviors for several iterations. What other kinds of unproductive loops could be recognized? How would you do so?

5.5 Conclusion

In this chapter, we explored feedback control, including proportional and proportional-derivative feedback, which is the foundation for many process control applications in the world. The basis of feedback control is monitoring the state of a system and continuously providing a "negative correction" to move the system from its current state to the setpoint state of the feedback loop. Negative feedback is a powerful tool for building systems that perform correctly regardless of external environmental forces or internal performance variances.

Then we experimented with two different models of robot control: sequential control and reactive control.

Many devices in the world are based on sequential control models. Consider the ubiquitous automatic teller machine (ATM). Its various subsystems—a card reader, input/output terminal, bill counter, and bill dispenser—must work in tandem in a prescribed way for the machine to function properly. But ATMs have been known to fail for absurd reasons. Documented cases include an ATM that ran out of $20 bills; when a customer made the maximum withdrawal, the bill counter spat out a large number of $10 bills—too many for the bill dispenser to handle. Then some bills got stuck inside the machine, shunted to an emergency overflow chute rather than to the customer's hands.

Partly this is because any given ATM isn't designed by one engineer or even one engineering firm. Different pieces of the ATM system are subcontracted out to various firms, and if the firm that doles out the job did not completely consider every possible fashion that the subcomponents could interact with one another, there is the potential for failure.

These types of failures also occur because contemporary engineered systems are incredibly complex, consisting of myriad parts with exponentially increasing possibilities for unexpected interactions and then failures.

The moral here is not that the sequential model of control should be discarded—it is used effectively in multitudes of applications—but rather the need for a respect for the complexity that arises in real-world systems.

Reactive and behavioral control is a powerful and different way to think about control; it is biologically inspired and ideal for situations that are so complicated with unanticipated interactions that closed-form descriptions of the solution are not viable.

6 *Advanced Sensing*

This chapter presents a collection of sensor technologies more sophisticated than those presented in the main portions of this book, along with a discussion of various approaches to using sensor data in robot programs. The chapter consists of a series of sections, each of which deals with specific sensor technology. In the last section, several approaches to interpreting sensor data are presented.

In order, here are the contents of this chapter:

- *Quadrature shaft encoding* is a technique for measuring the rotation of axles that maintains accurate counts even when the axle's direction of rotation changes. This is a more sophisticated and powerful way to monitor rotation than was presented earlier.

- Earlier in the book, *infrared sensing* was used for simple proximity measures. Here we explore its use as a communications method, as well as more accurate ways to use it for measuring proximity.

- *Ultrasonic distance sensing* is studied as another way to glean distance information.

- A method of *optical distance sensing*, more accurate than the infrared methods in this chapter, is revealed.

- Techniques of *sensor data processing*, including maintaining histories of sensor trends, are discussed.

Throughout this chapter, the techniques presented are accompanied by driver code mostly written in 68HC11 assembly language. The driver code is in general accompanied by copious notes on its operation. The hope is that the reader can both learn about the specific challenge of supporting the sensor technology in question while also being informed of more general design techniques involving this low-level code. It is often the case that sensors require assembly language or other low-level support, and the collection of varied sensors with drivers presented in this chapter make up a good base of the programming techniques that are involved. It may be helpful to review the information in Appendix A when working through the code examples.

6.1 Quadrature Shaft Encoding

In chapter 3, we explored the use of break-beam sensors to perform shaft encoding—a way of keeping track of the rotation of an axle (see Section 3.8). In the basic shaft encoder method presented there, we were able to measure how far an axle had rotated and how fast it was going, but we could not tell when the axle changed direction. In this section, we study a more advanced technique known as *quadrature encoding*, which allows us to know the precise rotational position of an axle (as well as its velocity)—even when the axle changes its direction of travel.

224

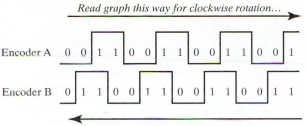

Read graph this way for clockwise rotation...

Encoder A   0   0   1   1   0   0   1   1   0   0   1   1   0   0   1

Encoder B   0   1   1   0   0   1   1   0   0   1   1   0   0   1   1

...Read graph this way for counter-clockwise rotation

FIGURE 6.1 Encoder Bit Streams for Quadrature Encoding

In the quadrature encoding technique, two encoders are mounted onto the same shaft, providing encoding streams that are one-quarter cycle (90 degrees) out of phase. One can imagine the encoder data streams standing still and traversing them forward or backward depending on the rotation of the shaft. Because of the 90-degree phase angle of the data streams, from any given position, only one encoder bit changes at a time. Depending on which bit changes, the direction of rotation can be determined.

Quadrature shaft encoding is used in a variety of robotic applications. It excels for position monitoring of "trapped systems," where the mechanics of a system limit travel between known stop positions. Examples of this type of system are rotary robot arms, where encoders are used to measure joint angles, and cartesian robots, where the rotation of a long worm screw moves a rack back and forth. Quadrature shaft encoding is also used to measure the motion of robot wheels as part of dead-reckoning robot positioning systems. By accumulating the result of a robot's wheels driving it along a surface, an estimate of overall translational movement can be made.

In the shaft encoding method explained earlier, a rotating shaft is equipped with a single break-beam sensor. By frequently monitoring the waveform from the sensor encoder, transitions can be counted, yielding a rotational position. In the quadrature method, a pair of encoders is used on a single shaft. The encoders are aligned so that their two data streams are one-quarter cycle (90 degrees) out of phase. When rapidly sampling the data from the two encoders, only one of the encoders will change state at a time. Which encoder changes determines the direction that the shaft is rotating. Figure 6.1 illustrates the idea.

To interpret a quadrature waveform, the pair of encoder signals is continuously monitored. Each iteration the signals are checked, and the current state of the encoders is compared with a previous state (which is recorded from the last time the signals were checked). Assuming the waveforms are checked frequently enough, *only one of the two encoders may change state between iterations*. This is the key to determining which direction the shaft is rotating (Figure 6.2).

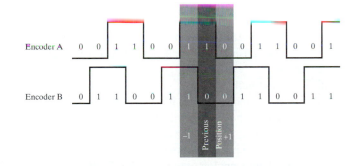

Encoder A   0   0   1   1   0   0   1   1   0   0   1   1   0   0   1

Encoder B   0   1   1   0   0   1   1   0   0   1   1   0   0   1   1

−1   Previous Position   +1

FIGURE 6.2 Example of a State Transition in Quadrature Data Stream

Suppose the encoders were previously at the position highlighted by the dark band (i.e., Encoder A as 1 and Encoder B as 0). The next time the encoders are checked, if they moved to the position AB = 00, the position count is incremented. If they moved to the position AB = 11, the position count is decremented.

A table of the four "previous state" possibilities (encoder AB = 00, 01, 10, or 11) and the four "current state" possibilities may be constructed. Each entry in the table corresponds to either no change (previous and current states are the same), a one-bit change (causing the count value to be incremented or decremented), or a two-bit change (which means something went wrong). Figure 6.3 shows a sample state transition table.

The remainder of this section presents construction techniques for building the mechanical portion of a quadrature encoder, explains the workings of a software driver, and presents exercises for further exploration.

FIGURE 6.3 State Transition Table for Quadrature Encoding

The state transition table spells out the transition rules for all possible state changes in the encoder data stream. If previous state and current state are the same, then there has been no change in position. Any single-bit change corresponds to either incrementing or decrementing the count. If there is a double-bit change, this corresponds to the encoders being misaligned or having moved too fast in between successive checks—an illegal transition.

Current State

		00	01	10	11
Previous State	00	0	+1	−1	′
	01	−1	0	′	+1
	10	+1	′	0	−1
	11	′	−1	+1	0

0 = no change
−1 = decrement count
+1 = increment count
′ = illegal transition
"01" = encoder A is 0, encoder B is 1

6.1.1 Construction Notes

Quadrature encoders may be built from scratch, scavenged from computer mice, or purchased as original equipment manufacturer (OEM) components. Let's consider each of these options in turn.

Figure 6.4 illustrates how to use a LEGO pulley wheel and two break-beam sensors in the quadrature configuration. The pulley wheel is just a convenient device to perform the function of alternately breaking and opening the light beams; any disk with holes or notches in it can serve equally well. Similarly, break-beam sensors can be the "U"-shaped integral variety or a pair of discrete LED emitters and detectors. The key is in the alignment, creating the quarter-cycle phase shift between the two encoders.

FIGURE 6.4 Using LEGO Pulley Wheel in Quadrature Encoding Configuration

A LEGO pulley wheel may be used with two break-beam optosensors to build a quadrature encoder. The two optosensors must be placed so that they are 90 degrees out of phase in reading the position of the wheel. In the diagram, the "A" encoder is fully blocked, whereas the "B" encoder is in the transition between being blocked and being open.

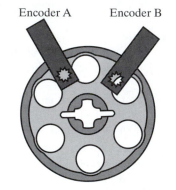

Encoder A   Encoder B

Quadrature shaft encoders are routinely used in computer mice to track the movements of the mouse ball. Each mouse has two quadrature encoders in it: one for horizontal ball movement, and the other for vertical ball movement. As shown in Figure 6.5, each encoder consists of an LED transmitter, a dual optical receiver, and a slotted wheel to interrupt the light beam.

When using either a hand-built encoder, such as that made with a LEGO pulley wheel, or an encoder based on mouse parts, it's important to shield the encoder optics from ambient light. Otherwise a burst of bright light could flood the detectors, causing the encoder to fail unexpectedly.

In the break-beam encoder application discussed earlier in Section 3.8, the break-beam sensors were plugged into analog inputs of the 68HC11. The driver presented here requires that the break-beam encoders are plugged into digital inputs; this will allow the encoder values to be sampled more frequently without incurring the overhead of the analog-to-digital conversion. For this reason, it is necessary that the light and dark (i.e., open and blocked) states of the encoder produce voltages that are amenable to the 68HC11's digital inputs. Specifically, the break-beam waveform should go at least as low as one volt and at least as high as four volts in normal operation.

It's also possible to buy a high-performance, enclosed quadrature shaft encoder module, such as the Clarostat model shown in Figure 6.6. Commercial encoders are very

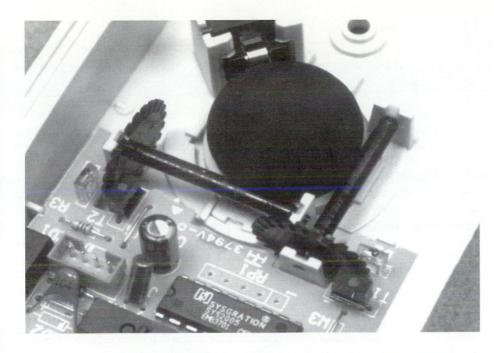

FIGURE 6.5 Close-Up of Quadrature Encoders in Computer Mouse

A standard computer mouse employs a pair of quadrature encoders to keep track of the mouse ball's movement. On either side of each slotted wheel encoder is a clear-colored LED emitter and a black-colored photodetector housing. Inside each photodetector housing are *two* detector elements precisely aligned to provide the quarter-cycle phase angle.

FIGURE 6.6 Clarostat Series 600 Optical Rotary Encoder

A commercial enclosed quadrature encoder typically operates off of a +5v supply and has two digital outputs providing the encoder stream.

easy to work with because they are optically shielded and nicely encased, ready to be mounted into a project. Also, commercial encoders, such as the Clarostat series 600, typically operate from a +5v supply and provide the encoder outputs on two digital signal lines. (For the Clarostat series 600, the red wire is +5v, the green wire is ground, and the yellow and orange wires are the encoder signals.)

The Clarostat series 600 is a very high-resolution device, providing 128 pulses per encoder channel per revolution—which are interpreted as 256 counts per revolution. By contrast, the six-hole LEGO pulley wheel encoder generates 12 pulses per channel per revolution, or 24 counts per revolution. Clarostat also makes lower resolution encoders.

On the down side, commercial encoders tend to be a little large and stiff and are somewhat pricey (about $40 each in unit quantities). The high-resolution models, rotating at higher speeds, can easily turn too fast for the 68HC11 driver code to keep up!

6.1.2 Driver Code

The technique for interpreting quadrature encoder signals is to repeatedly check the encoder state, looking for transitions and incrementing or decrementing a saved encoder count. A listing of a sample driver program, `qencdr10.asm`, is shown in Figures 6.7, 6.8, and 6.9.

To perform its periodic function of checking the encoder values, the driver "patches itself" into the Timer 4 interrupt, which is already set up by the Interactive C runtime software to operate at 1,000 Hz. This interrupt runs the "SystemInt" routine, which controls various system services during Handy Board operation, such as motor pulse width modulation (PWM) and LCD screen printing.

Figure 6.10 illustrates the patching technique. Initially, the TOC4 interrupt vector (at address $BFE2) points at the SystemInt routine, which terminates in an `RTI` return-from-interrupt instruction. The encoder routine is not linked into the interrupt structure.

The encoder routine installs itself by taking the pointer to the SystemInt routine out of the TOC4 vector location and storing the pointer into a `JMP` instruction located at the very end of the encoder routine. Then it replaces the TOC4 vector with a pointer to itself. When it's all done, on each interrupt, the new encoder routine runs first and then the original SystemInt runs.

The actual code to perform the vector patching is just four lines, beginning at the label `subroutine_initialize_module` (Figure 6.7). First, the D register is loaded from the TOC4 interrupt vector, yielding the pointer to the SystemInt routine (`ldd TOC4INT`). This pointer is then stored into the `jmp` instruction at the end of the encoder routine (`std interrupt_code_exit+1`). Then the pointer to the start of the encoder routine is loaded into the D register (`ldd #interrupt_code_start`). Finally, this pointer is stored back at the TOC4 vector location (`std TOC4INT`).

In principle, any number of additional periodic routines may attach themselves to the SystemInt routine in this fashion, with each one installing itself ahead of the previous one. As such, the TOC4 interrupt becomes a good shared resource for routines that wish to run periodically. As long as there are not so many routines that the whole system begins to bog down, this is an excellent way for any periodic driver to operate without having to use up the limited resources of another 68HC11 interrupt vector.

Working through the driver code, let's begin back at the top of the file, which has various constant definitions, including `system_time_lo`, which is defined to be $14. This location is used by the Interactive C runtime 68HC11 software to keep track of elapsed time in milliseconds. By checking this value, it is possible to tell how much time has elapsed. This is used in the velocity calculation, which performs a velocity measure about 16 times per second (every 64 times the routine is called).

Next are allocations for four memory variables used by the encoder routine. The first two begin with the text `variable_`, which makes them accessible from the C language portion of the Interactive C system. Here is how the four variables are used:

`variable_encoder10_counts` Current position of the encoder. Accessible from C as `encoder10_counts`.

`variable_encoder10_velocity` Current velocity of the encoder. Accessible from C as `encoder10_velocity`.

`encoder_state` The low two bits of this byte are the previous state of the encoder—00, 01, 10, or 11.

`last_counts` Encoder counts value from the last time the velocity was calculated.

After the declarations, the initialization routine is presented. When Interactive C loads binary modules, the code at label `subroutine_initialize_module` (if present) is

```
********************************************************************
* quaden10.asm                                                     *
*                                                                  *
* quadrature shaft encoder driver                                  *
* connect encoder to digital inputs 10 and 11                      *
*   (low two bits of digital input port)                           *
*                                                                  *
* Fred Martin        fredm@media.mit.edu       28 October 1996     *
********************************************************************


* 6811 registers
PORTA           equ     $1000
TOC4INT         equ     $BFE2       ; Timer Output Compare 4


* digital inputs
DIGIN           equ     $7000


* zero-page global variables
system_time_lo  equ     $14

        org     MAIN_START


* IC-accessible variables
variable_encoder10_counts           fdb     0
variable_encoder10_velocity         fdb     0


* internal variables
encoder_state                       fcb     0
last_counts                         fdb     0


* install module into 1 kHz IC system interrupt on TOC4
subroutine initialize_module:
        ldd     TOC4INT                 ; ptr to original vector
        std     interrupt_code_exit+1   ; install for our exit
        ldd     #interrupt_code_start   ; ptr to our routine
        std     TOC4INT                 ; install at TOC4 int


* reset encoder variables
        ldd     #0
        std     variable_encoder10_counts
        std     variable_encoder10_velocity
        std     last_counts

        ldaa    DIGIN
        anda    #3              ; mask low bits
        staa    encoder_state

        rts
```

FIGURE 6.7 Quadrature Encoder Driver qencdr10.asm, 1 of 3

FIGURE 6.8 Quadrature Encoder
Driver qencdr10.asm, 2 of 3

```
* encoder interrupt code:
*    check for transition every time called (1000 Hz)
*    calculate velocities at about 16 Hertz (ex-
actly: 1000 / 64 Hz.)
interrupt_code_start:
        ldx     #encoder_table

* get shaft encoder bits
        ldab    DIGIN
        andb    #3                  ; mask low bits
        pshb                        ; save it
        lslb                        ; times 2
        abx

* add in last state, rotated up 3 bits
        ldab    encoder_state
        lslb
        lslb
        lslb
        abx

* get increment from table
        ldd     0,X

**** optional clicking *****
** comment out to silence **
        beq     encoder_add
        pshb
        ldab    PORTA
        eorb    #8        ; piezo bit
        stab    PORTA
        pulb
****************************
encoder_add:
        addd    variable_encoder10_counts
        std     variable_encoder10_counts

* save new state
        pulb
        stab    encoder_state

* calc velocities every 64 calls
        ldaa    system_time_lo+1        ; lowest byte
        anda    #%00111111              ; mask off two high bits
        bne     interrupt_code_exit

* velocities are ticks since last interrupt
        ldd     variable_encoder10_counts
        subd    last_counts
        std     variable_encoder10_velocity
        ldd     variable_encoder10_counts
        std     last_counts

interrupt_code_exit:
        jmp     $0000    ; value poked in by init routine
```

```
encoder_table
* previous state 00
        fdb     0
        fdb     1
        fdb     -1
        fdb     0
* previous state 01
        fdb     -1
        fdb     0
        fdb     0
        fdb     1
* previous state 10
        fdb     1
        fdb     0
        fdb     0
        fdb     -1
* previous state 11
        fdb     0
        fdb     -1
        fdb     1
        fdb     0
```

FIGURE 6.9 Quadrature Encoder Driver qencdr10.asm, 3 of 3

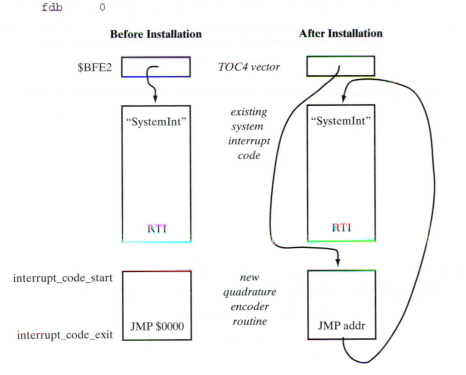

Before Installation

$BFE2

"SystemInt"

RTI

interrupt_code_start

interrupt_code_exit

JMP $0000

After Installation

TOC4 vector

existing system interrupt code

"SystemInt"

RTI

new quadrature encoder routine

JMP addr

FIGURE 6.10 Patching the System Interrupt with Encoder Routine

automatically executed. This routine performs the vector patching just discussed, initializes the four variables, and exits.

Listed in Figure 6.8 is the main encoder routine—the portion that is patched in by the initialization, and runs 1,000 times per second. Its first action is to load the X register with a pointer to the encoder table (shown in Figure 6.9). Then the B register is loaded with the current encoder bits, shifted left by one bit position. The B register thus contains the number 0, 2, 4, or 6 depending on the encoder value and is then added to the X register pointer.

Next the previously saved encoder state is added into the X register, this time shifted up by three bit positions (multiplied by eight). Thus, the previous encoder state acts a pointer to the proper table block, and the current encoder state chooses one item from that block. The X pointer is then dereferenced, loading the table value (0, −1, or +1) into the D register.

Next is a block of code that will generate a "click" on the Handy Board's piezo beeper if the D register is not zero (i.e., if there has been a change in the encoder position value). This click code is quite useful for debugging, but can be disabled by commenting out the code and rebuilding the driver's ICB file. The click code works by exclusive-ORing a "1" with the output bit in the PORTA register that controls the piezo voltage, thus toggling the piezo pin.

After the click code, the offset in the D register is added to the tally of encoder counts. The current encoder state, which was saved when it was first examined, is stored into the `encoder_state` variable for the next time through the routine.

Last is the calculation of the velocity. This is only done when the lowest six bits of the lowest byte of the system time are zero—in other words, once every 64 iterations of the encoder loop, or about 16 times per second. The velocity is calculated by subtracting the saved count reading from the last velocity measure from the current count value; then the current count value is stored into the `last_counts` variable. More frequent updates to the velocity measure can be made; smaller velocity readings will result.

The routine exits with a jump instruction. The source code shows a location of 0 as the destination of the jump, but remember that the address of the original SystemInt routine (or possibly the address of the last patched routine) is stored in this jump instruction by driver's initialization routine. This technique allows dynamic loading of drivers, but requires that the actual driver code is stored in RAM so that the code may be self-modifying, rewriting itself at run time.

6.1.3 Using the Driver

The `qencdr10.asm` driver assumes that the quadrature signals will be plugged into the two lowest bits of the Handy Board's digital input port. These bits are digital inputs 10 and 11 as labeled on the board. As mentioned earlier, it is important that the break-beam sensor hardware produce valid signals for digital inputs, with logic lows not higher than 1 volt and logic highs not lower than 4 volts.

To load the driver, type "`load qencdr10.icb`" at the IC prompt. On loading, the variables `encoder10_counts` and `encoder10_velocity` are defined in the C environment. These values may be used just like any other C variable. For example, to print the current encoder counts, try:

```
printf("counts %d\n", encoder10_counts);
```

The velocity variable is used in the same fashion.

To reset the encoder count to zero, simply set the variable to zero:

```
encoder10_counts = 0;
```

Note that there may be a spike in the velocity value when then encoder counts are reset. For example, if the encoder counts are 10000 and then reset to 0, the next velocity calculation will reflect this instantaneous jump in encoder position! The velocity calculation after the faulty one will be accurate again.

6.1.4 Quadrature Encoder Exercises

1. *Hysteresis.* In the simple encoder method, the analog waveform of a single enco-der channel is sampled and high/low transitions are counted (Section 3.8). In this

method, hysteresis is used to prevent false triggering when the encoder transitions between the high and low states. Why is hysteresis not employed in the algorithm for quadrature encoding?

2. *Additional drivers.* Modify the `qencdr10.asm` code for additional quadrature encoders plugged into digital input positions 12/13 and 14/15.

3. *Higher performance.* The encoder routine fails when the encoder state changes so rapidly that the encoder moves two positions in between calls to the encoder routine. Because the encoder routine operates at 1,000 Hz, the maximum rate the routine can support is 1,000 counts per second.

   For high-resolution encoders rotating at higher speeds, this might not be adequate. One solution is to increase the number of times per second that the encoder routine runs, but this can add excessive background computation to the 68HC11 system, reducing the amount of CPU time for the main robot behavior program.

   An alternate solution is to redefine the "illegal transition" states in the encoder table. If the encoders have moved two states in between checks, it's a good bet that they are turning fast. Rather than just leaving the encoder tally untouched when one of these double transitions occurs, the routine can add a +2 or −2 to the count tally—*based on the sign of the stored velocity.*

   Modify the encoder routine to function as described, and verify whether the software can now keep up with a more rapid stream of encoder pulses.

4. *Proportional-derivative control.* Perform the set of experiments described in Section 5.2, *Proportional-Derivative Control*, which require the use of a quadrature encoder.

6.2 Infrared Sensing

In chapter 3, we used a simple form of infrared (IR) sensing. An IR emitter LED provided a beam of light, which was either

- reflected off the surface and picked up by an IR detector (reflectivity sensing), or
- aimed directly at an IR detector, but interrupted by a disk with a cut-out, alternately allowing and blocking the light from passing (break-beam sensing).

This type of IR sensing is exactly analogous to using a light bulb, candle flame, or other constant light source with a visible-light photocell sensor. The sensor simply reports the amount of overall illumination, including both ambient (e.g., room) lighting and the light from the light source.

In this configuration, IR transmitters and detectors offer advantages over resistive photocells. They are quicker to respond to light changes, so they are well suited to the break-beam shaft encoding application (as discussed in the earlier chapter and previous section). They are more sensitive, so with proper shielding from ambient light sources can detect small changes in lighting levels.

There is yet a more powerful way to use IR sensing. By rapidly turning on and off the source of light, a technique called *modulation*, the source of light can be easily picked up from varying background illumination—even if the actual amount of modulated light is very small. Great insensitivity to background ambient lighting can be accomplished. This is how television remote controls work; IR LEDs in the remote control transmit rapid flashes of light, which are decoded by a device in the television.

The advent of widespread use of IR remote control has made the demodulating circuits (the device in the TV) quite inexpensive and easy to use. What previously required several integrated circuits is now available in a single package and at low cost (about US$3 in

FIGURE 6.11 GP1U52 and
GP1U52 IR Demodulators

IS1U60   GP1US2

small experimental quantities). Figure 6.11 shows two common IR demodulators, the
IS1U60 and the GP1U52, both manufactured by Sharp.

Let's explore the variety of ways that this commercial IR technology can be put to
use in robotic applications.

6.2.1 Modulation and Demodulation

The basic principle of IR modulation is that, by flashing a light source at a particular
frequency, the flashes of light at that same frequency can be detected (demodulation)
even if they are very weak with respect to overall lighting conditions.

Figure 6.12 illustrates this process. The upper graph indicates an IR LED being turned
on in two successive bursts. Each burst consists of a number of very rapid on–off pulses
of light (modulation). The lower graph shows the output from the IR detector. During
the rapid on–off bursts, the demodulator indicates "detection"; in between the bursts, the
demodulator sees no IR activity and indicates "no detection."

In other words, when the detector "sees" the flashes of light, it indicates "true."

There are a few details worth considering, however. Most important, the demodulator
is tuned to a specific frequency of light flashes. Commercial IR demodulators can be
obtained for a variety of frequencies, ranging from about 32 kHz to 45 kHz. All of these
frequencies are high enough to avoid interference effects from common indoor lighting
sources, like florescent lights.

In the experiments here, we assume the use of a demodulator tuned to 40 kHz (40,000
flashes per second). As indicated in the figure, this corresponds to a flash period of 25
μsec (0.000025 seconds). This means that the sum of the "on time" and "off time" for
each flash must be 25 μsec. (It happens that it is not critical that the on and off time be
exactly equal; if each flash consisted of a 10 μsec on pulse and a 15 μsec off interval,
that would work fine.)

Another detail in the diagram is the voltage level output of the IR demodulator.
Notice that it outputs five volts when there is no detection and zero volts during detection.

FIGURE 6.12 Idealized Response
of Infrared Demodulator

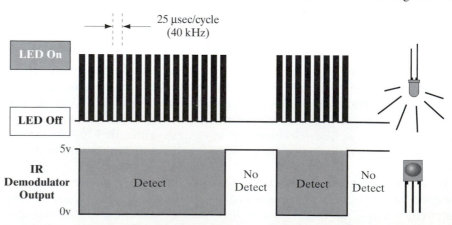

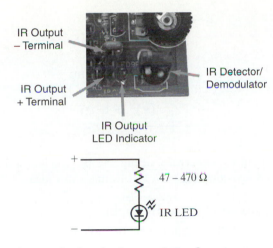

FIGURE 6.13 Handy Board IR Output Port, Indicator LED, and Detector

IR Output – Terminal

IR Detector/ Demodulator

IR Output + Terminal

IR Output LED Indicator

47 – 470 Ω

IR LED

FIGURE 6.14 Minimal Circuit for IR LED Emitter

In the minimal circuit for an IR LED emitter, the IR LED is wired in series with a resistor. The resistor serves to limit the amount of current through the LED, thus determining its brightness and distance from which it can be detected. Without the resistor, the LED will illuminate too brightly and will burn out.

This response—negative true logic—is characteristic of most commercial IR demodulator devices. This is worth noting as a detail that can be frustrating when you're trying to debug a circuit!

Notice that the caption for Figure 6.12 indicates that this is an idealized representation of the demodulation process. Indeed, the diagram obscures an effect that, although not important in the next few experiments, is important later. The diagram suggests that the IR demodulator detects the IR light bursts immediately as they occur. This is not actually true; in practice, the demodulator must receive several cycles of light, usually 5 to 10, at the proper frequency before indicating detection. This property is discussed later on in this chapter.

The Handy Board's IR Transmit Circuit

The Handy Board includes special hardware for generating the 40 kHz "carrier" frequency needed for IR transmission, as well as a power transistor for driving IR LED emitters. Here we explain how to use the Handy Board's IR output and defer the discussion of how the circuit works to Appendix A.

The Handy Board's IR output circuit is controlled by the 68HC11's timer output 2. This output is mapped to Bit 6 of the 68HC11's Port A register, which is located at address 0x1000. So, for example, to turn on the IR output, one can execute the following command from Interactive C:

```
bit_set(0x1000, 0x40);
```

After running this command, the visible red LED near the IR output port should light up (see Figure 6.13). This indicates that the Handy Board is powering the IR output. Remember, however, that the IR output is not just "on," but rather is turning on and off—modulating—at a frequency of 40 kHz.

Connecting a Single IR LED

Figure 6.14 illustrates how to connect an IR LED emitter to the Handy Board's IR output. As shown in the schematic, a resistor must be used in series with the IR LED. This resistor limits the amount of current through the LED; values in the range of 47 ohms (brightly lit) to 470 ohms (moderately lit) are typically used.

The Handy Board's IR output port generates a 5-volt level, and typical LEDs, including IR LEDs, require about 2 volts to operate. Therefore, it's possible to put two LEDs in series, with one current-limiting resistor.

A good practical idea is to wire a standard red or green LED in series with the infrared LED. This way, it's easy to tell when power is running through the LED circuit because

FIGURE 6.15 Suggested Circuit for Infrared LED Emitter

In the suggested circuit for an IR LED emitter, a visible LED is wired in series with the IR LED and current-limiting resistor. The visible LED—any standard red or green one will do—greatly facilitates debugging by lighting up when the circuit is powered.

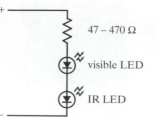

the visible LED will light up. Otherwise, debugging IR circuits can be difficult because infrared light is indeed invisible! Figure 6.15 illustrates this idea.

Detecting Continuous Modulated IR Light

With either of the previous LED circuits (single IR LED or IR LED plus visible LED), it's possible to begin experimenting with infrared detection. First, build the IR LED/resistor assembly (see Appendix B.3 for construction notes). Plug it into the Handy Board's IR output port and execute the `bit_set()` command required to enable the IR transmission:

```
bit_set(0x1000, 0x40);
```

The red IR output LED indicator should turn on; if your LED transmitter has a series visible LED, this should also light. If your transmitter does not have the visible LED, make sure the cathode end of the IR LED is plugged into the negative terminal of the Handy Board's IR port.

Next, run the following line of code. This will poll the Handy Board's IR detector and set the state of motor output 0 based on it. If the Handy Board IR detector indicates no IR detection, the motor output will light its green LED; if the detector registers IR the red output will be lit:

```
while (1) {if (peek(0x1000) & 4) fd(0); else bk(0);}
```

This test makes use of the fact that the Handy Board's IR detector is connected to Bit 2 of the 68HC11's Port A register, which is located at address `0x1000`. The loop repeatedly tests Bit 2 by "AND'ing" together (using the "`&`" operator) the byte at address `0x1000` with the number 4, which is `00000100` in binary. This yields either binary `00000100` or `00000000`—decimal 4 or 0—depending on the state of the relevant bit. The `if` statement then accepts 4 as true, running the `fd(0)` command, or 0 as false, running the `bk(0)` command.

Now, when the IR transmitter is aimed at the Handy Board's IR detector, the motor 0 output should light the red LED. Try it and notice that IR light bounces off many surfaces. Hence, if your IR LED is very bright, it might be difficult to *not* allow the IR detector to sense the IR energy! Unplug the IR transmitter to check whether the motor 0 output is continuously red, indicating detection.

Running this little test-and-display loop, the Handy Board becomes a portable IR detector. Try out various sources of modulated IR light; for example, remote controls for various consumer electronics devices. Most are compatible with the Handy Board's IR detector.

Also notice that various other illumination sources produce large amounts of IR energy. Light from halogen lamps and direct sunlight (even through tinted office windows) have large amounts of IR energy and overwhelm the IR detector (although they are not modulated at 40 kHz). Experiment with these light sources to learn about the limitations of the IR emitter/detector technology.

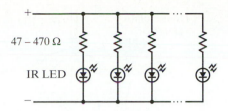

FIGURE 6.16 Correct Method of Connecting Multiple IR LEDs

To connect multiple IR LED transmitters to the Handy Board's output, provide each LED with its own current-limiting resistor.

Connecting Multiple IR LEDs

The Handy Board's IR output circuit is capable of driving many LED transmitters as long as they are connected properly. Figure 6.16 illustrates how multiple IR LEDs should be connected to the single Handy Board output driver.

Notice that each parallel strand of LEDs has its own current-limiting resistor. This is necessary because of the electrical properties of LEDs: When an LED begins conducting electricity, the voltage differential across its terminal drops slightly. Thus, if the LEDs were connected directly in parallel, as in Figure 6.17, the first LED that began conducting would drop in voltage and then receive all of the through current.

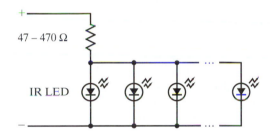

FIGURE 6.17 Incorrect Method of Connecting Multiple IR LEDs

This method of connecting multiple LEDs will *not* work. When power is applied, the first LED to conduct drops in voltage and accepts all of the through current. Provide an individual resistor for each parallel LED strand as illustrated in Figure 6.16.

Each parallel strand may have multiple LEDs wired in series, however. For example, Figure 6.18 shows three strands, one of which has a pair of LEDs in series (one IR and one visible). This is acceptable practice because each resistor provides the appropriate current through the corresponding strand of one or more LEDs.

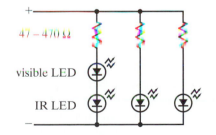

FIGURE 6.18 Mixed One- and Two-LED Per Strand Wiring

The example shows correct wiring that mixes one or two LEDs per parallel strand. The first strand has two LEDs: one visible and one IR. The second and third strands have just the IR LED. The wiring works properly because each strand has its own current-limiting resistor.

It is also possible to have different amounts of power through each parallel LED by having differently valued resistors for each.

6.2.2 Proximity Sensing

Using the simple modulated output of an IR LED and an IR demodulator, it's possible to build an effective *proximity sensor*. With a proximity sensor, the light from the IR emitter is reflected back into detector by a nearby object, indicating whether an object is present. This is just like the simple (not modulated) reflectance sensors discussed in Section 3.6.

Figure 6.19 illustrates the idea. An LED emitter and detector are pointed in the same direction so that when an object enters the proximity of the emitter–detector pair, light from the emitter is reflected off the object and into the detector.

FIGURE 6.19 Proximity Sensing Concept Drawing

With proximity sensing, the light from an LED emitter reflects off an object in the proximity and into an LED detector.

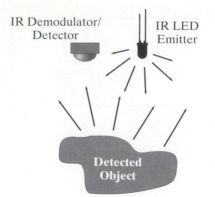

This kind of simple true–false proximity sensing is an ideal application for modulated/demodulated IR light sensing. Compared to simple reflected light magnitude sensing, modulated light is far less susceptible to environmental variables like amount of ambient light and reflectivity of different objects.

6.2.3 Using Proximity Sensors

The Emitter

When constructing a proximity sensor, it is necessary to shield the light from the emitter from directly entering the detector. Especially because most IR detectors are extremely sensitive, with auto-gain circuits that amplify minute levels of light, shielding can be a real issue. If light from the emitter can bleed directly into the detector, the sensor will be rendered useless.

One of the simplest and most effective ways to shield the emitter LED is with black heat-shrink tubing. The tubing can be placed around the base of the LED emitter and extend straight outward. After shrinking the tubing, it can be cut to length with a scissors, providing an easy way of tuning the amount of light output.

The Detector

There are two common varieties of modulated IR detectors: the highly integrated type used on the Handy Board, and the older, but more common, "tin can" type. (See Figure 6.20 for a photograph of these two styles.)

Both detectors produce a digital output than can be simply connected to the Handy Board. The detectors require a 5-volt power supply, which can be provided from any of the Handy Board's sensor connectors. The detector's digital output is then wired to a Handy Board signal input (analog or digital). (Full construction notes for wiring IR emitters and detectors are provided in Appendix B.)

The completed IR emitter/detector pair is shown in Figure 6.21. The emitter plugs into the Handy Board IR output port, and the detector plugs into any Handy Board sensor port. To test the sensor, let's use a simple program that turns on the Handy Board's

FIGURE 6.20 Two Styles of IR Detector/Demodulator

On the left is the modern, highly integrated IR detector manufactured by Sharp Electronics. On the right is the older "tin can" style, which is still widely used and more readily available.

FIGURE 6.21 Completed IR Emitter/Detector Pair

beeper if the detector registers "true" and turns it off otherwise. Plug the detector into digital sensor port 7 and run the following sequence of commands from the Interactive C command line:

```
set_beeper_pitch(1000.);                /* beep at 1000 Hz. */
bit_set(0x1000, 0x40);                  /* turn on IR output */
while (1) {if (digital(7)) beeper_on(); else beeper_off();}
                           /* beep based on the state of the IR detector */
```

Now bring your hand in front of the sensor and the Handy Board should beep.

6.2.4 IR LED Exercises

1. *Current through LED/resistor circuits.* Mentioned earlier is the need for a series resistor in LED driver circuits, which limits the current through the LED. In this exercise, we explore this matter in greater depth.

   (a) Assume the two-LED/one-resistor circuit shown in Figure 6.15, that each LED has a normal voltage drop of 2.0 volts, and that this circuit is to be plugged into the Handy Board's standard +5v IR output driver. What value of resistor is needed to obtain a current of 20 mA through the LEDs when the driver circuit is turned on? Show your calculations.

   (b) Build the circuit and plug into a regulated +5v supply (either the Handy Board's own sensor voltage supply or a bench power supply). Measure the voltage drops across the LEDs and the resistor, and determine the current through the circuit. Does it match your calculated result? Why or why not?

   (c) What will the *average* current through your LED/resistor circuit be when plugged into the Handy Board's IR output driver? Hint: Remember the 40 kHz modulation.

2. *Infrared noise sources.* There are many everyday sources of IR light that can interfere with IR proximity sensing. Experiment with sunlight (outdoor and through windows), florescent lighting, incandescent lighting, and halogen lighting.

   (a) Which (or all) of these cause spurious signals on the IR demodulator? Use tone feedback (or red/green motor LED) feedback on the Handy Board to determine when the IR demodulator indicates detection.

   (b) Using an oscilloscope to observe the IR demodulator output, repeat the tests. Is there any periodicity or other regularity in the interference from any of the illumination sources? If so, describe.

3. *Detection range.* Different objects having different amounts of reflectivity to IR light should be detectable at different distances. For instance, a shiny white card should be visible at a much further distance than a dull black object, which might not be detectable at all.

   With your standard IR emitter–detector pair, experiment with detection ranges of common objects and describe your results.

4. *Wall following and obstacle avoidance.* With one IR proximity sensor, write a wall-following routine for *HandyBug*. Compare its functionality to earlier wall followers based on nonmodulated IR reflectivity.

   Add another IR proximity sensor facing forward and add a behavior so that *HandyBug* avoids running into obstacles in its path. Compare the types of obstacles that IR avoidance is successful with versus touch sensing. Add a behavior to *HandyBug* to enable touch sensing obstacle avoidance as well.

6.2.5 Advanced IR Proximity Sensing

The proximity sensing discussed so far provides only binary data: Is there an object in view of the sensor or is there not? Although this is certainly a useful sensor to have, it's also quite limited. It would be much more powerful to know *how far away* an object is.

Although this would seem obvious, it is somewhat tricky to coax distance information from commercial IR demodulators. Remember that they are designed to receive IR data communications from hand-held remote controls. From the point of view of the engineer who designs these IR demodulators, it should work equally whether the user is a few inches or tens of feet away. Indeed these common IR demodulators include high-gain amplifiers that convert both weak and strong IR signals into stable levels to be fed into the frequency detection circuitry.

Nevertheless, there are still techniques available for extracting signal strength information, which translates into range data. The two techniques we discuss here are:

- Tapping into the IR demodulator circuit and measuring a voltage that corresponds to the signal strength.

- Detuning the IR emitter's modulation frequency, looking for the point at which the IR demodulator loses detection.

Inside the IR Demodulator

Figure 6.22 is a functional block diagram of IR demodulators made by Sharp Electronics; other manufacturers' demodulators have a similar architecture. As a prelude to experiments that take advantage of its "undocumented" peculiarities, let's examine how it works in some detail.

The sequence of information flow is from the left side of the diagram to the right. First, the infrared photodiode (1) receives infrared signals that are amplified (2) and limited (3).

FIGURE 6.22 Block Diagram of Sharp Electronics IR Demodulator

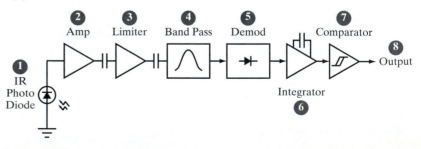

This normalized signal is then run into a band pass filter (4), which allows only a specific frequency of signal (e.g., 40 kHz) to pass through. Actually, this is an idealization of the band pass filter's performance; real band pass filters have a center frequency for which signals pass through best, and then a sloping curve that describes how much off-center frequencies are attenuated.

The Gaussian-shaped illustration in the band pass filter diagram suggests this attenuation curve. Ultimately, this means that even if an IR demodulator is tuned to a specific center frequency, it will detect other frequencies, with a desensitized response as the frequency moves farther away from the center point.

After the band pass, the signal contains predominantly a wave at the center frequency of the band pass or no signal at all. This wave is then rectified by the demodulator (5). The demodulator is just a diode that turns the wave into a series of positive pulses.

These pulses are fed into the integrator (6), which has a capacitor to store a brief history of incoming pulses. The more regular the pulse stream (corresponding to a steady signal at the center frequency of band pass), the larger the output of the integrator.

The integrator's output is given to the comparator (7), which measures it against an internal threshold. When the integrator's signal is above a threshold, the comparator signals "true" at the output (8); otherwise it signals "false."

The $\varPi$ symbol in the comparator block diagram indicates that the comparator functions with hysteresis (i.e., it has a bit of a latching function when interpreting the integrator's output). In a function with hysteresis, there are two separate thresholds: one for a rising input and one for a falling input. When the input is rising, it must reach above a higher threshold to be registered as high; when it is falling, it must fall below a lower threshold to be registered as low. By putting hysteresis in the comparator, small fluctuations of the input signal—which might happen to be about a single threshold, if there were just one—are ignored.

Armed with this information about how IR demodulators work, let's explore two different ways of obtaining signal-strength information from them.

Tapping Analog Signal Levels

As shown in Figure 6.22, the signal between the integrator and comparator represents the strength of the received and filtered modulated IR light. On many commercial IR demodulators, this signal—the integrator output—is present as a circuit trace on the demodulators' printed circuit board.

Figure 6.23 shows the inside of the Sharp GP1U52 IR demodulator, pointing to the printed circuit board trace that carries the demodulated signal strength information. The voltage level on this signal is an indicator of how much modulated energy the IR sensor

Top side of
Sharp GPIU52x

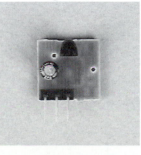

Bottom side of
Sharp GPIU52x

Analog Singal
Strength tap

FIGURE 6.23 Sharp GP1U52 IR Demodulator and Signal Strength PCB Trace

is receiving. On a typical GP1U52 sensor, this voltage varies from 1.7v (no signal) to 2.5v (strong signal).

This signal-strength level was never designed to drive external circuitry, however, and it is very sensitive to noise and electrical loading. The signal may be readily measured by a high-impedance digital voltmeter or oscilloscope probe, but it cannot be connected to a normal Handy Board analog input. This is because of the 47K pull-up resistor connected from each Handy Board analog sensor input to the +5v supply. The pull-up resistor creates too much of a load for the output of the IR demodulator's integrator component, and the circuit stops functioning.

There are several options for interfacing the integrator signal to the Handy Board. One is to remove the 47K pull-up resistor on a particular Handy Board sensor input and run the integrator signal to that input. It is easy enough to remove a pull-up resistor by cutting the printed circuit board (PCB) trace that connects the Handy Board sensor input pin to the corresponding pull-up resistor, which is part of the RP3 resistor pack. The relevant PCB traces are located on the underside of the Handy Board (the solder side), so they may easily be cut.

Of course, modifications to the Handy Board are inconvenient because then one must remember which analog inputs have had their pull-up resistor disabled. Most other sensors (e.g., the simple photocell light sensor) require the onboard pull-up resistor to function properly.

Another method of interfacing the GP1U52 signal-strength output is to build a simple circuit that buffers the IR demodulator from the Handy Board's pull-up resistor. The operational amplifier, or op-amp, is a common and inexpensive device that can be used to build such as circuit.

Figure 6.24 shows a schematic for such an op-amp circuit, using the LM358 op-amp—a simple and cheap operational amplifier that comes as two op-amps in an eight-pin DIP package. One of the two op-amps available is used in a configuration known as the "voltage follower." In the circuit, the input voltage (i.e., the signal from the IR demodulator) is wired to the op-amp's + input, and the op-amp output is connected back to its − input in a feedback configuration. This wiring causes the op-amp output to track (or follow) the voltage on the + input (see sidebar "How to Use Op-Amps").

This circuit works fine. However, because the sensor's signal-strength level only varies from 1.7 volts to 2.5 volts, much of the potential resolution of the 68HC11's analog-to-digital converter is wasted. Specifically, the 1.7-volt level corresponds to a digital reading of about 87, and 2.5 volts is about 128 (the zero-to-5v input is mapped to an output byte from 0 to 255). Thus, the whole range of the sensor is about 42 counts, or only 16% of the entire possible range.

FIGURE 6.24 Op-Amp Follower Circuit with Sharp GP1U52 Sensor

When used in the "voltage follower" configuration (the output tied to the − input), the op-amp's output follows its + input. Because the output is capable of driving a fair bit of current, the circuit acts as a buffer between sensitive devices and low-impedance circuits.

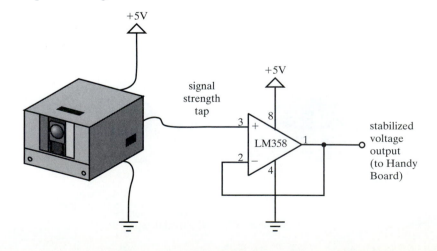

Figure 6.25 shows a dual op-amp circuit that amplifies the GP1U52's voltage level to a wider band within the zero-to-5v analog input range. The circuit conveniently uses both op-amps in the LM358 package.

Here's how the circuit works. The first stage is just the voltage follower shown in Figure 6.24. This produces the 1.7v-to-2.5v output on Pin 1 of the '358 (for the GP1U52 sensor; other IR demodulators with a similar internal signal-strength level might produce a different voltage range).

This signal is not directly amplified because it would soon reach off the scale of the output of the '358. Instead, three 1N4148 diodes are used to "subtract" a fixed amount from this signal. This works because each diode has a characteristic voltage drop of 0.6 volts; three of them in series will produce a voltage drop of 1.8 volts.

The 1K resistor is wired from the cathode (minus) end of the diode triplet to ground. This resistor is necessary to draw some current through the diodes and thereby produce the desired 0.6v drop each. If only minute amounts of current are flowing through the diodes (i.e., the amount that would be required by an op-amp alone), not enough current would flow to produce the voltage drop.

This corrected voltage is fed into the second op-amp stage (Pin 5). This second op-amp is wired in what is know as the "noninverting amplifier" configuration. The voltage gain of the op-amp is $1 + R_2/R_1$. If the recommended values of 1K for R_1 and 3.3K for R_2 are used, the circuit will have a gain of 4.3. The maximum output of the circuit will be when the IR demodulator produces a 2.5v signal level. After the 1.8v diode drop, this yields 0.7 volts, which multiplied by 4.3 is 3.01 volts, the maximum output of the whole circuit. Thus, the sensor works over a solid 60% of the possible range of the analog inputs—a large improvement over the 16% of the raw sensor value.

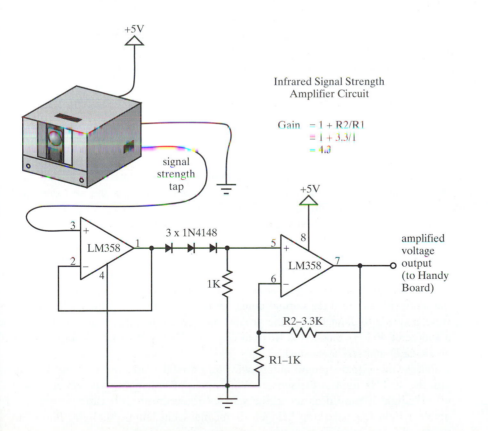

Infrared Signal Strength
Amplifier Circuit

Gain $= 1 + R2/R1$
      $= 1 + 3.3/1$
      $= 4.3$

FIGURE 6.25 Op-Amp Follower Plus Amplifier with Sharp GP1U52 Sensor

How to Use Op-Amps

The operational amplifier is essentially an amplifier with a very large gain; typical op-amps have a gain factor of about 10,000. In other words, what the op-amp does is take the voltage level at the + input and subtract the voltage level at the − input, multiply this voltage by 10,000, and put that result on its output.

Of course, the op-amp can't produce a voltage higher than its supply voltage or lower than ground. So if used simply as a voltage difference multiplier, the output will typically swing to the rails—a voltage difference of just 0.0005 volts between the two inputs will result in a full-scale output voltage swing (assuming a +5v supply). In fact, op-amps are often used as *comparators* in this open-loop mode. If the + input is greater than the −, the output will be +5v; if the + input is less than the −, the output will be 0v (again assuming a +5v supply).

In the voltage follower configuration shown in Figure 6.25, the op-amp output is tied to the − input. This creates a feedback loop in which the output will follow the + input. Suppose the + input is 2.5v and (for whatever reason) the output were 0v—the + minus − input would be a large positive value, and the output would be driven to the positive voltage supply rail (+5v). Then the + minus − input would become a negative value, and the output would be driven to 0v. The oscillatory process quickly dampens out, and the op-amp finds a stable state where the output voltage is essentially equal to the input voltage.

As described by Horowitz & Hill in *The Art of Electronics* as the first golden rule of op-amps, the output does whatever it can to make the voltage difference between the two inputs (essentially) equal to zero. This simple rule will go a long way toward understanding op-amp circuits.

Why not use a larger gain in the second stage to bring the maximum output closer to 5 volts? The answer lies in a limitation in the the LM358 chip: It can only produce an output voltage as high as its supply voltage *minus 1.5 volts*. Thus, with a 5-volt supply, the best a '358 can do is 3.5 volts. So a gain of about 4 to 5 is the best one can use unless it is desired to chop off the top end of the signal's range—possibly a valid design decision to gain greater sensitivity along the lower portion of the range.

Exercises

1. *Measuring the signal-strength level.* Disassemble a GP1U52 sensor and connect a wire to the point shown in Figure 6.23. Re-assemble the sensor, running this wire out alongside of the three normal connection pins. Apply +5v power to the sensor (remembering to connect both the ground pin and the metal case to ground) and get a source of 40 kHz modulated IR light (e.g., the Handy Board's IR output port with an IR LED and series resistor).

   Connect your signal-strength output wire to a digital voltmeter or oscilloscope and aim the 40 kHz light at the sensor. What range of voltage do you observe as the 40 kHz light is moved closer to the sensor? Experiment with various sources of ambient light (e.g., desktop halogen or incandescent lamps, sunlight, florescent light)—do they interfere with the signal-strength reading?

FIGURE 6.26 Dead-Bug
Construction of GP1U52
Sensor/LM358 Op-Amp Circuit

2. *Building the voltage-follower circuit.* On a breadboard, construct the voltage follower circuit shown in Figure 6.24. Verify that the op-amp output follows the positive op-amp input. Connect a sample load—a 1K resistor from the op-amp output to +5v—and verify that the output level is unaffected.

3. *Building the amplifier circuit.* Construct the voltage follower plus amplifier circuit shown in Figure 6.25. What is the range of output voltage you observe at the second stage (Pin 7)? Try using a larger resistor for R_2—say, 10K—and describe the results.

4. *Dead-bug construction.* Figure 6.26 shows a sample method of building the sensor/op-amp circuit for use on a robot. This building technique is known as "dead-bug construction" because the integrated circuit is mounted upside-down, legs-in-the-air, like a dead insect. The other components are wired directly to the chip's pins.

   Build a sensor using the dead-bug technique or prototyping perfboard. Also construct an IR LED with series resistor and shrink-wrap tubing to limit the beam emissions. Mount this pair so as in the reflectance-sensor configuration on *HandyBug*.

5. *Wall following.* Use your new ranging sensor to construct a wall-following program. At what distance can the sensor detect an object? How immune is the device to ambient light?

Detuning the Transmission Frequency

The IR demodulator's band pass filter establishes the frequency at which *most* sensitive, but demodulators will detect IR at frequencies other than the center frequency—at lessened sensitivity. It's possible to take advantage of this property by emitting constant amounts of IR energy at different frequencies and determining at which frequency the IR detector stops responding. The farther away from the center frequency that detection still occurs, the stronger the IR energy must be.

To implement this idea, an additional IR transmission circuit should be used. This is because the Handy Board's built-in IR transmission circuit has its frequency determined by hardware (a resistor-capacitor pair), so it cannot be used as a variable-frequency driver. A standard 68HC11 output can provide enough power to drive a single LED. However, with a transistor driver, multiple LEDs can be operated from one 68HC11 output (Figure 6.27). The transistor amplifies the 68HC11's output (limited to 20 mA) to enough power to drive IR LEDs at full strength.

FIGURE 6.27 Transistor Driver IR Transmitter Circuit

This circuit shows how to use a general-purpose NPN transistor as a power driver for an LED transmitter. The 68HC11 output can directly drive 20 mA of current (enough for one LED), but this circuit allows several LEDs to be controlled from the 68HC11 pin. When the 68HC11 output goes high, current flows through the base-emitter circuit (with 1K resistor), turning the transistor on. Then large amounts of current, limited by the resistor in the LED circuit, flow through the transistor's collector-emitter, turning on the LED.

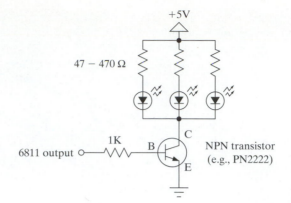

Next, software drivers are required to modulate the 68HC11 output at the desired frequency. This is a bit tricky because frequencies in the range required (20 kHz–40 kHz) will take all of the 68HC11's attention to produce directly (remember that the standard 40 kHz modulation of the Handy Board's IR output is done by a hardware circuit external to the 68HC11).

The 68HC11 can produce lower frequency tones using interrupt drivers, which operate "in the background" of the normal processing of the chip. For example, the audio beeper driver, which requires oscillations in the range of about 100 to a few thousand Hz, uses this approach. Several of the 68HC11 pins are special "timer output" lines that can be programmed to more or less automatically produce waves of this frequency range.

Generating a higher frequency wave, such as the frequencies required by the IR demodulator, requires a different programming method. All of the 68HC11's attention is used to produce the high-frequency output; all other processing is suspended for the duration of the signal. This is not an ideal method, but it is the only way that will work without providing additional hardware outside of the 68HC11 to generate the high-frequency signals.

To get precise control over the timing of the output wave involves a programming technique known as *cycle counting*. Many microprocessors, including the 68HC11, have the property that all instructions execute in a fixed number of machine cycles. Thus, by carefully counting the number of cycles for each instruction in a piece of code, it is possible to precisely determine the amount of time the code will take to execute.[1]

Procedurally, the method for generating a square wave is as follows:

> *begin loop*
> > *set output bit to "1"*
> > *delay for $\frac{1}{2}$ of the square wave time*
> > *set output bit to "0"*
> > *delay for $\frac{1}{2}$ of the square wave time*
> *end loop*

Let's build an example around generating a 15 kHz square wave. The Handy Board's 68HC11 has an 8 MHz crystal, but internally the 68HC11 divides each instruction into four phases so the "machine clock" runs at 2 MHz. That means the 68HC11 executes

---

[1]   Microprocessors used in contemporary desktop computers do not have this deterministic cycle-countable design because of speculative execution, pipelining, and other advanced features of the microprocessor architecture. Most eight-bit microprocessors designed for embedded control, however, have a simpler architecture and the cycle-counting method can be used.

2,000,000 machine cycles per second. However, a typical instruction uses two to seven machine cycles, so (on average) the 68HC11 will execute between 150,000 and 1,000,000 instructions per second.

But we need precise counts of instruction timing to generate our 15 kHz square wave. This is not a problem because the documentation for the 68HC11 tells exactly how many machine cycles each instruction takes up.

Now let us convert the 15 kHz timing into machine cycles. If the square wave is to oscillate at 15,000 cycles per second (i.e., 15 kHz), then each cycle takes up about 0.0000667 seconds or 66.7 microseconds (μs). The 68HC11 machine clock runs at 0.0000005 seconds/cycle—or 0.5 μs per cycle. Thus, each period of the 15 kHz square wave must take up 133.3 machine cycles of the 68HC11 (133.3 machine cycles × 0.5 μs per cycle = 66.7 μs, the period of the 15 kHz square wave).

Of course, we cannot have a fractional machine cycle, so we must round the desired 133.3 cycles into either 133 or 134. The choice is not critical because we do not need precisely a 15 kHz result; that number was an arbitrary choice at one step along the continuum away from the 40 kHz center frequency of our IR demodulators!

Figure 6.28 is the actual assembly code to implement the 15 kHz square wave. (This is an excerpt from the complete driver, an Interactive C binary module, by filename `khz15pd2.asm`.) The driver is written to use an output bit from the 68HC11's Port D register, which is wired to the Handy Board's SPI connector as the output line. Let's go through the code line by line to understand how it works.

```
loop    bset    portd,x pdbit   ; 7 cycles= 3.5 us
        bsr     kill29          ; 29 (6 for bsr + 23 more)
        bsr     kill29          ; 29
        nop                     ; 2 making 67 so far
        bclr    portd,x pdbit   ; 7
        bsr     kill29          ; 29
        bsr     kill20          ; 20
        nop                     ; 2
        brn     loop            ; 3
        decb                    ; 2
        bne     loop            ; 3
*                               ■ 133 total
...
kill29  pshx                    ; 4
        pulx                    ; 5
kill20  pshx                    ; 4
        pulx                    ; 5
        rts                     ; 5
```

FIGURE 6.28 Timing Loop for 15 kHz Square Wave

The first line is `bset portd,x pdbit`, which is a Bit SET instruction. This sets the output bit specified by the `pdbit` constant (which was defined earlier in the driver) in the 68HC11's Port D register. In other words, this is the instruction that causes the 68HC11 pin to be set to a logic 1, or +5v. The `bset` instruction uses seven machine cycles, or 3.5 μs.

Next is `bsr kill29`, which is a Branch to SubRoutine instruction. `kill29` is a subroutine (shown in the program listing after the main loop) that was written to take up 20 machine cycles. (It does this because of its design, not because of its name!) As indicated in the comment field, the subroutine only burns up 23 cycles, but the act of calling it uses up an additional 6, so 29 are used.

The first line of the `kill29` subroutine is `pshx`, the PuSH X register instruction. This instruction places the value of the X register on the 68HC11 stack. (The

stack is a data structure supported in hardware by microprocessors for temporary data storage and subroutine calling.) The next instruction is `pulx`, the PULl X register instruction, which takes a value from the stack and stores it in the X register. Taken as a pair, these two instructions have the effect of doing nothing—the X register has the same value it started with, and the stack is restored to its original state—but nine cycles are used in the process. Because the `pshx` and `pulx` instructions are both just one byte long, this pair is a very compact way of consuming nine cycles.

This push–pull operation is repeated for another nine cycles, and then the subroutine terminates in an `rts` (ReTurn from Subroutine) instruction, which returns control following the instruction that called the subroutine. The `rts` takes five cycles to execute. Thus, 23 cycles are used for the subroutine plus six to call the subroutine, making for 29 (as advertised in the name of the subroutine).

Next up is `nop`, which is a No Operation instruction. This instruction does just what it says—no operation, or nothing at all. But it takes two cycles to decode and do nothing.

At this point, we have used 67 cycles, which is half-way through the square wave. So the next instruction is `bclr portd,x pdbit`, which is a Bit CLeaR instruction. This sets the output bit to logic zero (0 volts) in a complementary fashion to the beginning `bset` instruction. Seven cycles are used.

Next are two calls to the cycle-eating subroutine: one to `kill29` and another to `kill20`, which bypasses the first push–pull pair to yield 20 cycles burned.

Following this is another `nop` and then `brn loop`, which is a Branch Never instruction. For reasons of symmetry, the 68HC11's branching instructions—which can branch based on an arithmetic result being zero, not zero, greater or less than zero, and so on—includes a "branch never" instance. Here we use this curious instruction to simply eat three cycles. It will never branch to `loop`, the beginning of our program, and we do not want it to.

Next is `decb`, DECrement register B. Before beginning the cycle loop, the B register is loaded with a number (from 0 to 255 because the B register is eight bits) indicating how many times to go through the loop. This instruction decrements (subtracts one) from the register value; when it is zero, the loop will be exited. Two cycles are used by the `decb` instruction.

Immediately after decrementing the count is the `bne loop`, which means Branch Not Equal to zero. Based on the status of the last instruction—the `decb` instruction—the `bne` causes the computer to branch to the named location if the result was *not* zero. Used here, this instruction will close the loop until the B register is counted down to zero. It takes three cycles to perform the conditional jump. The cycle count total for the entire loop is then 133 cycles.

In the full driver (shown in Figure 6.29), some clean-up code immediately follows the end of the loop (the `bne loop` instruction).

Using the Detuned Driver

The full 15 kHz driver is shown in Figure 6.29 as an assembly language source code for an ICB (Interactive C Binary) module. When assembled using an IC Binary assembler, an `.icb` file is produced, which, when loaded into the IC environment, defines a new function callable from C code. For our example IR transmitter driver, the function specification is:

```
int khz15pd2(int cycles)
```

The `khz15pd2()` function takes one integer as the argument of the number of cycles (at 15 kHz) to transmit. This is parameterized to allow experimentation with different cycle counts. IR receivers may respond in different ways depending on how long a burst

FIGURE 6.29 ICB Driver Source
for 15 kHz Square Wave Output

```
************************************************************************
* khz15pd2.asm                                                        *
*                                                                     *
* uses: transmits 15 kHz square wave on Port D, bit 2 (MISO)          *
*       takes argument: number of cycles to transmit                  *
*       (0= 256 cycles, 1 = 1 cycle, 255= 255 cycles)                 *
*       returns: port A in high byte and digital inputs in low byte   *
*                                                                     *
* Fred Martin     fredm@media.mit.edu        18 June 1997             *
************************************************************************

pdbit    equ     4          ; bit of port D to be used

digins   equ     $7000      ; digital inputs

base     equ     $1000      ; 6811 register base
porta    equ     $1000
portd    equ     $1008
ddrd     equ     $1009

         org     MAIN_START

subroutine_khz15pd2
         sei                    ; disable interrupts
*                               to gain complete control of CPU
         ldx     #base
         bset    ddrd,x pdbit   ; enable Port D bit for output

* B register contains count argument
* 15 kHz is 66.67 usec per oscillation
* 6811 runs at 0.5 usec per machine cycle
* inner loop is 133.3 (round to 133) machine cycles
loop     bset    portd,x pdbit  ; 7 cycles= 3.5 us
         bsr     kill29         ; 29 (6 for bsr + 23 more)
         bsr     kill29         ; 29
         nop                    ; 2 making 67 so far
         bclr    portd,x pdbit  ; 7
         bsr     kill29         ; 29
         bsr     kill20         ; 20
         nop                    ; 2
         brn     loop           ; 3
         decb                   ; 2
         bne     loop           ; 3
*                               = 133 total
...
kill29   pshx                   ; 4
         pulx                   ; 5
kill20   pshx                   ; 4
         pulx                   ; 5
         rts                    ; 5
```

FIGURE 6.30 Pinout of Handy
Board's SPI/Port D Connector

FIGURE 6.31 Pinout of Handy
Board's Digital Input Bank

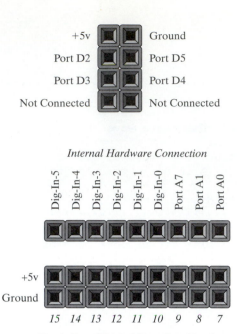

of modulated light they receive. The driver creates its modulated output on Bit 2 of the
68HC11's Port D register.

The function's return value, as indicated by the comment in the source code shown
in Figure 6.29, is a 16-bit value with the high byte being value of the Port A register
(immediately after the square wave transmission) and the low byte as the digital input
latch. This allows use of an IR receiver plugged into any of the positions of the Handy
Board's digital input bank (which are shared between 68HC11 Port A register pins and
the digital input latch). Immediately after the IR transmission, an IR receiver will still
output a "true value" (logic level 0) and this value will be reported by the transmission
routine.

Here is an example of how to use the routine. The transistor transmission circuit
shown in Figure 6.27 is used, with the control signal leading to the base of the transistor
(through a resistor) plugged into the 68HC11's Port D register, Bit 2. This pin is available
on the Handy Board's SPI connector, a 2×4 header bank located immediately above the
coax charge jack along the right-hand edge of the board. Figure 6.30 shows the pinout
of this connector, which includes four Port D pins, power, and ground.

Now connect an IR receiver to any of the digital input bank pins. Figure 6.31 shows
the mapping between the digital input connector and 68HC11/Handy Board circuitry; the
right-most three pins are connected to the 68HC11's Port A register, while the left-most
six pins are connected to the Handy Board's digital input latch. (The other two pins of
that latch are connected to the Handy Board's two user pushbutton switches.)

For the purposes of this example, we assume the use of Handy Board input 10, which
is connected to Bit 0 of the digital input latch. Because the `khz15pd2()` function reports
the digital input latch in the low byte of its return value, we test Bit 0 of this value to
determine the state of the IR sensor.

For example, enter the following at Interactive C's command line:

```
while (1) {if (!(khz15pd2(0) & 1)) beep();}
```

Let's unpack that one-liner. Beginning in the center is the call to the `khz15pd()` driver,
with an argument of 0. This causes the driver to send 256 cycles of oscillation, after
which it reports the digital input latch in the low byte of its return value. This value

is bitwise-ANDed with 1, using the & bitwise AND operator. This results in a 1 or 0 depending on whether the lowest bit of the return value (i.e., sensor input 10) was set.

Because IR demodulators are negative-true (i.e., they produce zero volts on detection and +5 volts when not detecting), we need to invert the sense of the result. That is the purpose of the exclamation point, which is C's logical-NOT operator. Thus, the condition for the `if` statement is the opposite of the bit value; if the bit were zero, the `if` statement is true, and the if-action, a `beep()` command, runs. Concluding, the Handy Board repeatedly sends out an IR pulse and, if the IR detector sees it, the Handy Board beeps.

Experiment with the performance of the transmitter–detector pair—is it noticeably different than the performance when the transmitter is operated from the Handy Board's internal 40 kHz modulation circuit?

Detuning Exercises

1. *Cycle counting.* The 68HC11's `nop` no-operation instruction, which is one byte long and takes two cycles to execute, is the classic way to create a delay in a program. But in the example driver program `khz15pd2.asm` shown in Figure 6.29, various tricks are used for creating delays of a specific number of cycles. For instance: the `brn` branch never instruction (two bytes for three cycles), and the pair of `pshx` and `pulx` instructions (nine cycles in only two bytes).

   Using 68HC11 programming reference materials, find optimal (defined as the fewest number of bytes) methods for delays of four, five, six, seven, and eight cycles. Your solutions must not affect any of the 68HC11 registers.

2. *Drivers at other frequencies.* Based on the model of the 15 kHz driver, write drivers to modulate the IR output frequency at several other points (e.g., 5 kHz, 10 kHz, and 20 kHz). Make use of the tricks you found in the previous exercise to get the cycle-counting delays right.

3. *Putting it together.* Using this collection of drivers and an IR emitter/detector reflective pair, write a C program that calls the drivers in order. The program should report the first driver to fail to yield detection. This should be a crude measure of the strength of IR energy reflected into the detector, and hence a distance sensor for objects of constance reflectivity.

   Experiment with the final product—does it work? What are its limitations and affordances?

6.2.6 Infrared Communications

Communications is one of the most prevalent applications of IR light; practically all television and consumer electronics come with an IR remote control nowadays. In this section, we learn how these IR communications schemes work and how they can be put to use for robotic applications.

Let's begin by examining in greater detail the performance characteristics of the IR demodulator devices. Then we study the signals from a Sony-brand remote control and reverse-engineer the Sony protocol. In the process, we create programs for the Handy Board to receive and transmit Sony-format IR signals.

Detailed Characteristic of IR Demodulators

In Section 6.2.1 of this chapter, we presented an idealized graph of the performance of the IR demodulator devices we have been using. In the graph (Figure 6.12), the IR demodulator "instantly" detected the presence of light modulated at 40 kHz; the IR output went low (because these are active-low devices) for exactly the duration of the 40 kHz "tone-burst" of light.

Of course, this perfect response is impossible. When the IR sensor first sees periodic flashes of light, it can't "know" before it has received at least a few flashes if the light is blinking at the proper frequency. If the sensor just acknowledged "true" whenever it saw flashing light, it would not be very discriminating, and the whole benefit of the 40 kHz modulation would be lost.

So there necessarily is a lag time from when the oscillations begin and when the sensor responds. Figures 6.32 and 6.33 show actual signals measured from the Sharp IS1U60 and GP1U52 IR demodulators, respectively.

In the graphs, the upper trace is the enable line to the Handy Board's IR transmit transistor, showing 12 bursts of IR light spaced 25 microseconds part—in other words, a burst of 40 kHz light lasting a total of 300 microseconds. In each graph, the lower trace shows the response of the particular IR sensor. For each of the two sensors, there are two graphs: one with a strong IR signal and one with a weaker signal.

There are several things to notice in looking at the set of four graphs. First, it takes at least three cycles of IR light—i.e., three "blinks"—to trigger the sensor. When the signal is weaker, it takes eight or nine blinks (at the proper frequency) to trigger the sensor. In the graphs, the Handy Board output trace shows that the first IR pulse is a little longer than all of the rest. This is due to the oscillation getting started.

Second, notice that the "recognized" pulse is of varying length and extends beyond the period of time that the IR light-blinks are being transmitted. Of the four graphs, the shortest recognition period was nearly 300 microseconds long (a weak signal on an IS1U60) and the longest was about 480 microseconds (a strong signal on the IS1U60).

FIGURE 6.32 Burst Response of Sharp IS1U60 IR Demodulator

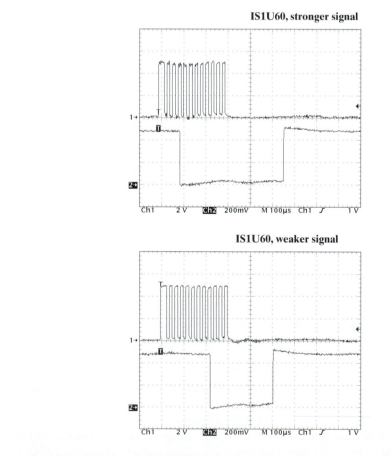

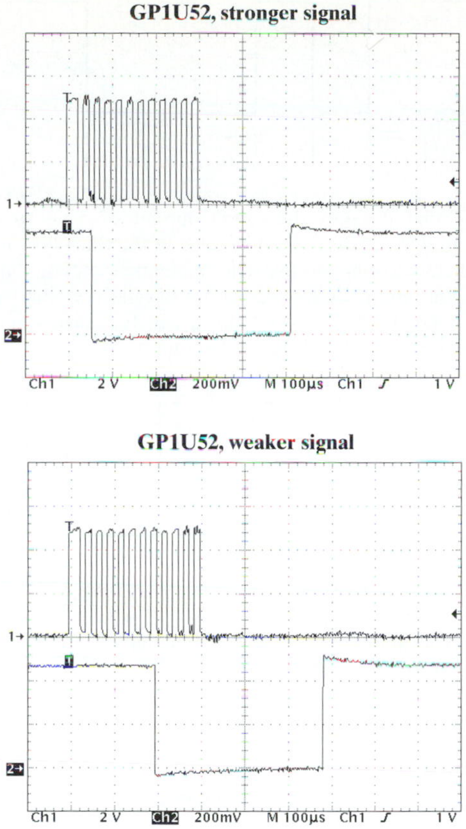

GP1U52, stronger signal

GP1U52, weaker signal

FIGURE 6.33 Burst Response of Sharp GP1U52 IR Demodulator

In other words, depending on signal strength, a 300 microsecond IR-transmit period may result in a received pulse that varies between 300 and 500 microseconds in duration. This uncertainty has implications in the method used for transmitting a stream of data using the IR communications path.

Based on these characteristics, let's explore how IR communications may be accomplished.

Serial Data Transmission Methods

Consider the two methods of transmitting data presented in Figure 6.34. In the first method, entitled *bit frames*, each bit is necessarily the same length of time, and the signal is sampled in the middle of each bit's "frame" to determine whether the bit is a one or a zero. This method works well when the bit stream signal can be accurately reproduced at the receiver's end of the communications channel; it is the method used for the standard communications between a computer and a modem (see Appendix C on Serial Communications and Data Collection).

The second method (shown in the lower half of the figure) is named *bit intervals*. In this method, the *elapsed time between transitions* in the signal determines whether a bit is a one or a zero. This method is good when it is difficult to control the exact shape of the bit stream signal across the communications path—as is the case with IR modulation and demodulation. Because of the properties of the IR demodulator, the width of the received pulse does not match the width of the transmitted pulse, and it would be difficult to transmit the bit-frame-style waveform accurately.

The bit interval method, thus, is an excellent match for the properties of IR transmission. The falling edges (marked with a ▼ symbol) are generated when the IR receiver

FIGURE 6.34 Two Methods of
Serially Transmitting Data

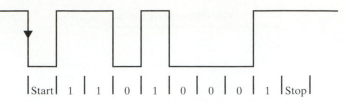

|Start| 1 | 1 | 0 | 1 | 0 | 0 | 0 | 1 |Stop|

Bit Frames: Each bit takes the same amount of time to transmit. Synchronization is based on the falling edge of the Start bit (marked by the ▼); after that, following bits are determined by sampling the signal in the middle of the time period when the bit is valid (i.e., the bit frame). This method is good when the waveform can be reliably transmitted across a wire or other communications medium.

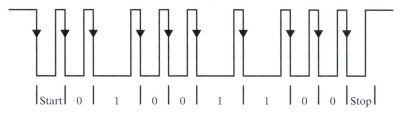

|Start| 0 | 1 | 0 | 0 | 1 | 1 | 0 | 0 |Stop|

Bit Intervals: The amount of time between falling edges determines whether a bit is a zero or a one. In this example, zeroes are represented by a short interval, and ones are represented by a longer interval. There is a short interval at the beginning to act as a start of frame, and a transition at the end to allow the last bit, a zero in this case, to be specified. This method is good when it is difficult to control the exact shape of the wave-form across the communications path.

"sees" a burst of modulated IR light, and the interval between these bursts can then be used to encode the one and zero bits.

Because of these performance considerations, most commercial IR remote controls use the bit interval method to encode key press data. For instance, consider the keystroke waveforms shown in Figure 6.35 from the seven, eight, and nine keys of a Sony TV remote. We reverse-engineer these waveforms—easily captured by a digital storage oscilloscope, or as worked out in an exercise later, by the Handy Board itself—and figure out how Sony chose to encode numbers in its IR signals. We make the assumption of the bit interval method to facilitate the reverse-engineering process.

Sony-Format Infrared Communications

Figure 6.36 takes a closer look at the timing of the seven–key press. In the annotated signal snapshot, three different pulse lengths are evident: a "start bit," which is 3.0 milliseconds (ms) long, and data bits of 1.2 and 1.8 ms. At this point, we don't know whether the 1.2 ms interval represents the 1–bit and the 1.8 ms represents the 0–bit or vice versa. This is indicated in the figure by the two possible interpretations of the bit stream.

Additionally, from just looking at the bit stream from one key, we can't be sure whether the protocol is most-significant bit first or least-significant bit first. To figure this out, as well as correspondence of the bit timing to ones and zeroes, it's necessary to look at a few more key signals.

As shown in Figure 6.35, let's look at the eight and nine keys, with the assumption that these keys have encodings that follow in sequential order starting with the seven-key. In other words, we assume that the seven, eight, and nine keys have sequentially increasing internal codes.

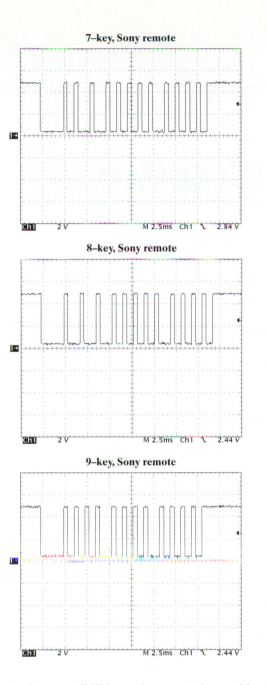

FIGURE 6.35 Keystroke Waveforms from Sony Remote Control

Figure 6.37 tabulates these possibilities and converts the resulting bit stream interpretations into their decimal values.

When the bit streams are interpreted least-significant-bit (LSB) first, the seven, eight, and nine keys fall into a sequential encoding (see the decimal values column). With most-significant-bit first interpretation, the encodings are scattered about. It's thus fairly evident that the LSB encoding is the method used. (The bit stream for the nine key happens to be a palindrome, so it resolves to the same number whether the bits are read left-to-right or right-to-left!)

The next question is the mapping between pulse intervals (1.2 and 1.8 millisecs) and bit values (0 and 1). This is not evident from the data on hand because both interpretations result in sequential encodings for the key presses we've examined. It may be surmised

FIGURE 6.36 Detailed Timing of the Sony IR 7–Key

In this detailed look at the timing of the seven key from a Sony-format IR remote, three different pulse intervals are revealed: a "start bit" of 3.0 milliseconds (ms) and data bits of 1.2 and 1.8 ms. It's not yet clear whether the 1.2 ms data bit represents a "1" and the 1.8 ms a "0" or vice versa.

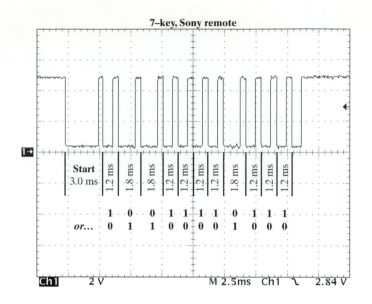

FIGURE 6.37 Two Possible Bit Stream Interpretations for seven, eight, and nine Keys

Timing	Key	The Bits	Decimal Value	
			LSB First	MSB First
1.2 ms is 1–bit; 1.8 ms is 0–bit.	seven key	1 0 0 1 1 1 1 0 1 1 1	1913	1271
	eight key	0 0 0 1 1 1 1 0 1 1 1	1912	247
	nine key	1 1 1 0 1 1 1 0 1 1 1	1911	1911
1.2 ms is 0–bit; 1.8 ms is 1–bit.	seven key	0 1 1 0 0 0 0 1 0 0 0	134	776
	eight key	1 1 1 0 0 0 0 1 0 0 0	135	1800
	nine key	0 0 0 1 0 0 0 1 0 0 0	136	136

that the second option in the table (1.2 ms as the 0–bit, 1.8 ms as the 1–bit) is more likely because it maps the increasing sequence of keys seven, eight, and nine to increasing rather than decreasing decimal values.

Indeed, this is correct; the Sony format represents the 0–bit as a 1.2 ms interval, and the 1–bit as a 1.8 ms interval. As it happens, the 11–bit sequence is divided into eight data bits followed by three "device" bits. The device bits are used to select different target electronics units—the VCR, television, or CD player. Each of these uses the same data bit encoding for many of the keys, like the numeric keys, and the device bits determine which piece of electronics responds to the IR signal.

Figure 6.38 summarizes the properties of the Sony-format IR communications scheme.

FIGURE 6.38 Summary of Sony-Format IR Protocol

		Sony Infrared Remote Protocol
Bit Interval	Start Bit	3.0 ms
	0–Bit	1.2 ms
	1–Bit	1.8 ms
Bit Format	Order	LSB First
	First 8 Bits	Key Data
	Next 3 Bits	Device Data (e.g., 000 = TV)

Receiving Sony IR Signals on the Handy Board

Based on this understanding of the Sony IR protocol, it's possible to write a program for the Handy Board to decode signals from Sony remote controls—or another Handy Board that transmits with the same scheme (see Section 6.2.6).

In this section, we examine an assembly language driver program that uses the Handy Board's built-in IR receiver to decode Sony-format signals. The actual assembly language code uses some fairly sophisticated tricks—it's possibly the most advanced assembly language code presented in this book—so don't worry if it seems confusing, it is.[2] First we present the algorithm, and then we walk through the assembly code.

Figure 6.39 presents the Sony IR decoding algorithm in simplified form. The program is installed as an interrupt routine, meaning it is automatically called by the 68HC11 whenever the Handy Board's IR sensor detects a burst of IR modulated light (see the sidebar, "Timing and Interrupts").

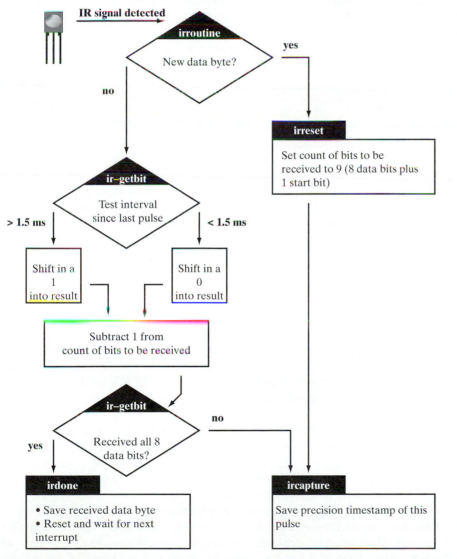

FIGURE 6.39 Simplified Algorithm for Decoding Sony IR Protocol

---

2   The IR decoder routine is contributed by Brian Silverman, a colleague and friend, who among other things is a master assembly language programmer. In addition to writing the decoding routine, Brian did much of the research of the IR technology presented in this section.

Timing and Interrupts

The 68HC11 has extra hardware on the chip that allows it to perform powerful timing functions in the background while processing the normal instruction stream.

There is a 16–bit timing register, named the TCNT register, that continually increments, keeping track of elapsed time at a rate of 2,000,000 counts per second (assuming an 8 MHz oscillator, as has the Handy Board). This TCNT register can be used to "time stamp" events on the 68HC11's special timer input lines.

The Handy Board's IR receiver is connected to timer input 1, one of these special timer inputs. By configuring the control registers associated with this timer input, the 68HC11 will perform two functions automatically and in the background of normal operation: (1) it will record the value of the TCNT register at the exact moment of a transition on the timer input line, and (2) it will schedule an interrupt routine to be executed as soon as possible after the transition on the input line has occurred.

The IR reception routine takes full advantage of these two capabilities. The routine is set up to activate when a "falling edge" occurs; in other words, when the Sharp IR receiver latches onto an IR burst. The 68HC11 takes the time stamp reading and schedules the IR reception routine to execute a short bit of time later.

The time stamp function is critical because there can be variable delays between the event (i.e., the IR reception) and the interrupt routine being called. For example, if the 68HC11 is presently in the middle of executing a different interrupt routine, the IR reception routine will have to wait until the other routine is done before the IR routine gains control. Because of the time stamping function, however, the IR routine can still know the precise point in time when the IR receiver triggered detection.

The first piece of the program, in the diamond entitled irroutine, checks whether the routine is already in the middle of parsing a keypress data byte or whether this is a new data byte. If it is a new data byte, then control goes to irreset, which establishes initial parameters for reading in the byte: 9 bits to be received (8 data bits plus the start bit). Then control passes to ircapture, which records the timestamp of the current IR burst for measuring the interval from the last burst the next time through the routine.

If irroutine has already started to receive a byte, then control continues with irgetbit, which interprets the current bit. The interval between the current IR burst and the last IR burst is measured. If it is greater than 1.5 ms (e.g., the 1–bit, which is 1.8 ms), then a 1–bit is shifted into the result. If the interval is less than 1.5 ms (e.g., the 1.2 ms 0–bit), then a 0–bit is shifted into the result.

Next, the count of bits to be received is decremented and checked. If all bits have been received, then irdone saves the result and finishes, ready for the next IR data transmission. If all bits have not been received, the control goes to ircapture, which records the time stamp of the current pulse for measuring the length of the subsequent IR pulse when it occurs.

This algorithm is the essence of the actual IR routine, which is distributed as sony_rcv.asm. What has been left out of the block diagram is a set of tests for resetting the whole algorithm if (for some reason) IR reception is interrupted in the middle of receiving a particular byte and for suppressing detections that occur too rapidly (e.g., the autorepeat that occurs when an IR remote key is held down).

Next, we look at how to use the driver and then explain its inner workings in detail.

Using the Sony Receive Driver   After loading the `sony_rcv.icb` driver program, the following functions are available for use:

int sony_rcv_init(int enable) This function turns on or off the IR receive processing. Call with an argument of one to enable IR reception or with a zero argument to disable reception (i.e., `sony_rcv_init(1)` enables IR reception, and `sony_rcv_init(0)` disables it). The routine is off by default after being loaded; it should be turned off when it is not being used because it consumes some processing power.

Return value is its argument.

int sony_rcv(int dummy) This is the function for retrieving the received data from the routine. The function reports two things packed into one 16–bit return value.

The low byte is the actual IR data received by the IR routine. This may be a value from 0 to 255.

The high byte is the number of IR bytes received since the last call to `sony_rcv()`. If this amount is zero, then no IR data have been received since the last call, and the value reported in the low byte is the same value as the last time it was checked.

If the high byte is one, then exactly one new IR data byte has been received, and its value is reported in the low byte.

If the high byte is greater than one, then some bytes have been received whose values are lost. The high byte count will increment with each byte received until it reaches 255, at which point it will no longer count. It will stay at 255 until reset by a call to the receive function.

`sony_rcv()` must be given a dummy argument, which is necessary but is ignored. For example, use `sony_rcv(0)`.

The following code may be used to extract the upper and lower bytes from the return value:

```
int i, count, data;

i= sony_rcv(0);        /* get info from IR routine */
data= i & 0xff;        /* most recently received data */
count= i >> 8;         /* bytes received since last call */
```

Figure 6.40 shows a listing of `remctrl.c`, a simple program for *HandyBug* that demonstrates IR remote control. With this simple demo program, you can drive *HandyBug* around the room with a Sony remote control. The two, four, six, and eight keys make *HandyBug* go forward, left, right, and backward, respectively.

The main loop of the program calls the IR receive routine, checks if any new data came in (`count > 0`), and then calls a movement routine (from the `turtle.c` library) based on the keystroke.

The Driver Code   Figures 6.41 and 6.42 list the driver routine for receiving the Sony-format IR signals. Let's walk through the code to understand how it works.

After the constant declarations and variable definitions, the code begins at the label `subroutine_initialize_module`. This routine is automatically called by Interactive

FIGURE 6.40 Listing of remctrl.c

```
/* remctrl.c:  sample LEGObug program for responding to IR sig-
nals */
/* requires turtle.c, sony_rcv.icb */

/* Fred Martin  August 18, 1997 */

void main() {

  int data, count, ir;

  sony_rcv_init(1);                     /* enable IR reception */

  while (1) {
    ir= sony_rcv(0);

    data= ir & 0xff;                    /* mask data field */
    count= ir >> 8;                     /* get count field */

    printf("count %d data %d\n", count, data);

    if (count > 0) {
      if (data == 129) forward();    /* 2 key */
      if (data == 131) left();       /* 4 key */
      if (data == 133) right();      /* 6 key */
      if (data == 135) backward();   /* 8 key */
      sleep(0.5); stop();            /* go for 1/2 sec */
    }
  }
}
```

C when the driver loads and is used to install the driver into the 68HC11 software system. Two routines are installed. First, a routine named ir_routine is installed as the interrupt routine for Timer Input 1. Timer Input 1 is the 68HC11 input where the Sharp IR sensor is attached; when the sensor receives a signal, the ir_routine program is automatically called by the 68HC11 interrupt facility.

Second, the program millisec_routine is installed on the Timer Output 4 interrupt. This timer interrupt is already used by the Interactive C runtime code on the 68HC11 as a periodic routine that runs 1,000 times per second. The millisec_routine essentially "piggybacks" itself in front of the existing routine so that the new millisec_routine is called before the existing routine. (This technique is discussed in further detail in Section E.3.12.) Both routines are still called 1,000 times per second.

Next comes the millisec_routine, which is used by the main ir_routine program to keep track of elapsed time in milliseconds. This code increments the ir_timer variable each time it is called. There is a trick in the millisec_routine's counting, however: Once it reaches 255 milliseconds, ir_timer doesn't "roll over" to zero, but rather stays at the 255 mark. Also, the routine clears the ir_data variable (which keeps track of the incoming IR data byte) if the timer attempts to overflow. This resets the main IR routine if the reception of an IR data byte is interrupted while it is in progress.

At the start of the continued listing in Figure 6.42 is the main ir_routine. The first two instructions clear the interrupt flag, a housekeeping measure that is necessary to allow the routine to be called again the next time the Sharp IR sensor detects a signal.

The next three program lines, before the irreset label, check the elapsed time since the last IR data bit was received. If four or fewer milliseconds have elapsed, then control

```
*************************************************************
* sony_rcv.asm:  decodes the Sony format IR protocol       *
*                                                          *
* by Brian Silverman                 (bss@media.mit.edu)   *
* modified for Handy Board by Fred Martin (fredm@media.mit.edu) *
* August 15, 1997                                          *
*************************************************************


TIC1      EQU      $1010    ; Timer Input Capture register 1
TFLG1     EQU      $1023    ; main Timer interrupt Flag register 1
TCTL2     EQU      $1021    ; Timer Control register 2
TMSK1     EQU      $1022    ; main Timer interrupt Mask register 1


TOC4INT   EQU      $E2      ; Timer Output Compare 4
TIC1INT   EQU      $EE      ; Timer Input Capture 1

          org      MAIN_START

ir_timer                    fcb      0   ; time since last bit
ir_shift                    fcb      0   ; received data in progress
ir_phase                    fcb      0   ; bits left to receive
ir_count                    fcb      0   ; #bytes rcv'd since last check
ir_data                     fcb      0   ; full data byte as received
last_captured_input         fdb      0   ; timestamp of last bit

subroutine_initialize_module:
          ldx      #$bf00             ; pointer to interrupt vectors

* install IR detection routine
          ldd      #ir_routine
          std      TIC1INT,X

* install millisec routine
          ldd      TOC4INT,X
          std      millisec_exit+1    ; record previous vector
          ldd      #millisec_routine
          std      TOC4INT,X          ; install new vector


          rts

* count up to 256 ms to receive single IR byte;
* otherwise clear incoming data
millisec_routine
          inc      ir_timer
          bne      millisec_exit
          dec      ir_timer         ; ir_timer is 255 now


millisec_exit
          JMP      $0000    ; this value poked in by init routine
```

FIGURE 6.41 Listing of sony_rcv.asm (1 of 2)

FIGURE 6.42 Listing of
sony_rcv.asm (2 of 2)

```
* the ir routine is called whenever a falling edge
* (i.e., beginning of valid ir signal) is received
ir_routine
          ldaa    #4
          staa    TFLG1           ; clear tic1 interrupt flag

          ldaa    ir_timer
          cmpa    #4
          bls     irgetbit        ; get bit if < 5 ms have elapsed
irreset   ldaa    #9              ; capture 9 bits (8 data + 1 start)
          staa    ir_phase
          bra     ircapture

irgetbit  ldaa    ir_phase        ; if ir_phase is zero, don't read bit
          beq     ircapture       ; didn't get 5ms gap between bytes
          ldd     TIC1
          subd    last_captured_input
          cmpd    #3000
          ror     ir_shift        ; shift carry bit into answer
          dec     ir_phase
          bne     ircapture       ; continue until all bits read

irdone    ldaa    ir_shift
          coma                    ; ones complement the answer
          staa    ir_data
          inc     ir_count
          bne     ircapture
          dec     ir_count        ; max out at 255

ircapture ldd     TIC1
          std     last_captured_input
          clr     ir_timer
          rti

* returns IR value received since last call
subroutine_sony_rcv:
          ldd     ir_count        ; count + data in D
          clr     ir_count
          rts

* call with 1 to turn on; 0 to turn off
subroutine_sony_rcv_init
          ldx     #$1000
          tstb
          beq     sony_off
          bset    TMSK1,X $04     * enable tic1 interrupt
          bset    TCTL2,X $20     * on falling edges (i.e., IR detects)
          bclr    TCTL2,X $10
          clr     ir_count
          clr     ir_data
          rts
sony_off
          bclr    TMSK1,X $04
          rts
```

continues with `irgetbit`. Otherwise, `irreset` resets the system to receive a new data byte by storing a nine in `ir_phase`, the variable that keeps track of how many bits to receive.

At `irgetbit`, the `ir_phase` variable is checked; if this is zero (meaning that a complete data byte has been received, but there has not been a 4 millisecond interval needed for a reset), then the system ignores the bit. Otherwise, the bit is valid, and the next few lines of code calculate the interval between the last IR pulse and the current one to determine whether it is a 1–bit or a 0–bit.

This code for testing whether the interval between IR pulses is less than or greater than 1.5 milliseconds is tricky. First, the time stamp of the current IR pulse is loaded into the D register. The time stamp of the last IR pulse (`last_captured_input`) is subtracted; this yields the interval between the bits. Then the value 3,000 is subtracted (the `cmpd #3000` instruction), with the result landing in the carry bit: one if the interval between the IR pulses was less than 3,000 timing units and zero if it was greater than 3,000 timing units.

Why the value 3,000, and what is the carry bit? Let's explore the 68HC11 timer system and the arithmetic system in a bit more detail to answer this.

The 68HC11 timer system keeps track of elapsed time by counting 2,000,000 ticks per second (see sidebar, "Timing and Interrupts"). Thus, one tick is $\frac{1}{2}$ of a microsecond, and 3,000 ticks is 1.5 milliseconds.

This value (3,000 counts or 1.5 milliseconds) is used to discriminate between the 1.8 millisecond 1–bit and the 1.2 millisecond 0–bit. The value is subtracted from the interval value using the `cmpd` "Compare D Register" instruction. The `cmpd` instruction performs a subtraction and throws away the "answer," but sets the 68HC11's *condition code register* based on the result. The condition code register keeps track of characteristics of numerical operations: whether a result was zero, greater than zero, or less than zero (as well as some other things).

The condition code register has several "flags," which are set or reset after a numerical operation to indicate particular results. For instance, there is the Z (zero) flag, which is set if the result is zero. Additionally, there is the C (carry) flag, which is set when a subtraction requires a carry from the most significant bit—in other words, if the result of the subtraction is less than zero.

In our case, the `cmpd` instruction causes the C flag to be set if the interval between IR pulses minus 3,000 is less than zero. Thus, the carry bit is set to one if there was an interval smaller than 1.5 milliseconds.

Memory or Register Operand

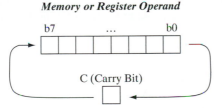

The next instruction after the compare instruction is `ror ir_shift`—the "Rotate Right through Carry" instruction. As shown in Figure 6.43, this instruction moves the carry bit into an operand byte. In this instance, the operand is the `ir_shift` memory location, which will hold the final answer after all the shifting is done.

Thus, each time an IR pulse is received, the pulse interval is calculated, the carry bit is set to a one or a zero depending on the length of the interval, and the the carry bit is rotated into position in an answer-in-progress byte (`ir_shift`). After all eight data bits have been shifted into `ir_shift`, we are done, and the final received byte is present in `ir_shift`.

FIGURE 6.43 Rotate Right Through Carry Instruction

In the *Rotate Right through Carry* instruction, the value of the carry bit is moved into the high bit of the operand byte, all of the bits in the operand byte are shifted down by one position, and the low bit of the operand moves into the carry.

The routine continues at `irdone`. Here the result is copied from `ir_shift` into `ir_data`. The `ir_count` variable, which keeps track of the total number of received bytes, is incremented, ready to be reported by the `sony_rcv` subroutine.

The last two pieces of the code are the `sony_rcv` and `sony_rcv_init` modules. These are both prefixed with the label "`subroutine_`" so that the Interactive C software system will recognize them as routines that can be called from the C-language environment.

The `sony_rcv` routine loads the D register with the `ir_count` memory location. The D register, however, consists of two 8–bit registers, the A register and the B register. When loading a 16–bit register from memory, like the D register, the 68HC11 loads the high byte from the memory location specified and the low byte from the next address in memory. Because `ir_data` follows `ir_count` in memory, the A register gets loaded with the value of `ir_count`, and the B register gets the value of `ir_data`. Thus, the single `ldd ir_count` instruction is really a shorthand for a two-instruction sequence `ldaa ir_count` and `ldab ir_data`. Tight assembly language programming is the result of setting things up so that shortcuts like this can be used.

After loading the return values into the D register, the `ir_count` variable is cleared and control is returned to Interactive C with the `rts` "Return from Subroutine" instruction.

The `sony_rcv_init` module sets up the 68HC11 timer control registers for proper functioning with the needs of the entire IR reception driver. In particular, the timer input 1 interrupt is enabled and set up to trigger when a falling edge signal (i.e., a transition from logic one to logic zero)—which indicates the onset of an IR burst—is received.

IR Receive Routine Exercises

1. At `irreset`, the `ir_phase` variable is loaded with the value 9 to allow the routine to receive nine pulses (one for the start bit and eight for the data bits). The start bit is then just interpreted as another data bit and shifted into the result byte (`ir_shift`). What happens to the start bit?
2. Before the final `ir_shift` value is loaded into `ir_data` (at `irdone`), it is complemented using the `coma` instruction. This instruction changes zeroes to ones and vice versa. Why is this done?
3. Rewrite the IR receive routine to measure the length of the start and data bits and reject a byte if the bits are not received at the proper timing. Devise a test to determine whether the more "finicky" routine is better able to receive noisy or weak IR signals without error.
4. Modify the IR receive routine to automatically buffer incoming IR data. Modify the `sony_rcv` routine to fetch received bytes from the buffer. Add a routine to flush the buffer.

Transmitting Sony IR Signals from the Handy Board

This section presents the design of an interrupt-based driver for transmitting 8–bit bytes over IR using the Sony protocol described in this chapter. First, the use of the driver is explained; then the internal workings of the driver are dissected in a similar fashion as was the IR receive routine.

Using the IR Transmit Routine   The routine is provided in the file `sonyxmit.asm`, with the Interactive C binary file `sonyxmit.icb`. After loading the `.icb` file into Interactive C, one function is defined:

```
int sony_xmit(int data)
```

The function takes one argument: the data byte to be transmitted. The upper byte of the argument is ignored; the lower byte holds the data.

The routine schedules the data byte to be transmitted out the Handy Board's IR output, using the Sony IR data transmission format, and returns immediately with a return value equal to the data being transmitted.

If a transmission is in progress when `sony_xmit()` is called, the routine returns the value −1, indicating that no action was taken.

Example: An IR Beacon   The `sony_xmit()` function may be called in a tight loop, enabling a robot to continually broadcast a value for other robots to see. For example, use the following function:

```
void beacon (int data) {
  while (1) {
    sony_xmit(data);
    defer();
  }
}
```

The `sony_xmit()` routine inserts a 5 msec space before the transmission of each data byte so that bytes will not run together if transmitted in rapid succession. This `beacon()` routine should be launched as its own process, using Interactive C's multitasking capability, so that other robot activities may operate in addition to the beacon function; for example,

```
...
start_process(beacon(5));
...
```

in the set-up code of a robot's program will launch the beacon process in the background of main robot corporation.

The `defer()` command tells Interactive C that it may give another process its turn after scheduling the data byte for transmission. Because each Interactive C process normally receives 5 msec of real time when it has its turn, the `defer()` invocation allows this time to not be wasted. Because each data byte takes about 15 msec to transmit, but almost no time to schedule, the beacon function would be continually wasting its 5 msec time slice if it were not for the `defer()` command.

How the IR Transmit Routine Works   Transmitting an IR byte takes a fair bit of time from the 68HC11's point of view. The start bit takes 3 msec, and each data bit takes either 1.2 msec (0–bit) or 1.8 msec (1–bit). Thus, an average data byte takes $3 + 8 \times 1.5 = 15$ msec to transmit. The 68HC11 executes 2,000 instruction cycles per msec, so 30,000 instruction cycles fit into the time that it takes to send one byte of IR data! (Typical 68HC11 instructions consume two to four cycles each, so we are talking about approximately 10,000 instructions per data byte.)

Clearly, we do not want the 68HC11 locked in the byte loop waiting for time to elapse as it generates the IR output waveform. For this reason, the Handy Board includes a hardware circuit to perform the carrier modulation of the IR signal (which occurs rapidly at 40 kHz or 25 microseconds per oscillation), so the 68HC11 only has to generate the millisecond-time-scale pulse modulation that represents the IR data.

This is a perfect job for interrupts, and the driver presented here uses the 68HC11's *output compare* interrupt to generate precise waveforms in a similar manner that the IR receive driver used the *input capture* facility to precisely time incoming signals.

The 68HC11's output compare mechanism works as follows. For each of the timer output pins (the IR output circuit is connected to timer output 2), there is a timer output

compare register and timer control register. When the 68HC11's free running primary timer register (TCNT) increments until it matches a timer output compare register, then that timer's hardware output pin immediately changes state. The pin may be set to go high, go low, or toggle (go from high to low or from low to high depending on where it started) depending on the setting in the timer control register. Additionally, a timer interrupt routine associated with that timer pin is scheduled to be executed as soon as possible after the TCNT/timer output compare register match.

This is wonderful because it means that a driver routine can *schedule output pin transitions ahead of time* and then return control to the normal instruction processing, knowing that the output transition will occur precisely at that future point in time. Further, when the time does come, the driver routine is automatically called again, allowing it to schedule the next transition for when it should then occur.

This is the technique used by the IR output driver to allow the IR output byte to be transmitted in the background of normal program execution. The portion of the driver called directly from Interactive C, sony_xmit(), simply sets up a series of events to be handled by the driver's interrupt routine and then immediately returns control back to Interactive C. From the standpoint of the Interactive C program, sending a single IR byte takes essentially no time to execute because all that the sony_xmit() routine does is *schedule the IR transmission to occur*.

Here is how the IR output routine works. The actual transmission of the output signal is broken up into 20 sequential phases (see Figure 6.44). The first phase is a 5 msec gap inserted to separate data bytes that might be transmitted in rapid succession. When this phase ends, the interrupt routine begins counting down the 20 next steps, beginning with a delay to establish the positive-going IR pulse that is the start of the IR transmit sequence. When the next interrupt occurs, the phase is decremented to 19, and the rising edge to signal the 3 msec start bit interval is scheduled. Phase 18 is the width of that IR pulse; at Phase 17, the first data bit interval is scheduled. This process continues until the last IR pulse for the last data bit is scheduled at Phase 1. When the interrupt occurs for phase 1, the routine finishes, by setting the phase to 0 and disabling the interrupt, until a new transmission sequence is scheduled by the sony_xmit() setup routine.

With this strategy in mind, let's walk through the IR transmit code shown in Figures 6.45 and 6.46. It may be helpful to refer to Figure 6.48, which summarizes the various timer registers that are used frequently throughout the code.

The first section of code declares constants for the registers that will be used, and TOC2INT, the address of the timer output 2 interrupt vector. The constant PULSE is declared to be 1,200; this corresponds to 0.6 msec, which is the length of each IR burst.

Two memory variables are allocated: ir_phase, which (as discussed earlier) keeps track of the progress of the IR output signal, and ir_data, which holds the actual bits being transmitted.

The initialize_module subroutine, which is automatically called by Interactive C when the driver is loaded, only has to do a couple of things. First, it installs the driver's

FIGURE 6.44 20-Phase Infrared Transmit Driver

The IR interrupt routine checks the value of the ir_phase variable to determine whether to schedule a rising or falling edge for the next interrupt and when that edge should occur. After each interrupt, ir_phase is decremented; when it reaches zero, the routine is finished.

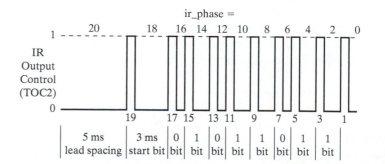

```
*********************************************************************
* sonyxmit.asm:  Transmits 8-bit Sony format IR bytes            *
*                                                               *
* by Fred Martin (fredm@media.mit.edu), August 28, 1997         *
*********************************************************************

CFORC     equ       $100b    ; Timer Compare Force Register
TCNT      equ       $100e    ; Timer Counter Register
TOC2      equ       $1018    ; Timer Output Compare Register 2
TFLG1     equ       $1023    ; main Timer interrupt Flag register 1
TCTL1     equ       $1020    ; Timer Control register 1
TMSK1     equ       $1022    ; main Timer interrupt Mask register 1


TOC2INT equ       $bfe6    ; Timer Output Compare 2 Interrupt Vector


PULSE     equ       1200     ; positive-going IR pulse = 0.6 msec

          org       MAIN_START

ir_phase            fcb       0        ; countdown in transmit sequence
ir_data             fcb       0        ; outgoing byte

subroutine_initialize_module:
          ldd       #ir_routine       ; pointer to driver routine
          std       TOC2INT           ; store at interrupt vector
          clr       ir_phase          ; so we can get going
          rts

* transmits value in B register;
* returns -1 if transmission is already in progress, or
* value called with if successful.
subroutine_sony_xmit:
          ldaa      ir_phase          ; check status
          beq       xmit_setup
          ldd       #$ffff            ; -1 return value
          rts
* make sure that IR transmitter is off;
* set phase countdown to 20;
* create 5 millisecond byte separation delay at start of byte.
xmit_setup
          stab      ir_data           ; store data out byte
          ldx       #$1000            ; pointer to register base
          bset      TCTL1,X $80
          bclr      TCTL1,X $40       ; set IR output to go low
          ldaa      #$40              ; select TOC2 output
          staa      CFORC,X           ; force compare -> output goes low
          staa      TFLG1,X           ; clear interrupt flag
          ldaa      #20               ; initial phase
          staa      ir_phase
          ldd       TCNT,X
          addd      #10000            ; 5 millisecond delay
          std       TOC2,X
```

FIGURE 6.45 Listing of sonyxmit.asm (1 of 2)

FIGURE 6.46 Listing of
sonyxmit.asm (2 of 2)

```
                bset    TCTL1,X $C0      ; set IR output to go high
                bset    TMSK1,X $40      ; enable TOC2 interrupt
                clra                     ; clear A register for return
                ldab    ir_data
                rts
ir_routine
                ldx     #$1000
                ldaa    #$40             ; select TOC2 output
                staa    TFLG1,X          ; clear interrupt flag

                ldaa    ir_phase
                cmpa    #1
                bne     ir_continue
* phase is 1; that means we're done.
* disable interrupt, set phase to zero, and return.
                bclr    TMSK1,X $40      ; disable TOC2 interrupt
                bra     ir_finish        ; phase decremented to 0
* if phase is even, generate constant-length IR pulse;
* if phase is odd, generate variable-length gap based on data bit,
*       unless phase is 19---generate 3.0 millisecond start bit.
* decrement phase and return.
ir_continue
                rora                     ; odd/even bit in carry
                bcs     ir_odd
* phase is even; set up falling edge for PULSE/2000 millisec-
onds later
                ldd     TOC2,X
                addd    #PULSE
                std     TOC2,X
                bset    TCTL1,X $80
                bclr    TCTL1,X $40      ; set IR output to go low
                bra     ir_finish
* phase is odd
ir_odd  ldaa    ir_phase
                cmpa    #19
                bne     ir_databit
* generate gap for start bit
                ldd     TOC2,X
                addd    #6000-PULSE      ; 3.0 ms minus pulse length
                bra     ir_sendbit
* generate gap for data bit
ir_databit
                ldd     TOC2,X
                ror     ir_data          ; move lowest data bit into carry
                bcs     ir_onebit
                addd    #2400-PULSE      ; 1.2 ms minus pulse length
                bra     ir_sendbit
ir_onebit addd  #3600-PULSE              ; 1.8 ms minus pulse length
ir_sendbit
                std     TOC2,X
                bset    TCTL1,X $C0      ; set IR output to go high
ir_finish
                dec     ir_phase
                rti
```

Timer Control Register 1 ($1020)

OM2	OL2	OM3	OL3	OM4	OL4	OM5	OL5

OMx–OLx	Action
00	none; timer is general-purpose output
01	toggle OCx output line
10	clear OCx output line
11	set OCx output line

FIGURE 6.47 Timer Control Register 1

The timer control register 1 (TCTL1) determines what action is taken when the free-running TCNT matches a timer's compare register. By setting a pair of bits, a timer output may be set to take no action, toggle, go low, or go high when a match occurs.

ir_routine address at the timer output 2 interrupt vector so that the routine will be called automatically by the 68HC11's interrupt system. (The IR output circuit is connected to timer output 2.) Also, it clears the ir_phase memory location so that the first time a byte is transmitted, the driver will accept it. (Variables declared in Interactive C binary modules are not automatically initialized by Interactive C, so this step is necessary.)

FIGURE 6.48 Summary of Timer Control Registers

Name	Address	Function
TCNT	0x100e	Free-running timer counter register. Increments continually at the rate of 2,000,000 counts per second.
TMSK1	0x1022	Timer mask register 1. Setting bits in this register enables particular timer interrupts to occur.
TCTL1	0x1020	Timer control register 1. Determines activity on timer output pin when TCNT register matches timer output compare register: no action, output toggles, output set, or output cleared.
TFLG1	0x1023	Timer flag register 1. Timer flag is set when interrupt occurs; must be cleared before a subsequent interrupt an occur.
TOCx	0x1016 0x1018 0x101a 0x101c 0x101e	Five timer output compare registers. When value of free-running TCNT register matches one of these, the corresponding interrupt is generated.
CFORC	0x100b	Counter force compare register. Used to explicitly force a compare action independent of matching of TOCx and TCNT registers.

Next comes the sony_xmit subroutine, which is called by the user from Interactive C. The routine checks if an IR transmission is already in progress, which is indicated by the ir_phase variable being nonzero. If a transmission is in progress, the routine exits without doing any further work, returning a value of −1 to Interactive C to let the user know that the requested byte will not be transmitted.

If all is clear, the sony_xmit routine proceeds to set up the byte for transmission. The following sequence occurs:

- The byte to be transmitted is stored in the ir_data variable.
- The IR output is set to go low (just in case it was left on by some previous operation) by putting a "10" in the two high bits of the TCTL1 register (see Figure 6.47).
- The timer output 2 is forced to compare (thus setting it low) by writing to the CFORC register with a 1 bit in the position corresponding to the TOC2 register control. This step is necessary to ensure that the interrupt system is fully reset.
- The interrupt flag for the TOC2 register is cleared by writing a 1 to the corresponding bit position of the TFLG1 register. This allows a subsequent interrupt to be processed properly.

- The number 20 is stored as the initial `ir_phase` value.

- The current time value of the `TCNT` register is read, the number 10,000 is added to it, and this result is stored as the time at which the first timer interrupt of the sequence will occur. Because the `TCNT` register increments at the rate of 2,000,000 counts per second, 10,000 corresponds to a delay of 5 milliseconds, which is thus inserted before the transmission of each IR data byte.

- The IR output is set to go high when this interrupt occurs by writing a "11" into the two high bits of the `TCTL1` register (see Figure 6.47 again).

- The timer 2 interrupt is enabled by writing a 1 into the corresponding bit position of the `TMSK1` register. This register allows particular interrupts to be selectively enabled and disabled; when the routine is finished sending the data byte, it will turn itself off by clearing this bit in the `TMSK1` register.

- As the return value to Interactive C, the high byte of the D register is cleared (`clra`) and the low byte is loaded back with the value that is to be transmitted (`ldab ir_data`). Then the routine returns control to Interactive C.

Now we are ready to look at the interrupt routine, `ir_routine`. This routine is automatically called by the 68HC11 after the `TCNT` time matches the value stored in the `TOC2` register, and the `TOC2` output pin has been set or cleared (depending on a setting of the `TCTL1` register).

The first thing the `ir_routine` does is clear its interrupt flag (done by writing a 1 into the proper bit position of the `TFLG1` register) so that a subsequent interrupt may occur.

Next, it checks the value of the `ir_phase` variable. If it is one, then the routine has finished transmitting the data byte, and all that is left to do is disable itself (by clearing the appropriate bit in the `TMSK1` register), decrement the `ir_phase` to zero (so the `sony_xmit` routine can schedule another byte), and exit.

If the phase is not zero, then the routine checks whether the phase is even or odd:

- If the phase is even, then the routine has been entered after the rising edge at the beginning of an IR burst, and it schedules a falling edge for 0.6 msec later (as defined by the `PULSE` constant).

    Thus, the routine produces constant-length IR bursts at variable spacing—defining either a start bit, 1–bit, or 0–bit—rather than variable-length bursts with constant gaps as was observed in the signal from the Sony remote control. The method used by the routine is more conservative of IR energy and is equally effective at communicating with the Handy Board's own decoding routine.

- If the phase is odd, then the routine has been entered following the falling edge at the end of an IR burst. It then schedules a rising edge a certain period of time later, thus defining a start bit, 1–bit, or 0–bit depending on this length of time.

    - If the phase is 19, then the start bit is scheduled at 3.0 msec − 0.6 msec = 2.4 msec later.

    - Otherwise, the data bit is scheduled: if a 1–bit, then 1.8 msec − 0.6 msec = 1.2 msec later; if a 0–bit, then 1.2 msec − 0.6 msec = 0.6 msec later.

IR Communications Exercises

1. *Communicating with consumer electronic devices.* The `sony_xmit()` function as it is provided *cannot* communicate with Sony consumer electronic devices because it does not transmit the device selection bits as discussed earlier (Section 6.2.6). Modify the `sonyxmit.asm` driver to transmit additional bits so that it can indicate with Sony consumer electronics units. Using the Handy Board and various sensors,

design a system to turn on the television in your room whenever someone sits down on the couch.

2. *Other consumer IR formats.* Using the reverse-engineering techniques presented in this section, capture and reverse-engineer other manufacturers' IR remote formats. To capture the foreign IR signals, use a digital storage oscilloscope or write an assembly language driver for the Handy Board to sample, store, and upload data from its IR input. Write driver code to transmit and/or receive these formats.

3. *Beacon systems.* Implement the IR beacon system as presented. Write a program to allow one robot to track another using the beacon system for location sensing.

4. *Robot dance troupe.* Give two (or more) robots bidirectional IR capability, and choreograph a robotic dance among them.

5. *Additional IR receivers.* Rewrite the `sony_rcv.asm` IR reception driver to work with timer inputs 2 and 3, which are broken out to Handy Board digital inputs 8 and 7, respectively. Plug additional IR receivers into these inputs.

6. *Noise-resistant proximity sensor.* Using external IR transmitters and receivers, implement a noise-resistant proximity sensor by transmitting a particular number and looking for it to be reflected back into the adjacent IR receiver.

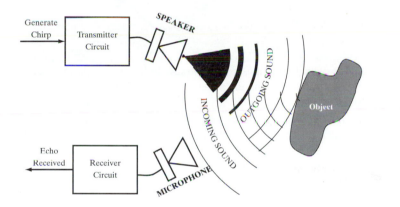

FIGURE 6.49 Ultrasonic Ranging Block Diagram

To perform ultrasonic ranging, a transmitter circuit causes an ultrasonic burst, or "chirp," to be emitted from a speaker element. This sound travels out to an object and is reflected back into a receiver circuit, which is tuned to detect the specific frequency of sound emitted by the transmitter.

By measuring the elapsed time from when the chirp is emitted to when the echo is received, the distance may be calculated. In normal room temperature, sound travels about 1.12 feet per millisecond or 0.89 milliseconds per foot. Because the sound has to go out to the object and then back to the receiver, 1.78 msec of elapsed time corresponds to an object at one foot's distance from each of the emitter and receiver.

So the distance to the target object (in feet) is the time it takes for a chirp to make a round trip (in msec) divided by 1.78.

6.3 Ultrasonic Distance Sensing with the Polaroid 6500

In this section and the following one, we explore two different technologies for measuring the distance from a sensor to an object: *ultrasonic ranging*, which measures the time of flight for a sonar "chirp" to bounce of a target and return of the sensor, and *optical ranging*, which uses a lens and a linear position sensor to detect the incident angle of a spot of light shone on the target. These techniques provide much greater accuracy than the ranging techniques presented in the previous IR sensing section.

Compared with the speed of microprocessor circuits, sound travels through the air incredibly slowly, moving at the rate of about one foot per millisecond. Because sound easily reflects off objects—that is, it creates echoes—it is a relatively straightforward task to create a device that produces a sound and waits to see how long it takes for that sound to return as an echo. So simply by emitting a "chirp" and timing how long it takes that chirp to return, we can get a radarlike measurement of how far away the nearest object is from the sensor.

Figure 6.49 illustrates this idea. In the block diagram, there is an ultrasonic speaker transmitter, with a digitally controlled drive circuit that produces a quick burst of ultrasound, and an ultrasonic microphone receiver, which recognizes when the proper echo is received. To measure distance, one must simply trigger the emitter and then measure the elapsed time until the receiver indicates that an echo is detected.

FIGURE 6.50 The Polaroid 6500
Series Ultrasonic Ranging
System

Such a device was first popularized by the Polaroid Corp. in a camera that used ultrasonic ranging to measure the distance from the camera to the subject for the control of an auto-focus system. Contemporary cameras typically use IR auto-focus systems, which are smaller, cheaper, and use less power, but Polaroid's ultrasonic auto-focus technology encouraged the use of ultrasonic ranging in many industrial and robotics applications.

Polaroid continues to sell their ultrasonic ranging system as an original equipment manufacturer (OEM) kit—that is, an unpackaged board-level technology to be designed into products by engineers. This is also ideal for use by students, hobbyists, and researchers, and the remainder of this section explores the use of Polaroid's ultrasonic ranging system.

Figure 6.50 shows the commercially available Polaroid 6500 Sonar Ranging System. It consists of two components: a single board that holds all of the electronics, and one ultrasonic transducer, which acts as both the speaker and microphone.

The ranging system is easily interfaced to a microprocessor circuit (such as the Handy Board's) using just two or three simple digital control signals. In the simplest operational mode, only two signals are used: INIT, an input to the ranging board that generates a sonar chirp, and ECHO, an output that indicates when the reflected chirp is received. All that the controlling circuit needs to do is raise the INIT signal and measure how much time elapses until the ECHO signal goes high. The distance from the sensor to the nearest object is directly proportional to the time it takes the sonar chirp to be reflected; twice as far, then twice as long. With the use of a third signal, very close distances may be measured.

There are a number of details about the operation of the Polaroid system that are instructive to know.

Signal Gain. As sound disperses through the air, its volume falls off at the square of the distance. For the purposes of ultrasonic ranging, the sound must then reflect off a surface, which introduces yet more dispersion as the sound travels back to the transducer. The net result is that an echo from a far away object may be one millionth the strength of an echo from a nearby object.

Bat Radar

It is now commonly known that bats use a radarlike form of ultrasonic ranging to navigate as they fly. In a fashion similar to the ultrasonic sensing discussed in this section, bats send out various high-frequency ultrasonic wails and listen for their echoes, using this information to build a three-dimensional representation of space.

The initial research that suggested that bats had this capability was conducted at the same time as the work in electromagnetic radar was starting (around 1940). Apparently, the scientists who were working on radar were not at all happy to believe that the lowly bat might have capabilities that surpassed their own ingenuity. As reported by Donald Griffin and recounted in Richard Dawkins' *The Blind Watchmaker*, "Radar and sonar were still highly classified developments in military technology, and the notion that bats might do anything even remotely analogous to the latest triumphs of electronic engineering struck most people as not only implausible but emotionally repugnant."

Dawkins went on to explain that the bat's ability to echolocate with sound should seem a lot like vision to us. That is, the components of a bat's brain that generate cries and process echoes must create a representation of the world in a very similar fashion as the visual cortex of most mammals' brains process light. So the fact that a bat can "see" with sound should be no more or less surprising than the fact that we can "see" with light. It's just the unfamiliarity that makes it so impressive.

To deal with this variance in signal strength, the Polaroid 6500 board includes a variable gain amplifier that is automatically controlled through 12 gain steps, increasing the circuit's gain as time elapses while waiting for an echo to return. As the gain is stepped up, the amplifier becomes progressively more selective, amplifying best around the chirp frequency of 50 kHz.

Transducer Ringing. The Polaroid ultrasonic system uses one transducer as both the transmitter "speaker" and the receiver "microphone." The transducer is designed to be especially efficient at the chirp frequency of 50 kHz. Because the emitted and detected frequencies are the same, it makes sense to use a single transducer element.

The only drawback to this approach is the ringing problem: After transmitting the outgoing chirp (at very high power because echoes may be weak), the transducer can have residual vibrations or ringing that may be interpreted as the echo signal. By keeping the initial circuit gain low, the likelihood of false triggering is lessened. Additionally, however, the controller board applies a blanking signal to completely block any return signals for the first 2.38 millisec after the ultrasonic chirp is emitted. This limits the default range to objects 1.33 feet and greater (because the reflection from objects closer than 1.33 feet would be received in less than 2.38 millisec).

For detection of objects in this close-up range, the 6500 board provides a "blanking inhibit" (BINH) input that may be used to disable the blanking at any point after the transmitted chirp. This works as long as one does not turn off the blanking so soon that the residual ringing is detected. Generally, the 2.38 millisec/1.33 foot default is fairly conservative, and the blanking may be disabled early enough to detect objects down to a few inches.

Operating Frequency and Voltage. The Polaroid ultrasonic system operates at a frequency of 49.4 kHz. Each sonar "chirp" consists of 16 cycles of sound at this frequency.

The 49.4 kHz value was chosen to provide good directionality and range. The higher the frequency of sound, the shorter its wavelength and the more directional it is. (When setting up a home stereo system, the low-frequency "subwoofer" may be placed nearly anywhere in the room, but high-frequency "tweeters" must be arranged so that they face the listening area.)

The Polaroid board generates a chirp signal of 400 volts on the transducer. This high voltage is necessary to produce an adequate volume of chirp so that the weak reflected signals are of enough strength to be detected. *It is important to recognize that this high voltage is present on the transducer terminals, so that care may be taken not to touch the transducer terminals while the ultrasonic device is operating!*

Sound Reflection

When sound strikes an irregularly shaped object, like a couch or a person's leg, it produces a collection of reflected sounds, diffusing outward in many different directions. When sound strikes a long flat surface, like a wall, however, it reflects cleanly, like a beam of light reflecting off a mirror.

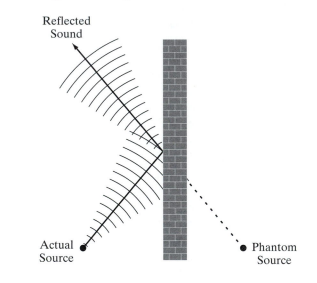

This phenomenon can be heard while standing near the wall of a large building. Often a sound will seem to come from behind the wall, even inside of the building. As indicated in the diagram above, a sound source will create a directed reflected beam of sound. To the ear, this produces a "phantom sound"—a sensorily consistent location for the actual sound to have originated.

For robots using sonar in office buildings, this effect can be problematic. A sonar chirp can strike the wall of hallway, reflect off with little or no sound aimed back at the sonar transducer, and be lost forever!

The 400-volt signal is of a low enough current rating that it is unlikely that real injury from the shock will result. Often, however, injury from shocks occurs from the reflex recoil of moving away from the electrical source. So please be aware that the Polaroid ultrasonic transducer can deliver an electrical shock.

Electrical Noise. Because of the high amplification involved, especially as the board ramps up the gain as it waits for distant echoes to return, the system is very sensitive to electrical noise in the power circuit, especially the type that is caused by DC motors. The Polaroid engineers recommend that all high current electronic and electromechanical activity be suspended while sonar readings are in progress. If it is not feasible to keep motors off when taking sonar readings, it may be necessary to provide the sonar module with its own power supply, isolated from the power supply of the robot's motors.

6.3.1 Connection Diagram

The remainder of this section explains how to electrically connect the Polaroid 6500 Series Ultrasonic Ranging System to the Handy Board, and it provides two different driver programs to demonstrate its usage.

In addition to the 6500 series Polaroid module, the following components and materials are required:

- six (6) 1N5401 diodes (3A current capacity)
- one (1) 1K resistor
- 0.1 μF capacitor
- 22 AWG gauge solid hookup wire

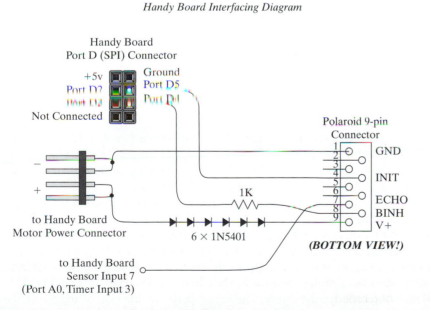

POLAROID ULTRASONIC RANGING SYSTEM

Handy Board Interfacing Diagram

Handy Board
Port D (SPI) Connector

+5v   Ground
Port D7   Port D5
Port D6   Port D4
Not Connected

Polaroid 9-pin
Connector

1
2 GND
3
4 INIT
5
6 ECHO
7 BINH
8 V+
9

1K

to Handy Board
Motor Power Connector

6 × 1N5401

(BOTTOM VIEW!)

to Handy Board
Sensor Input 7
(Port A0, Timer Input 3)

FIGURE 6.51 Wiring Diagram for Polaroid 6500 Sonar Board

Please note that the Polaroid 9-pin connector is illustrated from a bottom view, as if you were holding the connector in your hand looking at its pins. The six 1N5401 diodes, which are wired in series, drop the motor battery voltage from around 9v to the required 6v.

Figure 6.51 shows how the Polaroid Ranging Module is connected to the Handy Board. For the three wires that are plugged singly into the Handy Board (i.e., to Handy Board Port D5, Port D4, and Sensor Input 7), use 22 gauge solid hookup wire. For the motor power connector, use the same wiring technique as for typical Handy Board sensor devices.

FIGURE 6.52 Connection Board Between Polaroid Unit and Handy Board

In the lower right is a standard DB–9 connector, which accepts the flex-cable connector supplied with the Polaroid unit. Along the upper edge are the six 1N5401 diodes.

It may be helpful to use a 0.1-inch breadboard to mount the diodes and make the connections to the special 9–pin connector that comes with the Polaroid board. Figure 6.52 shows a sample mounting method. A standard DB–9 connector is used to allow the Polaroid 9–pin connector to plug in without soldering.

Install the 0.1 μF capacitor in the C7 position on the sonar board.

6.3.2 Basic Driver Code

Here is a basic version of code to drive the sonar board. This first driver performs the task of triggering the sonar ping and measuring the interval before the echo is received.

First, the initialization code:

```
void sonar_init() {
    bit_set(0x1009, 0x30);      /* ddrd */
    bit_set(0x1021, 1);         /* at tctl2, */
    bit_clear(0x1021, 2);       /* set tic3 for rising edge */
}
```

The first `bit_set` instruction changes two bits in the Port D Data Direction (DDRD) register to establish the two Port D pins as 68HC11 outputs. These two pins are used to control the sonar's transmit pulse (Port D5, connected to the sonar INIT pin) and user-adjustable blanking (Port D4, to the sonar's BINH pin).

The second pair of `bit_set` and `bit_clear` instructions modifies the settings in the 68HC11's TCTL2 register, telling timer input 3 pin to trigger on rising edges. This pin is connected from the sonar's ECHO signal, which rises from 0 to 1 when the return sonar pulse is received.

The `bit_set` and `bit_clear` operations are used—rather than `poke` instructions—so as not to affect the settings of any other bits in these two 68HC11 registers.

Next is the code for the driver. The driver performs the task of triggering the sonar pulse by bringing high the INIT signal and then measuring elapsed time until the ECHO signal goes high. Because the ECHO signal is plugged into a 68HC11 timer input, the timer subsystem is used to automatically capture the time value when the ECHO signal goes high. This is the purpose of the earlier settings to the TCL2 register in the initialization routine. Therefore, all the main driver needs to do is record the global time value when

Name	Address	Function
PORTA	0x1000	Port A pins. The ECHO signal from the Polaroid sonar is connected to the lowest bit of Port A, which is also Timer Input 3.
PORTD	0x1008	Port D pins. When pins are configured as outputs, setting a bit in this register causing the corresponding pin to go high; clearing the bit makes the pin go low. Two Port D pins are used to drive the Polaroid sonar's INIT and BINH inputs.
DDRD	0x1009	Data Direction Register for Port D. Setting a bit in this register causes the corresponding Port D pin to be configured as an output; clearing the bit sets the pin to be an input.
TCNT	0x100e	Free-running timer counter register. Increments continually at the rate of 2,000,000 counts per second.
TIC3	0x1014	Timer Input Capture 3 register. When the timer input is triggered (see TCTL2), the value of TCNT is immediately copied into the TIC3 register.
TCTL2	0x1021	Timer Control register 2. Determines what kind of signal causes timer input pin to respond. For the sonar driver, timer 3 is set to capture TCNT on rising edges (of the ECHO signal).

FIGURE 6.53 68HC11 Control Registers Used in Sonar Driver

the INIT signal is raised, clear the timer, wait until the ECHO signal goes high, and then calculate the total elapsed time by looking at the captured time value in the timer input's register:

```
int sonar_sample() {
    int start_time;

    poke(0x1023, 1);                /* clear tic3 flag */

    start_time= peekword(0x100e);   /* capture start time */
    bit_set(0x1008, 0x20);          /* trigger pulse */

    while (!(peek(0x1000) & 0x1)) { /* wait until receive echo */
        if ((peekword(0x100e) - start_time) < 0) {
            /* if too much time has elapsed, abort */
            bit_clear(0x1008, 0x20);
            return -1;
        }
        defer();                    /* let others run while waiting */
    }

    bit_clear(0x1008, 0x20);        /* clear pulse trigger */

    return peekword(0x1014) - start_time; /* tic3 has time of echo */
}
```

Let's go through the code in detail. First, an integer variable, start_time, is created to keep track of the starting time of the sonar ping. Next, the TIC3 flag (for timer input capture 3, the pin that is connected from the ECHO signal) is cleared, by writing a "1" into its bit position in the TFLG1 register.[3] The timer is now set up to capture the global time value when the ECHO signal goes high.

Next the start time is stored from the global TCNT time register (address 0x100e). Then the sonar pulse is triggered by setting bit 5 (the 0x20 value) in the Port D register.

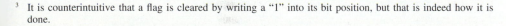

3   It is counterintuitive that a flag is cleared by writing a "1" into its bit position, but that is indeed how it is done.

Now the routine enters a while loop, waiting for the ECHO pulse to go high. Remember, the real work is going to be done by the 68HC11 timer subsystem, which will automatically capture the exact TCNT value when the ECHO pulse is received. The purpose of this while loop is mostly to just wait for that value to be captured so the sonar_sample() routine can report it. Also, the while loop checks if too much time has elapsed; if so, it returns an error value of −1.

Notice that the while loop includes a call to defer() each time through the loop. This yields control to any other C processes that might be running. The precision timing is being done by the underlying 68HC11 timer system, so this while loop can be sloppy and just occasionally check whether the operation has completed or timed out. Because of this, the while loop does not waste much processing time while it is waiting for the sonar ping to return.

The remainder of the routine cleans up by turning off the pulse trigger and returns the total elapsed time by subtracting the starting time value from the echo time captured in the timer input capture 3 register.

6.3.3 Driver with Close-Up Capability

The Polaroid module normally blanks the receive input for the first 2.38 milliseconds (corresponding to a distance of 1.33 feet) after a ping is produced so that the sensor does not detect residual ringing of the sonar transducer after the transmit pulse. This default mode of operation then limits the sensor to detect distances of 1.33 feet and beyond.

This limitation may be overcome with the use of the BINH, or Blanking INHibit, input. The module will accept receive echo signals as soon as the BINH input is taken high. Some blanking interval is needed; however, it can be much shorter than 2.38 milliseconds, allowing targets much closer than 1.33 feet to be detected.

The following routine extends the earlier sonar_sample() by turning on the blanking inhibit 0.5 milliseconds after the sonar ping is generated. This allows the sensor to detect objects down to a few inches.

```
int sonar_closeup() {
    int start_time;

    poke(0x1023, 1);                    /* clear tic3 flag */
    start_time= peekword(0x100e);
    poke(0x1008, 0x20);

    while ((peekword(0x100e) - start_time) < 1000);

    bit_set(0x1008, 0x30);              /* turn on BINH and INIT */

    while (!(peek(0x1000) & 0x01)) {
        if ((peekword(0x100e) - start_time) < 0) {
            /* if too much time has elapsed, abort */
            bit_clear(0x1008, 0x30);
            return -1;
        }
        defer();
    }

    bit_clear(0x1008, 0x30);

    return peekword(0x1014) - start_time;    /* 0x1014 is tic3 */
}
```

6.3.4 A Test Routine

The following test routine may be used to demonstrate proper operation of the Polaroid sonar device. Note the 50 millisecond delay between successive calls to the sonar driver; some delay between sonar pings is necessary for the device to operate properly.

```
void sonar_display()
{
    sonar_init();

    while (1) {
        int result;
        result= sonar_sample();
        if (result != -1) printf("%d\n", result);
        else printf("*******\n");
        msleep(50L);
    }
}
```

6.3.5 Converting Time Measurements to Actual Distance

Sound travels approximately 1.1 feet per millisecond in average atmospheric conditions at room temperature. Because the sonar ping must travel out to the target and back to the sensor, one must use the round-trip travel time when calculating from time to distance.

For example, the Polaroid 6500's blanking interval is 2.38 milliseconds. According to the Polaroid manual, this corresponds to a distance of 1.33 feet (the closest object the sensor can measure without using the blanking inhibit feature). This distance can be confirmed by multiplying the 2.38 msec by the travel rate of 1.1 ft/msec, yielding a total travel of 2.618 feet, which divided by two indicates an object about 1.31 feet from the ultrasonic transducer—close enough to the nominal 1.33 foot value.

6.3.6 Sonar Exercises

1. *Converting elapsed time counts to distance readings.*
   The sonar routines presented here report elapsed time in the 68HC11's TCNT units, which count at the rate of 2,000,000 counts per second, or 0.5 microseconds per count. Thus, for example, a reading of 10,000 corresponds to a time of 5 millseconds.

   (a) Assuming that sound travels 1.1 feet per millisecond, write a formula to convert from TCNT units to distance to target (in feet).
   (b) Assuming that sound travels 34 centimeters per millisecond, write a formula to convert from TCNT units to distance to target (in centimeters).

2. *Robot navigation.*

   (a) Mount the Polaroid ranging unit onto the *HandyBug* (see Figure 6.54). Determine the extent to which operating the *HandyBug*'s drive motors affects sonar readings.
   (b) Write a control program to drive *HandyBug* around without crashing into objects.
   (c) Mount the sonar transducer on a shaft driven from a servo motor, and write software to enable *HandyBug* to search for and then drive toward open spaces in its navigation routines.

3. *Multisonar interference.* Using two robots, each of which has its own sonar navigation system, characterize the nature of the interference (or lack of it) between the two sonar systems.

FIGURE 6.54 The *HandyBug*
Equipped with Polaroid Sonar
Module

4. *Mapping.* Combine a sonar unit with a robot that has shaft encoders on its wheels
(to measure displacement as it moves), and create a demonstration application of a
robot that can map its surroundings.

6.4 Optical Distance Sensing with the Sharp GP2D02

In Section 3.6, we discussed the reflective optosensor, which may be used to perform
crude proximity and distance measurements. In the simple reflective scheme, an emitter
LED sends a beam of light that is reflected off a target; a detector LED measures the
strength of the reflection, which provides a crude measure of the target's proximity to
the sensor device.

The simple reflective optosensor is not very useful as a general purpose distance-
measuring device. It only works well when the sensor is very close to the target (usually
an inch or less), and still it is greatly affected by ambient lighting conditions and the
reflectivity of the target.

Enter Sharp Electronics with its GP2D02 optical distance sensor, shown in Figure 6.55.
This device combines a modulated IR emitter with a detector assembly that includes a
focusing lens and a "position-sensitive detector."

Figure 6.56 illustrates how the sensor works. An IR emitter LED projects a spot of
modulated light onto the target surface. The light from this spot is focused by a detector
lens onto a special linear position-sensitive detector element. Depending on the distance
from the sensor unit to the target surface, the angle of incoming reflected light will
change, and the spot of light will be projected to a different point along the position
sensor. Thus, the location of the spot on the sensor corresponds to the distance to the
target.

The device's output is the position of the reflected spot. As long as the target is
sufficiently reflective so that the spot is registered by the detector, the resultant reading
is independent of the target's actual reflectivity. By contrast, the IR ranging methods
presented earlier in the chapter all are affected by the target's innate reflectivity.

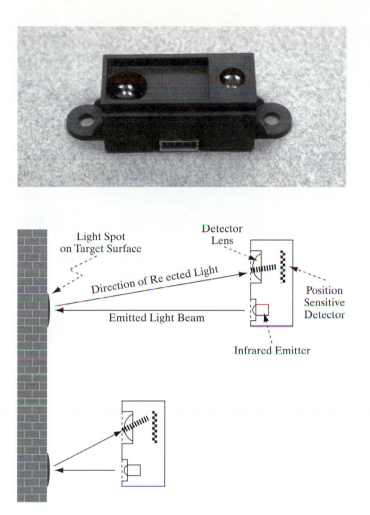

FIGURE 6.55 Photograph of Sharp GP2D02 Optical Distance Sensor

FIGURE 6.56 Operation of the Sharp GP2D02 Optical Distance Sensor

The Sharp GP2D02 distance sensor works by measuring the *incident angle* of a reflected beam of IR light. In the diagram, the emitted light beam creates a light spot on the target surface. This spot is picked up by the detector lens, which focuses the light spot along the position-sensitive detector. As indicated in the lower diagram, when the sensor unit is closer to the target, the incident angle of the reflected light changes and so does the position of the projected spot. The position-sensitive detector reports the location of the light spot, which thus corresponds to the distance from the sensor unit to the target.

6.4.1 Connection Diagram

The Sharp GP2D02 uses a digital interface. There is one input line and one output line. The input line is used to tell the device to take a reading and synchronize the clocking of data on its output line. The sensor uses a standard +5v power supply.

Figure 6.57 illustrates a method of interfacing the Sharp 2D02 sensor with the Handy Board. Two spare digital I/O pins from the Handy Board's SPI port (the Port D register) are employed to operate the sensor: Pin D2 drives the sensor's input, and D3 receives the sensor's output.

Notice the 1N914 diode in the path of the connection from Pin D2 to the input of the sensor. This is required because the GP2D02 device employs an unusual "open drain" input circuit, meaning that one must ever drive a +5v voltage to the input pin. The diode allows Pin D2 to pull the sensor's input low (to zero volts); when D2 is high, the diode blocks the voltage from driving the sensor input. There is a pull-up resistor internal to the sensor on its input line to assert the +5v level.

6.4.2 Construction Notes

The Sharp GP2D02 uses an unusual 4–pin connector (Japan Solderless Terminal Co. #S4B–ZR). If it is difficult to locate this or a compatible connector, the connector may be desoldered from the sensor, and wires may be soldered into the connector's mounting holes.

FIGURE 6.57 Wiring Diagram for Sharp GP2D02 Optical Distance Sensor

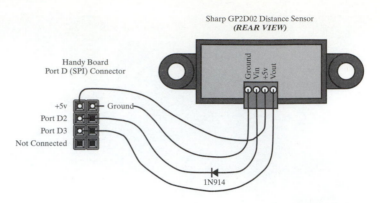

To remove the connector, first carefully cut away as much of the connector's plastic housing as is convenient using a razor knife. Then individually desolder and remove each of the four connector pins. After the last pin is removed, the remaining plastic connector housing will just lift away. Finally use a desoldering pump to remove solder from the mounting holes.

The diode shown in the wiring diagram may be mounted directly on the sensor in the proper hole. Make sure to mount the anode end toward the sensor so that the cathode (banded end) faces toward the Handy Board.

Double-row male pin header may be used to fashion the connector that plugs into the Handy Board. After soldering the terminals, bend the cable so that it leads out perpendicular to the connector and will fit underneath the LCD screen. Squeeze a glob of hot glue onto the connector plug to serve as a strain relief and electrical insulator.

Figure 6.58 shows the completed sensor ready to be plugged into the Handy Board.

6.4.3 Sensor Communications Timing

Figure 6.59 shows the timing chart for operating the sensor. The GP2D02's V_{in} input both enables the sensor and acts as a clock to serially shift the sensor reading out the V_{out} output.

The process for taking a reading is as follows. First, V_{in} must be taken low for at least 70 milliseconds to allow the sensor to power-up and perform the actual measurement. Then the V_{in} line can begin clocking rapidly to make the result data available on the V_{out} line. After one initial set-up clock pulse, the data, beginning with the most significant bit of the result byte, are available on each rising edge of the V_{in} clock.

FIGURE 6.58 Sharp GP2D02 Sensor Wired to Handy Board Plug

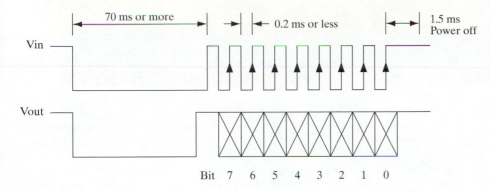

FIGURE 6.59 Sharp GP2D02
Timing Chart

To operate the sensor, first the V_{in} line is brought low for at least 70 milliseconds, during which time the sensor turns on and takes a reading. Then V_{in} is clocked to read the result out the V_{out} line. Each bit of the result is valid in between the falling edges of the V_{in} clock, and readings are taken on the rising edge of V_{in} (as indicated by the arrowheads). The data bits are presented most significant bit first. If a new measurement cycle is not begun 1.5 milliseconds after the final clock pulse, the sensor goes into a power-saving mode.

After clocking out the last data bit, the V_{in} line should be left high to allow the sensor to enter a power-saving mode in which it draws only 3 μA of current. (When taking a sensor reading, the GP2D02 consumes about 22 mA.) After 1.5 ms of idle time, the sensor automatically switches to the power-save mode.

6.4.4 Driver Code

Based on this understanding of the communications protocol of the Sharp GP2D02, here we present a driver program written as a pair of a C language "wrapper" function and an Interactive C assembly language module. Here is the following C function from the file gp2d02.c:

```
/*
   gpd202.c: wrapper for gp2d02.icb driver for Sharp GP2D02
   Fred Martin (fredm@media.mit.edu) 1/1/98
*/

int gp2d02_sample() {
    bit_clear(0x1008, 0x04);    /* turn on sensor */
    msleep(70L);                /* let it take reading */

    return gp2d02_talk(0);      /* clock in the result */
}
```

The gp2d02_sample() function is called by the user to take a sensor reading. First, it clears the Port D2 bit that is connected to the sensor's V_{in} line, turning the sensor on and initiating the sensor's operation. Then a delay of 70 milliseconds is performed, allowing the sensor to do its work. Then the gp2d02_talk() assembly language driver is called, which does the "hard" work of clocking in the result.

In Figure 6.60 is the gp2d02_talk() routine, contained in the file gp2d02.asm. (To load the driver pair into the Interactive C environment, the file gp2d02.lis is provided.) Let's examine how the gp2d02.asm program does the job.

After the constant definitions, the first code section is subroutine_initialize_module, which is automatically called when the driver is loaded. This section establishes the Port D2 pin as a 68HC11 output, and it makes sure that its state is high so the sensor is disabled until the main driver is called.

Next is the main subroutine_gp2d02_talk routine. After disabling interrupts (the sei instruction), the real work is done. The set-up pulse is transmitted to the sensor with a pair of bit set and bit clear instructions. Then the B register, which is used to build up the incoming data byte, is cleared, and the A register, which is used to count iterations through the loop reading in the data bits, is set to eight.

FIGURE 6.60 Listing of gp2d02.asm

```
******************************************************************
* gp2d02.asm                                                    *
*                                                               *
* uses: reads data byte out of Sharp GP2D02 optical distance sensor *
*       assumes output to Sharp is Port D2, input from Sharp is D3   *
*                                                               *
* Fred Martin        fredm@media.mit.edu        1 January 1998  *
******************************************************************

        BASE    equ     $1000   ; register base
        PORTD   equ     $1008   ; Port D data register
        DDRD    equ     $1009   ; Port D data direction register

        GPOUT   equ     $04     ; output to Sharp GP2D02
        GPIN    equ     $08     ; input from Sharp GP2D02

                ORG     MAIN_START

subroutine_initialize_module:
        ldx     #BASE   ; ptr to regs
        bset    PORTD,X GPOUT
        bset    DDRD,X GPOUT
        rts

subroutine_gp2d02_talk:
        ldx     #BASE   ; ptr to regs
        sei             ; disable interrupts for precise timing

* perform setup pulse
        bset    PORTD,X GPOUT
        bclr    PORTD,X GPOUT

        clrb            ; B reg will have answer
        ldaa    #8      ; loop 8 times to get data out
gploop  brclr   PORTD,X GPIN gpl50       ; test sensor output
        incb            ; if bit was high, add to result

gpl50   bset    PORTD,X GPOUT
        bclr    PORTD,X GPOUT

        deca
        beq     gpdone
        aslb            ; shift result up
        bra     gploop

gpdone  bset    PORTD,X GPOUT    ; disable sensor on exit
        cli             ; re-enable interrupts
        rts             ; A is zero, B has result
```

The data-in loop (at label `gploop`) begins by testing the state of the sensor output using a branch-if-bit-clear (`brclr`) instruction. If the incoming bit is zero, then the branch instruction is taken, skipping over the increment-B-register instruction. If the incoming bit is zero, the branch fails, and the B register is incremented, placing a "1" in its lowest bit position.

The loop continues at label `gp150` and clocks the sensor. Now the loop counter register (Register A) is decremented; if it is zero, the loop is exited by branching to `gpdone`.

If there are remaining bits to be clocked in, the result register (register B) is shifted upward with an arithmetic-shift-left (`aslb`) instruction. This places a zero in the lowest bit position and moves all other bits to the next higher bit position. Thus, the most significant bit—which is clocked in first into the lowest bit position of the B register—ends up in the highest bit position when everything is done.

At the loop exit label `gpdone`, all that remains to be done is turn on the Port D2 pin controlling the sensor (thus allowing the sensor to enter its low-power mode), reenable the 68HC11 interrupts, and return. By the design of the Interactive C assembly subroutine interface, the value in the D register (high-byte A register, low-byte B register) is returned to the C program. In this case, the high byte, which should be zero because there is only an 8–bit result, is already zero—because the A register was used for the loop counter, which exited when the count went to zero. The result byte is all ready to go in the B register.

Notice the distribution of functionality between the C language and assembly language portions of the driver. The C language portion is used mostly to perform the 70 millisecond delay after turning on the sensor. This is well suited for the C environment because (a) the 70 ms value is not critical—if it runs a little longer than that, there will be no impact on sensor performance; and (b) other Interactive C processes can run during the 70 ms delay, which is good because 70 ms is a relatively long period of time to the 68HC11.

Complementarily, the high-speed, timing-critical portion of the job is well suited to the assembly language environment. By turning off the interrupts, the driver assumes full control of the 68HC11. This is appropriate for this application because (a) the communications between the CPU and the sensor could fail if an interrupt occured during the data-clocking operation, and (b) the complete communications exchange happens fairly quickly so there is little consequence to the rest of the 68HC11 system for having the interrupts disabled during the communications interval.

6.4.5 Optical Ranging Exercises

1. *Relationship between sensor reading and actual distance.* The Sharp GP2D02 is rated to measure distances between 10 and 80 cm. By experimental measurement, verify these values and characterize the relationship between measured reading and actual distance—is it a linear response or some kind of curve?

2. *Ambient light immunity.* Experiment with different forms and brightnesses of ambient lighting (e.g., florescent, incandescent, halogen, sodium, sunlight) and describe the performance of the sensor.

3. *Modulation frequency.* To achieve its immunity from ambient lighting, the GP2D02 modulates its IR LED output. Using a photodiode or phototransistor to measure the IR emissions, determine the modulation frequency.

4. *Wall following.* The GP2D02 is ideal for tracking walls. Using a single GP2D02 sensor mounted on the *HandyBug*, write a program to have it follow along a wall. Try different setpoints of the nominal distance from the wall—what is the farthest distance from the wall that yields reliable results? Compare this to other sensor technologies.

FIGURE 6.61 Photograph of *HandyBug* with Line Sensor

5. *Maze running.* Using multiple GP2D02 sensors, it should be possible to drive down the center of a maze "hallway."

   (a) Construct a maze environment for the *HandyBug*. The walls should be far enough apart to allow *HandyBug* to maneuver easily.

   (b) Modify the provided gp2d02.asm drive to use other digital I/O pins on the Handy Board (e.g., timer output 3 [Port A5], located on the expansion header, and any of the digital inputs).

   (c) Using two GP2D02 sensors, write a program so that *HandyBug* drives forward maintaining equal distance between two walls of the maze.

6. *Other applications.* Invent some other uses for the GP2D02 sensor.

6.5 Sensor Data Processing

A big part of getting robot programs to function as intended lies in the interpretation of sensor data. If a robot's sensors are not performing or responding to the world as expected, it is very difficult to have the robot react properly.

In this section, we explore a set of issues relating to the interpretation of sensor data, including sensor calibration and sensor data-filtering techniques.

6.5.1 Line Following as a Reference Activity

We use line following as an example robot activity for looking at these issues. As shown in Figure 6.61, our line-following activity is based on the turtle-style robot chassis (e.g., the *HandyBug*) with one downward-facing reflectance sensor. The robot performs on a light-colored surface on which a dark line has been placed (e.g., electrical tape).

To follow the line, the robot waddles back and forth across the line, switching direction each time it has completely crossed over. An Interactive C program to describe this behavior is the following:

```
void line_follow() {
    while (1) {
        waddle_left();
        waituntil_on_the_line();
        waituntil_off_the_line();
        waddle_right();
```

```
        waituntil_on_the_line();
        waituntil_off_the_line();
    }
}
```

For the *HandyBug*, `waddle_left()` is accomplished simply by turning the right-side motor on forward, and `waddle_right()` is the left-side motor on. Here, we are interested in the sensor functions: How do `waituntil_on_the_line()` and `waituntil_off_-the_line()` work?

Line-Following Exercise

Before reading further, implement line following on your *HandyBug* based on the `line_follow()` function just presented.

6.5.2 Fixed Thresholding

The simplest, and often quite effective, way to interpret sensor values is with *fixed thresholding*. With this method, the sensor reading is compared with a setpoint value. If the reading is less than the setpoint, then the robot is assumed to be in State A (e.g., "on the line"); if the reading is greater than the setpoint, then the robot is in State B ("off the line"). The process converts a continuous sensor reading—like a light level—to a digital state, much like a touch sensor is either pressed or not.

With the line-following task, suppose the downward-facing reflective light sensor yields a reading of about 10 when aimed at the floor and 50 when aimed at the line. It would then make sense to choose the midpoint value of 30 as the setpoint for determining whether the robot is on the line.

Using the setpoint value of 30 and the fixed thresholding method, we can write the two line-sensor routines `waituntil_on_the_line()` and `waituntil_off_the_line()` as follows. Note that `line_sensor()` is a function that returns the current value of the light sensor aimed downward:

```
void waituntil_on_the_line() {
    while (line_sensor() < 30);
}

void waituntil_off_the_line() {
    while (line_sensor() > 30);
}

int line_sensor() {
    return analog(0);
}
```

The `waituntil_` routines each consist of a single while statement, which repeatedly tests the sensor value, exiting when a sensor reading crosses the predetermined threshold. The `waituntil_on_the_line()` routine loops while the sensor reading indicates that the robot is still on the floor (i.e., when the sensor reading is less than 30). The `waituntil_-off_the_line()` routine does the converse, looping while the sensor reading indicates the robot is still on the line (when the sensor reading is greater than 30).

6.5.3 Parameterized Fixed Thresholding

Simple fixed thresholding can be reliable, but what if the setpoint value needs to change under different operating conditions? In the example so far, the setpoint value is hard coded into two different routines—an approach that clearly does not scale as the program complexity increases.

FIGURE 6.62 Graph of Line-Following Performance Run

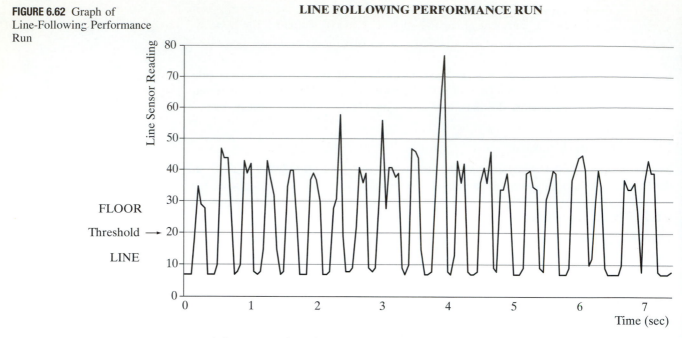

LINE FOLLOWING PERFORMANCE RUN

A better way is to break out threshold setpoints as named variables or constants and then refer to them by name in the actual routines. For example, the `waituntil_` routines would be rewritten as:

```
/*
  if using Interactive C 3.1 or higher, use
  #define LINE_SETPOINT 30
*/
int LINE_SETPOINT= 30;

void waituntil_on_the_line() {
    while (line_sensor() < LINE_SETPOINT);
}

void waituntil_off_the_line() {
    while (line_sensor() > LINE_SETPOINT);
}
```

Now when the setpoint needs to be changed, there is one clearly specified point in the program for this to be done.

6.5.4 Thresholding with Hysteresis

Simple thresholding works best in a perfect world—in other words, if sensor data are extremely reliable. Of course, this is often not the case, and there are a variety of sources of noise and other degradations of sensor performance. In our line-following example, variances in ambient lighting and surface texture of the floor can easily create unexpected and undesired glitches in sensor readings.

Figure 6.62 shows a graph of line-sensor readings over a typical line-following performance run. Notice that, although overall the data are fairly reliable, there are occasional spikes where the floor reading was much higher than usual. Also, there are places where the line detection (values less than 20, the setpoint in this case) seems unreliable.

In a less well-behaved situation, suppose experimentation reveals that, during travel across the floor surface, occasional pulses (when the robot runs over a bump, for instance) may spike the readings into the range of the line. When the robot is on the line, shiny spots may reflect as well as the floor, dropping the sensor readings up into the range of the floor.

A simple threshold will not work under these conditions because there is no single setpoint that is immune from glitches. Instead, two setpoints can be used. When the robot is looking for the line, it would wait for a strong dark reading, meaning the robot is right over the center of line. Then it would switch to looking for the floor, requiring a strong light reading, meaning it had completely left the line. With this strategy, the robot is less likely to accidentally trigger off a dark spot on the floor or a light spot on the line:

```
int LINE_SETPOINT= 35;
int FLOOR_SETPOINT= 10;

void waituntil_on_the_line() {
    while (line_sensor() < LINE_SETPOINT);
}

void waituntil_off_the_line() {
    while (line_sensor() > FLOOR_SETPOINT);
}
```

This technique imposes *hysteresis* on the interpretation of sensor values, meaning that the prior state of the system (e.g., on the line or off the line) affects the system's movement into new states. Having two setpoints to interpret the sensor reading makes it possible to require a very strong dark to recognize the line and a very strong light to recognize the floor. We have seen hysteresis used previously (Section 3.8, where it was used to cleanly interpret the waveform from a shaft encoder).

Hysteresis Thresholding Exercises

1. *Choosing threshold setpoints.* Set up the *HandyBug* with a line-following task and experiment with different values for the LINE_SETPOINT and FLOOR_SETPOINT thresholds. What values give the best performance? What values generate more line-tracking errors?

2. *Failure modes.* Explain a typical failure that occurs when using the hysteresis method versus the single threshold method.

6.5.5 Calibration by Demonstration

In the previous examples, the threshold setpoints were hard coded into the program. Parameterizing them as constants or variables makes it easier to modify their values, but adjusting the setpoints still requires editing source code and reloading the robot's program.

Instead of hard coding, another approach is to install manual calibration routines whereby the robot can be physically positioned over the line and over the floor and a threshold setpoint directly captured in the actual performance context. This has the advantage of easily adapting the robot's program for differing performance situations, trying out a variety of setpoints, and allowing a program to be written without knowing in advance what the correct setpoint values are. The following Interactive C code demonstrates how this may be done:

```
int LINE_SETPOINT= 100;
int FLOOR_SETPOINT= 100;
```

```
void main() {
    calibrate();
    line_follow();
}

void calibrate() {
    int new;
    while (!start_button()) {
        new= line_sensor();
        printf("Line: old=%d new=%d\n", LINE_SETPOINT, new);
        msleep(50L);
    }
    LINE_SETPOINT= new; /* accept new value */
    beep(); while (start_button());  /* debounce button press */
    while (!start_button()) {
        new= line_sensor();
        printf("Floor: old=%d new=%d\n", FLOOR_SETPOINT, new);
        msleep(50L);
    }
    FLOOR_SETPOINT= new;   /* accept new value */
    beep(); while (start_button());  /* debounce button press */
}
```

The line_follow() and line_sensor() routines are the same as in past versions of the example. The calibrate() routine is new; its job is to guide the process of setting threshold setpoints for the line and the floor.

The first while loop lets the users select a setpoint for the line, and the second one for the floor. The while loops each cycle through capturing a line-sensor reading, printing it on the LCD screen (along with the original setpoint value) and waiting briefly to keep the screen from flashing. The loops exit when the Start button is pressed, saving the new value in the setpoint variable.

To use the calibration routines, position the robot over the line when the display is prompting for the line threshold value. Notice that the value may be sharply higher when the reflectance sensor is positioned directly over the center of the line versus when it is near to the edge of the line. It is usually best to capture a value that is somewhere in between the value near the edge of the line and at the center of the line. If the absolute maximum value is selected, the robot will have trouble tracking the line in the actual performance because it might not obtain that maximum value while it is in motion. Similarly, for the floor threshold, it is often desirable to capture a value slightly higher than the minimum value that may be possible.

This "show me" calibration method can be a huge improvement over fixed and hard-coded calibration methods, especially when setpoints are easily parameterized and when they need to change over different operating conditions.

Calibration by Demonstration Exercises

1. *Optional calibration.* As it is written, the example calibration routine forces the selection of a new setpoint value even if the old one was desired. Write a modified calibration function that allows the user to accept a new value with the Start button, or exit without changing the setpoint when the Stop button is pressed.
2. *Automatic selection of operating mode.* Until this point, our examples have assumed that the line follower is operating on a light floor with a dark line and that the reflectance sensor returns smaller values with more light. Modify the example program to automatically perform properly if either of these characteristics is reversed.

6.5.6 Persistent Calibration

One problem with the "show me" calibration method is that the robot must be recalibrated each time the program is run—every time the Handy Board is turned off and on. If there are more than just a few parameters to establish, this can be quite time-consuming and annoying.

What is needed is a way to specify that variable values should persist through power cycling of the Handy Board. Because the contents of the Handy Board's main memory are preserved when the board is turned off and on—the battery-backed RAM keeps the robot's program intact when the Handy Board is turned off—it is a simple matter to allow variables to keep their values.

Interactive C provides a feature, called *persistent variables*, that allows any global variable to be specified as persistent, which will cause it to maintain its value when the board is turned off and on. This is accomplished simply by prefixing the global variable declaration with the keyword `persistent`. For example, the declaration

```
persistent int i;
```

creates a persistent integer named `i`. The initial value of a persistent variable is indeterminate—it is whatever happens to be the contents of the memory locations that are assigned to it—but after being set, persistent variables maintain their value until specifically assigned a new value by the user's Interactive C program.

Persistent Calibration Exercise

Persistent calibration. Declare the setpoint variables `LINE_SETPOINT` and `FLOOR_-SETPOINT` as persistent, and then use your modified calibration routine to allow optional calibration of their values. Verify that the variables maintain their values when the Handy Board is power-cycled, and that your calibration routine allows you to accept the old value when beginning a new line-following run.

6.5.7 Sensor Histories

To this point, all of our examples have required manual calibration of a robot's sensors. In other words, for a robot's program to operate properly, it has been necessary for a person to decide what action will be taken when a sensor value reaches a particular point (e.g., what value "off the line" means so that the robot should change direction).

In this section, we explore a technique whereby sensor thresholds may be determined automatically and can dynamically adjust to changing operating conditions. This and related methods have the opportunity to make robot behavior much more robust in the face of the variability and uncertainty of the real world.

Continuing with the line-following example, we add code that keeps track of the minimum and maximum values detected during the course of the line-following activity. By automatically setting the line-detection value to be the midpoint of the minimum and maximum, the line following can be accomplished without prior knowledge of what these values are. Further, if the robot is brought into a new environment (a different floor surface or different lighting) where the sensor values change, the same program can be used.

Figure 6.63 shows a sample program to automatically calculate a midpoint between the ongoing maximum and minimum values and use this midpoint as the line threshold. How well does this idea perform?

In practice, not very well. The trouble is that the maximum values recorded as the robot passes over the line are much higher than typical line values. This pushes the

FIGURE 6.63 Listing of
lineauto.c

```
/*
    lineauto.c:  automatically set line thresholds
    based on maximum and minimum readings
*/

int line, LINE_THRESHOLD;
int max=0;
int min=255;

void main() {
    start_process(display());
    line_follow();
}

void line_follow() {
    while (1) {
        waddle_left();
        waituntil_on_the_line(); waituntil_off_the_line();
        waddle_right();
        waituntil_on_the_line(); waituntil_off_the_line();
    }
}

void waituntil_on_the_line() {
    while (line_sensor() < LINE_THRESHOLD);
}

void waituntil_off_the_line() {
    while (line_sensor() > LINE_THRESHOLD);
}

int line_sensor() {
    line= analog(0);
    if (line > max) max= line;
    if (line < min) min= line;
    LINE_THRESHOLD= (max + min) / 2;
    return line;
}

void waddle_left() {
    fd(3); off(0);
}

void waddle_right() {
    fd(0); off(3);
}

void display() {
    while (1) {
        printf("max %d min %d thresh %d line %d\n",
                max, min, LINE_THRESHOLD, line);
        msleep(50L);
    }
}
```

FIGURE 6.64 Listing of
`linehist.c`

```
/*
   linehist.c:  automatically set line thresholds
   based on average sensor reading
   requires senshist.lis package
*/

int line[50];    /* buffer to hold sensor history */
int LINE_THRESHOLD;

void main() {
    start_process(compute_and_display());
    line_follow();
}

void line_follow() {
    while (1) {
        waddle_left();
        waituntil_on_the_line(); waituntil_off_the_line();
        waddle_right();
        waituntil_on_the_line(); waituntil_off_the_line();
    }
}

void waituntil_on_the_line() {
    while (line_sensor() < LINE_THRESHOLD);
}

void waituntil_off_the_line() {
    while (line_sensor() > LINE_THRESHOLD);
}

int line_sensor() {
    return current_value((int)line);
}

void waddle_left() {
    fd(3); off(0);
}

void waddle_right() {
    fd(0); off(3);
}

void compute_and_display() {
    install_sensor_history(line, 0, 3);
    while (1) {
        LINE_THRESHOLD= sensor_average((int)line);
        printf("thresh %d line %d\n",
                LINE_THRESHOLD, current_value((int)line));
        msleep(50L);
    }
}
```

threshold value well up into and sometimes over the value that will be seen by the sensor as the robot crosses over the line. Hence, the robot does not see the line, and line-following fails.

It would be possible to rewrite the averaging operation (presently in the `line_sensor()` function) to weight the threshold nearer to the minimum value. But finding the proper amount of weighting is likely to be situation-dependent and thus is not clearly better than manually choosing a setpoint.

The problem is that just having minimum and maximum sensor values is not enough to effectively calculate a good threshold. What is needed is a whole history of past sensor values, allowing the calculation of (for instance) the *average* sensor reading.

The remainder of this section presents a set of assembly language drivers for precisely this purpose.

The Interactive C library files `senshist.icb`, `senshist.c`, and `sensproc.icb` (which may be loaded with the single list file `senshist.lis`) contain a set of functions for keeping a running history of sensor values (sampled at adjustable intervals) and reporting various characteristics of the sensor readings, such as all time maximum, all time minimum, current recorded maximum, current recorded minimum, and current average value.

The drivers work by installing an interrupt routine that periodically samples the sensor values and stores them in a buffer. Other functions, such as the current maximum or current average functions, iterate through the stored values to calculate their results.

The drivers require that the user declare a global array in Interactive C, which acts as the buffer in which the sensor values are stored. For each sensor that is to be observed, there must be a corresponding global array in which to store its history of values.

Let's first look at an example of the sensor history drivers in operation, define precisely how they are used, and then look at how they work.

Figure 6.64 shows the auto-thresholding line follower rewritten using the sensor history functions. At the start of the listing is a declaration for `line[]`, an integer array of 50 items. In this array are stored the recorded values of the line sensor.

The `line_sensor()` function is rewritten to use the new `current_value()` library function. This function takes as argument the sensor history array and returns the current (most recent) stored value.

The only other changes are in the new `compute_and_display()` function. This function initializes the history-taking process with a call to `install_sensor_history()`. This function takes three arguments: the array in which to store the history (in this case, `line`), the sensor port to be monitored (0, the port we have been using for the line sensor example), and the frequency with which to monitor the sensor (in this case, 3, which corresponds to about 8 samples per second).

After installing the monitor for the line sensor, the `compute_and_display()` function enters an infinite loop, alternately computing the line threshold with a call to the new `sensor_average()` function and displaying current threshold and line-sensor reading.

How does the line-seeking robot perform? Now the automatic threshold calculation works, and the line-following performs quite well. Notice that the threshold continues to change as the robot tracks the line. There are some interesting "emergent" behaviors if the robot does not immediately find a line: If it drives on the floor long enough, the average value will become the floor value and the robot will start driving straight ahead, as if it were looking for a line. Also, the algorithm becomes more sensitive to imperfections in the floor as the threshold gets closer to the base floor value.

Sensor History Routines

After loading the `senshist.lis` file set, the following functions are defined:

```
int install_sensor_history(int sensor_array[],
                           int sensor_number,
                           int frequency)
```

Installs background monitoring on sensor port `sensor_number`, using `sensor_array[]` for storage, at rate `frequency`.

The sensor array must be a global integer array of at least eight elements. The number of samples stored is a function of the size of the sensor array, according to the following formula:

number of samples = (size of array − 7) × 2

The `sensor_number` should be a number from 0 to 6, corresponding to Handy Board sensor inputs 0 to 6. For testing purposes, the user knob may be monitored by providing 7 as an argument.

The rate of sampling is according to the following table:

Frequency Argument	Sampling Frequency
0	62.5 Hz
1	31.25 Hz
2	15.625 Hz
3	7.8125 Hz
4	3.906 Hz
5	1.953 Hz
6	0.977 Hz
7	0.488 Hz
8	0.244 Hz

Up to seven sensor-monitoring arrays may be installed using the `install_sensor_history()` function. The return value is nonzero (the array pointer) if the installation was successful or zero if not.

`clear_history(int array_ptr)`

Clears all data in the sensor history array indicated by `array_ptr` and resets recorded all-time maximum value to 0 and all-time minimum value to 255. *Sensor monitoring must have already been installed before this function is used.*

The array pointer must be coerced to an integer before passing it to this function. For example:

```
int sensor_data[20];
```

/ monitoring of `sensor_data` array must be installed before `clear()` function is used */*

```
void clear() {
  clear_history((int)sensor_data);
}
```

```
reset_history_frequency(int array[], int frequency)
```

Changes sampling rate of sensor array already installed for monitoring according to the same frequency table shown previously. *Sensor monitoring must have already been installed before this function is used.*

```
alltime_min(int array_ptr)
```

Returns minimum sensor reading recorded since monitoring was installed on ar-ray_ptr array (or since the last time it was cleared).
The array pointer must be coerced to an integer before passing it to this function.

```
alltime_max(int array_ptr)
```

Returns maximum sensor reading recorded since monitoring was installed on ar-ray_ptr array (or since the last time it was cleared).
The array pointer must be coerced to an integer before passing it to this function.

```
sensor_min(int array_ptr)
```

Returns minimum sensor reading presently recorded in sensor array.
The array pointer must be coerced to an integer before passing it to this function.

```
sensor_max(int array_ptr)
```

Returns maximum sensor reading presently recorded in sensor array.
The array pointer must be coerced to an integer before passing it to this function.

```
current_value(int array_ptr)
```

Returns current (most recently recorded) value in sensor array.
The array pointer must be coerced to an integer before passing it to this function.

```
sensor_average(int array_ptr)
```

Returns average of sensor values currently recorded in sensor array.
The array pointer must be coerced to an integer before passing it to this function.

Sensor History Code

The sensor history package is split into three files, with an Interactive C `.lis` file to tie them together:

senshist.asm With object code in senshist.icb, this file installs interrupt-driven code to sample sensor data periodically and store it in global arrays.

**Sensor History Array
Data Structure**

Memory Offset			Array Index
+0		*array size*	–
+2		*(unused)*	0
+4	*timing mask*	*sensor port*	1
+6	*sensor maximum*	*sensor minimum*	2
+8		*data start ptr*	3
+10		*data end ptr*	4
+12		*ring start ptr*	5
+14		*ring end ptr*	6
+16	*sensor data*	*sensor data*	7
	sensor data	*sensor data*	

FIGURE 6.65 Sensor History Array Specifications

Sensor data are stored in the Interactive C array beginning with the eighth element of the array (at array index 7). In the first through seventh array locations (array indices 0 through 6), values relevant to the operation of the sensor history routines are stored, including pointers that implement a ring buffer for tracking where in the array each recorded sensor value should be stored.

`senshist.c` This file contains C-language wrapper functions for calling the routines defined in `senshist.icb`.

`sensproc.asm` With object code in `sensproc.icb`, this file contains routines that analyze the data stored in the sensor history arrays, calculating (for instance) maximum, minimum, and average values.

Following, the code from each of these files is presented and explained.

Senshist.asm

The Interactive C array is used as a ring buffer to store the sensor values. As sensor values are recorded, they are stored in consecutively higher memory locations. Once the end of the array is reached, it automatically wraps around back to the beginning of the memory segment (hence the name "ring buffer"). Two pointers are used to implement the ring buffer: one to point at the end of the buffer, where the next datum will be stored, and one to point at the start of the buffer, where the old datum is available. The Interactive C array is partitioned primarily into space for the sensor data, with other locations reserved for the two ring pointers and other housekeeping functions.

Figure 6.65 shows how the `senshist.asm` routines use the array. Note that Interactive C defines an array to include the length of the array (as a two-byte value) at the memory address pointed to by the array pointer. This value is defined by the Interactive C software system when the array is first declared and is hidden from the Interactive C programmer—the first element of the array (at index 0) immediately follows this length word.

The length information is typically used during array accesses to ensure that all array accesses are within the bounds of the array. Here, however, the `senshist.asm` driver uses the array length to figure out how much space it has to store sensor data in the array that is given to it.

After the length word, the next seven words (14 bytes) are used by the sensor history routines for various housekeeping functions:

Unused argument. At offset +2 (the 0th element of the array) is an unused word, reserved for operations in which an argument (other than the pointer to the array)

might need to be passed between the Interactive C and assembly language environments.

Timing mask. At offset $+4$ is the timing mask, used to determine the interval between successive sensor samples. This is the high byte at array index 1.

Sensor port. At offset $+5$ is the sensor port number to be sampled. This is the low byte array index 1.

Sensor maximum. At offset $+6$, the all-time sensor maximum value is recorded. Each time a sensor is sampled, the new sensor value is compared with the stored maximum; if the new value is larger, it is stored back.

Sensor minimum. In a similar fashion, at offset $+7$ from the array base, the all-time minimum sensor value is recorded.

Data start pointer. At offset $+8$ is a pointer to the starting address of where sensor data are stored. This value is needed when the ring pointers wrap around, and it is calculated once when the array is initialized for all subsequent use.

Data end pointer. At offset $+10$ is a pointer to the end of the array, one byte beyond the last place where the sensor data may be stored. As with the Data Start Pointer, this value is calculated when the array is initialized for subsequent use.

Ring start pointer. At offset $+12$ is the start pointer for the ring buffer of sensor data.

Ring end pointer. At offset $+14$ is the end pointer for the ring buffer of sensor data.

Sensor data. Beginning at offset $+16$ is the actual sensor data.

There are three sections in the `senshist.asm` code: initialization of the module, a section to install a new sensor history array, and the section called at interrupt time to process the history arrays that are already installed. Let's briefly consider how each piece of code does its job.

Looking at the code for `senshist.asm`, which follows shortly, after the constant definitions for 68HC11 registers are constant definitions for the array record as just discussed. Then some memory definitions are made, including seven bytes for storing a master pointer list of up to seven pointers. The install routine places each array pointer that is installed into this list. At interrupt time, the interrupt routine walks through this list, dealing with each sensor array installed here in turn.

After the pointer list is the initialization code. This code patches the 1,000 Hz interrupt on timer output 4, as has been done in previous examples. It zeroes out the master pointer list and then returns.

The next code segment is in the installation routine, which is used to install a given sensor history array. This routine finds the first empty slot in the master list of array pointers, installs the array it is given into that list, initializes the array, and returns. Initializing the array consists of setting up its Data Start and Data End pointers, Ring Start and Ring End pointers, and initial maximum and minimum values.

The final code segment is the actual interrupt code. This is the code that does the work of recording sensor values into the history arrays. For each array installed in the master pointer list, the routine samples the sensor value specified in the array and records the value in the array's buffer.

Following is the listing of `senshist.asm`.

```
**********************************************************************
* senshist.asm                                                      *
*                                                                   *
* sensor history package                                           *
*                                                                   *
* Fred Martin        fredm@media.mit.edu        7 February 1998     *
**********************************************************************
```

```
* 6811 registers
PORTA           equ     $1000
ADCTL           equ     $1030     ; A/D Control/status Register
ADR1            equ     $1031     ; A/D Result Register 1
TOC4INT         equ     $BFE2     ; Timer Output Compare 4

* zero-page global variables
system_time_lo  equ     $14

* array data structure offsets
A_LENGTH        equ     0         ; # of elements in A
A_ARG           equ     2         ; unused at present
A_TMASK         equ     4         ; timing mask
A_SENSNUM       equ     5         ; sensor number
A_MAX           equ     6         ; alltime max sensor val
A_MIN           equ     7         ; alltime min
A_DATASTART     equ     8         ; ptr to beginning of data area
A_DATAEND       equ     10        ; ptr to end of data area
A_RINGSTART     equ     12        ; ring of data start
A_RINGEND       equ     14        ; ring of data end
A_DATA          equ     16        ; start of actual sensor data

        org     MAIN_START

* internal data structures
local_time      fcb     0         ; low byte of (sys time / 16)

plist_start     fdb     0         ; ptr list of sensor data arrays
                fdb     0         ; 2
                fdb     0         ; 3
                fdb     0         ; 4
                fdb     0         ; 5
                fdb     0         ; 6
plist_end       fdb     0         ; 7

* install module into 1 kHz IC system interrupt on TOC4
subroutine_initialize_module:
        ldd     TOC4INT                 ; ptr to original vector
        std     interrupt_code_exit+1   ; install for our exit
        ldd     #interrupt_code_start   ; ptr to our routine
        std     TOC4INT                 ; install at TOC4 int
* zero out list of installed array ptrs
        ldx     #plist_start
        clra
clrloop staa    0,x
        inx
        cpx     #plist_end+1
        bne     clrloop
        rts


subroutine__install_sensor_history
* find 1st empty slot in ptr list
        pshb
        psha                            ; save incoming array ptr
        ldx     #plist_start
```

```
instlp  ldd     0,x
        beq     install
        inx
        inx
        cpx     #plist_end+2
        bne     instlp
* ran out of slots - abort and return 0
        pulx
        clra
        clrb
        rts
* install, init, and return
install pula
        pulb
        std     0,x
* set up DATASTART and DATAEND ptrs
* D has ptr to array; copy to X
        pshb
        psha
        pulx
* start of data = x + A_DATA
        addd    #A_DATA                    ; D already has array ptr
        std     A_DATASTART,x
* end of data = x + (array count * 2) + 2
        stx     A_DATAEND,x
        ldd     A_LENGTH,x
        lsld
        addd    #2
        addd    A_DATAEND,x
        std     A_DATAEND,x

* put array ptr back in D, and
* fall into subroutine_clear_history to finish init and return
        xgdx

subroutine_clear_history:
* D has ptr to array; transfer to X
        pshb
        psha
        pulx
* set RINGSTART and RINGEND to point at DATA
        addd    #A_DATA
        std     A_RINGSTART,x
        std     A_RINGEND,x
* set min and max
        clra
        staa    A_MAX,x
        ldaa    #255
        staa    A_MIN,x
* return with array addr for confirmation
        xgdx
        rts

interrupt_code_start:
* first check if low 4 bits of system time are zero
* (max frequency 62.5 Hz)
```

```
        ldd     system_time_lo
        andb    #%00001111
        bne     interrupt_code_exit

* save "local time" -- sys time shifted down 4 bits
        ldd     system_time_lo
        lsrd
        lsrd
        lsrd
        lsrd
        stab    local_time

* for each array in plist, do it
        ldx     #plist_start
plistlp ldd     0,x
        beq     interrupt_code_exit
        bsr     do_array
        inx
        inx
        cpx     #plist_end+2
        bne     plistlp

interrupt_code_exit:
        jmp     $0000    ; value poked in by init routine

* D is ptr to array
* X is ptr into array ptr list; must be preserved on return
do_array
* save X, transfer D into X
        pshx
        xgdx
* check mask with local time
        ldaa    local_time
        anda    A_TMASK,x
        bne     a_done

* take sensor reading
        ldaa    A_SENSNUM,x
        staa    ADCTL
* wait 30 cycles for analog reading to happen
        ldab    #6              ; 2
waitlp  decb                    ; 2
        bne     waitlp          ; 3
        ldaa    ADR1            ; get analog read
* store A into array
        bsr     ring_insert
* test for max:  if A - current MAX > 0, have new max
        cmpa    A_MAX,x
        bcs     testmin
        staa    A_MAX,x
testmin cmpa    A_MIN,x
        bcc     a_done
        staa    A_MIN,x

a_done  pulx
        rts
```

```
* Structure of Ring Buffer
*
* if RINGSTART=RINGEND, there is no data
* insert data at RINGEND and then advance it, so RINGEND always point
*   where the next datum will go
* if RINGEND advances beyond end of array size, point it at A_DATA
* if RINGEND advances into RINGSTART, advance RINGSTART
* if RINGSTART advances beyond end of array size, point it at A_DATA

* A has byte to insert
* X is ptr to array
ring_insert
        psha       ; save sensor value
        ldy        A_RINGEND,x
        staa       0,y
        iny
* if y = DATAEND, must reset y to DATASTART
        cpy        A_DATAEND,x
        bne        storeend
        ldy        A_DATASTART,x
storeend
* y now has legit value for new RINGEND
        sty        A_RINGEND,x
* check if y equals RINGSTART; if so, advance RINGSTART
        cpy        A_RINGSTART,x
        bne        ri_done
* advance RINGSTART
        ldy        A_RINGSTART,x
        iny
        cpy        A_DATAEND,x
        bne        storestart
        ldy        A_DATASTART,x
storestart
        sty        A_RINGSTART,x
ri_done pula       ; restore sensor value
        rts
```

Senshist.c

In the file `senshist.c` are "wrapper functions" that simplify the interface to the assembly language routines. Most important is the `install_sensor_history()` function, shown in the listing that follows.

This function accepts an array pointer, sensor number, and frequency specification as arguments. The sensor number and frequency value are stored directly into the array, and then the array pointer is passed to the assembly function `_install_sensor_history()`. Note the leading underscore to distinguish the assembly function from the C language one.

The frequency argument is used as an index into an array with a series of increasing bit masks that determine the interval between successive sensor samples.

Following is the listing of `senshist.c`.

```
/* senshist.c:  driver functions for senshist.asm */
/* Fred Martin   fredm@media.mit.edu    6 feb 1998 */

int _freq_table[]= {0b00000000,     /* 0-> 62.5 Hz */
                    0b00000001,     /* 1-> 31.25 Hz */
                    0b00000011,     /* 2-> 15.625 Hz */
```

```
                    0b00000111,    /* 3-> 7.8125 Hz */
                    0b00001111,    /* 4-> 3.906 Hz */
                    0b00011111,    /* 5-> 1.953 Hz */
                    0b00111111,    /* 6-> 0.977 Hz */
                    0b01111111,    /* 7-> 0.488 Hz */
                    0b11111111};   /* 8-> 0.244 Hz */

/* arguments:
    array_ptr[]   integer array of not fewer than 8 items
    sensor_num    0 to 6 sensor input to keep history (7 is knob)
    frequency     rate of sensor sampling (see table above)
*/
int install_sensor_history(int array_ptr[],
                           int sensor_num,
                           int frequency) {
    if (frequency > 8)  {
        printf("freqency out of range\n");
        return -1;
    }
    array_ptr[1]= sensor_num + (_freq_table[frequency] << 8);
    return _install_sensor_history((int)array_ptr);
}

/* to change frequency after history is installed */
int set_history_frequency(int array_ptr[], int frequency)  {
    if (frequency > 8)  {
        printf("freqency out of range\n");
        return -1;
    }
    array_ptr[1]= (array_ptr[1] && 0xff) + (_freq_table[frequency] << 8);
}

/* functions in senshist.asm
    clear_history(int array_ptr)        erases all data in history array

    functions in sensproc.asm
    alltime_min(int array_ptr)          smallest value ever recorded
    alltime_max(int array_ptr)          largest value recorded
    sensor_min(int array_ptr)           smallest value presently recorded
    sensor_max(int array_ptr)           largest value presently recorded
    current_value(int array_ptr)        last sample taken
    sensor_average(int array_ptr)       average of presently recorded vals
*/
```

Sensproc.asm   The `sensproc.asm` contains code to process data in a sensor array, returning results like average, maximum, and minimum values.

In the code listing, the first two functions are subroutines for returning the all-time maximum and minimum values. These functions simply retrieve these values out of the proper location of the array because the all-time maximum and minimums are maintained when the sensor data are stored. These two functions could have been written in C, but it is more compact to use assembly code.

Next is the `current_value` function. This uses the `get_last_datum` subroutine, which checks the Ring End pointer to retrieve the last sensor value stored.

Next is the `current_min` function. This iterates through the sensor data, using `get_last_datum` to begin and then `get_prev_datum` to cycle through the sensor data.

Notice this latter subroutine sets the carry bit to indicate when there are no more sensor data.

The current_max and sensor_average functions follow a similar form as the current_min function: A call to get_last_datum is used to begin, followed by successive calls to get_prev_datum to iterate through the sensor data. When get_prev_datum returns with the carry bit set, there are no more data.

Last are the utility routines get_last_datum and get_prev_datum. The Y register is used as a pointer to the sensor data because the X register is used as a pointer to the base of the array.

Following is the listing of sensproc.asm:

```
*********************************************************************
* sensproc.asm                                                     *
*                                                                  *
* sensor history data processing package                          *
* analyzes data captured by senshist.asm                          *
*                                                                  *
* Fred Martin        fredm@media.mit.edu        7 February 1998    *
*********************************************************************

* array data structure offsets
A_LENGTH        equ     0       ; # of elements in A
A_ARG           equ     2       ; argument to various history fcns
A_TMASK         equ     4       ; timing mask
A_SENSNUM       equ     5       ; sensor number
A_MAX           equ     6       ; alltime max sensor val
A_MIN           equ     7       ; alltime min
A_DATASTART     equ     8       ; ptr to beginning of data area
A_DATAEND       equ     10      ; ptr to end of data area
A_RINGSTART     equ     12      ; ring of data start
A_RINGEND       equ     14      ; ring of data end
A_DATA          equ     16      ; start of actual sensor data


        org     MAIN_START

temp    equ     *               ; data storage
count   fdb     0               ; temp and count are the same
sum     fdb     0

subroutine_alltime_max:
        xgdx
        ldab    A_MAX,x
        clra
        rts

subroutine_alltime_min:
        xgdx
        ldab    A_MIN,x
        clra
        rts

subroutine_current_value:
        xgdx
        bsr     get_last_datum
        clra
```

```
                rts

subroutine_current_min:
                xgdx
                bsr        get_last_datum
                stab       temp
cmi_loop bsr    get_prev_datum
                bcs        cmi_done
                cmpb       temp
                bpl        cmi_loop
                stab       temp
                bra        cmi_loop
cmi_done clra
                ldab       temp
                rts


subroutine_current_max:
                xgdx
                bsr        get_last_datum
                stab       temp
cma_loop bsr    get_prev_datum
                bcs        cma_done
                cmpb       temp
                bmi        cma_loop
                stab       temp
                bra        cma_loop
cma_done clra
                ldab       temp
                rts


subroutine_sensor_average:
                ldx        #1
                stx        count
                xgdx
                bsr        get_last_datum
                clra
                std        sum

avg_lp   bsr    get_prev_datum
                bcs        avg_done
                pshx
                ldx        count
                inx
                stx        count
                pulx
                clra
                addd       sum
                std        sum
                bra        avg_lp

avg_done ldd    sum
                ldx        count
                idiv
                xgdx

                rts
```

```
* iterators for search through ring buffer
* X must point to array start
*
* get_last_datum
*       sets up Y as ptr through ring
*       returns datum in B
* get_prev_datum
*       clears carry if got datum; sets carry if done
*       returns datum in B
get_last_datum:
        ldy     A_RINGEND,x

get_prev_datum:
        cpy     A_DATASTART,x    ; check for wrap
        bne     gnd_ok
        ldy     A_DATAEND,x      ; wrap backward
gnd_ok  dey                      ; count backward from RINGEND
        ldab    0,y
        cpy     A_RINGSTART,x    ; check for last
        bne     gnd_clc
        sec
        rts
gnd_clc clc
        rts
```

Sensor History Exercises

1. *History duration.* In the last line-following example, the sensor history feature was used to set the line threshold as the average of all of the sensor readings in the history array. In the code, the array was declared as `int line[50]`, and the sensor history routine was installed at 7.8125 Hz. How many seconds of sensor readings does it take to fill the sensor history buffer?

2. *Wall following.* Use the average-value strategy demonstrated in the line-following program to make a wall follower.

3. *A stuck robot sensor.* Mount a photocell or other ambient light sensor so that it is facing outward, toward the back or side of the robot. Install a sensor history array for the light sensor with a history buffer of 5 seconds or more. If at any point the maximum and minimum values in the history buffer are the same, the robot is likely to have not moved for at least the length of time represented by the buffer.

4. *Digital sensors.* Modify the sensor history routine to keep track of digital sensors by storing digital input port byte (read at address `0x7000`) into the history array. What sort of reporter functions would be valuable for monitoring digital sensors? Implement them.

5. *Other analysis functions.* In the file `sensproc.asm`, several functions for analyzing sensor histories are available: minimum, maximum, and average. Depending on the application, various other measures of sensor data would be useful (e.g., the number of oscillations about a centerpoint, standard deviation, duration above a threshold, etc.). Describe an application that could use one of these (or any other) data measures. Using the `get_last_datum` and `get_prev_datum` subroutines, write assembly code to implement your instrument.

6. *Motor states.* In addition to monitoring sensor histories, it can be helpful to know the recent history of motor output states—to determine whether the robot is stuck in a loop, for example. This is easily done by capturing and storing the motor control

byte, a memory global used by the Interactive C software system to control motors at interrupt time. At memory location `0x0e`, the high four bits indicate whether each of the four motor outputs is on or off, and the low four bits indicate direction for the corresponding motor.

This idea of monitoring the commanded output state of the robot has been explored in chapter 5. In this exercise is a method for extracting such information without needing to modify the robot's control program.

Sensor Data Processing Conclusion

In this section, we have seen a progression of methods for interpreting sensor into actionable behaviors:

- fixed thresholds hard coded into program logic,
- fixed thresholds parameterized and broken out into constant or variable definitions,
- calibration by demonstration, and
- dynamic, self-adjusting algorithms.

All of these methods can coexist in a given robot's design as long as the virtues and limitations of each are recognized. There are instances where a fixed threshold will do the job reliably and simply, and hopefully too one can recognize design problems in which an adaptive solution is best.

APPENDIX

A

Inside the Handy Board Design

This appendix provides a comprehensive introduction to the 68HC11 microprocessor and the Handy Board circuit design. The intent is to provide an in-depth tutorial in working at the lowest levels of the Handy Board system—programming the 68HC11 in assembly language and talking directly to the Handy Board's hardware subsystems.

In the first section, "Introduction to Microprocessors and the 68HC11," the general scheme of the 8-bit microprocessor is presented, along with information specific to the 68HC11 design. The second section, "Introduction to Assembly Language Programming," presents an overview of the process of writing and running assembly language programs. This is explained by means of example programs, as well as introducing the digital sensor port, one of several Handy Board subsystems to be treated in detail.

The third section, "The 68HC11 with the Handy Board Hardware," systematically explains all aspects of the Handy Board hardware design, including the motor ports, analog inputs, the LCD screen, serial communications, and infrared (IR) communiations. Live 68HC11 code is presented for interfacing with each subsystem.

The final two sections are short references: "The AS11 Assembler" provides details on using the standard 68HC11 assembler software, and "Differences Between A and E Series 68HC11 CPUs" notes some details between these two very similar models of the 68HC11 chip.

A.1 Introduction to Microprocessors and the 68HC11

The modern microprocessor was invented by Intel in the 1970s—the company that is now the powerhouse that produces the hugely successful line of Pentium processors. Intel had won a contract to design a chip to operate a hand-held electronic calculator; rather than make a chip that could only be a calculator; they designed the Intel 4004, a fully programmable microprocessor.

At first, no one thought microprocessors would be good for much of anything (other than calculators). Now they're ubiquitous, and run the range from 25¢ versions inside mice and toasters to top-of-the-line models that drive desktop supercomputers.

A.1.1 Bits, Bytes, and Characters

Because we have 10 fingers, most people think in base 10, or decimal, numbers. In computers, information is represented with voltages, and it is most convenient for the voltage levels to represent only two states: a one or a zero. Thus, computers process binary digits, or bits.

For convenience, microprocessors group bits together into words. The first microprocessor operated on a word composed of four bits. Today, many small microprocessors

308

FIGURE A.1 Some Numeric Conversions

Binary	Decimal	Hex
%0000	0	$0
%0001	1	$1
%0010	2	$2
%0011	3	$3
%0100	4	$4
%0101	5	$5
%0110	6	$6
%0111	7	$7
%1000	8	$8
%1001	9	$9
%1010	10	$A
%1011	11	$B
%1100	12	$C
%1101	13	$D
%1110	14	$E
%1111	15	$F
%10000	16	$10
%11100011		$E3
%10011100		$9C
%11111111	255	$FF
	256	$100
	1024	$400
	65535	$FFFF

use eight-bit words called *bytes*. More powerful processors used for desktop machines operate in words in 32-, 64-, or 128-bit chunks.

In an eight-bit numeral, 256 different states can be represented because $2^8 = 256$. Programmers use these 256 states to represent different things. Some common usages of a byte of data are:

- a natural number from 0 to 255;

- an integer in the range from -128 to $+127$;

- a character of data (a letter, number, or printable symbol).

When programmers need to represent larger numerals, they group bytes together. A common grouping is two bytes, often called a (16-bit) *word*. A word can have 65,536 different values because $2^{16} = 65,536$.

Decimal numbers are painful to use when talking about binary information. To make life easier, programmers started to use the base 16 *hexadecimal* (or *hex* for short) numbering system when talking about bits, bytes, and other binary data.

The hexadecimal system uses 16 different digits to represent each place value of a numeral. The letters A to F are used to represent the values of (decimals) 10 to 15, respectively. Using hex, one would count as follows: 0, 1, 2, 3, 4, 5, 6, 7, 8, 9, A, B, C, D, E, F, 10, 11, ... etc. This is wonderful because a hex digit (of 16 possible states) is equivalent to four bits exactly. Then a byte can be represented by exactly two hex digits and a 16-bit word by four hex digits.

In this chapter, we use the following conventions, which are used in Motorola's software tools for working with the 68HC11 processor. *Binary* numbers are specified by the prefix %. *Hexadecimal* numbers are specified by $. *Decimal* numbers don't have a prefix. (Other conventions are used in the computer world—for instance, in the C language, the prefix 0x specifies a hexadecimal number.)

Examine some of the numeric conversions in Figure A.1. Notice that four bits equal one hex digit. This is helpful in converting binary to hex. Notice some entries

FIGURE A.2 Table of ASCII Characters.

Values from 32 to 126 are the printable character set, whereas values from 0 to 31 and 127 are nonprinting control characters. To form the value of a character in hex, use the column as the upper half of the byte and the row as the lower half (e.g., capital "A" is $41 or 65 decimal).

	$0-	$1-	$2-	$3-	$4-	$5-	$6-	$7-
$-0	NUL 0	DLE 16	space 32	0 48	@ 64	P 80	` 96	p 112
$-1	SOH 1	DC1 17	! 33	1 49	A 65	Q 81	a 97	q 113
$-2	STX 2	DC2 18	" 34	2 50	B 66	R 82	b 98	r 114
$-3	ETX 3	DC3 19	# 35	3 51	C 67	S 83	c 99	s 115
$-4	EOT 4	DC4 20	$ 36	4 52	D 68	T 84	d 100	t 116
$-5	ENQ 5	NAK 21	% 37	5 53	E 69	U 85	e 101	u 117
$-6	ACK 6	SYN 22	& 38	6 54	F 70	V 86	f 102	v 118
$-7	BEL 7	ETB 23	' 39	7 55	G 71	W 87	g 103	w 119
$-8	BS 8	CAN 24	(40	8 56	H 72	X 88	h 104	x 120
$-9	HT 9	EM 25	) 41	9 57	I 73	Y 89	i 105	y 121
$-A	LF 10	SUB 26	* 42	: 58	J 74	Z 90	j 106	z 122
$-B	VT 11	ESC 27	+ 43	; 59	K 75	[91	k 107	{ 123
$-C	FF 12	FS 28	, 44	< 60	L 76	\ 92	l 108		124
$-D	CR 13	GS 29	- 45	= 61	M 77	] 93	m 109	} 125
$-E	SO 14	RS 30	. 46	> 62	N 78	^ 94	n 110	~ 126
$-F	SI 15	US 31	/ 47	? 63	O 79	_ 95	o 111	DEL 127

don't have their decimal values filled in. This is to make the point that it's easy to transcribe between binary and hexadecimal representation, but using decimal is often cumbersome.

A byte can be used to represent one character of information. A standard has been devised for this: the American Standard Code for Information Interchange standard (ASCII code). ASCII is pretty much the standard for representing the English character set, including upper- and lowercase letters, numbers, and typical punctuation (like !@#$%&*()). An old IBM standard, the EBCDIC code, is largely defunct, but modern computer scientists have devised a 16-bit international character set called *Unicode*.

Figure A.2 shows the table of the ASCII codes. The high bit of a byte is not part of the ASCII code, so there are actually only 128 ASCII characters, using the values $00 to $7F.

Printable characters start at $20 (32 decimal). The codes from $0 to $1F are used for line-oriented terminals for things like cursor control, line feeds, and communications protocol. Knowing the ASCII characters becomes important if you want to display a message over the serial line or on the LCD screen. Then it is necessary to deal with printable characters as bytes using the ASCII codes.

A.1.2 Memory Map

Microprocessors store their programs and data in memory. Memory is organized as a contiguous array of *addresses* or locations for storing data. In the 68HC11, each memory address contains eight bits of data.

The entire amount of memory that a processor can access is called its *address space*. The 68HC11 has an address space of 65,536 memory locations, corresponding exactly to 16 bits of address information. This mean that a 16-bit numeral can be used to point at, or address, any of the memory bytes in the address space of the 68HC11. Thus, four hexadecimal digits (4 bits per digit × 4 digits) can exactly specify one memory location (in which there will be one byte of information).

Most of the 68HC11's address space is unallocated, allowing for devices such as external memory to be addressed. For the version of the 68HC11 chip in the Handy

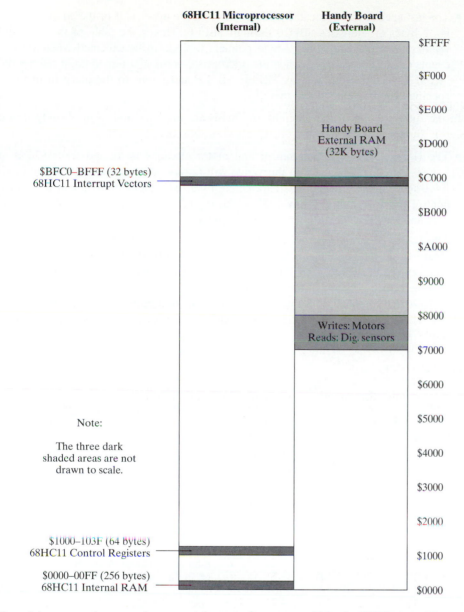

**68HC11 Microprocessor
(Internal)**

**Handy Board
(External)**

$FFFF

$F000

$E000

Handy Board
External RAM
(32K bytes)

$D000

$BFC0–BFFF (32 bytes)
68HC11 Interrupt Vectors

$C000

$B000

$A000

$9000

$8000

Writes: Motors
Reads: Dig. sensors

$7000

$6000

$5000

Note:

$4000

The three dark
shaded areas are not
drawn to scale.

$3000

$2000

$1000–103F (64 bytes)
68HC11 Control Registers

$1000

$0000–00FF (256 bytes)
68HC11 Internal RAM

$0000

FIGURE A.3 Memory Map of
68HC11 Microprocessor in
Handy Board System

Board, however, there are three special areas of memory within the 68HC11, as illustrated
in Figure A.3. The portion of the memory map specialized by the 68HC11 chip is shown
in the left column of the diagram:

- Reading from the beginning of memory at the bottom of the diagram, there are 256
  bytes of internal random access memory (RAM) located from the very start of the
  address space, at $0000, to $00FF.

- The next block is located about 4,000 bytes later, at address $1000. Here, there
  are 64 bytes of special purpose control registers—the *register bank*—which are
  used for controlling the various hardware features of the 68HC11 microprocessor. From the point of view of the 68HC11 processor core, these registers appear as if they were just part of memory; the standard instructions for reading
  and writing memory are used to test and set the values of the various
  registers.

- The last special block, located midway through the upper half of the address space, is 32 bytes at addresses $BFC0 through $BFFF. This is the table of the *interrupt vectors*, in which are stored 2-byte pointers to code to be executed when various events occur. For example, when the microprocessor is first turned on, it fetches the "RESET vector" from address $BFFE–$BFFF and jumps to the place in memory specified by the value stored there.[1]

In the right column of the diagram, the hardware implemented in the Handy Board design is shown in relation to the 68HC11's address space:

- The Handy Board's digital sensor and motor circuitry is located from $7000 to $7FFF. Any memory reads in this range will retrieve the values of six digital input lines and the two user buttons as a single byte. Any memory writes in this range control the four motor outputs. (How the digital sensor and motor ports work is explained in more detail later in this appendix.)

- The Handy Board's external RAM is located from $8000 to $FFFF. The Handy Board is designed so that when board power is turned off, the contents of this memory are preserved. This means a project can hold its program when the board is turned off, ready to run the next time the board is turned on.

    Note that the 68HC11's interrupt vectors overlap a portion of the external memory. This means that this portion of the external memory is necessarily used to store those interrupt vector values.

A.1.3 Registers

A microprocessor does its work by moving data from memory into its *internal registers*, processing them, and then copying them back into memory. These registers are like variables that the processor uses to do its computations. There are two different types of registers: *accumulators* and *index registers*.

Accumulators are used to perform most arithmetic operations, like addition, subtraction, or performing logical and bit operations (and, or, invert). Results of such operations are often placed back into a register; for example, an instruction may add something to the "A" register and place the sum back into that same register. It's for this reason that the name accumulator is appropriate for these register type: They accumulate the results of ongoing computations.

FIGURE A.4 Programmer's Model of 68HC11 Registers

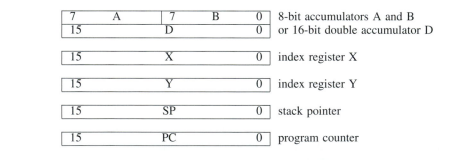

Index registers are used to point at data located in memory. For example, in the add operation just described, the addend (the number getting "added in" to the sum) might be indexed by the "X" register, meaning that the X register is being used to indicate the address of the data in memory.

---

[1] In normal 68HC11 designs, the interrupt vectors are located at the very top of the address space, from $FFC0 to $FFFF. In the Handy Board design, however, the 68HC11 is operated in "special mode," which causes the interrupt vectors to be relocated to the $BFC0–$BFFF area. The reason for using special mode is discussed in Section A.3.7.

Figure A.4 shows the "programmer's model" of the registers of the 68HC11, summarizing the processor's registers set. The 68HC11 has two accumulators, labeled A and B. Each are 8-bit registers: They hold one byte of data.

The general purpose index registers are the X and Y registers. These are 16-bit registers and are most commonly used to address data in memory.

The A and B registers can be used together as a 16-bit arithmetic register, in which case they are named the D register. As indicated in the diagram, the A register forms the "high bits," or most significant digit, in this mode.

The Stack Pointer (SP) register is used to store the location of the *program stack*. The stack, which is explained in detail later, is used for temporary storage of data and to store the return address when a subroutine is called.

The Program Counter (PC) is used to keep track of the current instruction being executed. The PC is automatically incremented as the microprocessor proceeds through the instruction stream.

A.1.4 Evaluation Sequence

When a microprocessor runs a program, it advances sequentially through memory, fetching and executing one instruction at a time. The PC register keeps track of the address of the instruction currently being executed. The microprocessor automatically advances the PC to the next instruction after it is finished executing the current one.

Let's look at typical instruction: Load a number into the A register. The machine code for this instruction is (in hex): 86 nn, where nn is the byte to be loaded into the register. The hex value $86 is called the *operational code (op-code)* that signifies the "load A register" instruction.

Instructions may be one, two, three, or four bytes long depending on what their function is. When the microprocessor encounters the byte $86 in the instruction stream, it interprets it and knows, "I'm going to fetch the next byte of data and load that into my A register." After the microprocessor evaluates the first byte of an instruction, it knows how many more bytes it needs to fetch to complete the instruction if it is longer than one byte. Then it executes the next instruction, and so on ad infinitum.

Instructions take varying numbers of *machine cycles* to execute depending on their complexity. The 68HC11 in the Handy Board operates at a frequency of 8 megahertz (MHz) or 8 million cycles per second. This frequency is divided into four clock phases to yield a machine cycle rate of 2 million machine cycles per second. The period of a machine cycle is then 0.5 microseconds (μsec), so an instruction that requires three machine cycles will take 1.5 μsec of real time to execute.

In general, longer instructions (those needing two, three, or four bytes) take longer (more machine cycles) to execute, although there are some exceptions to this rule. The "Load A register with a number" instruction is an example of a two-cycle instruction.

A.1.5 Machine Code Versus Assembly Language

People often speak of *machine code, object code*, and *assembly language*. These terms all refer to the same thing: the program that is executed directly by the microprocessor. However, these terms refer to that program in different states of development:

- *Machine code* usually refers to the raw data stored as a microprocessor's program. This is commonly described in the hexadecimal notation we've been using.

- *Object code* is basically the same as machine code, although it often refers to the file that represents the bytes to be run on the microprocessor.

- *Assembly language* is a set of *mnemonics*, or names, and a notation that is a readable yet efficient way to write down the machine instructions. Usually a program that is written in assembly language is processed by an *assembler program* that converts the mnemonic instructions into machine code. This output from the assembler program is often called the *object code*, which can then be executed directly by the microprocessor.

In the 68HC11 assembly language, the "Load A register" instruction mentioned earlier is written as follows:

```
LDAA    #$80
```

The word "LDAA" is the assembly language mnemonic for "LoaD Accumulator A." Then the #$80 is the hexadecimal value to be loaded. Because the A register is a one-byte register, the value to be loaded must be in the range of 0 to $FF inclusive; $80 is chosen at random.

When a 68HC11 assembler program processes an input file, it knows the mnemonics for all of the 68HC11 instructions, plus their corresponding op-codes. It uses this information to create the object code file. The assembly process is a straightforward, mechanical operation. Each assembly-language instruction is converted to one machine-language instruction (although that instruction may be one to four bytes in length).

An assembler program is not nearly as complex as a C-language compiler, for example, because there is little dependence across instructions in assembly language source code. Assemblers typically have features to make writing assembly programs easier. These features allow symbolic labels for constant values, arithmetic expressions, and binary, decimal, and hexadecimal conversions (among other functions).

Use of the development tools for 68HC11 assembly language is described in Section A.2. Rather than present an overview of assembly language all at once, 68HC11 instructions are introduced throughout this appendix in a progressive fashion.

A.1.6 Addressing Modes

In the previous example (LDAA #$80), the hex value $80 is loaded into the A register. This method of loading data into the register is called *immediate addressing* because the data to be loaded are located "immediately" in the instruction. The pound-sign character "#" specifies the immediate addressing mode.

There are other ways to address data bytes that need to be operated on. These different methods are known as *addressing modes*. Other than the immediate addressing mode, most addressing modes provide ways of accessing data that are stored somewhere in memory.

The *extended addressing mode* is a one way to access data stored in memory. In this mode, the 16-bit address of a memory byte is specified in the instruction. For example, the instruction

```
LDAA    $1004
```

will load the A register with the contents of memory location $1004. This instruction uses three bytes of memory: One byte is the op-code, and two more bytes are needed to specify the 16-bit memory address.

The *direct addressing mode* is similar to the extended mode, but works only for data stored in the first 256 bytes of the chip's address space, from addresses $00 to $FF (also known as the *zero page* of memory). This happens to be the 68HC11's internal RAM, as shown in Figure A.3. Thus, the direct mode is used to store and load data to the internal RAM.

In the direct mode, only one byte of address data is required to specify the memory address because it is known to be in the first 256 bytes of memory. Instructions using direct addressing may require only two bytes: one for the op-code and one for the address information. These instructions execute in fewer cycles as a result of this savings. The 68HC11 assembler will automatically choose the direct addressing mode if the address specified is in the range $00 to $FF. Extended addressing could also be used to access this portion of memory, but it would rarely be preferable.

The *indexed addressing mode* uses the X or Y register as a pointer into memory. The value contained in the index register and an offset byte are added to specify the location of the desired memory byte or word.

Let's look at an example to make this clear. Suppose the X register currently has the value $1000. Then the instruction

```
ldaa     0,X
```

will load the A register with the contents of location $1000, and the instruction

```
ldaa     5,X
```

will load the A register with the contents of location $1005.

The offset value is contained in one byte of data, and only positive or zero offsets are allowed. As such, only offsets in the range of 0 to 255 decimal are possible.

Why would a programmer use the indexed addressing mode when the extended addressing mode will access the desired byte directly?

One reason to use the indexed modes, with their associated offset bytes, is when repeatedly accessing locations from a particular region of memory. For example, the 68HC11 special register area begins at location $1000 and ends at location $103F. Suppose there were a series of instructions that accessed the registers located in this area. We could then set up the X register as a *base pointer*—pointing to the beginning of this area of memory (we'd load the X register with $1000: LDX #$1000). Then we can use the two-byte indexed instructions to do a series of loads, stores, or whatever to the locations in this region in which we were interested.

This is good programming practice because each indexed instruction saves a byte over the extended instruction. Once the cost is paid of loading the X register with the base address (a three-byte instruction), each use of an indexed instruction will save code space and execution time.

Indexed addressing is most useful, however, when working with an array of data records of the same format. Then one can set up an index register to point at the base of each data record and use indexed-offset operations to access individual fields of that record. To move to the next record, only the index base pointer needs to be changed, and the offsets will then access the fields in the subsequent record.

Finally, there are a few instructions that do not support the extended addressing mode (they support only direct and indexed addressing), so if one must work with a byte not in the direct addressing area, then indexed addressing must be used.

Here is a summary of all of the addressing modes that are supported on the 68HC11 architecture:

Immediate Data are part of the instruction itself. This mode is specified with the use of the prefix "#" before the data byte or word. Example: ldaa #$80 loads the A register with the hex number $80.

Direct Data are located in the zero page (the 68HC11 internal RAM from addresses $0000 to $00FF). One byte is used to specify which RAM location is to be used. Example: staa $80 stores the A register to the memory location $0080.

Extended Location of data is specified by a 16-bit address given in the instruction. Example: `staa #$1000` stores the contents of the A register at memory location $1000.

Indexed Location of data is specified by the sum of a 16-bit index register (register X or Y) and an offset value that is part of the instruction. Example: `ldaa 5,X` loads the A register with the memory byte located at the address that is the sum of the value currently in the X register and 5 (decimal). Offsets range in value from 0 to 255.

Inherent Data are "inherent" to the microprocessor and do not require an external memory address. Example: `tab` transfers the contents of the A register to the B register. No external memory address is required.

Relative Location is specified by an offset value from the address of the instruction currently being executed. Example: `bra 5` causes a branch that skips five bytes ahead in the instruction stream. Relative addressing is only used in branching instructions. Offsets range in value from -128 to $+127$, allowing jumps both forward and backward in the instruction stream.

A.1.7 Data Types

The 68HC11 supports a few different data types or ways to represent numbers. Most high-level languages support many data types, such as integers, floating point numbers, strings, and arrays. In assembly language, the programmer is given only "the bits" and must build more complex data types from scratch (i.e., with libraries of subroutines).

The 68HC11 has two data types: 8-bit numbers and 16-bit numbers. This means that there are instructions that process numbers of length 8 bits (bytes) and there are instructions that process numbers of length 16 bits (words).

A.1.8 Arithmetic Operations

Microprocessors give the programmer a standard set of arithmetic and logical operations that can be performed on numeric data.

The 68HC11 is a particularly nice processor because it provides instructions that work on both 8-bit data values (such as the A or B registers or memory bytes) and 16-bit data values (such as the X and Y index registers). Earlier processors provided only 8-bit operations; the programmer had to write subroutines libraries to get 16-bit ones.

The 68HC11 supports the following instructions:

Addition for both 8-bit and 16-bit values.

Subtraction for both 8-bit and 16-bit values.

Multiplication of two 8-bit values to yield a 16-bit result.

Division of two 16-bit values to yield an integer or fractional result.

Increment of both 8-bit and 16-bit values. The increment operation adds one to its operand.

Decrement of both 8-bit and 16-bit values. The decrement operation subtracts one from its operand.

Logical AND for 8-bit values. This instruction performs a bit-wise "and" operation on two pieces of data. The result of an AND operation is 1 if and only if both of its operands are 1 (e.g., `%11110010` ANDed with `%11000011` yields `%11000010`).

Logical OR for 8-bit values. This instruction performs a bit-wise "or" operation on two pieces of data. The result of an OR operation is 1 if either or both of its operands is 1.

Logical Exclusive OR for 8-bit values. The result of an exclusive-OR operation ("EOR") is 1 if either, but not both, of its inputs are 1.

Arithmetic Shift operations on 8-bit and 16-bit values. The Arithmetic Shift operation moves all the bits in an operand to the left or right by one bit position. This is equivalent to a multiplication or division by 2 (respectively) on the operand.

Rotation operations on 8-bit values. These are similar to the shift operations except that the bit that gets shifted out of the high or low bit position (depending on the direction of the rotate) gets placed in the bit position vacated on the other side of the byte (e.g., rotate right (ROR) of %11011001 produces %11101100).

Bit-wise Set and Clear operations on 8-bit values. These operations set or clear bits at specified bit positions within an eight-bit data byte.

Clear operations on 8-bit memory bytes or registers. This instruction is equivalent to writing a zero into the memory location or 68HC11 register, but does so more quickly.

There are a few more arithmetic instructions not mentioned here, but they are relatively obscure.

A.1.9 Signed and Unsigned Binary Numbers

Various methods of representing numbers are commonly used by microprocessors. Depending on the method, the same string of 1s and 0s that comprise a byte or word can represent two different numbers. The 68HC11 implements the most common of these representations: *unsigned* binary format and *two's-complement signed* binary format.

The unsigned format is used to represent numbers in the range from 0 to 255 (one byte of data) or 0 to 65,535 (one word of data). This is the most simple way of representing data. The earlier discussion of converting binary numbers into decimal equivalents assumed unsigned numbers. The limitation of the unsigned format is that values less than zero cannot be represented.

Here are some unsigned binary numbers and their decimal equivalents:

Binary	Decimal
%0000	0
%0001	1
%0010	2
%0011	3
%0100	4
%0101	5
%0110	6
%10011100	156
%11100011	227
%11111111	255

Signed values are represented using the *two's complement* binary format. In this format, a byte can represent a value from −128 to +127, and a word can represent a number from −32,768 to +32,767.

The highest bit (most significant or left-most bit) of the number is used to represent the sign. A "0" in the high bit indicates a positive or zero value, and a "1" in the high bit indicates a negative value.

If the number is positive or zero, then the signed representation is exactly equivalent to the unsigned one. For example, the largest binary number representable in a byte using the signed format is %01111111. The leading zero is the sign bit, indicating a non-negative number; the seven ones that follow are the significant digits.

If the number is negative, then the following algorithm determines its value: Invert the significant digits (change zeros to ones and ones to zeros) and add one. Put a minus sign in front of the number and that is the equivalent value.

For example, consider the signed number %10011011. This is a negative number because its high bit is one. To find its value, we take the significant digits (%0011011) and invert them, obtaining %1100100. We add one and obtain %1100101. This value converted to decimal is 101; thus, the original number was equal to −101.

For another way of understanding the two's complement representation, think about subtracting 1 from 0. The result is a number with ones in all of the bits because that is the number that when one is added to it "rolls over the odometer" and produces zero. Thus, %11111111 is equal to −1, %11111110 is −2, %11111101 is −3, and so on. Counting backward, the smallest negative number representable in one byte is %10000000, which is −128 decimal.

The great value of two's complement notation is that conventional unsigned arithmetic can be used to add and subtract numbers in two's complement notation, producing correct two's complement values. Thus, with one set of arithmetic routines, the 68HC11 can handle both unsigned and signed numbers; it's up to programmers to be consistent in their use of numeric formats.

A.1.10 Condition Code Register and Conditional Branching

Whenever the 68HC11 performs any type of arithmetic or logical operation, various *condition codes* are generated in addition to the actual result of the operation. These condition codes indicate whether the following events happened:

- The result of the operation was zero.
- The result of the operation overflowed the 8- or 16-bit data word that it was supposed to fit in. This condition is based on interpreting the data operands as two's complement values.
- The result was a negative value. Example: subtracting 50 from 10.
- The result generated a *carry* out of the highest bit position. This happens when two numbers are added and the result is too large to fit into one byte.

There is a special register in the 68HC11 called the *condition code register* (CCR) where this information is kept. Each condition is represented by a one-bit *flag* in the CCR; if the flag is 1, then the condition is true. The CCR has eight flags in all (four more in addition to the four mentioned).

Each flag has a name: The zero flag is called Z, the overflow flag is V, the negative flag is N, and the carry flag is C.

The usefulness of these flags is that programs may branch depending on the value of a particular flag or combination of flags. For example, the following fragment of code will repeatedly decrement the A register until it is zero. This code fragment uses the "branch if not equal to zero" instruction (BNE) to loop until the A register equals zero.

```
loop    DECA            * decrement A register
        BNE     loop    * if not zero, jump back to "Loop"
        ...             * program execution continues here
        ...             *    after A is zero
```

An entire set of these conditional branching instructions allows the programmer to test whether the result of an operation was equal to zero, not equal to zero, greater than zero, less than zero, and so on.

Some of the conditional branching instructions are designed for testing results of two's complement operations, whereas others expect to test results of unsigned operations. As mentioned earlier, the same arithmetic operations are used regardless of whether the data being operated on are considered signed or unsigned. The way that one must interpret the condition codes of the result is different. Different 68HC11 branch instructions may be used to perform this interpretation properly:

BEQ: **Branch if Equal to Zero** Branch is made if Z flag 1 (indicating a zero result). Applicable to both signed and unsigned data.

BNE: **Branch if Not Equal to Zero** Branch is made if Z flag is 0 (indicating a nonzero result). Applicable to both signed and unsigned data.

BLO: **Branch if Lower** Branch is made if the number in the register was lower (smaller) than the number subtracted from it. Applicable when using unsigned data.

BHI: **Branch if Higher** Branch is made if the number in the register was higher (larger) than the number subtracted from it. Applicable when using unsigned data.

Other branching instructions work with signed data and check the proper combination of flags to tell whether results are greater or less than zero.

One important thing to remember about branching instructions is that they use the *relative addressing mode*, which means that the destination of a branch is specified by a one-byte offset from the location of the branch instruction. As such, branches may only jump forward or backward a maximum of 128 bytes from the location of the branch instruction.

If it is necessary to branch to a location further away, the conditional branch instructions should be used in combination with a JuMP instruction (JMP), which takes an absolute two-byte address for the destination. The destination of a JMP instruction may thus be anywhere in memory. Use the conditional branch instruction to jump to (or around) a JMP instruction that jumps to far-away locations.

A.1.11 Stack Pointer and Subroutine Calls

All microprocessors support a special type of data structure called the *stack*. A stack stores data in a last-in, first-out (LIFO) method.

To visualize the stack, one may imagine a dishwasher who is washing a sink full of dishes, placing each finished dish on top of a pile of already washed dishes. At the same time, a server is removing dishes from the pile. The dish that is removed by the server is the last dish that the dishwasher placed on the pile. In this way, the stack of dishes implements a LIFO algorithm.

The stack on the 68HC11 works the same way. Instead of a stack of dishes, the 68HC11 stores bytes in a contiguous area of memory. Instead of a dishwasher and a server, the 68HC11 uses a special register, called the *stack pointer* or *SP*, to keep track of the location of the stack in memory.

When a value is placed on the stack (called a *stack push*), the value is stored in memory at the current address of the stack pointer. Then the stack pointer is advanced to the next position in memory.

When a value is taken off the stack (called a *stack pull*), the stack pointer is regressed to the last location stored, and then the value at that memory location is retrieved.

The stack has many different uses. One use is temporary storage of data. Suppose there is a number in the A register to be stored and then retrieved a few instructions later. One could push it on the stack (PSHA) to save it and later pull it off the stack (PULA) to restore it.

The data in several different registers may be temporarily stored and retrieved in this way. It's important to remember that data go on and come off the stack in reverse order.

If data are stored with a `PSHA` and then a `PSHB` (push A register, push B register), they must restored with the sequence `PULB`, `PULA` (pull B register, pull A register).

The most important use of the stack is involved with *subroutines*. Subroutines are pieces of code that may be called or executed by the main program. In this way, they are like utility routines that the main program uses.

For example, suppose a program often has a need to execute a delay, simply waiting $\frac{1}{10}$ of a second. Rather than repeatedly writing the code to perform the delay, it can be written just once, as a subroutine. Then whenever the main code needs to execute the delay, it can just call the subroutine.

The key thing about executing a subroutine properly is knowing where to return when it finishes. This is where the stack comes in. When a subroutine is called, the 68HC11 automatically pushes the *return address*—the place to continue after the subroutine is done—onto the stack. Then it branches to begin executing the subroutine.

When the subroutine is finished, the 68HC11 pulls the return address directly off the stack and branches to that location.

One may think, "Well, we don't need a stack for this; we could just have one particular location where the return address is stored. We could just look there when returning from a subroutine."

Actually, that is not a bad solution, but using the stack gives special power: It enables *nested subroutine calls*. What happens when a subroutine calls a subroutine? If a stack is being used, the second return address simply gets pushed on top of the first so that the first return address remains intact. In the other method, the first return address would be overwritten and destroyed when the second subroutine call occurred. It can be seen that advanced computer science ideas like recursion are based on this principle of a stack.

One detail worth mentioning about the stack's implementation on the 68HC11 is that the stack builds *downward* in memory. That is, when a number is pushed on the stack, the stack pointer is actually *decremented* to point to the next available memory location. This is somewhat counterintuitive, but it doesn't matter in how the stack functions.

Because the stack is a dynamic structure, it must be located somewhere in RAM. As shown in Figure A.3, the 68HC11's internal RAM is located from addresses $0000 to $00FF. It's customary to initialize the stack at the *top of RAM* because, as the stack grows, it moves downward in memory. In a single-chip 68HC11 system, this would be address $00FF. In the Handy Board, there is external RAM from $8000 to $FFFF, so address $FFFF may be used.

A good way to crash the processor is to repeatedly push a value on to the stack and forget to pull it off. If this mistake is made inside a program loop, all of RAM will easily be filled with garbage. When a subroutine attempts to return to its caller, the return address will be nowhere in sight.

Just remember: Each stack push must be matched with a stack pull. Each subroutine call must be matched with a return from subroutine. Leave enough space in memory for the stack to grow depending on how many nested subroutine calls your program may execute.

A.1.12 Interrupts and Interrupt Routines

Interrupt routines are a type of subroutine that gets executed when special events happen. These special events are often called *interrupts*, and they may be generated by a variety of sources. Examples of things that may generate interrupts are: a byte coming in over the serial line, a programmable timer triggering, or a sensor line changing state.

When an interrupt happens, the 68HC11 stops what it is doing, saves its local state (the contents of all registers), and processes the interrupt. Each interrupt has code associated with it; it is this code that is executed when the interrupt occurs.

Multitasking

Interrupts may be used to give the appearance that the 68HC11 is doing several things at once. There are several reasons for this:

- The main code doesn't have to know when an interrupt occurs. This is because after the interrupt finishes, control is returned to the main code exactly where it left off. No information is lost.

- The interrupt servicing process is automatic. In this way, it's different from a subroutine call, which must be explicitly done each time it is required.

- Many interrupts can be enabled at the same time. Whenever they occur, they are serviced. Many "background jobs" can be taken care of independently of each other.

If multiple interrupts are being used, it is possible for an interrupt to occur *during the servicing* of a different interrupt routine. Typically, interrupting an interrupt routine is not a good idea. The 68HC11 deals with this nested interrupt condition by queing up the interrupts and, based on a predetermined interrupt priority scheme, processing them sequentially as each interrupt routine finishes.

In their usage of the stack, interrupts are implemented quite like subroutines. When an interrupt call is processed, however, the state of *all* of the 68HC11 registers is saved on the stack, not just the return address. This way, when the interrupt routine returns—using the special RTI (return from interrupt) instruction—the processor can continue executing the main code in exactly the same state that it left it.

Interrupt Vectors

When an event causing an interrupt occurs, the 68HC11 must know where the code associated with that interrupt is located. An *interrupt vector* points to the starting address of the code associated with each interrupt. When an interrupt occurs, the 68HC11 first finds its associated interrupt vector and then jumps to the address specified by the vector.

These interrupt vectors are "mapped" into specific areas of system memory. In the Handy Board's implementation, the 68HC11 maps the interrupt vectors from $BFC0 to $BFFF. Two bytes are needed for each interrupt vector; thus it may be calculated that the 68HC11 has ($BFFF − $BFC0 + 1) ÷ 2, or 32 total interrupt vectors.

The location of each interrupt vector is predetermined. For example, the RESET interrupt is generated when the system reset button is pressed. The RESET vector is located at addresses $BFFE and $BFFF. When the Handy Board is powered on, the 68HC11 jumps to the location specified by the pointer contained in those two bytes. Because turning on the board should restart the microprocessor, the reset vector usually points to the start of the main code.

Those who are familiar with the 68HC11 may be surprised to be told that the interrupt vectors are located from $BFC0 to $BFFF. Indeed, in the 68HC11's "normal mode," the interrupt vectors are located from $FFC0 to $FFFF. In the Handy Board design, however, the 68HC11 is operated in its "special mode," which has the side effect of relocating the interrupt vectors to the $BFC0–$BFFF area. The rationale for using special mode is explained in Section A.3.7 on the LCD screen interface.

A.2 Introduction to Assembly Language Programming

In this section, we learn how to write complete assembly language programs for the Handy Board, assemble them into downloadable code, and then download and run them. It's not particularly complicated, but there are numerous little details that one must know to get things to work. By the end of this section, you should feel comfortable writing small assembly language programs for the Handy Board. The following section in this Appendix provides further detail about the Handy Board's hardware design and writing assembly language drivers.

A.2.1 Development Cycle

The basic process for developing assembly language programs for the Handy Board is as follows:

1. *Write* the assembly language source code and save it as a plain-text file with a ".asm" file name extension.
2. *Process* the source code file with a program known as an *assembler*. The assembler program converts the source file into an output *object file* containing the machine language bytes and the locations in memory where they are to be loaded. The object file has a file name extension of .s19 or .hex and contains a plain-text (ASCII) representation of the bytes.
   If there are no assembly errors, continue to the next step; otherwise modify the source code file and try again.
3. *Download* the object file to the Handy Board using the standard downloader tools that are used to download Interactive C's runtime object file (pcode_hb.s19) to the Handy Board.
4. *Run* the program! Hopefully it will do what you expect, but probably not. If changes are needed, start over the first step, modifying the original source file.

Let's look at each of these steps in a bit more detail, working through a first full example in the process.

A.2.2 Write the Source Code

There are a number of popular editors for composing code, including formatting assembly code. The most important property of a "programmer's editor" includes the ability to save unadulterated, plain-text ASCII files not augmented with word processors' formatting codes. Also useful are auto indent and parenthesis balancing—features to help organize the visual and logical presentation of code.

For the Windows 95/98/NT operating system, some of the more popular ones include:[2]

- *NotePad by Microsoft.* Distributed with the Windows operating system, so it's no surprise that NotePad is popular. NotePad is not the most powerful or convenient editor, but in a pitch it will do.

- *TextPad by Helios Software Solutions.* Excellent, full-featured shareware text editor for Windows.

For the Macintosh, some of the more popular editors include:

- *SimpleText by Apple Computer.* Distributed with the Macintosh operating system, SimpleText is a basic tool for editing text files. Its native file format is a plain ASCII file (font styling and other word processing characteristics are hidden away in resources that won't interfere with the assembler program) and it is easy to use. On the down side, it does not support auto-indent or other helpful programming features.

- *Alpha by Pete Keleher.* A powerful, easy-to-use shareware programmer's editor for the Macintosh. Provides option of using Emacs-like editing control keystrokes.

---

[2]   See the *Resources* appendix for information on locating this software.

```
* asmtest1.asm, a first assembly language test program

        org $8000          define program origin at address $8000

        ldaa #$f0          ; load the value $f0 into the A register
        staa $7000         ; store the A reg to $7000, the mo-
tor port!

loop    bra loop           ; loop endlessly here to terminate

        org $bffe          ; location of 68hc11 "RESET" vector
        fdb $8000          ; "form double byte" to start of program

        end
```

FIGURE A.5 Listing of asmtest1.asm

- *BBEdit by Bare Bones Software, Inc.* A powerful, easy-to-use text editor for the Macintosh. Comes in free "lite" and full commercial versions. BBEdit excels in regular-expression handling and general text editing functions.

After setting up your computer system with an appropriate text editor, refer to Figure A.5, which shows a listing of asmtest1.asm. Type the sample program into the text editor and save the code with a file name of asmtest1.asm.

Let's go through this program line by line to understand how it works. The first line,

```
* asmtest1.asm, a first assembly language test program
```

is a comment. Notice the use of the asterisk ("*"). If there is an asterisk as the very first character at the beginning of a line, then the whole line is treated as a comment.

Next is

```
        org $8000          define program origin at address $8000
```

This tells the assembler program where in memory to deposit the code that it assembles. The example uses address $8000 because that's the first location in the Handy Board's external memory. The org command (for "origin") is known as an assembler *pseudo-operation (pseudo-op)* because it is not actually a 68HC11 instruction. Rather, it's a directive to the assembler program.

Notice one other thing about this statement line. There is no delimiting character between the code of the statement—org $8000—and the comment that follows it. In fact, no delimiter is necessary; the assembler program is very line-oriented and will happily ignore anything after it parses one single valid instruction per program line.

Despite this "capability" (of ignoring everything after a valid instruction), many programmers use a semicolon or asterisk to precede their comments, even when one is not needed. In the remainder of the example, semicolons are used before comments to make things easier to read.

Next there is the first actual code of the program:

```
        ldaa #$f0          ; load the value $f0 into the A register
```

This instruction loads a value into the A register (ldaa = load accumulator A). Because the value field contains the pound sign "#" character, the instruction treats the value as immediate data—that is, the very number to load. The dollar sign "$" specifies the hexadecimal number format. Thus, the instruction loads the hex value $f0 (decimal 240) into the A register.

Next is a store instruction:

```
staa $7000       ; store the A reg to $7000, the motor port!
```

This instruction stores the value in the A register into the location specified $7000. This is the location of the Handy Board's motor output latch. The upper four bits of the A register determine which motor ports are on, and the lower for bits determine the motors' direction. Because the value is $F0 (upper four bits all on), all four motors will be turned on. The direction bits being zero corresponds to the direction in which the green LED is lit.

In the next instruction, the program terminates by branching endlessly to the same point—a branch to itself:

```
loop    bra loop         ; loop endlessly here to terminate
```

This endless loop is important because the 68HC11 must always be doing *something*! If one wishes a program to terminate, a simple way to do this is to put the 68HC11 into a harmless loop from which it cannot exit. Hence, the "branch to self" construct.

Next in the program listing is another origin command:

```
org $bffe         ; location of 68hc11 "RESET" vector
```

The address, $bffe, is the location of the 68HC11's RESET vector. When the 68HC11 powers up, it fetches a two-byte pointer from this location and jumps to that address to begin executing its program. Thus, it is necessary to put the address where one would like the 68HC11 to begin execution at the RESET vector location. This is done by the next line:

```
fdb $8000         ; "form double byte" to start of program
```

This line employs the `fdb` pseudo-operation, "form double byte." This pseudo-op takes a numeric argument and deposits two bytes into the instruction stream to represent it. In this usage, the value $8000 is deposited, which will be fetched as the RESET vector—a pointer to the start of the program, which was `org`'ed earlier at address $8000.

The last line of the program declares the end of the assembly file:

```
end
```

This statement is optional; nothing bad will happen if the end is omitted.

A.2.3 Assemble the Source Code

Now that the `asmtest1.asm` file is ready, let's run it through the 68HC11 assembler program. The assembler walks through the `.asm` source file, translating each line of assembly code into bytes to be loaded into 68HC11 memory. The assembler also obeys the pseudo-operations (like `org`, which tells the assembler where in memory the translated bytes should go) and resolves symbolic references (like the `loop bra loop` statement).

The assembler produces two output files: an `.s19` file, which is the image of the bytes to be loaded into memory, and a `.1st` list file, which is an annotated listing of the source `.asm` file. The `.1st` file shows the resulting machine code (i.e., the program bytes) alongside each line of the original source code.

Let's go ahead and run the assembler and then look at the two resulting files.

Assembler Versions

There are a number of both free and commercially available 68HC11 assemblers. The free assembler provided by Motorola, `as11`, is perfectly functional and is available in

```
0001                    * asmtest1, a first assembly language test program
0002
0003 8000                      org $8000        define program origin at address $8000
0004
0005 8000 86 f0                ldaa #$f0        load the value $f0 into the A register
0006 8002 b7 70 00             staa $7000       store the A reg to $7000, the motor port!
0007
0008 8005 20 fe   loop  bra loop               branch here to terminate
0009
0010 bffe                      org $bffe        location of 68hc11 "RESET" vector
0011 bffe 80 00                fdb $8000        "form double byte" to start of program
0012
0013                           end
```

FIGURE A.6 Listing of asmtest1.lst, Assembled Output of asmtest1.asm

source code form, so it has been ported to a variety of computer platforms. The following specific instructions will assume the use of the Motorola as11 assembler.

Windows   The as11.exe application is a DOS program and should be executed from a command-line shell.

The syntax for running the assember is simply:

```
as11 filename.asm
```

You must specify the full file name, including the .asm suffix.

This basic invocation will cause the assembler to produce the .s19 memory image file, but not the annotated .lst listing file. To additionally produce the listing file, issue the command as:

```
as11 filename.asm -l > filename.lst
```

The "-l" flag causes the assembler to write the listing to the standard output (i.e., the console), and the "> filename.lst" redirects it into a file named filename.lst.

Macintosh   The 68HC11 assembler is available for the Macintosh as an application named xasmhc11. The application provides a dialog box for configuring the assembler options (such as producing the listing file) and then a menu item and keyboard shortcut for assembling the source file. If the "output listing to file" dialog option is checked, the assembler automatically produces the .lst annotated listing file.

Unix   The Unix versions of the 68HC11 assembler are based on the source for the DOS version and follow the same command-line syntax as the DOS version.

The Annotated Listing File

Figure A.6 shows the resultant annotated listing file after assembly. Let's examine it in detail.

- In the first column, each line of the source code is sequentially numbered.
- The second column shows the target memory address for that line's piece of code.
- Next the assembled bytes for that line's instruction are shown.
- Finally, the line of the original source code is copied into the listing file.

By looking at the assembly listing, it's often easy to pick out the machine language op-codes for each instruction. For instance, at Line 5 of the listing, the instruction ldaa #$f0 is assembled into 86 f0. This is readily parsed: 86 is the op-code for ldaa, and f0 is the immediate argument of the instruction.

FIGURE A.7 Listing of
asmtest1.s19, Object of
Assembly of asmtest1.asm

```
S10A800086F0B7700020FEBA
S105BFFE8000BD
S9030000FC
```

FIGURE A.8 Analysis of S19 File
Format

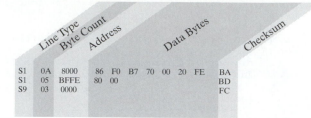

When debugging assembly language programs, reading through the listing file can be a big help in understanding what's going on. Make sure that you and the assembler agree on the meaning of your code!

A.2.4 Download the Object File

Figure A.7 shows asmtest1.s19, the assembler's object file. This is the file that is downloaded into the 68HC11's memory using any of the standard Handy Board downloader programs.

Note that the .s19 consists of printable ASCII characters. In fact, the .s19 format uses a hexadecimal encoding to represent each byte of the memory image. This makes it easy to view the .s19 file directly in any text editing program.

The S19 File Format

Just looking at the plain listing of the .s19 file, the file may seem rather cryptic, but it actually has a fairly straightforward format. Figure A.8 shows the same asmtest1.s19 file with spaces inserted between the hex digits so that the structure of the file is revealed.

The first two characters of each line indicate the *line type*, either S1 for a normal data line or S9 to indicate the last line of the file (hence the "S19" moniker for the file format).

The next two characters represent the *byte count* (as a hexadecimal number) for that line. For instance, the first line of the file has a byte count of 0A, or 10 bytes. Note that the byte count includes the address bytes and the checksum byte.

Next is the memory address at which to load the subsequent data. The memory address is specified as a four-digit hex value, which represents a two-byte or 16-bit address. The first line of the file specifies a target address of 8000, which is the result of our specification of a program origin of $8000 back in the assembly source file.

Next are the data bytes. The first line contains seven bytes, beginning with 86 F0, the result of assembling the ldaa #$f0 instruction. On second are two data bytes, 80 00, which correspond to the RESET vector being directed to address $8000.

Last on each line is a checksum byte. *The checksum calculation includes the byte count, address, and data bytes.* The checksum is obtained by adding together all of these bytes, taking the low byte, and subtracting it from $ff.

Downloading

Let's go ahead and download the asmtest1.s19 file to the Handy Board. Follow the standard download procedure as if you were downloading the Interactive C operating program pcode_hb.s19: Put the board into bootstrap mode by holding down the Stop button while turning it on, and then run the downloader, choosing the asmtest1.s19 file.

This will be a quick download because the file has only nine data bytes!

A.2.5 Run the Program

Run the program by turning the Handy Board off and then on. The four motor LEDs should light green as the result of the control byte $F0 being deposited into the motor latch hardware. That's all that should happen...not too exciting, but then again, this is a full-fledged standalone machine code program!

Following are two more example programs. The first of these introduces subroutines and delay loops; the second shows how to access the digital sensors and buttons at the hardware level.

A.2.6 Delay Loops and Subroutines

In this example, we introduce two new things: the use of the stack to perform subroutine calls, and a delay loop to introduce a human-visible delay into a program. Figure A.9 shows the second example program, `asmtest2.asm`.

```
* asmtest2.asm, demonstrating subroutines and delay loops

        org $8000        define program origin at address $8000

start   lds #$ffff       ; define program stack at very top of memory

again
        ldaa #$f0        ; load the value $f0 into the A register
        staa $7000       ; store the A reg to $7000, the motor port

        jsr delay        ; insert delay

        ldaa #$ff        ; other motor direction
        staa $7000       ; write to motor port

        jsr delay

        bra again        ; repeat indefinitely

delay   ldx #0           ; put zero into X register
delaylp dex              ; subtract 1 from X
        bne delaylp      ; loop until zero again (65536 times)
        rts              ; return from subroutine

        org $bffe        ; location of 68hc11 "RESET" vector
        fdb start        ; "form double byte" to start of program

        end
```

FIGURE A.9 Listing of `asmtest2.asm`

The program's main loop, which begins at the label `again`, sets the four motor outputs on in the green direction (as in the previous example), then delays for a bit, sets the motors to the red direction, delays again, and then repeats. Thus, the overall effect is to flash the four motor LEDs back and forth from green to red.

The Stack

Looking at the code, in the line after the `org` pseudo-op, there is a new instruction, `lds`, for "load stack pointer." As discussed earlier, the stack is a data structure used when calling subroutines: The return address is pushed onto the stack, and the program execution jumps to the subroutine entry point. When the subroutine wishes to return, it executes the `rts` return from subroutine instruction, which pops the return address from the stack and execution continues there.

The `lds #$ffff` instruction is important because the stack must be located somewhere in memory, and the default value of the stack pointer register is undefined. If one were to call a subroutine before establishing the location of the stack, the stack pointer register could easily be pointing somewhere undesirable (either a location that was not memory or a location in memory where executable program code was located) and the program would crash.

The stack grows downward in memory. Therefore, in the example, we have chosen $FFFF, the very top of the Handy Board's external RAM, as the starting point or the "top of the stack." As data are pushed on the stack, the stack pointer register is decremented to make room for the data.

As a general practice, one must be careful that the stack will not collide with anything else in memory. Executable code grows upward in memory as there is more and more of it. If one has a very large program (or if the stack grows very large), it's conceivable that the stack could move into the same place as the code resides. The stack operations would happily overwrite program code, and when program execution moved into the place where code was supposed to be, stack data would be there and a crash would result.

With the Handy Board there is the added complication that the 68HC11 reset vectors are located directly in the middle of the external RAM. (The vectors are located at addresses $BFC0 to $BFFF, and memory runs from $8000 to $FFFF.) A simple organization for dealing with this is to keep executable code at addresses under $BFC0 and data such as the stack above address $C000. This works fine as long as both executable code and program data are each less than 16K in size.

A Delay Subroutine

Continuing with the example, the stack is only used when a subroutine is called, which happens twice at the `jsr delay` instruction.

Let's look at the delay subroutine. First, the X register is loaded with a zero. Then the delay loop begins. The X register is decremented. Then the result is tested for zero. If the result were not zero, the program branches back to the top of the loop (`bne delaylp`). If the result were zero, then the subroutine returns.

Remember that the X register holds 16-bit value—a number from $0000 to $FFFF. Thus, the first time through the loop, the value will be decremented from $0000 to $FFFF. So the decrement/test loop will run 65,536 times before the X register is zero again.

Cycle-Counting Exercise

Try out `asmtest2.asm` on your Handy Board: Assemble, download, and run it. The motor LEDs should flash back and forth between all-green and all-red states. If you plug a motor into any of the motor ports, it should repeatedly change direction, going back and forth.

How long is the interval between the two states? The core loop of the delay subroutine consists of two instructions: `dex` and `bne delaylp`. Each 68HC11 instruction takes up a fixed number of machine cycles to execute; by determining these values and counting the cycles in the delay loop, the exact duration of the delay may be calculated.

1. By turning on the cycle-counting option in the 68HC11 assembler program or referring to technical documentation, determine the number of cycles the `dex` and `bne` instructions use.
2. Calculate the duration per iteration of the delay loop based on the fact that the 68HC11 in the Handy Board operates at a rate of 2 million machine cycles per second.

Digital Input Latch at Memory Location $7000

Start Button	Stop Button	Sensor Input 15	Sensor Input 14	Sensor Input 13	Sensor Input 12	Sensor Input 11	Sensor Input 10
Bit 7	Bit 6	Bit 5	Bit 4	Bit 3	Bit 2	Bit 1	Bit 0

FIGURE A.10 Bits on the Digital Input Latch

The two user buttons and six of the digital sensor inputs form a byte that can be accessed by reading the value of memory location $7000. The two high bits of the byte are the Start and Stop user buttons, and the six lower bits are sensor inputs 10 to 15.

3. Calculate the total duration of the delay loop.
4. Rewrite the `delay` subroutine to take 10 times as long to execute.

A.2.7 Digital Sensors and the User Buttons

Our final example program of this section demonstrates how to test the value of the digital sensor port and user buttons. In a similar fashion as the motor output latch, the digital sensor values may be obtained simply by reading the memory location $7000.

The Digital Input Latch

Earlier, to control the motors, we wrote a byte to memory location $7000. The Handy Board's hardware is set up to intercept that operation, and the byte is written to a latch that controls the motor chips.

Similarly, the Handy Board has an input latch whose value can be read by reading the memory location $7000. A hardware latch on the Handy Board is connected to the two user buttons (Start and Stop) and six of the digital sensor inputs (sensor ports 10 to 15). When memory location $7000 is read, these eight bits are composed into a byte that is read from the 68HC11 memory bus. Figure A.10 illustrates how these eight signals are formed into the single byte of information.

Because of the way the Handy Board's hardware is designed, each of these eight signals defaults to a logic one if nothing is connected. Thus, reading the location $7000 will result in a value of 255 (hex $FF) if neither of the buttons is pressed and no sensors are connected. Therefore, to check whether the Start button is pressed, we wait until its bit location becomes a zero. The Start button is bit 7, the high bit of the digital latch byte.

Reading the Digital Input Latch

Figure A.11 shows a listing of `asmtest3.asm`—a sample program that shows how to test the digital latch byte. The program is largely the same as the previous example, except that instead of the motor outputs flipping back and forth on their own, the program waits for the Start button to be pressed before changing motor state.

This is done in the three lines immediately into the `waitforpress` subroutine. First, the digital latch byte is read into the A register (`ldaa $7000`). Then the number $80 is logically AND'ed with the latch byte value. This has the effect of setting all of the lower seven bits to zero while preserving the value of the eighth bit—the bit representing the state of the Start button.

The result (which gets placed back into the A register) will be $80 if the Start button is *not* pressed (remember, the bits default to a one) or zero if the Start button is pressed. The next instruction tests the result of the And operation: If it is not zero (meaning button not pressed), then control jumps back to the `waitforpress` label and the button state is tested again.

If the result were zero, then program execution continues into a delay, which waits a little while before returning control to the main loop. Back at the main loop, the motor state is flipped and the `waitforpress` subroutine is called again.

FIGURE A.11 Listing of asmtest3.asm

```
* asmtest3.asm, demonstrating digital sensor input

            org $8000

start   lds #$ffff

again
            ldaa #$f0
            staa $7000

            jsr waitforpress       ; wait until Start button pressed

            ldaa #$ff
            staa $7000

            jsr waitforpress

            bra again

waitforpress
            ldaa $7000     ; load A with value of digital input latch
            anda #$80      ; mask off all but Start button bit
            bne waitforpress ; loop until pressed

            ldx #0
delaylp dex
            bne delaylp

            rts

            org $bffe
            fdb start

            end
```

Digital Sensor Exercises

1. *Other ports.*

   • Change the program so that the motors flip state when a touch switch plugged into sensor port 10 is pressed.

   • Now change the program so the port 10 sensor *and* the Start button must be pressed together for the waitforpress subroutine to return.

2. *Button debouncing.* The delay loop in the waitforpress subroutine gives the human operator a chance to release the button before the main loop calls waitforpress again. If the button is held down, the motors will flip state back and forth continuously. This may not be a desired behavior.
   Remove the fixed delay and modify the example program so that the button must be released for the motor state to change again.

A.3 The 68HC11 with the Handy Board Hardware

This section dives into the actual hardware design of the Handy Board as it centers around the 68HC11 microprocessor. We begin with a hardware overview of the 68HC11,

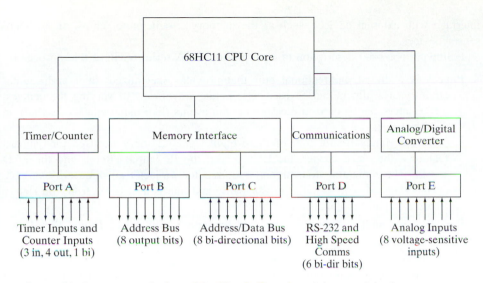

continue with the memory design of the Handy Board, and then explain the motor, sensor, and other circuits.

A.3.1 Architecture of the 68HC11

The 68HC11 chip includes many features that in previous microprocessors had to be implemented with hardware external to the microprocessor. Some of these features include:

- serial line input and output
- analog to digital converters
- programmable timers
- counters

This section explains how to use these advanced features of the 68HC11.

Register Block

The 68HC11 uses a particular area of memory to interface with these special functions. This area of memory is called the *register block* and is located from addresses $1000 to $103F.

The general method of controlling the various features of the chip is by reading and writing data to the different registers in the register block. Because the register block is mapped into memory, the typical 68HC11 instructions for reading and writing data to any area of memory are used into interact with these registers.

Block Diagram of 68HC11

Figure A.12 shows a simplified block diagram of the 68HC11 architecture for the A series of chips. (Other series of chips include additional hardware not present on the more simple A series.)

As shown in the diagram, the 68HC11 CPU core communicates with several hardware units, including a timer/counter modules, the memory addressing interface, a communications module, and an analog-to-digital converter.

There are five communications "ports" corresponding to these four subsystems (the memory interface uses two ports). With the exception of the communications port, each port has eight pins. When data are written to a particular port, *those data appear as voltage levels on the real pins connected to that port*. In this way, the 68HC11 can interface with external devices, such as the memory circuit, motor chips, or off-board sensor devices.

Following is a brief description of each port on the A series 68HC11 microprocessor.

Port A is a digital, bidirectional port that provides specialized timer and counter circuitry. The timers can be used to generate waveforms of varying frequencies; the counters can be used to measure certain events (like rising edges of signal) on the input lines.

In the Handy Board, four of these eight signals Port A are used for onboard features—the piezo beeper, the IR receiver, the IR output circuit, and the LCD screen. The remaining four signals are free for project use; three are available on the Handy Board's digital sensor bank, and one is accessible from the Handy Board's Expansion connector.

Port B is a digital port that may be used for output only. In the Handy Board, this port acts as the upper half of the address bus for interfacing with the 32K external memory.

Port C is a digital, bidirectional port. In the Handy Board, this port is used for the multiplexed lower memory address + data bus.

Port D is a bidirectional port dedicated to communications functions. Two of the Port D pins are used for RS-232 communications with a desktop computer, while the remaining four pins are open on the Handy Board design. These latter four pins are intended for implementing a high-speed network between 68HC11s and other microprocessor devices, but they may also be used for general purpose digital input and output applications.

Port E is an analog input port; an analog-to-digital converter integral to the 68HC11 chip converts voltages on this port to 8-bit numbers available to the CPU. In the Handy Board, seven of these eight pins are wired to the analog sensor connector, while the eighth pin is connected to a user knob.

The 68HC11 has an operating mode, called *single chip mode*, in which Ports B and C serve as general purpose inputs and outputs. In this mode, the memory interface circuitry is bypassed—the 68HC11 can't address external memory—but the programmer has full control of the Port B and C pins. In the other operating mode, *expanded mode*, the 68HC11 uses Ports B and C as the interface to external memory.

A.3.2 Microprocessor and Memory

At a basic level, a computer consists of a microprocessor, which executes instructions, and a memory, in which those instructions (and other data) are stored.

Figure A.13 shows a block diagram of these two components. The diagram shows four types of wires that connect the microprocessor and the memory:

Address Bus. These wires are controlled by the microprocessor to select a particular location in memory for reading or writing.

The Handy Board's memory chip is a 32K RAM; fifteen wires ($2^{15} = 32,768$) are needed to uniquely specify a memory address for reading or writing.

Data Bus. These eight wires are used to pass data between the microprocessor and the memory, one byte at a time. When data are written to the memory, the microprocessor drives these wires; when data are read from the memory, the memory drives the wires.

Read/Write Control Line. This single wire is driven by the microprocessor to control the function of the memory. If the wire is +5v, then the memory performs a read operation. If the wire is 0v, then the memory performs a write operation.

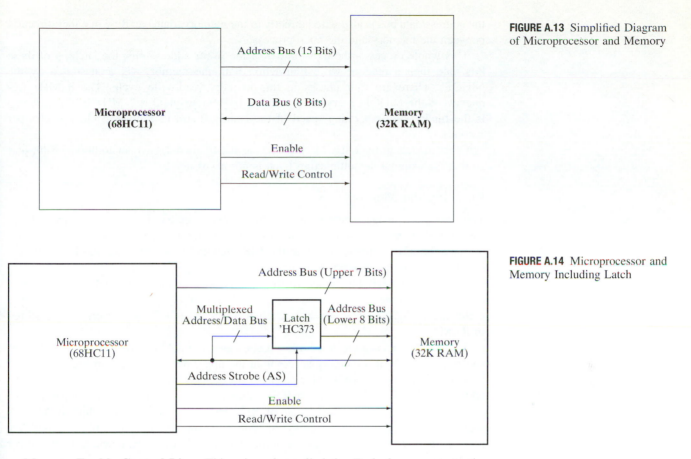

FIGURE A.13 Simplified Diagram of Microprocessor and Memory

FIGURE A.14 Microprocessor and Memory Including Latch

Memory Enable Control Line. This wire, also called the *E clock*, connects to the enable circuitry of the memory. When the memory is enabled, it performs either a read or write operation as determined by the read/write line.

Multiplexing Data and Address Signals

Things are a little more complicated in the particular microprocessor that is used in the Handy Board (the A1 version of the Motorola 68HC11). With this 68HC11, the eight data bus wires take turns functioning as address wires as well.

When a memory location is needed (for reading or writing), first the data wires function as address wires, transmitting the eight lower order bits of the address. Then they function as data wires, either transmitting a data byte (for a write cycle) or receiving a data byte (for a read cycle).

The memory needs to help deal with the split personality data/address bus. This help comes in the form of an 8-bit latch. This chip (the 74HC373) performs the function of latching or storing the lower 8 address bits so that the memory will have the full 15-bit address available for reading or writing data.

Figure A.14 shows how the latch is wired. The upper seven address bits are normal and run directly from the microprocessor to the memory. The lower eight bits are the split personality or, more technically, *multiplexed* address and data bus. These wires connect to the inputs of the latch and also to the data inputs of the memory.

An additional signal, the *Address Strobe* output of the microprocessor, tells the latch when to grab hold of the address values from the address/data bus.

When the full 15-bit address is available to the memory (7 bits directly from the microprocessor and 8 bits from the latch), the read or write transaction can occur. Because the address/data bus is also wired directly to the memory, data can flow in either direction between the memory and the microprocessor.

This whole process—the transmitting of the lower address bits, the latching of these bits, and then a read or write transaction with the memory—is orchestrated by the 68HC11. There are four phases in this memory read/write cycle. The 8 MHz frequency of the 68HC11's crystal is divided by four to yield a 2 MHz E clock, which is the fundamental operating speed of the Handy Board (2 million E clock cycles per second).

Other models of the 68HC11 chip, such as the F1 model, have an additional 8-bit port so that the external demultiplexing latch is not necessary.

Enabling the Memory

The next piece of the memory story is the enable circuitry. Because the Handy Board uses a 32K memory chip and the address space of the 68HC11 is 64K, it is necessary to place the 32K of memory within the 64K area and make sure that the RAM chip is enabled only for addresses within the desired 32K range.

Because the 68HC11's reset vectors are located in the upper half of its address space, it's sensible to locate the 32K of RAM in this upper half so vectors (especially the RESET vector, which is fetched when the 68HC11 is reset) can be stored in RAM.

To do this, we must create circuitry that enables the RAM chip, "turning it on," so to speak, if and only if a memory access is in the upper half of the 64K range.

Remember that the 68HC11 references an address by asserting a value on its 16 address lines, A0 to A15. To test if it's looking for an address in the upper half of memory, one can simply test the state of A15, the highest order address line. If A15 is a logic one, then the lower 15 address bits (A0–A14) specify an address in the upper 32K part of the address space. If A15 is zero, then the address is somewhere in the lower 32K.

To enable the memory chip only for address in the upper 32K, all that is necessary is to AND together the A15 line with the 68HC11's *E Clock*, a synchronization signal generated by the 68HC11 that controls all memory operations. This is illustrated in Figure A.15.

In the diagram, two signals from the 68HC11—the E clock and the A15 address line—are connected to the RAM chip's enable line through a two-input NAND gate. The NAND (Not–AND) gate is used instead of an AND gate because typical memory chips have a "negative true" enable, meaning they are enabled with a logic zero (0 volt) signal. The NAND gate's output is zero (think "true") only when its two inputs are true, so this is the right choice here.

FIGURE A.15 Enabling the Memory, Simplified Diagram

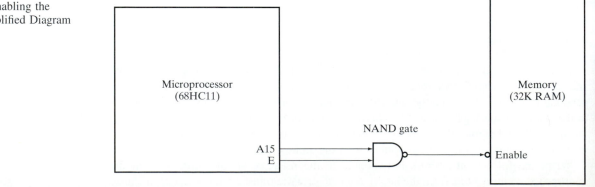

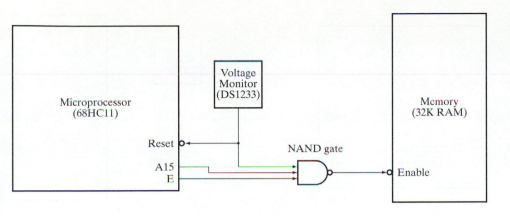

FIGURE A.16 Enabling the Memory with Power Switch Protection, Logical.

The output of the DS1233 chip is NANDed with the two control signals from the 68HC11 (A15 and the E clock enable). When all three of these signals are logic one, the memory is enabled for operation.

Memory Power Switching Protection

The final part of the memory explanation is logic to save the memory contents during power down. The memory enable design is slightly more complicated than the two-input NAND gate solution shown in Figure A.15. The Handy Board preserves the contents of its RAM when the board is turned off and then on again. To accomplish this, two additions are made to the memory circuitry:

1. The RAM chip is provided with power even when the rest of the Handy Board is switched off.
2. The RAM chip's enable input is turned off when the 68HC11 power supply is invalid.

We discuss the former of these additions later in Section A.3.9. Here let's discuss how to turn off the RAM enable when the 68HC11 power is invalid and why that's important.

The key reason to disable the RAM when 68HC11 power is invalid (typically defined as less than 4.5 volts) is that the behavior of the 68HC11 is undefined in this circumstance. When system power is climbing up from 0 volts to 5 volts when the board is switched on, and as it is falling from 5 volts down to 0 volts after power is switched off, the 68HC11 may do unpredictable things—including writing garbage all across RAM contents.

The solution to this problem is simple: Employ a voltage monitoring chip that asserts a reset signal (logic zero) all during power up and as soon as the system voltage falls below 4.5v. The Handy Board uses the Dallas Semiconductor DS1233, a simple and inexpensive device. As shown in Figure A.16, the output of the DS1233 is applied both to the memory enable circuit and to the 68HC11's reset line.

By sending the voltage monitor's output to the 68HC11, the microprocessor is prevented from running when the system voltage is invalid. Because the "voltage-safe" signal is also applied to the enable circuitry of the RAM, the memory is further protected against activity of the 68HC11 during these power-up and power-down "danger zones."

Figure A.17 shows the final design that it implemented on the Handy Board. This is functionally identical to the three-input NAND design shown in Figure A.16, but builds the triple NAND from three dual NANDs. This is because dual NANDs come four in a package, and the remaining gate is used in the IR transmit circuit (discussed in Section A.3.6). Thus, two different parts of the Handy Board design (the memory enable and the IR transmit oscillator) are implemented with just one integrated circuit package. This kind of optimization is often found when one gets to the final level of implementing a design; having a breadth of knowledge of the full range of components available is essential in making these decisions.

FIGURE A.17 Enabling the Memory with Power Switch Protection, Actual.

In the actual implementation, three 2-input NAND gates are used instead of one 3-input NAND. Because the 2-input NAND gates come four to a package, the extra one is available and is used in the Handy Board's IR transmit circuit.

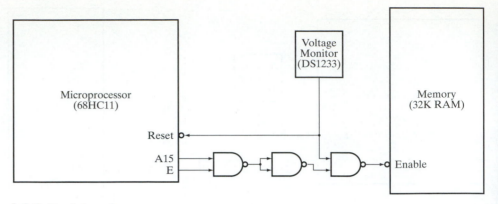

A.3.3 Peripherals

So far we have seen how a memory can be connected to a microprocessor. In a circuit like the one of the Handy Board, the microprocessor must interact with devices other than the memory—for example, motors and sensors.

Often microprocessors intended for control applications, such as the 68HC11, come with additional pins that may be used to connect to physical inputs and outputs. For instance, the 68HC11 has eight analog input signals (Port E) that are used in the Handy Board design to interface with the knob and provide seven user sensor ports.

The 68HC11 also has a bank of eight counter and timer lines. Four of these are uncommitted: Three inputs are available as user sensor ports (digital inputs 9 to 11), and one output is available on the expansion bus connector.

The remaining four of these signals are used for special purpose hardware on the Handy Board. Pins are used to control the LCD screen, beeper, and IR output, and one input pin receives the signal from the onboard IR sensor.

For connecting to additional peripherals—that is, the motors and digital inputs—the Handy Board uses a traditional solution: 8-bit latches for input and output. These latches are connected to the memory bus of the 68HC11 so that they appear like a location in memory. Then the act of reading from or writing to one of these memory locations causes data to be read from or written to a latch—to which the external devices are connected.

Figure A.18 illustrates this idea. Two 8-bit latches are connected to the 68HC11 data bus: a 74HC374 output latch for driving the motor circuit, and a 74HC244 input latch for receiving information from digital sensors.

The other piece of this story is address decoding—circuitry that decides when a memory access should go to the latches. We've already seen the address decoding for the RAM, which looks at the highest address bit (A15), thus putting the 32K of RAM into the upper half of the 68HC11 address space. We also saw that writing to address $7000 controls the motors and reading from address $7000 receives a byte of information from the digital sensors. The Address Decoding Circuitry suggested in Figure A.19 is what makes this happen. An address decoding module looks at the address lines, the read/write line, and the 68HC11's E clock and decides whether to enable the Motor Output latch (for a write) or the Digital Input latch (for a read).

This technique of placing peripheral interface chips into the memory address space of the processor is called *memory mapping* because the latches are "mapped" to a particular address in the processor's memory.

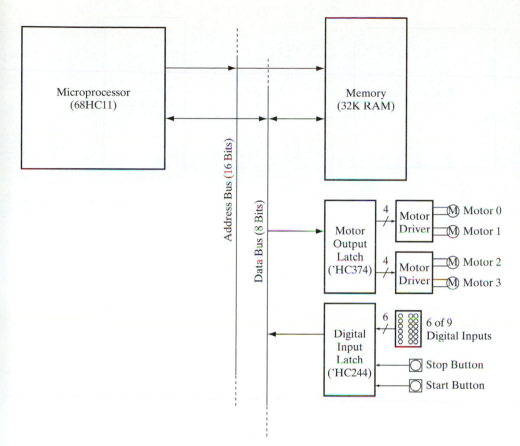

FIGURE A.18 68HC11, Memory, and Motor/Sensor Peripherals Block Diagram, Simplified.

For the 68HC11 to control motors and receive information from sensors, digital output and input latches are connected to the 68HC11's memory bus. The motor driver circuits are connected to a Motor Output Latch, which receives a byte of information from the memory bus; the digital sensor circuits drive a Digital Input Latch, which puts a byte of information onto the 68HC11 memory bus.

In the following discussion, we see how both the 32K RAM memory and the digital input and output latch chips share the address space of the 68HC11.

Memory Mapping with the 74HC138 Chip

The Handy Board solves the address decoding problem with essentially one chip—the 74HC138 3-to-8 address decoder (see Figure A.20). In the 74HC138 operation, a binary number of three digits (the *select inputs*) causes one of eight possible outputs to be selected (the *control outputs*). The chip also has three *enable inputs*, all of which must be enabled to make the chip become active.

The outputs of the 74HC138 chip control the sensor input and motor output latches shown in Figure A.19. The 74HC138 determines when these latches are activated, either to read data from the data bus (in the case of the 74HC374 motor output latch) or write data onto the data bus (in the case of the 74HC244 sensor input latch).

Enable Inputs   The enable inputs of the 74HC138 determine *when the chip will become active* and thereby turn on one of the input or output latches. These enable inputs are critical because the 74HC138 must not become active at the same time as the RAM chip. If it did, then two devices (the RAM and perhaps a 74HC244) would attempt to drive the data bus simultaneously, causing a problematic situation called *bus contention*.

FIGURE A.19 Address Decoding Circuitry Controls Peripheral Latches.

The Address Decoding Circuitry looks at the Address Bus and combines this with information from the E Clock and Read/Write Line to determine when to enable the Motor Output Latch or Digital Input Latch.

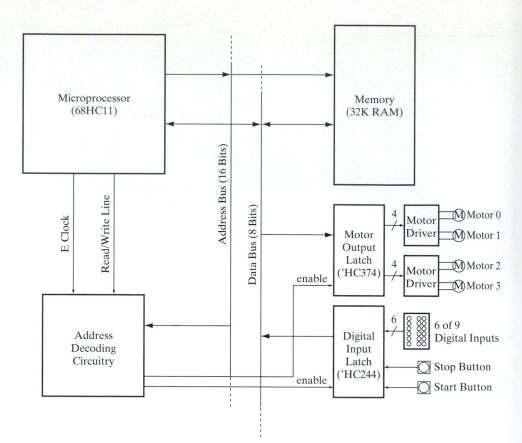

As shown in Figure A.21, A15, which is the highest order address bit, is connected to a *negative enable* of the 74HC138. Thus, A15 must be *zero* to enable the chip. Because the RAM is enabled only when A15 is one (putting the RAM into the upper half of the 68HC11's address space), there is no chance that the 74HC138 and the RAM could be active at the same time.

~A14, which is an inverted signal of A14, is connected to a second negative enable of the 74HC138. Thus, when A14 is one, ~A14 is zero, and the G2-A enable is true. So A14 must be one to activate the 74HC138. So far, the 74HC138 is enabled when A15 is zero and A14 is one (expressed in binary addresses of the form `01xx xxxx xxxx xxxx`)—any address between $4000 and $7FFF.

The final enable input is positive true and is connected to the 68HC11 E clock. When A15 is zero and A14 is one, the E clock will turn on the 74HC138 at the appropriate time for standard 68HC11 read/write cycles.

Select Inputs   Given that the 74HC138 is enabled, the A, B, and C inputs determine which device connected to its outputs will be activated. A, B, and C form a binary number (C is the most significant bit) to determine the selected output.

The A13 and A12 address bits and the 68HC11 read/write line make the selection. Suppose A13 and A12 are one. The read/write line makes the final choice. This line is one for a read and zero for a write. If a read operation is in progress, then the ABC inputs will form the number 7, and the Y7 output will be activated. As shown in Figure A.21, this output connects to the digital input 74HC244 chip. So the 74HC244

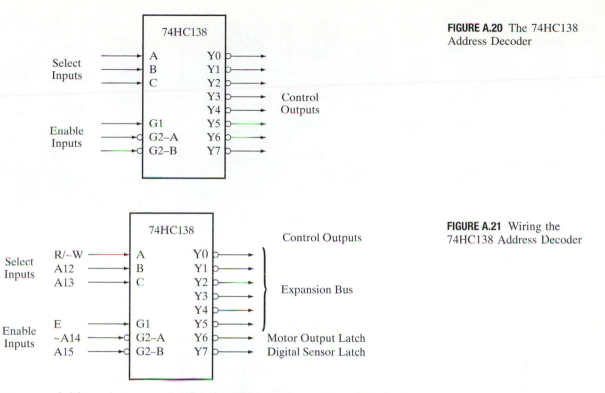

FIGURE A.20 The 74HC138
Address Decoder

FIGURE A.21 Wiring the
74HC138 Address Decoder

chip will turn on and drive a byte onto the data bus. The read operation will complete with this byte having been read from the location in 68HC11 address space that was selected.

Notice that address bits A0 to A11 have no effect on the operation just described. As long as A15 is zero and A14, A13, and A12 are one, a read operation will cause the 74HC138 to turn on the digital input 74HC244 chip to write a byte onto the data bus. Thus, the digital input chip is selected by a read from any address from $7000 to $7FFF. This is fairly wasteful of the address space of the 68HC11, but keep in mind that the only circuitry required to arrange this solution was the 74HC138 chip.

Suppose a write operation were to occur in that same range of memory. The relevant upper four address bits would have the same values, but the read/write line would be zero (indicating the write operation). Thus, the 74HC138 ABC inputs would form the number 6 and output Y6 would be activated. Y6 is connected to the 74HC374 chip that controls the motors; thus, the 74HC374 would latch the value present on the data bus during the write operation.

As shown in Figure A.21, most of the 74HC138 outputs are still available for future expansion. The Handy Board Expansion Board includes a circuit with one 74HC374 chip connected to the Y0 output. Outputs Y1 to Y5 are left free for further expansion use.

System Memory Map

Figure A.22 summarizes the memory map solution that has been implemented for the Handy Board.

The 32K RAM takes up half of the total address space of the microprocessor. As indicated in the map, it is located in the upper 32K of the microprocessor's memory, from addresses $8000 to $FFFF.

FIGURE A.22 68HC11 System
Memory Map

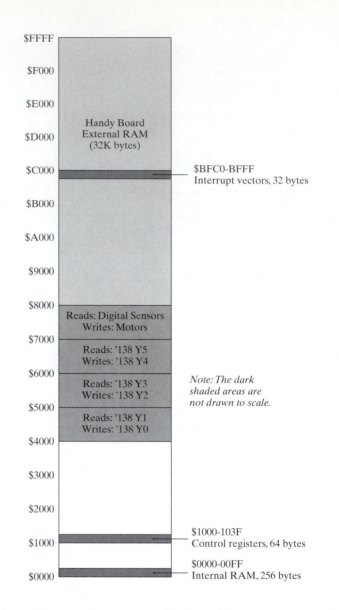

The four digital input and output ports are mapped at locations starting at $4000, $5000, $6000, and $7000.

There is a small area of memory that is internal to the 68HC11 chip. This memory consists of 256 bytes located at the start of the address space, from locations $00 to $FF.

The 68HC11 also has a bank of 64 internal *special function registers* located at addresses $1000 to $103F. These registers control various hardware features of the 68HC11 (the analog inputs and serial communications are two examples).

68HC11 and Memory Schematic

Figure A.23 presents the schematic of the 68HC11, memory, address decoding, and supporting main circuitry on the Handy Board Processor Board. Most of the circuitry depicted in this schematic has already been discussed, including the memory interface circuit (with power protection and enable) and the 74HC138 select circuit.

The remainder of this section presents details on the digital input and output circuit wiring.

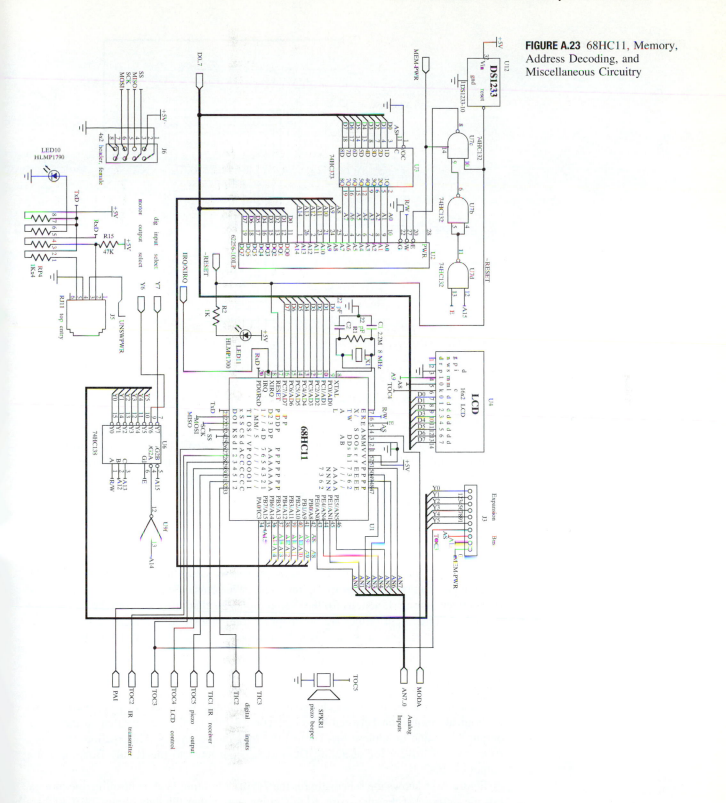

FIGURE A.23 68HC11, Memory, Address Decoding, and Miscellaneous Circuitry

FIGURE A.24 Digital Input Circuit

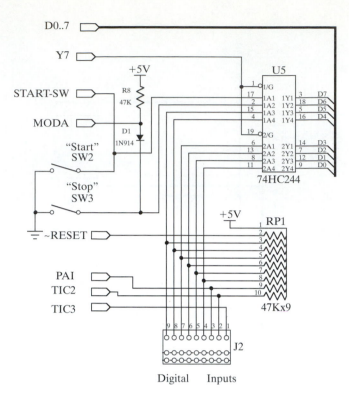

Digital Inputs

Figure A.24 shows the digital input circuitry. U5, a 74HC244 chip, is used to latch an 8-bit word of sensor inputs and drive the 68HC11 data bus with that value when the chip is selected.

The 74HC244 chip has two halves that may be separately enabled. The Y7 select is connected to both enable inputs so that both halves of the chip are always selected simultaneously.

The two upper bits of the 74HC244 are connected to the two user buttons (START and STOP). The lower six bits are connected to the digital input header.

The lower three bits of the input header are connected to timer inputs of the 68HC11. These inputs can be used to precisely measure waveforms or simply for digital input. The Interactive C library functions for the digital inputs insulate the user from the fact that the nine pins on the input header are not mapped contiguously to one location in memory.

RP1, a 47K resistor pack, acts as pull-up resistors to the inputs of the 74HC244 chip, making the default values of the inputs one.

Motor Outputs

In Section 4.3, basic theory of electronic motor control is presented. Here we focus on the logical connection between the eight control bits (which are written to the motor output latch) and how these bits control the four motor drivers. This section presents a simple set of drivers for operating DC motors connected to the Handy Board's motor output circuit.

Figure A.25 shows the schematic for the 74HC374 output latch controlling the motors. For the purpose of the discussion to this point, notice that the data inputs 74HC374 are connected to the 68HC11 data bus. The Y6 select signal from the 74HC138 connects to the clock input of the 74HC374. When Y6 is activated, the 74HC374 latches the value present on the data bus, and these bits then control the motor circuit.

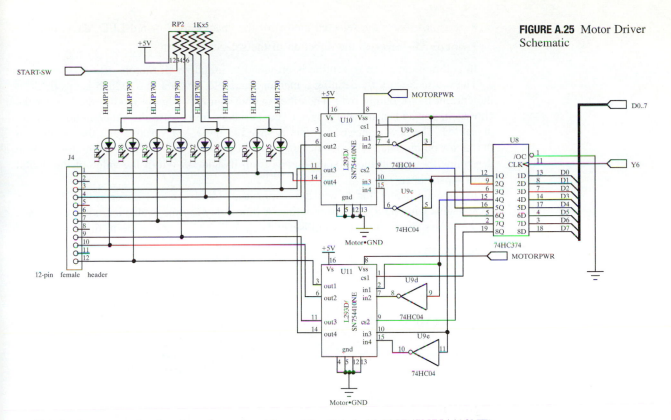

FIGURE A.25 Motor Driver Schematic

This latch presents its signals to the motor driver chips (labeled L293D/SN754410NE). There are two sorts of signals: enable signals, which run to the motor chips' inputs labeled `cs1` and `cs2` (chip selects 1 and 2), and direction signals, going to inputs labeled `in1` through `in4`:

- the upper four output bits of the 74HC374 (`5Q` through `8Q`) control motor enable state (i.e., whether the motors are on or off), and
- the lower four output bits (`1Q` through `4Q`) control motor direction.

Because the motor driver chips have two "direction" inputs per motor (either motor terminal can be driven high or low), the four lower latch bits control direction with the help of four inverters. For each motor, one direction signal from the latch is connected straight to one direction input and inverted to the other. This makes certain that a given motor will always be commanded to one direction or the other once it is enabled.

The following diagram summarizes the motor control latch's operation:

Bit 7	6	5	4	3	2	1	0
Motor 3 enable	Motor 2 enable	Motor 1 enable	Motor 0 enable	Motor 3 direction	Motor 2 direction	Motor 1 direction	Motor 0 direction

Following is an example set of driver routines for basic motor control. The subroutines accept a motor number in the A register—a value from 0 to 3—and provide the following functionality:

- `motoron`—turns the selected motor on.
- `motoroff`—turns the selected motor off.
- `motorfd`—sets the selected motor for the "forward," or green-LED, direction.

- motorbk—sets the selected motor for the "backward," or red-LED, direction.
- motorrd—reverses the direction of the selected motor.

In addition, an alloff routine is provided to initialize all motors off.

The routines work by defining a memory variable, motorbits, which keeps track of the current motor output byte. Then the routines can individually modify the bits for the chosen motor and, using the motorbits variable, make sure the other motor bits are preserved. The new motorbits state is saved in the RAM variable and then written to the motor output latch. (Remember that it's not possible to read from the motor latch to determine the current motor state—reads from its address return the value of the digital input sensor latch!)

In the code listing, the drivers are demonstrated with the mainloop calls. The driver code begins with the alloff subroutine. A time delay routine is also included: delayms, which delays for a number of milliseconds as indicated by the value in the X register.

```
* mtrdrive.asm
* sample motor interface library

MOTORS   equ     $7000   ; address of motor chip latch

         org     0

motorbits rmb    1       ; copy of motor state bits
*                        ; high 4 bits are on/off, low 4 are dir

         org     $8000

start
         lds     #$ff    ; set up stack for subroutines

         bsr     alloff          ; initialize motors off

mainloop
         ldaa    #0
         bsr     motoron         ; turn on motor 0

         ldx     #500
         bsr     delayms         ; wait 0.5 sec

         ldaa    #0
         bsr     motoroff        ; turn off motor 0

         ldx     #500
         bsr     delayms         ; wait 0.5 sec

         ldaa    #0
         bsr     motorrd         ; reverse motor 0 for next time

         ldaa    #3
         bsr     motorbk         ; set motor 3 for backward

         ldaa    #3
         bsr     motoron         ; turn on motor 3

         ldx     #500
         bsr     delayms         ; wait 0.5 sec
```

```
        ldaa    #3
        bsr     motorfd         ; set motor 3 for forward

        ldx     #500
        bsr     delayms         ; wait 0.5 sec

        ldaa    #3
        bsr     motoroff        ; turn off motor 3

        bra     mainloop        ; repeat

* resets motors to off
alloff:
        clra
        bsr     store_motors

* call with motor to be turned on in A
motoron:
        bsr     select_onoff_bit
        oraa    motorbits       ; turn on selected on/off bit
        bra     store_motors

motoroff:
        bsr     select_onoff_bit
        coma                    ; invert to all 1's except selected bit
        anda    motorbits       ; set selected bit to 0
        bra     store_motors

* "forward" direction has dir bit off
motorfd:
        bsr     select_dir_bit
        coma
        anda    motorbits       ; set selected bit to 0
        bra     store_motors

* "backward" direction has dir bit on
motorbk:
        bsr     select_dir_bit
        oraa    motorbits
        bra     store_motors

* reverse the direction (rd) by exclusive-OR'ing the dir bit
motorrd:
        bsr     select_dir_bit
        eora    motorbits
        bra     store_motors

* accepts motor byte in A;
* writes it to motorbits variable and hardware latch
store_motors:
        staa    motorbits
        staa    MOTORS
        rts

* selects on/off bit from motor number
```

```
* takes 0 to 3 in A, returns 0: $10, 1: $20, 2: $40, 4: $80 in A
select_onoff_bit:
        inca                        ; make range of A from 1 to 4
        ldab    #$08                ; motor 0 position after one shift
sob20   lslb                        ; shift B up by one bit position
        deca
        bne     sob20
* B has answer
        tba                         ; transfer B to A
        rts


* selects dir bit from motor number
* takes 0 to 3 in A, returns 0: $01, 1: $02, 2: $04, 3: $08 in A
select_dir_bit:
        inca                        ; put range of A from 1 to 4
        clrb                        ; clear result
        sec                         ; set carry, will get rotated into B
sdb20   rolb                        ; B is $01 after one rotate
        deca
        bne     sdb20
        tba
        rts


* delays specified num of milliseconds (from X register)
* returns with X = 0, B = 0
delayms:
* delay 1 ms, or 2000 cycles
        ldab    #222                ; 9 in loop x 222 = 1998
dms20   decb                        ; 2 cycles
        nop                         ; 2 cycles
        nop                         ; 2 cycles
        bne     dms20               ; 3 cycles
* test X and repeat till done
        dex
        bne     delayms
        rts


        org     $bffe               ; reset vector
        fdb     start
```

A.3.4 Analog Inputs

The 68HC11 has on-chip circuitry to perform an analog-to-digital signal conversion. In this operation, a voltage from 0 to 5 volts is linearly converted into an 8-bit number (a range of 0–255). This feature is one of the many that make the 68HC11 very well suited for control applications.

The 68HC11 has eight of these analog input pins, known as the Port E register. In the Handy Board design, seven of these are available sensor inputs (sensor ports 0–6), and one is wired to the user knob.

In the actual hardware implementation, the 68HC11 has only one analog-to-digital conversion circuit, but this circuit can perform a conversion on the voltage present on any of the eight Port E pins. There are several 68HC11 registers used to control the analog subsystem:

- `ADCTL`, the analog-to-digital control and status register. This register determines which operating mode the A/D subsystem will use when performing conversions and which input pin(s) will be converted.
- `ADR1`, `ADR2`, `ADR3`, and `ADR4`, the result registers. These hold the conversion results.
- `PORTE`, the digital register associated with the analog input pins. This register shows the readings of the analog inputs as digital values (greater than 2.5v is 1, less than 2.5v is 0).
- `OPTION`, a general system configuration options register. To enable the analog-to-digital subsystem altogether, the high bit of the `OPTION` register must be set to one.

The basic procedure for performing an analog-to-digital conversion is as follows:

1. Enable the A/D subsystem by setting the high bit in the `OPTION` register. (This only has to be done once in the operation of a whole program.)
2. Write the number of the input pin to be converted (in the range 0–7) into the `ADCTL` register.
3. Wait 32 machine cycles for the analog conversion process to take place.
4. Read the answer out of the `ADR1` register.

This procedure uses the simplest operating mode of the A/D subsystem—single conversion of one input pin. There are other modes that convert four different pins in a batch or repeatedly convert pins. For information on these modes, see the Motorola *M68HC11 Reference Manual* [Sec96].

Figure A.26 shows a listing of `analog.asm`, a demonstration program of the analog-to-digital conversion process. The code converts the knob reading and then writes this value to the motor port. Run the program and turn the knob; the motor LEDs should flash in a pattern as the knob value varies.

When writing your own assembly code, make sure to remember to set that high bit in the `OPTION` register. The analog-to-digital system will not work until that bit is turned on!

A.3.5 The Serial Line Circuit

The Handy Board communicates with a host computer over an RS-232 serial line. "RS-232" refers to a standard protocol for communications between computers and peripherals, first designed for computers to interface with modems.

As illustrated in Figure A.27, the basic RS-232 connection consists of three wires:

- *TxD*, transmit data, is used by the computer to send data to the modem;
- *Rxd*, receive data, is used by the computer to receive data from the modem; and
- *GND*, signal ground, is used as the zero-volt reference for the other two signals.

Note that the definition of what's TxD and what's RxD depends on whose side you're on. If you're the computer, then you transmit on your TxD and receive on your RxD (of course). The same is true for the modem. But the computer's TxD and the modem's RxD are the same wire, so when you say "the TxD line" you've got to specify which side is transmitting. Lots of serial problems arise when the computer's and modem's TxDs (or RxD) are inadvertently wired together. One side's TxD must go to the other side's RxD and vice versa.

The actual RS-232 standard involves several more wires for conveying various status information (some of these are known as "handshaking lines"), but the data themselves are transmitted on the two one-way TxD and RxD wires.

FIGURE A.26 Listing of
analog.asm, Analog Input
Demonstration Program

```
* analog.asm demonstration of analog conversion

ADCTL    equ      $1030    ; A/D Control/Status register
ADR1     equ      $1031    ; A/D Result register 1
OPTION   equ      $1039    ; System Configuration Options register

         org      $8000

start
         lds      #$ff             ; establish stack for subr calls

         ldx      #$1000           ; register base ptr
         bset     OPTION,X $80     ; enable A/D subsystem!

loop
         ldab     #7               ; knob is port E7
         bsr      analog           ; get analog reading
         stab     $7000            ; write it to motor port
         bra      loop

analog
         stab     ADCTL            ; begin analog conversion
* wait 32 cycles for analog reading to happen
         ldaa     #6               ; 2
waitlp   deca                      ; 2
         bne      waitlp           ; 3
         ldab     ADR1             ; get analog read
         rts                       ; b has reading, a has 0

         org      $bffe            ; reset vector
         fdb      start
```

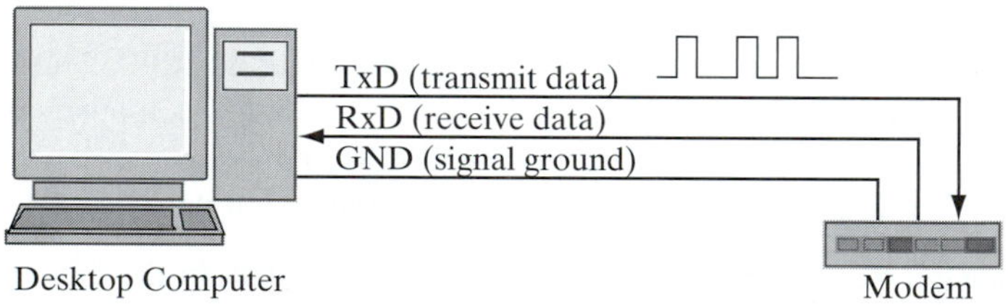

FIGURE A.27 Desktop Computer
and Modem Using RS-232
Communication

TxD (transmit data)
RxD (receive data)
GND (signal ground)

Desktop Computer   Modem

Protocol

In the RS-232 system, a "logic zero" is indicated by a +15 volt signal with respect
to ground, and a "logic one" is indicated by a −15 volt signal. Note that this is different from standard digital logic levels, in which a logic zero is 0v and a logic one
is 5v!

The communications method is known as "serial" because data are transmitted one
bit at a time or serially (i.e., in order). Figure A.28 illustrates the RS-232 signal format, indicating the RS-232 voltage levels and the "TTL level," which convey the same
information in the 0 to 5v range. In the diagram, the format of one byte of data is illustrated. First, notice that the serial line "idles high," meaning that when no data are being
transmitted, the line is at the logic one voltage.

The duration of each of the bits is specified by the *baud rate* of the serial
communication—the number of bits per second (bps). For example, if the communication is 9,600 baud (or 9,600 bps), then each bit is exactly $\frac{1}{9600}$ of a second in duration.

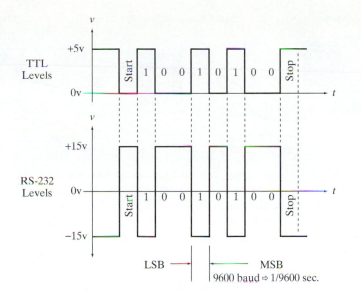

FIGURE A.28 Byte Format and Voltage Levels of RS-232 Communication.

The serial line idles with a logic one voltage level. The data byte begins with a "start bit," which is sent with the logic zero voltage. Then eight data bits are transmitted, least significant bit first. Finally there is a stop bit, which consists of one bit's width of the logic one voltage. The value being transmitted in the diagram is $29 or 41 decimal.

The transmission of a byte begins with a "start bit," which is sent at the logic zero voltage and lasts for one bit-time.

Then the data for the given byte are transmitted, least significant bit first.

Finally, a stop bit is produced, which is always a logic one.

Sometimes an additional error-checking bit, known as the *parity bit*, may be included (after the data bits but before the stop bit). The parity bit may be "even parity" or "odd parity." If it's even parity, then all of the data bits plus the parity bit (taken one at a time) should add to an even number.

In the example transmission in the diagram, there is a start bit, followed by eight data bits, followed by a stop bit. This format is known as "N–8–1": no parity, eight data bits, and a stop bit that's one bit long in duration. Sometimes the stop bit may be 1.5 or 2 bits long.

So, for example, "E–7–1" would mean even parity, seven data bits, and one bit-time stop bit. The N–8–1 format is by far the most common presently in use, although occasionally one finds devices that communicate differently.

Hardware

The 68HC11 chip includes a hardware module to generate waveforms compatible with the RS-232 systems. (This module is sometimes referred to as a UART for "universal asynchronous receiver/transmitter.") Because the 68HC11 operates at TTL, or 0 to 5v levels, it requires external circuitry to convert its own signals to the RS-232 voltages.

The Handy Board uses the Maxim MAX232 serial transceiver to solve the voltage problem. This chip is located on the Handy Board's separate Serial Interface and Battery Charger board. Figure A.29 illustrates how the Serial Interface Board sits between the desktop computer and the Handy Board performing the voltage conversion.

One of the difficulties in generating RS-232 signals is obtaining the negative voltage required to transmit a logic one. However, it turns out that the specified −15 volts is not required: −10 volts will do for most applications, and some modern computers use −5 volt levels.[3]

---

[3] Desktop computers differ by platform in how tightly they adhere to the official serial line specification. For instance, nearly all Intel-compatible PCs accept zero volts as a valid "logic one" (remember logic one should be a negative voltage). Macintosh computers, on the other hand, require at least −2v for the logic one level. This causes problems if circuit designers reduce the serial spec to simply a 0 to 5v range, which is then accepted by the PC but rejected by the Mac.

FIGURE A.29 Desktop Computer, Serial Interface, and Handy Board

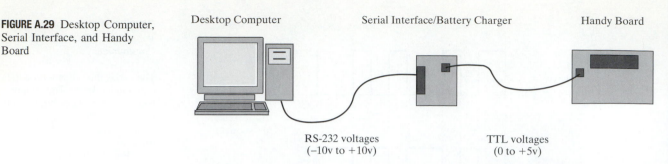

A circuit called a *charge pump* is used to generate this negative voltage. A charge pump consists of two capacitors and a switch. One of the capacitors is charged to a positive voltage by the main power supply. Then the terminals of this capacitor are switched to the terminals of the second capacitor. The first capacitor discharges rapidly into the second, charging it negatively with respect to system ground. This process is switched rapidly, and a steady negative voltage supply is produced in the second capacitor.

The MAX232 uses two charge pumps. The first is used to double the system voltage of +5 volts to obtain a +10 volt supply that more closely matches the RS-232 standard. The second charge pump inverts this +10 volts to obtain a −10 volt supply. As shown in Figure A.30, the schematic for the Serial Interface, capacitors C10, C11, C12, and C13 are used by the Maxim chip in its charge-pump circuit.

Software

The 68HC11 has several registers that are used to control its built-in UART. In the 68HC11 documentation, this subsystem is referred to as the *Serial Communications Interface* (SCI).

The SCI control registers are:

BAUD The baud rate control register, at address $1028. Sets the serial communications speed.

SCCR1 The SCI control register 1, at address $102C. Determines how many data bits are transmitted per byte.

SCCR2 The SCI control register 2, at address $102D. Contains enable bits for the receiver and transmitters, and interrupts generated on receive and transmit.

SCDR The SCI data register, at address $102F. This is the register that contains the actual communications data.

SCSR The SCI status register, at address $102E. Contains various status and error code bits.

In typical use, one would initialize the SCI system at the beginning of the program and then use primarily the SCDR register for transmitting and receiving data and the SCSR register for determining when outgoing data are finished or incoming data are available.

Figure A.31 is an example program that demonstrates how to use these registers to send and receive characters through the 68HC11's serial port.

Let's examine the program in detail. Here is where the SCI system is enabled and initialized for 9600–N–8–1 communication:

```
        ldaa    #$30    ; value for 9600 baud with an 8 MHz xtal
        staa    BAUD
        ldaa    #$0c    ; turn on xmit and rcv enable bits
        staa    SCCR2
```

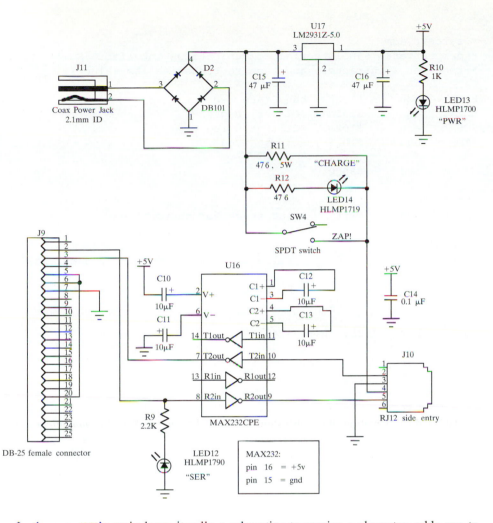

In the program's main loop, it calls a subroutine to receive a character, adds one to the value that's received, and then transmits the new value back:

```
loop    bsr     rcv_char
        inca
        bsr     xmit_char
        bra     loop
```

The routine to transmit a character waits for any previous characters in progress to finish by testing Bit 6 of the SCSR register. When this bit is a one, the previous transmit operation is complete. The new transmission is initiated simply by writing the desired value to the SCDR register:

```
xmit_char:
        ldab    SCSR    ; first check if ready
        andb    #$40    ; bit 6 is transmit complete flag
        beq     xmit_char ; wait until TC flag is 1
        staa    SCDR    ; transmit A register
        rts
```

The routine to receive a character waits for a character to appear by testing Bit 5 of the SCSR register. When this bit is a one, the character is retrieved from the SCDR register. The act of retrieving the character automatically clears the flag in the SCDR:

FIGURE A.31 Serial Line Test
Program

```
* sertest.asm
* demonstrates 68HC11 serial communications interface (SCI)
* receives a character, and then re-transmits its value + 1

BAUD     equ       $102b ; baud rate reg
SCCR2    equ       $102d ; SCI ctrl reg #2
SCSR     equ       $102e ; SCI status reg
SCDR     equ       $102f ; SCI data reg

         org       $8000

start
         lds       #$ff      ; set stack for subroutines

* initialize SCI
         ldaa      #$30      ; value for 9600 baud with an 8 MHz xtal
         staa      BAUD
         ldaa      #$0c      ; turn on xmit and rcv enable bits
         staa      SCCR2

loop     bsr       rcv_char
         inca
         bsr       xmit_char
         bra       loop

* send char in A register (destroys B register)
xmit_char:
         ldab      SCSR      ; first check if ready
         andb      #$40      ; bit 6 is transmit complete flag
         beq       xmit_char ; wait until TC flag is 1
         staa      SCDR      ; transmit A register
         rts

* get char into A register
rcv_char:
         ldaa      SCSR      ; first check if ready
         anda      #$20      ; bit 5 is receive data register full flag
         beq       rcv_char  ; wait until RDRF flag is 1
         ldaa      SCDR      ; get rcv'd char (auto-clears RDRF flag)
         rts

         org       $bffe     ; RESET vector
         fdb       start
rcv_char:
         ldaa      SCSR      ; first check if ready
         anda      #$20      ; bit 5 is receive data register full flag
         beq       rcv_char  ; wait until RDRF flag is 1
         ldaa      SCDR      ; get received char (auto-clears RDRF flag)
         rts
```

Testing

To try out the sertest program, load it into the Handy Board and then power cycle
the board to run the program. Then open a terminal emulator program on the development computer. Set the serial communications parameters to 9,600 baud, no parity,

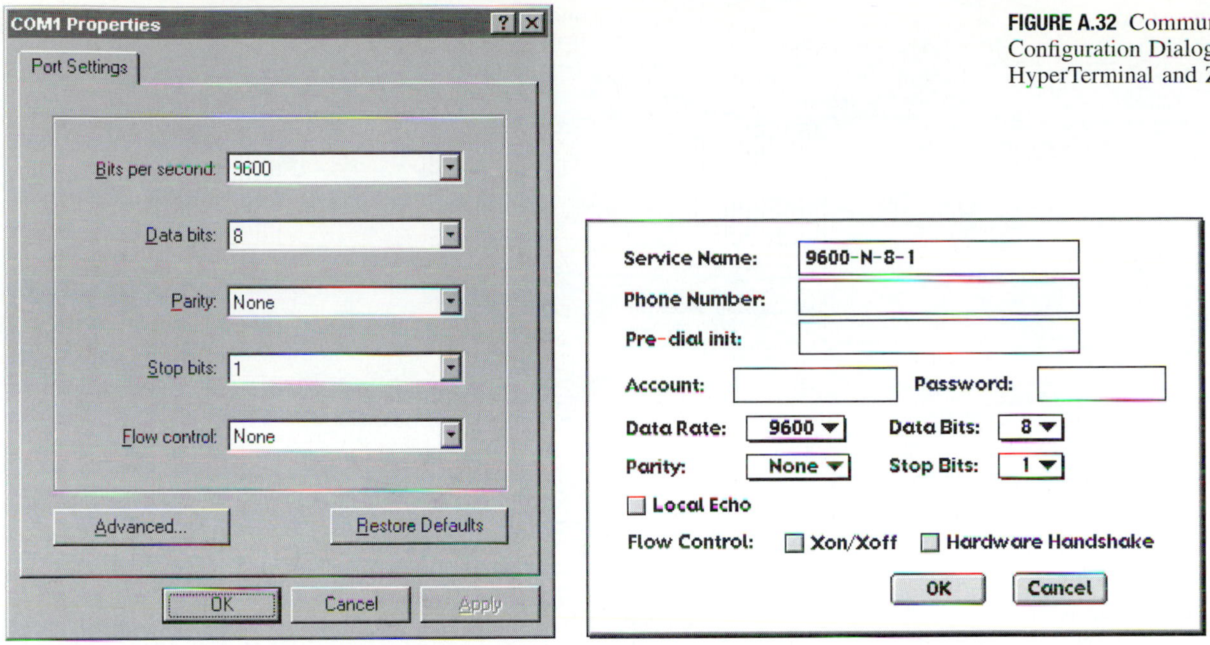

FIGURE A.32 Communications Configuration Dialogs for HyperTerminal and ZTerm

eight data bits, and one stop bit. Figure A.32 illustrates the appropriate configuration dialogs for two popular terminal emulators—*HyperTerminal* for Windows and *ZTerm* for Macintosh.

When in terminal emulator main screen, type a few characters on the keyboard. They should be echoed back by the Handy Board, incremented by one position in the ASCII table each time (e.g., if you type an "A," you should see a "B" typed back). Refer to the ASCII chart on page 310 to make sure you're getting the right thing.

The two routines at the core of this example (`xmit_char` and `rcv_char`) can serve as the basis for a more expanded use of serial communications.

A.3.6 The Infrared Transmission Circuit

The Handy Board includes a circuit for generating a modulated output signal for driving an IR LED. This IR LED emits light that can be detected by any of a number of common IR detectors, including the Sharp IS1U60 that's mounted on the Handy Board. Use of these sensors is detailed in Section 6.2; here the IR transmission circuit is explained.

The Sharp GP1U60 sensor, and others like it (commonly used in TVs, VCRs, and other devices controlled by IR), is sensitive to *modulated* IR light. These sensors detect the presence of IR light that is blinking on and off at a particular rate. The GP1U52 sensor is tuned to 38,000 Hertz (38 kHz).[4]

The 38 kHz signal is too high for the 68HC11 to comfortably generate directly. It would be possible for the processor to create this frequency, but it would require a dead-loop in which the processor did this and nothing else. Hence, an oscillator circuit is present on the Handy Board to generate a 38 kHz signal; a 68HC11 output is then used to switch this oscillator on and off.

Figure A.34 shows a block diagram of the IR transmit circuit. A 38 kHz oscillator is controlled by a resistor-capacitor pair. The output of this oscillator is gated with a control signal from the 68HC11 to produce a waveform that is a 38 kHz oscillation when the

---

[4] Note that this is different from more recently available IR sensors, often referred to as "IRDa sensors," because of their compliance with the Infrared Data Association specification. These IRDa parts directly interpret pulses of IR light into a digital waveform. So the 38 kHz signal, which is received by the IS1U60 as simply a "logic true," would be output by an IRDa sensor as a 38 kHz square wave.

FIGURE A.33 Square Wave Consisting of Bursts of 40 Khz Signals

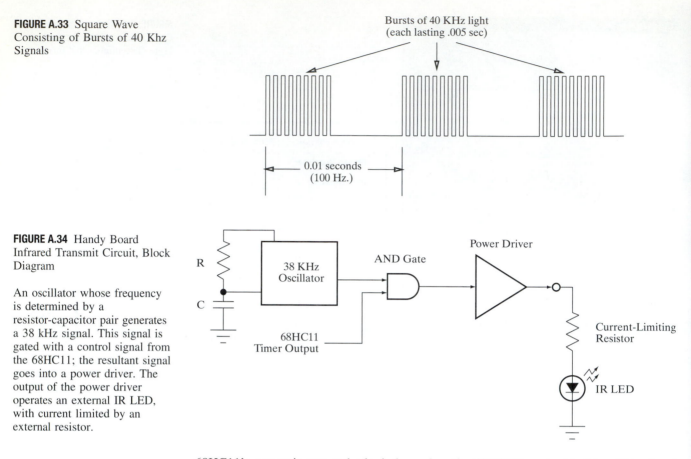

Bursts of 40 KHz light
(each lasting .005 sec)

0.01 seconds
(100 Hz.)

FIGURE A.34 Handy Board Infrared Transmit Circuit, Block Diagram

An oscillator whose frequency is determined by a resistor-capacitor pair generates a 38 kHz signal. This signal is gated with a control signal from the 68HC11; the resultant signal goes into a power driver. The output of the power driver operates an external IR LED, with current limited by an external resistor.

R

C

38 KHz
Oscillator

AND Gate

Power Driver

Current-Limiting
Resistor

IR LED

68HC11
Timer Output

68HC11's output is true and a logic low when the 68HC11's output is false. This signal is then run through a power driver and used to light the IR transmit LED.

In Figure A.35, the full circuit schematic for the IR subsystem is illustrated. The oscillator is built with one NAND gate from the 74HC132 package and enabled via the 68HC11's TOC2 output. In the actual circuit, this NAND gate forms both the oscillator and the controlling AND gate of the block diagram.

The 74HC132 is a special kind of NAND (not-AND) gate called a Schmitt trigger, which requires the input voltages for low and high logic levels to have a gap between them (e.g., 0.9 volts for logic low and 2.0 volts for logic high). This voltage differential must be built up or discharged on C6 through R4, the resistor-capacitor timing pair, hence causing the desired oscillation.

For example, suppose TOC2 is high, enabling the oscillation. If Pin 3 output is high, current will flow into C6 through R4. When C6 charges to 2.0 volts, the input on Pin 1 will become true, causing Pin 3 output to become false. Then current will flow *out* of C6 through the resistor and into the gate. When the voltage on C6 drops below 0.9 volts, resulting in a logic zero on Pin 1, Pin 3 output will become true again, causing the process to repeat. The result is a square wave on Pin 3 output, with its frequency determined by the charge rate of the C6 capacitor through the R4 resistor. The capacitor C6 is specified as a polypropylene capacitor, a type that is known for its relatively precise capacitance value. Likewise, R4 is specified as a 1% precision value.

Note that two different values are indicated for R4—3.83K Ω or 6.81K Ω. It so happens that different types of 74HC132 chips have slightly different voltage threshold properties. Depending on which type of 74HC132 is employed, different resistance must be used. The 3.83K Ω or 6.81K Ω value covers all varieties of 74HC132s encountered so far.

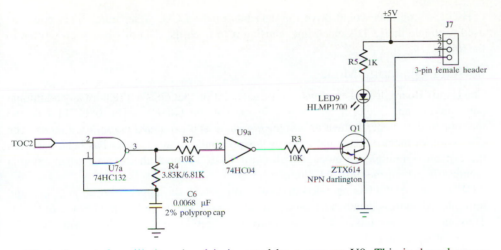

Next, the gated oscillation signal is inverted by a gate on U9. This is done because the 74HC132 chip is always powered on, even when the Handy Board is switched off, because the other gates on the 74HC132 are part of the battery-backed memory circuit. When the Handy Board is off, Pin 3 output of the oscillator will be high (the TOC2 input from the 68HC11 will be low because the 68HC11 *is* switched off). R7 limits how much current can flow into U9 in this case and, because U9 inverts, the transistor drive that follows is definitely off when the board is switched off.

Q1 is a power Darlington transistor—two transistors in one package. This provides a high gain, allowing a tiny amount of current from U9 to switch large amounts of current through IR LEDs.

The final drive LEDs are connected from the Handy Board's +5 volt supply to the collector of Q1. On the board is a low-current visible red LED to indicate the status of the IR transmit circuit. J7, a header connector, allows external IR LEDs to be connected to the same drive transistor.

Please note that an external IR LED must have a current-limiting resistor wired in series with the LED, just like the R5/LED9 indicator pair. Section 6.2.1 shows diagrams for attaching LEDs to the Handy Board's IR output.

A.3.7 The LCD Display

The first 14 pins of the Handy Board's Expansion Bus are designed to be compatible with a 14-pin standard LCD interface. A variety of character-based LCD devices with different screen sizes use this standard interface.

The LCD interface standard is fairly simple, consisting of the following signals:

- An 8-bit data bidirectional bus,
- two mode select input signals,
- a clock line,
- a voltage reference for contrast adjustment,
- +5 volt logic power, and
- a signal ground.

Reading and writing data to an LCD are much like reading and writing data to latches or memory. There is one problem, however: LCDs only work at data transfer rates up to 1 MHz. The 68HC11 in the Handy Board operates at 2 MHz—too fast for most LCDs.

One solution to the speed problem would be to use a 74HC374-type latch between the 68HC11 and the LCD. The 74HC374 could be written to at the full bus rate of the

68HC11; its outputs would drive the data bus of the LCD. A separate signal could be used to toggle the LCD's clock line, causing it to latch the data that had been written to the 74HC374.[5]

68HC11 Operating Modes

The Handy Board instead employs an unusual solution that does not require any additional parts, taking advantage of an obscure feature of the 68HC11. The 68HC11 has two main operating modes known as *single chip mode* and *expanded multiplexed mode*. The discussion of memory read and write cycles presented in this chapter has been based on the expanded multiplexed mode, which is the 68HC11 mode that is used when external memory is part of the 68HC11 circuit.

When the 68HC11 is operated in single-chip mode, the upper 8-bit address bus and multiplexed address/data bus become general purpose inputs and outputs of the 68HC11. Thus, in single-chip mode, it is possible for the 68HC11 to communicate with the LCD under software control.

There is a problem with this, however: When the 68HC11 is placed into single-chip mode, it can no longer execute a program from its external RAM. In fact, as far as the 68HC11 is concerned, there *is no external memory* anymore.

The 68HC11 has 256 bytes of internal RAM, however, from which it can execute a program when in single-chip mode. Thus, a software driver executing out of internal RAM could perform a transaction with the LCD and then switch back to expanded-multiplexed mode, returning control to the main program in external memory.

The obscure feature mentioned is not that the 68HC11 has both of these modes, but the idea of dynamically switching between them. To talk to the LCD while preserving the expanded-memory architecture, it's necessary to switch back and forth between expanded mode (for normal operation) and single-chip mode (for talking to the LCD). This requires the use of the 68HC11's *special test* mode, which is very much like the normal operating mode with the exception that the interrupt vector bank is moved from its normal range of $FFC0 to $FFFF to the special test range of $BFC0 to $BFFF.

Based on this idea, here is the solution that has been implemented:

1. Start by copying a software driver from external system memory into the 256 bytes of internal 68HC11 memory.
2. Begin execution of the driver program located in internal memory:

   - Place the 68HC11 into single-chip mode; external memory disappears.
   - Execute a low-speed transaction with the LCD by directly controlling the data bus via software.
   - Place the 68HC11 into expanded-multiplexed mode.
   - Return to the main program in external memory.

3. Continue normal program execution.

Sample LCD Driver

Following is a listing of a demonstration driver for using the LCD screen. The program includes the following subroutines:

lcdinit which copies the LCD driver into internal memory and initializes the LCD,

lcdcls which clears the LCD screen,

putchar which writes a single character to the LCD screen, and

putstr which writes a zero-terminated character string to the LCD.

---

[5] This solution assumes that one does not need to read status data back from the LCD.

A main program demonstrates the driver by displaying the message `Press start...` on the LCD, waiting until the Start button is pressed, and then displaying `Goodbye!` and terminating.

Following is the full source code listing and then a commentary that explains the code.

```
* lcdtest.asm
* demo of LCD driver located in 68HC11 internal memory

PORTA     equ      $1000
PORTC     equ      $1003    ; Port C latched data register
PORTB     equ      $1004    ; Port B data register
DDRC      equ      $1007    ; Data Direction register for port C
HPRIO     equ      $103c

          org      0
* label for zero page location of driver
lcdwrite

          org      $8000

start     lds      #$ffff             ; establish stack at top of RAM

          bsr      lcdinit            ; transfer LCD driver and init LCD

          ldx      #string1           ; point at first string
          bsr      putstr             ; write it to LCD!

waitstart ldaa     $7000              ; wait till user presses
          anda     #$80               ; the start button
          bne      waitstart

          bsr      lcdcls             ; clear the LCD
          ldx      #string2           ; point to 2nd string
          bsr      putstr             ; write it!

die       bra      die                ; we're done

string1 fcc        'Press start...'
        fcb        0

string2 fcc        'Goodbye!'
        fcb        0


* putstr: call with X pointing to zero-terminated string
putstr  ldab       0,x                ; fetch char
        beq        putstr90           ; test for done
        bsr        putchar            ; write to LCD
        inx                           ; increment ptr
        bra        putstr             ; try again
putstr90 rts

* putchar: writes B as a single char to the LCD
putchar
        pshx                          ; save X register
```

```
        ldaa    #2                      ; control for normal char
        jsr     lcdwrite                ; call LCD driver routine
        pulx                            ; restore X register
        rts

* lcdinit: call to load driver and clear LCD screen
lcdinit
        bsr     loaddriver              ; intall driver into zero page
        ldd     #$0038                  ; 8-bit operation, 2-line display
        jsr     lcdwrite                ; do it
        ldab    #%00001100              ; display on, cursor & blink off
        jsr     lcdwrite
* fall into lcdcls

* lcdcls:  call to clear LCD screen
lcdcls
        ldd     #$0001      ; home and clear screen
        jsr     lcdwrite
        ldab    #$06        ; set to increment char loc & cursor pos
        jsr     lcdwrite
        ldab    #$02        ; home cursor
        jsr     lcdwrite
        rts

* loaddriver: copy driver to zero page memory
loaddriver
        ldx     #driverstart            ; point to source
        ldy     #lcdwrite               ; destination
load20
        ldaa    0,x
        staa    0,y                     ; copy one byte
        inx
        iny                             ; increment ptrs
        cpx     #driverend
        bne     load20                  ; until done
        rts

* zero page LCD driver
* copy to zero page RAM, then call with A=command byte, B=data
* X and Y regs are destroyed in use
driverstart
        xgdy                            ; save args in y
        ldx     #$1000
        bclr    HPRIO,x %00100000       ; put into single chip mode
        bclr    PORTA,x %00010000       ; turn off LCD E line
        clr     DDRC,x                  ; make port C input
lcdready
        ldaa    #1
        staa    PORTB                   ; read operation from LCD
        bset    PORTA,x %00010000       ; strobe LCD on
        ldaa    PORTC,x                 ; get status
        bclr    PORTA,x %00010000       ; strobe LCD off
        anda    #$80                    ; bit 7 is busy flag
        bne     lcdready

        ldaa    #$FF
```

```
        staa    DDRC,x                  ; make port C output
        xgdy                            ; restore args
        staa    PORTB,x                 ; high byte is control
        stab    PORTC,x                 ; low byte is data
        bset    PORTA,x %00010000
        bclr    PORTA,x %00010000       ; write to LCD

driverexit
        bset    HPRIO,x %00100000       ; put into expanded chip mode
        rts                             ; return
driverend


* reset vector
        org     $bffe
        fdb     start
```

After the 68HC11 register equates, the label lcdwrite follows an org directive at address 0. lcdwrite is thus located in the 68HC11's internal RAM area; this is where the LCD communications driver will get copied. (If these drivers are included as part of a larger program that also uses locations in zero page RAM, the lcdwrite label should follow other allocations in the zero page RAM area.)

At address $8000, the main program begins. After establishing the stack pointer register, the program calls the subroutine lcdinit, which copies the driver at the location of the label lcdwrite and then uses the driver to reset and initialize the LCD.

The main program continues by setting up the X register to point at the address string1. After the main program's code, the message Press start... is located at label string1 (using the fcc "form constant character" directive).

After the X register is set up, the putstr routine is called. This will copy each character of the string to the LCD.

Next the three lines of code by waitstart will loop until the user presses the Handy Board's start button.

Then the lcdcls routine is called, clearing the LCD's screen. The X register is pointed at string2, Goodbye!, and this string is printed. Then the main program terminates with an indefinite dio loop.

Now let's look at the driver routines, beginning with the putstr function. This routine steps through the characters pointed at by the X register, calling putchar on each one until it finds a zero.

The putchar function is the first one to actually interact with the LCD driver directly. It sets up the A register with the number 2, which will be applied as control signals when writing data to the LCD. This control value tells the LCD to accept the data as a character to be displayed. The character is already located in the B register (as set up by the putstr function); then the LCD driver is actually called (jsr lcdwrite). The putchar function saves and restores the X register around the call to the LCD driver because the driver destroys it.

The lcdinit routine is next in the code listing. This routine calls loaddriver, which does the work of copying the LCD driver at the lcdwrite location. Then lcdinit performs some control operations, telling the LCD to use 8-bit communications mode and two-line mode. Notice that the A register, which becomes control pins to the LCD, is set to zero (ldd #$0038).

lcdinit falls into lcdcls, which performs additional control operations on the LCD to clear the screen.

Next is the loaddriver function. This copies the driver, located in main memory at driverstart, to the location specified by lcdwrite.

Finally is the code for the driver, located at the label `driverstart`. Remember this code will be copied into the 68HC11's internal memory and executed from there (at `lcdwrite`).

The driver begins by saving the D register, which contains the control and data information to be written to the LCD, in the Y register (`xgdy`, eXchanGe D and Y registers). The X register is then set to point at the register bank base address of $1000.

Next the 68HC11 is put into single-chip mode by clearing a bit in the HPRIO register. (HPRIO, the "Highest Priority" register, is primarily used in setting the priority of various interrupts, but also includes the bit for switching between single-chip and expanded modes.)

Then Port C, which in expanded modes is the multiplexed address/data bus, is set to be inputs so that information can be read from the LCD.

Beginning at `lcdready` is a loop that queries the LCD to determine whether it is busy. (Some LCD operations, like clear screen, take several milliseconds to complete so the driver must occasionally wait for the LCD to get ready.) The value 1 is put on the Port B register, which is the upper eight bits of the address bus, and whose lower two bits are connected to control pins of the LCD. This signals a read operation.

Then a bit on Port A is toggled. This bit is wired to the LCD's enable clock. This is the bit that ideally would have been wired to a 74HC138 select output were it not for the fact that LCDs are too slow to keep up with the natural bus rate of the 68HC11. In between toggling the enable bit, the byte of status information is read from Port C. If the high bit of this byte is 1, then the LCD is busy and the loop recycles.

When the LCD indicates that it's ready, Port C is established as outputs for writing a byte to the LCD. The subroutine's arguments are restored from the Y register to the A and B registers (`xgdy`) and put out to the LCD in Ports B and C, respectively. The LCD clock line (off Port A) is toggled and the information is thus written to the LCD.

To exit, the routine sets the bit in the HPRIO register, restoring expanded mode, and then executes a return-from-subroutine.

This driver code may be used as is for basic LCD operation. For more advanced operation, consult a reference manual for the Hitachi HD44780 LCD controller. It happens that nearly all character-based LCD screens have control chips that are clones of this standard LCD control chip. Information on the HD44780 and its operating modes is readily available online.

The LCD driver used in Interactive C is slightly more complicated than the one presented here. Rather than writing all of the characters in a print statement to the screen directly (as does the `putstr` routine), Interactive C buffers the characters to be printed to the LCD. Once per system interrupt (i.e., 1,000 times per second), an interrupt routine unspools a single character to the LCD. This allows `printf` statements to return control to the main program quickly, and the whole process operates transparently to the Handy Board system user.

A.3.8 Piezo Beeper and Interrupt Routines

This section explains how to generate tones using the Handy Board's built-in piezo beeper. This discussion also introduces the practical use of interrupt routines.

The Piezo Beeper Output Line

The Handy Board's beeper is connected to Pin 31 of the 68HC11 microprocessor (see Figure A.23). This pin is Bit 3 of Port A and is also known as the Timer Output 5 (TOC5) pin. Graphically, on Port A, it's:

```
* beeptest.asm beeper demonstration program

PORTA    equ     $1000              ; Port A register

PIEZO    equ     8                  ; position of beeper line

         org     $8000

start
         lds     #$ff               ; initialize stack
         ldx     #$1000             ; ptr to register base
loop     bset    PORTA,x PIEZO      ; set the beeper pin high
         bsr     delay              ; half-wave delay
         bclr    PORTA,x PIEZO      ; set the beeper pin low
         bsr     delay
         bra     loop

delay    clra
delaylp  deca
         bne     delaylp
         rts

         org     $bffe              ; reset vector
         fdb     start
```

FIGURE A.36 Listing of
beeptest.asm, Piezo Beeper
Test Program

	Bit 7	6	5	4	3	2	1	0
PORTA	PAI	TOC2	TOC3	TOC4	**TOC5**	TIC1	TIC2	TIC3

the pin shown in bold as **TOC5**.

To generate a tone on the beeper, all that one needs to do is toggle the TOC5 pin back and forth from one to zero.

Figure A.36 shows a listing of `beeptest.asm`, a demonstration program for making a tone. In the core loop of the program, the TOC5 piezo line is alternately set high and low, with a call to a delay subroutine between each transition:

```
loop     bset    PORTA,x PIEZO      ; set the beeper pin high
         bsr     delay              ; half-wave delay
         bclr    PORTA,x PIEZO      ; set the beeper pin low
         bsr     delay
         bra     loop
```

The constant `PIEZO` has been equated to 8, which puts a one in the appropriate bit position for TOC5. Bit set `bset` and bit clear `bclr` instructions are used to set and clear the piezo bit. These bit-wise instructions have only direct (zero memory page) and indexed addressing modes, so the X register is set up to point at the register base and the indexed addressing mode is used.

The length of the `delay` subroutine determines the pitch of the tone that is generated. Each half-wave of the output signal is determined by how long the `delay` routine takes to execute. The longer the delay, the lower the pitch.

Beeper Exercise

Cycle counting. Using the cycle-counting techniques discussed in Section 6.2.5, determine the frequency of the tone generated by the `beeptest.asm` program.

FIGURE A.37 Life Cycle of an Interrupt Routine.

The complete "life cycle" of an interrupt routine's execution is illustrated. During the execution of a program's main code, an external event occurs that generates an interrupt (#1). The 68HC11 then saves all processor registers (#2) and fetches the interrupt vector depending on which interrupt it was (#3). This vector points at an interrupt routine, and execution begins there (#4). When the interrupt service routine has completed its work, it signals that it's done by executing the RTI return from interrupt instruction (#5). Then the 68HC11 restores all of the registers from the stack (#6) and picks up execution of the main code where it left off (#7).

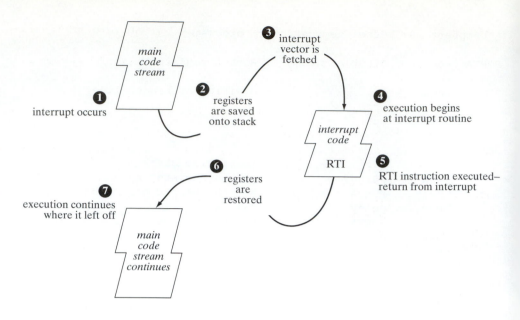

Overview of Interrupts

In the simple `beeptest` example, all of the 68HC11's attention is devoted to generating the tone. This is fine if one only wants to be playing a sequence of single pitches, but in general this is a poor solution.

A better method is to use the 68HC11's interrupt facility. Special hardware that's part of the 68HC11's timer and counter subsystem is coupled to the 68HC11's interrupts. The hardware allows the TOC5 output pin to automatically toggle state after a particular period of time has elapsed, and also to generate an interrupt to run a piece of code that can schedule the next toggle point. With this method, the main flow of 68HC11 code is only bothered on transitions of the output signal, and the half-wave timing is handled by the timer subsystem rather than a hard-coded delay routine.

To generate tones in this fashion, interrupts are used to schedule each transition point. As an overview of the interrupt process, Figure A.37 illustrates the "life cycle" of how the 68HC11 evaluates an interrupt routine. The sequence of events is as follows:

1. During the flow of execution of the main code, an interrupt is generated. There are a variety of sources of interrupts, ranging from system reset, to signals on pins of the microprocessor changing state, to internally generated sources like timing events. As soon as the instruction that's executing when the interrupt occurs finishes, handling of the interrupt begins.
2. The first step in processing the interrupt is to save the current execution state, which is represented by the collection of data in the 68HC11's registers (A, B, X, Y, the program counter, and the status register). These are pushed onto the stack to be restored later at the end of interrupt handling.
3. Next, the interrupt type is determined, and the corresponding interrupt vector is fetched. Each interrupt type has a location in memory for its vector. The vector must contain a two-byte address pointer to the location in memory where the code for that interrupt is.
4. The 68HC11 begins executing code at the address specified by the interrupt vector. The interrupt routine now has the chance to do its work.

5. When the interrupt routine is done, it executes the RTI (return from interrupt) instruction.
6. To perform the return from interrupt, the 68HC11 restores the machine registers from the stack.
7. Execution then continues back in the main code, with the instruction that followed the last one executed before the interrupt was processed.

From the point of view of the main code, it never even realized that this whole interrupt process has occurred. All that has happened is that some time has been lost, as if the main code took a tiny nap and didn't realize it.

Of course, interrupt processing is insignificant only if the main code is not timing-critical. If the main code is performing a task that needs precise timing, interrupts can destroy the performance of this work. It's often necessary to disable and then reenable interrupt processing around a timing-sensitive task.

But as long as the interrupt handlers are short, most functions of the main code can be periodically interrupted for tiny intervals without consequence.

The Timer Subsystem

To produce tones with interrupts, we'll make use of the 68HC11's timer subsystem. The timer subsystem consists of three major components:

- A free-running timer, named TCNT (timer counter). TCNT is a 16-bit counter that's continuously counting as long as the 68HC11 is running. Its default count rate is 2 counts per microsecond, or 2,000,000 counts per second. (Keep in mind that as a 16-bit number, TCNT can only count from 0 to 65,535 before overflowing back to 0.)

- Output compare registers, which can be programmed with a value that triggers an interrupt when TCNT counts up to match the predefined output compare value. When this match occurs, two events are triggered: The corresponding output pin can be set to immediately change state (go high, go low, or toggle), and an interrupt can be generated (which will be processed shortly thereafter).

- Input capture registers, which capture and store the value of the TCNT register at the precise moment when an input pin changes state. Additionally, an interrupt may be generated for further processing of the event. (The IR decoding routines discussed in Section 6.2.6 use the input capture facility.)

To generate tones, the output compare mechanism is used. The piezo pin is programmed to toggle state each time the output compare match occurs, and the output compare register is used to establish the half-wave delay of the resulting tone. Each time the TCNT match occurs, the piezo pin clicks and an interrupt is generated. The routine that is then called sets up the output compare register for the next half-wave transition.

Several registers in addition to the TCNT register are used to control this process:

- TCTL1, timer control register #1. This register determines what happens to the output pin when a timer match occurs. The pin may be set to take no action, go high, go low, or toggle state.

- TMSK1, timer mask register #1. This register determines whether an interrupt is generated (in addition to the action specified by the TCTL1 setting).

- TFLG1, timer flag register #1. This register contains flags that are set when the corresponding interrupt routine is called. These flags must be cleared to allow the interrupt routine to get called the next time there is a timer match.

- TOC5, timer output compare register #5. This is the register for the piezo pin, which is connected to timer #5. When the main TCNT timer value matches the value in this register, the pin change actions specified by `TCTL1` and the interrupt enabled by `TMSK1` are generated.

`TCTL1` controls four output timers, TOC2 to TOC5. For each of these, two bits (OM and OL) determine which of the four actions will be taken on a successful match according to this table:

OMx	OLx	action taken upon successful compare
0	0	no action
0	1	toggle OCx output line
1	0	clear OCx output line to zero
1	1	set OCx output line to one

The high two bits of `TCTL1` affect TOC2 (timer output 2), the next two bits TOC3, the next two, TOC4, and the lowest two, TOC5:

Bit 7	6	5	4	3	2	1	0
OM2	OL2	OM3	OL3	OM4	OL4	OM5	OL5

TCTL1

`TMSK1` determines whether an interrupt is generated when a timer match occurs (for output timers) or an input edge is detected (for input counters). The following shows how the timer and counter bits are mapped within the `TMSK1` register:

Bit 7	6	5	4	3	2	1	0
OC1i	OC2i	OC3i	OC4i	OC5i	IC1i	IC2i	IC3i

TMSK1

If the bit in `TMSK1` is set to one, then the corresponding interrupt is enabled. (On reset, all bits are automatically set to zero.)

`TFLG1` has a similar structure to `TMSK1`. When the interrupt occurs, the corresponding flag in `TFLG1` is set. This flag must be cleared for the interrupt to happen again.

Bit 7	6	5	4	3	2	1	0
OC1f	OC2f	OC3f	OC4f	OC5f	IC1f	IC2f	IC3f

TFLG1

Interrupt Code for the Piezo Beeper

With this information, we're ready to write code that generates tones using interrupts. Interrupt-based code can be difficult to write and debug because of this fairly large collection of details, all of which must be handled properly or nothing works.

Figure A.38 shows a listing of `beepint.asm`, an interrupt-based program for creating tones on the piezo beeper. Each line of the program is necessary to cause the whole interrupt process to work correctly, so let's go through the example in detail.

The first few lines of the program establish equates for the registers that will be used:

```
* beepint.asm beeper demonstration program using interrupts

TCNT    equ     $100e           ; Timer Counter register
TOC5    equ     $101e           ; Timer Output Compare 5 register
TCTL1   equ     $1020           ; Timer Control register 1
TMSK1   equ     $1022           ; Timer Mask register 1
TFLG1   equ     $1023           ; Timer Flag register 1

PIEZO   equ     8               ; position of beeper line
```

```
* beepint.asm beeper demonstration program using interrupts

TCNT    equ     $100e           ; Timer Counter register
TOC5    equ     $101e           ; Timer Output Compare 5 register
TCTL1   equ     $1020           ; Timer Control register 1
TMSK1   equ     $1022           ; Timer Mask register 1
TFLG1   equ     $1023           ; Timer Flag register 1

PIEZO   equ     8               ; position of beeper line

        org     $8000

start
        lds     #$ff            ; initialize stack
        ldx     #$1000          ; ptr to register base

        bset    TCTL1,x %00000001
        bclr    TCTL1,x %00000010 ; set TOC5 to toggle

        bset    TMSK1,x PIEZO   ; enable TOC5 interrupt

        cli                     ; globally enable interrupts

loop    bra     loop            ; main loop does nothing!

beepisr
        ldd     TOC5            ; get the last compare value
        addd    #1000           ; add 1000 (500 microseconds)
        std     TOC5            ; store back for next compare

        ldaa    #PIEZO          ; other method to clear
        staa    TFLG1           ; the TOC5 flag

        rti                     ; return from interrupt

        org     $bfe0           ; TOC5 interrupt vector
        fdb     beepisr         ; beeper interrupt service routine

        org     $bffe           ; reset vector
        fdb     start
```

FIGURE A.38 **FIGURE A.38** Listing of beepint.asm, Interrupt-Based Beeper Program

Each of the registers discussed is defined, along with PIEZO, which puts a one in the position of the beeper line in the TFLG1 and TMSK1 registers.

In the next section, the program location is established at the beginning of Handy Board RAM ($8000), the stack pointer is set to the top of 68HC11 internal RAM ($ff), and the X register is set up to point to the register base.

```
        org     $8000

start
        lds     #$ff            ; initialize stack
        ldx     #$1000          ; ptr to register base
```

It's critical to set up the stack pointer because interrupts push the whole register set on the stack, so everything will fail if the stack isn't set up. Setting X to the register bank allows the use of the bit set and bit clear instructions that follow.

In the next two lines, the action taken on successful compare is programmed into the TCTL1 register. We would like the beeper pin to toggle each time there is a timer match so that a square wave is generated. Thus, a "01" must be written into the control pins for TOC5. This is done with a bit set and a bit clear instruction:

```
bset     TCTL1,x %00000001
bclr     TCTL1,x %00000010 ; set TOC5 to toggle on interrupt
```

Next, we must enable the interrupt on successful match. This is to allow the interrupt routine to run; the interrupt routine is responsible for setting up the next match each time:

```
bset     TMSK1,x PIEZO    ; enable TOC5 interrupt
```

Note that the TMSK1 flag is "cleared" by *setting the appropriate bit to one*. This odd practice is simply an idiosyncracy of the 68HC11 interrupt flag mechanism, but one that can cause no end of frustration if the detail is forgotten.

The last set-up action is to *globally enable interrupts*. The cli (clear interrupt inhibit flag) instruction does this. It's a common and frustrating problem to forget this step and then wonder why it appears like nothing's happening. That would be because nothing *is* happening because you forgot to enable interrupts altogether. So remember, turn the entire interrupt facility on with the cli instruction!

```
cli                      ; globally enable interrupts
```

The set-up is now done, and all the real work will be done at interrupt time. The 68HC11 must be doing something for its main program, however! Here's where we'll just build the simple endless loop:

```
loop    bra     loop             ; main loop does nothing!
```

It's kind of ironic to be working so hard to make the processor do nothing. Of course, the interrupt routine is where the action happens.

The interrupt routine comes next in the code listing. It performs three actions:

1. Establish the next output compare match value.
2. Clear the interrupt flag so another interrupt can be generated.
3. Return from interrupt.

Here's the full interrupt routine:

```
beepisr
        ldd     TOC5             ; get the last compare value
        addd    #1000            ; add 1000 (500 microseconds)
        std     TOC5             ; store back for next compare

        ldaa    #PIEZO           ; other method to clear
        staa    TFLG1            ; the TOC5 flag

        rti
```

To establish the TOC5 compare value, the current value of TOC5 is retrieved, 1,000 is added, and the result is stored back to TOC5. This 1,000 determines the frequency of the resultant pitch. It's 1,000 "TCNT units," where TCNT normally runs at 2,000,000 ticks

Address	Purpose
$BFC0	reserved
$BFC2	reserved
$BFC4	reserved
$BFC6	reserved
$BFC8	reserved
$BFCA	reserved
$BFCC	reserved
$BFCE	reserved
$BFD0	reserved
$BFD2	reserved
$BFD4	reserved
$BFD6	SCI serial system
$BFD8	SPI serial transfer complete
$BFDA	Pulse Accumulator Input Edge
$BFDC	Pulse Accumulator Overflow
$BFDE	Timer Overflow
$BFE0	Timer Input Capture 4/Output Compare 5 (TI4O5)
$BFE2	Timer Output Compare 4 (TOC4)
$BFE4	Timer Output Compare 3 (TOC3)
$BFE6	Timer Output Compare 2 (TOC2)
$BFE8	Timer Output Compare 1 (TOC1)
$BFEA	Timer Input Capture 3 (TIC3)
$BFEC	Timer Input Capture 2 (TIC2)
$BFEE	Timer Input Capture 1 (TIC1)
$BFF0	Real Time Interrupt (RTI)
$BFF2	/IRQ (external pin or parallel I/O) (IRQ)
$BFF4	/XIRQ (pseudo non-maskable interrupt) (XIRQ)
$BFF6	Software Interrupt (SWI)
$BFF8	Illegal Opcode Trap
$BFFA	COP failure
$BFFC	COP clock monitor fail
$BFFE	system reset (RESET)

FIGURE A.39 Table of 68HC11 Interrupt Vector Locations

per second (500 μsec per tick). So 1,000 establishes a half-wave of 0.0005 seconds, or a full cycle of 0.001 seconds, or a pitch of 1,000 Hertz.

To clear the interrupt flag, a one bit must be written into the appropriate spot in the TFLG1 register. Earlier this was done with a bset instruction. Here it's done by putting the number with the correct bit set into the A register and then writing the A register to TFLG1. Either way works; just remember that, to clear the flag, you must write a one to the bit in question.

The interrupt routine finishes by executing the rti instruction.

There is one more crucial step. The *interrupt vector for TOC5 must be established.* This vector tells the 68HC11 where in memory to go to execute the interrupt service routine (i.e., the beepisr code we just looked at) when the timer output counter #5 match occurs.

The vector for the TOC5 timer happens to be located at $bfe0 in the 68HC11 memory map. (Figure A.39 lists all of the interrupts and their corresponding vector locations.)

The following code establishes the pointer to `beepisr` and also the reset vector to the start of the program:

```
org     $bfe0           ; TOC5 interrupt vector
fdb     beepisr         ; beeper interrupt service routine

org     $bffe           ; reset vector
fdb     start
```

Don't forget this critical step of establishing the interrupt vectors—otherwise the 68HC11 will start executing garbage and crash as soon as that interrupt fires.

There is a lot more to know about the output timer and input counter systems, and the other interrupts that are part of the 68HC11 design. Please read the *M68HC11 Reference Manual* published by Motorola, which contains a wealth of detailed information about the 68HC11 design [Sec96].

A.3.9 Power and Battery Charging

The Handy Board operates all of its circuits—including the microprocessor and the motors—from one 9.6-volt battery pack. Here is an explanation of how its power circuit and battery charger are designed.

Power

Figure A.40 is a schematic of the power subsystem. There are several power points noted on the schematic:

- **UNSWPWR**, for unswitched power, is a terminal that's connected to the battery even when the board is switched off. This terminal is where the battery charging circuit plugs in.

FIGURE A.40 Handy Board Power Circuit Schematic

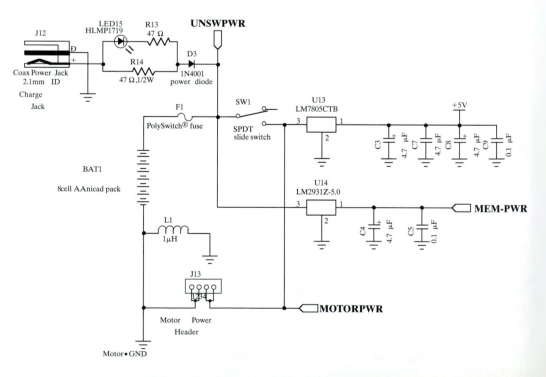

Note that even at the unswitched power terminal, all current must run through F1, the PolySwitch resettable fuse. This protects the battery against potential short circuit, which could be very dangerous because the primary power source is a nickel cadmium battery.

- **MOTORPWR**, motor power. This terminal is switched on and off via the main power switch (SW1), and is protected through the fuse, but otherwise is a direct source of current from the battery.

- **+5v**, the primary voltage supply for logic voltage. This power supplies the 68HC11 and all of the 74HCxx parts on the Handy Board, excepting the memory circuit (see following). This +5v supply also provides power to external sensors. The primary supply is switched on and off by SW1.

    This supply is provided by U13, a 7805 regulator. This part can provide up to approximately one ampere of current. It is what is known as a "linear regulator"; it dissipates the difference between its input voltage and its output voltage directly as heat. For instance, considering the input voltage is 9.6v and the output voltage is 5v, the voltage differential is then 4.6v. If the maximum one ampere of current is flowing, the power dissipation is $P = V \times I$ or 4.6 watts. This is quite a lot and enough to make the regulator literally burning hot. So one should be careful to not implement sensor circuits that draw too much current or U13 will overheat.

- **MEM-PWR**, memory power. The memory power circuit provides power to the RAM and its associated logic chips at all times, even when the board is switched off. For this reason, the memory power circuit has its own regulator—U14—and it taps the battery voltage before the switch. Thus, U14 is able to provide a regulated +5 volts to the memory circuit regardless of whether the Handy Board is switched on or off.

Each of the two regulators has its own set of *bypass capacitors* on its output (for U13—C3, C7, C8, and C9; for U14—C4 and C5). These capacitors help smooth out voltage fluctuations as the various components of the circuit change state and draw current.

L1, the iron-core inductor, provides some isolation between the logic ground and the motor ground. This helps prevent inductive voltage spikes that may be generated from motors from entering the logic portion of the circuit. In many hybrid micropro-cessor/motor circuits, it's important to provide complete electrical isolation between the motors and the microprocessor (using optical switches and separate power supplies, for instance). The Handy Board makes the compromise of keeping the motors and the mi-croprocessor on the same power source, which means that some motors may generate too much electrical noise to coexist with the 68HC11. If the 68HC11 resets when a motor is turned on or reversed, it's a good indication that the motor is too noisy (or the battery needs to be recharged).

Battery Charging

The Handy Board includes a built-in, eight AA cell, nickel cadmium rechargeable battery pack. There are two ways to charge this battery:

- Plug an adapter directly into the Handy Board; or
- Plug an adapter into the Serial Interface/Charger Board and run the telephone cable between the Interface/Charger and the Handy Board.

The latter choice has two options: normal charge and "zap charge." This section explains how each of these methods operates.

FIGURE A.41 Basic Battery
Charging Circuit

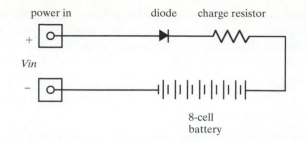

Modern rechargeable nickel cadmium batteries ("nicads") are an appealing design choice because they are inexpensive, high capacity, have a reasonable lifespan (circa 1,000 charges and 2 years), and are simple to charge. On the negative side, they can exhibit a "memory effect" (if they are never fully discharged, they lose the capacity that's not exercised) and are an environmental hazard (cadmium is a heavy metal and must be considered toxic waste when it is discarded). Despite the negatives, nicads are an excellent general purpose power source.

The charging circuit for nicads can be quite simple: A known voltage source and a current-limiting resistor is sufficient. The standard charge rate for nicads is $C/10$, where C is the ampere-hour capacity of the battery. For example, the standard battery pack used with the Handy Board has a capacity of 0.5 ampere-hours, or 500 mAh (milli-ampere-hours), so delivering a steady 50 mA to the cells is a safe charge rate. This will recharge fully depleted cells in 12 to 14 hours, and batteries may be left on the $C/10$ charge rate indefinitely without any adverse overcharging effect.

Figure A.41 shows the basic circuit. The charge voltage, V_{in}, is applied from the left. A diode protects against reverse polarity, which could be dangerous.[6] A "charge resistor" limits the current that can flow into the battery pack.

The only trick is calculating the proper values for the V_{in}, the charge voltage, and the charge resistor. The main criterion of the circuit is the amount of current flowing, which should be about 50 mA (the $C/10$ charge rate). Also, we know that the V_{in} voltage must be equal to the sum of the voltage drops across the diode, resistor, and battery pack. Of these, first and last are known, and the second is a function of the charge current:

- The voltage drop across a diode has a nominal value of 0.6 volts. In practice, 0.75 volts is typical.

- The voltage drop across a resistor is a function of its value and the current flowing through it: $V = IR$. We know that I should be 0.050 A.

- The voltage on the battery pack actually does not fluctuate too much from full charge to empty. The nominal battery voltage is 9.6 volts (1.2 volts per cell × 8 cells); a typical range will be between 9v (full discharge) and 11v (full charge, during charge).

Let's continue the design by fixing V_{in}, the charge voltage. We assume the use of a 12-volt, 500 mA DC adapter. Now this device does not provide a regulated 12v supply. Rather, it provides a voltage that varies inversely with current; when drawing 500 mA of current, it will provide 12v, but when drawing less than 500 mA, the voltage will be higher. The open-circuit voltage (voltage when it's delivering no current) of such an adapter is typically around 16.5v, so let's estimate that it will provide about 15v when delivering 50 mA.

Now we have all the information we need to pick the resistor. The voltage drop across the resistor should be 15v (V_{in}) − 0.75v (diode drop) - 11v (battery pack voltage),

---

[6] In a reverse-polarity situation, the battery would discharge quickly through the charge voltage, overheating and destroying the charge-limiting resistor and/or itself.

or 3.25v. Then the value of the resistor will be $R = V/I$ or $R = 3.25/0.050 = 65$ ohms.

The actual value specified in the circuit is 47 ohms. The discrepancy is explained by observation of the V_{in} charge voltage; in practice it's about 14.4 volts. This yields a voltage drop of about 2.7v on the resistor, corresponding to a charge rate of $I = V/R$ or 57 mA—a little high, but still fine.

Please note that the current specification of the adapter is critical. A 12v, 200 mA adapter would provide less than 14.4 volts when 50 mA were being drawn, so the voltage would fall and so would the charge rate. Conversely, a 12v, 1 A adapter would provide substantially more than 14.4v at 50 mA, resulting in a too-high charge rate.

There is one other parameter of the charge resistor that must be accounted for: its power rating, specified in watts. Power is volts × amps; for our charge resistor, we have (approximately) 3 volts and 0.05 amps, making 0.15 watts of power flowing through the thing. Please note that most of the resistors on the Handy Board are one-eighth watt. What would happen if we employed one of these in the charging circuit?

The resistor would get very hot—hot enough to burn itself up, char the circuit board, and roast any fingers that might be nearby. So at least a 0.25-watt resistor is called for, but the design specifies a 0.5-watt model. This allows a bit of a margin for when the battery pack voltage is quite low and extra current will be flowing (i.e., at full discharge), and also prevents the component from operating at high temperatures as a matter of course. It's always wise to overdesign when possible.

The full power schematic, including the Handy Board's built-in charge circuit, is shown in Figure A.40. Notice that the charge indicator light (LED15) is hanging (along with its own current-limiting resistor, R13) off the charge resistor R14. From the earlier discussion, we know that there will be a bit under 3v on the R14 when the battery is charging; this voltage drop is then used to power the charge indicator LED.

The charge circuit that's built into the Serial Interface/Charger Board (Figure A.30) is pretty much the same. There are a few small differences in the circuit:

- The power adapter is initially run through a full-wave bridge rectifier, normalizing any polarity to work properly. On the Handy Board, there's only one diode, which will block reverse polarity. The Interface board can use either polarity coming in.

- There is a charge rate switch that can short out the current limiting resistor (R11, in this case), thereby bypassing it. In this "Zap Mode," current is limited only by what the power adapter can deliver (about 500 mA if the proper adapter is used) and by the full-wave bridge (which is rated for 1 amp). In practice, about 200 to 300 mA of charge current will flow in Zap Mode, enough to charge the battery fully in 2 to 3 hours.

    Zap Mode should be used with care because after the battery is fully charged (as evidenced by it getting warm), overcharging will occur, which will definitely shorten the life of the battery.

- The R11 charge-limiting resistor is specified at 5 watts rather than $\frac{1}{2}$ watt as on the main Handy Board. This is to protect against accidental use of the wrong kind of RJ11 cable between the Interface/Charger Board and the Handy Board. A telephone-style (inverting) cable is specified, but if a network-style (noninverting) cable is used, then the battery tries to charge the charge circuit, causing large current flows that were easily burning out a half-watt R11. Using the wrong cable is still problematic, but now R11 typically survives the ordeal.

A.4 The AS11 Assembler

The assembler program freely distributed by Motorola is named `AS11`. Other 68HC11 assemblers are available, but this section contains information specific to Motorola's assembler.

A.4.1 Labels

The assembler has a facility to generate symbolic labels during assembly. This lets one refer to the location of an instruction using a label rather than by knowing its exact address.

The assembler does this by using a two-step assembly process. In the first step, the lengths of all instructions are determined so that memory usage may be calculated and labels values assigned. In the second step, instructions that used labels have their values filled in because those labels are now known.

Here is an example of a program that uses a symbolic label:

```
loop      ldaa      #$ff      * load A with 255
          deca                * decrement A register
          bne       loop      * branch to Loop if not zero
```

Labels must begin in the first character position of a new line, and label definitions may optionally end in a colon (`:`) (which is ignored).

A.4.2 Arithmetic Expressions

The assembler supports the following arithmetic operations, which may be used to form values of labels or instruction arguments:

+	addition
-	subtraction
*	multiplication
/	division
%	remainder after division
&	bitwise AND
|	bitwise OR
^	bitwise Exclusive-OR

Expressions are evaluated left to right and there is no provision for parenthesized expressions.

Constants are constructed with the following syntax:

'	followed by ASCII character
$	followed by hexadecimal constant
%	followed by binary constant

A.4.3 Assembler Pseudo-Operations

An assembler program typically has its own set of commands, called *pseudo-operations* or *pseudo-ops*, used to direct the assembly process. These pseudo-ops seem like real 68HC11 instructions, but they are interpreted as control information to the assembler rather than assembled into machine code.

ORG

The `ORG` pseudo-op, for ORiGin, specifies the location for the assembler to deposit the resulting object code. For instance,

```
org      $8000    ; start of the HB's RAM
```

will establish the start of the Handy Board's 32K of RAM as the position for subsequent code.

EQU

The EQU pseudo-op is used to EQUate a symbolic label to a numeric value. Equates are commonly used for fixed values like the locations of 68HC11 control registers and other numeric constants.

The following illustrates usage of the EQU pseudo-op to specify some of the 68HC11 register locations:

```
PORTA   EQU     $1000   * Port A data register
RESV1   EQU     $1001   * Reserved
PIOC    EQU     $1002   * Parallel I/O Control register
PORTC   EQU     $1003   * Port C latched data register
PORTB   EQU     $1004   * Port B data register
```

In coding, the programmer may then use the label name rather than the numeric value:

```
        ldaa    PORTB   * equiv. to LDAA $1004
```

FCC

The FCC, "Form Constant Character" pseudo-op, deposits a text string into the object code. This can be used to store messages in memory.

The following excerpt illustrates usage of the FCC pseudo-op:

```
        FCC     'Hello world!'
```

FCB and FDB

The FCB, "form constant byte," and FDB, "form double byte" pseudo-ops, deposit a single-byte or two-byte word into the object code. They are used to insert data that are not part of a 68HC11 instruction.

Example:

```
        FCB     $FF
        FDB     $1013
```

RMB

The RMB, "reserve memory block" pseudo-op, takes an argument and skips that many bytes ahead in the stream of output. It's used to leave a gap in the object code that will later be filled in by the program while it's running, typical for RAM-based variables.

```
        RMB     10      * reserve 10 bytes
```

A.4.4 Comments

A *comment* is defined as

- any text after all operands for a given mnemonic have been processed,
- a line beginning with * up to the end of line, or
- an empty line.

The * is a special character, however, that can also mean "the address of the current instruction." Thus, the following sequence will create an infinite loop:

```
        bra     *
```

Feature	Difference	Impact
Internal RAM	The A series 68HC11 has 256 bytes of internal RAM ($00 to $FF), whereas the E series has 512 bytes ($00 to $1FF).	The Interactive C software was written for the A series and ignores the extra RAM between $100 and $1FF.
Bootstrap Sequence	During bootstrap download, the A series chip reads exactly 256 bytes into internal RAM before executing those bytes. The E series reads up to 512 bytes, but begins execution early if it detects a four-character time gap between the bytes.	Some bootstrap software written for the A series chip must be modified to be compatible with the E series bootstrap sequence. (This software is a utility on the desktop host computer.)
Port A Counter and Timer Pins	In the A series chip, Port A includes 4 output pins, 3 input pins, and 1 bidirectional pin. In the E series, all of the Port A pins may be bidirectional.	The E series version of Port A is a strict superset of that of the A series. All software written for the A series works properly without changes, and the Handy Board user has the option of reconfiguring unallocated Port A pins as they wish.
Clock Speed	The maximum speed of the A series chip is 2 MHz (with an 8 MHz crystal). The maximum speed of the E series is 3 MHz (with a 12 MHz crystal).	Although it is possible to replace the crystal on the Handy Board and obtain faster execution speeds, it is not recommended. Timing-critical code, which is distributed throughout the Interactive C software system, would need to be modified (including, e.g., baud rate of communications with the host computer).

A.5 Differences Between A and E Series 68HC11 CPUs

Motorola has discontinued the A series of the 68HC11 since the time when the Handy Board was first designed. This is not a problem because the E series of the 68HC11 provides a superset of the functionality of the A series chip; when stock of the A series chips runs out, Handy Boards can be built with E series chips.

The table on the preceding page presents the differences between the two series of 68HC11s, and explains their significance to the Handy Board user.

Construction Techniques

This appendix describes construction techniques for:

- Using DC motors with the Handy Board, including making motors compatible with the LEGO Technic building system.
- Using servo motors with the Handy Board, including modifying servo motors for continuous rotation.
- Wiring an infrared transmitter and receiver.
- Wiring adapter cables for using LEGO motors and sensors with the Handy Board.

B.1 DC Motor

The Handy Board includes drivers for up to four DC motors. These drivers supply 9v with current limited to 600 mA or 1 A (depending on the variety of motor chip used in the Handy Board).

B.1.1 Motor Compatibility

All motors made by the LEGO Group (the 9v standard motor, 9v gear motor, and 9v micro motor) and many hobby motors are compatible with the Handy Board.

To determine whether a given hobby motor is compatible, first check its voltage rating. If it is 9 to 12v, it may be compatible. If it is 3 to 6v, it is not likely to be compatible.

Aside from the voltage rating, the motor's maximum current draw is important. The maximum amount of current that a motor can draw is known as its *stall current*; it is the amount of current drawn when the motor is completely stalled.

A good way to get an estimate of how much current this will be at the Handy Board's rated 9v supply level is to measure the motor's resistance using a standard VOM (volt-ohm meter), and apply the Ohm's Law formula *current = voltage* divided by *resistance*. Set the meter to its most sensitive resistance scale (typically, 0 to 200 ohms), apply the probes to the motor terminals, and gently rotate the motor shaft by hand until the smallest possible reading is obtained. The idea is to find the static position of the shaft that results in the smallest reading and take that as the measurement.

If this reading is 9 ohms or more, then the motor should be compatible with the Handy Board. (At 9 volts, a 9 ohm reading would mean a current draw of 1 amp, the maximum the Handy Board can deliver.) If the reading is less than 4 ohms, the motor will probably draw too much current and will not work.

Please be aware that the Handy Board is not compatible with 3v to 4.5v motors found in many toy cars. These inexpensive motors are extremely noisy from an electrical standpoint; also, they typically will draw several amperes of current, thereby overloading the Handy Board's motor drivers and causing the board to reset. The Handy Board also is not compatible with motors used in high end radio control cars. These motors are designed to draw huge amounts of power—25, 50, or more amperes of current.

B.1.2 Motor Wiring

Figure B.1 shows how to wire a motor to a tenth-inch pin header for use with the Handy Board. Use the construction method described in Section 3.2 for wiring the connector.

B.1.3 Interfacing Hobby Motors to the LEGO Technic System

Hobby DC motors may readily be adapted for use with LEGO Technic materials. There are two aspects to the conversion:

- A LEGO gear or pulley wheel must be installed on the motor shaft.
- At the proper spacing for interfacing with other gears, the motor must be attached to LEGO plates.

Please refer to Figure B.2 in the following discussion.

Attaching LEGO Gear to Motor Shaft

Most DC motors have a narrow metal rod as their drive shaft. The diameter of this drive shaft must be widened in order for a LEGO gear to fit snugly around it.

An ideal way to add diameter to the motor drive shaft is with two layers of $\frac{3}{32}$" heat-shrink tubing. Put one length over the shaft and then shrink it. The second length should fit snugly over the first before shrinking. Shrink the second length, and then press a LEGO gear onto the shaft immediately, *before the heat-shrink cools off.*

When the heat-shrink cools, it will harden. By having pressed the LEGO gear onto the heat-shrink while it was still pliable, the heat-shrink will tightly grab the LEGO gear.

Because most DC motors spin at a high RPM, it's best to use a gear that will provide the best gear reduction on the motor shaft. This means either the 8–tooth gear, a worm gear, or the small pulley wheel.

Fixing the Motor to a LEGO Plate

After the gear is attached, the motor should be glued or otherwise affixed to a LEGO plate. The trick here is to make sure the motor is at a proper spacing to interface properly with other LEGO gears. For this, the use of a motor mounting jig is highly recommended.

Figure B.2 shows a sample motor mounting jig, built using various LEGO elements. Two 40–tooth gears are positioned on either side of the 8–tooth gear that is mounted on the motor shaft.

The motor itself is attached to a 2×4 LEGO plate. Depending on the dimensions of the motor, it may be necessary to shave off the studs on the plate. The goal is to get the shaft of the motor in a perfect horizontal line with respect to the centers of the reference gears (the 40–tooth gears) when viewed head on.

To attach the motor to the LEGO plate, use either twin-tube epoxy or double-sided foam tape.

FIGURE B.2 Motor Mounting Jig

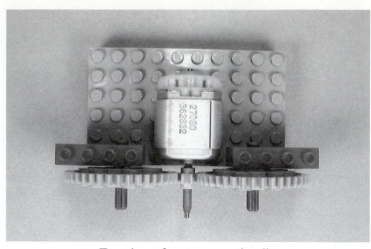

Top view of motor mounting jig

Front view of motor mounting jig

Twin-tube epoxy is a glue that is typically packaged in a dual syringe. Press the plunger of the syringe, and measured portions of the two components of the glue are ejected. Mix these two fluids thoroughly, and the glue is ready to be used. It is best to clean the motor surface well before gluing, possibly scratching the surface with a razor knife.

When epoxy sets, it is a hard, substantial glue that makes a solid and permanent bond. Its primary disadvantage is that it takes a little while to set and it is a toxic substance. Make sure that the gluing area is well-ventilated and wash hands after using the glue.

Depending on the variety, twin-tube epoxy can take anywhere from five minutes to an hour to set. Quick-setting five-minute epoxy is recommended.

Double-sided foam tape is easy to use and provides an instant bond. Over time, the tape dries out and the bond becomes nearly permanent.

On the other hand, double-sided tape does not have as strong a bond as epoxy, especially for the first week or so that the tape is applied.

Experiment—maybe a combination of double-sided tape and epoxy, or some other method entirely, will work best in your application. Don't waste your time with hot-glue, though. It makes a poor bond initially, and will almost certainly fail when in use: the motor will heat up and melt the glue!

B.2 Servo Motors

This section explains how to wire servo motors for use with the Handy Board and how to convert a servo motor for continuous rotation.

B.2.1 Electrical Interface

Figure B.3 illustrates the method for connecting the servo motor to the Handy Board. The ground lead of the servo motor is connected to the motor ground port of the Handy Board. A 4.8v supply is provided from an external power source. The signal lead of the servo runs to one of the Handy Board's servo control outputs.

To provide servo power, it is best to use an external power supply, such as four AA cells or C cells. This is what's illustrated in the figure. Alternately, one may use the Handy Board's own +5v supply to provide power to at most one servo motor. Another option is to use the diode-chain method of dropping the Handy Board's 9.6v battery to about 6v. This method is described in the section on using the Polaroid ultrasonic sensor in Chapter 6 (see Figure 6.51).

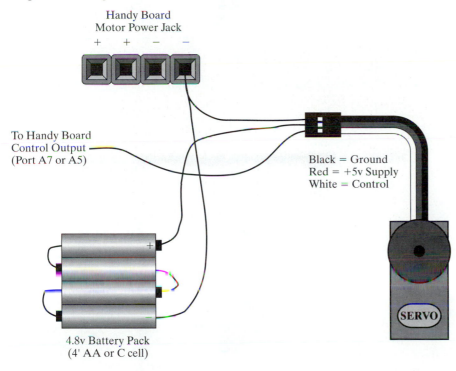

FIGURE B.3 Servo Motor Wiring Diagram

B.2.2 Continuous Rotation

Most servo motors provide approximately 180 degrees of rotation. In other words, the output shaft rotates back and forth with a sweep of travel of about 180 degrees. A special type of servo, known as the *winch servo*, rotates continuously. With this type of servo, the control signal specifies the speed and direction of rotation, rather than the desired angular position. The winch servo is useful for a wide variety of applications, including being suitable as a robot's main drive motors.

It is easy to convert a conventional servo motor to a winch servo motor. In this operation, the servo's feedback potentiometer is replaced by a pair of fixed resistors. The resistors serve to mimic the center position of the potentiometer; when the control signal deviates from center, the servo's control electronics drive the motor one way or the other

FIGURE B.4 Futaba S148
Modifications for Continuous
Rotation

Futaba S148 servo motor control board showing feedback potentiometer

Motor control board with two resistors installed in place of potentiometer

in a vain attempt to get the servo to move away from center. The result is that the servo spins continuously with user-controllable speed and direction.

In the following instructions for making this modification, refer to Figure B.4.

- Remove the four screws from the back of the servo.
- Remove the back panel of the servo; then, gently remove the front panel, making sure none of the gears fall on the ground.
- Remove three of the gears from the front of the panel, exposing two small screws which hold the motor to the servo package.
- Remove the two motor mount screws.
- Gently pull the servo control board out of the servo package. It may be helpful to push from the lower shaft, which is the potentiometer.
- Carefully desolder the potentiometer from the servo control board.
- Install two 2.2K resistors in place of the potentiometer. Each resistor goes from an outer hole to the center hole of the three potentiometer mounting holes, so the center hole has a lead from each of the two resistors inserted.
- Reassemble the servo.

  In removing the feedback potentiometer, the limit stops that prevented the servo drive shaft from rotating continuously are also removed.

B.3 Infrared Sensor and Transmitter

Figure B.5 shows how to wire a Sharp GP1U52 sensor for use with the Handy Board. Note that the metal case of the sensor must be wired to signal ground; this allows the sensor to reject noise.

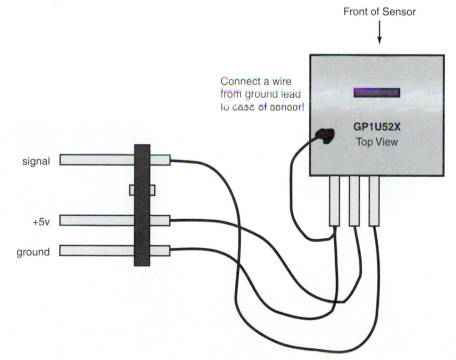

FIGURE B.5 Sharp GP1U52X Wiring Diagram

FIGURE B.6 Infrared Transmitter
Wiring Diagram

The diagram shows an IR
transmitter that uses an IR LED
in series with a visible LED.
The visible LED then provides
a clear cue when the IR transmit
function is active. This visible
LED may be omitted if desired.

Choose the resistor value based
on the desired brightness of the
IR output. The smaller the
resistor, the brighter the IR
light.

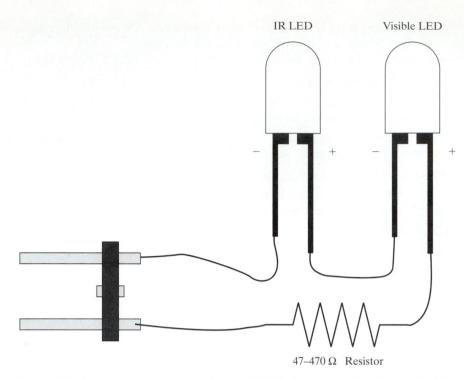

Figure B.6 shows how to wire an infrared LED for use in the Handy Board's IR
transmit output. The diagram shows the recommendation of using a visible LED in
series with the IR LED to act as a transmit-active indicator.

B.4 LEGO Adapter Cables

Figure B.7 shows how to build an adapter for using standard LEGO motors with the
Handy Board. Take a LEGO motor cable and cut it in half, yielding connectors for two
such cables.

FIGURE B.7 Handy Board Motor
Output to LEGO Motor Adapter
Wiring Diagram

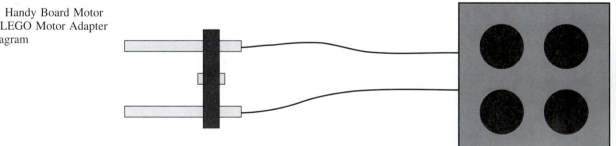

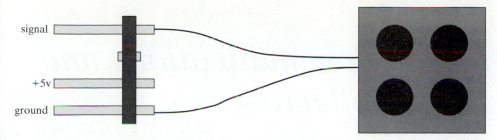

signal

+5v

ground

Figure B.8 shows how to build an adapter for using LEGO sensors with the Handy Board. As with the motor adapter, use half of a LEGO motor cable for making this adapter.

APPENDIX

C

Serial Communications and Data Collection

This appendix explains how to collect data on the Handy Board and upload it to a host computer for processing using the Interactive C environment. There are at least two ways to upload sensor data from the Handy Board:

1. Sensor data are printed to the serial line in real time.
2. Sensor data are collected and stored in the Handy Board's memory and later uploaded to the serial line.

The first method is ideal when the data do not need to be sampled too quickly because the sampling rate is limited by the serial transfer speed or when the amount of data being collected is so great as to exceed the Handy Board's memory.

The second method is best for capturing a short burst of rapidly changing data or when it is desired to leave the Handy Board in a remote location for the data collection process.

The appendix begins with an explanation of the Handy Board's serial line hardware and software protocol and then discusses the two data collection methods.

C.1 Serial Line Interaction

Interactive C uses its own low-level protocol for interacting with the Handy Board; this protocol allows it to do things like write to and write from the Handy Board's memory while the Handy Board is executing Interactive C programs. The runtime system resident on the Handy Board responds to this protocol at all times. Because of this, characters cannot simply be sent to the Handy Board's serial line because the runtime system will trap them and take action.

There is a hook in the runtime system for disabling its own responses to serial activity. By putting a nonzero value in a dedicated global memory location, the runtime system's low-level response to serial line activity can be temporarily disabled. From the host computer side, it will appear to Interactive C that the board is not connected because it will no longer respond to the built-in serial protocol.

After disabling the protocol, writing to the serial line is done by interacting with built-in 6811 serial port registers. The *Serial Communications Data Register* (SCDR) is located at address 0x102f. This is a bidirectional register: If data are stored to this register, the 6811 transmits it as serial output; when a serial character is received, it is retrieved by reading from the same register. Additionally, the *Serial Communications Status Register* (SCSR) is located at address 0x102e; bits in this register indicate when the serial port is busy (e.g., whether it is in the middle of receiving or transmitting a character). Before sending or receiving a character, it is prudent to check the SCSR to determine whether the 6811 serial port is ready.

The Interactive C library file `serialio.c` provides wrapper functions for interacting with the serial port. The following functions are defined in `serialio.c`:

FIGURE C.1 Listing of
serialio.c

```
/*
    serialio.c

    allows user Interactive C programs
    to send and receive serial data
*/

/* allows user programs to receive serial data */
void disable_pcode_serial()
{
    poke(0x3c, 1);
}

/* allows board interaction with IC on host computer */
void enable_pcode_serial()
{
    poke(0x3c, 0);
}

void serial_putchar(int c)
{
    /* wait until serial transmit empty */
    while (!(peek(0x102e) & 0x80));

    /* send character */
    poke(0x102f, c);
}


int serial_getchar(int c)
{
    /* wait until a character is received */
    while (!(peek(0x102e) & 0x20));

    /* return it */
    return peek(0x102f);
}
```

void disable_pcode_serial() Disables the functioning of the 6811 runtime system's response to incoming serial characters. It is necessary to call this function
so that user programs receive incoming serial data; otherwise incoming data are
trapped by the runtime system serial protocol.
After this function is called, it will appear to Interactive C on the host computer
that the Handy Board is not connected.

void enable_pcode_serial() Enables the functioning of the low-level serial protocol.

void serial_putchar(int char) Waits until any previous character being transmitted has finished and then transmits the low byte of the integer variable char
over the Handy Board's serial output.

int serial_getchar() Waits until a serial character is received and returns it in
the low byte of the return value. There is a one-character hardware serial buffer,
so if a character is received before this function is called, it will be returned. If

FIGURE C.2 Listing of
serxmit.c

```
/*
      serxmit.c

      serial transmit test program
      each time start button is pressed,
        transmits the 96-character ASCII set
      set communications parameters to 9600-N-8-1
*/

void main()
{
    int i;

    disable_pcode_serial();

    while (1) {

        printf("Press Start     button to begin\n");
        start_press();

        printf("Transmitting...\n");

        for (i= 32; i< 128; i++)
          serial_putchar(i);
    }
}
```

two or more characters are received in between calls to the serial_getchar()
function, however, all but the first one will be lost.

Figure C.1 shows a listing of the serialio.c file.

C.2 Connecting to a Terminal Program

A terminal emulator program is typically used for receiving serially transmitted data. As
a test program for establishing a connection between the Handy Board and a terminal
emulator on the host computer, a test program, named serxmit.c, is provided (the
program listing in Figure C.2). The program requires the serialio.c library to load
the test program into the Handy Board and type "load serxmit.c serialio.c" at
the Interactive C prompt.

The serxmit.c program consists of a single function, main(), which is run when
the Handy Board is reset. It calls the function disable_pcode_serial() so that the
Handy Board does not interpret any accidental characters that might be sent from the
host computer. Then the program enters an infinite loop, which:

1. Prints a message to the LCD screen telling the user to press the Start button.
2. Calls the library function start_press(), which waits for the Start button to be
   pressed.
3. Transmits the 96 printable characters of the ASCII[1] character set, beginning with
   Code 32, a space, and ending with Code 127, a tilde ("~").

[1]   The American Standard Code for Information Interchange, a 7-bit code that defines printable and control
      characters in computer text files.

After loading serxmit.c, run it either by typing "main();" at the Interactive C command line or by turning the Handy Board off and then on. Quit Interactive C before pressing the Start button, however: The Interactive C application will become confused by the unexpected characters that the main() function will send over the serial line.

To receive data from the Handy Board, use a simple terminal emulator program appropriate for the host computer platform. A program that provides minimal interpretation of the incoming serial data and has a feature for capturing received data to a text file is desirable. Set the serial communications parameters to 9,600 baud, 8 data bits, 1 stop bit, and no parity (i.e., 9600-N-8-1).

Boot up the terminal emulator and make sure its serial port is set for the same one that Interactive C uses to communicate with the Handy Board. Then press the Start button on the Handy Board. The Handy Board will take less than a second to transmit the 96 characters of ASCII data, which should then appear in the terminal emulator window:

Each time the Start button is pressed, another string of these characters should be displayed in the terminal emulator window. If this does not happen, check the communications settings and the choice of serial port.

To reconnect the Handy Board to Interactive C, it is necessary to *prevent the main() function from running*. This is because main() calls disable_pcode_serial(), which causes the Handy Board to ignore Interactive C's attempts to synchronize to it! There are two ways to restore the Handy Board to normal operation:

1. Re-initialize the Handy Board with the pcode_hb.s19 runtime system using the appropriate boot loader program (e.g., *DL*, *HBDL*, *6811 Downloader*, etc).
2. Power-on the Handy Board with the Start button *held down*. This prevents the Handy Board from taking the default action of running the main() function.

Because there is no reason to suspect that the Handy Board's memory is corrupted, bootloading with the pcode_hb.s19 file is not necessary. Just hold down the Start button while turning on the Handy Board and then Interactive C will be able to communicate with it normally.

C.3 Printing to the Serial Line

To print numbers to the serial line, there must be a conversion between the numeric value and the textual representation of that value. Interactive C's built-in printf() function provides such an operation for displaying values on the Handy Board's LCD screen, but a similar function does not exist for printing values to the serial line.

Instead, the library file printdec.c provides a convenient function, printdec(), which takes an integer as input and prints its value as a decimal number over the serial line. A listing of the function is shown in Figure C.3.

As an example of how to use the printdec() function, we can write a program that continuously prints the value of analog sensor 0 to the serial line. Such a program is shown in Figure C.4, contained in the file analogpr.c. This file requires the printdec.c and serialio.c libraries, so load it in Interactive C with the command "load analogpr.c printdec.c serialio.c".

When run, the analogpr.c program continuously prints the value of analog sensor 0 to the serial line. There are a pair of tricks in the code listing worth noting. After calling printdec() to print the sensor value, the program outputs the values 10 and 13 to the serial line. This is done using serial_putchar() so that the data are sent as control characters, not as the textual representation of the numbers "10" and "13." When interpreted by the terminal emulator, the 10 causes a line feed and the 13 causes a carriage return. Thus, the terminal program moves the cursor to the next screen line and the sensor data numbers line up in a column.

FIGURE C.3 Listing of
printdec.c

```
/*
  printdec.c

  routine to output an integer value
  as a decimal number over the serial line

  requires serialio.c

*/

/* prints number over serial line */
void printdec(int n)
{
  int leading_digit= 0;
  int dig, div;

  for (div= 10000; div= div/10; div> 0) {
    dig= n/div;
    n= n - dig*div;
    if (dig || leading_digit) {
      _printnum(dig);
      leading_digit= 1;
    }
  }
}

/* prints digit from 0 to 9 over serial line */
void _printnum(int n)
{
  serial_putchar(n + '0');
}
```

FIGURE C.4 Listing of
analogpr.c

```
/*
  analogpr.c

  continuously prints analog sensor 0 over serial line

  requires printdec.c, serialio.c
*/

void main()
{
  disable_pcode_serial();

  while (1) {
    printdec(analog(0));
    serial_putchar(10);
    serial_putchar(13);

    /* wait 0.1 sec between each print */
    msleep(100L);
  }
}
```

The other trick is to delay using the `msleep()` function in the inner loop of the display routine. This slows down the rate at which the Handy Board broadcasts the sensor data to allow the terminal emulator program to keep up on its screen display.

Connect a sensor to analog port 0, boot up the terminal emulator, and run the `analogpr.c` program. The sensor data should be continuously displayed on the host computer screen.

C.3.1 Exercises

1. Write a function that accepts a zero-terminated character array (i.e., a string) as input and prints the contents of the string to the serial line.
2. The ASCII code for the tab key is 9 decimal. Modify the `analogpr.c` example to print the values of two sensor ports per line in a tab-delimited format.

C.4 Capturing Data

For quickly changing data, the final piece of the puzzle is storing sensor data in the Handy Board's memory for later printing to the serial line. This allows a much faster capture rate because the speed is limited only by the speed of Interactive C, rather than the relatively slow serial communications rate.

Capturing data is easily done by using array variables in Interactive C. The sample program `datacoll.c`, shown in Figure C.5, illustrates the method.

A global array variable, `data[]`, is declared. In the example program, this is given a size of 1,000 elements. The core routine, `collect_data()`, simply iterates through the elements of the array, storing a successive data sample in each one. This takes approximately 2 seconds, yielding a data rate of 500 samples per second. This can be slowed down by inserting a delay statement in the loop. Speeding it up would require rewriting the data-taking loop in assembly language.

The `main()` routine allows the user to trigger the data collection and data dump modes by pressing the Start button. In an actual application, one could use a sensor to trigger the data collection routine.

The `dump_data()` routine outputs the data stored in the array to the serial line, using the line-feed/carriage-return technique mentioned earlier. It does not have a delay in the print loop because it is assumed that the terminal emulator program will be capturing the data to a text file. The data will probably stream in faster than the screen display can keep up, but as long as there is an adequate buffer for incoming serial characters in the host computer, data will not be lost. If it appears that data are getting lost, a delay statement should be inserted in this routine's loop.

After being saved to a text file, the sensor data can be loaded into a spreadsheet program for graphing and analysis.

C.4.1 Exercises

1. Using Interactive C's `seconds()` function, which reports elapsed time since system reset as a floating point number, obtain a more accurate measurement of the basic data collection rate in the `collect_data()` function.
2. Modify the trigger condition for collecting data in the `datacoll.c` example so that it begins when activity is detected on the sensor.
3. Based on the exercise in the previous section, modify `datacoll.c` so that it collects data from two sensors simultaneously and outputs the data in tab-delimited format.

FIGURE C.5 Listing of datacoll.c

```
/*
  datacoll.c
  data collection and printing

  requires printdec.c, serialio.c
*/

int SAMPLES=1000;
char data[1000];

void main()
{
  disable_pcode_serial();

  printf("press Start to  collect data\n");
  start_press();
  collect_data();
  beep();

  printf("press Start to  dump data\n");
  start_press();
  dump_data();
  beep();

  printf("done.\n");
}

void collect_data()
{
  int i;

  for (i= 0; i< SAMPLES; i++) {
    data[i]= analog(0);
    /* to slow down capture rate, add msleep here */
  }
}

void dump_data()
{
  int i;

  for (i= 0; i< SAMPLES; i++) {
    printdec(data[i]);
    serial_putchar(10);          /* line feed */
    serial_putchar(13);          /* carriage return */
  }
}
```

D

Handy Board Specification

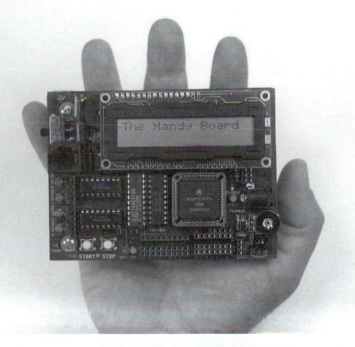

The Handy Board is a hand-held, battery-powered microcontroller board ideal for personal and educational robotics projects. Based on the Motorola 68HC11 microprocessor, the Handy Board includes 32K of battery-backed static RAM, outputs for four DC motors, inputs for a variety of sensors, and a 16×2 character LCD screen. The Handy Board runs Interactive C, a cross-platform, multitasking version of the C programming language.

The Handy Board is distributed under MIT's free licensing policy, in which the design may be licensed for for personal, educational, or commercial use with no charge.

D.1 Specifications

The Handy Board features:

- 52-pin Motorola 6811 microprocessor with system clock at 2 MHz.
- 32K of battery-backed CMOS static RAM.
- two L293D chips capable of driving four DC motors.
- 16 × 2 character LCD screen.

- two user-programmable buttons, one knob, and piezo beeper.
- powered header inputs for seven analog sensors and nine digital sensors.
- internal 9.6v nicad battery with built-in recharging circuit.
- hardware 38 kHz oscillator and drive transistor for IR output and onboard 38 kHz IR receiver.
- 8-pin powered connector to 6811 SPI circuit (1 Mbaud serial peripheral interface).
- expansion bus with chip selects allows easy expansion using inexpensive digital I/O latches.
- board size of 4.25 × 3.15 inches designed for a commercial, high-grade plastic enclosure that holds battery pack beneath the board.

D.2 Ports and Connectors

Figure D.1 shows a labeled view of the Handy Board's ports, connectors, inputs, and outputs. In the following, each of these is briefly described.

1. **Power Switch.** The power switch is used to turn the Handy Board on and off. The Handy Board retains the contents of its memory even when the board is switched off.

FIGURE D.1 Labeled Handy Board Diagram

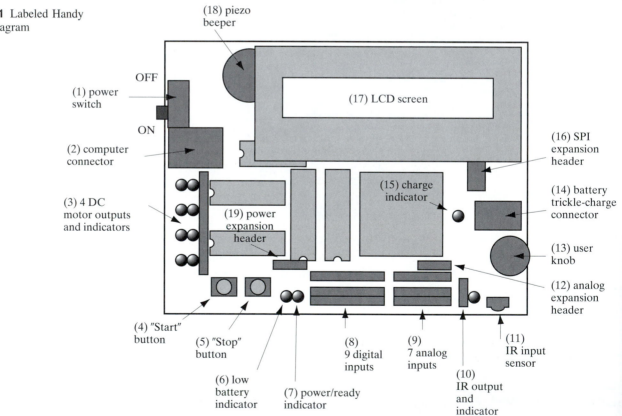

2. **Computer Connector.** Via this RJ11 connector, the Handy Board attaches to a desktop computer (using the separate Interface/Charger Board).

3. **4 DC Motor Outputs and Indicators.** The Handy Board's four motor outputs are located at this single 12-pin connector. Each motor output consists of three pins;

the motor connects to the outer two pins and the center pin is not used. Red and green LEDs indicate motor direction. From top to bottom, the motor outputs are numbered 0 to 3.

4. **Start Button.** The Start button is used to control the execution of Interactive C programs. Also its state may be read under user program control.

5. **Stop Button.** The Stop button is used to put the Handy Board into a special boot-strap download mode. Also its state may be read under user program control.

6. **Low Battery Indicator.** The red Low Battery LED lights when for a brief interval each time the Handy Board is switched on. If this LED is on steadily, it indicates that the battery is low and that the CPU is halted.

7. **Power/Ready Indicator.** The green Power/Ready LED lights when the Handy Board is in normal operation and flashes when the Handy Board is transmitting serial data. If the board is powered on and this LED is off, then the Handy Board is in special bootstrap mode.

8. **9 Digital Inputs.** The bank of digital input ports is here. From right to left, the digital inputs are numbered 7 to 15.

9. **7 Analog Inputs.** The bank of analog input ports is here. From right to left, the analog inputs are numbered 0 to 6.

10. **IR Output and Indicator.** The IR output port is here. The red indicator LED lights when the output is enabled.

11. **IR Input Sensor.** The dark green-colored IR sensor is here.

12. **Analog Expansion Header.** The analog expansion header is a 1×4 connector row located above analog inputs 0 to 3.

13. **User Knob.** The user knob is a trimmer potentiometer whose value can be read under user program control.

14. **Battery Trickle-Charge Connector.** The battery charge connector is a coaxial power jack to accept a 12-volt signal for trickle-charging the Handy Board's internal battery.

15. **Charge Indicator.** The yellow charge indicator LED lights when the Handy Board is charging via the coaxial power jack.

16. **SPI Expansion Header.** The SPI expansion header is a 2×4 pin jack that allows connection with the 6811's *serial peripheral interface* circuit. See the CPU and memory schematic diagram for a pin-out of this connector.

17. **LCD Screen.** The Handy Board is provided with a 16×2 LCD screen that can display data under user control.

18. **Piezo Beeper.** The Handy Board has a simple piezo beeper for generating tones under user control.

19. **Power Expansion Header.** The power expansion header is a 1×4 pin jack that provides access to the unregulated motor power and ground signals.

D.3 Battery Maintenance

The Handy Board has a 9.6v, 600 mA battery pack consisting of eight AA-cell nickel-cadmium rechargeable batteries.

D.3.1 Battery Charging

There are three ways to charge the internal battery:

1. *Adapter plugged directly into the HB.* Just plug the adapter into the power jack on the HB and the yellow "CHARGE" LED on the HB will light. This is a trickle-charge mode, which means that (1) the Handy Board will fully charge in about 12 to 14 hours, and (2) the HB may be left in this mode indefinitely.
2. *Adapter plugged into the Serial Interface/Battery Charger board; HB connected via telephone wire; "NORMAL CHARGE" mode selected.* The yellow "CHARGE" LED on the interface board will light. This is a trickle-charge mode, which means that (1) the Handy Board will fully charge in about 12 to 14 hours, and (2) the HB may be left in this mode indefinitely.
3. *Adapter plugged into the Serial Interface/Battery Charger board; HB connected via telephone wire; "ZAP CHARGE" mode selected.* The yellow "CHARGE" LED on the interface board will *not* light. The ZAP CHARGE will fully charge the HB's battery in just 3 hours, *after which time the battery will become warm and should be removed from charge or placed into either of the two trickle-charge modes.*

When using one of the trickle-charge modes, the Handy Board should be turned off so that the charge current goes toward charging the battery and not simply running the board. In Zap charge, there is enough charge current to operate the board and charge the batteries at the same time (assuming that the board is not driving motors or other external loads).

D.3.2 Adapter Specifications

The specifications of the Handy Board's DC adapter are as follows:

- 12-volt, 500 mA DC output
- 2.1 mm inside, 5.5 mm outside diameter barrel-type plug
- center conductor negative

Most "universal" type adapters will work properly at one of their settings. Look for the yellow charge LED to light up indicating proper charge (make sure the Charge Rate switch is set to "Normal" mode).

Please be careful not to get an adapter that is *overpowered*. Problems have been reported using adapters that are rated for 1 to 2 amps.

Also do not use an adapter that is underpowered or undervoltage. A 9-volt adapter will appear to work—the charge LED will light—but it won't be able to charge the battery for more than a few minutes' worth of power.

D.4 Part Listing

Circuit: hbsch12
Date: Thursday, November 30, 1995 - 9:58 AM

Device Type	Num.	Value	References	Price Ea.	Catalog No.	Supplier
8 cell AA nicad pack	1		BAT1	19.28	P227-L024-ND	Digikey
2% polyprop cap	1	0.0068 uF	C6	0.49	P3682-ND	Digikey
monolithic cer cap	4	0.1 uF	C5 C7 C9 C14	0.21	P4917-ND	Digikey
mini radial 'lytic	4	10uF	C10 C11 C12 C13	0.08	P6248-ND	Digikey
monolithic cer cap	2	22 pF	C1 C2	0.18	P4841-ND	Digikey
telephone cable	1	4-wire	CAB1	1.60	17MP007	Mouser
tantalum	2	4.7 uF	C4 C8	0.29	P2011-ND	Digikey
mini axial 'lytic	2	47 uF	C15 C16	0.29	P5972-ND	Digikey
mini axial 'lytic	1	470 uF	C3	0.65	P6305-ND	Digikey
power diode	1	1N4001	D3	0.15	333-1N4001	Mouser
signal diode	1	1N914	D1	0.15	333-1N914	Mouser
bridge rectifier	1	DB101	D2	0.62	DB101-ND	Digikey
AC or DC adapter	1	12v, 500mA	DC1	3.95	100087	Jameco
CPU board enclosure	1		ENCL1	5.12	537-402-RD	Mouser
interface enclosure	1		ENCL2	1.94	400-5043	Mouser
PolySwitchfi fuse	1		F1	1.32	RUE250-ND	Digikey
Coax Power Jack	2	2.1mm ID	J11 J12	0.34	CP-002A-ND	Digikey
RJ11 top entry	1	6/4	J5	1.08	154-UL6642	Mouser
RJ12 side entry	1	6/6	J10	1.28	154-UL6661	Mouser
10-pin female header	1		J3			
12-pin female header	1		J4			
14-pin female header	1		J14			
14-pin male header	1		J15			
3 pcs 9-pin female hdr	1		J2	[FEMALE HEADER IS CUT		
3 pcs. 7-pin female hdr	1		J1	FROM 36-PIN HEADER		
3-pin female header	1		J7	LISTED AT END OF PAGE]		
4-pin header	2		J8 J13			
4x2 header, female	1		J6			
DB-25 female connector	1		J9	1.54	152-3425	Mouser
iron core inductor	1	1 uH	L1	0.84	M7010-ND	Digikey
high-eff red LED	7	HLMP1700	LED1 LED2 LED3 LED4	0.282	HLMP-1700QT-ND	Digikey
			LED9 LED11 LED13			
hi-eff yellow LED	2	HLMP1719	LED14 LED15	0.282	HLMP-1719QT-ND	Digikey
hi-eff green LED	6	HLMP1790	LED5 LED6 LED7 LED8	0.282	HLMP-1790QT-ND	Digikey
			LED10 LED12			
NPN darlington	1	ZTX614	Q1	0.59	ZTX614-ND	Digikey
	2	10K	R3 R7	0.0235	10KEBK-ND	Digikey
	3	1K	R2 R5 R10	0.0235	1KEBK-ND	Digikey
	1	2.2K	R9	0.0235	2.2KEBK-ND	Digikey
	1	2.2M	R1	0.0235	2.2MEBK-ND	Digikey
1% precision res	1	2.94K	R4	0.11	2.94KXBK-ND	Digikey
trimpot	1	20K	VR1	0.72	569-91AR-20K	Mouser
	3	47K	R6 R8 R15	0.0235	47KEBK-ND	Digikey
	2	47	R12 R13	0.0235	47EBK-ND	Digikey
	2	47 , 1/2W	R11 R14	0.06	47H-ND	Digikey
	1	1Kx4	RP4	0.21	592-8A-1K	Mouser
RPACK6	1	1Kx5	RP2	0.16	592-6S-1K	Mouser
RPACK9	2	47Kx9	RP1 RP3	1.27	L03 10C 47K	Mouser
14-pin DIP socket	2		DIP4 DIP5	0.57	ED3114-ND	Digikey
16-pin DIP socket	4		DIP6 DIP7 DIP8 DIP9	0.65	ED3116-ND	Digikey
20-pin DIP socket	2		DIP1 DIP2	0.81	ED3120-ND	Digikey
28-pin DIP socket	1		DIP3	1.13	ED3728-ND	Digikey
52-pin PLCC socket	1		PLCC	2.03	A2123-ND	Digikey
piezo beeper	1		SPKR1	1.90	P9957-ND	Digikey
SPDT slide switch	1		SW1	4.47	CKN5006-ND	Digikey
SPDT switch	1		SW4	1.10	SW101-ND	Digikey
pushbutton switch	2		SW2 SW3	0.20	P8006S-ND	Digikey
32K static CMOS RAM	1	62256-100LP	U2	3.95	42833	Jameco
hex inverters	1	74HC04	U9	0.29	570-CD74HC04E	Mouser
quad Schmitt NANDs	1	74HC132	U7	0.46	511-M74HC132	Mouser
3-to-8 decoder	1	74HC138	U6	0.46	570-CD74HC138E	Mouser
tristate bus driver	1	74HC244	U5	0.70	570-CD74HC244E	Mouser
transparent octal latch	1	74HC373	U3	0.68	570-CD74HC373E	Mouser
octal latch	1	74HC374	U8	0.61	570-CD74HC374E	Mouser
voltage monitor	1	DS1233-10	U12	1.25	manufacturer	Dallas Semi
infrared demodulator	1	IS1U60	U15	3.00	manufacturer	Sharp
motor driver	2	L293D	U10 U11	3.00	manufacturer	SGS-Thomson
voltage regulator	2	LM2931Z-5.0	U14 U17	0.90	LM2931Z-5.0-ND	Digikey
voltage regulator	1	LM7805CTB	U13	0.53	NJM7805FA-ND	Digikey
RS232 converter	1	MAX232CPE	U16	1.95	24811	Jameco
6811 microprocessor	1	MC68HC11A1FN	U1	8.00	manufacturer	Motorola
16x2 LCD	1	Hitachi	U4	8.00	LM052L	Timeline
microproc crystal	1	8 MHz	X1	2.32	332-5080	Mouser
female strip header	4			1.10	929974-01-36-ND	Digikey
male strip header	1			0.76	929834-01-36-ND	Digikey

D.5 Printed Circuit Board Layouts

D.5.1 Handy Board Component Side

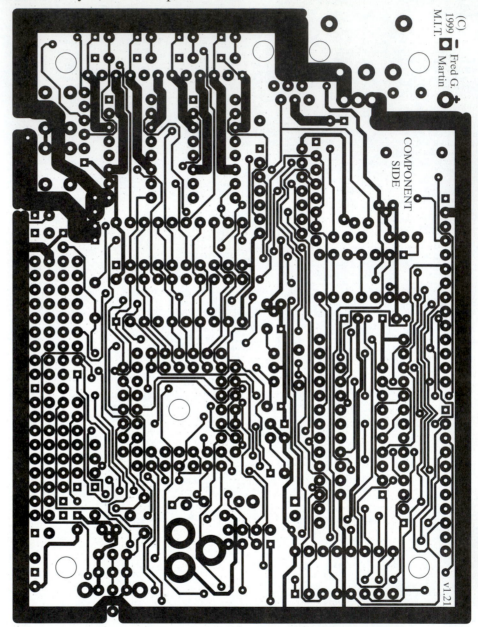

D.5.2 Handy Board Solder Side

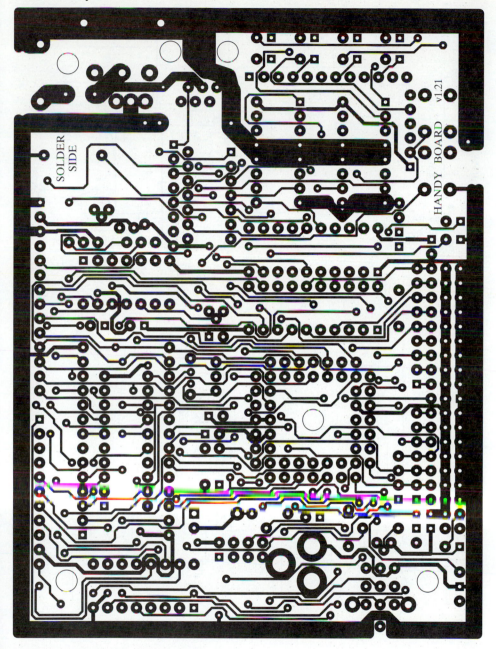

D.5.3 Handy Board Silkscreen

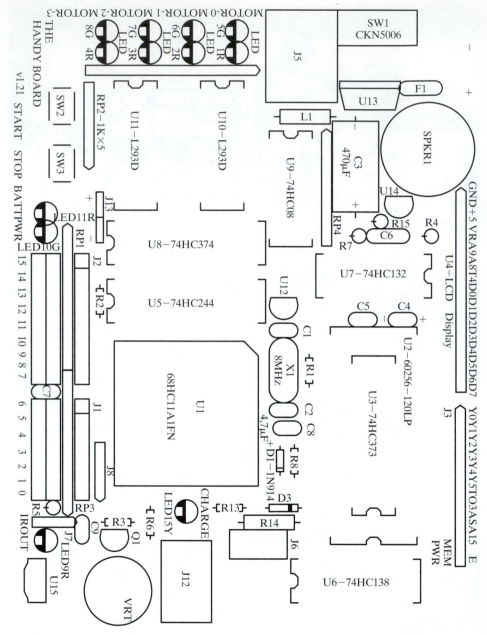

D.5.4 Interface/Charger Board Component Side

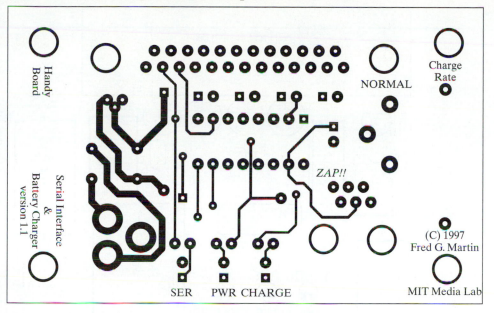

D.5.5 Interface/Charger Board Solder Side

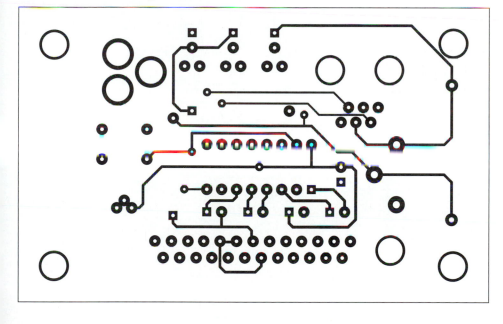

D.5.6 Interface/Charger Board Silkscreen

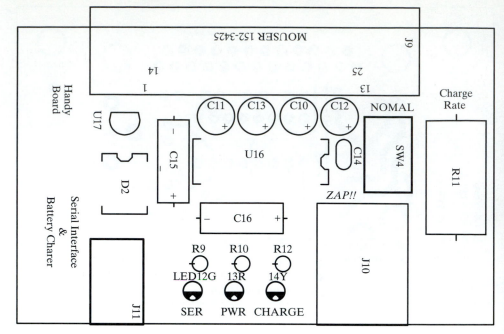

Interactive C Reference

E.1 Quick Start

Here are the steps to getting started with the Handy Board and Interactive C:

1. Connect the Handy Board to the serial port of the host computer using the separate Serial Interface board. The Serial Interface board connects to the host computer using a standard modem cable; the Handy Board connects to the Serial Interface using a standard four-wire telephone cable.
2. Put the Handy Board into bootstrap download mode by holding down the STOP button while turning on system power. The pair of LEDs by the two push buttons should light up and then turn off. When power is on and both of the LEDs are off, the Handy Board is in download mode.
3. Run the appropriate downloader for the host computer platform and download the file `pcode_hb.s19`.
4. Turn the Handy Board off and then on, and the Interactive C welcome message should appear on the Handy Board's LCD screen.
5. Run Interactive C.

E.2 6811 Downloaders

There are two primary components to the Interactive C software system:

- The *6811 downloader program*, which is used to load the runtime 6811 operating program on the Handy Board. There are a number of different 6811 downloaders for each computer platform.

- The *Interactive C application*, which is used to compile and download IC programs to the Handy Board.

This software is available for a variety of computer platforms/operating systems, including MS-DOS, Windows 3.1/Windows 95, Macintosh, and Unix. The remainder of this section explains the choices in the 6811 downloaders.

E.2.1 Overview

The 6811 downloaders are general purpose applications for downloading a Motorola hex file (also called an S19 record) into the Handy Board's memory. Each line hex file contains ASCII-encoded binary data indicating what data are to be loaded where into the Handy Board's memory.

For use with Interactive C, the program named "`pcode_hb.s19`" must be present in the Handy Board. The task of the downloaders, then, is simply to initialize the Handy Board's memory with the contents of this file.

An additional purpose of the downloaders is to program the 6811's "CONFIG" register. The CONFIG register determines the nature of the 6811 memory map. For use with Interactive C, the CONFIG register must be set to the value `0x0c`, which allows the 6811 to access the Handy Board's 32K static RAM memory in its entirety. Some downloaders automatically program the CONFIG register; others require a special procedure to do so. Please note that programming of the CONFIG register *only needs to be done once* to factory-fresh 6811s. It is then set in firmware until deliberately reprogrammed to a different value.

Another consideration related to downloaders is the type of 6811 in use. The Handy Board can use both the "A" and "E" series of 6811. These two chip varieties are quite similar, but not all downloaders support the E series' bootstrap sequence. (The E series chips have more flexibility on their Port A input/output pins and can run at a higher clock speed.)

E.2.2 Putting the Handy Board into Bootstrap Download Mode

When using any of the downloaders, the Handy Board must first be put into its bootstrap download mode. This is done by first turning the board off and then turning it on *while holding down the STOP button* (the button closer to the pair of LEDs to the right of the buttons). When the board is first turned on, these two LEDs should light for about $\frac{1}{3}$ of a second and then both should turn off. The S\textsc{top} button must be held down continuously during this sequence. *When the board is powered on and both of these LEDs are off, it is ready for bootstrap download.*

E.2.3 MS-DOS

Two downloaders are available for MS-DOS machines: *dl*, by Randy Sargent, and *dlm*, by Fred Martin.

dl is compatible only with the A series of 6811 and automatically programs the CONFIG register. Type "`dl pcode_hb.s19`" at the MS-DOS prompt.

dlm is compatible with both the A and E series of 6811, but does not automatically program the CONFIG register. Type "`dlm pcode_hb.s19 -256`" to download to an A series chip and "`dlm pcode_hb.s19 -512`" to download to an E series chip.

Neither *dl* nor *dlm* runs very well under Windows. It is generally necessary to run them from a full-screen DOS shell to get them to work at all. Under Windows, *hbdl* is recommended instead.

E.2.4 Windows 3.1 and Windows 95

hbdl, by Vadim Gerasimov, is the recommended Windows 6811 downloader. *hbdl* features automatic recognition of both A and E series 6811s and automatic programming of the CONFIG register.

To use *hbdl*, run the `hbdl.exe` application and select the "`pcode_hb.s19`" file for download. Make sure the text box for the CONFIG register has the value "`0c`."

E.2.5 Macintosh

There are two choices available for the Macintosh: *Initialize Board*, by Randy Sargent, and *6811 Downloader*, by Fred Martin.

Initialize Board features automatic programming of the CONFIG register, but only works with A series 6811s. It comes in two versions: one using the modem port and one using the printer port.

To get *Initialize Board* to use the Handy Board's `pcode_hb.s19` file, one must edit its STR resources to name this file. Then using it is just a matter of double-clicking on the application icon.

6811 Downloader features automatic recognition of both A and E series 6811s. To program the CONFIG register, one must select the "download to EEPROM" option and then download the `config0c.s19` file.

6811 Downloader may be run by double-clicking on the application icon and selecting a file for download or by dragging the file to be downloaded onto the application icon.

E.2.6 Unix

The *dl* downloader, written by Randy Sargent, is available for a number of Unix platforms, including DECstations, Linux, Sparc Solaris, Sparc Sun OS, SGI, HPUX, and RS6000.

This downloader only works with the A series of 6811 and supports automatic programming of the CONFIG register.

E.3 Interactive C

Interactive C (IC for short) is a C language consisting of a compiler (with interactive command-line compilation and debugging) and a runtime machine language module.

In a traditional C compiler, the C-language source code is converted directly into instructions that will run on the target microprocessor. Interactive C, however, uses a different approach: The user's C code is converted into instructions for a specially designed virtual machine. On the Handy Board, written in 68HC11 machine language, is a program that interprets these instructions. This program then implements the virtual machine for which the Interactive C compiler has produced code.

There are several motivations for this alternative architecture. First, it is easier to construct a compiler for a simplified virtual machine than an actual microprocessor like the 68HC11. Second, compiled programs are represented much more compactly in the virtual machine language than the native code, which maximizes the use of the Handy Board's memory. Third, the virtual machine makes runtime error checking a possibility. Finally, the particular virtual machine architecture we chose greatly simplified the job of implementing the multitasking portion of the system.

The primary drawback to this virtual machine approach is execution speed. In general, a native code compiler can produce code that runs about 10 times faster than Interactive C's virtual machine system. For typical robot programming, however, truly time-sensitive portions of code, like sensor driver routines, should be implemented directly in machine language anyhow. Interactive C is more than sufficiently fast for the main control structures and also provides a facility for easily incorporating machine language drivers into a C-language program.

It is interesting to note that the virtual machine approach has enjoyed a renaissance of late. Originally pioneered on IBM mainframes as a technique for maintaining compatibility with earlier architectures, the virtual machine approach was popularized in many implementations of the Pascal programming language. Today's Java language specification is based on a virtual machine implementation.

Features

Interactive C implements a subset of the full C-language specification. The features included in the free version are:

- Functions with a return value, procedures with no return value, arguments to functions and procedures, global and local variables.
- Standard C control statements: `if`, `else`, `for`, `while`, `break`, and `continue`.
- Four data types: 16-bit integers, 32-bit integers, single-byte characters, and 32-bit floating point numbers.
- One-dimensional arrays of numeric data and character strings.

IC was designed and implemented by Randy Sargent with the assistance of Fred Martin. This manual covers the freeware distribution of IC (version 2.852).

E.3.1 Using IC

When IC is booted, it immediately attempts to connect with the Handy Board, which should be turned on and running the `pcode_hb.s19` program.

After synchronizing with the Handy Board, IC compiles and downloads the default set of library files and then presents the user with the "`C>`" prompt. At this prompt, either an IC command or C–language expression may be entered.

All C expressions must be ended with a semicolon. For example, to evaluate the arithmetic expression $1 + 2$, type the following:

```
C>  1 + 2;
```

(The underlined portion indicates user input.) When this expression is typed, it is compiled by IC and then downloaded to the Handy Board for evaluation. The Handy Board then evaluates the compiled form and returns the result, which is printed on the IC console.

To evaluate a series of expressions, create a C block by beginning with an open curly brace "{" and ending with a close curly brace "}". The following example creates a local variable `i` and prints the sum `i+7` to the Handy Board's LCD screen:

```
C>  {int i=3; printf("%d", i+7);}
```

IC Commands

IC responds to the following commands:

- **Load file.** The command `load` *<filename>* compiles and loads the named file. The Handy Board must be attached for this to work. IC looks first in the local directory and then in the IC library path for files.

  Several files may be loaded into IC at once, allowing programs to be defined in multiple files.

- **Unload file.** The command `unload` *< filename >* unloads the named file and redownloads remaining files.

- **List files, functions, or globals.** The command `list files` displays the names of all files presently loaded into IC. The command `list functions` displays the names of presently defined C functions. The command `list globals` displays the names of all currently defined global variables.

- **Kill all processes.** The command `kill_all` kills all currently running processes.

- **Print process status.** The command `ps` prints the status of currently running processes.

- **Help.** The command `help` displays a help screen of IC commands.

- **Quit.** The command `quit` exits IC. In the MS-DOS version, CTRL-C can also be used.

Keystroke	Function
CTRL-A	beginning-of-line
CTRL-B	backward-char
←	backward-char
CTRL-D	delete-char
CTRL-E	end-of-line
CTRL-F	forward-char
→	forward-char
CTRL-K	kill-line

FIGURE E.1 IC Command-Line Keystroke Mappings

Line Editing

IC has a built-in line editor and command history, allowing editing and reuse of previously typed statements and commands. The mnemonics for these functions are based on standard Emacs control key assignments.

To scan forward and backward in the command history, type CTRL-P or ↑ for backward and CTRL-N or ↓ for forward.

Figure E.1 shows the keystroke mappings understood by IC.

IC does parenthesis-balance-highlighting as expressions are typed.

The Main Function

After functions have been downloaded to the Handy Board, they can be invoked from the IC prompt. If one of the functions is named main(), it will automatically be run when the Handy Board is reset.

To reset the Handy Board *without* running the main() function (e.g., when hooking the board back to the computer), hold down the START button when turning on the Handy Board. The board will reset without running main().

E.3.2 A Quick C Tutorial

Most C programs consist of function definitions and data structures. Here is a simple C program that defines a single function, called main.

```
void main()
{
    printf("Hello, world!\n");
}
```

All functions must have a return value; that is, the value that they return when they finish execution. main has a return value type of void, which is the "null" type. Other types include integers (int) and floating point numbers (float). This *function declaration* information must precede each function definition.

Immediately following the function declaration is the function's name (in this case, main). Next, in parentheses, are any arguments (or inputs) to the function. main has none, but an empty set of parentheses is still required.

After the function arguments is an open curly brace "{". This signifies the start of the actual function code. Curly braces signify program *blocks* or chunks of code.

Next comes a series of C *statements*. Statements demand that some action be taken. Our demonstration program has a single statement, a printf (formatted print). This will print the message "Hello, world!" to the LCD display. The \n indicates end-of-line.

The `printf` statement ends with a semicolon ("`;`"). *All* C statements must be ended by a semicolon. Beginning C programmers commonly make the error of omitting the semicolon that is required at the end of each statement.

The `main` function is ended by the close curly-brace "`}`".

Let's look at another example to learn some more features of C. The following code defines the function *square*, which returns the mathematical square of a number.

```
int square(int n)
{
    return n * n;
}
```

The function is declared as type `int`, which means that it will return an integer value. Next comes the function name `square`, followed by its argument list in parenthesis. `square` has one argument, n, which is an integer. Notice how declaring the type of the argument is done similarly to declaring the type of the function.

When a function has arguments declared, those argument variables are valid within the "scope" of the function (i.e., they only have meaning within the function's own code). Other functions may use the same variable names independently.

The code for `square` is contained within the set of curly braces. In fact, it consists of a single statement: the `return` statement. The `return` statement exits the function and returns the value of the C *expression* that follows it (in this case "n * n").

Expressions are evaluated according to a set of precendence rules depending on the various operations within the expression. In this case, there is only one operation (multiplication), signified by the "`*`", so precedence is not an issue.

Let's look at an example of a function that performs a function call to the `square` program.

```
float hypotenuse(int a, int b)
{
    float h;

    h = sqrt((float)(square(a) + square(b)));

    return h;
}
```

This code demonstrates several more features of C. First, notice that the floating point variable h is defined at the beginning of the `hypotenuse` function. In general, whenever a new program block (indicated by a set of curly braces) is begun, new local variables may be defined.

The value of h is set to the result of a call to the `sqrt` function. It turns out that `sqrt` is a built-in function that takes a floating point number as its argument.

We want to use the `square` function we defined earlier, which returns its result as an integer. But the `sqrt` function requires a floating point argument. We get around this type incompatibility by *coercing* the integer sum (`square(a) + square(b)`) into a float by preceding it with the desired type in parentheses. Thus, the integer sum is made into a floating point number and passed along to `sqrt`.

The `hypotenuse` function finishes by returning the value of h.

This concludes the brief C tutorial.

E.3.3 Data Types, Operations, and Expressions

Variables and constants are the basic data objects in a C program. Declarations list the variables to be used, state what type they are, and may set their initial value. Operators specify what is to be done to them. Expressions combine variables and constants to create new values.

Variable Names

Variable names are case-sensitive. The underscore character is allowed and is often used to enhance the readability of long variable names. C keywords like if, while, etc. may not be used as variable names.

Global variables and functions may not have the same name. In addition, local variables named the same as functions prevent the use of that function within the scope of the local variable.

Data Types

IC supports the following data types:

16-bit Integers   16-bit integers are signified by the type indicator int. They are signed integers and may be valued from $-32,768$ to $+32,767$ decimal.

32-bit Integers   32-bit integers are signified by the type indicator long. They are signed integers and may be valued from $-2,147,483,648$ to $+2,147,483,647$ decimal.

32-bit Floating Point Numbers   Floating point numbers are signified by the type indicator float. They have approximately seven decimal digits of precision and are valued from 10^{-38} to 10^{38}.

8-bit Characters   Characters are an 8-bit number signified by the type indicator char. A character's value typically represents a printable symbol using the standard ASCII character code.

Arrays of characters (character strings) are supported, but individual characters are not.

Local and Global Variables

If a variable is declared within a function or as an argument to a function, its binding is *local*, meaning that the variable has existence only that function definition.

If a variable is declared outside of a function, it is a global variable. It is defined for all functions, including functions that are defined in files other than the one in which the global variable was declared.

Variable Initialization   Local and global variables can be initialized when they are declared. If no initialization value is given, the variable is initialized to zero.

```
int foo()
{
  int x;         /* create local variable x
                    with initial value 0    */
  int y= 7;      /* create local variable y
                    with initial value 7    */
  ...
}

float z=3.0;     /* create global variable z
                    with initial value 3.0  */
```

Local variables are initialized whenever the function containing them runs.

Global variables are initialized whenever a reset condition occurs. Reset conditions occur when:

1. New code is downloaded;
2. The `main()` procedure is run;
3. System hardware reset occurs.

Persistent Global Variables

A special *uninitialized* form of global variable, called the "persistent" type, has been implemented for IC. A persistent global is *not* initialized on the conditions listed for normal global variables.

To make a persistent global variable, prefix the type specifier with the key word `persistent`. For example, the statement

```
persistent int i;
```

creates a global integer called `i`. The initial value for a persistent variable is arbitrary; it depends on the contents of RAM that were assigned to it. Initial values for persistent variables cannot be specified in their declaration statement.

Persistent variables keep their state when the Handy Board is turned off and on, when `main` is run, and when system reset occurs. Persistent variables, in general, will lose their state when a new program is downloaded. However, it is possible to prevent this from occurring. If persistent variables are declared at the beginning of the code, before any function or nonpersistent globals, they will be reassigned to the same location in memory when the code is recompiled, and thus their values will be preserved over multiple downloads.

If the program is divided into multiple files and it is desired to preserve the values of persistent variables, then all of the persistent variables should be declared in one particular file and that file should be placed first in the load ordering of the files.

Persistent variables were created with two applications in mind:

- Calibration and configuration values that do not need to be recalculated on every reset condition.
- Robot learning algorithms that might occur over a period when the robot is turned on and off.

Constants

Integers

Integers may be defined in decimal integer format (e.g., `4053` or `-1`), hexadecimal format using the "`0x`" prefix (e.g., `0x1fff`), and a non-standard but useful binary format using the "`0b`" prefix (e.g., `0b1001001`). Octal constants using the zero prefix are not supported.

Long Integers

Long integer constants are created by appending the suffix "`l`" or "`L`" (upper- or lowercase alphabetic L) to a decimal integer. For example, `0L` is the long zero. Either the upper- or lowercase "L" may be used, but uppercase is the convention for readability.

Floating Point Numbers

Floating point numbers may use exponential notation (e.g., "`10e3`" or "`10E3`") or must contain the decimal period. For example, the floating point zero can be given as "`0.`", "`0.0`", or "`0E1`", but not as just "`0`".

Characters and Character Strings

Quoted characters return their ASCII value (e.g., `'x'`).

Character strings are defined with quotation marks (e.g., `"This is a character string."`).

Operators

Each of the data types has its own set of operators that determine which operations may be performed on them.

Integers   The following operations are supported on integers:

- **Arithmetic.** addition +, subtraction -, multiplication *, division /.
- **Comparison.** greater-than >, less-than <, equality ==, greater-than-equal >=, less-than-equal <=.
- **Bit-wise Arithmetic.** bit-wise-OR |, bit-wise-AND &, bit-wise-exclusive-OR ^, bit-wise-NOT.
- **Boolean Arithmetic.** logical-OR ||, logical-AND &&, logical-NOT !.

  When a C statement uses a boolean value (e.g., if), it takes the integer zero as meaning false and any integer other than zero as meaning true. The boolean operators return zero for false and one for true.

  Boolean operators && and || stop executing as soon as the truth of the final expression is determined. For example, in the expression a && b, if a is false, then b does not need to be evaluated because the result must be false. The && operator "knows this" and does not evaluate b.

Long Integers   A subset of the operations implemented for integers are implemented for long integers: arithmetic addition +, subtraction -, and multiplication *, and the integer comparison operations. Bit-wise and boolean operations and division are not supported.

Floating Point Numbers   IC uses a package of public-domain floating point routines distributed by Motorola. This package includes arithmetic, trigonometric, and logarithmic functions.

The following operations are supported on floating point numbers:

- **Arithmetic.** addition +, subtraction -, multiplication *, division /.
- **Comparison.** greater-than >, less-than <, equality ==, greater-than-equal >=, less-than-equal <=.
- **Built-in Math Functions.** A set of trigonometric, logarithmic, and exponential functions is supported as discussed in Section E.3.9.

Characters   Characters are only allowed in character arrays. When a cell of the array is referenced, it is automatically coerced into an integer representation for manipulation by the integer operations. When a value is stored into a character array, it is coerced from a standard 16-bit integer into an 8-bit character (by truncating the upper eight bits).

Assignment Operators and Expressions

The basic assignment operator is =. The following statement adds 2 to the value of a.

```
a = a + 2;
```

The abbreviated form

```
a += 2;
```

could also be used to perform the same operation.

All of the following binary operators can be used in this fashion:

```
+   -   *   /   %   <<   >>   &   ^   |
```

Increment and Decrement Operators

The increment operator "++" increments the named variable. For example, the statement "a++" is equivalent to "a= a+1" or "a+= 1".

A statement that uses an increment operator has a value. For example, the statement

```
a= 3;
printf("a=%d a+1=%d\n", a, ++a);
```

will display the text "a=3 a+1=4."

If the increment operator comes after the named variable, then the value of the statement is calculated *after* the increment occurs. So the statement

```
a= 3;
printf("a=%d a+1=%d\n", a, a++);
```

would display "a=3 a+1=3" but would finish with a set to 4.

The decrement operator "--" is used in the same fashion as the increment operator.

Precedence and Order of Evaluation

The following table summarizes the rules for precedence and associativity for the C operators. Operators listed earlier in the table have higher precedence; operators on the same line of the table have equal precedence.

Operator	Associativity
() []	left to right
! ~ ++ -- - (*type*)	right to left
* / %	left to right
+ -	left to right
<< >>	left to right
< <= > >=	left to right
== !=	left to right
&	left to right
^	left to right
|	left to right
&&	left to right
||	right to left
= += -= etc.	right to left
,	left to right

E.3.4 Control Flow

IC supports most of the standard C control structures. One notable exception is the case and switch statement, which is not supported.

Statements and Blocks

A single C statement is ended by a semicolon. A series of statements may be grouped together into a *block* using curly braces. Inside a block, local variables may be defined.

There is never a semicolon after a right brace that ends a block.

If-Else

The if else statement is used to make decisions. The syntax is:

```
if  ( expression )
   statement-1
else
   statement-2
```

expression is evaluated; if it is not equal to zero (e.g., logic true), then *statement-1* is executed.

The else clause is optional. If the if part of the statement did not execute and the else is present, then *statement-2* executes.

While

The syntax of a while loop is the following:

```
while  ( expression )
   statement
```

while begins by evaluating *expression*. If it is false, then *statement* is skipped. If it is true, then *statement* is evaluated. Then the expression is evaluated again, and the same check is performed. The loop exits when *expression* becomes zero.

One can easily create an infinite loop in C using the while statement:

```
while (1)
   statement
```

For

The syntax of a for loop is the following:

```
for  ( expr-1 ; expr-2 ; expr-3 )
   statement
```

This is equivalent to the following construct using while:

```
expr-1 ;
while ( expr-2 )  {
   statement
   expr-3 ;
}
```

Typically, *expr-1* is an assignment, *expr-2* is a relational expression, and *expr-3* is an increment or decrement of some manner. For example, the following code counts from 0 to 99, printing each number along the way:

```
int i;
for (i= 0; i < 100; i++)
   printf("%d\n", i);
```

Break

Use of the break provides an early exit from a while or a for loop.

E.3.5 LCD Screen Printing

IC has a version of the C function printf for formatted printing to the LCD screen.

The syntax of printf is the following:

```
printf( format-string , [ arg-1 ] , ..., [ arg-N ] )
```

This is best illustrated by some examples.

Printing Examples

Example 1: Printing a message. The following statement prints a text string to the screen.

```
printf("Hello, world!\n");
```

In this example, the format string is simply printed to the screen.

The character "\n" at the end of the string signifies *end-of-line*. When an end-of-line character is printed, the LCD screen will be cleared when a subsequent character is printed. Thus, most printf statements are terminated by a \n.

Example 2: Printing a number. The following statement prints the value of the integer variable x with a brief message.

```
printf("Value is %d\n", x);
```

The special form %d is used to format the printing of an integer in decimal format.

Example 3: Printing a number in binary. The following statement prints the value of the integer variable x as a binary number.

```
printf("Value is %b\n", x);
```

The special form %b is used to format the printing of an integer in binary format. Only the *low byte* of the number is printed.

Example 4: Printing a floating point number. The following statement prints the value of the floating point variable n as a floating point number.

```
printf("Value is %f\n", n);
```

The special form %f is used to format the printing of floating point number.

Example 5: Printing two numbers in hexadecimal format.

```
printf("A=%x  B=%x\n", a, b);
```

The form %x formats an integer to print in hexadecimal.

Formatting Command Summary

Format Command	Data Type	Description
%d	int	decimal number
%x	int	hexadecimal number
%b	int	low byte as binary number
%c	int	low byte as ASCII character
%f	float	floating point number
%s	char array	char array (string)

Special Notes

- The final character position of the LCD screen is used as a system "heartbeat." This character continuously blinks back and forth when the board is operating properly. If the character stops blinking, the Handy Board has crashed.

- Characters that would be printed beyond the final character position are truncated.

- The printf() command treats the two-line LCD screen as a single longer line.

- Printing of long integers is not presently supported.

E.3.6 Arrays and Pointers

IC supports one-dimensional arrays of characters, integers, long integers, and floating point numbers. Pointers to data items and arrays are supported.

Declaring and Initializing Arrays

Arrays are declared using the square brackets. The following statement declares an array of 10 integers:

```
int foo[10];
```

In this array, elements are numbered from 0 to 9. Elements are accessed by enclosing the index number within square brackets: `foo[4]` denotes the fifth element of the array `foo` (because counting begins at zero).

Arrays are initialized by default to contain all zero values; arrays may also be initialized at declaration by specifying the array elements, separated by commas, within curly braces. Using this syntax, the size of the array would not specified within the square braces; it is determined by the number of elements given in the declaration. For example,

```
int foo[] = {0, 4, 5, -8,  17, 301};
```

creates an array of six integers, with `foo[0]` equalling 0, `foo[1]` equalling 4, and so on.

Character arrays are typically text strings. There is a special syntax for initializing arrays of characters. The character values of the array are enclosed in quotation marks:

```
char string[] = "Hello there";
```

This form creates a character array called `string` with the ASCII values of the specified characters. In addition, the character array is terminated by a zero. Because of this zero termination, the character array can be treated as a string for purposes of printing (for example). Character arrays can be initialized using the curly braces syntax, but they will not be automatically null terminated in that case. In general, printing of character arrays that are *not* null terminated will cause problems.

Passing Arrays as Arguments

When an array is passed to a function as an argument, the array's pointer is actually passed, rather than the elements of the array. If the function modifies the array values, the array will be modified because there is only one copy of the array in memory.

In normal C, there are two ways of declaring an array argument: as an array or as a pointer. IC only allows declaring array arguments as arrays.

As an example, the following function takes an index and an array and returns the array element specified by the index:

```
int retrieve_element(int index, int array[])
{
    return array[index];
}
```

Notice the use of the square brackets to declare the argument `array` as an array of integers.

When passing an array variable to a function, use of the square brackets is not needed:

```
{
int array[10];

retrieve_element(3, array);
}
```

Declaring Pointer Variables

Pointers can be passed to functions that then go on to modify the value of the variable being pointed to. This is useful because the same function can be called to modify different variables just by giving it a different pointer.

Pointers are declared with the use of the asterisk (*). In the example

```
int *foo;
float *bar;
```

foo is declared as a pointer to an integer, and bar is declared as a pointer to a floating point number.

To make a pointer variable point at some other variable, the ampersand operator is used. The ampersand operator returns the *address* of a variable's value; that is, the place in memory where the variable's value is stored. Thus:

```
int *foo;
int x= 5;

foo= &x;
```

makes the pointer foo "point at" the value of x (which happens to be 5).

This pointer can now be used to retrieve the value of x using the asterisk operator. This process is called *de-referencing*. The pointer, or reference to a value, is used to fetch the value being pointed at. Thus:

```
int y;

y= *foo;
```

sets y equal to the value pointed at by foo. In the previous example, foo was set to point at x, which had the value 5. Thus, the result of dereferencing foo yields 5, and y will be set to 5.

Passing Pointers as Arguments

Pointers can be passed to functions; then functions can change the values of the variables that are pointed at. This is termed *call-by-reference*; the reference, or pointer, to the variable is given to the function that is being called. This is in contrast to *call-by-value*, the standard way that functions are called, in which the value of a variable is given to the function being called.

The following example defines an average_sensor function that takes a port number and a pointer to an integer variable. The function will average the sensor and store the result in the variable pointed at by result.

In the code, the function argument is specified as a pointer using the asterisk:

```
void average_sensor(int port, int *result)
{
  int sum= 0;
  int i;

  for (i= 0; i< 10; i++) sum += analog(port);

  *result=  sum/10;
}
```

Notice that the function is declared as a void. It does not need to return anything because it instead stores its answer in the pointer variable that is passed to it.

The pointer variable is used in the last line of the function. In this statement, the answer sum/10 is stored at the location pointed at by result. Notice that the asterisk is used to get the *location* pointed by result.

E.3.7 Library Functions

Library files provide standard C functions for interfacing with hardware on the Handy Board. These functions are written either in C or as assembly language drivers. Library files provide functions to do things like control motors, make tones, and input sensors values.

IC automatically loads the library file every time it is invoked. The name of the default library file is is contained as a resource within the IC application. On command-line versions of IC, this resource may be modified by invoking "ic -config". On the Macintosh, the IC application has a STR resource that defines the name of the library file.

The Handy Board's root library file is named lib_hb.lis.

Output Control

DC Motors   DC motor ports are numbered from 0 to 3.

Motors may be set in a "forward" direction (corresponding to the green motor LED being lit) and a "backward" direction (corresponding to the motor red LED being lit).

The functions fd(int m) and bk(int m) turn motor m on or off, respectively, at full power. The function off(int m) turns motor m off.

The power level of motors may also be controlled. This is done in software by a motor on and off rapidly (a technique called *pulse-width modulation*. The motor(int m, int p) function allows control of a motor's power level. Powers range from 100 (full on in the forward direction) to -100 (full on in the backward direction). The system software actually only controls motors to seven degrees of power, but argument bounds of −100 and +100 are used.

```
void fd(int m)
```
Turns motor m on in the forward direction. Example: fd(3);

```
void bk(int m)
```
Turns motor m on in the backward direction. Example: bk(1);

```
void off(int m)
```
Turns off motor m. Example: off(1);

```
void alloff()
```

```
void ao()
```
Turns off all motors. ao is a short form for alloff.

```
void motor(int m, int p)
```
Turns on motor m at power level p. Power levels range from 100 for full on forward to -100 for full on backward.

Servo Motor   The library routines generate output signals on Port A bit 7 and Port A bit 5. The former of these (Port A bit 7) marked Digital Input 9 on the Handy Board. The latter is a pin that is open and available on the HB Expansion Bus.

The routines provide a primitive but functional interface for controlling the position of the servo. For each servo, a global variable is set, generating a specific pulse train which acts as a desired position input to the servo. In order to make the servo "sweep" one must write C code to iterate values over the position global.

For maximum flexibility, the routines do not provide a "sanity check" to validate the value of the global being in a usable portion of the servo's range. For a typical servo, valid values range from 400 to 4800 (yielding pulse times of 0.2 to 2.4 milliseconds). Value outside of this range will cause the servo to overtax itself as it tries to reach a position that is not mechanically possible. You may wish to write your own wrapper functions for setting the control globals and rejecting out-of-bounds values.

Electrical

Servo motors require a 5 to 6 volt DC power supply (the red servo wire). This can be taken from the regulated +5v of the Handy Board if the servo's aren't doing too much work. Otherwise, a separate power supply is recommended. See Appendix B.2 for a wiring diagram.

Another alternative is to use the Handy Board's own 9.6v battery with a string of several 1N4001 diodes to drop the voltage down to around 6 volts. The 9.6v output is either of the two left-most pins of the four-pin connector header directly above the BATT/PWR LED's.

The ground for the servo leads (black wire) should connect to the Handy Board's motor ground, not its logic ground. The motor ground is either of the two right-most pins of the four-pin connector header directly above the BATT/PWR LED's.

The servo signal lead (white wire) connects to specific Handy Board digital outputs as described following.

Usage

The two drivers (`servo_a7.icb` and `servo_a5.icb`) must be loaded into IC, either at the command line or via a `.lis` file. The drivers may be loaded individually or together.

Each driver declares a global variable for setting the servo position and an initialization routine for turning the servo on and off.

`servo_a7.icb`

The servo control signal is generated on Port A bit 7, which is brought out as digital "input" 9 on the HB connector bank (this input line is converted to an output when driving the servo).

`int servo_a7_pulse` Integer global variable determining value of servo control signal. Units are 0.5 microsecond counts; e.g., a value of 3040 yields a pulse length of 1.52 milliseconds, which is just in the middle of a typical servo's range. The default value of this global is 2560, which is re-established on board reset.

`int servo_a7_init(int enable)` Function to enable and disable the servo output. Call with argument equal to one to enable, and zero to disable.

`servo_a5.icb`

The servo control signal is generated on Port A bit 5 (also known as Timer Output 3), which is brought out on the HB expansion bus (labeled "TO3").

`int servo_a5_pulse` Integer global variable determining value of servo control signal. Units are 0.5 microsecond counts; e.g., a value of 3040 yields a pulse length of 1.52 milliseconds, which is just in the middle of a typical servo's range. The default value of this global is 2560, which is re-established on board reset.

`int servo_a5_init(int enable)`

Function to enable and disable the servo output. Call with argument equal to one to enable, and zero to disable.

Sensor Input

`int digital(int p)`

Returns the value of the sensor in sensor port `p` as a true/false value (1 for true and 0 for false).

Sensors are expected to be *active low*, meaning that they are valued at zero volts in the active, or true, state. Thus, the library function returns the inverse of the actual reading from the digital hardware: If the reading is zero volts or logic zero, the `digital()` function will return true.

If the `digital()` function is applied to port that is implemented in hardware as an analog input, the result is true if the analog measurement is less than 127 and false if the reading is greater than or equal to 127.

Ports are numbered as marked on the Handy Board.

`int analog(int p)`

Returns value of sensor port numbered `p`. Result is integer between 0 and 255.

If the `analog()` function is applied to a port that is implemented digitally in hardware, then the value 0 is returned if the digital reading is 0, and the value 255 is returned if the digital reading is 1.

Ports are numbered as marked on the Handy Board.

User Buttons and Knob   The Handy Board has two buttons and a knob whose value can be read by user programs.

`int stop_button()`

Returns value of button labeled STOP: 1 if pressed and 0 if released.
Example:

```
/*  wait until stop button pressed  */
while (!stop_button()) {}
```

`int start_button()`

Returns value of button labeled START.

`void stop_press()`

Waits for STOP button to be pressed, then released. Then issues a short beep and returns.

The code for `stop_press` is as follows:

```
while (!stop_button());
while (stop_button());
beep();
```

`void start_press()`

Like `stop_press`, but for the START button.

`int knob()`

Returns the position of a knob as a value from 0 to 255.

Infrared Subsystem   The Handy Board provides an onboard IR receiver (the Sharp IS1U60), for IR input, and a 40 kHz modulation and power drive circuit, for IR output. The output circuit requires an external IR LED.

To use the IR reception function, the file `sony-ir.icb` must be loaded into Interactive C. This file may be added to the Handy Board default library file, `lib_hb.lis`. *Please make sure that the file* `r22_ir.lis` *is not present in the* `lib_hb.lis` *file.*

The `sony-ir.icb` file adds the capability of receiving IR codes transmitted by a Sony remote or a universal remote programmed to transmit Sony IR codes.

```
int sony_init(1)
```
Enables the IR driver.

```
int sony_init(0)
```
Disables the IR driver.

```
int ir_data(int dummy)
```
Returns the data byte last received by the driver or zero if no data have been received since the last call. A value must be provided for the `dummy` argument, but its value is ignored.

The IR sensor is the dark green component in the Handy Board's lower right hand corner.

Time Commands

System code keeps track of time passage in milliseconds. The time variables are implemented using the long integer data type. Standard functions allow floating point variables when using the timing functions.

```
void reset_system_time()
```
Resets the count of system time to zero milliseconds.

```
long mseconds()
```
Returns the count of system time in milliseconds. Time count is reset by hardware reset (i.e., turning the board off and on) or the function `reset_system_time()`. `mseconds()` is implemented as a C primitive (not as a library function).

```
float seconds()
```
Returns the count of system time in seconds as a floating point number. Resolution is one millisecond.

```
void sleep(float sec)
```
Waits for an amount of time equal to or slightly greater than `sec` seconds. `sec` is a floating point number.
Example:

```
/*  wait for 1.5 seconds  */
sleep(1.5);
```

```
void msleep(long msec)
```
Waits for an amount of time equal to or greater than `msec` milliseconds. `msec` is a long integer.
Example:

```
/*  wait for 1.5 seconds  */
msleep(1500L);
```

Tone Functions

Several commands are provided for producing tones on the standard beeper.

```
void beep()
```
Produces a tone of 500 Hertz for 0.3 seconds.

```
void tone(float frequency, float length)
```
Produces a tone at pitch `frequency` Hertz for `length` seconds. Both `frequency` and `length` are floats.

```
void set_beeper_pitch(float frequency)
```
Sets the beeper tone to be `frequency` Hz. The subsequent function is then used to turn the beeper on.

```
void beeper_on()
```
Turns on the beeper at last frequency selected by the former function.

```
void beeper_off()
```
Turns off the beeper.

E.3.8 Multitasking

Overview

One of the most powerful features of IC is its multitasking facility. Processes can be created and destroyed dynamically during runtime.

Any C function can be spawned as a separate task. Multiple tasks running the same code, but with their own local variables, can be created.

Processes communicate through global variables: One process can set a global to some value, and another process can read the value of that global.

Each time a process runs, it executes for a certain number of *ticks* defined in milliseconds. This value is determined for each process at the time it is created. The default number of ticks is five; therefore, a default process will run for 5 milliseconds until its "turn" ends and the next process is run. All processes are kept track of in a *process table*; each time through the table, each process runs once (for an amount of time equal to its number of ticks).

Each process has its own *program stack*. The stack is used to pass arguments for function calls, store local variables, and store return addresses from function calls. The size of this stack is defined at the time a process is created. The default size of a process stack is 256 bytes.

Processes that make extensive use of recursion or use large local arrays will probably require a stack size larger than the default. Each function call requires two stack bytes (for the return address) plus the number of argument bytes; if the function that is called creates local variables, then they also use up stack space. In addition, C expressions create intermediate values that are stored on the stack.

It is up to the programmer to determine whether a particular process requires a stack size larger than the default. A process may also be created with a stack size *smaller* than the default, to save stack memory space, if it is known that the process will not require the full default amount.

When a process is created, it is assigned a unique *process identification number* or *pid*. This number can be used to kill a process.

Creating New Processes

The function to create a new process is `start_process`. `start_process` takes one mandatory argument—the function call to be started as a process. There are two optional arguments: the process number of ticks and stack size. (If only one optional argument is given, it is assumed to be the ticks number, and the default stack size is used.)

`start_process` has the following syntax:

```
int start_process( function-call( ... ) , [TICKS] , [STACK-SIZE] )
```

`start_process` returns an integer, which is the process ID assigned to the new process.

The function call may be any valid call of the function used. The following code shows the function `main` creating a process:

```
void check_sensor(int n)
{
  while (1)
    printf("Sensor %d is %d\n", n, digital(n));
}

void main()
{
  start_process(check_sensor(2));
}
```

Normally when a C functions ends, it exits with a return value or the "void" value. If a function invoked as a process ends, it "dies," letting its return value (if there was one) disappear. (This is okay because processes communicate results by storing them in globals, not by returning them as return values.) Hence, in the prior example, the check_sensor function is defined as an infinite loop so as to run forever (until the board is reset or a kill_process is executed).

Creating a process with a nondefault number of ticks or a nondefault stack size is simply a matter of using start_process with optional arguments; for example,

```
start_process(check_sensor(2), 1, 50);
```

will create a check_sensor process that runs for 1 millisecond per invocation and has a stack size of 50 bytes (for the given definition of check_sensor, a small stack space would be sufficient).

Destroying Processes

The kill_process function is used to destroy processes. Processes are destroyed by passing their process ID number to kill_process according to the following syntax:

```
int kill_process(int pid)
```

kill_process returns a value indicating whether the operation was successful. If the return value is 0, then the process was destroyed. If the return value is 1, then the process was not found.

The following code shows the main process creating a check_sensor process and then destroying it 1 second later:

```
void main()
{
  int pid;

  pid= start_process(check_sensor(2));
  sleep(1.0);
  kill_process(pid);
}
```

Process Management Commands

IC has two commands to help with process management. The commands only work when used at the IC command line. They are not C functions that can be used in code.

```
kill_all
```
kills all currently running processes.

```
ps
```
prints out a list of the process status.

The following information is presented: process ID, status code, program counter, stack pointer, stack pointer origin, number of ticks, and name of function that is currently executing.

Process Management Library Functions

The following functions are implemented in the standard C library.

```
void hog_processor()
```
Allocates an additional 256 milliseconds of execution to the currently running process. If this function is called repeatedly, the system will wedge and only execute the process that is calling `hog_processor()`. Only a system reset will unwedge from this state. Needless to say, this function should be used with extreme care and should not be placed in a loop unless wedging the machine is the desired outcome.

```
void defer()
```
Makes a process swap out immediately after the function is called. Useful if a process knows that it will not need to do any work until the next time around the scheduler loop. `defer()` is implemented as a C built-in function.

E.3.9 Floating Point Functions

In addition to basic floating point arithmetic (addition, subtraction, multiplication, and division) and floating point comparisons, a number of exponential and transcendental functions are built into IC. These are implemented with a public domain library of routines provided by Motorola.

Keep in mind that all floating point operations are quite slow; each takes one to several milliseconds to complete. If Interactive C's speed seems to be poor, extensive use of floating point operations is a likely cause.

```
float sin(float angle)
```
Returns sine of `angle`. Angle is specified in radians; result is in radians.

```
float cos(float angle)
```
Returns cosine of `angle`. Angle is specified in radians; result is in radians.

```
float tan(float angle)
```
Returns tangent of `angle`. Angle is specified in radians; result is in radians.

```
float atan(float angle)
```
Returns arc tangent of `angle`. Angle is specified in radians; result is in radians.

```
float sqrt(float num)
```
Returns square root of `num`.

```
float log10(float num)
```
Returns logarithm of `num` to the base 10.

```
float log(float num)
```
Returns natural logarithm of `num`.

```
float exp10(float num)
```
Returns 10 to the `num` power.

```
float exp(float num)
```
Returns e to the `num` power.

```
(float) a ^ (float) b
```
Returns a to the b power.

E.3.10 Memory Access Functions

IC has primitives for directly examining and modifying memory contents. These should be used with care because it would be easy to corrupt memory and crash the system using these functions.

There should be little need to use these functions. Most interaction with system memory should be done with arrays and/or globals.

```
int peek(int loc)
```
Returns the byte located at address `loc`.

```
int peekword(int loc)
```
Returns the 16-bit value located at address `loc` and `loc+1`. `loc` has the most significant byte, as per the 6811 16-bit addressing standard.

```
void poke(int loc, int byte)
```
Stores the 8-bit value `byte` at memory address `loc`.

```
void pokeword(int loc, int word)
```
Stores the 16-bit value `word` at memory addresses `loc` and `loc+1`.

```
void bit_set(int loc, int mask)
```
Sets bits that are set in `mask` at memory address `loc`.

```
void bit_clear(int loc, int mask)
```
Clears bits that are set in `mask` at memory address `loc`.

E.3.11 Error Handling

There are two types of errors that can happen when working with IC: *compile-time* errors and *runtime* errors.

Compile-time errors occur during the compilation of the source file. They are indicative of mistakes in the C source code. Typical compile-time errors result from incorrect syntax or mismatching of data types.

Runtime errors occur while a program is running on the board. They indicate problems with a valid C form when it is running. A simple example would be a divide-by-zero error. Another example might be running out of stack space if a recursive procedure goes too deep in recursion.

These types of errors are handled differently, as is explained below.

Compile-Time Errors

When compiler errors occur, an error message is printed to the screen. All compile-time errors must be fixed before a file can be downloaded to the board.

Runtime Errors

When a runtime error occurs, an error message is displayed on the LCD screen indicating the error number. If the board is hooked up to IC when the error occurs, a more verbose error message is printed on the terminal.

Here is a list of the runtime error codes:

Error Code	Description
1	no stack space for start_process()
2	no process slots remaining
3	array reference out of bounds
4	stack overflow error in running process
5	operation with invalid pointer
6	floating point underflow
7	floating point overflow
8	floating point divide-by-zero
9	number too small or large to convert to integer
10	tried to take square root of negative number
11	tangent of 90 degrees attempted
12	log or ln of negative number or zero
15	floating point format error in printf
16	integer divide-by-zero

E.3.12 Binary Programs

With the use of a customized 6811 assembler program, IC allows the use of machine language programs within the C environment. There are two ways that machine language programs may be incorporated:

1. Programs may be called from C as if they were C functions.
2. Programs may install themselves into the interrupt structure of the 6811, running repetitiously or when invoked due to a hardware or software interrupt.

When operating as a function, the interface between C and a binary program is limited: A binary program must be given one integer as an argument and will return an integer as its return value. However, programs in a binary file can declare any number of global integer variables in the C environment. Also, the binary program can use its argument as a pointer to a C data structure.

The Binary Source File

Special keywords in the source assembly language file (or module) are used to establish the following features of the binary program:

Entry point. The entry point for calls to each program defined in the binary file.

Initialization entry point. Each file may have one routine that is called automatically on a reset condition. (The reset conditions are explained in Section E.3.3, which discusses global variable initialization.) This initialization routine is particularly useful for programs that will function as interrupt routines.

C variable definitions. Any number of two-byte C integer variables may be declared within a binary file. When the module is loaded into IC, these variables become defined as globals in C.

To explain how these features work, let's look at a sample IC binary source program listed in Figure E.2.

The first statement of the file ("ORG MAIN_START") declares the start of the binary programs. This line must precede the code itself.

The entry point for a program to be called from C is declared with a special form beginning with the text subroutine_. In this case, the name of the binary program is double, so the label is named subroutine_double. As the comment indicates, this is a program that will double the value of the argument passed to it.

FIGURE E.2 Sample IC Binary
Source File: `testicb.asm`

```
/* Sample icb file */

/* origin for module and variables */
ORG     MAIN_START

/* program to return twice the argument passed to us */
subroutine_double:
ASLD
  RTS

/* declaration for the variable "foo" */
variable_foo:
FDB     55

/* program to set the C variable "foo" */
subroutine_set_foo:
STD     variable_foo
  RTS

/* program to retrieve the variable "foo" */
subroutine_get_foo:
LDD     variable_foo
  RTS

/* code that runs on reset conditions */
subroutine_initialize_module:
LDD     #69
  STD     variable_foo
  RTS
```

When the binary program is called from C, it is passed one integer argument. This argument is placed in the 6811's D register (also known as the "Double Accumulator") before the binary code is called.

The `double` program doubles the number in the D register. The `ASLD` instruction ("Arithmetic Shift Left Double [Accumulator]") is equivalent to multiplying by 2; hence this doubles the number in the D register.

The `RTS` instruction is "Return from Subroutine." All binary programs must exit using this instruction. When a binary program exits, the value in the D register is the return value to C. Thus, the `double` program doubles its C argument and returns it to C.

Declaring Variables in Binary Files

The label `variable_foo` is an example of a special form to declare the name and location of a variable accessible from C. The special label prefix "`variable_`" is followed the name of the variable, in this case, "`foo`."

This label must be immediately followed by the statement `FDB <number>`. This is an assembler directive that creates a two-byte value (which is the initial value of the variable).

Variables used by binary programs must be declared in the binary file. These variables then become C globals when the binary file is loaded into C.

The next binary program in the file is named "`set_foo`." It performs the action of setting the value of the variable `foo`, which is defined later in the file. It does this by storing the D register into the memory contents reserved for `foo` and then returning.

After User Program Installation

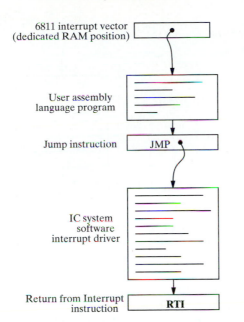

6811 interrupt vector
(dedicated RAM position)

User assembly
language program

Jump instruction — JMP

IC system
software
interrupt driver

Return from Interrupt
instruction — **RTI**

FIGURE E.3 Interrupt Structure Before User Program Installation

The next binary program is named "get_foo." It loads the D register from the memory reserved for foo and then returns.

Declaring an Initialization Program The label subroutine_initialize_module is a special form used to indicate the entry point for code that should be run to initialize the binary programs. This code is run on standard reset conditions: program download, hardware reset, or running of the main() function.

In the example shown, the initialization code stores the value 69 into the location reserved for the variable foo. This then overwrites the 55, which would otherwise be the default value for that variable.

Initialization of globals variables defined in an binary module is done differently than globals defined in C. In a binary module, the globals are initialized to the value declared by the FDB statement only when the code is downloaded to the 6811 board (not on reset or running of main, like normal globals).

However, the initialization routine is run on standard reset conditions and can be used to initialize globals, as this example has illustrated.

Interrupt-Driven Binary Programs

Interrupt-driven binary programs use the initialization sequence of the binary module to install a piece of code into the interrupt structure of the 6811.

The 6811 has a number of different interrupts, mostly dealing with its on-chip hardware such as timers and counters. One of these interrupts is used by the runtime software to implement time-keeping and other periodic functions (such as LCD screen management). This interrupt, dubbed the "System Interrupt," runs at 1,000 Hertz.

Instead of using another 6811 interrupt to run user binary programs, additional programs (that need to run at 1,000 Hz or less) may install themselves into the System Interrupt. User programs would then become part of the 1,000 Hz interrupt sequence.

This is accomplished by having the user program "intercept" the original 6811 interrupt vector that points to runtime interrupt code. This vector is made to point at the user program. When user program finishes, it jumps to the start of the runtime interrupt code.

FIGURE E.4 Interrupt Structure
After User Program Installation

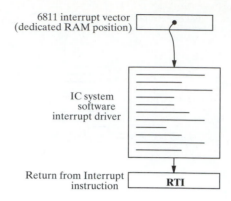

Figure E.3 depicts the interrupt structure before user program installation. The 6811 vector location points to system software code, which terminates in a "return from interrupt" instruction.

Figure E.4 illustrates the result after the user program is installed. The 6811 vector points to the user program, which exits by jumping to the system software driver. This driver exits as before, with the RTI instruction.

Multiple user programs could be installed in this fashion. Each one would install itself ahead of the previous one. Some standard library functions, such as the shaft encoder software, are implemented in this fashion.

Figure E.5 shows an example program that installs itself into the System Interrupt. This program toggles the signal line controlling the piezo beeper every time it is run; because the System Interrupt runs at 1,000 Hz, this program will create a continous tone of 500 Hz.

The first line after the comment header includes a file named "6811regs.asm". This file contains equates for all 6811 registers and interrupt vectors; most binary programs will need at least a few of these. It is simplest to keep them all in one file that can be easily included.

The subroutine_initialize_module declaration begins the initialization portion of the program. The file "ldxibase.asm" is then included. This file contains a few lines of 6811 assembler code that perform the function of determining the base pointer to the 6811 interrupt vector area and loading this pointer into the 6811 X register.

The following four lines of code install the interrupt program (beginning with the label interrupt_code_start) according to the method that was illustrated in Figure E.4.

First, the existing interrupt pointer is fetched. As indicated by the comment, the 6811's TOC4 timer is used to implement the System Interrupt. The vector is poked into the JMP instruction that will conclude the interrupt code.

Next, the 6811 interrupt pointer is replaced with a pointer to the new code. These two steps complete the initialization sequence.

The actual interrupt code is quite short. It toggles Bit 3 of the 6811's PORTA register. The PORTA register controls the eight pins of Port A that connect to external hardware; Bit 3 is connected to the piezo beeper.

The interrupt code exits with a jump instruction. The argument for this jump is poked in by the initialization program.

The method allows any number of programs located in separate files to attach themselves to the System Interrupt. Because these files can be loaded from the C environment, this system affords maximal flexibility to the user, with small overhead in terms of code efficiency.

FIGURE E.5 `sysibeep.asm`:
Binary Program That Installs
into System Interrupt

```
* icb file:  "sysibeep.asm"

    *
    *    example of code installing itself into
    *    SystemInt 1000 Hz interrupt
    *
    *    Fred Martin
    *    Thu Oct 10 21:12:13 1991
    *

#include <6811regs.asm>

    ORG      MAIN_START

subroutine_initialize_module:

#include <ldxibase.asm>
* X now has base pointer to interrupt vectors ($FF00 or $BF00)

* get current vector; poke such that when we finish, we go there
    LDD      TOC4INT,X            ; SystemInt on TOC4
    STD      interrupt_code_exit+1

    * install ourself as new vector
    LDD      #interrupt_code_start
    STD      TOC4INT,X

    RTS

    * interrupt program begins here
interrupt_code_start:
* frob the beeper every time called
    LDAA     PORTA
    EORA     #%00001000       ; beeper bit
    STAA     PORTA

interrupt_code_exit:
JMP      $0000     ; this value poked in by init routine
```

The Binary Object File

The source file for a binary program must be named with the `.asm` suffix. Once the `.asm` file is created, a special version of the 6811 assembler program is used to construct the binary object code. This program creates a file containing the assembled machine code plus label definitions of entry points and C variables.

The program `as11_ic` is used to assemble the source code and create a binary object file. It is given the file name of the source file as an argument. The resulting object file is automatically given the suffix `.icb` (for IC Binary). Figure E.6 shows the binary object file that is created from the `testicb.asm` example file.

Loading an ICB File

Once the `.icb` file is created, it can be loaded into IC just like any other C file. If there are C functions that are to be used in conjunction with the binary programs, it is

FIGURE E.6 *Sample IC Binary Object File:* `testicb.icb`

```
S116802005390037FD802239FC802239CC0045FD8022393C
S9030000FC
S116872B05390037FD872D39FC872D39CC0045FD872D39F4
S9030000FC
6811 assembler version 2.1  10-Aug-91
  please send bugs to Randy Sargent (rsargent@athena.mit.edu)
  original program by Motorola.
subroutine_double 872b *0007
subroutine_get_foo 8733 *0021
subroutine_initialize_module 8737 *0026
subroutine_set_foo 872f *0016
variable_foo 872d *0012 0017 0022 0028
```

customary to put them into a file with the same name as the `.icb` file and then use a `.lis` file to loads the two files together.

Passing Array Pointers to a Binary Program

A pointer to an array is a 16-bit integer address. To coerce an array pointer to an integer, use the following form:

```
array_ptr= (int) array;
```

where `array_ptr` is an integer and `array` is an array.

When compiling code that performs this type of pointer conversion, IC must be used in a special mode. Normally, IC does not allow certain types of pointer manipulation that may crash the system. To compile this type of code, use the following invokation:

```
ic -wizard
```

Arrays are internally represented with a two-byte length value followed by the array contents.

E.3.13 IC File Formats and Management

This section explains how IC deals with multiple source files.

C Programs

All files containing C code must be named with the ".`c`" suffix.

Loading functions from more than one C file can be done by issuing commands at the IC prompt to load each of the files. For example, to load the C files named `foo.c` and `bar.c`:

```
C> load foo.c
C> load bar.c
```

Alternatively, the files could be loaded with a single command:

```
C> load foo.c bar.c
```

If the files to be loaded contain dependencies (e.g., if one file has a function that references a variable or function defined in the other file), then the second method (multiple file names to one load command) or the following approach must be used.

List Files

If the program is separated into multiple files that are always loaded together, a "list file" may be created. This file tells IC to load a set of named files. Continuing the previous example, a file called `gnu.lis` can be created:

Listing of `gnu.lis`:

```
foo.c
bar.c
```

Then typing the command `load gnu.lis` from the C prompt would cause both `foo.c` and `bar.c` to be loaded.

File and Function Management

Unloading Files   When files are loaded into IC, they stay loaded until they are explicitly unloaded. This is usually the functionality that is desired. If one of the program files is being worked on, the other ones will remain in memory so that they don't have to be explicitly reloaded each time the one undergoing development is reloaded.

However, suppose the file `foo.c` is loaded, which contains a definition for the function `main`. Then the file `bar.c` is loaded, which happens to also contain a definition for `main`. There will be an error message because both files contain a `main`. IC will unload `bar.c`, due to the error, and redownload `foo.c` and any other files that are presently loaded.

The solution is to first unload the file containing the `main` that is not desired and then load the file that contains the new `main`:

```
C> unload foo.c
C> load bar.c
```

E.3.14 Configuring IC

IC has a multitude of command-line switches that allow control of a number of things. With command-line versions of IC, explanations for these switches can be gotten by issuing the command "`ic -help`".

IC stores the search path for and name of the library files internally; theses may be changed by executing the command "`ic -config`". When this command is run, IC will prompt for a new path and library file name and create a new executable copy of itself with these changes.

The Macintosh version of IC is configured by changing the values of STR resources using a utility like ResEdit.

APPENDIX

Robot Contests

The Handy Board and Interactive C were developed as part of the MIT LEGO Robot Design Competition. In this project, MIT undergraduates spend one month designing, testing, and debugging a fleet of autonomous robots which play against one another in a final contest event.

Robot contests like the MIT Robot Design project are a popular and exciting forum for engineering students and hobbyists to showcase their ideas. In this appendix we explore robot contests from both pedagogical and practical perspectives. Four different contest designs are presented and analyzed. Through this discussion, we will gain a greater understanding of the role of robot contests in learning, and how to create a challenging and successful contest.

F.1 Introduction

In this section we'll discuss two fundamental types of robot contests, consider the value of robot contests—and alternatives—as a pedagogical tool, and think about the larger social meaning of particular contest designs.

F.1.1 Why Robot Contests?

Design contests have a long tradition in engineering education. A well-designed challenge provides a structure for creative inquiry, focusing participants on interesting design problems.

The contest simulates real-world engineering constraints. Material resources can be limited by providing participants with a fixed kit of parts. A performance event establishes a time limit for completing one's work. What often comes as a surprise to most novice designers is that time is often a more limited resource than materials!

Contests also provide an exciting public forum for showcasing participants' work. Even when the competition rules officially recognize only the technical aspects of a robot's performance, an entertaining robot will rouse the audience. This excitement will not be lost on its designers.

F.1.2 Why Not Contests?

There are limitations of robot contests as a pedagogical tool. Students can innovate and be creative *within* the domain of the contest. But students are not being asked to think more broadly, considering robotics as a special case within the larger area of interactive, computational devices.

As an example alternative, Robbie Berg and Franklyn Turbak have created a *Robotic Art Studio* course at Wellesley College.[1] In this class, students create a variety of interactive robotic demonstrations, which are presented to the public in an art gallery

---

[1] http://www.wellesley.edu/Physics/robots/studio.html

opening-style event. Past projects in the class have included a xylophone player, various robotic pets, and a Venus flytrap flower. The most interesting of these projects involve the visitors as a participant in seeing the project in action—for example, a person can "feed" the Venus flytrap an "insect" hanging from a string, and then see the jaws of the flytrap close on it. In the context of the Robotic Art Studio, students get a unique opportunity to express creative technical *and* artistic ideas.

It's also important to provide students with a collegial, supportive learning environment. In a contest situation, students can take the competitive element too far, and there can be a tendency to keep ideas to themselves, working in isolation to protect a strategy, for example. A friendly, supportive atmosphere, in which students can freely collaborate can make a big difference in encouraging learning. In MIT contests, teams in recitation sections are not paired up against one another in early rounds of the contest, and valuable prizes are not offered to contest winners, to keep the competition on a friendly and fun rather than serious and important level.

More generally, the question of contests versus alternative like the Wellesley Robotic Art Studio boils down to constraints and freedom in promoting creativity. A well-designed contest has a lot of structure—there is a specific task that must be accomplished—but it should seem wide open, like there is an infinitude of ways that one could take in solving it. Correspondingly, a design project like "Make a interactive artwork that engages the viewer" allows for great creative leaps, but is supported by the specific materials that are provided (in this case, the Handy Board, LEGO mechanics, sensors, motors, and programming). In both contexts, there are simultaneous ingredients of something wide open with possibility, and something structured that can guide creativity.

F.1.3 Types of Contests

Fundamentally, there are two types of robot contests: single-robot events and multiple-robot events.

Single-robot events are solo performance runs; the obstacle course is a good metaphor for such contests. There is a task, and robots perform one at a time, attempting to accomplish the task. Typically, a robot's score is a based on the fraction of the task completed and how much time was consumed doing so.

Multiple-robot events involve two or more robots playing at the same time in the same environment. This can range from games where two robots are independently attempting to perform a task, to team events where multiple robots compete for limited resources, to demolition derby-type matches.

Multiple-robot games tend to be more interesting because of the possibility of robots interacting, and the implications for each robot's strategy because of this. When two robots meet, however, the most likely result is that they simply become entangled, effectively removing them both from the pursuit of other activity. This can be the intended result of one of the robot's strategy (c.g., score some points and get an early lead, then find the other robot and bang into it, keeping it from scoring), but more typically, robots accidentally collide and it's ultimately disappointing. Even in gladiator-style events, it's quite difficult for a robot to convincingly damage its opponents; little robots can do little more than push each other around, and as the "weight class" goes up, so does the amount of thick metal protection on each design.

So the challenge, as a contest designer, is to encourage *meaningful* multiple-robot interaction. This may be done with contests that encourage cooperation between robots, or require robots to play both offensively (scoring points for themselves or points against their opponent) and defensively (preventing such scoring).

Multiple-robot contests have the additional benefit that they allow for the possibility that there is not a single best design. In a single-robot contest, each robot's performance is reduced to a one-dimensional score; by ranking the scores one determines the "best" robot. In a multiple-robot challenge, however, it's possible that Robot A can defeat Robot B, Robot B can defeat Robot C, but the transitive is *not* true: Robot C can still defeat Robot A. (Think of the rock-scissors-paper game.) In real-world design problems there is not a single optimal solution, and the multiple-robot contest allows for such ambiguity.

F.1.4 Social Message

It is worth considering the social implications of promoting a particular robot contest. In recent years, concurrent with the popularity of so-called "professional" wrestling, there is interest in robotic gladiator contests. These robot demolition derbies are not only technically less interesting (the machines are remote-controlled, it being dangerous and difficult to build an autonomous destruction machine), but play into the lowest-common-denominator approach of the mass media.

Such destruction-oriented contests are certainly not suited for educational purposes. We have instead taken the approach of using sporting events like tennis or golf as inspiration for game play (not boxing or car-racing). In tennis or golf, skill is defined as being better able to play the game than one's opponent. Harming the opponent is explicitly *not* part of the game.

Many contests may use balls from a particular actual sport (ping-pong balls, golf balls, etc.) This lends naturally to employing that sport to help think about the robot version of the game—a robot golf that involves putting golf balls into holes, for example. For the contest's public audience, this is a nice way to build upon a familiar activity.

Entertainment value can be added to a robot contest by situating it in some kind of grand scenario. So robots aren't collecting golf balls; they're collecting treasure nuggets. If this helps make the game more interesting—and understandable—it's a fun addition.

Whatever contest and story is chosen, it's worth thinking about it from a social standpoint—what sort of message about the use of technology is the contest promulgating?

F.2 Sample Contests

In this section we'll look at four different robot contests. The full rules for each contest are included, followed by a discussion of the special qualities of each. These contests may be used exactly as presented, or serve as springboards for new contest designs.

The four contests are:

Kick the Can. An introductory, single-robot challenge that is easy to set up and encourages quick, starter robot designs.

Robo-Golf. A basic two-robot game. In *Robo-Golf*, the robots collect golf balls and try to deposit them into a single center hole.

Robo-Pong. Used in the MIT Robot Design course in 1991, *Robo-Pong* is a two-robot challenge in which the goal is to transport ping-pong balls to the other robot's side of the table.

Egg-Hunt. Designed at Case-Western Reserve University, the *Egg-Hunt* is a multiple-robot, team-oriented challenge in which the robots must perform for an extended period of time, collecting pastel-colored eggs while avoiding black ones.

F.2.1 Kick the Can

Kick the Can is a great introductory contest. It would make a good warm-up contest to introduce students to the whole process of design, performance, and testing, or as a final contest in a project where there were not a lot of time available for the design task.

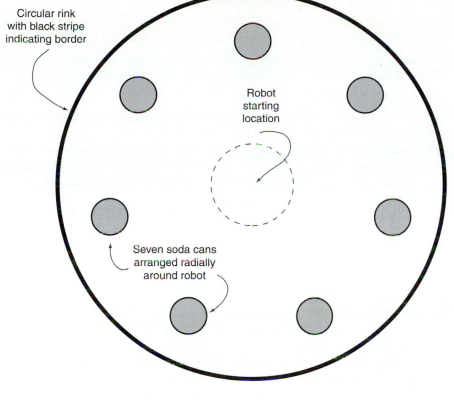

Circular rink
with black stripe
indicating border

Robot
starting
location

Seven soda cans
arranged radially
around robot

FIGURE F.1 Kick the Can Contest Diagram

Kick the Can is played on a flat surface demarked by a black circular line about four feet in diameter. The playing field may be built from white posterboard with the circular line drawn by a large marker pen or laid out with black electrical tape.

Kick the Can is played on a white circular rink demarked by a thick black line at the circumference. Seven 12 oz. cans of soda are placed in marked positions, arranged radially from the center. The goal is to remove soda cans from the inside the rink as quickly as possible.

Rules

The robot is placed in the center of the rink. When the round begins, the robot must attempt to remove the cans from the rink. The round ends when either all cans are removed from the rink, or one minute of time has elapsed (whichever comes first). The final score is the count of cans removed (if one or more remains), or the amount of time required to remove all of the cans. If no robot removes all of the cans, the robot removing the greatest number wins; otherwise, the robot which removes all the cans in the shortest time wins.

Figure F.1 illustrates the playing field.

Cans

- The soda cans are regular 12 oz. cans of carbonated soda, unopened. Beware of rough handling, which may cause cans to rupture and spray soda on your robot!

- The cans will be placed at designated positions in the playing field before the start of the round.

- Cans are declared outside of the rink when the entire can is beyond the inside edge of the playing field boundary, when the can is viewed from directly above.

- Once a can is declared outside the rink, it can not be counted as being inside, even it if rolls back. After being declared outside the rink, cans may be removed from the playing field at the judges' discretion.

Period of Play

- To set up the round, the contestant will place the robot in the designated starting circle. The contestant may choose the initial orientation of the robot.
- The powered portion of a round will last 60 seconds: After the machines are started, they will have 60 seconds to apply battery power to their motors.
- The round ends when all machines and cans come to rest.
- The start of the round will be indicated by a judge, upon whose signal the contestant will press a button on the robot to start play.
- The machines must have their own internal clock (software will be provided to do this) which cuts off power to the motors at the end of 60 seconds. Any machines that continue to supply actuator power after 60 seconds will be disqualified.

Control

- All entries must be solely controlled by their onboard computer. There can be no human intervention once the round begins.

Discussion

Kick the Can is simple contest; it can readily be solved by a robot with just a light sensor to detect the edge of the playing field. Such a robot could drive forward, hoping to catch a can, until it detects the playing field edge, at which point it would back up and turn, ready to head toward the next can.

There are many opportunities to make the game more interesting. The cans can be arranged less symmetrically, and the robot's initial starting orientation may be randomized. The number of cans and size of the rink may be varied.

It may be desirable to set a size limitation on robots, or a size limitation at the beginning of the round. Otherwise, robots can grow large arms to push multiple cans at the same time. On the other hand, this problem can be self-limiting: if a robot tries to push too many cans at once, it often does not have the traction or power to do so!

In short, even though *Kick the Can* is simple, it allows for a lot of design diversity—a good standard for evaluating any contest.

F.2.2 Robo-Golf

Robo-Golf is a two-robot challenge. The robots perform on a flat playing field about six by four feet in size. The goal is to collect golf balls and deposit them into the hole in the center of the playing field. Whichever robot ends up with more of its balls in the hole at the end of the one-minute round is the winner.

Rules

Goal and Scoring

- Figure F.2 shows the robot playing table. Please note that all measurements are approximate, and that your robot must perform on the actual table, not the idealized description of it.
- The goal of the game is to score more balls than your opponent. Rounds will last one minute each, and robots will have at least two rounds, against different opponents, in actual contest play.
- Game scores accumulate from round to round. That is, if you score three balls in your first round and five balls in your second round, your total score is eight. Therefore it is less important to win any particular round than it is to score well overall. During contest play, judges may elect to have a run-off against the best-

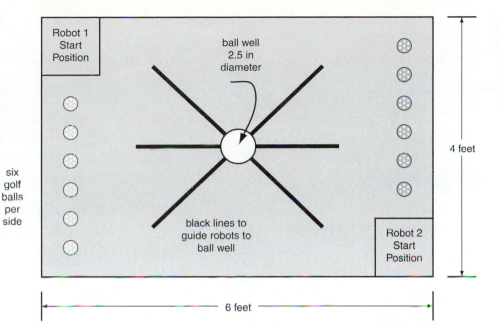

The *Robo-Golf* contest table is built from plywood. The table surface can be painted a light green color to suggest the golf greens. Underneath the ball well, a chute brings deposited balls to the front of the table, in view for the audience. A lamp mounted underneath the ball well lets robots know when they're in the proper position.

scoring robots, in which they may decide to reset all robots' scores to zero for the runoff. Judges may also elect to have a run-off in which previous scores are kept.

- The robot will be turned to one of four ninety-degree rotations, randomly chosen by a judge, before each contest round begins. Both robots will be turned to the symettrically same rotation before each round. E.g., if one robot is aimed toward its balls, the other will be also. Contestants must provide a marking on their robots to indicate which direction is the robot's "front."

The Robot

- Robots must fit fully within the marked robot start positions before the round begins. "Fitting fully" is defined as no portion of the robot being beyond the marked starting square from a birds-eye view of the field. There is no height restriction on robots before game play begins, and there is no size restriction on robots whatsoever after game play begins.

- Contestants will be provided with one LEGO MINDSTORMS Robotics Invention System (part #9719) and one RoboSports Expansion Set (part #9730). All robots must be built solely from the parts provided in these two kits. Nonfunctional decorative additions (e.g., LEGO minifigs) may be added at the discretion of the judges.

- No glue, tape, or adhesive materials of any form are allowed. Contestants found using such materials on their robots will be unceremoniously disqualified.

Contest Questions and Answers

- Q. Can you rebuild your robot between rounds?

    A. You may repair damage that your robot has sustained, but you cannot change the design of your robot.

- Q. Can you have multiple programs loaded onto your robot, and choose which one you would like to run depending on your opponent?

    A. Yes. You may select which one you will run after knowing who your opponent will be. However, you must select which program you will run before the random orientation is announced; you cannot deal with the random orientations by choosing a specific program.

- Q. Do I have control over my robot's placement within the starting square, given the specified orientation?

    A. Yes. You can place your robot however you like within the starting square (e.g., with its sensors touching the walls), as long as the robot is (1) facing the specified orientation, and (2) not protruding beyond the marked square.

- Q. Can I cut up or otherwise modify the LEGO elements provided?

    A. No. The LEGO elements must not be modified from their stock configuration.

- Q. Is the cardboard box and packaging material considered part of the kit for robot design purposes?

    A. No. The cardboard box and packaging materials are not part of the kit, and therefore may be used for decorative purposes only.

Discussion

Robo-Golf had an evident flaw that if all that mattered were winning single rounds, it would make sense to fetch and deposit just one ball quickly, and then block the hole from the opponent. If all participants were to gravitate to this design, it would make for a fairly boring final event.

Based on this observation, ball scores were allowed to accumulate between rounds. As stated in the rules, "it is less important to win any particular round than it is to score well overall." Thus, it became important that participants design their robots to score multiple balls in a round.

This was borne out in the final contest. All of the robots were designed to score repeatedly. There was a mixture of robots that would score one ball at a time before going back for more, and robots that attempted to collect most or all of the balls before heading toward the goal.

The initial orientation rule caused much consternation among the participants. Many hit upon the solution of using forward- and side-mounted touch sensors. They pressed their robot up against the corner of the table before the round started. Then the initial orientation could be deduced from which combination (or none) of the sensors was depressed.

Their code would then branch to a specific movement for each rotation. In a sense, this solution reduced the randomized rotation to a nuisance rather than a problem requiring more versatility in the fundamental design. A more complex initial rotation system might be required to cause students to consider how to make their robots more generally deal with uncertainty.

The multiple-program rule was added at the request of the students. They ended up not using it. It is an interesting idea to allow robots to run different programs based on the participants' assessment of their opponent. In practice, it's quite difficult to get just one program to work reliably. Still, in a contest of highly proficient designers, it could add a human strategy factor to the event.

F.2.3 Robo-Pong

Robo-Pong was developed for the 1991 version of the MIT Robot Design contest. *Robo-Pong* is a two-robot game in which the object is to transport balls onto the other robot's side of the table. The contest was described in detail as part of the discussion on control in Chapter 5. Please refer to a diagram of the *Robo-Pong* playing field on page 194.

Rules

Balls

- The balls will be practice golf balls. These are similar in weight to ping pong balls, but are slightly larger and have less bounce. They will be painted.
- There will be fifteen balls on the playing surface at the start of a round which will start at predetermined locations. Three balls will start at the top plateau. Each side of the table will have six evenly spaced balls in the player's flat area. There will be small depressions in the playing surface to hold the balls at the beginning of a round.
- The balls are inert and all have identical properties.
- Robots may gather balls "into" their body.
- The balls may not be altered or destroyed in any way.
- If a ball leaves the playing space, then the point at which it leaves the space (crosses the rim) will determine its permanent position on the playing field for scoring purposes. E.g.: if your robot pushes a ball off the opponent's side of the table, it counts as being permanently on that side of the table (for that round).

Period of Play

- The powered portion of a round will last 60 seconds: After the machines are started, they will have 60 seconds to apply battery power to their actuators (defined as motors and solenoids).
- The round ends when all machines and balls come to rest.
- The round will be started by the judges turning on the starting lights, located underneath the table in the center of each robot's starting circle, for the beginning 5 seconds.
- The contestants will place the machines on the playing field at a random angle with repect to the center per judges' instructions. The angle at which the machines will be placed will be the same for all machines during the same round, but will vary between rounds.
- The contestants will have 30 seconds to place their machines on the field from the time the judges call them.
- The contestants must stand a given distance away from the playing field. Any contestant that makes an attempt to touch their machine during the round of play will automatically be disqualified from the round.
- The machines must have their own internal clock (software will be provided to do this) which cuts off power to the motors at the end of 60 seconds. Any machines that continue to supply actuator power after 60 seconds will be disqualified.
- All rounds will have two robot players.
- Machines are not allowed to destroy their opponent's microprocessor board.
- Machines cannot try to destroy other machines' broadcast or detection beacons.

Scoring

- The winner(s) will be the machine with fewer balls on its side at the end of the round.

- A clear division between the two sides will be noted by having the surface of the two sides be painted in contrasting colors. Robots will be "told" which side they are starting on by the setting a DIP switch before the round begins. Dynamically, robots will be able to determine which side they are on by using reflectivity sensors aimed toward the playing surface.

Discussion

The *Robo-Pong* contest generated a nice variety of different designs. The most common was the "ball harvester," robots which collected the balls on their side of the table into U-shaped arms and then drove them onto the other robot's side of the table. Some of these harvesters held the balls inside their body, in which case the robot had to drive itself onto the opponent's side.

There was also a fair assortment of shooting robots. These fared less well since harvesters could recover most of the shot balls and bring them back to the shooter's side (few of the balls left the table in the "permanently scored against the opponent" fashion).

There were a couple of dual-robot strategies which combined a shooter robot and a blocking robot. These were difficult to accomplish, since getting just one robot to work properly is a challenge.

In retrospect, *Robo-Pong* had a design flaw which would have allowed a simple aggressor robot to win. The contest included an infrared beacon system which allowed robots to detect a direction vector toward the other robot. At the very start of the round, if a robot used this sensor to find the heading toward its opponent and drove straight toward it, it would push the middle ball on the plateau onto the opponent's side, and then be able to pin its opponent for the rest of the round. Such an "assassin" robot would have had a good chance of winning the whole event.

As it turned out, the simple assassin robot was not built. At least one team did field a robot based on this strategy, but it was a complex design that involved a radar-dish-like infrared detector that did not perform reliably enough to win the event.

A simple tweak to *Robo-Pong*'s rules would remove this problem: allow each robot's final ball tally to accumulate across trials, as described in the *Robo-Golf* contest. Then the assassin could win each round, but with only a margin of one ball, it would not be a viable long-term strategy.

F.2.4 Egg Hunt

The Case-Western Reserve University Egg Hunt competition is part of an undergraduate design course offered there [BCD99][2]. In this contest, teams of robots attempt to gather pastel-colored eggs into their own goal while avoiding black eggs. Each contest round lasts ten minutes—much longer than most other contests. The playing field is also quite large, measuring over 23 feet long and 11 feet wide (see Figure F.3).

Rules

Arena

- The Egg Hunt takes place in an octagonal arena with "nests" at either end (Figure F.3). The walls of the arena will be 12 inches high and painted flat black. The floor of the arena will be gray indoor-outdoor carpet.

- Each nest will be 3 feet wide by 2 feet deep and will be painted flat white. The nests have their own flat white floors to distinguish them from the arena carpeting. Across the entrance to each nest will be a metal strip (also painted flat white) that

---

[2] The course and contest were developed by Randall D. Beer, Hillel J. Chiel, and Richard F. Drushel. The contest rules and description are reprinted here with permission.

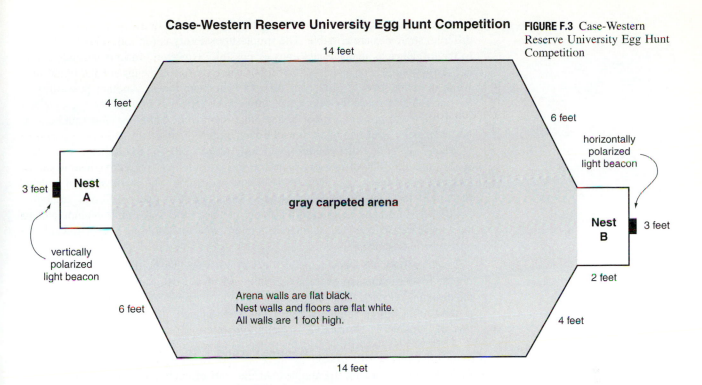

Case-Western Reserve University Egg Hunt Competition

FIGURE F.3 Case-Western Reserve University Egg Hunt Competition

14 feet

4 feet

6 feet

horizontally polarized light beacon

3 feet

Nest A

gray carpeted arena

Nest B

3 feet

vertically polarized light beacon

2 feet

Arena walls are flat black.
Nest walls and floors are flat white.
All walls are 1 foot high.

6 feet

4 feet

14 feet

will be high enough to prevent eggs from rolling out of the nest on their own, but which should not impede the free passage of robots.

- At the back of each nest will be a polarized incandescent light. The light in one nest will be vertically-polarized and the other will be horizontally polarized. You will be supplied with polarizing filters for the light sensors on your robot. You will find it necessary to utilize a robust scheme that is as insensitive as possible to changes in the ambient light.

- At the beginning of each round, each team will be assigned a polarization direction (and therefore a home nest). Thus, you should design your robot so that it can easily be switched from a horizontally polarized to a vertically polarized home nest and vice versa.

Eggs

- The arena will contain 40 pastel-colored eggs and 10 flat-black eggs randomly scattered throughout. These colors are chosen to simplify detection using the available light sensors.

- The object of the competition is for each team to gather as many pastel eggs as possible in its nest, while avoiding gathering black eggs. The winner of a round is the team with the higher score.

- In scoring, pastel eggs are worth $+1$ point, while black eggs are worth -4 points. The ratio of pastel/black eggs and their respective point values are deliberately chosen such that a completely random egg collection strategy results in a zero score. That is, if you gather all 50 eggs, your score is $40 + (-4 \times 10) = 0$.

Teams

- Robots will work in teams of two. We will choose the teams to create what we deem is the best balance.

- Since your team will be scored on the final contents of its home nest only, many different strategies are possible. The simplest possibility is for both robots on a team to try to gather as many pastel eggs as possible. However, various specializations are also possible. For example, one robot can try to gather eggs for the home nest while the other tries to steal eggs from the opponent's nest. Another possibility is for one robot to guard the home nest while the other robot forages for eggs. Or one robot can try to prevent a robot on the other team from gathering eggs (but be sure not to mistake your teammate for an opponent!).

    Recall our policy that you are financially responsible for any damage you cause to the controller boards or LEGOs before you consider too aggressive a strategy! In addition, since black eggs actually deduct points, it might be worthwhile to attempt to deposit them in the opponent's nest. There are also many different strategies for transporting eggs, from carrying them one at a time in a simple manipulator to carrying a set of them in an internal storage area to "shooting" them toward the nest from a distance.

- "Cloned" robots are forbidden. Each group must design, build, and debug its own unique robot. Teams are expressly prohibited to build two identical robots, whether the design is recycled from an existing mid-semester robot or is novel. While cloning a good robot design improves Egg Hunt performance, past experience has shown that this strategy is destructive to group dynamics.

Contest Format

- Each round will last for 10 minutes. At the start of each hunt, each team of robots will be placed side by side in front of its home nest.

- You should detect stalled motors and respond accordingly, because you will not be allowed to touch your robot once a round has begun. We reserve the right to free stuck robots as we deem necessary to keep the contest interesting and to avoid damage to the controller boards. We will not interfere with any strategy whereby one robot is actively preventing another from making progress, as long as there is no immediate danger to the controller boards.

Discussion

Egg Hunt is different from the other contests described here in two important ways. It takes place over an extended period of time—10 minutes versus a minute or less for the other contests. Also, *Egg Hunt* builds multiple-robot play into the contest, requiring each team to collectively build two robots (which must be different).

Both of these reasons make *Egg Hunt* particularly interesting from a pedagogical perspective. In terms of encouraging participants to build effective robots, *Egg Hunt* forces designers confront reliability concerns that can be missed with shorter contests. Many of the MIT contents are effectively solved with what I have called "sequential" robots—ones which perform a series of steps and fail badly if any of these steps goes wrong. Even if students agree that this is not a robust design, with a contest that's limited to one minute rounds (and can actually be won in ten seconds or less of playing time), it's hard to argue against such designs. With its ten minute run time, large playing field, and spatially distributed game objects, *Egg Hunt* encourages students to think about robots that are more like creatures than machines.

The team aspect of *Egg Hunt* also adds a lot to the design space. Each *Egg Hunt* game consists of four robots, working in two teams of two, created by four groups of students, also aligned in two teams of two groups. As described by Rich Drushel, one of *Egg Hunt*'s founders, this allows for a great richness of strategies:[3]

---

[3] From "Rich's Hints & Kinks for LEGO 375/475," `http://www.eecs.cwru.edu/courses/-`

- *Two independent pastel egg collectors.* Neither robot depends upon the other in any way. This approach maximizes offense and is the most robust, because it is functionally redundant: if one robot breaks down for any reason, the other still can collect eggs for a positive team score. Note: the strategy of constructing 2 identical "clone" robots is expressly forbidden.

- *One pastel egg collector, one black egg collector.* One robot increases the team's positive score, the other "poisons" the opponent. The robots can be completely independent, but there is a potential danger: if the pastel egg collector breaks down, there is no way to generate additional positive scores for the team (unless the black egg collector can somehow learn of its teammate's predicament and switch strategies).

- *One pastel egg collector, one opponent-nest blocker.* This strategy combines offense (increasing your own positive score) with defense (preventing your opponent from increasing its positive score by blocking its nest). It is risky in that a failure of the egg collector means that your team can win only through luck (e.g., you already got some pastel eggs in your nest before the collector failed) or through your opponent's stupidity (e.g., it accidentally puts some pastel eggs into your nest). Two competing teams which employ this strategy, assuming each deploys it successfully against the other, generate a dull 10-minute standoff.

- *One black egg collector, one home-nest blocker.* This is the strategy for those who like trenches and wars of attrition. You put black eggs into your opponent's nest while preventing him from doing the same thing to you. The only way you can win is with a score of You: zero, Opponent: minus-something. The reason this is riskier than the pastel-collector/opponent-nest-blocker strategy is that black eggs are far less numerous than pastel eggs. Again, it's brutal to watch if two teams use this strategy against each another. You're totally at the mercy of your opponent if the black egg collector breaks down—you can win only if your opponent makes a mistake.

At MIT, there is now an established culture of the quick one-minute contest format. This would make it a challenge to introduce a more authentic contest format like the *Egg Hunt*. If starting a contest tradition from scratch, the extended play period and team format of *Egg Hunt* is worth serious consideration.

F.3 Contest Rule Analysis

The contest rules provide a general framework for guiding participants' project work. Thus designing the contest is a sort of meta-design which shapes the design experience the contest participants will have. In this section, we explore how details in contest rules matter.

F.3.1 Materials

In the context of a course, it's often a good idea to provide all participants with the same kit of materials, and require robots to be built only from materials in that kit. This focuses participants' efforts on figuring out what to do with the materials they are given, rather than trying to hunt down some unusual artifact. Of course, it's essential that the robot-building kit be complete and matched to the contest game:

- *All entrants will be given an equal amount of LEGO and other supplies including:*

  1. *An ample supply of LEGO, including beams, axles, gears, wheels, and other parts from the LEGO Technics line.*

---

2. *A robot controller board suitable for use as the brain of the robot, and software for developing programs on it.*
3. *Motors.*
4. *Sensors, including but not limited to IR detectors, touch sensors, and photocells.*
5. *String, rubber bands, wire, solder, and glue.*

Courses based on the use of LEGO materials must ensure that the LEGO materials are used properly. Most important, this means prohibiting participants from using glue to hold their robots together. This is for at least two reasons: (1) to make sure that the LEGO parts can be reused at the end of the course, and (2) to encourage participants to understand the properties of the LEGO system—making their robots strong through intelligent application of those ideas, rather than bypassing them with glue:

- *Only LEGO parts and connectors may be used as robot structure.*

- *LEGO pieces may not be glued together.*

Building on the aesthetic of the LEGO system, we have often prohibited participants from modifying the LEGO parts, considering this a sort of going outside the bounds of the LEGO system. There are two exceptions: (1) gluing LEGO pieces to a motor or sensor to allow it be mounted *as part of* the LEGO system, and (2) an exception clause of the gray baseplate, which does not have LEGO studs underneath and hence would not be that useful unless it were modified:

- *LEGO pieces may not be altered in any way, with the following exceptions:*

    1. *The gray LEGO baseplate may be altered freely.*
    2. *LEGO pieces may be modified to facilitate the mounting of sensors and actuators.*
    3. *LEGO pieces may be modified to perform a function directly related to the operation of a sensor.*

- *A non-LEGO part may be attached to at most 5 LEGO parts via glue.*

- *No lubricants may be used. This would include silicone spray, oils of any sort, or solid lubricants such as Vaseline.*

Electrical wire is part of the kit, so participants are clearly told that it cannot be used for structural purposes (e.g., wrapping wire around an assembly to hold it together):

- *Wire may only be used for electrical purposes. Wire may not be used for structural purposes.*

In early years of the MIT Robot Design contest, we had a subpar assortment of LEGO wheels. The biggest wheels had quite poor traction, so we handed out fat rubber bands and created an exception to the gluing rule:

- *Rubber bands may be glued to LEGO wheels or gears to increase the coefficient of friction.*

We were worried that these rubber bands would be too powerful if used to build slingshots or other such devices:

- *Only the LEGO rubber bands and thin rubber bands may be used to provide stored energy.*

F.3.2 Design

Provide a deadline after which changes to the robot design cannot be performed. This helps participants refrain from making counterproductive design alterations:

- *Contestants may not alter the structure of their entry once the contest has begun, but may repair broken components between rounds if time permits.*

- *Contestants must submit the final version of the code to be run on their robot the night before the day of the contest. The robot code cannot be changed after this point. The submitted code will be available to be reloaded onto the robot in the case of a controller board failure.*

- *Robots will be impounded the evening before the final contest. Contestants cannot make design changes to the robots after this point.*

F.3.3 Robot Size

Some contest specifications provide implicit limitations to robot size—if a robot has to move through a maze, the width of the passageway will determine a robot's maximum length and width. Also, if participants are building from a particular kit of parts, those parts can be assembled into a robot only so big.

Often, however, explicit size constraints should be provided. For example, in the maze case, one may wish to prohibit robots from looking down at the walls. This would require an explicit vertical size constraint.

A nice compromise between explicit and implicit size limitations is to require robots to be within a certain size at *the beginning* of a contest round, but allow them to expand under their own power after the round has begun. This makes it much more challenging to deploy a large robot, helping to temper strategies based on large size.

For example:

- *The dimension of the robot may not exceed an imaginary 1 foot cube at the start of each round. Robots may be tested by placing a clear cubical box (12 inch inner dimensions) over the robot while the robot is stationary on a flat surface. No parts of the robot may press against the inside walls of this box.*

- *Robots may expand in size (under their own control) once the round has begun.*

On the other hand, one may wish to prohibit oversized robots altogether, lest participants get too engaged in the purely mechanical side of the design project.

F.3.4 Multiple-Robot Entries

On occasion, students' design solutions to a contest will involve multiple robots working as a team. For instance, in the *Robo-Pong* contest, one team developed a pair of robots: one robot which traversed its ball area and shot balls to the other robot's side of the table, and a second robot that drove up to the center plateau and attempted to prevent the opposing robot from interfering with its ball-shooting sidekick.

These designs are necessarily complicated; it's hard enough to get one robot functioning properly, no less two coordinated robots. There is an additional problem, though: if there is only one controller board per robot kit, these robots must carry wires between the multiple robot bodies. Intentionally or not, these wires can easily ensnarl the opposing robot and are generally a nuisance.

One compromise is to require multiple pieces of a given robot entry to be contiguously connected via LEGO parts. This allows participants who wish to create multiple-robot designs to do so, but limits the problem of wire harnesses.

- *Entries may not drag wires between two or more structurally separate parts of their robot, unless those wires are part of a LEGO chain link between the various parts of the robot.*

By contrast, the *Egg Hunt* contest is based on the idea of multiple robots cooperating. In the contest, though, each group constructs a single physical entity, so the sort of problem noted here does not apply.

F.3.5 Creativity Rule

To encourage participants who have unusual ideas that can not be satisfied with the stock robot kit, an "electronic creativity" rule may be included:

- *Entries must be built completely from kit parts, with the following exception: Contestants may spend up to $10 for the purchase of electronic components used in their design. No single part may cost more than $2. Contestants must show receipts upon request.*

A low-dollar-value limit should be established to keep student financial resources from becoming a factor. Another way of implementing this idea is to give each team some "virtual cash" that may be used to buy from a predetermined stock of special parts.

F.3.6 Starting the Round

Some mechanism must be employed to make sure all robots start the round at the same time. The simplest way to do this is have a judge give a countdown; when the judge reaches "go," participants press a start button on their robots.

A more sophisticated approach may be taken. In the MIT Robot Design contests, we have standardized on a method of embedding lights (flashlight bulbs or LEDs) into the robot playing table. Robots are placed above the lights; when the lights are turned on, the round is started.

- *The round will be started by the judges turning on the starting lights, located underneath the table in the center of each robot's starting circle, for the first one second of the round.*

To reduce the likelihood that purely mechanical solutions to a contest will be viable, robots may be rotated to a randomized starting position at the beginning of each round.

- *The contestants will place the machines on the playing field within the designated starting circles. A random orientation for the starting of the round will be selected by the judges. Both machines will have the same random orientation. The machines must be placed at that random orientation within the starting area.*

In the MIT contests, we have settled on four possible rotations (at 90 degree increments) for the randomized position. Participants tend to write special-case code for each of the rotations, sometimes using the robot beaconing system (described below) to obtain a vector to the other robot and thereby deduce their rotation. The intention of the randomized orientation is to encourage students to consider more robust control strategies. As mentioned in the *Robo-Golf* discussion, this is not always effective, though it still does force students to deal with some explicit uncertainty.

F.3.7 Robot Beaconing

Since the 1991 contest year, the MIT Robot Design project has employed a beaconing system for its contests (which since that time have always involved two robots). The beacon system consists of an infrared transmitter which each robot must carry, and a detection system provided to each team. The detection system includes four sensors for detecting the infrared emissions of the other robot.

The technology includes a modulation scheme where each robot transmits a signal on a different frequency. As long as a robot's sensors are optically shielded from its own transmitter, it can reliably detect the signals from the other robot.

From a rules standpoint, the beaconing system requires that robots mount their beacons in a known location that won't be obscured, and that the beacons operate properly:

- *All robots are required to carry an infrared transmitter. This transmitter acts as a beacon so that robots can locate each other on the playing field.*

- *The infrared beacon must be capable of broadcasting infrared (IR) light modulated at either 100 Hertz or 125 Hertz with a 40,000 Hertz carrier. Hardware and software is provided to do this.*

- *Machines failing to meet the infrared transmission specification or in any way modifying or jamming their transmission frequency during the round of play will be disqualified.*

- *Judges will assign frequencies for IR emitters to the machines in the beginning of each round by setting the robot's DIP switch 1. If the switch is one, the robot must broadcast 100 Hertz infrared light. If the switch is zero, the robot must broadcast 125 Hertz infrared light. Software will be provided to do this.*

- *The IR broadcasting beacon must be located at exactly 18″ (eighteen inches) above the surface of the playing field when mounted on the robot. The beacon and its mounting pole are exempted from the robot size limitation rule.*

- *The beacon must be located so that its center is never more than four inches (measured horizontally) from the geometric center of the microprocessor board.*

- *The beacon cannot be deliberately obstructed, or be designed in such a way that accidental obstructions are probable. This implies that robots may not extend farther than 18″ vertically.*

Typically, many more teams have plans to use the beaconing system than do those who ultimately field a robot which tracks the opponent robot. When it is successfully used, the beacon system leads to exciting contest behaviors. For example, in the *Robo-Pong* contest, one of the dual-robot designs had its blocker move back and forth to block the opponent.

There is a fair bit of overhead in supporting the beacon system; in addition to providing the hardware and software, robots must be tested for proper emissions during the contest itself. Beacons have the potential to add a lot to a game, but they must be wholeheartedly supported by the staff running the contest.

F.3.8 Playing Field Features

All of the contests described here have special features built into the robots' environment to make the contest task tractable. These features include:

- Black lines, such as the circumference in *Kick the Can* and the guide-lines in *Robo-Golf*.

- Surface shading, such as the black and white painted sides in *Robo-Pong*, and the arena/nest distinction in *Egg Hunt*.

- Inclined surfaces, as in *Robo-Pong*.

- Polarized light markers, as in the nest lights in *Egg Hunt*.

- Object shading, as in the eggs in *Egg Hunt*.

In order to be useful, each of these features would be paired with corresponding sensors in the robot design kit. For example, inclination sensors were part of the *Robo-*

Pong kit, but would be unnecessary for the other contests. Good reflectance sensors would be especially helpful for reading the eggs in *Egg Hunt*.

The polarized lights described in the *Egg Hunt* contest are an example of an active environment object. Polarizing film is placed in front of normal incandescent lamps. The two "nests" are marked with polarizing film rotated at two different orientation. Robots can then use simple photocell sensors in the configuration described in Chapter 3 (see page 115) to find the desired nest.

Thoughtful design of these environmental features is crucial to the quality of the robots that are built for a contest. If robots do not have features to interact with, participants are likely to create dead-reckoning sorts of strategies, which tend to be brittle and prone to failure. In a well-designed contest, students are provided with a collection of sensors well-matched to the performance environment of the robot.

F.3.9 Practical Concerns

Don't design a playing field that will take an unreasonable amount of time to construct, or won't be mobile after it's built. It's likely that a local science museum or school will want to hold a robot contest with your students' robots, and it would be best if the playing field could travel.

Make sure that markers used to paint black lines are visible to robots' infrared sensors. Some black markers are actually invisible in the infrared spectrum (that is, they don't absorb infrared light, so the reflective properties of surface being marked are not changed). Try a blue marker if black markers are not working.

Don't forget the audience when designing a game. It should be easy for the audience to see what actions robots are performing, and how the scoring is progressing. For instance, in *Robo-Golf*, when balls are deposited into the hole, a chute underneath the table brings them out to the front of the field for all of the audience to see. Ideally, the goal of the game should be simply stated, so that the audience can follow the action.

Consider lighting issues if the playing field will be moved for the contest itself. Students are likely to design control software with implicit assumptions based on ambient lighting conditions. If the playing field is moved to a new location, or subjected to camera lighting, many robots will be incapacitated.

If the performance lighting is expected to vary from the development lighting, provide students with various forms of spotlighting for experimentation in the lab. The best scenario is having the development environment match the performance environment, but if this isn't feasible, provide ample ways for students to vary the lighting in the lab.

F.4 Conclusion

Good contest design is itself a hard design problem. The contest shapes the sorts of problems that will be encountered by its students. Contests embody ideas about technology, demonstrating the capabilities of robots and challenging how we think about robots. A good contest sparks a whole range of creative solutions, and leaves everyone feeling successful. In a good contest, even if you are not the contest champion, you've had a winning learning experience.

APPENDIX

Resources

Apple Computer, Inc. *1 Infinite Loop, Cupertino, CA 95014, USA*
phone *(408) 996–1010*
`http://www.apple.com/`
Apple Macintosh operating system; SimpleText text editor.

Bare Bones Software, Inc. `http://www.barebones.com/`
BBEdit programmer's text editor for the Macintosh.

Dunfield Development Systems. *P.O. Box 31044, Nepean, Ontario K2B 8S8, Canada*
`http://www.dunfield.com/`
Creator of Micro-C, a low-cost, high-quality C compiler for the 68HC11 and other microprocessors.

Gleason Research. *P.O. Box 1494, Concord, MA 01742, USA*
phone: *(800) 265–7727, fax (978) 287–4170*
`http://www.gleasonresearch.com/`
Authorized distributor of Handy Boards. Will ship to domestic and international destinations.

Handy Board. `http://handyboard.com`
Information on Handy Board and Mini Board robot controllers.

Harvard Associates. *10 Holworthy Street, Cambridge, MA 02138, USA*
phone *(617) 492–0660, fax (617) 492–4610*
`http://www.harvassoc.com/`
United States distributor of the Roamer robot.

Helios Software Solutions. *P.O. Box 019, Longridge PR3 2GW, England*
phone *+44 (1772) 786373, fax +44 (1772) 786375*
`http://www.textpad.com/`
Creator and distributor of the TextPad programmer's text editor for Microsoft Windows.

ImageCraft. *P.O. Box 64226, Sunnyvale, CA 94088–4226, USA*
phone *(650) 493–9326, fax (650) 493–9329*
`http://www.imagecraft.com/`
Creator of ICC11, a low-cost, high-quality 68HC11 C compiler.

Images Company. *P.O. Box 140742, Staten Island, NY 10314, USA*
phone *(718) 698–8305, fax (718) 982–6145*
`http://www.imagesco.com/`
Distributor of AGE bend sensor.

Jameco Electronics *1355 Shoreway Road, Belmont, CA 94002, USA*
phone *(650) 592–8097, fax (650) 590–2503*
`http://www.jameco.com/`
Distributor of AGE bend sensor and many other electronic and robotic supplies.

LEGO Dacta. *DK-7190 Billund, Denmark*
fax +45 75 35 43 85
http://www.lego.com/dacta/

MCM Electronics. *650 Congress Park Drive, Centerville, OH 45459–4072, USA*
phone (800) 543–4330, fax (800) 765–6960
http://www.mcmelectronics.com/
Large retail distributor of electronic components and tools. Specializes in service parts for the consumer electronics industry.

Microsoft Corporation. *One Microsoft Way, Redmond, WA 98052–6399, USA*
http://www.microsoft.com/
Microsoft MS-DOS, Windows 3.1, 95, 98, NT, and 2000 operating systems; Note-Pad text editor.

Model A Technology. *2420 Van Layden Way, Modesto, CA 95256, USA*
phone (209) 575–3445, fax (209) 575–2750
http://www.techeducation.com/
United States distributor of *fischertechnik* building system.

Motorola Semiconductor Products Sector.
http://www.mot-sps.com/
Technical information and software for the 68HC11 microprocessor.

Newton Research Labs. *14813 NE 13th St., Bellevue, WA 98007, USA*
phone (425) 643–6218, fax (425) 643–6447
http://www.newtonlabs.com/
Creator of commercial version of Interactive C.

Patrick Hui. *Flat-E 13/F Yik Hon Bldg., 72–78 Java Road, North Point, Hong Kong*
phone (852) 2563–8511, fax (852) 2851–0804 c/o Patrick Hui
http://home.hkstar.com/~huip/
Authorized distributor of Handy Boards.

Pete Keleher. *8006 Barron Street, Takoma Park, MD 20912*
http://alpha.olm.net/
Creator and distributor of Alpha text editor for the Macintosh.

Pitsco-LEGO Dacta. *P.O. Box 1707, Pittsburg, KS 66762*
phone (800) 362–4308, fax (888) 534-6784
http://www.pitsco-legodacta.com/
Pitsco is a joint venture company of the LEGO Group and is the exclusive distributor of LEGO Dacta products in the United States.

Radio Shack. *Regional stores located across the United States.*
http://www.radioshack.com/
The ubiquitous consumer electronics and hobbyist parts retailer. Great for snagging transistors, wire, and LEDs within an hour's time.

Valiant Technology. *3 Grange Mills, Weir Road, London, SW12 0NE, UK*
phone +44 181 673 2233, fax +44 181 673 6333
Designer and manufacturer of the Roamer, a programmable educational robot.

References

Randall D. Beer, Hillel J. Chiel, and Richard F. Drushel. Using autonomous robotics to teach science and engineering. *Communications of the Association of Computing Machinery*, 42(6):85–92, June 1999.

Valentino Braitenberg. *Vehicles: Experiments in Synthetic Pyschology*. MIT Press, Cambridge, MA, 1984.

Rodney A. Brooks. A robust layered control system for a mobile robot. *IEEE Journal of Robotics and Automation*, RA(2):14–23, April 1986.

Richard Dawkins. *The Blind Watchmaker*. W.W. Norton & Company, New York, 1987.

Nira Granott. *Microdevelopment of Co-construction of Knowledge During Problem Solving: Puzzled Minds, Weird Creatures, and Wuggles*. PhD thesis, Massachusetts Institute of Technology, Epistemology and Learning Group, 20 Ames Street, Cambridge, MA 02139, 1993.

Fred G. Martin. *Circuits to Control: Learning Engineering by Designing LEGO Robots*. PhD thesis, Massachusetts Institute of Technology, MIT Media Laboratory, 20 Ames Street Room E15–315, Cambridge, MA 02139, 1994.

Otto Mayr. *The Origins of Feedback Control*. MIT Press, Cambridge, MA, 1970.

Seymour Papert. *Mindstorms: Children, Computers, and Powerful Ideas*. Basic Books, New York, 1980.

Seymour Papert and Cynthia Solomon. *Twenty things to do with a computer*. Logo Memo 3, Massachusetts Institute of Technology, 20 Ames Street Room E15–315, Cambridge, MA 02139, 1971.

Motorola Semiconductor Products Sector. *M68HC11 Reference Manual*. Motorola Semiconductor Products Sector, http://www.mot-sps.com/, 1996.

W. Grey Walter. A machine that learns. *Scientific American*, pages 60–63, August 1951.

Norbert Wiener. *Cybernetics: Control and Communication in the Animal and the Machine*. Technology Press, Cambridge, MA, 1948.

Index

A

Accumulators, 312
Active braking, 147–149
  in action, 149
  H-bridge, 148
Actual differential photocell sensor
  schematic, 113
Adapter cables, 382
Adaptive controllers, 190
Addition, 316
Address bus, 332
Address decoding circuitry
    controls peripheral
    latches, 338
Addressing modes, 314–316
  direct, 315
  extended, 316
  immediate, 315
  indexed, 316
  inherent, 316
  relative, 316
Address signals, 333
Address space, 310–312
Address strobe, 333
Alltime_max, 296
Alltime_min, 296
Ambient light
  correcting for, 125
Ambient light immunity, 285
Amplifier circuit
  building, 245
Analog.asm
  listing of, 348
Analog expansion header
  Handy Board, 393
Analog function, 82
Analog inputs, 24
  Handy Board, 393
  68HC11, 346–347
  sensors, 98
Analog sensors, 23–25
Analog-to-digital conversion, 98
Angled brick
  Handy Bug 9645, 30
Annotated listing file, 325–326
Anode, 151

Arithmetic expressions
  AS11, 372–373
Arithmetic operations, 316–317
Arithmetic shift operations, 317
Armature, 139
Array pointers
  passing, 428
AS11 assembler, 372–373
ASCII characters, 310
Asmtest2.asm
  listing of, 327
Asmtest3.asm
  listing of, 329
Assembler pseudo-operations
  AS11, 372
Assembler versions, 324–325
Assembly code
  implement 15 kHz square wave, 247
Assembly language, 313–314
  vs. machine code, 313–314
  programming, 321–330
    delay loops and subroutines,
      327–328
    development cycle, 322
    digital sensors and user
      buttons, 329
    downloading object file, 326
    run, 327
    source code assembly, 324
    source code writing, 322–323
Attenuation curve, 241
Audio taper, 117
  defined, 117
  vs. linear taper, 117
Average sensor reading, 294
Axle
  Handy Bug 9645, 29, 32
  Handy Bug 9719, 55
Axle connector
  Handy Bug 9719, 56
Axle extender
  Handy Bug 9645, 32
  Handy Bug 9719, 56
Axle joiner, 168
Axle locked through beam, 167

B

Band pass filter, 241
Barcode decoding, 120
  reflective sensor, 120
Base pointer, 315
Basic driver code
  sonar board, 276
Basic encoder counting algorithm
  flowchart, 132
BASIC language, 9
Basic robotic sensors, 96–138
Bat radar, 273
Battery charging, 368–370, 394
Battery maintenance
  Handy Board, 394
Battery trickle-charge connector
  Handy Board, 393
BAUD
  SCI, 350
Beacon systems, 271
Beam, 104
BEAM robotics, 81
Beeper
  exercise, 361
Beepint.asm
  listing of, 365
Behavior
  defined, 210
Behavior-based control, 191, 192
Bend sensor outrigger, 176
Bend sensors, 115–116
Bevel gear, 164
  Handy Bug 9645, 29, 31
  illustration using, 165
Big Trak, 5
Binary numbers, 309
  signed and unsigned, 317–318
Binary object file, 427
Bit frames, 253
  illustrated, 254
Bit intervals, 253
  illustrated, 254
Bits, 308–310
Bit SET instruction, 247
Bit-wise set and clear operations, 317
Black peg, 158–159

Blinks, 252
Block diagram
    68HC11, 331
Body syntonicity, 9
Bonnemain, 2
Braitenberg, Valentino, 4
Braitenberg light-seeking behavior
    programming, 85–86
Braitenberg vehicle 1, 76
Braitenberg vehicle 2b, 76–79
Braitenberg vehicles, 75–86
    coding, 80–82
Branch never instruction, 248
Branch to subroutine instruction, 247
Break-beam configuration, 110
Break-beam encoder application, 226
Break-beam optosensor
    construction diagram, 130
    technology, 120
    types, 128
Break-beam sensor, 119, 127–131, 132
    building, 129
    built from discrete components, 129
    exercises, 130
    interfacing, 129
    object detection, 130
    quadrature configuration, 226
B register, 231
Brick, 11
    Handy Bug 9645, 30
    Handy Bug 9719, 54
Brick with arch
    Handy Bug 9719, 54
Brooks, Rodney, 91, 208, 220
Bugcad.c
    listing of, 88
Bugs trapped in a jar, 88
Building outward
    from vertical wall, 168
Bump counter, 92
Bumper contact switch, 105
Bumper switch, 105
Burst response, 252
Button debouncing, 330
Bytes, 308–310

C

Cadmium-sulfide photocell sensor, 80
Calibrate routine, 176, 289
Calibration
    by demonstration, 289
    exercises, 290
Capturing data, 389–390
Caster design, 171
Catch
    Handy Bug 9719, 56

Cathode, 151
C (common), 105
CdS photocells, 80
C functions
    defined, 27
Chain link, 164
Chain link drive, 164
Characters, 308–310
Charge
    battery, 368–370, 393–394
    indicator
        Handy Board, 393
    pump, 350
Charger board
    component side, 399
    silkscreen, 400
    solder side, 399
Chassis
    Handy Bug 9645, 36–40
Checksum calculation, 326
Chirp, 271, 274
C-language compilers, 16
Clarostat series 600 optical rotary
    encoder, 227
Classical control, 190
Clear history, 295
Clear operations, 317
Click, 232
Close-up capability
    driver, 278
Cmpd instruction, 263
Comment
    defined, 373
Commercial enclosed quadrature encoder,
    227
Commercial encoders, 227
Common, 105
Communication
    IR light, 251
Communications configuration dialogs,
    353
Comparator, 241
Comparator functions, 241
Computer connector
    Handy Board, 393
Computer mouse
    quadrature encoders, 227
Conditional branching, 318–319
Condition code register, 263, 318–319
Connecting
    to a terminal program, 386–387
Connection board
    between Polaroid unit and Handy
        Board, 276
Connector, 101
    wiring
        four basic steps, 101

Connector peg, 158–159
    with axle
        Handy Bug 9645, 32
        Handy Bug 9645, 32
        Handy Bug 9719, 56
    with stud, 169
Connell, Jonathan, 220
Conservation of work, 144
Constructionist learning, 7–9
Construction notes
    Sharp Gp2DO2, 281–282
Construction techniques, 376–383
Contact sensing
    touch, 104
Contemporary robotics
    history of ideas, 1–17
Continuous modulated IR light
    detecting, 236
Continuous rotation
    servo motor, 379–381
    servo motors, 156
Control, 174–223
    types of, 193
Control registers
    used in sonar driver, 277
Control waveform
    generating, 155
Counter
    bump, 92
    encoder, 132
    Handy Bug 9645, 32
    program, 313
C programming, 16
Crank
    Handy Bug 9645, 32
Crank parts
    Handy Bug 9645, 49
Cross axle
    Handy Bug 9719, 56
Cross-bracing, 158–160
Crown gear, 164
Current, 99
Current-limiting resistor, 355
Current state, 225
Current_value, 296
Cybernetics, 1–4, 4
Cycle counting, 251, 361
    exercise, 328
Cycle-eating subroutine, 248

D

Dacta's Technology Resource Set, 29
Danger zones, 335
Data
    Handy Board, 384–390
Data bus, 332

Data direction register for port D,
    125–126
    function and address, 277
Data end pointer, 298
Data-in-loop, 285
Data start pointer, 298
Data structure, 214–215
    stack, 319
Data types, 316
DB-9 connector, 276
DC motors, 139–143
    construction techniques for, 376–378
    outputs and indicators
        Handy Board, 393
    wiring diagram, 377
DDRD (data direction register for
        port D), 125–126
    function and address, 277
Dead-bug construction, 245
Dead-reckoning
    robot positioning systems, 225
Debugging, 25
Decb instruction, 248
Decimal numbers, 309
Decoding Sony IR protocol
    algorithm, 257
Decrement, 316
Decrement register B, 248
Delay loops, 327
Delay subroutine, 328
Deliberative control, 191, 192
Demodulation, 234
Derivative term
    exercises, 189
    performance graphs, 188–190
Desired state, 175
Detailed timing
    Sony IR 7-key, 256
Detection range, 240
Detector, 238–239
    determination, 124
    Handy Board, 235
Detector photodiode/phototransistor,
    119–126
Detuned driver
    exercises, 251
    using, 248–250
Differential photocell. See also Photocell
    circuit, 111
    exercises, 114
    sensor, 111–114
        wiring construction, 112
    wiring diagram, 14
Differential photocell sensor
    schematic, 113
Digi-Comp computer, 6
Digital input circuit, 342

Digital input latch, 329
    reading, 329
Digital inputs, 24
    Handy Board, 393
    sensor ports, 96–99
Digital sensor
    exercises, 330
Digital sensors, 23–25, 96, 329
    sensor history exercises, 306
Digital voltmeter, 244
Diodes, 151
Direct addressing mode, 314
Direct encoder reading and interpreted
        encoder state
    graph of, 135
Direction logic, 147
    action, 148
Disable (pid) command, 210
Discrete infrared LED and
        phototransistor, 128
Division, 316
Double-sided foam tape, 378
Download, 21
    object file, 328–329
6811 downloaders, 401
Downloading, 326
Drebbel's furnace, 2
D register, 232
Driver
    using, 232
Driver chip
    limits of
        exercises, 152
Driver code, 228–232, 259–264,
        283–285
Driver pins
    servo motor, 155
Driver program
    listing of, 229–231
Driver qencdr10.asm, 229–231
Driver routines
    servo motor, 155
Driver schematic
    Handy Board motor, 343
Driver software, 135–136
Driverstart, 360
Dual photocell sensor
    building, 114
Dump_data routine, 178, 389
Duty cycle, 23

E

ECHO signal, 276
Educational technology, 1
Egg-hunt, 432, 438–441

Elapsed time
    counts to distance, 279
    function, 92
    between transitions, 253
Electrical interface
    servo motor, 379–381
Electrical noise, 275
Electronic control, 146–153
    exercises, 151–152
Emergence, 90
    exercises, 92
Emitter, 238
    determination, 124
Emitter LED, 119–126
Enable, 147
    action, 148
Enable input
    74HC138, 337–340
    motor spin, 150
Enabling the memory, 334
Enabling transistors, 147–148
Encoder bit streams
    for quadrature encoding, 225
Encoder clicks, 132
    counting, 131
Encoder_counter, 132
Encoder data stream, 225
Encoder library routines, 136
Encoder routine, 228
    system interrupt, 231
Encoder_state, 132, 228
Encoder?_velocity, 135
EQU, 373
Evaluation sequence, 313
Exit conditions, 199–206
Expanded multiplexed mode, 356
Extended addressing mode, 314
External sensor
    Handy Board, 99
Eye-like sensor grids, 80

F

Failure modes, 90
Falling edge, 258
FCB, 373
FCC, 373
FDB, 373
Features
    Handy Board, 13–14
Feedback
    negative, 77
    positive, 78
Feedback control, 1–4, 174–181
    exercises, 179
Feedback system, 175
    block diagram, 174

Files
  Handy Board/interactive C, 25–26
First program, 71–74
Fischertechnik, 16–17
Five-stage reduction, 162
Fixed thresholding, 287
Flags, 263
Floating point (FP) operations, 201
Floor turtles, 74
Formatted print, 27
Form constant byte, 373
Form constant character, 373
Form double byte, 373
FP operations, 201
Frequency wave
  programming method, 246
Full-width stop bush
  Handy Bug 9645, 32
  Handy Bug 9719, 56
Functions
  Handy board/interactive C, 25–26
Fusion, 207
Futaba S148, 156
Futaba S148 modifications
  continuous rotation, 380
Futaba S148 servo motor
  with mounting horns, 153

G

Gain, 184
Ganging, 144
  multiple gear reduction
    method, 146
Gear ganging concept, 161
Gearing, 143–146, 159–162
  exercise, 146
Gear mounter, 168
Gear physics, 144
Gear rack, 166–167
  Robot Gripper, 172
  using, 167
Gear reduction, 145
  Handy Bug 9719
    motor, 54
    technic motor, 52
  servo motor, 153
Gears
  meshing, 145–146, 162
Gear teeth
  designing, 145
Geartrains, 161–163
  design, 167–171
  Handy Bug 9645, 37, 40
  sample LEGO, 162
Generator
  exercises, 151

Generic Sensor Device Connection, 97
Gentle turning algorithm, 179
Go straight mode, 203
Gp2d02.asm
  listing of, 284
GP1U52 IR demodulators, 234
Granott, Nira, 89
Graph interpretation, 186
Gray peg, 158–159
Groucho's cornering algorithm, 197
Groucho's robot
  schematic of, 196
Groucho's sequential ball harvester
    strategy, 195
  exercises, 197–198

H

Half-radius round gears, 161
Hand-built encoder, 226
Handy Board, 12–14
  connect, 20–28
  connectors, 392–396
  design, 308–374
  digital inputs, 24
  features of, 13–14
  H-bridge circuit, 151
  H-bridge driver, 150–152
  infrared transmit circuit, 355
  interactive C, 20–28
  LCD screen, 25
  library function, 24
  main function, 26–28
  ports, 392–394
  printed circuit board layouts, 396–400
    silkscreen, 398
    solder side, 397
  sensor ports, 97
  specifications, 391–400
    DC adapter, 394
  test program, 25
  wiring diagram, 392
  workstation computer, 27
Handy Board's Analog and Digital Sensor
    Banks, 97
Handy Board Sensor Input Circuitry, 97
Handy Board Sensor Plug Pin-Out, 101
Handy Bug, 20, 28–71
  movement routines, 218
Handy Bug 9645
  robot completed, 51
  step-by-step instructions, 28–52
Handy Bug 9719
  completed, 71
  step-by-step directions, 50–71
H-bridge
  active braking, 148

H-bridge circuit
  with enable and direction logic, 148
  Handy Board, 151
  motor driver, 146, 147–149
  speed control, 150
H-bridge driver
  Handy Board, 150–152
  transistors, 146
H-bridge motor driver circuit, 146
H-bridge operating motor
  clockwise direction, 147
  counterclockwise direction, 147
68HC11, 12, 308–321
  analog inputs, 346–347
  architecture, 330–332
  block diagram, 331
  chip, 16
  CPUs
    A vs. E series, 375
  digital inputs
    volt, 226
  with Handy Board hardware, 330–373
  interrupt vector, 228
  memory, address decoding, and
      miscellaneous circuitry, 341
  memory and motor sensor
      peripherals block
      diagram, 337
  memory map, 311, 339–340
  memory schematic, 340
  operating modes, 356
  port A, B, C, D, E, 332
  register block, 331
  registers
    programmer's model, 312
  software, 350–352
  system memory map, 339–340
74HC138
  address decoder
    wiring, 339
  chip, 337–340
  enable inputs, 337
  memory mapping, 337–340
  negative enable, 338
  select inputs, 338
Heat shrink tubing
  installing, 102
Helping hands tool, 102
Hex, 309
Hexadecimal, 309
Hinged bumper switch, 105
History duration
  exercises, 306
Hybrid control, 191, 192
HyperTerminal, 353
Hysteresis, 135, 232, 241
  comparator, 241

Hysteresis thresholding, 288
    exercises, 289

I

ICB driver source
    for 15 kHz square wave output, 249
ICB file, 232
ICC11, 16
Ideal differential photocell sensor
    schematic, 112, 113
Idealized response IR
    demodulators, 234
If else statements, 92
Illegal transition states, 233
Immediate addressing, 314
Increment, 316
Indexed addressing mode, 315
Index registers, 312
Indicator LED
    Handy Board, 235
Infrared communications, 251–270
    exercises, 270–271
Infrared demodulation
    detailed characteristic, 251–252
Infrared demodulator, 234
    functional block diagram, 240–241
Infrared detector
    card, 123
    Handy board, 236
Infrared devices, 123
Infrared emitter/detector pair, 239
Infrared energy, 236
Infrared input sensor
    Handy Board, 393
Infrared LED
    exercises, 239
    negative terminal, 236
Infrared light
    reflective optosensors, 120
Infrared modulation, 234
Infrared noise sources, 239
Infrared output and indicator
    Handy Board, 393
Infrared output port
    Handy Board, 235
Infrared photodiode, 240
Infrared proximity
    sensing, 240–251
    exercises, 244–245
Infrared receive routine
    exercises, 264
Infrared remote control, 233
Infrared sensing, 233–270
    exercises, 270–271
Infrared sensor
    Sharp GP1U52, 381–382

Infrared transmit circuit, 353–354
    block diagram
        Handy Board, 354
    Handy Board, 235
Infrared transmit driver
    20-phase, 266
Infrared transmit routine
    description, 265–266
    using, 264
Infrared transmitter, 236
    wiring diagram, 382
Initialize_module subroutine, 266
INIT signal, 276
Input capture facility, 265
Input signal
    servo motor, 153
Integrated IR detector, 238
Integrator, 241
Integrator signal
    interfacing, 242
Intentionality, 175
Interactive C, 12, 15–16
    application, 401
    arrays, 413
    binary object file, 428
    binary programs, 423–428
    commands, 404
    compile-time errors, 422
    configuring, 429
    constants, 408
    control flow, 410–411
    creating new processes, 419–420
    electrical, 416
    error handling, 422
    features, 403–404
    file and function management, 429
    floating point functions, 421
    and Handy Board, 20, 28
    infrared subsystem, 417–418
    interrupt-driven binary programs,
        425–428
    LCD screen printing, 411–412
    library functions, 415
    line editing, 405
    list files, 428
    memory access functions, 422
    multitasking, 419
    operators, 409–410
    output control, 415
    passing pointers, 414
    pointer variables, 414
    process management commands,
        420–421
    programs, 428
    prompt, 21–22
    quick C tutorial, 405–407
    reference, 401–429

runtime errors, 422
    sensor input, 417
    time commands, 418
    tone functions, 418–419
    user buttons and knob, 417
    variable names, 407
    variables, 407–408
    versions, 15
Interactivity, 15
Interface/charger board
    component side, 399
    silkscreen, 400
    solder side, 399
Interface potentiometers, 117
Interfacing hobby motors, 377
Internal registers, 312
Interrupt based beeper program, 365
Interrupt routines, 258, 320, 362
Interrupts, 320
    overview, 362
Interrupt vectors, 312, 321
Int serial, 385
Inverter
    Handy Board, 151
IR. See Infrared
Ircapture, 258–263
Ir_count, 264
Irdone, 258–263
Irgetbit, 257–263
Irreset, 258–263
Irroutine, 258–263
IS1U60 IR demodulators, 234
Iterations, 225

J

JMP instruction, 228
Joint angles
    measuring, 225

K

Keystroke waveforms, 255
Kick the can, 432–434

L

Labels
    AS11, 372
Last _counts, 228
Last-in, first-out (LIFO) method, 319
Lcdcls routine, 359
LCD display, 355–359
LCD driver, 356–359
Lcdinit routine, 359
LCD printing, 82
Lcdready, 360
LCD screen
    Handy Board, 393

LDAA, 314
Least-significant-bit (LSB), 255
LED
    emitter and detector, 237
    wiring
        port D pin, 125–126
Left-hand switch construction, 107
Left routines, 178
LEGO. *See also* individual part
LEGO 99719, 50
LEGO brick
    single unit illustrated, 157
LEGO design, 157–171
    clichés, 172
    exercises, 172–173
    gearing, 159–167
    mechanism, 167–171
    structure, 157–158
LEGO/Logo, 9–10
    project, 10
LEGO technic, 10, 16–17. *See also*
        individual part
    cost and stability, 16
    system, 12
LEGO Turtle robot
    schematic drawing, 28
LIFO method, 319
Light and touch
    exercises, 87
    sensitivity
        program, 86
Light-avoiding program, 112, 113
Light box, 115
Light readings
    to motor commands, 83
Light-seeking
    exercises, 85
    program, 112
Light sensor
    Braitenberg, 80
    circuit, 108–111
        building it, 109–110
    conversion function, 84
    exercises, 81
    readings, 83–84
    shield, 82
Light-shielding
    exercise, 83
Limit sensing, 104
Linear potentiometers, 116
Linear taper
    vs. audio taper, 117
    defined, 117
Lineauto.c
    listing of, 292
Line following
    exercise, 287

performance run
    graph of, 288
    reference activity, 286–287
Line_follow routines, 290
Linehist.c, 293
Line_sensor routines, 290
Lisp, 8, 14
LM 358 chip, 244
Load accumulator A, 314
Load A register, 313, 314
Load driver function, 359
Lock an axle
    stop bush, 170
Logical AND, 316
Logical exclusive OR, 317
Logical OR, 316
Logo language, 8
Logo turtles, 9
Looking around, 212
Loop exit label, 285
Low battery indicator
    Handy Board, 393
Lower frequency tones
    69HC11, 246
LSB, 255
LSB encoding, 255

M

Machina docilis, 4
Machina speculatrix, 4
Machine clock, 246
Machine code
    vs. assembly language, 313–314
Machine cycles, 313
Macintosh, 325
    downloader, 402
Main encoder routine, 231
Male header
    soldering, 103
Mapping, 310–312, 337–340
    sonar exercises, 280
Mayr, Otto, 1
Maze running, 286
Mechanism, 167–171
Medium pulley wheel
    Handy Bug 9645, 32
Memory, 332–334, 334
Memory enable control line, 333
Memory location
    number, 310
Memory map, 310–312
    68HC11, 339–340
    74HC138, 337–340
Memory power switching protection, 335
Memory schematic
    68HC11, 342

Memory wires, 79
MEM-PWR, 369
Meshed bevel gear, 165
Meshing gears, 145–146
Metasens.c
    listing of, 93
Meta-sensing, 91–92
    exercises, 92
Microchip PIC series, 14
Microprocessors, 308–321
    and memory, 332–334
        diagram, 333
Microseconds, 155
Microswitch, 105
    mounting, 104
    wiring diagram
        normally closed, 107
        normally open, 105, 106
Milliseconds, 155, 201
Millisec_routine, 260
Mindstorm, 8
Mini Board, 14
MIT Robo-Miners contest
    table design, 219
MIT 6.270 robot design competition,
        11–12
Modified motor cables
    Handy Bug 9645, 38
Modified turning routines, 179
Modulated IR detectors
    varieties, 238–239
Modulated output, 237
Modulation, 233, 234
Modulation frequency, 285
Monitoring
    inner loop, 203–205
Motor, 22–23
    adapter
        wiring diagram, 382
    compatibility, 376
    direction, 23
    driver chips
        Handy Board, 150
    functions, 83–84
    Handy Bug 9645, 30, 39
        mounting, 37
        shafts, 40
    and one sensor, 76
    outputs
        74HC374, 342–344
    plugging in, 22, 71
    speed measuring, 141–142
    spin
        enable input, 150
    torque measuring, 140–141
    wiring, 377
Motorola, 15. *See also* individual part

Motorola break-beam sensor, 131
Motorola 68HC11. *See* 68HC11
Motorola MOC70F1 infrared break-beam
    optosensor, 129
MOTORPWR, 369
Movement abstractions, 7
MS-ODS
    downloaders, 402
Multiple IR LEDs
    connecting, 237
Multiple worm gears, 166
Multiplexed address, 333
Multiplexing data, 333
Multiplication, 316
Multisensor vehicles, 78
Multisonar interference
    sonar exercises, 279
Multitasking, 15, 321
    introduction to, 209

N

NC (normally closed), 105
Negative enable
    74HC138, 338
Negative feedback, 77
Nested subroutine calls, 320
Newline, 27, 82
Noninverting amplifier configuration, 243
Nonlinear connections, 79
NO (normally open), 97, 105
No operation instruction, 248
Normalizing
    exercises, 85
Normally closed, 105
Normally open, 97, 105
Nose, 114
Numeric conversion, 309

O

Object code, 313–314
Object detection
    reflectance sensors, 120
Object file
    download, 326
Obstacle avoidance, 72–73
Obstacle-avoidance
    exercises, 73
Ocko, Stephen, 9
Off-center frequencies, 241
Offset error, 187
Ohm's law, 99–100
    exercise, 101
    photocells, 113
Op-amp follower circuit, 242
Op-amp follower plus amplifier, 243

Op-amps
    use, 244
Open drain, 281
Operating frequency, 274
Operating modes
    68HC11, 356
Operating voltage, 139, 274
Operational code, 313
Optical distance sensing, 280–287
    exercises, 285–286
Optical distance sensor
    Sharp GP2DO2, 281
Optically shielded photocell light
    sensors, 82
Optically shielding nose, 112
Optical ranging
    exercises, 285–286
Optical shields, 110
Opto-electronic computer mice, 133
ORG, 372
Origins of Feedback Control, 1
Oscillation, 184
Oscilloscope, 244
Output compare interrupt, 265
Outrigger, 176
Overshoot, 184

P

Papert, Seymour, 4, 7, 74
Parallel strand
    LEDs, 237
Parameterized fixed thresholding, 287
Parker, Michael, 11
Part listing
    Handy Board, 395
Patches itself, 228
Patching
    system interrupt, 231
Patching technique, 228
PC, 313
PD control
    system for testing, 182
PD loop, 188
Periodic turn, 212–213
Peripherals, 336
Persistent calibration, 291
    exercise, 291
Phantom sound, 274
20-phase infrared transmit driver, 266
Photocell
    elements, 112
    exercises, 11
    interfaced, 108
    vs. phototransistors, 121
    resistors, 111–114
    voltage divider circuit, 109

Photocell circuit
    single, 108–111
Photocell sensor, 111–114
    attaching, 99
    light shields, 11
    mounted, 110
    optical shields, 82
    single
        wiring diagram, 109, 110
    wiring diagram, 109–110
Photo resistors, 80
Phototransistor, 129
    current flow diagram, 122
    vs. photocell, 121
PID command, 210
PID control, 190
Piezo beeper
    Handy Board, 393
    interrupt code, 364–369
    output line, 360
    test program, 361
Piezo pin
    toggling, 232
4-pin connector, 281
Pinion, 167
Piston rod, 171
    Handy Bug 9645, 32
Plate
    Handy Bug 9645, 31
    Handy Bug 9719, 55
Plate with slide
    Handy Bug 9719, 56
Plegobug.c
    listing of, 218
Polarized light beacons, 14
Polarized light seeking, 114–115
Polarized shields, 115
Polarizing filter, 115
Polarizing light filters
    principle, 14
Polaroid 9-pin connector, 275
Polaroid 6500 series ultrasonic ranging
        system, 272
    connection diagram
        Handy Board, 275–276
Polaroid 6500 sonar board
    wiring diagram, 275
Polaroid sonar device
    test routine, 279
Polaroid 6500 sonar ranging
        system
    exercises, 279
Polaroid's polarizing light filters
    principle, 14
Polaroid ultrasonic ranging system
    Handy Board interfacing
        diagram, 275

Port A
    function and address, 277
    68HC11, 332
    register
        piezo voltage, 232
Port B
    68HC11, 332
Port C
    68HC11, 332
PORTD, 125–126
Port D
    data direction register, 125–126, 285
    data register, 125–126
    68HC11, 332
    pins, 125–126
Port D data direction register (DDRD),
    125–126
Port D data register (PORTD), 125–126
Port E
    68HC11, 332
Ports, 71
    Handy Board, 392–394
Position-sensitive detector, 280, 281
Positive feedback, 78
Positive-going pulse, 153
Potentiometer, 116
    LEGO mounting ideas, 118
    mounting, 118
    schematic symbol, 117
    wiring diagram, 117, 118
Power, 23, 368
Power expansion header
    Handy Board, 393
Power/ready indicator
    Handy Board, 393
Power switch
    Handy Board, 392
Premature exits, 202–203
Previous state, 225
Printed circuit board layouts
    Handy Board, 396–400
Printf, 27, 82
Printing
    exercises, 389
    to the serial line, 387–389
Print messages and values, 26–27
Prioritization algorithm, 214–217
    data structures, 216
Prioritization code, 216
Prioritization program, 211
Prioritization scheme, 212
Priority-based control program, 213–220
Priority diagram
    reactive Groucho program, 221
Priority level, 210
Priorty.c
    listing of, 217

Process
    defined, 210
Process identifier, 210
Process number, 210
Programmable brick, 10
Programmer's model
    of 68HC11 registers, 312
Proportional control, 182–183
Proportional controller, 186
    graph interpretation, 186
Proportional-derivative control, 179–182,
    188, 233
Proportional gain, 184
Proprioceptive sensing, 205
Proximity sensing, 237
    concept drawing, 238
Proximity sensors, 238–240
Pseudo-operation, 323
Pulley wheels, 163
    Handy Bug 9645, 29
    illustrated, 164
    quadrature configuration, 226
    in quadrature encoding configuration,
        226
    sizes, 163
Pull-up resistor, 242
Pulse width modulation (PWM), 23, 149
PUL1 X register instruction, 248
Pushbutton schematic
    normally open, 105
    wiring diagram, 106
Pushbutton switch, 105
    wiring diagram, 105
Push-pull operation, 248
Putchar function, 359
Putstr routine, 359
PWM, 23, 149

Q

Quadrature configuration
    break-beam sensor, 226
Quadrature data stream
    state transition, 226
    state transition table, 226
Quadrature encoders, 224
    construction notes, 226–228
Quadrature shaft encoding, 133, 224–233
    exercises, 232–233
Quality technologies QRB1114 infrared
    reflective optosensor, 124

R

Radio control cars, 17
RAM, 311
Random access memory (RAM), 311
Random avoid, 92

Randomness, 87–90
    exercises, 89
Ranging system, 272
Reactive control, 190, 191, 192, 206–222
    exercises, 221–223
    using, 219–220
Reactive Groucho program
    priority diagram, 221
Reactive robotics approach, 208
Reactive robot program diagram, 207
Read/write control line, 332
Receiving
    Sony IR signals, 256
Recent_bumps, 92
Recognized pulse, 252
Red belt
    Handy Bug 9645, 32
Reflective optosensor, 118–126, 124, 280
    applications, 120–121
    building, 122–125
    construction diagram, 124
    device types, 119
    exercises, 126–128
    interfacing, 121–122
    shaft encoders, 136
    surface feature detection, 120
Reflective sensor, 119
    interface diagram, 121
    rotational shaft encoding, 120
Register bank, 311
Register block
    68HC11, 331
Registers, 312–313
Relative addressing mode, 319
Remctrl.c
    listing of, 260
Reserve memory block, 373
Reset history frequency, 296
Reset_timer, 92
RESET vector, 312
Resistance, 99
Resistive bend sensor, 116
Resistive position sensors
    exercises, 115–118
Resnick, Mitchel, 9
Resources, 447–448
Return address, 320
Return from subroutine
    instruction, 264
Revolutions per minute
    (RPM), 141–142
Right-hand switch construction, 107
Right routines, 178
Ring end pointer, 298
Ring start pointer, 298
RMB, 373
Roamer, 5

Robo-golf contest, 432–436
Robo-pong contest, 190–193, 432, 436–438
Robo-pong contest table, 194
Robot
    Braitenberg vehicles, 75–86
    contests, 430–446
        rule analysis, 441–446
        types, 431–432
    control
        approaches to, 191
        vocabulary, 210
    emergence and meta sensing, 89–94
    first program, 71–74
    Handy Bug, 28–71
    interactive C
        and Handy Board, 20–28
    light and touch sensitivity, 86–87
    moving, 139–173
    or creature, 76
    positioning systems
        dead-reckoning, 225
    randomness, 87–89
Robot.c, 27
Robot Gripper, 172, 173
    gear rack, 172
Robotics, 1–4
    basic sensors, 96–138
    contemporary
        history of ideas, 1–17
Rotate right through carry
    instruction, 263
Rotational force, 140
Rotational position, 225
Rotational potentiometers, 116
Rotational shaft encoding
    reflective sensor, 120
Rotational velocity, 140
Rotation operations, 317
Round brick
    Handy Bug 9645, 30
    Handy Bug 9719, 54
Rounded sensors, 79
Round gears, 163
    four sizes, 160–161
Round quality, 78
RPM, 141–142
Rpm.c
    listing of, 143
RS-232 serial line, 347
RS-232 system
    hardware, 349
    protocol, 348
Rubber band
    Handy Bug 9719, 56
Run the program, 327

S

Sanity check
    servo motor, 155
Sargent, Randy, 11, 15
SCCR1
    SCI, 350
SCCR2
    SCI, 350
SCDR, 385–386
    SCI, 350
SCI, 350–352
Screen turtles, 74
SCSR
    SCI, 350
Seconds
    vs. mseconds, 201
    routine, 214
Seering, Warren, 7
Seesaw physics, 144
Select inputs
    74HC138, 338
Self-tuning, 190
Senshist.asm, 297
    listing of, 298–302
Senshist.c, 302
    listing of, 302–303
Sensor, 96–137
    adapter
        wiring diagram, 383
    building, 101
    communications
        timing, 282
    data, 298
        graph, 131
        processing, 286–303
        processing exercises, 306
    exercises and projects, 137
    fusion, 207
    Handy Board, 23–25
    history, 291–294
        array data structure, 297
        array specifications, 297
        code, 296–300
        exercises, 306
        routines, 295, 297–298
    input
        circuit effects, 112, 113
        plugging into, 24
    interfacing, 96–101
    maximum, 298
    minimum, 298
    monitoring, 295
        arrays, 295
    mounting, 103–104
    photocell performance, 110
    plugging in, 71

ports
    digital inputs, 96–99
    reading
        and actual distance, 285–286
Sensor_average, 296
Sensor_max, 296
Sensor_min, 296
Sensproc.asm, 303
    listing of, 304–306
Sequential control, 190–191
Sequential program
    subloops, 195–196
Sequential strategies, 194
Serial communications data register (SCDR), 385–386
Serial communications interface (SCI), 350–352
Serial data transmission methods, 253
Serial line circuit, 347–352
Serial line interaction, 385–386
Serial line test program, 352
Serial peripheral interface, 125, 393
Series resistance, 99
Series Resistance Circuit, 100
Servo a5.ice, 156
Servo a7.ice, 156
Servo control signal, 152–153
Servo motor, 152–157
    construction techniques, 379–381
    exercises, 157
    pulse repetition interval, 154
    pulse width positioning
        waveforms, 154
    schematic diagram, 153
Servo pulse widths, 155
S19 file
    analysis format, 326
SGS Thomson L293D, 150
Shaft encoder, 104, 130–137
    built from LEGO parts, 131
    construction, 137
    counting, 131–133
    data, 131
    description, 130
    driver software, 134–136
    exercises, 134, 137
    measuring velocity, 136–137
Shaft encoders
    construction, 136
Sharp electronics IR demodulator, 240
Sharp GP2DO2, 280–287
    connection diagram, 281–282
    construction, 281–282
    driver code, 283–285
    optical distance sensor
        operation, 281
        wiring diagram, 282

Sharp GP2DO2 (*continued*)
    sensor wired to Handy Board plug, 282
    timing chart, 283
Sharp GP1U52X
    wiring diagram, 381
Shield
    emitter LED, 238
    encoder optics, 226
    light sensors, 82
    nose, 112
    optical, 110
    optical photocell sensor, 82
    photocell light sensors, 82
    photocell sensor, 11
    polarized, 115
Show me calibration method, 290
Shrinking
    tubing, 102, 103
Signal gain, 272
Signal-strength level, 242
    measuring, 244
Silverman, Brian, 10, 11, 257
Single chip mode, 356
Single-disk shaft encoder diagram, 130
Single IR LED
    connecting, 235
Single-photocell circuit, 108–111
Single-photocell sensor
    wiring diagram, 109
Single Resistor Ohm's Law Example, 99
Skid plate
    Handy Bug 9719, 56
Sleep statement, 82
Small pulley wheel
    Handy Bug 9719, 56
Software, 447–448
Software driver, 134
Software interface
    servo motor, 155
Soldering
    male header, 102, 103
Solomon, Cynthia, 9
Sonar
    board
        basic driver code, 276
    chirp, 274
    device
        test routine, 279
    exercises, 279
    ranging system
        exercises, 279
Sony-format infrared communications,
    254–257
Sony-format IR protocol, 256
    decoding algorithm, 257
Sony IR 7-key
    detailed timing, 256

Sony IR signals
    receiving, 256
Sony_rcv.asm
    listing of, 261–262
Sony_rcv routine, 264
Sony receive driver
    using, 259–260
Sonyxmit.asm
    listing of, 267–268
Sonyxmit subroutine, 266
Sound
    reflection, 274
    traveling speed, 271
Speed, 23
    control
        H-bridge circuit, 150
Spike-cancelling diodes, 150, 152
SPI (serial peripheral interface), 125
    expansion header
        Handy Board, 393
SP register, 313
Squareness, 159
Square quality, 78
Square wave, 248, 354
Stability, 15
Stack, 327–328
Stack pointer, 319
Stack pointer (SP) register, 313
Stack pull, 319
Stack push, 319
Stall current, 140
Stall torque, 140
Start button
    Handy Board, 393
State transition
    quadrature data stream, 225
Stepdiff.c, 112, 113
    listing of, 113
Stop bushes, 162, 163
    to retain an axle, 169
    trapping an axle, 169
Stop button
    Handy Board, 393
Stranded
    wire, 101
Stripping
    wire ends, 102
Structure
    LEGO, 157–158
Stuck in a loop, 91
Subroutine, 327–328
    calls, 319
Subroutine_initialize_module, 259
Subsumption architecture, 208
Subtraction, 316
Supplies and suppliers, 447–448
Supporting axles, 162

Surface feature detection
    reflective optosensors, 120
Switch connect
    digital input circuit, 97
Switch construction
    left- and right-hand, 107
Switches
    hinged bumper, 105
    illustrated, 104
    reporting the value, 98
    touch bumper contact, 105
    wired, 98
Switch sensor, 104–107
    application examples, 107
    completed plug, 104
    construction, 105
Switch Sensor Circuit, 98
Symmetry
    motors, 142
Sysibeep.asm
    listing of, 427
SystemInt routine, 228
System memory map
    68HC11, 339–340

T

Table design
    MIT Robo-Miners contest, 219
Tapping analog signal levels, 241–244
Task
    defined, 210
Task.c
    listing of, 213
TCL2 register, 276
TCNT
    function and address, 277
    register, 258
TCTL2
    function and address, 277
Technic beam
    Handy Bug 9645, 29, 30
    Handy Bug 9719, 54
Technic plate
    Handy Bug 9645, 31
    Handy Bug 9719, 55
Teletype interface, 9
Terminal emulator program, 386–387
Texas Instruments SN754410, 150
Three pulse width modulation waveforms,
    149
Three-terminal potentiometer wiring, 117
Three-terminal switch schematic, 105
Thresholding
    exercises, 289
    with hysteresis, 288
Threshold setpoints
    choosing, 289

TIC3
   function and address, 277
Tilden, Mark, 81
Tilden's BEAM robots, 81
Time measurements
   converting, 279
Timeouts, 200–201
   detection, 206
   exercises, 206
Timer.c
   listing of, 94
Timer control register 1, 269
Timer output 4 (TOC4)
      interrupt, 228, 260
Timer output 5 (TOC5)
      pin, 360
Timer subsystem, 363
Time stamp function, 258
Timing functions, 258
Timing loop
   for 15 kHz square wave, 247
Timing mask, 298
Tinning
   wire ends, 102
Tiny time, 155
Tire
   Handy Bug 9645, 32
   Handy Bug 9719, 56
Tire hub
   Handy Bug 9645, 32
   Handy Bug 9719, 56
Toaster control, 183
TOC4 interrupt, 228
   vector, 228
TOC5 pin, 360
Toft, Allan, 10
Toggle joint, 170
   with free or locked axle, 170
Tone-burst, 251
Tooth crown gear
   Handy Bug 9645, 31
Tooth gear
   Handy Bug 9645, 29, 31
   Handy Bug 9719, 55
   meshing with crown gear, 165
Torque, 140
   defined, 144
   gears, 145
Touch
   exercises, 87
Touch bumper
   mounted
      Handy Bug 9645, 49
Touch bumper contact switch, 105, 106
Touch.c
   listing of, 86
Touch sensitivity program, 86

Touch sensor
   avoidance strategy
      meta-sensing, 91
   Handy Bug 9645, 30
      bumper constructs, 47
      gears, 42–44
   Handy Bug 9719, 54
   program, 72–73, 86, 87
      reload, 90
   routine, 210
   task, 210
Transducer ringing, 273
Transistors
   and breaking, 149–150
   H-bridge driver, 146
   H-bridge operating motor, 147
Translational movement, 225
Transmission frequency
   detuning, 245–249
Transmitting data, 253
Trapped systems, 225
Triangular driver, 150
TRS-80 computer, 7
Turtle, 4, 9
Turtle.c
   listing of, 75
Turtle movement, 74, 75
   exercises, 74
Twin-tube epoxy, 378
Two motors and two sensors, 76–79
Two possible bit stream
      interpretations, 256
Two-terminal potentiometer, 118

U

Ultrasonic burst, 271
Ultrasonic distance sensing
   exercises, 279
   with Polaroid 6500, 271–275
Ultrasonic ranging block diagram, 271
Ultrasonic ranging system
   Handy board interfacing
      diagram, 275
Unicode, 310
Unix, 325
   downloader, 403
UNSWPWR, 368
Unused argument, 297–298
Upload, 21
   Handy Board, 384–390
Usage
   servo motor, 156
User buttons, 329
User knob
   Handy Board, 393

V

Valiant Technology, 5
Variable_encoder10_counts, 228
Variable_encoder10_velocity, 228
Vector patching
   code to perform, 228
   routine, 231
Veer left mode, 203
Veer right mode, 203
Velocity
   calculation of, 232
   graph, 188
   measuring, 136
Versions
   interactive C, 15
Visible LED, 236
Void disable_pcode_serial, 385
Void_enable, 385
Void_serial, 385
Voltage, 98–99
   break-beam waveform, 226
   divider, 98, 100
   divider relationship, 108
   follower, 242
   follower circuit, 245
   safe, 335
Voltage Divider Circuit, 100

W

Wallfola.c
   listing of, 177–178
Wall following, 175–179, 245,
      285, 306
   algorithm performance graphs,
      180–181
   run experiment, 178
Wall tracking
   reflective sensor, 120
Walter, W. Grey, 4, 74
Wandering, 212–213
Water clocks, 2
Watt, James, 3
Watt's governor, 3
Weird creatures, 89
Wiener, Norbert, 4
Windows, 325
Windows 3.1
   downloader, 402
Windows 95
   downloader, 402
Wire
   stranded, 101
Wire ends
   stripping and tinning, 102
Wire type, 101

Wiring
  connector
    four basic steps, 101
  differential photocell sensor, 112
  74HC138 address decoder, 339
  LED port D pin, 125–126
  motor, 377
  switches, 98
  three-terminal potentiometer, 117
Wiring diagram
  DC motors, 377
  differential photocell, 14
  Handy Board, 392
  infrared transmitter, 382
  microswitch
    normally closed, 107
    normally open, 105

motor adapter, 382
photocell sensor, 109–110
Polaroid 6500 sonar
    board, 275
potentiometer, 117
pushbutton switch, 105
sensor adapter, 383
Sharp GP2DO2
    optical distance
    sensor, 282
Sharp GP1U52X, 381
single photocell sensor, 109
Word, 309
Work
  defined, 144
Workstation
  definition, 20

Worm gear, 165–166
  Handy Bug 9645,
    31, 40
  Robot Gripper, 173

X

X pointer
  dereferenced, 232
X register, 313

Z

Zap mode, 371
Zero flag, 318–319
ZTerm, 353

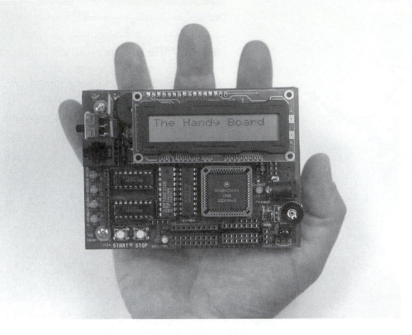